The Wednesday Boys

A Definitive
Who's Who of
Sheffield Wednesday
Football Club
1880-2005

Printed & Published by Pickard Communication

ISBN 0 9547264 9 9
Published & Printed by in 2005 by Pickard Communication

Pickard Communication
10-11 Riverside Park
Sheaf Gardens
Sheffield S2 4BB

Telephone 0114 275 7222 or 275 7444
Facsimile 0114 275 8866
email books@pickardcommunication.co.uk
www.pickardcommunication.co.uk

The Wednesday Boys

ACKNOWLEDGEMENTS

The Authors would like to offer heartfelt thanks to the countless individuals who have helped make this publication possible.

Our biggest thank you goes to fellow historian and Wednesday season ticket holder Michael Grayson who diligently checked our work, making corrections and even adding items where necessary.

Also thanks to Jason's partner Michelle Tilney who helped proof read the whole book and to John's son, Andrew, for helping his father search through Wednesday's archives and photocopy material during the early stages of the project. Also thanks to Jason's parents, Doreen and Ken, and John's wife, Jill, who spent hours helping him with letters to the ex players and daughter Jess, who gave invaluable support and help during the two and half years it has taken to bring this work to print.

Many, many more people have been only too happy to help and below is a small list, apologies to anybody we have missed:

Mike Davage (statistician extraordinaire), Jim Creasy, Garth Dykes, Keith Farnsworth, James Cockings (thanks for the texts), Steve Linley, Steve Clarke, Dave Green, Keith Howard, Terry Grocutt, Nick Johnson, Paul Joannou, Richard Lindsay, Clive Nicholson, Gary Chalk, Michael Dynes (thanks for finding Mirocevic), Stuart Basson, Tony Brown, Roger Walsh, Steve Wade, Leigh Edwards, John Quinn, Malcolm Brodie, Tony Bluff, Keith Rogers, Viv Brown, John Litster, Peter Cullen, Geoff Wilde, John Marsden, The staff of Sheffield Local Studies Library, Colin Jones, David McGregor, Jim McAllister, Elaine Murphy, Joan Smith, The Staff at Sheffield Wednesday (especially Andrea Neville) and at the training ground, the many players and players' relatives that helped with career details.

A big thank you also to Steve Chu, Sheffield Wednesday Communication Manager, and his colleagues Francis Hall and Mark Brailsford for their help and allowing the loan and permission to use some of Sheffield Wednesday's photographs.

Also to Denis Clarebrough, Craig Swift, Keith Littlewood and John Higginbotham and various players for the loan of photographs. Plus thanks to Steve Ellis, the official Wednesday photographer, for permission to use his photographs.

Finally, many thanks to Michael Liversidge and Chris Pickard at Pickard Communication who made this book become a reality.

DEDICATIONS:

To my wife Jill, son Andrew and daughter Jess and also to my Mother Mary
A special word of appreciation to the late Norma Lane,
whose support and help in tracking down ex-players was appreciated.

John Brodie

To my parents; Doreen and Ken,
my girlfriend Michelle
and her daughter Kayleigh Tilney.

Jason Dickinson

KEY TO STATISTICS:

Lge	-	Football League/Premier League
FAC	-	F.A.Cup
FLC	-	Football League Cup
Euro	-	FAIRS/UEFA/Intertoto Cup
Other	-	Full Members Cup/ Play Offs
N/C	-	Non Contract
Q/E	-	Quarter Ending
(T.)	-	Transfer Tribunal
Sun.	-	Sunday side
Amat.	-	Amateur
WWI/2	-	World War One/Two

All statistics up to and including 5th August 2005

Contents

Sheffield Wednesday players
alphabetically listed

ADAMS, Stephen 'Steve' 2005-

Born: 25 September 1980 Plymouth
(6ft, 11st 10lbs - 2004)
Debut: 19 March 2005
v Colchester United
League One Away
Total League
& Cup Appearances 8+2 Goals: 0

Career Details:

Plymouth Argyle	6 July	1999
WEDNESDAY	9 March	2005 £50,000

Like most managers, a change in employment usually results in a former player joining the manager's new club and Paul Sturrock was no exception. The signing of Kenwyne Jones and Chris Adamson - former Southampton & Plymouth players respectively - was then followed by the capture of defensive midfielder Steve Adams from the Devon club. The former Plymouth boys player had fallen out of favour at Home Park after having amassed 176 appearances in almost six years as a professional. During that period he was an invaluable member of the Argyle side that won the old Third Division in 2002 and then ran away with today's League One in 2004. The one-club man was known as a tactically aware player - who specialised in sitting in front of the back four to neutralise any attacking thrusts - and was a regular in the Championship for the Pilgrims prior to making the long move north. The Owls boss had given Adams his league debut and he jumped at the chance to sign a contract until June 2007 despite Wednesday being a division lower. Thankfully that situation was soon rectified as Wednesday earned promotion to the Championship with Adams amongst the matchday sixteen for the Cardiff Play Off Final.

ADAMSON, Christopher 'Chris' 2005

Born: 4 November 1978 Ashington
(5ft 11ins, 11st - 2004)
Debut: 12 March 2005
v Blackpool League One Home
Total League
& Cup Appearances: 1+1 Goals: 0

Career Details:

West Bromwich Albion	2 July	1997
IK Brage		1999 Loan
Mansfield Town	30 April	1999 Loan
Halifax Town	1 July	1999 Loan
Plymouth Argyle	10 January	2001 Loan
Halesowen Town	December	2002 Loan
St Patricks	April	2003 Free
Solihull Borough	20 January	2005 Free
WEDNESDAY	28 January	2005 Free
Released	30 June	2005
WEDNESDAY	11 July	2005

Much travelled goalkeeper who joined the Owls as back up to first choice David Lucas. His career had started at West Brom where he was mainly second choice, amassing just 14 senior appearances after having signed from trainee in July 1997. His league debut came in April 1998 and over the seasons that followed he was loaned to five different clubs including a spell in Swedish football before moving into Irish soccer near the end of the 2002-03 season. He remained in Eire football for eighteen months before returning to the UK to re-start his career in non-league football with West Midlands outfit Solihull Borough. However he played only a handful of games before Paul Sturrock signed Adamson for a second time; he had played under the Owls boss during his Plymouth days. An early injury to David Lucas handed Adamson his debut in the home win over Blackpool and he retained his place for the draw at Colchester United, impressing the travelling Owls fans with a competent display. However, the arrival of loanee Paul Gallacher then saw the Northeast born stopper drop to the subs bench where he remained for the rest of the season, warming the bench for the Play Off Final after Gallacher had returned to Carrow Road. Uniquely he was released by Wednesday only to be re-signed a few days later.

AGOGO, Manuel "Junior" 1996-2000

Born : 1 August 1979 Accra, Ghana
(6ft 1ins, 12st, 12lbs – 2000)
Debut: 9 August 1997
v Newcastle United
Premier League-Away
Last Appearance:
13 March 1999
v Leeds United
Premier League-Home
Total League
& Cup Appearances: 0+3 Goals: 0

Career Details:

Leary Constantine Club		
WEDNESDAY	8 October	1996
Oldham Athletic	13 July	1999 Loan
Chester City	2 September	1999 Loan
Chesterfield	12 November	1999 Loan
Lincoln City	17 December	1999 Loan
Contract cancelled	28 January	2000
Chicago Fire	24 February	2000
Colorado Rapids	April	2000
San Jose Earthquakes	12 June	2001 Player trade*
Queens Park Rangers	March	2002 Non Contract
Barnet	13 June	2002
Bristol Rovers	1 July	2003 £110,000

*Exchange for Chris Carrieri

Quicksilver forward Junior Agogo was born in North Africa but at the age of ten his family moved to London. It was while living in the Capital that Junior started to play competitive football and at the tender age of fourteen could be found playing in an open age men's league. This was where Owls youth coach Ricky Hill spotted his promise and invited Junior to Sheffield – in September 1996 – for a week's trial. He duly impressed the club's coaching staff and soon after put his signature to his first professional contract. The pacy forward quickly became established in the Owls Northern Intermediate side, scoring ten times in 29 games during the 1996-7 campaign, and duly made his first reserve team appearance in February 1997 at Oldham Athletic. He was a complete unknown to the majority of Owls fans when David Pleat handed him a surprise place on the substitutes bench at St. James' Park on the opening day of the following season. His Premiership debut duly came when replacing Guy Whittingham with just 13 minutes remaining but after his brief taste of top flight soccer Agogo dropped back into reserve and youth team football where he netted 8 times in 31 appearances as Wednesday's youngsters won the Northern Conference of the F.A. Premier Youth League.

However, with his opportunities seemingly limited at Hillsborough he spent the majority of what proved to be his final season at the club almost exclusively on loan at several sides in the lower divisions of English football. He made a big impression at Chester City, scoring six times in only ten games, but despite offers to drop down the divisions on a permanent basis he decided to emigrate to the United States – initially to pursue a modelling career through his mother's agency. The Owls agreed to cancel his contract in January 2000, although retaining his UK registration, and in March – after scoring three times in six pre season games – was awarded a pro contract by Major Soccer League club Chicago Fire. However before he could trade shoulders with Fire's other new signing Hristo Stoickhov he was almost immediately traded as a cost cutting measure to fellow MSL club Colorado Rapids for the 2000 season. Junior top scored for the Rapids with eleven goals in the 2001 season before in June 2001 he joined San Jose Earthquakes in a player exchange with Chris Carrieri.

He returned to England in the spring of 2002, joining Second Division club Queens Park Rangers on a non-contract basis where he appeared in two league games. However despite Rangers wanting to keep him Agogo decided to try his luck elsewhere and with help from his advisor Ricky Hill - Agogo's one time Youth coach at Hillsborough- he made the switch to Conference club Barnet in June 2002 to link up with ex-Owls manager Peter Shreeves. After finishing top scorer for Barnet in 2002/3 he moved back into the Football League in the summer of 2003, signing for Third Division side Bristol Rovers.

ALEXANDERSSON, Niclas Jens 1997-2000

Born : 29 December 1971
Halmstad, Sweden
(5ft, 9ins., 11st 7lbs – 2000)
Debut: 20 December 1997
v Chelsea
Premier League Home
Last Appearance: 14 May 2000
v Leicester City
Premier League Home
Total League
& Cup Appearances: 85 + 3 Goals: 12

Career Details:

Vessigbro BK		
Halmstads BK	June	1988
IFK Gothenburg	1 January	1996
WEDNESDAY	5 December	1997 £750,000
Everton	19 July	2000 £2.5m
West Ham United	11 September	2003 Loan
IFK Gothenburg	1 July	2004 Free

CAPS (@SWFC):
SWEDEN FULL (14) v Tunisia 10/02/99, v Luxembourg 27/03/99, v Poland 31/03/99, v Eire 28/04/99, v Austria 18/08/99, v Bulgaria 04/09/99, v Luxembourg 08/09/99, v Poland 09/10/99, v Italy 23/02/00, v Denmark 26/04/00, v Spain 03/06/00, v Belgium (EC) 10/06/00, v Turkey (EC) 15/06/00, v Italy (EC) 19/06/00

It was Ron Atkinson who first brought right-sided midfield attacker Niclas Alexandersson to English football, from his Swedish homeland in the winter of 1997. The winger was Big Ron's first signing during his second spell as Wednesday boss and like Roland Nilsson – his previous signing from Scandinavia – the Swede proved to be an excellent capture who thanks to a series of committed displays would quickly repay his bargain price tag and in the process endear himself to Owls fans.

Although virtually unknown to insular English supporters Alexandersson already boasted Champions League experience with crack Swedish outfit IFK and possessed over thirty full caps for his country. Alex had joined IFK on New Year's Day 1996 – for what was a Swedish domestic transfer record – and within a few months had a Championship medal in his grasp to complement the Swedish Cup winners medal earned a year earlier with his home town club Halmstad. In addition during his career in Sweden Niclas also won a multitude of International honours which included 15 U-21 caps, 12 Olympic appearances and a Swedish Player of the year award in 1995. On his arrival at Hillsborough Alexandersson made a great first impression – failing to taste defeat in the first seven games he started – but unfortunately received a serious knee injury in the January 1999 home game with Wimbledon that put him on the sidelines for almost six months. After successfully returning from that setback he went on to become one of the club's most consistent performers over the next two seasons and along with Alan Quinn was debatably the only bright spot during the relegation season of 1999-00 (for which Alex was named player of the season).

However, such was his form, combined with the financial problems that engulfed Wednesday after demotion, that it was obvious he would not be at Hillsborough much longer and after playing three times for Sweden in Euro 2000 it was Everton who captured his signature to make sure he remained a Premiership player. Unfortunately he joined a side that would struggle near the foot of the league in his first season which combined with a series of injuries meant his debut campaign on Merseyside was not a happy one for the affable Swede. He helped the Merseyside club to avoid the drop in 2001-2 before appearing in all of his country's four games in Korea/Japan 2002. Fell out of favour with Everton boss David Moyes early in the 2003-4 season, joining managerless Division One side West Ham on a month's loan.

ALJOFREE, Hasney 2004

Born: 11 July 1978 Manchester - (6ft 12st 2lbs – 2004)
Debut: 25 September 2004 v Wrexham League One Away
Last Appearance: 2 October 2004 v MK Dons League One Home
Total League & Cup Appearances: 3 Goals: 0

Career Details:

Bolton Wanderers	2 July	1996
Dundee United	9 June	2000 Free
Plymouth Argyle	30 August	2002 Free
WEDNESDAY	23 September	2004 Loan

It was somewhat ironic that defender Hasney Aljofree arrived on loan to help Wednesday during an injury crisis only to subsequently return to Home Park early after suffering a serious shoulder injury himself. The centre half was signed for a third time by Paul Sturrock, on the Scot's first day in charge at Hillsborough, and showed why the new Wednesday boss held him in such high esteem by performing admirably in his three games, showing terrific passing skills and a gritty determination – he played the latter stages of his final game without being able to use his left arm.

His career had started as a trainee at Bolton Wanderers but he failed to became established and after 22 games was signed by Sturrock for the first time when moving North to Dundee United. Two seasons later he followed his old boss to Plymouth Argyle and the utility defender with a great left foot would appear in 26 games as Argyle won the Second Division Championship in 2004. Aljofree – whose exotic surname came from his father who was born in Singapore but also had Saudi Arabian roots – missed the start of the 2004-5 season after undergoing a cartilage operation and moved to Wednesday to help regain fitness.

ALLAN, William 1891-97

Born: 1870 Montrose
(5ft 11ins., 12st - 1894)
Died: February 1948
Newcastle-upon-Tyne
Debut: 3 September 1892
v Notts County Division One Away
Last Appearance: 11 January 1896
v Blackburn Rovers Div One Home
Total League &
Cup Appearances: 118* Goals: 0
*** Also appeared in 7 Football Alliance League games**

Career Details:
Montrose Belmont, Aberdeen Orion, Victoria United

WEDNESDAY	December	1891
Victoria United		1897
Millwall Athletic	26 February	1898
Montrose	14 September	1899
Camelon	8 March	1900
East Stirlingshire	29 March	1900
Montrose	12 August	1901

Tall custodian William Allan joined the Owls from non-league Victoria United, making his Wednesday debut in the Football Alliance League at home to Lincoln City in December 1891.When Wednesday signed him it was discovered that the club did not have any boots big enough to fit the Scot so a local cobbler had to work through the night to make a pair so Allan could play the following day! The following season he was between the sticks for the club's opening game in the Football League – at Notts County in September 1892 – and was ever present for three seasons as Sheffield Wednesday adapted to life in their new surroundings. At his peak Allan was one of the country's best goalkeepers, his chief attributes being his coolness and the power and precision with which he could beat the ball away – it was said that Allan only "had to spread his feet out" to keep out any ground shot.

Amongst his more intimate Sheffield friends, Allan was known as "William the Silent"and he was probably speechless when he was forced into reserve team football in January 1896 when James Massey took his place! The reason, however, later came to light as in the home game with Burnley in early January 1896 he had taken a heavy knock to his leg but told no one and subsequently aggravated the injury a week later against Blackburn Rovers. When Allan reported for the following game he could hardly walk and therefore Massey- despite himself having a broken finger –

took his place. Allan's descent from first team football was indeed swift and at the start of the 1896/7 campaign he even lost his place in the reserve team and it was perhaps no surprise that he left Olive Grove before the season had reached its conclusion. After a short spell back in Scotland he joined Southern League side Millwall Athletic in 1897 – making his debut in March 1898 – and in total played 33 competitive games for The Lions before being released in the summer of 1899. His brother was transferred to Owlerton in 1895 but failed to appear in Wednesday's first eleven. After retiring from football he became a professional golfer and in the 1920s was employed as a bowls green keeper.

ALLEN, John William Alcroft "Jack" 1927-31

Born: 31 January 1903 Newburn, Newcastle
(5ft 9½ ins, 12st, 1927)
Died: 19 November 1957 Burnopfield, Co. Durham
Debut: 9 April 1927 v Aston Villa Division One Home
Last Appearance: 24 January 1931 v Barnsley F.A.C. Away
Total League & Cup Appearances: 114
Goals: 85

Career Details:

Prudhoe Castle (West Tyne)		
Leeds United	February	1922
Brentford	August	1924
WEDNESDAY	8 March	1927 £750
Newcastle United	8 June	1931 £3,500
Bristol Rovers	November	1934 £200
Gateshead	August	1935 £100
Ashington		1936

Prolific scorer Jack Allen is without doubt one of the greatest players to don the number 9 shirt in the club's long history. His arrival in 1927 was another vital piece of Bob Brown's jigsaw that would eventually see the Owls crowned Football League Champions twice within the next three seasons. Allen had started his career in local N-East soccer before signing professional forms at Leeds United, aged 19. He would start only two games for the West Yorkshire club before a move to London club Brentford where he would start to make his name. In three seasons at the Griffin Park club he netted 24 times in 54 league games – from inside forward - and this earned the Geordie a move into the big time at First Division Wednesday. Unfortunately for Allen his time at Brentford was spoilt by the abuse he received from the fans. It got so bad at one point that manager Harry Curtis would not play him in home games and even wrote to the local paper asking the supporters to give his player a fair crack of the whip!' Despite this Allen was a vital part of Brentford's memorable Cup run to the last sixteen in 1928 and the revenue that generated, along with the subsequent transfer fee paid by Wednesday, built a new stand at Griffin Park which was no doubt populated by those same fans who had criticised Allen!

Allen actually failed to score in his first five games at Wednesday and even found himself on the sidelines at the start of the 1927/8 campaign. However he was recalled – scoring on his comeback at home to Cardiff City in September 1927 – and would go on to score nine times in seventeen league games as Wednesday pulled off the "Great Escape". The confidence gained by the side from that remarkable escape from relegation continued into the following season and after Allen switched to Centre Forward – in October 1928 – both he and Wednesday never looked back with Jack scoring 35 times in just 37 games as the Owls won the title. He added an incredible 39 goals to his personal tally as the Owls walked away with the Championship in 1929/30 but incredibly the arrival of Jack Ball in the summer of 1930 meant Allen was dropped to the reserve team! The rigid 2-3-5 formation employed at that time in English football meant there was only one spot available in the first eleven for the traditional Number Nine and unbelievably – from a modern perspective – this meant the top scorer in arguably Wednesday's greatest ever side spent almost all of the 1930-1 season in the Central League team (he scored seven times in a Sheffield Invitation Cup tie versus Rotherham United Reserves in November 1930) and his apparent unhappiness was shown in February 1931 when he was placed on the transfer list. He netted 20 times for the free scoring reserves in that 1930-1 campaign but appeared in only eight first team games as Wednesday failed to complete a hat-trick of Championship successes.

Allen was an aggressive player, noted for his deadly left foot and exceptional pace, but there was not room for two big name Centre Forwards at Hillsborough and after almost re-joining Leeds United in March 1931 – only a knee injury curtailing a £3200 move – he returned to his roots in the summer of 1931 to join Newcastle United. After a difficult first few months on Tyneside, Allen recaptured his form and he went on to earn a winners medal when scoring both goals in the 1932 F.A.Cup Final as the Magpies beat Arsenal at Wembley – his first goal causing a furore of controversy as the cross from which he netted was judged by many to have already crossed the line before reaching Allen - it quickly went down in Wembley folklore as the "over the line incident". When he eventually left St. James' Park for Bristol Rovers his personal tally was an impressive 41 goals in just ninety games. Allen, whose brother Ralph played for several Football League clubs including Fulham, Charlton & Reading, stayed only briefly in the West Country and was soon heading back home to complete his playing career with short spells at Gateshead and then Ashington before hanging up his boots in February 1936. After retiring from football he became "Mien Host" at the Travellers Rest at Burnopfield.

ANDERSON, Vivian Alexander "Viv" 1991-93

Born: 29 July 1956 Nottingham
(6ft, 11st 1lbs – 1992)
Debut: 12 January 1991
v Hull City Division Two Away
Last Appearance: 15 May 1993
v Arsenal F.A.Cup Final
Total League &
Cup Appearances: 83+13 Goals: 13

Career Details:

Nottingham Forest	1 August	1974
Arsenal	3 August	1984 £250,000
Manchester United	9 July	1987 £250,000(T)
WEDNESDAY	9 January	1991 Free
Barnsley	3 June	1993 Free
Middlesbrough	23 July	1994 Free

Viv Anderson was nearing the end of a glittering, accolade filled career when Ron Atkinson brought his vast experience to Wednesday's promotion push from the old Second Division in 1991. Before moving to Hillsborough, Anderson had been mainly associated with his first club Nottingham Forest where he won the first of thirty full caps for England – he was the first coloured player to be capped by his country – and in all played in a mammoth 430 games for the City Ground club, netting 22 times. During his time in Nottingham the right back won League Championship, European Cup and League Cup winners medals as Forest, under the inspirational managership of Brian Clough, rose from the Second Division to become one of the finest teams in European football. Anderson was widely regarded as one of the finest defenders of his generation and after over a decade at Nottingham Forest – he had originally signed apprentice forms in November 1972 after being turned down by Sheffield United– he left for George Graham's Arsenal.

At Highbury he was part of the side that surprisingly beat Liverpool to win the 1987 League Cup but in the summer that followed Viv was again on his travels as Alex Ferguson took him to Manchester United for a transfer tribunal agreed fee of a paltry £1/4m. In his first season at Old Trafford he helped United to runners-up spot behind Champions Liverpool and a year later earned his only F.A.Cup winners medal despite not taking part in the Final replay victory over Crystal Palace. By this time Anderson was effectively just a squad player at United and in January 1991 Ferguson allowed him to leave on a free transfer to join promotion-chasing Wednesday. His transfer was thought by many to be a short term acquisition but the fiercely competitive Anderson stayed over two years at Wednesday, giving the club sterling service, and on many occasions led from the back as captain. He initially replaced the stricken Roland Nilsson at right back but had to sit out the League Cup Final win over Manchester United as he was cup-tied, having played for the Red Devils in an early round. Anderson had spent his entire career at right back but in the two seasons that followed he proved a more than capable centre-half and in fact captained the Owls from that position at Wembley in both the League & F.A.Cup Finals of 1993.

The tall, commanding player also had the useful knack of weighing in with the odd important goal and in all he was a vital player in what was arguably the club's best post-war side. Anderson's attitude on the pitch marked him out as obvious managerial material and it was no surprise when he left – along with Danny Wilson – to become player-manager at neighbours Barnsley in the summer of 1993. It was therefore a surprise to many that he experienced a poor first season at Oakwell and only a year after joining he resigned to become assistant manager to ex-team mate Bryan Robson at Middlesbrough. Despite retiring from playing in 1994 Anderson was still officially registered as a player and during the season that followed he had to turn out twice for Boro as an emergency centre-half as injuries and suspensions took their toll. However, after his side won promotion back to the Premier League at the end of the season he finally retired from playing, bringing the curtain down on a professional playing career of over twenty years. Anderson was awarded the MBE in January 2000 but along with Robson he left Boro in June 2001 after Terry Venables had been brought into the club to help stave off relegation. He now runs a sports travel agency while also acting as a Goodwill ambassador for the Football Association.

ANSTISS, Henry Augustus "Harry" 1926-27

Born: 22 August 1899 Hampstead
(5ft 9ins, 11st 7lbs – 1926)
Died: 9 March 1964 Isleworth
Debut: 28 August 1926
v Sheffield United Div One Home
Last Appearance:
12 February 1927 v Huddersfield Town
Division One Home
Total League &
Cup Appearances: 12 Goals: 5

Career Details:

Hammersmith Athletic		
Brentford	August	1920 Amateur
Brentford	November	1920 Professional
Millwall	May	1922 £650
Watford	June	1923 £150
Rochdale	June	1924 Free
WEDNESDAY	6 July	1926 £1000
Port Vale	18 February	1927 Fee/ Player exchange
Swansea Town	May	1931
Crewe Alexandra	July	1933
Gillingham	July	1934
Tunbridge Wells Rngs	September	1935
Cray Wanderers	January	1937

Inside forward Harry Anstiss enjoyed a long and varied career that spanned almost all of the inter-war period and encompassed eleven different sides from Division One down to non-league football. As a youngster he took part in Schoolboy International trials but was found to be nine days too old to play for his Country! His early playing career was spent in non-league football after having survived the battle of Jutland in 1916 – when British forces engaged the German sea fleet. Anstiss signed amateur forms for Brentford soon after the end of the hostilities and was quickly elevated to professional status by the Griffin Park club.

In two seasons Anstiss netted a superb 19 times in just 42 league games, this form prompting a "big money" move to London neighbours Millwall where he would stay for just one season, scoring only three times in 21 league and cup games. Incidentally his move across London, along with Brentford team mates Alf Amos and George Pither, took place in order to help the Griffin Park club stave off bankruptcy! Another brief spell at Watford followed (22 games, 5 goals) before he found a niche at Division Three (North) side Rochdale, where in two seasons he netted 43 times in just 76 games. This prolific scoring, albeit at a lower grade club, persuaded Owls boss Bob Brown to take a chance and he gave the Londoner his first taste of top flight football. His debut came in the cauldron that is a Sheffield derby and he started eleven of the opening thirteen games in 1926-7 before eventually losing his place. After several months of reserve team football he made a goal scoring comeback at Huddersfield Town in February 1927, a week after hitting a hat-trick for the reserves, but within a week he had departed Hillsborough for Vale Park with Port Vale's highly rated Alf Strange travelling in the opposite direction.

His spell at Wednesday would prove to be his only taste of Division One football as he spent five seasons in the Potteries, netting 38 times in 109 league games, winning a Division Three (North) Championship medal in 1930. A combined total of eighteen league goals in 94 games for three further clubs brought the curtain down on his professional career before his playing days finished where they had started – in non league soccer.

ANTHONY, G. "Nudger" 1874-82

Born:
Debut: 5 November 1881
v Providence F.A.Cup Away
Last Appearance: 2 December 1882
v Lockwood Brothers
F.A.Cup Away
Total League &
Cup Appearances: 5 Goals: 3

Career Details:

Local	
WEDNESDAY	1874
Local	1883

Forward Nudger Anthony was a Wednesday hero of the Victorian age, appearing in many of the early games in the Sheffield district that helped to advance the cause of Association football. One of those early games of note came in October 1879 when the football loving public were amazed by the sight of floodlight football. The progressive Sheffield association had arranged for the experimental game to take place at Bramall Lane and erected two high-powered lights behind each goal. The Sheffield fans loved the novelty and saw the Blues – containing Wednesday heroes of old such as Bob Gregory & William Stacey – beat Anthony's Reds which boasted Owls legend Billy Mosforth in their ranks. Anthony also played in several early Sheffield v Glasgow games as well as for the infamous Zulu team (a side that started out life playing a benefit game for dependants of those killed in the Zulu War but was so successful that is was eventually banned by the Sheffield F.A. after news reached them that several players were receiving remuneration for their services). The attacker first appeared in an Owls shirt in the 1870s with his competitive debut coming at Sheffield club Providence in the F.A.Cup, netting the second goal in a 2-0 win for Wednesday. He went onto to appear in four more F.A.Cup ties – netting in the 12-2 Bramall Lane win over Spilsby in November 1882 – before making a goal scoring final appearance in the 6-0 Cup win at Lockwood Brothers a month later. The season of 1882-3 proved to be his final one on the Owls books, his farewell appearance coming in April 1883 against a local team called Surrey FC. One curiosity surrounding Anthony related to his debut game when he netted but actually did not score! His second half shot was actually heading goalwards but was then handled by a defender only for the referee to give the goal regardless!

ANTOINE-CURIER, Mickael 2003

Born: 5 March 1983 Orsay, France
(6ft, 12st 4lbs – 2003)
Only Appearance: 22 Nov 2003 v Luton Town Division Two Home
Total League & Cup Appearances: 0+1 Goals: 0

Career Details:

Nice		
Paris St.Germain		
Nancy		
Preston North End	29 November	2000 Free
Nottingham Forest	22 June	2001 Free
Mansfield Town	7 February	2003 Trial
Brentford	10 March	2003 2-month loan
Released	30 June	2003
Oldham Athletic	8 August	2003 Free
Kidderminster Harr's	19 September	2003 N/C
Rochdale	23 September	2003 N/C
Released	17 November	2003
WEDNESDAY	21 November	2003 N/C
Released	15 December	2003
Notts County	19 February	2004 1-month contract
Released	10 March	2004
Grimsby Town	19 March	2004 Free
Released	30 June	2004
SK Vard Haugesund	July	2004 Free

Forward who arrived on trial in November 2003 to boost an Owls squad that was depleted by injury and suspension. His debut came in a reserve game at Bramall Lane where the Frenchman had a mixed time, seeing his late penalty saved and having a goal disallowed. It was therefore a surprise when Chris Turner not only signed the youngster on non-contract terms - just twenty-four hours before the home game with Luton Town – but also gave him a place on the subs bench. The ex-France U-18 International duly entered the fray late in the game but made little impression and soon dropped out of the matchday sixteen and after a handful of second team games was released.

His brief appearance at Wednesday was another blow for the pacy and gangly attacker whose career had never really taken off since moving into English football. He had originally started his career in French soccer – he was born 25 miles South-West of Paris – before moving across the English Channel to join Preston North End on a free transfer. However he failed to make a senior appearance for the Lancashire club and hopes of a change in fortunes at Nottingham Forest were soon dashed as despite being a reserve team regular he also failed to make a first team appearance – the closest being an unused sub in a League Cup tie versus Kidderminster Harriers. After finally making his league debut while on loan at Brentford, Antoine-Curier looked to have finally made an impact on the English game when scoring three times in eleven games. Unfortunately he could not replicate that breakthrough at Forest and was released in the summer of 2003. This left the forward in search of an employer and over the first half of the 2003-4 season he appeared for four different league sides - scoring against Wednesday in August for Oldham Athletic - which included a 27 minute sub appearance for Kidderminster against Lincoln City. After leaving Hillsborough he spent a brief time at Notts County before his short-term deal was cancelled after a breach of club discipline. He was then on Grimsby Town's books before signing for Haaugesund, who play in the second tier of Norwegian football. Incidentally he created a record in the 2003-04 season as no player in the history of English League football has played for six different sides in the same domestic campaign.

ARANALDE, Zigor 2005

Born: 28 February 1973 Ibazza, Guipuzcoa, Spain
(6ft 1ins, 13st 5lbs - 2005)
Debut: 29 March 2005
v Huddersfield Town
League One Away
Last Appearance: 2 April 2005
v Tranmere Rovers
League One Home
Total League
& Cup Appearances: 1+1 Goals: 0

Career Details:

SD Eibar		1990
Merbella		1993
Seville		1995
Albacete		1996
CD Logrones	1 August	1999
Walsall	11 August	2000
Contract cancelled	23 March	2005
WEDNESDAY	24 March	2005 Free
Released	30 June	2005
Carlisle United	5 July	2005

When Zigor Aranalde joined the Owls on a short-term contract he became the first Spanish player to sign for the club in their long history. He had previously spent almost five seasons at fellow League One club Walsall before his contract was cancelled by mutual consent just 24 hours before moving to Hillsborough. During his time at the Saddlers he was mainly utilised at left back and it was in this position that he made his Owls debut in the defeat at Huddersfield Town. His rival for the left back position, Paul Heckingbottom, was then rested for the home game with Tranmere Rovers just four days later and Aranalde made his full debut. However his hopes of impressing were dashed when he was controversially sent off early in the second half and the subsequent suspension meant he was a peripheral figure as Wednesday enjoyed play off success.

ARMITAGE, Harold A. "Harry" 1920-22

Born: 16 August 1901 Sheffield
(5ft $7^1/_2$ ins, 11st 7lbs – 1921)
Died: 1973 Sheffield
Debut: 2 May 1921
v Bristol City Division Two Home
Last Appearance: 18 March 1922
v Port Vale Division Two Away
Total League &
Cup Appearances: 3 Goals: 0

Career Details:

Hathersage		1919
WEDNESDAY	June	1920 Free
Bristol Rovers	19 May	1922 Free
Lincoln City	11 August	1926 Player exchange
Scarborough Town	August	1927

Young full back Harold Armitage arrived at Hillsborough in the summer of 1920. He brought with him a good reputation in local football, having just won the Sheffield Amateur league with Hathersage FC and boasting the ability to play in both full back positions. However, despite the Owls fortunes being at a low ebb – following the disastrous relegation season of 1919-20 – Harry struggled to win a place in the Owls Division Two side and had to be content with a regular place in Wednesday's Midland League side. Whilst playing for the second string he won a Sheffield Challenge Cup winners medal in March 1921 when Barnsley reserves were beaten 2-0 at Bramall Lane. His chance at first team level came at the end of that season, appearing in the final two games of the campaign, but at the beginning of the 1921-2 season found himself back in the reserves where he would remain for the remainder of his Owls career. The Sheffielder did make a further solitary first team appearance before in May 1922 he moved to the West Country to sign for Third Division (South) club Bristol Rovers. He came to the fore at Rovers and the tough tackling and fearless defender was a regular for four seasons, captaining the Pirates in 1925-6, totalling 122 appearances before moving back up North to sign for Lincoln City. Whilst in Bristol he had also played cricket for Stapleton CC in the summer of 1923. His move to Sincil Bank saw Josiah Barrett travel in the opposite direction but for the majority of his spell at City Armitage found himself a deputy to Bissett and appeared in only nine games for The Imps before leaving league soccer to sign for non-leaguers Scarborough Town.

ARMITAGE, Leonard 'Len' 1914-20

Born: 20 October 1899 Sheffield
(5ft 9½ ins, 11st 7lbs – 1920)
Died: 1972 Wortley, Sheffield
Debut: 19 September 1919
v Notts County Division One Away
Last Appearance: 18 October 1919
v Blackburn Rovers Div. One Away
Total League
& Cup Appearances: 3* Goals: 0
***Also appeared in**
15 Wartime games, scoring 6 goals

Career Details:

Sheffield Forge and Rolling Mills		
Walkley Amateurs		
Wadsley Bridge		
WEDNESDAY	March	1914
Leeds United	June	1920
Wigan	May	1923
Stoke	March	1924
Rhyl Athletic	October	1932
Port Vale	November	1932 Free

Whole hearted centre-forward Len Armitage was a star of schoolboy football, helping Sheffield boys win the English Schools Trophy in 1914, and looked set to follow in the footsteps of his famous grandad, Tom, who not only played cricket for Yorkshire but was in the first team ever to be capped at Test level for England, during the inaugural Ashes tour to Australia in 1876. His outstanding form in schoolboy football meant several clubs were chasing his signature but he rejected all other advances to sign for his hometown club Sheffield Wednesday in 1914. His first senior outing came in November 1917 at home to Barnsley and after sitting out the 1918-19 season he re-appeared at first team level early in the following season, playing three times but failing to find the net. This was after Lincoln City signed him in August 1919 without the Owls knowledge and the transfer was subsequently cancelled after Wednesday appealed to the league management committee. The Owls were experiencing one of their worst seasons in their history – recording only seven wins as they finished adrift at the foot of the table – and unfortunately for Armitage he became another statistic as a multitude of forwards were tried in a desperate attempt to stop the losing run.

The Owls were in no position to persevere with youngsters so it was quickly back into the reserves for Len and at the end of the season he was one of an astonishing 21 players who were released or transferred by Wednesday as they cleared the decks for a season in Division Two. The attacker's destination was league new boys Leeds United and although he failed to make the team for United's opening league game he did have the distinction of netting the new club's first goal in league football, a week later at Elland Road against South Shields. After 14 goals in 53 appearances for the West-Yorkshire club Armitage had a brief spell at Division Three (North) side Wigan Boro where the 'strong as a bull' and fearless forward netted a terrific 21 goals in just 28 league games – incidentally his time in Lancashire was tinged with tragedy as in December 1923 his brother Tom was injured while playing a reserve team game for Wednesday at Hillsborough and five days later he died in hospital, aged just 24.

This scoring form preceded a move to the Potteries and Stoke FC where Len would enjoy the best days of his career, remaining at the Victoria Ground for almost eight years. Stoke were a second division side when Len joined but the addition of the suffix "City" in 1925 proved unlucky as the newly named Stoke City suffered immediate relegation! However, with Armitage now a regular City immediately bounced back, winning the Division Three (North) title and by the time Len left the Potteries he had made 200 appearances, scoring 19 times – the relatively low goal tally being attributed to the fact that later in his career Armitage was more at home at centre-half than centre-forward. His form saw him tour South Africa in 1929 with an F.A.XI but after leaving Stoke – who kept his league registration – he played briefly at non-league outfit Rhyl Athletic. However, he could not stay away from the Potteries for too long and just four months after leaving City he returned….to sign for arch rivals Port Vale! The now rugged centre-half played 13 times for Vale but after losing his place through a knee injury in March 1933 he could not fight his way back into the first eleven and was released in May 1934.

ARMSTRONG, Steven Craig 2002-05

Born: 23 May 1975 South Shields
(5ft 11ins, 12st 10lbs – 2002)
Debut: 16 February 2002
v Watford
Division One Home
Last Appearance:
14 February 2004
v Hartlepool United
Div Two Home
Total League
& Cup Appearances: 34+6 Goals: 1

Career Details:

Nottingham Forest	2 June	1992 Trainee
Burnley	29 December	1994 Loan
Bristol Rovers	8 January	1996 Loan
Bristol Rovers	28 March	1996 Loan
Gillingham	18 October	1996 Loan
Watford	24 January	1997 Loan
Watford	14 March	1997 Loan
Huddersfield Town	26 February	1999 £750,000
WEDNESDAY	15 February	2002 £100,000
Grimsby Town	23 February	2004 Loan
Contract cancelled	18 January	2005
Bradford City	20 January	2005
Notts County	July	2005 Trial
Cheltenham Town	July	2005

Hard running left sided midfielder signed by Terry Yorath early in 2002 to help stiffen up the central area as Wednesday faced another fight to avoid the drop into Division Two. Made his debut at left back but after only eight games picked up an injury that saw him miss the end of the season. In the following season he struggled to hold down a regular place, despite netting his first goal for the club at home to Rotherham United in August 2002, and figured only briefly under the managerial reign of Chris Turner as a persistent calf injury left him on the sidelines. Under new manager Paul Sturrock he fared little better and after failing to play a first team game for almost a year his contract was cancelled by mutual consent, ending a disappointing stay at Hillsborough.

The North East born player had started his career as a trainee at Nottingham Forest where in his first five years as a professional he made only a handful of appearances and spent several spells out on loan to various Football League clubs. Finally in 1997-8 Craig broke into the Forest first eleven, appearing mainly at left back in a total of 26 league and cup games, and such was his impressive form that Dave Bassett picked him for the Nationwide League U-21 side that faced their Italian counterparts at Charlton in March 1998. He won a first Division Championship medal as Forest returned to the Premiership but unfortunately he found his status revert back to "squad member" in the following campaign and despite winning a call up the England U-21 side as an over age player could not regain a regular first team spot as Forest struggled in the top flight.

He eventually became First Division Huddersfield Town's most expensive defender when he moved to Yorkshire for a sizeable fee in February 1999 after only 49 games and two goals in a seven-year stay at the City Ground. He immediately impressed for the Terriers and was a mainstay in 1999-0 as Steve Bruce's side made a push for the play-offs. The burly Armstrong's decisive tackling was a strong part of his game and he combined this with quality passing and effective headwork when he was switched to centre half from left back late in the season. The Terriers suffered a shock last day relegation in 2001 and in Division Two Armstrong mainly filled a position on the left side of midfield but saw his season interrupted for three months by a severe ankle injury. Returned to the fold and won several man of the match honours before moving to Hillsborough for a cut-price fee in 2002.

ARMSTRONG, Harold A. 1907-09

Born: 1885
(5ft 7ins, 10st 7lbs – 1907)
Debut: 26 October 1907
v Liverpool
Division One Away
Last Appearance: 26 September 1908
v Newcastle United
Div One Home
Total League
& Cup Appearances: 6 Goals: 0

Career Details:

Southwick Club		
WEDNESDAY	Apr	1907
Released		1909

Right winger Harry Armstrong was signed from Sunderland non league club Southwick in the summer of 1907, joining a long line of North-East players to join Wednesday from the area. Future Owls boss Bob Brown was the Owls scout in the region at the times and it's probable his recommendation brought the 21 year-old wing man to Sheffield. In his first season at Wednesday Harry was a mainstay of the club's reserve side who were crowned Midland League Champions – Armstrong netting thirteen times as the second string scored 109 times in just 38 games!

His sole first team start in 1907-8 came in a 3-0 loss at Liverpool but his fortunes took a decided upturn at the start of the following campaign as Harry started the first five games in which the Owls were unbeaten, winning three. However, that was as good as it got for Armstrong as Billy Lloyd took his place for the 3-0 loss at Sunderland and he failed to appear for the club's first eleven again. It was therefore back to the reserves for Armstrong and he scored one further goal in Midland League football before drifting out of senior football in 1909.

ARMSTRONG, Joseph Williams 'Joe' 1921

Born: 10 October 1892 Blaydon, Tyne & Wear
(5ft 8ins, 11st 7lbs – 1921)
Died: 14 May 1966 Southwick, Cosham
Debut: 3 September 1921
v Barnsley
Division Two Away
Last Appearance: 5 November 1921
v Fulham
Division Two Home
Total League
& Cup Appearances: 7 Goals: 0

Career Details:

Hedgefield		
Scotswood	May	1913
Portsmouth	24 December	1913
WEDNESDAY	20 May	1921
Norwich City	28 Nov.	1921*
Clapton Orient	September	1922 Trial
Bournemouth & Boscombe	19 June	1923
Portsmouth Trams	May	1924

*Part of deal that brought George Gray to Hillsborough

Joe Armstrong was a player who was signed twice by Wednesday's legendary manager Bob Brown. He first secured the forward's signature when secretary-manager at Southern League Portsmouth who Armstrong joined from North East junior football. He was signed on Christmas Eve, making his debut two days later in the Boxing Day derby game at close rivals Southampton, and would give Pompey good service in an eight year stay that was interrupted by the horrors of World War One. The Blaydon born attacker served in the Army in The Great War, alongside two of his four brothers, and was injured in the hand although he was the lucky one as one brother was gassed and the other was killed in the fighting.

Armstrong played Southern League football for the South Coast club immediately before and after the hostilities, winning a Division One Championship medal in 1920 - in Portsmouth's final season as a non-league club before the whole of the Southern League Division One effectively became the new League Division Three (South).

Armstrong, who was primarily an inside right but was equally at home at centre-forward, netted 15 times in 32 games in that Championship winning season while in Portsmouth's debut season of league soccer he appeared 13 times, scoring twice, before losing his first team place just before Christmas 1920. By now Bob Brown had returned North to take over the managerial reigns at Hillsborough and Armstrong was soon to follow, along with Emil Thompson, in May 1921. The Owls were still recovering from a disastrous first season after the War and Brown was initially trying to steady the ship with what was almost a completely new set of players. Many players were signed with varying degrees of success and Armstrong found it difficult to make the step up to Division Two football after having spent the majority of his playing career in non-league football. He would play only seven times for the Owls first team, losing his place to James McIntyre and soon after was involved in a deal that brought George Gray to Hillsborough with Armstrong returning South to sign for Division Three (South) Norwich City.

He initially joined City on loan until the end of the season, at which point Wednesday granted him a free transfer, completing the move in April 1922. His stay in Norfolk was also brief as after just 22 appearances (8 goals) he was released, to be followed by an unsuccessful trial at Clapton Orient. He came back into league soccer thanks to ex-Wednesday goalkeeper Harry Kinghorn who signed him for Bournemouth where his tenure was again somewhat brief, lasting only a season, as a poor scoring rate of only two goals in 29 league games led almost inevitably to his release in May 1924. It was at this point Joe – whose unique middle name was actually his mother's maiden name - said goodbye to professional football, gaining employment at Portsmouth trams. He did not however hang up his boots totally as he played regularly for the works side and stayed with the company until ill health eventually forced his retirement.

ASHLEY, John Albert "Jack" 1935-45

Born: 13 October 1912 Clowne
(5ft 11ins, 12st – 1935)
Died: 25 December 1992
Debut: 18 April 1936
v Stoke City Division One Away
Last Appearance: 29 April 1939
v Tottenham H. Div Two Home
Total League
& Cup Appearances: 117* Goals: 3
***Also appeared in**
125 Wartime games, scoring 2 goals

Career Details:

Clowne Miners Welfare		
Markham Colliery		
Shirebrook	December	1926
Clowne Miners Welfare		1931
Notts County		1931 Trial
Shirebrook		1932 Amateur
Bolsover Colliery		1933
Mansfield Town	June	1933 (Amateur Feb 33)
WEDNESDAY	3 September	1935 £1,200

Before arriving at Hillsborough, right back John Ashley had played for many years in Derbyshire non-league soccer and had failed to impress in a short trial period at Notts County. However, after signing professional forms at Mansfield Town his career started to blossom and his excellent form for the Stags meant that after 74 League and Cup games he left for a higher grade of football with Wednesday and Wolverhampton Wanderers the clubs chasing his signature. Thankfully it was Wednesday boss Billy Walker who secured Ashley's services, the Owls paying Town what at the time was a record fee for Mansfield of £1,200.

Ashley would actually make his league debut for Wednesday at left back and even appeared at centre-forward in his debut season but eventually settled into the right back spot, competing with Joe Nibloe for the position. His debut for the Owls first eleven was certainly a baptism of fire as he was called upon to mark the legendary winger Stanley Matthews but Albert was outstanding as Wednesday beat Stoke 3-0 to preserve their first division status. He played the final ten games of the 1936-7 season in that right back role – after having earlier netted three times in consecutive games when again being deployed as an emergency centre-forward – and would not be dislodged for the remainder of the pre War period. Ashley was equally adept with both feet - said to "work the offside trap well"- and he missed only one of the 50 league and cup games played by Wednesday in 1938-9 as they agonisingly missed out on promotion to Division One on goal average to neighbours United.

He appeared in the opening three league games of the abandoned 1939-40 season and for the remainder of the War continued to appear regularly for the Owls in regional soccer – the definite highlight being his appearance in the 1943 War Cup Final against Blackpool. During the hostilities Ashley worked as a miner in the Worksop area and after hanging up his boots in 1945 he continued with this occupation until his retirement. The name of John Ashley however continued to be seen in league football as his nephew of the same name went on to play for both York City and Chesterfield. Incidentally during his time in football Ashley was known as either Jack, Albert or even Jumbo – reason for the latter nickname being a mystery!

ATHERTON, Peter 1994-2000

Born: 6 April 1970 Orrell
(5ft 11ins, 13st 12lbs – 1997)
Debut: 20 August 1994
v Tottenham Hotspur
Premier League Home
Last Appearance: 14 May 2000
v Leicester City
Premier Lge Home
Total League
& Cup Appearances: 251 Goals: 9

Career Details:

Wigan Athletic	12 February	1988
Coventry City	23 August	1991 £329,000
WEDNESDAY	3 June	1994 £800,000 (T)
Bradford City	4 July	2000 Bosman Free
Birmingham City	12 February	2001 3-months Loan
Halifax Town	July	2005

If you were to ask any fan at the end of the 1990s which player held the record for the most Premier League appearances then it is unlikely the name of Peter Atherton would have readily come to mind. However he did in fact hold the record after playing 114 times in the top flight for Coventry City and adding over 200 games to that tally while at Hillsborough.

Atherton had started his career at his local club Wigan, signing apprentice forms after impressing for both Wigan and England schoolboys, and made his league debut in October 1987 still four months before turning professional. He quickly became established in the Latics first eleven, playing a defensive midfield role, and his form in two F.A.Cup ties against Coventry City indirectly led to his move into the Premier League. The Sky Blues manager Terry Butcher was highly impressed with Atherton in those Cup ties and tried on several occasions to secure his signature before finally succeeding in the summer of 1991. His new signing had been named player of the year for two years running prior to his Highfield Road transfer and he quickly became a mainstay of the City team, winning his sole England U-21 cap in 1992 versus Turkey. Atherton was named player of the season in 1993 but a year later was out of contract and Wednesday boss Trevor Francis swooped to secure his signature, effectively as a direct replacement for the sadly departed Roland Nilsson.

However the signing of Dan Petrescu just before the season's kick off meant that Atherton would start his Owls career in the unfamiliar position of centre-half. It was David Pleat who switched Athers back to right back and he remained there until eventually metamorphosing into a deep lying defensive midfielder. It was in this position that Atherton captained the club for four seasons and arguably produced his most consistent form. He revelled in the tough tackling defensive role and although a somewhat unspectacular performer he was certainly missed on the very rare occasions when he was absent. During his final season of 1999-00, when the Owls suffered relegation from the Premier League, Atherton reverted back to centre half but after a turbulent season he refused Wednesday's offer of a new contract when his old one expired on 30th June 2000. He therefore became a free agent and just three days later moved back into the Premier League to sign for Bradford City on a Bosman free transfer.

He appeared at both right-back and centre-half for The Bantams during his first season but after being a regular in the side he found himself suddenly out of favour in February 2001 following the arrival of new manager Jim Jefferies. Within two days of being dropped to the subs bench he was on his way out of Valley Parade, on loan to Trevor Francis's Birmingham City until the end of the season. Under his old Wednesday manager Atherton played ten league games, helping City to the Division One play-offs where he played in both semi-final ties against Preston, only being denied a Final place when City conceded an agonising injury time goal in the second leg at Deepdale.

He returned to Bradford in the summer of 2001 but then experienced an unaccustomed injury prone season as persistent knee problems meant Atherton made just one solitary appearance. He returned to fitness late in 2002 to regain his first team spot under new manager Nicky Law.

ATKINSON, Dalian Robert 1989-90

Born: 21 March 1968 Shrewsbury
(6ft 1ins, 12st 10lbs – 1990)
Debut: 19 August 1989
v Norwich City
Division One Home
Last Appearance: 5 May 1990
v Nottingham Forest
Division One Home
Total League
& Cup Appearances: 45 Goals: 15

Career Details:

Ipswich Town	4 June	1985
WEDNESDAY	7 June	1989 £450,000
Real Sociedad	1 August	1990 £1.75m
Aston Villa	11 July	1991 £1.6m
Fenerbahce	1 August	1995 £500,000 ($650,000)
Manchester City	1 August	1996 7-day trial
Metz	October	1996 Trial
Manchester City	19 March	1997 Free (Loan 21/01/97)
Everton	October	1997 Trial
Sheffield United	February	1998 Trial
Barnsley	26 August	1998 Trial
Al Ittihad	December	1998
Taejon Citizen	April	2001 Loan
Chonbuk Hyundai Motors		2001

CAPS (@SWFC) England "B"(1) v Eire 27/03/90

Striker Dalian Atkinson exploded onto the Hillsborough scene in Ron Atkinson's first full season as manager. The strong, bustling and pacy forward arrived as a virtual unknown to Owls fans but his rocket like shooting soon endeared him to the Hillsborough faithful – a hat-trick in the club record 8-0 league cup romp at Aldershot perhaps the highlight - as he forged a partnership with David Hirst. Unfortunately the duo could not find the net frequently enough to save the Owls from relegation in his first season and when Spanish side Real Sociedad offered Wednesday a club record £1.75m for his services Big Ron took the money and re-invested with the purchases of Danny Wilson and Paul Williams.

Atkinson's record of one goal in every three games won him England "B" honours during his sole season at Sheffield 6 and it was a shock to many supporters when his namesake sold him following the Owls demotion. However the Atkinsons would not be apart for long as after a successful one-year stay in Spain – scoring 12 times in 30 appearances - Dalian returned to England to sign for an Aston Villa side who had just appointed Ron as manager following his acrimonious departure from Wednesday. Dalian – who had started his career as a trainee at Ipswich Town and scored 21 times in 68 games for the Tractor Boys - made his Villa debut on a highly charged afternoon at Hillsborough when the fixture computer brought his new side to his old club on the opening day of the new campaign. Unfortunately for Owls fans it was the old boys who had the last laugh as a goal from Atkinson helped the visitors to come from 2-0 down to win 3-2 to the dismay of angry home fans.

He could not quite recapture his Hillsborough form in his time at Villa Park, although he did score 36 times in 114 league and cup games and won a League winners medal in 1994 , with injuries and loss of form blighting what proved to be his final season. In 1994 he decided to try his luck abroad, signing for Turkish club Fenerbache, but he was reported to be badly out of shape on his arrival in Turkey and criticism only waned briefly when he scored a dramatic hat-trick in the highly charged local derby against arch rivals Galatasaray. He went on to net a respectable 10 times as Fenerbache lifted the League Championship but his Turkish adventure turned sour in his second season as he fell into dispute with the club – not making a single appearance in 1996-7 - and even Aston Villa had to call in FIFA in April 1997 to force the Turks to pay the outstanding $400,000 from Atkinson's fee of $650,000. When his contract expired he spent several unsuccessful trial periods at a variety of clubs both in England – playing league football during a brief spell at Manchester City - and on Continental Europe. Finally he found a home in the unlikely surroundings of Middle East football, signing for Saudi Arabian club Al Ittihad in 1998, winning the Asian and Saudi Cup in 1999 with his new side. A very short spell on loan in South Korea's K-League followed as despite scoring in what proved to be his only game his off the field antics meant he was sent back by Taejon. He would later return in 2001 to play seven times, scoring once for fellow South Korean side Chonbuk, before returning home to retire from senior football.

AVEYARD, Walter 1938-47

Born:11 June 1918 Hemsworth
(5ft $10^{1}/_{2}$ ins, 10st 10lbs – 1938)
Died: 16 July 1985 Blackpool
Debut: 5 January 1946
v Mansfield Town
F.A.Cup Away
Last Appearance: 5 October 1946
v Bradford Park Avenue
Division Two Home
Total League
& Cup Appearances: 10* Goals: 5
***Also appeared in 1 Wartime game**

Career Details:

Denaby United		
WEDNESDAY	17 October	1938 (Amat: 25/08/38)
Birmingham City	14 April	1947 £1,000
Port Vale	17 June	1948
Accrington Stanley	1 March	1952
Released	1 May	1953

Inside forward Walter Aveyard was one of hundreds of players who would lose the best years of their playing career to World War. In Aveyard's case it was the 1939-45 conflict that interrupted his career and unlike many of his contemporaries he did not even kick a ball once during the hostilities whilst serving throughout the conflict as a Company Sergeant Major in the A.P.T.C. (Army) and also being on active duty in the extreme heat of Burma.

The Owls had brought him from local non-league football just before the war and he would become a regular for the club's reserve side, making his debut on 22nd October 1938 in the second team's draw at Preston North End. He was primarily thought of as an inside-forward but in almost every game he played for Wednesday it was at centre-forward that Walter was deployed and he finished the 1938-9 season as joint top scorer for the reserves - with 13 goals – after an almost ever present run from his debut until the end of the season. The Yorkshire born attacker returned to Hillsborough in the autumn of 1945 and netted five times for the reserves as they won the Central league for the second time in their history, netting an amazing 112 goals on the way to the title! His competitive first team bow would also take place in that season as he was drafted in for the Third Round Cup tie at minnows Mansfield Town. The first leg at Field Mill finished goalless -the Cup was played over two legs for the first and only time in 1946 – but Aveyard netted in the 5-0 second leg romp at Hillsborough and also scored in the 5-1 home win over York City in the next round. Strangely although a regular in the Owls F.A.Cup side he could not break into the Football League North side, with the likes of Doug Hunt and Jack Lindsay blocking his path, making only a solitary appearance.

He finally made his league bow in the season that followed but despite netting an impressive three goals in just four games he just could not win a regular place in a Wednesday side that were struggling to avoid the unthinkable drop into regional Division Three football. The Owls tried several different permutations in attack in an attempt to find a winning formula and it seems Aveyard was simply just unlucky not to have been given an extended run in the side as he continued to score for the reserves – netting six more in 1946-7 - but was only a bit player on the first team scene. He eventually departed for fellow Second Division side Birmingham City and netted three times in seven matches for The Blues as they lifted the Championship in 1948 – poor old Walter not receiving a medal as he had not played enough games!. His most successful spell in league football came next at Port Vale where he netted 26 times in 103 games and had the distinction of scoring the first ever goal at Vale Park, netting the only goal of the game against Newport County in August 1950. He later moved to then league club Accrington Stanley for a four-figure fee who released him in May 1953 after 24 league appearances and four goals.

AYRES, George Alexander 1924-26

Born: 5 September 1901
Islington, London
(5ft 8ins, 11st – 1924)
Died: 17 January 1983
Seaford, East Sussex
Debut: 3 May 1924
v Manchester United
Division Two Home
Last Appearance: 17 October 1925
v Derby County Div. Two Home
Total League
& Cup Appearances: 26 Goals: 11

Career Details:

RAF Cranwell		
Charlton Athletic	February	1924 (amat. Dec 1922)
WEDNESDAY	2 May	1924
Blackpool	17 May	1926 £350

Inside right George Ayres was still serving in the Royal Air Force when he played for Charlton Athletic as an amateur. He would eventually sign professional forms in February 1924 – after being discharged from the forces – and in his time at The Valley would appear 33 times for Charlton's first eleven, scoring five times.

Ayres was one of the rare breed of sportsmen who excelled at two disciplines and when he moved North to Sheffield in May 1924 he was actually on Surrey Cricket Club's ground staff, although he did not make any first class appearances for the County. His impact at Wednesday was immediate, scoring on his debut as Manchester United were beaten 2-0 at Hillsborough in the final game of the 1923-4 season. He appeared in the unfamiliar centre forward role in that first game but reverted to the No.10 shirt in the following campaign with the definite highlight being a hat trick in the 3-0 home win over Stockport County in September 1924.

The Owls would finish 14th in Division Two in Ayres' first full season and he was in and out of the side as the club struggled to field a settled side. He would also net 10 times for the club's reserve side in 24-5 – a feat he repeated the following season – and looked to have finally secured a regular first team spot in the autumn of 1925 when he scored four times in as many games as Wednesday picked up eight points to climb to second spot in Division Two. However a poor display in the a 4-1 loss at Derby County in the next game saw Ayres dropped and inside-left Harold Hill switch wings to take his place. That effectively signalled the end of George's career at Hillsborough as Wednesday did not look back with Hill in the side – he would net 12 times in just 21 games – and Ayres was languishing in the Central League side as the Owls won the Championship in May 1926.

A move to Blackpool came next for Ayres where he netted four times in 33 games before injury forced his early retirement from professional football at the end of the 1927-28 season. He then returned home to become both football and cricket coach at Stamford school in 1929 as well as coach at Surrey County Cricket club.

BAILEY, Gavin Joseph 1995-96

Born: 10 October 1976
Chesterfield
(5ft 9½ ins, 11st 7lbs – 1995)
Only Appearance:
24 June 1995
v FC Basel
Intertoto Cup Away
Total League
& Cup Appearances: 0+1 Goals: 0

Career Details:

Derby County		1992 Schoolboy
WEDNESDAY	2 June	1995
Hallam	September	1995 Loan
Hallam	February	1996 Loan
Matlock Town	8 March	1996 Loan
Colwyn Bay		1996 Loan
Hallam	March	1996 Loan
Mikkeli Palloiljate		1996 Loan
Sheffield Hallam University		1997
Hallam		1997
Stocksbridge Park Steels	October	1997
Worksop Town	August	1999
Sheffield Club		2000
Hallam	Summer	2002

Pacy forward Gavin Bailey first came to prominence whilst playing for both Chesterfield and Derbyshire boys. His promise persuaded Derby County to capture his signature on schoolboy forms but it was with Sheffield Wednesday that he signed as a YTS trainee in 1993. His breakthrough at Hillsborough came in his second season when Gavin netted 22 times for the Owls youth side, effectively guaranteeing him a pro contract, which was duly signed in June 1995. Within a few weeks he was making the trip to Switzerland as part of a depleted Owls first team squad for the Intertoto Cup meeting with FC Basel. The teenager was handed a spot on the bench and with just four minutes remaining Bailey replaced fellow debutant Richard Barker for his only taste of first team duty.

Unfortunately for Bailey that brief Intertoto Cup appearance did not prove to be a springboard to further first team chances as under new manager David Pleat he would only make two substitute appearances for the reserves, spending the majority of the 1995-6 campaign on loan at a variety of local non league clubs as well as a one month – a shoulder injury cutting short his stay to three weeks - loan spell in Finland with Premier League side M.P. Along with several other young professionals he was released at the end of the that season and subsequently attended college whilst playing Central Midlands League football with Sheffield Hallam University and then Northern Counties East League football with Sheffield based club Hallam.

He secured a two-year contract at Unibond League Stocksbridge Park Steels in 1997 and after scoring regularly moved into the Premier Division with Worksop Town. However a back injury at Worksop kept him on the sidelines and a bad shoulder injury sustained at his next club Sheffield persuaded Gavin to retire from playing. However in the summer of 2002 he was back for a fourth spell with Hallam, scoring twice in the first four games of the new season before injury again put him on the sidelines. Off the field Bailey had been unemployed for two years but is now Fitness Leader at the Esporta Health and Fitness Club in Sheffield, having secured the required qualifications at Norton College in Sheffield.

BAILEY, Ian Charles 1982-85

Born: 20 October 1956
Middlesbrough
(5ft 9ins, 11st 12lbs – 1982)
Debut: 28 August 1982
v Middlesbrough
Division Two Home
Last Appearance:
9 April 1983 v Bolton Wanderers
Division Two Away
Total League
& Cup Appearances: 45 Goals: 0

Career Details:

Middlesbrough	18 October	1974
Doncaster Rovers	22 November	1976 Loan
Carlisle United	17 February	1977 Loan - 6 weeks
Bolton Wanderers	November	1981 Loan
WEDNESDAY	5 August	1982 £80,000
Blackpool	18 October	1984 Loan - 6 weeks
Bolton Wanderers	15 March	1985 Non-contract

Stylish left back Ian Bailey was a vital member of Jack Charlton's side that reached the F.A.Cup semi-final in 1983, playing in every round including the 5-0 Sixth Round win over Burnley at Hillsborough. However he was fated not to play in that Highbury meeting with Brighton as just one week before the Cup-tie, tragedy struck at Bolton when Bailey suffered a broken leg. Not only would the injury rob Charlton of one of his best defenders but for Bailey it would effectively mark the end of his Wednesday career as although he recovered from the fracture to became a reserve team regular in 1983-4 the Owls were under new management – Howard Wilkinson having taken over from Charlton – and he was unable to win back his first team spot. The arrival of Irish International Nigel Worthington in February 1984 did little to improve his position and after a spell on loan at Blackpool, Bailey and Wednesday agreed to terminate his contract by mutual consent on 8th March 1985.

A week after leaving Hillsborough Bailey signed non-contract forms with Bolton Wanderers, playing seven league games, before leaving in the summer of 1985 to commence training as a physiotherapist. This marked the end of a playing career that had started as a youngster back in his hometown of Middlesbrough at Easterside Junior School and Bertram Ramsey School. His talent at schoolboy level led to appearances for Middlesbrough boys and eventually to a pro contract at First Division Middlesbrough – managed at the time by one Jack Charlton. The youngster had started his career as a centre-forward before switching to the left wing but it was only when England and Boro physio Harold Shepherdson moved him to left back for a trial game that he found his true position. It was at full back that he would make his league debut in December 1975 as Boro beat Tottenham 1-0 at Ayresome Park – ex-Owl John Hickton scoring the winner.

Over the next couple of seasons Bailey spent two spells on loan in order to gain further league experience although a scheduled spell, during the summer of 1977, in the North American Soccer League with Minnesota Kicks never materialised. The 1977-8 campaign proved to be the breakthrough season for Bailey as by Christmas 1977 he was firmly established as first choice left back and remained so until surprisingly leaving to sign for his old boss Jack Charlton at Wednesday, after 169 games and two goals for Boro. Incidentally his form in 1978 won him an U-21 cap against Yugoslavia when he was an unused sub. After bringing the curtain down on his playing career Bailey was appointed physio at Sheffield United in July 1986 and later in the decade moved to Rotherham United where he remains today.

BAIRD, Walter Young 1934-35

Born: 3 January 1913 Cambuslang, Glasgow
(5ft 8¼ ins, 10st 4lbs – 1934)
Only Appearance: 17 November 1934
v Preston North End Division One Home
Total League & Cup Appearances: 1 Goals: 0

Career Details:

Lesmahagow		
Partick Thistle	February	1933
Larkhall Thistle		
WEDNESDAY	7 April	1934 £110*
Hamilton Academicals	May	1935 £200
Morton	June	1936
Doncaster Rovers	May	1938

*£50 +£60 if makes a first team appearance

Left back Walter Baird joined the Owls in the spring of 1934 from Scottish Junior club Larkhall Thistle- Owls manager Billy Walker personally travelling to Scotland to secure his signature. His debut in an Owls shirt came in the reserve team's final game of the 1933-4 season – a 4-1 defeat at Aston Villa in May 1934 – and he started the following campaign as first choice full back for the reserves - effectively understudy to Ted Catlin. The 1934-5 season of course not only saw the Owls lift the FA.Cup but also finish third in the top flight so it was perhaps understandably difficult for the newcomer to break into Wednesday's first team with Catlin and Joe Nibloe seemingly taking turns at left back – the latter tending to switch wings when the former was unavailable.

However in November 1934 Walter – who had come to Hillsborough with Scottish schoolboy and Junior International honours to his name – got his big chance when not only Catlin was unavailable but regular right back Tom Walker was also missing. Therefore Owls manager Billy Walker had no choice but to pitch the youngster in against a Preston side containing centre forward Jack Palethorpe – who would sign for Wednesday within a matter of weeks - and one Bill Shankly who became quite famous on the red side of Liverpool! The youngster had a steady debut – clearing a late header off his goal line to ensure Wednesday held on to their 2-1 lead – but seven days later it was back to the reserves for Baird to continue his apprenticeship in English football. He was a regular for the second team during the remainder of the season but unfortunately come May time Wednesday decided not to retain him and Baird returned home to Scotland, signing for league club Hamilton. Three years later he returned to South Yorkshire to sign for Doncaster Rovers but failed to make a league appearance for Rovers.

BAKER, Peter Robert 1954-61

Born: 24 August 1934 Walthamstow
(5ft 8ins, 11st 8lbs – 1957)
Debut: 4 September 1957
v Newcastle United
Division One Home
Last Appearance:
8 March 1958
v Sunderland Division One Away
Total League
& Cup Appearances: 12 Goals: 0

Career Details:

Tottenham Hotspur		Amat.
WEDNESDAY	19 November	1954
Queens Park Rangers	28 February	1961 £1,500
Romford	July	1964 Free
Monarch Sport F.C.	cs	1967

London born right back Peter Baker first won representative honours with Southend schools in the late 1940s and it was this early promise that persuaded Tottenham to sign him on amateur forms in 1949. While on Spurs books as an amateur Baker completed his national service and it was while playing for the Army that Ted Catlin – Owls scout and one time Wednesday full back – spotted Baker. After learning that Spurs had not offered professional terms to the youngster he duly invited Baker to Hillsborough for a trial. This was in September 1954 and seven weeks later he joined the club's professional ranks.

The inexperienced youngster spent the early years of his Wednesday career in the "A" team before eventually stepping up to reserve team football. After becoming a Central League regular his first team debut duly arrived although it needed a flu epidemic to sweep through Hillsborough to dislodge regular full back Ron Staniforth! The virus that hit the club at the start of the 1957-58 season decimated Wednesday's first team – causing several games to be called off - but it created a window of opportunity for Baker which would see him enjoy a good run in Wednesday's First Division side. However Baker, who was short in stature but carried enough weight to make up for it, soon found himself back in the reserves with both Jack Martin and Staniforth seemingly ahead of him in the right back queue. He did make a comeback – playing at left back – in the famous FA Cup tie at Old Trafford when Wednesday faced United in their first match since the Munich Air disaster. However that run in the side lasted only four games and the arrival of Peter Johnson in the late 1950s effectively ended his Hillsborough career, eventually moving back to London and signing for Queens Park Rangers in 1961. Incidentally it is often stated that he was the cousin of another Spurs full back called Peter Baker but this was in fact incorrect!

His stay at Loftus Road lasted almost three years – making 28 league and cup appearances – before in 1964 he signed on semi-professional terms for crack non league side Romford while at the same time starting his own decorating business. He was now living in Southend – one of his two sons was an apprentice at the towns professional club – and after leaving the semi-pro game in 1966 played amateur football for Monarch Sports in the Southend District League – after gaining a permit from the Football Association. He finally retired in 1969 to concentrate on his business that flourishes today although its founder retired in 1999.

BALL, John Thomas 'Jack' 1930-33

Born: 13 September 1907
Banks, nr Southport
(5ft 10ins, 11st 10lbs – 1930)
Died: 2 February 1976 Luton
Debut: 8 September 1930
v Chelsea Division One Home
Last Appearance: 23 December 1933
v Stoke City Division One Away
Total League &
Cup Appearances: 135 Goals: 94

Career Details:

Banks Juniors		
Croston FC		1924 Trial
Southport	25 August	1925 (amat.Dec 1924)
Darwen	8 September	1927
Chorley	18 January	1928
Manchester United	6 May	1929
WEDNESDAY	29 July	1930 £1300
Manchester United	29 December	1933 *
Huddersfield Town	21 September	1934
Luton Town	26 October	1934
Excelsior Roubaix	23 May	1936
Vauxhall Motors (Luton) cs		1937
St Albans City		

* In part exchange for Neil Dewar (Ball valued @ £2000)

Free scoring centre forward Jack Ball was the last in a long line of lethal pre war attackers who had helped to make Wednesday one of the great powers of English football. The line of descendancy had started with Andrew Wilson at the turn of the Century and was followed by the likes of David McLean, Jimmy Trotter and then the man Jack Ball was bought to replace – Jack Allen.

Jack Ball's playing career had started in the modest surroundings of Southport minor football where while captain of his local team Banks Juniors he won his first medal – The Southport & District Shield. In his spare time the youngster was a keen fisherman, once catching seven salmon on the River Ribble, and also enjoyed sea fishing for mackerel. It is then perhaps no surprise to learn that on leaving school the teenager went to work for his father – a fishmonger who also sold groceries in his Southport shop. However the young Ball still loved to play football on his days off and after scoring seven times in just three matches for West-Lancashire League Croston he was offered a trial by the town's Football league club. He was eventually signed as an amateur by Southport - turning professional in the following year - and many times found himself playing at full back and even on one occasion in goal! However times were hard for The Sandgrounders and after Ball netted seven times in 25 games he was allowed to leave, signing for Darwen. However his new club then found themselves short of money and after only half a season Ball was again on the move – this time to Lancashire Combination side Chorley.

It was at Chorley that Ball's career really started to flourish as in eighteen months at the Lancashire club he helped them to back-to-back Lancashire Combination titles in 1928 and 1929 - scoring an astonishing 58 times in just 42 games during his first full season! Not surprisingly this lethal finishing alerted several league clubs with Southampton, Portsmouth and Manchester United all hot on his trail. However it was Louis Rocca of the latter club who won the race – helped no doubt by taking a taxi ride with Ball one Sunday that lasted all day and in the process managed to shake off all his other suitors! Like the majority of his previous clubs his stay at Old Trafford was brief despite the fact he finished second top

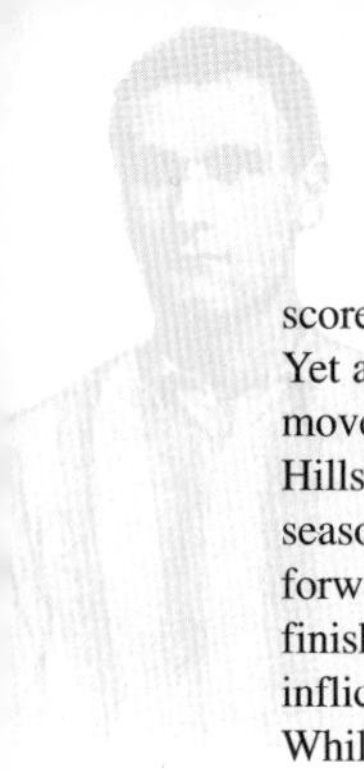

scorer in his solitary campaign with 11 goals from just 23 games. Yet again though financial problems hit his employers and he moved again, this time across the Pennines to Wednesday. At Hillsborough, Ball was a huge success, finishing top scorer in every season he pulled on the blue and white shirt, and legendary centre forward Jack Allen was hardly missed – such was Ball's clinical finishing. One only has to speculate what damage could have been inflicted on opposition defences if the pair had played together! While at Wednesday Jack was known for his splendid sportsmanship and devotion to club interests – once surprising some astonished deaf and dumb fans by communicating with them in sign language! He showed 100% commitment every time he pulled on an Owls shirt and with him leading the line Wednesday continued to ride high in the top division although sadly for Ball honours eluded him with just a Charity Shield runner-up medal to his name. During his penultimate season at Hillsborough Ball also set a record that stood for almost fifty years as after being appointed designated penalty taker he netted ten from fifteen in 1932-33 – a record that would not be broken until Mark Smith scored one more in 1979-80. Incidentally Ball had always been attributed with netting 11 times from the spot in that season but in fact during the home game with Wolves in March 1933 he netted from the rebound after the keeper saved his first kick. It was the arrival of new manager Billy Walker in 1933 that effectively signalled the end of Ball's goal-laden Hillsborough career as the new man at the helm was determined to obtain Neil Dewar from Manchester United. Unfortunately for Ball - and in hindsight for Wednesday as well – Walker decided it was the top scorer who would have to leave in order to prize the Scotsman from the clutches of Old Trafford.

Therefore Ball returned to Manchester where he experienced an unhappy and brief second spell before returning to Yorkshire to sign for Huddersfield Town. His somewhat nomadic career then took another strange twist as a fallout over the terms of his contract saw Ball leave after only four weeks to sign for Luton Town. At Town he rediscovered his scoring boots – netting 30 times in 31 games during his debut season – but is perhaps more famous for the game he did not play in! This occurred in April 1936 when Ball and his deputy were unfit to take their place for the league game with Bristol Rovers at Kenilworth Road and Luton were forced to play wing half Joe Payne at centre forward. He proceeded to net ten times to re write football history!! His second season at Kenilworth Road was badly affected by an ankle injury and he was still struggling for fitness when he signed as player-coach for French club Excelsior – after Luton had originally vetoed the move. He returned to Luton in 1937 to gain employment at Vauxhall Motors and for a while was player-coach to the works team before retiring from playing. He later coached Biggleswade Town – until the outbreak of War – and worked for almost twenty years at Vauxhall before joining a wholesale-manufacturing chemists, while working as a masseur in his spare time until he retired. The final years of his life were spent helping behind the bar at his son's public house, where the regulars must have lapped up his stories of his incredible goal scoring feats of the 1930s.

BALLAGHER, John 1957-61

Born: 21 March 1936 Dukinfield
(5ft 9½ ins, 11st 5lbs – 1958)
Debut: 30 August 1958
v Ipswich Town Division Two Away
Last Appearance: 7 February 1959
v Leyton Orient Division Two Away
Total League & Cup Appearances: 3 Goals: 0

Career Details:

Dukinfield Town		1954
WEDNESDAY	23 February	1957
Doncaster Rovers	6 February	1961*
Gillingham	July	1962
Thanet United	October	1964
Margate		1964
Folkestone		1966
Ramsgate		1967

*Ballagher + £7,000 exchanged for Meredith

At schoolboy level John Ballagher represented North East Cheshire and his first club was local Cheshire League side Dukinfield Town where he played as an amateur for three years. However his appearances in that period were somewhat limited as he also spent two years in the RAF, doing his National Service. This took him to Cyprus for twenty months, which effectively put his football career on hold, as he had no opportunity to play any organised soccer whilst in the forces. However after being de-mobbed the inside left arrived at Hillsborough for a trial late in 1956 and duly signed amateur forms for Wednesday in December. A move to the professional ranks was next for Ballagher and a regular spot in the club's reserve side followed a Central League debut in April 1957.

Unfortunately for Ballagher his direct competition for a first team spot at Hillsborough was the rapidly emerging John Fantham and he was never more than a squad player. His first team appearances all occurred during the Owls promotion season of 1958-9 – being victorious in all three – but it was the reserve team where he spent the majority of his Wednesday career and a healthy goal haul of 39 in four seasons persuaded neighbours Doncaster Rovers to take him to Belle Vue with John Meredith coming to Hillsborough as part of the deal. He made an immediate impact at Rovers, scoring eight times in 16 Division Four games, including his first senior hat trick on the final day of the season. A change of status to part-time professional came with his next move to Gillingham where he won a Division Four Championship medal in 1964 and added 40 league appearances to his career tally, netting a further ten times to bring an end to his league career.

During his time at Wednesday and Doncaster Rovers John had studied part-time at various colleges to qualify as a gas engineer and this had become his full time profession after moving to Kent – working five years for the South East Gas Board and then 22 years for the British Oxygen Company before his eventual retirement. However he continued to pull his boots on at non-league level and over a period of four years played for four different Kent non-league sides – winning the Kent Senior Cup in 1966 with Folkestone - before retiring in 1968 after a spell at Southern League Ramsgate.

BANNISTER, Gary 1981-84

Born: 22 July 1960
Collins Green, Warrington
(5ft 8½ ins, 11st 3lbs – 1981)
Debut: 29 August 1981
v Blackburn Rovers
Division Two Away
Last Appearance: 12 May 1984
v Cardiff City Division Two Away
Total League &
Cup Appearances: 142+1 Goals: 66

Career Details:

Coventry City	10 May	1978
Detroit Express	April	1980 Loan
WEDNESDAY	27 July	1981 £80,000
Queens Park Rangers	26 July	1984 £200,000 (T)
Coventry City	10 March	1988 £300,000
West Bromwich Albion	9 March	1990 £250,000
Oxford United	19 March	1992 Loan
Nottingham Forest	1 August	1992 Free
Stoke City	21 May	1993 Free
Released	May	1994
Hong Kong Rangers		1994
Lincoln City	14 September	1994 Free
Darlington	4 August	1995 Free
Porthleven		1996
Released	November	1997
Porthleven	July	1998

CAPS (@SWFC) – ENGLAND U-21 (1) v Poland 07/04/82

Pacy, razor sharp forward Gary Bannister was a big favourite with fans in the early 1980s, being arguably Jack Charlton's best signing while in charge at Wednesday. The diminutive Bannister – who had dropped down a division to join the Owls after failing to break into City's first eleven – netted a superb 22 goals in his debut season at Hillsborough and incredibly matched this tally in the remaining two years of his contract at Wednesday. This prolific goal scoring of course made him the club's top scorer in those three seasons and he became the first Owls player since Jack Ball, in the early 1930s, to net in excess of twenty goals in three successive seasons in a blue and white shirt.

With Bannister in their side Wednesday enjoyed several great Cup runs – F.A.Cup semi finalists in 1983 and consecutive League Cup quarter-final appearances – while in league football The Owls twice narrowly missed out on promotion back to the top flight before finally achieving the feat in what proved to be Bannister's final season at Hillsborough. After returning to the top flight it was expected that Bannister would remain in Wednesday colours so it was therefore a great disappointment to both the fans and the club when he rejected a new deal at Hillsborough and elected instead to move to fellow top-flight outfit Queens Park Rangers. The tribunal decided fee was a record for Wednesday but was no compensation to supporters who would have to wait several years until the arrival of David Hirst to lavish their affections on another number nine.

The goals continued to flow at Loftus Road – he won a League Cup runners up medal in 1986 - and after scoring 72 times in 172 games he returned for a second spell to Coventry City. Unfortunately for Bannister this was no more successful than his first spell and with competition from old Wednesday nemesis David Speedie he appeared in only 44 games for City, netting just 13 times. Twenty goals in two seasons at West Brom followed before his career was seemingly resurrected when he appeared in the majority of Nottingham Forest's Premier League games during the 1992-3 season. However this proved to be a last taste for "Banno" of top-flight football as several transfers later – and after a short spell in the Far East – he found himself appointed player-coach at Division Three side Darlington. Ironically it was here – in the twilight of his career - that Bannister would enjoy one of the most memorable moments of his career when his eleven goals from a new midfield role helped The Quakers to the 1996 Division Three Play-Off Final at Wembley. In front of over 43,000 his side lost one-nil to Plymouth Argyle but this proved to be a fitting finale to Bannister's professional career as soon after he was advised by a specialist to retire due to a serious neck injury. However this was not the end of his playing career as in the summer of 1996 he surprisingly signed for South-Western League club Porthleven. He played for the club as an amateur while on business in the area, where he owned several guesthouses, but in November 1997 returned to Darlington in a coaching capacity. He would eventually settle in the Southwest and was still appearing for Porthleven, as his fortieth birthday loomed large on the horizon.

BANNISTER, Keith 1945-53

Born: 27 January 1923 Sheffield
(5ft 10ins, 11st 4lbs – 1946)
Debut: 25 December 1946
v Bury Division Two Away
Last Appearance: 6 September 1952
v Charlton Athletic
Division One Home
Total League
& Cup Appearances: 78* Goals: 0
***Also appeared in 2 Wartime games**

Career Details:

Sheffield YMCA		
York City		1943 Guest
WEDNESDAY	17 February	1945
Chesterfield	19 June	1953 £750
King's Lynn		1954 Free
Macclesfield Town		1958 Free

After signing for Wednesday as a 14 year-old schoolboy in 1937 Keith Bannister would spend the majority of his next fifty years attached to the club in some capacity. After gaining experience in local football with Sheffield YMCA he stepped up to amateur status with Wednesday in 1941 but by now the Second World War was dominating public life and Bannister would serve in the RAF for five years until 1946. Despite being in the forces the half back still managed to play football and in fact appeared in 24 games for York City as a guest in 1943 before signing his first professional contract with Wednesday three months before VE Day in 1945. His senior debut for Wednesday came at Lincoln City in February 1945 – he signed pro on his way home from the game when Wednesday stopped for a meal - but after the end of the hostilities Bannister found himself a reserve team regular, appearing in only two first team games in the first two post war seasons of league football.

However, after several Division Two starts at left half back a move to left back came during the 1949-50 season before in the winter of 1950 he finally looked to have secured a regular first team spot – at right back. However a bad injury at Newcastle in February 1951 effectively ended his season and after regaining his fitness Bannister was back in the reserves. However in October 1951 secretary-manager Eric Taylor made an inspired decision when he called up Bannister and his great friend Derek Dooley for their first appearances of the season. The rest as they say is history as both were ever present until the end of the campaign with Dooley setting a club goal scoring record and the two-footed Bannister captaining the side to the Division Two Championship. However tough-tackling Bannister then enjoyed a terrible year, which started when he tore ligaments in his knee during a pre season practise match. This allowed Norman Jackson to start the season at right back and although Bannister replaced him for the 3-0 home loss to Charlton in September 1952 he was himself then replaced by Vin Kenny and that marked the end of his Owls career, as he never played another first team game for the club. A season at Division Three (North) club Chesterfield followed before he dropped into non-league football with King's Lynn – who Wednesday won 4-3 against in April 1958 in a benefit match for their old captain. His final club proved to be Cheshire League Macclesfield Town whom he captained to Cheshire Senior Cup success against Hyde United in 1960 before finally hanging up his boots to take a rep's job with an internal partitioning company. He later joined an insurance company – being a partner in the firm in later life – but his link to Wednesday was still strong and in 1961, on the recommendation of Derek Dooley – he was appointed part-time coach to the club's youth side who played in the Hatchard League.

He remained at Hillsborough in a coaching capacity until the summer of 1967 when he became a scout before working as a match analyser for Jack Charlton. In March 1983 he was appointed sports and recreation manager with his duties including the sports hall and training ground hire. He remained at Hillsborough in this capacity until retiring in 1989 when he moved to the United States to be near his daughter. Incredibly while over there Keith - now in his late 60s - played for a San Diego based over 40s team called Born Again Rovers while he was a paid coach for Valhalla College U-16 side, which under his leadership won the league title. After experiencing life in California, Bannister returned to Sheffield to enjoy his retirement and still watches the Owls as he enters his ninth decade.

BARGH, George Wolfenden 1935-36

Born: 27 May 1910 Clitheroe
(5ft 7½ ins, 11st 6lbs – 1935)
Died: 13 September 1995 Preston
Debut: 9 September 1935
v Bolton W. Division One Home
Last Appearance: 19 February 1936
v Derby County Division One Away
Total League
& Cup Appearances: 5 Goals: 0

Career Details:

Fulwood Amateurs		
Garstang		
Preston North End	February	1928
WEDNESDAY	8 May	1935
Bury	27 August	1936 £500
Chesterfield	June	1939
Shelbourne		1939-40 Guest
Aldershot	December	1939 Guest
Blackburn Rovers	January	1940 Guest
Accrington	April	1940 Guest
York City		1940 Guest
Linfield		1942 Guest
Bury	September	1946

Inside forward George Bargh started his playing career in Lancashire non-league football before signing a professional contract for Second Division Preston North End in 1928 – he had previously played for the club's reserve team at the tender age of 15 when still an amateur. Operating as an inside-left Bargh made his debut for Preston at West Brom in November 1928 and over the following seven seasons he was a regular member of the first team although only once – in 1931-2 – did he appear in over 25 league games in a season for The Lilywhites. In his time at the Deepdale club Bargh tended to alternate between the inside forward role on both wings and it was in the inside-right role that he first came to the attention of Owls manager Billy Walker when appearing in 23 top-flight games after earning promotion from Division Two in 1934. In fact Wednesday tried to sign Bargh during that 1934-5 season but it was not until the summer of 1935 that he became a Wednesday player after having scored 42 times for Preston in 142 league games.

He joined an Owls side who just eleven days earlier had lifted the FA.Cup at Wembley and found that competition for a first team spot would be extremely fierce with the likes of Ron Starling – the man who had just captained Wednesday to that Cup success – and Jack Surtees the men in possession! Not surprisingly he was unable to dislodge either man from their position and his first two appearances came when both missed a solitary game through injury. He would spend the majority of what proved to be his sole season at Wednesday in the club's reserve side, scoring three times as they finished second from bottom in the Central League. His other first team starts showed his versatility as they came on the right wing, at half back and in his old spot of inside-left but just when the inside-right role seemed up for grabs Wednesday bought Tom Grosvenor to fill the role and this effectively meant the end of Bargh's Hillsborough career.

A transfer to Bury ended his 15-month spell at Wednesday and at Gigg Lane he was a regular member of the Shakers first eleven, scoring 13 times in 89 games before joining Chesterfield. However only a few days after joining the Derbyshire club England declared War on Germany and the hostilities saw League football suspended. During the early years of the War, Bargh played occasional games as a guest for a variety of clubs – appearing ten times for York City – and when competitive football was re-introduced he returned for a second spell at Bury. However he was now in the twilight of his playing career and would play only one league game before retiring from professional football. He was appointed youth coach at his old club Preston in July 1955 – he had been in charge of the third team since September 1947 - and led the youngsters to the F.A.Youth Cup Final in 1960 when they drew at Chelsea before losing at home in front of over 27,000 fans. He later became Chief coach until his retirement in the mid 1970s.

BARKER, Richard 1993-96

Born: 20 May 1975 Sheffield
(6ft, 11st 6lbs – 1996)
Debut: 24 June 1995
v FC Basel Intertoto Cup Away
Last Appearance: 8 July 1995
v Gornik Zabrze
Intertoto Cup (sub) Home
Total League
& Cup Appearances: 1+1 Goals: 0

Career Details:

WEDNESDAY	27 July	1993
Doncaster Rovers	28 September	1995 Loan
Ards	13 January	1996 Loan
Linfield	23 August	1996 £40,000
Brighton & Hove Alb.	19 December	1997 Free
Macclesfield Town	5 July	1999 Free
Rotherham United	3 January	2001 £60,000
Mansfield Town	25 November	2004 Free

Hard running forward Richie Barker is the perfect example of a player who seemed to have failed to make the grade in professional football, only to bounce back and prove his doubters wrong by going on to carve out a successful league career. The Sheffield born attacker had signed apprentice forms with Wednesday in 1991- after impressing for England schoolboys – and slowly worked his way through the club's youth system to sign professional forms in the summer of 1993. He was never a prolific scorer in his early years at Wednesday but grabbed the headlines late in the 1994-5 season when in an incredible burst of scoring he netted 15 times in just 12 reserve team games, including three hat tricks in five games, to finish the season as Central League top scorer with twenty goals. It was without doubt that this sudden rush of goals earned Barker a place in the almost scratch squad that travelled to Switzerland for the Intertoto Cup in the following summer. He duly made his debut in Basel and retained a squad place when all the majority of the senior pros returned for the next match. A sub appearance versus Polish side Gornik at Millmoor was followed by a loan spell at neighbours Doncaster Rovers – making his league debut – and then a further loan spell at Irish club Ards. While in Ireland Barker scored freely, netting seven times in twelve games – including a hat trick in a 10-0 Cup romp over Crookstown United – but when returning to Sheffield he had to be content with reserve team football after failing to break into Wednesday's Premiership squad.

It was becoming obvious that Richie would need to move to get first team football and so it was back across the Irish Sea to sign on a permanent basis for Linfield. He eventually returned to English league football with Brighton – scoring his first league goal – before a highly successful spell at league new boys Macclesfield Town had many clubs chasing his signature. He netted 23 times in 53 games for The Silkmen before joining Rotherham United for a Bosman inspired cut-price fee early in 2001. He spent the majority of his first two seasons at The Millers on the subs bench, scoring only four times, although his first game back at Hillsborough proved truly memorable as he netted an unbelievable last minute winner. He experienced a distinct change of fortune as Rotherham consolidated in Division One during 2002-3, earning a regular role in the first eleven and reaching double figures in the goals column.

BARRASS, Matthew Williamson 1925-26

Born: 14 February 1899 Preston Colliery, nr North Shields
(5ft 8½ ins, 11st 7lbs – 1925) Died: 24 June 1953 Manchester
Debut: 21 March 1925 v Middlesbrough Division Two Away
Last Appearance: 17 April 1926 v Clapton Orient Div Two Home
Total League
& Cup Appearances: 49 Goals: 14

Career Details:

Seaham Harbour Bible Class		
Dawdon Colliery		
Seaham Harbour		1918
Blackpool		1919
WEDNESDAY	16 March	1925 £1950
Manchester City	30 June	1926 £1750
Ashton National		1933 Free

When mercurial inside forward Matt Barrass arrived at Hillsborough in March 1925 it was with a remit to save Wednesday from the unthinkable drop into regional Division Three football. Thankfully he helped the Owls achieve that particular goal and then his superb displays in 1925-26 – as vice captain to Frank Froggatt – contributed to Wednesday's capture of the Division Two Championship. Barrass was a highly accomplished player who combined outstanding passing ability with vision and was seen as the brains behind the Wednesday attack. Although not a dominant player Barrass could still force the tempo of a game with his eye for an opening – his speciality was the reverse pass – and he set up countless goals for prolific scorer Jimmy Trotter during that Championship winning season, also netting a fair share himself from inside right – he missed only the final two games of the season - as the Owls regained their top flight spot six years after being relegated.

As a teenager the Northeast born attacker had actually had trials for Sunderland as a goalkeeper but it was as an outfield player that his first experience of organised football came in the Wearside

League with Dawdon Colliery. The outbreak of War saw the teenager join the Royal Artillery as a Gunner and after surviving the bloody conflict he returned home to sign for another Wearside League club – Seaham Harbour. After winning the Championship in 1919 a move into league soccer came with a transfer to Blackpool where he netted 53 times in 180 appearances for the Bloomfield Road club. Three of those goals had come at Hillsborough on Christmas Day 1924 when Wednesday crashed 6-2, their heaviest home defeat until the early 1990s, and it was not long after that Owls manager Bob Brown stunned Blackpool fans by taking their club captain across The Pennines. Unfortunately for Wednesday fans they would only see the midfield schemer in a Wednesday shirt for one full season as Matt was unhappy with the terms offered by the club and decided to stay in Division Two, returning to Lancashire to sign for Manchester City.

Within two years City won the Championship themselves although by now Matt had dropped from the forward line, playing as a half back. After City gained First Division status Barrass would miss only two games in their first two seasons, finishing eighth and third, but part way through the 1930-1 campaign he lost his place to Matt Busby and in the three seasons that followed only made a further ten first team appearances- taking his Manchester City total to 170. It was at this point that Barrass joined Manchester non-league club Ashton National as well as opening a fish and chip shop in Chorlton-Cum-Hardy. He would stay only a season with Ashton before retiring from competitive football and after running the chip shop for several years Barrass later was the licensee at two public houses in Manchester – The Justice Birch Hotel in West Gorton and the Tamworth Hotel in Hulme. During the Second World War Matt worked as a government inspector in Newton Heath and when he died at the age of 54 he was employed as a storekeeper in a factory at Trafford Park, Manchester. The Barrass name however lives on as his great grandson – Matt - currently plays for Bury while his son Malcolm enjoyed a highly successful career with Bolton Wanderers and Sheffield United which saw him play in the "Matthews Final" of 1953 and win three full caps for England - thankfully a feat his father just lived to see.

BARRETT, Earl Delisser — 1998-99

Born: 28 April 1967 Rochdale
(5ft 10ins, 11st 7lbs – 1997)
Debut: 28 February 1998
v Derby County Premier League Away
Last Appearance: 3 October 1998
v Middlesbrough Premier League (Sub) Away
Total League
& Cup Appearances: 10+6 Goals: 0

Career Details:

Manchester City	26 April	1985
Chester City	1 March	1986 Loan
Oldham Athletic	24 November	1987 £35,000
Aston Villa	25 February	1992 £1,700,000
Everton	30 January	1995 £1,700,000
Sheffield United	16 January	1998 Loan
WEDNESDAY	24 February	1998 Free
Released	30 June	1999

It was Ron Atkinson - Earl Barrett's old boss at Aston Villa - who brought the ex-England International to Hillsborough in 1998 during his second stint as Wednesday manager. Big Ron had originally splashed out to take the right back to Villa Park after he enjoyed great success with Oldham, appearing in 217 games, winning a League Cup runners up medal in 1990, a Division Two Championship medal in 1991 and becoming one of only four players in the club's long history to win a full England caps – the first of his three caps coming alongside fellow debutant David Hirst against New Zealand in 1991. In addition he was also capped at "B" and U-21 level while at Boundary Park and proved a highly versatile player, appearing in a variety of positions including striker.

The pacy, enthusiastic Barrett had originally signed apprentice forms at Manchester City in April 1984 but appeared in only four matches for The Citizens prior to his short transfer across Greater Manchester to neighbours Oldham Athletic. His career was at its peak when Atkinson took him to Birmingham and while with Villa Barrett won the League Cup in 1994 before another big money move reacquainted him with old manager Joe Royle at Everton. Barrett experienced a turbulent debut – being sent off in a stormy match at Newcastle United – but his sterling displays at full back saw off the challenges of both Matt Jackson and Marc Hottiger to become first choice at Goodison Park. Unfortunately, after playing in the Third Round for Aston Villa and therefore Cup-tied, he was forced to watch from the sidelines as Everton won the F.A.Cup in May 1995 before a serious knee injury saw him absent for the majority for the 1995-6 campaign. He returned to the fold to become a regular in the season that followed and remained in the side until making his final appearance in January 1998, just two weeks before joining Sheffield United on loan. Incidentally his farewell Goodison Park appearance was also the final game in an Everton shirt for Andy Hinchcliffe who soon after was also signed by Ron Atkinson for the Owls.

It was when Barrett was just about to start a second month on loan at Bramall Lane that Wednesday pounced to take him across the City on a free transfer, as a direct replacement for broken leg victim Ian Nolan. He immediately brought experience and consistency to the right back spot but somewhat ironically he would suffer a similar fate to Nolan in October 1998 when a serious injury to his left knee in a game at Middlesbrough put him on the sidelines. He would fail to play another game in a Wednesday shirt due to the severity of the injury and after being released by Danny Wilson at the end of his contract he was forced to announce his retirement from the professional ranks in December 1999. After hanging up his boots Barrett has worked with the young community and become heavily involved in various campaigns to eradicate racism from football, speaking at various conferences in the UK and abroad.

BARRETT, Graham Philip Robert — 2005

Born: 6 October 1981 Dublin
(5ft 10ins, 11st 7lbs, 2005)
Debut: 26 March 2005
v Torquay United
League One Home
Last Appearance: 7 May 2005
v Bristol City
League One Home
Total League
& Cup Appearances: 5+1 Goals: 1

Career Details:

Arsenal	14 October	1998
Bristol Rovers	15 December	2000 Loan
Crewe Alexandra	11 September	2001 Loan
Colchester United	14 December	2001 Loan
Brighton & Hove Albion	28 August	2002 3-month loan
Coventry City	1 July	2003 Free
WEDNESDAY	24 March	2005 Loan
Released	11 May	2005

Attacker Graham Barrett made a dream start to his Owls career when scoring on debut in the League One draw with Torquay United. He had joined on transfer deadline day from Coventry City where he was out of favour despite having appeared in 31 league games during the previous season. Despite arriving from Arsenal as a forward Barrett was mainly used by City on the right side of midfield where he impressed the City faithful with a series of hard running displays and excellent crossing ability, combined with a willingness to tackle back. However he had to be content with reserve team soccer in the next season and looked to resurrect his career when joining Wednesday on loan until the end of the season. Sadly the six-timed cap Eire International could not follow up his encouraging debut display for the Owls and made little impression in five more senior appearances for the club. His parent club announced his release - on the same day as ex-Owl Kevin Pressman - in early May and Wednesday decided not to pursue a full transfer.

BARRICK, Dean 1988-91

Born: 30 September 1969 Hemsworth
(5ft. 9ins, 11st 4lbs – 1989)
Debut: 27 March 1989
v Newcastle Utd Division One Away
Last Appearance: 31 March 1990
v Tottenham H Division One Home
Total League
& Cup Appearances: 11 Goals: 2

Career Details:

WEDNESDAY	7 May	1988
Rotherham United	13 February	1991 £50,000 (T)
Cambridge United	11 August	1993 £50,000
Preston North End	11 September	1995 £10,000 + Paul Raynor
Bury	3 July	1998 Free
Ayr United	19 February	1999 Loan
Doncaster Rovers	8 May	2001 Free
Hereford United	25 March	2002 Loan
Nuneaton Borough	28 February	2003 Free
Hucknall Town	July	2003 Free

Until Lloyd Owusu scored with his first touch against the Blades in September 2002 it was Dean Barrick who could lay claim to the most dramatic senior debut for the club. Arguably though Barrick's feat – scoring with his first touch after just four minutes in a vital relegation clash at Newcastle United - is perhaps more praiseworthy as the game was actually his league debut after having come through the youth ranks at Hillsborough. He was signed by the Owls as an apprentice on 1st July 1986, after impressing for both Wakefield and West Yorkshire boys, and the left sided midfielder was thrown into the fray by newly appointed manager Ron Atkinson for the vital St.James' Park clash. The Owls won that game 3-1 and he enjoyed an eight game run in the side during which he scored a spectacular long-range effort in a heavy defeat at Liverpool.

Unfortunately as Big Ron revamped the Wednesday squad Barrick found himself playing mainly reserve team football for the next two seasons – making eighteen appearances for the second string side as they won the Central league in 1991. He made only three further first team appearances, with the left-wing partnership of Phil King and Nigel Worthington blocking his path to the first eleven and would eventually move for a tribunal decided fee to neighbours Rotherham United. It was in the old Third Division with the Millers that he started to establish himself in league football and won a Championship medal with the Millmoor club in 1992. His consistency brought him over a hundred games for both Rotherham and his next club Cambridge United where he captained the side in 1994-5,being voted player of the year.

A move to Preston North End came next and in his first season, after having now switched to left back, he again won a Third Division Championship medal and in total played in 109 league games for the Deepdale club, the highest tally at any of his five league clubs. After being released by The Lilywhites at the end of the 1997-8 campaign Barrick signed for Bury on a Bosman free transfer and after 47 league games – interrupted by an eleven game loan spell at Scottish league Ayr United – the hard working Barrick was released to drop out of league football to sign for Conference club Doncaster Rovers. While playing part-time for Rovers he completed a Sports Science Degree at Alsager College in Manchester and was a regular for Rovers until losing his place to Chris Beech in February 2003, subsequently moving to fellow Conference club Nuneaton on a free transfer. He later joined ambitious Conference North club Hucknall Town where was appointed manager in September 2004. Led Hucknall to the 2005 FA Trophy final but not only experienced defeat but also suffered a broken leg which ended his playing career. He now teaches in a Doncaster School.

BARRON, George Ward 1903-05

Born: 4th Quarter 1883 Darlington (5ft 9ins, 11st – 1903)
Only Appearance: 6 May 1903 v Bury Div One Away
Total League & Cup Appearances: 1 Goals: 0

Career Details:

Wallsend Park Villa		
WEDNESDAY	18 March	1903 £25
Released	19 March	1905

Inside left George Barron was yet another example of a player brought to the club by North East scout Bob Brown, who of course would eventually become one of the greatest managers in Wednesday's history. The speedy 20-year old attacker earned a living as a brass finisher before signing for Wednesday at the latter end of their Championship season of 1902-3 and would actually make his debut – just over two weeks after signing professional for Wednesday - on the right wing after Wednesday were denied the services of Harry Davis due to an injury sustained in an International game on the previous Saturday. Being handed his debut for a re-arranged game at FA Cup Finalists Bury must have been daunting for the youngster and after firing an early chance wide he saw little of the ball and like his team mates must have been shell-shocked as the Owls Championship challenge received a setback following a 4-0 loss.

In hindsight throwing the inexperienced youngster into the hurly burly of the top flight was perhaps a mistake and not surprisingly Barron then dropped completely out of the first team picture and struggled to even secure a place in the club's very strong Midland league side, which won both the Championship and Sheffield Challenge Cup in 1903. An additional problem for Barron was that at the time Wednesday boasted two of the best wingers in their long history with the aforementioned Davis on the right and legendary left-winger Fred Spiksley on the opposite flank and it was extremely hard for the youngster to make a real impression on the first team. Even in the reserves Barron was faced with competition from the likes of George Simpson and after two years Wednesday decided he was surplus to requirements and was released, dropping out of league soccer altogether.

BARRY-MURPHY, Brian 2003-04

Born: 27 July 1978 Cork, Ireland
(5ft 11ins, 13st 3lbs – 2003)
Debut: 1 February 2003
v Wolverhampton W. Division One Home
Last Appearance: 8 May 2004
v Queens Park Rangers Div. Two Home
Total League
& Cup Appearances: 64+3 Goals: 0

Career Details:

Cork City		
Preston North End	3 August	1999 Free
Southend United	11 February	2002 Loan
Hartlepool United	30 October	2002 2-month loan
WEDNESDAY	31 January	2003 Free
Released	30 June	2004
Bury	13 July	2004 Free

Left back Brian Barry-Murphy made an immediate good impression on Owls fans with his confident displays after joining from fellow First Division club Preston North End. He had just completed a two month loan spell at Hartlepool United and his move to Hillsborough meant he had been signed for two different clubs in the same season by the same manager – Chris Turner having secured his loan from Preston back in October 2002, just days before moving to take over at Wednesday. His combative displays and superb tackling down Wednesday's left flank made Owls fans initially wonder why he was only ever a peripheral figure at Deepdale, where despite captaining The Lilywhites reserves to the Championship in 2001-02 he appeared in only five first team games and was even loaned out to bottom division side Southend United to gain more first team experience.

The former Republic of Ireland U-21 and youth International found himself back in the reserves at the start of the following season but his chance of first team football came at Third Division leaders Hartlepool where he was a regular before being recalled by Preston boss Craig Brown in late December 2002 after they were hit with a suspension and injury crisis. Barry-Murphy duly appeared twice in Preston's first team in January 2003 but it was clear this was just a temporary measure and when Wednesday approached his employers they agreed he could leave on a free to join the Owls relegation fight. The ex-Cork City player proved in his early weeks that he could be the long term solution to the problematic left back position which had seen several players – the majority out of position – tried in an attempt to plug the gap. Like the Owls he struggled for form in Division Two but remained a regular, showing a versatility to his game by appearing on several occasions in a midfield role. However he was one of thirteen players released at the end of the disastrous 2003-4 campaign as Chris Turner slashed the playing staff.

BARTLETT, William John "Billy" 1902-10

Born: 13 April 1878 Noars Yard, Newcastle
(5ft 8ins, 10st 7lbs – 1902)

Died: 6 August 1939 Belfast
Debut: 22 February 1904
v Notts County Division One Home
Last Appearance: 19 March 1910
v Sheffield Utd Division One Home
Total League
& Cup Appearances: 199 Goals: 3

Career Details:

Brandling		
Gateshead NER		
WEDNESDAY	27 March	1902 £45
Huddersfield Town	25 April	1910 £250*
Linfield	July	1912
Retired		1918

*Joint fee with Hamilton

They say the secret of comedy is timing and Wednesday used this skill to sign half back William Bartlett from under the noses of his local club Newcastle United. The highly skilful Bartlett had been earning rave reviews whilst playing for non league Gateshead NER – who he had joined after initially playing as a sixteen year-old for a local junior club – and looked set to sign for the Magpies. However literally just a few hours before he was set to move to St.James' Park in stepped Wednesday and Arthur Dickinson secured his signature with the Owls paying just £25 with the promise of a further £20 if he was re-signed for 1902-03.

It proved a valuable capture for the Owls as after serving a two-year apprenticeship in Wednesday's Midland League reserve side – winning Sheffield Challenge Cup and Midland league Championship medals in 1903 - the Geordie developed into a more than capable understudy for left half back Herrod Ruddlesdin and his initial first team starts would come as a direct replacement for "Ruddy". An injury to Ruddlesdin at the start of the 1904-5 season saw Bartlett enjoy an eight game run in the side but it was back to the reserves when his rival was available. However Billy – whose brother Albert played for both Bradford City and Park Avenue - had made his mark and later in the season Wednesday were forced to reshuffle their defence and with Ruddlesdin temporarily moving over to right half back in came Bartlett on the left – he never looked back from this point and poor old Ruddy never did get his No. 6 shirt back!

Over the next five seasons Bartlett was an automatic choice – forming a defensive trio with Tommy Crawshaw and Ruddlesdin and later with Crawshaw and Tom Brittleton - as Wednesday strived to follow up their back-to-back title wins of 1903-4. However the highlight for Bartlett came when he won an F.A.Cup winners medal in 1907 when the Owls beat Everton to lift the famous old trophy. After the Cup success Bartlett – who had a reputation as a player who hardly ever conceded fouls such was his expert timing – appeared in the North v South International trial match in January 1908 and remained in the Owls first team until Wednesday made a poor start to the 1909-10 campaign. He was one of three players axed after a heavy defeat at home to Bury and it marked the beginning of the end for the classy half back as despite regaining his place later in the season (appearing once at outside-left!) he was soon displaced and in April he joined Huddersfield Town, in a joint deal that also took Hamilton to a side that at the time were still playing non league football. He stayed two seasons in West Yorkshire – playing in the club's first ever Football League game in September 1910 and was almost ever present for two seasons before a surprise move took him across the Irish sea.

He signed for Linfield and certainly found the Irish air very much to his liking, especially as a multitude of honours flowed his way including an Irish League Championship medal in 1914, three Irish Cup winners medals in 1913,1914 and 1916, an Irish League cap during the 1912-13 season and the County Antrim Shield in 1913. When his playing career came to a close in 1918 Bartlett remained in Ireland, becoming assistant trainer at Linfield where he looked after the second team Linfield Swifts. He was appointed senior trainer at fellow Irish League club Distillery in 1921, three years later took the position of Blackburn Rovers scout in what had now become known as Northern Ireland and would remain on the Emerald Isle for the remainder of his life.

BART-WILLIAMS, Christopher Gerald 1991-95

Born: 16 June 1974
Freetown, Sierra Leone
(5ft 11ins, 11st 10lbs – 1992)

Debut: 23 November 1991
v Arsenal Division One Home
Last Appearance: 7 May 1995 v
Manchester United Premier League Away
Total League
& Cup Appearances: 115+41 Goals: 24

Career Details:

Leyton Orient	18 July	1991
WEDNESDAY	15 November	1991 £575,000*
Nottingham Forest	1 July	1995 £2,500,000 (T)
Charlton Athletic	3 December	2001 Free
Ipswich Town	10 September	2003 Loan
Ipswich Town	11 December	2003 Free
Released	30 June	2004
Leeds United	July	2004 Trial
Apoel Nicosia	20 September	2004 Free
Marsaxlokk	August	2005

*Initial £350,000 + three further £75,000 payments after 25 game intervals

CAPS (@ SWFC)- ENGLAND "B" (1) v N.Ireland 10/05/94

ENGLAND U-21 (14) v Spain 08/09/92, v Norway 13/10/92, v Turkey 11/11/92, v Denmark 08/03/94, v Russia 29/05/94, v France 31/05/94, v Belgium 05/06/94, v Portugal 07/06/94, v Portugal 06/09/94, v Austria 11/10/94, v Eire 15/11/94, v Eire 27/03/95, v Latvia 25/04/95, v Latvia 07/06/95

When 17 year-old midfielder Chris Bart-Williams joined the Owls he was widely regarded as one of English football's brightest jewels and it was thought only a matter of time before he won full International honours for his adopted country. The classy playmaker was actually born in Africa but after moving to London with his family when still an infant all his early football experience came in the capital, starring for both Haringey and Middlesex boys. He soon attracted the attention of Leyton Orient and signed YTS forms, making his league debut while still a trainee. His silky passing skills and mature displays in the centre of midfield – which had already brought him England Youth honours – soon had the Premier League scouts flocking to Brisbane Road and only four months after signing his first professional contract he was elevated into the top flight with Wednesday.

It was expected Bart-Williams – who was unsurprisingly nicknamed Bartman by the Wednesday fans - would be eased gradually onto the first team scene but Trevor Francis thought differently and he handed the teenager a shock debut just over a week after arriving at Hillsborough, in a deal that took Chris Turner to Leyton Orient. The youngster duly produced an astonishing debut display, considering his tender years, playing a starring role in the home game with Arsenal and he would go on to appear regularly in his first season at Wednesday – winning the

Barclays "Young Eagle of the month" in December 1991. In every subsequent season at Wednesday he would start more games than in the previous campaign and before reaching the age of twenty had appeared in over one hundred games for the club, including a brief appearance in 1993 F.A.Cup Final replay loss to Arsenal – replacing an exhausted Roland Nilsson with just a minute of extra time remaining. Although lacking pace Bartman's quality on the ball was obvious to all and during his time at Wednesday he won a multitude of England Under-21 caps and in April 1994 received a shock call up to Terry Venables England "training squad".

On many occasions Bart-Williams was asked to play a forward role and responded with some excellent displays, the highlight being a hat trick in the home game with Southampton at Easter 1993. However despite all his plaudits it was felt by many that he had yet to really fulfil his early promise and when he decided to leave - under freedom of contract in the summer of 1995 - it seemed excellent business for the Owls when the transfer tribunal ordered Nottingham Forest to pay the not inconsiderable sum of £2.5m for the 21 year-old – the fee being one of the highest ever set by tribunal. However many fans did akin the sale to selling the crown jewels and it would probably be fair to say that in the decade following his departure the Owls failed to adequately replace his creativity. After initially failing to settle at Forest, Bart-Williams soon became established in a midfield role, helping his side to the First Division Championship in 1998 and an immediate return to the Premier League after suffering relegation in 1997. He signed a lucrative new contract at Forest in June 1998 but after suffering relegation again in 2000 financial problems engulfed the club and as a cost cutting measure Bart-Williams returned to the top flight – joining Charlton Athletic on loan – a move that was made permanent on 27th January 2002. After a mixed spell at The Valley, Bart-Williams was released and after failing to win a deal at Leeds United he surprisingly signed for Cypriot club Apoel. In the summer of 2005 he signed a 3 year contract at Maltese side Marsaxlokk.

BECKETT, Albert 1885-87

Born: 1st Quarter 1867
Only Appearance: 5 November 1887
v Long Eaton Rangers F.A.Cup Away
Total League & Cup Appearances: 1 Goals: 0

Career Details:

Local	
WEDNESDAY	1885
Local	1887

Right half back Albert Beckett was one of the Victorian players who helped Wednesday forge a reputation as Cup fighters in their early years. His first appearance for the club came in April 1885 when he played in a benefit game for ex-Owl Arthur Malpas at Lockwood Brothers' Eccleshall Road ground. He was a regular during 1885-6, winning The Lord Mayor's Silver Cup competition and the Wharncliffe Charity Cup as Wednesday asserted themselves as top dogs in Sheffield. He was probably denied an F.A.Cup appearance in the following season when Wednesday forgot to send in their entry before the required deadline but he did net his first goal for the club in December 1886 – versus Attercliffe in a Wharncliffe Charity Cup tie held at Bramall Lane. He appeared in the Final of that competition – losing 3-0 to Staveley – but won a Sheffield Challenge Cup medal in March 1887 when Wednesday beat Sheffield Collegiate 2-1.

The season that followed was a major one in the club's history as they obtained their first proper ground and Albert played in the opening game at Olive Grove when the famous Blackburn Rovers shared eight goals in front of a "bumper" 1,500 crowd. Beckett continued to appear regularly for Wednesday, although his only F.A.Cup appearance came in a 2-1 win in Derbyshire, before his final appearance in a friendly against Lincoln City in late November 1887. After hanging up his boots Beckett worked as a surgical instrument fitter.

BEDFORD, Lewis 1925-26

Born: 1899 Aston, (5ft 6ins, 10st 7lbs – 1925)
Died: 29 June 1966 Birmingham
Debut: 29 August 1925 v Fulham Division Two Home
Last Appearance: 17 October 1925 v Derby Co Div. Two Home
Total League & Cup Appearances: 11 Goals: 2

Career Details:

West Bromwich Albion	March	1921
Walsall	June	1922
WEDNESDAY	20 August	1925 £575
Walsall	17 September	1926 £200
Nelson	March	1927
Walsall	February	1928
Luton Town	June	1928
Walsall	December	1929
Bloxwich Stollers		1931
Walsall Wood		

The name of left-winger Lewis Bedford was inexorably linked with Walsall Football Club as he spent an unprecedented four spells at the Midlands club, all inside a decade! His career had started with West-Midlands rivals West Bromwich Albion, signing amateur forms for The Baggies in November 1920 before turning professional six months later. He would only appear three times in league football for Albion before deciding to revert to part-time status on joining Walsall at the beginning of the 1922-3 campaign. The first of his 142 appearances for Walsall came at the start of that season and Bedford would spend four seasons at The Saddlers before deciding to turn professional again, joining Bob Brown's revolution at Hillsborough. The legendary Owls manager was slowly rebuilding the side after their horrendous immediate post war season and the pacy forward – who had a welcome tendency to cut in from the wing and have a shot at goal – made an immediate impact by scoring on his debut as Wednesday won 3-0 on the opening day of the season.

This encouraging start meant he retained his first team spot for the next ten games but competition for places at Hillsborough was getting fiercer and he would lose his place to Arthur Prince following the 4-1 home defeat to Derby County. Unfortunately for Lewis he could not dislodge his wing rival and even in the reserves was forced to switch to the right wing following the outstanding form of teenage newcomer Jack Wilkinson. The continued good form of Prince, and later Wilkinson, ensured Lewis would never again get a sniff of first team football as Wednesday stormed to the Second Division Championship. In the summer Bedford moved back to the West Midlands to re-sign for Walsall and over the next few years would move continuously around the lower leagues before dropping into non-league soccer at Bloxwich Strollers - following seven goals in thirty-two games at Division Three (South) club Nelson and fifteen goals in forty-nine league games at The Hatters. Bedford would eventually retire in May 1940 after almost a decade in minor football and it was perhaps fitting that his final club would be based in Walsall.

BEECH, George 'Jack' 1896-1904

Born: 2nd Quarter 1892 Sheffield
Debut: 5 April 1897
v Nottingham Forest Div. One Home
Last Appearance: 4 April 1904
v Everton Division One Away
Total League
& Cup Appearances: 22 Goals: 5

Career Details:

Attercliffe Sports Club	cs	1893
WEDNESDAY	August	1896
Barnsley	May	1904 £50
Released		1906

In the history of Sheffield Wednesday inside forward George Beech was perhaps the most patient player as over an eight-year period he was a consistent goal scorer for the club's reserve team but appeared in only twenty-two games for the first team – his best run in the side coming at the end of the 1901-2 season when he played in the final seven games. Of course at the time his rivals for the No.10 jersey were many of the greatest players of Wednesday's early league years – names such as Harry Davis, Alec Brady, Jock Wright and Jack Malloch – and it was no surprise that Jack would play the majority of his football at Wednesday in the second eleven.

His record in reserve team football was in fact quite remarkable as in those eight seasons Beech's goal tally would reach double figures in every campaign as Wednesday won a multitude of honours which included consecutive Sheffield Association League Championships in 1900 and 1901 plus Midland League Championship wins in 1898 and 1903 – Jack also won a Sheffield Challenge Cup winners medal in 1903. In total the inside right netted almost 150 times at reserve team level, his first goals coming in the 8-1 win over Staveley back in December 1896, and grabbed several hat tricks, four of which came in the 1899-0 season when he scored four goals in one game and hit five in a 16-0 romp over Wombwell Town. In modern parlance Beech would perhaps be classed as squad player although unlike the modern footballer he seemed quite content to score regularly for the reserves and make the odd first team start. His appearances in the League side came mainly at his favoured inside-left spot – scoring from this position on his debut before being dropped for the next game - but he also played at inside right and centre forward in an era when Wednesday challenged for all the major honours in the English game. After eight years loyal service Wednesday did not retain his services at the end of 1903-4 and he joined neighbours Barnsley where he would score eleven times in 69 league and cup games for The Tykes before retiring from league football.

BEESON, George 1929-34

Born: 31 August 1906 Clay Cross, Derbyshire (5ft 10ins, 12st 2lbs – 1932)
Died: 6 January 1999 Wishaw, Birmingham
Debut: 2 November 1929
v Leicester City Division One Home
Last Appearance: 24 March 1934
v Huddersfield Town Division One Home
Total League
& Cup Appearances: 75 Goals: 0

Career Details:

North Wingfield Rangers		
New Upton		
Clay Cross		
Chesterfield		1927
WEDNESDAY	16 March	1929 £1250
Aston Villa	11 August	1934 £500+Joe Nibloe
Walsall	June	1938
Hull City	September	1944 Guest

CAPS (@ SWFC)
Football League (2) v Irish League 1933, v Irish League 1934

When George Beeson arrived at Hillsborough from neighbours Chesterfield it was as understudy to regular right back Tom Walker and it's a role that he would serve for the majority of his time at Wednesday. In fact Beeson would play less than twenty first team games in his first three full seasons at the club and it was not until 1932-33 that he looked to have secured an automatic spot, missing only seven league games in the whole season. It was during this purple patch that his superb form won him representative honours – he was also named reserve for the full England team against Ireland in 1934 - but within a year Walker had reclaimed his first team place and Beeson was on his way back to his native Birmingham, as part of the deal that brought Scottish International Joe Nibloe to Hillsborough.

Beeson – the youngest of thirteen children – had actually played in goal during his schooldays and like the majority of his contemporaries worked at the local pit after leaving school. Thankfully his talent with the round ball took him away from the dangers of such work – his father and a brother were killed in an explosion at the pit head – and after appearing for various non league sides he signed as an amateur for Chesterfield in 1927, turning professional soon after. Incidentally he is one of only two Clay Cross players to have played for Aston Villa – the other, William Morris, having captained Villa to F.A.Cup success before The Great War. He would spend two years at Saltergate, appearing in 46 competitive games - before financial pressures forced the Derbyshire club to sell him to a Wednesday side who weeks later would clinch the first of back-to-back League Championships – Beeson would play three games in the second success but not enough to earn a medal.

After failing to nail down a regular place at Hillsborough his first season at Aston Villa proved traumatic as they suffered relegation to Division Two and by the time they reclaimed their top flight position – in 1937 – Beeson was out of the first team picture after seventy league games for The Villains. He would then spend two years at Walsall before joining the Royal Air Force as a P.T. Instructor for the duration of World War Two – playing twenty games as a guest during 1944-5 for Hull City while he was billeted in Filey. After hostilities ended he was sent by the F.A. to coach in Denmark, Sweden and Norway, only turning down the offer to move to the latter country due to a lack of suitable housing. Back in Birmingham he worked in George Ellison's factory, coaching the works football team to a variety of local honours, and even played for Boldmere St.Michaels when he was over fifty years old. He continued to keep fit into his late 80s by training with the various amateur sides his son – also called George - managed and also helped out in the furniture shop his son owned.

BELL, Derek Martin 1976

Born: 30 October 1956 Wyberton, Lincolnshire
(5ft 10ins, 11st 5lbs – 1975)
Debut: 24 March 1976
v Chesterfield Division Three Home
Last Appearance: 10 April 1976
v Wrexham Division Three Away
Total League
& Cup Appearances: 5 Goals: 1

Career Details:

Derby County		1972 App.
Halifax Town	May	1975
WEDNESDAY	11 March	1976 Loan
Barnsley	26 October	1978 £30,000
Lincoln City	22 November	1979 £33,000
Chesterfield	August	1983 £8,500
Scunthorpe United	January	1984 Free
Boston United	March	1986 Free
Spalding United	December	1986 Free
Lincoln United	August	1987

Forward Derek Bell was a player who spent his entire career in the bottom two divisions, being a consistent scorer at a variety of clubs. His playing career had started as an associate schoolboy at First Division Derby County in 1971- after he'd impressed for Lincolnshire schools - but after progressing to apprentice status a year later he could not make the last step to the professional ranks and dropped down the leagues to sign for Halifax Town. He netted twenty-one goals in 112 league games for The Shaymen and it was while at the West Yorkshire club that Wednesday manager Len Ashurst brought him to Hillsborough on loan, with a view to a full transfer. At the time the Owls were fighting a desperate rearguard action to avoid relegation to the basement division and Bell would play five times, scoring his only goal in 4-2 defeat at Preston North End, but did not impress sufficiently enough for Wednesday to follow up their initial interest and he returned to Town at the end of his one month loan period.

He would return to South Yorkshire on a full transfer over two years later but his destination was not Hillsborough but Oakwell where he scored an impressive twenty times in just forty-six league games for The Tykes. He would continue to score regularly in league football before dropping into the Conference to join Boston United on a part-time basis in 1986. After leaving the pro game Bell would drive H.G.V's for three years before being appointed scout at York City in 1990 – a position he held for three years while also managing haulage company G.F.Fisher's Sunday league team. In October 1994 Bell was promoted to Youth Team coach/Chief Scout at City and then assistant manager in 1996, while later in his career had spells on the backroom staff at both Lincoln City and Wigan Athletic.

BELL, Lawrence Stanley T. "Lawrie" 1895-97

Born: May 1875 Dumbarton
(5ft 9ins, 10st, 8lbs – 1896)
Debut: 2 September 1895
v Everton
Division One Away
Last Appearance: 17 April 1897
v Bury Division One Home
Total League
& Cup Appearances: 53 Goals: 13

Career Details:

Langbank		
Dumbarton		
Third Lanark		
WEDNESDAY	May	1895
Everton	July	1897 £200
Bolton Wanderers		1898
Brentford		1902
West Bromwich Albion	June	1904
Hibernian	May	1905

The Owls had competition from Everton for the services of centre forward Lawrie Bell but the teenager decided to sign for Wednesday and duly gave the Merseyside club a taste of what they missed by scoring on his debut on the new season's opening day - at Everton! The youngster had risen to prominence in Scottish football first with Dumbarton and then Third Lanark and at the time became the youngest player to move across the border to Sheffield since the imports began with James Lang in the late 1870s. Bell had played for the Scottish League while at Dumbarton and his superb shooting and dribbling skills endeared him to the Olive Grove faithful. His clever play and distribution to his wing-men looked to have permanently solved Wednesday's problem at No.9 – inside forward Harry Davis having spent the majority of the previous season in the position – and he played a major part as Wednesday won the FA.Cup in 1896. His appearance in the Final against Wolves made him the youngest player so far to play in the glamour final and at the time he was described by a local scribe as the "best centre-forward Wednesday have had in modern football".

After experiencing an outstanding first season at Wednesday it was perhaps not a surprise that the youngster struggled to repeat his display in 1896-7 and could only net three times from twenty-three league and cup games, although any absences were due to injury rather than poor form. Despite not scoring prolifically in his second campaign it was still a shock to Owls fans when in July 1897 he finally did join Everton, two years after he had snubbed them to sign for Wednesday. At Everton, Bell quickly rediscovered his goal scoring form – netting 15 times in just 28 games – as The Toffeemen finished fourth in the top flight and reached the FA.Cup semi-finals. Feelings amongst Everton fans during the summer of 1899 must have been similar to Wednesday fans two years earlier when their exciting centre forward was not re-signed, leaving instead for Second Division Bolton Wanderers. He would net 23 times in his debut campaign for Bolton as they finished runners-up to Champions Wednesday but despite this record he was duly converted into a right-winger in the following season! A broken leg suffered against Newton Heath (a.k.a. Manchester United) in a Manchester Senior Cup tie in April 1902 did little to interrupt his career with Bolton and by the time he left for Brentford, Lawrie had scored 45 goals in 103 league and cup games for The Wanderers. After a short spell at West Bromwich Albion, Lawrie returned to his homeland to sign for Hibs and would eventually retire from football in 1911. His brother Jack played for Everton, New Brighton & Preston North End and made history by becoming the first Chairman of the PFA and also Preston's first manager.

BELLAS, John Edward 'Jack' 1920-23

Born: 16 September 1895
Bishop Auckland
(5ft 8½ ins, 11st 7lbs – 1920)
Died: 23 August 1977 Peasley, Notts
Debut: 9 October 1920
v Leeds United Division Two Home
Last Appearance: 5 May 1923
v Port Vale Division Two Away
Total League
& Cup Appearances: 51 Goals: 0

Career Details:

Shildon Athletic		
WEDNESDAY	24 September	1920 £250
Mansfield Town	15 June	1923 £500
Coventry City	17 January	1925 £350
Heanor Town	30 July	1926
Sutton Junction	August	1927
Peasley College	September	1929
New Houghton Church	December	1929

Following the disastrous relegation season of 1919-20 Wednesday released an unprecedented number of players and it was up to new manager Bob Brown to re equip Wednesday for life in the Second Division. The Owls had started the new season with newcomer John Dunn in the right back role but Brown decided fairly quickly that a further change was needed so he raided non-league Shildon to sign 25 year-old Jack Bellas on professional forms. His league debut would come soon after and Jack would move confidently into league soccer, missing only four more games until the end of the season as Wednesday recovered from relegation to finish in mid table. However during the close season Bellas met with what seemed a minor accident when he fell down some stairs but the injury to his leg meant the highly regarded defender missed the start of the season and as a consequence failed to make a single first team appearance at right back - his only two starts coming somewhat strangely at inside left! After recovering his fitness, and despite competition from George Gray, the crack darts player would re-claim the right back berth during his third season at Hillsborough but the arrival of future England International Billy Felton in January 1923 effectively ended his Wednesday career. The new man came straight into the side at left back but it was the emergence of the outstanding left back Ernie Blenkinsop that provided the mortal blow to Bellas' Wednesday career as Felton soon switched wings and the pair would play for many years as full back partners.

He spent the last few weeks of his Owls career in the club's reserve side as they lifted the Midland League Championship and it would be to a fellow Midland League club that Jack would be sold in the summer that followed. His move to Mansfield Town was effectively a free transfer as F.A. rules of the day stated that no fee was due if the buying club was a non-league team – it would be his next club Coventry City who had to cough up the £500 fee! The back enjoyed a successful time at Mansfield Town – winning back-to-back League Championships – and his form saw Coventry City take him back into League football just over eighteen months after he had departed. Ever present from signing until the end of the season he would start to drift out of first team contention early in the next campaign and eventually returned to Midland league soccer after 34 appearances for The Sky Blues.

The remainder of his career was spent in non-league football – the change in the offside law not helping the somewhat slow paced Bellas'chances of returning to the football league – while he worked at Peasley Colliery until his retirement. On his death Jack's ashes were scattered over the pitch at Mansfield Town's Field Mill ground – perhaps reflecting his affinity with a club where he enjoyed his greatest success.

BENNETT, David Anthony "Dave" 1989-91

Born: 11 July 1959 Manchester
(6ft, 11st 2lbs – 1988)
Debut: 25 March 1989
v Queens Park Rngs
Div. One Home
Last Appearance: 7 April 1990
v Southampton
Division One Home
Total League &
Cup Appearances: 23+8 Goals: 1

Career Details:

Manchester City	2 August	1977
Cardiff City	25 September	1981 £120,000
Coventry City	21 July	1983 £125,000 (T)
WEDNESDAY	23 March	1989 £250,000
Swindon Town	19 September	1990 £50,000
Shrewsbury Town	21 November	1991 Loan
Nuneaton Boro	March	1994 Free
Stamford		Free
Hinckley Athletic	September	1995 Free
Atherstone United	February	1996 Free
Stamford		Free
Telford United	September	1997 Free
Sutton Coalfield Town	cs	1997 Free
Corby Town	December	1997 Free
Stockingford AA/ Pig & Whistle		1999 Free

Winger Dave Bennett is perhaps best remembered for his part in Coventry City's fairytale FA.Cup win in 1987, scoring one of the goals that saw hot favourites Spurs beaten 3-2 at Wembley. His best days were certainly at City and when he arrived at Hillsborough on deadline day 1989 he was seen by the majority of Wednesday fans as a short term signing by new manager Ron Atkinson, bringing experience to his relegation threatened side. The new signing certainly played his part in that fight to escape the dreaded drop, appearing in the final ten games of the season, but it would be fair to say that his star had been dimmed somewhat by a broken leg he suffered in March 1988 and after flitting in and out of the side in the next season he eventually moved to Swindon Town.

Unfortunately for Bennett this transfer proved the beginning of the end of his professional career as he suffered another leg break in only his second game for Town. This run of bad luck continued unabated however as after regaining fitness he went on loan to Shrewsbury Town where he broke his leg for a third time, in only his second appearance, and then to complete a miserable two years suffered a fourth break in 1992 pre season training at Swindon Town. This final fracture probably convinced Bennett that his professional career was at an end after 332 league appearances for six clubs over a fifteen-year period. He had originally signed apprentice forms for his local side Manchester City in June 1977, turning pro just over a year later, and enjoyed an extended spell in their first team in the early 1980s culminating in an appearance in the 1981 F.A.Cup Final defeat to Tottenham Hotspur. Within four months of receiving that runners-up medal he was sold to Cardiff City where he scored eighteen times in seventy-seven league appearances before moving back to the Midlands to sign for perennial First Division strugglers Coventry City. It was at City that he hit the heights, forming a deadly partnership with Cyrille Regis and David Phillips which took The Sky Blues to the aforementioned Cup win – he also netted in the semi-final win against Leeds United at Hillsborough – and his brilliant close control mesmerised many a full back in the two hundred plus games he played for City.

After his professional career was ended through injury Bennett retired only to make a 1994 comeback in non-league football at Nuneaton Boro. Over the next five years he would play for a wide variety of non-league sides in the Midlands area with his debut for Corby Town certainly one he would remember as he hit a hat-trick only for his new side to lose 6-5 in an incredible game at Grantham Town! He had his first experience of coaching as player-coach at Atherstone United and as he passed his fortieth birthday could still be found playing Saturday football and for his local pub side on a Sunday! He continues to also play charity games around the country as well as fulfilling various coaching duties and some media work.

BENNETT, William 'Mickey' 1889-91

Born: 2nd Quarter 1863 Rotherham
(5ft 4½ ins, 10st 8lbs – 1890)
Died: 13 September 1919 Mexborough
Debut: 20 January 1890
v London Swifts
F.A.Cup Home
Last Appearance: 29 March 1890
v Blackburn Rovers
F.A.Cup Final
Total League
& Cup Appearances: 5* Goals: 4
***Also appeared in 21 Football Alliance League games**

Career Details:

Rotherham Town		
Mexborough Town	cs	1884
Doncaster Rovers		1888
WEDNESDAY	August	1889
Mexborough Town		1891

It was with his village side that forward Mickey Bennett first came to prominence, becoming a local hero in April 1886 when his two goals against Heeley secured the much sought after Sheffield Challenge Cup for the first time in Mexborough's history. After moving to neighbouring club Rotherham Town in 1888 the free scoring inside forward would again help his side to lift the area's premier trophy – scoring in the semi-final and also netting in the Bramall Lane final as Town beat Staveley 2-1. His swashbuckling form in local football persuaded Wednesday to sign Mickey and he would first appear in blue and white favours during the club's first practise game of the new season in August 1889. However this was the first season of Alliance League Football and with Wednesday having built a formidable squad to cope with the new concept of league football Bennett would start his Wednesday career in the second team.

However it soon emerged that Mickey had signed for both Rotherham Town and Wednesday for the 1889-90 season and he was subsequently banned for a year! Thankfully this was later reduced to just two months and in November 1889 he made his first team debut – in a friendly at home to Burton Swifts. An Alliance League debut at home to Long Eaton Rangers followed two weeks later and Bennett would score from a new centre forward position in a 9-1 rout. From this moment Mickey was an automatic choice for the remainder of the season, missing only four first team games as Wednesday not only won the Alliance League Championship but also reached the Final of the F.A.Cup for the first time in their history. Unfortunately the Final against Blackburn Rovers proved a somewhat sobering experience for Bennett and his teammates as the Lancashire club won 6-1, although Mickey did have the consolation of being the first ever Wednesday player to score in a Final – his brother Walter appeared in three F.A.Cup Finals for Sheffield United while another brother, Harry, was a former Barnsley captain. On his day he was described as a "brilliant footballer" and "superb header of the ball" so it was therefore a surprise that he would only make six Alliance League appearances for the club in 1890-91 – in a season when The Owls finished bottom of the league - mainly in a left wing role, and at the season's end returned to his old club Mexborough. He could be found working in a glass foundry at the turn of the Century and passed away in 1919 at the age of 56 having entered Wednesday's history books as one of the club's early goal scoring heroes.

BENTLEY, Harold "Harry" 1909-20

Born: Sheffield 1891
(5ft 8ins, 11st –1913)
Debut: 14 April 1914
v Oldham Athletic
Division One Away
Last Appearance: 17 April 1920
v Aston Villa
Division One Away
Total League
& Cup Appearances: 53* Goals: 3
***Also appeared in**
13 Wartime games, scoring 3 goals

Career Details:

Heeley Friends		
WEDNESDAY	April	1909 £10
Brighton	10 June	1920 £250
Swindon Town	August	1922 £350

Versatile defender Harry Bentley joined the Owls from local non-league football – the club donating the handsome sum of £10 to Heeley in July 1909 - and had to wait patiently for almost five years before making his senior bow. His consistent form in the club's Midland League side eventually won him a first team chance but after establishing himself in the Football League eleven his career was interrupted by the First World War.

He spent the majority of the hostilities in France with the Royal Field Artillery, returning home occasionally to appear in Wartime soccer for Wednesday. When regional football ended at the end of the War the Owls experienced a horrendous season – culminating in relegation from Division One – and for Bentley it was a mixed season as he could not secure a regular place, making 18 starts. A change of scenery was perhaps needed and this occurred in the summer of 1920 when he made the long trip South to sign for Brighton. He appeared in seventy league and cup games for the Seagulls – including an appearance in their first ever football league game in August 1920 - before winding up his professional career with eleven league games for Swindon Town.

BENTLEY, Willis 1882-85

Born: Sheffield
Debut: 6 January 1883 v Nottingham Forest F.A.Cup Away
Last Appearance: 3 January 1885
v Nottingham Forest F.A.Cup Away
Total League & Cup Appearances: 5 Goals: 1

Career Details:

Exchange	
WEDNESDAY	1882
Owlerton	1885-89
Sheffield United	1890

When teenager Willis Bentley joined the Owls they were still an amateur club slowly establishing themselves as top dogs in the City of Sheffield. His first ever appearance in a Wednesday shirt would come in the 2-2 draw at Trent Bridge in an F.A.Cup tie against Nottingham Forest and for the next two seasons Willis would be a regular in the side – winning local Cup competition the Wharncliffe Charity Cup in 1883 and finishing runners-up two years later. Bentley – who played in a variety of position including half back, full back and inside forward - made his final appearance in a November 1885 friendly defeat at home to Derby County before moving to pastures new.

As well as appearing for the Owls, Willis was employed as a tutor/warder in the South Yorkshire Asylum – after starting his working life as a Steel tilter – where he taught patients football and cricket. His wife Hannah was a nurse – they married in June 1887 – but sadly for the couple only one of their four children lived beyond the age of three years, a not uncommon occurrence in Victorian England. After ending his playing career Bentley helped with the development of Owlerton based side Channing Rovers – coaching alongside Billy Betts around the turn of the Century.

BERESFORD, Marlon 1987-92 & 2001

Born: 2 September 1969 Lincoln (6ft 1ins, 13st 6lbs – 2000)
Debut: 13 January 2001 v Blackburn Rovers Div. One Away
Last Appearance: 10 Feb 2001 v Wimbledon Division One Away
Total League & Cup Appearances: 4 Goals: 0

Career Details:

WEDNESDAY	23 September	1987
Bury	25 August	1989 Loan
Ipswich Town	29 September	1989 Loan
Northampton Town	27 September	1990 Loan
Crewe Alexandra	1 March	1991 Loan
Northampton Town	15 August	1991 3-month loan
Burnley	28 August	1992 £176,000*
Middlesbrough	10 March	1998 £500,000
WEDNESDAY	12 January	2001 Loan
Wolverhampton W.	18 August	2001 Loan
Burnley	31 January	2002 Loan
York City	5 August	2002 Free
Burnley	5 September	2002 Free
Released	30 June	2003
Bradford City	15 September	2003 one-mth contract
Released	16 October	2003
Luton Town	24 October	2003
Barnsley	26 January	2004 Free
Luton Town	1 July	2004 Free

* Including 20% sell on clause

When Marlon Beresford signed his first professional contract with Wednesday in 1987 he would have had one ambition – to play first team football for the Owls. However he could not have possibly guessed that it would take him over thirteen years to achieve the feat! That incredible gap – and with it a unique place in Wednesday history – occurred due to the fact that when Beresford was first earning rave reviews in the reserves his competition for a first team spot came from Chris Turner and the emerging Kevin Pressman. Not surprisingly the highly rated youngster found his chances of first team football somewhat limited and it would be while on loan at variety of lower division clubs that Beresford would get his first taste of league football – his league debut coming for Bury. His debut for Northampton Town in September 1990 did not make him a popular figure in the household of long serving Town keeper Paul Gleasure as he was unceremoniously dropped to make way for the loanee – after 229 consecutive games for the Cobblers!

It was becoming obvious to all that Beresford was too good to be just a third choice and the situation became untenable in the summer of 1991 when new manager Trevor Francis inexplicably spent a club record fee to add England goalkeeper Chris Woods to his roster. The sale of Turner soon afterwards offered some hope for the youngster but following another loan spell at Northampton – he would play twenty-eight league games for Town in two spells – the inevitable parting of ways came in the following close season after Marlon had turned down an offer of a lucrative new contract. His move across the Pennines – for a fee decided by transfer tribunal after The Owls asked for £150,000 and Burnley offered just £50,000 - would finally secure permanent first team football for Beresford and over the next six years he would play 294 games for The Clarets, becoming a huge crowd favourite and building a reputation as the best goalkeeper outside of the Premier League – such was his popularity that a fanzine entitled "Marlon's gloves" was named after the stopper! However with a Bosman free transfer looming on the horizon Burnley decided to cash in their prize asset – he had been named P.F.A keeper of the year for two seasons running in 1992-3 and 1993-4 - and Beresford moved into the top flight at Bryan Robson's Middlesbrough. Unfortunately it was here that his career stalled somewhat as in four years at the Riverside Beresford appeared in only ten league games for Boro, eventually regressing into the situation he was originally in at Hillsborough – as third choice keeper.

It was during his penultimate season at Middlesbrough that Paul Jewell would bring Beresford back to Hillsborough for a loan spell. However despite backing up his reputation for shot stopping the old boy would experience a disappointing time on his return as Wednesday lost all four games he appeared in; he netted an embarrassing own goal in his final game at Wimbledon and when he returned to the shadows at Boro he left The Owls bottom of Division One – his final game would also be the last match for boss Jewell who was sacked soon after. After a loan spell at Burnley he was released by Boro in the summer of 2002 before signing a short-term contract at York City. However his next move took him back to Turf Moor for a third spell, signing for the season after initially joining on a month long contract. He stayed only a season though and after Burnley leaked 89 times in league soccer – including an incredible seven at home to Wednesday – he was released. Further spells at Luton and Barnsley followed before re-signing for the former on a two-year deal which also gave Beresford coaching duties with The Hatters young keepers.

BESWETHERICK, Jonathan Barry "Jon" 2002-04

Born: 15 January 1978 Liverpool
(5ft 11ins, 11st 4 lbs – 2002)
Debut: 10 August 2002
v Stoke City
Division One Home
Last Appearance: 7th March 2004
v Chesterfield Division Two Away
Total League
& Cup Appearances: 12+4 Goals: 0

Career Details:

Plymouth Argyle	27 July	1996
WEDNESDAY	29 May	2002 Free
Swindon Town	21 February	2003 Loan
Macclesfield Town	15 January	2004 Loan
Released	30 June	2004
Bristol Rovers	July	2004 Trial
Kidderminster Harriers	4 November	2004 N/C
Released	5 January	2005
Forest Green Rovers	7 January	2005 N/C

Although born in Merseyside it was in deepest Devon that Jon Beswetherick would begin his professional football career, the left back originally signing as a trainee at Home Park before turning pro in the summer of 1996. His debut for Plymouth came in October 1997 – as a late sub in the 2-1 defeat at Gillingham – but it was a while before Jon could break into the Argyle side, totalling only two sub appearances in his first two years in the professional ranks. The breakthrough did come though in 1998-9 as Beswetherick appeared in almost half of Argyle's Third Division games before becoming an automatic choice for the remainder of his Plymouth Argyle career – missing only two games from the start of 1999-00 campaign until September 2001. By the time Terry Yorath took him North to Sheffield the scouser had totalled 146 league games for the Pilgrims and had just won a Division Three Championship medal.

He was one of several summer signings made by Yorath in an attempt to improve Wednesday's fortunes in Division One but unfortunately for both player and manager the move proved a disappointment to all concerned as despite showing promise in pre season Beswetherick struggled to adapt to life in the higher grade and after starting the first four league games of the new season was dropped to the reserves. He returned in January 2003 for the disastrous 4-1 loss in the F.A.Cup at Gillingham but his next taste of league football would come while on loan at Second Division Swindon Town. After a month in Wiltshire he returned to Hillsborough to play out the remainder of the season in Wednesday's reserve team while he fared little better in his second season at Hillsborough, being nothing more a squad player and spending a loan period at Third Division Macclesfield Town. After being released he struggled to make an impression in the lower reaches of the Football League and eventually joined Conference club Forest Green on non-contract after being released by League Two strugglers Kidderminster Harriers.

BETTS, William 'Billy' 1883-95

Born: 26 March 1864 Sheffield
(5ft, 7ins. 11st 2lbs – 1890)
Died: 8 August 1941 Sheffield
Debut: 6 January 1883
v Nottingham Forest
F.A.Cup Away
Last Appearance: 13 April 1895
v Preston North End
Division One Away
Total League
& Cup Appearances: 83* Goals: 4
***Also appeared in 60 Football Alliance League games**

Career Details:

Pitsmoor (Christchurch)		
Parkwood Rovers		
Clarence		
Pyebank Rovers		1881
Heeley	March	1882
WEDNESDAY		1883
Lockwood Brothers		1883
WEDNESDAY		1887
Retired		1895

CAPS (@SWFC)
ENGLAND Full (1) v Wales 23/02/89

There is no doubt that "Old Warhorse" Billy Betts was one of Wednesday's greatest players of the Victorian era, playing in many games that shaped the early history of the club. From appearing in many of the club's early F.A.Cup ties he would go on to appear not only in the opening game at Olive Grove but in Wednesday's debut fixtures in both the Football Alliance and Football League, not to mention the first ever meeting with Sheffield United in 1890! The outstanding centre back first appeared for Wednesday on Boxing Day 1882, in a 5-0 friendly win at Brigg Town, but at the time he was attached to the Pyebank club with whom he played for against The Owls just four days later! He had joined Wednesday – for what proved to be only a brief spell – after first rebuffing several efforts to sign him.

He had first played football while at school and although he would later make his name as one of the outstanding centre-half backs of his generation it was at full back that he first played organised football with local club Pitsmoor. After making appearances for Parkwood – the reserve side of crack local outfit Burton Star – and Clarence his first local honour was won with Pyebank when they lifted the Sheffield Challenge Cup in 1882. The teenager would appear in several local Cup Finals in the years that followed – his first final appearance had come in 1882 when playing as a guest for Heeley they lost 5-0 to a certain Sheffield Wednesday in the Wharncliffe Final! He would however win the competition with his next club Lockwood Brothers – where he first switched to half back after regular Jack Housley lost form – and again lift the Sheffield Challenge Cup as his side rose to become a major threat to Wednesday's dominance in Sheffield soccer. The situation reached crisis point in 1886-7 when an administrative blunder resulted in Wednesday failing to apply in time to play in that season's F.A.Cup – this coupled with their refusal to turn professional meant the likes of Betts and several Wednesday players would appear for the new boys in the Cup and threaten the very existence of The Owls.

Thankfully Wednesday would bow to the inevitable and in 1887 duly turned professional with a certain Billy Betts one of the first players to sign. This would start an association with the club that would last almost ten years and see Betts appear over 300 times for Wednesday in a wide variety of games. He enjoyed a hugely successful first season at Olive Grove, as Wednesday completed the Sheffield Challenge and Wharncliffe Charity Cup double, and over the next five seasons was almost ever present as Wednesday progressed from friendly games to the Alliance league and ultimately to the Football League. During the Owls three years in the Alliance League Betts would miss only six of the sixty-six games played – being ever present in 1889-90 as the Championship was brought to Sheffield. In the same season Wednesday reached their first F.A.Cup Final – losing to Blackburn

Rovers with Betts in the side – and in the following year he would play in the 12-0 win over Halliwell – the club's record win of all time. His talents were also not only exclusive to the football field as Betts was a cricketer of considerable ability and even appeared for Yorkshire colts during the close season. His reputation was of a player made of solid steel and this was perhaps no more personified than during a game at Olive Grove when Billy broke his nose but after ten minutes in the dressing room returned to finish the game!

Incredibly despite playing professionally for Wednesday, Betts also worked for a living and after starting his working life as a file cutter was eventually employed as a stoker at Neepsend Gas Works in Sheffield, where he worked during the week before being ready on a Saturday to do battle on the football field. After helping Wednesday become established in The Football League the centre-back – who was a superb header of the ball and dominated the field of play – was rewarded with a benefit game against Liverpool in April 1894 before hanging up his boots after losing his place to another future Wednesday legend – Tommy Crawshaw. He later combined his full time job with working as the club's groundsman and after helping the club's "A" team in 1921-22 he was appointed assistant trainer in July 1922. His family connection with the club would not be completely cut when he finally retired as his grandson Dennis Woodhead played over two hundred times for the club during the 1940s and early 1950s.

BINGLEY, John 'Jack' 1876-82

Born:
Debut: 8 January 1881
v Turton F.A.Cup Away
Last Appearance: 5 November 1881
v Providence
F.A.Cup Home
Total League
& Cup Appearances: 2 Goals: 0

Career Details:

Local	
WEDNESDAY	1876
Park Grange	1882

When Wednesday first started their rise to prominence in the early days of Sheffield football several players provided the backbone for success. One such player was forward Jack Bingley who helped Wednesday to win the Sheffield Challenge Cup in its first two seasons of competition – 1877 and 1878 – while he also won a winners medal in 1882 plus lifted the Wharncliffe Charity with the Owls in 1879 – again in its inaugural season. He was a regular when the Owls – or as they were known then, The Blades - first entered the new national F.A.Cup competition in 1880 although he missed the opening fixture at Blackburn Rovers, playing in the club's second ever tie.

By the time Wednesday reached their first F.A.Cup semi-final in 1882 Bingley was out of the first team picture and would eventually move on to Sheffield side Park Grange – playing against his old club in January 1884 when he helped them to a 3-1 Wharncliffe Cup win at Bramall Lane.

BINGLEY, Walter 1955-58

Born: 17 April 1930 Sheffield
(6ft, 11st 10lbs – 1955)
Debut: 3 September 1955
v Bristol Rovers
Division Two Home
Last Appearance: 26 October 1957
v Sunderland
Division One Home
Total League
& Cup Appearances: 39 Goals: 0

Career Details:

Meynell Road Youth Club		
Eccleshall Business Mens Team		
Bolton Wanderers	April	1948
WEDNESDAY	May	1955 £500
Swindon Town	3 January	1958 £1,150
York City	August	1960
Halifax Town	July	1963
Released	June	1965
Selby Town	December	1965
Released	February	1966

Despite playing all his junior football in Sheffield it was Bolton Wanderers who would capture his signature from under the noses of the two Sheffield professional clubs. The left back had initially impressed for Sheffield boys – while playing his youth football at Meynell Road until aged 16 – and it was while playing local non-league football that the Lancashire club took him to Burnden Park. However Walter experienced a frustrating time with Wanderers, starting only six first team games in a seven-year stay – with a Central League Championship medal in 1955 no real consolation for lack of opportunities in the Football League side.

After being transferred back to the City of his birth Bingley appeared in twenty-one league games during 1955-56 to qualify for a Division Two Championship medal but unfortunately for Bingley his role at Hillsborough was simply one of stand in for regular full back Norman Curtis and with his rival fit in the season that followed Bingley would play only four times. After missing only one of the opening fourteen games of the following season the return of fit again Curtis again saw Walt relegated to the reserves where he remained until moving to Swindon Town early in the New Year. He would spend two and a half seasons in Wiltshire, appearing in 101 games for Town, before playing out his league career back in Yorkshire at York City and Halifax Town. At the former club he missed only six games in a three-year period, scoring his first ever league goals in 1962-3 after being appointed the club's penalty taker. He also helped City to the quarter-finals of the League Cup in 1962 and the steady and reliable full back would provide sterling service for City in a new role of right back.

After retiring from full time football Walter played briefly at Yorkshire league Selby Town before being appointed trainer-manager of fellow league club Hampton Sports, a Sheffield based works team. He led them to the runners-up spot in 1966 while he also did some scouting, helping several local players to sign for league teams. Bingley – who captained the Army Team at Lichfield while doing his National Service – worked alongside fellow ex-Owl Ron Capewell for Whitbread Brewery in Sheffield until his retirement.

BINKS, Sydney "Sid" 1922-24

Born: 25 July 1899
Whitworth, nr Bishop Auckland
(5ft 10ins, 12st – 1920)
Died: 4 February 1978
Beauchief, Sheffield
Debut: 26 August 1922
v Rotherham County
Division Two Away
Last Appearance: 27 September 1924
v Manchester United
Division Two Away
Total League
& Cup Appearances: 83 Goals: 33

Career Details:

Spennymoor United		
Sunderland		Trial
Bishop Auckland		
WEDNESDAY	8 May	1922
Huddersfield Town	28 September	1924 £750 + E.Richardson
Blackpool	2 October	1925
Portsmouth	July	1927
Southend United	June	1928
Fulham	February	1929
Heart of Midlothian	August	1930 Trial
Chesterfield	September	1930
Rotherham United	April	1933
Ashington	August	1933

Centre-forward Sid Binks was a rare example of a player who would achieve great success on the football field despite not having played the game until joining the Royal Naval Air Service at the age of seventeen! He had started his working life as a baker in his native North-East but his career would take a dramatic turn during the War years as, on the advice of a fellow serviceman, he took up football to get out of "dirty jobs". Binks played throughout the conflict in a centre forward role for the services football team – he was a mechanic in the forces, flying over enemy territory on several occasions. After being de-mobbed he returned to his old job but the football bug had bitten and he would sign amateur forms for Northern league club Spennymoor United before scoring twice in a trial spell at Sunderland – he decided not to sign as this would have meant him having to leave home and give up his job!

It was the move to legendary non-league giants Bishop Auckland that really lighted the touch paper of Binks' career as with The Bishops he not only won back-to-back Amateur Cups, scoring in both the 1921 and 1922 Finals as Bishop Auckland became the first club to retain the trophy, but also England Amateur International caps, the first coming in November 1921 against Wales. By this time he was an amateur at Hillsborough, having signed in October 1920, and it needed Bob Brown's persuasive tongue to finally secure his signature on a professional contract with Sid receiving wages of £5, a rise of £2 on his usual weekly wage. His impact at Hillsborough was immediate, scoring in his first two games as Wednesday topped the table early in the 1922-23 campaign, and he netted sixteen times in his debut campaign as an Owls side still rebuilding after the traumatic relegation in 1920 finished in a respectable eighth spot. The strong and bulky Binks netted three hat-tricks in his time at Wednesday – including a four-goal haul at home to Crystal Palace in December 1923 – so it was therefore a surprise when the prolific scorer left for neighbours Huddersfield Town in a deal that brought Ted Richardson to Hillsborough. Luckily for Wednesday his replacement Jimmy Trotter would become one of the club's greatest No.9s but Binks' career stalled somewhat at Leeds Road as he played only four times for Town as they won consecutive League Championship under their legendary manager Herbert Chapman – Sid did however have the consolation of being awarded a medal for his bit part in the success. After failing to become a regular at Town he moved to Blackpool where he would appear at both centre half and centre forward in fifty-five games before failing to make a first team appearance at Portsmouth and having a short spell at Southend. During his time at Fulham he was astonishingly placed on the transfer list after refusing to play for their cricket side and on leaving London spent just one month North of the Border at Hearts.

It was his old Hillsborough team mate Teddy Davison – then manager of Chesterfield – who took him to Saltergate and he scored fifteen times in 43 games for the Derbyshire side, winning the Third Division North Championship in 1931, before a knee injury brought an end to his professional career. It was at this point, in the summer of 1932, that Sid returned to Hillsborough for a brief spell as assistant trainer – covering for the incapacitated Sam Powell - before putting on his boots again to play league football for Rotherham United and then non-league football back in his native Northeast. That marked the end of a career that could easily have ended while at Wednesday as at the time his friends tried to persuade Sid – who was a superb sprinter – to give up football for the racetrack! In those days professional sprint meetings – held at Sheffield United's old training ground at Ball Inn – were well attended by fans, bookmakers and backers while on Binks' first appearance he bet 50p on himself and duly won £3 and the 1st prize! He did however decide to stick with football and after his career finished Binks would return to Sheffield where he would run a bakery for thirty years.

BINNEY, Charles 'Chas' 1919-23

Born: 24 February 1901 Sheffield
(5ft 8ins, 11st 6lbs– 1920)
Died: 3 March 1952 Sheffield
Debut: 15 November 1919
v Derby County
Division One Home
Last Appearance: 26 December 1922
v Bradford City
Division Two Away
Total League
& Cup Appearances: 43 Goals: 6

Career Details:

Leadmill St.Mary's		
Leadmill St Mary's Old Boys		
WEDNESDAY	October	1919 £10/10s
Released	May	1923
Worksop Town		1925
Wombwell Town	September	1926
Frickley Colliery	June	1927

Attacker Charlie Binney joined the Owls from local non-league football after his form alerted both of Sheffield's professional clubs to his potential. It was the blue and white side of the City that secured his signature and Wednesday's faith looked to have been justified when he impressed greatly on his debut, netting twice for the reserve side in September 1919. Within six weeks of signing pro he had replaced Harvey in the first eleven but this was during the traumatic relegation season of 1919-20 and he could do little to stop his side tumbling out of the top flight. The three seasons that followed saw Binney involved less and less in Wednesday's league side – dropping from 17 appearances to just 3 in 1922-23 – and he became a reserve team regular, winning a Sheffield Challenge Cup winners medal in 1921 and a Midland League Championship medal two years later – he also worked as a cashier in a local firm during this period.

However his league career effectively finished in dramatic fashion in May 1923 when Binney suffered a nervous breakdown and became seriously ill. A move away from the smoke of the City helped his recuperation and in October 1924 it was reported that he had almost recovered and was leading an outdoor life on the outskirts of Sheffield. Eventually – two years after becoming ill – Binney re-launched his career and played for top local non-league sides before retiring from the game

BIRCH, Arnold 1919-23

Born: 12 July 1891 Grenoside, Sheffield
(6ft 1ins, 11st – 1922)
Died: 6 January 1964 Grenoside, Sheffield
Debut: 30 August 1919
v Middlesbrough
Division One Home
Last Appearance: 6 January 1923
Blackpool
Division Two Away
Total League
& Cup Appearances: 29* Goals: 0
***Also appeared in**
29 Wartime Games

Career Details:

Tankersley Colliery		
Grenoside		
1st Royal Naval Brigade		1914-18
Be Quick		1917
WEDNESDAY	August	1919
Chesterfield	June	1923 £100 + C.L.Roberts
Denaby United	29 September	1927
Grenoside Sports	March	1930

Fearless and clever goalkeeper Arnold Birch started his playing career at Colliery side Tankersley where was he employed as a 'filler' – he had started his working life at the age of only thirteen at Smithywood Colliery. At the outbreak of war Arnold joined the 1st Royal Naval Brigade but within five weeks was captured at Antwerp and had to spend the rest of the conflict interned in Holland. While in captivity Birch continued to play regularly in the inter-battalion matches organised inside the camps and with the special permission of the camp commandant was also allowed to play twelve times for Groningen based Dutch side Be Quick. He made such an impact in local football that in 1918 Birch actually played twice for the North Netherlands select side, including one appearance against his own internment camp!

Due to a family bereavement he was allowed home on a month's parole in March 1917 and duly signed amateur forms for Wednesday – incidentally he had first appeared as a trialist during the 1914 pre season public practise game at Hillsborough. After being demobbed in February 1919 he returned to work at Tankersley Colliery but soon after signed professional forms for Wednesday – the Owls donating five guineas to Grenoside in August 1919 – and during the disastrous relegation campaign of 1919-20 shared the custodian duties with Wednesday legend Teddy Davison.

Unfortunately for Birch it was his goalkeeping rival who saw off the challenge of his young pretender to become re-established at first team level and Birch had to be content with being a regular in the club's Midland League side, in addition to an occasional senior appearance when Davison was unavailable. The arrival of Jack Brown – another outstanding goalie signed by the club in the pre war years – in February 1923 effectively signalled the end of his Hillsborough career and the following summer saw a move to neighbours Chesterfield. Incidentally Wednesday signed his brother Wally from Luton Town in July 1930 although Arnold's younger sibling failed to appear in the Owls league side. Arnold also ran the line during the home game with Bury in April 1921 after the appointed official failed to turn up!

At Saltergate he enjoyed a run of 125 consecutive league and cup appearances and in 1923-24 set a unique Football League record when he scored five times from the penalty spot! This amazing run of games ended in January 1926 and within a year he'd lost his place to Bernard Bilcliff. His next transfer took Birch to Midland League Denaby United where he was a member of the side that reached the First Round of the F.A.Cup for the first time in the club's history in 1927 - losing 3-2 to League club Southport at Tickhill Square. After his professional career came to a close in 1930 – he had been suspended by Denaby after showing his displeasure at being relegated to the reserve side - Birch joined Sheffield based company Newton Chambers while continuing to play football back at his old club Grenoside. However a serious illness in 1935, necessitating several operations, ended his playing career and also saw a change of employment at Chambers to gateman. He later worked as a telephonist and for the last 11 years, until his retirement at the age of 66, he was employed as night telephonist.

BIRKS, Graham 1960-64

Born: 25 January 1942 Sheffield
(5ft 9ins, 10st 13lbs – 1961)
Debut: 1 September 1962
v West Bromwich Albion
Division One Home
Last Appearance:
24 November 1962
v West Ham United
Division One Home
Total League
& Cup Appearances: 4 Goals: 0

Career Details:

Stocksbridge Works		1958
WEDNESDAY	12 January	1960
Peterborough United	May	1964 £1000
Southend United	January	1966
Chester City	10 October	1969 £2500
Port Elizabeth City		1972
Fleetwood Town		
Worksop Town		
Buxton		
Matlock Town		1982

In simple terms Graham Birks' time at Hillsborough equated to just over four years of reserve team football as he tried, ultimately unsuccessfully, to dislodge the indomitable Don Megson from the left back role. He had originally joined the Owls as an amateur in May 1959 at the age of seventeen and continued to play for his local side Stocksbridge Works until joining the Owls professional ranks in the following year. After breaking into the reserve side in August 1960 the youngster then went on to set a quite remarkable record which saw him play in 59 consecutive games for the reserves – from December 1960 to April 1962 – during which time he won a Central league Championship medal in 1961 and became firmly established as Number two to Megson. Injuries to his rival gave Birks several first team starts during the early part of the 1962-3 season but he was never really going to dislodge "Meg" on a permanent basis and an inevitable parting of ways came in the summer of 1964 when he moved to Peterborough United.

The first team football he craved came at London Road where he made 34 league appearances for The Posh before enjoying his most productive spell in league football at his next club, Southend United. In a three and a half year stay at United he avoided injury to clock up an impressive 140 league and cup appearances for the Roots Hall club, the majority in the bottom division as United continuously just missed out on the promotion spots. His time at Chester added a further seventy-three league appearances to his career tally before a spell in South African soccer. When he returned home to Sheffield, Birks continued to play non-league football until his retirement in 1983 and until the age of 51 regularly played for Johnny Quinn's All Stars in charity games. Away from football he was employed by Bass brewery as a sales manager, until his retirement in 1997, while for three months Birks was a caddy for golf professional John Mellors on the European Tour.

BLACKHALL, Raymond "Ray" 1978-82

Born: 19 February 1957 Ashington
(5ft 10ins, 11st 7lbs – 1981)
Debut: 22 August 1978
v Doncaster Rovers
League Cup Away
Last Appearance: 4 May 1982
v Rotherham United
Division Two Away
Total League
& Cup Appearances: 140 Goals: 1

Career Details:

Newcastle United	August	1974
WEDNESDAY	18 August	1978 £25,000
Contract Cancelled	31 May	1982
IK Tord	8 July	1982 Free
Mansfield Town	November	1982 Free
Released	May	1983
Carlisle United		1984 Trial
Blyth Spartans	September	1984

When right back Richard Walden – who had been ever present in 1977-78 campaign– left the club in controversial circumstances during the summer of 1978 it caused a major headache for Jack Charlton. In fact he was forced to start the new season with teenage centre half Peter Shirtliff filling in at right back while Big Jack looked for a capable successor to Walden. Thankfully a week after the season kicked off tough tackling, attacking full back Ray Blackhall arrived at Hillsborough after falling out of favour at his home town club Newcastle United – where he had made 47 first team appearances. He had started as a trainee at St.James' Park and not for the first or last time Jack Charlton's eye for a player would prove sound as over the next three seasons Blackhall would be a regular member of the Owls side as the club hoisted themselves out of the old Third Division in 1980 and consolidated in the second tier of the English game.

After joining the club Blackhall became an immediate first choice and was ever present until suffering a serious knee injury - in a

February 1979 friendly at Guernsey Club Vale Recreation – which meant a premature end to his debut season. After regaining fitness he helped Wednesday to promotion and then missed only one game during his first season in the higher grade – after a wages dispute was settled in June 1980 when he signed a new contract. However the emergence of all action full back Mel Sterland meant Blackhall would be in and out of the side in 1981-2 and after asking for a transfer in March 1982 he was released when his contract expired. At this point he decided to accept the offer of a short-term contract at Swedish club IK Tord of Jankoping, where he stayed until returning to the UK in November to join Mansfield Town. He added a further fifteen league appearances to his career tally while at Field Mill and after an unsuccessful trial at Carlisle United returned to his native northeast to sign for Northern League giants Blyth Spartans. By this time Blackhall had secured full time employment in the Steel Industry but his career would then take a completely different route as he would move to Kensington to join the Police force!

BLAIR, Andrew 1984-86

Born: 18 December 1959 Kirkcaldy
(5ft 8ins, 10st 5lbs – 1984)
Debut: 25 August 1984
v Nottingham Forest
Division One Home
Last Appearance:
26 February 1986
v Derby County
F.A.Cup Away
Total League
& Cup Appearances: 75 Goals: 7

Career Details:

Coventry City	October	1977
Aston Villa	August	1981 £300,000
Wolverhampton W.	October	1983 Loan
WEDNESDAY	7 August	1984 £60,000
Aston Villa	13 March	1986 £120,000
Barnsley	March	1988 Loan
Northampton Town	October	1988 Free
Naxaar Lions	December	1988 Free
Kidderminster Harriers	July	1989

During his time as Wednesday manager, Howard Wilkinson resurrected the careers of many players, one such individual was Scotsman Andy Blair. The midfielder had arrived at Hillsborough after a big money move to Aston Villa from neighbours Coventry City had not really worked for either party. His debut for Villa actually came at Wembley when he replaced Dennis Mortimer in the 1981 Charity Shield draw with Spurs but he would experience a frustrating time at Villa Park and although winning European and Super Cup medals in 1982 both were as a non-playing sub and in a three-year stay he would start only twenty-four league games, plus nine as a substitute. This contrasted greatly with his spell at Coventry City where his form won him five Scotland U-21 caps and meant he was a first team regular after initially impressing Sky Blue scouts with his displays for Bedworth Juniors and Warwickshire County Schools. After joining City as an apprentice in July 1976 he would remain for five years before financial problems at Highfield Road meant a move across the Midlands to the newly crowned Champions.

After his cut price move to Hillsborough Blair would enjoy a great first season at Hillsborough as Wednesday took the First Division by storm, following their promotion to the top flight the previous season. He would miss only one league game during the campaign and in November 1984 wrote himself into the record books when netting a hat-trick of penalties in the 4-2 League Cup win over Luton Town at Hillsborough – becoming the first player in Wednesday and League Cup history to achieve the feat. However in sharp contrast to his debut campaign Blair's second season started badly – he was injured in the first game of the season – and gradually got worse! After an absence of several weeks he returned to first team duty and was a regular until a fateful F.A.Cup tie at Derby in February hastened his exit from Hillsborough. He was substituted at half-time after his error had gifted County an equalising goal and the subsequent row with Wilkinson saw Blair dropped from the first team and within three weeks on his way back to Birmingham, surprisingly re-joining Aston Villa.

Unfortunately for Andy his second term at Villa Park was totally ruined by injury - at one point he spent 14 months on the sidelines with a serious knee injury. When he left Villa he had appeared in only a handful of games and following three matches at Northampton Town spent six months in the sunnier climbs of Maltese soccer. However his knee could not now stand up to the rigours of professional football and after a spell with Conference club Kidderminster he was forced to retire in 1990. In the same year he opened a children's playschool in Coventry with his wife and later had a somewhat disastrous two-month spell managing Racing Club Warwick before tendering his resignation. He eventually became Commercial Manager at Bedworth United and that experience enabled him to open his own sports shop in the Midlands, which he runs today while still occasionally playing for Aston Villa Old Boys.

BLAIR, James "Jimmy" 1914-19 & 1919-20

Born: 11 May 1888 Glenboig,
Lanarkshire
(5ft 9ins, 11st 7lbs – 1920)
Died: 28 February 1964 Sheffield
Debut: 26 September 1914
v Bradford Park Av Div One Home
Last Appearance: 13 November 1919
v West Ham United Div One Away
Total League
& Cup Appearances: 61* Goals: 0
***Also appeared in 5 Wartime games**

Career Details:

Bonnyrigg Thistle		
Glasgow Ashfield		1906
Clyde		1908
WEDNESDAY	14 May	1914 £1975
Clydebank		1915 Guest
Glasgow Rangers	August	1916 Guest
Alloa United	August	1919
WEDNESDAY	24 October	1919 £250
Cardiff City	19 November	1920 £3500
Bournemouth & Boscombe United	24 December	1926 £3900
Sheppey United	July	1933 Player/manager

CAPS (@ SWFC):
SCOTLAND FULL (2) v Ireland 13/03/20, v England 10/04/20

Scottish International Jimmy Blair was without doubt one of the finest left backs to ever wear a Wednesday shirt. Unfortunately his stay in Sheffield was not the great success the club's hierarchy had hoped for when they paid what was then a club record to bring him South of the Border just before the outbreak of War. The start of those hostilities obviously interrupted his Hillsborough career although two motorbike accidents in his first season meant he started less than half of the league games in his debut season.

However it was obvious to all that this cool, clever and reliable defender was an outstanding talent and The Owls had been fortunate to capture his signature as he had been chased by many top clubs on both sides of Hadrian's Wall – after initially impressing for non-league club Ashfield where he won junior International honours. For Wednesday fans though they would see little of his talents as he spent the majority of the War back in his homeland – guesting initially for Clydebank before playing 93 Wartime games for Glasgow giants Rangers, winning a Championship medal in 1918. In the summer of 1919 football returned on a proper national footing and it was fully expected that Blair would return to Sheffield to re-start his English League career but the Owls were in a for a big shock when the stopper refused to sign and instead turned out for junior club Alloa United. The reason behind the shock move was that Blair had asked for the war period to count towards his benefit but as he had not played in requisite number of matches Wednesday were not allowed by the rules to come to such an arrangement. Later he stated that in addition to his weekly pay he wanted additional work at about £4 per week. The two parties eventually came to an agreement- one concession made by Wednesday was that Blair could train in the evenings - and he returned to Hillsborough in October 1919 although to add salt into Wednesday's wounds they had to pay the non league club a fee to get him back!

During the calamitous relegation season of 1919-20 Blair was one of the few bright spots and during the season won two full caps for his country, the second in England's classic 5-4 win over Scotland at a rain soaked Hillsborough in April 1920. Unfortunately Blair remained unsettled in Sheffield – his lack of a house and the ongoing wrangling over his benefit both being contributory factors - and in November 1920 he was placed on the transfer list. Sadly for Wednesday fans the brilliant and polished left full back was subsequently transferred to Cardiff City for a club record fee – quickly coming back to haunt Wednesday as his third and fourth games for City were against The Owls with the Welshmen winning both one-nil!

He prospered at Ninian Park and would play over 200 times for the South Wales club – in addition to winning six more full caps for Scotland – and would help them to promotion to Division One in 1921 and then captain them in their 1925 F.A.Cup Final defeat to Sheffield United – Jimmy was thrice a Cup Final loser as he was Scottish Cup runner up with Clyde in both 1910 and 1912. Incredibly at the age of 38 City made a £400 profit when he moved to Bournemouth on Christmas Eve 1926 and after a further 61 league games for the Cherries Blair was appointed manager in 1928, returning to Cardiff in November 1932 for a two-year tenure as a coach. After almost twenty years as a licensee from 1928 to 1948 in Cardiff and Cowbridge he eventually returned to Sheffield in the 1950s to live with his daughter – his Sheffield born son Doug was a top player at Cardiff City while his other son Jim played for Blackpool, Bournemouth and Orient – and became a season ticket holder at Hillsborough. However ill health meant he spent 14 weeks in a Sheffield hospital in late 1963 where he passed away two months later.

BLATSIS, Con 2000-01

Born: 6 July 1977 Melbourne, Australia
(6ft 3ins, 13st 7lbs – 2001)
Debut: 30 December 2000
v Huddersfield Town Division One Away
Last Appearance: 10 February 2001
v Wimbledon Division One Away
Total League & Cup Appearances: 8 Goals: 0

Career Details:

Clarinda		
Bulleen		
VIS		
AIS		
South Melbourne		
Olympiakos		Trial
Nottingham Forest		Trial
Derby County	8 August	2000 £150,000
WEDNESDAY	29 December	2001 Loan
Colchester United	15 March	2002 N/C
Koceali Spor	5 August	2002 Free
St Patrick's Athletic	March	2004 Free
Coventry City	July	2004 Trial
FC Twente	August	2004 Trial
South Melbourne		2005

Antipodean defender Con Blatsis spent two months on loan at Wednesday during the 2000-1 campaign, making an impressive debut in the final game of the old year as The Owls kept a clean sheet for the first time since October. The tall centre-half – who could produce a giant long throw in – had first played football with a variety of minor clubs back home in Australia before appearing in the 1997 World Youth Cup tournament while on South Melbourne's books. It would be his appearance for that club against Manchester United in Brazil during the much-derided World Club Championship in January 2000 that would alert European clubs to his talents - Premier League Derby County duly capturing his signature in the following summer.

Soon after signing a three-year deal at County he won his first full cap for the Socceroos against South Korea, having already earned International caps at U-20 and U-23 level. However he would make only two Premiership starts for The Rams before International commitments – appearing for his Country in the 2000 Olympic games in Sydney - and injury saw him fade from the first team scene. After regaining fitness Blatsis arrived at Hillsborough with no work permit required – Blatsis holds an EU passport due to his Greek ancestry – and would be a regular as Paul Jewell tried to stave off relegation to Division Two. However he would return to Derby on what has become known as Black Monday when with Wednesday bottom of the league not only was Jewell sacked but Chairman Howard Culley also resigned! Back at Derby the Aussie's fortunes did not improve and after failing to break into the first team he was released in February 2002.

He would join Second Division Colchester United on a non-contract basis soon after, making his debut twenty-four hours later in a one-nil home loss to Huddersfield Town. However after becoming a free agent in the following summer he looked set to move to the Far East but instead switched to Turkish football, signing a two-year contract with top-flight club Koceali Spor. However his time in Turkey soon turned into a nightmare as after months of contractual non-compliance, mainly involving non payment of salary, he was forced to take his club to the FIFA Dispute Resolution Chamber. In April 2004 the long running case was finally decided in Blatsis' favour with the Australian being awarded substantial damages against Koceali Spor and also his freedom from contract. Before the verdict Blatsis had already played a handful of games for Irish Republic side St Pats and attended trials at Championship club Coventry City and Dutch side Twente in 2004 pre season but failed to secure a contract.

BLENKINSOP, Ernest 1923-34

Born: 20 April 1902 Cudworth
(5ft 8½ ins, 11st 8lbs – 1923)
Died: 24 April 1969 Sheffield
Debut: 27 January 1923
v Bury
Division Two Away
Last Appearance: 10 March 1934
v Wolverhampton Wanderers
Division One Home
Total League
& Cup Appearances: 424 Goals: 5

Career Details:

Cudworth United Methodist Club		
Cudworth Village		
Hull City	21 October	1921 £100
WEDNESDAY	20 January	1923 £1150
Liverpool	15 March	1934 £6500
Cardiff City	November	1937 £400
Buxton		1939
Halifax Town		1940 Guest
Bradford Park Avenue	May	1940 Guest
Bradford City	October	1940 Guest
Hurst		WW2 Guest

CAPS (@SWFC) – ENGLAND Full (26) v France 17/05/28, v Belgium 19/05/28, Ireland 22/10/28, Wales 17/11/28, v Scotland 13/04/29, v France 09/05/29, Belgium 11/05/29, Spain 15/05/29, Ireland 19/10/29, Wales 20/11/29, v Scotland 05/04/30, v Germany 10/05/30, Austria 14/05/30, Ireland 20/10/30, Wales 22/11/30, v Scotland 28/03/31. France 14/05/31, Belgium 16/05/31, Ireland 17/10/31, Wales 18/11/31, Spain 09/12/31, Scotland 09/04/32, Ireland 17/10/32, Wales 16/11/32, Austria 07/12/32, Scotland 01/04/33

FOOTBALL LEAGUE (8) v Scottish league, Irish league 1928, v Scottish League 1929, v Scottish League 1930, v Scottish League 1931, v Scottish League, Irish League 1932, v Scottish League 1934

Of the many left backs to have served the club in their long history Ernest Blenkinsop is widely regarded as the greatest of them all. In over ten years in Wednesday colours the stylish and polished defender was a key figure as Wednesday rose from the lower reaches of the Second Division to become established as one of the top sides in the English game, winning back-to-back Championships in the late 1920s/early 1930s. In the process "Blenky" gained 26 caps for his country to become the second most capped England International in the Owls history – a figure only bettered by Ron Springett thirty years later. The outstanding full back was idolised by Wednesday fans for his impeccable positional play, superb timing in the tackle and great distribution and his move to Liverpool in 1934 was without doubt one of the most sensational transfers in The Owls history - at the time of the sale Blenkinsop was captain of the Owls and still a current International. His departure was totally unexpected by fans and player alike and most supporters pointed the finger of blame at manager Billy Walker as many thought he saw Blenkinsop – who was training to become a coach - as a threat to his own position and decided to act first by transferring Ernie for a club record fee.

As a boy Blenkinsop played for Barnsley Road Council School but after leaving and going down the mines he thought his playing days were over. However almost three years after last kicking a ball he decided to join Cudworth United Methodist Club, winning the Barnsley Sunday School League Championship in his first season After a year he moved to Cudworth Village FC where he played with his brother, sometimes exchanging positions with his sibling and playing at inside left.

However it was at left back that old Barnsley manager H.P.Lewis, then manager of Hull City, spotted him playing against Wath Athletic and he moved to Hull for £100 (and so the story goes 80 pints of beer) in 1921. City thought little of his prowess as a defender though and at one point even tried him at centre forward but the major problem for the youngster was he was understudy to regular left back Matt Bell and played only a handful of games in his two years by the Humber. He was actually in The Tigers reserves when Bob Brown brought him to Hillsborough but the legendary manager's eye for talent yet again provided the club with a diamond as Ernie would quickly establish himself in the first eleven. His debut would actually be at right back but for his home debut against Barnsley in a the F.A.Cup a week later – in front of a then record Hillsborough crowd of over 66,000 – he was switched to the opposite flank and would remain there for the rest of his career. After being ever present in his second season at Wednesday "Blenky" would miss part of the next season due to injury and then could not win his first team place back due to the form of Billy Felton and new boy William Inglis. However the ice-cool defender produced such outstanding form in the reserves that he was recalled to the side and was never deposed. As Wednesday won the Division Two title in 1926 Ernie formed a great full back partnership with Billy Felton and later combined with outstanding right back Tommy Walker in the Division One title winning years.

Such was the high esteem that Ernie was held in at Hillsborough that when he returned with his new club Liverpool in April 1934 he was not only given a standing ovation by the crowd but the Wednesday players lined up before the game to clap him onto the pitch and the band played "See the Conquering hero comes"! After 71 games for Liverpool, Blenkinsop would spend two years at Cardiff City – being player-coach in his second year – before retiring from league football in May 1939. He would continue to make occasional appearances for a variety of clubs during the War while in 1941 could be found coaching Sheffield FC and was appointed a part-time scout by the Owls in 1942. In the same year, after having to give up his job in the steelworks due to ill health, he went into the public house trade on the advice of ex-Owl Billy Marsden. After firstly becoming Mein Host at the Mason's Arms in Crookes "Blenky" moved to take over the Sportsman's Inn in Crosspool in 1950 and it was here that he died suddenly while serving a customer in 1969 – in the same period he had also acted as a scout for Sheffield United during Joe Mercer's tenure as manager. In his later years Blenkinsop loved a game of golf – playing off scratch at one point – and a week before he passed away won his club championship to ensure he remained a winner in all of his sporting endeavours.

BLINKER, Reginald Waldi "Regi" 1996-97

Born: 4 June 1969 Paramaribo, Surinam
(5ft 8ins, 11st 7lbs – 1997)
Debut: 6 March 1996
v Aston Villa
Premier League Away
Last Appearance: 7 May 1997
v Leicester City
Premier League Away
Total League & Cup Appearances: 27+18 Goals: 3

Career Details:

Delfia DHC		
Feyenoord		1986
Den Bosch	December	1988 Loan
WEDNESDAY	1 March	1996 £275,000
Glasgow Celtic	5 August	1997 £1,500,000
Den Haag	July	2000 Trial
Bolton Wanderers	July	2000 Trial
RBC Roosendaal	1 August	2000 Free
Sparta Rotterdam	17 June	2001 Free
S.V.Deltasport	July	2003 Free

The distinctive dreadlocks of Regi Blinker were a familiar sight around Hillsborough for a seventeen-month period after arriving from Dutch giants Feyenoord near the end of the 1996-7 season. His debut could not have been more spectacular as he netted two superb goals as Wednesday lost 3-2 in a midweek fixture at Villa Park. This ensured he achieved instant cult status amongst Owls fans and it was not long before you could purchase "Regi wigs" in the club's superstore! However despite the fact that he boasted superb close control and was a real entertainer he suffered from the flaw that affects all but those wingers of International class – inconsistency. After his initial impact had subsided he played a part in Wednesday making a dream start to the next season – they spent several weeks atop the Premier League – before effectively spending the remainder of the campaign on the subs bench. His cause was certainly not helped in November 1996 when he was banned by World Governing body FIFA after Italian side Udinese complained that he had signed a declaration of intent to join them – two months before leaving to join Wednesday for a Bosman effected cut price fee. Ironically in December 1996 – while still suspended - he was called into a Dutch provisional squad for the home friendly with Belgium, along with teammate Orlando Trustfull, but could not add to his three full caps for his country. His career had originally started in his adopted homeland of Holland– he was born in the Dutch colony of Surinam and moved to Europe at the age of nine - before hitting the big time with Rotterdam club Feyenoord where he netted 45 times in 238 games.

The ban was lifted after fifteen days with the Italian side being found guilty of improper conduct although Blinker was still handed a hefty fine of 75,000 Swiss Francs (around £35,700). Despite not being a regular in the side the enigmatic winger remained a big crowd favourite and many fans were disappointed when he was used as a makeweight in the deal that brought Paolo Di Canio to Hillsborough in the summer of 1997. However the move was certainly great business for Wednesday as they sold the South American born player for over five times the amount they had paid for him. In his first season at Celtic Park, Blinker was in and out of the side but still won a League Championship medal as his team stopped fierce rivals Glasgow Rangers from recording ten consecutive titles. Not unlike his time at Hillsborough Regi was never a regular in Scotland and eventually returned home to sign for newly promoted Dutch side RBC- following unsuccessful trial spells in Holland and England. After two years at Sparta he dropped out of the Dutch professional leagues to sign for semi-pro side Deltasport.

BLONDEAU, Patrick **1997-98**

Born: 27 January 1968
Marseilles, France
(5ft 8ins, 11st 6lbs – 1997)
Debut: 9 August 1997
v Newcastle U
Premier League Away
Last Appearance: 8 November 1997
v Bolton Wanderers
Premier League Home
Total League
& Cup Appearances: 5+1 Goals: 0

Career Details:

Martingues		
Monaco		1989
WEDNESDAY	24 June	1997 £1,800,000
Bordeaux	14 January	1998 £1,200,000
Marseilles	1 August	1998
Watford	12 July	2001 Free
Créteil	1 August	2002 Free

Over the years Sheffield Wednesday have made a few gaffs in the transfer market and the signing of French International Patrick Blondeau was perhaps the most disastrous signing of them all! The full back had come to Sheffield with a glowing reputation after an eight year stay in the South of France had culminated in a 1997 Championship success with Monaco and two full caps for his country – he appeared in 148 league games for Monaco after starting his playing career with one goal in fifty league games for Second Division Martigues. The Owls hierarchy had travelled to France in late April 1997 but it would be several weeks before he put his name to a contract. However from this point onwards it was all downhill for Blondeau as he failed to settle and perhaps more importantly failed to adapt to the pace of the English game – being sent off in his fifth match after being caught out of position. Fans could have perhaps forgiven his poor form as Wednesday made a disastrous start to the new season but when he started to openly criticise both the club and the City of Sheffield he quickly lost all support.

It was David Pleat who brought Patrick to Hillsborough but from the opening game at St.James' Park it was obvious he would struggle to cope in a 4-4-2 formation – he was used to playing in a wing-back role – and was frequently exposed at right back as Wednesday struggled. That poor form would see Pleat sacked in early November and a week later Blondeau would make his final appearance as a late substitute, in a midfield role, in Peter Shreeves' only game in charge. By this time the Frenchman was on borrowed time – following his media outbursts – and after a few reserve outings would return to his homeland to put an end to the whole sorry episode that had cost the Owls an incredible £100,000 for every appearance Blondeau made in a blue and white shirt! He would then play just nine times for his next club Bordeaux before signing for home town club Marseille, appearing for them in the 1999 UEFA Cup Final 3-0 defeat to Italian side Parma. After appearing in 58 league games for Marseille – helping them consolidate in the French top division - he was one of several big name signings brought to Watford in the summer of 2001 by high profile manager Gianluca Vialli. However despite signing a three-year deal Blondeau would stay only one season – appearing in 24 league games.

BOLDER, Robert John "Bob" **1977-83**

Born: 2 October 1958 Dover
(6ft 3ins, 13st 13lbs – 1978)
Debut: 27 December 1977
v Rotherham United
Division Three Home
Last Appearance: 14 May 1983
v Crystal Palace
Division Two Home
Total League
& Cup Appearances: 224 Goals: 0

Career Details:

Dover Athletic		1974
WEDNESDAY	9 March	1977 £1,000
Liverpool	4 August	1983 £125,000
Sunderland	21 September	1985 £30,000
Luton Town	21 February	1986 Loan
Charlton Athletic	10 August	1986 £40,000
Margate		1994
Dagenham & Redbridge		1995 £3,000

The history of football is littered with instances of players being rejected by clubs only to gain fame elsewhere. One such player was Bob Bolder who was rejected by Charlton Athletic – after several trials – with the reason being that he was too small. However when he left school he started to work on a farm and promptly shot up to over six feet tall before starting to play Southern League football with Dover Athletic. It was while playing there that he was recommended to the Owls and after a week's trial Wednesday paid a bargain fee for his services to bring him North.

The teenager quickly established himself as second choice keeper at Hillsborough but faced stiff competition from crowd favourite Chris Turner for the No.1 jersey. However Jack Charlton was convinced that Turner's lack of inches counted against him and therefore Bolder took his place with "Big Jack" initially facing a barrage of criticism from disgruntled fans. However the well built and excellent shot stopper would eventually win the fans over – helped by his rivals transfer to Sunderland in 1979 – and become established as first choice as the Owls won promotion from the old Third Division in 1980. An appearance in the 1983 F.A.Cup semi-final defeat to Brighton would prove to one of Bob's final games in a Wednesday shirt as in the summer that followed he was one of four senior players who shocked the club by rejecting new contracts. Bolder had been ever present for Wednesday since October 1980 – a run of 133 consecutive games – but when a dream move to Liverpool emerged as a possibility it is not surprising that Bolder signed for the Anfield giants.

Unfortunately for Bolder his move to Liverpool did not really advance his career as he might have hoped as he failed to start a first team game. His new club completed the treble of League, League Cup and European Cup in his first season and Bolder did win a European Cup medal a year later when he was reserve in the final but he simply found it impossible to dislodge the eccentric Bruce Grobbelaar. After a spell out through injury Bolder would join Sunderland on loan – a move that eventually became permanent – and after 29 league games spent a short spell on loan at Luton Town where he failed to make a first team appearance. His final move in league football saw his career path turn full circle as he returned to Charlton Athletic and thankfully for Bob his fortunes changed for the better as at The Valley he became a regular and would play 296 times, including an appearance at Wembley in the Full Members Cup Final, to finally banish any doubts he might have had about leaving Hillsborough. His final game for Charlton would come in February 1993 and just over two years later he decided to retire from league soccer, signing for Conference club Dagenham & Redbridge. A month before leaving the full time game Bolder was rewarded with a benefit game contested between the two clubs where he enjoyed his greatest success – the Owls travelling to Charlton in April 1995 to play out a 3-3 draw – and would play a further 37 times for Dagenham before leaving in September 1995 to become goalkeeping coach at Charlton. He later became football in the Community Officer for The Valiants – a role he still holds today.

BOLLAND, William Thomas "Tommy" 1907-09

Born: December 1884 Darlington
(5ft 8½ ins, 10st 6lbs - 1909)
Died: 3 January 1967 Swindon
Debut: 18 January 1908
v Notts County
Division One Away
Last Appearance: 20 March 1908
v Bradford City
Division One Home
Total League
& Cup Appearances: 13 Goals: 1

Career Details:

Washington United		
WEDNESDAY	29 April	1907 £20
Swindon Town	May	1909
Bath City	cs.	1921

Left winger who arrived from Northeast non-league football just a week after Wednesday had beaten Everton to lift the F.A.Cup. Outside left in that Cup winning side was George Simpson and it was the role of his understudy that Bolland served during his two years at Hillsborough. The new boy would twice get a taste of first team football in his debut season – due to Simpson's absence – but would play the majority of that campaign in the club's reserve side – scoring three times as Wednesday won the Midland League Championship.

Despite Simpson starting only ten league games in the following campaign Tommy still found himself in the second team as both Frank Foxall and Oliver Tummon emerged from that same reserve side to share left wing duties with Simpson. Even the shock sale of the senior man to West Brom in March 1909 still effectively left Bolland as third choice and it was not a surprise when he returned to non-league football – signing for Southern League Swindon Town. He certainly must have been missed around Hillsborough as the fine athlete was also a self-defence expert and fine juggler – he entertained the crowds in the latter capacity at an Owlerton St.John's concert in May 1908!

He would stay over ten years at Swindon Town – playing for many years alongside future Owls centre-forward Jack Burkinshaw - during which time his new club established themselves as one of the outstanding sides in the Southern League before the whole top division was voted en-bloc into the Football League just after the First World War. Town would finish runners-up for a second consecutive season during Tommy's first campaign – also reaching the semi-finals of the FA.Cup where it needed red-hot favourites Newcastle to end their march to the Final. He would then play his part as a year later Swindon not only lifted the Championship but also grabbed yet more national headlines by reaching the last eight of the Cup, this time losing 3-1 at Chelsea. In fact during Tommy's time in Wiltshire, Swindon Town's record in the Cup was quite remarkable as they again reached the last four in 1912 where they must have rubbed their hands when drawing Second Division Barnsley at Stamford Bridge. Unfortunately it was The Tykes year and they would win in a reply on the way to their solitary Cup win. However, The Robins could console themselves with a second Southern League Championship in 1914 – Tommy appearing in 37 games and scoring four times, before finally being rewarded with that elusive Football League place. Unfortunately by this time Bolland was in his mid-30s and would appear in only six league games for Swindon in that debut season in the League before finishing his career back in the Southern League with Bath City.

BOLSOVER, Henry 1900

Debut: 12 March 1900 v Burton Swifts Division Two Home
Last Appearance: 17 March 1900
v Woolwich Arsenal Division Two Home
Total League & Cup Appearances: 2 Goals: 0

Career Details:

Sheffield FC		
Sheffield United	16 March	1894
Sheffield FC		1894
WEDNESDAY	5 March	1900
Sheffield FC		

Goalkeeper Henry Bolsover was one of a handful of players who remained amateur throughout their career – the most famous Owls player being Bolsover's contemporary and Sheffield Club team mate Vivian Simpson. It was while playing with Sheffield Club that Henry would achieve his greatest success when in 1904 "The World's oldest club football club" did the City proud by reaching the Final of the famous F.A.Amateur Cup. After overcoming non-league giants Bishop Auckland 5-2 in the Derby semi-final Sheffield club would go on to beat Southerners Ealing 3-1 at Bradford with Bolsover between the sticks to earn his winners medal.

Four years earlier he had signed league forms for Wednesday – he also played two senior games for Sheffield United during the 1893-4 season - during their second division season of 1899-00 and was called up for his first taste of league football when regular keepers James Massey and William Mallinson were both unavailable. The Owls won 6-0 on his debut and five days later Henry was again between the sticks as Woolwich Arsenal were beaten 3-1 at Hillsborough, in a season when the Owls incredibly won all eighteen home games in the league! However that proved to be his final first team appearance and it was soon back to local football for Bolsover.

BONVIN, Pablo Facundo 2001-02

Born: 15 April 1981 Concepcion del Uruguay, Argentina
(5ft 8ins, 11st 8lbs – 2001)
Debut: 21 August 2001 v Bury League Cup Away
Last Appearance: 9 March 2002 v Gillingham Division One Home
Total League & Cup Appearances: 9+21 Goals: 5

Career Details:

Gimnasia y Esgrima		1992
Ferro Carril Oeste		1993
Boca Juniors		1996
Newcastle United		2000 1-year loan
WEDNESDAY	20 August	2001 Loan
Loan Return	22 April	2002
Racing Club	February	2003 Loan
Argentinos Junior	January	2004 Free

The somewhat cosseted life of today's Academy players must have seemed just a pipe dream to Pablo Bonvin when the youngster started on the long road to being a professional footballer. It was at the age of eleven that Pablo joined his first club but he stayed for only one year before moving to Buenos Aires club Ferro – 200 miles from his home! His devoted parents would make the eight-hour round trip on a regular basis so he could play for Boca's youth side, but from the age of just fourteen Pablo lived on his own in the sprawling capital of Argentina. His commitment was rewarded with a professional contract at Boca and it was while playing in a tournament in Ireland that he was spotted by Newcastle scouts and experienced English football for the first time.

He would spend his year on loan as a regular in United's reserve side but the skilful attacker could not break into The Magpies first team squad and after returning home he arrived at Wednesday on trial in early August 2001. He quickly endeared himself to the Hillsborough faithful after a starring role on this first appearance – a 1-0 home win over the previous seasons UEFA Cup runners-up Alves – and two weeks later Wednesday secured him on loan from Boca for the rest of the season. During his time in Sheffield Pablo certainly provided some much needed flair for a struggling Wednesday side but despite netting five times his inability to stamp his authority on a game and lack of real physical presence meant he was not offered a contract by the club when his loan period expired. He duly returned home to play out the final year of his contract at Boca, hoping to finally make a league start for the Argentinean giants. However he could not break into the Boca first team and so joined Ossie Ardiles' Buenos Aires based team Racing Club on long-term loan. He later joined National B – the second tier in Argentina – side Argentinos and finished top scorer in 2003-4 with 17 goals as his new club finished third in the overall standings and secured runners-up spot in the 2004 closing Championship.

BOOTH, Andrew David "Andy" 1996-2001

Born: 6 December 1973 Huddersfield
(6ft, 12st 6lbs – 1996)

Debut: 17 August 1996
v Aston Villa
Premier League Home
Last Appearance: 17 March 2001
v Burnley
Division One Home
Total League
& Cup Appearances: 143+11 Goals: 34

Career Details:

Huddersfield Town	1 July	1992
WEDNESDAY	4 July	1996 £2,700,000
Tottenham Hotspur	30 January	2001 Loan
Huddersfield Town	22 March	2001 £175,000

Despite spending almost five years at Wednesday the name of Andy Booth will forever be linked with that of his hometown club Huddersfield where in two spells he appeared in over two hundred games, achieving cult status amongst Terriers fans. It was his initial spell at Town that first alerted many bigger clubs to his promise as in a four year period he scored 64 times in 144 games – winning three England U-21 caps - with Liverpool one of many sides linked with a possible transfer away from West Yorkshire. However it was Owls manager David Pleat who paid Town the highest transfer fee in their history to bring the tall and powerful Booth to Hillsborough in the summer of 1996.

The newcomer would enjoy a successful first season in the top flight, netting a praiseworthy thirteen times as Wednesday surprised their fans by finishing in seventh spot, just outside a UEFA Cup spot. He also made a cameo appearance on the last day of the season when following Matt Clarke's controversial sending off he went between the sticks and made several good stops – including one with his face! However the old fashioned style centre –forward would then experience several mixed seasons at Hillsborough with injury, loss of form and simply playing for a side on the slide all contributing to a relatively poor goal tally. Despite not being blessed with pace Booth proved himself a brave and wholehearted player who possessed terrific ariel ability but it would be fair to say he never really proved himself in the higher grade of football and after a surprise loan move to Tottenham – no doubt linked with Spurs Director of football David Pleat – he would return to Huddersfield Town late in the 2000/1 season.

Unfortunately despite scoring in his first game back at Huddersfield Booth would suffer heartache on the final day of the season when an unlikely set of results – all three relegation rivals won while Town lost – condemned them to demotion from Division One. After just missing out on the play-offs a year later – Andy netting 11 times in 36 league games- the following season was quite simply an unmitigated disaster from start to finish. Not only did Town suffer a second relegation in three years but also injury meant Booth would spend large chunks of the season on the sidelines and could only watch as a financial crisis engulfed the club - culminating in Town going into administration in March 2003 and suffering relegation to Division Three a month later.

BOSWORTH, Samuel 1899

Born: 2nd Quarter 1877 Basford
Debut: 4 March 1899 v Everton Division One Home
Last Appearance: 22 April 1899 v Preston N E Division One Away
Total League & Cup Appearances: 7 Goals: 0

Career Details:

Long Eaton Rangers		
Loughborough Town	September	1898
Derby County	December	1898 £100
WEDNESDAY	22 February	1899
Released		1899
Whitwick White Cross	October	1901
Ilkeston United		

The appearance of right-winger Sam Bosworth in Wednesday's final few games of the 1898-99 season is somewhat of a mystery. What is known is that he arrived from Derby County in February 1899 after having made just two league appearances for The Rams in December 1898. It's also known that he joined a club in turmoil as Wednesday were not only staring relegation from Division One in the face but also their very existence was under threat as they were just about to lose their ground at Olive Grove and had not secured a new home.

Under these somewhat gloomy circumstances Bosworth replaced regular outside right William Dryburgh to play all but one of the final eight games of the season, appearing in the last ever match played at Olive Grove – against Newcastle United in April 1899. He also played in the second instalment of that historic two-part game against Aston Villa when the two sides played the final ten minutes in March after the original game had been abandoned due to bad light back in November 1898! However he not could help Wednesday avoid the drop and then quite simply disappeared from the record books – strangely he failed to make a single appearance in the club's reserve side either before or after his first team games - and later played for Midland League club Whitwick White Cross

BOWLING, Ian 1995

Born: 27 July 1965 Sheffield
(6ft 3ins, 14st 8lbs – 1996)
Only Appearance:
24 June 1995
v FC Basel
UEFA Intertoto Cup Away
Total League
& Cup Appearances: 1 Goals: 0

Career Details:

Frecheville CA		
Stafford Rangers		
Denaby United		
Gainsborough Trinity	August	1987 Free
Lincoln City	23 October	1988 £2000
Hartlepool United	17 August	1989 Loan
Kettering Town	February	1990 Loan
Bradford City	25 March	1993 Loan
Bradford City	27 July	1993 £27,000 (T)
WEDNESDAY	June	1995 N/C
Mansfield Town	8 August	1995 Free
Kettering Town	17 October	2000 Free
Worksop Town	15 May	2003
Stalybridge Celtic	5 December	2003 Loan
Hucknall Town	September	2004 Loan
Matlock Town	13 January	2005 Loan

Giant goalkeeper Ian Bowling was one of several players signed by the Owls on a non-contract basis just for the Intertoto Cup tie in Switzerland against Basel – this was after Wednesday had decided to enter the tournament at the last minute but found they had a distinct lack of players to choose from as the majority were still on vacation! This is why the squad that travelled for the first group game was a motley bunch of young pros and lower league journeymen who had been released by their clubs at the end of the previous season. For Bowling it was his first appearance for a club in his home City since playing for his first club, Northern Counties East League side Frecheville Community Association.

After moving up the non-league ladder with transfers to first Stafford Rangers and then Gainsborough Trinity Bowling eventually entered the professional ranks at Lincoln City where in a injury interrupted five-year stay he appeared in 59 games for The Imps. After a spell at Bradford City his most successful time in league soccer would come immediately after his European adventure with Wednesday when he signed for Mansfield Town. During the majority of his four-year stay at Field Mill he played in precisely two hundred first team games, forging a reputation as a superb shot stopper and penalty saving expert – he saved five spot kicks during 1996-7. However he continued to suffer rotten luck with injuries – breaking his arm and undergoing two knee operations in 1999-00 – and when a domestic accident left him with a broken toe early in the following season he lost his place to veteran Bobby Mimms and soon after moved into Conference football at Kettering Town.

Since joining Kettering Town – where in later years he played under the managership of ex-Owl Carl Shutt – Bowling has been undisputed No.1 but in March 2002 his injury jinx struck again. However this time he almost lost his life as after colliding with a post during the home game with Tiverton Town, Bowling suffered a fractured skull. This was bad enough but later in hospital he had an emergency operation to remove blood clots that had formed following the collision. Thankfully after a spell in hospital he made a full recovery and returned to the first team, playing in the majority of Kettering's games as they suffered relegation from the Conference in 2003. Later moved to Worksop Town but lost his place to Dave McCarthy, prompting a loan move to Unibond rivals Stalybridge.

BOWNS, George Henry — 1883 & 1885

Born: 1859 Sheffield
Debut: 12 February 1883 v Notts County F.A.Cup Away
Last Appearance: 31 October 1885 v Long Eaton Rangers Away
Total League & Cup Appearances: 2 Goals: 0

Career Details:

Pyebank	
WEDNESDAY	1883
Pyebank	
WEDNESDAY	1885
Clinton	1889
Sheffield United	1890

The name of George Bowns first appeared in Sheffield football under the colours of Pyebank Club. A stonemason by trade Bowns would spend the majority of his career with Pyebank but over a two-year period would also make fleeting appearances for Wednesday. Incredibly he would actually appear in only three matches for the Owls in total, two being F.A.Cup ties and the other Bob Gregory's benefit games at Bramall lane in April 1883. In those days of course – when every player in Sheffield was supposedly amateur – a footballer could swap clubs at will and Wednesday – like many other clubs – used that to their advantage by recruiting the best local talent when it was F.A.Cup time! That would partly explain why George, whose father ran a public house on Brunswick Road, played so few games for the club although he did make appearances in the club's annual Athletic Sports Days.

Later in his career Bowns would play for local club Clinton while in January 1890 he became one of the first players to appear for both City sides when he lined up for United against Derby Midland in a friendly game – playing alongside ex-Wednesday legend Billy Mosforth. After hanging up his boots George would work as a builder and contractor in the Brightside area of Sheffield and would steadfastly remain a batchelor well into his forties!

Incidentally some records show a G.H.Bownes and simply a Bown playing F.A.Cup football for Wednesday in the 1880s – neither name was in fact correct as it was George Bowns who played in both matches.

BRADBURY, Lee Michael — 2002-03

Born: 3 July 1975 Cowes, Isle of Wight
(6ft 2ins, 13st 10lbs – 2002)
Debut: 26 December 2002 v Nott'm Forest Division One Home
Last Appearance: 4 April 2003 v Wimbledon Division One Home
Total League & Cup Appearances: 10+1 Goals: 3

Career Details:

East Cowes Victoria		
Cowes Sports		
Army and Combined Services		
Portsmouth	14 August	1995 Free/£300
Exeter City	1 December	1995 Loan
Manchester City	1 August	1997 £3,000,000
Crystal Palace	29 October	1998 £1,500,000
Birmingham City	25 March	1999 Loan
Portsmouth	14 October	1999 £380,000
WEDNESDAY	24 December	2002 Loan
Loan Return	3 January	2003
WEDNESDAY	26 February	2003 Loan
Loan Return	6 April	2003
Derby County	14 August	2003 Loan
Loan Return	21 August	2003
Derby County	21 November	2003 Loan
Walsall	25 March	2004 N/C
Released	19 May	2004
Oxford United	26 June	2004

In December 1994 Wednesday raided Portsmouth to bring to Hillsborough a highly rated ex-Army forward to aid their fight against relegation. That player was Guy Whittingham and incredibly eight years later Lee Bradbury mirrored his predecessor by not only making his debut on Boxing Day but also helping Wednesday to a much-needed victory. However that is where the similarities ended, as Whittingham was a pure out-and-out goalscorer whereas Bradbury was a hard running, physical forward who led the line with aplomb. He had severed his Army connections in 1995 – after serving four and a half years as a Rifleman in the Prince of Wales regiment - to enter professional football with Portsmouth and quickly became established as one of the brightest young talents in the game, winning three England U-21 caps and the 1997 Player of the year accolade at Pompey.

After bursting onto the scene Bradbury's career looked set to soar when he was transferred to Manchester City in a multi-million pound deal but this was where Lee's career stalled somewhat as in an unhappy spell he netted eleven times in 46 games before City took a fifty-percent loss in selling him to Crystal Palace. After failing to recapture his form at either Selhurst Park or Birmingham City it was back to Portsmouth in the autumn of 1999 where he quickly found the familiar surroundings to his liking to get back into the goal-scoring groove. However in December 2001 he suffered the first serious injury of his career – knee ligament damage during a game at Millwall – that would effectively put him out of the game for a year. It was partly to help him regain fitness that Pompey manager Harry Redknapp allowed Bradbury to join Wednesday on a month's loan but his bravery in the third match of that spell – at Rotherham United on New Year's Day – saw injury again put him on the sidelines when he damaged shoulder ligaments after throwing himself in front of the ball to stop the Millers grabbing an equaliser.

This meant he returned to Fratton Park just a few days into his loan spell but several weeks later he was back at Hillsborough for a second loan period with Wednesday bottom of the table and Portsmouth top! With his fitness now almost fully returned Bradbury would make a greater impact in this second month and would net three times, his first a brave header in a 5-1 win over Coventry City – before an injury crisis at Portsmouth ruled out any chance of Chris Turner securing his services for the a further month. Ironically his first game back in a Portsmouth shirt would come against Wednesday at Fratton Park – his first appearance in a Pompey shirt for sixteen months – and inevitably he would net although his old club had the last word by grabbing a dramatic injury time winner. Joined Derby County on loan in August 2003 but had the misfortune to suffer a fractured foot during his first week at Pride Park, sidelining him for at least six weeks.

BRADLEY, Martin — 1910-11

Born: 4th Quarter 1886
Wolstanton, Staffs.
(5ft 8ins, 12st – 1908)
Died: 4th Quarter 1958 Hemsworth
Debut: 15 October 1910
v Bury
Division One Away
Last Appearance: 28 January 1911
v Notts County
Division One Away
Total League
& Cup Appearances: 2 Goals: 0

Career Details:

South Kirkby		
Grimsby Town	April	1908
Mexborough	May	1909
WEDNESDAY	13 April	1910 £110*
Bristol Rovers	June	1911 £50

*Joint fee

Inside right Martin Bradley arrived at Wednesday with the daunting task of displacing stalwart Harry Chapman from the first team. However the old campaigner was actually coming to the end of his illustrious career and during Bradley's spell at Hillsborough would depart for pastures new, effectively meaning his first team spot was up for grabs. However it would not be Bradley who filled Chapman's boots as after failing to impress in his two first team starts Wednesday promptly signed Marr Paterson to fill the role! That meant -in what proved to be his only season at Wednesday - Bradley would have to be content with playing Midland league football for the club's reserves where he finished second top scorer with twelve goals in 1910-11 as runners-up spot was secured.

His actual transfer to Wednesday has one reaching for the calculator as although he was playing non-league football with Mexborough Town it was Grimsby Town – who held his league registration form - that the Owls paid a joint fee to of £85 for him and Teddy Glennon. To complicate matters further Wednesday also paid Mexborough a joint fee of £70 for Bradley and Laurie Burkinshaw while in the following season paid a further £60 after the players "proved a success"! It was with Grimsby that the attacker enjoyed his best days in league soccer, appearing in 28 league games and netting six times, but after failing to make the grade in Division One football at Wednesday he would drop into non-league soccer with Southern League Bristol Rovers. His brother James enjoyed greater success than his sibling, playing for Liverpool, Stoke and Reading and earning a League Championship with the Merseyside club in 1906.

BRADSHAW, Carl — 1986-88

Born: 2 October 1968 Sheffield
(6ft 11st – 1987)

Debut: 29 November 1986
v Queens Park Rangers
Division One Away
Last Appearance: 27 September 1988
v Blackpool
League Cup Away
Total League
& Cup Appearances: 25+19 Goals: 7

Career Details:

WEDNESDAY	11 August	1986
Barnsley	23 August	1986 Loan
Manchester City	29 September	1988 £100,000
Sheffield United	7 September	1989 £50,000
Norwich City	28 July	1994 £500,000
Wigan Athletic	3 October	1997 Free
Scunthorpe United	11 July	2001 Free
Alfreton Town	July	2002 Free
Released	June	2005

CAPS (@SWFC)
ENGLAND Youth (4) v Brazil, Hungary, France, Thailand 1986

If the Wednesday first team debut of Carl Bradshaw's contemporary Dean Barrick – who scored with his first touch – was out of a comic book then Bradshaw own debut was almost unreal as he scored at Oakwell after just 38 seconds of the 1986-7 season. However one small fact differentiated him from Barrick as on that opening day Wednesday were actually playing at Charlton Athletic and it was for Barnsley that he made a dream start to his Football League career! The teenager had joined the Tykes on loan just two weeks after signing professional forms for Wednesday and would play five further games before returning to Hillsborough to continue his football education. He had originally impressed while appearing for Sheffield Boys, playing at every level from under-11 to under-15 and earning an English Schools Trophy winners medal in 1984. In addition he was a regular for both South Yorkshire and Yorkshire boys and this promise eventually led to him signing apprentice forms at Wednesday in 1985.

Although for the majority of his career Bradshaw would play at full back it was as a forward that he first made his mark in league football at Wednesday, making a goal scoring debut on Queens Park Rangers' plastic pitch in November 1986. He would enjoy a highly successful first campaign as a pro at Wednesday, appearing in sixteen games, scoring five times and winning the club's Young Player of the Year award. However the aggressive Bradshaw then became a regular on the subs bench and in fact started only nine further league games before moving to Maine Road in a transfer that brought Imre Varadi back to Wednesday for a second spell. Within a year however he was on his way back to Sheffield to sign for his boyhood heroes Sheffield United and it was at Bramall Lane that he became established in a new right back role – appearing in over 150 games for the Blades and helping them to swap places with Wednesday at the end of the 1989-90 season. However it was problems off the field of play, which then started to dog Bradshaw's career, and after encountering problems in his home City he moved to Norwich City where in September 1997 he was handed a six-week jail sentence after being found guilty of assaulting a taxi driver.

He was released from jail early but forty-eight hours later was freed by Norwich City only for Second Division Wigan Athletic to offer Carl a chance to restart his career. He would remain on Wigan's books for four seasons – appearing in 140 games and captaining the club to Auto Windscreen Cup glory in 1999 – before completing his league career with a midfield role at basement club Scunthorpe United. After being released by The Iron in April 2002 the now vastly experienced Bradshaw joined highly ambitious Unibond club Alfreton Town, helping them to promotion from Division One in the club's first season back in the league.

BRADSHAW, Francis 'Frank' — 1905-10

Born: 31 May 1885 Sheffield
(5ft 9½ ins, 11st 10lbs – 1907)

Debut: 23 April 1906
v Everton
Division One Home
Last Appearance: 19 February 1910
v Notts County
Division One Home
Total League
& Cup Appearances: 95 Goals: 40

Career Details:

Oxford Street Sunday School		1897
WEDNESDAY	January	1905
Northampton	May	1910 £700*
Everton	November	1911 £1,250
Arsenal	8 June	1914

*Including £500 paid by Everton – for his league forms - after Bradshaw was transferred from Northampton to Everton

CAPS (@SWFC) –
ENGLAND Full (1) v Austria 08/06/08
Football League (2) v Scottish League , Irish League 1909
International Trial (1) v North v South 27/01/08

In quite simple terms big, strong and wholehearted inside forward Frank Bradshaw was one of the most brilliant footballers Sheffield has produced in its long history. One can only imagine what heights his career could have reached if he had not been constantly dogged by injury during his almost twenty-year career as a professional. His playing career had started in the Sheffield Sunday School League with Oxford Street and he would spend several years in their colours while pursuing his chosen profession as a silversmith. However his talents required a larger audience and after signing amateur forms for Wednesday early in 1904 he started to form a reputation in the club's reserve side, playing in the strong Midland League competition. After scoring his first goal for Wednesday in the reserve fixture at Doncaster Rovers in February 1904 Bradshaw would net over twenty goals for two consecutive seasons as the Owls won the Midland League Championship in 1906, completed the Wharncliffe Charity League double and also finish runners-up in the 1905 and 1906 Sheffield Challenge Cup Finals – he would score an amazing eight times in a January 1906 Cup win against Hoyland Common, two weeks before playing his part in an 18-0 Sheffield Cup romp!

His superb form for the second team eventually earned Frank a first team call up and he was probably a bit miffed when after scoring twice on his debut he was not retained for the final game of the season five days later! However the "big, dashing and clever" attacker then spent several months on the sidelines because of injury – at one point it was feared he would not make the grade due to a knee injury received during a practise game – only to bounce back into first team contention just at the right time. This was in February 1907 and over the next two months Bradshaw would retain the number eight shirt as Wednesday reached the F.A.Cup Final against Wolves, the inside right being the youngest member of the Cup Final team at age 23. The Owls of course won the trophy and over the next two years Bradshaw was at the peak of his game as Wednesday finished fifth in two consecutive seasons. His form earned him several representative honours which included a full England cap in Vienna which, despite netting a hat trick in an 11-1 romp, would prove to be his solitary cap – he received a call up February 1909 for a game versus Ireland but had to pull out due to injury and was never picked again.

Not surprisingly Bradshaw was a great favourite with Hillsborough fans and they must have been dismayed when his career looked over in 1910 after a season of persistent injury problems with his knee cartilage restricted him to only a dozen appearances. It was at this point that the Wednesday hierarchy decided it was time for him to move on and promptly sold him to Southern League Northampton Town for a knock down fee. However player-manager at Town was a young Herbert Chapman – who would become one of the greatest club managers the English game has seen – and he immediately sent Bradshaw to a specialist in London which would effectively save his career. He repaid the Cobblers by leading them to runners-up spot in 1911 but would stay only one season in non-league soccer as with his fitness problems seemingly over he was soon back in Division One with Everton- also helping them to second spot. In his first full season at Goodison Park he missed only four league games, netting ten times and was reacquainted with his old Southern League rivals when playing for the Football League against then in 1912. His final club proved to be Arsenal where he played until May 1923 – thirteen years after Wednesday thought his career was finished – appearing in over 300 games for the Gunners, including over a hundred in Wartime soccer. Later in his career Frank played at half back and actually finished his playing days as a full back when his knee injuries finally took their toll. After retiring he was appointed manager of Football League club Aberdare Athletic but would stay only eleven months – hauling the financially stricken club into a mid table spot after they had finished second bottom the previous season. He would leave in April 1924 and until 1938 acted as coach for the Football Association in Somerset before retiring to Taunton after working at Bristol Aeroplane Co. until he was 72 years old.

BRADSHAW, Paul 1976-78

Born: 2 October 1953 Sheffield
(5ft 6ins, 10st 4lbs – 1978)

Debut: 25 September 1976
v Wrexham
Division Three Away
Last Appearance: 7 March 1978
v Chester
Division Three Home
Total League
& Cup Appearances: 72+2 Goals: 11

Career Details:

Burnley	October	1970
WEDNESDAY	23 September	1976 £19,444
Retired	31 October	1978
Hallam	September	1980
Frickley Athletic		1981

Winger Paul Bradshaw sadly saw his flourishing career at Wednesday cut short by a serious knee injury, which after two unsuccessful operations forced his retirement from the game at the relatively tender age of just 25. He had arguably enjoyed the best days of his career when still a teenager as the ex-Sheffield and Yorkshire boys player won two England Schoolboy caps in 1969 and then when on the books of Burnley earned thirteen England Youth caps, winning International tournaments in Czechoslovakia in 1971 and in Spain a year later. This was after he had elected to join Burnley despite having trained with both professional clubs from the City of his birth.

His seven years at the Turf Moor club – he signed apprentice forms in 1969 – would be frustrating for Bradshaw as he made only thirteen appearances at first team level and when the chance came to re-launch his career under Len Ashurst took the opportunity to return to Sheffield. Division Three football was much more to the pacy wingman's liking and the uncle of ex-Wednesday keeper Matt Clarke quickly became a popular player at Hillsborough, missing only a handful of games before injury wrecked his career. The Owls played a benefit game for him against Leeds United in 1979 by which time Bradshaw had launched himself into a schools coaching career that he maintained for twenty years until 1999. During that period he also worked as an insurance salesman and in 1991, after qualifying to be a teacher after a four-year course, he took a teaching job at a Sheffield school. In the early 1980s he twice made comebacks in non-league soccer but his knee could not take the strain so he finally retired in January 1981. Returned to senior non-league football in December 2003 when being appointed assistant manager at Northern Premier League side Stocksbridge Park Steels. He now teaches at Silverdale School in Sheffield.

BRADY, Alexander "Alec" 1892-99

Born: 2 April 1865
Cathcart, Renfrewshire
(5ft 5½ ins, 11st 6lbs – 1896)
Died: 19 October 1913 Renton
Debut: 3 September 1892
v Notts County Division One Away
Last Appearance: 28 January 1899
v Stoke FC F.A.Cup Home
Total League
& Cup Appearances: 178 Goals: 39

Career Details:

Dundee Harp		
Renton		
Partick Thistle		1888
Sunderland	September	1888
Burnley	October	1888
Sunderland	May	1889
Everton	November	1889
Broxburn Shamrock		1890 Loan
Glasgow Celtic		1891
WEDNESDAY		1892
Clydebank	10 August	1899
Renton	14 August	1901

The story of Alec Brady's signing from Glasgow giants Celtic in 1892 not only shows the passion that football can arise but also gives a curious insight into 19th Century life. Since professional football began there had been many cross border raids by English clubs in search of Scottish talent and it would be fair to say these advances were not welcomed by our Scottish friends! It was therefore with some trepidation that Wednesday secretary Arthur Dickinson must have travelled to Glasgow in the hope of securing the signature of not just Brady but this teammate Jack Madden. However both players were secured and he managed to get them to Sheffield despite pressure being exerted at Glasgow Station in an attempt to "persuade" them not to leave! That was not the end of the story however as it emerged a Roman Catholic Priest had been despatched from Glasgow so Wednesday put both players into hiding – Brady being secreted in Boston, Lincolnshire. Unfortunately for Wednesday the priest found Madden and he returned to Glasgow – he was sent off for fighting in Celtic's opening league game of the new season – but the cloak and dagger tactics paid off in Brady's case and the brilliant inside forward would make his debut at Notts County in September 1892 – the club's first ever game in the Football League.

The diminutive and unselfish attacker was thought by many to be one of cleverest players of his era and there was no doubt that Brady possessed outstanding ball control and a passing ability rare for his time. During his years in Sheffield, Alec would form a great left wing a partnership with the legendary Fred Spiksley and was prominent as Wednesday established themselves in league soccer and won the F.A.Cup for the first time in their history in 1896, Brady appearing in the Final against Wolves. Although not a prolific scorer Brady however can be credited as being the first player to score a hat-trick in league football for the club, netting his treble against Derby County in October 1893. He was also indirectly instrumental in ending the ridiculous practise of clubs appealing after the event in order to get Cup-ties replayed. After playing in the January 1893 F.A.Cup tie versus Derby County – which Wednesday won – the Rams protested that Brady was ineligible and they were subsequently granted a replay with the Wednesday man being suspended. The Derbyshire club won the replay but Wednesday protested against Steve Bloomer and controversially another game was ordered which Wednesday won at Olive Grove. This led to a change in the law that stated teams had to send player lists to their opponents before any Cup-tie was played.

Despite his great form for Wednesday he would never earn an International call up for his country and when he returned home to join non-league Clydebank in the summer of 1899 could quite rightly be classed as one of the finest players never to have been capped by Scotland. He had actually started his career in Scottish junior football and the move to Olive Grove was in fact the start of a second spell in English football as he had first come to the fore with Sunderland and Burnley before missing only one game for Everton as they won the League Championship in 1891 – incidentally he was suspended for two months in September 1889 after signing for both Burnley and Everton at the same time! He was lured back to Scotland after scoring 20 times in 34 games for the Toffeemen and in his only season at Celtic made a huge impression, helping them to runners-up spot behind Dumbarton and scoring six times in five games as the famous Glasgow club won the Scottish Cup for the first time in their history – beating Queens Park in a replay after the first game was abandoned due to crowd disorder! After finishing his playing career Brady worked on the banks of the Clyde as a Ship's caulker but after undergoing a serious operation in August 1913 he was sent £20 by Wednesday after his doctor stated he would be unable to work again - he passed away soon after.

BRANDON, Harold "Harry" 1890-98

Born: 1871 Kilbernie, Ayrshire
(5ft 5ins, 12st 2lbs. – 1896)

Debut: 17 January 1891
v Halliwell
F.A.Cup Home
Last Appearance: 16 April 1898
v Wolverhampton Wanderers
Division One Away
Total League
& Cup Appearances: 172* Goals: 16
***Also appeared in**
29 Football Alliance League games

Career Details:

Haywood Wanderers		
Paisley St. Mirren		1890
Glasgow Clyde		1890
WEDNESDAY	12 December	1890
Chesterfield Town	18 October	1898

CAPS (@SWFC) –
Football Alliance League (1) v Football League 1891

At various times during the 1890s Wednesday could call upon four members of the Brandon family and it was whole-hearted, one hundred percent competitor Harry who was without doubt the most successful. After learning his football trade with Lanarkshire junior side Heywood he moved to St.Mirren – winning the Paisley Charity Cup in 1890 – but after a few months was on the move again, signing for Glasgow club Clyde. However the wanderlust would strike again and he eventually arrived at Olive Grove in December 1890 – just two months after his cousin Bob joined Wednesday. The halfback made his debut in a Wednesday shirt in the first ever meeting with Sheffield United, in December 1890, but possibly because the Owls did not want to alert their rivals to his presence in Sheffield he actually played under the pseudonym of Todd!

He made such an impression in that first game that he was carried shoulder high from the pitch and from that day forward Harry was an automatic first choice, appearing for Wednesday on their debut in the Football League in September 1892, having made his competitive debut for the Owls in the club record 12-0 win over hapless Lancashire side Halliwell eighteen months earlier. Although playing most of his Wednesday career in his best position of right half back Harry could be described in modern parlance as a utility player as while with the Owls he played in every position on the field of play – including between the sticks in a reserve match – and was a huge favourite with Wednesday fans of the time, especially after he was a member of the side that brought the F.A.Cup to Sheffield for the first time in 1896. Once described as a "very useful player although rather rash" Harry never hesitated in shooting for goal when the opportunity arose and his commitment to the cause was perhaps typified by an incident at Olive Grove when he had to leave the field to change his boots. However Wednesday were under the cosh and he returned to the pitch in his stocking feet to clear the ball several times while bootless!

Brandon – whose father came over from Ireland and married a Scots lass – drew a three thousand crowd to his benefit game against Notts County in December 1897 and completed his playing career with a short spell at neighbours Chesterfield, making twenty appearances for the Spireites before retiring from the game. Incidentally local press reports at the time suggested that Chesterfield were so keen to sign Harry that they waiting at his door at dawn on the day he became available! Later in life he worked at Barnsley Colliery and in September 1919 could be found coaching Thursday club Silverwood.

BRANDON, Robert "Bob" 1890-91

Born: 1866 Kilbirnie, Scotland
Debut: 17 January 1891 v Halliwell F.A.Cup Home
Last Appearance:
14 February 1891 v West Bromwich Albion F.A.Cup Home
Total League & Cup Appearances: 2* Goals: 1
***Also appeared in 16 Football Alliance League games**

Career Details:

Clyde		
WEDNESDAY	October	1890 Free
Released		1891

Strangely, like his cousin Harry, Bob Brandon's first appearance in a Wednesday shirt was actually under an assumed name when he played with the pseudonym of Brown in the friendly at Wolves in October 1890. He netted Wednesday's third goal in the 3-3 draw at Molyneaux and scored again a week later on his Football Alliance League debut, in a 5-3 loss at Birmingham St.George. The centre-forward would play a total of sixteen Alliance league games for the club in 1890-1 as Wednesday's attempt to retain the Championship ended in disastrous fashion as they ended the season in bottom spot! This poor league form was probably a factor in the fact that this proved to be his one and only season at Wednesday although during the campaign he would appear alongside Harry in the historic first meeting with Sheffield United and also net his only competitive goal during the 12-0 Cup romp against minnows Halliwell – the Owls biggest winning margin in their history. He was released in the summer of 1891 and later worked as a shale miner back in Scotland.

BRANDON, Thomas "Tom" 1891-93

Born: 26 February 1869 Kilbirnie, Scotland
(5ft 10½ ins, 11st 10lbs – 1896)
Debut: 23 January 1892 v Bolton Wanderers F.A.Cup Home
Last Appearance: 3 April 1893 v Notts Co. Division One Home
Total League & Cup Appearances: 38* Goals: 2
***Also appeared in 11 Football Alliance League games**

Career Details:

Clippsons		
St.Johnstone		1885
Port Glasgow Athletic		1886
Renfrew Athletic		
St.Mirren		1887
Blackburn Rovers	August	1889
WEDNESDAY		1891
Nelson	September	1893
Blackburn Rovers	13 December	1893
St.Mirren		1900

Uncompromising right back Tom Brandon holds a special place in the history of Sheffield Wednesday as he was not only the captain on the day the Owls made their debut in the Football League but is also credited with scoring the only goal of the game in the victory at Notts County. He had arrived at the club a year earlier, joining his brother Jim and cousin Harry, after a controversial move from Blackburn Rovers where he had won a Football League cap and an F.A.Cup winners medal just a few months earlier. He was lured across the Pennines with the promise of a public house – which ironically he never got – and perhaps not surprisingly Rovers furiously objected to this and after complaining to the league Wednesday were put on the Football League's own "black list" for a time. However they did nothing to stop the move and during Wednesday's final season as a non-league club Tom appeared in eleven Football Alliance league games, missing the middle part of the campaign through injury, plus numerous friendlies and minor games.

In the summer that followed the Owls were of course elected into the First Division of the Football League and Tom would be one of only two players to appear in all thirty league games in that debut campaign, the other being goalie William Allan. His two goals in that season came on the opening day and on the final day – the latter helping to beat Notts County and ensure Wednesday avoided the "test matches" which were used to decide promotion and relegation – a forerunner of today's play-offs. He may not have been the most cultured full back in the club's history – using his big and burly frame to the full – but he was certainly effective and it was a big blow when he refused to re-sign for Wednesday in the summer of 1893, after the Owls failed to grant him permission to transfer back to Blackburn Rovers. At this point Tom started to play as a professional for non-league Nelson - F.A. rules stated he was allowed to do so and the club holding his league registration could not intervene – but a furious Wednesday appealed to the F.A that they had not granted permission, therefore breaking F.A.rules! However the F.A decided he could play for Nelson after all and advised Wednesday they would have to take legal action if they wanted to stop him! The whole sorry episode ended in December 1893 when Brandon and the club settled their differences and the brave, battling defender got his wish of a move back to Blackburn Rovers – a transfer that rankled for many years with the club elders.

Back at Rovers he would give sterling service to the club, taking his appearance tally to an impressive 245 league and cup games, and his consistency was finally rewarded when being capped at full International level by Scotland in 1896. He left Lancashire at the turn of the Century, returning home to play out his career at St.Mirren, before it is believed he emigrated to the U.S.A. He is known to have been living in Rhode Island in 1904 but certainly returned home as Tom was working in the Lanarkshire coalfields six years later.

BRANFOOT, Ian Grant 1965-69

Born: 26 January 1947 Gateshead
(5ft 10ins, 12st 2lbs – 1966)
Debut: 9 May 1966
v Burnley Division One Home
Last Appearance: 22 November 1969
v West Bromwich Albion
Division One Away
Total League
& Cup Appearances: 37+4 Goals: 0

Career Details:

Redheugh Boys Club		
Gateshead FC		
WEDNESDAY	12 July	1965
Doncaster Rovers	17 December	1969*
Lincoln City	30 July	1973 £7,500

*Branfoot & Irvine exchanged for Wilcockson

Came to Hillsborough as a teenager from ex-league club Gateshead with a good reputation, having appeared for both Gateshead and Durham boys in addition to earning International caps for the Association of boys clubs. The youngster would go straight into the Owls reserve side and after becoming quickly established was given his first taste of First Division football in the final game of the season – following an injury to regular left half back Gerry Young. Over the next three seasons Branfoot would prove himself an able deputy to the stalwart Young although many of his first team starts would come in a variety of positions, including outside-left and almost every defensive position. However this "no nonsense" player simply could not nail down a regular first team slot and eventually moved to South Yorkshire neighbours Doncaster Rovers in a deal that brought Harold Wilcockson to Hillsborough.

The solid and dependable Branfoot found the lower reaches of the Football League more to his liking and totalled an impressive 156 league appearances for Rovers before moving further east to sign for Lincoln City. It was at City that Branfoot would get his first real experience of coaching – being appointed player-coach in 1976 after helping The Imps to the Division Four Championship under the stewardship of one Graham Taylor. He would twice be named in P.F.A divisional teams in his time at Lincoln and when he retired to become assistant manager at Sincil Bank in July 1977 had totalled 166 competitive games for City, mainly at right back, scoring eleven times. After a year as No.2 he joined Southampton as youth team coach, remaining in that capacity until being appointed assistant manager at Reading in July 1983. After being appointed manager at Elm park in January 1984 he would experience a real roller coaster spell in the hot seat which started with tremendous success – Reading were promoted to Division Three at the end of his first season and two years later stormed to the Division Two Championship to earn a place in the second tier of English football for the first time in over sixty years. On limited resources Branfoot kept Reading in Division Two for a season but relegation came in 1988 with a shock victory at Wembley in the Simod Cup Final perhaps only small consolation for Royals fans. The almost inevitable sack came in October 1989 and for the next eighteen months Branfoot was chief coach at Crystal Palace, before jumping back on the managerial merry-go-round to take over at old club Southampton in June 1991.

It would be fair to say his time at The Saints was a disappointment to all concerned and he received merciless criticism from the terraces as Southampton struggled near the foot of the Premier League. This strong vocal opposition to his managership combined with poor results led to a parting of ways after three years at the helm. He was then, somewhat surprisingly, appointed boss at Fulham but fared little better and in February 1996 resigned to become general manager with the Cottagers near the foot of Division Three. He eventually left to become chief scout at Swansea City in October 1997 but within days of joining was elevated to assistant manager after manager Mickey Adams resigned just thirteen days into the job! After six months in South Wales Branfoot linked up briefly at the Football Association with old Wednesday team mate Howard Wilkinson before in March 1998 moving back to his native Northeast after landing the plumb job of Academy Director at Sunderland.

BRANNIGAN, Kenneth 1986-88

Born: 8 June 1965 Glasgow
(6ft , 12st 4lbs – 1986)
Only Appearance: 3 January 1987
v Leicester City Division One Away
Total League & Cup Appearances: 1 Goals: 0

Career Details:

St.Marys Calton		
Queens Park		1981
WEDNESDAY	18 June	1986 Free
Stockport County	21 August	1986 2-month loan
Doncaster Rovers	17 December	1987 3-month loan
Released	30 June	1988
St.Mirren		1988 3-month trial
Kilmarnock	15 October	1988 Free
Released	January	1989
Falkirk	February	1989 Free
East Stirlingshire	17 November	1989 £15,000 (T)
Stranraer	22 November	1991 £15,000 (T)
Stenhousemuir	25 July	1995 £15,000
Clydebank	29 March	1996 £15,000
Partick Thistle	2 June	1999 Free
Clydebank		2000 Free
Berwick Rangers	September	2001 Free
Stirling Albion	January	2002 Free
Clydebank	4 November	2001 Free
Airdrie United	2 August	2002 Free
Queen's Park	January	2003 Free

It would interesting to know who was more surprised when Wednesday signed centre half Kenny Brannigan – the player or the Wednesday fans! To say the Glaswegian was an unknown to Owls supporters would be a rather formidable understatement as at the time Brannigan was playing part-time football for famous old Scottish amateur club Queens Park, in the lower reaches of the Scottish League, and only his wildest fantasies could he have dreamt of signing for an English First Division club. However that is exactly what happened to the youngster after 131 appearances for the Hampden Park based club with manager Howard Wilkinson considering him as "one for the future" and immediately sending him on a two-month loan spell at Stockport to gain some valuable experience. His English league debut came at County but it was not long before he was presented with his big chance at Wednesday – an injury crisis meaning the Owls had little choice but to throw Brannigan in for a baptism of fire at Filbert Street. Unfortunately for the Scot his debut – alongside fellow "one game wonder" David Tomlinson - was traumatic as Wednesday crashed 6-1 to The Foxes. The uncompromising centre half was probably quite relieved to be taken out of the firing line and dropped back into reserve team football and this is where he would remain for the remainder of his Wednesday career – his only additional experience of league football coming during a fifteen game loan spell at Doncaster Rovers.

After being released in the summer of 1988 the rugged defender earned a contract at Kilmarnock – after an unsuccessful trial spell at St.Mirren – but was sensationally sacked by his club in February 1989 after having head butted team mate Derek Cook just three minutes into a league game with Queen of the South! However he was almost immediately signed by Falkirk and over the years that followed played for a wide variety of clubs in the lower reaches of Scottish League football, whilst building a small business empire that had started when he first signed professional for Wednesday. After initially being involved in property Brannigan invested his money wisely and by the time he reverted back to part-time status in 2000 owned a string of taxicab firms, food stores and even a public house. His first taste of management came during a third spell at crisis torn Clydebank where he was player-manager briefly just before the club became defunct. They were taken over by Airdrie United and Kenny was appointed player-coach although he only appeared once for the new club before jumping at the opportunity to return to the club where it all started, Queens Park. He was officially appointed into a new player-manager role – although Kenny was only expected to play mid-week games for the reserves if needed - on 15th January 2003, over sixteen years after he had left for Sheffield. He watched from the stands as his new charges lost a two-goal lead in his first game in charge to share six goals with East Stirlingshire and must have reflected on how his career had truly come full circle. Unfortunately his fiery temper again let Brannigan down at Queen of the South as at the beginning of the 2004-5 season he was sacked after striking a supporter!

BRANSTON, Guy Peter Bromley 2004

Born: 9 January 1979 Leicester
(6ft, 13st 12lbs – 2004)
Debut: 7 August 2004 v Colchester United
League One Home
Last Appearance: 11 December 2004
v Brentford League One Home
Total League &
Cup Appearances: 12+1 Goals: 0

Career Details:

Leicester City	3 July	1997
Rushden & Diamonds	November	1997 Loan
Colchester United	9 February	1998 Loan
Colchester United	7 August	1998 Loan
Plymouth Argyle	20 November	1998 Loan
Lincoln City	10 August	1999 Loan
Rotherham United	15 October	1999 £50,000
Wycombe Wanderers	15 September	2003 Loan
Peterborough United	25 February	2004 Loan
WEDNESDAY	1 July	2004 Free
Peterborough United	30 December	2004 Loan
Oldham Athletic	18 February	2005

Whole hearted centre half Guy Branston started his career with hometown club Leicester City, playing under Chris Turner while a youth team regular for the Foxes. After turning professional he found his first team opportunities virtually non existent and a league bow came while on loan at Colchester United. Several loan spells followed and despite failing to make a senior appearance for Leicester he was sold for a fee to Division Three Rotherham United. The old-fashioned style 'rugged' centre half then enjoyed the best period of his career, helping the Ronnie Moore inspired Millers to a meteoric rise from the basement division to current Championship level in consecutive seasons. His competitive style saw Branston sent off twice in the early days of his league career and he continued to fringe with disciplinary problems at Millmoor, once receiving his marching orders after a tunnel incident and even managing to punch a whole through a dressing room door after being handed a red card! However he was a firm favourite with Rotherham supporters and scored 13 times in 116 competitive games before falling out of favour during the 2003-4 season.

He appeared in only eight league games for the Millers as they maintained their Championship status in 2004 and played the majority of his first team football while on loan - initially at Wycombe and then Peterborough. He then made a surprise move to Hillsborough in the summer of 2004 and seemed set to partner Graeme Lee at the heart of the Owls defence in Chris Turner's totally revamped side. However he lost out to youngster Patrick Collins for the opening day fixture and then received his marching orders at Tranmere Rovers for an off the ball incident. His subsequent suspension and then a niggling injury disrupted his early months at Wednesday and he was then sent out on loan by new manager Paul Sturrock to help regain fitness. However on his return he was told he was not guaranteed a first team place and eventually moved on a free transfer to League One rivals Oldham Athletic after a disappointing short spell at Hillsborough.

BRASH, Archibald T. 1894-98 & 1899-00

Born: 1873 Uphall, Linlithgow
(5ft, 4ins, 10st 7lbs – 1894)
Debut: 1 September 1894
v Everton
Division One Away
Last Appearance: 28 April 1900
v Middlesbrough
Division Two Home
Total League
& Cup Appearances: 131 Goals: 23

Career Details:

Paisley St Mirren		
WEDNESDAY	4 July	1894
Crewe Alexandra		1898
WEDNESDAY	3 May	1899
Leicester Fosse	20 June	1900 £110
Aberdeen	12 August	1901

At the time of his transfer to Hillsborough the diminutive Archie Brash was considered to be one of the finest players Scotland had to offer and the 21 year-old winger would live up to this billing during two spells in Sheffield. He was one of three Scots to join the club in the summer of 1894 – the others being fellow countrymen Bob Ferrier and Bob Petrie – and their arrival, along with that of future captain Tom Crawshaw, would transform Wednesday's fortunes to such an extent that two years after joining, Brash held an F.A.Cup winners medal in his hand after victory over Wolves at Crystal Palace. The tricky and speedy right winger was a thorn in the side of many an opponent and was instrumental in that Cup success, netting a brace in the quarter-final win over Everton and scoring in the semi-final draw with Bolton before his quickly taken throw-in allowed Fred Spiksley to net in the first minute of the final. He formed a deadly, although somewhat lightweight, right wing partnership with Bob Ferrier but lack of brawn was more than made up for with fleet of foot and downright cleverness that had the Owls fans roaring their approval.

Brash – one of the smallest players in the club's history – eventually lost his place to William Dryburgh early in 1898 and would then spend a season in non-league football with Crewe before returning to Wednesday a year later, playing in the opening game at Hillsborough in September 1899. While Brash had been away Wednesday had not only lost Olive Grove but also their First Division status but with Archie back in the side the Owls romped to the Second Division Championship, winning all seventeen home games along the way. However in April 1900 he was placed on the transfer list and soon after transferred to Leicester Fosse where he really did not live up to his big reputation, although during a great spell of form he netted four times against Burton Swifts in December 1900. After leaving Fosse he returned home to Scotland to join Pittodre based non-league side Aberdeen – one of three sides who in 1903 amalgamated to form the present day club. After hanging up his boots Brash returned to Paisley to work the family business as a cotton reel maker.

BRATLEY, George William 1933-34

Born: 17 January 1909 Wickersley, Rotherham
(5ft 11ins, 12st – 1933)
Died: First Quarter 1978 Sheffield
Debut: 11 February 1933 v West Brom Alb Division One Away
Last Appearance: 25 March 1933 v Portsmouth Division One Away
Total League & Cup Appearances: 3 Goals: 0

Career Details:

Rotherham St. Peters		
Rotherham YMCA	March	1929
Rotherham United	April	1929
WEDNESDAY	9 February	1933 £850 +E V Wright
Rotherham United	26 January	1934
Gainsborough Trinity	19 July	1934
Bath City	July	1935
Barrow	August	1936
Swindon Town	June	1938
Tunbridge Wells Rgrs	February	1939

*Wartime guest for Brighton & Hove Albion, Crystal Palace, Halifax Town, Hull City, Leeds United, Oldham Athletic & York City

Centre half George Bratley was actually six-goal top scorer for Rotherham United when he arrived at Hillsborough early in 1933. He was described as "useful in defence and effective in forward roles" but it was at centre half-back where George played throughout the majority of his Wednesday career – with the likes of Jack Ball, Ellis Rimmer and Ron Starling in advanced positions he had little chance to impress in an attacking role! His first team debut came only forty-eight hours after his transfer from the Millers – where in two spells he appeared in 103 games, scoring 12 times – and he would fill in on three occasions over the six weeks that followed for first team regular Tony Leach. However it was in Wednesday's Central league side that Bratley played most of his football while at Hillsborough, even reverting back to a centre-forward role at Christmas 1933 just before transferring back to Rotherham United in January 1934.

He would again become a fixture in the Millers side as they finished second bottom in Division Three (North) but in the summer that followed switched allegiance to divisional rival Barrow. After 82 games (9 goals) for the Cumbrians the defender would drop into non-league soccer for four years before returning to league soccer at Swindon Town just before the outbreak of World War Two.

BRAYSHAW, Edward 'Teddy' 1884-91

Born: 2nd Quarter 1863 Kirkstall
(5ft 6½ ins, 11st 8lbs – 1890)
Died: 20 November 1908 Wortley
Debut: 8 November 1884
v Long Eaton Rangers
F.A.Cup Away
Last Appearance: 14 February 1891
v West Bromwich A.
F.A.Cup Home
Total League
& Cup Appearances: 21* Goals: 0
***Also appeared in**
30 Football Alliance League games

Career Details:

All Saints	1882
Pyebank	1882
Walkley	1883
WEDNESDAY	1884
Lockwood Brothers	1886-87
Sheffield Rovers	1887
Retired	1891
Grimsby Town	1892

CAPS (@ SWFC)
England Full (1) v Ireland 05/02/1887

A resourceful and dependable player who was both influential and instrumental in the Owls switch from amateur to professional status in the 1880s. The left back was a true stalwart of Sheffield football, first playing for the Sheffield FA in 1884 while with his second club Walkley. He joined Wednesday in the same year, first appearing in a friendly at Aston Villa in September, and played 24 times in his debut campaign. Over the years that followed Brayshaw – whose father was a well known Sheffield detective - would win a variety of local honours with the club, starting with a Wharncliffe Charity Cup success in 1886 and then a Sheffield Challenge Cup win a year later – Teddy netting the late winner against Sheffield Collegiate at Bramall Lane. It was at the then home of Yorkshire County Cricket club that just a few weeks before Brayshaw won his one and only cap for his country – he was so proud of the feat that he wore the cap several times during subsequent games – including an F.A.Cup tie at Nottingham Forest in 1888!

However despite repeating the Sheffield Cup win a year later all was not well at Wednesday, the situation not helped in 1886-7 when the club secretary failed to send in their FA.Cup entry in time to play in the competition. During that season Brayshaw- along with several other Wednesday men – appeared for Lockwood Brothers in the Cup – and in 1887 he was one of the "rebel" group who formed a team called Sheffield Rovers as the Owls still refused to turn professional. His new side played the requisite solitary game so they could apply for the following season's F.A.Cup and with Teddy on the committee Rovers were on the verge of adopting professionalism. With Wednesday's very existence now under threat they bowed to the pressure and after turning professional their new rivals Rovers played their second match before disbanding. It was perhaps ironic that Brayshaw, like so many of his contemporaries, remained amateur throughout his career, being a carpenter by trade. Now back under the wing at Olive Grove – he had played in the opening game at the new ground in September 1887 – his career continued to flourish as Wednesday became a dominant force in local football and started to come to national prominence.

A second Wharncliffe Charity Cup success came his way in 1888 before Wednesday enjoyed an outstanding 1889-90 campaign, winning the inaugural Football Alliance League Championship and reaching the F.A.Cup Final for the first time in their history. The outstanding full back missed only four of the 22 games in that title-winning season – appearing in the first ever Alliance game at home to Bootle in September 1889 – but could do little to stop Blackburn Rovers putting six past Wednesday in the Cup Final! As injury started to take its toll he began to drift from the first team scene in the season that followed – playing twelve Alliance league games – although he was a member of the eleven who thrashed Halliwell 12-0 in January 1891 – the club's biggest ever win. His career finally ended in that year due to several small broken bones in his left foot and despite an attempted comeback with Grimsby Town he was forced to retire in 1892. By this time he was a publican – having joined the trade in 1889 – and continued to be so until 1907 when he was forced to retire through ill health. Unfortunately his health deteriorated and he passed away at the age of just 45 after spending just over twelve months in a South Yorkshire Asylum.

BREEDON, John Norman 'Jack' 1930-35

Born: 29 December 1907 South Hiendley, Barnsley (5ft 9½ ins, 11st 7lbs – 1930)
Died: 2nd Quarter 1977 Leeds
Debut: 27 December 1930
v Newcastle United
Division One Away
Last Appearance: 5 May 1934
v Stoke City
Division One Home
Total League
& Cup Appearances: 47 Goals: 0

Career Details:

Hemsworth West End		
South Hiendley Amateurs		
Barnsley	September	1928
WEDNESDAY	20 November	1930 £1200
Manchester United	9 July	1935 £350
Burnley		WW2 Guest
Rochdale		WW2 Guest
Bolton Wanderers	March	1942 Guest
Manchester City	March	1945 Guest
Burnley	26 October	1945

Like many of his peers Jack Breedon starting his working life at the local pit after leaving school at the age of 14. He worked five years at New Monkton Colliery, near Barnsley, before being signed professional by the Tykes from Barnsley Junior League side South Hiendley. However the consistency of Gale ensured Jack made only a single first team appearance for Barnsley in his debut season and would play only four times in 1929-30 as their neighbours Wednesday won the league Championship. It was not until the start of November 1930 that Breedon finally replaced Gale but incredibly he would play only three matches before Bob Brown took him down the A61 to Hillsborough. His role at Wednesday was without doubt as deputy to the outstanding Jack Brown and in his five seasons at the club Breedon proved himself a more than capable replacement – his first run in the side starting in March 1931 after Brown broke his thumb at Middlesbrough. A variety of injuries to Brown ensured that Jack would end his Wednesday career with a healthy number of appearances although a wrist injury that required surgery ruined his final season at Hillsborough; he appeared in only fourteen reserve games during 1934-5.

His transfer to Manchester United started a long association with the Old Trafford club where somewhat strangely he only established himself during wartime football. During his first three seasons at United – when they were promoted twice and relegated once – Breedon played only a bit part and it was not until the final season of Pre War soccer that Jack enjoyed an extended run at first team level. Throughout his career he had generally been regarded as second choice and in peacetime football totalled less than one hundred league appearances at three clubs over an eleven-year period. However this all changed once war had been declared as Breedon started between the sticks in the aborted league campaign of 1939-40 and remained there for five years – except for single appearances as a guest for Bolton and Manchester City - totalling 164 appearances. His form during the hostilities was at times quite spectacular but when peace broke out he moved to Burnley. He made only four appearances for the Lancashire side in regional football before turning down an offer to become manager of Division Three (North) club New Brighton because his wife did not want to leave their Leeds home!

His did eventually secure a post closer to home when being appointed Halifax Town boss in August 1947 but his time at The Shay was not a happy one as Town struggled near the foot of the table, twice having to apply for re-election. Despite wholesale changes in playing staff he was unable to improve matters and finally resigned in November 1950 saying "the club had been in the doldrums when I arrived and had continued to stay there, in view of this I feel a parting of ways should be". He showed his loyalty to Town by staying until a successor could be appointed before spending several years scouting for Bradford City. A nine-month spell as manager at Bradford Park Avenue ended in October 1955 after several poor results and Jack would stay in West Yorkshire to scout for Leeds United in the early 1960s before retiring.

BRELSFORD, Charles W. "Chas" 1912-19

Born: 1890 Darnall, Sheffield
(5ft 7ins, 11st – 1913)
Debut: 9 November 1912
v Oldham Ath. Division One Home
Last Appearance: 7 February 1914
v Liverpool Division One Away
Total League
& Cup Appearances: 7* Goals: 0
***Also appeared in**
88 wartime games, scoring 1 goal

Career Details:

Kilnhurst Town		
Buxton		
WEDNESDAY	March	1912 £30*
Sheffield United	December	1918 Guest
South Shields	July	1919
Castleford Town	January	1921
Mansfield Town	August	1923

*Fee paid to Kilnhurst

Chas Brelsford was a member of the famous Sheffield family that provided players for both City clubs in the period either side of the First World War – his brother Tom played for Wednesday while his other sibling Bill made over five hundred appearances for The Blades, winning the F.A.Cup with United in 1915. Of the three footballer brothers Chas made the least impact on league football, starting just seven first team games for Wednesday in this preferred position of left back. Competition for the full back slot came initially from "man in possession" Jimmy Spoors but following the arrival of the outstanding Jimmy Blair his league career effectively came to a close.

With his two rivals both unavailable in wartime soccer Chas would be a regular for Wednesday during regional football, also making a couple of appearances as a guest alongside his brother Bill for United. After the Great War came to a close he signed for League new boys South Shields but failed to appear in Division Three (North) football for the Horsley Hill club in their debut season of league soccer. After failing to break into the league side Chas moved to non-league Castleford Town early in 1921. He later played alongside ex-Owl Jack Bellas at Midland League Mansfield Town, winning two Championships with The Stags, before a broken leg suffered during 1926-7 led to his retirement after 120 games.

BRELSFORD, Thomas William 'Tom' 1924-25

Born: 12 April 1895
Attercliffe, Sheffield
(5ft 9ins, 11st 4lbs – 1920)
Died: September 1946 Sheffield
Debut: 10 March 1920
v Liverpool
Division One Away
Last Appearance: 15 March 1924
v Oldham Ath
Division Two Away
Total League
& Cup Appearances: 122* Goals: 6
***Also played in**
52 Wartime games, scoring two goals

Career Details:

Wombwell Town		
Castleford Town		
WEDNESDAY		1919
Barrow	16 July	1924
Rotherham United	May	1925 £150
Wombwell Town	March	1927

Left half-back Tom Brelsford served in the Army in World War One - stationed for a time in India- but also played over fifty games in Wartime soccer for Wednesday who he had initially joined at the age of 17 - before signing his first professional contract in 1919. For the majority of his time at Hillsborough Brelsford – who played in Wartime as a wing forward but soon developed into a robust half back - was a first team regular, only briefly losing his place to Robert Eggo at the start of the 1920-1 season. He remained so until March 1923 when he suffered a broken leg in the home game with Wolves. On his return to fitness he quickly regained a first team spot but competition from youngster Oliver Levick and the arrival of future England International Billy Marsden eventually led to his departure to league side Barrow.

Incredibly on the day Tom was released by Wednesday – at the end of 23-4 season - his brother William was released by Sheffield United after having played the small matter of 417 league and cup games for the Blades! The brothers were part of famous trio – their brother Ben having played two seasons for Wednesday without breaking into the first eleven. Tom spent less than a year in Cumbria - the travelling from his Sheffield home was probably a major factor in his short stay – and after 31 league starts for Barrow he returned to South Yorkshire. His move to Millmoor was actually a little piece of history as he became the first ever signing of the new Rotherham United club which had emerged from the merger of Rotherham County and Thornhill United. He would score twice in 36 games for the Millers during his one and only season before retiring from league football in May 1926.

BRETNALL, Charles "Oscar" 1913-20

Born: Chesterfield 1888/89
(5ft 8½ ins, 11st – 1920)
Only Appearance:
19 January 1920 v Darlington F.A.Cup Home
Total League & Cup Appearances: 1 Goals: 0

Career Details:

Sheffield FC		
Midland Athletic		1910
Worksop Town		
WEDNESDAY	August	1913 £10
Rotherham County		WW1 Guest
Lincoln City		1920
Worksop Town	May	1921
Denaby United		1922
Rotherham County		1923

Centre Forward Oscar Bretnall spent the majority of his career in local non-league football except for a spell as a professional at Hillsborough. His early days were spent in Sheffield amateur football before joining the Owls in August 1913 with Wednesday donating the princely sum of £10 to his last club pro club, Midland Athletic. He was a regular for Wednesday's Midland League side during 1919-20, scoring four times, and got his first team chance for the replayed F.A.Cup tie against non-league Darlington at Hillsborough. However this proved to be his only appearance in an Owls first eleven shirt as Wednesday crashed out of the competition in one of the most embarrassing Cup exits in their long history. At the end of that disastrous season – Wednesday finished bottom of Division One – he was one of an amazing 21 players not retained by the club as they undertook a huge clear out.

From Hillsborough he moved to Midland League side Lincoln City where despite finishing top scorer in 1920-1 with twenty goals he stayed for only one season as after trying on several occasions Worksop Town finally got their man and he signed for The Tigers for a second spell. Away from football Bretnall was well known in local circles as an excellent lawn tennis player.

BRIEN, Anthony James "Tony" 1995

Born: 10 February 1969 Dublin, Eire
(5ft 11ins, 11st 9lbs – 1995)
Only Appearance: 24 June 1995
v FC Basel Intertoto Cup Away
Total League & Cup Appearances: 1 Goals: 0

Career Details:

Leicester City	13 February	1987
Chesterfield	16 December	1988 £90,000
Rotherham United	8 October	1993 Free
WEDNESDAY	June	1995 N/C
West Bromwich Albion	13 July	1995 Free
Mansfield Town	16 February	1996 Loan
Chester	22 March	1996 Loan
Hull City	15 August	1996 Free
Stalybridge Celtic	January	1998 Free
Bromsgrove Rovers	August	1999 Free
Stourbridge		1999 Free
Alfreton Town	December	1999 Free
Staveley	February	2000 Free

The June 1995 Intertoto Cup fixture in Switzerland caused the Owls to sign several players on a non-contract basis to simply enable them to fulfil the fixture. One such player was centre half Tony Brien who was probably best known for a spell at Chesterfield where he appeared in 239 competitive games for the Spireites. His career had started as a youth trainee at Leicester City, helping The Foxes to the 1987 F.A.Youth Cup semi-final while also winning Youth caps for the Republic of Ireland. The composure he showed at youth level was then repeated at first team level at both right back and centre half as manager Bryan Hamilton gave him a first taste of league football. However despite his initial impact the teenager found he could not gain a regular first team spot under new manager David Pleat and so moved to Saltergate for what was a sizeable fee for a reserve player. He would of course enjoy his best years in league football while at Chesterfield before a 55-game spell at Rotherham United preceded his brief appearance in the blue and white shirt.

After his experience of European football Brien returned to the UK to sign for Alan Buckley's West Brom, mainly as a squad player. A combination of factors, including injury, meant he appeared only four times for the Baggies before eventually dropping down two divisions to join Hull City. He left Boothferry Park during the disastrous campaign of 1997-8 to sign for ex-Owl Mel Sterland at Conference side Stalybridge Celtic but his professional career was coming to a close – mainly due to an arthritic hip – and he was forced to revert to part-time status in January 1998. He would make only three more Conference starts for Celtic after retiring from the full-time game – while training to be a Commercial pilot – and would play the remainder of his career in non-league soccer while pursuing a career outside the game. He later became an executive at rapidly expanding Chesterfield based company GBL International – makers of alcoholic drink VK Vodka Kick – who sponsored the away shirt of Chesterfield in 2001/2 and also became Barnsley's main shirt sponsors in 2003.

BRIGHT, Mark Abraham 1992-97

Born: 6 June 1962 Stoke
(6ft 12st 12lbs – 1996)
Debut: 12 September 1992
v Nottingham Forest
Premier League Away
Last Appearance: 2 September 1996
v Leicester City
Premier League Home
Total League &
Cup Appearances: 148+22 Goals: 70

Career Details:

Leek Town		
Port Vale	15 October	1981 Free
Leicester City	19 July	1984 £66,000 (T)
Crystal Palace	13 November	1986 £75,000
WEDNESDAY	11 September	1992 £875,000
Millwall	13 December	1996 Loan
Sion	17 January	1997 £70,000*
Charlton Athletic	4 April	1997 Free

*Fee never paid

The Owls side of the early 1990s was without doubt one of the best teams in the club's long history and forward Mark Bright fully played his part in the entertaining football that side produced. The Staffordshire born attacker had started in local non-league football before two spells in league football at Port Vale and Leicester but he really came to the fore as part of the Wright-Bright double act at Crystal Palace - actually outscoring the higher profile Ian Wright during their prolific partnership, netting an outstanding 114 times in 286 games for The Eagles. Wright was the first to be sold – to London neighbours Arsenal – and soon after Trevor Francis brought Bright to Hillsborough in a deal that took £500,000 rated Paul Williams to Selhurst Park.

Thankfully Bright was no less prolific at Wednesday, finishing top scorer in four consecutive seasons, and would eventually net close to a goal every two games while in Sheffield – he was coveted by many clubs with a £1m bid from Everton rejected by Wednesday in August 1993. He was a superb header of the ball and a true penalty box predator who in his time at Wednesday probably netted only once from outside the penalty area – a spectacular long range strike at Wimbledon in a League Cup tie. He thrived on the brilliant service provided by the likes of John Sheridan and Chris Waddle and will always be remembered with fondness by Owls fans for netting the extra time winner against Sheffield United in the 1993 F.A.Cup semi-final at Wembley! The many injuries to David Hirst meant the pair rarely played together in what for Wednesday fans surely would have been a dream attack but Bright did form a lethal partnership during 1992-3 with Paul Warhurst which produced 38 goals. However despite this scoring record the arrival of David Pleat saw Mark become more of a squad player than a regular – Marc Degryse and Darko Kovacevic keeping him on the sidelines – but at least he would end his Owls career on a high with his final appearance coming as a sub in the home game with Leicester City which left Wednesday top of the Premier League – unfortunately for Bright he was double Cup runner up while at Hillsborough and also lost in the 1990 F.A.Cup Final while at Palace – his only winners medal came at Palace in the Zenith Data Cup!

He eventually left Hillsborough early in 1997 but his destination was a surprise to all as he signed for little known Swiss club Sion. However the transfer proved to be a disaster for all concerned as Bright was subsequently banned from making his debut after Wednesday complained to FIFA that Sion had failed to pay the first instalment of his transfer fee - his new club were therefore refused International clearance and Bright was sat kicking his heels. Ironically by the time Wednesday started legal proceedings against Sion, in April 1997, he had returned to the UK, signing on transfer deadline day for First Division Charlton Athletic. After Charlton paid Wednesday £30,000 to settle the problem Bright would enjoy an Indian summer at The Valley and after marrying actress and pop singer Michelle Gayle would help The Addicks to a dramatic 1998 promotion play off win at Wembley to earn a Premiership place. He duly retired in 1999 to concentrate on his radio based media work which saw him reunited with old striking partner Ian Wright as well as being a match summariser for Radio Five Live.

BRISCOE, James Patrick "Jim" 1946-47

Born: 14 October 1923 Swinton,
Nr. Rotherham
(6ft 1ins, 12st – 1946)
Debut: 12 October 1946
v Manchester City
Division Two Away
Last Appearance: 4 January 1947
v Plymouth Argyle Division Two Away
Total League
& Cup Appearances: 5* Goals: 3
***Also appeared in 1 Wartime game**

Career Details:

Raith Rovers		1944 Guest
WEDNESDAY	August	1946
Gainsborough Trinity	July	1947 Free
Ramsgate		1948
Margate		1953

Forward Jim Briscoe joined Wednesday as an amateur in 1940, making his debut on Christmas Day 1943 in the 1-1 draw with Sheffield United at Bramall Lane – his only first team appearance for the club during the hostilities. Throughout the war he served in the Fleet Air Arm section of the Royal Navy, stationed at Donbristol in Scotland – allowing him to make guest appearances for Raith Rovers – and appeared several times for the services in representative games. One such appearance was a high profile game against Holland in the Olympic Stadium, Amsterdam that drew an incredible crowd of 132,000 for what was the first "International" since the start of the war in 1939. His appearance for a combined services team against Glasgow Rangers in October 1945 in Hannover, Germany made the Scottish club's history books as his hat-trick in the match is recorded as the first by an Englishman against the Ibrox club!

After being offered a professional contract by Portsmouth manager Jack Tinn while he was still in the forces Jim declined and on returning to Sheffield signed professional terms for Wednesday – he had reminded the Wednesday management of his qualities when scoring twice on his sole appearances for the reserves during the 1945-6 season. On his league debut he came up against Manchester City's legendary keeper Frank Swift and after Wednesday trainer Sam Powell had told the debutant to "irritate Frank as much as possible" Jim duly netted after 65 minutes although Wednesday would lose the game 2-1 – at the end he shook hands with Swift (which Jim said "wrapped twice around mine") and after having made himself a nuisance to the big goalie Swift commented "they all try that on their first match against me". Despite scoring twice more in only four more appearances – plus four in a dozen reserve team games – the centre-forward could not win a regular place in a struggling Wednesday side that almost dropped into Division Three(North) football, and in the following summer signed for Midland League Gainsborough Trinity.

In his first four games for Trinity they netted 15 goals – Jim scoring nine times – but after breaking his leg in the next match Briscoe did not play again for the Northolme club. A move to Kent League Ramsgate was next for Briscoe where he continued to score frequently as his new club completed the Kent League/Division One Cup double in 1948-9 while his seasonal tally of 55 goals still stands as a record today. The ex-Yorkshire boys player would play over 200 times for the club before ending his career at Margate in 1958 after over one hundred appearances. After hanging up his boots Jim concentrated all his energies on the manufacturing of amusement arcade machines but in the 1968 he was appointed manager of Stevenage Athletic – starting an association with football in the town that continues today. He remained in charge until 1973 while three years later was a founder member of current Conference side Stevenage Borough – he is still the President of their supporters club. His son and grandson were both brought up as Wednesdayites and travel North to Hillsborough on a regular basis, maintaining a link with the club that commenced almost sixty years earlier. Incidentally when the Owls played Stevenage in a pre-season friendly in July 2000 his grandson, Sam, was the Wednesday mascot!

BRISCOE, Lee Stephen 1994-2000

Born: 30 September 1975 Pontefract
(5ft 11ins, 10st 9lbs – 1996)
Debut: 5 February 1994
v Tottenham Hotspur
Premier League Away
Last Appearance: 9 May 2000
v Arsenal
Premier League Away
Total League
& Cup Appearances: 55+35 Goals: 1

Career Details:

WEDNESDAY	22 May	1994
Manchester City	20 February	1998 Loan
Burnley	12 July	2000 Free
Released	30 June	2003
Preston North End	22 July	2003 Free

CAPS (@SWFC) –
ENGLAND U-21 (5) v Croatia 23/04/96, v Belgium 24/05/96, v Angola 28/05/96 v Brazil 01/06/96, v Switzerland 01/04/97

It was while still a teenager that left-winger Lee Briscoe first burst onto the Hillsborough scene under the managership of Trevor Francis – replacing Ryan Jones at White Hart Lane as a half-time sub while still a trainee. He did not disgrace himself in such exalted surroundings and it was no surprise when he was offered, and signed, a professional contract at the end of the season. Despite early appearances coming on the left side of midfield it was actually at left back that Briscoe would become a first team regular under new boss David Pleat, appearing thirty times for Wednesday during 1995-6. However after recording several appearances for the England Under-21 side the youngster's career was effectively put on hold due to a series of persistent injures that severely limited his opportunities at first team level.

After finally recovering his fitness the left-footed Briscoe found his path to first team football blocked by the likes of Andy Hinchcliffe, Mark Pembridge and Dejan Stefanovic. A spell on loan at Manchester City brought Lee his first goal in League football and his return to Hillsborough was a disappointment to new City boss Joe Royle who had seen Briscoe bring balance to his side and perform impressively in the role of over lapping full back. However Briscoe did return to Sheffield, hoping to finally make the expected breakthrough at Hillsborough at either left back or left wing. Always full of endeavour and commitment he just could not find the consistency to impress new boss Danny Wilson and despite scoring a spectacular late winner against Arsenal – a goal totally overshadowed by the Di Canio incident with the referee – he would play only a bit part for the remainder of his Owls career.

It was obvious to all that a change of scenery was required if the West Yorkshire player's career was to progress and this duly occurred in the summer of 2000 when after rejecting a new contract offer from Wednesday he signed for Division One club Burnley on a Bosman free transfer. His first season at Turf Moor was disrupted by injury but he was then an almost ever present – failing to start only three league games in 2001-2 – to become firmly established in the side. Used both as a left back and left winger by Burnley boss Stan Ternent his game showed a distinct improvement – particularly the tackling and distribution side of his game – and even added goal scoring to his armoury when netting twice from the subs bench during the 5-2 home win over Walsall. Nicknamed "Brisser" at Burnley he remained a first choice during 2002-3 – now with over one hundred appearances to his name - as The Clarets reached the quarter-finals of the F.A.Cup and finished just above the relegation zone in Division One. However the defensive record showed 89 goals conceded and Briscoe was one of several players released at the end of the season by manager Stan Ternant as he looked to re-build for the next season.

BRITTLETON, James Thomas "Tom/Tommy" 1905-20

Born: 23 April 1882 Winsford
(5ft 9½ ins, 12st 4lbs – 1913)
Died: 22 February 1955 Winsford
Debut: 14 January 1905
v Bury
Division One Home
Last Appearance: 1 May 1920
v Oldham Ath.
Division One Home
Total League
& Cup Appearances: 372* Goals: 33
***Also appeared in**
129 wartime games, scoring 10 times

Career Details:

Winsford Juniors		1892
Winsford Celtic		1894
Winsford United		1896
Stockport County	January	1902
WEDNESDAY	6 January	1905 £300
Stoke	21 May	1920 Free
Winsford Celtic		
Winsford United	9 July	1925 Free

CAPS (@ SWFC) –
ENGLAND Full (5) v Ireland 10/02/12, v Wales 11/03/12, v Scotland 23/03/12, v Scotland 05/04/13, v Wales 16/03/14
Football League (2) v Scotland 1910 v Ireland 1913

When playing at the peak of his game half back Tom Brittleton was once described as "the perfect footballer". There is no doubt he was one of Wednesday's greatest ever players as in a career which spanned fifteen years the one time record signing was an automatic choice as the Owls challenged for honours in league and cup football. In modern parlance Brittleton would probably be described as a defensive midfielder as it was in the old position of right half back that the Cheshire born player rose to national prominence through a series of classy displays characterised by tireless running, superb tackling, unselfish play and terrific shooting ability.

He had started to forge a reputation – as a smart and clever inside right - while playing for Stockport County in both the Second Division and the Lancashire Combination League - and it was after County had played a game at Ashton in December 1904 that the referee wrote a report to Wednesday singing his praises! The Owls acted immediately and after their first offer of £200 for his services was rebuffed they upped their bid and prevailed as hard up County agreed to the sale – much to the dismay of their supporters! Wednesday would pay a record transfer fee of £300 for the 22 year-old – fifty-percent more than they had paid for previous record buy Andrew Wilson five years earlier! The move to First Division Wednesday completed Brittleton's gradual rise through the ranks that had started when he began playing organised football on leaving school at the age of 14. At his second club Winsford Celtic, Tom was a real "jack of all trades" as he appeared in every position, including goalkeeper, before signing for the senior club in the town. While at Cheshire League Winsford United Brittleton gained several Cheshire Amateur Cup winners medals and in one year appeared in three district finals. It was while appearing for United that a Stockport fan, whose girlfriend was from Winsford, noticed his skills and it was he who recommended the teenager to the County hierarchy. Soon after the 19 year-old signed amateur forms for County, while continuing to work at the Winsford Salt Works, although he was perhaps not totally committed to the Stockport cause as on one occasion he was due to play for County but did not turn up, playing instead in a Cheshire Amateur Cup tie for Winsford!

However after signing professional forms for County his priorities switched to Stockport and after making his league debut in December 1902 he appeared in forty-five league games, scoring ten times, before County failed to gain re-election in 1904. They bounced back into the League by winning the Combination in 1905 but by then Tom had moved across the Pennines after making fourteen appearances at inside right. Brittleton – who was one of the first exponents of the long throw in – would quickly make his Wednesday debut in that position, mainly due to the absence of regular No.8 Harry Chapman, but over the seasons that followed would eventually move back through the ranks and prove an outstanding replacement for Herrod Ruddlesdin. While wearing the famous blue and white shirt Tommy would help the Owls to FA Cup success in 1907 and during his time at Hillsborough would win a multitude of representative honours, including full England caps, although when asked by the F.A. in 1911 to tour South Africa the strong willed Brittleton politely refused the offer in order to stay at home and spend his summer at the waterside with a fishing rod! It was not without reason that Tommy was once described as "the biggest home bird you could ever meet".

It was a credit to Brittleton's fitness that he continued to play in the Owls first team into his late thirties – his England debut did not come until his 31st year – and when he appeared for the final time at the age of 38 years and 8 days he became one of the club's oldest ever player – only beaten at the time by the emergency appearance of trainer Jerry Jackson in 1923. After giving the Owls superb service he was rightly rewarded with a free transfer in May 1920 and after initially looking set to re-join Winsford United – he was already living back in Winsford by this time after Wednesday agreed he could move back home in 1919 - he surprisingly signed for league club Stoke. It is actually part of Brittleton family folklore – although no records have been traced to support this - that he actually re-signed for United and they received a small fee when he moved almost immediately to the Potteries club. Amazingly he played a further five seasons for Stoke – being appointed player-coach in 1921 - helping them to promotion from Division Two in 1922 and even turning down their offer of the manager's job so he could continue playing! After finally retiring from league soccer at the age of 45 he made the almost inevitable move to take over as player-manager at Winsford United while gaining employment at I.C.I. When he finally stopped playing Tom became the landlord of the Navigation Inn in his hometown while his son, John Thomas junior, followed in his father's footsteps by playing league football for Aston Villa.

BROADBENT, Albert Henry 1955-57

Born: 20 August 1934 West Bromwich
(5ft 11ins, 12st, 8lbs - 1956)
Debut: 20 August 1955
v Plymouth Argyle
Division Two Home
Last Appearance: 26 October 1957
v Sunderland
Division One Home
Total League
& Cup Appearances: 83 Goals: 17

Career Details:

Greet Green Juniors		1948
Dudley Town		1949
West Bromwich Albion		Trial
Notts County		Trial
Notts County	March	1952
WEDNESDAY	5 July	1955 £7,400*
Rotherham United	24 December	1957 **
Doncaster Rovers	June	1959 £2,000
Lincoln City	November	1961
Doncaster Rovers	January	1963
	Exchange for Bob Rooney	
Bradford Park Avenue	October	1965 £4,500
Hartlepool United	February	1967 £3,000
Rotherham United	March	1968
Scarborough		1968
Arbourthorne EA	October	1969 (Sun.)
Brunsmeer Athletic		(Sun.)
Sheffield Waterworks		1977

*£6800 + £50 for every Division two goal scored in 1955-6!
*Broadbent + £6000 for Peter Johnson

Left-winger Albert Broadbent first started to play organised football at George Salter school in Birmingham and appeared in local football before signing a professional contract with Notts County as a seventeen-year-old. This tall, lean and hard-boned winger quickly became a regular at Meadow Lane – after serving his two years National service between 1950 and 1952 - and was amongst County's leading scorers in 1954-55, prompting Wednesday secretary-manager Eric Taylor to pay a sizeable fee to bring him to Hillsborough. The Owls were rebuilding after relegation from Division One and Broadbent was one of four new players – Roy Shiner, Ron Staniforth and Don Gibson being the others – to make their debut for the club in the opening day 5-2 win over Plymouth Argyle. The new men would play a big part during the season as Wednesday lifted the Second Division championship, no more so than Albert who netted twelve times in 42 games as well as creating many of Shiner's 33 league goals. Broadbent possessed pace, superb ball control plus a fierce shot and appeared regularly for the club in the top-flight until surprisingly being sold to neighbours Rotherham United in a deal that brought full back Peter Johnson to Wednesday.

The move to Millmoor effectively meant the end of Albert's top-flight career and over the decade that followed he would play for a wide variety of lower league clubs, taking his career appearance tally to over five hundred games – including over two hundred times for Doncaster Rovers in two spells at Belle Vue. His league career finally came to a close after failing to make a first team appearance during a second spell at Millmoor – after having played under the unique management style of Brian Clough at Hartlepool United – and was subsequently appointed as second team trainer at Millmoor. However the high profile appointment of Tommy Docherty as United boss soon saw Albert unemployed, prompting a move to Midland League Scarborough. In July 1969 he returned to Wednesday after being appointed coach but remained only until June 1970

After leaving the professional game he ran his own window cleaning business but such was his fitness and enthusiasm for the game that at the age of 42 could be found playing on a Saturday for Heeley, on a Sunday for Brunsmeer and also appearing for Derek Dooley's all star charity side – known to have played for all three one weekend! Unfortunately a hip problem forced a premature end to his working life - he would eventually have both hips replaced – and he lives out his retirement in the Sheffield area.

BROLLY, Thomas Henry "Tom" 1933-35

Born: 1 June 1912 Belfast
Died: June 1986 Sutton, Surrey
(5ft 9ins, 11st – 1933)
Debut: 14 October 1933
v Derby County
Division One Home
Last Appearance: 10 March 1934
v Wolverhampton Wanderers
Division One Home
Total League
& Cup Appearances: 2 Goals: 0

Career Details:

Linfield		
Crusaders		
Glenavon		
Lurgan		
Linfield		
WEDNESDAY	8 May	1933 £125
Millwall	18 July	1935
Aldershot		1940 Guest
Linfield		1940 Guest
Northampton Town	November	1943 Guest

Half-back Tom Brolly signed for Wednesday after impressing against them whilst playing as a guest for Linfield in a friendly game, in Belfast in May 1933. However the jump from Irish league football to England's First Division proved somewhat troublesome for the cool and composed defender and he would play out almost his entire Wednesday career in the reserves, appearing just twice at first team level. Considering the competition the young Irishman faced at Hillsborough – Tony Leach, Alf Strange and Horace Burrows to name just three right-half backs on the club's books at the time– it was not surprising that he failed to secure a first team spot and subsequently moved to Division Three (South) club Millwall.

At the South London club the tough-tackling defender became a veritable stalwart, appearing in 260 games, scoring 11 times, for the Lions either side of World War Two. During that time the all-round sportsman – he played tennis, cricket and golf in his spare time - showed his versatility by playing in all three half-back positions and during an association that lasted fifteen years he earned a Division Three (South) Championship medal in 1939 and four full International caps for Northern Ireland between 1937 and 1939. Just before the outbreak of war a successful cartilage operation saved Tom's career and ensured he could join the Army, becoming a P.E.Instructor. During the hostilities he played occasionally including four games for Aldershot and two goals in two appearances for Northampton Town while in November 1940 he was appointed captain and player-coach of Linfield. Nicknamed "the professor" during his playing days, Brolly was thirty-four when peacetime football returned but he still captained Millwall until retiring from professional football in 1950. He was subsequently trainer at Crystal Palace and then Chelmsford City before leaving the game to take employment with the G.P.O.

BROMBY, Leigh David 1998-2004

Born: 2 June 1980 Dewsbury
(6ft 1ins, 12st 7lbs – 2001)
Debut: 23 December 2000
v Wolverhampton Wanderers
Division One Home
Last Appearance: 17 April 2004
v Blackpool
Division Two Away
Total League
& Cup Appearances: 117+3 Goals: 2

Career Details:

Liversedge		
WEDNESDAY	9 July	1998
Mansfield Town	10 December	1999 Loan
Norwich City	24 February	2003 Loan
Sheffield United	1 July	2004 Free

Tall, commanding centre half Leigh Bromby looked to have a sparkling career at the top of the English game ahead of him after impressing greatly during his debut season at Wednesday. He was linked with a move to several Premier League clubs but unfortunately the constant struggles of the Wednesday team saw the youngster's confidence suffer and a loss of form saw him dropped to the reserves during the early months of the Chris Turner reign. A loan move to First Division rivals Norwich City certainly helped the situation and when City failed to make an offer for his services on a permanent basis he returned to Wednesday, re-appearing in the first eleven for a shock win at league leaders Portsmouth.

Before his form started to stutter Leigh's career had been on an ever upwards spiral from making his debut for Northern Counties East league side Liversedge in September 1997 – ironically in Sheffield at Stocksbridge Park Steels - to signing a professional contract with the Owls. The ex-England schoolboy and Youth International was scouted by several clubs while at Liversedge but it was Wednesday who secured his signature and Leigh was outstanding as the U-19 Academy side reached the 1999 Play-Off Final, losing only to a last minute goal at Upton Park against West Ham United. He duly graduated to the reserves in the season that followed and enjoyed his first taste of league football during a highly successful loan spell at Mansfield Town – such was his impact that Town wanted to make the move permanent but Wednesday refused. After eleven games for the Stags he returned to Hillsborough only for injury to dash his hopes of making a first start in an Owls shirt.

After almost six months on the sidelines Bromby was back in first team contention and finally made his long awaited bow against Wolves although frustratingly this lasted only 43 minutes before injury forced him off the field! However he retained a first team spot for the next game and was a regular for eighteen months – signing a two-year contract extension in February 2000 – thanks to a series of confident and unruffled displays, at centre half and both full back positions, which augured well for the future. After becoming a first team regular again during the disappointing 2003-4 season he was one of thirteen players released by Wednesday as they tried desperately to halt the almost never ending slump.

BROOMES, Marlon Charles 2001-02

Born: 28 November 1977 Birmingham
(6ft, 12st 12lbs – 2002)
Debut: 15 December 2001 v Gillingham Division One Away
Last Appearance: 21 April 2002
v Wolverhampton W. Division One Home
Total League & Cup Appearances: 19+1 Goals: 0

Career Details:

Blackburn Rovers	28 November	1994
Swindon Town	22 January	1997 Loan
Queens Park Rangers	25 October	2000 Loan
Grimsby Town	7 September	2001 Loan
WEDNESDAY	12 December	2001 Free
Released	30 June	2002
Burnley	July	2002 Trial
Preston North End	7 August	2002 Free
Stoke City	3 August	2005
		Exchange for L. Neal

The story of Marlon Broomes could easily be described as "the one that got away" as after joining the club on a short term contract in December 2001 he was an ever present and gave a series of sterling defensive displays as Wednesday fought off relegation from Division One. His early appearances for The Owls were in the uncustomary role of right back but once he moved into the middle Wednesday looked a far better defensive unit and it was a blow to fans when financial restrictions meant the club were unable to offer him a new contract when his deal ran out in the summer of 2002. After his contract expired Broomes trained for the majority of the pre season period with Burnley – even appearing on the club's pre season team photo - but surprisingly he actually moved, on a Bosman free transfer, to First Division rivals Preston North End after the Turf Moor club stalled on a contract!

The ex-England U-21 International had spent the majority of his career at Premier League Blackburn Rovers where after making an initial impact he was pushed down the pecking order through a combination of injury and several big money signings by a Jack Walker banked Rovers team – Blackburn won the Premier League title in Broomes first season as a professional. However in almost seven years at Ewood Park he could never claim to be anything more than a squad player, appearing in only 38 competitive games for Rovers, as well as appearances on loan at Swindon and Queens Park Rangers. His loan spell at Grimsby Town looked set to end in a permanent deal but the Mariners board could not raise the necessary finances and Wednesday stepped in to secure his services until the end of the season.

BROWN, Robert Christopher "Bobby" 1974-76

Born: 24 November 1953 Plymouth
(5ft 7ins, 11st 4lbs – 1975)
Debut: 24 August 1974
v Bristol Rovers
Division Two Home
Last Appearance: 13 September 1975
v Swindon Town
Division Three Away
Total League
& Cup Appearances: 17+4 Goals: 3

Career Details:

Chelsea	August	1972
WEDNESDAY	1 July	1974
Aldershot	7 February	1976 Loan
Boston United		1976
Sheffield Polytechnic	October	1976
Thionville		1980

Bobby Brown was a regular in Chelsea's Football Combination side but had yet to appear for the Blues first team before Wednesday boss Steve Burtenshaw brought him to Hillsborough during the close season of 1974. The midfielder cum forward started the new season in the first team squad at Hillsborough – making a debut appearance as a sub in the second match of the campaign – but unfortunately for the Devonian he was a member of one of the club's worst sides in their history and was in and out of the team as the club plunged into Division Three for the first time. Despite the drop in status Bobby was an even more peripheral figure in the lower division and played only three times more for Wednesday before dropping out of league football altogether to join Northern Premier League side Boston United. While playing under Howard Wilkinson at York Street, Brown also started a teacher training course at Sheffield polytechnic and played several times for the Polytechnic's second team as well as appearing for Boston United.

However after scoring for Boston United in the April 1980 F.A.Trophy semi-final his career took a completely new route as he signed for French club Thionville! He has remained in France ever since, first coaching at Caen before being appointed at Dunkerque in February 1998. He remains in their employment today having been appointed general manager in 2002.

BROWN, John Henry 'Jack' 1923-37

Born: 19 March 1899 Worksop
(5ft 10ins, 12st 6lbs – 1935)
Died: 9 April 1962 Sheffield
Debut: 21 April 1923
v Coventry City
Division Two Away
Last Appearance: 20 March 1937
v Liverpool
Division One Home
Total League
& Cup Appearances: 507 Goals: 0

Career Details:

Netherton United		
Worksop Wesley		
Worksop Town		1919
WEDNESDAY	23 February	1923 £360
Hartlepool United	17 September	1937

CAPS (@SWFC):
ENGLAND Full (6) v Wales 12/02/27, v Scotland 02/04/27, v Belgium 11/05/27, v Luxembourg 21/05/27, v France 26/05/27, v Ireland 19/10/29

Football League (2) v Scottish League 1927, v Irish League 1930

In Wednesday's long history the club has been truly blessed with many outstanding goalkeepers, several of whom stayed between the sticks for many, many years. The likes of Jack Lyall, Teddy Davison, Ron Springett and most recently Kevin Pressman – to name but a few - have all upheld Wednesday's fine tradition in the goalkeeping department but Jack Brown holds a special place in that list as he is one of only three players – Andrew Wilson and Alan Finney being the others – to have played over five hundred times for the club.

The big and broad shouldered keeper had started his working life – like so many of his peers – as a miner at the local (Manton) Colliery and it was not until the age of seventeen that Jack – who was born within sight of Worksop Town's old ground – took an active part in football. It was at this point that he joined Netherton United – a side that played friendly matches in the Worksop district – and would play many times for the junior club in his regular position - of centre forward! However in 1919 fate took a hand as his side were short of a goalie for a game against a Mansfield team and asked Brown to go between the sticks. He stayed there for the remainder of the season and was subsequently spotted by Worksop Town who signed him at the start of the 1919-20 season. Within three years Brown was widely regarded as the best goalkeeper in the Midland League – and by definition one of the best outside of the Football League – and it was an heroic performance for The Tigers in January 1923 that brought Wednesday boss Bob Brown knocking on Town's door. The Nottinghamshire club had battled their way through the early rounds of the F.A.Cup to be rewarded with a trip to First Division Tottenham Hotspur but few expected anything other than a heavy defeat for the plucky minnows. However in one of the most amazing results in the history of the old competition Worksop held Spurs to a 0-0 draw with Brown truly outstanding. The replay was lost 9-0 but Jack had made a name for himself and a few weeks later moved to Hillsborough to act as understudy to another Wednesday great – Teddy Davison.

He did not have to wait long for his debut but it is a little known fact that in May 1924 Brown's Wednesday career almost ended before it had really begun. The Owls were poised not to re-sign Jack for the 1924-5 campaign but with No.1 Davison out of action with a broken arm Wednesday suddenly found themselves without a goalkeeper for the County Cup Final against Sheffield United at Hillsborough. They were trying to sign Carr from Newport County but this move was delayed so the club had no real choice but to re-sign Brown for another season – suffice to say that although Carr did eventually sign it was Jack Brown who would prove to be the long term replacement for Davison. In his early days Brown had his critics – it was said he did not get down to low shots and did not like it when forwards "mixed it" – but these quickly disappeared as by the end of the decade Jack radiated the confidence that club and International honours can give to a player.

The brilliant and spectacular goalie was ever present during the Owls Division Two Championship season of 1925-6 and after earning caps for his country missed just a solitary game when winning back-to-back League Championship medals in 1929 and 1930. During his career at Wednesday Jack missed only a handful of games, his longest absence coming in the early part of 1927-8 when a broken figure saw Mellors step into his shoes for a nine-game spell. After adding an F.A.Cup winners medal to his collection in 1935, followed by a Charity Shield winners medal a few months later, the courageous and fearless Brown remained first choice for the club right until March 1937 when newcomer Roy Smith took his place. By this time though Jack was at veteran stage – his final appearance in the Owls first team came a day after his 38th Birthday – and at the end of the season was put on the transfer list, accompanied by a small transfer fee to aid his hopes of a move. However it took longer than expected for Brown to get a new club but after eventually signing for Division Three (North) Hartlepool United he would play only one game – a defeat to Gateshead – before being released after just two weeks in the Northeast to retire from the game. After leaving the game Jack owned an off licence in Sheffield before managing a public house for several years and later owned a newsagents shop opposite – of all places - Bramall Lane! His final job was at Sheffield Drill and Twist Company (which later became Dorma Tools – now the site of a giant supermarket at Handsworth) but Jack would sadly pass away before having a chance to enjoy his retirement having entered club history as one of Wednesday's all time greats.

BROWN, James 1892-94

Born: Scotland
Debut: 2 January 1893 v West Bromwich Albion
Division One Home
Last Appearance: 26 December 1893 v Burnley
Division One Home
Total League & Cup Appearances: 10 Goals: 0

Career Details:

Dundee	
WEDNESDAY	1892
Released	1894

Left back James Brown was one of several signing made by Wednesday in preparation for their first season of league football. He arrived at Olive Grove from Scottish football and during that debut season of league soccer was rival to Jack Darroch for the full back position – a duel won by the latter who appeared in thirteen games to Brown's two. Therefore Brown had to be content with reserve team football, helping Wednesday to the Sheffield & District League title in 1893, before playing another eight First Division games in 1893-4 as Wednesday consolidated in the top-flight. However the arrival of outstanding full back Ambrose Langley in 1893 effectively signalled the end of his Hillsborough career and in 1894 was not re-signed by the club.

BROWN, Robert N "Sparrow/Bob" 1891-94

Born: August 1870 Cambuslang, Glasgow
(5ft 6½ ins, 10st, 10lbs – 1893)
Debut: 23 January 1892 v Bolton Wanderers F.A.Cup Home
Last Appearance: 26 March 1894 v Preston North End
Division One Away
Total League & Cup Appearances: 55* Goals: 8
***Also appeared in 12 Football Alliance League games**

Career Details:

Blantyre Thistle		
Cambuslang		
WEDNESDAY	November	1891
Scottish Football		1893
Third Lanark		1894
Bolton Wanderers	18 June	1895
Burnley	March	1897 Loan
Released		1903

When 21 year-old attacker Robert Brown first arrived in Sheffield his impact was immediate, scoring four times as Wednesday won five games in a row. His debut came in a 4-1 friendly win over Sheffield United at Olive Grove in November 1891 while five days later he netted on his Alliance League bow as Walsall Town Swifts were beaten – the first of twelve Alliance League appearances for Brown in what would prove to Wednesday's final season as a non-league club. Incidentally his only hat trick for the club came in that competition against Small Heath in January 1892.

The Scotsman – who started his career as a left-winger at Cambuslang – was a deft and somewhat dainty forward (hence his nickname of "Sparrow") who possessed great dribbling skills and a superb shot. After appearing at inside right in the club's first ever league fixture – in September 1892 at Notts County – he remained in that unaccustomed role for almost all of the season, missing only a handful of games as Wednesday adapted to league life. However he ran into trouble at the start of the following season when after playing back in Scotland during the close season he was suspended for one month in September 1893. When the suspension expired Brown found that Harry Davis had taken his place at inside right and after a few games on the sidelines the clever inside left – who had a knack of side-stepping opponents – came back into the side but at right half-back! He remained in this new role for the remainder of the campaign – except for the odd positional change which included a solitary appearance at that favourite position of outside left –and looked set to be a mainstay of the club's early league years. However in the summer of 1894 he promptly left Sheffield, returning home to get married, and would play a season with Third Lanark.

He returned to England a year later, signing for Bolton Wanderers, and appeared in Wanderers first ever game at Burden Park. In total Brown appeared in 136 competitive games for Bolton, scoring 14 times, and won promotion to Division One with Wanderers in 1900 when they finished just two points behind Divisional Champions Wednesday. During his time in Lancashire, Sparrow was once loaned to struggling neighbours Burnley until the end of the season – he played just four games and then went back to Bolton!

After hanging up his boots in 1903 he gained employment as an insurance agent.

BRUCE, Alex 2005

Born: 28 September 1984 Norwich
(6ft, 11st 7lbs)
Debut: 12 March 2005
v Blackpool
League One Home
Last Appearance: 29 May 2005
v Hartlepool United Play Off Final
Total League
& Cup Appearances: 8+1 Goals: 0

Career Details:

Manchester United Academy		
Blackburn Rovers		
Oldham Athletic	22 December	2004 Loan
Birmingham City	27 January	2005
Loan recall	9 March	2005
WEDNESDAY	10 March	2005 Loan
Loan return	30 May	2005

When injuries started to deplete the Owls defensive ranks late in the 2004-05 season Paul Sturrock turned to utility player Alex Bruce. The youngster - son of former Manchester United centre half Steve Bruce - joined the Owls on loan in somewhat unique circumstances as he was recalled from a loan period at Oldham to sign for Wednesday just 24 hours later. The man who recalled him was actually his father who six weeks previously had actually signed Bruce from Blackburn Rovers whilst he was still on loan at Boundary Park! The twenty-year-old took a few games to adjust to life in League One - a red card in his fourth game not helping the acclimatisation - but by the end of the season his highly impressive displays at right back showed why his father had taken Bruce to Birmingham City. The former Old Trafford trainee and Stockport boys player had only made his league debut a few months earlier, whilst in Oldham colours, but ended the campaign on a real high when Bruce was in the Wednesday side that beat Hartlepool United to secure Championship football at Hillsborough.

BRUCE, Robert Frederick "Bob" 1935-36

Born: 29 January 1906 Paisley
(5ft 6ins, 11st 5lbs – 1935)
Debut: 12 October 1935
v Derby County
Division One Home
Last Appearance: 9 November 1935
v Leeds U
Division One Away
Total League
& Cup Appearances: 5 Goals: 0

Career Details:

St.Anthonys (Glasgow)		
Aberdeen	June	1924
Middlesbrough	31 January	1928 £4500
WEDNESDAY	10 October	1935 £2500
Ipswich Town	6 August	1936 Free
Mossley	10 August	1938 Free

When Aberdeen manager Paddy Travers first discovered Robert Bruce he suggested to a friend that he would make the same impact on Scottish football that his namesake made on Scotland's history! This comparison was of course impossible for the youngster to live up to but football's version of Robert the Bruce did develop into an exciting and accomplished forward who was equally adept at either centre or inside forward. After starting in junior football the teenager quickly became an automatic choice at Aberdeen, being a member of the Dons side that undertook a trail blazing pre season tour to South Africa in 1927, and in January

1928 became the only Aberdeen player to score a hat-trick in a Scottish Cup tie but still end up on the losing side.

However within a few days of that feat he was treading the well-worn path to England – after netting 28 goals in just 24 games for Aberdeen - to sign for Middlesbrough where he served the Teeside club with distinction for eight seasons, appearing in 253 games and netting 72 times – including a hat-trick in a 10-3 rout of Sheffield United! After initially being criticised by Boro fans – he was bought for a club record fee to replace Boro legend Jacky Carr – Bob won over many of his detractors with a series of outstanding displays, helping the club to promotion from Division Two in 1929 before earning his solitary full cap for Scotland in November 1933 against Austria in Glasgow. However he was still described by Boro fans as being "inconsistently inconsistent" – he had asked for a transfer in 1930 after being constantly barracked by his own supporters – and after losing his place at the start of the 1935-6 season moved to Wednesday to provide competition for Ron Starling.

The Owls of course had just won the F.A.Cup with Starling a pivotal player in the success so it was indeed a daunting task for Bruce to displace his rival for the No.8 shirt. His only appearances would come in a five game spell when Starling was absent but after Wednesday lost 7-2 at Leeds United in the final game of the sequence Bruce found himself playing Central league football for the remainder of the season, scoring twice. After less than a year at Hillsborough Bob moved to a Southern League Ipswich Town side - Wednesday not receiving a fee as Town were a non-league club – who had just turned professional in an attempt to gain Football league status – a feat they achieved just two years later. After ending his professional career Bruce was appointed player-manager at Mossley in the final peacetime season before the outbreak of World War Two.

BRUNT, Christopher 'Chris' 2004-

Born: 14 December 1984 Belfast
(6ft 1ins, 11st 8lbs - 2004)
Debut: 17 March 2004
v Bournemouth
Division Two Home
Total League
& Cup Appearances: 39+19 Goals: 7

Career Details:

St Andrews		
Middlesbrough		2001
Released	January	2004
Cardiff City		Trial
WEDNESDAY	2 March	2004 Free

CAPS (@ SWFC)
N.Ireland Full (2) v Switzerland 18/08/04, v Germany 04/06/05
N.Ireland U-23 (1) v Serbia & Montenegro 27/04/04
N.Ireland U-21 (1) v Scotland 08/02/05

When teenager Chris Brunt made his Owls debut he was immediately tarred with the rather unfair tag of being the next Chris Waddle. The similarities between the former Middlesbrough Academy player and the ex-England International were obvious - both being tall and slim with a rather ungainly playing style - and hopes for the youngster were raised when on his full home debut Brunt crashed home a spectacular goal from the edge of the area. His form in those early weeks certainly gave great encouragement to the Owls fans - he was voted player of the month for April 2004 - and given a new year contract by Chris Turner to reward his promising start to life in league football. As is usually the case with young players the Irishman then experienced a mixed 2004-05 season which saw him flit in and out of the side as his form fluctuated - competition from Matt Hamshaw meaning Brunt was never an automatic choice.

His career had started at Belfast boys club St Andrews but after failing to earn a professional contract with Premier League Middlesbrough he underwent trials at the likes of Glasgow Rangers and Cardiff City before Wednesday took a gamble on his talents. Despite being the archetypical inconsistent winger Brunt showed enough to earn his first full cap for Northern Ireland - entering the field as an 81st minute substitute during his country's 0-0 draw with Switzerland in Zurich - and was back in the Owls side in time for the successful play off campaign. His deflected goal in the semi-final at Brentford almost guaranteed his place in the Cardiff Final and he played his part as Wednesday beat Hartlepool United to move up a division.

BRYANT, Stephen Paul "Steve" 1976

Born: 5 September 1953 Islington
(5ft 8ins, 10st 4lbs – 1976)
Debut: 25 August 1976 v Northampton Town
Division Three Home
Last Appearance: 11 September 1976
v Swindon Town Division Three Away
Total League & Cup Appearances: 2+1 Goals: 0

Career Details:

Birmingham City	July	1971
WEDNESDAY	23 August	1976 Loan
Northampton Town	2 December	1976 £5000
Portsmouth	21 March	1979 £20,000
Northampton	28 March	1982
Australian football		

Londoner Steve Bryant was originally a winger of extreme promise but played most of his early career at left back, only converting to a midfield role in the latter stages of his Birmingham City career after losing his first team place to Archie Styles. He had joined The Blues as an apprentice in 1970 – after appearing for Middlesex boys – and after serving his time in the reserve side broke into City's league side part way through the 1974-5 campaign. He played in all but one of the final seventeen games of the season but after being mysteriously dropped for the F.A.Cup semi final against Fulham at Hillsborough - he played in the replay defeat – his confidence was visibly knocked and after starting the following season with the number three shirt he dropped out of favour, only reappearing occasionally in a variety of unaccustomed roles.

After totalling forty-two appearances for Birmingham, Bryant was brought to Hillsborough by Len Ashurst early in the 1976-7 season for a one-month loan spell. In his short stay at Wednesday Steve reprised his schoolboy role of left winger but after the Owls crashed 5-2 at Swindon in what proved to be his final appearance he returned to St.Andrews, transferring to Northampton Town soon after. In two spells at The Cobblers Bryant appeared over one hundred times in league soccer and also played in 111 league games for Portsmouth before ending his playing career in the rather more sunnier climes of Australia

BULLEN, Lee 2004-

Born: 29 March 1971 Edinburgh
(6ft 2ins, 12st 7lbs - 2004)
Debut: 7 August 2004
v Colchester United
League One Home
Total League
& Cup Appearances: 52 Goals: 7

Career Details:

Dunfermline Athletic		Youth
Penicuik Athletic		
Meadowbank Thistle	10 January	1990
Stenhousemuir	January	1991
Whitburn		
Stanmore CYC	January	1992
Kui-Tan	January	1993
Golden AA		
South China AA		
PAE Kalamata	January	1998
Dunfermline Athletic	3 January	2000
WEDNESDAY	24 May	2004 Free

When Lee Bullen arrived at Wednesday in May 2004 he was virtually unknown to the majority of Owls fans. However in the roller coaster season that followed the totally committed Scot would enjoy somewhat of an 'Indian summer' as he was ever present in League One football for Wednesday and on May 29th 2005 enjoyed the high point of a varied career when as captain he lifted aloft the Play Off trophy in front of 40,000 ecstatic Owls fans. During the season Bullen - who was brought to the club as a right back - had played in several defensive positions and even netted in consecutive games when pushed up front. New manager Paul Sturrock did not initially rate the hard working Scot as defensive material - mainly due to his propensity to make careless errors - but his outstanding displays in the final few games of the season - from centre half - saw Bullen offered a new contract soon after the Millennium Stadium triumph.

His journey to that sunny Cardiff day had started back in Lothian schools football before he was signed to Dunfermline's youth side. However he failed to make the progression to professional status and would pursue his playing career on a part-time basis for Meadowbank Thistle whilst working for the Edinburgh Building Society. However in 1991, after a spell in Scottish junior football at Whitburn, Bullen made the move down under, signing for Australian club Stanmore. The transfer was just the start of a nomadic career that over the ensuing years saw Bullen ply his trade in Hong Kong and Greece before returning home to Scotland. While in the Far East the wholehearted attacker - he was a forward for the majority of his career - appeared six times for the Hong Kong national side with the highlight coming in 1996 when he was part of the Golden XI side that faced a touring England side. He spent five years in the Far East before a spell in Greece with PAE Kalamata preceded a move back home to sign for Dunfermline Athletic. The highlight of his Pars career came in 2004 ,when he appeared as a sub in the Scottish Cup Final loss to Glasgow Celtic, while he totalled 151 games for the Fife based club, netting 24 times.

BURCHILL, Mark James 2003-04

Born: 18 August 1980 Broxburn, Scotland
(5ft 8ins, 10st 2lbs – 2003)
Debut: 26 December 2003 v Port Vale Division Two Home
Last Appearance: 17 January 2004
v Swindon Town Division Two Home
Total League & Cup Appearances: 4+1 Goals: 0

Career Details:

Celtic Boys Club		
Glasgow Celtic	3 June	1997
Birmingham City	22 September	2000 Loan
Ipswich Town	22 January	2001 Loan
Portsmouth	24 August	2001 £600,000
Dundee	31 January	2003 Loan
Wigan Athletic	21 August	2003 Loan
WEDNESDAY	24 December	2003 Loan
Loan return	19 January	2004
Rotherham United	24 September	2004 Loan
Hearts	28 January	2005
Dunfermline	6 July	2005

Pacy, diminutive forward who arrived on loan from Premier League Portsmouth mid way through the 2003-4 season. Made a bright start to his Owls career – his running off the ball creating space for others – but after failing to score in five games he returned early to Fratton Park after receiving an injury in his final game for Wednesday. The move to Hillsborough was seen as a further chance to re-launch a career that had started with great success at Glasgow Celtic where Burchill scored a superb 25 times in just 64 appearances, with over half of those games coming from the subs bench. Fifteen Scottish U-21 and six full caps followed before two loan spells in English football preceded a move to First Division Portsmouth.

He made a terrific start on the South Coast, scoring four times in his first five games, but a freak training accident resulted in damage to a cruciate ligament that sidelined Burchill for the remainder of the season. After regaining fitness Burchill found himself out of favour, despite again netting four goals in five matches, and spent the final months of his 2002-3 season on loan at Dundee, helping the Dens Park club to the First Division Championship.

BURGESS, Harry 1929-35

Born: 20 August 1904 Alderley Edge, Cheshire
(5ft 8ins, 11st 7lbs – 1929)
Died: 6 October 1957 Wilmslow
Debut: 14 September 1929
v Aston Villa
Division One Home
Last Appearance: 20 February 1935
v Liverpool
Division One Away
Total League
& Cup Appearances: 233 Goals: 77

Career Details:

Wilmslow Albion		
Alderley Edge		
Stockport County	August	1925 Amat.
Sandbach Ramblers		1925 Loan
Stockport County	March	1926 Full-time
WEDNESDAY	21 June	1929 £3500
Chelsea	15 March	1935 £4000
Brentford		1939-40 Guest
Reading		1939-40 Guest
Fulham		1939-40 Guest
Southampton		1939-40 Guest
Stockport County		1940-41 Guest

CAPS (@SWFC) –
ENGLAND Full (4) v Ireland 20/10/30, v Scotland 28/03/31, v France 14/05/31, v Belgium 16/05/31

Inspirational inside left Harry Burgess was an key member of the Wednesday side that challenged for England's major honours in the early 1930s.With the creative attacker in their ranks the Owls won the League Championship in 1930 - by a record margin – with Burgess also winning representative honours, scoring four times for England in four appearances as well as hitting a brace in his only appearance in an International trial match. His signing by Bob Brown was a catalyst for a quite remarkable burst of scoring by Wednesday as in every one of Harry's first three seasons at Hillsborough the Owls scored over one hundred league and cup goals! The Cheshire born forward contributed greatly himself to that goal rush– finishing second top scorer to the legendary Jack Allen in the 1930 title success – and provided the ammunition for the likes of Allen and Jack Ball to score almost at will to delight Hillsborough regulars of the time. His goal in the 1930 Charity Shield Final was not enough to overcome Arsenal but this was only a sideshow to the bread and butter of league football where Harry excelled, becoming a firm crowd favourite.

He remained an automatic choice for five years but the sudden departure of manager Bob Brown and appointment of Billy Walker as his replacement dramatically altered his fortunes. The Christmas Day 1934 home game with Birmingham proved to be the beginning of the end for Burgess at Hillsborough as although he scored he was also injured and missed the next day's game. However this led to him having a row with Walker and he subsequently played only three of the next ten league games – trialist Jack Surtess taking his place – before being transferred to Chelsea, a move that dismayed many Owls fans. A certain Bob Brown was scouting for the Londoners at the time and Harry would re-join his old boss at Stamford Bridge after Brown recommended his undoubted talents to Chelsea boss Leslie Knighton. The move of course denied Harry a chance of an F.A.Cup winners medal – he was transferred twenty-four hours before the semi-final win over Burnley – but the long striding inside-forward would serve Chelsea royally in the seasons up to the War, appearing in 155 competitive games for The Pensioners and scoring 37 times – including three goals when Chelsea knocked Wednesday out of the F.A.Cup in 1939 after a three game fifth round tie. It was testament to Harry's fitness that at all of the three league clubs he served he missed only a handful of games in a career that spanned almost fifteen years – ironically after brief guest appearances for a wide spectrum of clubs in wartime soccer an ankle injury actually forced his retirement in 1945.

The injury brought an end to a career that had begun at non-league Wilmslow Albion, where he played while working as a carpenter. It was actually while turning out for his village side that he was scouted by Stockport County, initially signing part-time professional forms for The Hatters who immediately sent him to Sandbach Ramblers, to aid Harry's development. After signing as a full time pro at Edgeley Park, Harry made a huge impression, scoring an outstanding 28 goals in just 35 games from centre forward in his first full season at County in 1926-7. This prolific scoring diminished when he dropped to inside right but incredibly he netted an almost unprecedented – from a left wing position - 31 times in 1928-9. This outstanding scoring of course alerted the big boys and after highly successful spells at both Wednesday and Chelsea he would return North when war was declared in 1939, serving in the police force for the duration of the hostilities. After retiring from football he served as a clerk of works for the Ministry of Defence before moving back to Cheshire to take a public house in Wilmslow. Burgess - a keen cricketer and golfer – also worked as a foreman joiner but unfortunately passed away at the relatively early age of 53 in his beloved Cheshire.

BURGIN, Andrew "Andy" 1964-67

Born: 6 March 1947 Sheffield
(5ft 8ins, 9st 9½lbs – 1964)
Debut: 9 January 1965
v Everton
F.A.Cup Away
Last Appearance: 16 January 1965
v Liverpool
Division One Home
Total League
& Cup Appearances: 3 Goals: 0

Career Details:

Hillsborough Boys Club		
WEDNESDAY	9 March	1964
Rotherham United	August	1967 Free
Detroit Cougars	March	1968 Free
Rotherham United	25 October	1968 Free
Halifax Town	December	1968 Free
Blackburn Rovers	September	1974 Free

Generally players tend to excel at one particular sport but as a fifteen year-old Andy Burgin appeared regularly for Sheffield boys at both football and cricket, also representing England schools and Yorkshire boys at the summer game. In the bat and ball game Burgin was an all rounder while in the winter pastime he was a good tackling right back who boasted great positional sense and versatility – he appeared at inside forward for his Langsett Road school team, at right back for Sheffield boys and at wing half for Hillsborough Boys Club! After signing apprentice forms for Wednesday in August 1962 he progressed quickly, becoming one of the youngest players ever to appear in reserve team football for the club when playing against Stoke City in 1962-3 at the age of just 16 years and 10 days. In the same season he had helped the Youth team to reached the semi-finals of the F.A.Youth Cup – appearing in the last four loss to Liverpool – and it was not long before Wednesday promoted him to the professional ranks – manager Vic Buckingham securing his signature in the Burgin's front room, a mile from Hillsborough, over a homemade Bilberry pie!

The teenager – a relative of Sheffield United goalie Ted Burgin - seemed set for a long career in league football but a traumatic debut in January 1965 perhaps effected his confidence as after regular full back Brian Hill was injured he was thrown in at the deep in front of almost 45,000 at Goodison Park. The Owls secured a 2-2 draw but the youngster had the misfortune to put through his own goal and after playing in the replay loss at Hillsborough four days later made what would prove to be his final first team appearance for the Owls – and a third against a team from Liverpool - in a defeat at Anfield on the following Saturday. First choice Hill regained his place in the following game and the later emergence of Wilf Smith meant Burgin had to be content with reserve team football until his career at Wednesday – which had burnt so brightly in its early days – ended in disappointment with his release by the club in the summer of 1967. He subsequently signed a twelve-month contract – commencing in March 1968 - with FIFA affiliated Detroit Cougers of the North American League, where ex-Arsenal and Millwall player Len Julians was manager. As Burgin had time to spare before departing for the US he signed monthly contacts at Rotherham United – playing for a modest weekly sum – as a direct result of his personal friendship with the Millers acting boss Fred Green. After playing nine times for United he departed for Detroit, pleas from new boss Tommy Docherty for him to stay falling on deaf ears.

He was to stay only six months across the pond before returning home to sign, initially on loan, for Halifax Town. When his Detroit contract expired – in March 1969 - his move to The Shay was made permanent and Burgin would enjoy the most successful years of his league career at Town, appearing in 243 league games at right back, before joining his final league side, Blackburn Rovers. In his first season at Ewood Park he helped Rovers to the old Division Three Championship but after exactly fifty competitive games for the club fate took a hand as during a match at Southampton in September 1975 he collided with teammate Mike Hickman, suffering a serious leg injury that eventually forced his early retirement in January 1977. After leaving the pro game Andy ran a public house for six and a half years before two and a half years as a health club manager. He now works as a caretaker at a private school in Blackburn.

BURKINSHAW, John Dean Lewis 'Jack' 1913-20

Born: 12 May 1890 Kilnhurst
(5ft 8ins, 12st – 1920)
Died: 2nd Quarter 1947
Wortley, Sheffield
Debut: 1 September 1913
v Bolton Wanderers
Division One Away
Last Appearance: 14 January 1920
v Darlington
F.A.Cup Away
Total League
& Cup Appearances: 61* Goals: 10
***Also appeared in**
95 Wartime games, scoring 39 goals.

Career Details:

Kilnhurst Town		
Grimsby Town	February	1908
Rotherham Town	May	1909
Swindon Town	May	1910
WEDNESDAY	30 May	1913 £150
Barnsley	October	1917 Guest
Rotherham Town		1919
Bradford Park Avenue	26 May	1920
Accrington Stanley	16 June	1921
Denaby United		1921
Wath Athletic		1922
Chicago (US)		

Powerful attacker Jack Burkinshaw started his football career in local non-league football before spending just over a year at Grimsby Town where he netted three times in five appearances. He then dropped out of league football to play for Midland League Rotherham Town and then Southern League Swindon Town. His signing for Swindon came after one of the most unusual trials as he was invited to play for Town in a friendly in Paris! In fact his time in Wiltshire – where he played alongside ex-Owl Tommy Bolland - coincided with a golden period for Town as they lifted the Southern League Championship in 1911 and reached the semi-finals of the F.A.Cup a year later – the last time they achieved this feat.

He eventually returned to Yorkshire to sign for Wednesday and at Hillsborough started at inside right and in his debut campaign grabbed eight goals in 34 league and cup appearances. Burkinshaw was bold and bulky and had a reputation for creating chances for himself but was then kept out of the side by Teddy Glennon and it was not until December 1914 that Jack returned to the first team fold after scoring three hat-tricks for the Owls reserve side in the Midland League. He would net 24 goals for the second team in that season but only appeared eight times for the first eleven before the outbreak of War put a stop on his league career. During wartime soccer Jack moved to centre forward and scored freely in regional football until national football returned in 1919. Unfortunately for both Burkinshaw and Wednesday the first Post War season was a disaster as the Owls were relegated from Division One and, although appearing in 18 games, Jack struggled in a poor side and was played out of position at either wing half or inside right.

However as the Owls dropped from Division One Burkinshaw – brother to Laurie and Ralph - remained in the top flight as he subsequently signed for Bradford Park Avenue in the summer of 1920, after being one of 16 players released by Wednesday. Unfortunately a year later he suffered relegation from Division One for the second consecutive season as Avenue were promptly relegated at the end of the 1920-1 season! He stayed only twelve months in West-Yorkshire – scoring twice in 23 appearances - before completing his English league career at Accrington, adding a further 31 games to his career tally. After dropping out of league soccer he spent time in the US, playing for Chicago, and in September 1927 was reported to be still living in the US but suffering from failing eyesight.

BURKINSHAW, Laurence 'Laurie/Lol' 1910-15

Born: 2 December 1893 Kilnhurst
(5ft 6½ ins, 11st 6lbs – 1913)
Died: 2nd Quarter 1969 Mexborough
Debut: 23 September 1911
v Notts County
Division One Away
Last Appearance: 25 April 1914
v Tottenham Hotspur
Division One Home
Total League
& Cup Appearances: 25 Goals: 7

Career Details:

Kilnhurst Town		
Mexborough Town		
WEDNESDAY	30 April	1910 £65*
Rotherham Town	June	1914
Stalybridge Celtic	19 March	1915 £225**
Barnsley		WW1 Guest
Kilnhurst Town		WW1 Guest
Rotherham Town		WW1 Guest
Kilnhurst Town	August	1918
Birmingham FC	August	1919
Halifax Town	June	1922
Mexborough Town	August	1923

*Owls paid joint fee of an initial £70 plus £60 if they succeeded for Burkinshaw/Bradley.
**Fee paid to Wednesday

Winger Laurie Burkinshaw arrived at Hillsborough in the summer of 1910 from local football and spent his first season at the club playing for the reserve team in the Midland League – scoring seven times as the Owls finished runners-up to Grimsby Town's first team. Over the next two seasons Laurie remained a second team regular – finishing top scorer in 1912-13 with fifteen goals – whilst making occasional first team appearances when automatic choice Sam Kirkman was absent. Despite scoring on his home debut in September 1911 he was soon back in the reserves and it was not until his brother Jack signed in the summer of 1913 that Laurie experienced his best season at Wednesday – appearing in sixteen games for the club as they just escaped relegation from the top-flight. The brothers appeared together for the first time on Boxing Day 1913 and both scored to set a record that still stands today – they are the only siblings to net in the same game for the club as although some records state Harry and Tom Brandon were brothers (they scored in the same game in 1893) they were in fact cousins!

Although Laurie experienced his most successful season at Wednesday in 1913-14 it was only as a replacement for right wing regular Kirkman and when The Owls decided not to re-sign him at the end of the season Laurie dropped into non-league football, joining Rotherham Town. During the war the keen cricketer appeared for several different clubs as a guest before re-entering league football with Birmingham when national soccer returned. At the St.Andrews club he scored 12 goals in 75 appearances – winning a Second Division Championship medal in 1921 – before the skilful winger completed his league career back at Halifax Town, becoming a popular figure with the fans when appearing in 26 games during his sole season with the West-Yorkshire club. His playing career ended back on home territory in South Yorkshire while he remained in the region after hanging up his boots to work at Swinton in the Steel industry. Incidentally his playing career was interrupted by a 12-month jail sentence after Lol, along with others, was found guilty of assaulting a police officer!

BURRIDGE, Ben James Herbert 'Bert' 1926-30

Born: 11 March 1898
Beamish, Co.Durham
(5ft 9ins, 11st 8lbs – 1926)
Died: 22 December 1977 Oldham
Debut: 26 August 1926
v Sheffield United
Division One Home
Last Appearance: 28 December 1929
v Portsmouth Division One Home
Total League
& Cup Appearances: 26 Goals: 0

Career Details:

Oxhill Villa		
Houghton Rovers	August	1920
Annfield Plain		
Darlington	November	1921
WEDNESDAY	23 June	1926 £1200
Oldham Athletic	7 June	1930 £460
Macclesfield Town	August	1931 Free
Hyde United	June	1933 Free
Hurst	June	1934 Free
Ashton National		WW2 Guest

Whole hearted half back Bert Burridge joined an Owls side that were on the up under the inspirational leadership of Bob Brown – Wednesday had been crowned division two champions two months earlier - and he initially came as competition to established first team players Arthur Lowdell and Billy Marsden. He had caught Wednesday's eye – possibly during a scouting mission to watch his team mate Mark Hooper – while impressing for Darlington where he appeared in 96 games over a five-year period, scoring seven times. Although he had missed almost all of Darlington's promotion season of 1924-5 he was a regular as they retained their newly gained Division Two status and played twice against Wednesday –including the March 1926 meeting when Wednesday slumped to a shock 5-1 defeat at Darlington.

Both Hooper and Burridge would eventually wear the blue and white stripes but it was the latter who appeared first, making a surprise debut in the opening game of the 1926-7 season when Lowdell was absent through injury. It was a tough baptism for Burridge as over 43,000 were inside Hillsborough to see derby rivals United win 3-2 – his initial experiences of Division One football must have left him shell shocked as two days later he was in the side that crashed 7-2 at Spurs! He made two further appearances in that debut season – at centre half-back and inside-left – while he gained valuable experience in the tough surrounds of the Central league – a competition at the time that probably rivalled the lower divisions of the Football League. After appearing in all but one of Wednesday first fifteen games of the 1927-8 season it looked like Burridge was becoming an established first team player but unfortunately this proved not to be the case as of those games the Owls won only two, slumping to the foot of the table. Change was needed and Bob Brown acted by bringing Norman Smith to Hillsborough in December 1927 – as direct replacement for Burridge.

This meant it was back to reserve team football for Bert, as over the next three seasons he would make only eight first team appearances as the defensive trio of Strange-Marsden-Leach led Wednesday to consecutive league Championships. In Central League football Burridge captained Wednesday to the Championship in 1929 before eventually leaving for Oldham Athletic where frustratingly he could not break up the regular half back combination, playing only six games in his sole season at Boundary Park. After dropping into Cheshire non-league football at Macclesfield Bert helped Town to the Cheshire League and Cup double in 1932 – he also was a regular as the Silkmen retained the League title a year later. Following a spell at Hyde he moved to non-leaguers Hurst, being appointed player-manager in June 1935 before joining the club's committee in January 1938.

BURROWS, David 2002-03

Born: 25 October 1968 Dudley
(5ft 9ins, 11st 8lbs – 2002)
Debut: 9 March 2002
v Gillingham
Division Two Home
Last Appearance: 14 December 2002
v Gillingham
Division One Home
Total League
& Cup Appearances 23 Goals: 0

Career Details:

West Bromwich Albion	8 November	1986
Liverpool	20 October	1988 £550,000
West Ham United	17 September	1993 £2,500,000*
Everton	6 September	1994 Exchange for T Cottee
Coventry City	2 March	1995 £1,100,000
Birmingham City	4 July	2000 Free
WEDNESDAY	8 March	2002 Free
Released	30 June	2003
Studley BKL	August	2003

*Joint fee with Mike Marsh

Vastly experienced left back David Burrows was brought to the club by Terry Yorath to help the Owls fight against relegation. The position of left back had a been a major problem all season – Leigh Bromby, Derek Geary and even midfielder Craig Armstrong occupying the position – but after signing on a short term contract Burrows made the spot his own and was faultless as Wednesday just managed to retain their First Division status. He was rewarded in June 2002 with a one-year contract but after being a regular in the first two months of the 2002-3 campaign suffered a hairline fracture of his collarbone in the home game with Leicester City, putting him on the sidelines for two months. During that period of inactivity Burrows was given the caretaker manager role – along with Chief Scout Bill Green – for the home game with Derby County in the aftermath of Yorath's resignation. He returned to his rehabilitation after Chris Turner took over the managerial reins but after making a comeback in December the injury jinx struck again when a serious hamstring injury brought a premature end to his season. The injury would bring an end to his Owls career as Burrows was one of eight players released by the club in May 2003 following relegation to Division Two.

His transfer to a struggling First Division side was a long way from the heady days at Liverpool when during 193 competitive appearances for the Reds he won a multitude of honours, including a League Championship medal in 1990 and an F.A.Cup winners medal two years later, before moving to West Ham in a deal that saw Julian Dicks move to Anfield. It was in West Ham colours that Wednesday fans – before his move to Hillsborough – perhaps best knew Burrows, as he was the unfortunate full back who was teased and tormented by Chris Waddle in the December 1993 five-nil romp. Poor old Burrows was at one point left on his backside by the mercurial winger in a game that has entered Wednesday folklore as "Waddle's game". After relatively short spells at both The Hammers and Everton he moved for a large fee to Highfield Road where his consistency at left back helped City to retain their membership of the Premier League. It was while at Coventry that Burrows actually came within hours of transferring to Wednesday as in November 1997 Ron Atkinson agreed terms with the tough tackling defender in a deal that would have seen Mark Pembridge moving to the Midlands as part of the deal. However the Welshman decided against the move and it would be over four years before Burrows finally joined the Owls.

During his time at Coventry Burrows became more of an orthodox full back – at Liverpool he tended to play the role of an attacking full back – but was no less effective in his 129 appearances for The Sky Blues. After playing the majority of his career in the top-flight a move to First Division Birmingham City came next before the ex-England U-21 and "B" International signed for the Owls - his seventh football league club. After retiring from professional football in the summer of 2003 he decided to move to France but in the interim signed for his ex-Albion team mate Nicky Cross at Midland Alliance League side Studley BKL.

BURROWS, Horace 1931-42

Born: 11 March 1910 Sutton-in-Ashfield
(5ft 10 ins, 11st – 1931)
Died: 22 March 1969 Sutton-in-Ashfield
Debut: 27 December 1932
v Manchester City
Division One Home
Last Appearance: 29 April 1939
v Tottenham Hotspur
Division Two Home
Total League
& Cup Appearances: 260* Goals: 8
***Also appeared in**
49 Wartime games, scoring 1 goal

Career Details:

Sutton Junction		1929
Coventry City	February	1929 Trial
Mansfield Town	May	1930
WEDNESDAY	1 May	1931 £200
Millwall		1941-2 Guest
Retired		1942
Ollerton Colliery		

CAPS (@SWFC) –
ENGLAND Full (3) v Hungary 10/05/34, v Czechoslovakia 16/05/34, v Holland 18/05/35

After breaking into the Owls side part way through the 1932-33 season, stylish and skilful left half-back Horace Burrows was an almost ever present until the outbreak of war in 1939, missing only a handful of games. In fact such was his consistency and fitness that between April 1933 and March 1936 the crisp tackling and hard working half-back played in 136 consecutive games for Wednesday. In the two seasons that followed injury did keep Horace out for short spells but he returned in the final season before the war to be ever present as Wednesday just missed out on promotion back to the top-flight. During his time in the blue and white shirt Burrows – known for his tenacious and constructive play - was a member of the side that lifted the F.A.Cup at Wembley in 1935 and his superb passing ability marked him out as the club's best wing half since the outstanding Billy Marsden.

His career had started in his home county of Nottinghamshire for whom he won schoolboy honours before spending two years with local non-league side Sutton Junction. A move into league football at Coventry City came next but after failing to make a league appearance for The Sky Blues he dropped back into non-league soccer, signing for Midland League Mansfield Town. He won his first medal while at Mansfield – the Notts Senior Cup in 1931 – but perhaps his most significant appearance in a Stags shirt came in a low key Yorkshire mid-week game against Wednesday at Hillsborough. It was here where he first impressed the Hillsborough hierarchy and manager Bob Brown's eye for a player yet again proved true after Wednesday snapped Burrows up a month before Town were elected into the Football League.

At the outbreak of the War, Horace continued to play for Wednesday while running a sports outfitters shop back in his home village of Sutton-in-Ashfield – a vocation he continued until closing the shop in January 1942 to join the Sherwood Foresters Regiment. He was initially posted to India but was quickly sent to the Middle East and was subsequently injured in the arm during the battle of Al Alamein. His final appearance in a Wednesday shirt had come in October 1941 but he would play several games for Millwall as a guest later in the season before effectively hanging up his boots. After being de-mobbed Horace re-opened his sports shop in November 1945 and also made a playing comeback as player-manager at Notts club Ollerton Colliery. He ran his shop until his death in 1969 – in his spare time Horace loved to play golf and had a low, single figure handicap – and it is still trading today, ran by his son. The Burrows name continued in the Football League after Horace's retirement as his son Adrian played for several clubs including Mansfield Town and Plymouth Argyle.

BURTON, Henry Arthur "Harry" 1902-09

Born: 3rd Quarter 1881
West Bromwich
(5ft 10½ ins, 12st – 1907)
Died: 28 August 1923 Sheffield
Debut: 10 October 1903
v Wolverhampton W.
Division One Away
Last Appearance: 27 March 1909
v Manchester City
Division One Away
Total League
& Cup Appearances: 198 Goals: 0

Career Details:

Huntsman's Garden Schoolboys		
Attercliffe FC		
WEDNESDAY	August	1902 £10
West Bromwich Albion	28 March	1909 £850*
Scunthorpe & Lindsay United	May	1912 Free

*Joint fee with G. Simpson

Despite being born in the West Midlands, Harry Burton spent his boyhood years in Sheffield, attending Darnall Road School. His first experience of senior football came with local non-leaguers Attercliffe, from where he arrived at Wednesday in the summer of 1902. He initially came as an understudy to the great Ambrose Langley but injury soon ended the old campaigners career and Burton stepped straight into his shoes. His lightening dashes and deadly tackling soon made him a greatly feared opponent and at his peak the two-footed left back was regarded as the fastest back in the English game. His form was such that Langley was not missed and after initially breaking into the side in October 1903 he ended his debut season with a League Championship medal, also playing for Wednesday in their F.A.Cup semi-final defeat to Manchester City.

He quickly formed a full back partnership with Willie Layton and would be a first team regular for several years, helping Wednesday to win the F.A.Cup in 1907 – before experiencing a disastrous afternoon in February 1909 against minnows Glossop North End. The Second Division club were rank underdogs but poor old Harry managed to score in his own goal and miss a penalty at the other end as North End shocked the Owls one-nil to reach the last eight. It was perhaps coincidence but within a month Harry – along with George Simpson – was on his way to West Bromwich Albion in a move that caused a great stir in Sheffield football. This was mainly because Albion were fighting for promotion from Division Two – ironically Harry's own goal would deny Albion promotion as they missed out by one fifty-sixth of a goal!

At The Hawthorns Harry immediately settled into his usual left back role although part way through the following season a change to right back occurred before a cartilage injury ended his Football League career after 36 games. He subsequently played a season for Scunthorpe & Lindsay United in their debut campaign in the Midland League but his knee could not stand up to the rigours of competitive football and he was forced to retire altogether from the game. After retiring from football Harry returned to Sheffield where he gained employment but kept active with a variety of sporting pastimes – being a member of Darnall Hockey Club for a year before becoming a valued member of the Sitwell Park Golf Club. Unhappily he died at the relatively young age of 42 only ten years after ending his playing career.

BURTON, Kenneth Owen "Ken/Kenny" 1967-73

Born: 11 February 1950 Sheffield
(5ft 8ins, 11st 6lbs – 1971)
Debut: 30 November 1968 v Stoke City
Division One Home
Last Appearance: 26 February 1972 v Burnley Division Two Away
Total League & Cup Appearances: 58+4 Goals: 2

Career Details:

WEDNESDAY	11 February	1967
Chesterfield	8 March	1973 Loan
Peterborough United	March	1973 Loan
Chesterfield	July	1973
Halifax Town	September	1980 Free
Alfreton Town	July	1981
Worksop Town	August	1983
Sheffield Club		1985
Burton Albion	December	1985
Retford Town		1986

CAPS (@ SWFC) –
ENGLAND Youth (3) v Bulgaria, Holland, Russia 1968

Although originally a wing half Kenny Burton was converted to full back early in his Wednesday career. He signed apprentice forms for the club in July 1965 and within three months – and still only 15 years old – was pressed into an emergency appearance for the reserve team. After his shock Central League start it was back to youth football for Burton and it would not be until December 1967 that he re-appeared at reserve level, playing in seven consecutive games from left back. The youngster's big chance came in the following season as with stalwart Don Megson absent through injury Burton enjoyed two spells in the first team and would subsequently start the relegation season of 1969-70 as the first choice left back at Hillsborough. He remained so for two seasons but after Wednesday's disastrous 5-1 home defeat to Bristol City in August 1971 he was unceremoniously axed and made only a solitary substitute appearance during the remainder of his Wednesday career. Burton, whose father Ernie played for the Owls without making a first team appearance, saw his left back spot go to Dave Clements and after playing four games for Peterborough while on loan he was released by the Owls in the summer of 1973.

After a two-month trial at Chesterfield he was given a contract in September 1973 and perhaps proved a point to the Owls management by being almost ever present at the Saltergate club, appearing in 266 league and cup games for The Spireites. The tough tackling, although somewhat one-footed, player eventually completed his league career at Halifax Town before joining Midland League outfit Alfreton Town. Over the next five years Kenny appeared for a variety of non-league clubs while being employed as a postman in Sheffield, a job he still holds today.

BUTLER, Barry 1952-57

Born: 30 July 1934 Stockton
(6ft, 12st – 1954)
Died: 9 April 1966 Sprowston, Norwich
Debut: 2 January 1954
v Burnley
Division One Home
Last Appearance: 19 February 1955
v Blackpool
Division One Away
Total League
& Cup Appearances: 36 Goals: 1

Career Details:

Stockton West End		
Billingham Minors		
South Bank Juniors		
South Bank		
Middlesbrough		Trial
Dundee		Trial
WEDNESDAY	20 September	1952 £300
Norwich City	17 August	1957 £5,000

Over the years there have been countless examples of a player being sold by a club only to achieve greater success elsewhere. One such player was centre half Barry Butler who after leaving Hillsborough in 1957 made a mammoth 349 appearances for Norwich City, including a run of 208 consecutive games which was only broken when he appeared for an F.A.XI side! The ex-Stockton and North Riding schoolboys player led City to the F.A.Cup semi-finals in 1959 – when they were still a Third Division side – and a year later helped The Canaries earn promotion to Division Two. At the time Butler was widely considered the best uncapped centre-half in the country and this view was enhanced in 1962 when Norwich beat Rochdale over two legs to win the Football League Cup. At City he was an inspirational captain – regarded as one of the club's greatest ever players – and had to overcome a variety of injuries that included a broken leg, fractured cheekbone, fractured wrist and even a bout of pneumonia. The club's player of year award is named the Barry Butler Trophy and even now his name stands for all that is good about a professional footballer.

His achievements at Carrow Road must have left Wednesday wondering if they hade made a major error in letting Butler leave Hillsborough after he had failed to become established in five years in Sheffield. He had originally signed as a part-time professional in early September 1952 from Northern League South Bank – the same club that provided Wednesday with Ted Catlin – after having played for a variety of minor clubs whilst working as an apprentice electrical fitter at ICI Billingham – he gained employment there after leaving Richard Hind Secondary school where he captained both the cricket and football teams. After three "A" teams games with Wednesday he was signed as a full-time professional and after serving his apprenticeship in the reserves got his chance in January 1954 thanks to an injury to Cyril Turton. This was the start of a run in the side that stretched to nineteen consecutive games, including an appearance in the F.A.Cup semi-final defeat to Preston North End at Maine Road. He also made several first team appearances in the season that followed but the signing of Don McEvoy in December 1954 effectively signalled the end of his Wednesday career and he would start only three more games – including a game at centre-forward in his final appearance – before spending the remaining two years of his Owls career in the Central league side.

After qualifying as an F.A.Coach in 1963 Butler was appointed player-coach at City for the 1966-67 season but he could not take the position as he was tragically killed – at the age of just 42 - when his car collided with a bus late at night.

BUTTERY, Edward "Ted" 1877-82

Born
Died:
Debut: 18 December 1880
v Blackburn Rovers
F.A.Cup Away
Last Appearance: 15 March 1882
v Blackburn Rovers
F.A.Cup S/F
@ Manchester
Total League
& Cup Appearances: 11 Goals: 0

Career Details:

WEDNESDAY	1876
Released	1882

Defender Tom Buttery was one of many players who helped advance the club in its early amateur days, appearing in several games that represented "firsts" for the club - from the first Sheffield Challenge Cup win in 1877 – a thrilling 4-3 win over Heeley - to the first F.A Cup tie in 1880 – a stunning 4-0 win at Cup stalwarts Blackburn Rovers. He also claimed a place in Sheffield football history by appearing in the City's inaugural Floodlit game in October 1878 – facing his brother Tom – and during his years with Wednesday won several local honours including four Sheffield Challenge Cups and two Wharncliffe Charity Cups while his final competitive appearance in an Owls shirt came in Wednesday's first ever appearance in the last four of the English Cup.

BUTTERY, Thomas "Tom" 1880-83

Born:
Died:
Debut: 18 December 1880
v Blackburn Rovers
F.A.Cup Away
Last Appearance: 5 February 1881
v Darwen
F.A.Cup Away
Total League
& Cup Appearances: 2 Goals: 0

Career Details:

Exchange	1879
WEDNESDAY	1879
Lockwood Brothers	1883
Preston North End	1884

When Tom Buttery played alongside his brother Ted in the club's first ever F.A.Cup tie, in December 1880, he not only ensured a place in Wednesday's early history but also gained - with his brother - the distinction of being the first siblings to play competitive football for the club – the famous Clegg brothers having just appeared in friendly games. The Cup win at Blackburn was in fact only Tom's second appearance for Wednesday – his first coming in March 1879 when he and his brother helped the club to a 3-2 win over Heeley to secure the inaugural Wharncliffe Charity Cup – and in fact he would play only occasionally for Wednesday.

Tom would actually spend the majority of his career at Sheffield based teams Exchange and Lockwood Brothers - Wednesday actually providing the opposition for the latter in February 1884 for Buttery's benefit game.

CALLAGHAN, John 1895-96

Born: Scotland
Debut: 4 January 1896 v Burnley Division One Away
Last Appearance: 12 September 1896 v West Bromwich Albion Division One Home
Total League & Cup Appearances: 4 Goals: 2

Career Details:
Hunslet

WEDNESDAY	Close season	1895
Contract cancelled	December	1896

Although three of John Callaghan's four appearances for Sheffield Wednesday were actually at right half-back it was at inside forward where the Scotsman played the majority of his 18-month career at Olive Grove. His first appearance for the club saw him net twice as the reserves beat Attercliffe 8-0 in September 1895 and he would net eleven times for the second eleven during the 1895-6 season as they finished third in both the Sheffield Challenge Cup and Wharncliffe Charity Cup Leagues. However despite appearing regularly for the reserves in this attacking role it was as a replacement for Olive Grove stalwart Harry Brandon that Callaghan made his senior bow at half back in the two-nil defeat at Burnley, early in 1896.

He would stand in twice more for Brandon during the season but his biggest impact on Wednesday's league history came at the beginning of the following season when he was drafted in for the home game with West Brom, in the accustomed position of inside-left. The versatile Callaghan duly netted twice in a 3-1 win to further his cause for first team selection but unfortunately his goal scoring feat did not cut much ice with The Owls selection committee and in the following game – which Wednesday lost four-nil – the number 10 shirt was handed to first team regular Alec Brady and Callaghan never played another league match for the club, his contract being cancelled three months later.

CAMERON, Daniel "Danny" 1971-76

Born: 9 November 1953 Dundee
(5ft 8ins, 11st 4lbs – 1974)
Debut: 24 October 1973
v West Bromwich Albion
Division Two Away
Last Appearance: 27 September 1975
v Crystal Palace
Division Three Away
Total League
& Cup Appearances: 38 Goals: 1

Career Details:

WEDNESDAY	1 July	1971
Colchester United	6 February	1975 Loan
Preston North End	14 April	1976 Free
Dundee	August	1981 Free
P.G.Rangers	February	1983
Hellenic	March	1983

Right back Danny Cameron signed for Wednesday straight from school after his talents were spotted by the club's Scottish scout while appearing for Dundee boys – he was also picked on three occasions for Scotland boys but failed to earn a cap. His reserve team debut – in April 1970 at Maine Road – came while he was still an apprentice but after signing pro forms in the following summer Cameron spent two seasons as a Central League regular, creating competition for first team right back Peter Rodrigues. He finally made his league bow for the club in 1973 and his debut season in the first eleven proved to be his best – appearance wise- as in a five-year stay at Hillsborough he could never quite shake off the tag as Rodrigues' understudy. During that debut season Cameron enjoyed a six game spell on the left wing but in Wednesday's disastrous relegation season of 1974-5 his appearances were distinctly infrequent. However his big chance came following Rodrigues' departure in the summer of 1975 and Cameron duly started the first eleven games of Wednesday's first ever season of Division Three football. Unfortunately fate then took a hand and an injury in Steve Burtenshaw's last game as Wednesday boss meant Danny was not able to impress new manager Len Ashurst and in the spring moved to Preston on a free transfer – following a five-game loan spell at Hereford United.

He found a niche at Deepdale and after helping The Lilywhites to promotion from Division Three in 1978 he took his appearance tally to 122 before a short spell back in his hometown at Dundee. He then started a love affair with South Africa, which saw Danny play for Johannesburg club P.G.Rangers and Cape Town side Hellenic. After hanging up his boots in March 1985 – following three broken legs in an eighteen month period - Cameron worked in the South African glass industry until returning home to Scotland in February 1996. He lived in the Dundee area for over three years, as a self employed courier, but much preferred the lifestyle in the Southern Hemisphere and after returning to Cape Town in May 1999 he now runs a furniture delivering business. He also coached local amateur teams for a time but eventually was forced out of the game due to a chronic knee problem.

CAMPBELL, James 'Jimmy' 1911-20

Born: 1886 Newhaven, Edinburgh
(5ft $8^{1}/_{2}$ ins, 11st 7lbs – 1913)
Died: May 1925 Edinburgh
Debut: 18 February 1911
v Bury
Division One Home
Last Appearance: 10 March 1920
v Liverpool
Division One Away
Total League
& Cup Appearances: 156* Goals: 3
***Also appeared in 7 Wartime games**

Career Details:
Leith Athletic

WEDNESDAY	February	1911 £450*
Huddersfield Town	15 May	1920
Edinburgh St.Bernards	March	1921

* Joint fee with Paterson

CAPS (@ SWFC): Scotland Full (1) v Wales 03/03/13

Left half-back James Campbell arrived in February 1911 along with Leith team mate Paterson and was an immediate success, appearing in the final thirteen games of the season as Wednesday finished sixth in Division One. He arrived at Hillsborough with a reputation as one of Scotland's finest young players and this proved to be correct as his polished displays soon started comparisons with Sheffield United's legendary half-back Ernest Needham. Incredibly from making his debut in February 1911 Campbell would be ever present for Wednesday until December 1913, a run of 116 consecutive league and cup games.

His superb form earned him an International call up in 1913 but then, like so many of his contemporaries, Campbell lost some of the best years of his playing career to World War One. Being a reservist, Campbell was called up as soon as war was declared – leaving Wednesday for the front in September 1914- and was immediately sent abroad. He was later wounded in action at which point he was transferred back to Woolwich in London where he made harnesses. However he returned to the front line in 1916 and on his return to Wednesday's first team in the immediate post war era it was obvious his long years in the Army had dimmed his play as he struggled to adjust to league football in peacetime.

He appeared in just over half of the clubs games in the relegation season of 1919-20 but just could not recapture his old International form and eventually moved onto Yorkshire neighbours Huddersfield Town – being signed by ex-Owl Ambrose Langley. Unfortunately he would appear in only one game for The Terriers before returning to his native Edinburgh as he started to suffer health problems. He subsequently joined non-league side St Bernard's but he was forced to retire early from football as his health deteriorated and he sadly passed away at the tender age of 38 in May 1925.

CAMPBELL, Philip Anthony "Phil" 1979-81

Born: 16 October 1961 Barnsley
(5ft 8ins, 10st 7lbs – 1980)
Only Appearance:
13 September 1980
v Bristol City
Division Two Home
Total League
& Cup Appearances: 0+1 Goals: 0

Career Details:

WEDNESDAY	15 October	1979
Barnsley	summer	1981 Trial
Scarborough	May	1981 Free
Frickley Athletic		

While appearing for both Barnsley and South Yorkshire boys forward Phil Campbell trained once a week at his local club Barnsley but looked set to miss out on a career in professional football after the Tykes decided not to take him on apprentice terms. However supply teacher Robin Livsay – who also coached Wednesday's U-18 side – came to his school and soon after, in June 1978, Campbell signed apprentice forms at Hillsborough. A member of the highly successful F.A.Youth Cup side of 1979-80, that provided many future first team players, the teenager soon became established in the club's reserve side and made his first team bow in September 1980 – appearing for just eleven minutes as a late substitute for Gordon Owen. Unfortunately that brief cameo appearance proved to be his only taste of league football as he subsequently dropped out of the matchday squad and played reserve team soccer until an unsuccessful month's trial at Barnsley.

After being freed by The Owls the youngster joined Alliance Premier League Scarborough but his stay was brief, returning to South Yorkshire to finish his playing career at Frickley Athletic. He eventually retired from competitive football at the South Elmsall club as he was – and still is – a self employed plumber and did not want to run the risk of being injured.

CAPEWELL, Ronald "Ron/Lofty" 1950-54

Born: 26 July 1929 Sheffield
(6ft 4ins, 14st 8lbs - 1952)
Debut: 6 September 1952
v Charlton Athletic
Division One Home
Last Appearance: 9 September 1953
v Bolton Wanderers
Division One Away
Total League
& Cup Appearances: 30 Goals: 0

Career Details:

Arbourthorne Boys Club		
Kiveton Park		
Midhill W.M.C.	September	1949
Wednesday	10 December	1949 Amat.
WEDNESDAY	25 February	1950
Hull City	July	1954 £500
King's Lynn	July	1955
Goole Town	July	1956
Hyde United		1958
Stalybridge Celtic		1961
Mossley		1962

Giant goalkeeper Ron "Lofty" Capewell arrived at Hillsborough as a result of a tip off received by Wednesday, while Ron was playing representative football for the Army during his national Service. The source of the information was Ron's neighbour who told Wednesday of the Army's high opinion of the Sheffielder. On hearing the stories of his good form secretary-manager Eric Taylor invited the youngster for trials at Hillsborough and after initially signing as an amateur he soon turned professional. Capewell had started his playing career at local Sheffield youth side Arbourthorne – while working as an apprentice bricklayer - before making a handful of appearances for Yorkshire League Kiveton Park as well as attending trials for the Yorkshire boy's club representative team. After completing his two years National Service in the Medicinal Core – winning the Army National Cup on the football field – Capewell started work as a roof tiler while playing for Midhill Working Mens Club – on East Bank Road in Sheffield - immediately prior to signing professional forms for Wednesday.

After serving his apprenticeship in The Owls' second and third teams Capewell became established as No.2 to Dave McIntosh and when his rival suffered a broken leg in September 1952 "Lofty" was given his big chance. In fact he would play in 26 consecutive league and cup games for Wednesday as they consolidated in the top-flight after winning the Second Division Championship. However when "Mac" had regained his fitness Capewell dropped back into reserve team football until earning a second chance in the early stages of the following season when McIntosh again suffered a broken bone – this time his arm. Unfortunately his stay lasted only four games this time as Brian Ryalls took his place, effectively relegating Capewell to third choice status. By now a knee injury was also hampering his first team chances – a cartilage operation failing to totally cure a knee problem that meant he developed fluid on the knee – and after moving to Hull City he played only a single game, keeping a clean sheet, before dropping out of League soccer altogether.

When his professional career ended in 1957 Capewell began working as a stonemason at Sheffield firm James Longdens – owed by a Wednesday director of the same name – while playing part-time for a variety of high profile non-league clubs, before retiring at the end of the 1962-3 season. He later worked for sixteen and a half years as a delivery driver for Whitbreads Brewery – along side fellow ex-Owl Walter Bingley – before retiring.

CAPPER, Alfred "Freddy" 1913-21

Born: 1st Quarter 1891
Knutsford, Cheshire
(5ft 9ins, 11st – 1921)
Died: 31 October 1955 Winnington
Debut: 26 September 1914
v Bradford Park Avenue
Division One Home
Last Appearance: 26 February 1921
v Hull City
Division Two Away
Total League
& Cup Appearances: 62* Goals: 4
***Also appeared in**
63 wartime games, scoring 9 times

Career Details:

Winnington Park School		
Winnington Bible Class		
Northwich Church Lads		
Northwich Victoria		
Manchester United	June	1912
Witton Albion	May	1913
WEDNESDAY	April	1913 £160*
Manchester City	December	1916 Guest
Brentford	9 August	1921 £100

* Including £60 to Manchester United for league registration

Speedy attacker "Freddy" Capper joined the Owls from Lancashire Combination side Witton Albion, where he'd netted 29 times as they won the Division Two Championship. The forward had been only one season in Cheshire after a year at Manchester United where England International George Wall had ensured he only made a solitary first team appearance for The Red Devils. He had originally arrived at Old Trafford from Witton's cross town rivals Northwich Victoria where despite not being a regular, or even having scored a goal, he was spotted by Manchester United scouts and taken into League football.

Soon after arriving at Hillsborough he quickly established himself in the Owls first team, helped no doubt by netting on his debut as Bradford Park Avenue were thrashed 6-0. It was an outside right role that Capper mainly occupied in his time at Wednesday but like so many of his contemporaries he would find his career put on hold with the outbreak of war. He did play frequently for Wednesday during the war – while doing war work in Sheffield - but a sole guest appearance for Manchester City in December 1916 grabbed all the headlines as he scored an amazing five times as City thrashed Blackburn Rovers 8-0! He would struggle to re-establish himself when the hostilities ended and eventually moved on to Brentford where his league career came to a close after 96 league games and five goals for the Londoners.

CARBONE, Benito 1996-99

Born: 14 August 1971
Bagnara Calabra, Italy
(5ft 6ins, 10st 8lbs – 1998)
Debut: 19 October 1996
v Blackburn Rovers
Premier League Home
Last Appearance: 19 September 1999
v Newcastle United
Premier League Away
Total League
& Cup Appearances: 96+11 Goals: 26

Career Details:

Torino		1989
Reggina	July	1990 Loan
Casertana	July	1991 Loan
Ascoli	July	1992 Loan
Napoli	July	1994
Inter Milan	August	1995
WEDNESDAY	14 October	1996 £3,000,000
Aston Villa	21 October	1999 £250,000
Bradford City	10 August	2000 Free
Derby County	18 October	2001 Loan (to 10/01/02)
Middlesbrough	8 February	2002 Loan (to 12/05/02)
Como	26 July	2002 £800,000
AC Parma	12 September	2003
Catanzaro	June	2004 Free

Highly talented but temperamental attacker Benito Carbone was the club's record signing when David Pleat brought him to Hillsborough in the autumn of 1996 from Italian giants Inter Milan. The diminutive forward had started his career as a seventeen-year old at Turin side Torino from where he was farmed out to several other League sides in order to gain valuable experience. He made such an impact during his season with Ascoli that he was recalled and "Beni" enjoyed an outstanding season during 1993-4 in Torino colours. By now he had amassed twenty U-21 caps for Italy and with his star in the ascendancy he transferred to the Deep South, signing for Napoli. He had the unenviable task of replacing the recently departed Diego Maradona but his form was such in the heel of Italy that Carbone moved again in the following summer, this time to Italian giants Inter Milan. In just over a season at The San Siro the skilful Carbone became a big hit with The Tifosi but the majority of his appearances would come from the subs bench and a move to England – and regular first team football – came at the right time after having scored 30 times in 218 Italian League games for seven different clubs.

Although arriving as a right winger Beni was played as an out-and-out striker in his debut season at Wednesday, as well as occupying a role in "the hole", playing just behind the front two. His whole-hearted play and unexpected work rate endeared him to the Hillsborough faithful and he spearheaded a seventh place finish in that debut season. However the arrival of compatriot Paulo Di Canio saw Carbone on the subs bench on several occasions although the departure of Pleat and arrival of Ron Atkinson ensured a first team place for the flamboyant twosome. He remained a first team regular under Danny Wilson – scoring some truly spectacular long-range goals along the way – until 1999 when his Wednesday career unravelled in spectacular style. He had already ran into trouble in the previous pre season when arriving late but his days were truly numbered when he refused to be a sub in the game at Southampton in August 1999 – famously calling a taxi and leaving to catch a place home to Italy! This behaviour signalled the end of his Wednesday career – his popularity with Owls fans was now at rock bottom – and he completed a acrimonious departure to Aston Villa in October 1999 – Wednesday recouping only a fraction of the huge fee (the second biggest purchase in Wednesday's history) they paid Inter in return.

He stayed at Villa Park less then twelve months as after appearing in the 2000 F.A.Cup Final defeat to Chelsea – after scoring five times in six matches on the way to Wembley – he failed to agree a new contract and became one of several big money buys by Bradford City as they tried to ensure a second season in the Premier League would not end in relegation back to the Football League. However City failed to stay up although Carbone became a big favourite with Bantams fans – despite being dropped and placed on the transfer list by new manager Jim Jefferies in January 2001 after he had previously been ever present. To Carbone's credit he turned down a move to Middlesbrough to fight for his place at City and after a five game absence took his seasonal tally to 36 games. He showed all his best attributes to City fans – pace and outstanding close control being just two – and the player of the year trophy was deservedly won. He was rated by Bantams fans as one of the greatest players in the club's history but after relegation his pay packet became a milestone around City's neck and as they desperately tried to cut costs Beni was loaned out to Derby County. He appeared alongside fellow Italian Fabrizio Ravanelli while at Pride Park but after retuning to Valley Parade after three months he duly blotted his copybook by again refusing to be a substitute – a fine of two weeks wages ensued. A further loan spell at Middlesbrough looked set to end in a permanent deal but Boro boss Steve McLaren decided against the transfer and as Bradford City plunged into administration Carbone found he was effectively sacked as all contracts were cancelled. Therefore after a somewhat turbulent career in English football he returned to Italy, signing for Serie A new boys Como, only to suffer relegation in his debut season alongside old club Torino. Following relegation he moved back into the Italian top-flight when signing for Parma before moving to hometown Serie B club Catanzaro, signing a 4-year contract and being made captain.

CARGILL, David Anderson "Dave/Darkie" 1956-58

Born: 21 July 1936 Arbroath, Scotland
(5ft 9ins, 11st 2lbs – 1956)
Debut: 19 September 1956
v Chelsea
Division One Away
Last Appearance: 19 February 1958
v Manchester United
F.A.Cup Away
Total League
& Cup Appearances: 13 Goals: 0

Career Details:

Arbroath YC		
Burnley	July	1953
WEDNESDAY	18 September	1956 £5,000
Derby County	25 April	1958 £4,250
Lincoln City	December	1960 £3,265
Arbroath	February	1962

It was while playing for Arbroath High School and starring for Arbroath Youth Club that winger Dave Cargill first started to attract interest from clubs South of the Border. This led to him joining First Division Burnley straight from school in 1951, signing professional forms two years later. Unfortunately for the youngster he was in direct competition for a first team spot with England International left winger Brian Pilkington and unsurprisingly managed only five first team appearances for the Turf Moor club before Wednesday manager Eric Taylor brought him to Hillsborough from The Clarets reserve side.

He was still serving his National Service when he joined Wednesday, signing full time forms on being de-mobbed in December 1956, and while serving in the R.A.F. appeared in representative football for both the R.A.F. and Fighter Command. His debut for Wednesday came just twenty-four hours after joining – a 0-0 draw at Stamford Bridge – and for the remainder of the season would compete with Albert Broadbent for the left-wing role, appearing in nine top-flight games as Wednesday consolidated after the previous season's promotion. However his hopes of securing a regular first team spot were severely hit when Alan Finney switched wings and with Broadbent still going strong Cargill moved to Derby County – as a direct replacement for ex-Owls winger Dennis Woodhead.

He enjoyed a modicum of success at The Baseball Ground, starting 56 leagues games and scoring eight times, before a short spell at Lincoln City where he played ten times during the 1961-2 season. However he then rejected The Imps offer of a new deal and went back to Arbroath although he could not play any senior football as City still held his playing registration. Lincoln eventually released him in February 1962 and over the next four years – until his retirement in 1966 – he was outstanding for his home town club, even attracting interest from the Scottish International selectors. After hanging up his boots Cargill started work in the licensing trade and is now a bar manager in Arbroath.

CARR, Christopher 'Chris' 2004

Born: 14 December 1984 Newcastle
(5ft 11ins, 12st 6lbs – 2004)
Debut: 1 May 2004
v Luton Town
Division Two Away
Last Appearance: 8 May 2004
v Queens Park Rangers
League One Home
Total League
& Cup Appearances: 0+2 Goals: 0

Career Details:

West Denton		
Sunderland Academy		
Newcastle United Academy		
WEDNESDAY	25 March	2004 Free
Contract cancelled	22 December	2004
Hartlepool United	January	2005 Trial
Macclesfield Town		Trial
Queen of the South	24 March	2005

Confident central defender who signed from Newcastle's reserve side, after a successful trial. The former Newcastle boys player had previously captained the Geordies Academy side to the Championship and was immediately given the same role with the Owls reserve side, appearing in the team that won the Pontins League Cup in May 2004. His first team debut came as a late substitute at Kenilworth Road but seven days later he had the misfortune to slice the ball into his own net during his home debut against QPR. The arrival of Guy Branston and Patrick Collins pushed the teenager down the pecking order and he failed to make the matchday sixteen during the following season, which resulted in his contract being cancelled by mutual consent

CARR, Franz Alexander 1989-90

Born: 24 September 1966 Preston
(5ft 7ins, 10st 12lbs – 1989)
Debut: 26 December 1989
v Liverpool
Division One Away
Last Appearance: 21 March 1990
v Manchester United
Division One Home
Total League
& Cup Appearances: 11+3 Goals: 0

Career Details:

Blackburn Rovers	30 July	1984
Nottingham Forest	2 August	1984 £100,000
WEDNESDAY	22 December	1989 3-month loan
West Ham United	11 March	1991 Loan
Newcastle United	13 June	1991 £250,000
Sheffield United	12 January	1993 £120,000
Leicester City	8 September	1994 £100,000
Aston Villa	10 February	1995 £250,000
Reggiana	23 October	1996 Free
Everton	October	1997 Trial
Bolton Wanderers	31 October	1997 3-month loan
West Bromwich Albion	12 February	1998 Loan
Pittsburgh Riverhounds		

Mercurial winger Franz Carr enjoyed two spells in the City of Sheffield, both initially on loan for three months. He first played in the City for Wednesday during Ron Atkinson's first season in charge and his electric pace down the right immediately had a positive effect on The Owls results – Wednesday losing only four of the fourteen games he played as they moved towards mid-table security. However Wednesday fans who fully expected his move to be made permanent, when his loan period expired, were in for a shock as he surprisingly snubbed a £500,000 move to Hillsborough, returning instead to Forest's reserve team (Wednesday subsequently winning only one more game to suffer last-day relegation). It would be over four years before he signed a permanent contract, again after a three-month loan period, but this time with neighbours Sheffield United – five days after playing against Wednesday in the FA.Cup semi-final at Wembley!

As a teenager he was quick enough to be offered an Athletics Scholarship in the USA but it was football he chose, starting as a trainee in 1982 at Blackburn Rovers. He signed after impressing for Lancashire boys but he would experience one of the shortest professional careers on record while at Rovers as just three days after signing a contract he was snapped up by Brian Clough, moving to the City Ground for a large fee. However it was at Forest that Carr made his name, appearing in 160 games and earning nine England U-21 caps, a Full Members Cup winners medal in 1989 and League Cup winners medal in 1990. At the majority of his clubs Carr had a tendency to drift in and out of the first team picture – consistency was not his strong point – and it could be argued that he never really managed to earn a regular place at any of his thirteen clubs – with the possible exception of Nottingham Forest. It was this inconsistency that ensured he would appear for a variety of clubs in the years that followed, including a spell at Newcastle where he was nicknamed "Roadrunner".

After leaving Aston Villa in 1996 he had a trial at Italian side Reggiana, signing on a free transfer a month later, making his debut at Perugia in January 1997. However he would spend only a year in Reggia before returning home to train with Everton while struggling to obtain release from his contract at Reggiana. After three months on loan at Bolton Wanderers he was finally given a free by his Italian employers and subsequently won a short-term deal at West Brom. However his career was now coming to a close and after a spell in US soccer he opened a Bistro back in his adopted home of Nottingham. He later sold this establishment and in October 1999 became a licensed football agent.

CATLIN, Arthur Edward "Ted" 1930-45

Born: 11 January 1911 South Bank, Nr Middlesbrough
(5ft 10ins, 10st 10lbs – 1935)
Died: 28 November 1990 Sheffield
Debut: 28 March 1931
v Leicester City
Division One Home
Last Appearance: 29 April 1939
v Tottenham Hotspur
Division Two Home
Total League
& Cup Appearances: 227* Goals: 0
***Also appeared in**
96 wartime games, scoring 1 goal

Career Details:

Middlesbrough		Amateur
South Bank		
WEDNESDAY	13 November	1930
Charlton Athletic		1941-2 Guest
Stockport County		1941-2 Guest
Released		1946

CAPS (@SWFC) –
ENGLAND Full (5) v Wales 17/10/36, v Ireland 19/10/36, v Hungary 02/12/36, v Norway 14/05/37, v Sweden 17/05/37

Football League (1) v Scottish League 1936

It is widely accepted that Ernie Blenkinsop was the greatest left back to play for Wednesday in their long history. It was therefore a huge challenge for youngster Ted Catlin when he arrived at Hillsborough in 1930, initially as an amateur, to act as understudy to "The Prince of full backs". It was a task that the one time South Bank player attacked with gusto and by the time of his retirement in 1946 Catlin had joined Blenkinsop as one of the greatest full backs to wear the famous blue and white shirt. His rise to prominence at Hillsborough was a slow process, as Ted had to serve a long apprenticeship in the club's reserve side –playing over eighty Central league games over a four-year period. His debut came when Blenkinsop was one of three men missing because of England duty and his second appearance for Wednesday was one Catlin would want to quickly forget – a 9-3 thrashing at Everton in October 1931!

However happier days were just around the corner for Ted as the shock transfer of Blenkinsop to Liverpool in March 1934 opened the first team door wide open and Catlin did not need a second invitation to make the left back spot his own for the remainder of the pre-war period. The peerless defender would become an integral member of the side that lifted the F.A.Cup a year later and such was his form that several England caps followed even though Wednesday suffered relegation in 1937- incidentally in the same year Ted, along with two other men, saved two young girls from drowning in the North Sea after they swam out from a deserted beach to haul the girl's sinking boat back to the shore. He remained a first team regular as Wednesday just missed out on promotion from Division Two in 1939, despite spending time in a Sheffield hospital in December 1938 when the car he was driving in alongside team mate Bill Fallon skidded off Penistone Road and crashed into a telegraph pole!

When war broke out in 1939 Catlin joined the Army, becoming a sergeant, and was subsequently posted to Scotland in 1940 (appearing for the Forfarshire Junior Association team) before being sent south of the border – allowing him to guest for both Stockport and Charlton Athletic. Throughout the hostilities Catlin continued to play for Wednesday and after being invalided out of the Army due to stomach trouble in the 1943 he returned to Sheffield to work in a local munitions factory. During this period he was an almost ever present in wartime soccer for Wednesday, playing 71 games in two seasons, and appeared in 1943 War Cup Final defeat to Blackpool, although he missed the second leg due to a serious injury that looked to have finished his career. However Catlin recovered to regain his first team spot and must have been delighted in September 1944 when -in what proved to one of his final appearances for Wednesday – he scored his only goal for the club in the 6-1 home win over Notts County. As his playing career came near to its conclusion Catlin became licensee of the Kelvin Grove Hotel in Sheffield in March 1944 and after giving way to youngster Hugh Swift in 1945 Catlin finally retired in 1946 after almost fifteen years at Wednesday.

Catlin, whose father played rugby for both Driffield and Hull, actually played in goal during his juvenile years and on leaving school he worked as an assistant operator in a cinema – the late night screenings ensuring he played no football for two years. However after being out of work for a year Ted gained employment on the Railways, checking goods as they came in and out of Middlesbrough, and had to get up at five o'clock on a Saturday so he could play football in the afternoon (incidentally Catlin was also a keen cricketer and once took nine wickets in an innings while playing for the Middlesbrough docks team). It was at this point that Catlin switched to full back and he was soon a "schoolboy" star at Boro, where he had signed amateur forms. However it was with Wednesday that Ted made his name and he remained in Sheffield for the majority of his life, being appointed Wednesday scout in August 1947 while later running The Anvil public house in Stannington and The Magnet in Southey Green. In August 1957 he was appointed Chief Scout at Wednesday but early in 1958 was effectively sacked and demoted to a part-time scouting role after "failing to fulfil his duties". After an unsuccessful short spell running a boarding house in Blackpool he returned to Sheffield in September 1965, taking over as Mein Host at The Rose and Crown in Wadsley, near Hillsborough. He remained in the licensing trade for the rest of his life – passing away in 1990 while he was serving behind the bar.

CAWLEY, Thomas Edward "Tom" 1880-92

Born: 2 January 1860 Sheffield
(5ft 9ins, 10st – 1890)
Died: 28 January 1933 Sheffield
Debut: 5 November 1881 v Providence F.A.Cup Away
Last Appearance: 23 January 1892 v Bolton W. F.A.Cup Home
Total League & Cup Appearances: 37*
Goals: 22
***Also appeared in 49 Football Alliance League games**

Career Details:

St.Michael's Juniors	1875
Parkwood/Burton Star	1878
WEDNESDAY	1880
Lockwood Brothers	1886-7

Although Victorian forward Tom Cawley did not appear in league football his significance in the history of Sheffield Wednesday cannot be understated, his actions off the field of play arguably having a greater impact than his on the field contribution. It was in 1887 that Tom, along with other top Wednesday players, formed a side called Sheffield Rovers in direct response to Wednesday's reluctance to bow to calls for them to turn professional. A meeting was subsequently held for Rovers to discuss turning professional but before the vote was taken it was Tom Cawley who stood up and addressed the meeting, asking that Wednesday be given one more chance to join the move to pro status. Thankfully his plea led to The Owls bowing to the inevitable and in hindsight was one of the most significant moments in the club's history – if they had decided not to turn professional it's likely the name of Sheffield Wednesday would not have survived into the 20th Century, never mind the 21st Century.

As a player Tom Cawley earned a reputation for being scrupulously fair with his skill and superb ball control making him stand out in an era of "kick and rush" football. He was greatly respected by his peers and played for over ten years in Wednesday colours – apart from brief appearances for the aforementioned Sheffield Rovers and also Lockwood Brothers – after first appearing for the club in an October 1880 challenge match versus Queens Park at Bramall Lane. His interest in the new game of Association football had started in his schooldays when he watched Parkwood Springs before joining his first club St.Michael's Juniors. In 1878 this team was renamed Burton Star and he continued to play in all their major matches whilst also playing occasionally for Parkwood in local cup games. He was one of the men behind the famous "Zulu" team that enjoyed great popularity between 1879 and 1882 and after becoming established in the Wednesday side he appeared in the opening game played at Olive Grove in 1887 and won a variety of local Cup winners medals, including four Wharncliffe Charity Cup triumphs and back-to-back Sheffield Challenge Cup wins. However the club was now slowly outgrowing local football and as Wednesday started to make an impact on the National stage Cawley was a major player, scoring on a regular basis as the club reached their first F.A.Cup semi-final in 1882, won the inaugural Football Alliance League Championship in 1890 and won through to their first F.A.Cup Final in the same year. Cawley – who could adapt to any position due to his use of brain more than brawn – finished with a losers medal as Wednesday lost that 1890 Cup Final to Blackburn Rovers and in the same year Tom enjoyed a benefit game versus Stoke to mark his ten years service.

He was a true all round sportsman - a keen and excellent cricketer who also won several medals for running – and played 28 representative games for the Sheffield Football Association as well as appearing in an International Trial match in 1889 - his four goals in that game failing to persuade the selectors to give him a cap for his country! After retiring in 1892 Cawley was appointed coach to Wednesday's reserve side and eventually gained an assistant trainer role to Charles Parramore. During the First World War his son Tom Cawley junior guested for Wednesday while in December 1920 Cawley senior was appointed as "advisor" to the club's Board of Directors.

CHALMERS, Bruce 1892-95

Born: 1868 Lanarkshire, Scotland
(5ft 8ins, 12st – 1896)
Debut: 24 December 1892 v Newton Heath
Division One Away
Last Appearance: 23 December 1894 v Everton Division One Away
Total League & Cup Appearances: 28 Goals: 1

Career Details:

Caldervale		
Albion Rovers		1886
Derby County		1890
Albion Rovers		1891
WEDNESDAY	December	1892
Albion Rovers	6 November	1895

Left half-back Bruce Chalmers joined Wednesday during their first season in the Football League, immediately replacing Albert Mumford for the remainder of the campaign. The Scotsman had previously enjoyed a short spell in English football at Derby County and his form in his debut season at Olive Grove ensured he started the 1893-4 campaign as first choice for Wednesday. However the emergence of James Jamieson saw Chalmers demoted to the reserves in the autumn of 1893 and he would play only a handful of games at first team level for the club over the next twelve months before moving back to Scotland in 1895 – his final appearance coming in an 8-1 thrashing at Everton.

His working career had incredibly began as an underground coalman at the tender age of thirteen while he started to play football on a regular basis in this late teenage years, winning representative honours with Lanarkshire for three successive years, starting in 1887. In his final season at Albion Rovers, before moving to Sheffield, he won both the 1892 Ayrshire and Larkhall Charity Cups.

CHAMBERLAIN, Mark Valentine 1985-88

Born: 19 November 1961
Stoke-on-Trent
(5ft 8½ ins, 10st 7lbs – 1985)
Debut: 14 September 1985
v Arsenal
Division One Away
Last Appearance: 22 April 1988
v West Ham United
Division One Home
Total League
& Cup Appearances: 40+48 Goals: 10

Career Details:

Port Vale	1 May	1979
Stoke City	24 August	1982 £125,000
WEDNESDAY	11 September	1985 £300,000 (T)
Portsmouth	22 July	1988 £200,000
Brighton & Hove Albion	20 August	1994 Free
Aidrieonians	August	1995 Trial
Exeter City	11 August	1995 Free
Fareham Town	April	1997
Andover	August	1998
Fareham Town		
Fleet Town		2002-3

Pacy, attacking winger Mark Chamberlain enjoyed a rapid rise to stardom that saw him transformed from a Division Four player to a full England International inside a twelve-month period. His career had started as an apprentice at local club Port Vale in 1977 and after three years as a pro at Vale Park he moved to local rivals Stoke City for a record fee for a basement division player. His impact at City was quite remarkable as after barely half a dozen games his brilliant dribbling skills earned him an England call up – he had only previously been capped at schoolboy level – and his flying header after just three minutes of his first game against Luxembourg in November 1983 was the quickest goal ever scored by an England debutant – his goal was literally a textbook strike as it is now included in an F.A.Coaching manual! Over the next two years Chamberlain won seven more full England caps, plus four U-21 caps, while at club level he appeared in 125 games for The Potters, scoring 18 times. However Stoke's relegation in 1984-5 saw Chamberlain unsettled and he duly moved back into the top-flight to sign for Howard Wilkinson's Wednesday – the fee decided by tribunal after City asked for £750,000 and The Owls offered just £175,000!

His first appearance for Wednesday came from the substitute bench and that was certainly a taste of things to come for Chamberlain as in his first season at Hillsborough, Wilkinson used him almost exclusively in that role (24 of 27 games were as a sub), much to Wednesday fans frustrations. He loved to run at defenders and was certainly a crowd favourite but as his frustrations grew he lost his way somewhat and in the final analysis simply could not secure a regular first team place in three years at Wednesday. Like many wingers he was a confidence player and being a perennial sub under Wilkinson meant Owls fans never really saw the form that won him England honours.

After rejecting a new contract in May 1988 he moved to Portsmouth three months later and would play over 150 games for Pompey before ending his league career playing at right-back – under ex-Owl Peter Fox's management at Exeter City. After leaving St.James' Park he started working as a salesman but in April 1997 returned to football, becoming player-manager at Dr.Martens Southern Division side Fareham Town. He stayed over a year at Town before a two-month playing stint at Andover ended when he returned to Fareham in a playing capacity. Chamberlain – whose brother Neville played league football for several clubs including both Potteries sides - was still appearing regularly in Wessex League football for Town in 2001- while managing the side - but in December of that year was asked to step down as manager, ending a second spell in charge. He now works full-time for Southampton as one of their Academy coaches.

CHAMBERS, Adam Craig 2004

Born: 20 November 1980 West Bromwich
(5ft 10ins, 11st 8lbs – 2004)
Debut: 21 February 2004 v Rushden & Diamonds Division 2 Away
Last Appearance: 1 May 2004 v Luton Town Division Two Away
Total League & Cup Appearances: 9+3 Goals: 0

Career Details:

West Bromwich Albion	8 January	1999
WEDNESDAY	20 February	2004 Loan
Loan Return	May	2004
Released	9 February	2005
Kidderminster Harriers	24 March	2005

Energetic midfielder who spent three months on loan at Wednesday during the disappointing 2003-4 campaign. Although Chambers had appeared in fifteen senior games during the previous season his Baggies career had stalled somewhat and had only a solitary substitute appearance to his name on arriving at Hillsborough. He showed himself to be a pacy, combative central midfield player on his debut – he was not adverse to 'putting his foot in' – but as his loan spell progressed he failed to build on that promising start and was eventually dropped before returning to Albion before the end of the season. Chambers – whose twin brother James is also on Albion's books – first enjoyed a prolonged run in the side during the 2001-02 season when he appeared in 39 league and cup games as Albion earned promotion to the Premier League under Gary Megson.

CHAPMAN, Henry "Harry" 1899-1911

Born: 19 January 1878
Kiveton Park, Sheffield
(5ft 6ins, 11st 7lbs –1907)
Died: 29 September 1916
Debut: 16 February 1901
v Blackburn Rovers
Division One Home
Last Appearance: 28 January 1911
v Notts County
Division One Away
Total League
& Cup Appearances: 299 Goals: 100

Career Details:

Kiveton Park		1896
Worksop Town		1898
Grimsby Town		1898 Trial
Attercliffe		
WEDNESDAY		1899
Hull City	27 April	1911 £200

The outstanding Harry Chapman was without doubt unsurpassed as Wednesday's best inside-forward in the period before the First World War. His attributes were many – he was a tremendous worker, extremely fast and imaginative with an acute tactical brain – and fully deserved the tag as "the finest inside-forward of his day not to be capped". The fact that his country never capped Harry could be attributed to the simple fact that his rival for an England jersey was one Steve Bloomer – a true legend of the game who was a fixture in the national side for a decade. However in club football Chapman had no peers – his all round game was thought even better than Bloomer's – and he was indeed a rare breed of player for his time – one who could play in several positions including attack and defence. His tireless work often saw him doing the job of two men – this earned him great respect among fans and fellow players – and Harry's enthusiasm was well documented. In fact on his first appearance in a Wednesday shirt – in the club's public practice game at The Niagara Grounds in August 1899 – his somewhat over zealous tackling promoted Ambrose Langley to let him know in no uncertain terms that it was not the done thing in pre season games!

His dynamic making and taking of goals made Harry a huge favourite with the early Owlerton crowds but he was not a sole performer. His partnership with right-winger Harry Davis was truly devastating with the diminutive duo nicknamed "the marionettes"; such was their harmony together. In his first season at Wednesday Harry won both Sheffield Association and Wharncliffe League Championship medals with the reserves and it was his form at second team level that eventually led to his debut, initially as a replacement for the injured Jock Wright at inside-left. However it was inside-right Pryce who was actually dropped so Harry could retain his place for the next game, effectively ending the Scotsman's career at Wednesday! From that point on Chapman was a cornerstone of one of Wednesday's most successful periods in their history, his 28-goal haul over two seasons helping Wednesday to consecutive league Championships in 1903 and 1904 while he was in the side that beat Everton to win the 1907 F.A.Cup – Harry's winner in the quarter-final against Liverpool led to him being chaired off the field by ecstatic Wednesdayites.

Chapman – whose brother was of course the legendary Huddersfield Town and Arsenal manager Herbert – was also known as a great trainer and his fitness and courage was no more shown in February 1908 when after breaking his collar bone at Aston Villa he missed only two games before returning to the first team fold! He remained an automatic first choice well into his early 30s and after leaving in 1911 – after being appointed player-coach at Hull City - still played for two more seasons before a broken knee cap, suffered in a reserve team game in September 1912, brought an end to his illustrious playing career. He was then appointed secretary at Hull in March 1913 but within a month was elevated to manager when ex-Wednesday legend Ambrose Langley tendered his resignation. Under his management The Tigers topped Division Two in January 1914, only to fall away and finish seventh, but in September 1914 Harry was forced to resign due to ill health. Unfortunately his story had a sad end as two years later, aged just 38, he died from the dreaded tuberculosis, followed soon after by his wife, leaving two orphaned children who probably grew up not knowing the indelible memory their father had left with Wednesday fans of his era.

CHAPMAN, Lee Roy 1984-88

Born: 5 December 1959 Lincoln
(6ft 2ins, 13st 3lbs – 1984)
Debut: 25 August 1984
v Nottingham Forest
Division One Home
Last Appearance: 7 May 1988
v Liverpool
Division One Home
Total League
& Cup Appearances: 183+4 Goals: 78

Career Details:

Stoke City	August	1976 App.
Stafford Rangers	August	1977 Loan
Stoke City	22 June	1978 Pro.
Plymouth Argyle	5 December	1978 Loan
Arsenal	25 August	1983 £500,000
Sunderland	29 December	1983 £200,000
WEDNESDAY	12 July	1984 £100,000
Niort	30 June	1988 £290,000 (T)
Nottingham Forest	October	1988 £350,000
Leeds United	1 January	1990 £400,000
Portsmouth	11 August	1993 £250,000
West Ham United	11 September	1993 £250,000
Southend United	13 January	1995 Loan
Ipswich Town	19 January	1995 £70,000
Leeds United	11 January	1986 Loan
Swansea City	28 March	1996 Free

An old fashioned style centre-forward whose terrific heading ability was ideally suited to the Owls style of play during his time at Hillsborough. After having started as a trainee at Stoke City – playing three games on loan at Stafford Rangers while still a trainee – Chapman's career had been on an upward curve for several years before a disastrous big money move to Arsenal in the summer of 1983. His time in North London was cut short but he experienced no better fortunes at his next club Sunderland and when Howard Wilkinson brought him to Hillsborough it would be fair to say his career was on the crest of a slump. Despite never being the most graceful of players Chapman's no-nonsense attitude endeared him to fans – voting him player of the year in 1986-7 - and in hindsight his goals record while in a Wednesday shirt was quite remarkable – scoring almost a goal every two games. He regularly finished top scorer and even started to improve his technique on the floor so it was therefore a surprise when he refused a new contract and signed for obscure French Division Two (South) side Niort, after a £600,000 move to Greek club PAOK Salonika had fallen through.

His time in France was as farcical as it was brief as after the two clubs failed to agree a transfer fee a UEFA tribunal set a figure of £290,000. However his new club were financially embarrassed at the size of the fee and simply could not afford to pay Wednesday unless they sold Chapman back to an English side! This is what they duly did – at a nice tidy profit – and Lee found himself back in the First Division quicker than he could ever have imagined. The move back to England was the beginning of a golden period for Lee as in his first season at Forest he won both Full Members Cup and League Cup winners medals – his first honours in the game –before earning both Division Two and Division One Championship medals under his old boss Howard Wilkinson at Leeds United in the early 1990s – coming back to haunt Wednesday in January 1992 when netting a hat-trick at Hillsborough. A marriage to TV star Leslie Ash lifted his off the field profile considerably but after leaving Leeds his career slowly wound down as he had spells at several different clubs in his final three years as a professional until retiring in May 1996 – with a career tally of 253 goals in 679 games. At this point Lee – whose father Roy was a prolific scorer for both Aston Villa and Lincoln City - opened a bar called Barfly in South Kensington and after doubling his money when selling it three months later he opened a Members' Bar and Non-Members restaurant called Teatro in Soho, London – a joint venture with his wife. In the summer of 2000 he opened a second Teatro establishment in Leeds (this later closed down) and also opened a restaurant in Clapham called SO.UK. As well as building his bar and restaurant empire Lee also worked for satellite sport channels.

CHAPMAN, William " Billy" 1923-26

Born: 21 September 1902 Murton
(5ft 6½ ins, 9st 6lbs – 1923)
Died: 2 December 1967 Murton
Debut: 15 March 1924 v Oldham Athletic Division Two Away
Last Appearance: 25 October 1924
v South Shields Division Two Away
Total League & Cup Appearances: 4 Goals: 0

Career Details:

Murton Celtic		
Murton		
Hetton		
Murton Democratic Club		
Sunderland		Trial
WEDNESDAY	May	1923
Manchester United	27 April	1926 £250
Watford	June	1928
Murton Colliery Welfare	August	1934 Free

Despite being on Wednesday's books for three years right winger Billy Chapman made little impression on the first team scene – being kept out by the excellent form of Welsh International winger Rees Williams. He had originally arrived at Hillsborough on trial in April 1923, signing a professional deal in the following month, and started his first season in the reserve team – playing in the club's first ever-home game in the Central League against Aston Villa in September 1923. He remained a reserve regular throughout that debut campaign – his two first team appearances both occurring when Williams was absent – and this pattern was repeated throughout his Owls career as legendary manager Bob Brown slowly found a winning formula. Known to be a fast, tricky and consistent winger Billy eventually moved on to Manchester United at the end of Wednesday's Division Two Championship winning season of 1925-6.

Unfortunately for Chapman – who was known for his lightening speed of acceleration when running onto the ball - he again found himself cast in the role of understudy at Old Trafford, initially to Joe Spence and then, somewhat ironically, to one Rees Williams who had moved from Wednesday! This meant he played only 26 times for The Red Devils before enjoying his best spell in league football while at Watford. In a six-year stay at Vicarage Road he forged a great right wing partnership with Tommy Barnett and appeared in 233 league and cup games for The Hornets before returning home to his roots when signing for Murton Colliery Welfare. He had first played football for Murton Council School and although originally playing at full back he became an outside-right by accident, playing in this position during his early days in the Hetton District Church League. As a schoolboy Billy was a keen supporter of Sunderland but when he gained employment on leaving school as a coalminer in the Durham pits his playing activities ceased completely. However he later re-launched his career at Murton Celtic – winning the Seaham League Championship in his debut season – and after an unsuccessful trial at Sunderland found his way to Wednesday. Contemporary reports of Billy suggest he had a somewhat unique trick when running at speed – he seemed to back heel the ball without actually stopping, causing the marking player to either hesitate or stop completely! After his time at Watford, Chapman played well into his mid-30s at Murton, eventually retiring mid-way through the 1937-8 season.

CHEDGZOY, Sydney "Syd" 1937

Born: 17 February 1911 Liverpool
(5ft 9½ ins, 11st, 4lbs – 1937)
Died: 17 January 1983 Liverpool
Debut: 28 August 1937 v Chesterfield Division Two Away
Last Appearance: 16 September 1937
v Tottenham Hotspur Division Two Home
Total League & Cup Appearances: 4 Goals: 0

Career Details:

Orwell Wednesday		
Wavertree	January	1928
New Brighton	February	1928 Amat.
Burscough Rangers	August	1929 Trial
Everton	April	1929
Burnley	May	1933
Millwall	May	1934
Runcorn	May	1935
Halifax Town	May	1936 Trial
Runcorn	September	1936
WEDNESDAY	13 May	1937 Free
Runcorn	20 October	1937 Free
Swansea Town	May	1938
New Brighton		1939-42 Guest
Cardiff City		1942-43 Guest
Tranmere Rovers		1942-43 Guest
Aberman		WW2 Guest

It would perhaps be fair to say that the signing of right-winger Syd Chedgzoy was a gamble that did not pay off for Wednesday manager Billy Walker. The son of ex-Everton and England International player Sam had brought scouts flocking to Runcorn in the previous season when he netted an amazing 29 times from the right wing as his side lifted the Cheshire League Championship trophy. It was Wednesday who took the risk of bringing him into the professional game but after starting four of the opening six Division Two games of the 1937-8 season he was quickly discarded and returned to Runcorn after less than six months as a Sheffield Wednesday player.

Unfortunately for Syd this pattern of boom and bust was repeated throughout his league career, beginning at Burnley where he appeared in only five league games, netting once. Three more games followed at Millwall before spells at Runcorn and Halifax Town (staying only four weeks at The Shay). After failing to establish himself at Wednesday he tried again to crack league football at Swansea Town and in fact appeared in eighteen league games for The Swans, scoring twice before War ruined his chances of further progress. He later played wartime football for several clubs, including 26 games at New Brighton.

CLARKE, Harry Maurice 1957-58

Born: 29 December 1932 Newcastle
(5ft 8½ ins, 11st – 1959)
Only Appearance:
12 October 1957
v Blackpool
Division One Home
Total League
& Cup Appearances: 1 Goals: 0

Career Details:

Darlington	July	1951
WEDNESDAY	August	1957
Hartlepool United	August	1958
South Shields	July	1962
Horden Colliery Welfare	July	1963
Stockton	July	1969

Inside-forward Harry Clarke was a teenage star at his first club Darlington, making his league debut on Boxing Day 1950 against Bradford City whilst still at school. He would in fact make twenty-one appearances for The Feethams club before signing professional forms – he had joined as an amateur in September 1950 – and before being put on the transfer list in 1957 had scored 27 times in

149 appearances. He was actually put on the transfer list with a £1,500 price tag on his head but after a successful appeal to the Football League was granted a free transfer and duly arrived at Hillsborough for a two-month trial in August 1957.

He signed part-time professional forms for Wednesday on 12th October, just three hours before his making his top-flight debut in the 3-0 home loss to Blackpool, but his promise was never fulfilled at Wednesday and he played only a handful of reserve team games – in addition to that sole first team game – before moving back to the lower leagues to sign for Hartlepool United. The ex-Darlington and Durham County Boys player actually remained a part-time professional throughout his career as he was training to be an architect. His studies meant his national service was deferred until he reached the age of 26 and when enlisting for the Army a Wednesdayite recruitment officer told him to go into the R.A.F. as he could play football all the time and it was easier to get time off to play League football! The Owls fan was right as Harry played for his R.A.F. unit team, The Command Team and was even selected to play representative football against an F.A.XI at Norwich in 1959 – injury sadly denying him the opportunity.

Throughout his national service Harry was almost an ever present for Hartlepool - finishing top scorer in successive seasons – and when he left for South Shields in 1962 had scored a praiseworthy 43 times in 124 senior appearances for United. Until his retirement from football in 1971 Harry played in local northeast non-league soccer and scored over 150 goals as he won a variety of honours. After finishing with professional football he worked as an architect until his retirement.

CLARKE, Matthew John "Matt" 1996-99

Born: 3 November 1973 Sheffield
(6ft 4ins, 12st 8lbs – 1998)
Debut: 11 May 1997
v Liverpool
Premier League Home
Last Appearance: 27 September 1997
v Aston Villa
Premier League Away
Total League
& Cup Appearances: 2+2 Goals: 0

Career Details:

Rotherham United	28 July	1992
WEDNESDAY	10 July	1996 £325,000
Bradford City	5 July	1999 Free
Bolton Wanderers	20 March	2001 Loan
Crystal Palace	7 September	2001 £1,350,000

Although born in Sheffield it was with near neighbours Rotherham United that he forged a reputation as one of the best young keepers in the game. In four seasons as a professional at Millmoor, Clarke amassed 142 league and cup appearances for the Millers, captaining the side to Auto Windscreens Cup success at Wembley in 1996. The tall goalkeeper – who was rather unsurprisingly nicknamed "Matt the Cat"- had superb shot stopping abilities and this combined with his athleticism meant he was destined for a higher grade of football than Rotherham could at the time provide for him. He duly moved the short distance to Hillsborough soon after his Wembley success, initially as understudy to first choice Kevin Pressman, hoping to challenge for the No.1 jersey and become an established Premier League keeper.

However life does not always go exactly to plan and it was almost a year before he made his first team bow, as a sub in the final home game of the season against Liverpool when Pressman was forced off injured. However his debut proved to be a massive anti-climax as only ten minutes after entering the field of play he was taking an early bath as referee David Ellerey controversially sent him off for handling the ball outside of the area – TV replays showed this was in fact not the case. Forward Andy Booth became Wednesday's third goalie in the game and Clarke had to wait until September before again replacing the injured Pressman after just 22 minutes of the home game with Coventry City. Unfortunately his first full game at Hillsborough saw Clarke concede five as Derby County ran riot and soon after Danny Wilson brought Czech International Pavel Srnicek to the club – effectively meaning Matt was demoted to third choice status.

The inevitable parting of the way came when Clarke's contract expired in the summer of 1999, triggering a Bosman free transfer move to Premier League new boys Bradford City. He moved to City as second choice to Gary Walsh but after being given his chance at Anfield in November 1999 performed superbly to keep his rival on the bench. A medial knee ligament injury suffered at Watford in January 2000 meant two months on the sidelines but on recovering his fitness Matt was recalled to the side, playing until the end of the season as City just managed to retain their Premier League status. His form during the early part of the following campaign saw calls for him to receive an England call up but the arrival of new manager Jim Jefferies in December 2000 changed all this as Clarke was dropped – along with several other high salaried players including ex-Owl Benito Carbone. A transfer request followed and the confident and imposing keeper then played eleven games on loan at Bolton Wanderers, helping them to promotion to the Premier league via the play-offs. However the full transfer to Wanderers never materialised and it was Division One club Crystal Palace who paid a huge fee to take Clarke to South East London. After conceding seven goals in his first two games Clarke became the club's undisputed No.1 keeper as Palace strived to regain their place back in the Premier League but sadly in April 2004 he was forced to retire, aged just 30, due to a knee injury. He is now working as a property developer.

CLEMENTS, David "Dave" 1971-73

Born: 16 September 1945 Larne, Northern Ireland
(5ft 8ins, 12st – 1972)
Debut: 31 August 1971
v Middlesbrough
Division Two Away
Last Appearance: 25 August 1973
v Swindon Town
Division Two Away
Total League
& Cup Appearances: 87 Goals: 0

Career Details:

Portadown		
Wolverhampton Wanderers	January	1963 £8,000
Coventry City	July	1964 £1,500
WEDNESDAY	27 August	1971 £55,000
Everton	20 September	1973 £62,500
New York Cosmos	January	1976
Denver Caribous	August	1977
Colorado Rapids		1978

CAPS (@ SWFC) –
NORTHERN IRELAND Full (13) v USSR 22/09/71, v USSR 13/10/71, v Spain 16/02/72, v Scotland 20/05/72, v England 23/05/72, v Wales 27/05/72 v Bulgaria 18/10/72, v Cyprus 12/02/73, v Portugal 28/03/73, v Cyprus 08/05/73, v England 12/05/73, v Scotland 16/05/73, v Wales 19/05/73

For a boy from Larne in Northern Ireland Dave Clements packed a lot into his football career, including multiple caps for his Country, over three hundred top-flight games in England, playing alongside Pele in New York and even managing Northern Ireland for a while. His varied career had started as a striker at Irish league side Portadown from where Wolves paid a sizeable fee to bring the seventeen-year old youngster across the Irish Sea. However, after failing to play a senior game for Wolves they decided to cut their losses and he moved to Midlands neighbours Coventry City at a knock down price. It was at City that boss Jimmy Hill blooded him in the reserves and then introduced him into Division Two football – Clements making a stunning impact by netting eight times in ten league games. Soon after he would win the first of his 48 full caps for Northern Ireland – he already had Youth caps, one Amateur Cap and three U-23 caps – and he was a regular as City won

promotion to Division One for the first time in their history. He was a keenly determined midfielder who possessed a tremendous shot in his left foot and during his time at Highfield Road became a big crowd favourite with Sky Blues fans. Therefore it was a shock when he dropped down a division to sign for Derek Dooley's Wednesday in 1971, after 30 goals in 247 games for City.

Despite having played all his league football in midfield it was at left back that Clements was switched by Dooley early in his first season and over the next two years he missed only a handful of games as Wednesday tried in vain to get back into the First Division. While at Hillsborough he continued to pile up Northern Ireland caps – captaining his country in many – and his commanding displays for club and country meant it was only a matter of time before he moved back into the top-flight of the English game. This duly occurred a week into the 1973-4 campaign when future N.Ireland boss Billy Bingham took him to Goodison Park, immediately moving Clements back into a midfield role. At Everton he matured into an influential midfield playmaker whose superb passing skills set up many an attack for the Toffeemen and played a total of 98 times for the Merseyside club, scoring eight goals. It was during one of these games that he discovered he had been appointed manager of his country, a role he retained until a move to US football effectively cost him the position. However the financial rewards in the NASL and the chance to play alongside Pele were ample consolations and he stayed with Cosmos for six months before being appointed player-manager at Denver Caribous, who were set to join the NASL in the following April. He finished his playing career in America at Colorado Rapids but instead of returning home to the 30-acre farm he had bought for his retirement when he was a teenager, he instead settled in the States. He started his post-football career by running an Irish Goods Store in Georgetown, Colorado but after selling this business now earns his living in St.Peters, Missouri.

CLOUGH, Nigel Howard — 1997

Born: 19 March 1966 Sunderland
(5ft 10ins, 12st 3lbs – 1997)
Debut: 17 September 1997 v Grimsby Town League Cup Away
Last Appearance: 24 September 1997
v Derby County Premier League Home
Total League & Cup Appearances: 2 Goals: 0

Career Details:

AC Hunters (Sun.)		
Heanor Town		
Nottingham Forest	15 September	1984
Liverpool	7 June	1993 £2,275,000
Manchester City	24 January	1996 £1,500,000
Nottingham Forest	12 December	1996 Loan
WEDNESDAY	11 September	1997 Loan
Burton Albion	23 October	1998 Free

Experienced a brief and unsuccessful spell on loan at Wednesday under the managership of David Pleat. The ex-England International joined from struggling Division One outfit Manchester City but it was a case of out of the frying pan and into the fire for Clough as Wednesday sat second bottom in the Premier League with manager Pleat already starting to feel the pressure. There was no doubt that Clough's star was on the wane when he made the surprise switch to Hillsborough and he was obviously short of confidence, failing to make any impact in two disastrous results for Wednesday - an embarrassing two-nil defeat at Grimsby Town in the League Cup and an equally calamitous 5-2 home thrashing by Derby County.

He of course experienced his most productive spell in club football under his father Brian's managership at Nottingham Forest, where after joining from Midland league Heanor Town he amassed 130 goals in 399 games for the City Ground club. During his time at Forest Nigel won many honours, including two League Cup winners medals, two Full Members Cup winners medal and an F.A.Cup runner-up medal in 1991. He was also capped fourteen times at full level by England – in addition to 3 "B" caps and 15 U-21 caps – as at his peak Clough was one of the most intelligent playmakers in the game with his subtle touches creating countless chances. However despite a good start to his Anfield career – a brace on the opening day of the 1993-4 campaign against the Owls giving him a dream start – he quickly became known as an expensive misfit and he failed to nail down a regular place at Liverpool. He looked to resurrect his career at both Manchester City and back on loan at his old side Forest but could just not recapture his International form. After a disastrous time at Maine Road, City paid up the remaining nine months of his £250,000 a year contract in October 1998 and he left after having failed to appear for City since the final day of the 1996-7 season.

He subsequently followed in his father's footsteps by entering club management with Southern League Burton Albion. He took a player-manager role at the Derbyshire club and in his second season led The Brewers to runners-up spot in the Premier Division whilst also capturing the Southern League Cup. Albion finished runners-up again in 2001 but following a switch across the non-league pyramid he finally steered them into the Conference League when Burton ran away with the 2002 Northern Premier League Championship. His charges retained their newly won Conference status in 2002-3 and it seems only a matter of time before Clough Jnr. follows his father into the world of Football League management.

COBIAN, Juan Manuel — 1998-99

Born: 11 September 1975
Buenos Aires, Argentina
(5ft 9ins, 10st 10lbs – 1998)
Debut: 15 August 1998
v West Ham United
Premier League Home
Last Appearance: 1 May 1999
v Nottingham Forest
Premier League Away
Total League
& Cup Appearances: 8+2 Goals: 0

Career Details:

Boca Juniors	1 August	1997
Huracan Corrientes		1997 Season loan
WEDNESDAY	11 August	1998 £250,000
Barnsley	July	1999 Trial
Bolton Wanderers	July	1999 Trial
Charlton Athletic	5 August	1999 Free
Released	22 September	1999
Aberdeen	2 November	1999 Free
Swindon Town	7 July	1999 Free
Contract cancelled	23 January	2003
Club Deportivo Linares		2003
Club Atletico Almagro		

Pacy, diminutive right back Juan Cobian was a surprise capture by Danny Wilson just days before the start of the 1998-9 season. He arrived at Hillsborough from famous Argentinean side Boca Juniors where he had played alongside the likes of Diego Maradona, Claudio Canigga and Juan Veron, signing a one-year contract with a one-year option in the hope of succeeding in the Premier League. A tip off from an International agent had alerted Wednesday to his availability and after flying over for a successful trial he was offered a deal which was swiftly completed in time for Juan to make his English League debut on the opening day of the new season – no work permit was required as Cobian held dual nationality, holding an EU passport thanks to an Italian Grandfather. The tough defender, who speaks perfect English after earning a degree in the language at Buenos Aires' English University, had originally joined Boca at the tender age of ten and gradually progressed through the various age groups to make his senior debut at the age of nineteen. He would play fifteen times at senior level for Argentina's top club – also appearing at U-15, U-18 and U-23 level for his country – but as competition became fierce he was sent out on loan to Rhuracan in 1997-8, appearing in 38 games before crossing the Atlantic to the UK.

After starting seven of the first eight Premier League games in his first English league season Cobian would spend the majority of the remainder of the campaign on the subs bench as Peter Atherton made the right-back spot his own. At the end of the season Wednesday decided not to exercise their one-year option and Juan was released, immediately being taken to Oakwell on trial by Dave

Bassett. However he was released by Barnsley and eventually signed for Premier League Charlton, failing to make a first team appearance for the Valiants before making the long journey North to join Scottish Premier League club Aberdeen. The change of scenery failed to re-launch Juan's career and after playing only four games for The Dons he became one of Colin Todd's first signings as boss of Swindon Town – after Wednesday had tried to re-sign him. Unfortunately his fortunes hit rock bottom in Wiltshire where in two and half years at Swindon he appeared in only nine competitive games, only playing for one minute during the 2001/2 league campaign! Even a scheduled trial at League new boys Boston United in December 2002 was called off due to poor weather and in January 2003 his contract was cancelled by mutual consent, leaving him a free agent. A move to Spanish football came next for the much-travelled South American, signing for CD Linares who play in the Country's regional Third Division – Group 4 of Division B. He returned to his homeland in 2005, signing for Premera club Atletico Almagro.

COCKROFT, Joseph "Joe" 1945-48

Born: 20 June 1911 Barnsley
(5ft 7ins, 10st 12lbs – 1948)
Died: 12 February 1994
Debut: 5 January 1946
v Mansfield Town
F.A.Cup Away
Last Appearance: 16 October 1948
v Grimsby Town
Division Two Home
Total League
& Cup Appearances: 97* Goals: 2
***Also appeared in 198 wartime games, scoring 13 goals**

Career Details:

Yorkshire Paper Mills		
Barnsley Old Boys		
Barnsley		Trial
Ardsley Athletic		
Wombwell Town		
Rotherham United		1931
Gainsborough Trinity		1932
West Ham United	March	1933
Chesterfield		1940 Guest
WEDNESDAY		1940-45 Guest
Huddersfield Town		1941 Guest
WEDNESDAY	21 September	1945 £750
Sheffield United	5 November	1948 £4,000
Wisbech Town		1949

Despite having been born in Barnsley it was with London club West Ham that polished wing-half Joe Cockroft made his name. After playing in local non-league football during the early years of his career it looked like his chances of forging a Football league career had disappeared when Rotherham United released him, after only three games. However The Millers loss proved to be West Ham's gain as after a spending a successful month's trial at Upton Park – he was a Gainsborough Trinity player at the time – he was signed, making his debut on Good Friday 1933 in the one-nil loss at Chesterfield. Incredibly Joe would go on to play in the next 217 games for The Hammers – a club record – and was presented with a cigarette case and lighter by the West Ham Directors to mark the feat when his astonishing run ended in April 1938. Such was his consistency that he was picked in an International trial match for England versus The Rest in 1936 and was in the Hammers side that beat Blackburn Rovers to win the Football League War Cup in 1940 - in total he made 263 peacetime appearances for United.

It is doubtful that Joe would ever have returned to South Yorkshire if his home had not been badly damaged in the London Blitz of 1941 but return he did – much to West Ham's disappointment - to work at Edgar Allen's Steelworks in Sheffield. While working in the City Joe guested for both Chesterfield and Huddersfield but it was with Wednesday that he played the majority of his wartime football, making his debut at Bramall Lane on Christmas Day 1940. After making more appearances in Wartime football than any other Wednesday player – including the 1943 War North Cup Final defeat to Blackpool, scoring a penalty in the first leg – he was officially transferred near the end of the hostilities. He was signed in a player-coach role and just over a year later – in October 1946 – Joe was appointed as a local coach in the Football Association's new soccer coaching in schools initiative (he also spent the summer of 1948 coaching in Finland under the F.A. banner). In the same year Joe played for the Football League against the Army and in the immediate post-war years was a mainstay of Wednesday's Division Two side. However after losing his place to Keith Bannister in October 1948 Cockroft asked for a transfer and twenty-four hours later made the shock switch to neighbours United – the first direct transfer between the clubs since Billy Mosforth way back in 1889!

His move to Bramall Lane was seen by many as a major risk, not least because at the age of 37 he became the oldest player to make his First Division debut. In fact the doom merchants were proved right as Joe would play only twelve games in United colours – also missing two penalties – before dropping out of the league completely to become player-manager at Wisbech Town. He remained three years in The Fens, retiring in April 1952 after the Owls sent a side to play a benefit match for him. He was then briefly a publican before moving back to Sheffield to work in the printing industry until his retirement.

CODD, Ronald William "Ronnie" 1953

Born: 3 December 1928 Sheffield
(5ft 10ins, 11st 2lbs – 1953)
Debut: 21 March 1953
v Chelsea
Division One Away
Last Appearance: 28 March 1953
v Manchester United
Division One Home
Total League
& Cup Appearances: 2 Goals: 0

Career Details:

Meynell Road YC	September	1946
Bolton Wanderers	March	1950
WEDNESDAY	16 March	1953 £2,500
Bolton Wanderers	30 June	1953 Free
Barrow	October	1953 Free
Peterborough United	June	1956 Free
Spalding United		1957 Free
Burton Albion		1959 Free
Hyde United		1960 Free

Centre-forward Ronnie Codd was involved in one of the strangest transfers in Wednesday's history. It was ironic that he came from Bolton's reserve team as the first possible replacement for the stricken Derek Dooley as both had attended the same Meynell Road school and had been such firm friends as boys that they took family holidays together! His £12,500 move to Hillsborough was dependent upon medical reports about a long standing knee injury and whether this could stand up to the rigours of First Division football. The joint verdict by club doctor Andrew Stephen and Sheffield specialist Mr.F.W.Holdsworth was no and Codd seemed set to return from whence he came without appearing for the Owls. However when the clubs met in March 1953 they agreed that Codd could stay at Hillsborough until the summer, with Wednesday paying a small fee for his services, and if they were happy with his fitness they could pay the outstanding balance of his transfer fee. In hindsight the purchase of a reserve team striker with a knee injury would seem somewhat foolhardy and this proved the case as he would appear only twice for Wednesday's first team – the Owls failing to score in either – before playing out his "loan" spell in the reserves.

His career had started in schoolboy football – playing along side Albert Quixall - and after finishing his education Ronnie started work as an accountant, whilst playing for several minor sides in the Sheffield area. His playing career really started to flourish when he signed for Meynell Road as he was spotted by Bolton

Wanderers scout Steve Shepard - subsequently joining the Lancashire club's ground staff. The teenager started his National Service in January 1947, joining the R.A.F., and whenever he could get a Saturday off played for Bolton's "A" team. It was in the services that Codd first experienced problems with his knee as after being injured while playing for the R.A.F. he underwent a cartilage operation. He left the forces in 1949 to turn professional with Bolton and experienced a baptism of fire on his debut when he was picked ahead of legendary forward Nat Lofthouse for the home game with Arsenal in December 1950! The home crowd groaned at his selection but after he had set up two goals in a 3-0 win the local newspaper headlines was "Codd cures groaners". However he was never a regular at Bolton, appearing in only two more games on his return from Wednesday – taking his career tally at the Burden Park club to just thirty-one.

He eventually moved down the divisions to sign for Barrow but after requiring a second knee operation his league career came to a close after scoring eleven times in forty-five matches for the Cumbrian club. After signing for Midland League Peterborough United Ronnie re-activated his accountancy career while at his next club – Eastern Counties League Spalding United – a third operation was required, this time to remove a small piece of cartilage. At Spalding he could be found playing at inside-left, partnering ex-Newcastle United player George Hair, but when the club slashed their wage bill at the end of the 1958-9 season it became uneconomical for Codd to travel to deepest Lincolnshire. He therefore signed for Southern League Burton Albion where in his one season Codd was almost ever present, scoring 16 goals in 49 appearances as The Brewers finished second from bottom. His final club would prove to be Cheshire League Hyde United as ongoing knee problems finally led to his retirement in 1961 – he would only play the occasional charity game from that point onwards. A full time move into the Accountancy profession came when he hung up his boots although he did keep active by joining Dronfield Cricket club. He later played for ten years at Parkhead CC and is now retired and living in Sheffield – he was a season ticket holder at Wednesday for many years.

COLE, William 1897-1901

Born:
Debut: 17 September 1898
v Bolton Wanderers Division One Away
Last Appearance: 19 January 1901
v Notts County Division One Away
Total League & Cup Appearances: 10 Goals: 1

Career Details:

WEDNESDAY	June	1897
Worksop Town		1901

Of all the players to have played League football for Wednesday William Cole is perhaps the biggest mystery of them all. What is known in that he arrived at Olive Grove in 1897, making his debut for the club's reserve team in the 3-0 United Counties League win at Sheepbridge Works in September of the same year. He would solely play second team football in his first season - winning a UCL Championship medal - appearing in the main at inside-right although he also played at both centre-forward and inside-left. He netted five times for the reserves in that season and got his first team chance early in the following campaign, scoring with a header only for it to be disallowed for offside in a 0-0 draw at Bolton Wanderers.

Unfortunately for Cole the Owls were experiencing their worst season since entering the league in 1892 and by April had suffered not only relegation to Division Two but also lost their home at Olive Grove. To compound matters for Cole his favoured position of inside-right had been taken by Harry Davis so it was on the right wing and at right back that he would make three further appearances in the 1898-99 season – scoring in the 1-1 draw at Nottingham Forest in January 1899. With John Pryce the man in possession of the No.8 shirt during Wednesday's Second Division Championship winning season of 1899-00 Cole was switched to right-back on a permanent basis by the Owls hierarchy and quickly became established as understudy to Billy Layton. In his new role Cole was almost ever present as the reserve team celebrated the clubs new ground at Owlerton by incredibly losing only once in 37 competitive games to win three trophies – the Sheffield Challenge Cup, Sheffield Association League and Wharncliffe Charity Cup League. It was the same story for Cole in the next season as just two defeats and 110 goals saw the Championship of the newly expanded fifteen-team Association league retained. However despite making three further league appearances, due to Layton's absence, he probably knew he would never replace his rival and therefore moved to Midland Counties League Worksop Town in 1901.

COLEMAN, Anthony George "Tony" 1969-70

Born: 2 May 1945 Crosby, Liverpool
(5ft 8ins, 11st 6lbs – 1969)
Debut: 4 October 1969
v Ipswich Town
Division One Away
Last Appearance: 22 April 1970
v Manchester City
Division One Home
Total League
& Cup Appearances: 27+1 Goals: 2

Career Details:

Marine		1960
Stoke City	18 August	1961 App.
Ellesmere Port Town		1962
Tranmere Rovers	8 October	1962
Preston North End	19 May	1964 £10,000
Bangor City		1965
Doncaster Rovers	19 November	1965
Manchester City	16 March	1967 £12,000
WEDNESDAY	1 October	1969 £15,000
Blackpool	27 July	1970 £12,000
Cape Town		1972
Durban City		1973
Southport	8 November	1973
Stockport County	14 June	1974 £5,000
Macclesfield Town		1976

Although his impact at Hillsborough was limited the career of left-winger Tony Coleman is perhaps the most fascinating and eventful of any player who has pulled on the famous blue and white shirt. After finishing his education Coleman worked on the Mersey tugboats while playing Lancashire Combination football for Marine. However he was then signed as an apprentice by Stoke City but lasted only seven months before being sacked by City in March 1962 for disciplinary reasons! It was back to non-league football at Cheshire League Ellesmere Port next – while working as a fireman on the railways – before signing a professional contract with Tranmere Rovers, following a successful trial period. Coleman's league debut came at Liverpool's unofficial third club but after just eight games he was sold to Lancashire rivals Preston North End.

However at Deepdale his ill discipline surfaced again and after one goal in five league games his club lost patience and it was back to non-league soccer! This time Coleman started work as an apprentice plumber – while playing for Bangor City – but his roller coaster career was just about to hit the heights as within four years the original T.C. had won an F.A.Cup and League Championship medal! This dramatic rise started when Bill Leivers took him to Doncaster Rovers, putting him straight into the side that won the Fourth Division title six months later – incidentally in May 1966 Coleman was suspended for twenty-eight days by the F.A. after he swung a punch at referee John Pickles as he left the field after being sent off! His explosive form with the ball for Donny alerted Manchester City to his talents and he duly moved to Maine Road – incredibly on joining City Coleman was quoted, in all seriousness, that the problem with moving to Maine Road was that City went on close season foreign tours, therefore denying T.C. one of his great pleasures in life – selling ice cream on the beach at Crosby!!

At City the stockily built winger, who was sharp on Scouse humour and of course no stranger to problems was famously described by Chief Coach Malcolm Allison as "like a nightmare of a delirious probation officer". He could certainly be described as a "character "but this mattered little to City fans as his performances down the left wing left a trial of bewildered, bruised and booked full backs in his wake, helping City to the 1968 League Championship. The 1969 F.A.Cup triumph followed but the inevitable parting of ways came in October 1969 – after 16 goals in 102 games - when Danny Williams brought him to relegation threatened Wednesday. At Hillsborough, Tony played just à solitary season, his moment to remember coming in what proved to be his final league appearance when he netted the equaliser in the famous relegation decider against his old club in April 1970 – he played twice more at Hillsborough in the end of season Anglo-Italian Cup, being sent off in the home game with Napoli! Defeat to Manchester City of course meant Division Two football for Wednesday but Coleman by this time had moved to Blackpool before a spell in South African football – earning Championship and Castle Cup winners medals with Cape Town in 1972. Before quitting professional football at the age of just 30 he played a total of 53 games for Southport and Stockport County, ending his playing career at Northern Premier League Macclesfield Town. After leaving the Cheshire club T.C. ran a café in Waterloo – in his native Liverpool – before moving to Australia. He currently lives in Brisbane and works for the Queensland Railways.

COLEMAN, Simon 1993-94

Born: 13 June 1968 Worksop, Notts.
(6ft, 10st 8lbs – 1996)
Debut: 4 December 1993
v Liverpool
Premier League Home
Last Appearance: 10 September 1994
v Nottingham Forest
Premier League Away
Total League
& Cup Appearances: 16+5 Goals: 1

Career Details:

Mansfield Town	27 July	1985
Middlesbrough	26 September	1989 £600,000
Derby County	15 August	1991 £300,000
WEDNESDAY	30 November	1993 £250,000
Bolton Wanderers	5 October	1994 £350,000
Wolverhampton Wanderers	2 September	1997 Loan
Southend United	20 February	1998 Free
Rochdale	10 July	2000 Free
Released	29 May	2002
Ilkeston Town	August	2002 Free
Hyde United	13 March	2003 Free

The loan signing of centre-half Simon Coleman by Owls boss Trevor Francis was a surprise to many Wednesday fans and when his move was made permanent on 18 January 1994 it was perhaps a bigger surprise as the no frills defender had only played a bit part in Wednesday's Premier League side. However it was an injury in early January to regular left back Nigel Worthington that probably prompted the full transfer, Coleman appearing in five consecutive games in the unaccustomed full back role. Despite this run in the side Coleman – who had a tendency to go forward for set pieces - was never anything more than a squad player in his time at Wednesday and never really endeared himself to the Owls fans who were more accustomed to the silky skills of Des Walker!

He had arrived at Hillsborough with an impressive record to his name that had began with 113 games at Mansfield Town, prompting a big money move to Middlesbrough. In two years at the Ayresome Park side he played seventy games and that consistency brought another move – this time to Premier League Derby County. Again the tall stopper was a integral part of the Rams side and played over a hundred times before dropping into the lower leagues to sign for Southend United on a free transfer. He eventually dropped out of league football after two years at Rochdale and after a short time with Southern League Ilkeston Town switched across the non-league pyramid to sign for Unibond Premier League strugglers Hyde United. He retired from playing in May 2003 and now works as 'Head of Football Development' at Garibaldi College in Mansfield.

*Date of birth confirmed with player

COLLIER, William 1924-25

Born: 11 December 1892 Kirkcaldy, Scotland
(5ft 10ins, 12st – 1924)
Died: 17 April 1954 Dunfermline
Debut: 30 August 1924
v Crystal Palace
Division Two Away
Last Appearance: 14 March 1925
v Port Vale
Division Two Home
Total League
& Cup Appearances: 14 Goals: 0

Career Details:

Raith Rovers	14 August	1912
Kirkcaldy United		1915 Loan
Victoria Hawthorns		Loan
Cowdenbeath		Trial
WEDNESDAY	9 June	1924 £510
Kettering Town	18 May	1925 Free*
Dartford		1929 Free

*No fee as Kettering non-league club

Not many players could say they had been shipwrecked while on club duty but centre-back William Collier could! In the summer of 1923 he set sail, along with his Raith Rovers teammates, in the "Highland Loch" steamer, bound for Buenos Aires, Argentina. The club's destination were the Canary Islands for a series of friendly games but in early morning on July 1st the players and officials were awoken by a terrific crash during a violent storm. It transpired the ship had run aground on a sandbank near Corruedo, Northern Spain and it was everybody overboard! A fishing boat rescued all the squad – many of who were still in their pyjamas – and after a few days in emergency accommodation their journey was completed on a passing P & O. liner. Incidentally also on board was William Inglis who moved to Hillsborough along with Collier in 1924.

The big and hefty stopper – today's defensive midfielder – had signed for Raith Rovers in 1912 but played little before joining the Army in 1914 - serving with distinction in the famous Black Watch and winning the D.C.M. at the Battle of the Somme in 1916. After the War, Bill returned to Starks Park and within two years had won his solitary cap for Scotland – in February 1922 versus Wales. He was a member of the Raith team that included the legendary "famous five" forward line that included future Preston and Arsenal legend Alex James. Unfortunately Raith did not have the resources to hold onto such talents and all five were eventually sold, along with Collier and Inglis. It was Wednesday boss Bob Brown, who was slowly building a side at Hillsborough that would win both Second and First Division Championships within the next five years, who brought the former to Sheffield. In the previous season Tom Brelsford and Oliver Levick had shared duties at left half-back but with the former sold to Barrow and the latter out of favour it was Collier who Brown hoped would cement a place in the Owls Division Two side. However despite starting nine of the first eleven games of the new campaign he was displaced by William Powell and the die was cast near the end of the season when – following another mini-run at first team level – Billy Marsden dropped back to half-back, a move that would eventually bring him England honours in that position. Incidentally in November 1924 Collier turned down a chance to play football in the US.

With such competition for places Wednesday let Collier move to non-league Kettering Town in 1925 where he became both coach and Captain. He enjoyed great success at The Poppies leading them to consecutive fourth placed finishes in the Eastern Division of the Southern league before winning the section in 1927 (and the play-off 5-0 against Western winners Bristol City reserves). After he turned down an offer to become manager at his old club Raith Rovers in the summer of 1927 the Eastern section title was retained in 1928 – surprisingly losing at home to Plymouth reserves in the play-off – before Bill moved to fellow Southern league outfit Dartford as player-manager in 1929. His new side had finished near the foot of the league in 1928-9 but with Collier in charge he built a side that within two years had won the Divisional title and then beaten Exeter City reserves to claim the overall Championship. After retiring he later ran a public house in Dunfermline, where he passed away in the mid-1950s.

COLLINS, John Lindsay 1976

Born: 21 January 1949
Bedwellty, Wales
(5ft 8ins, 10st 10lbs – 1976)
Debut: 14 August 1976
v Grimsby Town
League Cup Away
Last Appearance: 2 November 1976
v Rotherham United
Division Three Home
Total League
& Cup Appearances: 11 Goals: 0

Career Details:

Tottenham Hotspur	March	1966
Portsmouth	12 May	1971 £20,000
Dallas		1973
Halifax Town	12 August	1974 £8,000
WEDNESDAY	14 July	1976 £3,000
Barnsley	2 December	1976 £3,000
Kidderminster Harriers	July	1980 Free
Baltimore	August	1980 *

* Six-a-side Professional club

Left-back John Collins was a Swansea boys and Welsh Schoolboy International before signing apprentice forms for First Division Tottenham Hotspur in April 1964. Soon after being elevated to the professional ranks at White Hart Lane he appeared twice in League soccer for Spurs but with competition for first team places fierce he would spend the remainder of his time in North London playing Combination football with Tottenham reserves – from where he earned five Welsh U-23 caps in the late 1960s. A change of scenery was needed and a move to Portsmouth saw the left footed Collins achieve his goal of regular first team football, playing eighty-seven times over three seasons at Fratton Park (gaining two more U-23 caps) before signing for Halifax Town. He was first choice full back at The Shay but after relegation from Division Three in 1976 Collins was brought to Hillsborough by Len Ashurst to fill the problem position.

In the previous season the left back spot had been shared by three different players but with only Jimmy Mullen remaining from the trio after a summer clearout reinforcements were required and so the Welshman moved to Hillsborough. However despite starting the first three games of the season – the Owls being unbeaten in all three – he soon found he was in direct competition with Mullen for a first team spot. It's a duel he may have eventually won but this became academic when compatriot Dave Rushbury arrived from Swansea City in November 1976 and was immediately installed as first choice left back. Within weeks Collins was on loan to neighbours Barnsley, a move that was made permanent in February 1977. In fact his best spell in League soccer would come at Oakwell, playing over one hundred games for The Tykes and earning promotion from Division Three in 1979. He moved to non-league Kidderminster Harriers in the summer of 1980 but after playing a few pre season games for "Kiddy" decided to accept an offer to play for a professional indoor six-a-side team based in Baltimore, USA. While in America John did some coaching before moving back to the United Kingdom and entering the licensing trade – managing hotels and public houses. He is now thought to be running a Hotel in Southern Ireland.

COLLINS, Patrick Paul 2004-

Born: 4 February 1985 Newcastle
(6ft 2ins, 12st 8lbs – 2004)
Debut: 7 August 2004
v Colchester United
League One Home
Total League
& Cup Appearances: 29+4 Goals: 1

Career Details:

Sunderland		
WEDNESDAY	27 May	2004 Free
Swindon	1 August	2005 Loan to 31/12/05

CAPS (@SWFC)

England U-20 (1)	v Holland 10/10/04

Defender Patrick Collins initially arrived at Hillsborough on trial in March 2004, after being told by Sunderland he would not be offered a professional contract. Whilst a trainee at the Wearside club the tall and athletic defender had won caps at U-18 level for England and looked set to make his first team bow after being recalled from a tournament in Eqypt - by manager Howard Wilkinson - to join the Sunderland senior squad. However he failed to make the matchday sixteen and in the spring of 2004 underwent trials at eight different sides, including Glasgow Celtic and Birmingham City, before signing for Chris Turner. With no league experience under his belt it was expected Collins would be left in the reserves to develop but a pre season injury crisis saw the youngster thrust onto the first team frame for the opening game of the season. He was one of the bright spots of a miserable day and over the next few months Collins proved somewhat of a revelation as he started the first 25 games of the new season, mainly appearing at right back with the occasional switch to central defence.

A minor injury saw the youngster lose his place just before Christmas and it would be early April before Collins started another league game. He then became a squad regular for the remainder of the season and his now trademark surging runs from full back were an occasional feature as Wednesday went all the way to Cardiff to the League One Play Off Final. The still inexperienced Collins was handed a place on the subs bench for the showpiece occasion and entered the fray for the final fifteen minutes of normal time - subsequently playing extra time and being on the field to celebrate the highlight of his fledgling career as Wednesday won promotion to the Championship

COLLINS, Wayne Anthony 1996-98

Born: 4 March 1969 Manchester
(6ft, 12st – 1997)
Debut: 17 August 1996
v Aston Villa
Premier League Home
Last Appearance: 28 December 1997
v Leicester City
Premier League Away
Total League
& Cup Appearances: 19+15 Goals: 6

Career Details:

Lancaster City		
Maine Road		
Winsford United		
Crewe Alexandra	29 July	1993 £10,000
WEDNESDAY	31 July	1996 £600,000
Fulham	23 January	1998 £400,000
Preston North End		2001 Trial
Crewe Alexandra	9 August	2001 Free
Contract cancelled	26 March	2003
Stockport County	7 July	2003 Trial

Utility player Wayne Collins arrived at Hillsborough after a superb season for Crewe where he appeared in forty-two league games from right back – taking his Crewe tally in that first spell to an impressive 147 games. He had joined the professional ranks at a relatively late stage, after playing in northwest non-league soccer for many years – appearing under the name of Wayne Grant for the whole period. His move from Crewe to Premier League Sheffield Wednesday was certainly welcomed by his old club Winsford as the Cheshire club had wisely inserted a sell on clause when he first moved to Gresty Road and the £88,000 they subsequently received wiped out all their debts in one go!

Under the tutelage of Dario Gradi at Crewe, Collins developed into an excellent lower division player, equally at home in midfield or at full back. It was in the former position that Wayne would play the majority of his games at Wednesday, after making his debut on the opening day of the 1996 season in the 2-1 win over Aston Villa. He was ever present as the Owls made a sensational start to the season – topping the Premier League for the only time in their history – but unfortunately for Wednesday and Collins he was injured after just six games and could only watch from the sidelines as David Pleat's side slipped from the summit. It would be several months before Collins regained his fitness and with the likes of Orlando Trustfull and Regi Blinker newly arrived he could not force his way back into the team – starting only two more league games after returning from injury. In the following campaign he developed a useful knack of scoring – five of his six goals in a Wednesday shirt came in 1997-8 – but his days looked numbered in December 1997 when new manager Ron Atkinson withdrew him at Filbert Street after Collins had himself entered the fray from the subs bench.

In fact he did not play another game for Wednesday and a month later joined the gravy train to Kevin Keegan's big spending Fulham. A Division Two Championship medal came his way in 1999 and in March 2000 he won International caps for The Cayman Islands. As Al Fayed's resources powered Fulham to the Premier League Collins' first team involvement decreased and during the The Cottagers Division One Championship season of 2000-1 he appeared in only five league games before being released in the summer of 2001 when his contract expired. He duly returned to his first professional club and stayed there until his contract was cancelled by mutual consent in March 2003.

CONWELL, Anthony "Tony" 1949-55

Born: 17 January 1932 Bradford
(5ft 9½ ins, 11st 7lbs – 1954)
Debut: 19 August 1953
v Manchester City
Division One Home
Last Appearance: 12 February 1955
v Portsmouth
Division One Home
Total League
& Cup Appearances: 47 Goals: 0

Career Details:

Bradford North Wing YC		
Bradford Rovers		
WEDNESDAY	15 January	1949
Huddersfield Town	18 July	1955 *
Derby County	June	1959 £6,000
Doncaster Rovers	2 July	1962 Free
Released	5 May	1964

* Conwell and Marriott exchanged for Shiner and Staniforth

After starting his career in Bradford non-league football – while training to be a bricklayer – full back Tony Conwell joined the Owls as a part-time professional at the tender of age of sixteen in 1949. He was elevated to full-time status just two weeks later and over the next four-seasons served his football apprenticeship in the club's junior and reserve sides, as well as doing his two-years National Service. His speed and keen tackling at right back made him a difficult opponent for any winger to overcome and he was handed a first team chance at the start of the 1953-4 season – in preference to Vin Kenny. He would go on to miss only two of the first twenty-three league games of the season before Kenny took his place just before Christmas 1953. He was given another run at first team level during the relegation season of 1954-55 but the arrival of Jack Martin in February 1955 effectively brought the curtain down on his Wednesday career and in the following summer he was one of four players involved in a swap deal that took him to First Division neighbours Huddersfield Town.

He enjoyed a highly successful time at Leeds Road – becoming a favourite with Town fans due to his whole-hearted attitude – and played over one hundred times before joining Derby County. He also appeared in over one hundred games for The Rams but by this time was starting to feel the effects of an arthritic problem in his hips and eventually left on a free transfer – a move that shocked County fans. Despite his fitness problems Tony played several starring roles at his next club Doncaster Rovers, including a display in September 1962 that kept Birmingham City's newly capped England player Mike Hellawell quiet. Unfortunately two months later in the home F.A.Cup tie against Tranmere Rovers Conwell had the misfortune to suffer not only a broken leg but also a dislocated ankle – injuries that put him on the sidelines for the remainder of the season. He recovered however to play nineteen games in the season that followed, appearing mainly at left back plus a one-game stint at centre-forward, before the arthritis brought a premature end to his league career – in later life he would have both hips replaced.

He made a solitary appearance for a non-league club back in his home City of Bradford before retiring from soccer to take a job with a Doncaster based concrete manufacturing firm that was owned by a Rovers Director. He later sold liquid fertilizer to the farming trade for a year before moving back to Bradford where he bought a milk round. After four years of early mornings Tony returned to his original trade of bricklaying, a trade he was employed in until his retirement in 1996.

COOKE, Terence John "Terry" 2000-01 & 2003-04

Born: 5 August 1976 Birmingham
(5ft 7ins, 9st 9lbs – 2001)
Debut: 23 September 2000
v Preston North End
Division One Home
Last Appearance: 8 May 2004
v Queens Park Rangers
Division Two Home
Total League
& Cup Appearances: 35+8 Goals: 3

Career Details:

Manchester United	1 July	1994
Sunderland	29 January	1996 Loan
Birmingham City	28 November	1996 Loan
Wrexham	30 October	1998 Loan to 09/01/99
Manchester City	14 January	1999 £1,000,000
Wigan Athletic	7 March	2000 Two-month loan
WEDNESDAY	19 September	2000 Loan
Loan Return	28 November	2000
WEDNESDAY	15 December	2000 Loan
Loan Return	2 January	2001
Grimsby Town	28 March	2001 Loan
Sheffield United	March	2002 Trial
Loan Return	22 April	2002
Grimsby Town	5 July	2002 Free
Released	30 June	2003
Bury	July	2003 Trial
WEDNESDAY	8 August	2003 Free
Released	30 June	2004
Chesterfield	July	2004 Trial
Barnsley	August	2004 Trial
Peterborough	September	2004 Trial
Kidderminster Harriers	October	2004 Trial
Oldham Athletic	October	2004 Trial
Colorado Rapids	24 March	2005 Free

Old fashioned style winger who experienced two spells on loan at Hillsborough before signing on a permanent basis in 2003, following a successful pre season trial. He was initially brought to Hillsborough by new manager Paul Jewell as Wednesday struggled to adapt to life outside of the Premier League and like the majority of wingers he was an inconsistent performer – excellent one week, anonymous the next. He had a tendency to hug the touchline and occasionally produced the form that had made him a teenage starlet at Old Trafford during the mid-1990s. He had joined Manchester United straight from school as a trainee in July 1992 – having been with their centre of excellence from aged 13 – and was part of the United Youth side that won the 1995 F.A.Youth Cup against Tottenham Hotspur – Cooke scoring both goals as the two-legged final finished two-a-piece – United winning on penalties. The right-winger had already won eight caps for England at U-18 level and would earn four U-21 caps in 1996 as he became established in United's reserve side. Central League Championship medals would follow in 1996 and 1997 but he simply could not make the big breakthrough into Alex Ferguson's first team – making only nine competitive appearances for United - and in almost five years as a professional at Old Trafford Cooke played the majority of his first team football while on loan at a variety of clubs – he missed the whole of the 1997-8 season through injury.

In almost five years as a professional at Old Trafford, Cooke had played only thirty first team games at five different clubs and it was obvious a move was needed if his career was to progress. This duly happened in April 1999 as following a successful three-month loan spell at cross-City rival Manchester City he signed for a fee that rose by £400,000 to £1m following City's dramatic promotion from Division Two. In one of the most sensational play-off finals ever City scored twice in the last two minutes to take the game with Gillingham into extra-time and Cooke would net one of the subsequent penalty kicks as his new club won 3-1 in the shoot out. He played the best football of his career during his early years at Maine Road - becoming the darling of the Manchester City fans – with his direct, pacy wing play usually climaxing in an accurate cross. He also proved to be a danger at set pieces – once scoring twice at Reading with efforts from outside the area – and looked set to be a fixture in the side after signing a three-year contract. However he was unable to find the consistency required during City's 1999-00 Division One promotion campaign and following the home game with Huddersfield Town in November 1999 became the "forgotten man"- dropping into reserve team football before asking to be placed on the transfer list in February of the following year. His fall from Division Two hero to Division One zero had indeed been dramatic and after starting only six games in his first full season at Maine Road he failed to make a single appearance during the club's Premier League campaign. In fact his only first team soccer during that period came while on loan at Wigan (ten appearances), Wednesday and Grimsby Town (three games) – somewhat mirroring his experiences at Old Trafford. After playing a small part in keeping both Wednesday and Grimsby in Division One he became a free agent in 2002 and duly returned to Blundell Park, signing a one-year contract. After a mixed year on the East Coast he was given a chance by Chris Turner to resurrect his career back at Wednesday and he duly put pen to a one-year deal in August 2003. Made a great start to his third spell at Wednesday but a broken leg and then medial ligament damage affected his form and fitness and Cooke was released in the summer of 2004.

COOPER, Alfred 'Alf' — 1919-20

Born: Brampton, Manchester
Debut: 20 September 1919
v Notts County
Division One Away
Last Appearance: 4 October 1919
v Sheffield United
Division One Away
Total League
& Cup Appearances: 3 Goals: 0

Career Details:

Manchester United		
Hartington Colliery		
Middleton		
WEDNESDAY	September	1914
Rotherham Town	July	1920

The disastrous 1919-20 season saw Wednesday use a record number of players – forty-three in total - and many made only very brief cameo appearances before disappearing from view. One such individual was tricky winger Alf Cooper who started three consecutive games, including two derby games against the Blades, but simply failed to make a lasting impression and was one of twenty-one players cleared out at the end of the season following relegation. He had signed league forms just before World War One started after having failed to make the grade at Manchester United before dropping into non-league soccer with Middleton. The left-winger served in the Army during the Great War and had to recover from two bouts of rheumatism to gain a place in Wednesday's first team. He eventually joined Yorkshire neighbours Rotherham Town but remained in non-league football for the rest of his senior career.

COOPER, Anthony — 1919-20

Born: 7 April 1893 Sheffield
(5ft 9ins, 12st)
Died: 12 November 1974 Chesterfield
Only Appearance: 20 September 1919
v Notts County Division One Away
Total League & Cup Appearances: 1 Goals: 0

Career Details:

Beighton FC		
Birmingham		
Hardwick Colliery		
WEDNESDAY	May	1919
Barnsley		

Like his namesake, Anthony Cooper appeared briefly for the Owls during the relegation season of 1919-20 when he was one of four players to make their only appearance for the club, before being released. He had joined in pre season but struggled to even become a Midland League regular so it was therefore a surprise when given his top-flight chance in the away game at Notts County. Unfortunately he failed to impress as Wednesday extended their winless start to the season to six games and he dropped out of contention completely before signing for Barnsley – failing to make a league start for the Tykes. One curiosity about Cooper was that his surname was actually Routledge!

COOPER, Joseph "Joe" — 1921

Born: 1899 Newbold, nr Chesterfield
(6ft, 11st 12lbs)
Died: 22 January 1959 Cleethorpes
Only Appearance: 7 May 1921 v Bristol City Division Two Away
Total League & Cup Appearances: 1 Goals: 0

Career Details:

Sheepbridge Works		
Saltley College		
West Bromwich Albion		1919 Amat.
WEDNESDAY	5 May	1921 Trial
Chesterfield	24 June	1921
Notts County	March	1923 £1,500
Grimsby Town	September	1924 £1,000
Lincoln City	July	1932

Joe Cooper holds a unique place in Wednesday's long history as he is the only player to appear in a league fixture for the club while only on trial. His solitary appearance came in the final game of the 1920-1 season – a one-nil win in the West Country – before joining neighbours Chesterfield seven weeks later. A schoolteacher by profession Cooper had first played football for Derbyshire club Sheepbridge Works, while attending Dronfield Grammer School. He continued his education in Birmingham, playing for his college side, and after a trial with West Brom he signed amateur forms for the Hawthorns based club. However he failed to appear in league football for The Baggies and after obtaining his release from scholastic duties at Saltley College he joined Bob Brown's Wednesday side in the final week of the season.

Soon after making his solitary appearance for Wednesday Joe took up a teaching post in Chesterfield and subsequently signed professional forms for The Spireities. Chesterfield had just re-gained their league status and over the next two seasons the centre-forward would lead the line with distinction, scoring 12 times in 53 league games. His cultured play attracted the attentions of several possible suitors and it was Notts County who won the chase for his signature – agreeing to pay Chesterfield a fee that equalled their club record. However throughout his football career Joe continued to work as a teacher and this part-time status obviously brought it's own problems with training and availability. This caused County to become frustrated and when they asked him to turn fully professional in the summer of 1924 his refusal led directly to a transfer to Grimsby Town.

However this transfer proved highly beneficial for Joe as he experienced his best spell in League football at Cleethorpes as Town rose from regional football to Division One inside three years. It was from inside-right that Cooper appeared in thirty league games for Town in 1924-5, scoring eleven times, and matched that tally in 1925-6 as the Division Three (North) Championship came to Blundell Park. He remained a regular as Town adjusted to their new surroundings in Division Two and scored five times in just nine league games as The Mariners won promotion to Division One for the first time in their history in 1929 – unfortunately Joe was badly hurt in a January 1929 Cup Tie versus old club West Bromwich Albion and was on the sidelines for ten months. He regained his fitness to make a First Division debut in November 1929 and played in the final six games of the season when Town performed a remarkable escape from relegation – winning five of those matches to avoid the drop by a single point – the only defeat of the sequence coming against Sheffield Wednesday! In the season that followed, the versatile Cooper switched positions again – this time to inside-left – and despite his teaching commitments appeared in twenty league games as Town retained their lofty status for another season. He appeared regularly again in 1931-2 – taking his Grimsby tally to 48 goals in 167 games – but following Town's relegation at the end of the season moved the short distance to Lincoln City. After a season at Sincil Bank he retired at the age of 33 to concentrate on his teaching career. Incidentally during his time at Grimsby Town Joe proved himself a fine cricketer and for several years captained the town's side

COOPER, Sedley 1931-36

Born: 17 August 1911 Garforth, nr Leeds
(5ft 8½ ins, 10st 12lbs – 1931)
Died: 23 February 1981 Garforth, nr Leeds
Debut: 28 October 1933
v Wolverhampton Wanderers Division One Away
Last Appearance: 9 November 1935
v Leeds United Division One Away
Total League & Cup Appearances: 19 Goals: 4

Career Details:

Carlton Athletic		
Halifax Town	November	1928
WEDNESDAY	9 June	1931 £1050
Huddersfield Town	June	1936 £750
Notts County	March	1937
Lincoln City		WW2 Guest
Torquay United		WW2 Guest

The unenviable task of trying to dislodge the incomparable left-winger Ellis Rimmer fell to Sedley Cooper during his five years at Hillsborough. The youngster had joined the Owls after having played in all of Halifax Town's games during the 1930-1 season – he played 79 times for the West Yorkshire club - and was seen as a possible long-term replacement for Rimmer. Unfortunately for the newcomer his rival had an incredible fitness record and Rimmer was ever present in the Owls first eleven during Cooper's first two seasons at Hillsborough. Therefore Sedley had to be content with being a reserve team regular and hoping that his first team chance would eventually arise – he scored eleven times in that debut Central League season and in his career at Wednesday ended with a tally of 49 goals in almost 150 reserve team appearances.

The understudy finally got his chance in the autumn of 1933 when Rimmer was sensationally dropped to the reserves and despite suffering a 6-2 defeat on his debut Cooper proved himself an able deputy- scoring in the 3-2 defeat at Huddersfield Town in his third appearance. However after a six-game run Rimmer was re-called – in the final game before new manager Billy Walker took over – and it was back to the Central League for Sedley until an injury to his rival late in the season provided him with another five-game run in Division One football. The 1933-4 season proved to be Cooper's best at Wednesday as in addition to double-figure league appearances he also finished top scorer for the second team – netting twelve times. During the Owls F.A.Cup winning season of 34-5 Cooper proved his versatility by making several first team appearances on the right wing but during his final two years at Hillsborough had to be content with a stable diet of reserve team football before being transferred to neighbours Huddersfield Town – incidentally his final appearance proved even worse than his debut as this time Wednesday were thrashed 7-2!

His stay at Town lasted only nine months as after appearing in just five games – failing to taste victory – he moved to Division Three (South) side Notts County. He appeared regularly for County as they struggled to extricate themselves from mid table anonymity and before the advent of war had netted 14 times in 56 league games.

COOPER, William 1887

Born:
Only Appearance: 15 October 1887 v Belper Town F.A.Cup Away
Total League & Cup Appearances: 1 Goals: 0

Career Details:
WEDNESDAY

Although right-winger William Cooper played occasionally for the club over a four-year period he only played in one competitive game for Wednesday - a 3-2 F.A.Cup win at Belper in October 1887. He had first appeared in Wednesday colours in a 3-0 friendly defeat at Port Vale back in December 1885 and over the next four seasons appeared somewhat infrequently on the club's team sheet – of the line-ups that were recorded from the period he can be credited with sixteen appearances in a Wednesday shirt. His final appearance came in September 1888 – on the opening day of the new season - in a 3-1 Olive Grove defeat to West Bromwich Albion.

COX, Brian Roy 1979-82

Born: 7 May 1961 Sheffield
(6ft 1ins, 11st 10lbs – 1981)
Debut: 17 October 1978
v Oxford United
Division Three Home
Last Appearance: 7 October 1980
v Blackburn Rovers
Division Two Home
Total League
& Cup Appearances: 26 Goals: 0

Career Details:

WEDNESDAY	19 February	1979
Huddersfield Town	18 March	1982 £10,000
Mansfield Town	5 August	1988 £25,000
Hartlepool United	August	1990 Free
Buxton	November	1992
Centre Spot (Sun.)		1996-7

Before signing apprentice forms for Wednesday in June 1977 goalkeeper Brian Cox had played for a variety of local juniors teams including the Three Feathers U-13s, Throstles U-14s, Beighton U-15s and finally for the club's nursery side Middlewood Rovers. Within a year of arriving at Hillsborough the ex-Sheffield boys player had signed a professional contract – his debut had occurred when he was still a trainee – and following Chris Turner's transfer to Sunderland in the summer of 1979 Cox became firmly established as No.2 to Bob Bolder. The great shot stopper played fifteen times during the Owls Division Three promotion campaign of 1979-80 but it was not until moving to Huddersfield Town that his career blossomed.

He initially joined The Terriers on loan for the final fourteen games of the 1981-2 season and when the move was made permanent in August 1982 would go on to appear in exactly 250 competitive games for Huddersfield Town in a six-year stay. He helped Huddersfield to the promotion from Division Three in 1983 and when his outstanding display for Town back at Hillsborough in October 1983 earned his side a draw his popularity increased still further at Leeds Road. After leaving Huddersfield he dropped into lower league football – earning promotion from Division Four with Hartlepool United in 1991 – before playing a handful of Northern Premier League games for Buxton. After finishing with football he was unemployed for two years, volunteering as a driver for "Dial A Ride" charity. He later played a few games in the Meadowhall Sunday League before running betting shops in the City – he now works for a tributary of the NHS.

COYLE, Robert Irvine "Roy" 1972-74

Born: 31 January 1948
East Belfast, N.Ireland
(5ft 8ins, 10st 13lbs – 1974)
Debut: 16 December 1972
v Blackpool
Division Two Away
Last Appearance: 20 August 1974
v Scunthorpe United
League Cup Away
Total League
& Cup Appearances: 47+3 Goals: 3

Career Details:

Glenavon		
Lomond Star		
Ballyclare Comrades		
Ballymena United		
Glentoran		
WEDNESDAY	10 April	1972 £10,000
Grimsby Town	3 October	1974 £15,000
Linfield	19 November	1975 Free

CAPS (@ SWFC) –
NORTHERN IRELAND Full (5)
v Portugal 28/03/73, v Cyprus 08/05/73, v Wales 19/05/73, v Bulgaria 26/09/73, v Portugal 14/11/73

Although capped five times by Northern Ireland it was as a manager that Roy Coyle achieved his greatest successes. His record at managerial level in Northern Ireland is truly remarkable as from being appointed player-manager at Linfield in November 1975 to the end of the 2002-3 season he has won twelve League Championships – including six in a row at Linfield in the 1980s – five Irish Cups and an astonishing 31 other trophies! This incredible record includes countless league and cup doubles as Coyle entered the history books as one of the greatest managers in the history of Irish football – he continues to add to his list of honours today as only defeat in the 2003 Irish Cup Final denied Glentoran a domestic clean sweep of the four major honours – League Championship, Cup, Antrim Shield and League Cup. That haul in 2002-3 made it thirteen trophies for Coyle since he moved to the Belfast giants in December 1997, continuing a run of success that started back in 1977 when Linfield won the County Antrim Shield. He stayed at the Ulster based club for almost fifteen years before leaving in April 1990 and subsequently was appointed manager at Ards in October of the same year. However Roy – whose son Darren was briefly on the books of Everton - would stay only one season as in May 1991 he was on the move again – this time to Derry City. He "only" won a League Cup while at City and subsequently returned to Ards for a second spell as manager in October 1993.

Before he scaled the heights in management Coyle had enjoyed a playing career that had started in schools football, firstly at Euston Primary School and then Orangefield School. After finishing his education Coyle joined Glenavon, starting a playing career in Irish League soccer that would bring him two Championship medals with Glentoran in 1970 and 1972 as well as representative honours which included eleven Northern Ireland amateur caps and an Irish league cap against England. Ironically it was Linfield, where he would achieve unsurpassed success as manager, who rejected Coyle at the age of 14 and after a variety of spells at several local teams he even considered emigrating to Australia to play football for a team called George Cross. However in March 1972 he arrived at Hillsborough for a two-week trial and when this proved a success was offered a contract by Owls boss Derek Dooley, which he duly signed soon after. Six months later the hard working midfielder – who was an excellent man-marker – had become a regular in the Owls Division Two side and within a matter of weeks won the first of his five full caps for his Country– four coming as a substitute. He appeared in half of the Owls matches during the eventful season of 1973-4 before spending two years at Grimsby Town where injury restricted him to just 26 appearances – incidentally his testimonial game at Linfield in January 1987 came against a Spurs side that contained Chris Waddle.

CRAIG, James Philips "Jim" 1972-74

Born: 30 April 1943 Glasgow
(6ft 1ins, 11st 10lbs – 1973)
Debut: 27 January 1973
v Portsmouth
Division Two Away
Last Appearance: 29 September 1973
v Crystal Palace
Division Two Home
Total League
& Cup Appearances: 5+1 Goals: 0

Career Details:

Glasgow University		
Glasgow Celtic	7 January	1965
Hellenic F.C.	May	1972 £10,000
WEDNESDAY	7 December	1972 Free
Contract Terminated	8 March	1974

One match in the career of right-back Jim Craig not only ensured his place in Celtic folklore as a member of the "Lisbon Lions" but also his place in British football history. This occurred on 25 May 1967 when Celtic beat Italian side Inter Milan 2-1 in Portugal to become the first British side to lift the European Cup. That historic victory was the major prize for Craig during a trophy laden seven-year career at Celtic Park that included seven consecutive League Championship medals, four Scottish Cups, three Scottish League Cups plus a full cap for his country in 1968. It was a remarkable career in Scottish football for the uncompromising full back who had actually turned down the chance of joining Celtic at the age of sixteen so he could continue his studies at Glasgow University, joining in 1965 when he had qualified as a dentist.

Throughout his career Jim combined running his dentist practise with playing football but the former took a back seat when he was persuaded by ex-Arsenal player George Eastham – manager at South African club Hellenic - in 1972 to move to the Southern Hemisphere. He spent an enjoyable full season in South Africa before returning to Scotland in October 1972 and was contacted soon after by Second Division Wednesday with a view to moving to Hillsborough. Craig had several offers on the table from German sides but he wanted to play in English football so the ex-Scotland schoolboy International joined Derek Dooley's squad. Unfortunately the move did not prove a success as Craig made little impact at first team level and after fifteen months in Sheffield it was mutually decided by Club and player to cancel his contract so Craig could concentrate on the dentistry practise he had set up in Sheffield. A move to become manager at Irish club Waterford broke down in July 1974 due his wife's illness and he has remained in the UK ever since, continuing his dentistry while undertaking a variety of media work. This has included journalistic work – he published a history of Celtic in 1999 – work for Radio Glasgow and Radio Scotland while he now splits his time between dentistry and Celtic's web site.

CRAIG, Robert McAllister "Bobby" 1959-62

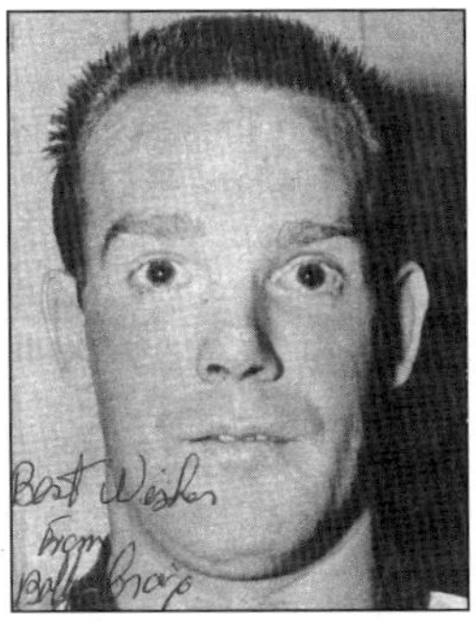

Born: 8 April 1935 Airdrie
(5ft 4ins, 10st 12½ lbs – 1961)
Debut: 21 November 1959
v Leeds United
Division One Away
Last Appearance: 24 February 1962
v Chelsea
Division One Away
Total League
& Cup Appearances: 99 Goals: 28

Career Details:

Bicester		
Blantyre Celtic		
Third Lanark	23 November	1955
WEDNESDAY	18 November	1959 £7,750
Blackburn Rovers	13 April	1962 £17,500
Glasgow Celtic	24 October	1962 £15,000
St Johnstone	6 August	1963 £12,000
Oldham Athletic	13 March	1964 £5,000
Toronto City	13 May	1965 Free
Johannesburg Wanderers		1966
Third Lanark	4 February	1967

Even though diminutive attacker Bobby Craig played in Wednesday colours for less than three years that was in fact his second longest spell at any club in a somewhat nomadic career. He had first come to prominence while playing for Airdrie boys and continued to play while serving his National Service in the R.A.F – while stationed in Oxford he appeared for non-league side Bicester. On his return to Scotland, Bobby spent four years in the Scottish League with Third Lanark before deciding to try his luck in English football when Wednesday boss Harry Catterick came knocking on his door – moving South after drawn out negotiations.

His impact at Wednesday was immediate, netting five times in his first five games including a home debut goal in the 7-0 romp over West Ham. The newcomer proved himself a dynamic player, always on the move, who one minute was threading passes through to a spearhead centre-forward and in the next jinking his way through a bewildered defence. He had the ability in either foot and looked a more than capable successor to Redfern Froggatt but unfortunately the inside-right also had a few negatives which included unpredictability and inconsistency while he was also said to lack the correct attitude to fulfil his truly immense potential. His superb displays and twelve goals in 1960-1 helped the Owls to their best post-war finish – runners-up to the Tottenham double side – but new manager Vic Buckingham never really took to the ginger-haired attacker and in November 1961 Craig turned down the chance of a £25,000 move to Blackburn Rovers. During his time at Wednesday he also helped them to an F.A.Cup semi-final in 1960 and captained Sheffield against Glasgow in 1962 – ironically while with Third Lanark in 1955 he captained Glasgow against Sheffield! However the cunning and stocky forward did eventually join the Lancashire club with Buckingham drafting Colin Dobson into the Wednesday side as his replacement.

His rumoured poor attitude would perhaps explain why over the next few years he flitted from club to club, staying less than twelve months at teams in England, Scotland, Canada and South Africa. After three goals in just eight games for Blackburn he made a Scottish Cup Final appearance for Celtic – losing to Rangers in a replay – before failing to hold down a regular place at Second Division strugglers Oldham Athletic. After leaving Boundary Park he played for a while alongside Stanley Matthews for Canadian side Toronto City and after a spell in Africa his career turned full circle when he re-signed for his first club Third Lanark. After hanging up his boots Bobby moved back to Canada and worked with Toronto Parks as a gardener until his retirement. He still keeps fit by going to the local gym but in hindsight must regret that his football career was one of massive potential that was never fulfilled.

CRAIG, Thomas Brooks "Tommy" 1969-74

Born: 21 November 1950 Glasgow
(5ft 7ins, 11st 7lbs – 1970)
Debut: 12 May 1969
v Tottenham Hotspur
Division One Home
Last Appearance: 14 December 1974
v Oldham Athletic
Division Two Home
Total League
& Cup Appearances: 228+5 Goals: 40

Career Details:

Avon Villa		
Drumchapel Amateurs		1965
Aberdeen	November	1967
WEDNESDAY	7 May	1969 £100,000
Newcastle United	20 December	1974 £120,000
Aston Villa	25 January	1978 £270,000
Swansea City	20 July	1979 £150,000
Carlisle United	March	1982
Hibernian	October	1984 £6,000

CAPS (@SWFC) – SCOTLAND U-23 (1)
v England 13 /03/74

It is said the secret of comedy is timing but this adage could equally apply to football as the Wednesday career of midfielder Tommy Craig can illustrate. The ex-Glasgow boys player is without doubt one of Wednesday's greatest players but unfortunately for Owls fans, the club and Craig he signed at the start of the blackest period in Wednesday's long history as they plummeted from the top-flight to the edge of Division Four inside a handful of seasons. The teenager had started in amateur football in his native Glasgow, joining the Aberdeen ground staff in 1966, and received early plaudits when making his first team debut aged just sixteen. He was also captain of the Scotland's Youth side – after having played for his Country at U-15 level - and was once described by the Dons manager as "the complete footballer – capable of walking into any team in England". His old boss proved to be right but neither he nor Craig could have foreseen how quickly that theory would be tested as in May 1969 the football world was shocked when eighteen year-old Craig moved to Wednesday in a deal that not only broke the British transfer record for a teenager but was also the club's record buy. At the time Wednesday were managerless and it was secretary Eric Taylor who negotiated the deal – fighting off competition from Aston Villa - for the flame-haired midfielder.

The teenage star who possessed an outstanding left foot and powerful shot used his experience of almost sixty first team games at Aberdeen – which included European matches – to slot immediately into the Owls First Division side, appearing in forty-three games in the season that followed. Unfortunately Wednesday were relegated in his first full season at Hillsborough and Craig would not play in the top-flight until leaving for Newcastle in 1974. Over the next five years Tommy would be the jewel in the crown of a struggling side, playing under three different managers as Wednesday slid towards Division Three. He had initially overcome the enormous pressure such a price-tag can heap upon a player and scored regularly during his time at Wednesday and although he was often accused of lacking bite he was still generally regarded as a player of real talent in an Owls side bereft of such quality. He had certainly been unlucky to have signed for a club on the slide – one can only speculate how he would have faired in a better side - and no Owls fans could have begrudged Craig a move back into Division One when in December 1974 Wednesday boss Steve Burtenshaw decided he was an expensive luxury, selling him to Newcastle United.

It was probably true that he had started to stagnate during his later months at Hillsborough – as Wednesday constantly struggled – but the move to St.James' Park re-ignited Tommy's career as he revelled in his new surroundings, developing into a highly influential player who was equally adept at supplying both short and long passes while scoring many long range goals and becoming the club's penalty expert. The move clearly gave a true indication of his class as Tommy quickly became a firm favourite with United fans and would captain Newcastle at Wembley in their 1976 League Cup Final loss to Manchester City. While at Newcastle he won his only full Scotland cap, plus several U23 caps and even an U-21 cap as an over age player – ironically his last cap at any level came at U-21 level when he was 26 years old! His time on Tyneside ended – after 28 goals in 157 games - with a club record sale to Aston Villa but unfortunately for Tommy his time at Villa Park was ruined by injury and inside eighteen months he had moved onto second Division Swansea City. He played nineteen times during City's historic season of 1980-1 – when the Welsh side won promotion to the top-flight for the only time in their history – but did not start a game in Division One football for The Swans, eventually leaving for Carlisle United in the spring of 1982. After completing his English league career in Cumbria Craig returned to Scotland, joining Hibs as player-coach. Before his playing career came to an end Tommy played in the 1985 Scottish league Cup Final before being appointed assistant manager at Hibs. This was the launch of a successful coaching career – although he had briefly been assistant manager at Carlisle from July 1982 - that saw Craig appointed caretaker manager at Easter Road from November 1986 until his departure to Celtic in February 1987 to take over as assistant to Billy McNeill. During his time as No.2 at Celtic Park the Green and White Hoops won the double in 1988 and also captured the Scottish Cup in 1989. However when Liam Brady appointed Joe Jordan as his assistant in 1993 Craig was appointed Youth development officer. In 1995 Tommy returned to Aberdeen as coach and achieved immediate success as The Pittodre side won the League Cup. He also doubled up as Scotland U-21 manager in that period before moving onto the Newcastle United coaching staff in April 1998, where he is still employed today.

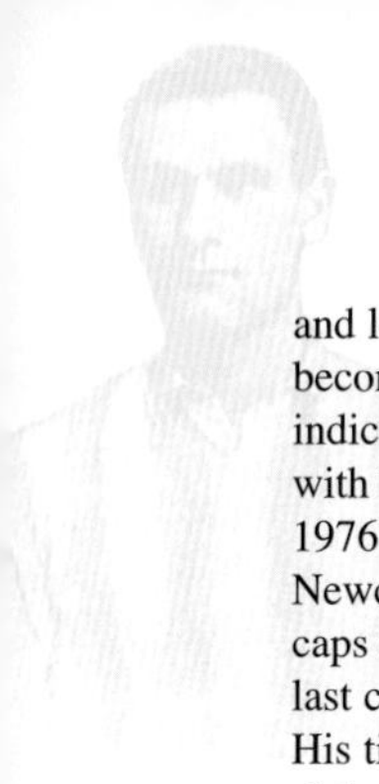

CRANE, Anthony Steven "Tony" 1999-2003

Born: 9 September 1982 Liverpool
(6ft 1ins, 12st 6lbs – 2000)
Debut: 13 September 2000
v Nottingham Forest
Division One Home
Last Appearance: 29 March 2003
v Watford
Division One Home
Total League
& Cup Appearances: 28+33 Goals: 5

Career Details:

WEDNESDAY	9 September	1999
Grimsby Town	1 July	2003

CAPS (@ SWFC) – England U-18 (1) v Luxembourg 27/04/00

The phrase "utility player" could have been invented for Tony Crane as in his four seasons as a professional at Hillsborough he played in all three positions in the so called spine of the team - centre-half, central midfield and centre-forward. He first burst onto the first team scene under the managership of Paul Jewel following the Owls relegation from the top-flight, playing in the hard-running, tough tackling midfield role that he had developed in the club's academy teams. He played in twenty-two games in that debut season – twelve as sub – and would only miss three reserve games – his debut having come in April 1999 - as he proved his fitness and form. However the following campaign proved a disappointment to the Liverpool born player who had moved to Sheffield when just a toddler. He started only four league games and despite again missing only three reserve team games seemed to have slipped backwards in the pecking order for a first team spot.

The 2002-3 campaign saw Crane first tried at both centre-half and as a forward and in what proved to be his final season at Hillsborough he was almost exclusively used in either of those roles. Crane – who had joined the club's Academy at the age of 14 – impressed greatly on the club's pre-season tour of Sweden (scoring three in as many games) and duly won a place on the bench for the opening game of the season. However it was not until the arrival of new manager Chris Turner in November 2002 that Crane started a first team game, going on to enjoy an eleven game run in the side at centre-half. However a nightmare first forty-five minutes at home to Reading in January 2003 ended his best ever sequence in the first team and Danny Maddix took his place. However his strength and ariel power always ensured Tony was a useful man to have on the bench and after scoring a late equaliser as a sub at Derby he repeated the feat when played from the start as a forward at Bradford in the following month – incidentally his first goal for the club was easily his best – a tremendous 30-yard drive at Watford in November 2000.

Unfortunately despite playing twenty times during the Owls relegation season Crane could still not be considered anything other than a squad player and this was probably a factor in his surprise decision to reject the Owls offer of a one-year contract. He therefore joined the mass exodus of players from Hillsborough as Chris Turner tried to re-build for Division Two. Soon after leaving Wednesday the youngster joined fellow Division Two side Grimsby Town on a three-year contract.

CRANSON, Ian 1988-89

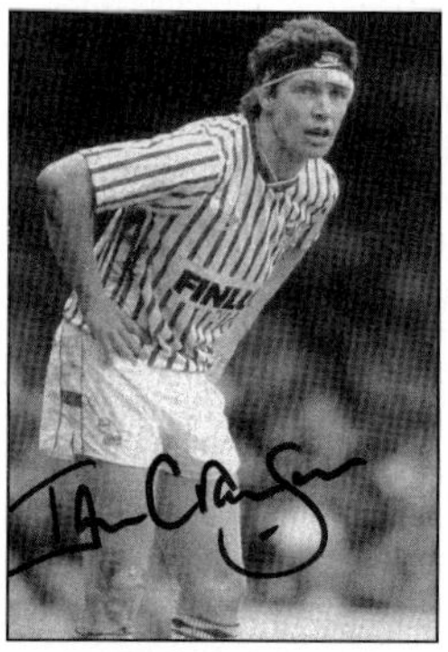

Born: 2 July 1964 Easington
(5ft 11ins, 11st 7lbs – 1988)
Debut: 26 March 1988
v Norwich City
Division One Away
Last Appearance: 1 April 1989
v Millwall
Division One Home
Total League
& Cup Appearances: 34+1 Goals: 0

Career Details:

Horden Colliery U-18		1979
Ipswich Town	7 July	1982
WEDNESDAY	22 March	1988 £475,000
Stoke City	21 July	1989 £480,000

Commanding centre-half Ian Cranson's career at Wednesday was brief as he never really settled after moving to Hillsborough on deadline day in 1988 for a hefty fee. After gaining schoolboy honours with East Durham the northeast born defender played a year in senior youth football with Horden Colliery before moving to East Anglia to start his apprenticeship with Ipswich Town. At Portman Road he built a sizable reputation that included five U-21 caps for England and one hundred and seventy first team games for Town. Under both Howard Wilkinson and his successor Peter Eustace the stopper was an ever present but following the arrival of Ron Atkinson in February 1989 Cranson found himself increasingly on the fringes of the first team and it was no real surprise when he became Stoke City's record signing.

It proved to be money well spent however for The Potters as Cranson would give sterling service to City, appearing in over 300 hundred first team games and winning the Autoglass Trophy in 1992 followed by the Second Division Championship a year later. He was named player of the year in 1993-4 and also won three other supporters accolades in his time at The Victoria Ground before in November 1996 – following a series of knee injuries – he had to abandon his latest comeback attempt after two reserve games and officially retire from professional football. After a while away from football Cranson joined Stoke's Centre of Excellence in 1998 and after coaching at Academy U-19 level became Assistant Academy Director, a role he combined with reserve team manager. However after fourteen years at City he was released in May 2003.

CRAPPER, Christopher 'Chris' 1905-07

Born: 3rd Quarter 1884 Rotherham
(5ft 10ins, 11st – 1905)
Died: 2nd Quarter 1933 Hemsworth
Only Appearance: 23 April 1906
v Everton
Division One Home
Total League
& Cup Appearances: 1 Goals: 0

Career Details:

South Kirkby		
WEDNESDAY	6 May	1905 £125
Grimsby Town	July	1907 £25
South Kirkby		

There are many different reasons why a player cannot fulfil their potential and it was injury that ruined the League career of Owls full back Chris Crapper before he had reached his twentieth birthday. The defender, who was equally at home in either full back positions, had originally joined Wednesday from local soccer and was a regular at left back as Wednesday's reserve team won the Midland Counties League in 1905-6, scoring 111 goals in the process! It was at the latter end of that campaign that Crapper appeared in what proved to be his only game for the club, against newly crowned F.A.Cup holders Everton at Owlerton – Wednesday winning 3-1 – when regular full back Harry Burton was absent.

The teenager continued to gain experience in the second team during the following season but sadly 1907 proved a particularly unlucky year for Crapper as a knee injury suffered at Wednesday effectively ended his chances of replacing Burton in the Owls Division One side and then after a transfer to Grimsby he suffered a broken leg that forced his retirement from the professional game altogether. After ending his League career Chris returned to play in the Sheffield Association League for first love South Kirkby although his ill luck with injuries meant the speedy back could not over exert himself in non-league football. He passed away at the age of 48 in 1933.

CRAWSHAW, Percy 1899-1905

Born: 3rd Quarter 1879 Sheffield
Debut: 31 December 1899
v Chesterfield
Division Two Away
Last Appearance: 31 December 1904
v Middlesbrough
Division One Home
Total League
& Cup Appearances: 9 Goals: 0

Career Details:

Worksop Town	
WEDNESDAY	1899
Contract cancelled	1905

Right half-back Percy Crawshaw certainly came from good footballing stock as in addition to his England International brother Tommy he could also point to sibling George who served Worksop Town for many years – Percy actually played one of his early games in Wednesday colours back at Worksop in a Sheffield Association league game that doubled as George Crawshaw's benefit game. After joining Wednesday in the summer of 1899 Percy was almost ever present as his new side walked away with the treble of Sheffield Challenge Cup (ironically against Worksop Town and his brother George) Wharncliffe Charity Cup League and the aforementioned Association League – Wednesday losing only one of thirty-eight games and repeating the feat of the senior team by winning every home game.

Over the next five seasons Percy proved himself a loyal clubman, helping Wednesday to a multitude of local honours at reserve team level including the Association League in 1901, Midland Counties League & Sheffield Challenge Cup in 1902, Wharncliffe Cup and Challenge Cup in 1903 and the Wharncliffe Cup again in 1905. In the days before agents Percy was quite happy to ply his trade at second team level with the added bonus of occasional appearances at first team level – as replacement for the outstanding back Bob Ferrier. He remained Ferrier's understudy until late in 1905 – his final first team appearance having come in the 5-0 Owlerton rout of Middlesbrough - when he was forced to retire due to a football injury. On New Year's Eve 1905 his contract with Wednesday was cancelled by mutual consent after he took control of a public house on The Moor in Sheffield.

CRAWSHAW, Thomas Henry "Tommy" 1894-1908

Born: 27 December 1872 Sheffield
(5ft, 11ins, 12st – 1896)
Died: 25 November 1960 Sheffield
Debut: 1 September 1894
v Everton
Division One Away
Last Appearance: 7 March 1908
v Sheffield United
Division One Home
Total League
& Cup Appearances: 465 Goals: 26

Career Details:

Park Grange		
Attercliffe		1891
Heywood Central		1893
WEDNESDAY	24 April	1894
Chesterfield Town	June	1908
Castleford	January	1910

CAPS (@SWFC) –
ENGLAND Full (10) v Ireland 09/03/95, v Ireland 07/03/96, v Wales 16/03/96, v Scotland 04/04/96, v Ireland 20/02/97, v Wales 29/03/97, v Scotland 03/04/97, v Ireland 09/03/01, v Wales 29/02/04, v Ireland 12/03/04

FOOTBALL LEAGUE (8) v Scottish League 1895, v Scottish League 1897, v Scottish League, Irish League 1899, v Irish League 1902, v Irish League 1904, v Irish League 1905, v Irish League 1908

Of all the players who helped forge the club in its early league years the name of Tommy Crawshaw has become legendary. The inspirational captain not only led Wednesday to consecutive League Championships in 1903 and 1904 but also helped the Owls to F.A.Cup wins in 1896 and 1907 – earning a unique place in club history as the only Wednesday player to win two Cup winners medals. He enjoyed a truly outstanding career at Wednesday as in addition to the aforementioned major honours Tommy also led the Owls to the Division Two Championship in 1900 - in the club's first season in their new home at Owlerton – and won a multitude of representative honours, including several full caps for his Country and countless appearances for the Sheffield Football Association. An outstanding header of the ball, Crawshaw was described as a "glorious spoiler of the opposition" and his wholehearted attitude to the game – he was always guaranteed to give 100% every game - made him a huge favourite with fans at first Olive Grove and then Owlerton. The centre half-back was a speedy and tireless worker but it was his natural leadership qualities that made Tommy a giant amongst men – he was a captain who led by example, never lacking courage or determination, and never thought the cause lost until the final whistle.

The strong-willed Sheffielder had started his playing career in local football but arrived at Wednesday from Manchester League Heywood Central, fresh from netting a rare own goal as his side had lost 4-2 to Bury in the Manchester Senior Cup. He was brought to Wednesday as a long-term successor to another great captain of the club's early days – Billy Betts – and made his debut on the opening day of the 1894-5 season. Within a year Tommy had become both an established top-flight player and an England International and would remain a fixture in the Owls side for the next thirteen seasons as Wednesday became established as one of the greatest teams of the era. The Ferrier-Crawshaw-Ruddlesdin back-line of the early part of the Century was feared throughout the land and proved a major factor in the many honours than came the club's way in that period. Part way through the Cup winning season of 1906-7 Tommy passed his 36th Birthday, but it was hard to tell as he used all his enthusiasm and experience to lead Wednesday all the way to Crystal Palace where, although touted as underdogs to Everton, Tommy rallied his troops to record a glorious victory. That season would prove to be Tommy's last as a regular – father time finally starting to have an effect – and although he appeared in fourteen Division One games in 1907-8 his loyalty was rewarded with the granting of a free transfer in April 1908- incidentally his final game proved particularly memorable for Tommy as it was a two-nil derby win over The Blades!

However Crawshaw was held in such high esteem that there were no shortage of clubs willing to employ the clean living ex-Owl and he eventually signed for neighbours Chesterfield – it was said that the announcement of his capture at the club's AGM is thought to have been the only factor that won Football League re-election for Chesterfield that summer! After a season at the Saltergate club he signed – along with ex-Wednesday team mate Jamieson - for Castleford before being employed as Glossop secretary until 1914. After the Great War Tommy owned a newsagents shop in of all places Bramall Lane while he later ran the Sporting Group public house near Hillsborough and then the Yorkshireman in the City centre. Sadly after retiring from the licensing trade Tommy struggled to make ends meet and in 1952 it was reported he was depending upon public donations to survive. However on hearing of his plight Wednesday deposited £50 in his bank account (roughly equivalent to ten weeks wages now) which he was allowed to draw at £1 per week! Thankfully Tommy got back on his feet and lived another eight years before passing away in Wharncliffe Hospital, aged 88.

CRESSWELL, Richard Paul Wesley 1999-2000

Born: 20 September 1977 Bridlington
(6ft, 11st 8lbs - 1999)
Debut: 3 April 1999
v Coventry City
Premier League Home
Last Appearance: 28 August 2000
v Blackburn Rovers
Division One Home
Total League
& Cup Appearances: 8+28 Goals: 3

Career Details:

Bridlington Rangers		
York City	15 November	1995
Mansfield Town	27 March	1997 Loan
WEDNESDAY	25 March	1999 £950,000
Leicester City	1 September	2000 £750,000
Preston North End	10 March	2001 Loan
Preston North End	18 July	2001 £500,000

CAPS (@SWFC) – ENGLAND U-21 (3) -
v Hungary 27/04/99, v Sweden 04/06/99, v Bulgaria 08/08/99

It would have been difficult to know who was more excited when highly rated England U-21 International Richard Cresswell moved to Hillsborough on deadline day 1999- the player or his Wednesday supporting mother! He was actually on International duty at Southampton for an U-21 game against Poland when Danny Wilson captured his signature – he did not play any part in the game as manager Peter Taylor, who later signed him from Wednesday for Leicester City, thought his mind would not be fully on the match! The move to Hillsborough was a welcome surprise for Cresswell after he had scored 24 times for his first professional club York City from making his League debut back in January 1996. The youngster made a favourable impression during his early weeks at Wednesday – scoring the winner in the May 1999 home game with Liverpool – but started only two games in the Owls relegation season as big money signings Gilles De Bilde and Gerald Sibon were given preference. He was therefore cast in the role of substitute and during the season came off the bench an amazing twenty-two times, scoring twice, without being given a decent run in the side. His frustration must have grown when he started the opening game of the next season on the right wing although did not have long to grow accustomed to his new role as within thirteen seconds Kevin Pressman was sent off and Chris Stringer brought on with Cresswell the man sacrificed - therefore sharing with Pressman the record of the shortest first team appearance in Wednesday's history!

However salvation was at hand for Cresswell in the form a shock move back into the Premier League, joining Leicester City. Unfortunately is was a case of out of the frying pan into the fire for the hard-running attacker as he again found his opportunities limited and after scoring just once during 2000-1 for The Foxes went out on loan to Division One side Preston North End. It was at Deepdale that Richard was finally allowed a run in the side and he rewarded David Moyes by helping Preston into the end of season play-offs. The Lilywhites lost out to Birmingham City in the semi-finals but Cresswell had impressed enough for Preston to sign him on a permanent basis during the following summer. Over the next two seasons Cresswell showed a real poachers instinct in front of goal and finished top scorer in both 2001-2 and 2002-3 with sixteen league and cup goals in each campaign. He was also voted player of year in the former season and came back to haunt Wednesday in March 2003 when he netted the winner at Hillsborough – one of 46 appearances he made in the season under the new managership of Craig Brown. He then experienced a barren season before finishing top scorer in 2004-05 with 21 goals, as Preston reached the play-off final.

CRINSON, William James 'Bill' 1906-08

Born: 1883 Sunderland
(5ft 11ins, 12st – 1906)
Debut: 5 January 1907 v Manchester City
Division One Away
Last Appearance: 8 April 1908 v
Middlesbrough Division One Away
Total League & Cup Appearances: 4
Goals: 0

Career Details:

Southwick Club		
WEDNESDAY	April	1906
Huddersfield Town	June	1908
Brighton & Hove Albion	June	1909
Sunderland Rovers	September	1913

Goalkeeper Bill Crinson was another player who came from the breeding grounds of northeast non-league soccer that had served Wednesday so well in the years before World War One. He arrived at Owlerton after having experienced great success at County Durham amateur side Southwick, winning the Wearside League and Sunderland Shipowners Cup double in both 1905 & 1906. Following the departure of goalie Richard Jarvis in the previous year the Owls needed a new custodian to play the role of understudy to regular No. 1 Jack Lyall and it was Crinson who would fill the position for the next two years. Unfortunately for the newcomer, Lyall was almost ever present between the sticks for Wednesday for eight years during the early part of the century and Bill would have to be happy with having to be a regular in Wednesday's Midland League side – winning a championship medal in 1908. He did make an occasional first team start but soon after conceding six goals at Manchester City in April 1908 Wednesday returned to the northeast to bring a certain Teddy Davison to Owlerton.

The arrival of a player that would develop into one of England's best goalkeepers marked the end of Crinson's career in Sheffield and soon after he joined newly formed Huddersfield Town making history by playing in their first ever competitive fixture – a North Eastern League game at South Shields Adelaide in September 1908. He would play 26 times for the fledgling club in that first season but a move to Southern League Brighton saw Bill back in the situation he found himself in at Hillsborough – the role of understudy, this time to Albion legend Bob Whiting. In a four year stay on the south coast he would appear in only nine first team games for Albion before returning to his native county to sign for Sunderland Rovers. He was appointed secretary at Sunderland Comrades in 1918 while occasionally scouting locally for his old club Brighton.

CRUICKHANK Alexander 1926-27

Born: 12 August 1900 Haddington, East Lothian
(5ft 7½ins, 10st 0lbs – 1926)
Debut: 13 September 1926
v Birmingham City Division One Away
Last Appearance: 18 September 1926
v Blackburn Rovers Division One Away
Total League & Cup Appearances: 2 Goals: 0

Career Details:

Port Glasgow Athletic		
Derby County	January	1924
Merthyr Town	May	1925
WEDNESDAY	8 June	1926
Annfield Plain	August	1927 Trial
Guildford City	August	1927
Merthyr Town	June	1929
Swindon Town	June	1930

When right winger Alex Cruickshank arrived at Hillsborough in the summer of 1926 the Owls were still celebrating the Division Two Championship success of the previous season. In the summer of 1925 Cruickshank had showed his prowess with the willow by scoring over 600 runs for his native Scotland and was brought to Hillsborough by Bob Brown as competition on the football field to first team regular Rees Williams - strangely both came from the same somewhat obscure source of perennial Division Three (South) strugglers Merthyr Town. The club's first capture from the Welsh side had been an ever present on the right wing for Wednesday for four seasons and it looked a difficult task for the newcomer to dislodge him. However, he was given an early chance when Williams was absent in the early stages of the new season and helped Wednesday to two away draws before dropping back into reserve team football.

He stayed a reserve team regular until well into the New Year but the arrival of Mark Hooper made sure his days were numbered as Williams was dropped into the second team and Alex left to kick his heels on the sidelines. His final appearance in a Wednesday shirt came in the reserves' February 1927 home win over Huddersfield Town and in the summer he dropped out of league football to sign for Southern League Guildford City. After helping the now defunct non-league side to two mid table finishes he re-entered league soccer at Division Three (South) side Swindon Town.

CUNNINGHAM, Anthony Eugene "Tony" 1983-84

Born: 12 November 1957 Kingston, Jamaica
(6ft 1ins, 13st 7lbs – 1983)
Debut: 11 November 1983 v Fulham Division Two Away
Last Appearance: 12 May 1984 v Cardiff City Division Two Away
Total League & Cup Appearances: 30+3 Goals: 5

Career Details:

Laferyettie FC (Sun.)		
Kidderminster Harriers		1976
Stourbridge		1977
Lincoln City	11 May	1979 £12,500
Barnsley	23 September	1982 £80,000
WEDNESDAY	9 November	1983 £100,000
Manchester City	12 July	1984 £100,000
Newcastle United	7 February	1985 £75,000
Blackpool	4 August	1987 £25,000
Bury	2 August	1989 £40,000
Bolton Wanderers	28 March	1991 £70,000
Rotherham United	14 August	1991 £50,000
Doncaster Rovers	July	1993 Free
Wycombe Wanderers	24 March	1994 £5,000
Released	30 June	1994
Gainsborough Trinity	September	1994 Free

West Indian born striker Tony Cunningham started his playing career in West Midlands Sunday league football but it was not long before the tall bustling centre-forward moved into semi-professional football with Kidderminster Harriers – he continued to play part-time while completing his engineering apprenticeship. His high work rate and no holds barred attitude to the game ensured he would be a fans favourite wherever he played and after a successful year at Aggborough he first started to attract the attention of Football League scouts while scoring regularly for Stourbridge. It was not long before Tony was experiencing league soccer as in a spell at Lincoln City he led the line well and scored on average a goal every four games – helping The Imps to promotion from the Fourth Division in 1981. This form persuaded Barnsley manager Norman Hunter to take Cunningham to Oakwell and the likeable attacker was unfazed by the higher-grade football – such that when new Owls boss Howard Wilkinson was looking to bolster his promotion chasing squad he came knocking on Barnsley's door.

The ex-Wolverhampton boys player's arrival added much needed aggression to the Owls attack and alongside the silky skills of Gary Bannister and Imre Varadi he proved to be an ideal target man as Wednesday finally re-claimed their place in the top-flight of English football after a fourteen-year absence. It was therefore a surprise when on the same day Lee Chapman arrived at Hillsborough (an event not unconnected) Cunningham went out of the exit door – joining Manchester City. He was therefore denied a chance of playing First Division football but after a short spell at Maine Road he finally played top-grade football in Newcastle United colours. Over the next decade Cunningham continued to play League football for a wide variety of mainly Northern based sides, appearing at Wembley in Bolton's play-off defeat to Tranmere Rovers in 1991 before winning promotion from Division Two with Rotherham United a year later. In his time at Doncaster Rovers Cunningham was both player-coach and for a spell caretaker manager while his professional playing career finally came to an end at league new boys Wycombe Wanderers in 1995 – at the age of 36 after he had completed a business studies degree at Huddersfield University. After over five hundred senior appearances for eleven different league sides he then returned to Lincoln to take employment as a legal executive, later qualifying as a solicitor.

CURRAN, Edward Terance "Terry" 1979-82

Born: Kinsley, Nr.Pontefract
20 March 1955
(5ft 10ins, 11st 3lbs – 1980)
Debut: 31 March 1979
v Watford
Division Three Away
Last Appearance: 15 May 1982
v Norwich City
Division Two Home
Total League
& Cup Appearances: 135+3 Goals: 39

Career Details:

Doncaster Rovers	July	1973
Nottingham Forest	28 August	1975
Bury	13 October	1977 Loan
Derby County	17 November	1977 £50,000
Southampton	17 August	1978 £60,000
WEDNESDAY	29 March	1979 £85,000
Sheffield United	28 July	1982 £100,000 (T)
Everton	December	1982 Loan
Everton	September	1983
Orebro	April	1985
Huddersfield Town	July	1985
Panionios	July	1986
Hull City	October	1986 Trial
Sunderland	November	1986
Matlock Town	July	1987 Trial
Grantham Town		1987 N/C
Grimsby Town	October	1987
Chesterfield	March	1988
Goole Town	November	1989

It would be fair to say the 1970s were the worst decade in the club's long history and fans brought up on stories of great players and glorious games were starved of both. With the exception of Tommy Craig supporters had no one to lavish their affections on but this all changed in March 1979 when Owls boss Jack Charlton persuaded Terry Curran to drop down two divisions to sign for Wednesday. The flamboyant winger – whose attitude certainly bordered on arrogant - was a real showman and he immediately endeared himself to the Hillsborough faithful- within months you could collect tokens from the local paper that could be redeemed for a glossy poster of the player fans affectionately labelled "T.C."!

By the time he arrived at Hillsborough, Curran had already appeared for five different league clubs – playing in 166 league games - after having joined hometown side Doncaster Rovers in 1973. His brief spells at all five – he won promotion to Division One under Brian Clough at Forest in 1977 - was mirrored throughout his career by the maverick forward and in fact his three-year stay in Sheffield was easily the longest time he spent at any club in a professional career that spanned over fifteen years.

He had turned his back on a possible League Cup Final appearance for Southampton to move North and would prove to be arguably Charlton's best signing – a definite case of the right player at the right time. During his time in the blue and white stripes Curran experienced many moments of note with a much re-played spectacular goal at Bramall Lane at Easter 1980 making him an all time hero on one side of Sheffield! His twenty-four goals during the promotion season of 1979-80 did little to dampen that popularity (he was named in the P.F.A. Division Three team) although his controversial sending off at Oldham in September 1980 made all the wrong headlines as the infamous riot that ensued caused the F.A. to close all Hillsborough's standing areas for three matches and fine T.C. £100. At his best the flying winger was irresistible with supporters calling for him to be called up to the full England squad – a Curran fan club was started and he even recorded his version of "singing the blues" which flew off the shelves of local record stores!

However Curran's rebellious nature ensured a parting of ways was almost inevitable and after falling out with Jack Charlton several times during the 1981-2 season the situation came to a head in December 1981 when Big Jack's criticism had T.C. on the verge of asking for a move. The two did settle their differences with Curran agreeing to stay until the end of the season but when his contract expired in the summer his choice of destination caused yet more controversy, becoming only one of a handful of players to move direct to Sheffield United from Hillsborough. The move to Bramall Lane was certainly a shock to the system for Wednesday fans but Jack Charlton's emotion was anger when a Football League tribunal ordered that The Blades should just pay £100,000 for his services – the Owls had asked for £250,000 while United offered just £50,000! No doubt a few Owls fans were quite happy that his spell across the City was an unproductive one and within a year he had joined top-flight Everton. During Everton's Championship winning season of 1984-5 Curran played nine times – unfortunately not enough to win a medal – before trying his luck abroad with Swedish club Orebro. Over the years that followed T.C. could not rediscover the form he showed at Wednesday and played for several different sides – including a short time in Greek football – before dropping into non-league soccer. A player-manager role at Goole Town did not last long as after scoring seven times in 14 games he finally hung up his boots in December 1988 to bring the curtain down on a varied and eventful career. If his spell in charge on Humberside had been brief his stint as boss at Manchester club Mossley was even shorter as he was sacked in December 1992 after just five weeks in charge, following seven consecutive defeats and 27 goals conceded!

After finishing his playing career Curran worked at a pallet business near Leeds before buying the "The Woodland" transport café on the A1 - the property boasted a large tract of land and T.C. set up his own pallet business behind the café. The café was later turned into a Motel and then an Italian restaurant before in 2001 he sold the whole enterprise to a property developer, retiring on the proceeds.

CURRY, Robert "Bob" 1936-39

Born: 2 November 1918 Gateshead
(5ft 7½ins, 9st 6lbs – 1937)
Died: 23 June 2001 Halstead, Essex
Only Appearance: 18 September 1937
v Aston Villa
Division One Home
Total League
& Cup Appearances: 1* Goals: 0
***Also appeared in**
7 wartime games, scoring 1 goal

Career Details:

WEDNESDAY	10 October	1936
Gainsborough Trinity	21 June	1939
Bradford Park Avenue	March	1940 Guest
WEDNESDAY		1940-41 Guest
Sheffield United		1943
Leeds United	March	1944 Guest
Mansfield Town		1944-45 Guest
Colchester United	July	1946
Clacton	June	1951
Halstead Town		1954

Inside-left Bob Curry holds a record that is probably unique in the history of league football – his first appearance in league soccer was actually illegal as he was unregistered at the time! This occurred during his three-year spell at Hillsborough when after appearing in what proved to his only Wednesday first team game - at Villa Park in October 1937 – it transpired that he was actually unregistered at the time and the Owls were subsequently censured and fined two guineas. He had originally joined the club's ground staff in 1936 – while training to be a joiner – but in his first season Wednesday were relegated from the top-flight as many old stars retired and were not adequately replaced. It was certainly a period of transition and it was perhaps this upheaval that resulted in Curry being tried in the problem position of inside-left, which had been vacant since Ronnie Starling's departure. However he failed to impress as Wednesday lost 2-1 so it was back to reserve team football until he was released at the end of the 1938-9 season.

During the summer of 1939 he signed for non-league side Gainsborough but would play almost no football in the early years of World War Two as after having signed up with the T.A. during his time at Hillsborough, Curry was one of the first to be called up into the Army once Mr.Hitler invaded Poland. During his time in the forces he did play occasionally for his unit team but whilst on active duty was "blown up" and medically discharged with injuries and shell shock. After leaving the Army, Curry began driving wagons for the Jubilee Brewery in Sheffield and soon after signed for Sheffield United – appearing in twenty games during wartime soccer for the Blades. After the hostilities ended Bob dropped back into semi-pro football at Southern League Colchester United and enjoyed four successful seasons at Layer Road before United were voted into the Football League in 1950 – despite having only finished runners-up in the previous season to ex-league side Merthyr. Before entering league soccer Bob had won a Southern League Cup winners medal in 1948 while in the same season he had scored in every round of the F.A.Cup up until Colchester's brave exit at eventual finalist Blackpool in the last sixteen. After appearing in the "U's" first ever game in league football he played in 34 senior fixtures – scoring thirteen league goals - for United in that debut season before dropping back into non-league football as player-coach at Clacton.

Four months after joining Clacton he was elevated to a player-manager role and held a similar position at his final club Halstead Town – retiring from the latter at the age of 42 to return to his trade as a joiner. His son – also called Robert - was later on the books of both Southend and Colchester but after becoming a successful builder bought a golf course where his father worked as odd job man during his latter years. His grandson Paul also became a professional sportsman – being the club pro at the Five Lakes Golf Club.

CURTIS, Norman William 1950-60

Born: 10 September 1924
Dinnington, Nr.Worksop
(5ft 8½ins, 11st – 1950)
Debut: 25 November 1950
v Bolton Wanderers
Division One Home
Last Appearance: 6 February 1960
v Everton
Division One Home
Total League &
Cup Appearances: 324 Goals: 21

Career Details:

Gainsborough Trinity		
WEDNESDAY	23 January	1950 £1250
Doncaster Rovers	25 August	1960 £1,000
Buxton	August	1961

After starting his working life as a butcher's boy in his native Dinnington, Norman Curtis joined the Royal Navy in December 1942, working as a wireless operator/air gunner throughout the duration of the hostilities. Thankfully despite spending a total of 324 hours airborne – mainly acting as escort to the Far East aircraft carrier fleet – he survived the hostilities and on returning home was given a trial at Midland League Gainsborough Trinity. This proved successful and after moving to the Lincolnshire town he gained employment at a local engineering works in addition to playing part-time for Trinity- winning a Midland League Championship medal in 1949.

A move to Hillsborough was next for Curtis – although he lived in Gainsborough throughout his Wednesday career - and his progress was such that within a year he was making his First Division debut in a 4-3 home defeat to Bolton Wanderers. The two-footed Curtis was a quiet man off the field but on the pitch he was a fearless bundle of energy who scared the living daylights out of many an opposing winger, being blessed with natural speed and the ability to recover well and tackle decisively. It was Hugh Swift who Curtis replaced at left-back and after fighting off competition from Vin Kenny he became established as first choice for almost all of the 1950s – winning Division Two Championship medals in 1952, 1956 and 1959. He did occasionally play at right-back – notably in the 1954 F.A.Cup semi-final defeat to Preston North End - and was also the club's emergency goalkeeper. Incredibly in an August 1953 game at Preston, Norman saved two penalty kicks after replacing broken arm victim Dave McIntosh although he did concede five goals as Wednesday lost six-nil! However it was his technique of taking penalties that earned Curtis the nickname of "Cannonball" as when the Owls were awarded a spot-kick a forward would place the ball on the spot so that Norman could run from the other half and hit the ball as hard as possible! This method certainly entertained the fans and of the 24 penalties he took in a Wednesday shirt Curtis scored 19 with the others hitting the woodwork!

The hard but fair Curtis – who played as a wicketkeeper batsman for Lincolnshire during the summer months – eventually lost his place late in 1959 to another outstanding defender, Don Megson, and after playing throughout Wednesday's yo-yo years, moved to neighbours Doncaster Rovers as player-manager. He appeared in forty-four competitive games for Rovers during the 1960-1 season but internal politics led to his resignation in July 1961 after the club's Chairman decreed that no members of the youth side could be picked for the first team without his permission, even if Norman thought the player worthy of a place. The other members of the board failed to back Norman so he promptly resigned, being appointed player-manager at Buxton a month later. After joining Doncaster he had opened a sports shop back in Gainsborough and ran this for several years while continuing to play for Buxton – facing the Owls at the age of 39 in a benefit game played in April 1964. After selling his business he later worked as a sales rep for Carlsberg – while living in Harrogate - until retiring to York.

CUSACK, David Stephen "Dave" 1974-78

Born: 6 June 1956 Thurcroft, Rotherham
(6ft 2½ins, 14st 2lbs – 1976)
Debut: 11 October 1975
v Millwall
Division Three Home
Last Appearance: 12 August 1978
v Doncaster Rovers
League Cup Away
Total League
& Cup Appearances: 106+3 Goals:1

Career Details:

WEDNESDAY	7 May	1974
Southend United	3 September	1978 £50,000
Millwall	March	1982 £40,000
Doncaster Rovers	22 July	1985 £40,000 (T)
Rotherham United	23 December	1987 Free
Copenhagen Ball Klub	May	1988 Free
Boston United	August	1988 Free
Doncaster Rovers	August	1989 N/C
Kettering Town	June	1992 Free
Harworth Colliery Institute		1992
Grays Athletic		1993
Dagenham & Redbridge	August	1994
Ford United		1995
Heybridge Swifts	January	1996
Basildon United		1997

Although centre-half Dave Cusack played over one hundred games for Wednesday it was his incredible managerial record that made the headlines as a combination of several factors saw him sacked on no fewer than five occasions before he had reached the age of forty! In fact the situation got so bad that he bought his own club – Basildon United in 1997 to avoid it happening again! The tall and rugged defender had originally joined Wednesday straight from school in June 1973, signing professional forms inside twelve months, and after breaking into the Owls Third Division side was an automatic choice as first Len Ashurst and then Jack Charlton started to turn the club around. The emergence of Mark Smith eventually saw Cusack leave for Southend United where he enjoyed a successful four-year stay, totalling an impressive 212 games and winning a Division Four Championship medal in 1981 as well as being named in the P.F.A.Divisional team in the first two seasons of the 1980s.

His peers again named him after moving to Millwall – in the Lion's Division Three promotion season of 1984-5 – before he returned to South Yorkshire to sign for Doncaster Rovers in July 1985. It was that transfer that triggered his amazing managerial run as in October 1985 he was appointed player-manager at Belle Vue. As with his previous three clubs, Cusack again played in over a hundred games for Doncaster but this came to an abrupt end in December 1987 when he was dismissed. Almost immediately he was appointed to an identical position at Rotherham United but this tenure was somewhat briefer as after playing just eighteen games for the Millers he was given his cards in April 1988. He gained relief from his early managerial misfortunes by just playing in Danish football and then at Conference side Boston United. He was actually at York Street for two years – although he did play a single league game for Doncaster Rovers as a non-contract player – and was given the managerial reins in January 1990, replacing George Kerr. He decided to take a rest from playing during the 1991-2 season to concentrate on management but this patently failed as in May 1992 he was surprisingly sacked after sixty-seven games for United! After swapping positions with Kettering Town's Peter Morris in June 1992, Cusack's luck really ran out as just three months later The Poppies went into receivership and the ex-Rotherham Boys player was given another P45.

This was followed with a successful playing spell at Harworth Colliery - appearing in the game that brought the Championship to the Worksop club – before he captained Grays Athletic to Essex Senior Cup success in 1994. He then jumped back into the managerial frying pan at Dagenham & Redbridge but again got his fingers burnt – being sacked thirteen months later. After completing his playing career at Isthmian League sides Ford United and Heybridge Swifts – his sole appearance for the latter coming in a title decider – he was appointed joint manager at Basildon United. He later became Director/Owner of the Essex club and was known to occasionally play if his side was short – once being pulled out of the bar to keep a clean sheet after the goalkeeper did not turn up! His career took another turn in August 1998 after being appointed Chief Executive at then League side Scarborough but lady luck again deserted Cusack as in November of the same year ex-Rotherham United supremo Anton Johnson bought a majority shareholding in the East coast club and Cusack was again unemployed. Unfortunately his next piece of misfortune was far more serious than simply losing his job as in 1999 he broke his neck in a car crash and spent many months out of action. Thankfully he eventually recovered and now works as Project Fire Manager at a fire proofing company.

DAILEY, James "Jimmy" 1946-49

Born: 8 September 1927 Airdrie, Scotland
(5ft 10ins, 12st – 1946)
Died: 14 January 2002 Weymouth
Debut: 16 November 1946
v West Bromwich Albion
Division Two Home
Last Appearance: 22 January 1949
v Leeds United
Division Two Away
Total League
& Cup Appearances: 41 Goals: 25

Career Details:

Wolverhampton Wanderers		1943 Amat.
Third Lanark		1945
WEDNESDAY	12 November	1946 Free
Birmingham City	10 February	1949 £8,500
Exeter City	August	1952 £6,000
Workington	November	1953 £4,000
Rochdale	October	1957 £2,000
Weymouth	July	1959
Bath City	July	1961
Poole Town		1961
Bridport		

Purely based on a goals-per-game ratio the Wednesday career of Jimmy Dailey was comparable with the likes of Jack Ball, Jack Allen and Derek Dooley. However the ex-Scottish International schoolboy was playing in an age where the 2-3-5 formation was still rigidly adhered to and when Clarrie Jordan came to the club in February 1948 the prolific Scotsman was relegated to the reserves. This was despite a record that had seen Dailey net 23 times in just 32 league games, including a hat-trick against Spurs in March 1947 and a tremendous five-goal haul at home to Barnsley in September of the same year – he would play only five more games for Wednesday following Jordan's arrival, even those appearances being as a replacement for his absent rival.

The centre-forward started his career as an amateur at Wolves but as he was not old enough to sign professional forms for the Black Country club he returned home to Scotland, signing for League side Third Lanark just as the Second World War came to an end. Amazingly his arrival at Hillsborough was actually on a free transfer and after he had scored thirteen times in his first thirteen games for Wednesday, many other clubs must have been on the phone to Third Lanark asking if they had any other such prolific giveaways! After losing his place to Jordan, Jimmy of course was effectively out in the cold at Hillsborough so a move was always on the cards - this duly occurred early in 1949 although despite his destination seeming set to be Arsenal he was in fact the first signing of new Birmingham City manager Bob Brocklebank. Amazingly he failed to score in his first eight games for City – playing alongside future Owl John Jordan – and although he finished the following season as top scorer with nine goals it was a terrible campaign as Birmingham finished bottom of Division One. For the remainder of his time in the West Midlands, Jimmy only appeared occasionally at first team level and it would surely have been a relief when his disappointing stay at St.Andrews ended with a transfer to the West Country.

In his only full season at Exeter City he finished top scorer with twelve goals – The Grecians finishing near the foot of Division Three (South) in 1952-3 – and continued that pattern by finishing top scorer at Workington for three consecutive seasons until signing for Rochdale. At Spotland Dailey repeated his Hillsborough five-goal haul for Rochdale - against Hartlepool United in November 1957 – and by the time Jimmy dropped into non-league soccer in 1959 he had scored 127 league goals in 325 games since leaving Wednesday. He, of course, finished top scorer in his debut campaign at Weymouth and continued to score freely in semi-professional football until retiring from playing after a spell at Bridport in the early 1960s. However he remained involved in the game until 1974 after having managed the Dorset Youth Clubs U-21 side, Portland and Dorchester Town. He later ran a sports shop in Weymouth before retiring to the sunnier climes of Alicante, Spain. Unfortunately his story has an unhappy ending as in September 2001 Jimmy was brought back from Spain as he was suffering from Alzheimer's disease, passing away soon after in a local nursing home. Incidentally his name lives on in the world of football as his grandson – also called Jimmy – had trials for the England U-16 side in 2000 and must have made his grandad a proud man.

DARLING, Malcolm 1977

Born: 4 July 1947 Arbroath
(5ft 7½ins, 10st – 1977)
Debut: 3 September 1977
v Bury Division Three Away
Last Appearance: 10 September 1977
v Shrewsbury Town
Division Three Home
Total League
& Cup Appearances: 2+1 Goals: 0

Career Details:

Errol Juniors	September	1961
Luncarty Juniors	August	1962
Blackburn Rovers	27 October	1964
Norwich City	22 May	1970 Player-exchange
Rochdale	6 October	1971
Bolton Wanderers	25 September	1973
Chesterfield	22 August	1974
Stockport County	2 March	1977 Loan
WEDNESDAY	25 August	1977 Trial
Hartlepool United	22 September	1977 Trial
Morecambe	October	1977
Bury	4 March	1978 N/C
Morecambe	April	1978
California Sunshine	May	1979
Darwen		1981

Although Malcolm Darling's time at Wednesday was somewhat brief he could boast a long – if perhaps unspectacular – league career that ended at Bury on a non-contract basis after 360 games in league football. However the ex-Perthshire schoolboys player had already played over three hundred of those games when arriving at Hillsborough on a month's trial and it would be fair to say that his career was firmly in the doldrums when Len Ashurst offered him an olive branch. Before signing apprentice forms for Blackburn Rovers the somewhat lightweight attacker had earned his living as a joiner, while playing in Scottish junior football, but failed to fulfil his early promise at Ewood Park and eventually moved on to start a nomadic career that was mainly restricted to the lower divisions of English league football.

During his short time at Wednesday, Darling played in three consecutive games but after failing to impress sufficiently he soon moved to Hartlepool United for a similar trial period. However he then dropped into Northern Premier League football with Morecambe and after playing some soccer in the US retired from playing after a spell at non-leaguers Darwen – his final games in league football coming at Bury. After hanging up his boots Darling managed Great Harwood Town for a period before working as a production controller for twenty years. He is now employed as a workshop supervisor for adults with learning difficulties.

DARROCH, John "Jack" 1891-95

Born: 1872 Dumbarton, Scotland
(5ft 6½ins, 10st 7lbs – 1896)
Died: 24 November 1949 Dundee, Scotland
Debut: 15 October 1892
v Blackburn Rovers Division One Away
Last Appearance: 9 December 1893
v Aston Villa Division 1 Away
Total League
& Cup Appearances: 20* Goals: 0
***Also appeared in 12 Alliance League games**

Career Details:

Renton		
Vale of Leven		
WEDNESDAY		1891
Dundee	April	1895
Bury	4 May	1896 £50
Blackburn Rovers	5 December	1901
Dundee	August	1902

Full back who was known as the cleanest 'dirty' player – he had a knack of running alongside an opponent before sending him tumbling head over heals with the referee unable to see how he had fouled him! He had originally arrived from Scottish junior football in the summer of 1891 and was in and out of Wednesday's Alliance League side in 1891-2, in the club's last season as a non-league side. He earned a Sheffield Challenge Cup runners-up medal in March 1892 – Wednesday Wanderers losing to Sheffield Strollers (United's reserves) – and started the next season in the second team as Albert Mumford entered the record books as Wednesday's first left back in League football. However his chance came in October 1892 and Jack was on the winning side in his first four games as Wednesday made a great start to their Football League life.

As in the previous season Jack also played regularly for the reserve side as they lifted the inaugural Championship of the Sheffield & District League in 1893 but despite a handful of first team games during 1893-4 – all at right-back – Darroch would play out his final two years at Olive Grove as understudy to newly established first teamers Jack Earp and Ambrose Langley. After retaining the Sheffield & District League Championship in 1894 he won a Sheffield Challenge Cup League Championship medal a year later before returning to Scotland, signing for Dundee. However he soon returned to England – the Owls receiving the £50 fee as they held his registration - and would enjoy a highly successful spell at Bury, playing in 156 games for the Lancashire club and winning several honours including the F.A.Cup in 1900, two Manchester Senior Cups and a Lancashire Senior Cup – incidentally he was nicknamed "Joe" at Bury. After a short spell at Blackburn Rovers he returned to play out the rest of his career at Dundee, retiring in the 1907 close season. On ending his football career Jack started working for Dundee Corporation Baths and was still employed there well into the 1930s although it is known he lived in the United States for a while as in 1912 it is recorded in Bury's minute books that they forwarded him £10 as a gift to alleviate his hardship!

DAVIES, Brian 1964-68

Born: 21 August 1947 Doncaster
(5ft 8ins, 11st 7lbs – 1966)
Debut: 2 May 1966
v Chelsea
Division One Home
Last Appearance: 14 September 1966
v Rotherham United
League Cup Home
Total League
& Cup Appearances: 4 Goals: 1

Career Details:

WEDNESDAY	24 August	1964
Contract Cancelled	11 April	1968
Baltimore Bays		1968
Boston Beacon		1968
Doncaster Rovers	September	1968 Trial
Released	23 October	1968

When teenage inside forward Brian Davies scored on his senior debut for the club he looked set to join the long line of outstanding players to emerge from Wednesday's youth ranks. However for the youngster that goal against Chelsea proved to be the highlight of a professional career that had promised so much after he had become the youngest ever player to represent Doncaster boys. In fact as a youngster Davies could have chosen athletics instead of football as he was a fine sprinter – this natural speed ensured that on his Wednesday debut he impressed greatly with his all round skill, pace and determination. He also possessed a good shot and after making his debut would play two further games as Wednesday rested various players in advance of the F. A. Cup Final meeting with Everton.

However he played only one more senior game for the club – Wednesday's first ever in the League Cup – early in the following season and after eighteen months of reserve team football decided to try his luck in the North American Soccer League after the Owls agreed to cancel his contract. He initially played for Baltimore in the States but when they folded he moved to Boston. During his time with Boston, Davies reached a cup final – he scored the winner in extra time – but suffered a serious hip injury that effectively brought the curtain down on his pro career; whilst he was receiving treatment for the injury he was told he would never play professional football again. However on his return to the United Kingdom he spent a month on trial at Doncaster Rovers but after breaking down in training decided to abandon any comeback hopes. At this point he joined the RAF, as a physical educational instructor, working in that role for four years until becoming station warrant officer and eventually a parachute instructor based at Bicester in Oxfordshire. During his early years in the forces Davies played for the Combined Services football side but every time he stepped up training in an attempt to re-launch a professional career he broke down again due to the hip injury.

DAVIES, George 1950-56

Born: 1 March 1927 Rednal, Nr.Oswestry
(6ft, 13st 7lbs – 1950)
Debut: 14 April 1951
v Bolton Wanderers
Division One Away
Last Appearance: 5 March 1955
v Everton
Division One Home
Total League
& Cup Appearances: 109 Goals: 2

Career Details:

Llanymynech		
Oswestry Town		1950
WEDNESDAY	9 June	1950 £2,050
Chester	July	1956 £600
Wellington Town	November	1957

A baker by trade, George Davies had started his senior playing career in the Oswestry & District League before signing professional forms with Oswestry Town near the end of the 1949-50 season. However he never actually made an appearance for his new club as Wednesday swooped – giving Oswestry a more than welcome quick profit – with the initial fee of £2000 rising by £50 after fifty league starts although an agreed additional sum of £500 for an International appearance was of course never paid. The Welshman was a tall, strong and forceful player who usually played in a left-half role although his first team debut actually came as a replacement for Eddie Gannon on the opposite side of the defensive half-back trio.

Over the next five years the well-built defender competed for a first team spot with the likes of Doug Witcomb and the aforementioned Gannon, playing in a promotion campaign from Division Two (1952), two relegation seasons (1951 and 1955) and an F.A.Cup semi-final in 1954 against Preston North End. He proved to be an excellent defensive wing-half – who could often set up attacks by breaking quickly up field – and served the Owls well before eventually moving to Chester City after failing to make a first team appearance in 1955-6 for Wednesday. He appeared in a further fifty-five league games for City before retiring from professional football to join Cheshire League Wellington Town (now Telford United). After leaving soccer he returned to his previous trade as a baker and later started his own window cleaning business.

DAVIS, Henry "Harry" 1892-99

Born: cs 1873/74 Smethwick, nr Birmingham
(5ft 6½ins, 12st. – 1896)
Debut: 3 September 1892 v Notts County Division One Away
Last Appearance: 27 March 1899 v Stoke City Division One Away
Total League & Cup Appearances: 184
Goals: 42

Career Details:

Willesden Green Albion		
Summer Hall Sunday School		
Birmingham St.George's		
WEDNESDAY	Summer	1892
Retired		1899

Versatile forward Harry Davis was a mainstay of the Owls early years in League football, making his debut for Wednesday in the club's first ever league fixture at Notts County. He was described as "full of dash and a real bag of tricks" and was without doubt one of the most consistent players during the Owls period at Olive Grove, playing as left-wing partner to Fred Spiksley as the F.A.Cup was won for the first time in 1896. During his time at Olive Grove the sturdy attacker played in all five forward positions and as well as scoring frequently himself created countless chances for his fellow attackers.

The Midlands born player had started his career in youth football, before captaining a club called Summer Hall for two seasons. He was courted by both Aston Villa and Alliance League side Birmingham St.George and after picking the latter impressed sufficiently to be capped for an England side in 1891 – against a Canadian touring side at The Oval. In the same year Harry also won the Staffordshire Cup with St.George – beating Walsall 5-3 in the Final – and to cap a tremendous season led the Football Alliance League attack against The Football League in a representative game at Olive Grove. His goal in that game was probably a more than useful reminder of his talents to the watching Owls officials and when his club hit financial problems he was transferred to Wednesday – St.George were so short of cash in April 1892 that they wired Wednesday saying they could not afford to travel for an Alliance League game, the Owls paying their expenses in advance! Perhaps not surprisingly St.George disbanded in the mid-1890s. After being a first team regular at Wednesday for seven seasons the move to Owlerton in 1899 also signalled the end of Davis' Owls career and he retired from league football, becoming a wine storekeeper. Incidentally when Wednesday and Aston Villa played the famous "10½ min game" the two sides remained on the pitch to play a benefit game for Davis – this was after his original benefit game against Villa in January 1899 was poorly attended.

DAVIS, Henry "Harry/Joe Pluck" 1900-07

Born: November 1879 Wombwell, Barnsley
(5ft 4ins, 11st 10lbs)
Died: 18/19 October 1945 Sheffield
Debut: 3 February 1900 v Newton Heath Division Two Away
Last Appearance: 27 February 1907 v Sunderland F.A.Cup Away
Total League & Cup Appearances: 235
Goals: 67

Career Details:

Wombwell		
Ardsley Parish Church		1895
Barnsley		1897 £5
WEDNESDAY	22 January	1900 £200 + Simmons (Loan)
Released	April	1908

CAPS (@SWFC):
ENGLAND Full (3) v Ireland 14/02/03, v Wales 02/03/03, v Scotland 04/04/03
Football League (1) v Scottish League 1903

Like his namesake, Harry Davis was an automatic first team choice at Wednesday for several years but unlike his predecessor was fortunate enough to play during one of the club's golden periods. In over eight years in the blue and white stripes he won a variety of honours, including back-to-back League Championships in 1903 and 1904. The diminutive but highly courageous player – he was nicknamed "Joe Pluck" by Wednesday fans – had first come to prominence with Barnsley non-league side Ardsley who were so worried of losing his services that they persuaded Harry to sign professional forms at the tender age of fifteen. Their concerns were certainly not without foundation but it would be two years later before he progressed to League football at Barnsley, although their committee was divided about paying the mammoth £5 fee for an untried youngster! In the end the Oakwell club took the chance and were rewarded as Davis scored 25 times in 56 competitive games for The Reds before joining Second Division Wednesday part way through the 1899-1900 season – signing for forty times the fee Barnsley paid for his services with the deal also seeing Simmons going to Oakwell for the rest of the season and Wednesday agreeing to play a friendly at Barnsley.

During his early years at Hillsborough Harry was tried all along the forward line before settling into an outside right role that would see him picked for Sheffield against London and Glasgow before earning full caps for his country – being the first ever Barnsley FC product to reach international status. The little player with a big heart quickly became a huge favourite with Wednesday fans and his deadly right wing partnership with the outstanding Harry Chapman was a major factor in Wednesday's successes in the early part of the Twentieth Century – the pairing being dubbed "The Marionettes" by fans. The cool player who possessed a deadly shot was also a real entertainer and had the crowds roaring with laughter with his trick, when tackled, of sliding for ten yards or more with his arms and legs in the air! Unfortunately such was his whole-hearted commitment that Davis received various injuries in his time at Wednesday that saw him miss both the 1904 and 1905 F.A.Cup semi-finals. He also missed the run to the Final in 1907 as in the Third Round tie at Sunderland Harry had the misfortune to suffer a broken leg – following a clash with future Wednesday player English McConnell - which sadly brought a premature end to his playing career. He was even unable to attend the Cup Final win over Everton – although he can be found on subsequent team photos taken with the Cup – along with his crutches!

After retiring from the game he was appointed assistant trainer at Wednesday in 1907 but in February of the following year took over as licence of a public house at Wadsley Bridge, near Hillsborough. He remained in the pub trade until joining the 9th Battalion of the Army in October 1914 and after surviving the Great War ran a newsagents shop in Sheffield until his death.

DAVIS, John Leslie 1977

Born: 31 March 1957 Bethnal Green, London
(5ft.11ins, 12st 2lbs – 1976)
Only Appearance: 14 May 1977 v Oxford United Division 3 Home
Total League & Cup Appearances: 1 Goals: 0

Career Details:

Arsenal		1972 App.
Crystal Palace	July	1974
Gillingham	July	1975
WEDNESDAY	10 February	1977
Released	September	1977
Tipples		1980 (Sun.)

After starting as an apprentice at Arsenal, Londoner John Davis signed for Crystal Palace after the Gunners decided not to offer him a professional contract. Despite spending two years at Selhurst Park the defender failed to make a senior appearance for The Eagles and when they released him Davis was on the verge of giving up football to pursue a career in boxing – following in the footsteps of his father who was a top-class middleweight and later coached Olympic medallist Terry Spinks. However when Gillingham manager Len Ashurst offered him a trial at the Kent club the rugged defender impressed when scoring twice on his reserve team debut – in an unaccustomed role of striker. At Gillingham the ex-East London boys player finally made his league bow as a right-back but would appear in only three games before Ashurst – who had left to take over as manager at Wednesday – invited him to Hillsborough on trial in October 1976.

After several reserve team appearances at right-back he signed a contract with Wednesday in February of the following year and was given a first team chance in the final home game of the season. He actually played in midfield in his sole appearance for the club and must have struggled to impress as he was appearing in his fourth game in just nine days, due to a backlog of fixtures at reserve team level. He looked set to join Hartlepool United in August 1977 but when this deal fell through he played just a solitary reserve team game more for Wednesday before being released at the end of September 1977. This marked the end of his professional career as John moved back to his native London to work for the council. He later coached in schools – he played for six years with his local Sunday club - and was a security man at various London nightclubs before becoming a taxi driver.

DAVISON, John Edward "Teddy" 1908-26

Born 2 September 1887 Gateshead
(5ft 7ins, 11st 10lbs – 1913)
Died: February 1971 Wortley, Sheffield
Debut: 10 October 1908
v Bristol City Division One Home
Last Appearance: 20 December 1924
v Hull City Division Two Away
Total League
& Cup Appearances: 424* Goals: 0
***Also appeared in 11 wartime games**

Career Details:

Gateshead St.Chad's		
Gateshead Town		
WEDNESDAY	14 April	1908 £300
Mansfield Town	1 June	1926

CAPS (@ SWFC)
ENGLAND Full (1) v Wales 13/03/22

Goalkeeper Teddy Davison was without doubt one of Wednesday's greatest servants and in total spent almost forty years in Sheffield football as a player at Hillsborough and then manager at Sheffield United. The diminutive custodian had been spotted in non-league football by scout Bob Brown and the legendary future manager's eye for talent again ran true as within eighteen months Davison had replaced stalwart Jack Lyall in the Owls first eleven – he had originally arrived at Wednesday on trial but after saving a penalty in a practice game was signed. Incredibly he remained the Owls undisputed number one for almost fifteen years and it was not until the arrival of anther future legend – Jack Brown – that Teddy found his place under threat. By then Davison – who became the smallest ever England keeper when playing at Anfield against Wales in 1922 – had left an indelible mark on club history as one of their most talented and respected players – at the time he was one of the most popular players in the game and was held in high esteem by everyone in the sport. In fact such was his unswerving nature that he earned the nickname "Honest Ted" and long after he had retired his name still brought forth comments that "he was a sportsman and gentleman of the first order".

He had been brought up as one of nine children – called Edward the Seventh by his family – and started his working life in the composing room of a Newcastle paper. However after deciding to turn professional with Wednesday he never looked back as his courage, razor sharp reflexes and brilliant anticipation more than made up for his lack of inches. The gentle natured Teddy also kept a meticulous match by match diary which showed he appeared in 618 games in his career, being beaten 810 times, and also revealed he was somewhat of a penalty expert, saving 24 of 77 spot-kicks he faced, once saving two in one game! To his peers it was no surprise that he volunteered for active service in The Great War, landing at Le Harve, France in July 1916 with the Field Royal Artillery, Northumbrian Bridge. He spent the rest of the war in France – playing only twice during that period for Wednesday whilst home on leave – but thankfully survived the trenches to reclaim his position between the posts at Hillsborough. As well as his England cap Teddy – who possessed powerful arms and great strength - also earned three F.A. caps during a tour of Australia in 1925 and during his time in Sheffield was also picked eight times for the City's representative side.

His remarkable Wednesday career finally came to a close in 1926 when he took the position of player-manager at Midland League Mansfield Town – unfortunately he left Hillsborough without a trophy to his name, having joined a year after Wednesday's F.A.Cup win and failing to make a first team appearance during his final season in their Division Two Championship success. If as a player he had been outstanding his managerial career would reach the same heights as in his debut season at the Nottinghamshire club, Davison won a total of five trophies – the biggest prize being the Notts Senior Cup. He continued to perform with consistency between the sticks for Mansfield before suffering a broken rib in a County Cup game against Newark Town on New Year's Day 1927, ending a playing career during which he was never dropped. Exactly a year after his final appearance Teddy moved to neighbours Chesterfield as manager and subsequently led The Spireites to the Division Three (North) Championship in 1931.

He had quickly became established as one of the brightest young managers in the English game and it was no surprise when in June 1932 he accepted a lucrative offer to return to Sheffield as manager at United – replacing the great John Nicholson. Teddy would stay for twenty years at Bramall Lane, leading The Blades to the 1936 F.A.Cup Final and promotion from Division Two in 1939, denying his old club Wednesday in the process. His years at the heart of the City's football saw Davison dubbed "The George Washington of Sheffield soccer" but after winning the Football League North title in 1946 he suffered relegation from the top-flight in 1949 and after failing to gain an instant return left in August 1952 - he is perhaps best remembered by Unitedites as the manager who brought the legendary Jimmy Hagan to Bramall Lane for a paltry £2500 fee from Derby County. He returned to Chesterfield for a second spell as manager soon after and stayed at the helm until stepping down in May 1958 – at the age of 71 – to become chief scout. The highlight of his second stint at Saltergate came in 1956 when the club's Youth side – including Davison signing Gordon Banks – reached the Final of the F.A.Youth Cup where they lost in front of 26,000 at Saltergate to a Manchester United side also including a future World Cup winner – Bobby Charlton. After finally retiring Teddy spent his later years back in Sheffield, safe in the knowledge that he had made the greatest ever impact on Sheffield soccer.

DAVISON, Thomas Reay "Tommy" 1931-32

Born: 3 October 1901 West Stanley (5ft 11½ins, 11st 10lbs – 1930)
Died: 1 January 1971 Derby
Debut: 7 February 1931 v Bolton Wanderers Division One Away
Last Appearance: 6 February 1932
v Newcastle United Division One Home
Total League & Cup Appearances: 18 Goals: 0
Career Details:

Tanfield Lea Rovers		
Stanley United		1920
Durham City	August	1920
Wolverhampton Wanderers	June	1923
Derby County	July	1925
WEDNESDAY	5 February	1931 £4850*
Coventry City	28 July	1932 £1100
Rhyl Athletic	July	1935
Bath City	August	1936

* Joint fee with J.Stephenson

During his relatively short stay at Wednesday, Tommy Davison acted as understudy to outstanding centre half-back Tony Leach and enjoyed two mini-runs at first team level when his rival was absent. However he would spend most of his time in the club's reserve side until moving to Coventry City in 1932. His spell at the East Midlands club would actually be the most successful – appearance wise – in his career, playing in exactly one hundred league games for the Sky Blues, scoring five times. After controversially losing his place in the City side - following an off the field incident before a big F.A.Cup tie in January 1935 - he dropped into non-league football as player-coach at Rhyl Athletic before a three-year stint at Bath City led to his retirement just before the start of the Second World War.

His road to Hillsborough had started in his native northeast where he worked as a miner whilst playing local football. Davison – who was also a very good cricketer -eventually left the coalfield to play in Durham City's first ever season of League football – appearing in their opening fixture at fellow newcomers Southport in August 1921 – and totalled 62 league games for The Citizens before he was scouted by Wolves and signed by their manager George Jobey. At Molineux, Davison was a somewhat peripheral figure and in two seasons started only nine games – failing to play in the requisite number of matches to win a Division Three (North) championship medal in 1924. After George Jobey moved to take over as manager at Derby County one of his first signings was Davison and he quickly achieved success as County finished Division Two runners-up to Wednesday in his debut season. During the 1929-30 season Tommy was a regular as County again finished second to The Owls – this time in the top-flight – and in total played in 83 league games for Derby before he was signed part-way through the 1931-2 campaign by Bob Brown, along with team mate George Stephenson.

DE BILDE, Gilles Roger Gerald 1999-2001

Born: 9 June 1971 Zellik, Belgium
(5ft 11ins, 11st 6lbs – 2000)
Debut: 7 August 1999
v Liverpool
Premier League Home
Last Appearance: 6 May 2001
v Crewe Alexandria
Division One Home
Total League
& Cup Appearances: 59+9 Goals: 15

Career Details:

Zellik Sport		
RSC Anderlecht		Youth
Zellik Sport		
KHO Merchtem		
Eendracht Aalst		1990
RSC Anderlecht		1995
PSV Eindhoven		1997
WEDNESDAY	10 July	1999 £2,8000,000
Aston Villa	10 October	2000 2-month loan
RSC Anderlecht	21 July	2001 Free
SK Lierse	2 September	2003 Season-loan
Willebroek - Meerhof	27 June	2005

CAPS (@SWFC) – BELGIUM Full (8)
v England 09/10/99, v Italy 13/11/99, v Portugal 23/02/00,
v Holland 29/03/00, v Norway 26/04/00, v Denmark 03/06/00,
v Turkey 19/06/00, v Bulgaria 16/08/00

Came to Hillsborough with a reputation as the Belgian Cantona after being banned for a massive fifteen league games - plus a four month international suspension - after hitting an opponent during a game in his native Belgium, damaging his victim's eye and breaking his nose. After the game in December 1996 he was arrested – spending the night in cells - and after being taken to court by his victim De Bilde received a nine-month suspended jail sentence. This led to him being dubbed "The Beast of Belgium" and he was sold in disgrace to Dutch football, ending a successful time in his homeland that he seen De Bilde named Belgian player of the year in 1994 after having started his career in local football. He was rejected as a teenager by Anderlecht but a second shot at league soccer came at the age of nineteen when Gilles – then working for the Ministry of Justice in Brussels – signed for Second Division Eendracht Aalst. His goals record in Belgium league football was quite outstanding – sixty-seven in just over one hundred games – and he settled easily into Dutch football at PSV Eindhoven. The Dutch giants won the championship in De Bilde's first season – although he played in only seven games, scoring seven times- and he was mainly kept out of the side by two players who would go on to play in the English Premier League – Luc Niis and Ruud Van Nistelrooij.

That was the background to his move to Sheffield and Wednesday fans were fascinated to see a player who came with seventeen caps for his country and the nickname of "The Animal". Unfortunately that animal turned out to be a pussycat and he experienced a highly disappointing two years at Hillsborough as the club tumbled from the Premier League, becoming public enemy No.1 amongst Owls fans for his perceived lack of effort and commitment on the field of play. Despite the fact that he top scored for Wednesday during their relegation season - with ten league goals - it was obvious almost from the start that he was not cut out for the hurly-burly of English football and his laid back attitude made sure he was never in the running for the player of the year trophy! He was ever present during 1999-00 for the club but played less than half of the league games in the season that followed as Wednesday struggled at the wrong end of the First Division table. After failing to impress Aston Villa boss John Gregory during a loan spell at Villa Park he returned to Hillsborough and thankfully, for both player and Owls fans, he departed in the summer of 2001 after Wednesday decided to cut their losses, agreeing he could leave on a free transfer with still two years left on his highly lucrative contract. He subsequently signed a three year deal with his old club Anderlecht, appearing in almost one hundred competitive games until back and knee injuries finished his season early in April 2003. After a major fall out with Anderlecht in the summer of 2003 he was effectively frozen out of the first team picture – training with the youth squad. However a month later he joined fellow Belgium League side Lierse on loan for the remainder of the season. Retired to Marbella in Spain in 2004 but made a comeback with Belgium third division side Willebroek-Meerhof.

DEGRYSE, Marc 1995-96

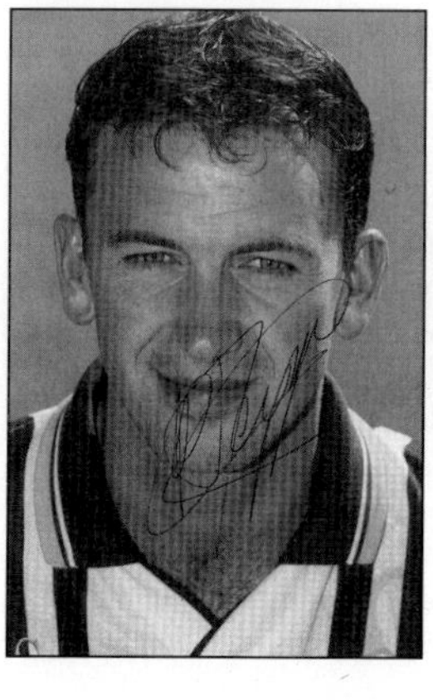

Born: 4 September 1965 Roeselare, Belgium
(5ft 8ins, 10st 9lbs – 1996)
Debut: 27 August 1995
v Newcastle United
Premier League Home
Last Appearance: 5 May 1996
v West Ham United
Premier League Away
Total League
& Cup Appearances: 34+4 Goals: 12

Career Details:

VC Ardoole		
Club Brugge KV		1980
RSC Anderlecht		1989 £1,500,000
WEDNESDAY	19 July	1995 £1,500,000
PSV Eindhoven	5 July	1996 £1,800,000
KAA Gent	April	1998
Germinal Beerschot Antwerpen		1999

CAPS (@SWFC) – BELGIUM Full (3)
v Denmark 06/09/95, v Cyprus 15/11/95, v France 27/03/96

The Wednesday career of Marc Degryse contrasted greatly with that of his fellow Belgian Gilles de Bilde and when he moved to Dutch football after just a season at Hillsborough many fans were disappointed at his departure. He had arrived with an impressive C.V. that included over fifty caps for his country plus in excess of 350 top-flight appearances for Belgian giants Brugge and Anderlecht. Born in the Flemish town of Roeselare, Marc spent his early teenage years playing trumpet in the local band while appearing for youth side Ardoole. He was eventually signed by Club Brugge, turning professional just before his eighteenth birthday, and made such an impression in his first season as a professional that National manager Guy Thys included him in the provisional 23-man squad for the 1984 European Championships in France. Even though he was one of three players who failed to make the cut for the tournament it was not long before the midfielder made his international debut – winning the first of 63 caps in September 1984 – and was a regular in both international and domestic football for over a decade. He missed out on the squad for Mexico 86 – after being dropped for a handful of games by Brugge – but had the consolation of his first medal – the Belgian Cup. The disappointment of missing out on the World Cup soon dissipated and Marc came back to score 22 times as Brugge won the league championship in 1988

After netting 93 goals in 182 league games he moved, for a record domestic transfer fee, to Anderlecht but suffered disappointment in his first season when finishing runners up in both the Belgium League and the European Cup Winners Cup. However a second championship medal came his way in 1991 and after again finishing runners-up to Brugge in 1992 Degryse – who had been converted to midfield from an out-and-out striker on moving to Anderlecht - would be instrumental as Anderlecht competed a hat trick of titles – he totalled 170 league games for RSC, scoring a superb 65 goals. He also won the Belgium Cup in 1994 and during a honours laden spell in his home country Marc was crowned footballer of the year on three occasions, played eleven consecutive seasons of European football and appeared in both the 1990 and 1994 World Cup Finals.

When Degryse arrived at Hillsborough – as one of David Pleat's first signings – the Owls were going through a transformation after just escaping relegation in the previous season and although he sometimes struggled to adapt to the pace of the Premier League the technically gifted Belgium enjoyed an encouraging debut campaign. When you consider he was often played out of position – being used mainly as a forward by Pleat – he performed admirably and showed himself to be an accurate passer of the ball and goal taker. His goals helped the Owls to avoid the drop for a second year running and it was a surprise when Wednesday sold him to Dutch side PSV Eindhoven after less than a year at Hillsborough. In his first season in Holland, Marc won the Dutch title in 1997 before returning home to Belgium for a short spell at Gent. His final club proved to be GBA where he enjoyed an Indian summer, winning his fourth Belgian player of the year award in 2000 – at the age of 34. He finally retired in July 2002 and after months of drawn out negotiations was appointed Technical Director at Club Brugge in May 2003.

DENT, Fred 1920-21

Born: 24 January 1896 Sheffield
(5ft 10ins, 11st 10lbs - 1928)
Died: 11 July 1983 Leeds
Debut: 20 November 1920 v Fulham Division Two Home
Last Appearance:
18 December 1920 v Leicester City Division Two Home
Total League & Cup Appearances: 4 Goals: 1

Career Details:

St Cuthberts		
Vickers		
WEDNESDAY	1 October	1920
Halifax Town	11 June	1921
Chesterfield	16 August	1923 Free
Mid Rhondda United	July	1924
Bristol City	May	1925
Exeter City	19 July	1926
Merthyr Town	16 May	1928
Norwich City	24 December	1928 Free
Swindon Town	17 May	1929
Luton Town	7 July	1930
Sheffield Employment Exchange	7 December	1931
Barnsley Ministry of Labour	February	1935

After starting his playing career in Sheffield junior football, Fred Dent spent the duration of World War One employed in war work at Vickers, also playing regularly for their works side. At the end of the hostilities Fred signed amateur forms for Wednesday, in 1919, and scored in his first two appearances for the reserves. He would play only a handful of second team games before signing professional forms early in the following season and repeated his trick of scoring on his debut for the reserves by netting on his first team debut in the three-nil home win over Fulham in November 1920. He initially took the place of Arthur Price at inside-left but after four games Dent himself was replaced when centre-forward Jimmy McIntyre switched positions. It was then back to reserve team football for Fred and his chances of a first team recall diminished even further when Wednesday brought Sam Taylor to the club early in 1921.

After just one season as a professional at Wednesday, Fred moved to Halifax Town where he played in their first ever Football League game against Darlington in August 1921. A week later he netted twice as the same side were beaten in Town's first home game and in total Dent scored 12 times in 39 league games before being granted a free transfer – the reason given being that the crowd's attitude towards him would not bring out his best form! A drop into Welsh non-league soccer revitalised his career and after netting 29 times for Mid-Rhondda in 1924-5 he was taken back into league football at Bristol City. Over the next few years Fred played for a variety of sides and proved a consistent and prolific scorer in lower league soccer, scoring 53 times in 118 games from his move to City until retiring from league football at Luton Town. He once scored a double hat-trick in a reserve game while at Exeter City although his best individual season came at Swindon Town – scoring 26 league goals from centre-forward. After hanging up his boots Dent returned to Sheffield to work in local government.

DEWAR, Neil Hamilton 1933-37

Born: 11 November 1908 Lochgilphead, Argyllshire
(5ft 11ins, 13st – 1933)
Died: 10 January 1982
Debut: 30 December 1933
v Manchester City Division One Home
Last Appearance: 1 May 1937
v Huddersfield Town Division One Away
Total League
& Cup Appearances: 95 Goals: 50

Career Details:

Lochgilphead United		
Third Lanark	October	1929
Manchester United	8 February	1933 £4,000
WEDNESDAY	29 December	1933 Nevin + Ball*
Third Lanark	19 July	1937 £1800

*Joint transfer value of £3000

Despite scoring more than a goal every two games in a Wednesday shirt Neil Dewar never quite settled at Hillsborough during four and a half years at the club. The intelligent, pencil thin centre-forward arrived after a short and unsuccessful spell at Old Trafford where Dewar could not adapt to the United playing formation. He had first come to prominence in Scottish football at Third Lanark where he signed his first professional contract after a successful trial – neither of the big Glasgow sides had deemed to give him a trial match! His impact at The Thirds was quite remarkable as he scored an incredible 124 goals in just four seasons, including forty in his debut season and 35 in just 37 games as Third Lanark finished fourth in Division One after having lifted the Division Two title in 1931. Dewar – who could shoot with tremendous power and direction – was described as a "scientific" player and the man known as Neilly Dewar in his homeland soon saw International honours come his way, starting with two Scottish League appearances. However it was his three caps for Scotland that brought him to the attention of English league managers and after he followed up a superb display against England at Wembley in 1932 with a hat trick against France in Paris he was one of the hottest properties in the British game.

His eventual transfer to Manchester United caused a sensation at the time as The Thirds had been inundated with offers for their prize forward ever since his display at Wembley. Arsenal, Portsmouth and Newcastle United were all on his trail but it was Second Division United who paid a substantial fee to take him south of the border. After his disappointing spell at Manchester United he was the first signing of new Wednesday manager Billy Walker although many fans would have questioned the judgement of trading prolific scorer Jack Ball as part of the deal! He went straight into the first team but it was off the field events that dominated the headlines in his early weeks at the club. Soon after moving across the Pennines Dewar eloped with the daughter of Manchester United director councillor A.E.Thomson, the couple marrying in a registry office after overcoming various paperwork difficulties. Such was the scandal and publicity over the affair that a few weeks after the wedding the United director resigned from the board! On the field of play Dewar scored regularly but when he did lose his place briefly in the 1934-5 season it coincided with the Owls run to the F.A.Cup Final, so it was Jack Palethorpe who wore the No.9 shirt in the Wembley win over West Bromwich Albion. He was back as first choice in the following campaign – scoring the winning goal as Arsenal were beaten to win the Charity Shield – but the Owls were in decline and the Scotsman suffered relegation from the top-flight in his final season at Hillsborough.

When moving back to Third Lanark his transfer fee was at the time the biggest paid in the Scottish club's history but the attacker – who started his working life as a trawler fisherman – played three more years in league football until retiring from the game in 1940. A well-known public speaker in Scotland, Dewar moved back to his home village of Lochilphead after finishing his playing career to work in the countryside, although in 1947 he could be found playing for a veteran side called the Old Crocks!

DI CANIO, Paolo 1997-99

Born: 9 July 1968 Rome, Italy
(5ft 9ins, 11st 9lbs – 1998)
Debut:
9 August 1997
v Newcastle United
Premier League Away
Last Appearance:
26 September 1998
v Arsenal
Premier League Home
Total League
& Cup Appearances: 46+2
Goals: 17

Career Details:

Lazio		1985
Ternana	July	1986 1-year loan
Juventus	July	1990 £3,000,000
Napoli		1993 Loan
A.C.Milan		1994 £1,500,000 + Alessandro Orlando
Glasgow Celtic	3 July	1996 £1,000,000
WEDNESDAY	8 August	1997 £4,500,000
West Ham United	28 January	1999 £2,000,000
Released	30 June	2003
Charlton Athletic	11 August	2003 Free
Lazio	11 August	2004 Free

The words temperamental, charismatic, volatile and spectacular are just four words in the English language that could be used to describe the unpredictable Italian with the magic feet. In fact a whole directory would be needed to fully describe the footballing career of the Roman – particularly since his move to British football – from his early days in youth football with Rinascita 79 and Pro Tevere Roma. After signing as a trainee for his boyhood heroes Lazio the right-winger won an Italian Youth Championship medal in 1986 and was voted the club's young player of the season three years later. However after failing to break into Lazio's first team he left for a year-long loan at minnows Ternana, appearing in 27 games to gain valuable league experience. On his return to the Italian capital Paolo still had to wait over a year before finally making his Serie A debut but would go on to appear in over thirty games for Lazio during 1988-9 and had become an established first team player at the Olympic Stadium when Turin giants Juventus paid a huge fee for his services.

He stayed three seasons at Juventus – scoring five goals in 78 league games – and although he won an Italian Cup runners-up medal in 1992 the definite highlight came a year later when Paolo played in both legs of the UEFA Cup Final success over German side Borussia Dortmund – Juve winning 6-1 on aggregate. The passionate and fiery Di Canio was a big crowd favourite at every club he played for and the ex-Italian U-21 International's next port of call was another of the country's giants – AC Milan. He won a European Super Cup medal in 1995 – Milan beating Arsenal over two legs – but unfortunately at The San Siro he spent the majority of his time warming the bench, being mainly used a sub as Milan won the Scudetto (Italian Championship) in 1996. He then moved to Celtic in the summer of 1996 but after thrilling the Parkhead crowd – scoring fifteen times in thirty-seven games - and being named Scottish PFA player of the year the departure of manager Tommy Burns seemed to unsettle the unpredictable Di Canio and after falling out with the Celtic board he failed to return for pre-season training – an action that would soon become well known to Wednesday fans!

It was while Di Canio was in this limbo situation that Owls boss David Pleat took a risk, making Paolo Wednesday's record signing on a £1m a year contract – the Owls paying £3m cash to Celtic as well as transferring £1.5m rated Regi Blinker. He quickly became a cult hero at Hillsborough, finishing top scorer in his first season and being voted player of the year after some quite spectacular play and outstanding goals – he also managed to get fined £1,000 in November 1997 for bringing the game in disrepute after showing his buttocks in a 1-1 draw at Wimbledon three months earlier! He continued to thrill Owls fans until that fateful day in September 1998 when - after being red-carded for the second time in his Wednesday career – he proceeded to push over referee Paul Alcock. The repercussions of his actions were of course immense and after immediately being suspended by the club he was charged with misconduct by the F.A. – eventually being banned for eleven matches and fined £10,000 following an October 1998 commission of enquiry at Bramall Lane. He was due to return to the fold for the Boxing Day home game with Leicester City but of course never did return to Hillsborough – being suspended, without pay, for two weeks in December after failing to return for training from his hideout in Italy. He duly sent a sick note for the whole month – citing stress as the reason for his absence – and although he did not seem to have a future in British football he eventually signed for West Ham, in a cut-price deal after agreeing to waive his rights to the wages Wednesday had stopped.

At Upton Park he continued his pattern of being loved by the fans but forever falling out with the management although he remained over four years in East London – his longest time at any side since his time at Lazio. On his day Paolo was one of the Premierships best players and was simply a revelation amongst Hammers fans – his skill, passion and creative genius making him the most popular West Ham player since the days of Trevor Brooking. "The sublime to the ridiculous" may be a cliché but it perfectly summed up Di Canio who one minute would take on a defence single-handed and the next literally sit down on the pitch, asking to be taken off. It was somewhat ironic – considering his brushes with authority - that Di Canio was awarded the UEFA Fair Play award in 1999, after failing to score after an opposition keeper was lying injured in the penalty area. His incredible volley for West Ham against Wimbledon won Paolo the 1999-2000 BBC goal of the season award and after starring in a 12-minute film called "Parallel Roads" he published his autobiography. Despite being linked with both Lazio and Manchester United Paolo remained with West Ham but his nine goals in nineteen games – taking his United tally to 51 goals in 141 games - during 2002-3 failed to save The Hammers from the drop. However this true entertainer remained in English football following his subsequent release by West Ham, signing for Charlton Athletic, before returning home to re-join Lazio in the summer of 2004.

DI PIEDI, Michele 2000-03

Born: 4 December 1980 Palermo, Italy
(6ft, 13st 5lbs – 2002)
Debut: 13 August 2000
v Wolverhampton Wanderers
Division One Away
Last Appearance: 17 January 2003
v Sheffield United
Division One Away
Total League
& Cup Appearances: 10+34 Goals: 7

Career Details:

Perugia		
WEDNESDAY	1 August	2000 Free
Mansfield Town	3 August	2002 Trial
Odd Grenland	30 August	2002 Loan
Bristol Rovers	21 February	2003 Loan
Contract cancelled	28 April	2003
A.S.Sora		2003
AFC Bournemouth	July	2004 Free
Apoel Nicosia	September	2004

Hard running Italian forward who was a surprise capture by Paul Jewell during the 2000-1 close season – after the long-haired attacker had greatly impressed during a trial period at Hillsborough. He made an immediate impact when scoring a spectacular long-range effort in a 1-0 win at Grimsby Town in August 2000 and throughout his debut season endeared himself to Wednesday fans with a series of wholehearted displays and outstanding goals. The youngster was Paul Jewell's first signing as Owls boss – he was a free agent when captured by Wednesday after being recommended by ex-Owls player Simon Stainrod – and Jewell's confidence in the Sicilian's abilities was reflected by the offer of a four-year contract.

Unfortunately his career at Wednesday would never fulfil the promise Di Piedi showed in that first season and under the subsequent managership of Peter Shreeves, Terry Yorath and later Chris Turner he became an increasingly peripheral figure. A series of persistent injuries disrupted his second season at Wednesday although his superb overhead kick in a League Cup tie against Sunderland in September 2001 won him the Nationwide goal of the month award. Throughout his time at Wednesday Di Piedi was never one to score tap-ins but his strike against Bradford City five days after the Sunderland game would prove to be his final goal in a Wednesday shirt. Despite regaining his fitness for the start of the following season he failed to make the squad for the opening day of the campaign and three weeks later left for a loan spell at Norwegian top-flight side Odd Grenland. He was mainly played out of position whilst on loan and was a playing sub as Odd Grenland won their Norwegian Cup semi-final. Unfortunately it was the subs bench where Di Piedi spent the latter weeks of his time in Scandinavian football, being an unused sub as his new club lost one-nil to Valerenga in the Cup Final.

He returned to Wednesday in November 2002 but bizarrely – due to new FIFA transfer rules – was unable to play competitive football for the Owls until the transfer window re-opened in January 2003! This ruling of course further hampered his chances of breaking into the first team at Wednesday and he would make only two first team appearances for the club under Turner before failing to make an impression during a loan spell at Division Three strugglers Bristol Rovers. At the end of the season – with his wife expecting their first child – his contract was cancelled by mutual consent and the Italian returned home to Italy, joining Serie C (Group B) side A.S.Sora.

DICKINSON, Walter 'Wally' 1922-23

Born: 22 December 1895 Sheffield
(5ft 8½ ins, 11st 8lbs – 1922)
Died: 5 February 1968 Sheffield
Debut: 18 November 1922
v Hull City
Division Two Away
Last Appearance: 20 January 1923
v Bury
Division Two Home
Total League
& Cup Appearances: 8 Goals: 0

Career Details:

Craven's Sports		
Barnsley		WW1 Guest
Southend United		WW1 Guest
Barrow		WW1 Guest
Bradford Park Avenue	August	1918
WEDNESDAY	June	1922 £250
Swindon Town	8 June	1923

Full back Walter Dickinson was originally plucked from Sheffield junior football early in the 1918-19 season by Bradford Park Avenue. During his time in Bradford, Wally – a player described as "clever but slow"- actually trained with Wednesday and at one point made seventy consecutive first team appearances for Avenue. However Wednesday boss Bob Brown was struggling to find a regular left back at Hillsborough and so Dickinson returned to the City of his birth during the close season of 1922, after 115 games for Bradford. The cool and calculating defender – whose son was tragically killed in the Second World War - started his time at Hillsborough in the reserves but after making his league debut enjoyed a seven-game run in the league side.

However his hopes of becoming a permanent fixture at Wednesday effectively disappeared when Ernie Blenkinsop arrived from Hull City in January 1923 – the outstanding left back making the position his own over the next decade. The Wednesday hierarchy decided Wally did not have the pace to act as understudy to Blenkinsop and after just a year at his hometown club he subsequently moved onto Division Three (South) club Swindon Town. However he found the lower league more to his liking and before retiring in 1930 had appeared in 230 league games for The Robins – developing a useful scoring knack which included seven goals during the 1927-8 season, out of a total of nineteen goals for Town.

DILLON, Francis Richard 1938-39

Born: 1st Quarter 1913 Bury
(5ft 8½ins, 10st 7lbs – 1938)
Debut: 29 October 1938
v Sheffield United
Division Two Away
Last Appearance: 4 March 1939
v Sheffield United
Division Two Away
Total League
& Cup Appearances: 9* Goals: 0
***Also appeared in**
3 wartime games, scoring 1 goal

Career Details:

Manchester North End		1936 Amat.
WEDNESDAY	10 May	1938
Released		1939
Rotherham United		1941-2 Guest

Little is known of right winger Francis Dillon although he is unique in Wednesday history as not only did his debut come in a the white heat of a Sheffield derby but his last appearance also came in the reverse fixture at Hillsborough – the Owls won one-nil at home and drew at Bramall Lane in a season when United pipped Wednesday to promotion by the slenderest of margins. The pacy winger had started his playing career as an amateur in Cheshire League football with Manchester North End and was brought to Hillsborough – aged 21 - by new manager Jimmy McMullen as competition for Len Massarella. However despite being on the losing side only twice in his eleven games in a blue and white shirt Dillon could not dislodge his rival from the number seven shirt and after just twelve months at Wednesday was released as war loomed. He spent the early years of the wartime working in a munitions factory and later played just a single game as a guest for Rotherham United.

DJORDJIC, Bojan 2001-02

Born: 6 February 1982 Belgrade, Yugoslavia
(5ft 10ins, 11st 1lbs – 2001)
Debut: 8 December 2001 v Millwall Division One Home
Last Appearance: 29 December 2001
v Norwich City Division One Home
Total League & Cup Appearances: 4+1 Goals: 0

Career Details:

Bromma Pojkarna (Sweden)		1998
Manchester United	16 February	1999 £1,000,000*
WEDNESDAY	7 December	2001 Loan
AGF Aarhus	1 September	2002 Season Loan
Loan Return	30 June	2003
Red Star Belgrade	July	2003 Season Loan
Glasgow Rangers	22 November	2004 Trial
Glasgow Rangers	27 December	2004 Free
Plymouth Argyle	June	2005

* Dependent upon appearances

When Swedish U-21 international winger Bojan Djordjic made his debut for Wednesday he looked a truly remarkable talent – not only did he supply the cross for The Owls goal but also hit the crossbar with an audacious 35-yard free kick that surprised everybody in the ground, including the opposition keeper! However that display from the pacy winger proved to be the highlight of his month on loan at Wednesday as the Yugoslavian born attacker – his father Branko was a former Red Star Belgrade and Yugoslavian international - contributed little in his remaining games. Admittedly he was playing in a Wednesday team that was struggling at the wrong end of the First Division table and perhaps had no real room for talents of a "luxury player" like Djordjic. However despite playing in a side bereft of quality he did disappoint fans with his displays and was eventually dropped to the subs bench before returning to Old Trafford

He had arrived at Wednesday with the image of yet another United starlet who was just about to roll off the conveyor belt of talent that had brought the likes of Giggs, Scholes and Beckham into the English game. He had joined United from Swedish football in February 1999 but was allowed to complete the season in his adopted homeland before moving to Manchester for pre season training. He was signed for a large fee – which could rise to £1m - but withstood the pressure of the price tag to be named young player of the year 1999-00 - his first full season at Old Trafford. He continued his education in United's reserve team and was rewarded with a first team debut in the final game of the following season while his only start in senior football for United came in a Worthington Cup tie at Arsenal, when United fielded an under strength side. The lack of first team opportunities led to his move to Wednesday soon after and in the summer that followed Bojan joined Danish side AGF, being almost ever present as his Scandinavian club finished mid-table in the 2002-3 Superligen. Later moved back to the former Yugoslavia on loan but returned to the UK to sign a six-month contract for Rangers, following a successful trial.

DOBSON, Colin 1957-66

Born: 9 May 1940 Eston, Middlesbrough
(5ft 8ins, 10st 10lbs – 1964)
Debut: 20 September 1961
v Arsenal
Division One Home
Last Appearance: 7 May 1966
v Nottingham Forest
Division One Away
Total League
& Cup Appearances: 195 Goals: 52

Career Details:

South Bank		
WEDNESDAY	November	1957
Huddersfield Town	27 August	1966 £20,000
Brighton & Hove Albion	January	1972 Loan
Bristol Rovers	3 June	1972 Free

CAPS (@SWFC)
ENGLAND U-23 (2) v Yugoslavia 29/05/63, v Rumania 02/06/63

After impressing for both Easton District and Yorkshire schoolboys, attacker Colin Dobson signed amateur forms for Wednesday in 1955, aged fifteen. He progressed to part-time professional status in November 1957 but stayed in his native northeast – completing his apprenticeship at a Middlesbrough ship building firm – until finally moving to Sheffield on becoming a full-time professional in July 1961. During those years he would travel down to Wednesday to turn out for the club's junior, "A" and reserve sides but soon after moving to the City was handed a first team debut, replacing mercurial inside-right Bobby Craig. Although the Scot returned to the side two games later Dobson retained his first team jersey, switching to the left wing so manager Vic Buckingham could accommodate the duo. Luckily though for Dobson the patience of Buckingham with the wayward Craig was at breaking point and when the latter was dropped in February 1962 Dobson was moved back into the inside-right position.

From that point Dobson became a fixture in the first team, becoming a firm favourite with Owls fans and missing only a handful of games over the next four years. During that period the diminutive but highly skilful forward played mainly as a left-winger and helped Wednesday to a Fairs Cup quarter-final meeting with Barcelona and contributed greatly to three consecutive sixth placed finishes in Division One. However a change of tactics by pragmatic manager Alan Brown in March 1966 – following England manager Alf Ramsey's lead of dispensing with the traditional winger – led to Dobson missing out on the latter stages of Wednesday's run to the F.A.Cup Final and in the following summer departed for pastures new. Incidentally while back in Sheffield soon after being transferred he met a club official who told him that there was an F.A.Cup runners-up medal at the club waiting for him, which he had forgotten about! During a successful six-year stay at Huddersfield Town, Dobson played in every forward position and was top scorer in several seasons – netting a healthy 52 times in 174 league and cup games for The Terriers. He won the Second Division Championship with Town in 1970 – ironically replacing his old club Wednesday in the top-flight – but after falling out of favour was unfortunate to suffer a broken leg whilst on loan at Brighton. His final league club proved to be Bristol Rovers where under manager, and ex-team mate, Don Megson he gained valuable coaching experience while completing his playing career with four goals in sixty-two league games-winning promotion from Division Three in 1974.

The player-manager role at Rovers was the start of a varied career off the field of play for Dobson, starting in May 1977 when he was appointed reserve/youth coach at Division One Coventry City. The Teeside native stayed at Highfield Road for just over six years - until August 1983 – before becoming first team coach at Port Vale in December of the same year. However he stayed only a season in the Potteries before leaving these shores for a two-year stint as coach in The Middle East. After a year in charge at Bahrain club

West Riffa – winning the Amir Cup - he moved to Al Rayyan in August 1985 where in his one season he took the Qatar based side to the Amir League and Cup double as well as winning the United Arab Emirates Championship. A year back in England as youth coach to Aston Villa followed but Dobson was soon dusting down his suitcase as a year later he joined Portuguese club Sporting Lisbon – also as youth team coach. He departed the beautiful City of Lisbon in November 1988 for the sunny climes of Gillingham, accepting a joint role of Chief Scout and Youth coach. His next engagement was as assistant youth team coach back at Coventry City before returning to the desert for a three-year spell as youth coach at Al Arabi of Kuwait. A nine-month stint as first team coach at Port Vale preceded his appointment as national youth team coach of Oman, winning the 1996 Asian Cup in Thailand soon after joining. A third stint at Coventry City – as Academy coach – started in January 1999 before he was appointed to his current position of chief Scout at Stoke City.

DODDS, Christopher "Chris" 1928-32

Born: 24 March 1904 Gateshead
(5ft 8½ ins, 11st 7lbs – 1928)
Died: 24 June 1990 Gateshead
Only Appearance: 22 November 1930
v Leicester City Division One Away
Total League & Cup Appearances: 1 Goals: 0

Career Details:

Greenfield Locomotive Ath.		
Middlesbrough	5 February	1926
Accrington Stanley	23 July	1926
WEDNESDAY	22 October	1928 £790
Colwyn Bay United	August	1931
Accrington Stanley	11 June	1932
Great Harwood Town	September	1936
Charter Street FC		

In the late 1920s/early 1930s the Owls could consistently field a start-studded line up that included many internationals. However for every Ernie Blenkinsop and Billy Marsden there would be a Chris Dodds – a player who spent three years in Wednesday's reserve side but was only called into first team action on one occasion. In fact his sole appearance came in quite extraordinary circumstances as in those days there was no rest for the top league so their best players could play international football – the matches were played mainly on a Saturday and if you lost half your side to call up it was tough luck! This happened to Wednesday in November 1930 when for the trip to Leicester the services of Alf Strange, Ernie Blenkinsop and Tony Leach were all required by England for a game against Wales in Wrexham. The Owls were therefore forced to reshuffle almost their whole defensive unit with Dodds being introduced at centre half-back and both Millership and Smith recalled. Thankfully such was the club's strength in depth – they were in second spot in Division One, looking to complete a hat-trick of League titles – that the England boys were hardly missed as Wednesday proceeded to thrash Leicester 5-2 at Filbert Street!

However it was back to Central League football for Dodds when Leach returned from International duty and in the summer that followed a move into non-league football at Colwyn Bay. A second spell at league side Accrington Stanley followed – he totalled nine goals in 157 games for Stanley – before finishing his playing career back in amateur football – reported to be still playing at the age of 43 for Charter Street in the Accrington League. His league career had actually started in his native northeast where after signing amateur forms for Boro in December 1925 he moved up to professional status three months later. However, after failing to make a league start at Middlesbrough Chris signed for Accrington where the forward - he was only moved to half-back during the 1927-8 season – spent most of his first season in the second team, netting twenty times. His excellent ball control and nimble footwork did earn him a Football League debut in December 1926 at Durham City but it was the change of position that advanced his first team chances – Dodds becoming a regular at perennial strugglers Stanley before signing for Bob Brown's Wednesday after just forty-one league games.

DONALDSON, O'Neill McKay 1995-98

Born: 24 November 1969 Birmingham
(6ft 1ins, 11st 8lbs – 1995)
Debut: 18 March 1995
v Manchester City
Premier League Away
Last Appearance: 8 November 1997
v Bolton Wanderers
Premier League Home
Total League
& Cup Appearances: 4+10 Goals: 3

Career Details:

Manchester United		Trainee
Hinckley Town		
Shrewsbury Town	13 November	1991 Free
Doncaster Rovers	10 August	1994 Free
Mansfield Town	23 December	1994 Loan
WEDNESDAY	10 January	1995 £50,000
Oxford United	30 January	1998 Loan
Stoke City	13 March	1998 Free
Torquay United	7 September	1998 Free
Released	30 June	2000
Halesowen Town	13 August	2001 Free
Stourport Swifts	11 September	2002 Free

After his surprise signing by Trevor Francis in January 1995 pacy forward O'Neill Donaldson seemed to be permanently on the fringes of the first team during his time at Wednesday. The ex-Manchester United trainee arrived on the day Manchester United bought Andy Cole from Newcastle United, having impressed greatly when scoring seven times in just five games while on loan at Mansfield Town. However while Cole would score freely and win many honours, Donaldson spent the majority of his time at Hillsborough playing Central League football – he scored 34 times for the second team and was top scorer for three seasons in a row. He always seemed too good for reserve team soccer but just could not win an extended run at first team level.

Frustrated with his lack of first team opportunities – and with several clubs said to be tracking him - Donaldson refused the Owls offer of a new contract in July 1997, going on week-to-week terms. However he stayed at Hillsborough and after another successful loan spell at Oxford United – scoring twice in six games – he looked set to move to Premier League neighbours Barnsley in March 1998. This move broke down though and he was eventually allowed to leave, somewhat surprisingly, on a free transfer to Stoke City. Unfortunately for Donaldson, City suffered relegation soon after he joined and after having only signed a short-term deal was subsequently released in the summer that followed. On the recommendation of ex-Wednesday team mate Chris Waddle he was signed by Devon club Torquay United but his league career finished in the summer of 2000 after an injury-ruined time which saw him score only three times in 32 appearances. He now combines a role in the media with his work in senior schools where Donaldson helps children with special needs and juvenile offenders – thanks to football and DJ classes – gain access to the National Curriculum.

DONNELLY, Simon Thomas 1999-2003

Born: 1 December 1974 Glasgow
(5ft 9ins, 10st 12lbs – 2001)
Debut: 7 August 1999
v Liverpool
Premier League Home
Last Appearance: 29 March 2003
v Watford
Division One Home
Total League
& Cup Appearances: 30+32 Goals: 8

Career Details:

Clyde Boys Club		1988
Queen's Park Boys Club		
Celtic Boys Club		
Glasgow Celtic	27 May	1993
WEDNESDAY	1 July	1999 Free
Released	30 June	2003 Free
Coventry City	1 July	2003 Trial
St Johnstone	1 August	2003 Free
Dunfermline Athletic	14 July	2004 Free

Creative midfielder Simon Donnelly arrived with Celtic team mate Phil O'Donnell in the summer of 1999 on a lucrative four-year "Bosman" inspired transfer. In his final season with Celtic, Donnelly helped the Scottish giants to runners-up spot behind Rangers and in five seasons as a professional at Celtic Park he was a consistent performer, appearing in 146 league games, scoring 30 times. While wearing the famous green and white hoops he won both Scottish League (1998) and Scottish Cup (1995) honours and was also capped eleven times at U-21 level for Scotland and ten times at full international level. It was this record that persuaded Wednesday manager Danny Wilson to sign Donnelly on a pre-contract agreement on 17 March 1999 with the full transfer taking place four months later when his existing contract expired.

At the time the capture of the two Scottish Internationals was hailed a major coup for Wednesday but unfortunately for everyone concerned the twosome would experience quite horrendous problems with injury that not only ruined their spell at Wednesday but also placed financial pressure on the club. Previous to joining the Owls, Donnelly – whose father Tom played for Rangers and Motherwell - had only been sidelined through injury once in his career – perhaps significantly for three months in his final season at Celtic – but his debut campaign at Hillsborough was badly disrupted by injury and despite making double figure sub appearances he started only four games. His first goal in a Wednesday shirt came in the dramatic 3-3 draw at Derby County in February 2000 but it could not stop Wednesday crashing out of the Premier League. Unfortunately the situation deteriorated even more for Donnelly in his second season at Wednesday as despite playing in a handful of pre season games he was injured again and became somewhat of a forgotten man as the Owls struggled to avoid the drop from Division One. After spending almost the whole season on the sidelines he eventually returned to first team action, appearing as a sub in the final three games of the season – netting a dramatic winner in the home game with Barnsley after coming off the bench.

This mini-run in the side gave fans hope that finally they would see the best of Donnelly and in fact over the final two years of his contract the forward's fitness record improved dramatically. He appeared in exactly half of the club's league fixtures in 2001/2 (starting fourteen games) and at times looked a real asset to the side – a superb brace at Millwall in March 2003 helping Wednesday to record a stunning win. However despite the fact that Donnelly possessed real vision and passing ability he was a somewhat lightweight player who was not really suited to the rigours of Division One football. Even when fit he struggled to break into the Wednesday side during his final season at Hillsborough and left in the summer of 2003 after a frustrating, disappointing and somewhat disastrous stay in Sheffield. After failing to earn a contract after a trial period at Division One Coventry City, Donnelly returned to his homeland to sign a one-year deal at St Johnstone and later penned another twelve-month deal at Dunfermline.

DOOLEY, Derek 1947-53

Born: 13 December 1929 Sheffield
(6ft 3ins, 12st 8lbs – 1948)
Debut: 11 March 1950
v Preston North End
Division Two Home
Last Appearance: 14 February 1953
v Preston North End
Division One Away
Total League
& Cup Appearances: 63 Goals: 63

Career Details:

Sheffield Y.M.C.A.		
Firth Park Y.M.		
Lincoln City	November	1945 Amat.
Denaby United		
WEDNESDAY	16 June	1947
Dundee United		1950 Guest

Like his predecessor Teddy Davison the name of Derek Dooley has entered the annals of Sheffield football as a man loved and respected on both sides of the City. However Dooley's playing career was of course dramatically cut short due to the tragic events of 14th February 1953 when the raw-boned attacker suffered a broken leg following a 50/50 challenge with Preston goalkeeper George Thompson. The fracture alone would not normally end a player's career but while Derek was lying in Preston Royal Infirmary his leg became infected with gas gangrene – it was thought the organism had entered his leg via the soil on the Deepdale pitch – and an SOS was sent out to Manchester Infirmary for a gangrene serum. Unfortunately even after receiving his injections Dooley's health slowly deteriorated and three days after the game his surgeon Mr.Garden took the momentous decision to amputate his right leg to save Derek's life. The news was a devastating blow for the youngster and stunned the football world that could hardly believe his whirlwind career had ended in such abrupt and tragic circumstances.

He had first played football at Owler Lane School and after leaving to start work as a trainee deaf aid mechanic played for both Sheffield YMCA and Firth Park. However on his fifteenth birthday Derek was picked to play for Lincoln City reserves in a game at Denaby United and was soon signed on amateur forms by the Lincolnshire club. During those years Derek trained two evenings a week at Bramall Lane – during one of these sessions he actually played for The Blades in a friendly game against Oak Folds – and manager of United at the time (one Teddy Davison!) tried unsuccessfully to sign the towering youngster. When not required by Lincoln, Derek appeared for both YMCA and Denaby United and once scored four times in a 6-1 win for the former in a Youth final. He was also picked to appear for a Sheffield and Hallamshire representative side but his career was about to take a different path, thanks in part to the English weather! The 1946-7 season was extended into June because of the worst winter on record but although professional contracts were extended by two weeks, amateur ones were not so Dooley became a free agent. He had played two Division Three (North) games for City and won the Lincolnshire Senior Cup but it was a reserve appearance against Denaby United at Sincil Bank that started the wheels of a transfer in motion. On the opposition side was ex-Wednesday player Walt Millership and after the game he asked the teenager if he would like to sign for Wednesday. Dooley said yes and so Millership informed Wednesday who sent Tommy Walker to watch Derek in a local Cup Final. Both Nottingham Forest and Wolves had scouts at the game but when Walker arranged for Dooley to meet Eric Taylor the move was just about sealed.

He duly signed part-time professional forms for Wednesday and soon started to score freely in reserve and "A" team soccer. The tall, red-haired, courageous and in his early days somewhat ungainly centre-forward found Yorkshire League football much to his liking - scoring three consecutive hat-tricks in December 1947 –and after making his Central League debut he netted his first goal – also in December 1947. His call up to do National Service in

February 1948 then put a brake on his career although while in the R.A.F. Derek did play services football and also in his first year appeared in the odd game back at Wednesday. However he was posted to Scotland in his second year and helped his station team reach the R.A.F. Cup Final two seasons running – he even played a game for Dundee United against St.Andrew's University. After being de-mobbed Derek returned to Wednesday's Central league side and a dozen goals in second team soccer – Wednesday turned down a £5,000 offer from Aston Villa after he impressed against them - during 1949-50 was enough to persuade Eric Taylor to hand Dooley a first team debut against Preston at Hillsborough. Unfortunately his league debut was a disappointing experience and it was back to square one after he failed to impress. However you cannot keep a good man down and he bounced back to score 49 times for the reserve and "A" teams in 1950-1, including all eight as Halifax Town were beaten 8-2 in a Yorkshire League fixture in September 1950.

He made a single appearance in 1950-1 at first team level, failing to score, but the big breakthrough came in October 1951 when with Wednesday struggling in mid-table and Dooley having scored 13 goals in 11 reserve games he was given a third chance to make his mark at Hillsborough. It was a opportunity he grasped with both hands and in the 31 games he played in that momentous season scored an astonishing 47 goals, setting a club goal scoring record that in all probability will never be beaten. With his great physical advantage, powerful shot in both feet, pace and quick eye for an opening Dooley terrorised every defender he faced as Wednesday stormed to the Second Division Championship. He became a true enigma in English football but initially found life in the higher grade hard and was dropped after four games – such was his popularity that thousands of fans decided to watch him score twice for the reserves at Bramall Lane than attend the home game with Charlton Athletic! He was only absent though for one game and on his recall scored 16 times in 25 league games as Wednesday consolidated in the top-flight. When his career was cut short the Owls not only lost a consistent goal scorer – one can only speculate what Dooley and Wednesday could have achieved if fate had not taken a hand – but the fans an idol and it is perhaps significant that two years after his accident crowds at Hillsborough had dropped by over 15,000 per game.

After spending weeks in hospital back in Sheffield, Dooley had his contract paid up until the end of the season by Wednesday before starting to write for a national newspaper, initially with a ghostwriter but eventually on his own. His testimonial match in March 1955 - between a Sheffield select side and a star-studded International eleven - was the first game played under floodlights at Hillsborough and in total his benefit earned Derek the not inconsiderable sum - by 1955 standards – of £15,000.

By then Dooley was working at Gunstone's bakery in Sheffield and spent eight years in their employment – eventually becoming assistant sales manager – while he took time out to train Wednesday's junior side in the evenings. He also started the Dooley All Star Team (handing the mantel to Johnny Quinn ten years later) and before taking over as Wednesday's inaugural development fund manager was twice the subject of TV programme "This is your life". On 29th January 1971 Dooley took charge of first team affairs from Danny Williams and as a manager Derek was a reflective, pipe-smoking figure who believed in attacking football. His side briefly topped Division Two early in the 1972-3 season with the likes of Willie Henderson and Brian Joicey lifting some of the gloom that had surrounded the club since relegation in 1970. Unfortunately the following season a combination of a mystery virus and loss of form saw Wednesday drop down the league. However just when Derek thought Wednesday were starting to turn the corner he was controversially dismissed on Christmas Eve 1973, to condemnation from all quarters – only for the timing if nothing else.

Not surprisingly the nature of his departure caused much bitterness in the Dooley household and it would be almost twenty years before he set foot back inside Hillsborough for a Wednesday game – in March 1992 in his capacity as managing director at Sheffield United. After leaving Wednesday Derek had worked for a sports footwear company as a sales rep before in November 1974 he accepted Sheffield United's offer of becoming Commercial manager. It started an association with the Blades that still exists today. He joined the board in 1983 - after recovering from a heart attack – and was appointed M.D. and Chief Executive in February 1986 before officially retiring in August 1992. However he returned to Bramall Lane during the Brealey debacle, taking over as Chairman and after being ousted through a boardroom buy out he returned for a second spell at the helm in November 1999. Dooley – who was made a freeman of the City in 1993 – eventually became Chairman of both Football Club and PLC boards and for his services to football was deservedly awarded an MBE in the 2003 New Year's honours list.

DOWD, Hugh Oliver 1974-79

Born: 19 May 1951 Lurgan, N.Ireland
(6ft 1ins, 13st – 1978)
Debut: 17 August 1974
v Oldham Athletic
Division Two Away
Last Appearance: 30 September 1978
v Swindon Town
Division Three Away
Total League
& Cup Appearances: 134+3 Goals: 0

Career Details:

Bessbrook Boys Club		
Newry Celtic		
Glenavon		1969
WEDNESDAY	10 July	1974 £20,000
Doncaster Rovers	8 August	1979 £14,000
Sheffield Club	July	1983

CAPS (@SWFC) – N.IRELAND Full (2)
v Norway 04/09/74, v Sweden 30/10/74

Unfortunately for tall centre-half Hugh Dowd he joined the Owls at the start of the club's worst ever season, as they tumbled into Division Three for the first time in their history. He had arrived from Irish football with eight amateur and one full international cap for his country – he was still playing as an amateur when capped for Northern Ireland against Wales in 1974. While with Glenavon he suffered an Irish Cup semi-final loss to Glentoran – Dowd conceding the decisive penalty – but spent most of his time in England, studying Physical Education and French at Manchester University. While furthering his education in Lancashire, Dowd turned down offers to join both Sunderland and Luton Town, only turning professional when Steve Burtenshaw took him to Hillsborough.

The imposing defender was a regular during the traumatic 1974-5 season – winning additional caps for N.Ireland – but injury meant he appeared in only thirteen league games in the following season as Wednesday came mightily close to a second successive relegation. However Hugh was then a regular for two seasons under the managership of Len Ashurst and then Jack Charlton before falling out of favour with the latter and moving to Fourth Division Doncaster Rovers in 1979 – at the time he was a record signing for Rovers. At Belle Vue, Hugh appeared in 94 league games before being released in the summer of 1983, joining Danny Begara's Sheffield Club on a part-time basis. By now he was employed by Sheffield City Council, initially as a mini bus driver, and over the next few years combined full time employment with playing spells at a wide variety of Sheffield junior league teams – he left Sheffield Club in 1985. He still works in the City, employed as a Community remand officer for the Youth Offending Team, involved in pre-sentence work with young offenders.

DOWLING, Michael 1910-11

Born: 30 March 1890 Jarrow-on-Tyne
(5ft 9ins, 12st 7lbs – 1910)
Died: 4th Quarter 1969 Rotherham
Debut: 17 September 1910
v Preston North End Division One Away
Last Appearance: 8 April 1911
v Nottingham Forest Division One Away
Total League & Cup Appearances: 7 Goals: 0

Career Details:

Paisley St. Mirren		
WEDNESDAY	June	1910 £40
Portsmouth	June	1911 £125*
Jarrow	August	1913
Lincoln City	July	1914
Ebbw Vale	June	1920

*Joint fee with Stringfellow

Well-built forward Michael Dowling arrived at Hillsborough with a glowing reputation as a right-winger who had also showed his versatility by playing in every position in the forward line at St.Mirren. The Englishman, with an Irish name, who was signed from a Scottish club would stay only a solitary season in Sheffield. He came as direct competition for first team regular Sam Kirkman but would spend most of his season playing Midland League football with Wednesday's reserves as they finished runners-up. His only goal for the club came in an Owlerton reserve outing against Gainsborough Trinity in October 1910 but at the end of the season he moved to Southern League Portsmouth – an up and coming manager by the name of Bob Brown making Dowling, and his team mate Stringfellow – amongst his first signings. After returning to his roots a year later – signing for North-Eastern league Jarrow - Dowling then spent six years at Lincoln City, serving in the Royal Navy during World War One, before ending his playing career at Southern League (Welsh section) outfit Ebbw Vale.

DOWNES, Stephen Fleming "Steve" 1969-72

Born: 2 December 1949 Leeds
(5ft 10ins, 12st 5lbs – 1971)
Debut: 26 December 1969
v Sunderland
Division One Home
Last Appearance: 21 August 1971
v Bristol City
Division Two Home
Total League
& Cup Appearances: 29+5 Goals: 5

Career Details:

Wolverhampton Wanderers		Trainee
Leeds M.D.B.C.		
Rotherham United	April	1967
WEDNESDAY	23 December	1969 £35,000
Chesterfield	10 August	1972 £10,000
Halifax Town	1 July	1974 Free
Blackburn Rovers	12 March	1976 Loan
Scarborough		1976
Gainsborough Trinity		1978

After impressing for both Leeds and Yorkshire boys attacker Steve Downes signed apprentice forms at First Division Wolves. However after failing to make the grade at Molineux he dropped into non-league soccer before being taken to Rotherham United by Fred Green. He duly enjoyed a very successful start to his professional career at Millmoor, netting eighteen times in 62 league games for the Millers, and it was this early promise that alerted First Division strugglers Wednesday to his attributes. After having had his first offer refused, Wednesday boss Danny Williams finally got his man after an increased bid was accepted and he pitched the youngster straight into the side on Boxing Day 1969. However despite Downes scoring in a 2-0 win it proved to be a false dawn as the youngster did not score again until the opening day of the following season, by which time Wednesday had been relegated from the top-flight.

In fact he would net only twice more in league soccer for Wednesday and a disappointing spell at Hillsborough ended when he was sold to neighbours Chesterfield at a big financial loss to the club – the move coming just weeks after he had turned down a £10,000 move to Peterborough United in order to stay and fight for his place. His scoring record in the lower leagues at Saltergate and then Halifax Town did improve – netting 23 times – although he failed to score during a six-game loan spell at Blackburn Rovers which signalled the end of his league career. After retiring from the professional game he spent two seasons at Northern Premier League Scarborough (an oft quoted spell at Matlock Town never took place) before injury ended his career after a further year at ex-League club Gainsborough Trinity. After retiring from the game, Downes started work as a sales rep, moving through the company to eventually become National Sales manager. After ten years he left and now runs his own electrical wholesale business in his native Leeds.

DRISCOLL, John Henry 'Jack' 1937-38

Born: 27 July 1909 Grays
(5ft 9ins, 11st – 1937)
Died: 7 October 1997 Wellington
Debut: 23 October 1937 v Manchester United Division One Away
Last Appearance: 11 January 1938 v Burnley F.A.Cup Away
Total League & Cup Appearances: 6 Goals: 2

Career Details:

Rodington FC		
Oakengates Town		
Oswestry Town	May	1932
Stourbridge		
West Bromwich Albion	November	1934
WEDNESDAY	28 May	1937 £300
Released		1938
Wellington Town	June	1938
Wrexham	February	1943 Guest

The Football League career of inside-left John Driscoll amounted to just five games at Sheffield Wednesday, after he had failed to break into the first team during a stint at West Bromwich Albion. His career had started in West-Midlands non-league soccer and he was brought to Hillsborough by Owls boss Billy Walker to fill the problematic position on the left side – a vacancy never properly filled since the departure of Ron Starling in January 1937.

However in his only season at Wednesday, Driscoll failed to secure a regular first team spot and had to be content with reserve team football for most of the season – scoring five times in sixteen Central league games. He was released by new boss Jimmy McMullen after a terrible season which had seen the Owls finish in seventeenth position in Division Two – the lowest finish in the club's history at that point.

DRIVER, Allenby 1936-46

Born: 29 September 1918 Clipstone
(5ft 10½ ins, 11st 4lbs – 1936)
Died: 31 March 1997 Grenoside, Sheffield
Debut: 1 January 1938
v Chesterfield
Division Two Home
Last Appearance: 11 February 1946
v Stoke City
F.A.Cup Home
Total League
& Cup Appearances: 12* Goals: 6
***Also appeared in**
35 wartime games, scoring 11 goals

Career Details:

Clipstone		
Mansfield Shoes		
WEDNESDAY	18 April	1936
Luton Town	5 October	1946 £4,000
Norwich City	5 January	1948 £4,000
Ipswich Town	16 January	1950 £3,000
Walsall	4 July	1952 Free
Corby Town	2 July	1953 Free
Frickley Colliery	August	1954

* Guested for Brentford, Crystal Palace, Watford, Millwall, Fulham, Brighton & Aberdeen in wartime football.

For many players the advent of the Second World War effectively signalled the end of their careers in the Football League. However Allenby Driver had time on his side – he was only twenty years old when War was declared – and after the hostilities had ceased continued to play football well into the late 1950s at a variety of clubs in league and non-league soccer. He had first come to the fore while starring for Mansfield and Notts boys before joining Wednesday on amateur forms in March 1936. After a season in "A" team football at Hillsborough – playing a solitary reserve team game in March 1937 – Driver finished the following campaign as reserve team top scorer, with nine goals to his name. A goal on his first team debut led to a mini three game run in the side for Allenby but it was soon back to the Central League where the youngster showed his eye for goal by finishing top scorer again – this time sharing the 13-goal mark with Walter Aveyard.

The form of Charlie Napier kept Driver in the reserves during 1938-9 and although he netted in both of his first team appearances – including a game at inside-right - his rival was firmly in possession of the first team jersey when the following season kicked off. However he was recalled to the first eleven for the third league game of the season but soon after War was declared and the whole Football League season was declared null and void. Throughout the War Driver served with the Army Royal Artillery Home forces - despite its name he did go overseas to both France and Germany – and played football for a wide variety of clubs on a guest basis, as well as appearing for Wednesday in regionalised football. When the F.A.Cup was restarted in 1945-6 Driver scored three times in four appearances as Wednesday reached the last sixteen but when league soccer returned a year later Red Froggatt blocked his path to first team soccer and early in the campaign Allenby left for Luton Town.

Thirteen goals in 45 appearances for Town preceded a similarly successful spell at Norwich City where he netted nineteen times in forty-nine appearances. The ball playing forward continued to hit the net on a regular basis at Ipswich Town – 25 in 86 league matches – before wrapping up his league career back in the West Midlands at Walsall. When his professional career came to an end he worked as a travelling salesman for a confectionary company for twenty years – finally hanging up his boots in 1958 after four years at Frickley Colliery – before spending the seven years until his retirement in the employment of Union Carbine back in Sheffield.

DRURY, George Benjamin 1934-38

Born: 22 January 1914 Hucknall, Notts.
(5ft 8ins, 11st 5lbs – 1934)
Died: 19 June 1972 Hucknall. Notts.
Debut: 7 November 1936
v Grimsby Town
Division One Home
Last Appearance: 5 March 1938
v Manchester United
Division Two Home
Total League
& Cup Appearances: 47* Goals: 11
***Also appeared in 29 wartime games, scoring 6 times**

Career Details:

Hucknall Colts		Trial
Hucknall Congregationals		
Hucknall Villa		
Loughborough Corinthians		1933
Heanor Town		1934
West Bromwich Albion		1934 Trial
WEDNESDAY	26 September	1934
Arsenal	10 March	1938 £7,000
West Bromwich Albion	26 October	1946
Watford	July	1948 £2,500
Linby Colliery	November	1950
Darlaston		
South Normanton		

* Guested for Wednesday, Aberdeen, Nottingham Forest, Liverpool, Doncaster Rovers, Notts County, Distillery, Burnley & Bury in wartime football.

The almost indecent speed of George Drury's sale to Arsenal not only stunned Hillsborough regulars but was also a shock for the player himself who did not know of the move until the day he was sold! The transfer of the highly promising inside-forward – seen as a vital player around which Wednesday could build for the future – caused a storm of controversy and quite unprecedented criticism of the club followed his big money move to Highbury – the signing was completed during the morning in London but the news was not released until the afternoon and then only in the Capital. The move even prompted Wednesday shareholders – a group not known for their militancy - to call for a protest meeting and this was only called off when the Owls subsequently entered the transfer market to sign Scottish International Charlie Napier from Derby County and Bill Fallon from Notts County.

His original move to Hillsborough was in fact one of pure chance as in late 1933 assistant manager Joe McClelland went to a Heanor Town game to watch a young player. He was however impressed by another forward and after twenty-four hours of ceaseless research he traced Drury to his home in Hucknall and subsequently signed him for Wednesday. He made an immediate impact in the club's third team – once netting four goals in a win over Sheffield United – and after breaking into the first team as a right-winger he became one of the few high spots in a season that ended in relegation for Wednesday. In what proved to be his final season at Wednesday, Drury played 25 times and showed his versatility by figuring in three games at right-half, three matches at left-half, two at inside-right and 17 times in his best position of inside-left. His undoubted talent and consistency marked him out – along with fellow inside-forward Jackie Robinson – as a real star of the future so it was perhaps understandable that with Wednesday struggling near the foot of Division Two, and the player not looking to move, that his sale proved to be so controversial.

Within weeks of joining Arsenal, Drury had won the League Championship although despite playing in the final eleven games of the season it was not sufficient to be awarded a medal. In the final season before the outbreak of war the outstanding attacker missed only a handful of games for the Londoners as they finished fifth in the top-flight. Unfortunately war then deprived league football of Drury's best years as while serving in the RAF he appeared for a wide spectrum of clubs, including several games back in the blue and white shirt. He actually played twice for the Irish Regional League against the League of Ireland during the 1943-44 season, while he was at Distillery. After being de-mobbed George only played four games in post –war league football for Arsenal before dropping down a division to sign for West Bromwich Albion. He experienced a mixed time at The Hawthorns club - scoring nine times in thirty-one games – before another disappointing spell at Watford brought the curtain down on his league career – he was signed for Watford by his old Gunners team mate Eddie Hapgood. After playing six years in non-league football Drury retired in 1954.

DRYBURGH, William 1897-99 & 1901-02

Born: 22 May 1876 Cowdenbeath, Scotland
Died: 5 April 1951 Kelty, Fife, Scotland
Debut: 1 September 1897 v Aston Villa Division One Away
Last Appearance: 22 March 1902
v Blackburn Rovers Division One Home
Total League & Cup Appearances: 50 Goals: 11

Career Details:

Cowdenbeath	6 August	1895
WEDNESDAY	August	1897
Millwall Athletic	July	1899
WEDNESDAY	1 May	1901
Cowdenbeath	7 August	1902
Tottenham Hotspur	15 December	1902
Lochgelly United		1903

Right-winger William Dryburgh initially arrived at Olive Grove as competition to the established Archie Brash but actually started his Wednesday career as first choice with his rival banished to the reserve side – Dryburgh scored on his debut, a feat he repeated for both Millwall and Tottenham Hotspur. The experience of Brash led to his recall after just three games but Dryburgh was back on New

Year's Day 1898 – in a centre-forward role – before again replacing Brash on the right wing for the final eight Division One games of the season. During his time out of the side Dryburgh had greatly impressed in reserve team soccer, netting thirteen times as Wednesday walked away with the Midland Counties League, but the next campaign proved a major disappointment to all concerned at Wednesday as the club suffered relegation for the first time in their short Football League career.

The Scot was not re-signed for Wednesday's first experience of Division Two soccer and subsequently moved to South London, signing for professional Southern League side Millwall Athletic. The pacy winger was a big hit at Millwall and in his first season missed only one F.A.Cup tie as The Lions reached the semi-finals for the first time in their history – in addition the South District Combination League was won while Millwall finished seventh in the Southern League. The attacker – known as Willie during his time in the Capital – took his appearance tally to 88 games (13 goals) before returning to Sheffield for a second spell. By now of course Wednesday had moved to Hillsborough but his first appearance on the new ground would be in the opening reserve game of the season – an astonishing 13-1 win over Derby County reserves. There was no Archie Brash to deny Dryburgh a first team spot now but the form of Harry Davis ensured Willie played only a bit part in the Owls season before being released and returning to Scotland. He was not out of English football for long though as six months later he returned to London, signing for Southern League Spurs. After scoring on his Christmas Day 1902 debut Dryburgh appeared in a total of 32 competitive games for Tottenham before ending his playing career back in his homeland at non-league Lochgelly United. He retired from the playing field in 1905 and was a miner for the rest of his working life.

DUNGWORTH, John William "Jack/Johnny" 1881-92

Born: 1866 Heeley, Sheffield
(5ft 6½ ins, 10st – 1890)
Debut: 31 October 1885 v Long Eaton Rangers F.A.Cup Away
Last Appearance: 29 March 1890
v Blackburn Rovers F.A.Cup Final
Total League & Cup Appearances: 17* Goals: 2
***Also appeared in 32 Alliance League games**

Career Details:

Meersbrook Rangers	
WEDNESDAY	1881
Retired	1892

Jack Dungworth was another example of a player who rendered great service to Wednesday in the Victorian age without registering a Football League appearance for the club. The right-half back was perhaps the earliest known example of a man marker as he would follow the opponent's star player around the pitch and made sure he did not get a kick – he was said to "stick to his man like a leech!" The stopper was born in the Sheffield district of Heeley – his father was a table knife hafter – and started his playing career with local club Meersbrook Rangers, playing in several local finals before joining Wednesday at the age of fifteen. The player who had "a kick like a mule" waited until an April 1884 friendly at Walsall Town to make his senior bow for the club and it was not until part-way through the next season that Jack became an established member of a Wednesday side that were emerging as a real force in Sheffield football.

Over the next five years Jack was a mainstay of an Owls side that won many local honours including the Wharncliffe Charity Cup in 1886 and 1888, The Heeley Silver Cup in 1887 and Sheffield Challenge Cup in both 1887 and 1888. However these successes paled into insignificance when you consider that Dungworth played through an era when Wednesday not only turned professional but also secured the their own home and joined their first organised league competition. Although the Owls turned pro in 1887 Dungworth remained amateur throughout his career and was ever present during the 1889-90 season when Wednesday won the inaugural Championship of the Football Alliance League and also reached the F.A.Cup Final for the first time – Jack failing to stem the Blackburn Rovers tide as the Lancashire side won 6-1 at Kennington Oval. That heavy defeat in the biggest game on the English football calender proved a nemesis for Dungworth as he appeared in only more ten Alliance games in the following season as Wednesday slumped from first to last place. The arrival of Harry Brandon pushed Jack further back in the pecking order and during the 1891-2 season he was restricted solely to appearances for The Wanderers – the name that the club's reserve side played under.

In April 1892 his loyalty was rewarded with a benefit game at Olive Grove when players from United and Wednesday appeared under the banner of "Scotch v English"- the Englishmen prevailing three-nil in front of a superb crowd of over seven thousand. It proved to be a fitting end to his career at Wednesday for the fine all round sportsman who was also an outstanding runner, being thought as unequalled in the UK at the two-mile mark – he competed for many years in local races and lost only once, to a certain Billy Mosforth in a 600 yards steeplechase! In total he won 125 major prizes on the track and continued to compete after hanging up his football boots to become manager of a Leivage works in Sheffield

DUNLOP, Walter 1892-93

Born: 1st Quarter 1862 Saddleworth
Only Appearance: 3 September 1892
v Notts County Division One Away
Total League & Cup Appearances: 1 Goals: 0

Career Details:

Local football	
WEDNESDAY	1892
Darwen	1893

Although little is known about winger Walter Dunlop he does hold a unique place in the history of Sheffield Wednesday as his sole appearance at first team level actually came in the club's inaugural Football League fixture. Despite making a winning debut Dunlop found his left wing place taken by the legendary Fred Spiksley for the club's first home game and Walter would play reserve team football for the remainder of the season, in his preferred role as a right-winger. After missing only a handful of second team games as Wednesday won the Championship of the Sheffield & District League, Dunlop was released at the end of the season, joining fellow Football League side Darwen. However he would play only six times in the top-flight for the Lancashire side before returning to the Sheffield area where he was employed as an "Iron Turner" – a job he held when Walter first joined Wednesday.

DUNN, John H. 1920-21

Born: 4th Quarter 1888, Eccles, Lancashire
(5ft 10ins, 12st)
Debut: 28 August 1920 v Barnsley Division Two Away
Last Appearance: 7 October 1920
v Nottingham Forest Division Two Away
Total League & Cup Appearances: 8 Goals: 0

Career Details:

Eccles Borough		
Leeds City	May	1913
Luton Town		1914
WEDNESDAY	July	1920 £600
Released		1921

Right back John Dunn arrived at Hillsborough in the aftermath of Wednesday's disastrous season of 1919-20 when they had suffered relegation from Division One, using a total of 43 different players. Almost half of those were actually released in the summer of 1920 and as new manager Bob Brown started to re-build he turned to Dunn to fill one of the full back positions. The newcomer had started his playing career with hometown club Eccles Boro where after winning the Lancashire Combination Championship in 1913 he moved into the Football League at Leeds City. He failed to break into the league side at City and subsequently spent six years at Southern League Luton Town – playing in wartime football for The Hatters - before arriving in Sheffield.

The Owls paid the non-league side a hefty fee for his services and it looked money well spent when Wednesday kept three consecutive clean sheets at the start of the 1920-1 campaign. However after appearing in the first eight games, Dunn was unceremoniously dropped to the reserve team with Jack Bellas taking his place and the full back never again played League football. He netted his only goal for the club, from the penalty spot, during a reserve team win over Mexborough and helped Wednesday to the Final of the Sheffield Challenge Cup although he missed out on the win over Barnsley that secured the trophy. After being released in the summer of 1921 it was reported in September of the same year that after undergoing a knee operation in Liverpool, Dunn had been told he would never play again and later received £800 compensation from the league fund.

EARP, Martin John "Jack" 1893-1900

Born: 6 September 1872 Nottingham
(5ft 9ins, 11st 12lbs - 1894)
Debut: 7 October 1893
v Stoke FC
Division One Away
Last Appearance: 31 March 1900
v Leicester Fosse
Division Two Home
Total League
& Cup Appearances: 174 Goals: 8

Career Details:

Nottingham Forest		Am.
Everton		1891 Am.
Nottingham Forest		1892 Am.
The Corinthians		1892 Am.
WEDNESDAY	29 September	1893
Stockport County	26 July	1900

CAPS (@SWFC)
Football League (1) v Irish League 1898

As the captain of Wednesday's first ever F.A.Cup winning team, Jack Earp will always hold a special place in the club's long history. Before joining Wednesday the highly principled Earp had played strictly as an amateur, enjoying two spells at his hometown club Forest as well as playing several games for famous amateur outfit Corinthians. In fact he initially signed for Wednesday on an amateur basis under an arrangement that would see Jack assist Mansfield Town when not required by the Owls. However just six days after signing forms for Wednesday he was given a free transfer by Nottingham Forest and immediately signed professional forms at Olive Grove. It did not take Earp long to break into the Owls first team and for the remainder of the decade he was a regular, becoming hugely popular with supporters and his fellow professionals. He was totally right footed but was also fast, plucky and without doubt one of the finest full backs in England at the time. He replaced Tom Brandon as right-back – forging an outstanding partnership with Ambrose Langley - and his brilliant form ensured Brandon was not missed as the Owls consolidated in league football.

It was his steadfast personality and tendency to get " stuck in" when required that made Earp obvious captain material and it was in this role that Jack led Wednesday to the 1896 F.A.Cup Final meeting with Wolves at Crystal Palace. A brace from Fred Spiksley ensured Earp would be the first captain to lift the new trophy – the previous one having been stolen from a Birmingham shop where 1895 winners Aston Villa had let it go on show – and enter Wednesday history as one of only three men to achieve the feat. Incidentally the presenting of the Cup finally confirmed to Wolves keeper Billy Tennant that Wednesday had been victorious, as he had not realised one of Spiksley's goals had actually rebounded from the net before he had cleared the ball up field. He somehow failed to see the teams kick off again and at the end of play remarked to Earp "when is the replay?" – he would not believe Jack when he told the crestfallen keeper that Wednesday had won! The outstanding Earp remained Wednesday captain until the traumatic season of 1898-99 when the Owls not only lost their First Division status but also their beloved Olive Grove. Incidentally although he was well respected Earp kept himself to himself and usually got changed in a local hotel before travelling to Olive Grove in a taxi! The move to pastures new at Owlerton also signalled the end of Earp's Wednesday career as he appeared in only five more games – including the first match at the new ground against Chesterfield in September 1899 – and was now effectively understudy to Willie Layton.

After being put on the transfer list in April 1900 Earp signed for league new boys Stockport County in a player-coach role and captained County in their first ever Football League game in September 1900 at Leicester Fosse. However after just seventeen games for County Jack was allowed to leave on a free transfer in January 1901 so he could emigrate to South Africa to join Major Baden-Powell's police force. He was still serving in the Southern Hemisphere in August 1910.

EATON, Walter 1904-05

Born: 3rd Quarter 1881 Sheffield
Only Appearance: 3 April 1905 v Derby County Division 1 Home
Total League & Cup Appearances: 1 Goals: 0

Career Details:

WEDNESDAY		1904
Released		1905

Reserve team right back who was given a trial game in a re-arranged home game with Derby County, late in the 1904-5 season. He appeared as a replacement for the absent Willie Layton but was back in the second team in time for the Derby game at Bramall Lane five days later. A halloware stamper by trade, Eaton was released at the end of the season.

EDMONDSON, James 'Joe' 1919-21

Born: 1st Quarter 1895 Tarleton, Lancashire
(5ft 11ins, 12st 8lbs – 1914)
Debut: 25 October 1919
v Manchester City
Division One Away
Last Appearance: 19 April 1920
v Bradford Park Avenue
Division One Home
Total League
& Cup Appearances: 14 Goals: 3

Career Details:

Leyland		
Leeds City	April	1914
Preston North End		1916/7
WEDNESDAY	17 October	1919 £1000
Swansea Town	22 June	1920 £500
Exeter City	September	1923

Forward Joe Edmondson joined the Owls, along with Arthur Price, from the disgraced Leeds City club. The forerunner of Leeds United were expelled from the league for financial irregularities and their whole playing squad were controversially sold off at a mass auction attended by over thirty clubs. Wednesday procured his signature despite competition from Aston Villa, Preston and Stockport County, convinced he would be good enough to help the Owls stave off relegation from Division One. The bulky Edmondson, who possessed a deadly shot, netted twice in a run of ten consecutive appearances after signing but then found himself dropped into the reserve team – where he remained until being released at the season's end as part of the mass clear out undertaken by Wednesday after demotion.

He had originally started his career in Lancashire minor football but slipped through Preston's hands to sign for Leeds City just before the Great War. He boasted a praiseworthy six goals in only eleven peacetime games for City – plus another ten in twenty wartime games – and Preston got an idea of what they missed when he scored a tremendous 27 goals in 30 games during 1916-17, when guesting for The Lilywhites. His career goal ratio continued to average more than one every two games at Swansea where thirty-three hit the opponents net in just sixty appearances. A disappointing season at Devon side Exeter City ended his league career and he retired in 1924.

EDWARDS, Leonard Owen "Len" 1951-54

Born: 30 May 1930 Wrexham
(5ft 10½ ins, 11st 10lbs – 1951)
Debut: 8 December 1951
v West Ham United
Division Two Away
Last Appearance: 15 December 1951
v Doncaster Rovers
Division Two Home
Total League
& Cup Appearances: 2 Goals: 0

Career Details:

Wrexham		Am.
Llay Welfare		
WEDNESDAY	13 January	1951 £115
Brighton & Hove Albion	16 March	1954
Crewe Alexandra	December	1955

Welshman Len Edwards started his playing career as an amateur with Wrexham but he played the majority of his early football at non-league side Llay Welfare. It was to the amateur side that the Owls paid a small fee to bring the 20 year-old to Hillsborough early in 1951. He started life in the club's Yorkshire League side before being promoted to reserve team football in August 1951. However after only a handful of Central league games he was handed his big chance in December 1951 when an injury to regular left half-back George Davies prompted manager Eric Taylor to call up Edwards. He duly made his first team debut at Upton Park and it could not have gone better as a Dooley inspired Wednesday thrashed West Ham United 6-0 – the highest margin of victory in an away league game in the club's history. Perhaps not surprisingly he kept his place for the following week's home match with Doncaster Rovers but it was then back to reserve team football as The Owls ran away with the Division Two Championship.

The red-headed defender spent the next two years toiling away in Central League football with little chance of breaking into the club's First Division side. A move to Brighton saw Len add six league appearances to his C.V. – he actually made his debut for The Seagulls at centre-forward – before enjoying his best spell in league soccer at Cheshire side Crewe Alexandra. He appeared in thirty-nine games for The Railwaymen before dropping out of league football in 1957.

EGGO, Robert Mollison "Bert" 1919-21

Born: 22 November 1895 Brechin
(5ft 9ins, 12st 7lbs – 1920)
Died: 23 May 1977 Sheffield
Debut: 17 February 1920
v Burnley Division One Away
Last Appearance: 18 December 1920
v Leicester City
Division Two Home
Total League
& Cup Appearances: 23 Goals: 0

Career Details:

Brechin		
Heart of Midlothian		
Dunfermline Athletic		1919 Trial
WEDNESDAY	24 December	1919 Free
Reading	15 June	1921 Nominal

Versatile defender Bert Eggo joined the Owls on Christmas Eve 1919 from Scottish football after having survived the carnage of World War One. During the hostilities Bert – who had started his working life in a butcher's shop – joined the famous Black Watch and saw active service in mainland Europe, being shot in the right wrist and subsequently hospitalised for a long spell. At the time Bert was on the books of Hearts who he had joined after playing amateur football for Brechin – a forerunner of today's Brechin City. After arriving in Sheffield, Bert had to watch from the sidelines for two months as his new team toiled away at the foot of Division One and would appear only four times in that relegation season, at right half back, before a change of division brought a change of luck as he found himself first choice at the start of the 1920-1 campaign. He would miss only one of the first twenty league games of the season but just when he seemed to be established his Owls career came to a juddering halt as a bout of pleurisy cost him his place to the emerging Tom Brelsford and he would never again play a first team game for the club!

He played out a season with the club's Midland League side but Wednesday probably had cause to regret their decision to let him go to Third Division (South) club Reading as he was an almost ever present at Elm Park – it was said later that Wednesday had indeed made a major mistake in letting him go for "the price of an old song". After appearing in every outfield defensive position for Reading he finally settled at right back in October 1923 and would captain The Royals to the Division Three (South) Championship in 1926 and an F.A.Cup semi-final in 1927. Incidentally part of his duty as captain was to shake hands with opposing captains but because of his war wound Bert had to use his left hand for the pleasantry because he had to wear a bandage on his right wrist as it was prone to swelling! He eventually lost his place to Percy Thorpe in 1928 and when he retired at the end of the season had amassed a pre war best tally of 312 games for Reading. He is widely regarded as the club's best ever right back and was given a richly deserved benefit game against Spurs that raised the handsome sum of £200.

After retiring from the game he became licensee of the "Ye Old Salutation Arms" in Reading before moving to take over at the quirkily named "The World Turned Upside Down" public house. In 1934 he played in a charity game at Reading's Greyhound stadium, which was the first floodlight game in the town but after the break up of his marriage Bert returned to his hometown of Brechin. He was quite a celebrity back in Brechin and became a man of leisure for many years until taking a kitchen assistants job in his local hospital, which he did until retiring from work. He eventually moved back to Sheffield to live with his family before passing away in 1977.

EKOKU, Efangwu Goziem "Efan" 2000-2002

Born: 8 June 1967 Manchester
(6ft 2ins, 12st – 2002)
Debut: 22 October 2000
v Birmingham City
Division One Home
Last Appearance: 6 April 2002
v Nottingham Forest
Division One Home
Total League
& Cup Appearances: 62+9 Goals: 21

Career Details:

Liverpool College		
Merton		
Sutton United	December	1988
Charlton Athletic		Trial
Bournemouth	11 May	1990 £100,000
Norwich City	26 March	1993 £500,000
Wimbledon	14 October	1994 £900,000
Grasshoppers Zurich	27 August	1999 £500,000
WEDNESDAY	20 October	2000 Free
Contract cancelled	10 September	2002 Free
Luton Town	24 September	2002 Trial
Rushden & Diamonds	October	2002 Trial
Brentford	27 March	2003 Free
Released	30 June	2003
Dublin City	31 August	2004 Free

Pacy forward Efan Ekoku started his career in non-league soccer despite having attended a non-football playing school where he excelled as both a sprinter and jumper. He actually played on the wing for Liverpool college Rugby team - representing Lancashire at the sport at the age of 16 - before turning down Sheffield United to sign for Bournemouth for a six-figure sum to take him into league football. He netted 25 goals in 75 appearances for the Dean Court club to alert higher division clubs to his potential and it was not long before Premier League Norwich City secured his services. During his relatively short spell at Carrow Road, Efan scored seventeen times in 45 games – including a famous four-goal haul in a 5-1 win at Everton in September 1993 – before moving to fellow top-flight outfit Wimbledon. During this time he earned five full caps for Nigeria (from where his nickname of the "Chief" originates) and he would enjoy his most prolific spell in English football while at Selhurst Park, netting 44 times in 153 competitive games for The Dons as they defied the critics to retain Premier League status. It was therefore a blow to Wimbledon fans when Ekoku asked for a transfer only a few games into the 1998/9 season and although he played out the season he did eventually move to Swiss club Grasshoppers in the following summer.

After finishing top scorer in his debut season in Switzerland, Ekoku became unsettled and jumped at the chance to return to England, signing for Paul Jewell's Wednesday side, initially on loan for the remainder of the 2000-1 season. He struggled for both fitness and form on his arrival at Hillsborough – two goals against Sheffield United in the league Cup buying Ekoku heaps of goodwill with Wednesdayites – but eventually gave a series of impressive displays to contribute seven league goals as the Owls staved off a successive relegation. After signing on a permanent basis on 27 July 2001 Efan was instrumental in Wednesday's run to the League Cup semi-final – scoring five goals in as many games – and again netted seven league goals as the Owls again fought their way out of danger at the foot of Division One. However he could not find the net on a regular enough basis and his contract was eventually cancelled by mutual consent so Ekoku could pursue a career in the media – he had previously co-hosted the BBC's coverage of the African Nations Cup tournament. After leaving Hillsborough he undertook unsuccessful trial periods at two sides before signing on a non-contract basis for Brentford, on transfer deadline day in 2003. He now sells insurance for a living.

ELLIS, Keith Duncan 1953-63

Born: 6 November 1935 Sheffield
(6ft $^3/_4$ ins,, 11st 12lbs – 1955)
Debut: 19 March 1955
v Preston North End
Division One Home
Last Appearance: 26 October 1963
v Aston Villa
Division One Home
Total League
& Cup Appearances: 118 Goals: 60

Career Details:

Edgar Allen's		
WEDNESDAY	9 April	1955
Scunthorpe United	4 March	1964 £7,300
Cardiff City	September	1964 £22,000 + Dick Scott
Lincoln City	September	1965

Despite not being quoted in the same breath as John Fantham and Bronco Layne, the scoring exploits of Keith Ellis were equally impressive as those of his contemporaries – Ellis netting at a rate of just over a goal every two games for Wednesday. The weighty six-footer was a real handful for opposition defenders, possessing a powerful shot, with his finest attribute being his superb heading ability. The Sheffielder had originally come to the Owls attention whilst playing in an Edgar Allen's inter departmental football tournament and after just six games in local football he was signed by Wednesday on amateur forms. However Ellis would then remain strictly amateur while he trained to be a draughtsman at a local engineering firm and it would in fact be two years before he signed professional forms for Wednesday. His first team debut came when he was still an amateur but after netting six times in six league games during the 1956-7 season, Ellis found his career put on hold when being called up for National Service in 1957.

He was assigned to the R.A.F. Intelligence service and spent a year in Cyprus although he kept in shape by playing for the forces at both Football and Cricket. When Ellis returned to Sheffield he found his opportunities limited – due to the great form of Roy Shiner – but when manager Harry Catterick gave Keith an extended run in the first team he was rewarded with two tremendous back-to-back seasons. As Wednesday finished fifth and then second in the old Division One Ellis boasted a 33-goal haul, which included a hat trick in the famous 7-2 F.A.Cup win at Old Trafford in February 1961. Unfortunately a clash of personalities then brought his career to a shuddering halt as after falling out with new manager Vic Buckingham the attacker played only a handful of first team games during the last two years of his time at Hillsborough. He eventually left for Division Three strugglers Scunthorpe United in 1964 that saw Ellis – nicknamed "the big

Yank" by his teammates – as a possible savour from relegation. The deal included an additional fee if United avoided relegation but unfortunately for Scunthorpe they had no reason to pay the additional sum, finishing rock bottom! Within two years of leaving Hillsborough, Ellis had retired altogether from professional football and initially became the landlord of a public house in Rotherham before working as a sales manager for a Brewery, a position he held until his retirement. However his working life did not stop on his retirement as he has subsequently undertaken marketing work for the brewery and also ran hospitality boxes for the company at Leeds United, Sheffield Steelers Ice Hockey and Wakefield Wildcats rugby League. When he can create some spare time Ellis plays golf while he still occasionally watches Wednesday.

ELLIS, Samuel "Sam" 1964-72

Born: 12 September 1946 Ashton-under-Lyne
(6ft, 11st 7lbs – 1966)
Debut: 4 April 1966
v Blackpool
Division One Home
Last Appearance: 7 September 1971
v Carlisle United
League Cup Away
Total League
& Cup Appearances: 179+3 Goals: 1

Career Details:

Andenshaw Grammer School		
Snipe Wanderers		
W.H.Smith, Manchester		
WEDNESDAY	12 September	1964
Mansfield Town	January	1972 £5,000
Lincoln City	12 May	1973 £7,000
Watford	1 August	1977 £15,000

CAPS (@SWFC) – ENGLAND U-23 (3)
v Wales 02/10/68, v Wales 01/10/69, v Russia 22/10/69

Half back Sam Ellis will always be remembered as the teenager who made his F.A.Cup debut in the 1966 Final against Everton, in only his eleventh appearance for the club. The appearance in the showpiece occasion of English soccer completed a remarkable rise from Manchester amateur League soccer for the flame-haired youngster who had joined Wednesday as a professional less than two years previously. He had actually looked set for a career in banking after leaving school but after a successful trial at Wednesday he quickly decided a professional football career would be more to his liking – strangely he did not request a trial at Hillsborough, he attended after a Manchester based Owls fan had written to Wednesday offering to pay for his trial period! It would prove a wise decision for Ellis as he would play in over 400 league games for four different league sides as well as carving out a long career in management after his playing days had finished.

The ex-England Youth International trialist had appeared in only a handful of reserve team games before being promoted to first team duty, following an injury to key defender Vic Mobley, in April 1966. The nineteen year-old retained his place for the final ten games of the league campaign and then the dramatic Cup Final loss to Everton. His consistent performances saw Ellis quickly become an established member of the club's First Division side and he was a regular throughout the remainder of the 1960s. However following relegation in 1970, Sam was in and out of the side and eventually left for Mansfield Town on loan in January 1972 to obtain some first team football. The move to Field Mill was made permanent in March 1972 and in 64 league games he netted a surprisingly high goals tally of seven – surprising when you consider he netted only once in over 150 games at Wednesday! At his next side Lincoln City the tall and powerful defender established a fine partnership with Terry Cooper as Graham Taylor's side ran away with the 1976 Division Four Championship. He was captain for the majority of his time at Sincil Bank and actually finished top scorer in 1974-5 with thirteen goals, thanks mainly to his role as designated penalty taker! He certainly made a big impression with City fans as he was twice voted player of the season, earning the nickname "Super Sam". After 33 goals in 173 appearances for Lincoln he followed manager Taylor to Watford in a player-coach capacity, winning another Division Four Championship medal before hanging up his boots in May 1979.

After three years on the coaching staff at Vicarage Road, as Watford surged through the divisions to reach the top-flight, Ellis left to become Blackpool manager in June 1982. On limited resources he achieved promotion from Division Four in 1985 but was eventually sacked in March 1989, being appointed boss at Lancashire rivals Bury two months later. He subsequently guided The Shakers to the Division Three play off Final a year later but in December 1990 accepted Peter Reid's offer to became his assistant manager at Manchester City. He stayed until August 1993 and later returned to Sincil Bank, initially as assistant manager in March 1994 before taking over as manager in May. He was dismissed in September 1995 after a string of poor results had left Lincoln bottom of Division Three and soon after returned to Bury for a second spell, this time as assistant manager. In almost four years at Gigg Lane he helped Bury reach Division One after successive promotions and also helped Burnley reach the second tier of English football in 2000 after being appointed in the summer of 1999 as assistant manager to his old Bury boss Stan Ternent. Remained for five years until The Clarets decided not to renew his and Ternent's contracts in May 2004 but a month later was back in football, as assistant manager to Kevin Blackwell at newly relegated Leeds United.

EUSTACE, Peter 1962-70 & 1972-75

Born: 31 July 1944 Sheffield
(5ft 11ins, 11st 9lbs – 1964)
Debut: 29 August 1962
v Leicester City
Division One Home
Last Appearance: 29 March 1975
v Millwall
Division Two Home
Total League
& Cup Appearances: 269+12 Goals: 26

Career Details:

Stocksbridge Works		1959
WEDNESDAY	1 June	1962
West Ham United	5 January	1970 £95,000
Rotherham United	9 March	1972 Loan
WEDNESDAY	14 August	1972 £13,900 (signed 10/11/72)
Peterborough United	7 May	1975 Free
WEDNESDAY	10 May	1976 Trial
Worksop Town	August	1976
Worksop Town	March	1977

It was ex-Owl Frank Slynn who first spotted Peter Eustace playing for his village side Stocksbridge Works in the old Yorkshire League – he became the youngest ever player to win a championship medal when his works side won the title in 1959. At the time Eustace was working at the local steel works as an apprentice mechanical engineer but quickly changed careers after signing apprentice forms for Wednesday in March 1961. He was elevated to pro status in the summer of 1962 and did not have to wait long for his senior debut – an unfortunate three-nil home loss to Leicester City. It took Eustace two seasons to gain a regular first team spot but his excellent form and general classy play ensured that he remained a first choice for many years. The tall and elegant defender/midfielder lent flair and grace to the Wednesday side and it remains a mystery why he was never capped at any level for his country – he was called into three England squads but failed to make an appearance. He was ever present – and a major factor - as Wednesday reached the 1966 Cup Final and when new manager Danny Williams was appointed in 1969 he stated that Eustace was the best player at the club – soon after he promptly sold him to West Ham for a then club record fee!

His stay at Upton Park was generally a disappointment for Eustace as he appeared in 43 games and even returned to South Yorkshire for a loan spell at Rotherham United. After six games for the Millers Derek Dooley then brought him back to Hillsborough, initially on a three-month loan arrangement. The move was made permanent in November 1972 but after an encouraging first season the Owls fortunes started to decline sharply and although Eustace played his heart out for Wednesday he could not stop the rot and left in the summer of 1975 after the Owls had dropped into Division Three for the first time in their history. After turning down an offer to play in the US he subsequently signed for Peterborough United and after a brief time back at Wednesday on trial he retired following two short spells at non-league Worksop Town – taking a job in the building trade at his father-in-law's firm in Stocksbridge.

He returned to the game in 1979 as coach at Sunderland and when his old Wednesday teammate Howard Wilkinson was appointed Owls boss in July 1983 it was Eustace who he chose to be his no.2. The duo achieved immediate promotion back to the top-flight after a fourteen year absence and led Wednesday to consecutive top eight finishes with a hard running, hard pressing game – Eustace and Wilkinson signed five-year contracts in December 1985. However lack of investment saw the Owls fortunes decline and when Wilkinson resigned to take over at Leeds United in October 1988 Peter was appointed caretaker manager. Victories in his two games in charge probably helped his claim for the job on a full time basis but it was clear Eustace was not first choice as Wednesday chased, and were rejected by several managerial targets. However on 28 October 1988 he was appointed manager at Hillsborough and in hindsight would have probably refused the offer if he knew that within 109 days he would be sacked – the shortest spell in charge of any manager at Wednesday. His disastrous reign saw the Owls win only one competitive fixture – an F.A.Cup tie at home to minnows Torquay United – and he encountered a multitude of problems with playing staff. The likes of Gary Megson, Imre Varadi (his wife famously phoning local radio to complain about Eustace), Alan Harper & Mel Sterland all threatening to leave or submit transfer requests – the latter furious when he was not given his captaincy back on return from injury. After a tide of criticism from the players about his methods and tactics the inevitable parting of ways came on 15 February 1989 when his brief spell as Owls boss was confined to the history books.

After a spell out of the game Eustace returned to football for brief coaching spells at Leyton Orient and Charlton Athletic before returning to Brisbane Road as assistant manager to Frank Clark in 1990, taking charge of first team affairs when Clark moved upstairs in July 1991. The O's just missed the play-offs in 1992 – selling their teenage star Chris Bart-Williams to his old club Wednesday in November 1991 – and after a poor run of results he was sacked for the second time in his managerial career in April 1994. After leaving Orient he became the licensee of a public house in the Derbyshire village of Hope until becoming West Ham United's Northern Scout in July 1999 – a job that entailed scouting for the Hammers in Scotland and Scandinavia. He later scouted for Portsmouth and after helping Wednesday out on an informal basis during the 2003-4 season he was appointed as Chief Scout in July 2004.

EVANS, Paul 2002-03

Born: 28 December 1973 Newcastle, South Africa (6ft 4ins, 14st – 2002)
Debut: 15 February 2003
v Derby County
Division One Away
Last Appearance: 18 March 2003
v Bradford City
Division One Away
Total League
& Cup Appearances: 7 Goals: 0

Career Details:

Wits University	January	1992
Leeds United	1 August	1995
Crystal Palace	18 March	1996 Loan
Bradford City	3 March	1997 Loan
Super Sports United		1997
Mamelodi Sundowns		2001
Jomo Cosmos	1 August	2001
WEDNESDAY	6 March	2002 12-day trial
Huddersfield Town	22 March	2002 Loan
WEDNESDAY	11 July	2002 Free
Released	30 June	2003
Crewe Alexandra	5 August	2003 Trial
Rushden & Diamonds	15 October	2003 N/C
Released	1 December	2003

Despite leaving his native South Africa to sign a professional contract with Leeds United in 1995 it would be over seven years before Paul Evans finally made his debut in English League football. After working his way into the No.2 position at Wednesday – proving himself a good shot stopper and equally adept at fielding crosses - his big chance came when first choice Kevin Pressman fell ill on the morning of the game at Derby County, meaning the giant goalkeeper was drafted in at the last minute. He proceeded to take his chance with both hands and his excellent form ensured that when his rival recovered, Evans retained the first team jersey. A terrible gaff in an away game at Leicester City did not seem to affect his confidence but just when he seemed to becoming a serious rival to long term goalie Pressman fate took a hand as a hairline fracture of the pelvis meant he was ruled out for the remainder of the season. Following the Owls relegation from Division One Evans was one of several players out of contract – he had been given a one-year deal in the previous year after having impressed while on trial in spring 2002 – and it was a surprise to many fans when the goalkeeper was not retained.

It closed another chapter on his career in England that had seen Evans appear for five different sides, two on loan, while trying to become established at Elland Road. The imposing keeper, who dominated his penalty area, had previously made history by appearing in the first ever games at both U-20 and U-23 for South Africa while before arriving in Sheffield he had won two full caps for his country – against Gambia and host nation Mali in a 2001 International tournament.

EVANS, Richard 2003-

Born: 19 June 1983 Cardiff
(5ft 9ins, 10st 4lbs – 2003)
Debut: 29 March 2003
v Watford
Division One Home
Total League
& Cup Appearances: 9+2 Goals: 1

Career Details:

Arsenal		Trial
Everton		Trial
Coventry City		Trial
Cardiff City		
Everton		
Birmingham City	summer	2002
Moor Green	December	2002 3-month loan
WEDNESDAY	27 March	2003 Free
Swansea City	December	2004 Trial
Colchester United	July	2005 Trial

Pacy winger Richard Evans was born in the Welsh capital city of Cardiff but moved to the village of Caerphilly when just a toddler. After playing his first organised football for his local side Evans moved to a junior side back in Cardiff where during a tournament in Aberystwyth he was spotted, subsequently having trials at several Premier League clubs. He eventually signed schoolboy forms for Everton – after having made several appearances in

Cardiff City's youth sides – but after they decided not to offer him a trainee position he instead signed a three-year scholarship with Birmingham City in 1999. At the end of that period he was duly signed as a professional but spent most of his first season in the professional ranks on loan at Dr Martens League side Moor Green – he appeared for the Welsh U-20 side against South Korea in February 2003 while appearing in thirteen games for the non-league side.

With competition fierce at newly promoted Birmingham City the Welshman knew his chances of first team football would be limited after returning to St.Andrews. Therefore with little chance of being offered a new deal the 19 year-old decided to switch to Hillsborough when Owls boss Chris Turner offered the youngster a contract until the end of the season. After impressing on debut with his speed and accurate crossing the left winger netted his first goal for the club in the astonishing 7-2 win at Burnley in April 2003 and was rewarded at the end of the season with a new one-year contract. After an impressive 2003 pre season he started the new campaign in the first team but unfortunately he suffered a cruciate ligament injury in a reserve game in late September, which meant the youngster spent the rest of the season on the treatment table. He returned to fitness early in the following season but was clearly not in new manager Paul Sturrock's plans, joining League Two club Swansea City on a two-week trial and returning to figure only occasionally at reserve team level.

EYRE, Claude Ronald "Ron" 1924-25

Born: 26 November 1901 Stanhill, Notts
(5ft 7½ ins, 12st – 1924)
Died: 18 August 1969 Bournemouth
Only Appearance: 22 March 1924
v Oldham Athletic Division Two Home
Total League & Cup Appearances: 1
Goals: 0

Career Details:

Stanhill Colliery		
WEDNESDAY	September	1923 1-month trial
WEDNESDAY	21 January	1924
Bournemouth		
& Boscombe United	2 January	1925 £100
Christchurch	May	1933
Bournemouth Electric		1937

If you consult the Rothmans football directory you may notice that in the Bournemouth section a certain Ron Eyre is listed as the record goal scorer in that club's long history. His tally of 202 league goals will almost certainly never be beaten and his incredible record of 259 goals in 367 competitive appearances for the Cherries marked him as one of the deadliest strikers in the inter war years. However before finishing top scorer for eight consecutive seasons on the South Coast the centre forward was actually on the books of Sheffield Wednesday. He had originally arrived at Hillsborough for a trial period from Nottinghamshire minor football and showed his eye for goal by finishing the 1923-4 season as Central League top scorer for Wednesday – his 14 goals including a treble in the 8-2 romp over Oldham reserves in March 1924. Ironically a week later he was again facing Oldham at Hillsborough as injury to Sid Binks saw Ron drafted in for his senior debut. Unfortunately the game was lost 2-1 and in the season that followed the goals dried up for Eyre – failing to score in a handful of reserve team games – and he was allowed to join Bournemouth, on loan, in January 1925 until the end of the season.

Manager at the time was ex-Wednesday keeper Harry Kinghorn and he must have been delighted when Eyre scored within five minutes of his league debut for Bournemouth – after having only met his team mates for the first time in the dressing room before the game at Luton Town! After Kinghorn made his new signing a permanent one in the summer of 1925 his faith was rewarded as Eyre broke every club scoring record on offer – his feat of scoring in seven successive games in 1927 was only bettered in the 2000-1 season when loan player Jermaine Defoe netted in ten consecutive matches. During his time in a Bournemouth shirt Ron twice returned to Hillsborough for F.A.Cup ties but found little joy as his new club lost 3-0 and 7-0! The Cherries finally released him in May 1933 and after gaining permission from Stanley Rous at the F.A. he was able to revert to amateur status and sign for non-league Christchurch – incidentally despite his goals, Bournemouth failed to finish higher than seventh position in Division Three (South) during Eyre's nine seasons at Dean Court!

After retiring from professional soccer in 1933 Ron worked for the West Hampshire Waterboard while his playing career included four years with his employer's works team (Christchurch) and two years at Bournemouth Electric before retiring in 1939. Throughout the duration of the War, Ron worked as an auxiliary in the Portsmouth fire service while in 1946 he became a foreman ganger of a construction department for the Southern Electricity Board – retiring in November 1966 at the age of 65. While working for the SEB he developed a reputation as a superb bowler for the cricket side and was well known locally for always wearing a cap – he only removed the headwear when going to bed! He was also a big fisherman – wiling away the hours at the waterside near his Christchurch home – before moving back to Bournemouth to live out his final years.

EYRE, Isaac J. 1903-04

Born: 1st Quarter 1875 Heeley, Sheffield
Only Appearance: 12 March 1904
v Stoke FC
Division One Home
Total League
& Cup Appearances: 1 Goals: 0

Career Details:

Sheffield Club	
WEDNESDAY	1903 Amat.
Released	1904

Sheffield club amateur who played several reserve games for the club during the League Championship winning season of 1903-04 as well as making a solitary first team start in the one-nil Division One win over Stoke at Owlerton in March 1904. The youngster – a stone finisher by profession - was given a chance during a five game period when regular centre forward Andrew Wilson was unavailable – Sheffield club team mates George Hoyland and Vivian Simpson were both tried in the position during the club record goal scorer's absence.

FALLON, William Joseph "Bill" 1938-46

Born: 14 January 1912 Dublin
(5ft 9½ ins, 11st 8lbs – 1938)
Died: 23 March 1989 Nottingham
Debut: 19 March 1938
v Barnsley
Division Two Away
Last Appearance: 29 April 1939
v Tottenham Hotspur
Division Two Home
Total League
& Cup Appearances: 51* Goals: 13
*** Also appeared in 2 wartime games**

Career Details:

St.Gates		
Brideville		
Dolphin		
Notts County		1933
WEDNESDAY	16 March	1938 £3000 + J.R.Roy
Shamrock Rovers	November	1939 Guest
Shelbourne		Guest
Dundalk		Guest
Notts County	June	1946 Free
Exeter City		1947
Peterborough United	July	1948

CAPS (@SWFC)
EIRE FULL (4) v Switzerland 18/09/38, v Poland 13/11/38, v Hungary 18/05/39, v Germany 23/05/39

With the outstanding career of left winger Ellis Rimmer coming to a close the Owls management knew that a ready made replacement was urgently needed as the club tried to claw their way out of the old Second Division. The Owls had recently appointed ex-Notts County manager Jimmy McMullan as their secretary-manager and it was to his old club that the new manager returned to bring Irish Free State International Bill Fallon to Hillsborough. The pacy and well built winger had started his career in junior Irish football before moving to Nottingham and enjoyed a successful time at the Meadow Lane club, appearing in 128 games for County, scoring 24 times. While at County, Fallon also won the first of his nine full caps for Eire although at the time he was playing in Division Three (South) football for The Magpies.

The popular winger was also a real character and often found himself in hot water with the County coaching staff, especially during cross country runs – he would at times catch the bus and wave to his team mates as he went past them! At one time he rode past the rest of the team on a kid's bike with the child sat on the crossbar! Fallon – who was deaf in one ear due to his childhood pastime of high diving – proved a big success at Wednesday, netting ten league goals during the 1938-9 season as Wednesday agonisingly missed out on a return to the top-flight – incidentally he missed a handful of games part way through the season when a car, also containing his team mate Ted Catlin, skidded on Penistone Road and crashed into a telegraph pole, the Irishman ending up in hospital. He formed an exciting left wing partnership with Scot Charlie Napier but like so many players of his era the advent of the Second World War brought a premature end to his first class career, Fallon returning home to Ireland in 1939 after a couple of games in wartime soccer for Wednesday. During the war Fallon guested for several clubs in the Dublin area and it is believed he appeared in seven wartime Internationals for Eire. He worked in munitions during the conflict and joined the I.R.A., although at the time the organisation could only boast sticks instead of guns.

He eventually returned to Sheffield when peace was declared but stayed only briefly, moving back to Notts County just before national soccer returned in 1946. He appeared in seventeen more games for County, netting three goals, before wrapping up his league career with a short spell at Exeter City. His final club proved to be Midland League Peterborough United where his playing career ended after he broke his collar bone, following a collision with Tony Hateley during a reserve game, ironically, against Notts County. When his playing days ended Bill had several jobs in the building trade and was part of the workforce that built the M1 motorway. He also coached local Nottingham sides such as Raleigh and Boots and on occasion would get his players to run around the pitch during evening training sessions. However sometimes his players would still be trudging around the pitch two hours later as Bill had gone to the pub!

FANTHAM, John 1956-69

Born: 6 February 1939 Sheffield
(5ft 8ins, 11st 7lbs – 1964)
Debut:1 February 1958
v Tottenham Hotspur
Division One Home
Last Appearance: 20 September 1969
v West Ham United
Division One Away
Total League
& Cup Appearances: 426+8 Goals: 166

Career Details:

WEDNESDAY	1 October	1956
Rotherham United	9 October	1969 £4,000
Macclesfield Town		1971

CAPS (@SWFC):
ENGLAND Full (1) v Luxembourg 28/09/61

ENGLAND U-23 (1) v Italy 02/11/60

Football League (3)
v Scottish League 22/03/61, v Irish League 01/11/61, v Italian League 08/11/61

Brilliant inside forward John Fantham was without doubt one of the most outstanding players to ever pull on the famous blue and white shirt, lying second only to the legendary Andrew Wilson in the goal scoring stakes. The attacker was brought up in Pitsmoor – the same breeding ground of Derek Dooley – and showed his all round sporting abilities at Burngreave Secondary Modern, winning a place in the Yorkshire boys side at cricket and also playing football and cricket for Sheffield boys. He later won wide repute as a golfer and nearly became a professional cricketer but it was football where he would make his mark as one of the finest talents the city of Sheffield has produced. He originally joined the Owls as a fifteen-year old and after one season as an amateur signed professional forms in 1956.

After gaining experience in the club's youth and reserve sides, Fantham made his first team debut at inside-right for the absent Albert Quixall but it would be on the opposite wing that Wednesday's post war record scorer would spend the majority of his career. The transfer of "golden boy" Albert Quixall to Manchester United in September 1958 provided the ideal opportunity for the teenage Fantham and he grasped the chance with both hands, remaining in the side for over ten years as the Owls won the Second Division Title in 1959, finished Division One runners-up to Spurs in 1961, reached the quarter-finals of the FAIRS Cup in 1962 and finished runners-up to Everton in the classic 1966 F.A.Cup Final. With veteran inside-left Redfern Froggatt coming to the end of his career it was the young pretender who took the number No.10 shirt – Froggatt switching to Quixall's old position on the opposite flank – and it would be Froggatt's post war goal scoring record that "Fants" would eventually better.

The strong, thrusting forward who possessed a powerful shot was also highly skilled in exploiting cross field passes and this combined with a true goalscorer's instinct make him a dangerous proposition for opposing defenders. Equally adept at scoring simple and spectacular goals, his consistent form quickly won John representative honours – in 1961 he played at U-23 and full level for England as well as touring New Zealand and the Far East with an F.A. side. It is fair to say that if Jimmy Greaves had been born in a different era than Fantham would surely have added to his sole full cap for England in the 4-1 Highbury win over minnows Luxembourg. His father John (known as Jack) played league football for Rotherham, Stockport, Chester and Exeter but it was John Fantham junior who proved to be the outstanding football talent in the family and his years at Wednesday saw him set a club scoring record that in all probability will never be beaten. Incidentally John's father tragically collapsed and died as he left the derby game with United in October 1958.

As well as being a fine football talent he also showed a head for business and while still at Hillsborough opened a hairdressing business that went from strength to strength. The outstanding marksman of his generation scored almost all of his goals in the top-flight and when his fifteen-year association with Wednesday finally came to a close he went with the good wishes and gratitude of Wednesdayites – it would be many years before Owls fans would watch a player who could score with such consistency. In two years at Millmoor he netted eight times in 51 games before ending his playing days after a brief spell at Macclesfield Town, retiring in 1972. After finally packing his shooting boots away, Fantham started his own machine tool business, which still runs today, while he did return to football in the mid-1980s when he became coach and later assistant-manager at Sheffield based non-league club Hallam. In his spare time Fantham is an outstanding golfer – he held the course record at Beauchief golf club for several years – and still plays today as he reaches a deserved retirement.

FAULKNER, David Peter 1992-96

Born: 8 October 1975 Sheffield
(6ft 1ins, 11st 12lbs – 1995)
Only Appearance: 24 June 1995
v FC Basel
Intertoto Cup Away
Total League
& Cup Appearances: 0+1 Goals: 0

Career Details:

WEDNESDAY	1 August	1992
Cape Cod Crusaders	May	1996 3-month loan
Darlington	8 August	1996 Free
Waterford		1997
Gainsborough Trinity		1997
Hallam		1997
Alfreton Town	September	1997
Hallam	December	1997
Gresley Rovers	July	1999
Sheffield FC		2000

Commanding centre-half David Faulkner first came to prominence with Sheffield boys before being picked to attend the F.A.National school at Lilleshall. After excelling at youth level for The Owls he was subsequently awarded a professional contract, soon after having signed YTS trainee forms. While at Hillsborough, Faulkner was a regular for England Youth – winning a total of 16 caps between the age ranges of U-15 to U-18 – but after quickly breaking into the reserve side at Wednesday he could not maintain his rapid progress and found himself in the Owls newly formed under-21 side.

His only first team appearance came in the much maligned Intertoto Cup when he replaced fellow one game wonder David German with thirteen minutes left of the game against Basel in Switzerland. After a spell on loan in US football he was released by Wednesday in the summer of 1996, signing a short-term deal at Darlington. His league debut came at Cambridge United in October 1996 but after only three more games for the Quakers he was released before the end of the 1996-7 campaign. After his professional football career ended Faulkner took temporary work before attending University to train as a teacher. While studying he played football for a wide variety of Unibond and Northern Counties East League clubs and after graduating now works as a P.E. teacher in the Hucknall area of Nottingham.

FEE, Gregory Paul "Greg" 1987-91

Born: 24 June 1964 Halifax
(6ft, 12st – 1991)
Debut: 29 August 1987
v Everton Division One Away
Last Appearance: 4 November 1989
v Nottingham Forest
Division One Away
Total League
& Cup Appearances: 20+11 Goals: 1

Career Details:

Northowram		
Bradford City	May	1983
Kettering Town	August	1984
Boston United	September	1986
WEDNESDAY	4 August	1987 £20,000
Preston North End	12 September	1990 Loan
Northampton Town	29 November	1990 Loan
Preston North End	4 January	1991 Loan
Leyton Orient	1 March	1991 Loan
Mansfield Town	28 March	1991 £20,000
Chesterfield	27 November	1992 Loan
Grantham Town		Loan
Stamford		Loan
Boston United	August	1993 Free
Telford United	September	1998 Free
Emley	August	1999 Free
Gainsborough Trinity	July	2000 Free
Harrogate Town	November	2000 Free
Hucknall Town	August	2001 Free

Tough, old-fashioned style centre half Greg Fee was plucked from the relative obscurity of Boston United by Howard Wilkinson and thrown immediately into top-flight football at Hillsborough. Considering the giant leap from non-league football to the top level of the English game the newcomer performed admirably and would go on to appear in over thirty first team games for Wednesday under three different managers. Of course Fee was never anything more than a squad player during his spell in the "big time" and his first team chances disappeared altogether when Ron Atkinson took over following the disastrous tenure of Peter Eustace – Greg only appearing once under "Big Ron" as a last minute sub at The City Ground, Nottingham.

The ex-West Yorkshire boys player had started his career as a trainee at Bradford City in September 1980 but after signing professional forms found his opportunities limited and eventually secured his release from City in order to study mathematics and sports studies at Loughborough University - touring Japan in 1985 and Yugoslavia in 1987 with the Great Britain student team. While furthering his education Fee played semi-professional football at Conference sides Kettering Town and Boston United and in fact only signed a contract for the latter, two weeks before moving to Wednesday. After emerging from University with a Bsc Honours degree he spent six years as a full time professional, four years at Hillsborough ending on transfer deadline day 1991 when he moved to Mansfield Town. After dropping back into non-league soccer in 1993 – re-joining Boston United – Fee became a teacher and after further studies at Sheffield University earned a Masters First degree in sports and exercise science. In June 1996 he was appointed Boston player-manager to replace the departing Mel Sterland and remained at York Street in that capacity until resigning in September 1998, joining Telford United in a purely playing role. In total Fee played 297 times for Boston United, scoring 49 goals, and during his time in Lincolnshire made three appearances for the Northern Premier League representative side as well as being an unused reserve for the England non-league side.

After reverting back to part-time status in 1993 Fee spent eighteen months as a teacher before becoming area manager for oil giants B.P. He remained in industry while playing under ex-Owl Jimmy Mullen's management at Telford United and after a year at Emley was handed the player-manager role at NPL Premier Division club Gainsborough Trinity in the summer of 2000. He stayed only briefly at Northolme, resigning in November 2000, and was then signed by old Wednesday trainer Mick Hennigan for Harrogate Town. In April 2001 he changed careers again when being appointed as the first ever National League Manager with a remit to look after the general well being of clubs and players in the non-league pyramid system. By now the studious Fee had achieved a full A coaching licence while working for the Football Association although he still continued to play – signing a one-year contract with NPL club Hucknall Town in August 2001 after impressing in training. Following a round of redundancies at the F.A. in April 2003 he was made redundant from his National League manager post. He subsequently left football and now runs a string of petrol stations in Sheffield and Barnsley.

FEELY, Peter John 1976-77

Born: 3 January 1950 City of London
(5ft 11ins, 12st 10lbs – 1977)
Debut: 16 February 1976
v Port Vale
Division Three Away
Last Appearance: 30 October 1976
v Mansfield Town
Division Three Home
Total League
& Cup Appearances: 21+3 Goals: 2

Career Details:

Tottenham Hotspur		
Ipswich Town		
Enfield		1968
Chelsea	May	1970
Bournemouth	1 February	1973 £1,000
Fulham	July	1974 Free
Gillingham	4 October	1974 £7,000
WEDNESDAY	13 February	1976 £8,000
Stockport County	11 February	1977 Loan
Released	9 May	1977
Norwegian football	June	1977
Slough Town		
Hong Kong football		

Although forward Peter Feely started his career at Spurs it was with Ipswich Town that he first came to prominence, being capped at England Youth level. Unfortunately he failed to make the grade at Portman Road and after being released started to re-build his career in non-league football at Isthmian League side Enfield. He enjoyed a highly successful two years at the North London side, winning the F.A.Amateur Cup at Wembley in 1968, and also earned three England amateur International caps. His success in amateur football persuaded Chelsea to tie Feely to his first professional contract but in almost three years at Stamford Bridge the Londoner played only five times and soon moved into lower league football at Bournemouth.

He again failed to make a lasting impression while at the Dean Court club and this time added only nine league games to his career tally before moving back to London – his stint at Fulham failed to even accrue a solitary appearance! By far his best spell in league soccer came at his next club Gillingham, where under Len Ashurst's management Feely netted 22 goals in only 41 league games. This sudden burst of scoring made him top of Ashurst's shopping list after his acrimonious move to the Hillsborough hot seat in October 1975 but although Feely seemed set to be his first signing for Wednesday the deal was put on ice after complications set in. He did eventually move to Sheffield but it took five months for the protracted transfer to be completed and unfortunately by that time his goals had seemingly dried up and he made little impact in Third Division football for a struggling Owls side. Near the end of his Hillsborough spell the attacker played two games on loan at Stockport County and after being released by Wednesday seemed set to return home and sign for League new boys Wimbledon. However he subsequently had a change of heart and left to fulfil a short-term contract in Norwegian soccer. After returning from Scandinavia, Feely reverted back to non-league soccer at Slough Town before a playing spell in Hong Kong. He earned a living in The Far East as a quantity surveyor and after buying land and property he became a millionaire when his assets were sold.

FELTON, William "Billy" 1923-29

Born: 1 August 1900 Heworth
(5ft 8ins, 12st 4lbs – 1924)
Died: 22 April 1977 Manchester
Debut: 1 January 1923
v Southampton
Division Two Home
Last Appearance: 23 February 1929
v Birmingham
Division One Away
Total League
& Cup Appearances: 164 Goals: 0

Career Details:

Pelaw Albion		
Pandon Temperance		
Pelaw Albion		
Wardley Colliery Welfare		1914
Jarrow		1917
Grimsby Town	January	1921
WEDNESDAY	1 January	1923 £1450
Manchester City	15 March	1929 £4800
Tottenham Hotspur	16 March	1932
Altrincham	September	1934

CAPS (@SWFC): ENGLAND Full (1) v France 21/05/25

During the Owls Division Two Championship campaign of 1925-6 the club could boast the best full back pairing in the whole division with "prince of full backs" Ernie Blenkinsop on the left side and robust and powerful Billy Felton on the right. The latter had originally joined the club in quite bizarre circumstances as on New Year's Day 1923 he was travelling with his Grimsby Town teammates for a game in Lancashire at Accrington. Somehow the Owls got in touch with Felton on route and not only did he sign but he made his debut for Wednesday at Hillsborough on the same day!

The superb tackler did not play much football at school but at the age of 14 started his working life as a miner at Wardley Colliery and within a few weeks was asked to play as a centre-forward for the pit side in the local Tyneside League. After moving to Jarrow he was converted into his true position of full back and after turning down offers from both Aston Villa and Newcastle United, Billy signed for Grimsby Town. He went straight into the side at Blundell Park and was in fact almost ever present, appearing in 43 league games – before Bob Brown swooped to take the highly rated Felton to Hillsborough. His debut actually came at left back – he was equally at home on either flank - and Billy would play his first four games in that position before Brown pulled off yet another masterstroke by capturing the signature of Blenkinsop just three weeks later.

Felton, who was so enthusiastic about his football that he once said he "would play football all day if they would let him", remained a first choice at Wednesday for the next four seasons and missed only a handful of games to earn the aforementioned championship medal in 1926. However following the move into a higher grade of football Felton struggled to hold down a regular place and after Tommy Walker became first choice right-back at the club, Felton would spend the majority of his final two seasons at Wednesday as a standby player in case either Blenkinsop or Walker were absent. His three games in the 1928-9 season were not sufficient to earn Felton a League Championship medal and he had in fact left for Manchester City before Wednesday had clinched the title. He perhaps proved a point to the Wednesday hierarchy by appearing in 28 top-flight games – in the main at left back - for City in his first full season at the Maine Road club. His new side finished in third spot in that season but after losing his place part way through the following season Felton eventually moved to Spurs where during his 146 games he captained the North London side to runners-up spot in Division Two in 1932. Incidentally in the Hillsborough game with Manchester United in March 1927 Felton ran the line after one of the officials failed to appear!

FERGUSON, Robert "Bobby" 1974

Born: 1 March 1945 Ardrossan, Scotland
(5ft 11ins, 12st 2lbs – 1974)
Debut: 10 February 1974
v Bristol City
Division Two Home
Last Appearance: 2 March 1974
v Hull City
Division Two Away
Total League
& Cup Appearances: 5 Goals: 0

Career Details:

Kilmarnock Amateurs		
Kilmarnock	June	1963
West Ham United	30 May	1967 £65,000
WEDNESDAY	8 Feb-3 March	1974 Loan
Released		1980
Adelaide City	January	1982

Despite attending a school that played only rugby and cricket, Bobby Ferguson went on to enjoy a long and successful football career on both sides of the border. His playing career started in earnest when he joined Kilmarnock Juniors straight from school while at the same time starting a five-year engineering apprenticeship. However his career of course would soon take a detour as he signed professional forms for the town's Scottish League side and never looked back, enjoying a highly successful four years at the Rugby Park club. Such was the youngster's outstanding form between the sticks at Kilmarnock that after earning eight youth caps and a Scotland U-23 cap he would eventually win seven full caps for his country during which time Killie won the League Championship in 1965 and reached the semi-final of the old Fairs Cup in 1967 – losing 4-2 on aggregate to Leeds United.

The goalkeeper's superb form of course alerted many clubs south of the border to his talents and after tracking him for several months it was First Division side West Ham United who paid a sizeable fee – then a British record for a keeper - to take the Scot to East London. His first team debut came on the opening day of the 1967 season – ironically against Wednesday – and in a 13-year stay at Upton Park he would appear in 276 league and cup games for the Hammers. During his time at Upton Park, Ferguson reached the League Cup semi-finals in 1972 – losing 3-2 to Stoke after a marathon four-game semi-final – and was first choice for the majority of that time, only suffering a lean time in the mid-1970s when he was kept out by Grotier and Day. It was during this time on the sidelines that Steve Burtenshaw brought Ferguson to Hillsborough, the goalie making his Owls debut in the home game with Bristol City which doubled as Burtenshaw's first home game in charge and Wednesday's first ever Sunday League fixture. He kept previous No.1 Peter Springett out of the side for five games but eventually returned to West Ham United where he remained until 1980.

At this point Ferguson emigrated to Australia and after acclimatising to his new surroundings, signed for Aussie side Adelaide City – he never played for Port Elizabeth which was previously thought. After retiring from football, in December 1983, he owned a scuba diving business but this was sold after five years when his best friend was tragically killed in a shark attack. He then bought a carpet business, selling carpets and floor tiles, but eventually sold this as well and now owns a chain of snack bars. Also in his spare time Bobby trains a Rugby Union club in Adelaide.

FERGUSON, Ronald Charles "Ronnie" 1975-76

Born: 9 February 1957 Accrington
(6ft 1ins, 12st 7lbs – 1975)
Debut: 9 November 1974
v York City
Division Two Home
Last Appearance: 12 April 1975
v Bristol City
Division Two Away
Total League
& Cup Appearances: 10+1 Goals: 1

Career Details:

WEDNESDAY	9 February	1975
Scunthorpe United	10 December	1975 Loan
Darlington	26 February	1976 Loan to June 1976
Darlington	1 July	1976 Free
Racing Jet Brussels	July	1980
La Louviere	July	1986

Striker Ronnie Ferguson had the misfortune to break into Wednesday's first team during one of the most horrendous seasons in the club's long history. The ex-Gainsborough and Lincolnshire boys player – he moved to Gainsborough at the age of five with his family - was given a debut by Steve Burtenshaw as the under pressure manager tried in vain to find a winning, and scoring, combination to pull Wednesday away from the lower reaches of the old Second Division. He had seemingly found the solution when the 17-year old scored on his debut as The Owls beat York City 3-0 at Hillsborough and soon after, having played in just ten reserve team games, Ronnie was called into the England Youth squad. The youngster was still an apprentice when he made his debut, not turning pro until four months later, and in his first four games Wednesday experienced a mini-revival by losing only once.

After this initial run of first team soccer Ronnie dropped back into the reserves and would only be recalled when the situation had reached crisis point – Wednesday only scored twice from December 29 1974 until the end of the season! Playing in such circumstances cannot have been helpful to the teenager's development and confidence, and it was perhaps no surprise that he failed to play another first team game in Wednesday colours following the inevitable relegation to Division Three. After a three-game loan spell at Scunthorpe, Ronnie eventually spent a successful four years at Darlington where in 127 competitive games he scored 22 times – including the late winner when Darlington knocked Wednesday out of the F.A.Cup in December 1976! Incidentally during his time at Darlington he actually quit professional football in March 1978 to work as a sales rep for Wrigley's spearmint gum. He remained out of the game for three months before returning to Darlo for pre season training. There then followed an eight-year spell in Belgium football, which ended in October 1988 when a contract dispute saw Ferguson return home to England. It took a year before the contract problems were resolved, by which time Ronnie had retired from football to concentrate on his current full time employment at a printing firm in Gainsborough.

FERRIER, Robert "Bob" 1894-1906

Born: 1874 Dumbarton (5ft 5ins, 10st 7lbs – 1896)
Died: 11 December 1947
Debut: 1 September 1894 v Everton
Division One Away
Last Appearance: 26 April 1905
v Newcastle United Division One Home
Total League & Cup Appearances: 329
Goals:20

Career Details:

L'Homme qui rit		
Dumbarton		
WEDNESDAY	summer	1894
Released	summer	1906

In the early years of Wednesday's league history the club regularly crossed Hadrian's Wall to snatch the best Scottish talent available and Robert Ferrier – known as "Rabbie" in his homeland - proved to be one of their greatest imports to the English game. He had started his playing career in local Dumbarton football – playing for a club with a French name that translated to "The man who laugh" – but was spotted by Wednesday scouts whilst plying his trade at the town's Scottish League club. He arrived in Sheffield during the summer of 1894 and in his first season impressed the Olive Grove faithful by working in tandem with Archie Brash down the Owls right-wing – the newcomer appearing at inside forward. Over the next twelve years he would become hugely popular with Wednesday fans as he proved to a be a tireless worker who not only possessed a "capital long shot" and close ball control but was also "fast and scientific". He was prone to dally at times when in possession but overall he would be a mainstay of the Wednesday side that established the club as a major force in the English game during the years before the First World War.

In his second season at Wednesday, Ferrier played in all but five league games but was crucially absent at the start of the F.A.Cup campaign and subsequently played only once in the competition as Wednesday reached their second Cup Final – he was named as reserve for the Cup Final win over Wolves and was one of thirteen players who travelled down to Crystal Palace. Despite missing out on the chance of a Cup winners medal he was soon an automatic choice again and would perform consistently on the right side until an F.A.Cup tie at Sunderland in 1898 when his career took another turn. The Owls were without stalwart left half-back Harry Brandon for the trip to the Northeast and it was Ferrier who stepped into his shoes as a temporary measure. However it quickly became apparent that Bob was ideally suited to the defensive role and that Wednesday had suddenly found a replacement for the ageing Brandon from within their own ranks.

Ferrier would prove truly outstanding in his new role and was a key player as Wednesday won the Second Division Championship in 1900 and then back–to-back Division One titles in 1903 and 1904. However tragedy struck for Bob in January of the latter year when his young wife passed away and although he recovered from that tragedy in his personal life to play first team football again for Wednesday he lost his place to Herrod Ruddlesdin part way through the 1904-5 season. After solely playing reserve team soccer in the following season – helping Wednesday to runners-up spot in the Midland League – Ferrier was released in the summer of 1906 and returned home to Dumbarton where he gained employment as a boilermaker at Denny's Shipyard. With shipbuilding being a reserve occupation Bob was not called up during the Great War and between the wars he scouted for Wednesday in Scotland. Incidentally both his son and grandson, both also called Bob Ferrier, enjoyed successful careers in the public eye – the former made a club-record 626 appearances for Motherwell, scoring over 200 goals, while the latter was a well-known sports writer for over forty years.

FINNEY, Alan 1950-66

Born: 31 October 1933 Langwith, Notts (5ft 8ins, 10st 7lbs – 1950)
Debut: 24 February 1951
v Chelsea
Division One Home
Last Appearance: 1 January 1966
v Leeds United
Division One Away
Total League
& Cup Appearances: 504 Goals: 88

Career Details:

Armthorpe Youth Club		
WEDNESDAY	31 October	1950 £50
Doncaster Rovers	13 January	1966 £3,500
Alfreton Town	30 June	1967
Doncaster Dentists		1968 (Sun.)

CAPS (@SWFC):
ENGLAND "B" (1) v Scotland 29/02/56
ENGLAND-23 (3) v Italy 20/01/54, v Scotland 08/02/56, v Scotland 26/02/57

As a young boy Alan Finney would walk the four miles to Belle Vue from his home village of Armthorpe to watch Doncaster Rovers play. He would one day play league football for Rovers but only after having served Wednesday with distinction for almost twenty years, from joining the Owls ground staff as a 15-year old in 1948 to his transfer to Doncaster early in 1966. He had achieved early prominence with both Doncaster and Yorkshire boys and was already attached to the Owls when he left school and started working as an apprentice coach and wagon repairer for British Railways. This was in fact a ploy by Wednesday to try and keep him from serving National Service and his manager at the time – a mad keen Owls fan - aided and abetted the cause by letting the youngster work just on a Monday and train with Wednesday the rest of the time! However when a new manager appeared on the scene Finney received a letter stating that unless his attendance improved he would lose his job!

He did eventually spend two years in the Royal Signals unit alongside fellow Wednesday starlet Albert Quixall, and the pair would be inexorably linked over the next few years as both made their first team debuts in the same game and played together for seven seasons before Quixall left for Manchester United. Until signing professional for Wednesday on his seventeenth birthday, Finney was allowed to play for his village youth club when not required for the Owls junior sides but was soon a reserve team regular for Wednesday, before breaking into the first eleven. His debut would come on the right wing, where he would spend the majority of his playing career at Hillsborough, and the pencil thin Finney went on to play over 500 games in the blue and white shirt to set a post war appearance record that will probably never be beaten by an outfield player. At his best the winger was highly elusive, tricky and boasted an attribute rare for wingmen – consistency. He of course became a big favourite with Owls fans, for his goals and creation of goals, and from being demobbed in 1951 to the mid-1960s he was an automatic choice. During that time he helped Wednesday to three Division Two Championships (1952, 55 & 59), two F.A.Cup semi-finals, a Fairs Cup quarter-final and was also ever present during the 1960-61 season when the Owls finished runners-up to the legendary Spurs double side – he also had the distinction of appearing in the first ever England U-23 International, against Italy in Bologna in January 1954.

Due to the Owls Cup run to Wembley in 1966, combined with World Cup matches at Hillsborough, Finney unfortunately missed out on his promised testimonial against Sheffield United with Wednesday instead playing Doncaster Rovers at Belle Vue on his behalf in May 1966. The game was strictly a no tackle match, coming just days after the Cup Final loss to Everton, and would perhaps explain why the match ended in a 6-5 win for Rovers! In his short time at Rovers, Alan won a Division Four Championship medal and after three goals in 34 games quit the professional game in the summer of 1967. He played another season in non-league football at Derbyshire club Alfreton Town before combining Sunday football with his job at Armthorpe Colliery. His responsibilities at the Colliery were wide ranging, from joining cables to being a paddy driver – the man who drives the miners to the coalface. However he was eventually introduced to the bookmakers business by his father-in-law and went on to run his own business in Doncaster.

FISH, Thomas "Tom" 1899-1903

Born: 2nd Quarter 1877 Birtley, C.Durham
Debut: 30 March 1901 v Everton Division One Home
Last Appearance: 25 January 1902 v Sunderland F.A.Cup Away
Total League & Cup Appearances: 8 Goals: 0

Career Details:

Birtley FC		
WEDNESDAY	30 May	1899 £10
Released		1903
Thornhole F.C.		1904

Centre half-back Tom Fish spent a total of four years at Wednesday, mainly as understudy to the great Herrod Ruddlesdin. He had originally arrived from Durham minor football, making his Owls debut in only the second match to be played on the club's new ground at Owlerton - the reserves' Association League encounter with Wombwell in September 1899. It would be at second team level that Fish would make his greatest impact while a professional at Wednesday, winning a multitude of local honours as Wednesday's reserves swept all before them in the years bridging the dawn of the Twentieth Century. In his first season he was almost ever present as the reserves won the Sheffield Association League, dropping only three points in the process, The Wharncliffe Charity Cup League and completed a treble when Worksop Town were beaten in the Final of the Sheffield Challenge Cup. The SAL League title was retained a year later, the Challenge Cup won in 1902 and finally the Midland Counties League Championship in 1903.

However his rival Ruddlesdin boasted an almost ever present record at first team level for Wednesday and Fish had only brief opportunities to further his cause in League football. After making just a sole appearance in 1900-01 he did enjoy a spell of five consecutive games in the season that followed but once Ruddlesdin was fit and well it was back to reserve team soccer for Tom. He never again played senior football for The Owls and was released in 1903, later dropping into non-league football.

FLEMING, John Ian Horea "Ian" 1979-80

Born: 15 January 1953
Maybole, Scotland
(5ft 8ins, 10st 7lbs – 1979)
Debut: 13 February 1979
v Southend United
Division Three Away
Last Appearance: 3 November 1979
v Barnsley
Division Three Home
Total League
& Cup Appearances: 17 Goals: 2

Career Details:

Craigmark Bruntonians		
Kilmarnock	August	1970
Aberdeen	December	1975 £50,000
WEDNESDAY	9 February	1979 £48,000
Dundee	8 February	1980 £45,000
Brechin City	October	1982

Despite starting his working life as an apprentice electrician, while playing part-time football with Kilmarnock, it would be as a professional footballer that Ian Fleming earned a crust for almost a decade. After qualifying as an electrician Fleming moved from Killie to Aberdeen for a large fee, after having earned a reputation as a goal poacher thanks to 51 goals. While in the "Granite City" the forward earned a League Cup winners medal in 1977 – although he did not play in the final – and was runner-up in the 1978 Scottish Cup Final, after having scored a hat-trick in the semi-final mauling of Partick Thistle.

His form for Aberdeen persuaded Wednesday boss Jack Charlton to bring Fleming to Hillsborough but his first few weeks at the club were badly disrupted after he was unfortunate enough to be injured on his debut – ex-Owl Dave Cusack the culprit – and required a cartilage operation. In reality the tenacious and diminutive striker never really recovered from that unfortunate beginning and struggled to make his mark on Division Three football while at Wednesday and it was no real surprise that in January 1980 he asked for a move, subsequently returning to Scottish football a few days later. At Dundee he scored within two minutes of his debut – against old club Kilmarnock – and stayed until being appointed player-manager at Brechin City at the tender age of 29 in October 1982. In his first season at the helm he led City to their highest ever finish in the Scottish League – Division Two Champions – and he remained in charge until 1987 when he departed following relegation back to Division Two. Incidentally his playing days had ended during the 1984-5 season so he could concentrate on the management side of the job.

Fleming – whose brothers Jim and Chris both played league football for Kilmarnock and Brechin City - then spent a year as manager of Icelandic club F.H.Hafnjaforder before two years as assistant-manager at Forfar Athletic and a year in the same capacity at Arbroath. In 1991 he was appointed at old club Aberdeen in a joint role of scout and under-14 coach. He now works for an electrical company as their sales and specification manager while also working as a scout for Aberdeen on a purely voluntary basis.

FLETCHER, Brough 1926

Born: 9 March 1893
Mealsgate, Cumberland
(5ft 7½ ins, 12st 4lbs – 1926)
Died: 12 May 1972 Bristol
Debut: 3 April 1926
v Hull City
Division Two Home
Last Appearance: 5 April 1926
v Stoke City
Division Two Away
Total League
& Cup Appearances: 2 Goals: 0

Career Details:

Clilton Colliery Welfare		
Shildon Athletic		
Barnsley	August	1914
WEDNESDAY	4 February	1926 £600
Barnsley	December	1926 £600

Almost the whole of inside forward Brough Fletcher's professional career was spent at Barnsley where in two spells totalling almost fifteen years he scored 83 goals in 332 appearances for the Oakwell club. Fletcher was a veritable pocket battleship style of player and his robust play made him a popular player amongst Tykes fans either side of the Great War – he played only two games for Barnsley in wartime football. His brief spell away from Oakwell came in 1926 when Owls manager Bob Brown brought Fletcher to Hillsborough, mainly to captain and coach the club's reserve side. However near the end of Wednesday's Second Division Championship season of 1925-26 Brown found his team diluted and called on the services of 33-year old Fletcher to replace the void left by the absent Arthur Prince. He would play two consecutive games in the No.8 shirt but before the year was out had returned to Oakwell in a "get your money back" deal.

He would play for three more years at Barnsley before being appointed to the coaching staff in May 1929 and on 5th May 1930 was promoted to trainer/manager – the first man to hold the post without the extra burden of secretarial duties. He had little money to spend and Barnsley were relegated from Division Two in 1932 after a spell of 34 years in the second tier of the English game.

However he subsequently took The Tykes back up in 1934, as Division Three (North) Champions, and led Barnsley to an F.A.Cup quarter-final meeting with Arsenal in 1936 before resigning a year later – on 25th January 1937. Incidentally it was reported that he had actually resigned in June 1934 to take over a business in the town but he was persuaded to reverse his decision and stay at the helm for Barnsley's first season back in Division Two.

After cutting his ties with Barnsley, Fletcher was appointed Chief Scout at Bradford Park Avenue but resigned in December 1937, being appointed Bristol Rovers manager a month later. Brough, who was also appointed as a temporary scout for Wednesday in September 1937, spent almost twelve years at Bristol Rovers and although failing to gain promotion did bring some quality players to the club. However he is not fondly remembered by Rovers fans as he was instrumental in selling Eastville to a greyhound racing company and in fact his tenure was ended abruptly in December 1949 as he was sacked following an F.A. inquiry into the sale of the ground. He joined Walsall in March 1952 but near the end of his first full season, and with The Saddlers bottom of the league, he resigned in April 1953 and retired to the West Country.

FLETCHER, Douglas "Doug" 1948-51

Born: 17 September 1930 Sheffield
(5ft 8½ ins, 10st 3lbs – 1950)
Debut: 11 April 1949
v Leicester City
Division Two Home
Last Appearance: 16 August 1949
v Cardiff City
Division Two Home
Total League
& Cup Appearances: 4 Goals: 0

Career Details:

Hillsborough Boys Club		
WEDNESDAY	4 February	1948
Bury	May	1951 £330
Scunthorpe United	July	1956 £2,775
Darlington	July	1958
Halifax Town	June	1959 N/C
Bath City		1960
Oughtibridge WMSC	March	1961
Goole Town		
Oughtibridge WMSC		

The incredible goal scoring feats of Derek Dooley may never have entered the annals of Hillsborough history if it was not for Doug Fletcher and a broken ankle! While the young striker was serving his National Service in the Army he had the misfortune to suffer a broken ankle in an October 1949 game against Cambridge University and it was this injury that directly led to the club calling off Derek Dooley's proposed transfer to Lincoln City! Unfortunately for Fletcher – who signed for Wednesday at the age of 17 from Hillsborough Boys Club – the injury badly disrupted his Wednesday career and in fact he never appeared in first team football again for the Owls. His only games at senior level had come earlier in the year as a replacement for the absent Clarrie Jordan, after having risen throughout the ranks at Hillsborough to become established as the centre forward's understudy.

When he had originally signed professional forms for Wednesday Fletcher actually held three welterweight boxing titles – ABA Junior, National Boys club and The Yorkshire Counties - and it must have been difficult for the teenager to decide which career to persue. However he plumped for professional soccer and despite failing to really make the grade at Hillsborough still enjoyed over ten years in league football at several lower league clubs after leaving Wednesday for Bury in 1951. At Gigg Lane, and his next three league sides, Fletcher totalled 60 goals in 194 league matches before dropping into non-league football at Bath City. He was soon back in Sheffield however, gaining employment at British Steel's Stocksbridge plant and in 1965 was appointed manager/trainer to the Works' Yorkshire League side – a position he held for eighteen months. He worked in the Traffic Maintenance department at Stocksbridge and remained in that capacity until his eventual retirement

FLETCHER, Henry 1880-81

Born: Sheffield
Only Appearance: 8 January 1881 v Turton F.A.Cup Away
Total League & Cup Appearances: 1 Goals: 0

Career Details:

Local	
WEDNESDAY	1880
Local	1881

Mystery surrounds the single appearance Henry Fletcher made in a Wednesday shirt back in 1881. The game against Lancashire club Turton was only Wednesday's second in the F.A.Cup and Henry had the pleasure of recording a win on his sole start for the club in competitive football. However no trace of Fletcher can be found either before or subsequent to the Cup tie and the mystery deepens even further as on the same day a Wednesday side faced Walsall at Bramall Lane where a certain H.Fletcher was listed in the Owls line up!

FORD, David 1963-69

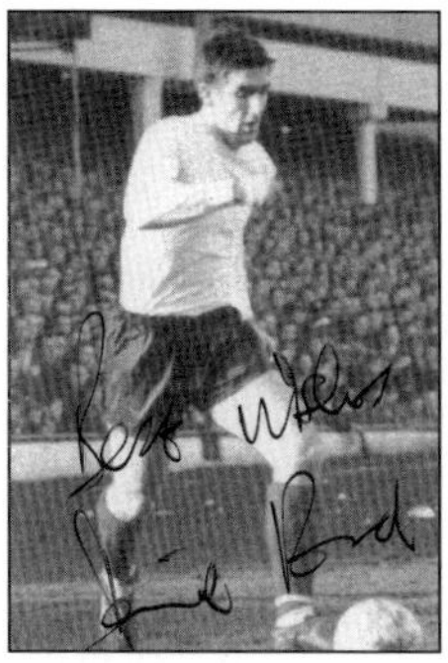

Born: 2 March 1945 Sheffield
(5ft 7ins, 10st 7½lbs – 1966)
Debut: 23 October 1965
v Sunderland
Division One Home
Last Appearance: 13 December 1969
v Leeds United
Division One Away
Total League
& Cup Appearances: 130+5 Goals: 37

Career Details:

WEDNESDAY	15 January	1963
Newcastle United	16 December	1969 £30,000*
Sheffield United	28 January	1971 **
Halifax Town	August	1973

*Deemed value in exchange with Jackie Sinclair
**Exchange for John Tudor

CAPS (@SWFC)
v England U-23 (2) v Wales 12/10/66, v Scotland 01/03/67

David Ford was an all round athlete at school, representing both Sheffield and Yorkshire Grammer schools at football and also his City and County at athletics – he was Sheffield Schools 100 yards champion. However on finishing his education Ford gained employment as a clerk at the Sheffield town hall and if his mother had not written to Wednesday to request a trial for her son a career in commerce could have followed for Ford. He duly signed for Wednesday on amateur forms in September 1961 and in January of the following year signed apprentice forms, playing in the club's youth side that was managed by Derek Dooley. Early success in his fledgling years at Wednesday included a run to the semi-finals of the F.A.Youth Cup in 1963 – losing to Liverpool – but unfortunately his career at first team level was blighted by injury and he could never fulfil his massive potential.

After progressing to reserve team football he made a big impression with his speed, resourcefulness and shooting ability but on making his senior debut in August 1964 – in a pre season friendly in Germany against Werder Bremen – Ford suffered a knee injury which put him on the sidelines for the remainder of the season. Thankfully he recovered from that setback to make his league debut in October 1965 – as the club's first ever substitute – and the outstanding forward quickly proved to be one of Wednesday's most mobile and exciting discoveries of the 1960s and an automatic choice for the next four years. He scored for Wednesday in the 1966 F.A.Cup Final loss to Everton and grabbed a treble in the 7-0 win over Burnley in May 1967 but in September 1967 tragedy struck when he was injured in a serious car crash in which his fiancée was killed. Apart from the emotional distress caused by the accident he was also put out of action for ten weeks and only returned to regular first team duty near the end of the campaign. His form dipped slightly near the end of the decade but it was still a disappointment to Wednesday fans when Danny Williams sold David to First Division Newcastle United in December 1969.

He stayed barely a year in the Northeast, making 26 league appearances, before returning to Sheffield to sign for neighbours United, helping the Blades to promotion to the top-flight in 1971.After 27 games at United he wound up his league career with a further 6 goals in 85 games at Halifax Town before retiring to start a plumbing and heating business back in Sheffield. This still thrives today while in the intervening years Ford has run the Wednesday Executive Club – also arranging away travel and match tickets for the same body – as well as playing on a regular basis for Johnny Quinn's All Stars Charity team.

FOX, Oscar 1943-50

Born: 1 January 1921 Sheffield
(5ft 8½ ins, 10st 9lbs – 1948)
Died: 15 January 1990 Sheffield
Debut: 12 October 1946
v Manchester City
Division Two Away
Last Appearance: 18 February 1950
v Brentford
Division Two Home
Total League
& Cup Appearances: 47* Goals: 4
***Also appeared in**
38 wartime games, scoring 4 goals

Career Details:

Wadsley Amateurs		
WEDNESDAY	9 October	1943
Mansfield Town	June	1950 £1,000

Although it was previously thought that Oscar Fox was born in the Derbyshire village of Clowne, he was in fact a Sheffielder – born at Braydon House in Walkley Lane on New Year's Day 1921. His first experiences of organised football came at Wisewood School – he also played for the men's cricket team later in life - and after playing local football with Wadsley Amateurs he duly signed professional forms for Wednesday during World War Two. His senior debut for the Owls came in April 1943 at Rotherham United and Fox was a regular in wartime football, appearing mainly at inside or outside-left.

It was in the latter position that Fox would play in post war soccer for the Owls, competing with the likes of Frank Slynn and Jackie Marriott while fitting in his two years National Service in the R.A.F. However he never really became established at Hillsborough in peacetime soccer and appeared in only nine games during the Division Two promotion season of 1949-50 before leaving for Mansfield Town. In his first season at Field Mill he appeared in 34 matches for Town as they finished runners-up to Rotherham United in the old Division Three (North), missing out on promotion as only the Champions went up. Fox would spend eight years at Mansfield, appearing in 247 league games, before retiring in June 1958, at the age of 37, when his contract expired. He was then appointed assistant to manager Sam Weaver but was fired in January 1960, along with Weaver, with Mansfield near the bottom of Division Three.

Oscar's father, also called Oscar, played for Bradford City just after the First World War and when his son's playing career finished Oscar jnr. gained employment at an Engineering works in Clay Cross, near Chesterfield, while also occasionally scouting for legendary Liverpool manager Bill Shankly.

FOX, Peter David 1975-78

Born: 5 July 1957 Scunthorpe
(5ft 11ins, 11st 8lbs – 1975)
Debut: 31 March 1973
v Orient
Division Two Home
Last Appearance: 2 November 1976
v Rotherham United
Division Three Away
Total League
& Cup Appearances: 52 Goals: 0

Career Details:

WEDNESDAY	23 June	1975
West Ham United	10 February	1977 Loan
Team Hawaii	May	1977 Loan
Barnsley	22 December	1978 2-month loan
Stoke City	3 March	1978 £15,000
Linfield	September	1992 Loan
Wrexham	23 March	1993 Loan to 02/04/93
Exeter City	15 July	1993 Free
Leek Town		2000

Although perhaps better known for his 409 League appearances in a fifteen-year spell at Stoke City, goalkeeper Peter Fox will always have a permanent place in Wednesday's rich history as the club's youngest ever player. This record was set back in 1973 when apprentice Fox, aged 15 years, 8 months and 26 days, was called into the breach when a goalkeeping crisis saw both Peter Grummitt and Peter Springett sidelined. The teenager had only signed apprentice forms in the previous July but showed remarkable ability to keep a clean sheet on his debut, although he did suffer a broken toe in the process. After his eventful day it was back to mopping the dressing room floor and cleaning the professional's boots until he returned to the side, still aged only seventeen, in December 1974 to play in the final twenty games of a traumatic relegation season – despite the teams poor form Fox was called into the England U-18 squad.

The ex-Scunthorpe and Lincolnshire boys player started the club's first ever season of Division Three football as understudy to newcomer Neil Ramsbottom but as in the previous campaign Fox came to the fore once the Christmas trimmings had come down, playing in the final 27 games of the season as Wednesday just avoided a catastrophic relegation to the basement division. However the emergence of Chris Turner and purchase of Bob Bolder greatly increased competition for the No.1 jersey and after the former became firmly established as first choice Fox asked for a move in November 1976, eventually leaving for West Ham on loan four months later. He played only three reserve team games for The Hammers before leaving for an enjoyable four month spell in the flourishing NASL, playing against the likes of Pele and Eusebio in the not unattractive surroundings of Hawaii! A further loan spell at the slightly less glamorous setting of Barnsley followed before the 20-year old cut his losses and moved to Stoke City in the search of regular first team football.

The transfer started a remarkable association with the Potteries club that saw Fox set the record for the most appearances by a City goalkeeper, a mammoth 477 games. He showed remarkable consistency throughout his career and was three times named player of the year as well as winning the Auto Windscreen Trophy in 1992 – beating Stockport County one-nil at Wembley. A Division Two Championship medal followed in 1993, playing in the final ten games of the season after earlier loan spells in Irish football and Welsh football, before he was appointed player and assistant manager at Exeter City in the summer that followed. Despite being at the veteran stage of his career Fox was named player of the year at City in both 1994 and 1995 and was a popular choice when appointed manager in June 1995. He remained in charge until parting company on 9th January 2000 and was subsequently employed as part-time goalkeeping coach at Huddersfield Town and Notts County – working two days a week at both. In addition he spent his Saturdays reporting on games for the Press Association before playing several games for Northern Premier League side Leek Town. He left Huddersfield and hung up his boots in 2001 and currently works full time as goalkeeping coach at Notts County.

FOX, William 1894-95

Born Scotland (5ft 10ins, 11st 8lbs – 1894)
Debut: 25 March 1895 v Small Heath Division One Away
Last Appearance: 22 April 1895
v West Bromwich Albion Division One Away
Total League & Cup Appearances: 4 Goals: 0

Career Details:

Carfin Club		
WEDNESDAY	22 December	1894
Released	April	1895
Carfin	3 September	1897
Albion Rovers	29 September	1899

Centre forward William Fox was signed on trial from Lanarkshire junior football, late in December 1894. His first appearance in a Wednesday shirt came five days later when Fox netted in the reserves' 10-0 romp over Rotherham Town reserves at Olive Grove. During the season he played a total of seven second team games and also appeared in four Division One games, initially as a replacement for Harry Davis at centre-forward. He also played at inside and outside right but when his trial period ended Wednesday decided not to offer him a contract for the new season and he dropped back into amateur football.

FOXALL, Francis 'Frank' 1907-10

Born: 2nd Quarter 1883 Sheffield
Debut: 4 April 1907
v Sheffield United
Division One Away
Last Appearance: 19 March 1910
v Sheffield United
Division One Home
Total League
& Cup Appearances: 44 Goals: 9

Career Details:

All Saints School		
Roundel FC		
Wombwell Town		1901
Doncaster Rovers		1902
Gainsborough Trinity		1903
WEDNESDAY	1 April	1907
Birmingham	July	1910 £150
Shrewsbury Town	August	1911

Left-winger Frank Foxall came from the same school as Teddy Brayshaw – Foxall winning the prestigious Clegg Shield in three successive seasons while playing for his school and also representing Sheffield boys. He was also somewhat unique in Wednesday history as both his first and last appearances for the Owls came in the white-hot cauldron of a Sheffield derby game. He had initially arrived from fellow League club Gainsborough Trinity – his brother Jack played for the Lincolnshire club as well as for Rotherham County – and was seen as direct competition for first team regular George Simpson. Foxall was a pacy and tireless player who possessed a tremendous hard shot and he looked to have displaced his rival from the left wing during the1908-09 season when Fred appeared in sixteen games to Simpson's ten.

However despite Simpson's shock transfer to West Brom in March 1909, Foxall could not become established at first team level and eventually Oliver Tummon and then George Robertson pushed him into Midland League football. His cause was probably not helped by his off the field problems, which culminated in a court appearance at Sheffield magistrates in January 1909. Foxall was charged with causing grievous bodily harm to a P.C.Limb after a police raid on a street betting racket that had seen his brother arrested. The policeman had been concussed and was off duty for several weeks but Foxall escaped a jail sentence, being fined £20. After leaving Wednesday, Foxall – who played at left back in his school days – spent three seasons at Birmingham where he netted three times in 22 games. His playing career finished at non-league Shrewsbury Town, hanging up his proverbial boots in 1913.

FRANCIS, Trevor John 1990-95

Born: 19 April 1954 Plymouth
(5ft 10ins, 11st 7lbs – 1992)
Debut: 3 February 1990
v Millwall
Division One Home
Last Appearance: 20 November 1993
v Coventry City
Premier League Home
Total League
& Cup Appearances: 38+51 Goals: 9

Career Details:

Ernesettle Youth Club		
Birmingham City	1 May	1971
Detroit Express	May	1978 Loan to Aug 78
Nottingham Forest	14 February	1979 £975,000*
Detroit Express	June	1979 Loan - August 79
Manchester City	3 September	1981 £1,200,000
Sampdoria	1 July	1982 £800,000
Atlanta	1 July	1986 £900,000
Glasgow Rangers	1 September	1987 £75,000
Queens Park Rangers	1 February	1988 N/C
WEDNESDAY	23 January	1990 N/C

*Fee rose to approx. £1.15m after various additions

Lightning fast attacker Trevor Francis was without doubt one of the greatest players of his generation, winning a multitude of honours which included 52 full caps for England and several domestic honours in three different countries. He will of course always be remembered as the first player to transfer for the magic £1m and at his peak combined superb dribbling skills with clinical finishing to score over 220 goals in over 700 appearances.

The ex-Plymouth boys striker had initially burst onto the scene as a 16 year-old at Birmingham City – becoming the youngest ever player to score four times in a match when netting against Bolton in 1971 – and would earn legendary status at St.Andrews by scoring 133 times for City in 329 games, helping The Blues to promotion from Division Two in 1972. His amazing self confidence remained with Francis throughout his career and he seemed unfazed when Brian Clough made him the first player to move for £1m in the UK – the basic fee was nudged over the magic £1m by VAT and levy. Typically for Clough he gave Francis his Forest debut in an "A" team fixture but the ploy rebounded when Forest were censured because he was not yet registered with the Football League! However a few weeks later Francis was the toast of Nottingham as on his European Cup debut – he was ineligible until the Final – he met a John Robertson cross at the far post to head home the only goal against Malmo FF to win European football's greatest prize.

In the following summer he spent a second loan spell in the NASL – scoring five on his first appearance – and when he left for Manchester City in 1981 Francis had added a European Super Cup medal to his haul – having missed the club's 1980 European Cup success through injury – as well as earning runners-up medals in both the Football League Cup and World Club Championship. Despite this his time at The City Ground was plagued by injury and he in fact appeared in less than one hundred games for Forest, scoring 37 times, although scoring the winning goal in a major European Final probably repaid his fee in full! While at Maine Road, Francis appeared for England in the 1982 World Cup Finals before moving to Italian football in the same year for another sizeable fee. He enjoyed a highly successful spell in Italian soccer – somewhat bucking the trend at the time on British exports to Serie A – and won the Italian Cup in 1986 before returning home to sign for Graeme Souness' Glasgow Rangers.

In a short six-month stay in Scotland he added a Scottish League Cup winners medal to his collection before returning to England to sign non-contract terms at Queens Park Rangers. This move eventually led to his first managerial appointment when in December 1988 Francis was handed the reigns following Jim

Smith's departure. He continued to score frequently while fulfilling his player-manager role at Rangers but his reign was somewhat controversial and he was dismissed in 1990, promptly being signed on a free transfer by Wednesday boss Ron Atkinson. Despite arriving at Hillsborough at the twilight of his career Francis could still turn a game single handedly and proved a potent substitute for Wednesday as they earned promotion in 1991 and won the League Cup – Trevor was an unused sub in the Final win over Manchester United. The acrimonious departure of Atkinson in the summer that followed opened the door for Francis and he was duly appointed to the vacant position on 18 June 1991. During his first season in charge he led Wednesday to their highest league position for 31 years and enjoyed four Wembley appearances in the season that followed although silverware agonisingly eluded Wednesday. He was named manager of the month twice during his time in the hot seat and brought several high quality players to Hillsborough, including the likes of Chris Waddle and Des Walker. However a series of high profile personality clashes with senior Owls players and a poor 1994-5 season led to his somewhat surprising departure on 20 May 1995. In retrospect his time at Hillsborough saw the Owls play some of the most attractive football in their entire history but this is tempered by the fact that Francis did inherit an outstanding side from his predecessor and the jury is still out as to how history will judge Francis' four years at the helm. After a spell out of the game he returned to his spiritual home of St Andrews in May 1996 and led City to several Division One play-off semi-finals without success. He was also in charge when The Blues lost on penalties to Liverpool in the 2001 League Cup Final at Cardiff but after a poor start to the following season he parted company in October of the same year. Was appointed Crystal Palace manager in December 2001 but after failing to take The Eagles back into the top-flight he left by "mutual consent" on Good Friday 2003 – a day before his 49th birthday. He now works as a pundit for Sky TV.

FROGGATT, Frank 1921-27

Born: 21 March 1898 Sheffield
(5ft 9ins, 11st 7lbs – 1921)
Died: 6 March 1944 Sheffield
Debut: 22 October 1921
v Bradford Park Avenue
Division Two Home
Last Appearance: 7 September 1927
v Manchester United
Division One Away
Total League
& Cup Appearances: 96 Goals: 1

Career Details:

Army football		
Rose Athletic		
Denaby United	April	1921
WEDNESDAY	13 October	1921 £650
Notts County	18 November	1927 £1000
Chesterfield	May	1931
Scarborough	August	1934
Manchester North End	September	1935

When Frank Froggatt was appointed captain of Wednesday in 1925 he not only became the first Sheffield born player to be given the honour since Tommy Crawshaw but also ended a patient wait that had seen the half back live in the shadow of England International George Wilson for several seasons. In fact Froggatt – who was known to be a fine header of the ball and dour tackler - had been a reserve team regular at Wednesday for over three years since being signed by Bob Brown from Midland League Denaby United in 1921 – his career had started in Attercliffe Alliance League soccer at Rose Athletic. He had made such an impact in his first reserve team game against Worksop Town that Brown gave him an immediate league debut the following Saturday when George Wilson was captaining England against Ireland at Belfast. However it proved only to be a taster for Froggatt and he would remain second-choice to his rival until the 1924-5 campaign when the pair vied for the pivotal half back role – Frank actually made several appearances at left half back during that season after converting to the role when his path to first team football was seemingly blocked by Wilson.

Thankfully for Froggatt the Owls sensationally sold George Wilson to minnows Nelson in the summer of 1925 and he grabbed his chance with both hands, being ever present as the Owls walked away with the Second Division Championship. Frank – father of Redfern and uncle of Portsmouth and England attacker Jack – revelled in the No.5 shirt and literally played a pivotal role in that golden season. However Wednesday lost their first three games back in the top-flight and the fifteen goals conceded probably persuaded Bob Brown that a change was needed immediately. His solution was to move Freddie Kean from right half back to the pivotal role, hand him the captaincy and drop Froggatt! It was a bitter blow to Frank and he played only once more in that season. In the following summer, a possible explanation for that poor early season form came when an operation on his nose cured persistent breathing problems and saw Frank regain all his old stamina and fitness.

Unfortunately Kean was now even more established in the first team than Wilson had previously been and after appearing in just two more first team games ex-Owl Horace Henshall signed Froggatt for his Notts County side. He enjoyed a successful spell in Nottingham, scoring one goal in 118 appearances, and helped his new club to promotion from Division Three (South) in 1931. His final league side proved to be Chesterfield where despite making an initial impact Froggatt eventually lost his place through injury and then to the emerging Allan Sliman. After ending his playing career in non-league football he retired to take employment at Fox's Steelworks at Stocksbridge in Sheffield. In August 1942, Frank was appointed as a part-time scout by the Owls but within two years he had sadly passed away at the age of only 45, leaving his 19 year-old son Redfern to continue the footballing dynasty.

FROGGATT, Redfern 1943-62

Born: 23 August 1924 Sheffield
(5ft 11ins, 11st 1lbs – 1948)
Died: 26 December 2003 Sheffield
Debut: 5 January 1946
v Mansfield Town
F.A.Cup Away
Last Appearance: 30 April 1960
v West Ham United
Division One Away
Total League
& Cup Appearances: 458* Goals: 148
***Also appeared in**
80 wartime games, scoring 17 goals

Career Details:

Sheffield Y.M.C.A.		
WEDNESDAY	11 November	1943
Stalybridge Celtic	August	1962

CAPS (@ SWFC):
ENGLAND FULL (4)
v Wales 12/11/52, v Belgium 26/11/52, v Scotland 18/04/53, v USA 08/06/53

ENGLAND "B" (1) v Switzerland 18/01/50

FOOTBALL LEAGUE (1) v Scottish League 25/03/53

Outstanding inside forward Redfern Froggatt followed in his father's footsteps by leading Wednesday to Division Two Championship success in 1959. However where his father only enjoyed one season of real success at Hillsborough his offspring became one of the greatest players in the club's history, third only to Andrew Wilson and John Fantham in the all-time goal scoring stakes. That title success was in fact his third Division Two Championship while at Hillsborough during the period in Wednesday's history that is commonly referred to as the "yo-yo years" – he also won the trophy in 1952 and 1956. Froggatt was a real all round player, being equally adept at scoring as well as making chances, and earned a reputation as a subtle and intelligent attacker who was always a danger to opposition defences.

The Sheffielder – who ironically played for Sheffield boys at cricket but not football – was an outstanding athlete at school and was spotted by Wednesday when his Sheffield YMCA side won a 5-a-side tournament in Millhouses Park in Sheffield. He duly joined the Owls ground staff in August 1942, aged seventeen, and while still working as a tool draughtsman he signed part-time professional forms in November 1943. His job was a reserved occupation so Redfern was not called up during the hostilities and he took advantage to cement his place in the side – his actual debut for Wednesday had come back in February 1943 when he played a one off trial game. When the war came to a close Redfern signed full time pro forms and for the next fourteen seasons he was an established first team player with only an occasional injury denying him a first team spot. That was apart from two periods in the 1950s when first Albert Quixall, and then Jackie Sewell challenged his first team place but Froggatt usually showed his versatility by changing position to ensure he remained in the starting eleven – a third of his goals came from the right wing although he is generally recognised as an inside-left. The early 1950s also saw Froggatt earn many representative honours – playing alongside his cousin Jack in all four of his England games – and if Wednesday had been playing top-flight football throughout the decade "Red" would surely have earned many more honours – his form was such that neighbours United cheekily offered £15,000 for his services which was quickly turned down!

After setting the club's post war record for goals and appearances – both figures were subsequently bettered by John Fantham and Alan Finney respectively – Red spent his final two seasons at Wednesday playing reserve team football and passing his great experience onto the club's younger players. However he was still a big draw and after retiring from professional football his debut for Cheshire League Stalybridge Celtic boosted their opening day of the season crowd to a bumper 2,200. Soon after Froggatt was given a well deserved benefit game against Dutch giants Ajax of Amsterdam and later in life Froggatt returned to Hillsborough as a volunteer commentator for local hospital radio. After finishing with football – after turning down a £1,500 a year offer from Irish club Derry City to become player-manager - he worked as a sales rep for an oil company and lived out his retirement in Sheffield. Incidentally the Froggatt family name re-emerged in the late 1960s when Red's son Paul played for Wednesday's youth side.

FRYE, John Marr 1961

Born: 27 July 1933 Ardrossan, Scotland
(5ft 7ins, 10st 8lbs – 1961)
Only Appearance: 7 March 1961
v Burnley
F.A.Cup Away
Total League
& Cup Appearances: 1 Goals: 0

Career Details:

Largs Rovers		
Ardrossan Winton Rovers		
Hibernian		1954
St.Mirren		£10,000
WEDNESDAY	9 January	1961 £3,500
Tranmere Rovers	6 October	1961 £2,000
Queen of The South		1962 £8,000
Hamilton Academicals		1963
Stranraer		1968 Free

The Sheffield Wednesday career of Scotsman John Frye lasted only nine months and saw the utility forward make just a solitary first team appearance for the club – a two-nil Cup quarter-final replay loss at Turf Moor in March 1961 – plus exactly 21 reserve team games as Wednesday won the Central league Championship. Frye – whose father Derek played for Queen of The South and holds the record of most goals in a season at Stranraer – learned his trade in Ayreshire junior football, winning the local cup competition with Largs Rovers, before breaking into League soccer at Edinburgh club Hibs.

A move to St.Mirren followed before Harry Catterick brought Frye to Hillsborough but he could not break into the Owls league side and was soon crossing The Pennines to sign for Tranmere Rovers. In fact his career at Wednesday had started off on the wrong foot as he was unable to play for three weeks after signing as he was serving a suspension after being sent off for St.Mirren against Ayr United in November 1960! To make matters worse he appealed to the Football League in September 1961 after Wednesday's new boss Vic Buckingham felt unable to offer Frye improved terms – after having not seen him play for the club. The League turned down Fry's appeal – saying they could not interfere – and with the relationship between Frye and Buckingham now somewhat soured the former was sold just two weeks later. Six goals in twenty-one games on the Wirral brought the curtain down on his English league career before he returned home to join Hamilton, winning promotion to Division One in 1965. His playing career ended at Stranraer and until his retirement in the late 1990s Frye worked as a tanker driver for oil company Shellmax/BP.

GALE, Thomas "Tommy" 1944-47

Born: 4 November 1920 Washington, County Durham
(5ft 10ins, 12st – 1946)
Died: 29 January 1975 Bath
Debut: 26 January 1946 v York City F.A.Cup Home
Last Appearance: 5 April 1947
v Coventry City Division Two Away
Total League & Cup Appearances: 13* Goals: 0
***Also appeared in 38 wartime games**

Career Details:
Fatfield Juniors

Gateshead		1939 Amat.
WEDNESDAY	April	1944 £10
York City	28 August	1947 £250
Scarborough	June	1949
West Stanley		1949
Bath City	November	1949 £3,000*
Salisbury		1957

* Fee set by York City but not paid as Bath were a non-league side

Half back Tom Gale was a real old fashioned gentleman player who is perhaps best remembered at non-league Bath City where in ten years as a player he appeared in over three hundred games, including two hundred consecutive games, and later became club chairman. His playing career had started in his native northeast where he signed amateur forms with Gateshead just as war broke out in Europe. After completing his apprenticeship as an electrical engineer Gale joined the Owls as a professional in April 1944 – his debut coming in September of the same year at home to Notts County – and would play over thirty times during the transitional season of 1945-46 alongside Joe Cockroft.

However Tommy would experience a traumatic season when regional football ceased as firstly he failed to agree a new contract with Wednesday and in November 1946 – despite being offered work and furnished accommodation by the Owls – he took employment as Washington Chemical Works! Under the terms of his existing contract he was therefore unable to play any football whatsoever but a change of heart came in January 1947 and Tommy sign a new professional deal. However he found his first team opportunities limited and after just six appearances in peacetime league soccer he left for York City in the summer that followed. The powerfully built stopper made his City debut in a 6-0 home win over Halifax Town and enjoyed two successful seasons at the Bootham Crescent club, appearing in 80 games and captaining the side on several occasions. While at York City he first showed his community spirit – working as a voluntary youth worker – and later spent many years helping out the scout movement in Bath. Described as a "perfect gentleman" Gale was never sent off in his career and his amiable personality made sure he was a highly respected figure in football circles.

After leaving York he spent a brief time at Scarborough before ending his days as a professional footballer to become an electrical engineer and civil servant with the admiralty in Foxhill, Bath. The move south also started a long association with the local non-league side City that only ended when he played the final two years of his career at Salisbury, retiring in 1959. In April 1970 Tommy was approached to form a new board at City, who were in financial crisis, and he was appointed along with two other new directors. However one of the newcomers was deemed too old by the Football League and the other was involved in an accident to leave new Chairman Gale to run the club virtually on his own! After steering the ship to calmer waters he quit after the club was taken over by a group of businessmen but retained a great interest until he collapsed - while playing squash – and passed away in the coronary unit of Bath hospital at the age of just 54.

GALLACHER, Paul 2005

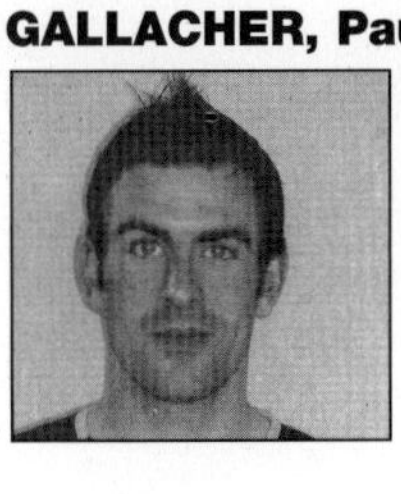

Born: 16 August 1979 Glasgow
(6ft, 11st 12lbs - 2004)
Debut: 26 March 2005
v Torquay United League One Home
Last Appearance: 7 May 2005
v Bristol City League One Home
Total League
& Cup Appearances: 8 Goals: 0

Career Details:
Dundee United Boys Club
Lochee United Juniors

Dundee United	2 September	1997
Airdrieonians	11 November	1999 Loan
Norwich City	2 July	2004 Free
Gillingham	10 December	2004 Loan
WEDNESDAY	18 March	2005 Loan
Loan return	13 May	2005

Experienced goalkeeper who was brought to the club by Paul Sturrock when the Owls lost the services of No. 1 David Lucas to injury. It was the Owls manager who had given Gallacher his senior bow at Dundee United back in February 2000 and the Glasgow born custodian would go on to record 138 appearances for the Tannadice club prior to a move into the Premiership during the summer of 2004. Gallacher - whose father, Jim, played for Clydebank and Arbroath - was capped on seven occasions for the full Scotland side while at Dundee United but found his road to first team football at Carrow Road firmly blocked by the outstanding Robert Green. A loan spell in the Championship at Gillingham followed for Gallacher and he had still to make a senior appearance for the Canaries when his old boss secured his services on loan. He was brought into the Owls side for the home draw with Torquay United and experienced a mixed time as he appeared in the final eight league games of the League One campaign. He was between the sticks as Wednesday secured a play off place with a dramatic win at Hull City but hopes of appearing in the end of season play offs were dashed on the season's final day when Gallacher was controversially sent off against Bristol City. The subsequent ban saw Gallacher unavailable for the play off trip to Brentford and he duly made an early return to Norwich City, just 48 hours before his parent club suffered relegation from the Premier League.

GALLACHER, Kevin William 2002

Born: 23 November 1966 Clydebank
(5ft 8ins, 11st – 2002)
Debut: 29 March 2002 v Coventry City Division One Home
Last Appearance: 21 April 2002
v Wolverhampton Wanderers Division One Home
Total League & Cup Appearances: 0+4 Goals: 0

Career Details:

Duntocher Boys Club	1 August	1982
Dundee United	1 January	1983
Coventry City	29 January	1990 £900,000
Blackburn Rovers	22 March	1993 £1,500,000
Newcastle United	1 October	1999 £500,000
Preston North End	17 August	2001 Free
WEDNESDAY	28 March	2002 Free
Released	28 April	2002 Free
Huddersfield Town	30 August	2002 Free
Released	17 October	2002

Scottish attacker who came from a real footballing family – both his father and grandfather played for Celtic and Falkirk while his uncle played for Dundee. When he arrived at Hillsborough on a short-term contract in the spring of 2002 Gallacher was attempting to kick start a career that had stalled after a loss of form and multitude of injuries. Previously the diminutive player had achieved great success in his native Scotland – appearing in the 1987 UEFA Cup Final loss to IFK Gothenburg for his first club Dundee United and consecutive Cup Final defeats – before becoming a record signing for Premier League Coventry City after scoring 40 goals in 190 appearances for The Tangerines.

While at City, Gallacher broke his leg twice but also regained his place in the full Scotland side, appearing in the 1992 European Championships in Sweden. He had previously won caps at Youth, U-21 and "B" level and when his top-flight career came to a close Gallacher could boast 53 full caps for Scotland. Despite his frequent injury set backs he remained a valuable player for Coventry City but they could not hold onto such a talent and big spending Blackburn Rovers took Gallacher to Ewood Park to link up with Alan Shearer. Unfortunately lady luck was again absent as a triple fracture of his leg effectively ended his Rovers career and after an impressive 53 goals in 170 games he left for Newcastle

United. After less than fifty games for United he dropped out of top-flight football for the first time in his career to join Preston but failed to make an impression as the injuries took their toll on his pace and fitness. It was the same story at Hillsborough as Wednesday struggled near the foot of Division One and he soon moved to Huddersfield Town where he was released as a cost cutting measure when The Terriers hit acute financial problems. After hanging up his boots Gallacher now works as a match summariser for a National Radio station.

GALVIN, Anthony "Tony" 1987-89

Born: 12 July 1956 Huddersfield
(5ft 9ins, 11st 5lbs – 1988)
Debut: 31 August 1987
v Coventry City
Division One Home
Last Appearance: 17 May 1989
v Norwich City
Division One Home
Total League
& Cup Appearances: 26+18 Goals: 2

Career Details:

Hull University		
Goole Town		
Tottenham Hotspur	January	1978 £30,000
WEDNESDAY	29 August	1987 £140,000
Swindon Town	28 July	1989 Free

CAPS (@ SWFC) – Eire FULL (9)
Luxembourg 09/09/87, v Bulgaria 14/10/87, v Romania 23/03/88
v Poland 22/05/88, v Norway 01/06/88, v England 12/06/88,
v USSR 15/06/88, v Holland 18/06/88, v Spain 16/11/88

The name of Tony Galvin will forever be associated with Tottenham Hotspur where the winger appeared in 375 games for the White Hart Lane club, scoring 47 times. He proved a no-frills and highly consistent foil to the outlandish talents of Glenn Hoddle and Ossie Ardiles and was an automatic choice after becoming established in the first team in early 1981. His route to North London was certainly different to the norm as the studious Galvin initially put his education before his professional career, playing for Hull University and non-league Goole while completing a B.A. in Russian Studies and later attending teacher training college. The West Yorkshire born attacker had represented his County and England schoolboys at U-18 level before winning a University Championship medal in 1977. At this point in his life a career as a professional footballer looked highly unlikely but this changed when a Spurs scout spotted the youngster playing for Goole at Buxton and took him to London for a trial.

He made such an impression on the Spurs management that he signed as a part-time professional soon after – Goole receiving a hefty fee for his services – and when his studies were completed Galvin signed as a full time pro in July 1978. This started a long association that saw Galvin win several major honours, including two F.A.Cups in 1981 and 1982 plus the UEFA Cup in 1984, under the astute managership of Keith Burkinshaw. An Irish grandfather also resulted in a call up for the Republic of Ireland national side and Galvin won the first of 29 caps for his adopted country in 1983. Incidentally while at Wednesday he appeared in the Euro 88 finals and played many games for Eire under the stewardship of ex-Owls boss Jack Charlton. He was subsequently brought to Hillsborough by Howard Wilkinson but his time in Sheffield was continually interrupted by injuries and he struggled to make a long-term impression on the Hillsborough faithful – incidentally his thirst for knowledge continued in Sheffield as Galvin took a part-time degree course in Leisure management, gaining a post graduate diploma at Sheffield University. On his day the deep lying and hard-working winger could produce a constant supply of quality crosses but it was no real surprise when new boss Ron Atkinson let Galvin move to Swindon Town – becoming the first signing of his old team mate Ossie Ardiles who had taken over at The County Ground.

He suffered an injury ruined first season at Swindon – as his new club earned promotion to the top-flight only to be demoted back down two divisions due to financial irregularities – and in February 1991 was appointed assistant-manager. When Ardiles departed for Newcastle soon after Galvin was appointed caretaker boss but when another ex-spurs teammate – Glenn Hoddle – was appointed manager he left to re-join Ardiles at St.James' Park. While on the backroom staff at Newcastle he turned down an offer to play part-time for Conference side Gateshead but in February 1992 a boardroom re-shuffle saw the pair dismissed to make way for new man Kevin Keegan. A reported move to became assistant-manager at West Brom in 1992 did not actually take place as instead Galvin fell back on his education to become a lecturer in Leisure and tourism at Hertford Regional college. In 1994 he started a two-year tenure as manager of Royston Town and in the same year was appointed Curriculum manager in leisure and tourism at the College of North West London, a position he holds today.

GANNON, Edward "Eddie" 1949-55

Born: 3 January 1921 Dublin, Eire
(5ft $9^1/_2$ ins, 11st 9lbs – 1949)
Died: 31 July 1989 Dublin
Debut: 12 March 1949
v Grimsby Town
Division Two Away
Last Appearance: 2 April 1955
v Cardiff City
Division One Home
Total League
& Cup Appearances: 219 Goals: 4

Career Details:

Star "O'Connell" Celtic		1939
Creighton Rovers		
Dublin Pearse Street		
Distillery		
Shelbourne		
Notts County	August	1946
WEDNESDAY	10 March	1949 £15,000
Shelbourne	21 April	1955 Free

CAPS (@SWFC)
Eire FULL (11) v Belgium 24/04/49, v Portugal 22/05/49,
v Sweden 02/06/49, v Spain 12/06/49, v Finland 08/09/49,
v Norway 26/11/50, v West Germany 04/05/52, v Austria 07/05/52,
v Luxembourg 28/10/53, v France 25/11/53, v Norway 07/11/54

Talented wing-half Eddie Gannon was a rare example of a player who rose to the top of his sport despite the incredible fact that he did not start to play organised football until the age of eighteen – the school he attended as a youngster did not play football. It was at this age that Eddie was spotted playing in a kick around by local youth side Star "O'Connell" Celtic who invited him for a trial. Gannon – whose father and father-in-law both played Irish league soccer – went straight into the club's first team and such was his progress that he was soon capped at Youth level for his country. He was later "transferred" to a mystery Sunday league team for the princely sum of five shillings and sixpence but was soon playing senior football with Distillery and Shelbourne. A League of Ireland Championship medal came his way in 1944 – he was also in the Shelbourne side that lost in the Irish Cup Final – and such was his outstanding form that he soon moved to English football, signing for Notts County when national football returned in 1946.

His progress continued at the Meadow Lane club – winning the first of 14 Eire caps in December 1948 against Switzerland in Dublin – and after 106 games the quiet, unassuming and studious Gannon moved to Hillsborough. The Owls had to fight off the attentions of Arsenal and Nottingham Forest for Gannon's signature but he proved an outstanding capture and would enjoy the best years of his career while in Sheffield. He was one of the trio of "Eddies" that were expensively assembled in the late 1940s (Kilshaw & Quigley completing the threesome) but proved excellent value for money as his attacking play from wing–half set up many goals for the likes of Derek Dooley. He had few superiors in his position and his strong half back play helped Wednesday to promotion from Division Two in 1950, the Division Two Championship in 1952 and an F.A.Cup semi-final appearance in 1954. In November 1950 he was forced to have all his teeth extracted after an on the field clash and his longing for his native Ireland manifested itself in March 1953 when Eddie asked for a transfer – in the latter part of his Owls career Gannon actually lived in Dublin and flew over for the games! In fact before moving back to Ireland permanently the Owls had to send an official to Dublin every summer to bring Eddie back after he'd spend the close season in Dublin! He was considered one of the game's real gentleman and his generous nature was typified during one of those summers back in Ireland when he donated all eleven – at that point - of his precious International jerseys to a fledgling youth side that could not raise the money to buy themselves a strip.

Eventually Wednesday granted Gannon his wish and in 1955 he was released from his contract to take up the position of player-manager at his old club Shelbourne. Despite being in his mid-thirties Gannon won another full cap for his country after re-joining the Dublin side and even represented the League of Ireland against the Football League in 1955. He later managed Irish side Bolton Athletic and for the remainder of his life worked for The Irish Power Company at Poolbeg Station, retiring at the age of 65.

GEARY, Derek Peter "Del" 1997-2004

Born: 19 June 1980 Dubin, Eire
(5ft 6ins, 10st 8lbs – 2000)
Debut: 19 September 2000
v Oldham Athletic
League Cup Away
Last Appearance: 8 May 2004
v Queens Park Rangers
Division Two Home
Total League
& Cup Appearances: 116+11 Goals: 0

Career Details:

Rivermount Boys		1989
Cherry Orchard		1996
WEDNESDAY	17 November	1997 £10,000
Released	30 June	2004
Stockport County	26 July	2004 Free
Sheffield United	22 October	2004 £25,000*

*Rising to £50,000 dependant upon appearances

Tenacious and enthusiastic full back who became a big crowd favourite after becoming an established first team player during the 2001-2 season – winning the player of the year trophy. The diminutive Dubliner had joined the Owls from Irish junior football back in 1997 after being spotted by Wednesday scout Harry O'Brien, arriving in Sheffield along with the likes of Alan Quinn. His compatriot was the first to break into The Owls league side but Geary made steady progress through the club's youth ranks and the jovial youngster eventually made his competitive bow in the 3-1 League Cup win at Oldham in September 2000. Football mad as a youngster, Geary supported Glasgow Celtic but after leaving school he did think about a career in the priesthood before deciding to follow his dream of becoming a professional footballer.

The whole-hearted overlapping full back played many of his early games at left back – his almost cult status at Wednesday aided by a sparkling display in that position in a League Cup tie versus Sheffield United - but it was at right back that he became an automatic choice under several different managers at Hillsborough. He proved an enthusiastic tackler and – considering his height – surprisingly adept in the air and although perhaps at times too committed in the tackle – indicated by several sendings off and countless yellow cards – the attacking full back became an integral part of the Owls side and undisputed crowd favourite. A combination of suspension and a long-term knee injury meant Del spent six months on the sidelines during 2003 – being unable to help as Wednesday suffered relegation to Division Two – but thankfully he recovered sufficiently to re-gain his first team spot at the start of the new season. Despite appearing in fifty senior games during the 2003-4 season 'Del' was one of thirteen players released after his contract expired and after a short spell at League One strugglers Stockport County he surprisingly re-joined former Wednesday team mates Leigh Bromby and Alan Quinn at Bramall Lane.

GEMMELL, Duncan 1891-92

Born: 1870 Glasgow (5ft 5ins, 10st 7lbs – 1892)
Debut: 23 January 1892 v Bolton Wanderers F.A.Cup Home
Last Appearance: 13 February 1892
v West Bromwich Albion F.A.Cup Home
Total League & Cup Appearances: 3* Goals: 0
***Also appeared in 25 Football Alliance League games**

Career Details:

Elderslee Rangers Swifts		
WEDNESDAY	March	1891
Woolwich Arsenal	June	1892

Scottish right winger who signed for Wednesday in their second season in the Football Alliance League. His first team debut for Wednesday came in the Alliance League game at Nottingham Forest in March 1891 and netted his first goal a week later as Birmingham St.George were beaten four-nil at Olive Grove. The forward played in the final twelve games of the 1890-1 season – the newcomer failing to stop Wednesday from finishing bottom of the table – and ended the season on a personal high when scoring a hat-trick in the 6-2 home win over Accrington in April 1891.

In what proved to be Wednesday's final season of non-league football Gemmell was a virtual ever-present in the Alliance League, missing only two of 22 games, and in total played in 55 games for the club during the season! However he was considered surplus to requirements when the Wednesday directors formulated their team for the advent of League soccer and Gemmell moved south to sign for Woolwich Arsenal. The Gunners were a non-league side at that time and he had probably caught their eye when scoring three times in the home and away friendly matches that the teams had played in the previous season. The North London side were elected into the Football League a year later and after signing League forms for Arsenal in June 1893 the Glaswegian appeared in the first five league games played by The Gunners, including their first ever fixture against Newcastle United in September 1893. He then dropped into the reserves and effectively remained there until being released in April 1894, falling out of league soccer altogether.

GERMAN, David 1995

Born: 16 October 1973 Sheffield
(5ft 10ins, 11st 7lbs – 1995)
Only Appearance: 24 June 1995
v FC Basel
Intertoto Cup Away
Total League
& Cup Appearances: 1 Goals: 0

Career Details:

WEDNESDAY		1989 Assoc. schoolboy
Halifax Town	June	1990 Trainee
Halifax Town	14 July	1992
WEDNESDAY	June	1995 N/C
Macclesfield Town	August	1995 Free
Ashton United		1995 Loan
Winsford United	February	1996 Loan
Winsford United	July	1996 Free
Leigh RMI	1 August	1999
Stalybridge Celtic	10 June	2002
Ashton United	16 March	2005 Loan

One of several players to join the Owls on a one-game basis in the summer of 1995, to help the club fulfil their UEFA Intertoto Cup tie in Switzerland. For the utility player it was a return to his roots as German had been brought up in the Sheffield district of

Handsworth and despite supporting United as a youngster had signed schoolboy forms with Wednesday in 1989. Despite captaining Sheffield boys for four years German was not offered a YTS contract by Wednesday but he did sign as a youth trainee at League side Halifax Town – after Owls Youth supreme Clive Baker had contacted the West Yorkshire club. He was actually still a YTS player when German made his league debut for Town and he would appear – mainly at right back – in 39 games for The Shaymen as they suffered relegation to the Conference in 1993.

He remained at Halifax as they adjusted to life outside of league soccer before being released in the summer of 1995. After his sole appearance for Wednesday he signed for Conference side Macclesfield Town but after falling out of favour with manager Sammy McIlroy he played a single game on loan at Ashton (breaking his toe to cut short the loan spell) before signing on a permanent basis for Cheshire side Winsford United. A spell back in the Conference with Leigh RMI followed – David winning a Unibond Championship medal in 2000 - before German signed for Unibond League side Stalybridge Celtic. After leaving full time football in the early 1990s German was employed in a variety of jobs – including postman and removal man – before starting work as a fireman in May 1998. He now works for the Greater Manchester fire service while living in West Yorkshire and in 2005 was picked to play for the GB Fire service team in a tournament in Ireland.

GIBSON, Thomas Richard Donald "Don" 1955-60

Born: 12 May 1929 Manchester
(5ft 9ins, 11st 2lbs – 1955)
Debut: 20 August 1955
v Plymouth Argyle
Division Two Home
Last Appearance: 19 September 1959
v Everton
Division One Away
Total League
& Cup Appearances: 84 Goals: 3

Career Details:

St Christoper's		
Manchester United	November	1946 Amat.
Manchester United	20 August	1947
WEDNESDAY	17 June	1955 £8,000
Leyton Orient	30 May	1960 £1,050
Buxton	June	1961 Free

Ex-marine commando Don Gibson joined the Owls from Manchester United in the summer of 1955 as Wednesday re-built their side following relegation from the top-flight. Unfortunately soon after joining he underwent a cartilage operation and this was indicative of the injury problems Gibson encountered during his five-year stay in Sheffield. The tough tackling and constructive wing half had made his name under the tutelage of Matt Busby at Manchester United where he progressed through the junior ranks to earn a regular place during the 1950-1 season, before winning a League Championship medal in 1952. He also appeared as a right-winger during his time at Old Trafford but it was at right wing half that Gibson was best known.

After a defensive re-shuffle saw Don lose his place at Manchester United he moved to Hillsborough and was almost ever present for Wednesday until a knee injury sustained at Swansea Town in January 1956 brought his season to a premature end. He had however played enough games to qualify for a Division Two Championship medal and in June 1956 he completed a memorable year by marrying Sheena Busby, daughter of his old manager at United. More injuries problems saw the strong, intelligent and fiery tackler restricted to just twelve games during the following season and he eventually lost his automatic first team place to the rapidly emerging Tony Kay. After enjoying a mini renaissance in the Owls Second Division championship season of 1958-9 – appearing in 23 league games – Gibson was only a bit player back in top-flight football and moved to Leyton Orient in the summer that followed.

Injury again dogged his spell in London and he spent the majority of his time as captain of the reserve side. He managed to add only eight games to his career tally while at the Brisbane Road club – he had appeared in 108 games for Manchester United – before spending six months as player-manager at Buxton before a knee injury brought an end to his playing career. After hanging up his boots Gibson ran a confectionary shop in Burnage, nr Manchester that he had bought back in 1951, selling sweets and signing autographs until retiring to Blackpool.

GILL, James "Jimmy" 1913-20

Born: 9 November 1894 Sheffield
(5ft 9ins, 11st 7lbs – 1913)
Died: 4th Quarter 1964 Sheffield
Debut: 25 December 1913
v Chelsea
Division One Away
Last Appearance: 17 April 1920
v Aston Villa
Division One Away
Total League
& Cup Appearances: 43* Goals: 10
***Also appeared in**
6 wartime games, scoring 3 times

Career Details:

Local		
WEDNESDAY	April	1913
Cardiff City	28 June	1920 £750
Blackpool	22 October	1925 £3,200
Derby County	February	1926 £3,200
Crystal Palace	May	1928
Scarborough Town	September	1930

Inside forward Jimmy Gill was still only a teenager when he made his First Division debut, just six months after being signed from Sheffield minor football. The youngster first came to prominence in local circles when appearing for Sheffield boys – later appearing for England boys as well - and it was his pace and vigorous play that persuaded The Owls to take a chance on the unproven local boy. Their faith was justified as Gill proved himself a more than capable performer in all of the forward positions, his debut coming at outside right and his other starts coming at outside left, inside right and even centre forward. Despite most of his early appearances coming on the left wing it was known he actually disliked playing in the position as he did not see enough of the ball, preferring to come inside and get involved in the play.

Like many of his teammates Gill's career was interrupted by the war and he would serve in the Army, thankfully surviving the hostilities to return to Wednesday's league side when national football returned in 1919. During the disastrous season that followed he was actually one of the few successes, scoring eight times in twenty-seven games, as Wednesday finished well adrift at the foot of the division. It must have therefore been a surprise to Wednesday fans when he was allowed to make history at Cardiff City by becoming their first ever signing after being admitted into the Football League – he subsequently netted the Bluebirds' first ever league goal and finished top scorer in his maiden season. The Owls must surely have quickly regretted their decision to let him go as at Cardiff he became an automatic choice and a major reason behind the Welsh club's immediate promotion to Division One and subsequent runners-up spot in 1924- their highest ever league finish. The exciting inside right – if given the ball he tended to go straight for goal and liked nothing better than trying to force his way through the opposition rearguard – also appeared for City in their 1925 F.A.Cup Final loss to Sheffield United and by the time he left for Blackpool in 1925 had played over two hundred times for Cardiff to enter the annals of their history as one of their greatest players. His stay on the West Coast was brief before moving to Derby County where, despite his pace fading, Jimmy still hit 36 goals in just over two seasons and finished Rams top scorer in 1926-7. His playing career ended in non-league soccer while he passed away at the age of seventy back in Sheffield.

GILLIES, Alexander 'Alex' 1897

Born: Scotland
Debut: 6 March 1897 v Burnley Division One Home
Last Appearance: 13 March 1897
v Wolverhampton Wanderers Division One Away
Total League & Cup Appearances: 2 Goals: 0

Career Details:

Lochgelly United		
Bolton Wanderers	October	1895
Ardwick	February	1896
Lochgelly United	8 May	1896
Heart of Midlothian	August	1896
WEDNESDAY	February	1897
Leicester Fosse	August	1897
Lochgelly United	29 March	1898
Dumbarton	23 April	1898
Lochgelly United	19 May	1899
Dumbarton	15 August	1899
Lochgelly United	15 May	1900

Centre forward Alex Gillies experienced a somewhat short, controversial and ultimately unsuccessful career in English football in the late nineteenth century. The attacker had started his playing career in his native Scotland, winning the East of Scotland Consolation Cup with non-league Lochgelly United in 1895, before signing for Bolton Wanderers later in the same year. His stay at the Lancashire club was brief – he appeared in only six league games for Wanderers – and following equally short stays in non-league football at Ardwick and then back in Scotland at Hearts he arrived at Olive Grove early in 1897. His first appearance in a Wednesday shirt came in a Sheffield & North Derbyshire League game at Bramall Lane in February 1897 – both sides playing their first teams for what was actually a reserve team fixture –and he would net his only goal for Wednesday in the same competition against Barnsley St.Peter's later in the season.

His two starts in league football came as a replacement for Harry Davis but he failed to impress the Wednesday hierarchy and was released at the end of the season. A move to fellow league side Leicester Fosse came next for Gillies and after initially making a favourable impression, making four competitive appearances for Fosse, his stay was dramatically cut short in February 1898 when he was one of several players dismissed in a disciplinary measure, following an alcohol related incident! It was therefore back across Hadrian's Wall for the No. 9 to end his career back at Lochgelly United after having failed to score a single goal in English league football.

GLEN, Robert "Bob" 1893-94

Born: 16 January 1875 Renton, Scotland
(5ft 5ins, 11st 7lbs – 1902)
Only Appearance: 9 September 1893
v Blackburn Rovers Division One Away
Total League & Cup Appearances: 1 Goals: 0

Career Details:

Renton		
WEDNESDAY		1893
Renton	4 April	1895
Glasgow Rangers	30 January	1897
Hibernian	May	1898 £100

Utility defensive player Bob Glen was a teenage sensation at his first club Renton, his debut for the Scottish League club occurring at the tender age of just sixteen. Incredibly the youngster would also captain Renton in the 1895 Scottish Cup Final loss to St.Bernard's and win two full caps for his Country before moving to Rangers in 1897. In between those successes however was a spell in English football at Wednesday after Glen's rave reviews persuaded The Owls to bring the eighteen year-old to Sheffield. He spent only a season in English football but his tender years probably contributed to the fact that he appeared in only a handful of games for Wednesday – including a solitary first team appearance at left halfback in a 5-1 defeat at Blackburn Rovers.

A return to his homeland saw Bob's career get back on track and after the aforementioned Cup Final appearance and caps for Scotland he enjoyed a highly successful eight-year stay at Edinburgh club Hibernian. A move from half back to full back saw Glen become a big crowd favourite at the Easter Road club and in 1900 he added two Scottish League caps and a third full appearance for Scotland to his curriculum vita. A Scottish Cup winners medal followed in 1902 and during a golden era in Hibs' history he helped them to a Championship win in 1903 plus numerous local honours such as the Glasgow Charity Cup, Roseberry Cup and McCrate Cup. Glen made his final appearance for Hibs in August 1906 and was rewarded with a benefit game in the following month. Unfortunately tragedy struck the Glen family in April 1907 when they lost their young baby and Bob was also taken into hospital for an emergency appendix operation. His old club Hibs duly presented Bob and his wife with a "generous cheque" in their "days of sorrow and financial difficulties".

GLENNON, Joseph Edward "Teddy" 1910-19

Born: 17 October 1889 Whitwick
(5ft 9 3/4 ins, 11st 10lbs – 1912)
Died: 26 June 1926 Ashby de la Zouch
Debut: 24 December 1910
v Oldham Athletic
Division One Away
Last Appearance: 17 April 1915
v Bradford City
Division One Away
Total League
& Cup Appearances: 133* Goals: 42
***Also appeared in**
118 wartime games, scoring 54 goals

Career Details:

Kilnhurst Town		
Grimsby Town	November	1907
Denaby United		1909
WEDNESDAY	13 April	1910 £60*
Rotherham County	July	1919 £700
Rotherham Town	August	1921

*Also paid a joint fee of £85 to Grimsby Town for Glennon & Bradley

Although a Denaby United player when he arrived at Hillsborough – having just won the prestigious Sheffield Challenge Cup with the Conisbrough based club – Teddy Glennon's Football League registration was in fact held by Grimsby Town for whom he had made his initial breakthrough into league soccer. The strong and forceful inside forward had appeared in ten league games for the Mariners before dropping back into Midland League football at Denaby but when given a second chance to shine in league soccer by Wednesday he repaid the Owls faith by becoming a highly consistent performer – the Owls paid a fee to Grimsby and also paid £35 to Denaby plus another £25 if he proved a success!

Teddy would play all his football at Wednesday in Division One after having initially helped the club's reserve side to runners-up spot in the Midland League in 1911 before becoming established at inside-right – proving a more than capable replacement for the legendary Harry Chapman. With the likes of David McLean and Andrew Wilson at the height of their powers the Owls were a force to be reckoned with in the seasons immediately before World War One and Glennon proved to be a valuable player who contributed as a goal maker and goal taker – he scored a total of 25 goals for Wednesday in back to back seasons when The Owls finished fifth and third in the top-flight. The Leicestershire born player was the top scorer in the Great War for Wednesday – including four goals at Bramall Lane in March 1918 when United were beaten five-nil - and was expected to be a vital member of the Owls league side when normal football returned in 1919. Therefore it must have a been a surprise and disappointment to Wednesday fans when the club let him join neighbours Rotherham County, a decision that was probably influenced by Teddy's move to become landlord of the Red Lion Hotel on Cambridge Street in Sheffield, despite the fact that Wednesday did not allow any of their professional players to be licencees!

The summer of 1921 saw Glennon join a select band of sportsmen to have played in both the Football League and cricket's County Championship when he scored a total of 12 first class runs for his native County of Leicestershire in four innings. In the same summer Teddy moved to neighbours Rotherham Town and in

November he took over the tenancy of the Nelson Hotel at Moorhead in Rotherham. Sadly despite his all round sporting prowess Teddy was struck down with illness in 1926 and after a long fight he passed away at the relatively tender age of 37.

GOODFELLOW, Derwick Ormond 1936-47

Born: 26 June 1914 Shilbottle. Northumberland
(6ft 1ins, 12st 7lbs – 1936)
Died: 9 December 2001 Alnwick
Debut: 17 September 1936 v Huddersfield Town Division One Home
Last Appearance: 4 January 1947 v Plymouth Argyle Division Two Away
Total League & Cup Appearances: 77* Goals: 0
***Also appeared in 22 wartime games**

Career Details:

Amble		
Gateshead	March	1935
WEDNESDAY	14 May	1936
Exeter City	September	1945 Guest
Middlesbrough	7 June	1947 £2000

Like so many players of his era a large part of Derwick Goodfellow's career was lost to the Second World War. In fact the conflict almost ended his professional career altogether as whilst serving with the Royal Marines the goalkeeper was wounded in the left arm and contracted the same gas gangrene what tragically ended the career of Derek Dooley. Thankfully though a dose of penicillin effectively saved his arm when it was touch and go whether it would have to be amputated to save his life. He therefore returned to Hillsborough to compete with Albert Morton and Roy Smith for the first team jersey – incidentally he wore a leather arm guard to protect the scar tissue around the wound but the referees association forbade him to wear the guard during matches.

The tall, agile keeper had originally arrived at Wednesday from Division Three (North) side Gateshead where Derwick had made his league debut and appeared in a total of 30 games for the perennial strugglers. He arrived at Hillsborough as understudy to the legendary Jack Brown but within twelve months had displaced his experienced rival, remaining first choice until he was himself replaced by Roy Smith part way though the 1938-9 campaign. It would be another six years before Goodfellow played football again, returning to competitive action during the transitional season of 1945-6 when he appeared for Wednesday in the Football League North and also played twelve games for Exeter City as a guest. When peacetime football returned in August 1946 it was Goodfellow who was in possession of the No. 1 jersey but after just four games he was dropped for Roy Smith and almost immediately Derwick was placed on the transfer list at his own request.

At the end of the season – after seven games in post war football – he moved back to his native Northeast, signing for Middlesbrough where he appeared in 39 league and cup games. Goodfellow eventually lost his place to Rolando Ugolini and looked set to move to Exeter City before the transfer broke down. However with Boro still holding his registration and a leg injury meaning he could not compete for a first team spot the tough keeper decided to take the position of steward at Bedlington Working Men's club. However just when Goodfellow thought his professional footballing days were over, Blackburn Rovers came calling and offered Middlesbrough £2,000 to take Derwick back into the Football League. After taking consideration of his poor fitness, Derwick felt that his long-term future in football was not tenable, and with the added responsibility of a young family it was important at the time to secure a livelihood to support his family. Thus he confided in Rovers officials about his injury problems and the move collapsed. Some weeks later Middlesbrough were approached by non-league side Ashington who wanted Derwick to guest for them as well as coaching local schoolboys. However Boro manager David Jack was still unhappy at Derwick refusing to move to Lancashire and Ashington were give a terse reply consisting of the words "Goodfellow's playing days are over", effectively barring Derwick any involvement in professional football for the rest of his life. He therefore remained as steward at Bedlington Club and was later landlord at the Walton Arms public house until his retirement in 1975. At the turn of the 21st Century Goodfellow was the oldest Sheffield Wednesday player still alive although he did pass away just under two years later, aged 87.

GOOING, William Henry 1895-97

Born: 1874 Penistone (5ft 9ins, 11st)
Died: 1969
Debut: 8 February 1896 v Small Heath Division One Away
Last Appearance: 7 March 1896 v Sunderland Division One Away
Total League & Cup Appearances: 3 Goals: 1

Career Details:

Penistone		
Wath		
WEDNESDAY	Summer	1895
Chesterfield		1897
Chesterfield	14 August	1899 £15
Woolwich Arsenal	November	1901 £80
Northampton Town		1905

Local born centre forward William Gooing joined the Owls in the summer of 1895 after impressing against Wednesday's reserve team for Wath. The inexperienced attacker enjoyed a highly encouraging debut season for the club, scoring over thirty times in reserve team football which included netting five in a game on no less than three occasions! In total Gooing blasted five hat tricks and it was this goal scoring that persuaded Wednesday to hand the youngster a league debut at Small Heath when Lawrie Bell was absent. He duly rewarded the club's faith by netting the Wednesday goal in a 1-1 draw and was given two further starts before the season reached its conclusion.

The goals dried up in what proved to be Gooing's final season at Wednesday – he netted only ten times in second team soccer – and in the following summer was allowed to join Midland League Chesterfield. William – who possessed great close control and vision – scored regularly for The Spireites for two seasons in non-league football before Wednesday were paid for his league registration when Chesterfield were elected into the competition for the first time in their history. Ironically The Spireites opening league fixture was also Wednesday's first ever game at their new ground of Owlerton and Gooing was at centre forward in that historic first league eleven for Chesterfield. He failed to score as Wednesday triumphed 5-1 but William would score 26 times in 71 League games before earning a transfer to Arsenal, helping the Gunners to promotion from Division Two in 1904. His goals record for Arsenal was quite remarkable – 44 in only 94 league games – and surely must have made Wednesday officials wonder if they should have persevered with the youngster a bit longer before letting him go! Unfortunately his playing career finished on a low as his new side Northampton Town finished bottom of the Southern League in 1906 before Gooing retired from the game.

GOSLING, William 1901-02

Born:
Debut: 23 March 1901 v Liverpool Division One Away
Last Appearance: 21 December 1901 v Small Heath Division One Away
Total League & Cup Appearances: 5 Goals: 0

Career Details:

Jarrow FC		
WEDNESDAY	February	1901 £100*

*Joint fee with Lyall, paid in two instalments

In would be fair to say the Wednesday career of right back William Gosling was full of controversy and ill discipline that effectively ruined his chances of forging a career in the top-flight of English football. He had originally arrived – along with outstanding goalkeeper Jack Lyall – from the fertile breeding ground of Jarrow Football Club and within a few weeks Gosling was taking his league bow at Anfield. Although he was mainly used in a right back role his debut at league level came as replacement for left back Ambrose Langley and he appeared in four consecutive games before dropping back into the reserve side to continue his apprenticeship.

Unfortunately the following season proved nothing short of a disaster for Gosling as despite being a Midland League regular, playing in a variety of positions including inside forward and also scoring seven times, it was off the field events that would prove his downfall. This started in February 1902 when he was suspended by Wednesday for one month after he had been found guilty by West Yorkshire magistrates of being drunk and disorderly on a public highway! To compound matters he then failed to report for a reserve game later in the season and the final straw came when he was suspended by Wednesday for "serious misconduct". Unsurprisingly he failed to appear in a Wednesday shirt ever again and was released in April 1902!

GOWDY, William Alexander "Bill" 1931-33

Born: 24 November 1903 Belfast
(5ft $7^1/_2$ ins, 10st 11lbs – 1931)
Died: 16 March 1958 Larne
Debut: 9 January 1932 v Tottenham Hotspur F.A.Cup Away
Last Appearance: 9 April 1932 v Portsmouth Division One Home
Total League & Cup Appearances: 2 Goals: 0

Career Details:

Duncan Olympic		
Highfield		
Crusaders		
Cliftonville		1926
Ards	May	1927 Amat.
Hull City	July	1929
WEDNESDAY	24 December	1931 £350
Contract cancelled	March	1933
Gateshead	12 April	1933
Linfield	August	1933
Hibernian	December	1935
Goole Town	July	1936
Altrincham	July	1937
Aldershot	June	1938
Hull City	August	1940 Guest

CAPS (@SWFC):
N.Ireland Full (1) v Scotland 12/09/32

During the Owls golden years of the late 1920s and early 1930s competition for places was fierce and several players who arrived with International caps to their name failed to make a lasting impression. This was true of half back William Gowdy who was signed from Hull City on Christmas Eve 1931 after having earned his first cap for Northern Ireland earlier in the same year. Bob Brown brought him to Hillsborough as competition for the likes of Alf Strange and Gavin Malloch but the task proved too great for Gowdy and he made just two first team appearances in fifteen months at Wednesday. He could not even earn a regular reserve team place either so it was no real surprise when in March 1933 Wednesday agreed with Gowdy to terminate his contract – the Owls paying him £20 for the privilege.

Within a few weeks Bill had joined league side Gateshead, being the first ever International to sign for the fledgling club, and when his new side advertised the fact their gate doubled on the day Gowdy made his debut. Unfortunately he appeared in only three more games for the Northeast side before returning home to Ireland in the summer of 1933 to sign for Linfield. His form back in Irish League football saw Bill earn three more caps for his country of birth – strangely he was a regular for Ireland but not always for his club - before a stroke of luck saw a move back across the Irish Sea to Hibs. After Linfield had turned down a large offer from Dundee for Gowdy's services the manager of Hibs visited the Emerald Isle to sign another player but instead went back to Scotland with Gowdy's signature, the Edinburgh club paying a substantial fee for his services.

Gowdy won his sixth and final Northern Ireland cap while at the Easter Road club before returning to English football to sign for Yorkshire League Goole Town. His final league appearances came at Aldershot while after guesting for Hull City in World War Two, Gowdy moved to California and for many years owned a ranch in Santa Monica.

GRANT, David "Dave" 1978-82

Born: 2 June 1960 Sheffield
(6ft, 12st 8lbs – 1978)
Debut: 17 December 1977
v Wigan Athletic
F.A.Cup Away
Last Appearance: 19 January 1982
v Crystal Palace
Division Two Away
Total League
& Cup Appearances: 147+3 Goals: 5

Career Details:

WEDNESDAY	17 February	1978
Oxford United	23 June	1982 Free
Chesterfield	September	1983 Loan
Crystal Palace	18 January	1984 Loan
Cardiff City	March	1984 Free
Rochdale	March	1985
Macclesfield Town		1987
Boston United	December	1988 £500

For many players their debut game in professional is one of the most memorable occasions of their whole career. Unfortunately for ex-Sheffield and Yorkshire boys full back Dave Grant his debut will be remembered for all the wrong reasons as non-league Wigan Athletic humiliatingly knocked the Owls out of the F.A.Cup. Thankfully for Grant – who had originally joined Wednesday as an apprentice in July 1976 – he soon put that bittersweet introduction to first team football behind him and when new boss Jack Charlton re-shuffled his pack it was Grant who replaced Dave Rushbury at left back. The youngster quickly became established in Division Three and while still a teenager the impressive newcomer had totalled over one hundred first team games in the famous blue and white shirt.

He helped the Owls out of the third tier in 1980 and was a more than able performer in the higher grade as Wednesday enjoyed a successful season back in Division Two. It was therefore a mystery to many fans when he fell out of favour early in the following campaign – being replaced by teenager Charlie Williamson - and was subsequently given a free transfer in May 1982. Two months later he joined Oxford United and later experienced a frustrating time on loan at Crystal Palace where a problem with his registration restricted him solely to reserve team appearances for The Eagles. After 25 games for Cardiff City and 97 matches for Rochdale, Grant dropped into non-league soccer at Macclesfield Town. After scoring four times in thirty-seven games for Town his playing career ended in Lincolnshire at Boston United where 35 appearances brought the curtain down on his senior career. After finishing with football, Grant held a variety of jobs, including working in the building trade, but unfortunately due to a knee injury sustained during his playing days he is currently unable to work.

GRAY, George William 1921-23

Born: 27 February 1896 Sheffield
(5ft 9ins, 12st 6lbs – 1921)
Died: 5 May 1962 Norwich
Debut: 3 December 1921
v Clapton Orient
Division Two Home
Last Appearance: 18 November 1922
v Hull City
Division Two Away
Total League
& Cup Appearances: 33 Goals: 0

Career Details:

Eastwood Bible Class		
Alfreton Juniors		
Grimsby Town	May	1919
Norwich City	26 October	1919 Amat.
Norwich City	27 August	1920 Pro.
WEDNESDAY	28 November	1921 £1300 + Armstrong
Released		1923

Despite spending his formative years in Sheffield football in would take a successful spell at Norwich City to bring George Gray's talents to the attention of his hometown club. After completing a Sheffield Amateur League Championship and Cup double with Eastwood, George's senior career started in vengeance at Southern League Norwich. Following the Canaries subsequent promotion into the Football League in 1920 he played in their historic first ever game and was an ever present as City finished sixteenth in Division Three. After missing only one first team game in two seasons at City, the Ecclesfield born right back missed the start of the 1921-22 campaign but soon after returning to first team duty was brought home to Sheffield by Owls boss Bob Brown.

He arrived at Hillsborough in a deal that saw Joe Armstrong travel in the opposite direction and over the next twelve months competed with the likes of George Prior and George Holmes for the right back role. Unfortunately Gray then suffered a serious knee injury, which forced his early retirement in 1923. At this point he moved back to Norwich, becoming licensee of the Fountain Inn Public House, and later became a crane driver until his retirement. His life however came to a sad end just after he had retired when he was found dead in his kitchen.

GRAYSON, Simon Nicholas 2000

Born: 16 December 1969 Ripon (6ft, 13st 7lbs - 2002)
Debut: 13 August 2000
v Wolverhampton Wanderers Division One Away
Last Appearance: 9 September 2000
v Wimbledon Division One Home
Total League & Cup Appearances: 5 Goals: 0

Career Details:

Leeds United	13 June	1988
Leicester City	13 March	1992 £50,000
Aston Villa	1 July	1997 £1.35m
Blackburn Rovers	29 July	1999 £750,000
WEDNESDAY	11 August	2000 Loan
Stockport County	12 January	2001 Loan
Notts County	6 September	2001 Loan
Bradford City	15 February	2002 Loan
Blackpool	20 July	2002 Free

Utility player Simon Grayson was brought to Hillsborough by Paul Jewell just forty-eight hours before the start of the 2000/1 season. The newcomer slotted into the side at right back but during his brief stay failed to stamp his authority on the side and Wednesday decided not to pursue a permanent move when Grayson's loan spell expired. He had originally made his name at Leicester City where after appearing in a total of 229 games he made a big money move to Aston Villa. In fact while at City the versatile defensive player helped The Foxes to promotion to the Premier League in 1994 – being appointed captain for the day when promotion was secured – and was also named player of the season by the fans of the East Midlands club. He also appeared in the 1992 Play off Final loss to Blackburn Rovers and in 1997 was again named player of the season as well as helping Leicester to League Cup glory, defeating Middlesbrough in the Hillsborough replay.

However his successful time at Leicester would contrast greatly with his experiences at both Aston Villa and Blackburn Rovers where Grayson simply failed to find the consistency in his game that would bring regular first team football. After his short spell at Wednesday, Grayson – who is co-owner of a bar in Leicester and whose brother Paul played County cricket for Yorkshire and Essex - ended the season on a three-month loan at First Division strugglers Stockport County and after being released by Rovers in the summer of 2002 signed a two-year deal at Division Two side Blackpool.

GREEN, Adam 2005

Born: 12 January 1984 Hillingdon
(5ft 9ins, 10st 11lbs – 2004)
Debut: 29 January 2005
v MK Dons
League One Away
Last Appearance:
12 February 2005
v Bradford City
League One Home
Total League
& Cup Appearances: 3 Goals: 0

Career Details:

Fulham	4 July	2003
WEDNESDAY	25 January	2005 Loan
Bournemouth	11 March	2005 Loan

Joined the Owls on loan from Premier League Fulham as a direct replacement for suspended left back Paul Heckingbottom. The highly rated attacking full back duly made his debut in a 2-2 draw at MK Dons and played twice more on the left side of midfield as the Owls drew at Oakwell and lost at home to Bradford City. The Londoner – who had made 10 senior appearances for Fulham - was calm and assured on the ball but struggled to adapt to the hustle and bustle of League One and returned to Craven Cottage with much needed experience of life in the lower leagues! In the previous summer Green had signed a new two-year contract at Fulham and is recognised as a star of the future.

GREEN, Albert Willis 'Willie' 1935-38

Born: 4th Quarter 1916 Sheffield
Debut: 21 November 1936
v Leeds United
Division One Home
Last Appearance: 16 September 1937
v Tottenham Hotspur
Division Two Home
Total League
& Cup Appearances: 6 Goals: 1

Career Details:

Dore FC		
WEDNESDAY	November	1935 £20
Barnsley	August	1938
Gainsborough Trinity	October	1939

Left-winger who spent three seasons at Hillsborough after arriving from local junior football. He was spotted by the Owls playing for Sheffield based village side Dore and was soon making his Central League debut for Wednesday, at home to Blackpool in November 1935. The Owls had donated the princely sum of £20 to his old side in the same month and Albert enjoyed a run of ten consecutive reserve team outings before dropping back into third team soccer.

The 1936-7 campaign proved to be the highlight of Green's professional career as not only did he finish second top scorer for the reserves with eleven goals but he also deputised on five occasions in league football for the legendary Ellis Rimmer. His only senior goal for Wednesday came in the November 1936 draw at Birmingham but Green's hopes of proving a long-term replacement for Rimmer were dashed in September 1937 when he was one of five players brought into the side for the home game with Spurs at Hillsborough. Unfortunately Wednesday slumped to a three-nil defeat and Green would spend the remainder of the season in the second team, scoring only three times, before moving to neighbours Barnsley.

GREEN, Ryan Michael 2002-03

Born: 20 October 1980 Cardiff
(5ft 7ins, 10st 10lbs – 2002)
Debut: 30 November 2002 v Wimbledon Division One Away
Last Appearance: 11 January 2003 v Reading Division One Home
Total League & Cup Appearances: 4 Goals: 0

Career Details:

Wolverhampton Wanderers	1 October	1997
Torquay United	2 March	2001 Loan
Millwall	19 October	2001 Free
Cardiff City	12 November	2002 Free
WEDNESDAY	27 November	2002 Free
Released	30 June	2003
Hereford United	31 July	2003 Free

Utility player Ryan Green holds the unique distinction of being the youngest ever full International for Wales. The Cardiff born player was aged just seventeen when he was picked to appear for Wales against Malta in the summer of 1998 and incredibly this occurred before the youngster had even made his Football league debut! At the time Green was on the books of Wolves, a club he had joined straight from school after being chased by a host of sides including Cardiff City, Norwich City and Blackburn Rovers, where under the youth team management of one Chris Turner he had earned rave reviews in junior and reserve team soccer. This led to Green being capped on sixteen occasions for the Welsh U-21 side over the ensuing years (under the managership of ex-Owls Academy Director Jimmy Shoulder) and he even won a second full cap despite only making a dozen appearances at first team level for the Black Country club.

Unfortunately Ryan could not maintain his rate of progress at Molineux and after a loan spell at Torquay he was signed for Millwall by his old Wolves boss Mark McGhee. He was put straight into The Lions first team at right back and retained that position for three months but after losing his place dropped into reserve team soccer, before moving to hometown club Cardiff City on a free transfer. His fortunes fared even worse at the Ninian Park club where Green made only one appearance – as a substitute in an LDV Vans Trophy game at Exeter City. After little more than a year at Cardiff he was Chris Turner's first signing for Wednesday and in four appearances for the club appeared at right back and on the right side of midfield. He initially signed a three-month contract at Hillsborough but despite this being extended until the end of the season he was one of 14 players released by Wednesday following relegation from Division One. In the summer of 2003 he signed a two-year contract at Conference side Hereford United.

GREENSMITH, Ronald "Ron" 1954-58

Born: 22 January 1933 Sheffield
(5ft $9^1/_2$ ins, 10st 7lbs – 1954)
Debut: 1 January 1955
v Aston Villa
Division One Away
Last Appearance: 9 October 1957
v Manchester City
Division One Away
Total League
& Cup Appearances: 6 Goals: 1

Career Details:

Bellhouse Road WMC		
WEDNESDAY	21 January	1954
York City	10 January	1958
Scarborough	July	1960
Bridlington Town		1963
Selby Town		1965

After completing his two years national service with the R.A.F. – appearing on a regular basis for the Bomber Command football side – inside-forward Ron Greensmith returned home to his native Sheffield to work for local firm Viners Limited. At the same time he also started to play for Shiregreen based side Bellhouse Road Working Men's Club and it was here that Wednesday scouts first noticed his talents. His junior side were dominant in local football and Greensmith was soon snapped up by Wednesday, making a second team debut in March 1954. Within a year of signing professional forms Ron was drafted into top-flight football – making his debut alongside fellow new boy Mike Turley in the 0-0 draw at Villa Park on New Year's Day.

Despite playing the majority of his football at inside forward it was actually on the left wing that Ron made his senior debut for Wednesday and strangely, despite playing in several forward roles for the Central league team, it was in this position where Greensmith played all his first team games for The Owls. Competition from Albert Broadbent ensured that Ron's best run in the first team was three consecutive games during the 1956-7 season and he eventually dropped down the divisions to sign for York City. The pacy forward was utilised on the wing at the Bootham Crescent club but after one goal in 43 games he moved, along with several City players, to non-league Scarborough. His playing career came to a close in 1966 - after a season at Yorkshire league Selby Town - and after turning down an offer to coach York schoolboys he gained employment at an engineering company in the city. He later worked for a soft drinks company and for the sixteen years before his retirement was employed on the railways.

GREENWOOD, Ross 2002-05

Born: 1 November 1985 York
(5ft 11ins, 11st 5lbs – 2004)
Debut: 22 September 2004
v Coventry City
League Cup Away
Last Appearance: 3 January 2005
v Wrexham League One Home
Total League
& Cup Appearances: 1+3 Goals: 0

Career Details:

WEDNESDAY	1 July	2002 Academy
Released	30 June	2005
Stockport County	July	2005 Free

Athletic, hard-working right back who was previously on the books of Manchester United. The energetic York-born performer possesses strong tackling ability and looks to get forward and attack whenever possible. Greenwood trained with the first team squad for the final two months of 2003-04 and was given a first team bow when his youth coach, Mark Smith, was handed the reins on a caretaker basis immediately following the dismissal of Chris Turner. He acquitted himself well at Highfield Road and made the senior subs bench on several occasions during the 2004-05 campaign, twice appearing in League One football. He returned to Old Trafford in May 2005 as part of the Owls reserve side that narrowly lost in the Pontins League Cup Final but hopes of a prolonged senior career at Hillsborough ended when the youngster was released soon after the Owls secured promotion to the Championship.

GREGG, Robert Edmund 'Bob' 1928-31

Born: 4 February 1904 Ferryhill, nr Sunderland
(5ft 9ins, 11st 4lbs – 1928)
Died: May 1991 Hounslow, Middlesex
Debut: 8 September 1928
v Sunderland
Division One Home
Last Appearance: 15 September 1930
v Chelsea
Division One Away
Total League
& Cup Appearances: 39 Goals: 7

Career Details:

Ferryhill Athletic		
Cornforth Juniors		
Winlaton Juniors		
Spennymoor United		
Chilton Colliery Welfare	cs	1925
Durham City		
Ferryhill Athletic	cs	1926
Darlington	September	1926 (Amat – Jul 26)

WEDNESDAY	12 May	1928 £730
Birmingham	2 January	1931 £3,250
Chelsea	September	1933 £1,500
Boston United	May	1938
Sligo Rovers	September	1940

Inside-forward Bob Gregg spent the early years of his playing career in local Northeast soccer before experiencing a rapid rise through the ranks which saw him win a Division One Championship medal within three years of turning professional at Division Three (North) side Darlington. The tricky forward joined Darlington in the summer of 1926, making his league debut for The Quakers at South Shields in December of the same year. He made only three league appearances for Darlington in that debut season but had clubs flocking to Feethams in the following campaign when Gregg scored 21 times in just 37 games from a predominantly inside-right position.

It was obvious that Darlington would not be able to retain his services and this proved the case as Owls boss Bob Brown added another piece to his jigsaw by capturing Gregg's signature. The newcomer was an instant hit at Hillsborough – he was switched to inside-left by Brown - and scored seven times in thirty league games as Wednesday won the League Championship for the third time in their history. The left –wing combination of Gregg and Ellis Rimmer provided many goals for prolific scorer Jack Allen but Bob Brown cared little for past form and the arrival of the outstanding Harry Burgess in the summer of 1929 effectively ended Gregg's first team days at Hillsborough. He would appear in only seven first team games for Wednesday in two further seasons at the club before being sold to Birmingham, early in 1931.

He went straight into The Blues first team and was a key player as his new club saved themselves from relegation from Division One – Gregg scoring against Wednesday in a two-nil win at St Andrews – and reached the 1931 F.A.Cup Final. Opponents in Birmingham's first showpiece final were local rivals West Brom but it was The Baggies who triumphed 2-1, Gregg scoring a superb goal after just six minutes which was controversially disallowed for offside. After taking his appearance tally to 75 games for the West Midlands club he subsequently moved to Chelsea but the talented Gregg failed to settle in London and after scoring 6 goals in 51 games dropped into non-league football at Boston United. His career came to a close in Irish league football, Gregg retiring in May 1944.

GREGORY, Anthony Gerard "Tony" 1986-90

Born: 21 March 1968 Doncaster
(5ft 8ins, 10st 10lbs – 1986)
Debut: 24 August 1985
v Manchester City
Division One Away
Last Appearance: 2 January 1989
v Coventry City
Division One Away
Total League
& Cup Appearances: 16+5 Goals: 1

Career Details:

Ridgewood Colts		1980-83
Middlewood Rovers		
WEDNESDAY	7 January	1986
Charlton Athletic	August	1989 Trial
Halifax Town	16 July	1990 Free
Buxton	February	1993
Emley	March	1994
Eden Grove Pinkney		1991-2003 Sunday

CAPS (@SWFC) –
England Youth (9) 1985 v Italy, Russia, Netherlands, Iceland, 1986 v Scotland Brazil, France, China, China Army

The history of professional soccer is littered with stories of "the next big thing" who for a variety of reasons then fail to fulfil their early promise. The Owls of course can boast several players in this category themselves, one being hard-running midfielder Tony Gregory. As a teenager Gregory captained Doncaster boys at every level from under-11 to under-15s, represented South Yorkshire boys and scored four times in 11 appearances for the England Youth side – playing alongside Paul Merson, David Hirst, Kevin Pressman & Andy Hinchcliffe. He joined the Owls on schoolboy forms in March 1983 and after signing apprentice forms in May 1984 made his top-flight bow at Maine Road, aged just 17. After signing professional forms Gregory started the 1986-7 season as first choice in Howard Wilkinson's side but after losing his place to Brian Marwood spent the remainder of the season in reserve team soccer, before touring Uruguay in the summer of 1987 with England Youth.

It was that foreign tour that effectively ended Gregory's promising career as he returned from South America with a hamstring injury, the cause of which was not diagnosed by either Wednesday or a specialist. Over the next two and a half years the midfielder struggled on with hamstring pain, making only fleeting first team appearances and failing to start a game under Ron Atkinson, before leaving for Fourth Division Halifax Town in the summer of 1990. It was at Halifax that his medical problem was finally diagnosed, a London specialist concluding that he was suffering from a severed hamstring! Corrective surgery meant Gregory spent thirteen months on the sidelines and unfortunately led to his retirement from the professional game – he later re-joined Town on a non-contract basis after gaining some semblance of fitness. He later tried to sue Wednesday's backroom staff for alleged negligence, the P.F.A. taking up his case, but because of a technicality the case never ran its course. A cartilage operation in 1992 further restricted his appearances for a Halifax side that had suffered relegation from the Football League and his injury woes continued in the following year when he tore ankle ligaments.

For over a year Gregory was unemployed but between August 1994 and July 2000 he worked in a warehouse while playing part-time at Northern Premier League sides Buxton and Emley. In the 1990s he also played, managed and coached Sunday league side Eden Grove, coached schoolboys at the Glyn Snodin Coaching School and also gained his F.A.coaching badge and UEFA's "A" licence coaching qualification. However after scrapping plans to train as a physiotherapist he instead qualified in 1999 as a chiropodist, starting his own practise soon after. This flourishes today although its success means Gregory can no longer use his coaching skills due to time pressures.

GREGORY, Robert 'Bob' 1873-84

Born: 3rd Quarter 1853 Sheffield
Died: October 1910 Sheffield
Debut: 18 December 1880
v Blackburn Rovers
F.A.Cup Away
Last Appearance: 1 December 1883
v Staveley
F.A.Cup Away
Total League
& Cup Appearances: 17 Goals: 14

Career Details:

Oxford FC (Sheffield)	
Hallam	1871-1888
WEDNESDAY	1873-84

Attacker Bob Gregory was described as a "loveable fellow" and in all probability was the first real crowd hero to fans of fledgling club The Wednesday. The centre-forward was an ever present during The Owls' early forays into the F.A.Cup, netting Wednesday's first ever goal in the competition on his way to a hat-trick in a 4-0 win at Blackburn Rovers. He would play in the next seventeen F.A.Cup ties played by the club, including the semi-final loss to old foes Blackburn in 1882, and became the first Wednesday player to score five times in a competitive fixture - achieving the feat at home to Spilsby in November 1882.

The talisman forward was hard to knock off the ball and a good dribbler – although described as lacking speed – but after becoming a regular for Wednesday in the late 1870s he was an automatic choice for several seasons, helping The Owls to a variety of local honours. These included the Wharncliffe Charity Cup in 1880, 1882 & 1883 plus The Sheffield Challenge Cup in 1881 and 1883 - Bob scoring five in the 8-1 Final romp over Ecclesfield in the former final. Gregory – who played cricket for Hallam in the summer months - also captained the club on numerous occasions and achieved representative honours in 1881 when he was picked for the North v South International trial game. His loyalty to Wednesday was rewarded in April 1883 when the club staged a benefit game at Bramall Lane, an over 25 side being matched against an under 25 side. After playing his final game for Wednesday he continued to assist Hallam until the late 1880s.

GREGSON, Colin 1977-79

Born: 19 January 1958
Newcastle-upon-Tyne
(5ft 7ins, 10st 6lbs – 1978)
Debut: 30 August 1977
v Blackpool
League Cup Away
Last Appearance: 12 October 1977
v Exeter City
Division Three Away
Total League
& Cup Appearances: 2+1 Goals: 0

Career Details:

West Bromwich Albion	19 January	1976
WEDNESDAY	July	1977 Free
Berwick Rangers	May	1979 Free
Adelaide		1979

Forward Colin Gregson spent three years as a professional in English football but failed to really make the grade at either West Brom or Wednesday. The ex-Newcastle boys player had originally joined Albion as a trainee in June 1974 and was a regular in the Baggies youth side that beat Wolves in 1976 to win the F.A.Youth Cup. He also helped West Brom's reserve side to runners-up spot behind Liverpool and to complete a successful season attended trials for the England U-18 side. However he could not make the jump to first team soccer and after failing to make a first team appearance was brought to Hillsborough by Len Ashurst.

His new manager gave Gregson a senior debut but unfortunately for the newcomer Ashurst was sacked early in the 1977-78 season and over the next two seasons the diminutive attacker often struggled to break into the club's reserve side. He was duly released to spend a season in Scottish football before accepting an offer to play in Australia. The newly wed Gregson spent a full season Down Under before hanging up his boots and returning to his birthplace to gain employment at Newcastle council, where he remains today.

GRIFFIN, William "Billy" 1957-62

Born: 24 September 1940 Bircotes, nr Worksop
(5ft 9ins, 10st – 1958)
Debut: 22 November 1958
v Cardiff City
Division Two Away
Last Appearance: 10 November 1962
v Aston Villa
Division One Home
Total League
& Cup Appearances: 37 Goals: 21

Career Details:

WEDNESDAY		1955 Ground Staff
Hillsborough Boys Club		1955-56
WEDNESDAY	24 September	1957
Bury	17 December	1962 £8,800
Workington	9 February	1966 *
Rotherham United	January	1969 £1,000
Cambridge City		1971
Frickley AF.C.		

*Griffin + £8,000 in exchange for Barry Lowe

It was purely a twist of fate that launched the career of livewire forward Billy Griffin. Wednesday manager Eric Taylor had travelled to watch a youngster play for Worksop boys but on arrival found that the lad in question had broken his arm. However he decided to stay and watch the game anyway and was highly impressed by a small 14 year-old inside forward called Griffin. A year later, on leaving school, the teenager agreed to join the Owls ground staff and then furthered his footballing education by spending a season at Hillsborough Boys Club. At the time Griffin was so slight of build that Wednesday placed Billy on a special diet and exercise programme, in an attempt to increase his ten stone weight! It was Harry Catterick who launched the youngster into league football and Griffin quickly became known as Billy "The Goal Kid" as his great turn of speed and fierce shooting brought him a flood of goals in several short spells in the first team. Incidentally his debut for Wednesday came against the club his grandfather had supported all his life – sadly Billy's grandfather passed away before his grandson's big day at Ninian Park.

Unfortunately therein lied the problem for Griffin as he struggled to nail down a regular place with competition from the likes of Bobby Craig and Derek Wilkinson – he once showed his desire to succeed by dashing back from his own wedding reception in Doncaster to score in a 2-0 win over Bolton in October 1960! His goals per game ratio was truly remarkable and his form was such that after scoring twice at West Ham in October 1961 he was pencilled in by some football writers to be picked for the next England International versus Northern Ireland! Of course a cap did not come his way and just over a year later he moved to Bury, although Wednesday secretary Taylor wanted him to stay, in search of regular first team soccer. He was approached "off the record" by Birmingham about a £45,000 transfer when he was on the books of Bury but remained in Lancashire, scoring 22 goals in 88 games for the Shakers. After a spell at Workington the versatile forward ended his Football league career at Millmoor before dropping into non-league football. After leaving the game he gained employment at Harworth Glass factory, later worked for the Milk Marketing Board and was employed by the shoe factory in Harworth until his retirement in 2000.

GROSVENOR Albert Thomas 1936-37

Born: 22 November 1908
Netherton, Nr Dudley
(5ft 11¼ ins, 11st 8lbs – 1936)
Died: 31 October 1972 Dudley
Debut: 19 February 1936
v Derby County
Division One Away
Last Appearance: 1 May 1937
v Huddersfield Town
Division One Away
Total League
& Cup Appearances: 23 Goals: 1

Career Details:

Tippity Green Victoria		
Vono Works		
West Bromwich Albion		1927 Trial
Wolverhampton Wanderers		1927 Trial
Stourbridge		1927
Birmingham	March	1928 Amat.
Birmingham	September	1928 Pro.
WEDNESDAY	13 February	1936 £3,650
Bolton Wanderers	11 May	1937 £3,000
Dudley Town		

It was the collapse of England International Joe Carter's transfer from West Brom to Wednesday that led directly to Thomas Grosvenor's move to Hillsborough. It was only 24 hours after the Carter deal had broken down that Wednesday boss Billy Walker swooped on Albion's neighbours to secure the signature of inside forward Grosvenor. The newcomer – who had won three full caps for England while at St.Andrews – had started his career in the Cradley Heath League with Tippity Green and later played for his works side when gaining employment at Vono Works. After unsuccessful trials at both West Brom and Wolves he eventually moved into senior non-league soccer at Birmingham League Stourbridge before the climb into professional football. His form at St Andrews soon brought International honours to Grosvenor although a broken leg suffered at Huddersfield in December 1933 meant he spent twelve months on the sidelines – he was generally a very sport orientated individual, being a fine runner and swimmer.

The highly gifted attacker – he was not a noted goal getter but was entertaining to watch due to his tremendous ball control, dribbling ability and knack of creating opportunities for team mates – was drafted straight into the Owls first eleven, scoring on his debut in a 3-1 loss at Derby County, and helped Wednesday to just avoid relegation from the top-flight. He had appeared in 115 games for The Blues but after starting well for Wednesday his place quickly went to emerging talent Jackie Robinson and after just over a season in Sheffield he moved to Bolton Wanderers. The tall, slim forward came from a real footballing family – his father was former Wolves player Sid while his brother Percy played for Leicester City and his younger brother Cliff was also on the books of The Foxes. The Second World War brought the curtain down on his professional career and after playing wartime football for non-league Dudley he retired from the game in May 1943. Later in life he became a sheet metal worker in Dudley while becoming expert at racing pigeons and also growing flowers and vegetables for exhibitions!

GRUMMITT, Peter Malcolm 1970-74

Born: 19 August 1942 Bourne
(5ft 11ins, 11st 5lbs – 1973)
Debut: 28 January 1970
v Coventry City
Division One Home
Last Appearance: 7 April 1973
v Millwall
Division Two Away
Total League
& Cup Appearances: 130 Goals: 0

Career Details:

Bourne Town		
Birmingham City		Trial
Notts County		Trial
Nottingham Forest	May	1960
WEDNESDAY	26 January	1970 £35,000
Brighton & Hove Albion	8 December	1973 Loan
Brighton & Hove Albion	8 January	1974 £6,000
Dover		1978
Worthing Town		1979

Goalkeeper Peter Grummitt started his career between the sticks at Central Alliance League side Bourne Town, from where he joined Nottingham Forest as an apprentice in September 1959. He signed professional forms in the following year and despite suffering an unfortunate first team debut – conceding an own goal without having touched the ball – he quickly became established as Forest's undisputed No. 1. This remained so for nine seasons during which time the brave and agile keeper won three England U-21 caps and represented the Football League. He is regarded by many as one of the best goalies never to have been capped – the closest he came was in 1968 when he was named understudy to Gordon Banks for a game versus Wales. He was again named understudy in 1969 but tragedy struck in the home game with Leeds United when the broken arm he suffered not only ended his England hopes but also brought the curtain down on his Forest career.

After recovering from the injury he could not regain his first team spot from Alan Hill and so after a mammoth 352 appearances for Forest he was taken to Hillsborough by Owls boss Danny Williams - a fall out with Forest manager Matt Gillies certainly hastening the move. During almost four years at Wednesday, Grummitt fought off competition from Peter Springett for the first team jersey, missing only one league game out of the ninety played by Wednesday from January 1970 until March 1972 – his form seeing Peter tour Australia with an F.A.XI in the summer of 1971. It was another injury that ended his run and despite starting the next season back as No.1 he did eventually lose out in the race with Springett, joining Brian Clough's Brighton on loan in December 1973. Grummitt – who had his brother Pip to thank for his career as his sibling always demanded that Peter went in the net when the kids played football – is regarded by Brighton fans as one of the greatest goalkeeper to ever play for The Seagulls as his heroic displays helped Albion to promotion from Division Three in 1977.

Unfortunately a knee injury – suffered against Tranmere Rovers in March 1977 – would signal the end for Grummitt as combined with a now arthritic hip he was forced to retire in December 1977, after 570 league games. He was awarded a benefit game at the end of the campaign and subsequently purchased a tobacconists and confectionary shop in Brighton - also spending two months as manager of Lewes, leaving after failing to secure a place on the club's board of directors. He made a playing comeback with Dover in 1978, lasting three months, before moving to Worthing Town as player and assistant manager. He eventually moved back to Nottinghamshire, starting work as a landscape gardener with the local council in Newark, while also lecturing the unemployed on careers. He later set up his own business as a landscape gardener but after two years was forced to retire due to the injuries he received during his playing career.

HALL, Alexander R. 'Sandy' 1891-93

Born: Scotland (5ft 9ins, 11st 8lbs – 1892)
Debut: 23 January 1892 v Bolton Wanderers F.A.Cup Home
Last Appearance: 3 April 1893 v Notts County Division One Home
Total League & Cup Appearances: 20* Goals: 2
***Also appeared in 16 Football Alliance League games**

Career Details:

Raith Rovers		
WEDNESDAY	October	1891
Raith Rovers		1893
Heart of Midlothian	9 April	1895
Dundee	18 May	1896
Tottenham Hotspur		

Robust and strong tackling half back Sandy Hall joined Wednesday during their final season as a non-league club and holds the distinction of playing in the club's first ever Football league fixture, at Notts County in September 1892. He had initially arrived at Olive Grove in the autumn of 1891, making his first start for the club in a friendly win at Rotherham Town in early November, and it was not long before he had replaced old warhorse Tom Cawley in Wednesday's back line. He played in the final sixteen Alliance League games of the season – The Owls ending the campaign in fourth position – and when League football came to Sheffield for the first time the Scot was an automatic choice.

His early successes had come with Raith Rovers – winning both the Fife Charity Cup and Fife and King Cup in 1891 – and he took to league soccer like a duck to water to help Wednesday make a great start to life in the big leagues. However following a three-nil reverse at home to Blackburn Rovers in November 1892 he was dropped to the second team and for the remainder of the season would play only occasionally for both the first eleven and reserves. In fact after losing his place to Albert Mumford the defender would appear in only five more league games for Wednesday, including the crucial last day win over Notts County that helped Wednesday avoid the dreaded test matches. This proved to be Hall's final game in a Wednesday shirt and in the summer that followed he returned north to re-sign for Raith Rovers. During his second spell at the Kirkcaldy based club he formed a half back line with Dall and Couper, which was said to be one of the finest in Britain. He later returned to English football to play two seasons at Southern League Tottenham – once playing in goal when the regular custodian was unavailable – before retiring in 1899.

HALL, Harry 1920-22

Born: 4th Quarter 1893 Newark
(5ft 9ins, 12st - 1921)
Debut: 11 December 1920 v Cardiff City Division Two Away
Last Appearance: 18 March 1922 v Port Vale Division Two Away
Total League & Cup Appearances: 31 Goals: 1

Career Details:

Gainsborough Trinity	cs	1910
Newark		
Long Eaton St.Helens		
Sheffield United	26 April	1913 £65
Worksop Town		
Long Eaton FC	November	1919
Ilkeston United	October	1920
WEDNESDAY	9 December	1920 £300
Lincoln City	February	1922
Gainsborough Trinity		
Newark Town	August	1922
Long Eaton St Helens		
Grantham Town	February	1924
Ransome & Marles	August	1927

Bulky centre-forward Harry Hall is one of the small band of players to have appeared for both of Sheffield's professional clubs. He had started his playing career as a sixteen year-old at Gainsborough Trinity and initially arrived in Sheffield to sign for The Blades just before the Great War. Competition was fierce at Bramall Lane for the youngster but he did start six senior games for United before the hostilities began and also a handful in wartime soccer. After scoring regularly during the 1919-20 season for the Derbyshire based club Long Eaton he moved up the non-league ladder to sign for Worksop Town and was soon transferred again, this time to Ilkeston United.

It was an impressive appearance for Ilkeston against the Owls in a friendly game that directly led to Hall's move back into the league at Hillsborough, Wednesday paying Town a record fee for the Derbyshire club. Hall had netted in every game he had played for Ilkeston and the Owls were so confident of his abilities that he was offered a two-year contract. Within 48 hours of signing for Wednesday he played in The Owls Second Division game at Cardiff City and after manager Bob Brown converted Harry into an inside-right role he was almost ever present for the remainder of the season, playing in 22 of the final 24 league games of the season. He was instrumental in a terrific second half to the season but was only a bit player during the 1921-2 campaign, playing most of his football in the reserves, finishing second top scorer with fifteen goals as the Midland League side finished in third spot. Competition from the likes of Arthur Lowdell and Sam Taylor kept Hall on the sidelines and he subsequently dropped out of senior football in the summer of 1922.

HAMILTON, Henry Gilhespy 1908-10

Born: 3rd Quarter 1887 South Shields
(5ft 8ins, 11st – 1908)
Died: 3rd Quarter 1938 South Shields
Debut: 22 January 1910 v Bristol City Division One Home
Last Appearance: 14 March 1910
v Tottenham Hotspur Division One Home
Total League & Cup Appearances: 7 Goals: 0

Career Details:

Craghead United		
WEDNESDAY	16 December	1908 £10
Huddersfield Town	April	1910 £250*
Southampton	May	1911
Belfast Celtic	March	1912
South Shields		1913

*Joint fee with William Bartlett

Inside forward who joined the Owls from northeast junior football after two successful trial periods in the reserves. He made an immediate impact at Wednesday, netting ten times for the reserves in the remainder of the 1908-09 campaign, and blossomed in the following campaign, notching 28 goals as the free scoring second team smashed 110 Midland League goals. His tremendous scoring in reserve team football was also rewarded with a mini run at first team level which saw Hamilton replace the absent Andrew Wilson and then deputise for Frank Rollinson in the Owls top-flight side. However before the season came to a close Hamilton was on his way to neighbours Huddersfield Town in a joint transfer with William Bartlett.

His career at non-league Huddersfield started in dramatic style as Hamilton scored a brace on debut and grabbed a hat-trick in the final game of the season. During the summer months his new club were elected into the Football League and it was Henry who scored the only goal as Town won at Bradford Park Avenue in Huddersfield's first ever league fixture. He continued to score on a regular basis for the West Yorkshire club, netting 18 times in only 22 games, and it was not long before he was on the move again. However his destination was certainly unexpected as he made the long journey to the South Coast, signing for Southern League Southampton. He experienced an unhappy time at The Saints and in March 1912 was banned "sine die", along with team mate Andrew Gibson, after what was described as "a serious breach of club discipline". A short spell in Irish football followed before Hamilton ended his playing career back in his hometown of South Shields.

HAMSHAW, Matthew Thomas "Matt" 1999-2005

Born: 1 January 1982 Rotherham
(5ft 9ins, 11st 9lbs - 2000)
Debut: 26 August 2000 v Grimsby Town
Division One Away
Last Appearance:
16 May 2005 v Brentford League One Play Off S/F Away
Total League & Cup Appearances: 45+43
Goals: 6

Career Details:

WEDNESDAY	1 January	1999
Released	30 June	2005
Stockport County	11 July	2005

CAPS (@ SWFC):
England U-18 (8)
v France 08/03/00, v Luxembourg 27/04/00, v Israel 01/09/00, v Andorra 07/10/00, Faeroe Islands 09/10/00, v Italy 11/10/00, v Belgium 16/11/00, v Poland 22/03/01

England U-20 (6)
v Finland 13/02/02, Portugal 10/04/02, v China 06/05/02, v Poland 10/05/02, v Brazil 14/05/02, v Japan 17/05/02

Exciting right-winger Matt Hamshaw joined the Owls on his fourteenth birthday and after appearing for England at under-15 level signed three-year scholarship forms at Hillsborough in the summer of 1998. It quickly became apparent however that Hamshaw would not be in youth football for long and within six months he had put his signature to a professional contract, joining on his seventeenth birthday. Caps at U-18 level for his country soon followed and Matt duly made the breakthrough at first team level at the beginning of the 2000-1 campaign. He went on to appear in 22 games during a highly promising debut campaign in senior football and consolidated his first team squad place in the following season as the Owls successfully fought relegation and reached the last four of the League Cup - Matt scoring a wonder goal in the Hillsborough quarter-final against Watford.

The tricky and pacy winger started the 2002/3 season on the subs bench and failed to start a game during Terry Yorath's short tenure as boss. However the slate was wiped clean with the arrival of Chris Turner and a series of sparkling displays saw Hamshaw become firmly established as Wednesday showed signs of recovery after an awful start to the season. Unfortunately just when he looked to have cemented a permanent place in the starting eleven, his career was put on hold after Matt ruptured his cruciate ligament during the home game with Nottingham Forest on Boxing Day 2002. It meant over nine months on the sidelines for the youngster but his ill luck continued during his comeback in the autumn of 2003 when the same injury in his right knee recurred, leaving Hamshaw on the sidelines for the remainder of the 2003-04 season. After regaining fitness Hamshaw enjoyed an extended run in the side under Paul Sturrock but his injury jinx struck again, leaving Hamshaw out of action for several weeks with a severe hamstring pull. He did return to help Wednesday to the Play Off Final but after failing a fitness test before the Cardiff showpiece his Owls career came to a close as the club announced his release just 48 hours later.

HANFORD, Harold "Harry" 1936-46

Born: 9 October 1907
Blaengwynfi, Wales
(5ft 10ins, 11st – 1936)
Died: 26 November 1995
Melbourne, Australia
Debut: 29 February 1936
v Leeds United
Division One Home
Last Appearance: 29 April 1939
v Tottenham Hotspur
Division Two Home
Total League
& Cup Appearances: 94* Goals: 1
***Also appeared in 8 wartime games**

Career Details:

Ton Pentre		
Blaengwynfi Juniors		
Swansea Town		
WEDNESDAY	25 February	1936 £3600+Leyland
Swansea Town	January	1940 Guest
Swindon Town		1939-40 Guest
Aberman	August	1943 Guest
Swansea Town		1944-45 Guest
Aberman		1944-45 Guest
Exeter City	May	1946
Haverfordwest		

CAPS (@ SWFC)
Wales Full (4) v N.Ireland 11/03/36, v Scotland 30/10/37, v England 17/11/37, v France 10/05/39

Halfback who arrived at Hillsborough primarily as understudy to Harry Millership. In fact within four days the ex-Swansea Captain – who already had three full Welsh caps to his name – was playing alongside Millership in the Owls back line and would play ten times to the end of the season, helping Wednesday to just avoid relegation from the top-flight. The former schoolboy International had started his career in Welsh non-league soccer before breaking into league football while on the books of Swansea Town, appearing in 201 Football League games for The Swans from making his debut in December 1927. His move to Sheffield saw Owls reserve Peter Leyland travel in the opposite direction while Wednesday also promised Town a friendly game as part of the transfer – this was played in September 1936.

During the following season Harry was a regular in the back line as The Owls suffered the dreaded drop but was only a peripheral figure during the club's first season back in the lower tier. However during the 1938-9 season Hanford enjoyed his most successful spell at Wednesday, appearing in the pivot role during 47 league and cup games. Unfortunately the war then intervened and Harry moved back to Swansea where he joined the police force for the duration of the conflict. When peace returned he was awarded a benefit by Wednesday but by this time Hanford was an Exeter City player where he would play a season before retiring from league football. He played a further year back in Welsh junior football before hanging up his proverbial boots in 1947 and later spent two seasons as assistant trainer at Northampton Town in the early 1950s before being appointed head trainer at Exeter City for the 1953-4 campaign. Soon after he opened his own physiotherapist practise in Swansea but later emigrated to Australia where he worked at the MEB power station. After passing away in 1995 his ashes were scattered over Swansea's Vetch Field pitch

HARDY, Robin 1958-65

Born: 18 January 1941 Worksop
(5ft 8ins, 12st 2lbs – 1963)
Debut: 16 October 1961
v Aston Villa
Division One Away
Last Appearance: 30 March 1964
v Arsenal
Division One Home
Total League
& Cup Appearances: 33 Goals: 1

Career Details:

WEDNESDAY	6 February	1958
Rotherham United	4 February	1965 £8,000
Cambridge United		1967 Free
Gainsborough Trinity		1971

Despite spending almost ten years on the Owls books, wing-half Robin Hardy was never anything more than an understudy to Tom McAnearney. The ex-Worksop and Notts Boys wing-half had originally signed amateur forms for The Owls back in August 1956 but had to wait over five years before getting his chance when McAnearney was absent for a Monday night game at Villa Park. After two further starts he returned to the reserves but was recalled for the return game with Villa and then enjoyed a run of thirteen straight games until the end of the season – including appearances in both legs of the Fairs Cup quarter- final with Spanish giants

Barcelona. Unfortunately this run of games proved nothing but a false dawn for Hardy as McAnearney remained first choice with the youngster making only fleeting appearances over the next three seasons.

His attributes included determination in the tackle as well as good ball distribution and it was these qualities that persuaded Rotherham United to take Hardy to Millmoor in 1965. Two seasons brought 41 league games and two goals before Hardy dropped into non-league soccer to join ambitious Southern League side Cambridge United. He made a big impact at The Abbey Stadium club and was named player of the year in 1969 as United won the Southern league Championship, the first of back-to-back title successes. His new club was voted into the Football League in 1970 and Hardy was a regular before dropping back into non-league soccer at the end of the season. After two spells in the licencing trade – while at Rotherham and Cambridge – Hardy now works for an engineering company back in his native Worksop.

HARGREAVES, Leonard "Len" 1929-31

Born: 7 March 1906 Kimberworth, Nr Rotherham
(5ft 11½ ins, 11st 2lbs – 1929)
Died: 3rd Quarter 1980 Sheffield
Debut: 16 March 1929
v Leicester City
Division One Home
Last Appearance: 23 March 1929
v Manchester United
Division One Away
Total League
& Cup Appearances: 2 Goals: 1

Career Details:

Blackburn Wesleyans		
Doncaster Rovers	March	1925
Sunderland	April	1927 £2000
WEDNESDAY	March	1929 £2700
Shelbourne	cs	1931 Loan
York City	cs	1931 Free
Workington	October	1931 Free
Doncaster Rovers	July	1932 Free
Luton Town	August	1933 Free
Peterborough & Fletton Utd	July	1934 Free

Although Len Hargreaves spent his early years in Sheffield Junior football with Blackburn Wesleyans – playing alongside former school teammate Tony Leach - it was with Doncaster Rovers that Len first made his breakthrough into league soccer. The tall left-winger, who had a reputation for scoring spectacular goals and possessing great ball control, made his competitive bow for Rovers in November 1925 and such was his fine form that after scoring twelve times in just thirty-six league games he was sold to top-flight Sunderland for a then Doncaster club record fee. Hargreaves was first choice for Sunderland during the 1927-8 campaign and coincidently also scored 12 times in 36 league games for the northeast side before losing his place to Adam McLean and subsequently moving to Hillsborough in the spring of 1929.

He joined an Owls side that were mounting an ultimately successful challenge for the First Division Championship and he would play twice during the run in, scoring in the 2-1 defeat at Manchester United, as stand in for first choice Ellis Rimmer. Unfortunately those two games proved to be the highlight of Hargreaves' time at Hillsborough as competition for places was so fierce during the 1929-30 season that Jack Wilkinson invariably kept Len out of the reserve team! Matters improved little during what proved to be his final season at Wednesday and in search of first team football he left for a short spell in the Irish Free State League with Shelbourne. This foreign adventure did not last long and after a brief time at York City he returned to Doncaster Rovers in the summer of 1932, appearing in a further 9 games before ending his playing days back in non-league football – after failing to play a first team game at his final league side, Luton Town. He had the distinction of scoring the first ever goal for the new Peterborough and Fletton United club and later in life worked as a locomotive fitter.

HARKES, John Andrew 1990-93

Born: 8 March 1967
Kearny, New Jersey, US
(5ft 10ins, 11st 10lbs – 1993)
Debut: 31 October 1990
v Swindon Town
League Cup Home
Last Appearance: 20 May 1993
v Arsenal
F.A.Cup Final – replay @ Wembley
Total League
& Cup Appearances: 95+23 Goals: 11

Career Details:

Kearny High School		
University of Virginia		
Missouri Athletic Club		1987
U. S. Soccer Federation		
WEDNESDAY	January	1990 Trial
Blackburn Rovers	August	1990 Trial
Glasgow Celtic	September	1990 Trial
WEDNESDAY	September	1990 Loan
WEDNESDAY	3 December	1990 $185,000
Derby County	17 August	1993 £800,000
U. S. Soccer Federation	27 October	1995 £600,000
West Ham United	28 October	1995 Loan
Washington D.C.United	March	1996
Nottingham Forest	20 January	1999 Trial
Nottingham Forest	27 January	1999 Loan
New England Revolution	3 March	1999
Columbus Crew	11 May	2001 *

*Exchange for Roland Aguilera + conditional draft pick

CAPS (@SWFC)
USA Full (12) v Eire 29/04/92, v Eire 30/05/92, Portugal 03/06/92, v Italy 06/06/92, v Saudi Arabia 15/10/92, v Brazil 06/06/93, v England 09/06/93, v Germany 13/06/93, v Jamaica 10/07/93, v Honduras 17/07/93, v Costa Rica 21/07/93, v Mexico 25/07/93

Although John Harkes spent less than three years at Hillsborough his impact was such that he is without doubt one of the most popular Wednesday players of the modern era. The engaging American – the son of Scottish parents who emigrated to New Jersey just before he was born – burst onto the English football scene in 1990 and quickly grabbed the headlines when scoring an astounding 35-yard goal past ex-England keeper Peter Shilton in a League Cup win at Derby County. Harkes was in a US training camp, preparing for Italia 90, when he initially arrived on trial early in 1990 and played several reserve games along with fellow American International Tony Meola. He returned to Wednesday on loan early in the 1990-91season– after having played in all three of the States' games in Italy - so Ron Atkinson could decide whether to pursue a full transfer. He duly became a fully-fledged Wednesday player and a switch to right back to cover long-term injury victim Roland Nilsson ensured Harkes would become a regular as Wednesday won promotion from Division Two and lifted the League Cup at Wembley. In the Final versus Manchester United Harkes was detailed to help the fit again Nilsson combat the threat of Lee Sharpe and the American almost ran himself into the ground to ensure Wednesday took the silverware back to Sheffield – his appearance at the famous old ground was one of many records he would break in his time in the blue and white shirt, including first US National to play in a major English Cup Final and also the first to score – he netted the Owls goal in the 1993 League Cup Final loss to Arsenal.

His rise to fame had started in the somewhat low-key surroundings of US high school and college football – playing in the same side as future US Internationals Tab Ramos and Tony Meola – before the hard-running midfielder spent a junior season at the University of Virginia. Within a year he was voted player of the season at the Missouri Club and in May 1987 played against Canada to win the first of 90 full caps for the US. He was subsequently contracted to the US Soccer Federation, from where Wednesday secured his signature for a bargain fee. After experiencing a memorable first season at Hillsborough, Harkes reverted back to his more accustomed midfield role in the campaign that followed as

Wednesday finished third in the top-flight to earn a UEFA Cup place. He remained a valuable squad player under Trevor Francis but after appearing in 47 games for Wednesday during 1992-3 – suffering double Wembley heartbreak along the way – he rejected two contract offers from the Owls and eventually moved to Derby County after having been on week-to-week terms since his contract had expired at the end of June 1993.

Unfortunately for Harkes – whose wife Cindi also played soccer to a high standard – his time at the Baseball Ground proved an unhappy one and after three goals in 85 games he returned home, being re-signed by his national federation. However within 24 hours John was back in the UK on loan at West Ham where he temporarily wound up his English League career before returning home again, to help launch the fledgling North American Soccer League. He achieved immediate success, appearing in 28 games and captaining DC United to the inaugural Championship – a title that was retained in 1997. Harkes just missed out on a hat-trick of title successes in 1998 when DC United lost in the play-offs while his International career continued to flourish – he was captain from March 1996 to March 1998 -until being sensationally axed from the France 98 squad. He returned to the National side in 1999 – appearing for the US in the new Confederations Cup competition – after a short spell under old boss Ron Atkinson at Nottingham Forest. A move to New England came next for John where he experienced an injury ravaged first season before leading Revolution to their highest ever league finish in 2000. His final club proved to be Columbus Crew where Harkes won the equivalent of the F.A.Cup in 2002 – beating L.A.Galaxy in the final – before finally retiring in May 2003. His final game saw John return to D.C.United to appear as a guest in their victory over a touring Spurs side in Washington, proving a fitting end to the career of arguably the most famous football player to originate from across the pond. After hanging up his boots Harkes returned to his old club D.C.United in February 2004 when being appointed Director of Youth development.

HARKNESS, Steve 2000-02

Born: 27 August 1971 Carlisle
(5ft 10ins, 11st 2lbs – 2001)
Debut: 30 September 2000
v Gillingham
Division One Away
Last Appearance: 28 April 2001
v Norwich City
Division One Away
Total League
& Cup Appearances: 30+2 Goals: 1

Career Details:

Carlisle United	23 March	1989
Liverpool	17 July	1989 £75,000
Huddersfield Town	24 September	1995 Loan
Southend United	2 February	1995
Benfica	9 March	1999 £750,000
Blackburn Rovers	8 September	1999 £400,000
WEDNESDAY	28 September	2000 £200,000
Contract cancelled	28 May	2002
Chester City	11 July	2002
Released	1 November	2002

Utility player Steve Harkness joined the Owls on a three-year contract early in the 2000-1 season after disappointing spells at both Blackburn Rovers and Portuguese giants Benfica. The ex-England Youth International had initially made the grade at his hometown club Carlisle United but it was ten years at Liverpool that brought his name to the fore. After only a handful of games for Carlisle he became a valuable squad member at Anfield where his fierce tackling and competitive spirit made the Cumbrian a favourite amongst Liverpool supporters. Unfortunately his all action style meant he was frequently on the treatment table – missing the whole of the 1996-7 season with a broken leg – but he fought back to become a regular for Liverpool during 1997-8, ostensibly at left back. However the following term proved a watershed in his Anfield career as Harkness' versatility proved a double-edged sword as he was utilised in several different positions and often relegated to the subs bench.

After a total of 139 games for Liverpool, Harkness made a surprise move to Portuguese club Benfica in March 1999, being signed by his old Liverpool boss Graeme Souness. However he stayed for only six months, as when Souness was fired it was not long before he was followed back to the UK by his small contingent of English players! It was not long though before the two joined up again at Blackburn Rovers where Harkness was stuck in the reserves until he briefly became a first team regular following Souness' appointment as manager in March 2000. Unfortunately when the Scot got his feet under the Ewood Park table it was back into the reserves for Harkness, prompting his signing by Paul Jewell for the Owls. In his first season at Wednesday Harkness proved he was not a player to shirk tackles – shown by a hefty collection of yellow cards – and was a regular under Jewell and then caretaker manager Peter Shreeves. However his second season at Wednesday was an unmitigated disaster for the likeable Harkness as he failed to even make the subs bench under the managership of Terry Yorath and the situation was so acute that the two parties agreed to cancel his contract by mutual consent in May 2002. He was subsequently signed as player-coach by old teammate Mark Wright for Chester City but in November 2002 he quit the Conference club in the hope of finding a league side.

HARPER, Alan 1988-89

Born: 1 November 1960 Liverpool
(5ft 8ins, 10st 9lbs – 1989)
Debut: 27 August 1988
v Luton Town
Division One Home
Last Appearance: 18 November 1989
v Derby County
Division One Away
Total League
& Cup Appearances: 35+4 Goals: 0

Career Details:

Liverpool	22 April	1978
Everton	1 June	1983 £100,000
WEDNESDAY	8 June	1988 £275,000
Manchester City	15 December	1989 £155,000
Everton	12 August	1991 £200,000
Luton Town	13 September	1993 Free
Burnley	11 August	1994 Free
Cardiff City	24 November	1995 Loan

Ex-Liverpool boys player who is one of only a handful of players to have been on the books of both senior Merseyside clubs. The versatile Harper was a regular in the Owls poor side of the late 1980s and was subsequently sold by Ron Atkinson in December 1989 when Big Ron performed major surgery on his side – the likes of Phil King, Roland Nilsson and John Sheridan arriving at Hillsborough.The steady but unspectacular Harper – who appeared at right back and on the right side of midfield in his time at Wednesday – was brought to Hillsborough by Howard Wilkinson after enjoying his most productive spell in league soccer at Everton - winning two League Championship medals and helping The Toffees to the 1986 F.A.Cup Final – scoring against Wednesday in the Villa Park semi-final.

The ex-England youth International had enjoyed early success in his career when winning the English Schools Trophy in 1975 and looked set for stardom after signing apprentice forms at Liverpool. He duly moved up to professional status but failed to make a first team appearance for The Reds and after five years made the surprise switch across Stanley Park to sign for Howard Kendal's Everton. The move of course provided a launch pad to his professional career and Harper would total 250 games for Everton in his two spells at the club. After finishing his playing career at Burnley he was appointed youth coach at Turf Moor but found himself out of work in 1996 after a new management team decided to bring in their own backroom staff. He subsequently re-joined Everton in a coaching capacity in 1997 but had to retire from the position in the summer of 2003 due to injury.

HARPER, Edward Cashfield "Ted" 1927-29

Born: 22 August 1901 Sheerness, Kent
(5ft 10ins, 11st 7lbs – 1927)
Died: 22 July 1959 Blackburn
Debut: 26 November 1927
v Derby County
Division One Away
Last Appearance: 2 March 1929
v Bury
Division One Home
Total League
& Cup Appearances: 22 Goals: 16

Career Details:

Whitstable Town		
Sheppey United		
Blackburn Rovers	May	1923
WEDNESDAY	24 November	1927 £4,400
Tottenham Hotspur	14 March	1929 £5,000
Preston North End	10 December	1931 £1,000*
Blackburn Rovers	September	1933

Free scoring centre forward Ted Harper may not have stayed long in Sheffield but he left an indelible mark on club history as the only Sheffield Wednesday player to score a hat trick on his league debut for the Owls. This amazing feat occurred just 48 hours after his big money move from Blackburn Rovers when Harper – replacing Jimmy Trotter in the No. 9 shirt – grabbed a treble in an amazing game at the Baseball Ground, Derby which Wednesday won 6-4. It continued a rich vein of scoring for the attacker who had first shot to prominence at the tender age of 18 when netting an astonishing 102 goals in Kent League football. After completing his apprenticeship as a shipwright Harper moved into League football - it cost Blackburn nothing more than the train fare from Sheppey to Lancashire to secure his signature.

The move from minor soccer into the First Division had little effect on Harper's incredible scoring as he netted 18 times during his debut season. A spell out of the side followed for the rather ungainly centre forward but he returned with a vengeance during the 1925-6 season, setting a Football League record of 43 goals as well as winning his sole England cap – against Scotland at Old Trafford in April 1926. Incidentally his top-flight scoring record would still stand today if the legendary Dixie Dean had not – with the aid of the change in the offside law – plundered sixty goals during the 1927-8 season! Although not the quickest or most skilful of players, Harper did possess that natural goalscorers instinct and this allied with great positional sense, the ability to shoot with either foot and tremendous courage made him one of the greatest centre-forwards of the inter-war years. It was therefore a blow to Rovers when he left for Bob Brown's Wednesday after netting 106 league goals in only 144 games, although the Lancashire side were amply compensated with a huge fee.

The Owls boss saw him as an ideal replacement for the ageing Jimmy Trotter and Harper went straight into a Wednesday side that were struggling at the foot of the First Division. After his dramatic debut Ted remained in the side throughout the winter months but a brave and inspirational move by Brown saw Harper dropped and Trotter reinstated as Wednesday stared relegation in the face. The move worked like a dream for Brown as Trotter netted seven times and Wednesday made one of the greatest escapes from relegation of all-time. However Harper was left to play the season out in reserve team football and when Jack Allen was converted to centre forward early in the following campaign it effectively spelt the end of Harper's Wednesday career. With English football using the rigid 2-3-5 formation there was no place in the side for Harper and after being stuck in the reserves for six months he asked for a transfer in February 1929, moving to Spurs soon after.

The return to first team football at Spurs re-ignited his goalscoring powers and Ted netted 62 goals in just 63 games before grabbing 67 in 75 at his next club Preston North End. It should be worth noting also that Harper scored on his debut for every club he played for – including a goal on his return to Blackburn Rovers – and set seasonal scoring records at Blackburn, Spurs and Preston.

After a short final playing spell at Rovers he joined the Ewood Park coaching staff in 1935, remaining on the payroll until May 1948. He subsequently worked for English Electric until his relatively early death in 1959.

HARRISON, W 1883

Born
Debut: 6 January 1883
v Nottingham Forest
F.A.Cup Away
Last Appearance: 13 January 1883
v Nottingham Forest
F.A.Cup Home
Total League
& Cup Appearances: 2 Goals: 3

Career Details:

Local		
WEDNESDAY	January	1883
Heeley		

A total unknown in the annals of Wednesday's history. Joined the Owls early in 1883, appearing in the 2-2 F.A.Cup draw at Nottingham Forest. He was one of several Wednesday players who Forest lodged protests against for ineligibility – the protest being dismissed by the F.A. before the game was replayed seven days later. By scoring twice in the second game at Bramall Lane Harrison took his tally to thrcc in just two games but promptly disappeared from the Wednesday scene without playing another first team game for the club.

HARRON, Joseph "Joe" 1923-25

Born: 14 March 1900 Langley Park, Co.Durham
(5ft $7^1/_2$ ins, 11st 2lbs – 1923)
Died: 19 February 1961
Debut: 15 March 1923
v Stockport County Division Two Away
Last Appearance: 25 October 1924
v South Shields Division Two Home
Total League & Cup Appearances: 64 Goals: 6

Career Details:

Langley Park		
Hull City	August	1920
Northampton Town	June	1921
York City	July	1922
WEDNESDAY	8 March	1923 £300
York City	September	1925 £200
Kettering Town	January	1926
York City		1926 Loan
Scarborough		1926
Barnsley	21 December	1928 £300
Dartford	August	1930

Diminutive winger who improved in leaps and bounds after joining the Owls – his fifth club although he was aged only 22 when arriving from York City. The left sided player had started his career in his native northeast at Northern League Langley Park before entering league soccer with Division Three (South) side Northampton Town. However he stayed only a season down south and was soon signed by fledgling club York City, who had only been formed in the previous May. His new side had been accepted into the Midland league, after unsurprisingly failing to win enough votes for direct membership into the Football League, and Harron entered City's history books as one of the eleven players who appeared in the club's first ever competitive fixture – away at Notts County reserves in September 1922.

After impressing greatly down the flanks for City – playing in the same side as his younger brother George - he subsequently became the first player to move from York for a transfer fee, Wednesday boss Bob Brown bringing the youngster to Hillsborough as he slowly reshaped the club's playing staff. Joe was drafted straight into Wednesday's Second Division side – replacing Horace Henshall on the left wing – and played in the final twelve games of the season, scoring his first goal on his home debut against South Shields. He remained an automatic choice during the following

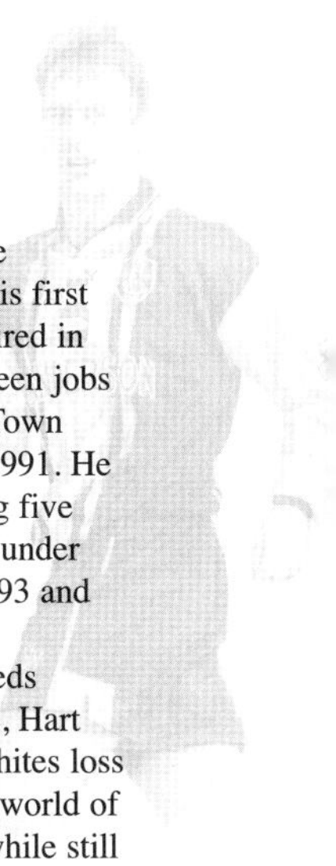

season, missing only four games, but the arrival of Arthur Prince in the summer of 1925 greatly increased competition for the prized first team spot. Harron started the new season in the No. 11 shirt, appearing in the opening eleven games, but after losing his shirt to Prince he spent the remainder of his time at Wednesday in the reserves before moving back to York City. A short spell in non-league football at Kettering preceded a third spell – this time on loan – at York City before Joe played, and scored, in Scarborough's first ever Midland League fixture against Mansfield Town in August 1927. He later made 28 appearances in League soccer for Barnsley before ending his playing days at Dartford – winning the Southern League Championship with the Kent club in 1931 before being appointed manager.

HART, Paul Anthony 1985-86

Born: 4 May 1953 Golborne, Manchester (6ft 2ins, 12st 3lbs – 1984)
Debut: 17 August 1985
v Chelsea
Division One Home
Last Appearance: 21 December 1986
v Newcastle United
Division One Home
Total League
& Cup Appearances: 60 Goals: 3

Career Details:

Preston North End		3-month trial
Whalley Range		
Stockport County	September	1970
Blackpool	18 June	1973 £25,000
Leeds United	9 March	1978 £330,000
Nottingham Forest	May	1983 £57,000
WEDNESDAY	17 July	1985 Free
Birmingham City	31 December	1986 £15,000
Notts County	30 June	1987 £15,000
Chesterfield	2 November	1988 Free
Grantham Town	23 January	1991

Imposing central defender Paul Hart followed the likes of Mike Pickering and Mick Lyons into Hillsborough, being a player of vast experience who joined Wednesday in the twilight of his career. On his debut for the club Hart actually played alongside Lyons – making a centre back pairing with a combined age of 65 – but thankfully the years had not diminished his defensive qualities and the Lancasterian appeared in 34 top-flight games during that debut season as the Owls finished a highly creditable fifth. The no-nonsense defender was recognised as one of soccer's hard men and in a career spanning almost twenty years many an opposition forward had reason to rue the day when they attempted to get past him! He was seen by many as just a short-term acquisition by Howard Wilkinson – Hart had been linked with player-manager jobs at Tranmere Rovers and Stockport County – but he would remain for the majority of his two-year contract to give Wednesday sterling service and captained the side for a time following Lyons'departure in November 1985.

He had first impressed as a schoolboy – representing Manchester boys at both football and cricket – and after writing to several league clubs asking for a trial he was given a chance with Preston before signing apprentice forms with Stockport County in June 1969. After signing pro at the Edgeley Park club he was soon a first team regular and after a further spell at Blackpool, Hart moved to Leeds United for a large fee. His reputation soared with the Yorkshire club and after five years at Elland Road he moved to Brian Clough's Nottingham Forest – playing in the infamous UEFA Cup semi-final defeat to Anderlecht in 1984, a tie in which it later transpired that the Belgium club had bribed the referee!

The old-fashioned stopper had played over five hundred league games before joining the Owls but his luck with injury came to an abrupt halt immediately on leaving Hillsborough as Hart had the misfortune to suffer a compound fracture of his leg, meaning his debut for Birmingham City would also prove to be his final game in a Blues shirt. After recovering his fitness he joined Notts County in a player-coach role – retiring from playing at the end of the 1987-88 season - before accepting his first managerial appointment as boss at Chesterfield in November 1988. He enjoyed a roller coaster time at Saltergate – relegation in his first season and a Play-Off Final defeat a year later – but was fired in January 1991 after results took a downturn. While in between jobs Hart played seven games for Southern League Grantham Town before joining old club Forest as coach in the summer of 1991. He started to forge a reputation as an outstanding coach during five years in charge of the Youth set up at Leeds United where under his leadership The Peacocks won the F.A.Youth Cup in 1993 and 1997 as well as producing the likes of Harry Kewell, Paul Robinson and Jonathan Woodgate. A fall out with then Leeds manager George Graham led to his departure in June 1997, Hart being appointed to an identical role back at Forest. The Whites loss was certainly Forest's gain as he continued to excel in the world of youth soccer, producing the likes of Jermaine Jenas who while still as teenager would move to Newcastle United for a £5m fee.

He was given another chance of management at senior level in July 2001 when following David Platt's departure from The City Ground, Hart was given the reins. He subsequently produced one of the most attractive sides in the First Division and reached the play –off semi-finals in 2003, losing over two legs to Sheffield United. However as financial problems hit the City Ground Hart was forced to sell many of his better players and with his hands tied was sacked in February 2004 with Forest in relegation trouble. However Hart was only out of work for a matter of weeks before being appointed manager at Second Division Barnsley in March 2004. Struggled to win over fans during almost twelve months at Oakwell, leaving by mutual consent on 4th March 2005 after the hoped for promotion challenge failed to materialise.

HARVEY, James Colin 1974-76

Born: 16 November 1944 Liverpool (5ft 8ins, 11st – 1975)
Debut: 14 September 1974
v Bolton Wanderers
Division Two Away
Last Appearance: 22 November 1975
v Macclesfield Town
F.A.Cup Home
Total League
& Cup Appearances: 48
Goals: 2

Career Details:

Liverpool Junior football		
Everton	November	1962
WEDNESDAY	12 September	1974 £66,666
Contract cancelled	1 May	1976

Classy midfielder who had enjoyed an outstanding career at his only other club Everton before joining Wednesday's fight against relegation in the disastrous 1974-5 season. Owls boss Steve Burtenshaw hoped that the vastly experienced Harvey would lead Wednesday to safety in the twilight of his career but unfortunately injury restricted his appearances to less than fifty and he was forced to retire in March 1976 – the two parties agreeing to cancel his contract by mutual consent in May of the same year.

It was a hip injury that brought an end to a career that had started in Liverpool youth football where he actually once had a trial for Everton's great rivals Liverpool. However after leaving school he was still unattached and started work as a clerk in the National Health Service - a position held for all of two weeks before signing for Everton. After serving his apprenticeship at the Goodison Park club, Harvey made a dramatic start to his first team career, being drafted into the Everton side for a volatile European Cup game against Inter in Milan! That tie in September 1963 was lost by a solitary goal but the experience proved invaluable for Colin and over the next few months he made a big impression on the Goodison Park regulars, showing himself to be a player of genuine quality and style. He was a real midfield dynamo, possessing superb passing ability and positional sense, and at his peak Harvey

was a delight to watch – being part of the midfield trio including Alan Ball & Howard Kendall that took Everton to the 1970 League Championship. In the same year of the title success he won his solitary England cap – against Malta – and during his long spell at Everton he won a variety of other club honours including an F.A.Cup winners medal in 1966 against the Owls!

After 384 games for Everton he finished his playing days at Hillsborough but he would soon be back in his home City, re-joining The Toffeemen as youth team coach in 1976. A progression to reserve team manager followed before in November 1983 – under ex-team mate Howard Kendall – he was appointed first team coach. He was later No.2 to Kendall and during a golden three-year period the duo steered Everton to two league Championships (1985 & 1987) an F.A.Cup win (1984) and a European Cup Winners Cup triumph (1985). Following Kendall's departure in the summer of 1987 Harvey was appointed manager in June but he experienced a relatively unsuccessful time in the hot seat – an F.A.Cup Final appearance in 1989 being his only real achievement – and was dismissed in October 1990 after just over three years in charge. Bizarrely he was only away from the club for six days as a certain Howard Kendall arrived for a second spell as boss and his first task was to bring Harvey back as assistant manager! After finally managing to prise himself away from Goodison Park he was briefly coach under Graeme Sharp at Oldham – resigning in February 1997 – and was assistant manager at Burnley from March 1997 until June 1997. The inevitable return to Everton saw Colin appointed youth supremo in 1997, a position he held until the summer of 2003 when his hip caused his early retirement.

HARVEY, Edward Lee 1919-21

Born: 3rd Quarter 1892 Sheffield
(5ft 8½ ins,, 10st 3¼lbs – 1919)
Died: May 1965 Sheffield
Debut: 1 September 1919
v Manchester United Division One Away
Last Appearance:
1 January 1921
v Leicester City Division Two Away
Total League
& Cup Appearances: 12 Goals: 0

Career Details:

Hallam		
Heeley		
WEDNESDAY	August	1919
Bristol Rovers	12 September	1921 £75
Retford Town	28 September	1924

Winger Edward Harvey first came to the notice of Wednesday fans when he made a surprise appearance in the old traditional curtain raiser to the season - the public trial match. His display in the 1919 version impressed the Wednesday management enough for him to be immediately offered a professional contract and Harvey would go on to make nine top flight appearances for the Owls – at outside left – in the disastrous campaign of 1919-20. He was one of only a handful of players to survive the mass clear out at the end of the season but would fail to gain a regular place in the Owls Second Division side – Jimmy Lofthouse barring his path. After a season of mainly reserve team football he moved to Bristol Rovers in the summer of 1921 but his early promise at Rovers soon faded and after just five games in a 12-month stay he returned north to sign for Retford Town.

Harvey continued to play non-league football with Town until he was forced to retire in July 1924 due to a serious knee injury. He would later hit the headlines for all the wrong reasons when in June 1934 he was found guilty at Leeds Court of obtaining money by false pretences. At the time he was working as a medical orderly and living in Barnsley.

HARVEY, William Henry Tompkins 'George/Billy' 1919-21

Born: 12 April 1896
Freemantle, Hampshire
(5ft 10½ ins, 11st – 1919)
Died: July 1970 South Africa
Debut: 25 October 1919
v Manchester City
Division One Away
Last Appearance: 17 April 1920
v Aston Villa
Division One Away
Total League
& Cup Appearances: 20 Goals: 1

Career Details:

Netley Schools		
Yorkshire Amateurs		
Duke of Wellington's Regiment		
South Shields		1918-19 Guest
Pembroke		
Bradford City		1918-19 Guest
WEDNESDAY	October	1919 Amat.
Birmingham	5 July	1921 Amat.
Southend United	August	1925

CAPS (@SWFC)
England Amateur (1) v Ireland 1919

In the early 1930s the Owls lost the outstanding talents of Billy Marsden after he was injured whilst on International duty. Unfortunately for Wednesday the same occurred with right-winger George Harvey although in his case it was an illness contracted on foreign shores that brought his Owls career to a close. He had first joined the Owls as a virtual unknown after having survived the horrors of the Great War – Harvey had enlisted in the army at the age of seventeen in 1914 and was wounded in the battle at Passchendale in 1917 – and was recommended to Wednesday when his regiment was sent to Sheffield. Lieutenant Harvey had no experience of senior football other than two games for South Shields in the 1918-19 Victory League and a solitary game for Bradford City but he made such an impact in his trial game for the reserves against Worksop Town that Wednesday immediately signed him on amateur forms.

Harvey – who had learned his football with school teams in Aldershot and Leeds – was drafted straight into Wednesday's first team 72 hours after signing and he made such an impression that an Owls official of the time, somewhat overenthusiastically, declared him to be the best right winger Wednesday have had since moving to Hillsborough! Within a week of signing for the Owls he was picked to represent England in the amateur International at Derby and after being de-mobbed in November 1919 he could concentrate on his club's desperate plight at the foot of the old First Division. Unfortunately the Owls situation was hopeless and Harvey would appear in twenty games as Wednesday ended the season with only seven wins to their name - his form ensured Harvey escaped the cull that resulted in an astonishing 21 players being released by the club in the summer that followed. However Harvey's career was just about to receive a huge setback as in the summer of 1920 – whilst on tour in South Africa with an F.A. representative team - he was taken ill after injuring his knee in a game. He was subsequently hospitalised after contracting pneumonia and it would be a year before he returned home to England, promptly signing amateur forms for Birmingham.

He eventually signed professional forms – in November 1921 - at the St.Andrew's club and after two goals in 79 games left for Southend United in the summer of 1925. However he stayed just a solitary season in Essex before returning to Birmingham as assistant secretary/reserve team manager in August 1926. Between March 1927 and May 1928 he held the reigns at The Blues – finishing 11th in his only full season in charge – before reverting back to his previous status as assistant. He was subsequently appointed secretary-manager at Second Division Chesterfield on 4th July 1932, after the departure of Wednesday legend Teddy Davison to take over at Bramall Lane. After suffering relegation with The Spireites in 1933 he led them to the Division Three (North) Championship in 1936 before taking over at Gillingham in June 1938, leading the Kent club to third place in the Southern League in the final season before war broke out again. Incidentally the pacy winger joined the small band of sportsman to have played First Class county cricket and League football when making a solitary appearance for Warwickshire – he was a medium pace bowler and middle order batsman. Later in life Harvey – who was also an excellent tennis player, swimmer, runner & three-quarter at rugby – returned to the Southern Hemisphere to live out the final years of his life.

HASLAM, Steven Robert "Steve" 1996-2004

Born: 6 September 1979 Sheffield
(5ft 11ins, 10st 10lbs – 2002)
Debut: 8 May 1999
v Liverpool
Premier League Home
Last Appearance: 28 February 2004
v Bristol City
Division Two Home
Total League
& Cup Appearances: 139+32 Goals: 2

Career Details:

WEDNESDAY	7 October	1996
Released	30 June	2004
Huddersfield Town	July	2004 Trial
Burton Albion	August	2004 Trial
Halifax Town	August	2004 Free
Northampton Town	27 August	2004 Free
Released	27 September	2004
Halifax Town	1 October	2004

CAPS (@ SWFC)
England U-20 (3)
v USA 05/04/99, v Cameroon 08/04/99, v Japan 11/04/99

England U-18 (5)
v Russia 27/10/97, v Russia 14/11/97, v Israel 12/02/98, v Cyprus 30/05/98, v France 01/06/98

High Green born utility player who spent almost eight years as a professional at Wednesday, the club he supported as a boy. From an early age the level-headed Haslam had been tipped to succeed in League football, representing England at all levels from under-15 to under-18, after having signed schoolboy forms at Hillsborough on his fourteenth birthday. He subsequently attended the short-lived National school at Lilleshall and within weeks of signing apprentice forms at Wednesday was elevated to professional status. His composure and leadership qualities ensured he was appointed captain of the youth side and in July 1997 the Owls blooded the youngster in senior football during their pre–season tour of the South-West.

At this point in Haslam's career he was predominantly a centre-half and it was in this position he excelled as Wednesday enjoyed a successful 1997-8 campaign in the Premier U-18 league. Within a year he was an automatic choice at reserve team level – playing all three games for England in the World Youth Championships in Nigeria - and his big break came in the Owls final home game of the season when he was asked to play in the unaccustomed position of right back. Since making his debut Haslam has played over 150 senior games for the club but only a handful have come in his natural position at the heart of the defence. His sheer versatility has ensured he has remained a first team squad regular although relations with supporters have occasionally became strained as Wednesday plummeted from the Premier League into Division Two. However he never let the criticism affect the likeable Haslam and after maturing into a defensive right back or holding midfielder he was a respected member – and only Sheffield born player - of Chris Turner's squad as they struggled to life in the lower divisions.

Unfortunately he failed to avoid the cull at the end of the 2003-4 season that saw thirteen out of contract players released as Wednesday started to re-build from scratch. He surprisingly struggled to find a club during last summer but eventually signed a contract with Conference club Halifax Town that included a 'get out' clause if a Football League club offered him terms. He would experience a traumatic spell at Halifax as after being harshly sent off on his debut he then scored an own goal on his second appearance and was probably quite happy when he was offered, and signed, a short term deal at League Two club Northampton Town, following a successful trial period.

HATFIELD, Samuel Ernest 'Ernie' 1927-30

Born: 16 January 1902 Basford
(5ft 10ins, 11st – 1929)
Only Appearance: 13 April 1929
v West Ham United
Division One Home
Total League
& Cup Appearances: 1 Goals: 0

Career Details:

Frickley Athletic		
Wombwell Athletic	July	1927
WEDNESDAY	3 November	1927 £100
Sheppey United	June	1929
Wolverhampton Wanderers	April	1930 £200
Southend United	May	1931
Dartford	August	1933
Upton Colliery	July	1934

Left back who spent three years at Wednesday after joining from nursery club Wombwell. Throughout his time at Hillsborough Hatfield had the unenviable task of being understudy to the incomparable Ernie Blenkinsop and made only a solitary first team appearance for Wednesday when "Blenki" was unavailable. The Owls made his only game memorable by thrashing West Ham United 6-0 at Hillsborough but seven days later it was back to reserve team football for Hatfield, where he stayed until moving to Wolves. During his time on the Owls books Hatfield was a regular in Central League football – winning a Championship medal in 1929 – and played over sixty times before the likes of George Beeson and Charles Wilson meant competition to gain just a second team place became too fierce.

He spent a season in the Black Country, appearing in four games for Wolves, before spending two seasons as a regular at Division Three (South) club Southend United where he totalled 57 appearances, scoring three times. Hatfield, who was a cabinet maker by trade, ended his playing career in non-league soccer at Southern League Dartford and then back in Yorkshire.

HAZEL, Desmond St Lloyd "Des" 1985-88

Born: 15 July 1967 Bradford
(5ft 10ins, 10st 4lbs – 1987)
Debut: 6 October 1986
v Stockport County
League Cup Away
Last Appearance: 30 April 1988
v Arsenal
Division One Home
Total League
& Cup Appearances: 6+2 Goals: 0

Career Details:

WEDNESDAY	15 July	1985
Grimsby Town	24 October	1986 2-month Loan
Rotherham United	13 July	1988 £45,000
Chesterfield	23 March	1995 £20,000
Guiseley A.F.C.	March	1997 Free
Joodalup	May	1997
Guiseley A.F.C.	October	1997

Tricky right-winger who came through the youth ranks to make his debut in the amazing 7-0 League Cup win against Stockport County at Maine Road. He failed to make another appearance during that season and it was not until Brian Marwood was sidelined early in the 1987-88 campaign that Hazel enjoyed his best spell at Wednesday – playing five consecutive games before dropping back into reserve team soccer. The ex-Bradford and West

Yorkshire boys player had previously enjoyed a successful nine-game loan spell at Grimsby Town and it was not until he dropped out of top-flight football to sign for neighbours Rotherham United that Hazel became a first team regular. At Millmoor, Hazel was a firm favourite with fans and in a seven-year stay – during which time he helped United to the Division Four title in 1989 - he played 291 times for The Millers, scoring 40 goals before making the short journey South to sign for John Duncan's Chesterfield.

The move to Saltergate proved a disappointment for Des as he found opportunities limited and after two seasons dropped out of league soccer to sign for Leeds based Northern Premier League team Guiseley. After moving into semi-professional football a variety of opportunities appeared for Hazel, starting with a spell as player-coach at Australian club Joodalup, before in March 1998 he received a shock call up for the national team of The Caribbean island of St. Kitts. The chance to play International football came through his parentage and Des took the chance with both hands, winning 16 caps for the paradise island between 1998 and 2000. During this period he also started to coach Bingley's Under-7 side as well as Bradford City's ladies team while he is currently employed as U-16 coach at Halifax Town's centre of excellence, while still occasionally appearing for Guiseley.

HEALD, Paul Andrew — 2002

Born: 20 September 1968 Wath-upon-Dearne
(6ft 2ins, 14st – 2002)
Debut:
22 January 2002 v Blackburn Rovers League Cup S/F Away
Last Appearance:
16 February 2002 v Watford Division One Home
Total League & Cup Appearances: 6 Goals: 0

Career Details:

Hoyland Common Falcons		
Barnsley		Trial
Sheffield United	30 June	1987
Leyton Orient	2 December	1988 £2,500
Coventry City	10 March	1992 Loan
Malmo FF	13 April	1992 Loan
Crystal Palace	13 August	1992 3-month loan
Leeds United	November	1992 Loan
Swindon Town	27 April	1994 Loan
Wimbledon	25 July	1995 £125,000
WEDNESDAY	22 January	2002 Loan
Loan return	4 April	2002

Goalkeeper who returned to his County of birth to help Wednesday out of a goalkeeping crisis in January 2002. On the previous Saturday the Owls had seen Kevin Pressman stretchered off in the game at Burnley and with his deputy Chris Stringer already on the treatment table were forced to send rookie goalkeeper Sean Roberts into the fray. Shorn of his two senior keepers, manager Terry Yorath secured the services of Heald just 24 hours before the semi-final at Ewood Park and the ex-Mexborough and South Yorkshire boys player remained in the side for the next six games until Pressman regained his fitness.

The tall keeper had started his playing career at youth side Hoyland Common Falcons – vying with future Nottingham Forest and Middlesborough stopper Mark Crossley for the gloves – and both Barnsley and Forest showed interest before Heald joined Sheffield United as a trainee in 1986. While at Bramall Lane he appeared regularly for Rotherham boys and also attended Wath comprehensive to study his "A" levels. After signing professional forms for The Blades he was unable to break into the first team and eventually left for Leyton Orient in 1988, starting a long association with the London side which would see Paul appear in 219 competitive games. He helped the "Os" to Division Two via the play offs in 1989 and was named player of the year in 1990 although he suffered ill luck with injury, breaking his back twice before undergoing major back surgery at The Princess Grace clinic, London in 1991. The procedure saw screws fitted into Heald's back which were removed in 1993 to be replaced with plates, nuts ands bolts – he returned to training in 1992 but earned the nickname of "Metal Mickey" from his team mates.

Heald – known for his superb reflex saves and safe handling – spent several spells out on loan to regain his fitness and confidence but in April 1993 suffered a fractured cheekbone which meant yet another operation. Thankfully he did eventually stay injury clear and his form for Orient persuaded Premier League Wimbledon to obtain his services as back up to Neil Sullivan. In five years as understudy to the Scottish International he appeared in 28 first team games but looked set to become undisputed No. 1 in 2000 after his rival transferred to Tottenham Hotspur. Unfortunately for Heald the Dons immediately went out and bought Kelvin Davis who was almost ever present for three seasons, leaving Paul to spend more time tending to the memorabilia business he owns in London. Sadly a serious knee injury forced his early retirement, at the age of 35, in February 2004.

HEARD Timothy Patrick "Pat" — 1983-84

Born: 17 March 1960 Hull
(5ft 9ins, 11st 5lbs – 1984)
Debut: 15 January 1983
v Middlesbrough
Division Two Away
Last Appearance: 25 September 1984
v Huddersfield Town
League Cup Home
Total League
& Cup Appearances: 30+3 Goals: 3

Career Details:

Everton	16 March	1978
Aston Villa	20 October	1979 £100,000 + J.Gidman
WEDNESDAY	13 January	1983 £50,000
Newcastle United	27 September	1984*
Middlesbrough	30 August	1985 £5,000
Hull City	27 March	1986 £5,000
Rotherham United	5 July	1988 Free
Cardiff City	20 August	1990 Free
Hull City		1992 N/C
Hall Road Rangers		1993
Brunei		1994

*Owls paid £40,000 + Heard in exchange for Ryan

The name Patrick Stewart usually brings to mind the Star Trek actor but there is another artist currently working the Northern club circuit of the same name as amazingly 1980s Wednesday midfielder Pat Heard appears under the same stage name as a hypnotist!! This somewhat bizarre change of career was actually achieved through PFA funding – Heard making his stage debut in 1997 – and helps supplement his income from his day job as manager of the pub-restaurant Friar Tuck's at Calow, Chesterfield.

His stage persona is a long way from a football career that started back in June 1976 when Heard signed apprentice forms for Everton, after having impressed for Hull and Humberside boys. He gained an England Youth cap while at Goodison Park but the midfielder only made a handful of first team starts for Everton – the majority of those out of position at left back – before moving to Villa Park in the late 1970s. However it was a case of out of the frying pan and into the fire for Heard as Villa were on the brink of the greatest back-to-back seasons in their long history which saw the League Championship come to Villa Park in 1981, followed by the European Cup a year later. With the likes of Gary Shaw, Dennis Mortimer and Trevor Morley already established in the Villa midfield it was an almost impossible task for Heard to break into the side and competition was so fierce that he failed to make a single appearance during the Championship season and although he did receive a European Cup medal it was solely as a non-playing substitute.

Thankfully for Heard, Owls boss Jack Charlton was a long–term admirer of his talents and after a twelve-month chase for his signature he brought the left-sided player to Hillsborough partway through the 1982-3 season, after 26 games for Villa. Big Jack put the newcomer out on the left wing and Heard responded by producing some terrific displays – showing himself to be a superb exponent of the inswinging corner kick – as the Owls reached the last four of the F.A.Cup and just missed out on promotion from

Division Two. That semi-final meeting with Brighton also gave Heard one of his more embarrassing moments as he – along with team mate David Mills – were famously left behind at the team hotel before the game when police ordered the Wednesday coach to set off early to avoid traffic congestion! Unfortunately just when he looked set to become an established first team regular Heard became one of several players who found themselves out in the cold when Howard Wilkinson replaced Charlton in the summer of 1983 – Heard appearing in just six league games during the Owls promotion season of 1983-4. It was then Jack Charlton – manager at Newcastle - who signed him for a second time and although he eventually lost his place in the Geordie line-up after 36 games it was to a youngster by the name of Paul Gascoigne!

A spell at home town club Hull City proved his most successful, appearance wise, as he played eighty games before winding up his league career as a non-contract player at Hull after a handful of games at Rotherham and Cardiff. Whilst playing for £100 a game during his final spell at Hull he was struck by the debilitating post viral syndrome ME and was unable to play for over 6 months. He returned to football with Northern Counties East League Hall Road Rangers in 1993 – later becoming player-coach – and then spent nine months playing for the Brunei national side in the Asian League. Unfortunately his marriage broke up following his spell in the Middle East and on returning to Hull he began working behind the bar at his brother's pub before gaining bar relief work. He eventually became mein host at "The Three Tuns" public house near Boothferry Park before moving to Chesterfield in 1998. Since February 2004 he has worked in Overseas Property management.

HECKINGBOTTOM, Paul 2004-

Born: 17 July 1977 Royston, Barnsley
(5ft 11ins, 12st - 2004)
Debut: 7 August 2004
v Colchester United
League One Home
Total League
& Cup Appearances: 41+1 Goals: 4

Career Details:

Manchester United		Trainee
Sunderland	14 July	1995
Scarborough	17 October	1997 Loan
Hartlepool United	25 September	1998 Loan
Bolton Wanderers		1999 Trial
Darlington	17 March	1999 Loan (to 09/05/99)
Darlington	1 August	1999 Free
Norwich City	3 July	2002 Free
Bradford City	3 July	2003 Free
WEDNESDAY	25 May	2004 Free

Former Barnsley and South Yorkshire boys full back who joined the Owls when his previous club, Bradford City, plunged into administration. The left back had been named 'player of the year' by City fans in 2003-04 but the well documented financial problems that hit the Valley Parade club meant all their contracted playing staff became available on free transfers. His signing proved an astute capture by Chris Turner as despite suffering indifferent form in his early weeks at Hillsborough Heckingbottom went on to become an automatic choice as the Owls won promotion via the play offs. His consistency and defensive solidity showed fans why he was originally a trainee at Old Trafford, playing in the same youth team as future Owl Terry Cooke. After being released by Manchester United he signed his first professional contract with Sunderland but in four seasons he failed to make the Black Cat's first team - all his league appearances coming during loan spells at a variety of lower league clubs.

It was at Darlington that Heckingbottom really became established in league soccer as he amassed 135 senior games, also showing his versatility by filling in when required at both centre half and in midfield. In his first season at the Feethams club Heckingbottom experienced the down side of play off football as at the Millennium Stadium he was on the wrong end of a Final defeat to Peterborough United. His form for Darlington eventually secured a move to Division One side Norwich City but he failed to displace left back Adam Drury and all of his seven league starts came in midfield prior to moving back to Yorkshire to sign for Bradford City. Heckingbottom - who used to attend Owls matches as a boy with his grandfather - was also voted 'player of the year' by his Bradford City teammates in his sole season at Valley Parade and will provide vital experience as the Owls look to consolidate in the Championship.

HEDLEY, Graeme 1978

Born: 1 March 1957
Easington, Co. Durham
(5ft 10ins, 10st 2lbs – 1978)
Debut: 25 February 1978
v Portsmouth
Division Three Home
Last Appearance: 25 March 1978
v Rotherham United
Division Three Away
Total League
& Cup Appearances: 6 Goals: 1

Career Details:

Middlesbrough	March	1975
WEDNESDAY	22 February	1978 Loan
Darlington	27 March	1979 Loan
York City	October	1981 Loan
Contract cancelled	March	1982
Hartlepool United	August	1984
Horden Colliery		
Whitby Town		1986

The playing career of midfielder Graeme Hedley was restricted solely to Northern clubs and in fact Sheffield was the farthest South the northeast born player roamed in a league career that lasted over a decade from joining Middlesborough as an apprentice in the early 1970s. In total he appeared in fifty games for Boro but despite possessing fine passing ability he was never a regular at Ayresome Park and was subsequently given a chance to resurrect his career by his ex-Boro boss Jack Charlton at Wednesday. He duly arrived on loan as the Owls struggled at the wrong end of the old Third Division but showed enough quality to suggest a permanent move was a mere formality. Unfortunately lady luck then played her hand and a broken ankle scuppered the chance of a full transfer, Hedley returning to Teeside to recuperate and re-acclimatise to reserve team soccer.

The ex-Durham boys player – instantly recognisable by his shock of blond hair - could actually have become a professional cricketer as in 1972 he played alongside David Gower and Mike Gatting for England schoolboys, scoring 75 from opening bat. He was later offered terms by Northants County Cricket Club but declined to sign trainee forms for Middlesborough, deciding instead to follow a football career. The break from Middlesborough came in March 1982 when with relegation from the top-flight looking an almost certainty Hedley was one of several players to have their contract's cancelled by mutual consent as the decks were cleared for life in the lower division. After a spell out of the game he netted nine times in 32 games for Hartlepool United in the 1984-5 season before dropping into non-league football. After leaving the full-time game Hedley started to work in the insurance business and is now branch manager for Pearl Assurance, based in Sunderland. He keeps fit however by appearing on a regular basis for the Middlesborough Over-35s five-a-side team whilst playing cricket for Bishop Auckland

HEESON, James 1884-85

Born: 1866 Soothill Nether, York
Only Appearance: 8 November 1884
v Long Eaton Rangers FA Cup Away
Total League
& Cup Appearances: 1 Goals: 0

Career Details:		
Mexborough		
WEDNESDAY	November	1884
Mexborough		

Believed to be a tin plateworker by trade, James Heeson spent his free time playing football in a time when professionalism was strictly frowned upon. He was actually a regular for Mexborough during the 1884-5 season but as was often the case in the early days of the F.A.Cup he was borrowed for the day by Wednesday to help fulfil their tie at Derbyshire club Long Eaton. Players could of course move around and play for whoever they desired in those amateur days and after helping Wednesday to a one-nil win he returned to Mexborough, never to appear for the Owls ever again.

HEMMINGFIELD, William Edmund 'Bill' 1898-99/1903-08

Born: 3rd Quarter 1875
Wortley, Sheffield
Died: 11 June 1953 Cleethorpes
Debut: 10 September 1898
v Nottingham Forest
Division One Home
Last Appearance: 25 April 1907
v Birmingham
Division One Away
Total League
& Cup Appearances: 47 Goals: 13

Career Details:		
Mexborough		
WEDNESDAY		1898
Grimsby Town	11 September	1899 £25
WEDNESDAY	May	1903 £75

Versatile player who started his Wednesday career as a centre-forward during the club's final season at Olive Grove, before moving to play at half back during a subsequent second spell. He had originally arrived from local football in the summer of 1898 and finished the season with highly creditable figures – considering it was his debut season in league soccer - of eight goals in twenty-two league games. However Wednesday suffered relegation for the first time in their short league history and Hemmingfield was not retained, moving instead to Second Division Grimsby Town. Incidentally his transfer fee was agreed at £75 but this was later reduced by the Football League committee, ensuring Wednesday made a big loss on his sale!

A second division championship medal came Bill's way in 1901 and he appeared in a total of 101 competitive games for the Mariners before Wednesday brought him back to Sheffield, in order to further strengthen a side that had just won the League Championship. Over the next five seasons Hemmingfield proved himself to be an early example of a utility player, appearing for Wednesday in six different positions, including half back and his old position of centre-forward. Unfortunately competition was fierce during one of The Owls' golden eras with the likes of Bob Ferrier and Tom Brittleton blocking his way to the first team at half back. Therefore the Sheffielder had to be content with reserve team football where his eight goals during the 1905-06 season helped the second team to the Midland League championship. He failed to make a first team appearance during his final season at Wednesday and retired from league football in the summer of 1908 – he later served as assistant trainer back at Grimsby Town during the Great War. His son was on Grimsby's books during the 1920s and Bill was coach at Town throughout the decade – he was the man who in 1927 found ex-Owl trainer Jerry Jackson dead in his Cleethorpes home. He also spent a spell at Wednesday as coach – between June 1928 and May 1929 – during which time the Owls won their third First Division Championship.

HENDERSON, William "Willie" 1972-74

Born: 24 January 1944
Baillston, Scotland
(5ft 4ins, 11st 2lbs – 1972)
Debut: 12 August 1972
v Fulham
Division Two Home
Last Appearance: 27 April 1974
v Bolton Wanderers
Division Two Home
Total League
& Cup Appearances: 50+6 Goals: 5

Career Details:		
Edinburgh Athletic		
Glasgow Rangers	24 January	1961
Durban City	2 May	1972 Free
WEDNESDAY	10 July	1972 £750
Miami Toros	29 April	1973 Loan
Contract cancelled	29 April	1974
Hong Kong Rangers	1 May	1974-1977
Carolina Hill	January	1977
Sliema Wanderers	March	1978 Trial
Airdrie		1978-79

There is now doubt that Scottish winger "Wee" Willie Henderson was one of the greatest characters to play for the Owls in their long history. When manager Derek Dooley brought him to Hillsborough in the summer of 1972 he was like a breath of fresh air to players and supporters alike with his infectious enthusiasm and tremendous wing play. He was a real throw back to wingers of pre war days and quickly became a huge favourite with fans as he bamboozled a variety of opposition defenders as Wednesday made a great start to the season. He was also notoriously short sighted and even wearing contact lenses during games had little effect – stories abound of Willie just getting his head down, running with the ball past defenders and only crossing when he saw the white of the touchline! Such was Henderson's impact in that debut season that almost thirty years later he is classed by many as a better maestro on the wing than the likes of Chris Waddle and Paolo Di Canio.

Great ball control allied with electric pace and outstanding dribbling ability helped the right-winger to win every domestic honour in Scotland during over a decade at Glasgow giants Rangers. Nicknamed the "Wee Blue Train" by Gers fans, Willie made his Rangers debut at the tender age of seventeen and became one of the youngest players to gain a full cap for Scotland when he represented his national side aged eighteen. He would appear in over 300 domestic and European games for Rangers, winning two league titles, five Scottish Cups and two Scottish League Cups as well as wearing the No. 7 shirt in the 1967 European Cup Winners Cup Final defeat to Bayern Munich. Henderson was undisputed first choice at Ibrox Park for ten years and it was not until the arrival of Scottish International winger Tommy McLean from Kilmarnock in 1971 that his place became under threat. The newcomer eventually took Willie's place part way through the 1971-2 campaign and it was not long before the diminutive wingman was on a plane to try his luck in South African football.

However his time in Durban was brief as Wednesday brought him to Hillsborough on a bargain free transfer – it later transpired he was not a free agent as was first thought so Wednesday paid a small transfer fee to cover various expenses. The 1972-3 season proved one of the better campaigns in a dismal decade and it was Henderson who helped put the smile back on the faces of Wednesday fans – he was without doubt Dooley's finest capture during his short tenure as manager. After spending his summer playing in North America injury would restrict Henderson's appearances in his second season at Wednesday as the Owls struggled to avoid the almost unthinkable drop into Division Three and after helping Wednesday to victory over Bolton that kept them up Willie announced he was leaving for a player-coach role in Hong Kong. He would remain in the Far East for almost four years and in 1975 actually played twice for the Hong Kong National side against Argentinean club Independiante and neighbours Red China. He left H.K.Rangers in 1977 – scoring against them on his debut for their great rivals Carolina Hill – before a mix up over his permit aborted a move to Maltese football in 1978.

After returning home to play just two league games for his hometown club Airdrie, Henderson then emigrated to Spain, living for eight years in Fuengirila, Nr Madrid, where he owned several public bars on the Costa Del Sol. He now lives back in Scotland's football capital, running his own bar as well as entertaining corporate clients on match days with Rangers. In 2003 Henderson featured in a TV programme about his career and stated that he enjoyed his time in Sheffield and found the people very friendly towards him.

HENDON, Ian Michael 2000-03

Born: 5 December 1971 Ilford
(6ft, 12st 10lbs – 2001)
Debut: 14 October 2000
v Portsmouth
Division One Away
Last Appearance: 16 November 2002
v Gillingham
Division One Away
Total League
& Cup Appearances: 53 Goals: 2

Career Details:

Tottenham Hotspur	20 December	1989
Portsmouth	16 January	1992 Loan
Leyton Orient	26 March	1992 Loan
Barnsley	17 March	1993 Loan
Leyton Orient	9 August	1993 £50,000
Birmingham City	23 March	1995 Loan
Notts County	24 February	1997 £50,000
Northampton Town	25 March	1999 £30,000
WEDNESDAY	12 October	2000 £40,000
Barnet	23 December	2002 Loan
Contract cancelled	23 January	2003
Peterborough United	24 January	2003 N/C
Barnet	14 May	2003 Free

Defensive utility player who looked set to enjoy a career in the top echelon of the English game after winning England Youth and U-21 caps while at Tottenham Hotspur. Unfortunately he could not earn a regular place in Premier League football and after only a handful of first team games for Spurs, in addition to several spells on loan in the lower divisions, he left for Leyton Orient in the summer of 1993. He found soccer further down the pyramid much more to his liking and over the years that followed Hendon carved out a reputation as one of the best defenders in the lower leagues – while at Northampton in 1999-00 he was named in the PFA divisional team for the third time in his career. Despite only spending eighteen months at The Cobblers the Londoner became a firm favourite with Town fans who were surprised when he was taken to Hillsborough by Paul Jewell, early in the 2000-1 campaign.

The tall and imposing Hendon was seen by Jewell as a ready made solution to a right back problem that had seen a variety of players fill the position, including loan player Simon Grayson. He duly appeared in thirty-three games for the Owls in that debut season – although at times he seemed to lack consistency in the higher grade - but persistent injury problems in the season that followed meant Hendon played only a handful of games. The emergence of Derek Geary then saw Hendon pushed out of the right-back slot – he later re-claimed the position when the young Irishman was switched to left back – but in December 2002 his Owls career hit the rocks when he was one of four players arrested after an incident at the club's Xmas party in Leeds. He was subsequently suspended by Wednesday on 12th December but despite Hendon being released without charge was sent out on loan to Peter Shreeves' Conference side Barnet to allow the situation to cool off. However in late January 2003 the two parties agreed to cancel his contract at Hillsborough – Hendon joining Division Two strugglers Peterborough United on a non-contact basis twenty-four hours later. After scoring once in seven games for Posh he moved back to Barnet on a permanent basis in May 2003 and in March 2004 was appointed joint caretaker manager – along with ex-Owl Danny Maddix – when Bees boss Martin Allen left for Brentford. He would later captain the North London club to the Conference title in 2005, securing a return to the Football League four years after suffering relegation.

HENRY, Gerald Robert 'Gerry' 1950-51

Born: 5 October 1920 Hemsworth
(5ft 8½ins, 11st 12lbs – 1950)
Died: 1 September 1979 Dewsbury
Debut: 18 February 1950
v Brentford
Division Two Home
Last Appearance: 22 September 1951
v Rotherham United
Division Two Home
Total League
& Cup Appearances: 40 Goals: 7

Career Details:

Outwood Stromcocks		
Leeds United	October	1937
Halifax Town	May	1940 Guest
Doncaster Rovers		1940-41 Guest
Huddersfield Town	April	1941 Guest
Manchester City	April	1941 Guest
Doncaster Rovers	March	1943 Guest
Bradford Park Avenue	November	1947
WEDNESDAY	17 February	1950 £8,000
Halifax Town	30 November	1951 £1,000

*Also guested for Leeds United, Barnsley, Bradford City, Bradford Park Avenue & Liverpool in WW2

The departure of Eddie Quigley in December 1949 and retirement of Alf Rogers through injury meant the Owls lost the services of two inside-right players inside a matter of weeks. To fill the void, Owls secretary-manager Eric Taylor brought Gerry Henry from Park Avenue and he made his debut 24 hours later as Wednesday shared six goals with Brentford at Hillsborough. The ex-Yorkshire boys player – he appeared in the same County side as Hugh Swift – had started his league career at Leeds United where during wartime soccer he netted 94 goals in 186 games for the West Yorkshire club. He continued to score regularly during a two-year stay at Park Avenue and after joining the Owls he helped them to promotion from Division Two in 1950.

However the arrival of the two Johns – Jordan and Sewell – meant Henry was in and out of the First Division side during 1950-1 and as his opportunities diminished he asked for a transfer in November 1951, leaving for Halifax Town a few days later. His first appearance for Town had occurred as a guest back in May 1940 – a 6-1 loss at Newcastle United – but his second game proved happier as on his league debut he helped The Shayman to beat Darlington 4-1. Two days later he was officially appointed player-coach and after manager Billy Wootton resigned in early February 1952 Henry was appointed caretaker boss. Two wins out of the next three games convinced the Halifax board he was the man for the job and after being officially appointed manager on 27 February he guided Town away from the re-election zone in Division Three (North). He dropped the player prefix from his managerial title during the 1952-3 campaign and was at the helm when Town defied all the odds to reach the Fifth Round of the F.A.Cup for only the second time in their history – bowing out at home to Spurs in front of a record Shay crowd of 36,885. Two seasons of struggle followed before in October 1954 – with his side propping up the division – Henry resigned his position. It is believed he then dropped out of the game completely and lived out his life in Gomersall, a district of Leeds.

HENSHALL, Horace Vincent 1922-23

Born: 14 June 1889 Hednesford, Staffs.
(5ft 9ins, 11st 7lbs – 1922)
Died: 7 December 1951 Nottingham
Debut: 9 December 1922
v Leicester City
Division Two Home
Last Appearance: 17 March 1923
v South Shields
Division Two Home
Total League
& Cup Appearances: 17 Goals: 1

Career Details:

Hednesford Victoria		amateur
Bridgetown Amateurs		
Aston Villa	May	1906
Notts County	November	1912
Barnsley		WW1 Guest
WEDNESDAY	12 June	1922
Chesterfield	June	1923

Vastly experienced left-winger who was signed by Bob Brown in the summer of 1922, primarily as player-coach to the Owls reserve side. It was a position he filled with great distinction – scoring three times as Wednesday won the Midland League Championship – but it proved only a part-time role as mid way through the season the Owls senior team found themselves short of left sided players and it was the services of Henshall that Brown called upon. He remained in the side from early December until early March and the 33 year-old – who boasted a terrific right foot shot - performed admirably before Joe Harron was drafted in from York City to fill the left sided berth.

His professional playing career had started back in 1906 when he signed professional forms for Aston Villa just before his 17th birthday. Eleven goals in fifty games was his record at Villa Park before Henshall left for Notts County in 1912- a year earlier he had represented the Football League against the Scottish League in Glasgow. He enjoyed a successful time at The Meadow Lane club, scored 29 times in 180 games – also appearing in 63 wartime games despite serving in the R.N.A.S during the hostilities – and won a Division Two Championship medal in 1914. After just a solitary season at Wednesday, Henshall wrapped up his league career at Chesterfield before being appointed secretary-manager at Lincoln City in May 1924. He presided over three mid table seasons while in charge at Sincil Bank but achieved greater success back at Notts County, leading the oldest league side to the Division Three (South) title in 1931. After seven years in charge he handed the reins to Charlie Jones in May 1934 and would serve County solely as secretary for a further ten months before leaving in 1935 to take over as landlord of the Navigation Inn near the ground.

HENSON, Philip Michael 1975-77

Born: 30 March 1953 Manchester
(5ft 10½ins, 10st 4lbs – 1975)
Debut: 8 February 1975
v Blackpool
Division Two Home
Last Appearance: 14 May 1977
v Oxford United
Division Three Home
Total League
& Cup Appearances: 72+8 Goals: 9

Career Details:

Brookdale Youth Club		
Manchester City	July	1970
Swansea City	19 July	1972 Loan
Loan return	17 October	1972
WEDNESDAY	5 February	1975 £44,000
Sparta Rotterdam	14 July	1977 £30,000
Stockport County	September	1978
Rotherham United	22 February	1980

Cool and confident attacking midfielder who was a welcome addition to Wednesday's struggling side in the mid-1970s. He had started his career at home town club Manchester City, joining from school in May 1969, but after turning professional appeared in only seventeen league games for City before being signed by Owls boss Steve Burtenshaw. He joined a Wednesday side already cut adrift at the bottom of the old Second Division and could do little to stop the Owls dropping into the third tier of the English game for the first time in their history. Over the next two seasons Henson was a consistent performer as Wednesday slowly started to steady the ship and it was this form that brought interest from abroad with Dutch side Sparta taking him to the lowlands on a one-year contract in the summer of 1977.

After a season in Holland he returned to the UK, joining Stockport County and was later Ian Porterfield's first signing as Rotherham United manager. He subsequently helped The Millers to the Division Three Championship in 1981 and appeared in a total of 92 league games, scoring seven times, before being appointed youth coach at Sheffield United in July 1986 – he had previously filled the role of player-coach and reserve team manager at Millmoor. After two years at Bramall Lane, Henson returned to The Millers in July 1988 to become assistant manager to Billy McEwan and was appointed boss in January 1991. In his first full season at the helm United won promotion from Division Four in 1992 and after keeping United in the higher grade he moved upstairs, being appointed chief executive in September 1994 when Archie Gemmell and John McGovern were hired as a joint management team. He is still employed in the role today as The Millers cope with life after Ronnie Moore.

HERBERT, David Ronald "Dave/Herbie" 1974-76

Born: 23 January 1956 Sheffield
(5ft 7ins, 10st 7lbs – 1974)
Died: 29 April 2002 Sheffield
Debut: 8 March 1975
v West Bromwich Albion
Division Two Away
Last Appearance: 19 April 1976
v Mansfield Town
Division Three Away
Total League
& Cup Appearances: 13+6 Goals: 4

Career Details:

Hackenthorpe Throstles		1969
WEDNESDAY	23 January	1974
Released	30 June	1976
Chesterfield	21 July	1976 2 month trial
Buxton		1976
Norton Woodseats		1981-87
Rawlinson Youth Club		1983-87 Sun.

Diminutive attacker who joined the club as an apprentice in July 1971, after being spotted in local Sunday football by Wednesday youth supremo George McCabe. In one remarkable season he netted 101 goals in just 18 games for Hackenthorpe Throstles and continued to score freely in the Wednesday youth side - netting 21 times during the 1973-4 campaign. The ex-Sheffield boys forward eventually made his senior debut for Wednesday at West Bromwich Albion in March 1975 but experienced a disappointing afternoon as The Baggies cruised to a 4-0 victory. He was perhaps unlucky to break onto the first team scene during one of the worst seasons in the Owls history and during his time at Wednesday it must have been difficult for the youngster to progress as The Owls seemingly lurched from one crisis to another. After figuring in fourteen Division Three games for Wednesday during the nerve-racking 1975-6 season he was one of the unlucky players who were released en masse at the end of the season after the drop into the basement division had just been averted.

An unsuccessful trial period at Chesterfield followed before Herbert dropped out of the professional game to join Northern Premier League Buxton. It started a five-year association with the Derbyshire club that saw Herbert become the club's all-time record goal scorer – netting 102 goals – before joining Dronfield based side Norton Woodseats in 1981. He later won a league championship medal under the management of Derek Dooley at Sunday club Rowlinson before osteo-arthritis in his knees led to surgery and the end of his playing days. Away from football he had been employed by Crown paints since 1977 and from 1994 to

2000 was manager-coach to the Dronfield AFC boys team – winning the league and cup double in 1999. Along with his son Matthew he also held season tickets at Hillsborough and it was tragic when his life was cruelly cut short at the age of just 46 after he lost a brave six-month battle against cancer, leaving a widow and two children.

HIBBERT, Henry Crookes 1907-08

Born: 1887 Dore, Sheffield (5ft 11ins, 12st)
Debut: 4 April 1908
v Blackburn Rovers Division One Home
Last Appearance: 18 April 1908
v Birmingham Division One Home
Total League & Cup Appearances: 2 Goals: 0
Career Details:

Hathersage		
WEDNESDAY		1907
Stockport County		1908
Lincoln City	July	1909
Rotherham County		1910
Sheffield United	April	1913
Chesterfield Town		1916

A player of some repute in the Sheffield Amateur League who spent just a solitary season at Wednesday, helping the reserve team to win the Midland League Championship in 1908. He was given two first team starts at centre half-back – a position the Owls had struggled to fill throughout the season due to the impending retirement of stalwart Tommy Crawshaw – and he later appeared in a single league game for Stockport County in the same position. His only goal in league soccer came during a four game spell at Lincoln City while he later joined The Blades, failing to make a senior appearance.

HICKTON, John 1961-66

Born: 24 September 1944
Brimimgton, nr Chesterfield
(5ft 11ins, 11st 6lbs – 1964)
Debut: 7 March 1964
v Aston Villa
Division One Away
Last Appearance: 9 May 1966
v Burnley
Division One Home
Total League
& Cup Appearances: 55+1 Goals: 20
Career Details:

WEDNESDAY	November	1961
Middlesbrough	23 September	1966 £20,000
Hull City	19 January	1977 Loan
Fort Lauderdale	May	1978
Staveley Works		1981

There are several players in the Owls history that have left the club to achieve greater success elsewhere. Of all those John Hickton is perhaps the one player that Wednesday in hindsight would not have released as after being sold to Middlesborough he achieved great success, becoming the Teeside clubs fourth all-time top goal scorer with a staggering haul of 185 goals in over 450 games – all this while his old club slid out of the top-flight and towards the Third Division.

The ex-Chesterfield and Derbyshire boys player was the Owls last ever groundstaff boy when he joined in 1959 – the following year's intake were classified as apprentices – and initially was utilised as either a full back or centre half during his early days at Wednesday. However after Youth team manager Derek Dooley converted Hickton to centre forward he started to score frequently and his career took a completely different path – ironically the ex-England boys trialist actually considered his best position to be at full back. In the autumn of 1961 he made headlines when grabbing nine goals against Stamford in an F.A.Youth Cup tie – also scoring five against Rotherham soon after – but it was actually at right back that he made his league bow later in that season. However this proved only a brief taste of league action and it was not until the Owls were struggling to score at first team level, early in the following season, that Alan Brown decided to try the youngster in the No.9 shirt. He duly netted ten times in two consecutive seasons, the highlight being a hat trick against Arsenal in December 1965, but after failing to convince Brown that he deserved a regular first team place subsequently left for Middlesborough in 1966.

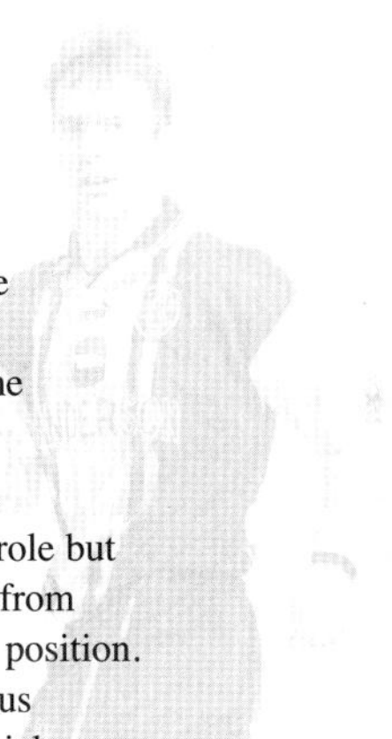

His career in the Northeast actually started in a defensive role but fifteen goals from centre forward as Boro won promotion from Division Three in 1967 left no doubt about Hickton's best position. Over the next six seasons the whole-hearted and courageous forward – he also possessed a powerful shot and terrific ariel ability - finished Middlesborough's top scorer and eventually helped Boro to the First Division in 1974 under future Wednesday boss Jack Charlton. By this time Hickton had been converted into a battering-ram style target man and even returned to a utility role in his latter years until trying his luck in NASL football in 1978. Unfortunately he suffered a broken leg in his second game there – after scoring on his debut – and this proved to be his final game as a professional.

On his return to England he trained with Hartlepool United – thanks to old team mate Willie Maddren who was coach at the time – but his leg could not stand up to the rigours of full-time soccer so he decided to retire. During this period he ran an off licence and newsagents shop in Redcar for eighteen months and although he is credited with appearing for Whitby Town, Hickton actually has no recollection of this occurring! In the early 1980s John moved back to his native Chesterfield to start work for an insurance company, until retiring in 2004. Incidentally after moving back to Derbyshire he played a handful of games alongside his brothers Roy and Dave at Staveley Works.

HILL, Brian 1955-67

Born: 6 October 1937 Sheffield
(5ft 8½ins, 11st 8½lbs – 1957)
Died: 5 April 1968 Sheffield
Debut: 2 March 1957
v Blackpool
Division One Away
Last Appearance: 4 May 1966
v Stoke City
Division One Away
Total League
& Cup Appearances: 121+1 Goals: 1
Career Details:

WEDNESDAY	9 April	1955
Bruges	June	1967 Free

Right back who joined Wednesday as an amateur in 1953 – he worked as a brick layer for Owls director James Longden at the time - before signing as a part-time professional two years later, not becoming a full-time player until the late 1950s. For the majority of his time at Wednesday, Hill had to be content with Central League football and in fact from making his debut in 1957 until 1963 he started only 28 games for the first team. It was the exemplary form of Peter Johnson that kept Hill in the shadows but the compactly built defender bided his time and was rewarded when keeping his rival out of the side for two seasons in the mid-1960s. Incidentally his brother Billy played for York City while his cousin Fred played for several clubs and was capped by England.

However the emergence of youngster Wilf Smith saw Hill lose his place at the beginning of the club's run to Wembley in 1966 and after another season of second team football the strong tackling player was allowed to leave by Wednesday. He was wanted by ex-Owl Tom McAnearney at Aldershot but decided instead to fly to Belgium to appear in a trial game for Bruges against Anderlecht. He subsequently signed a one-year deal and on returning home stayed with his parents back in Sheffield. It was here where tragedy struck as in April 1968 when at the tender age of just 30 he was found dead in his bedroom – it later transpired the cause was an enlarged heart.

HILL, Harold 1924-29

Born: 24 September 1899 Blackwell, Derbyshire
(5ft 5 ins, 9st, 7lbs -1926)
Died: 14 February 1969 Blackwell
Debut: 18 October 1924 v Coventry City Division Two Home
Last Appearance: 1 September 1928 v Blackburn Rovers Division One Away
Total League & Cup Appearances: 99 Goals: 40

Career Details:

Blackwell		
South Normanton		1915
New Hucknall Colliery		1919
Notts County	September	1919
WEDNESDAY	18 October	1924 £1700
Scarborough	28 June	1929
Chesterfield	May	1932
Mansfield Town	August	1933
Sutton Town		1934
Bolsover Colliery		1936

When manager Bob Brown needed an inside forward to replace broken leg victim Sam Taylor he raided Notts County for the services of diminutive attacker Harold Hill. The Owls had to pay a club record fee for County but it proved to be money well spent as Hill became an integral part of a Wednesday side that surged out of Division Two in 1926. Nicknamed the "Tom Thumb" of Hillsborough, Hill was a real wizard of the forward line who possessed cunning, great footwork and, considering his height, quite remarkable heading ability. He had the ability to play anywhere in the forward line and proved more than a match for many an opposition defender as Brown's patient team building finally came to fruition.

The native of Blackwell began his working life down the pit, playing for the village side in friendly games, before joining Clay Cross League side South Normanton at the age of sixteen. At the outbreak of war the league was disbanded – Harold still receiving a Championship medal – but the conflict in Europe then put a temporary halt to his career with Harold working as a miner until joining the machine gun corps in 1918. He played briefly in Army football during this period but upon demobilisation joined Central Alliance League club New Hucknall Colliery. After only four games for the Colliery side he was snapped up by Notts County and such was his impact at The Meadow Lane club that he finished top scorer in his debut season, netting 12 goals in thirty-three league appearances. Hill did not mind where he played as long as he was in the side and he allied superb ball control with a whole-hearted attitude to the game that endeared him to management and fans alike. It was these qualities that made him a hugely popular player during his time in Nottingham – he was so revered that in February 1925 he was presented with a gold "Albert medal" in appreciation of his loyal service – and after helping County to the Second Division Championship in 1923 he totalled 56 goals in 170 games before dropping down a division to sign for The Owls.

His capture was a real coup for Wednesday and in his second season Hill formed a great left wing partnership with Arthur Prince that was instrumental in taking Wednesday to the title. He subsequently showed his versatility over the two seasons that followed by switching between both inside-forward positions and it was not until the arrival of Jimmy Seed and Jack Allen that Harold moved to Midland League Scarborough in the summer of 1928. In his second season Scarborough won the Championship before Harold spent a short spell as player-coach at Chesterfield and was then appointed player/youth coach at Mansfield Town. Hill – whose son Arthur played for Chesterfield – returned to his original job as a miner when retiring from football, working until his retirement at B Winning colliery.

HILL, Haydn Henry Clifford 1934-36

Born: 4 July 1913 Cresswell, Derbyshire
(6ft 1ins, 11st 10lbs – 1935)
Died: 3 November 1992 Weymouth
Debut: 6 April 1935 v Tottenham Hotspur Division One Home
Last Appearance: 26 December 1935 v Everton Division One Away
Total League & Cup Appearances: 4 Goals: 0

Career Details:

Sutton Town		
Sheffield University		
Clowne Welfare		
Yorkshire Amateurs		
Worksop Town		
Chesterfield	March	1932
Sheffield United	April	1933
WEDNESDAY	December	1934
Clowne Welfare	January	1935
The Corinthians	November	1935
Yorkshire City	November	1935
Bournemouth and Boscombe	July	1936
Weymouth		1937

CAPS (@SWFC)
England Amateur (5) v Scotland, Wales, Ireland 1935, v Scotland, Ireland 1936

Goalkeeper Haydn Hill was a rare example of a player who remained amateur throughout his career. It was while studying for a Maths degree at Sheffield University that Hill helped the varsity football team to the Championship in 1933 and also played a handful of reserve team games for Chesterfield. It was while playing reserve team soccer for the Spireites that he was spotted by Blades boss Teddy Davison who signed the scholar on amateur forms – Hill playing both Northern and Yorkshire League football for United. During the 1934-5 season Hill was picked to play for the famous Corinthians and in addition to winning three amateur caps for England also signed for Wednesday - because he was on United's books the Owls had to gain their consent before he could appear for Wednesday. He subsequently started to train with the Owls and made his first team debut in the friendly versus FC Austria at Hillsborough in December 1934 – manager Billy Walker asked Hill if he was going to the game and when he said yes the Owls boss said "bring your boots as you are playing"!

Over the next two seasons Hill acted as back up to first choice keeper Jack Brown and made four top-flight appearances for Wednesday in that time – becoming the first amateur player since William Harvey in the early 1920s to appear in league football for the club. In July 1936 the F.A. University and England amateur international appeared for Great Britain in the 1936 Olympic games in Berlin and on his return became Maths master at Weymouth grammer school, while also signing amateur forms for Bournemouth.

HILLER, Carl 1883-88

Born: 3rd Quarter 1866 Sheffield
Debut: 1 December 1883 v Staveley F.A.Cup Away
Last Appearance: 30 January 1888 v Preston North End F.A.Cup Home
Total League & Cup Appearances: 5 Goals: 1

Career Details:

Heeley	1884-89
WEDNESDAY	1883-88

Strictly amateur "gentleman player" from the 1880s who came from an affluent family. Along with his brother Walpole he attended Harrogate Boarding school and while still a teenager made his debut for the Owls in a 3-1 Cup defeat at Staveley. Throughout the decade he was a regular for Heeley, occasionally stepping into the Owls F.A.Cup side when required. His solitary goal came in the one-nil win at Crusaders in December 1887.

HILLER, Walpole 1885-90

Born: 3rd Quarter 1867 Sheffield
Died: May 1928
Only Appearance: 3 January 1885
v Nottingham Forest F.A.Cup Home
Total League & Cup Appearances: 1* Goals: 0
***Also appeared in 3 Football Alliance League games**

Career Details:

Heeley	1884-88
WEDNESDAY	1885

Like his brother, Walpole Hiller was an educated individual who played sport purely as a pastime. He was in fact one of Sheffield's finest all-round sportsmen as he not only excelled at football but was also a fine cricketer and keen long distance swimmer. After ending his football career in the early 1890s he became an eminent cyclist of Sharrow Cycling Club and later served them as honorary secretary. Away from his sporting activities he worked as a solicitor in Sheffield.

HINCH, James Andrew 'Jim' 1977

Born: 8 November 1947 Sheffield
(6ft 3ins, 12st 9lbs – 1976)
Only Appearance: 10 December 1977
v Cambridge United
Division Three Away
Total League
& Cup Appearances: 0+1 Goals: 0

Career Details:

Club 62		1962
Shirebrook MW		1964
Wrexham		1965 Trial
Bradford Park Avenue		1967 Trial
Bangor City		1968
Bethesda		1968
Portmadoc		1969
Tranmere Rovers	March	1970
Plymouth Argyle	February	1971 Exchange for F.Molyneux
Hereford United	October	1973 £20,000
York City	July	1974 £11,000
Southport	March	1975 Loan
Los Angeles Skyhawks		1976 Loan
York City		1976
Los Angeles Skyhawks	May	1977 Loan
WEDNESDAY	18 October	1977 Trial
Barnsley	14 December	1977
Released	March	1978
California Surf		1979 & 1981
Frecheville Community Association		

Forward Jim Hinch could hardly be accused of being a home bird as in a playing career that spanned almost twenty years he appeared for an astonishing array of different teams. He would spend the first five years of his working life as an apprentice pattern maker in the dyeing trade while playing at halfback in non-league soccer – gaining his first honour in 1968 when winning the Welsh League with Porthmadoc. At that time he was only 5ft 5ins tall but amazingly he continued to grow until the age of 25, shooting up to well over six foot in height before arriving at Wednesday on trial in 1977. His career at Wednesday was one of the shortest on record as his only taste of first team football came in the final 29 minutes of a Third Division fixture at The Abbey Stadium, Cambridge.

His final tally in English league football was a quite respectable 63 goals in 261 games while his career came to a close in the USA where Hinch emigrated to in the early 1980s – in the latter part of the 1970s he spent several summers in the US, mainly playing ASL football for San Fernando Valley club LA Skyhawks – a side based just North of Los Angeles on the West Coast of America. He was league top scorer in the 1976 season and voted M.V.P. (most valuable player) while after a second spell at Skyhawks he moved onto California Surf who competed in the top pro league in the US – the North American Soccer League (NASL). After a knee injury sustained while at Surf brought his playing career to a premature end, Hinch gained a USSF 'A' coaching licence – the highest coaching qualification in the US – and was subsequently appointed assistant coach at California Surf. He later became assistant coach at San Diego Sockers and also coached at the California High School until retiring from football in 1983 – in 1977 he also ran coaching courses for schoolboys along with ex-Wednesday player Paul Taylor before launching his own soccer camps, which ran from 1978 to 1982.

After leaving football he launched a new career as a mortgage broker before forming his own company – Chelsea Mortgage – in 1986. His business still thrives today, supplying loans for US homebuyers and house builders.

HINCHCLIFFE, Alan Arthur 1953-59

Born: 8 December 1936
Staveley, Chesterfield
(5ft 10ins, 10st 7lbs – 1955)
Debut: 3 November 1956
v Bolton Wanderers
Division One Home
Last Appearance: 10 November 1956
v Leeds United
Division One Away
Total League
& Cup Appearances: 2 Goals: 0

Career Details:

Bakestone Moor		
WEDNESDAY	26 December	1953 £10
Chesterfield	July	1959
Alfreton Town		1960
Cresswell Colliery		
Matlock Town		
Cresswell Colliery		

Goalkeeper who joined the Owls as an amateur in May 1953, signing part-time professional forms just a week later. He had been spotted playing in Derbyshire amateur football – the Owls later donating the princely sum of £10 to his old club – and after breaking into the Central League side in December 1953 acted as No.3 to Les Williams and Dave McIntosh for several years in the 1950s. His first competitive first team game came in a County Cup tie at home to Rotherham United in October 1956 and on the following Saturday Hinchcliffe was called into first team action when both his rivals were ruled out through injury. He also started the next game but the return to fitness of McIntosh and then subsequent arrival of future England International Ron Springett pushed him even further down the pecking order, eventually leading to a transfer to hometown club Chesterfield.

After failing to make a first team appearance for the Spireites he reverted back to his previous part-time status and signed for Central Alliance League Alfreton Town. After failing to appear on a regular basis for the North Street club he dropped further down the football Pyramid, joining Yorkshire League Cresswell where after two spells he hung up his gloves to concentrate on a career in engineering. He eventually became a project engineer before retiring in 2000.

HINCHCLIFFE, Alfred G. 1920

Born: 26 August 1896 Wadsley Bridge, Sheffield
Only Appearance: 17 January 1920
v Everton
Division One Home
Total League
& Cup Appearances: 1 Goals: 0

Career Details:

Craven Sports	
WEDNESDAY	1920 Trial

Born a stone throws from the ground, goalkeeper Alf Hinchcliffe initially built his reputation while playing for Sheffield boys although it was somewhat critically said that he was "on the slow side but very sure". His only first team game for Wednesday came during the disastrous 1919-20 season when The Owls used a record number of players and suffered relegation from the top-flight. He appeared to have played his solitary game for the Owls on a purely trial basis – he did not appear in any other competitive game in a Wednesday shirt - before dropping back into local amateur football. Incidentally a goalkeeper called Arthur Hinchcliffe, who later played for Rochdale, is incorrectly credited as being the individual who played for the Owls. However the most amazing fact about goalie Hinchcliffe was that his only game for Wednesday came at left half back!

HINCHCLIFFE, Andrew "Andy" 1998-2002

Born: 5 February 1969 Manchester
(5ft 10ins, 12st 10lbs – 1998)
Debut: 31 January 1998
v Wimbledon
Premier League Home
Last Appearance: 12 January 2002
v Crewe Alexandra
Division One Home
Total League
& Cup Appearances: 96+1 Goals: 7

Career Details:

Manchester City	13 February	1986
Everton	17 July	1990 £800,000
WEDNESDAY	30 January	1998 £2,750,000
Retired	30 June	2002

CAPS (@SWFC)
England Full (2) v Switzerland 25/03/98, v Saudi Arabia 23/05/98

Sadly the Wednesday career of left back Andy Hinchcliffe will be most remembered for the final two years of his contract when horrendous injury problems saw the England International on the treatment table, appearing in only two games in his final season at Hillsborough. It was a far cry from Hinchcliffe's first two seasons at Wednesday when the classy defender looked to have finally solved the problem position of left back which had troubled The Owls since the departure of Nigel Worthington in the mid-1990s. A month before joining Wednesday, Hinchcliffe had looked set to sign for Tottenham Hotspur but after a fee had been agreed the deal dramatically collapsed due to a possible Achilles tendon injury. However Owls boss Ron Atkinson was confident in his fitness and duly paid Everton a large fee to bring Hinchcliffe to Hillsborough. He immediately added stability and sheer quality to the Owls rearguard, showing that he possessed a deadly left foot when scoring several spectacular goals from free kicks.

Despite winning the F.A.Youth Cup in 1986 with his first club Manchester City – in addition to gaining England Youth and U-21 honours – it wasn't until he moved to Goodison Park that Andy's career started to blossom. Under the stewardship of Howard Kendall he developed into one of England's finest left-sided players and was capped five times by his country, in the left wingback role that he occupied for the majority of his 227 games at Everton. He was part of the famous Everton "dogs of war" side that lifted the F.A.Cup in 1995 but after breaking into Glen Hoddle's England side early in the 1996-7 season he had the misfortune to sustain cruciate knee ligament damage in the home game with Leeds in December 1996. After returning to fitness he regained both his club and International place but a public disagreement with Kendall eventually led to his departure from Merseyside – a move mourned by Blues supporters, as Hinchcliffe had become a prolific creator of goals. Ironically Kendall had been boss at Manchester City when he sold Hinchcliffe to Everton in 1990 – in a deal that saw Neil Pointon move to Maine Road – and then subsequently bought and sold the player while in charge of Everton!

During his early days at Wednesday he became the first Owls player for five years to be capped at full level for England – he is also currently the last Wednesday player to earn the honour – but was playing in a side that was on the slide and after suffering relegation with The Owls in 2000 he was only a bit player in Division One as persistent knee problems made him Hillsborough's forgotten man. He did make several comebacks, lasting only seventeen minutes in what proved to be his final game for the club, before leaving Wednesday at the end of his 4 year contract, having prematurely retired at the age of 33 in March 2002.

HIRST, David Eric 1986-97

Born: 7 December 1967 Cudworth, Barnsley
(5ft 11ins, 13st 10lbs – 1997)
Debut: 23 August 1986
v Charlton Athletic
Division One Away
Last Appearance: 4 October 1997
v Everton
Premier League Home
Total League
& Cup Appearances: 309+49 Goals: 128

Career Details:

Barnsley	8 November	1985
WEDNESDAY	11 August	1986 £300,000
Southampton	17 October	1997 £2,000,000
Retired	25 January	2000
Brunsmeer Athletic	February	2000 (sun.)

CAPS (@SWFC)
England Full (3)
v Australia 01/06/91, v New Zealand 03/06/91, v France 19/02/92
England "B" (3)
v Switzerland 20/05/91, Spain 18/12/91, v Czechoslovakia 24/03/92
England U-21 (7)
v USSR 07/06/88, v France 12/06/88, v Denmark 13/09/88,
v Bulgaria 05/06/89, v Senegal 07/06/89, v Eire 09/06/89,
USA 11/06/89

There is no doubt that David Hirst was one of the greatest and most popular players to ever wear the famous blue and white shirt. At the height of his game Hirst was a truly outstanding attacker who if not for injury would surely have beaten John Fantham's post war goals record for the club. His tally of 128 for Wednesday placed "Hirsty" sixth in Wednesday's all time list while his pace, strength, deadly left foot and totally committed displays made him one of England's most feared strikers – such was his form that in May 1992 Wednesday rejected a British transfer record £4m offer from Manchester United for his services.

It's a little known fact that as a schoolboy Hirst actually had a two days trial with Wednesday where after his first morning's training he was asked his name by a club official and was told "we didn't think you had turned up". David's father, Eric, said that if they don't know you are here you might as well go home! Thankfully this experience did not influence his decision when in 1986 Owls boss Howard Wilkinson offered Hirst the chance to move into top-flight football after winning England Youth honours and appearing in just 29 games for his boyhood club Barnsley. The Owls boss had certainly recognised his huge potential and brokered a deal that saw Wednesday pay additional sums after thirty games and if Hirst was capped by England. The raw youngster made his debut for the club in a youth friendly at Humberside non-league outfit North Ferriby United in August 1986 but made a truly dramatic Hillsborough entrance just a few days later in the game with Everton. The match marked the opening of Wednesday's newly roofed Kop and that roof was almost lifted off when the teenager came off the subs bench to score with his first touch in front of the packed home end!

In his first three seasons at Wednesday Hirst was in and out of the side but after the arrival of Ron Atkinson his career made a great leap forward as Big Ron installed "Hirsty" as first choice striker. He rewarded his new boss by netting sixteen times during the 1989-90 season – winning the club's player of the year award – although he could not stop Wednesday from dropping out of the top-flight. Thankfully Wednesday spent only one glorious season in the lower tier and after being tied to a new three-year deal in July 1990 Hirst would enjoy the most prolific season in his career. Not only did he net 32 times – including a four-goal haul in the home game with Hull City – but he also won the League Cup at Wembley and was capped at full level for England, scoring in his second appearance against New Zealand. In February 1992 he led the England attack against France at Wembley but after being replaced at half time by a certain Alan Shearer the careers of both marksmen went in opposite directions.

It was a crude tackle by Arsenal's Steve Bould in August 1992 - which broke Hirst's ankle – that effectively brought an end to his International career and started the slow decline of Hirst's powers as a world-class striker. Even a half fit Hirst was better than anything Wednesday could produce in attack but from netting at Spurs in March 1992 until his transfer to Southampton in October 1997 Hirst scored only 28 times as persistent Achilles problems greatly restricted his appearances. He did however remain a hugely popular player – on his first comeback from injury in January 1992 almost ten thousand fans flooded into Hillsborough for a reserve team game – and he left Wednesday fans with a unforgettable moment when using his lethal left foot to score the equaliser against Arsenal in the 1993 F.A.Cup Final. It was one of many incredible moments Hirst gave to Wednesday fans and it was a sad day when he finally left for Southampton – the Saints paying a club record fee - in the hope that a change of surroundings would bring a change of luck. He duly regained fitness and form and typically scored a tremendous strike against Wednesday when The Owls won 3-2 at the Dell in November 1997. Unfortunately lady luck again deserted Hirst when in the 1998 pre season he tore knee ligaments in a freak training accident and was ruled out for the whole of the season. After failing to start a game for eighteen months Hirst sadly was forced to admit defeat – after nine goals in 32 games for The Saints - and announced his retirement from the professional game in January 2000. He immediately returned home to South Yorkshire and a month later was making his Sunday League debut alongside Chris Waddle for Dore based Sunday League club Brunsmeer – typically scoring the winner in a 2-1 win! After finally retiring altogether he is now a regular sight at Hillsborough on matchdays – helping with corporate entertaining – while also being heavily involved with fans organisation "The Owls Trust" and working for a Yorkshire based independent radio station.

HODDER, William 1890-91

Born: cs 1867
Died: 1st Quarter 1897 Nottingham
Debut: 31 January 1891 v Derby County F.A.Cup Away
Last Appearance: 14 February 1891
v West Bromwich Albion F.A.Cup Home
Total League & Cup Appearances: 2* Goals: 1
***Also appeared in 13 Football Alliance League games**

Career Details:

Notts Rangers		
Notts County		1888-89
Nottingham Forest	September	1889
Kidderminster Olympic	September	1889
WEDNESDAY		1890
Lincoln City		1891-93

Nineteenth Century left winger who was one of the immediate predecessors to the great Fred Spiksley. He was one of the first "outsiders" to play for the club, making his debut in September 1890 in an Olive Grove friendly versus Lincoln City, and speed was said to be always a great feature of his play. He had previously had spells at both Nottingham clubs although he appeared only once for Forest – netting twice in the club's first ever game in the Football Alliance League in September 1889. However the financial incentives offered by Kidderminster carpet baron George Taylor then persuaded Hodder to move to Birmingham League club Olympic where he enjoyed an outstanding season, scoring 36 times as his new club won the inaugural title without losing a game – Olympic were actually unofficial winners as a Championship was inexplicably not awarded as a handful of fixtures were not fulfilled! Included in that tremendous goal haul were a brace on his Olympic debut and six goals in a 25-0 Birmingham Senior Cup win over Hereford.

The two Kidderminster clubs – Harriers and Olympic – merged in the summer of 1890 but Hodder was a Wednesday player by then and was a regular until losing his place to Harry Woolhouse as Wednesday ended the season in bottom spot, moving to Lincoln City in the summer that followed. The former winner of the Sheffield sprint handicap in the 1880s spent two seasons in Lincolnshire but sadly just six years after playing F.A.Cup football for Wednesday he passed away at a very young age of 31.

HODGE, Martin John 1983-88

Born: 4 February 1959 Southport
(6ft 2ins, 13st 7lbs – 1983)
Debut: 27 August 1983
v Swansea City
Division Two Away
Last Appearance: 12 March 1988
v Manchester United
Division One Away
Total League
& Cup Appearances: 249 Goals: 0

Career Details:

Southport Trinity		
Plymouth Argyle	1 February	1977
Everton	1 July	1979 £135,000
Preston North End	13 December	1981 Loan
Oldham Athletic	22 July	1982 Loan
Gillingham	13 January	1983 Loan
Preston North End	23 February	1983 Loan
WEDNESDAY	22 August	1983 £50,000
Leicester City	26 August	1988 £250,000
Hartlepool United	7 August	1991 Free
Rochdale	12 July	1993 Free
Plymouth Argyle	10 August	1994 £10,000
Released	May	1996

When Martin Hodge arrived on loan from Everton just before the start of the 1983-4 season it was simply to act as cover for England U-21 goalkeeper Iain Hesford, who had signed from Blackpool in the summer. However on the opening day of the season Hodge was given the No. 1 shirt by Howard Wilkinson and incredibly he did not relinquish the position for over five years, ensuring that Hesford would never play a first team game for Wednesday! Such was his form and consistency that Hodge – who was signed permanently in September 1983 - played in 214 consecutive league games from making his debut at the Vetch Field, breaking the club record which had previously been held by pre war star Mark Hooper. He quickly became a crucial cog in Wilkinson's direct team that won promotion in 1984 – Hodge took the majority of free kicks in his own half – and his terrific shot stopping resulted in him being named as standby for the 1986 World Cup Finals in Mexico. Unfortunately with his bags packed – and England No. 3 Gary Bailey looking certain to be sent home injured – the Football Association decided at the last minute that he was not required, much to Hodge's understandable disappointment.

He had helped Wednesday to the last four of the F.A.Cup in the same year and seemed set to remain between the sticks for several more seasons before experiencing a torrid 1987-88 campaign. His confidence received a hammer blow when Coventry City keeper Steve Ogrizovic scored past him in October 1987 and a subsequent loss of form and spell out injured allowed youngster Kevin Pressman to stake his claim for a first team spot. The newcomer impressed sufficiently for Wednesday to allow Hodge to join Leicester City on loan but in his first game after transferring to Filbert Street on a permanent basis he pulled stomach muscles to leave him on the sidelines – it was several months before Hodge reclaimed his first team spot but overall his time in the East Midlands saw his form fluctuate and eventually he moved to basement division club Hartlepool United. His final league appearances came back at his first club Plymouth Argyle who he had initially joined as a trainee after a successful trial as a schoolboy. He was a first team regular for Plymouth at the tender age of 19 and was quickly snapped up by Everton – playing for the Toffeemen in 1980 F.A.Cup semi-final. Unfortunately competition for places was fierce at Goodison Park – Hodge had to compete with four other keepers including Neville Southall – and he would spend the majority of his time out on loan at a variety of lower league clubs.

During his second spell at Plymouth, Hodge combined a playing role with the youth team coaching duties and this valuable experience led to his return to Hillsborough in July 1996 when his old boss at Leicester City, David Pleat, appointed him the club's first ever full-time goalkeeping coach. He later experienced a torrid two seasons in charge of the reserve side and in June 2001 was promoted to first team coach. However when Terry Yorath departed on Halloween night 2002 Hodge was also dismissed. In January 2003 he returned to one of his old clubs, Rochdale, to become goalkeeping coach and in July 2004 was appointed to the same role at Leeds United.

HODGKISS, Thomas 1923-30

Born: 1904 Sheffield
(5ft 9ins, 11st – 1930)
Debut: 10 March 1928
v Burnley
Division One Home
Last Appearance: 17 March 1928
v Bury
Division One Away
Total League
& Cup Appearances: 2 Goals: 0

Career Details:

Wincobank CFC		
WEDNESDAY	November	1923
Reading	June	1930 £1000
Released	May	1932

Right back who essentially spent seven seasons at Wednesday as reserve to the likes of Billy Felton and Tommy Walker. He was actually unemployed when initially signing a professional contract with Wednesday – he was going to join the Army if The Owls decided not to sign him – and would loyally play out his Wednesday career in the reserves except for two top-flight appearances late in the 1927-8 season when the absence of Ernie Blenkinsop saw Walker switch to the left side, allowing Hodgkiss to play his only senior games. After helping the Owls to the Central League Championship in 1929 he moved to Reading where he started the 1930-1 season as first choice. He did eventually lose his place but returned to be The Royals regular right back in the following season, scoring his one and only league goal at Watford in November 1931.

HODGSON, David James 1988-89

Born: 1 November 1960 Gateshead
(5ft 10ins, 12st 2lbs – 1989)
Debut: 22 October 1988
v Southampton
Division One Away
Last Appearance: 21 January 1989
v Arsenal
Division One Away
Total League
& Cup Appearances: 7+5 Goals: 2

Career Details:

Redleugh Boys Club		
Ipswich Town/Bolton/**WEDNESDAY**		Trial
Middlesbrough	19 August	1978
Liverpool	8 August	1982 £450,000
Sunderland	24 August	1984 £125,000
Norwich City	18 July	1986 Free
Middlesbrough	27 March	1987 Loan
Jerez Club Deportivo	July	1987 Free
WEDNESDAY	28 July	1988 Free
Mazda Horoshima	17 July	1989 Free
Metz		1990 Free
Swansea City	March	1992 Loan

During his time as Wednesday boss Howard Wilkinson signed many players whose careers had seemingly seen better days only for them to turn their fortunes around in a Wednesday shirt. Unfortunately while he achieved several successes he did have a few failures and it would be fair to say David Hodgson was one of those. The midfielder had received great acclaim in the early stages of a career that had started as a trainee at Middlesbrough in August 1976 and over the next few years would become an established first team player for the Teeside club – earning six England U-21 caps and winning the 1982 European U-21 Championship. His major asset was searing pace – he was an all-round athlete who represented Gateshead and District boys at cross-county running and swimming – and along with Mark Procter and Craig Johnston they formed an exciting attacking midfield trio for Boro in the late 1970s.

He was also a superb crosser of the ball and his tireless work ensured popularity with Ayresome Park fans – an affection that was increased on the day he famously joined the supporters on the terraces when forced to miss a game through injury! Unfortunately for Boro fans relegation in 1982 meant Hodgson would follow the likes of Graeme Souness and Johnston away from Teeside. His destination – after 140 games for Middlesbrough - was League Champions Liverpool where in two seasons he failed to gain a regular place, having to cope with competition from Ian Rush and Kenny Dalglish. Despite this he did win several major medals at Anfield, including two Championships and a European Cup medal as a non-playing sub, and appeared in 47 games for Liverpool, scoring ten times. After leaving Merseyside Hodgson struggled to make an impact on league football – although he did appear for Sunderland in their 1985 League Cup Final loss to Norwich City – and after failing to even start a first team game for Norwich City he decided to move abroad in an attempt to revive a flagging career.

A season in Spanish football followed before he returned to England to sign for Wednesday but the Owls were struggling near the foot of the old First Division and the newcomer struggled to make an impact. It was therefore no surprise when he was released on a free in the following summer – signing for Japanese Second Division club Mazda, who were managed by Manchester United 1968 European Cup winner Bill Foulkes. He later added French football to his C.V. before ending a rollercoaster career with six games on loan at Swansea City. After ending his playing days Hodgson became a FIFA registered football agent before spells as coach and manager at Darlington. He was sacked as Darlington manager in July 2000 but after a spell out of the game he was appointed Darlington manager for a third time in October 2003.

HOLBEM, Walter 1905-11

Born: 4th Quarter 1884
Heeley, Sheffield
(5ft 8½ins, 11st – 1905)
Died: 18 June 1930 Ascot
Debut: 26 January 1907
v Preston North End
Division One Away
Last Appearance: 11 February 1911
v Liverpool
Division One Away
Total League
& Cup Appearances: 89 Goals: 0

Career Details:

Heeley Friends		
WEDNESDAY		1905 £10
Everton	31 August	1911 £500
St. Mirren		1913
Preston North End		1915
Southport Central		1915

After forging his reputation as a halfback in local Sheffield football, Walter Holbem was handed the daunting task of having to dislodge Wednesday legend Tommy Crawshaw from the centre of The Owls defence. After solely playing reserve team football in his first full season at Hillsborough Walter stepped into Crawshaw's shoes on several occasions over the two seasons that followed but it would be at left back that the Sheffielder would make his mark at Wednesday. It was the arrival of English McConnell in the summer of 1908 that saw Walter switched to left back, in direct competition with Harry Burton and he would play 26 league games in that 1908-9 season, mainly at left back although he did play several games at right back. He remained a regular in the next season, being sent off in the March 1910 derby meeting with United, but a fall out with the club effectively ended his Hillsborough career - he had demanded that his benefit game be played before and not after Christmas (the accepted rule was that players chose a game after Christmas when the colder weather meant a smaller crowd!).

He started the new campaign in the reserves and eventually moved to fellow top-flight side Everton where he experienced a poor first season as a series of knee problems restricted his appearances. In two years at Goodison Park, Holbem appeared in only eighteen games and after a brief spell at St.Mirren – the Scottish environment did not suit his wife and he quickly followed her back to their Southport home – his league career ended at Preston North End. After ending his playing days in non-league football Walter became a bookmaker but it was this profession that directly led to his tragic death in 1930. Holbem was working at an Ascot race meeting in June 1930 when during a violent thunderstorm he was knocked unconscious after a bolt of lightening struck his umbrella – he died soon after in hospital.

HOLLIDAY, Edwin "Eddie" 1962-65

Born: 7 June 1939 Royston, Barnsley
(5ft 10ins, 11st 8lbs – 1964)
Debut: 17 March 1962
v West Ham United
Division One Home
Last Appearance: 30 March 1964
v Arsenal
Division One Home
Total League
& Cup Appearances: 62 Goals: 14

Career Details:

Middlesbrough	7 August	1956
WEDNESDAY	16 March	1962 £25,000
Middlesbrough	16 June	1965
Hereford United	July	1966 Free
Workington	February	1968 Free
Peterborough United	July	1969 Free

Arguably Eddie Holliday's career had already peaked before he joined The Owls as when he was part of Middlesbrough's explosive attack in the 1950s – alongside Billy Day and Brian Clough – he'd wrought havoc amongst second division defences to win three full caps for England in addition to several U-23 and Football League caps. The fast and tidy winger – who was a superb crosser of the ball – had started on Middlesbrough's ground staff after joining from Royston Modern School at the age of fifteen but his form over the years that followed alerted many top-flight sides to his talents.

It was Wednesday boss Vic Buckingham who won the chase for his signature but at Hillsborough he was unable to reproduce his cap winning form and was in and out of the side – going on a week-to-week terms in July 1963 after turning down The Owls offer of a new contract. His also experienced off the field problems when in March 1964 he was found guilty of being drunk in charge of a car – Holliday being found asleep at the wheel of his car with the keys in the ignition. He final season saw Holliday fail to make a first team appearance for Wednesday and after asking for a transfer he was allowed to return to Teeside after a season of reserve team football at Hillsborough.

Unfortunately he could not rediscover his old form back on Teeside and Boro were relegated to the old Third Division at the end of the season. After taking his Boro tally to 25 goals in 169 games he left for Southern League giants Hereford United in the close season and spent two years at Edgar Street before re-entering league soccer at Workington. His career effectively ended with a badly broken leg when playing for Peterborough United against Exeter City in November 1969, retiring in September 1970 after failing to regain his fitness. A nephew of England International Colin Graingar he returned to his native Barnsley where he still resides, playing golf and following the "Sport of Kings".

HOLMES, Darren Peter 1993-96

Born: 30 January 1975 Sheffield
(5ft 8ins, 11st 3lbs – 1994)
Only Appearance: 24 June 1995 v FC Basel Intertoto Cup Away
Total League & Cup Appearances: 1 Goals: 0

Career Details:

WEDNESDAY	1 July	1993
Bangor City	2 March	1996 Loan
Cape Cod Crusaders	June	1996 Loan
Scunthorpe United	August	1996 Trial
Boston United	August	1996 Free
Notts County	August	1996 Trial
Lincoln City	September	1996 Trial
Emley	October	1996 N/C
Ponterfract Colleries	November	1996
Alfreton Town	July	1998
Hallam	July	1999
Gainsborough Trinity	October	2000
Sheffield Club	July	2002

Left sided midfielder who spent three years as a professional at Wednesday but failed to break into the Owls league side. He had joined as an apprentice in 1991 but after appearing in over seventy reserve games for Wednesday his only taste of senior football came in the fateful Intertoto Cup game in Switzerland when Wednesday effectively fielded a scratch side. After a loan spell in Northern Irish football he was loaned to US club Cape Cod – where he coached boys and girls in June 1996 – but was handed a free transfer in May 1996 – a surprise decision considering his consistent form for the second team. After leaving Wednesday he had several unsuccessful trials at a variety of league clubs before dropping into non-league soccer at Boston United.

He later played a handful of games under Ronnie Glavin's managership at Emley before settling into semi-professional football while forging a career outside of the game. He was top scorer at Hallam during the 1999-00 season and soon stepped up to Northern Premier League football at Gainsborough Trinity. After drifting out of the first team picture at the ex-league club Holmes signed League forms for Hallam (in non-league soccer you can play for different sides in different leagues) and later signed for Sheffield Club. Unfortunately he has experienced a torrid time with injuries and has hardly kicked a ball in anger for three years. He now works for LCV commercial vans, based on Middlewood Road in the shadow of The Owls training ground.

HOLMES, George William 1921-22

Born: 3rd Quarter 1896
Goldenhill, Staffordshire
(5ft $7^1/_2$ins, 12st – 1921)
Debut: 17 September 1921
v Notts County Division Two Home
Last Appearance: 13 March 1922
v Coventry City
Division Two Home
Total League
& Cup Appearances: 21 Goals: 0

Career Details:

Goldenhill Wanderers		
Leek Alexandra		
Ton Pentre		
Port Vale	August	1916
Merthyr Town	October	1920
WEDNESDAY	3 June	1921 £435
Wrexham	September	1922 £120

Strong, powerful right back George Holmes joined the Owls from Division Three (South) club Merthyr Town in Bob Brown's early days in charge of team affairs at Hillsborough. The ex-Port Vale player was aged 25 when he joined Wednesday and had played several games for Merthyr in the previous season in what was the Welsh club's first ever season in League football. He replaced Jack Bellas in the Owls Second Division side but would stay only fifteen months before dropping back into Southern section soccer at Wrexham. He missed only a single game after joining – appearing in 39 matches - but was surprisingly released at the end of the 1922-3 season, dropping out of league soccer altogether.

HOLSGROVE, John William 1971-75

Born: 27 September 1945 Southwark, London
(6ft 3ins, 12st 7lbs – 1972)
Debut: 14 August 1971
v Queens Park Rangers
Division Two Away
Last Appearance: 8 March 1975
v West Bromwich Albion
Division Two Away
Total League
& Cup Appearances: 114+1 Goals: 5

Career Details:

Arsenal		1960 Amat.
Tottenham Hotspur		1962 Amat.
Crystal Palace	February	1964
Wolverhampton Wanderers	1 May	1965 £18,000
WEDNESDAY	24 June	1971 £50,000
Stockport County	August	1975 Free
Contract cancelled	December	1975
Stalybridge Celtic	January	1976

Before signing his first professional contract at Crystal Palace in 1964, John Holsgrove spent the formative years of his career as an amateur inside forward at first Arsenal and then Spurs. He was on the Highbury ground staff for two years but had the misfortune to be offered a professional contract by Gunners boss George Swindon only for this to be withdrawn when Swindin was sacked! A phone call to Spurs boss Bill Nicholson secured a move to White Hart Lane where he stayed for a year while taking a job in Southwark Town Hall as a wages clerk. During this period the born and bred Londoner was capped by both London and England boys but when Spurs offered John only a semi-professional contract he decided to leave, signing for Dick Graham's Third Division Palace side.

His league debut came on the opening day of the 1964-65 campaign and Holsgrove would go on to net twice in twenty-two starts for The Eagles in an encouraging first season in league soccer. His teammate at the time was Ronnie Allen who promised Holsgrove that when he moved into management he would buy John for his side. He duly moved to Wolves as coach in the summer of 1965 and Holsgrove followed soon after – manager Andy Beattie taking him to Molineux solely on Allen's recommendation. It was the start of a successful six year stay in The Black Country for Holsgrove as he experienced a dramatic upturn in fortunes following a decision by Wolves boss Bill McGarry to convert the tall and powerful player into a centre half. From this moment on he never looked back – helping Wolves to promotion from Division Two in 1967 – between January 1967 and February 1969 Holsgrove started 97 consecutive league games. After gaining his first experience of top-flight football, injury then forced John out of Wolves' first team and after failing to dislodge his replacement, John McAlle, he was signed by Derek Dooley – the Owls boss making Holsgrove club captain.

During the Owls push for promotion in 1972-3 the newcomer was a veritable rock at the heart of Wednesday's defence but when a mystery illness swept through Hillsborough in the early stages of the following season Holsgrove was hit badly. He was absent from first team duty for six months of the season but did return to the side in March to help Wednesday just avoid the drop into Division Three. Unfortunately he never really recovered from his spell on the sidelines – his absence was complicated by a liver condition – and left at the end of the disastrous 1974-5 season with The Owls in Division Three for the first time. "Big John", who was said to ease stress by playing the guitar to a high standard, subsequently spent only six months at Stockport County before his contract was cancelled by mutual consent just before Christmas 1975. Holsgrove then played out the season in non-league soccer before retiring from the game and moving back to his London roots. He now lives in Camberley, Surrey where he is a finance manager with Lombard North Central.

HOLT, Grant 2003-04

Born: 12 April 1981 Carlisle
(6ft 1ins, 12st 7lbs – 2003)
Debut: 29 March 2003
v Watford
Division One Home
Last Appearance: 24 January 2004
v Peterborough United
Division Two Home
Total League
& Cup Appearances: 15+15 Goals: 4

Career Details:

Workington/Sunday football		
Halifax Town	16 September	1999 £10,000
Barrow	March	2000 Loan
Workington		2001 Loan
Barrow	February	2002 Loan
Released	May	2002
Sengkang Marine	summer	2002
Barrow	1 July	2002 Free
WEDNESDAY	27 March	2003 £7,500
Rochdale	30 January	2004 £10,000

Old fashioned style bustling centre forward who was plucked from the relative obscurity of Northern Premier League football by Chris Turner in the Spring of 2003. Holt made an immediate positive impression on the Hillsborough faithful and delighted the travelling fans when scoring his debut goal during the 1-1 draw at Brighton on Easter Monday. His strike could not stop Wednesday from the drop into Division Two where Holt remained a first team squad regular as The Owls tried to bounce back into Division One at the first attempt. Although not blessed with great finesse Holt was nevertheless a wholehearted player who could always be relied upon to give 100% commitment

He had first made an impact with Workington when the Northwest side lifted the Northern Premier League Division One title in 1999 and this form earned Holt a move into League soccer at Halifax Town. However he failed to adapt to league football and after netting once in eight games for Town he dropped back into non-league football to sign permanently for Barrow, after a summer of football in the Singapore League. He proceeded to net an impressive 54 goals in 113 games for Barrow – while working in a factory to earn a living – before a dream move to Hillsborough. Spent less than a year at Wednesday before dropping into Division Three during the January 2004 transfer window.

HOOPER, Mark 1927-39

Born: 14 July 1901 Darlington
(5ft 5ins, 10st, 7lbs - 1927)
Died: 9 March 1974 Sheffield
Debut: 22 January 1927
v Leicester City
Division One Home
Last Appearance: 9 October 1937
v Southampton
Division Two Away
Total League
& Cup Appearances: 423 Goals: 135

Career Details:

Cockfield Colliery		
Darlington	May	1924
WEDNESDAY	21 January	1927 £1950
Rotherham United	Summer	1939

Arguably the greatest right winger to play for the Sheffield Wednesday and without doubt one of the finest attackers never to be capped by his Country. In tandem with Ellis Rimmer on the opposite flank the double act were one of the main reasons behind the Owls golden years, which saw Wednesday win two league titles, one F.A.Cup and become one of the greatest teams in the English game. Although slightly built – Hooper wore only size 4 boots – he possessed the heart of a lion and was fearless against players who were taller and heavier. The diminutive winger was a real bag of tricks, deceptively fast, boasted great ball control and was an outstanding crosser of the ball, while also having the happy knack of meeting centres from the opposite wing - proven by his exceptional goal tally that would have put many centre forwards to shame. He also possessed a rapier like shot which left many keepers rooted to the spot as the ball flew past them into the net!

Considering all his tremendous attributes it was actually as a goalkeeper that Hooper – whose uncle Charlie Roberts played league soccer - started his playing career back in his native Northeast, winning consecutive league and cup doubles with Risecarr School in Darlington. When his education was complete Hooper gained employment as a furnace worker at Darlington Rolling Mills while also playing amateur football with Northern League club Cockfield. In only their second season in the Northern League Hooper's goals helped the pit village to third spot in 1923 while they were dubbed "Cockfield Wonder Village" by the press when reaching the semi-finals of the famous F.A.Amateur Cup – Hooper netting as his side lost 4-2 to Evesham Town in the last four clash at Bishop Auckland. His sparkling form soon alerted the region's bigger sides and after scoring five times in eleven games for Darlington's North Eastern League side he turned professional at the end of the 1923-4 season – incredibly at the same time Hooper was scouted by Wednesday boss Bob Brown whose eye for talent for once let him down when he stated that the wing-man was simply too small.

His opinion of Hooper was certainly to change over the next three seasons as 43 goals in 124 games helped Darlington win the Division Three (North) Championship in 1925 and consolidate in Division Two – Mark finishing top scorer with eighteen goals. A sparkling brace in a 5-1 win over Wednesday at Feethams in March 1926 also probably had Brown reassessing his decision and a year later he finally brought Hooper to Hillsborough. He quickly settled into the Owls First Division side – replacing Welsh winger Rees Williams – and would remain an automatic choice for almost a decade, becoming an idol of the Hillsborough crowd. Back-to-back League Championships followed in 1929 and 1930 and Hooper would set a club record of 189 consecutive games, a mark that was only bettered by Martin Hodge over fifty years later. Hooper, whose brother Chas signed from Darlington in 1929 but failed to make the Owls first eleven, went on to net Wednesday's second goal in the 1935 F.A.Cup win over West Brom and took his appearance tally to over four hundred games before the likes of Len Massarella started to threaten his first team spot in the late 1930s.

His cartilage was removed in May 1937 and in the following season Hooper acted as player-coach with the Owls "A" team as his career came to a dignified close. What proved to be his final appearance in a Wednesday shirt came in a May 1939 third team friendly at Stocksbridge Works after which he signed for The Millers as player-coach. The advent of war meant Hooper appeared in just a handful of games for Rotherham in the transitional wartime season of 1939-40 before he finally retired in 1940. He remained at Millmoor for the next eighteen years, initially as second team trainer and then first team, before retiring in 1958 following a major operation. In the early 1960s he also scouted for The Millers and Newcastle United while continuing to run his sweet and tobacconists shop on Middlewood Road – a corner kick from Hillsborough – that he first opened back in the early 1930s! He continued to serve a new generation of Wednesday fans – and no doubt tell stories of the glory days - from behind his counter until passing away in 1974.

HOPE, Robert "Bobby" 1976-78

Born: 28 September 1943 Bridge of Allan, Stirlingshire
(5ft 7¼ins, 11st 3lbs – 1976)
Debut: 18 September 1976
v Chesterfield
Division Three Home
Last Appearance: 3 December 1977
v Colchester United
Division Three Home
Total League
& Cup Appearances: 43+3 Goals: 9

Career Details:

Drumchapel Amateurs		
Sunderland		Trial
West Bromwich Albion	September	1960
Birmingham City	26 May	1972 £66,666
Philadelphia Atoms	April	1975 Loan
Contract cancelled	April	1976
Dallas Tornados	May-August	1976
WEDNESDAY	16 September	1976 Free
Dallas Tornados	April-August	1977 Loan
Dallas Tornados	April-August	1978 Loan
Bromsgrove Rovers	August	1978 Free

Diminutive midfielder who was a major star at West Bromwich Albion where he appeared in over four hundred games for The Baggies, making his debut at the tender age of sixteen. At his peak Hope was one of the most accurate passers of a ball in the English game and his talents not only helped Albion to win the League Cup in 1966 and the F.A.Cup in 1968 but also brought him two full caps for Scotland – he was also capped at schoolboy and U-23 level. He later moved onto Birmingham City but after failing to reproduce his Hawthorns form left after just 46 games for The Blues, following the golden path to the NASL.

After returning from a second spell in US football The Owls engaged his services and Hope enjoyed a consistent first season, scoring on his debut and remaining a first team regular. However after another spell in NASL soccer the strain of all year round football seemingly started to takes it toll as Hope experienced an injury plagued 1977-8 season, starting only five Division Three games. Another trip across the Atlantic followed but on his return Wednesday handed him a free transfer – Hope subsequently returning to the Midlands to sign as player-coach for Southern League Bromsgrove Rovers – winning the Midland Division title in 1985. The ex-Dumbartonshire boys player was elevated to manager in May 1979 and over the next fifteen years – interrupted by a short spell as boss at Burton Albion between August 1988 and October 1988 - led Rovers to the greatest spell in the club's history, leading them into Conference soccer in the early 1990s.

After turning part-time in the mid 1980s he took over a post office in Handsworth Wood and later in Boldmere – the pressure of running this business and travelling was actually the cause of his departure from Burton. His non-football activities also eventually led to his resignation as Bromsgrove manager in September 1994 as he channelled all his energies into a new sandwich business in Birmingham City Centre. He eventually owned a chain of sandwich bars, which were later sold when Hope was appointed Recruitment Officer at West Brom. He was later promoted to Chief Scout in June 2001 and now combines the role with running a newsagents shop in Walsall.

HORNE, Barry 2000

Born: 18 May 1962 St Asaph, Denbighshire
(5ft 9ins, 12st 2lbs – 2000)
Debut: 12 April 2000
v Wimbledon Premier League Away
Last Appearance: 14 May 2000
v Leicester City Premier League Home
Total League
& Cup Appearances: 7 Goals: 0

Career Details:

Deeside district teams		
Greenfield		
Liverpool University		
Rhyl		
Wrexham	26 June	1984 Free
Portsmouth	17 July	1987 £60,000
Southampton	22 March	1989 £700,000
Everton	1 July	1992 £675,000
Birmingham City	10 June	1996 £250,000
Huddersfield Town	13 October	1997 Free
WEDNESDAY	23 March	2000 Free
Kidderminster Harriers	11 August	2000 Free
Walsall	23 March	2001 Free
Released	1 June	2001
Belper Town	September	2001 Free

Although as a schoolboy Barry Horne came to Hillsborough for trials – he was also looked at by both Everton and Manchester United – he would not actually sign for The Owls until the latter end of a successful league career, almost fifteen years later. In fact he initially seemed destined for a career outside of the game as after staying on at school to earn A levels he then gained a First in Chemistry and a Masters degree in Engineering at Liverpool University – while appearing for the University football side he added the National University Trophy to his list of honours. His early football had been played in Welsh minor football – a team mate was Ian Rush – and he later appeared for Rhyl on a semi-professional basis (he did not play for Flint Town as is recorded in other publications).

However it was a Welsh Cup appearance for Rhyl against Wrexham that would alter Horne's career path as The Robins took him into the professional game at the age of 22. His non stop midfield displays quickly saw Horne elevated to Division One at Southampton in 1989 – after being named Portsmouth player of the season in both 1988 and 1989 - and Horne spent seven years in England's top-flight, serving The Saints and Everton with distinction. He lifted the F.A.Cup with Everton in 1995 and it was a surprise to Goodison Park regulars when he was sold at the end of the 1995-6 campaign as Barry had just retained his player of the season trophy! After a spell at Birmingham City Horne led by example at Huddersfield Town – captaining the side – before suffering a medial ligament injury on his 50th appearance for The Terriers.

After recovering from the injury Horne found himself out of favour with new manager Steve Bruce and his career seemed to be drifting to a close before Wednesday acting manager Peter Shreeves made a shock deadline day swoop to take him back into Premier League football – the Owls taking over his contract until the end of the season. Unfortunately despite a series of all-action displays he could not stop Wednesday from falling from the Premier League and at the end of the season signed for Jan Mobley's league newcomers Kidderminster – appearing in The Harriers first ever league fixture, at home to Torquay United in August 2000. Following a contract dispute with The Harriers the then PFA Chairman – he was the players union figurehead for four years from 1997 – finished his league career at Walsall. After scoring 35 goals in 575 league games and winning 59 full caps for Wales he dropped into non-league soccer at Northern Premier League Belper Town in 2001, finally hanging up his boots at Christmas 2001. He is currently attending teacher training college while working in the media as a match summariser for several organisations including SKY TV, BBC Radio Wales and BBC Radio Five Live.

HORNSBY, Brian Geoffrey 1978-82

Born: 10 September 1954
Great Shelford, Cambridgeshire
(5ft 8ins, 10st 11lbs – 1978)
Debut: 18 March 1978
v Lincoln City Division Three Away
Last Appearance: 5 December 1981
v Chelsea Division Two Away
Total League
& Cup Appearances: 120+4 Goals: 30

Career Details:

Arsenal	10 September	1971
Shrewsbury Town	19 May	1976 £20,000
WEDNESDAY	9 March	1978 £40,000
Chester	4 November	1981 Loan
Edmonton Drillers	22 March	1982 Loan
Carlisle United	September	1982 Free
Chesterfield	December	1983 Loan
Released	June	1984
IK Brage	July	1984
Spalding United	July	1989
Holbeach United	July	1990

Although Brian Hornsby attended schoolboy trials at both Bristol City and Leicester City it was North London giants Arsenal who signed the midfielder on schoolboy forms in 1969. He was elevated to apprentice in May 1970 and secured a professional deal a year later, making his senior debut for The Gunners in May 1973 after having shown his promise by winning England schoolboy and youth honours – he was a member of the side that lifted the "Little World Cup" in Italy in 1973. He had also won the F.A.Youth Cup in 1971 but Hornsby found life much harder as a pro and after appearing in just twenty-six games left for Shrewsbury Town in 1976. Incidentally in September 1973 he appeared as a substitute for the Gunners for all of three seconds!

He made a big impact at Gay Meadow and duly became Jack Charlton's first major capture when he moved to Hillsborough on deadline day. The left sided midfielder's first full season at Wednesday would easily prove to be his best as he finished top scorer with 21 goals, was named by his peers in the Division Three seasonal team and helped the Owls take his old club Arsenal to five games in an epic F.A.Cup saga. The goals dried up during the promotion season that followed, although he was a regular, but in the higher grade Hornsby was used sparingly by Charlton and following a loan spell at Chester he left for Canadian football, being signed by his old Arsenal Youth team boss Roger Thompson for Edmonton.

On his return to England a free transfer took him to Carlisle United but an unhappy spell at Brunton Park, where he fell out with manager Bob Stokoe, ended with a move to Swedish football. He returned home in December 1984 to spend Christmas back in Sheffield but a month later returned to play in the Swedish indoor league with a player-coach contract in his pocket for the 1985 summer season. He would actually stay almost five years in Scandinavia before returning home to work as a contractor for Cable & Wireless and complete his competitive playing career in non-league football – he was player-manager at Holbeach United for one season before retiring. For the last ten years Hornsby has played for the Arsenal Old Boy's team - running and managing the side in latter years – and once even had to call for the services of Chris Turner for a game in Monaco when they was short of a goalkeeper! He now earns a living running a business that sells sheds and summerhouses to the public.

HORROBIN, Thomas "Tom" 1960-63

Born: 8 August 1943 Askern, Doncaster
(5ft 7ins, 11st – 1960)
Debut: 29 September 1962
v Manchester United
Division One Home
Last Appearance: 10 November 1962
v Aston Villa
Division One Home
Total League
& Cup Appearances: 3 Goals: 0

Career Details:		
WEDNESDAY	August	1960
Frickley Colliery		1964
Askern Welfare		

Right back who joined The Owls ground staff as an amateur in March 1958 before being elevated to professional status at the start of the 1960-1 campaign. His reserve team debut came in September 1961 and over the next two seasons Tom became established as understudy to first team full back Peter Johnson. His first team debut could not have been more high-profile – at home to Manchester United – while what proved to be his final appearance was memorable for all the wrong reasons as Bronco Layne's controversial sending off led to crowd disturbances, including the Hillsborough pitch being covered with cushions thrown from the North Stand by disgruntled fans!

Somewhat surprisingly, after playing top-flight football at the tender age of nineteen – Horrobin was not retained at the end of the 1962-3 season, later signing for Frickley Colliery. Unfortunately his playing career did not last much longer as five operations on his knee cartilage failed to solve the problem and Horrobin was forced to retire. He later worked for seventeen years on the coalface at the same Armthorpe Colliery as Alan Finney before being employed at a Doncaster timber yard before being made redundant in 2000.

HOUNSFIELD, Reginald Edward 1902-03

Born: 3rd Quarter 1882 Hackentorpe, Derby
Debut:
3 October 1902 v Notts County Division One Away
Last Appearance:
4 October 1902 v Liverpool Division One Away
Total League & Cup Appearances: 2 Goals: 0

Career Details:		
Sheffield Club		Amat.
WEDNESDAY	March	1902
Derby County	October	1903
Released		1906

Flying right-winger who was still a Sheffield F.C. amateur player when making two senior appearances for Wednesday in the space of twenty-four hours. Reputed to be one of the fastest wingers of his day, Hounsfield remained amateur throughout his career and was an example of what would be called a "gentleman player" – an individual who came from the upper classes of English society and played the game purely for pleasure.

His education was spent at Repton Public School near Derby and his debut for The Owls came at Trent Bridge, Nottingham when regular Harry Davis was absent. The game was actually played on a Friday to coincide with the Nottingham Goose Fair and a hat-trick from Fred Spiksley ensured Reg made a winning 3-0 start. However twenty-four hours later Wednesday lost 4-2 at Liverpool and Hounsfield returned to amateur soccer. He later spent three seasons on Derby County's books, scoring four times in 26 league games before dropping out of league football altogether.

HOWELLS, Peter 1953-56

Born: 23 September 1932
Middlesbrough
(5ft 10ins, 11st – 1954)
Died: 16 January 1993 Middlesbrough
Debut: 6 November 1954
v Manchester City
Division One Home
Last Appearance: 7 April 1956
v West Ham United
Division Two Away
Total League
& Cup Appearances: 3 Goals: 1

Career Details:		
WEDNESDAY	10 October	1953
Hartlepools United	October	1956 Free

Outside-left who joined Wednesday as an amateur in July 1953, appearing in the club's Hatchard League side before stepping up to reserve team football during the 1953-4 season. He struggled to impact upon the first team scene during his three years as a professional at Hillsborough, making only three first team appearances, although he did score in the 3-3 draw at Upton Park in what proved to be his final senior game for Wednesday. A move into the lower leagues at Hartlepool also failed to ignite his career – Howells made only one solitary appearance for the Northeast side – and he subsequently drifted out of professional football.

HOYLAND, George A. 1904-05

Born:
Debut:
26 March 1904 v Manchester City Division One Home
Last Appearance:
17 December 1904 v Newcastle United Division One Away
Total League & Cup Appearances: 3 Goals: 1

Career Details:		
Sheffield Club		
WEDNESDAY	March	1904

One of three players who hold the distinction of having played top-flight football with Wednesday and also won the famous F.A.Amateur Cup with Sheffield Club. The latter feat was achieved in April 1904 when Club defeated Ealing 3-1 in the Bradford Final, George playing alongside fellow Wednesday players Henry Bolsover and Harry Potts. He would remain amateur throughout his career and occasionally helped the Owls when required – appearing in three different forward positions in his three games for the club, scoring in the 2-2 draw at Notts County in December 1904.

HUDSON, John "Jack" 1880-89

Born: 11 October 1860
Died: 21 November 1941 Worksop
Debut: 18 December 1880 v Blackburn Rovers F.A.Cup Away
Last Appearance:
31 October 1885 v Long Eaton Rangers F.A.Cup Away
Total League
& Cup Appearances: 16 Goals: 0

Career Details:	
Surrey (Sheffield)	1879-82
Owlerton	1880
Sheffield Club	1880
WEDNESDAY	1880-89
Walkley	1882
Heeley	1884
Lockwood Brothers	1886
Blackburn Olympic	1886
Sheffield United	1889-90

CAPS (@ SWFC)
ENGLAND Full (1) v Ireland 24/02/1883

One of several players who helped the club advance and flourish during the nineteenth Century. Hudson – an engraver by trade – was an outstanding halfback who played a key role in Wednesday's early successes in local Cup football. Like many of his contemporaries he played for several other Sheffield based teams during his career – his amateur status making this possible – having started as a teenager at The Surrey Club. He was a rock at the heart of the club's defence for several seasons – being described as "difficult to pass"- and was involved in many Wednesday "firsts", such as the club's first ever F.A.Cup tie in 1880, first Semi-final appearance in 1882 and the opening game at Olive Grove in 1887.

When Wednesday secretary Billy Littlehale fell ill in 1886 Jack –now club captain – took over the secretarial duties but the Owls failed to enter the F.A.Cup that year as the entry was posted too late! It was this error that almost brought the club to its knees in the following summer and Hudson was one of a group of players who successfully pleaded for Wednesday officials to adopt professionalism. He represented Sheffield on several occasions –

he was also a fine runner who won many prizes on the track - but injury saw his playing days come to an early close, allowing him to concentrate on a coaching and training career. Before retiring he was able to play in Sheffield United's first ever fixture before returning to Olive Grove, spending a short period as Wednesday's trainer/coach. He was later licensee of a public house in Wadsley Village, Sheffield and after his daughter married ex-Owls hero Jimmy Spoors spent the remaining years of his life at the Gateford Hotel in Worksop.

HUKIN, Arthur 1954-57

Born: 22 October 1937 Sheffield
(5ft 11½ins, 10st 11lbs – 1955)
Died: 21 November 1983 Bedford
Debut: 27 November 1954
v Leicester City Division One Away
Last Appearance: 27 December 1954
v Charlton Athletic Division One Home
Total League & Cup Appearances: 6 Goals: 3

Career Details:

WEDNESDAY	26 October	1954
Bury	29 March	1957 Free
Boston United	August	1957
Bedford Town	August	1959 £250
Corby Town	August	1963
Dunstable		1965

Although Arthur Hukin played several top-flight games for Wednesday while at Hillsborough it was in non-league soccer that he forged a reputation as one of the most prolific scorers outside of the Football League. He had originally joined the Owls straight from school, after having scored freely for Sheffield boys, and make a sensational first team debut when scoring twice in the 4-3 defeat at Filbert Street in November 1954. He retained that first team spot for five more games but then dropped back into reserve team soccer, remaining there until moving to Bury on a free transfer. He failed to play a first team game for The Shakers and while still a teenager he had to accept that his promising career in league soccer had already come to a close – he was also a fine sprinter in his younger days, representing Sheffield based Hallamshire Harriers.

He subsequently dropped into semi-professional football and was top scorer for two consecutive seasons at Boston United. After asking for a move he left for Southern League giants Bedford Town and scored over one hundred times before moving again, this time to Corby Town. He helped Town win the Merit Cup in his debut season and his partnership with Tommy Crawley - that brought 77 goals – was dubbed the "Tommy and Arthur show". In 1964-5 Corby won promotion to the Southern League Premier Division while Hukin finished his playing career at Dunstable. He died of cancer in 1983.

HULL, Gary 1974-77

Born: 21 June 1956 Sheffield
(5ft 9½ins, 12st 8lbs – 1975)
Debut: 21 February 1976
v Aldershot
Division Three Home
Last Appearance: 13 April 1976
v Shrewsbury Town
Division Three Away
Total League
& Cup Appearances: 6+2 Goals: 0

Career Details:

WEDNESDAY	7 May	1974
Released	June	1977
Mossley		1977
Buxton		1979
Worksop Town		1980
Burton Albion		1982

Ex-Sheffield boys player who signed apprentice forms at Wednesday in July 1971. Boasted a strong will and never-say die attitude but after signing professional struggled to make an impact at senior level for The Owls. The right back spent eighteen months as a pro before making his debut in the 3-1 home win over Aldershot and remained in the side for several weeks as Wednesday pulled off a remarkable escape from relegation. However it was then back to reserve team football for Hull before being released in May 1977, joining Northern Premier League Mossley. He now works in the building trade having retiring from playing back in 1983.

HULL, John Smellie 'Jack' 1936-37

Born: 22 April 1913 Motherwell
(5ft 8ins, 9st 12lbs – 1936)
Only Appearance: 12 February 1936
v Portsmouth Division One Home
Total League & Cup Appearances: 1 Goals: 0

Career Details:

Wishaw White Rose		
WEDNESDAY	February	1936
Released	April	1937

Scottish right halfback who spent just over a year as a professional at Hillsborough in the mid-1930s. Arrived on trial from junior soccer in January 1936 – making his Central League debut at home to Everton – and made such an impression that Owls boss Billy Walker gave Hull a shock league debut. On a rock hard, frozen pitch the young defender struggled to stamp his authority on the game and it was quickly back to second team football after Pompey had stolen a one-nil win thanks to a late goal. Hull's appearances in reserve team football were infrequent during the rest of his Owls career and he returned home at the end of the 1936-7 season.

HUMPHREYS, Richard John "Richie" 1996-2001

Born: 30 November 1977 Sheffield
(5ft 10ins, 11st 3lbs – 1997)
Debut: 9 September 1995
v Queens Park Rangers
Premier League Away
Last Appearance: 1 November 2000
v Sheffield United
League Cup Home
Total League
& Cup Appearances: 43+39 Goals: 8

Career Details:

WEDNESDAY	8 February	1996
Scunthorpe United	13 August	1999 Loan
Cardiff City	22 November	1999 Loan
Cambridge United	2 February	2001 Free
Hartlepool United	18 July	2001 Free

CAPS (@SWFC)
England U-20 (2)
v Ivory Coast 18/06/97, v Argentina 26/06/97
England U-21 (3)
v Poland 08/10/96, v Georgia 08/11/96, v Switzerland 01/04/97

Burst onto the first team scene at the start of the 1996-7 season when Wednesday won their first four games to go top of the Premier League. He had actually made his senior debut as a late sub at Loftus Road in the previous season – while still a YTS trainee – and appeared four more times after signing professional forms early in 1996. In his first season as a trainee Humphreys was utilised in a right midfield role but it was a position he was not comfortable with and he struggled to make an impression in youth team soccer. However after moving to centre forward in the following pre season he quickly impressed new boss David Pleat who blooded the teenager in the 3-1 "Steel City Cup" win at Bramall Lane.

A year later he was truly outstanding on the Owls pre-season tour of Holland – Dutch legend Marco Van Basten being one of many admirers – and he hit the ground running as the new season started to score three times in the first four Premier League games of the season, including an unstoppable half-volley versus Aston Villa and an outstanding individual goal against Leicester City. A five-year contract followed in October 1996 and England U-21 honours came next as Richie's career looked set to soar. However the bustling forward seemed to lose the edge to his game after playing in the stifling heat of Malaysia for England in the 1997 World Youth Cup – Ritchie failing to score a solitary goal during the 1997-8 season as Wednesday struggled to maintain their top-flight status. Sadly for Humphreys, Wednesday fans and the club his early promise had all but disappeared by the late 1990s – he failed to even make a first team appearance during Wednesday 1999-00 relegation season – and with his confidence all but non-existent he joined Cambridge United on trial in January 2001. Incidentally his final appearance in a Wednesday shirt came in the 2-1 League Cup win over The Blades in November 2000 – a torrid first half (playing at left back!) against Paul Devlin resulted in his substitution at half-time.

His career seemed on a downward spiral when Humphreys left Hillsborough but to his eternal credit he proceeded to turn his fortunes around to enjoy great success at Third Division Hartlepool United. Under the managership of ex-Owl Chris Turner, Humphreys was re-invented as an attacking midfielder and was a major factor as United won promotion in 2003 – Richie being named in the PFA Division Three team, chosen as the supporters "player of the year" and to complete a trio of accolades named "The North East Nationwide player of the year".

HUNT, Douglas Arthur 1938-46

Born: 19 May 1914 Shipton Bellinger, Hampshire
(5ft 10ins, 11st 8lbs – 1935)
Died: 30 May 1989 Yeovil
Debut: 5 March 1938
v Manchester United
Division Two Home
Last Appearance: 29 April 1939
v Tottenham Hotspur
Division Two Home
Total League
& Cup Appearances: 48* Goals: 31
***Also appeared in**
20 wartime games, scoring 7 goals

Career Details:

Winchester City		
Southampton		Amat.
Northfleet United		
Tottenham Hotspur	March	1934
Barnsley	March	1937 £1700
WEDNESDAY	1 March	1938 £3875
Brentford		1939-44 Guest
Tottenham Hotspur		1939-40 Guest
Aldershot		1941-42 Guest
Fulham		1944-46 Guest
West Ham United		1944-46 Guest
Clapton Orient	April	1946 £620
Gloucester City		1948-53

Centre forward who holds a unique place in Wednesday history as the only man to score six goals in a competitive fixture. He achieved the feat on 19 November 1938 during a 7-0 romp against Norwich City at Hillsborough – the goals coming after 17, 25, 39, 44, 65 and 87 minutes. A few days before the record breaking game Hunt had netted all four goals in a County Cup win over Rotherham United and his incredible month of scoring was completed a week after the City game when he had to settle for a mere three goals in Wednesday's 5-1 win at Luton Town. This burst of scoring was a major part of his 25-goal haul during the 1938-9 season as The Owls narrowly missed out on promotion back to the top-flight after two seasons in the lower tier.

He had originally joined late in the previous campaign after spells at Tottenham Hotspur and Barnsley. His career had started in Hampshire non-league football – filling the boots of Ted Drake at Winchester City - and it was here that Spurs scouts spotted his potential, assigning Hunt to their nursery side Northfleet. His first team debut came on Christmas Day 1934 and although he netted 6 times in 19 senior games for Spurs his time at the White Hart Lane club was mainly spent in the second team – he scored 56 times in just 74 reserve games. In pursuit of first team football he moved to Oakwell in the spring of 1937 and after netting 17 goals in 36 league games the tall and well-built attacker made the short trip to Hillsborough, signing for an Owls side that were struggling at the wrong end of the Second Division table. Wednesday had tried the likes of Harry Hanford and Jack Ashley at centre forward in a desperate attempt to solve their chronic goal scoring problems but Hunt's arrival provided the solution, his six goals in the final twelve games of the season leading the club to safety and setting up the exciting promotion chase of a year later.

Unfortunately the outbreak of war effectively ended Hunt's career at Wednesday as after making a handful of appearances during the transitional season of 1939-40 he returned to his native Hampshire, subsequently joining the Army. Throughout the war years he guested for a wide variety of clubs – winning the London War Cup in 1942 in Brentford's colours – before being de-mobbed and returning to Sheffield to pay five games in the Football League (North) competition during 1945-6. After being put on the transfer list in February 1946 he was appointed player-coach at Leyton Orient where Hunt showed he had lost none of his sharpness by finishing joint top scorer for Orient during the first season of peacetime soccer. In August 1947 he was given the assistant manager role at Brisbane Road but in June of the following year left to become player-manager at Southern League Gloucester City, remaining for five years before being appointed trainer-coach at Yeovil Town in September 1951. This preceded a move to Tonbridge as boss in January 1954 where Hunt would lead the Kent side to two Southern League Cup Finals in the 1950s, losing to Yeovil Town and Hereford United. He subsequently returned to Yeovil in 1958 and would spend an astonishing 28 years as trainer-coach before finally retiring in 1986.

HUNT, George Samuel 1946-48

Born: 22 February1910 Barnsley
(5ft 8¾ins, 10st 3lbs – 1935)
Died: 19 September 1996 Bolton
Debut: 9 November 1946
v Newcastle United Division Two Away
Last Appearance: 30 August 1947
v Tottenham Hotspur
Division Two Away
Total League
& Cup Appearances: 35 Goals: 8

Career Details:

Barnsley Regent St.Congretional		
Barnsley		Trial
Sheffield United		Trial
Port Vale		Trial
Chesterfield	September	1929
Tottenham Hotspur	6 June	1930
Arsenal	1 October	1937 £7,500
Bolton Wanderers	16 March	1938 £5,000
Liverpool		1940-1 Guest
Rochdale		1940-1 Guest
Luton Town		1940-1 Guest
WEDNESDAY	7 November	1946 £3,000
Bolton Wanderers	May	1948

Forward George Hunt was coming to the end of his career when he moved to Second Division Wednesday at the age of 36 in 1947. The pacy and direct forward had been a top-flight star in the 1930s after having finally broken into league soccer at Chesterfield – he had been rejected by several clubs and even four goals in a trial match for Sheffield United failed to convince the Blades of his qualities! It proved a major mistake for United as after just nine months at Saltergate (and just fourteen games) Hunt's promise was recognised by Tottenham and they took the born and bred Yorkshireman to North London, paying The Spireites a substantial fee for his signature.

He quickly became a huge crowd favourite at Spurs and his exciting solo runs, courageous play and prolific scoring eventually led to three full caps for England. After helping Spurs to promotion from Division Two in 1933 he went on to set a club scoring record of 138 goals that stood until the great Jimmy Greaves surpassed the mark in the 1960s. Hunt's goals came in only 198 games and it must have been a blow to Spurs fans when he became one of only a handful of players to transfer direct to fierce rivals Arsenal – this was after Hunt lost his first team place following the arrival of manager Jack Tresaden in 1935. His time at Highbury proved to be brief – he rated the Gunners 'too stuck up' – and after six months returned north to sign for Bolton Wanderers. Incidentally although he spent only six months at Arsenal he appeared in enough games to be awarded a League Championship medal.

He continued to play football throughout the war years, scoring 84 goals in 177 wartime games for Bolton Wanderers, and won the League North Cup with Wanderers in 1945. Soon after peacetime soccer returned Hunt was brought to Hillsborough by Eric Taylor as a short-term successor to the great Jackie Robinson at inside right. He netted seven times to help Wednesday avoid the almost unthinkable drop into regional football but the big-money arrival of Eddie Quigley in October 1947 effectively ended Hunt's Wednesday career and he was allowed to return to Bolton at the end of the season to become assistant trainer – his final appearance in a Wednesday shirt came at Spurs where he was given a rapturous reception by the home fans. He remained at Burnden Park in a variety of roles – including coach and chief scout – until September 1968 and spent the final years of his working life at Bolton Garage running the car wash. Hunt – whose grandfather Sam played for Barnsley and was Doncaster's first ever professional player – contracted Alzheimers in old age and sadly passed away after a five year battle with the disease.

HUNTER, Andrew S. 1909-10

Born: Belfast
Debut: 27 March 1909
v Manchester City
Division One Away
Last Appearance: 11 September 1909
v Bristol City
Division One Away
Total League
& Cup Appearances: 15 Goals: 3

Career Details:

Distillery		
Glentoran		
Belfast Celtic		
WEDNESDAY	24 March	1909 £205
Glentoran		1910

Irish right winger who went straight into Wednesday's Division One side after joining from Belfast Celtic. He had already won four full caps for his country but experienced an inauspicious start to his English league career as Manchester City thrashed Wednesday four-nil! However he retained his place for the remainder of the season but the emergence of Sam Kirkman early in the following campaign saw Hunter relegated to reserve team football. He duly netted seven times as Wednesday's Midland League side finished in fourth spot but returned to Ireland in the summer of 1910, signing for a second spell at Belfast side Glentoran. In October 1910 he had regained sufficient form to be picked for The Irish League against their English counterparts and in 1911 won both the County Antrim Shield and Charity Cup with Glentoran- later adding the New Irish Cup to his honours board in 1912.

HUNTER, John "Jack" 1880-82

Born: 1852 Sheffield
Died: 13 April 1903 Blackburn
Debut: 18 December 1880
v Blackburn Rovers
F.A.Cup Away
Last Appearance: 5 February 1881
v Darwen
F.A.Cup Away
Total League
& Cup Appearances: 3 Goals: 0

Career Details:

Heeley Youth	
Garrick (Sheffield)	1873-76
Millhouses	1875
Hallam	1876
Heeley	1877-82
Sheffield Albion	1879
Providence	1880
WEDNESDAY	1880-82
Blackburn Olympic	1882
Blackburn Rovers	1887
Heeley	1888-89

One of the greatest players of the Victorian age who occasionally played for Wednesday in the club's bigger cup ties of the early 1880s, including their first ever F.A.Cup tie, at Blackburn Rovers in 1880. Hunter was described as a genius half back and while playing for Sheffield club Heeley he won seven full caps for England – captaining his country against Wales in 1881 - as well as appearing nine times in representative games for Sheffield. He was also one of the first players from the City to exploit the rise of professionalism and got in to hot water early in his career when being one of the players who appeared in the famous "Zulu" matches – he was banned for what effectively was a professional undertaking but after apologising by letter to the Sheffield FA was reinstated on appeal.

However he would not remain amateur for long – he worked as a butcher and then a silver cutler while in Sheffield – as after facing Blackburn Olympic for Wednesday he was lured across The Pennines by the Lancashire club with a promise of a licensed house in the town. He therefore became a thinly veiled professional before it was legalised – his controversial transfer remained a sore point for Wednesday for many years – and was outstanding in Olympic's 1883 F.A.Cup Final win over Old Etonians. He later moved to cross town rivals Blackburn Rovers and played in the Rovers side that provided Wednesday with the opposition in the club's first ever game at Olive Grove in 1887. He later returned to his first love Heeley before retiring to become assistant trainer and then groundsman at Blackburn Rovers. Died, aged 52, but will always being remembered as a player who did more than anyone else to bring professionalism to Sheffield football.

HUTTON, Robert 1898-1902

Born: 1880/81 Ecclesall, Sheffield
Debut:
27 March 1899 v Stoke FC Division One Home
Last Appearance:
11 January 1902 v Notts County Division One Home
Total League & Cup Appearances: 5 Goals: 1

Career Details:

St. Andrews (Sheffield)		
WEDNESDAY	August	1898
Worksop Town		1900
WEDNESDAY		1901
Chesterfield	May	1902 £10
Worksop Town	August	1904

Centre forward who had two spells at Wednesday over a hundred years ago. Started his playing career in Sheffield junior football, joining The Owls when still a teenager in 1898 and was given a first team debut in one of the last games ever played at Olive Grove. Spent the majority of his time at Wednesday in the club's reserve side – finishing top scorer in 1901-2 with 23 goals – and helped Wednesday to the double of Sheffield Association and Wharncliffe Charity Leagues in 1900. Mid-way through his Wednesday career Hutton – who was a joiner by trade - spent a season at Worksop Town but returned to play a further season at Hillsborough before signing for Chesterfield. Appeared in eleven League and Cup games for the Spireites, scoring once, before returning to Worksop Town.

HYDE, Graham 1988-99

Born: 19 November 1970 Doncaster
(5ft 7ins, 11st 11lbs – 1996)
Debut: 14 September 1991
v Manchester City
Division One Away
Last Appearance: 22 August 1998
v Tottenham Hotspur
Premier League Away
Total League
& Cup Appearances: 164+54 Goals: 16

Career Details:

WEDNESDAY	17 May	1988
Birmingham City	5 February	1999 Free
Chesterfield	18 August	2001 Loan
Peterborough United	20 September	2002 Loan
Bristol Rovers	26 November	2002 Free
Released	30 June	2004
Hereford United	1 August	2004 Free
Worcester City	15 June	2005

Tenacious and wholehearted midfielder who endeared himself to Wednesday fans during the 1990s, thanks to his tigerish displays at the heart of The Owls engine room. He had progressed through the club's youth ranks to sign professional terms – after having helped the Wednesday youth side to success in the Northern Intermediate League Cup – and was given his debut by Trevor Francis in a one-nil win at Maine Road. He duly repaid the faith shown in his ability by appearing in seventeen games during that debut season as Wednesday just missed out on an unlikely Championship win and in the season that followed Hyde made substitute appearances in the two losses to Arsenal in the finals of both the F.A.Cup and League Cup.

In the next two seasons Hyde was a first team regular under Francis but following the arrival of David Pleat in the summer of 1995 his career stagnated somewhat as a combination of injury, poor form and the arrival of Mark Pembridge saw him flit in and out of the first team. Hyde – who won a Central League Championship medal with Wednesday in 1991- also encountered disciplinary problems during the 1997-8 season and a flurry of yellow cards not only resulted in several suspensions but also severely hampered his hopes of regaining a first team shirt. Under the managership of ex-team mate Danny Wilson he found his opportunities almost non-existent and after over a decade as a pro at Hillsborough Hyde moved to Birmingham City, signing for old boss Francis. Enjoyed an encouraging first full season at St.Andrews, appearing in 31 league games, but gradually fell from favour and after 58 league and cup appearances for The Blues joined Division Three strugglers Bristol Rovers. After being released in the summer of 2004 Hyde signed a one-year deal at Nationwide Conference club Hereford United.

IBBOTSON, Wilfred "Wilf" 1944-48

Born: 1 October 1926 Sheffield
(5ft 11½ins, 11st 10lbs – 1948)
Only Appearance: 22 November 1947
v Coventry City
Division Two
Total League
& Cup Appearances: 1* Goals: 0
***Also appeared in**
9 wartime games, scoring 1 goal

Career Details:

Firth Park FC		
WEDNESDAY	March	1944 Amat.
Mansfield Town	6 August	1948 £750
Goole Town		1949

Utility player who signed amateur forms for Wednesday during wartime football after impressing on trial in Sheffield Association League football for the club. Aged only seventeen when he signed, Ibbotson made his senior debut for Wednesday in March 1944 at home to Rotherham United and later signed part-time professional forms. He combined his football with employment as a draughtsman and his fifteen goals during the 1945-6 season helped Wednesday's second team to win the first post-war Central League Championship. He could usually be found at centre forward or on either wing but managed just a solitary first team competitive appearance for Wednesday – in a 3-1 defeat at Highfield Road – before eventually leaving for Mansfield Town. Made just three league appearances for The Stags before dropping into non-league football at Goole Town.

INGESSSON, Klas 1994-95

Born: 20 August 1968 Odeshog, Sweden
(6ft 1ins, 14st – 1995)
Debut: 10 September 1994
v Nottingham Forest
Premier League Away
Last Appearance: 4 November 1995
v Chelsea
Premier League Away
Total League
& Cup Appearances: 15+6 Goals: 2

Career Details:

IFK Gothenburg		1986
Mechelen		1990
PSV Eindhoven		1993
WEDNESDAY	6 September	1994 £800,000
Bari	9 November	1995 £1,000,000
Bologna	31 May	1998
Olympic Marseilles	28 June	2000 £3,000,000
Lecce	12 January	2001 Loan
Lecce	28 December	2001 Free
Elfsborg	January	2003 Trial
Odeshog		2003

CAPS (@SWFC)
Sweden FULL (2) v Iceland 07/09/94, v Hungary 26/04/95

Experienced and much-travelled midfielder who played for his country in both the 1990 and 1994 World Cup Finals, helping Sweden to third spot in the latter, and had already played football in three different countries before being signed by Trevor Francis early in the 1994-5 season. His career had started with nine goals in 53 league games for Swedish side IFK before a spell in Belgium football (28 goals in 99 games for Mechelen) and an unhappy time in Dutch soccer where he appeared in only twelve games for PSV Eindhoven. However his displays in central midfield for Sweden in USA 94 re-ignited interest in his qualities and when Wednesday swooped for his signature he seemed an excellent capture and a possible long-term successor to the recently departed Carlton Palmer. After protracted negotiations he joined the Owls with the undisclosed fee rumoured to be as high as £2m. However it later transpired to be a bargain £50,000 with a further £750,000 payable after a year.

Unfortunately for Ingesson he simply could not adapt to life in the Premier League and came over as a rather cumbersome figure to the majority of supporters. It was only when new manager David Pleat switched the giant Swede to centre half that his Wednesday career finally seemed to be kick started as he gave a series of encouraging displays. Somewhat ironically after probably his best display in a Wednesday shirt – playing in a sweeper role in a nil-nil draw at Stamford Bridge – Ingesson's Owls career came to a sudden close as 24 hours after rejecting a £800,000 bid Wednesday accepted a last minute £1m offer from Italian side Bari for his services. He would stay in Serie A for almost five years, appearing in 94 games for Bari and a further 64 for Bologna before moving to French football in the summer of 2000. Marseille paid a huge fee for his services but Ingesson would appear in only thirteen games for OM – alongside ex-Owl Patrick Blondeau – before returning to Italian football, initially on loan. While playing in Italy Ingesson had been constructing a luxury house in his hometown of Odeshog and after ending his top-class playing career in Italian football he duly returned to his place of birth, taking the role of player-manager at the Swedish minnows.

INGLIS, William White 1924-25

Born: 2 March 1897 Kirkcaldy, Fife, Scotland
(5ft 8$^{1}/_{2}$ins, 12st 7lbs – 1924)
Died: 20 January 1968 Sale
Debut: 8 September 1924
v Derby County
Division Two Away
Last Appearance: 14 March 1925
v Port Vale
Division Two Home
Total League
& Cup Appearances: 31 Goals: 0

Career Details:

Kirkcaldy United		
Raith Rovers		1917
WEDNESDAY	14 June	1924 £100
Manchester United	14 May	1925 £100
Northampton Town	June	1930

Right back signed by Bob Brown in the summer of 1924 from Scottish side Raith Rovers. At Rovers the sturdy defender had been club captain and on three occasions been named as reserve for Scotland, as well as playing in England v Scotland inter-league meetings. He was also involved in the amazing incident in 1923 when the ship taking Raith on a pre season tour of The Canary Islands was shipwrecked off the coast of Spain and all of the players had to abandon ship – including teammate and future Owls player Bill Collier!

His arrival in Sheffield resulted in regular right back Billy Felton being switched to the opposite flank and Inglis was a regular as Brown made further progress towards assembling a side that would take Wednesday out of the Second Division in 1926. However Inglis would spend only one season at Wednesday and could have departed even earlier as in November 1924 he received an offer to play football in the US at the lucrative terms of £14 a week in season and £7 in the close season. He eventually decided against moving across the Atlantic but Inglis – described as "not very speedy but boasting tremendous positional sense" - eventually left for Manchester United exactly eleven months after first crossing the border to sign for Wednesday.

He was primarily used as understudy to regular right back Charlie Moore during his time in Manchester, captaining United's reserve side for several seasons while making only 14 senior appearances for United. His playing career came to a close at the age of 38 after a two-year stay at Northampton Town brought 60 league appearances. He was then appointed assistant–trainer at The Cobblers in June 1932 before moving back to Manchester United in the same role in August 1934. He was later coach at Old Trafford and proved a patriarchal figure to the club's young players, including many of The Busby Babes, until retiring in August 1961 after 27 years on the club's backroom staff.

INGRAM, William "Billy" 1887-93

Born: 11 December 1866 Sheffield
(5ft 6ins, 9st 2lbs – 1890)
Died: 19 March 1949 Shiregreen, Sheffield
Debut: 19 December 1887
v Crusaders F.A.Cup Away
Last Appearance: 31 January 1890
v Derby County F.A.Cup Away
Total League
& Cup Appearances: 16* Goals: 8
***Also appeared in**
32 Alliance League games

Career Details:

Bethel Reds		
Attercliffe		1885-6
Clinton		1886-7
Lockwood Brothers		
Heeley		
WEDNESDAY	November	1886
Heeley		1893

First appeared for Wednesday in a friendly at Owlerton in November 1886 and over the next four seasons was a pivotal figure as the club became established as top dogs in the city and a force to be reckoned with in national football. The attacker netted the first of many hat-tricks for the club against Park Grange in December 1887 and was top scorer with 21 goals in the 1889-90 season as Wednesday won the inaugural Football Alliance League championship and also reached the F.A.Cup Final for the first time - Billy playing in the heavy defeat to Blackburn Rovers at Kennington Oval. He was less to the fore in the following season as Wednesday finished bottom but had the distinction of playing, and scoring, in the club's record 12-0 win against Lancashire side Helliwell in January 1891. Incidentally on the same day United lost 9-1 at home to Notts County to make 22 F.A.Cup goals in one day in the same City!

After Wednesday were elected to the Football League in 1892, Ingram had to be content with reserve team football but did net nine goals as the second string won the Sheffield & District League in 1893. He lived the rest of his life in the City and was a true died-in-the-wool Wednesdayite who visited Hillsborough every week to watch either the first team or reserves play- in December 1947 Billy told a group of Wednesday's players that "you ought to shoot more often, in our days we used to shoot if we had only half a chance".

Prior to his death Billy had an appendicitis operation but just after he once again began watching Wednesday play he caught a chill and sadly became the penultimate member of the 1890 Cup Final side to pass away – the surviving member was Hayden Morley who Ingram had met for the first time in 48 years at an October 1941 reunion! Billy's devotion to Wednesday was no more typified than on his death bed when Ingram asked "how have Wednesday gone on?". When being told they had beaten Nottingham Forest he said "That's good" and died.

IRVINE, Archibald "Archie" 1968-69

Born: 25 June 1946 Coatbridge, Lanarkshire, Scotland
(5ft 7½ins, 10st 8lbs – 1969)
Debut: 12 October 1968 v Queens Park Rangers Division One Away
Last Appearance: 22 November 1969 v West Bromwich Albion
Division One Away
Total League
& Cup Appearances: 31+3 Goals: 1

Career Details:

All Saint United		Amat.
Armadale Thistle Juniors		
Airdrieonians	July	1965
WEDNESDAY	25 September	1968 £15,000
Doncaster Rovers	17 December	1969 *
Scunthorpe United	August	1975
Spa Social		1976 Amat.

* Irvine and Branfoot exchanged for Wilcockson

Initially spotted in Scottish junior football, signing part-time professional forms for league club Airdrie in 1965 – he worked as a plasterer's labourer to supplement his football earnings. His new manager Ralph Collins soon converted Archie from inside forward to outside right and his skilful and aggressive displays on the right wing soon alerted scouts from south of the border to his potential. It was Wednesday who won the chase for his signature and after just three weeks of full-time training he was thrown into top-flight football by Owls boss Jack Marshall. The fast and tricky winger went on to appear in 25 games in his debut season but was in and out of the side at the start of the following campaign and the arrival of Jackie Sinclair signalled the end of his brush with First Division football.

He subsequently moved to Belle Vue in a multi-player swap deal and would enjoy a successful six-year stay at Rovers, captaining the side, winning back-to-back player of the year awards and scoring 16 goals in 228 league games. His professional career ended after a season at Scunthorpe at which point he moved back to the Sheffield area to work as a wagon driver for ten years – also playing on an amateur basis in local football. He then worked for fifteen years as a concrete floorer before taking early retirement.

JACKSON, Jeremiah "Jerry" 1923

Born:
Died: 22 July 1927 Cleethorpes
Only Appearance: 27 August 1923 v Port Vale
Division Two Away
Total League
& Cup Appearances: 1 Goals: 0

Career Details:

Burnley	
WEDNESDAY	1923

Although it has proven impossible to substantiate Jerry Jackson's actual date of birth what is known is that when the Owls trainer made his emergency appearance he was the oldest player to ever play for Sheffield Wednesday. Contemporary reports suggest that Jackson was actually aged 46 when he made his only appearance although research has suggested he could have been as old as fifty – a Jeremiah Jackson was born around 1873 in Burnley which would make him not only one of the oldest players to ever play league football but also the oldest to ever make his debut!

His appearance occurred in a mid-week fixture at Port Vale when Wednesday players Billy Felton and Rees Williams both missed the 1.48pm train from Sheffield station, leaving the Owls short of two players for the Division Two game. Travelling reserve Charlie Petrie filled one of the vacancies at halfback and Jackson pluckily agreed to fill in at outside right. He managed to centre the ball whenever he was unimpeded by opposition players but it became obvious that the pace of the game was beginning to tell and ten minutes before the break Jackson left the field. Five minutes later Wednesday went a goal behind and they played the rest of the game with ten men, losing two-nil, while the old trainer regained his breath!

His thirty-five minute appearance was Jackson's only taste of league football as despite being a professional with home town club Burnley in pre war football he failed to make a first team appearance for The Clarets, being appointed instead as second team trainer in 1907. He achieved success in his first season – winning promotion to the top-flight of the Lancashire League – and was promoted to first team trainer in 1910. He enjoyed a successful time in the years immediately prior to the Great War as Burnley won promotion to the top-flight in 1913 and then won the Cup in 1914. His training qualities were also recognised in October 1912 when he was appointed trainer to the Football League representative side for their inter-league game with The Irish league in Belfast.

During the First World War Jackson was trainer for Lincoln City before being appointed in the same capacity at Wednesday on 18th August 1920, working alongside manager Bob Brown for four years as The Owls tried in vein to win promotion from the old Second Division. He was paid one week's pay in lieu of notice in May 1924 and in July of the following year was appointed trainer at Reading. Whilst at Reading he suffered a stroke when returning from a game at Darlington and in June 1927 was installed as trainer at Grimsby Town. However before he could even take up his appointment he was found dead in his Cleethorpes lodgings, leaving a widow and six children.

JACKSON, Norman Edward 1948-54

Born: 6 July 1925 Bradford
(5ft 11ins, 10st 10lbs – 1951)
Debut: 7 April 1950
v Bury Division Two Away
Last Appearance: 4 April 1953
v Portsmouth
Division One Away
Total League
& Cup Appearances: 31 Goals: 0

Career Details:

Manningham Mills		
WEDNESDAY	18 October	1948 £25
Bristol City	19 June	1954 £750
Oldham Athletic	29 June	1956 Free

Full back who had the misfortune to have his Football League debut wiped from the record books when Wednesday's Division Two game at Coventry City in November 1949 was abandoned after 63 minutes due to fog! His first team chance had arisen when Eddie Gannon had failed to return in time from a funeral in Ireland and it would be almost six months before Jackson was given another chance, replacing the absent Doug Witcomb at left halfback for a goalless draw at Bury. His playing career had started at Dronmow Road School where he won a league championship medal before progressing to Bradford Amateur League football with Manningham Mills. After serving two years National Service in the Navy, playing for the unit football team, Jackson continued to combine amateur football in the winter months with playing local Bradford League cricket in the close season – he still played the summer sport during his time at Wednesday.

While on the books at Hillsborough, Norman was converted to right back and it would be in this position that he made all but one of his senior appearances for the club, initially standing in for Keith Bannister at the end of the relegation season of 1950-1. However Norman could never shake off the role of understudy to the likes of Bannister and Vin Kenny during over six years as a professional at Hillsborough and spent most of his time playing Central League football. His ten games during Wednesday's Division Two Championship season was not sufficient to earn him a medal and after getting a "dead leg" against Portsmouth in April 1953 he never played another first team game for The Owls – he would be dogged by knee trouble for the rest of his career which did not respond to treatment as at the time the club did not employ a qualified physiotherapist. Jackson even paid out of his own pocket to attend a clinic along with Clarrie Jordan and Cyril Turton but after leaving Wednesday he could play in only a handful of games for Bristol City as they won the Division Three (South) title in 1955.

His final club proved to be Oldham where after playing only twice for The Latics he underwent a cruciate knee ligament operation in January 1957 which back in the 1950s signalled the end of his playing career- he was released at the end of June 1957. After retiring from the game he was landlord for eight months at The Don Inn on Penistone Road before joining a Sheffield company that manufactured safety equipment – he eventually became a director at the company until retiring after 29 years service. In later life he played cricket for Coal Aston and Shiregreen and currently lives out his retirement in Sheffield.

JACOBS, Wayne Graham 1987-88

Born: 3 February 1969 Sheffield
(5ft 9ins, 10st 2lbs – 1989)
Debut: 18 August 1987 v Oxford United Division One Home
Last Appearance:
14 November 1987 v Luton Town Division One Home
Total League & Cup Appearances: 9+1 Goals: 0

Career Details:

WEDNESDAY	3 January	1987
Hull City	24 March	1988 £28,000
Rotherham United	5 August	1993 Free
Bradford City	5 August	1994 Free
Halifax Town	15 June	2005

A prime example of a player who failed to impress at Hillsborough but enjoyed a highly successful league career elsewhere. He had first come to prominence when winning the English Schools trophy with Sheffield boys in 1984 and duly joined Wednesday as an apprentice in July 1985, signing professional forms eighteen months later. It was Howard Wilkinson who gave the teenager his first taste of top-flight football – on the left side of midfield – and he later dropped back into an unaccustomed full back role. However he struggled somewhat in top class football and only fourteen months after turning pro dropped down the divisions to sign for Hull City. The move to The Tigers ignited his career and Jacobs would play in exactly 150 games from left back before returning to South Yorkshire to sign for Rotherham United. However after being ever present for just one season for The Millers he moved again, to Bradford City, and found the best form of his career. He helped City win the Division Two play-offs in 1996 and revelled in a new wing back role as his new club consolidated in the higher grade. He took over the captaincy in March 1997 and missed only two league games during the 1998-99 season when Bradford earned a fairytale promotion to the Premier League on the final day of the season. He then helped City stay in the top-flight for two seasons and was at Valley Parade for over ten years, approaching 350 appearances for The Bantams, and remained a valuable and consistent defensive utility player until finally being released in the summer of 2005.

A committed Christian, Jacobs worked for a charity in China before being appointed player/assistant manager at Conference club Halifax Town.

JAMESON, Joseph B. "Joe" 1905-10

Born:
(5ft 8ins, 11st – 1905)
Debut: 4 April 1907
v Sheffield United
Division One Away
Last Appearance: 27 February 1909
v Preston North End
Division One Away
Total League
& Cup Appearances: 7 Goals: 0

Career Details:

Wallsend Park Villa		
WEDNESDAY	April	1905 £50
Castleford	January	1910

Versatile defensive player who spent almost five years at Wednesday, primarily as reserve to the likes of Tommy Brittleton and Willie Layton. Proved a stalwart for the club in reserve team football – helping the second team to the Championship of the Midland League in 1908 – and made the occasional senior appearance for the club at either right back or right half back. Left for Midland League Castleford Town, along with Wednesday team mate Tommy Crawshaw, in early January 1910 and made his debut against Sheffield United reserves a few days later.

JAMIESON, James "Jim" 1893-99

Born: 1871, Cambuslang, Nr. Glasgow
(5ft 8ins, 11st 5lbs – 1896)
Debut: 2 September 1893 v Sunderland Division One Home
Last Appearance:
18 February 1899 v Sunderland Division One Home
Total League & Cup Appearances: 135 Goals: 3

Career Details:

Cambuslang	
Everton	
WEDNESDAY	1893
Released	1899

Owls stalwart from the late Nineteenth Century who was an automatic choice for five seasons after joining from Everton in 1893. Although he was described as having an "ugly style" he was however a tireless worker who would always play until the final whistle and proved himself an outstanding left halfback as Wednesday acclimatised to life in the Football League in the 1890s. He replaced Bruce Chalmers in the Wednesday line up and his work rate and heading ability were vital components in a formidable back line which also included Tommy Crawhaw and Harry Brandon.

Known locally as 'Dr Jim' he had the terrible misfortune in 1896 to miss out on an appearance in the F.A.Cup Final because of good weather! Jamieson had played in nearly every round of Wednesday's run to the Final against Wolves but his place was then dependent upon whether the ground was soft or hard – Jamieson was exceptionally good on soft grounds. Unfortunately there was little sign of rain in the days leading up to the big day and Jamieson's place agonisingly went to Charlie Petrie with Jim left to reflect on his ill fortune. Despite that disappointment Jamieson remained a consistent performer and first team regular for Wednesday until the arrival of Herrod Ruddlesin in 1898, Jamieson spending most of the 1898-99 campaign in the reserve side before being released at the end of the season.

JARVIS, Richard Thomas 1903-06

Born: 1880 Died 1924
(5ft 11ins, 11st 10lbs – 1903)
Debut: 2 April 1904
v Notts County
Division One Away
Last Appearance: 1 April 1905
v Notts County
Division One Home
Total League
& Cup Appearances: 6 Goals: 0

Career Details:

Whitwick White Cross FC		
WEDNESDAY	18 June	1903 £50
Hastings		1906
St Leonards		
Luton Town		

Goalkeeper who signed league forms for Wednesday in the summer of 1903 at the age of 23 and continued to play for Midland League club Whitwick W.C. when not required by The Owls – he in fact played against Wednesday's reserve side in September 1903! He eventually signed a professional contract in October of the same year – Wednesday paying a further £30 to his non-league side – and helped the second team to consecutive top four finishes in the Midland League in 1904 and 1905.

With Jack Lyall firmly in possession of the first team jersey, Jarvis did well to quickly become established as his understudy and stepped into his shoes on several occasions when his rival was unavailable – the high point coming on New Year's Eve 1904 when Jarvis was between the sticks as The Owls thrashed Middlesbrough five-nil at Hillsborough. He eventually dropped out of league soccer to spend the rest of his career in non-league football before passing away at the tender age of forty-four in 1924.

JEEVES, John 'Jack' 1883-84

Born: 2nd Quarter 1862 Sheffield
Only Appearance: 1 December 1883 v Staveley F.A.Cup Away
Total League & Cup Appearances: 1 Goals: 0

Career Details:

WEDNESDAY	1883

"Gentleman player" of the Nineteenth Century who appeared occasionally for Wednesday while studying medicine. His name first appears in a friendly against Darwen at the club's old Hunter's Bar ground in February 1883 and his only senior appearance came in the shock 3-1 F.A.Cup loss at Derbyshire club Staveley. After playing his final game for Wednesday in March 1884, Jeeves – who could usually be found playing at full back - seemingly hung up his boots and after passing his medical exams became a physician and an eminent surgeon.

JEFFERSON, Derek 1976

Born: 5 September 1948 Morpeth
(5ft 11ins, 10st 2lbs – 1976)
Debut: 2 October 1976
v Lincoln City
Division Three Away
Last Appearance: 30 October 1976
v Mansfield Town
Division Three Home
Total League
& Cup Appearances: 6 Goals: 0

Career Details:

Ipswich Town	2 February	1966
Wolverhampton Wanderers	2 October	1972 £88,000
WEDNESDAY	1 October	1976 Loan
Hereford United	4 November	1976 Loan
Hereford United	23 December	1976 £12,000
Boston (US)	April	1976 Loan
Washington Diplomats	May	1977
Hereford United	August	1977

Ex-Northumberland Boys defender who started his career in Suffolk at Ipswich Town, joining The Tractor Boys as an apprentice in July 1964. After appearing in 175 games for Town – winning a Division Two Championship medal in 1968 - he later moved for a large fee to top-flight Wolves from where, after losing his first team place, he eventually arrived at Hillsborough on loan. At the time The Owls were showing signs of revival in Division Three under Len Ashurst and Jefferson performed well as a short-term replacement for Dave Cusack at the heart of The Owls defence. When his loan spell expired he returned to Wolves but quickly joined Hereford United on loan where he would finish his league career, after two spells in North American soccer.

His second spell at Hereford United also involved coaching work and he was later reserve team manager at Birmingham City from November 1978 to 1983. He then left the world of football altogether to work for a drugs company until 1993 when he left to set up his own company dealing with sports pursuits.

JEMSON, Nigel Bradley 1991-94

Born: 10 August 1969 Hutton, Nr Preston
(5ft 10ins, 11st 10lbs – 1992)
Debut: 18 September 1991 v Norwich City Division One Away
Last Appearance: 3 May 1994 v Leeds Utd Premier League Away
Total League & Cup Appearances: 34+34 Goals: 11

Career Details:

Bamber Bridge Youth		
Preston North End	6 July	1987
Nottingham Forest	25 March	1988 £150,000
Bolton Wanderers	23 December	1988 Loan
Preston North End	15 March	1989 Loan
WEDNESDAY	17 September	1991 £800,000
Grimsby Town	10 September	1993 Loan
Notts County	8 September	1994 £300,000
Watford	1 January	1995 Loan
Coventry City	23 March	1995 Loan
Rotherham United	15 February	1996 Loan
Oxford United	23 July	1996 £60,000
Bury	5 February	1998 £100,000
Portuguese football		1999 Trial
Ayr United	21 July	1999 Free
Oxford United	27 January	2000 Free
Shrewsbury Town	18 June	2000 Free
Released	30 June	2003
Ballymena	15 October	2003
Ilkeston Town	August	2004 Free

Another example of a striker who enjoyed great success in the early days of his career only for off the field events to ensure his early promise was not totally fulfilled. In the case of striker Nigel Jemson a serious car accident in 1992 badly interrupted his career and although recovering to enjoy a lengthy career in league football it was in the lower divisions when he had looked capable of appearing at the top of the English game. His early football came in Preston youth soccer – he represented Penwortham as well as Preston Boys – before signing apprentice forms for his local side in August 1986. He made such an impact at the Deepdale club that Brian Clough subsequently took him to Nottingham Forest less than a year after Jemson had signed his first professional contract for North End – he had become one of the club's youngest ever players when making his debut as a 16 year-old trainee in May 1986.

Under Clough's tutelage at Forest, Jemson shot to national prominence when netting the only goal of the game in the 1990 League Cup Final against Oldham Athletic and won a solitary U-21 cap for England before leaving for Hillsborough after scoring roughly one goal in every three top-flight games for Forest. At his best Jemson was a lively all round forward, equally adept with his head as well as his feet, but after arriving at Wednesday with a big reputation his time at the club was a disappointment as a series of niggling injuries and the aforementioned traffic accident saw him net only nine league goals in three seasons. The definite highpoint of his Wednesday career came in October 1991 when he netted twice as a sub in a thrilling 3-2 win over Manchester United at Hillsborough but within a year he almost returned to The City Ground when a swap deal involving Kingsley Black broke down.

After seeing his transfer request granted in August 1993 Jemson eventually did return to Nottingham but it was County who secured his signature.

Since moving to Meadow Lane Jemson has played for a wide variety of clubs with differing degrees of success – while on loan at Rotherham United he scored both Wembley goals as The Millers beat Shrewsbury Town to win the 1996 Auto Windscreens Shield. Much to Rotherham fans disappointment he elected to sign instead for Oxford in the following summer and in his debut season for The U's Jemson netted 23 league and cup goals -the best season of his career. However he could not maintain that strike rate and returned north to sign for Bury. A spell in Scottish football followed before Jemson returned to Oxford and then spent three seasons at Shrewsbury Town. He grabbed national headlines in January 2003 when his double strike saw Town knock Everton out of the F.A.Cup but it would be a bittersweet season for The Shrews captain as his side were relegated from the Football League a few months later. He was released in the summer following demotion and was out of the game until signing a short term deal at Irish League side Ballymena United

JOHNSON, David Anthony 2002

Born: 15 August 1976 Kingston, Jamaica
(5ft 6ins, 12st 3lbs – 2002)
Debut: 5 February 2002 v Preston North End Division One Away
Last Appearance: 6 March 2002 v Wimbledon Division One Home
Total League & Cup Appearances: 7 Goals: 2

Career Details:

Manchester United	1 July	1994
Bury	5 July	1995 Free
Ipswich Town	13 November	1997 £800,000
Nottingham Forest	12 January	2001 £3,000,000
WEDNESDAY	5 February	2002 Loan
Burnley	12 March	2002 Loan
Sheffield United	10 March	2005 Loan

Pacy, livewire striker who seemingly re-launched his career after a successful loan spell at Wednesday. He was quickly becoming a multi-million misfit at Nottingham Forest where after joining from Ipswich Town he had struggled to find any real semblance of form. However following his time at Wednesday and a later loan spell at Burnley he gained some much needed confidence and duly scored a tremendous 29 goals in just 45 games during the 2002-3 season as Forest reached the Division One play-off semi-finals- to cap a memorable season he was named player of the year and also voted into the PFA divisional team.

It was this goal scoring form at Bury and Ipswich that brought Johnson 85 goals before joining Forest although he had initially failed to make a senior appearance for his first club Manchester United. The West Indian born striker won the F.A.Youth Cup with United in 1995 but after just a single year as a pro at Old Trafford he dropped down the divisions to sign for neighbours Bury. It was at Gigg Lane that Johnson started to show the form that would bring him an England "B" cap although during his time he could have played for Wales, Scotland or England! While at Ipswich only injury denied him a cap for Wales – at this time he had already appeared, and scored, for Jamaica – and it was later reported that both Scotland and England were enquiring about his eligibility. However it later transpired that Johnson was not eligible for any of the home countries and would have to be content with representing the country of his birth – he had won four caps for Jamaica up to 2003.

JOHNSON, David Alan 1989-93

Born: 29 October 1970 Dinnington, Nr Sheffield
(6ft 2ins, 13st 8lbs – 1990)
Debut: 18 January 1992 v Aston Villa Division One Away
Last Appearance: 20 April 1992 v Norwich C Division One Home
Total League & Cup Appearances: 5+1 Goals: 0

Career Details:

WEDNESDAY	1 July	1989
Hartlepool United	31 October	1991 2-month loan
Hartlepool United	20 November	1992 Loan
Lincoln City	20 August	1993 £32,000 (T)
Released	March	1996
Chesterfield	July	1996 Trial
Altrincham	September	1996 Free
Worksop Town	October	1996

Tall and powerful forward David Johnson came through the Owls youth ranks after having played his early football for Thorpe Salvin U-10s prior to spending three seasons with Rotherham United's Junior Reds. After signing schoolboy forms for Wednesday he represented Rotherham, South Yorkshire and Yorkshire boys and in July 1987 was offered, and signed, YTS forms for The Owls. He eventually became a Central League regular and was given his first team bow by Trevor Francis in a controversial win at Villa Park in January 1992. However, throughout his time as a professional at Hillsborough, Johnson faced a constant battle to become established at first team level, facing stiff competition from the likes of David Hirst, Paul Williams and Mark Bright. It was a fight he would eventually lose and after two loan spells at Hartlepool United he left for Lincoln City- his transfer fee decided by tribunal.

He would enjoy two terrific seasons as a right-sided attacker at City- scoring 20 times – and earned the nickname "Magic" after the famous American Basketball player. However his form totally deserted him in the 1995-6 season and after playing on a week-to-week contract he was released before the campaign had reached its conclusion. After joining non-league Altrincham he started to work for his father-in-law as a butcher but after three years at Worksop Town retired from senior football to move with his actress and dancer wife Sue to London. Whilst in London Johnson gained a Sports/Events Management B.A.degree.

JOHNSON, George Alfred 1929-32

Born: 20 July 1905 Ashington
(5ft 9ins, 11st – 1929)
Died: 26 May 1985 Reading
Only Appearance: 4 April 1931 v Blackpool Division One Away
Total League & Cup Appearances: 1 Goals: 1

Career Details:

Ashington Welfare		
Ashington	October	1914
WEDNESDAY	5 July	1929 £500
Reading	June	1932 £90
Watford	May	1937 Free

Centre forward who spent three seasons at Wednesday and was faced with the almost impossible task of dislodging scoring legend Jack Allen and later Jack Ball from the club's first team. In fact Johnson – who was plucked from junior football after netting 40 goals in two seasons for Ashington – played all his football for Wednesday in the Central League except for a solitary senior appearance at Bloomfield Road when, standing in for Ball, he netted in a 4-0 win. In his first season at the club Johnson netted a tremendous 29 goals as the free scoring reserves scored 114 but failed to make the top three! He added a further thirty goals in his remaining two seasons at the club and surely if Wednesday had not been in the midst of a real golden period in their history then Johnson would have played far more first team soccer.

However it was not to be for the consistent scorer and he moved to Division Three (South) side Reading in the summer of 1932. He had to wait until December to make his first team bow and promptly netted a hat trick on debut against Northampton Town. Inexplicably though Johnson would soon be converted into a tough tackling half back by the Reading management and hardly missed a game over the next five years – his only absence came when he tragically lost both his wife and daughter. He captained Reading in their 1935 F.A.Cup quarter-final loss to Arsenal and appeared in 179 senior games for The Royals before reverting back to a forward role for two seasons at Watford. He was taken to Watford to captain the club's reserve side but scored eight times in 22 league games from inside forward before the Second World War effectively ended his playing career.

After the hostilities were over he was appointed coach at Dutch side Krooger F.C in June 1946 and later in the same year was recruited by fellow Netherlands side Gauda, remaining there until November 1949. On returning to the UK he spent just a solitary month as scout for Chelsea before being appointed coach at Oxford City – he was later groundsman at the non-league side until his retirement.

JOHNSON, Jeffrey David 'Jeff' 1976-81

Born: 26 November 1953 Cardiff
(5ft 8ins, 11st 7lbs – 1978)
Debut: 14 August 1976
v Grimsby Town
League Cup Away
Last Appearance: 8 May 1981
v West Ham United
Division Two Home
Total League
& Cup Appearances: 206+5 Goals: 9

Career Details:

Clifton Athletic		
Manchester City	December	1970
Swansea City	19 July	1972 Loan
Loan return	April	1973
Crystal Palace	13 December	1973 £12,000
WEDNESDAY	1 July	1976 Free
Newport County	30 July	1981 £60,000
Gillingham	September	1982 £8,000 (T)
Port Vale	June	1985
Barrow	May	1986 Free

Without doubt one of the finest free transfer acquisitions in the club's history as when Wednesday boss Len Ashurst snapped him up, after Crystal Palace manager Malcolm Allison had somewhat hastily released him, he signed an experienced former Welsh U-23 International who provided sterling service to The Owls over the next five seasons to help Wednesday out of the Third Division. The stylish midfielder was an automatic choice for Ashurst and his successor Jack Charlton, duly winning the fans 'player of the year' accolade during the 1979-80 promotion season. He was still a regular first team member during the club's first season back in Division Two but in 1981 became the final player to be sold from the squad Jack Charlton inherited back in October 1977.

The ex-Welsh schoolboy and Youth International had started his career at Manchester City – after having signed schoolboy forms at Bristol Rovers - but after only six league games was sent on a long-term loan to Swansea City where he appeared in 39 games but failed to seal a permanent deal. However after a short loan spell at Crystal Palace he did secure a full transfer - joining on a permanent basis in January 1974 – and played 87 times for The Eagles before moving north to Hillsborough. The move to Newport County meant Len Ashurst signed him again and Johnson was an almost ever present before seeing out his league career at Gillingham and then Port Vale. His final club proved to be Northern Premier League outfit Barrow but a broken leg caused his retirement in 1986. He later obtained a PSV licence and is now a taxi driver in Manchester.

JOHNSON, Kevin Peter 1970-72

Born: 29 August 1952 Doncaster
(5ft 5ins, 10st 3lbs – 1971)
Only Appearance:
14 August 1971 v Queens Park Rangers Division Two Away
Total League & Cup Appearances: 0+1 Goals: 0

Career Details:

WEDNESDAY	27 July	1970
Southend United	September	1972 Free
Gillingham	27 February	1974 Loan
Workington	22 July	1974 £5,000
Hartlepool United	14 February	1975
Huddersfield Town	24 September	1976 £23,000
Halifax Town	10 August	1978 £25,000
Hartlepool United	1 January	1981*
Gateshead		1984
Pilkington Recreation		1986

* Exchange for Billy Ayre

Kevin Johnson's first team career at Wednesday is recorded as one of the shortest in the club's history – lasting only eighteen minutes after replacing Paul Taylor at Loftus Road in the opening game of the 1971-2 season. His brief appearance proved the highlight of an Owls career that had started in 1968 when the ex-Doncaster Boys player signed apprentice forms for the club. The inside forward slowly worked his way through the ranks to became a reserve team regular by the early 1970s but his taste of first team football proved no more than that as after making the match day twelve at QPR he never again made the subs bench, or for that matter the starting eleven. This inevitably led to his move away from Hillsborough in search of first team soccer, Johnson scoring once in 17 games at his next club Southend United.

For the remainder of the decade Johnson returned to his Northern roots, appearing for a wide variety of teams with varying degrees of success. He scored only once for then league side Workington and played over one hundred times in two spells at Hartlepool United. However his best years came in the late 1970s when at Huddersfield Town he netted 23 times and was named 'player of the year' in 1977-8. He then became Halifax Town's record signing and was again named 'player of the year' for the 1978-9 campaign although a broken leg suffered in September 1979 meant he missed almost all of the following season. When his professional career ended at Hartlepool in 1984 Johnson spent two years employed in the industrial diamond industry – working with diamond tipped tools – while also appearing for Gateshead in a player-coach role.

A move back to his hometown came next as he took over the Sun Inn public house at Scawsby, near Doncaster while also spending a season as player-manager at local non-league side Pilkington Recreation – he finished playing after a handful of games for an over-35 team in the Doncaster area. After two years as a publican Kevin – whose son married Alan Finney's daughter - moved back into industry at Polypipe and is currently employed as a quality control inspector at the company.

JOHNSON, Peter "Charlie" 1957-65

Born: 31 July 1931 Rotherham
(5ft 9ins, 10st 8lbs – 1961)
Debut: 25 December 1957
v Preston North End
Division One Home
Last Appearance: 2 January 1965
v Sheffield United
Division One Away
Total League
& Cup Appearances: 207 Goals: 6

Career Details:

St Beads Roman Catholic Youth		
The Tree Club Youth		
Rawmarsh Welfare		1948
Rotherham United		1952 P-Time
Rotherham United	March	1953 Pro
WEDNESDAY	24 December	1957 £6,000*
Peterborough United	1 July	1965

*Plus Albert Broadbent

Started playing in schoolboy football as a goalkeeper but soon became an outfield player where the seeds of his professional career were first sown. While a youngster Peter often played football in the street and Rotherham player Danny Williams often joined in, starting a life long friendship that would see the two play together at Millmoor and the future Wednesday boss act as best man when Peter married his first wife. After leaving school he combined a job as a baker/confectioner with appearing for Rotherham based non-league side Rawmarsh Welfare before starting his two-year stint of National Service. During his time in the Army, Johnson was a dispatch rider and later a driving instructor before being promoted to Lance Corporal. He also played regularly for his unit team and on being de-mobbed signed for The Millers on a part-time basis, progressing to a fully fledged professional in 1953.

He initially broke into The Millers first team at inside forward but would play the majority of his games at left back or half back before given a trial run at centre-forward early in 1956. Although not a roaring success in the No. 9 shirt he did net regularly, including a hat trick in the November 1956 meeting with Notts County, before dropping back into a defensive position in March 1957. The Owls had tried to sign Johnson back in 1954 – he refused as he only wanted to play for Rotherham – but finally got their man on Christmas Eve 1957 after he had appeared in 153 league games for his hometown club, scoring 23 times. The Owls new signing possessed great attacking flair allied with a keen sense of positional play and within twenty-four hours made his debut in a thrilling 4-4 draw with Preston at Hillsborough – the Owls last ever Christmas Day fixture.

He was not an immediate fixture at Wednesday until Ron Staniforth left in 1959 at which point 'Charlie' made the right back spot his own, being almost ever present for four seasons as Wednesday finished runners-up to Spurs in 1961 and finished in the First Division's top six in every season. Lightening fast and brave as a lion he proved an excellent Eric Taylor signing and as well as league success he helped The Owls to the F.A.Cup semi-final in 1960 and last eight of the Fairs Cup in 1962. However during the 1964 pre season tour of Germany Peter fell out with manager Alan Brown, over a non-footballing matter, and played only twice more for Wednesday although he was named 12th man on thirteen occasions (in the days before substitutes a player always travelled in case of injury or illness). Brian Hill took his first team place and Johnson left for Peterborough United at the end of a season of reserve team soccer. He added 42 league appearances to his career tally at London Road – incidentally he appeared as an emergency stand-in goalkeeper for both Peterborough and Wednesday –before retiring in 1967 to move back to Rotherham. Incidentally one curious statistic about Johnson was that he was part of three different sides, Rotherham, Wednesday & Peterborough, from three different divisions who scored seven times away from home in competitive matches.

He then owned a tailors shop in Rotherham for two years – while also playing occasionally for Derek Dooley's all-star charity side – before gaining employment at the Templeborough steel works as an auxiliary burner. He later worked in the furnace shop and is now living out his retirement with his second wife – his first wife passed away – and new young family.

JOHNSON, Thomas "Tommy" 2001

Born: 15 January 1971 Newcastle-upon-Tyne
(5ft 11ins, 12st 4lbs – 2001)
Debut: 8 September 2001 v Birmingham City Division One Away
Last Appearance:
16 October 2001 v Preston North End Division One Home
Total League & Cup Appearances: 9 Goals: 3

Career Details:

Notts County	19 January	1989
Derby County	12 March	1992 £1,300,000
Aston Villa	6 January	1995 £1,450,000
Glasgow Celtic	27 March	1997 £2,400,000
Everton	24 September	1999 Loan
WEDNESDAY	7 September	2001 3-month loan
Kilmarnock	20 December	2001 Free
Gillingham	6 July	2002 Free
Contract cancelled	31 January	2005
Sheffield United	9 February	2005
Scunthorpe United	13 June	2005

Lively and hard running attacker who shot to prominence at his first club Notts County under the management of Neil Warnock. His 57 goals – including strikes in consecutive Wembley play-off finals - in 146 competitive games for County led to seven England U-21 caps and a big money move to neighbours Derby County. He continued to score a goal every three games while in the East Midlands and his transfer value increased again when Aston Villa proved his next destination. A 1996 League Cup winners medal followed for the ginger-haired forward before a successful spell in Glasgow at Celtic brought a domestic League Championship in 2001, S.F.A.Cup in 2001 and League Cup in 2000.

Despite this success he actually appeared in only 48 games for The Bhoys and was allowed to join Everton on loan, making just three sub appearances for the Merseyside club. His career was certainly in need of a boost when he joined Wednesday on a three-month loan deal early in the 2001-2 campaign and Johnson impressed the Owls faithful with his forward play. Unfortunately the injury problems that badly affected his career in Scottish football again reared their ugly head part way through his time in Sheffield and he spent the final six weeks of his loan spell in the treatment room. Not surprisingly he was not offered a contract by Wednesday and he soon returned to Scotland to sign for Kilmarnock. Seven goals in only ten league games for Killie showed he had lost none of his poacher's instincts and a move back to England soon followed. A broken bone in his foot – following a collision with a teammate – interrupted his debut season at Gillingham and he was mainly used in a substitutes role – ironically one of only two league goals he scored came against The Owls in November 2002 in a 1-1 draw in Kent.

He remained in Kent for two further seasons before his contract was cancelled by mutual consent in January 2005. After turning down a move to Wycombe Wanderers he was appointed 'attacking' coach by his old boss Neil Warnock, on a contract until the end of the season. He also registered as a player although he was only seen as an emergency option if the Blades were hit by an injury crisis.

JOHNSTON, Allan 2002-03

Born: 14 December 1973 Glasgow
(5ft 11ins, 11st – 2002)
Debut: 14 December 2002 v Gillingham Division One Home
Last Appearance:
1 March 2003 v Preston North End Division One Home
Total League & Cup Appearances: 12 Goals: 2

Career Details:

Lenzie Boys Club		
Eastercraigs Boys Club		
Glasgow Rangers Juniors		
Tynecastle Boys Club	August	1989
Heart of Midlothian	23 June	1990
Rennes	1 July	1996 Free
Sunderland	1 April	1997 £550,000
Birmingham City	10 October	1999 Loan
Bolton Wanderers	27 January	2000 Loan
Glasgow Rangers	1 June	2000 Free
Middlesbrough	1 September	2001 £1,000,000
WEDNESDAY	13 December	2002 3-month loan
Kilmarnock	10 August	2004 Free

Scottish International winger who holds a unique place in the history of Sunderland Football Club as the player who scored the last ever goal at Roker Park. His spell at The Black Cats was without doubt the most successful and consistent period in his career, culminating in a fantastic 1998-99 season when Sunderland lifted the First Division Championship and Johnston not only won four full caps for his Country but was also named in the PFA Divisional team. However Johnston – nicknamed 'Magic' by Sunderland fans – then fell dramatically from grace as after refusing to sign a new deal offered in the summer of 1999 he was effectively frozen out of the first team picture by manager Peter Reid. Two loan spells followed before Scottish giants Rangers ended his turbulent season by taking him to Ibrox Park after 20 goals in 101 appearances for Sunderland.

He would appear in only nineteen games for Rangers, in just over a year in Glasgow, before returning to the northeast of England to sign for ambitious Middlesbrough. Johnston – a superb two-footed crosser of the ball who could turn a full back inside out on either wing – was a first team regular in his early months at Boro but slowly fell out of favour, leading to a loan move to Hillsborough. His pace and terrific wing player endeared him to Owls fans during three months in Sheffield but with a full transfer out of the question he returned to The Riverside hoping to re-launch a career that had started to stagnate. He had first come to prominence while at Hearts where fourteen goals in 94 games helped him gain four Scotland U-21 caps. After leaving Tynecastle Allan spent a year in French football before a sizeable fee took him to Sunderland while he returned to his roots in the summer of 2004, signing a three-year deal at Scottish Premier League side Kilmarnock.

JOICEY, Brian 1971-76

Born: 19 December 1945
Winlanton, Co. Durham
(5ft 11ins, 12st 2lbs – 1974)
Debut: 31 August 1971
v Middlesbrough
Division Two Away
Last Appearance: 20 March 1976
v Rotherham United
Division Three Away
Total League
& Cup Appearances: 160+6 Goals: 53

Career Details:

Clara Vale		1960 Amat.
Ashington		Amat.
Blyth Spartans		Amat.
Tow Law Town		Amat.
North Shields		1967 Amat.
Coventry City	June	1969 Free
WEDNESDAY	27 August	1971 £55,000
Barnsley	July	1976
Retired	February	1979
Frickley Athletic		1979
Matlock Town		1980-81
Royal Oak (Coal Aston)		1980 Sun.

The 1970s were a grim decade in the history of Sheffield Wednesday with goals at a premium but one man did hit the net on a regular basis – swashbuckling forward Brian Joicey. The ex-Blaydon boys attacker was actually still playing amateur football in his native northeast at the age of 23 and it was not until he hit the headlines with Northern League North Shields in 1969 that a professional career looked a possibility. The last year of the 1960s proved a real springboard to success for Joicey as his remarkable goal haul of 45 helped his club to a Northern League and cup double, a Northumbrian Senior Cup triumph and best of all an F.A.Amateur Cup win at Wembley against Sutton United – Joicey scoring the only goal of the match. To cap a remarkable year he was also picked to tour Japan in the summer with the famous Middlesex Wanderers (effectively the Great Britain Amateur team) whilst he also made his first appearance at Hillsborough when in April he netted four times as an F.A.Amateur XI beat a Universities Union side 6-0!

Despite making an initial impact in the professional game at Coventry City – his winning goal in a game versus Wolves took The Sky Blues into Europe for the first time - he was subsequently rescued from reserve team football by Derek Dooley in a move that also saw Dave Clements sign for The Owls. He quickly became a big crowd favourite at Hillsborough, scoring 16 times in his debut season, although it was a game in the following season for which he is probably best remembered when grabbing a treble to knock First Division Crystal Palace out of the F.A.Cup in a dramatic second replay at Villa Park. In the same season he also netted a hat trick against Orient and in total scored twenty league and cup goals as Wednesday lifted the Hillsborough gloom by spending the season in the top half of the Second Division table and reaching the last sixteen of the Cup. For Owls fans he also netted a vitally important goal in the desperate 1974-5 campaign, in which Joicey was plagued by injury, when scoring in the final minute against Oxford United at Hillsborough – the goal triggered wild scenes of celebration as incredibly it was the club's first goal for eight games!

Injury and loss of form saw Joicey finish his Owls career playing at centre half in reserve team football before moving to Barnsley on a free transfer – a 1976 deadline day £3,000 move to Port Vale having fallen through. He continued to score freely at Oakwell – 43 goals in 92 league games – but his professional career came to a dramatic close in November 1978 when during a game at York City he was kicked in the kidneys and later collapsed after suffering a stroke. He was forced to retire soon after but the spirited Geordie was soon back playing in non-league soccer while concentrating on his partnership in a car sales business based on Middlewood Road, next to The Owls training Ground. His playing days ended with the occasional appearance for Derek Dooley's All Star side while he later managed and coached his son's football team from U-11 to U-18s. He later sold his share in the car business and is now Corporate Sales Manager for Sheffield based Peter Brookes Honda while living in Dronfield.

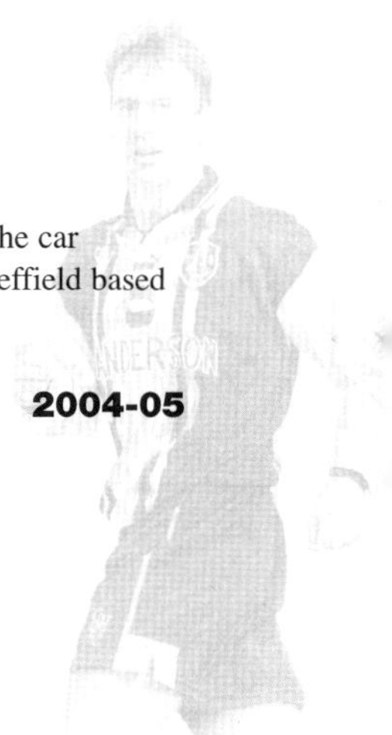

JONES, Kenwyne 2004-05

Born: 5 October 1984 Trinidad (6ft 2ins)
Debut: 19 December 2004
v Doncaster Rovers League One Away
Last Appearance: 15 January 2005
v Bournemouth League One Away
Total League & Cup Appearances: 7 Goals: 7

Career Details:

St Anthonys College		
Joe Public		
Vibe CT 105 W Connection		2002
Glasgow Rangers	April	2004 Trial
West Ham United		Trial
Southampton	1 July	2004 £150,000
WEDNESDAY	17 December	2004 Loan
Stoke City	14 February	2005 Loan

When virtual unknown Kenwyne Jones arrived from Southampton no one could have envisaged that a month later he would return to the South Coast having made the greatest impact of any loan player in the club's history. His record of seven goals in as many games helped the Owls to move from mid-table into a play off position and made supporters clamour for the club to secure his long-term signature from Southampton. However the Saints – no doubt influenced by his scoring at Wednesday - were not willing to deal and he returned after his first experience of league football. He scored for the Saints' reserve side a few days later and within a week made his Premier League debut – as a late sub, on the left hand side of midfield - in the 2-0 home win over Liverpool. However Jones was soon out on loan again, this time joining Championship club Stoke City for a three-month period.

His career had started back in his Caribbean homeland where Jones was initially a strong, aggressive and intelligent defender who could also play upfront. He quickly won International honours, being voted one of the outstanding defenders of the 2001 FIFA U-17 World Championships, which were held in Trindad & Tobago. His qualities soon started to attract interest from abroad and over the months that followed Jones attended trials at a variety of clubs including Manchester United, Middlesbrough, West Ham United, Tottenham Hotspur and Glasgow Rangers. A few months later he captained the U-20 side and the inevitable full cap for his country came in January 2003 when Jones faced Finland at the tender age of just nineteen. It was obvious a move into European club football was on the horizon for the tall and commanding Trinidadian and the move was made easier as Kenwyne qualified for a two-year commonwealth country visa, meaning no work permit was required. It was Premier League Southampton who won the race for his signature – Jones signing a pre contract with the Saints in April 2004 – and it was here that Paul Sturrock first recognised the versatility that Jones possessed. Although he was seen as a utility player before arriving at Hillsborough there is no doubt that he left as a fully-fledged striker after a loan spell that contributed greatly to the Owls eventual qualification for the play offs and subsequent promotion.

JONES, Ryan Anthony 1991-97

Born: 23 July 1973 Sheffield
(6ft 1ins, 13st 10lbs – 1996)
Debut: 3 March 1993
v Coventry City
Premier League Away
Last Appearance: 29 April 1995
v Southampton
Premier League Away
Total League
& Cup Appearances: 43+6 Goals: 7

Career Details:

WEDNESDAY	18 June	1991
Scunthorpe United	11 January	1996 Loan
Retired	12 March	1997
Worksop Town	January	1998
Glapwell	September	1999Loan
Colley WMC		2000-05 Sun.
Maltby Miners Welfare	August	2001
Parkgate		
Staveley	April	2002

CAPS (@SWFC)
Wales Full (1) v Estonia 23/05/94
Wales 'B' (1) v Scotland 02/02/94
Wales U-21 (4) v Romania 16/11/93, v Bulgaria 13/12/94 & 28/03/95, v Germany 25/04/05

Ryan Jones was a tall, powerfully built left sided midfielder who burst into the Owls Premier League side under the managership of Trevor Francis. He had initially joined the club straight from school, in July 1989, and after helping Wednesday to the Final of the F.A.Youth Cup in 1991 seemed a real prospect for the future. His first team chance duly came when a fixture pile up meant Francis was forced to blood several youngsters and he made such a good impression that Jones enjoyed a terrific 1993-4 season, appearing in 34 first team games, scoring seven times – including a memorable diving header that won a League Cup tie at QPR. A Welsh grandmother also meant he won several representative honours – he was brought into the Welsh set up by Terry Yorath who thankfully was not discouraged after phoning Ryan to enquire about his surname only to be met with a broad Yorkshire accent!

At the end of his 'breakthrough' season Jones signed a lucrative 5-year contract but unfortunately for the youngster his career then hit the rocks as a series of persistent injury problems kept him on the sidelines. A loan spell at Scunthorpe – scoring on his debut – improved his fitness but the youngster was fighting a losing battle and sadly a career that looked set to reach the heights was abruptly ended in March 1997 when he was forced to retire from the professional ranks after failing to recover from a serious ankle injury. During his final season at Wednesday Ryan managed his brother's side Wadsley Bridge in the Meadowhall Sunday League and it was in non-league football that he launched a comeback in 1998, in the reserve team at Worksop Town. After proving his fitness, although he was unable to train, Ryan moved into The Tigers first team and helped them gain promotion to the Northern Premier League top-flight in 1998. He later played Saturday and Sunday football for a variety of local sides while carving out an alternative career in insurance. He currently runs a car-hire firm whilst playing at centre half for Colley Working Men's Club in Sunday football.

JONES, Thomas John "Tommy" 1929-34

Born: 11 August 1908
Tonypandy, Glamorgan
(5ft 8½ins, 10st 12lbs – 1930)
Died: 29 August 1971 West Bromwich
Debut: 5 April 1930 v Liverpool Division One Away
Last Appearance: 14 April 1934 v Leicester City Division 1 Away
Total League & Cup Appearances: 29 Goals: 6

Career Details:

Mid-Rhondda		
Dundee		Trial
Tranmere Rovers	February	1926
WEDNESDAY	29 June	1929 £1500
Manchester United	16 June	1934
Watford	May	1935 £1500
Arsenal		1945 Guest
Guildford City	June	1946

CAPS (@SWFC)
Wales Full (2) v Northern Ireland 05/12/31, v France 25/05/33

Welsh International right winger who was limited to fleeting first team appearances due to the outstanding and almost injury free form of Mark Hooper. Throughout his Wednesday career the fast and tricky attacker – known to be not afraid to cut in from the wing and have a shot at goal -was never anything other than a stand in for Hooper but nevertheless gave loyal service in reserve team football, always performing admirably when called into the first team. His time at Wednesday did of course coincide with one of the best periods in the club's history but after failing to dislodge his nemesis Hooper he left for Manchester United in search of regular first team soccer. Unfortunately Jones – who started in non-league soccer before turning down Dundee to sign for Tranmere Rovers – experienced no real change in fortunes at Old Trafford as despite impressing in his early performances he drifted out of contention, eventually moving to Watford after 4 goals in 22 league and cup games for United.

The move to Vicarage Road proved his final transfer in league soccer as Jones would spend over eleven years on Watford's books, appearing in 137 peacetime games and playing more wartime matches than any other Watford player (241). Jones ended his playing career back in non-league football before being appointed trainer-coach at Tranmere Rovers in August 1946, moving to the same role at Workington seven years later. He was caretaker boss at Workington in September 1953 and subsequently moved to Birmingham City as assistant trainer in August 1958 and was then physio at neighbours West Bromwich Albion from 1966 until his retirement in 1971.

JONK, Wim 1998-2001

Born: 12 October 1966
Volendam, Holland
(6ft, 12st 2lbs – 1999)
Debut: 15 August 1998
v West Ham United
Premier League Home
Last Appearance: 19 August 2000
v Huddersfield Town
Division One Home
Total League
& Cup Appearances: 80+1 Goals: 5

Career Details:

RKAV Volendam		
FC Volendam		1986
Ajax Amsterdam		1988
Inter Milan	August	1993
PSV Eindhoven	August	1995
WEDNESDAY	6 August	1998 £2,500,000
Released	30 June	2001

CAPS (@SWFC)
Holland Full (1) v Denmark 18/08/99

Dutch playmaker who was Danny Wilson's first capture as Owls boss, the tall, rangy central midfielder treading the well-worn path that had previously brought Marc Degryse and Klas Ingesson from PSV Eindhoven. In the previous summer Jonk had played for Holland in their World Cup semi-final defeat to Brazil and his qualities were obvious when he settled into the Owls midfield – his vision reminding many fans of midfield master John Sheridan. He was ever present during his debut season, helping Wednesday to a mid table finish in the Premier League, but struggled to impose his talents in the following campaign as The Owls tumbled out of the top-flight. Unfortunately the situation only worsened for Jonk as a groin injury suffered in only the second game of the new season meant he spent the final year of his contract on the treatment table – an expensive injury for a now cash strapped Wednesday. At the end of his three-year contract Jonk retired altogether from professional football and after commentating on Dutch football for French TV company Canal Plus joined the board of home town club Volendam in April 2003.

Before moving to England Jonk had enjoyed great success in his homeland where his career had started in the small Dutch fishing village of Volendam at the local amateur side. He later progressed to the town's professional side and soon helped them to the Second

Division Championship before moving to Ajax after 28 goals in 59 games. After a three-season fight he became an Ajax regular during the 1991-2 season and after winning the UEFA Cup he added a Dutch Cup winners medal in 1993. By this time he had won the first of 49 full caps for Holland - starring in the 1994 World Cup Finals - and in the summer of 1993 left for Italian giants Inter in a big money transfer that also saw Dennis Bergkamp move to the The San Siro. However neither really settled in Milan although Jonk did score a spectacular 30-yarder in the 1994 UEFA Cup Final as Inter beat fellow Italians Torino on away goals to lift the trophy. After two years he was back in Holland and won the Dutch Cup again in 1996 before earning his first league championship medal a year later.

JONSSON, Sigurdur 'Siggi' 1985-89

Born: 27 September 1966 Ikranes
(6ft, 11st 7lbs – 1985)
Debut: 9 March 1985
v Leicester City
Division One Away
Last Appearance: 13 May 1989
v Middlesbrough Division One Home
Total League
& Cup Appearances: 64+9 Goals: 6

Career Details:

I.A.Akranes		1982
WEDNESDAY	11 January	1985 nominal
Barnsley	30 January	1986 2-month loan
Arsenal	27 July	1989 £475,000 (T)
Retired	January	1992
I.A.Akranes		1992
Orebro	January	1996
Dundee United	24 November	1997 £50,000
I.A.Akranes	April	2000
FH Hafnarfjarder	February	2001

CAPS (@SWFC)
Iceland Full (14) v Luxembourg 24/04/85, v Scotland 28/05/85, v Spain 25/09/85, v Eire 25/05/86, v France 10/09/86, v USSR 24/09/86, v East Germany 29/10/86, v France 29/04/87, v East Germany 04/06/87, v Norway 09/09/87, v USSR 31/08/88, v Hungary 21/09/88,v USSR 31/05/89, v Austria 14/06/89

When Icelandic midfielder Siggi Jonsson arrived in England he was only eighteen years old but was such a prodigious talent in his homeland that he was already capped at senior level by his country in addition to having won two domestic league championships and three Iceland cups. He came from a real footballing family, as his father was one of several brothers to play for Akranes while his uncle Rikhardur actually had a trial at Arsenal in the 1950s. It would be the younger Jonsson though who would become one of the greatest players in the island's history after learning his trade as an amateur at hometown club Akranes – a small fishing town with a population of only 5,000. He joined straight from school and showed his maturity and outstanding promise when being picked for the Iceland U-18 team when aged only fifteen.

The youngster had trials at both Anderlecht and Feyenoord but was actually recommended to Wednesday boss Howard Wilkinson by England manager Bobby Robson. It would be Wilkinson who won the race for the teenager and Jonsson duly arrived in December 1984 although he had to wait several weeks for a work permit before putting pen to a three-year contract. His first game in a Wednesday shirt actually came in a youth game and it would be several months before Siggi could reach the fitness levels of his teammates. A subsequent loan spell at Barnsley gave Jonsson valuable experience of the 'hurly-burly' of English league soccer and he slowly started to push his way into the first team picture at Hillsborough. Ironically his style of play was not really suited to the pressing play favoured by the man who brought him to Hillsborough and it wasn't until Wilkinson left that Jonsson's huge potential started to show. He scored some truly spectacular goals – a long range effort at Norwich City perhaps the most memorable – and there is no doubt he was one of the most naturally gifted players to appear for the club in the 1980s. However he was also dogged by injury and this continued after George Graham swooped to take Siggi to Highbury when he was out of contract in the summer of 1989. In fact he appeared in only nine games for Arsenal before a serious back injury looked to have brought an early end to his playing career.

However after several months of recuperation he came back into football at his old side in Iceland and after proving his fitness moved into Swedish football at Orebro. A move to Scotland came next for the rejuvenated Jonsson before two spells back in Iceland finally brought the curtain down on a varied career, which perhaps did not reach the heights that his talents deserved despite that fact that he won 66 full caps for Iceland. His first backroom role came at FH Hafnarfjarder where he was appointed assistant coach in 2001 before being promoted to manager a year later. In 2003 he was named new boss at Reykjavik side Vikingur who had just earned promotion to Iceland's top division.

JORDAN, Clarence 'Clarrie' 1948-55

Born: 20 June 1922 South Kirkby
(5ft 8ins, 11st 10½lbs – 1948)
Died: 24 February 1992 Doncaster
Debut: 7 February 1948
v Bradford Park Avenue
Division Two Home
Last Appearance: 18 September 1954
v Sheffield United
Division One Away
Total League
& Cup Appearances: 94 Goals: 36

Career Details:

South Kirkby Juniors		
Upton Colliery		
Doncaster Rovers	August	1939 P-Time
South Kirkby Colliery		1941
Aldershot		1942-3 Guest
Leeds United	October	1943 Guest
Birmingham City		1944-5 Guest
Derby County		1944-5 Guest
WEDNESDAY	4 February	1948 £3000 + Arnold Lowes
Retired injured	May	1955

Not long after Clarrie Jordan's birth his father died due to wounds received in the Great War and this signalled that life would not be easy for him in the South Yorkshire pit village of South Kirkby. However he soon learned how to 'look after himself' and earned the nickname 'Canny' while attending a local school and playing at full back for the newly formed South Kirkby juniors team. Jordan was an all round sportsman but it was football he loved most and he continued to develop, physically and mentally, after leaving school to work in the local pit. After moving to centre forward he once netted an astonishing 117 goals in just one season for the Pit side and during one of a handful of games for Upton Colliery was asked to sign for Leeds United. However Clarrie was a hometown boy and was soon taken under Fred Emery's wing at Doncaster Rovers, signing as a part-time professional just before the outbreak of war.

His mining job was a reserved occupation so Jordan was not called into the forces during the war and was therefore able to play on a regular basis for Doncaster Rovers while also guesting for several other sides. He made his senior debut for Rovers in May 1940 at Sheffield United and would score over sixty goals in Wartime soccer for the Belle Vue club - this was despite spending almost all of the 1941-2 season appearing for his pit side in local soccer. Every club he played for during wartime soccer wanted to sign him on a permanent basis from Rovers but Clarrie turned down all the overtures to remain loyal to his local club. One curiosity is that when he played twice for Aldershot in wartime soccer it was under the pseudonym of Brookes – replacing Tommy Lawton – and only returned to South Yorkshire when a local journalist uncovered the fact that he was 'only' a pit boy from Yorkshire!

When the war finally reached its end Jordan was still only a part-time player and he remained so during the incredible 1946-7 season when Rovers walked away with the Division Three (North) championship, setting a new points record of 72 and scoring 123 times. Jordan's personal haul was a remarkable 42, making the deadly centre forward the top scorer in English football in that first season of post war soccer. This form of course alerted many clubs to his talents and when Rovers were trying to avoid the drop in the following season they asked Clarrie to leave as Wednesday were offering a player plus cash for his services. He duly left his job at the pit to sign as a full-time professional at Hillsborough and would score regularly for Wednesday for the remainder of the decade. His four goal haul at home to Hull City in 1949 was a definite highlight but this display was not unconnected with the rough ride he subsequently received at Boothferry Park in the return game. The knee injury he received in that game made the rest of the season a struggle for Clarrie and he eventually needed an operation to correct the problem - after helping Wednesday to promotion from Division Two. Unfortunately by the time he returned to fitness both Hugh McJarrow and Jack Shaw had been brought into Hillsborough and Jordan would have to settle for a bit part role for the rest of his Owls career until arthritis in his knees caused an early retirement in 1955.

After hanging up his boots Jordan was appointed steward of the South Kirkby Coronation Working Men's Club, remaining there for 14 months before becoming landlord of the White Rose Pub in the Doncaster village of Rossington. In 1958 he became licencee of the Schoolboy Inn at Norton and would stay behind the bar until retiring in 1986. Sadly in later life diabetes meant he lost both legs to the disease before passing away at the age of 69 in 1992.

JORDAN, John William 'Bill/Johnny' 1950-51

Born: 8 November 1923 Bromley, London
(5ft 8ins, 11st 4lbs – 1950)
Debut: 23 September 1950
v Huddersfield Town
Division One Away
Last Appearance: 13 January 1951
v Charlton Athletic
Division One Away
Total League
& Cup Appearances: 11 Goals: 2

Career Details:

Bromley		
Grays Athletic		
West Ham United		1946 Amat.
Tottenham Hotspur	August	1947
Juventus	August	1948
Birmingham City	March	1949
WEDNESDAY	19 September	1950 £7,500
Tonbridge	June	1951
Bedford Town	July	1953

Inside forward who during World War Two served in the Royal Air Force, flying spitfires in the pivotal 'Battle of Britain'. When the hostilities came to an end Jordan played for both West Ham and Spurs as an amateur before joining the latter as a professional and appearing in 27 games, scoring ten times- including a double on his Spurs debut against Wednesday! Jordan – who was not a cousin of Clarrie Jordan as has previously been stated in other publications – was a great passer of the ball and possessed great control which was perhaps why he was involved in a ground breaking move to Italian giants Juventus after just a season at White Hart Lane. The move to Turin did not really work out though and he returned to England in the spring of 1949, signing for Birmingham City.

Eighteen months at the St Andrews club brought only 25 league starts before a brief spell at Hillsborough proved no more successful. He made an initial good impression at Wednesday but the arrival of record signing Jackie Sewell in March 1951 effectively ended his Owls career and after rejecting The Owls offer of a new contract in May 1951 he dropped into non-league football. After playing spells in Southern League football he ran a menswear shop until his retirement.

KAY, Anthony Herbert "Tony" 1954-62

Born: 13 May 1937 Sheffield
(5ft 8ins, 10st 7lbs – 1954)
Debut: 8 April 1955
v Bolton Wanderers
Division One Away
Last Appearance: 22 December 1962
v Everton
Division One Home
Total League
& Cup Appearances: 203 Goals: 10

Career Details:

WEDNESDAY	22 May	1954
Everton	27 December	1962 £60,000
Banned sine die	April	1965

CAPS (@SWFC)
England U-23 (7)
v Italy 07/05/59, v West Germany 10/05/59, v Scotland 02/03/60, v Holland 16/03/60, v East Germany 15/05/60, v Poland 18/05/60, v Israel 22/05/60

Football League (3)
v League of Ireland 04/11/59, v Irish League 01/11/61
v Italian League 08/11/61

Unfortunately for outstanding wing half Tony Kay his attributes on the field of play will always be overshadowed by the infamous bribes scandal of 1964 which would eventually see Kay, along with ex Owls team mates David Layne and Peter Swan, banned sine die by the Football Association. Like the majority of young boys his love of sport started to develop at school although it was actually rugby that was Tony's first love, only turning his attentions to football after being told he was too small to play the 15 a-side game. After impressing for Sheffield boys he was signed for Wednesday by pre war player Ted Catlin – the 1930s full back lived across the road from Kay – and spent two years on the club's ground staff before turning professional. The small ginger-haired defender had to wait three years to become an established first team player but he was then an automatic choice – his highly competitive nature, superb passing skills and tough tackling marking him out as one the country's finest players in his position.

He formed part of the famous back line that also included Tom McAnearney and Peter Swan which helped Wednesday to the Second Division title in 1959 and Division One runners-up spot behind the legendary Spurs double team in 1961. A multitude of representative honours also came his way before a shock move to Goodison Park in 1962 – his old Wednesday boss Harry Catterick paying a record fee for a half back to take Kay to Merseyside. His career continued to blossom at Everton – winning a Division One Championship medal in 1963 and what proved to be his sole senior cap for England against Switzerland in the same year. However his career came to an abrupt end in 1964 when he was implicated in a betting scandal that rocked the world of football. It was proven he was one of three Wednesday players who bet on The Owls to lose at Ipswich Town in 1962 and Kay served a four-month prison sentence before receiving a lifetime ban from all levels of football.

After being released from jail Kay tried to pick up the pieces of his life and worked as a bookmaker whilst playing for several local teams using a false name! In February 1967 Toronto Falcons of the outlawed North American Soccer League tried to sign him but Kay turned down the offer and instead emigrated to Spain in the following year. He worked in bars and played for a local team of ex-pats while in Spain but when his ban was lifted in 1972 he decided against making a comeback, remaining in Spain until returning to England in 1986. He gained employment running a sports centre in London and would play for the Arsenal old boys team until aged 61 – along with Tom Watt and Nick Berry he also had the somewhat dubious honour of forming the Eastenders charity football team in 1987! He now lives out his retirement probably still regretting the day when a moment of rashness cost him so dearly.

KAYE, Albert 1897-99

Born: 1875 Staveley
(5ft 8ins)
Died: September 1935
Debut: 11 September 1897
v Bury
Division One Away
Last Appearance: 25 February 1899
v Wolverhampton Wanderers
Division One Away
Total League
& Cup Appearances: 44 Goals: 13

Career Details:

Eckington		1895
WEDNESDAY		1897
Chatham		1899
West Ham United		1900
Stockport County	October	1903 £15
Belfast soccer		1904

Nineteenth Century centre forward who was spotted in local football by Wednesday, signing as a pro in the summer of 1897. He quickly broke into The Owls top-flight side and enjoyed an excellent debut season, scoring ten times in 27 games as Wednesday finished fifth in Division One. However the following season proved a disaster for both club and player as the former suffered relegation and lost their Olive Grove home while Kaye struggled for form and left before the season's end to sign for Kent non-league side Chatham.

He later signed for Southern League West Ham United who had just changed their name from Thames Ironworks. He had the distinction of playing in the first match under the club's new title – a 7-0 win over Gravesend in September 1900 – and scored five times in twenty games as The Hammers finished in sixth place and reached the final qualifying round of the F.A.Cup in their debut season in the competition. When Kaye moved back into the Football League at Stockport County the £15 transfer fee was paid to Wednesday – they still held his registration – but he stayed only briefly at Edgeley Park before moving to Irish football along with ex-West Ham team mate Walter Tranter.

KEAN, Frederick William "Fred" 1920-28

Born: 10 December 1898 or 3 April 1899 Sheffield
(5ft 8ins, 12st – 1935)
Died: 28 October 1973 Sheffield
Debut: 28 August 1920
v Barnsley
Division Two Away
Last Appearance: 8 September 1928
v Sunderland
Division One Home
Total League
& Cup Appearances: 247 Goals: 8

Career Details:

Soldiers and Sailors Federated Team		1918
Crookes United		
Sheffield Club		
Hallam		1919
Portsmouth		1919
WEDNESDAY	June	1920
Bolton Wanderers	13 September	1928 £5,600
Luton Town	June	1931
Sutton Town	13 November	1935

CAPS(@SWFC)
England FULL (7) v Belgium 19/03/23, v Scotland 14/04/23, v Wales 03/03/24, v N.Ireland 22/10/24, v N.Ireland 24/10/25, v Belgium 24/05/26, v Luxembourg 21/05/27

Football League (4) v Irish League 1923, 1925 & 1927, v Scottish League

Fred Kean was born in the Sheffield district of Walkley and such was his patriotism that as a teenager he lied about his age to join the forces during World War One. He was sent home when the authorities found out but they promptly called him up when he was old enough, Kean being conscripted to the Royal Naval Division. Thankfully he survived the horrors of The Great War and on being demobbed in 1918 he returned home to play non-league football back in Sheffield. In was in local football that he quickly developed as an inside forward and his form prompted a move to Southern League Portsmouth. However he appeared in only a solitary friendly for Pompey and was subsequently told by Portsmouth manager Bob Brown that he could secure Fred a move back to Sheffield – days later he signed for Wednesday and was introduced to The Owls new manager – one Bob Brown!

The Owls legendary manager obviously had big plans for Kean and he soon switched him to half back where Fred would truly excel, becoming a fixture at Hillsborough and winning several representative honours including seven of the nine full caps he would earn for England – he became the first Sheffield born player to play for England since Tommy Crawshaw in 1904. His upright playing stance made him akin to a guardsman and the fair-haired Kean was a real no nonsense defender who also liked to venture upfield to have a pop at goal. After helping Wednesday to the Second Division title in 1926 Kean took over the captaincy from Frank Froggatt but subsequently lost his first team place altogether to youngster Leach near the end of the 'Great escape' season of 1927-8 – he had turned down a £5,500 move to Tottenham in January 1928. The captaincy duly passed to Jimmy Seed and after Kean asked for a transfer he left for Bolton Wanderers in a club record sale, to the dismay of many Owls fans.

He scored once in 89 games for Wanderers and won the F.A.Cup in 1929 before transferring to Luton Town where after 117 league appearances he was appointed player-coach at Central Combination club Sutton Town in 1935. After his playing career ended Fred returned to Sheffield to become a publican in the city. Incidentally Kean had to live all his life with the bizarre rumour that he was drunk during a 6-2 Boxing Day home loss to Blackpool in 1924. Such was his poor form in the game that a wag in crowd said he must be drunk – the rumour spread like wildfire and even during his days as a licensee he was still asked about that day!

KELL, George 1920-22

Born: 13 July 1896 Gateshead
(5ft 9ins, 11st 7lbs –1920)
Died: April 1985 Sheffield
Debut: 3 February 1921
v Everton
F.A.Cup Home
Last Appearance: 26 February 1921
v Hull City
Division Two Away
Total League
& Cup Appearances: 6 Goals: 0

Career Details:

Allhusen Works		
WEDNESDAY	May	1920
Brentford	2 June	1922
Hartlepool United	July	1925
Gainsborough Trinity	May	1928

Full back who arrived from northeast non-league soccer in the summer of 1920. Spent his first season at Hillsborough as a reserve team regular in the club's Midland League side and earned a Sheffield Challenge Cup winners medal in March 1921 when Barnsley's second string were beaten 2-0 in the Bramall Lane final – his season also finished on a high when on the final day George netted his only goal for the club, in a 3-1 home win over Gainsborough Trinity. The following season saw Bob Brown shuffle his playing staff in order to find a winning solution and several different men were utilised in both full back roles. One such player was Kell who despite having lost his regular reserve team spot was called into action at left back for the Cup replay with Everton at Hillsborough. Despite Wednesday bowing out of the competition he retained his spot for the next game and then spent five games at right back before dropping out of first team contention as Jack Bellas and Harry O'Neill became established as the first choice full backs.

KENNY, Vincent "Mick/Vin" 1945-55

Born: 29 December 1924 Sheffield
(5ft 10½ins, 10st 12½lbs)
Debut: 14 September 1946
Leicester City
Division Two Away
Last Appearance: 12 February 1955
v Portsmouth
Division One Home
Total League
& Cup Appearances: 152 Goals: 0

Career Details:

Atlas and Norfolk Works		
WEDNESDAY	November	1945 Pro
Carlisle United	28 June	1955 £500

Vincent Kenny played for Longley School but despite several trials failed to make an appearance for Sheffield boys. However this did not affect his prospects and after impressing in Sheffield non-league soccer – playing for the works team of his employers Firth Brown - he was signed as an amateur in 1942, Wednesday beating the likes of Huddersfield Town, Arsenal and Everton to his signature. He became a part-time professional in 1943 but was then called into the armed forces, serving in the Royal Engineers and being involved in the D Day landings at Normandy in June 1944 and consequently fighting all the way through to Germany. On his return Mick – as he was known at Hillsborough – signed full time pro forms and would appear in exactly a third of the Owls league games in the first season of peacetime football. However he then spent over two years out of the first team, as Westlake and Swift were virtually ever present at full back.

Thankfully Kenny's patience was finally rewarded at the end of the 1948-9 season when injury to Westlake saw appearances at both left and right back for the Sheffield born defender. He started the following season as the club's first choice right back and remained there as The Owls won promotion from Division Two. A switch to left back came soon after and it was in this position that Mick helped Wednesday to the Second Division title in 1952 before reverting to his favourite position on the right side. A rather unwanted claim to fame for Kenny is that in January 1954 he became the first Wednesday player to be sent off in post war football after being entangled with Jimmy Hagan in a fierce F.A.Cup tie at Bramall Lane. This proved his final season as a regular at Hillsborough and the tough defender eventually moved onto Carlisle where in three seasons he appeared in 103 league games, scoring three times. While in Cumbria he still lived and trained in Sheffield and on leaving United he took employment with Sheffield based Sunblest Bakery as a salesman. He worked for thirty years before retiring and now lives out his retirement in the City at Loxley, occasionally being seen watching non-league football at Hallam FC.

KENT, Michael John "Mick" 1973-74

Born: 2 January 1951 Rotherham
(5ft 11½ins, 12st 3lbs – 1973)
Debut: 10 October 1973
v Bournemouth
League Cup Away
Last Appearance: 24 November 1973
v Oxford United
Division Two Home
Total League
& Cup Appearances: 5+1 Goals: 0

Career Details:

Rotherham United		1966 Juniors
Wath Wanderers		1967
Wolverhampton Wanderers	August	1968
Gillingham	11 March	1971 Loan
Highland Power		1972 Loan
Released	August	1973
WEDNESDAY	15 October	1973 Free
Released	1 May	1974
Johannesburg Rangers		1974
Barnsley		1975
Norwich City		1975
Worksop Town		1976
Spalding United		
Sutton Town		

The career of utility player Mick Kent was continuously dogged by injury from the moment he was advised to stop playing at the tender age of 15 when on Rotherham United's ground staff. The ex-Rotherham and Yorkshire boys player looked set for a career out of the game when he started work as a sheet metal worker but he later re-started his career at Wolves nursery club Wath Wanderers before signing pro forms at The Black Country club after just under two years in the steel industry. It was the start of a meteoric rise that would see Kent make his top flight debut while still a teenager but unfortunately his career quickly came to a shuddering halt as a mysterious pelvic injury meant he made only two sub appearances for Wolves. An eleven game loan spell at Gillingham eased Kent back into league football but a back injury then ruined a short spell in South African football at Highland Power.

He initially arrived at Hillsborough on trial – after being released by Wolves – and eventually won a short-term deal before making his debut as a sub during a nil-nil League Cup draw at Bournemouth. His luck again ran out at Hillsborough, as he was one of several players to contract a mystery virus that swept through the club in the autumn of 1973. After being released by The Owls Kent – whose brother Paul played league football for Norwich City, Cambridge United and Halifax Town - returned to South Africa but his shocking luck continued when suffering a broken leg on his debut for Johannesburg Rangers! On returning to England he trained back at Hillsborough – sustaining another broken leg – before making a comeback at Barnsley. He failed to make a senior appearance for The Tykes or his next club Norwich City and in the summer of 1976 became a sales representative. He continued to play non-league football during seven years as a sales rep before moving into the licensing trade, managing public houses and nightclubs – playing the odd game of football for his pub side. Kent – who was once married to comedian Charlie Williams' daughter – started employment as a driver/chauffeur for a holiday company in 1999, a job he still holds today.

KEY, Lance William 'Keysie' 1990-96

Born: 13 May 1968 Kettering
(6ft 3ins, 15st 1lb – 1995)
Only Appearance: 7 January 1995
v Gillingham
F.A.Cup Away
Total League
& Cup Appearances: 0+1 Goals: 0

Career Details:

Collingridge Kestrels		1984-86
Histon	August	1987
WEDNESDAY	13 April	1990 £10,000
York City	11 October	1991 Loan
Portadown		1993 3-month loan
Oldham Athletic	13 October	1993 Loan
Portsmouth	26 April	1994 Trial
Oxford United	25 January	1995 Loan
Lincoln City	11 August	1995 Loan
Hartlepool United	15 December	1995 Loan
Rochdale	2 March	1996 Loan
Dundee United	25 July	1996 Free
Tranmere Rovers	January	1997 Loan
Linfield		1997
Sheffield United	14 March	1997 Free
Rochdale	6 August	1997 Free
Northwich Victoria	21 December	1998 Loan
Northwich Victoria	2 March	1999 Free
Altrincham	February	2000 Loan
Kingstonian	28 June	2001 Free
Histon	September	2004 Free

Tall, athletic goalkeeper who joined Wednesday from Cambridgeshire non-league football along with team mate Shaun Sowden. His early years at Hillsborough saw Key gain experience in the Owls Central league side before spending several different spells on loan at a variety of Football league sides, making his senior debut for Oldham Athletic in October 1993. However throughout his time at Wednesday he was always behind the likes of Kevin Pressman and Chris Woods in the Hillsborough pecking order and appeared only once at first team level. This came in an F.A.Cup tie at Gillingham where he came off the subs bench to replace Pressman who had been red carded after conceding a penalty. Literally within seconds of his debut Key was picking the ball out of the net as the resultant spot kick was converted but he performed superbly in the second half to keep the Kent club at bay and secure The Owls passage to the next round of the Cup.

In fact Key was named as sub keeper for the opening thirty games of the 1994-5 season, due to Woods' injury problems, before returning to his usual diet of loan spells and occasional reserve team appearances – he played in only 54 second team games in six years at Wednesday. He eventually asked for a move in December 1995 and duly signed a two-year deal at Scottish Premier League side Dundee United. After just four games for the Tannadice club he moved into Irish soccer before making a surprise return to Sheffield football when signing for United as goalkeeper cover – after Linfield agreed to cancel his contract. His final spell in league football came at Rochdale before Key – whose brother Richard played for Cambridge United – started working for a stationery company in Sheffield while playing semi-professional football for Conference club Northwich Victoria. After being made redundant from his Sheffield job Key moved back to his home County, gaining employment as a chauffeur, and joining Kingstonian. He was voted players and supporters 'player of the year' in 2001-2 and made his debut for the England semi-professional side in February 2003 against Belgium. Incidentally his brother Richard was between the sticks for Fourth Division Swindon Town when they knocked top-flight Wednesday out of the League Cup in 1985. He returned to Histon as player-coach in 2004 and was in goal as the Cambridgeshire minnows knocked League Two side Shrewsbury Town out of the F.A.Cup.

KILSHAW, Edward Ainsworth "Eddie" 1948-51

Born: 25 December 1919 Prescot
(5ft 5½ins, 9st 7lbs – 1948)
Debut: 4 December 1948
v Luton Town
Division Two Away
Last Appearance: 11 April 1949
v Leicester City
Division Two Home
Total League
& Cup Appearances: 19 Goals: 1

Career Details:

Prescot Cables		
Bury	2 October	1937 £350
Manchester United	January	1940 Guest
WEDNESDAY	3 December	1948 £20,000
Released	May	1951

The story behind Eddie Kilshaw's move into league soccer is a true example of fate taking a hand. The teenager was playing for Lancashire Combination club Prescot Cables when Bury assistant manager Jimmy Porter drove past while giving a friend a driving lesson. He spotted Kilshaw and seven days later Bury boss Norman Bullock watched the youngster, Kilshaw eventually signing six months later as a part-time professional with The Shakers paying his club a sizeable fee. At this time Kilshaw was still employed as a laboratory assistant in chemical analysis at the Widnes ICI plant – he had joined straight from school at the age of 16 – as well as studying for a BSc degree in Chemistry. He would eventually leave ICI to concentrate on his football career but crucially – in hindsight – he continued his studies to gain the degree.

After just five games in Bury's reserve side he was promoted to the first eleven, making his debut on his 18th Birthday – Christmas Day 1937 against Tottenham Hotspur. The diminutive, tricky and skilful right-winger was an automatic choice for the remainder of the pre war period and before joining the R.A.F. in 1940 guested in six games for neighbours Manchester United. He trained as a pilot in the forces and spent the majority of the war in the Far East flying Sunderland 'flying boats'. On one occasion, as co-pilot taking a Catalina from Scotland to an Atlantic base, the plane crashed due to poor weather conditions in the Western Isles, killing three of the crew. Miraculously several of the crew survived, including Eddie, and they managed to find the only cottage on a deserted island where they took cover until being rescued by the Navy.

Despite the trauma of war Kilshaw started post war soccer in the best form of his career and soon several clubs were looking to prise away Bury's star asset. It would be Eric Taylor who won the race, paying a British record fee for a winger to bring Kilshaw to Hillsborough after 17 goals in 149 games for Bury. Incidentally a poor telephone connection at the time had many thinking that the Wednesday had paid £20,060 for his services that would have made Kilshaw the most expensive player in British football by the handsome sum of £10! The ex-Prescot Grammar School captain had come a long way but sadly tragedy struck after less than twenty games in an Owls shirt when in the home game versus Leicester City in April 1949 he suffered a snapped cruciate ligament. It's believed he was the first person in the country to have the ligaments sewn back together but the task of regaining his fitness proved impossible despite Kilshaw's best attempts – he spent many hours running up and down the Hillsborough grandstand steps in order to build up his leg muscles. A December 1949 medical report advised Eddie against playing in 'serious football' and sadly in May 1951 he had to admit defeat and retire from the game due to injury.

While he had been on the sidelines Eddie worked in a coal research lab to gain experience and after retiring from football attended Alsager Training College where he passed 'A' levels in Physics, Chemistry and Maths with distinction. He also gained a grade 'A' teaching diploma that thankfully would ensure the loss of his football career would not affect the earning potential of the studious Kilshaw. He was subsequently appointed head of science at Huyton Secondary Modern and hit the headlines in 1971 when coaching the unfancied Prescot and Huyton district team to English Schools Trophy success – they were the first non-City team to win the prestigious competition. After ending his teaching career at St Columba school he retired to live out his retirement in the Liverpool area.

KING, Jeffrey 'Jeff' 1979-82

Born: 9 November 1953 Fauldhouse, Edinburgh
(5ft 8ins, 11st – 1981)
Debut: 11 August 1979
v Hull City
League Cup Home
Last Appearance: 24 November 1981
v Barnsley
Division Two Home
Total League
& Cup Appearances: 65+3 Goals: 7

Career Details:

Fauldhouse United		
Albion Rovers	December	1972
Derby County	20 April	1974 £7,000
Notts County	8 January	1976 Loan
Portsmouth	12 March	1976 Loan
Walsall	26 November	1977 £12,500
WEDNESDAY	3 August	1979 £27,500
Hibernian	4 September	1981 Trial
Contract cancelled	5 January	1982
Sheffield United	13 January	1982 Free
Chesterfield	October	1983 N/C
Stafford Rangers	November	1983
Altrincham	February	1984

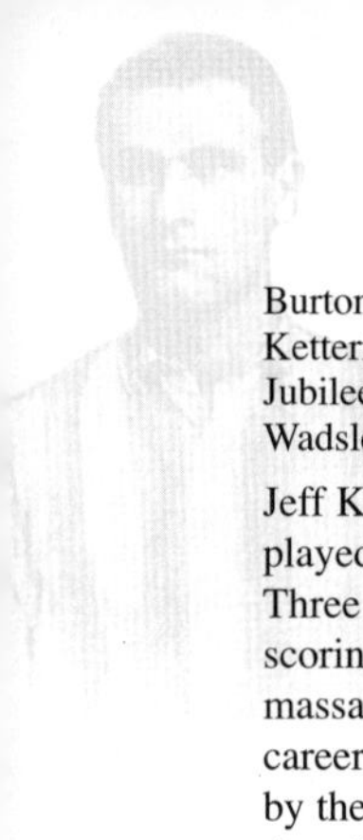

Burton Albion	August	1984
Kettering Town		1984
Jubilee Sports		
Wadsley Bridge		

Jeff King will always be remembered as a stylish midfielder who played a key role in Wednesday's promotion from the old Division Three in 1980, also earning the eternal gratitude of Owls fans by scoring a spectacular goal against United in the 'Boxing Day massacre' game. However after his superb debut season King's career at Hillsborough rapidly deteriorated to such an extent that by the summer of 1981 he had asked for a transfer on no more than three occasions! It was obvious he did not see 'eye to eye' with manager Jack Charlton and after an unsuccessful trial spell in his home city of Edinburgh at Hibs his contract was cancelled by mutual consent. His next move surprised football followers on both sides of the City divide as King became one of only a handful of players to transfer directly between Wednesday and United.

He subsequently helped the Blades to the Division Four Championship in 1982 before dropping out of senior football after a year at Chesterfield. After leaving the professional game King started work as a painter and decorator – a job he still does today – while winding down his playing career in non-league soccer.

KING, Philip Geoffrey "Phil" 1989-94

Born: 28 December 1967 Bristol
(5ft 10ins, 12st – 1989)
Debut: 4 November 1989
v Nottingham Forest
Division One Away
Last Appearance: 2 April 1994
v Everton
Premier League Home
Total League
& Cup Appearances: 154+5 Goals: 2

Career Details:

Exeter City	7 January	1985
Torquay United	14 July	1986 £3,000
Swindon Town	6 February	1987 £155,000
WEDNESDAY	3 November	1989 £400,000
Notts County	22 October	1993 Loan
Aston Villa	1 August	1994 £250,000
West Bromwich Albion	30 October	1995 Loan
Swindon Town	26 March	1996 Free
Blackpool	20 October	1997 Loan
Brighton & Hove Albion	19 March	1999 Free
Kidderminster Harriers	August	1999 Free
Bath City	July	2000 Free
Clifton FC		Sun.
Dolphin FC		Sun.
Cinderford Town	March	2004

CAPS (@SWFC)
England 'B' (1) v Switzerland 20/05/91

Popular full back who formed an almost telepathic understanding with Nigel Worthington which created one of the most feared combinations in the country during the Owls golden spell of the early 1990s. King was a steady and consistent player who was rarely found wanting with regard to his defensive duties and always liked to push forward whenever possible – his two goals proved this was not a frequent occurrence! He helped Wednesday to promotion and League Cup glory in 1991 but hit disciplinary problems in February 1992 when after a row with assistant manager Ritchie Barker he refused to play in the home game with West Ham United. He was fined two weeks wages by The Owls but the incident did not seem to affect his first team chances as King remained an automatic choice at left back – being named 'player of the year' in 1991-2.

Unfortunately injury then badly interrupted the following season - he suffered cruciate ligament damage at Highbury in August 1992 - and when Andy Sinton arrived in the summer of 1993 it was Worthington who was switched to full back, leaving King out in the cold. He went on a week-to-week contract in the summer of 1993 and actually left in November 1993 before returning a month later – he also got into hot water in March 1994 when he was fined by the FA for illegally selling F.A.Cup Final tickets. The ex-Bristol boys player – who started his career as a trainee at Exeter City – eventually moved onto Aston Villa where he famously netted the winning goal in a UEFA Cup penalty shoot out win over Inter Milan, He actually appeared in only 23 games for Villa and soon left for a second spell at Swindon Town – in his first stint he helped Town to Play off success over Gillingham at Wembley back in 1987 – before winding up his league career on the South Coast at Brighton. A Conference League Championship medal followed during a season at Kidderminster Harriers before King decided to retire in 2000. However he made a comeback with Bath City before becoming landlord at The Clifton public house in Swindon. He later moved to become landlord at The Dolphin Hotel and proved a popular host with Owls fans when the travelling hordes invaded Swindon on the opening day of the 2003-4 season. Played a one off game for Cinderford Town in March 2004 as a favour to the club's manager who is a personal friend.

KINGHORN, Henry McGill 1908-11

Born: 1881 Midlothian, Scotland
(5ft 6ins, 12st 11lbs – 1910)
Died: 16 April 1955 Montrose
Debut: 27 February 1909
v Preston North End
Division One Away
Last Appearance: 31 December 1910
v Tottenham Hotspur
Division One Home
Total League
& Cup Appearances: 25 Goals: 0

Career Details:

Arniston Rovers		
Alloa		
Leith Athletic		
WEDNESDAY	January	1909 £290
Released		1911

The Owls plucked diminutive goalkeeper Henry Kinghorn from Scottish non-league football during the early years of the Twentieth Century. He arrived as competition for Wednesday goalkeeping legend Teddy Davison and quickly became established as No.2, making his league debut in a 4-1 defeat at Deepdale just a month after signing professional forms for Wednesday. This proved just a taster for the Scot but he became a serious rival to Davison's first team place at the end of the following season – ironically just after he had asked for a transfer in February 1910 - when Kinghorn appeared in fourteen of the final fifteen league games of the season. He also started the first five matches of the 1910-11 campaign but Davison won back his place for Wednesday's first home win of the season and would remain first choice until the early 1920s.

After leaving Hillsborough Kinghorn became a scout for Arsenal before being appointed trainer-manager at Southern League Bournemouth & Boscombe in 1923, helping them to the Championship in the same year. In the summer that followed his new side were elected into the Football League and Henry remained in charge until dropping the manager suffix when Les Knighton was appointed sole manager in the summer of 1925 – not before Kinghorn had signed Ron Eyre from Wednesday, who would became the club's all-time record goalscorer! In March 1929, aged 48, he became the Cherries oldest ever player when making an emergency appearance on the left wing during a 0-0 draw at Brentford in a Division Three (South) fixture. He remained Bournemouth trainer until 1939 and was manager during the war years before leaving completely in May 1947 to return home to enjoy his retirement back in his native Scotland.

KINMAN 1887

Born: Sheffield
Only Appearance: 15 October 1887 v Belper Town F.A.Cup Away
Total League & Cup Appearances: 1 Goals: 1

Career Details:

WEDNESDAY	1887

A real mystery player whose name is even in doubt as contemporary match reports spelled it as either Kinman or Kinnion. However census records suggests that no one was born with the former surname in Yorkshire in the 19th Century but twelve men did boast Kinman as their family name. Of those only four were old enough to have played in the 3-2 Cup win at Derbyshire club Belper Town in 1887 and we will probably never know whether it was Albert, George, Joseph or Morris Kinman who wore the blue and white for that one and only time.

KIPPAX, Dennis Hobson 1946-48

Born: 7 August 1926 Sheffield
(5ft 8½ins, 10st – 1946)
Died: 18 May 1970 Sheffield
Only Appearance: 28 September 1946
v Millwall
Division Two Away
Total League
& Cup Appearances: 1* Goals: 0
***Also appeared in 11 wartime games, scoring 1 goal**

Career Details:

Stocksbridge Works		1942
WEDNESDAY	2 March	1946
Goole Town	24 August	1948
Released	6 May	1950
Stocksbridge Works	24 August	1950

Started his working life at the age of 14 as an apprentice engineer at Stocksbridge Works in Sheffield, gaining his first taste of senior football with the crack works team. Signed part-time professional forms for Wednesday in March 1946 – he continued to work at Stocksbridge - and made several appearances in the transitional 1945-6 season before being called up for National Service in May 1946. Despite serving in the Navy he continued to play regularly in the Owls reserve side and was given just one chance to shine in league football when he wore the No. 7 shirt in the 2-2 Division Two draw at Millwall in September 1946. However he could not make the desired impact at League level and eventually signed for Goole Town after being released in the summer of 1948.

After leaving Hillsborough Kippax reverted to part-time status – he completed his apprenticeship while in the Navy so could gain employment back at Stockbridge Works. After two seasons at Goole he returned to Yorkshire League football at Stocksbridge Works and remained a regular until hanging up his proverbial boots in May 1957 – his final game coming in a benefit match against The Owls. Throughout his adult life Dennis played cricket for the Stocksbridge Old Cricket Club but sadly he died young, aged just 43.

KIRBY, Eric 1950-52

Born: 12 October 1926 Sheffield
(5ft 8½ins, 11st 0½lbs – 1950)
Only Appearance: 3 February 1951
v Huddersfield Town
Division One Home
Total League
& Cup Appearances: 1 Goals: 0

Career Details:

Aughton Juniors		
WEDNESDAY	March	1950 £25 donation
York City	2 August	1952

Right half back who holds the unique distinction of being a 'one game wonder' for not one but two Football League clubs during his four seasons in professional soccer. A football career of any sorts seemed highly unlikely when after leaving school at the age of 14 Kirby gained employment as a centre lathe turner at Osborn Mushet Tools on Penistone Road in Sheffield. He subsequently started his two years of National Service in 1947 – joining the R.A.F. and playing regular football for Bomber Command, losing in the 1949 R.A.F. Cup Final. When being demobbed he returned to work and continued playing amateur football in local Sheffield soccer until The Owls signed Eric as an amateur in December 1949.

After signing professional forms his Central League debut came at Bury in April 1950 and Kirby was an 'A' team regular during the 1950-1 campaign as Wednesday recorded a Yorkshire League double. An injury to regular No. 4 Eddie Gannon handed Eric his big chance at first team level and he was not disgraced as The Owls won 3-2 at Hillsborough. Unfortunately that proved to be Kirby's only taste of top-flight football and in the season that followed he failed to even make an single appearance at reserve team level so it was therefore no surprise when he moved to Division Three (North) side York City. He fared little better at Bootham Crescent – appearing only once in a 2-1 home loss to Gateshead in November 1952 – and a serious knee injury eventually forced his early retirement from the game in 1954. After leaving York City he started work in the Research and Development department of Armstrong patents in York before returning to Sheffield in 1966 to re-join Osborn Mushet where he worked as a study engineer until his retirement.

KIRBY, George 1959-60

Born: 20 December 1933 Liverpool
(6ft, 12st 1lbs – 1959)
Died: 24 March 2000
Debut: 3 October 1959
v Bolton Wanderers
Division One Away
Last Appearance: 17 October 1959
v Tottenham Hotspur
Division One Home
Total League
& Cup Appearances: 3 Goals: 0

Career Details:

Longview Juniors		
Everton	June	1952
WEDNESDAY	13 March	1959 £8,000
Plymouth Argyle	7 January	1960 £3,250
Southampton	September	1962 £20,000
Coventry City	March	1964 £12,500
Swansea Town	October	1964 £11,500
Walsall	May	1965 £10,000
New York Generals		1967-69
Brentford	October	1968
Worcester City	June	1969

Although George Kirby spent less than a year at Hillsborough, appearing in only three first team games, his career as player and manager lasted over forty years and included spells in America, Iceland, The Far East and the Middle East! The strong and fearless forward, who vigorously pursued any scoring chance that came his way, netted over 120 goals for eight different league clubs in a playing career that started as a ground staff lad at Everton in August 1950. The ex-Prescot Schoolboys player appeared in only 26 games for The Toffeemen in almost seven years as a professional before Harry Catterick brought him to Hillsborough as competition for the likes of Keith Ellis. However the centre forward failed to make a lasting impact at Wednesday and a week into 1960 left for Plymouth Argyle in a move that saw Jim McAnearney also move in a £10,000 joint deal. Incidentally during his time at Everton he served the obligatory two years National Service, playing alongside the likes of Bobby Charlton, Duncan Edwards, Dave MacKay and Jimmy Armfield for the Army representative side.

He experienced a barren first season at the Devon club but hit top form thereafter and 39 goals in 104 games earned a transfer to Southampton. An F.A.Cup semi-final appearance against Manchester United followed in 1963 while he was once bizarrely booked when not retreating ten yards at his own sides' free kick! His robust style endeared him to the Saints fans – he once netted three goals in just four minutes against Middlesbrough in November 1962 - and quickly became a popular player at his next club, Coventry City, when netting a hat trick on his home debut. While at City he went into business as a part time insurance broker but on the field of play he fell out of favour after helping The Sky Blues to the Division Three (South) title in 1964. During two summers with North American Soccer League side New York General he boasted future Argentinean World Cup winning manager Cesar Menotti as his strike partner but retirement from the game came in 1969. In July of the following year he was appointed coach at Halifax Town but within a month was promoted to manager and duly led Town to the highest ever finish in their history – third place in the old Third Division – and a legendary win over Manchester United to lift the Watney Cup. After a highly successful debut season he was 'head-hunted' by Watford in the summer of 1971 but experienced a disastrous two-years in charge, only goal average saving The Hornets from successive relegations.

He was sacked in May 1973 before moving to Iceland where three years as I.A.Akranes boss saw Kirby win three National championships. In 1977 he moved to Kuwait side Khaitan before returning to Halifax Town in November 1978 for a second spell in charge – he was also a paid director and chief executive. Sadly he could not repeat the success of his earlier time in West Yorkshire and after Town were forced to seek re-election he was dismissed in July 1981. He was immediately appointed coach to Indonesian side Mercua Buana and twice took them to Championship play off finals only to fall at the final hurdle – incidentally his club were situated in Medan, on the island of Summatra. He remained in the tropics for over four years before three years in the Middle East at Al Fath of Saudi Arabia. His globetrotting finally ended with a final year back at Akranes before George returned to the UK in 1989 although he continued to work outside of the game. He was still scouting for QPR in the late 1990s but sadly lost a battle against cancer, passing away early in 2000.

KIRKMAN, Samuel 'Sam' 1909-20

Born: 3rd Quarter 1889 Bury
(5ft 7½ins, 11st – 1913)
Died: 2 November 1960 Blackburn
Debut: 18 September 1909
v Bury
Division One Home
Last Appearance: 1 May 1920
v Oldham Athletic
Division One Home
Total League
& Cup Appearances: 201* Goals: 40
***Also appeared in**
12 wartime games, scoring 4 goals

Career Details:

St Stephens F.C.		
St.Andrews F.C		
Ramsbottom		
Carlisle United	May	1908
WEDNESDAY	May	1909 £75
Southport Central		WW1 Guest
Mid Rhondda	June	1920 Free
Bury	September	1920 £500*
Wombwell	30 September	1922 Free

* Fee paid to Wednesday

When flying winger Harry Davis retired in 1907 The Owls searched in vain for a replacement, trying a variety of different players on the right side. Thankfully the purchase of Sam Kirkman solved the problem as he proved a fine forward who boasted an excellent turn of speed and was both goal maker and taker – his ratio of a goal every five games compared favourably with any winger in the club's history. His direct play and penchant for outstanding goals made him a big Owlerton favourite in the years immediately preceding the Great War and his combination with the likes of David McLean, Teddy Glennon and Andrew Wilson saw Wednesday agonisingly miss out on the 1913 League Championship.

At the start of World War One he joined the Army, working as a dispatch rider in the A.S.C transport section, but smashed the cartilage of his left knee when his motorcycle crashed while on duty in France. After a spell in Boulogne Hospital he was sent home to a Manchester institution and after a successful operation was recalled to active duty, later serving in The Far East where he managed to catch malaria! Thankfully he came through the war relatively unscathed – even finding time to play several games for Wednesday and appear as a guest centre half for Southport – but his top-flight football career was almost over as he appeared in only six games for Wednesday in the traumatic 1919-20 season. After relegation Kirkman was one of the men released in a mass clear out by the club and he subsequently joining Welsh non-league side Mid-Rhondda for a season. He re-entered league soccer with Bury – the transfer fee being paid to The Owls as they still held his league registration – but appeared in only one league game for The Shakers. He still trained with Wednesday while on the books at Bury and eventually moved back to South Yorkshire after being unable to reconcile his business interests in Sheffield – he was in the motor trade, owing a garage – to the necessity of living back in his hometown of Bury. He later joined Barnsley based non-league side Wombwell.

KIRKWOOD, Daniel 'Dan' 1926-28

Born: 24 December 1900
Dalserf, Lanarkshire
(5ft 10ins, 11st 10lbs – 1926)
Died: 20 October 1977 Stonehouse, Lanarkshire
Debut: 20 November 1926
v Aston Villa
Division One Away
Last Appearance: 11 February 1928
v Middlesbrough
Division One Home
Total League
& Cup Appearances: 19 Goals: 1

Career Details:

Ashgill YMCA		
Airdrieonians	September	1922
Glasgow Rangers	August	1923
St.Johnstone	October	1925 Loan
St.Johnstone	April	1926 Loan
WEDNESDAY	18 November	1926 £1500
Brighton & Hove Albion	12 June	1928 £500
Luton Town	October	1933 Free
Swindon Town	November	1933 Free

Inside right Dan Kirkwood was signed by Bob Brown from Glasgow giants Rangers part way through the Owls first season back in Division One after promotion in 1926. The club's regular in the number 8 shirt during that promotion season, Matt Barrass, had subsequently left and it was Harold Hill who was filling in until Wednesday could find a suitable replacement. It was therefore ex-Dalserf boys player Dan Kirkwood that Brown turned to and he was given an immediate debut in a 2-2 draw at Aston Villa just forty-eight hours after moving South. He quickly showed that he possessed splendid ball control and made a great start to his Hillsborough days when netting on his home debut in a 3-0 win over Cardiff City. He remained a first choice throughout the winter months but the signings of Alf Strange and Jimmy Seed effectively brought an abrupt end to his Owls career as Kirkwood would only make a single appearance during the following season before moving to the South coast in the summer of 1928.

The bulky and intelligent forward – whose brother Andy played for Rangers and St.Johnstone - had previously impressed the Brighton hierarchy when appearing against them for Wednesday in an F.A.Cup tie and he proved a great signing, scoring 82 goals in only 181 senior appearances for The Seagulls. His 63-goal partnership in the 1928-9 season with Hugh Vallance – Kirkwood netting 21 – is still a club record and he was truly a goal maker as well as a goal taker. It was only an injury that resulted in Dan being given a free transfer at the end of the 1932-3 campaign, Kirkwood subsequently spending only a few weeks at Luton before ending his career at Swindon Town. After ending his playing career Kirkwood returned to his original profession of coal miner while indulging in his hobby of crown green bowling – he won a County championship in his native Scotland.

KITE, Percy Albert 1920

Born: 3rd Quarter 1892 Warrington
(6ft 6ins, 12st 7lbs – 1920)
Died: 18 February 1960 Lymm
Only Appearance:
1 May 1920 v Oldham Athletic Division Two Home
Total League & Cup Appearances: 1 Goals: 0

Career Details:

Thelwall F.C.		
Eccles Borough		1914
Lancashire Tool F.C. (Lymm)		
Warrington	cs	1917
Manchester United	January	1917 Trial
WEDNESDAY	April	1920 Amat.
Lancashire Tool F.C. (Lymm)		1920
Mossley		Trial

By virtue of a sole appearance at the end of the disastrous 1919-20 season, giant goalkeeper Percy Kite has entered Wednesday history as the tallest ever Owls player. At 6ft 6ins he would be tall by 21st Century standards but in an era when players rarely measured six feet he must have proved a real oddity for those fans at Hillsborough when he ran out for his league debut. He had originally arrived on trial from Cheshire non-league football and was strictly amateur during his brief spell on The Owls books. Described as 'a very tall, slim and agile young man' he was rated as a goalkeeper of outstanding ability but played just one game for the club, in the final match of the season – a 1-0 home win over Oldham Athletic. He even failed to play any reserve games for the club and was not re-engaged in the summer, drifting back into amateur football.

KNIGHT, Ian John 1985-90

Born: 26 October 1966 Hartlepool
(6ft 2ins, 12st 4lbs – 1987)
Debut: 19 April 1986
v Aston Villa
Division One Home
Last Appearance: 28 January 1989
v Blackburn Rovers
F.A.Cup Away
Total League
& Cup Appearances: 27 Goals: 0

Career Details:

Barnsley	July	1983 App.
WEDNESDAY	17 July	1985 Free
Scunthorpe United	25 August	1989 Loan
Grimsby Town	11 January	1990 £15,000
Carlisle United	August	1992 N/C
Boston United	October	1993
Grantham Town	August	1994

CAPS (@ SWFC)
England U-21 (2) v Sweden 09/09/86, v Yugoslavia 11/11/86

Sadly for outstanding central defender Ian Knight his name will always be associated with one of, if not the worst, injury ever sustained in professional soccer. The reckless tackle by Chester's Gary Bennett in an F.A.Cup tie at Hillsborough in February 1987 was such that the sickening sound of breaking bone could be audibly heard in the stands. His horrific injuries were the worst seen by Owls physio Alan Smith and were to be more akin to a serious traffic accident than a game of football. The tackle effectively ended his highly promising career as his leg was fractured in seven different places and to this day Knight's right leg is an inch shorter than his left. It was fourteen months before Knight could kick a ball in anger and a further four before he returned to full training. His brave comeback was completed in October 1988 when he played for the reserves and he did manage a four game spell back in the first team early in 1989.

However hopes of a return to the form that had earned Knight England U-21 honours were slim and after a loan spell at Scunthorpe United he moved on a similar basis to Grimsby Town before being transferred permanently. Sadly he broke his leg twice more while at Blundell Park – including the first game after his full transfer – and was eventually forced to drop into non-league soccer before retiring in 1994. It proved an unhappy end to a sporting career that had started in his hometown where he represented Hartlepool boys at football, appeared for Cleveland at athletics and played basketball for the North of England. His footballing career had started as an apprentice at Oakwell but after The Tykes inexplicably decided not to offer Knight a professional contract in stepped Howard Wilkinson to bring the youngster to Hillsborough. He arrived initially on trial but his career was changed by Wednesday coach Mick Hennigan, who converted him to centre half from his usual midfield role. After quickly earning a first team call up he looked set for a glittering career before the fickle finger of fate intervened.

After being forced into retirement Knight was appointed assistant 'Football in the Community Officer' in 1994 back at Grimsby Town, taking over fully in January 1995. He returned to Wednesday in the same capacity in November 1996 but only stayed until July 1997 when he returned to Grimsby to became Youth team coach – incidentally in the same year his court case against Gary Bennett was concluded with Knight receiving undisclosed damages in an out of court settlement. He later became 'Director of Youth Football' at the Cleethorpes based club but was made redundant in May 2002 as a cost cutting measure.

KNIGHT, Leon Leroy 2002-03

Born: 16 September 1982
Hackney, London
(5ft 4ins, 9st 10lbs – 2002)
Debut: 17 August 2002
v Nottingham Forest
Division One Away
Last Appearance: 19 April 2003
v Grimsby Town Division One Home
Total League
& Cup Appearances: 16+11 Goals: 3

Career Details:

Chelsea	17 September	1999
Queens Park Rangers	9 March	2001 Loan
Huddersfield Town	23 October	2001 Six-month loan
WEDNESDAY	25 June	2002 One-year loan
Loan return	26 April	2003
Brighton & Hove Albion	24 July	2003 £100,000

Diminutive and pacy attacker who failed to settle during a season long loan from Premier League Chelsea. In the previous campaign he had netted seventeen times for Second Division Huddersfield Town – being named 'player of the season' and leading Town to the play offs - but for a variety of reasons could not make the same impact at Hillsborough, only showing glimpses of the form he produced while at the West Yorkshire club. After a bright start he became an increasingly peripheral figure under the management of Chris Turner and hardly figured in the match day squad after the Christmas decorations had been removed.

His career had started when he joined Chelsea on schoolboy forms at the age of thirteen, signing professional forms in 1999. To gain experience he was loaned out to West London neighbours QPR but returned to Stamford Bridge after failing to score in eleven league appearances. His only senior appearance for The Blues came in September 2001 when he replaced Gianfranco Zola during a UEFA Cup tie but the ex-England U-20 International found his opportunities increasingly limited as Chelsea added more and more foreign firepower to their multi-national strike force. Following the loan spells at The McAlpine Stadium and Hillsborough he joined Brighton on a similar arrangement in July 2003 but with QPR also tracking his availability the South Coast club made his move permanent in August 2003 – three goals in the opening four games of the new season no doubt influencing their decision. He continued to score freely for Brighton – totalling 27 goals by the season's end - and capped a tremendous season by scoring the winning penalty in the 2004 Play Off Final against Bristol City, leaving many Wednesday fans wondering what might have been if the young attacker had played on a more regular basis while in Sheffield.

KNIGHTON, Kenneth "Ken" 1973-76

Born: 20 February 1944, Kexborough, Nr. Barnsley
(5ft 9ins, 11st 5lbs – 1975)
Debut: 8 September 1973
v Nottingham Forest Division Two Away
Last Appearance: 6 December 1975
v Colchester United Division Three Away
Total League & Cup Appearances: 79+5 Goals: 4

Career Details:

Mexborough Rovers		
Wath Wanderers		
Wolverhampton Wanderers	25 February	1960
Oldham Athletic	18 November	1966 £12,000
Preston North End	22 December	1967 £35,000
Blackburn Rovers	4 July	1969 £45,000
Hull City	4 March	1971 £60,000
WEDNESDAY	2 August	1973 £57,777
To Staff	9 April	1976

When Ken Knighton joined his boyhood heroes Wednesday he was approaching the end of a career that had began at Mexborough Rovers, after impressing in Barnsley schools football. His working life had started as a trainee miner but after being signed by Wolves nursery club Wath Wanderers he was elevated to apprentice status for the Black Country club in July 1959. However in almost five and a half years as a professional at Wolves, Knighton appeared in only 16 first team games and therefore left for several short spells at three different Lancashire Football League sides. It was while at Blackburn Rovers that Wednesday boss Derek Dooley first tried to sign the central defender but it would be thirty months before Knighton finally became an Owls player, following a spell at Hull City after Rovers needed to sell to raise much needed funds.

He joined The Owls when results were poor and relegation a distinct possibility but Knighton's leadership, including the winning goal on the last day against Bolton to avoid the drop, helped Wednesday pull away from trouble. Joyous supporters carried him from the field after the Bolton game but unfortunately his captaincy could not save Wednesday from relegation in 1975 and this tough, determined and fearless defender wound up his playing career in 1976, being appointed coach to the club's Youth side. Incidentally a year earlier Knighton had spent a short time presenting sports and music programmes on fledgling local radio station Hallam! When Steve Burtenshaw was dismissed Knighton applied unsuccessfully for the managerial position and he was caretaker manager for one game in 1977 – a 1-0 home win over Chesterfield – before Jack Charlton's appointment.

In 1978 he left to take up a coaching position at Sunderland and in June of the following year was elevated to the manager's chair. However despite leading Sunderland to promotion to the old First Division in 1980 he was surprisingly sacked in April 1981 and spent a short time out of the game before re-entering the fray as boss at Orient in October 1981. He spent eighteen months in the job but left in May 1983 to concentrate on a career out of football – joining telecommunications company Plessey whilst also managing non-league Dagenham on a part-time basis. He led The Daggers to the third round of the F.A.Cup for the first time in their history in 1985 and later spent three years as boss at Trowbridge Town (1985-88) and two years at Somerset Senior League side Portishead (1991-93). Off the field of play he moved to Bristol based Mercury Communications in 1991 but after joining his next employer, London based COFTC, he severed all ties with football. He is now Director of Networking for Data Sharp, another telecommunications company based in Truro, Cornwall.

KOVACEVIC, Darko 1995-96

Born: 18 November 1973 Kovin, Yugoslavia
(6ft 1ins, 12st – 1995)
Debut: 23 December 1995
v Southampton
Premier League Home
Last Appearance: 8 April 1996
v Arsenal
Premier League Home
Total League & Cup Appearances: 9+8 Goals: 4

Career Details:

Radnicki Kovin		
Proleter Zrenjanin		
Red Star Belgrade	June	1994 £450,000
WEDNESDAY	11 December	1995 £2,500,000
Real Sociedad	18 June	1996 £4,600,000
Juventus	1 July	1999 £12,000,000
Lazio	1 September	2001 *
Real Sociedad	27 December	2001 £8,275,862 ($12,000,000)

*Exchange for Salas

CAPS (@SWFC)
Yugoslavia Full (4) v Romania 27/03/96, v Mexico 23/05/96, v Japan 26/05/96, v Malta 02/06/96

When tall, slim forward Darko Kovacevic left Wednesday in the summer of 1996 the club's supporters expressed surprise but hardly inundated the local media with cries of selling the crown jewels. In hindsight perhaps they should have, as that self same attacker would soon be scoring regularly at the top echelons of the European game and was involved in moves totalling over £20m! Before being signed by David Pleat he was one of the hottest properties in European football and it was regarded as a major coup when Wednesday secured his signature, along with compatriot Dejan Stefanovic, in a £4.5m double deal. The duo were actually signed in October but red tape almost caused the moves to be aborted before a work permit was finally received almost two months after the players had initially put their names to a contract. Kovacevic could already boast six full caps for his country in a career that had started in his hometown before grabbing 37 goals in just 51 games for next club Proleter. This form soon prompted a bargain move to Yugoslavian giants Red Star and he was an instant hit, crashing home 27 league goals as the Belgrade club won their twentieth League title and their domestic Cup – he scored an incredible 41 goals in only 45 games in that debut season!

This phenomenal scoring of course alerted many clubs all over Europe but his final destination proved to be Hillsborough for the traditional style centre forward who was absolutely unparalleled in the air. He was a real fighter, supreme finisher and excellent target man but these qualities were never shown to the full during what proved to be a short spell in Sheffield. He made a great start at Wednesday – scoring twice on his full home debut against Bolton Wanderers – but as he settled into life in English football was used sparingly by Pleat and in hindsight was never really able to show his true worth to the side. Perhaps Wednesday showed a lack of patience in letting Kovacevic move to Spanish football after such a short time at Hillsborough but they certainly had cause to regret the move – despite eventually receiving a club record £4.6m which was boosted by a sell on clause that brought an additional £2.1m. He was a huge hit at Real Sociedad and went on to represent his country in the 1998 World Cup Finals before injury cut short his tournament. Forty-one goals in only ninety-five Spanish League games then prompted Italian giants Juventus to make Darko their record signing in the summer of 1999, paying Sociedad a whopping $18m fee to take the forward to Turin.

He continued to score freely in the tough surroundings of Italian football and although not a Serie A regular still managed to grab 20 goals in 44 league and cup-ties in his debut campaign – including eleven in Champions League soccer. A move to Roman club Lazio followed – in exchange for Chilean forward Salas – but after failing to find the net he was loaned back to Real Sociedad in December 2001. Personal tragedy then hit Kovacevic as he lost his brother on New Year's Day 2002, a few days before his move back to Spain was rubber stamped with Sociedad paying another large fee. Kovacevic's 8 goals in 19 league games helped the struggling Spaniards avoid relegation and he was amongst the top scorers in the whole league during 2002-3 as his club finished runners-up to Real Madrid. He has now passed fifty caps for his country - now called Serbia and Montenegro – and continues to score regularly in International and domestic football to leave the Owls to regret even more the day they decided to let the powerful forward catch a plane to Spain.

KUQI, Shefki 2002-03

Born: 10 November 1976
Voqitern, Kosovo
(6ft 2ins, 13st 10lbs – 12002)
Debut: 12 January 2002
v Crewe Alexandra
Division One Home
Last Appearance: 20 September 2003
v Brighton & Hove Albion
Division Two Away
Total League
& Cup Appearances: 62+6 Goals: 19

Career Details:

Miki		1990
Kapa		1991
Miki		1992
MP		1994
HJK Helsinki		1997
FC Jokerit		1999
Wolverhampton Wanderers	November	2000 Trial
Stockport County	31 January	2001 £300,000
WEDNESDAY	11 January	2002 £700,000
Ipswich Town	26 September	2003 3-month loan
Ipswich Town	28 November	2003 Free*
Blackburn Rovers	1 July	2005 Free

CAPS (@ SWFC)
Finland Full (11) v South Korea 20/03/02, v Macedonia 18/04/02, v Latvia 22/05/02, v N.Ireland 21/08/02, v Wales 07/09/02, v Azerbaijan 12/10/02, v Yugoslavia 16/10/02, v N.Ireland 12/02/03, v Serbia & Montenegro 07/06/03, v Denmark 20/08/03, v Wales 10/09/03

During almost two years at Hillsborough barrel-chested forward Shefki Kuqi enjoyed a love-hate relationship with Owls fans. After arriving from Stockport County in January 2002 he became an instant hit with his 100% commitment and a never say die attitude that brought him six goals, helping Wednesday avoid relegation from Division One. However the Owls could not avoid the drop in 2002-3 and despite finishing top scorer with eight goals Kuqi experienced a decidedly mixed time as frustrated supporters questioned his overall attitude and finishing abilities. On any given Saturday he could either be booed or clapped by fans that debated his merits over a pre match pint. One fact that could not be denied was that he took a liking to Division Two football and when he surprisingly left for a loan spell at Division One side Ipswich Town he was top scorer with five league goals – he remained atop the Owls scoring chart for several months as Wednesday plummeted down the table.

Although born in Kosovo his playing career started in Finland where his family had emigrated when Shefki was thirteen years old. He first played for junior club Miki before actually appearing in the Finnish Division Four during a year at Kapa, scoring fifteen times. His old club Miki had become a senior side by the time Kuqi returned in 1992 and he netted 11 times in Second Division football before, aged 18, he earned a move to the Finnish top-flight with MP. Soon after he moved to HJK, playing Champions League football in his first season, but really hit the headlines at Helsinki club Jokerit where Shefki was league top scorer in 2000, Finnish 'footballer of the year' and won his debut cap for Finland against Belgium in 1999 – he had previously won 8 full caps for Albania, scoring once. A move away from his adopted homeland seemed a certainty and he looked set to move to Wolves following a trial period but returned home after Wanderers manager Colin Lee only offered him a six-month contract. However when Stockport boss Andy Kilner offered Kuqi a longer deal he did finally move into English football, becoming an instant favourite when scoring 6 times in 17 games to help County avoid the drop. Injury then scuppered a possible move to Premier League Blackburn Rovers – Stockport needed to sell to ease their financial plight – before new boss Carlton Palmer sold him to his old club Wednesday after the pair fell out. After a succesful spell at Ipswich he did finally join Blackburn Rovers, moving on a free transfer in the summer of 2005.

LAMB John William **1912-20**

Born: 4th Quarter 1893 Worksop
(5ft 11ins, 12st – 1912)
Debut: 22 September 1913
v Oldham Athletic
Division One Home
Last Appearance: 18 October 1919
v Blackburn Rovers
Division One Away
Total League
& Cup Appearances: 5* **Goals: 0**
***Also appeared in**
24 wartime games. Scoring 2 goals

Career Details:

Bolsover Colliery		
WEDNESDAY	6 April	1912 £35
Brentford	October	1915 Guest
Notts County		WW1 Guest
Brentford		WW1 Guest
St Bernards		WW1 Guest
Luton Town	20 May	1920 £200
Matlock Town		1921

Although signed as a centre forward John Lamb was soon converted to half back where he made a handful appearances for Wednesday during an eight year stay. The Great War of course interrupted his time at Hillsborough and Lamb served in the 'Football Battalion' during the war years. He was wounded at the Somme during the hostilities – recuperating in Edinburgh where he played for non-league side St Bernards - but thankfully recovered sufficiently to re-sign for the Owls for the 1919-20 season. Described as being 'rough and ready' he soon moved to Southern League Luton Town before dropping into non-league football.

LAMB, Walter Charles **1921-23**

Born: 8 August 1897 Tarleton, Nr Southport
(5ft 8½ins, 10st 9lbs)
Died: 1st Quarter 1973 Huddersfield
Debut:
29 August 1921 v Derby County Division Two Home
Last Appearance:
3 September 1921 v Barnsley Division Two Away
Total League & Cup Appearances: 2 Goals: 0

Career Details:

Liverpool (Res.)		
Fleetwood	April	1920
WEDNESDAY	August	1921
Swansea Town	August	1923
Southend United	May	1925
Rhyl FC	June	1926
Abergele	November	1931

Full back who appeared in consecutive league games for Wednesday soon after arriving on trial from non-league Fleetwood. After his month's trial Walter was signed to professional forms but had to be content with reserve team soccer until moving to Swansea Town. His fortunes improved little at the Welsh club and he appeared in only three games, all at left back, before joining his final league side Southend United. A solitary Division Three (South) appearance for 'The Shrimpers' brought the curtain down on his league career.

LANG, James J. 'Reddie/Jimmy' **1876-82**

Born: March 1851 Glasgow
Debut: 18 December 1880
v Blackburn Rovers
F.A.Cup Away
Last Appearance: 15 March 1882
v Blackburn Rovers F.A.Cup Away
Total League
& Cup Appearances: 5 Goals: 0

Career Details:

Glasgow Eastern	
Clydesdale	
Third Lanark	1876
WEDNESDAY	1876
Third Lanark	1877
WEDNESDAY	1879-82

James Lang is widely regarded as the first Scottish footballer to move South to specifically play football - he was preceded by another Scot named Peter Andrews but he was sent by his employers to work in Leeds, subsequently playing for Sheffield club Heeley. Lang first came to Wednesday's attention in February 1876 when playing for Glasgow against Sheffield at Bramall Lane and after impressing against Wednesday in a friendly for Clyesdale he was asked to become the club's first unofficial professional player. At the time professionalism was deeply frowned upon so in order to disguise his true vocation the skilful and energetic attacker was given employment by Wednesday official Walter Fearnhough in his Sheffield based knife-making firm – his job description included no duties at all and he was therefore free to read newspapers and play football!

He had initially come to prominence when winning a Scottish Cup runners-up medal with Clydesdale in 1874, a feat he repeated in 1878 when returning briefly to Scotland to play for Third Lanark. In his pre Wednesday years Lang combined his football career with employment at John Browns in the Clydebank shipyard and it was while working there in 1869 that he lost the sight in his left eye – a little known fact that was always kept secret to ensure any opponents could not take advantage of the fact. Just prior to moving south Lang won the first of his two full caps for Scotland and while in Sheffield he helped Wednesday to a variety of local honours including three Sheffield Challenge Cups and a Wharncliffe Charity Cup. He was also one of the eleven men who played in the Owls first ever F.A.Cup tie and was known to still be living in 1926, aged 75.

LANGLEY, Ambrose **1893-1905**

Born: 10 March 1870 Horncastle
(5ft 11½ins, 14st – 1896)
Died: 29 January 1937 Sheffield
Debut: 2 September 1893
v Sunderland Division One Home
Last Appearance:
19 December 1903
v Newcastle United Division One Home
Total League
& Cup Appearances: 318 **Goals: 14**

Career Details:

Horncastle Town		1885
Blue Star/Horncastle Gridirons		1886
Boston Town		
Grimsby Town	March	1889
Middlesbrough Ironopolis	April	1891
Everton		1893
WEDNESDAY		1893
Hull City	26 April	1905

CAPS (@ SWFC)
Football League (1) v Scottish League 1898

Left back Ambrose Langley started his career with hometown club Horncastle Town, making early headlines in 1886 when his side reached the Fifth Round of the F.A.Cup, losing 5-0 to Aston Villa. In the following season Langley was amongst several players who broke away to form a club called Blue Star, which they financed through collections and subscriptions - the youngsters each having to give a guarantee that their sister would make them each a shirt! – blue and white stripes being their choice of kit. About the same time a Mr Cook of Boston started a 'watch competition' for players under-18 and after entering the competition two gentleman of Horncastle took an interest in the side, providing much needed equipment for the fledgling club. A name change came next, to Horncastle Gridirons, after the gridiron which forms part of the town's coat of arms, and Langley's side went all the way to the Final but lost 3-2 to Grimsby Humber Rovers at Boston. While playing for Horncastle, Langley had secured employment as an apprentice photographer but after losing his job was signed on an amateur basis by Boston Town at the rather excessive sum of £1 per week expenses. His remuneration from Boston would soon get Langley into hot water as he later signed amateur forms for Grimsby Town – they secured him another position as a trainee photographer – who subsequently refused Boston permission to play Langley in a Lincolnshire Cup semi-final. The furious Boston officials reported to the FA that Grimsby were playing an amateur who was being paid a wage by Boston Town but this tactic rebounded upon Boston as after neither they or Langley could justify his expenses both were suspended for two weeks!

A move into the powerful Northern League came next for the tough, uncompromising full back when he signed forms for Middlesbrough Ironopolis. Two Championships followed for Langley while his side also reached the last eight of the F.A.Cup in 1893 before losing 7-0 at Preston North End. Immediately after the Cup exit Langley signed league forms for Everton but somewhat bizarrely they gave him a free transfer in the following summer after seeing him play again and stating that he was too slow! A move to Aston Villa then broke down when he refused to undergo a medical on his suspect knee and doubts were raised about his fitness when The Owls secured his signature in the summer of 1893. Thankfully these doubts proved to be totally unfounded as over the next eleven seasons Langley was a true colossus in defence, forming part of the famous 'three Ls' back line that also contained Lyall and Layton. Won the championships of Division One and Two while at Wednesday, as well as the F.A.Cup in 1896, and proved a veritable rock at the back on which many an opposition forward ran aground!

Langley was certainly a non-nonsense individual as not only was he sent off in the infamous F.A.Cup battle against Sheffield United in 1900 but during a game at Preston North End he lost his temper due to the constant barracking of one fan behind the goal. He decided to take a goal kick to get within reach of the supporter and duly swung his arm around, catching the poor individual in his face, giving him two black eyes! He was later summoned to appear at Preston Police Court but on day of trial paid £7 in settlement. The Lincolnshire product was a real fighter and it was these qualities that made him a huge Olive Grove and later Owlerton favourite and worthy successor to Jack Earp as captain. A bad injury sustained at Sunderland in 1903 saw Harry Burton take Langley's first team place and when regaining his fitness Ambrose was told by Wednesday to keep fit for first team duty without playing for the reserves – when he returned to the side he was understandably rusty due to lack of match practise. This effectively signalled the end of his playing career at Wednesday as after undergoing admin work and some scouting for the club he left when being appointed player-manager at Hull City in 1905.

His playing career would only last until December 1905 but he enjoyed a successful time purely as manager at Analby Road, almost leading The Tigers into the top-flight 1910 – was once said to have rowed across the Humber to beat a rival manager to a players signature! He left in 1912 and in April 1913 returned to Hillsborough to become assistant secretary to Arthur Dickinson on a £260 per year wage. During the war years Langley was appointed temporary trainer before moving to become Huddersfield Town boss in 1919. While in charge at Leeds Road he led Town to runners-up spot in Division 2 and to the Final of the F.A.Cup in 1920 – losing 1-0 to Aston Villa. He later resigned after his position became untenable after he strongly backed moves for The Terriers to move to Elland Road during the club's financial crisis of the early 1920s. He subsequently dropped out of football to take the Cricketers Arms on Bramall Lane and when he passed away was licensee of The Pheasant Hotel on London Road in Sheffield.

LAW, Alexander 'Alex' 1932-35

Born: 28 April 1910 Bathgate, West Lothian
(5ft 9ins, 11st 12lbs – 1932)
Debut: 9 December 1933
v Liverpool
Division One Away
Last Appearance: 6 April 1935
v Tottenham Hotspur
Division One Home
Total League
& Cup Appearances: 9 Goals: 4

Career Details:

Bathgate		
Fauldhouse United		
Bo'ness	April	1932 Loan
WEDNESDAY	4 June	1932 Free
Brighton & Hove Albion	19 June	1935 £250
Chester	June	1939

Centre forward who was a complete unknown when he arrived from Scottish junior soccer in the summer of 1932. However he enjoyed a fine first season at Wednesday where despite not making a first team appearance Law scored 27 times in reserve team football, including three hat tricks plus a four-goal haul in a 5-1 Central League win over Bolton Wanderers. Not surprisingly he finished second team top scorer and in his three seasons at the club netted 53 times in reserve football – he was also top scorer with seventeen goals in the 1934-5 campaign.

On the opening day of the 1933-4 campaign he suffered a broken collarbone for the fourth time in his career, which meant several weeks on the sidelines. However on his return he found Jack Ball had fallen out of favour and was soon on his way to Old Trafford, giving Law his first taste of league soccer. He grabbed the opportunity with both hands and duly impressed, scoring on his home debut and helping Wednesday to four wins and a draw in his first five games. Unfortunately for Law his manager Billy Walker was not totally convinced of his abilities and the arrival of Neil Dewar effectively signalled the end of his top-flight career after such a promising start. The attacker would appear in only one more senior game for the Owls – on the right wing – before moving to Brighton in 1935.

His ill luck with injury struck again on the south Coast when he suffered a broken leg in April 1936 but Law recovered to take his Albion tally to a highly creditable 40 goals in 74 games before signing for Chester just before the outbreak of World War Two. The pacy Law actually played in the first two league games of the 1939-40 season, scoring once, but these matches were subsequently expunged from the record books when the season was abandoned, just three games into the campaign.

LAWSON, William "Willie" 1969-71

Born: 28 November 1947 Dundee
(5ft 6ins, 10st – 1970)
Debut: 18 October 1969
v Burnley
Division One Away
Last Appearance: 22 September 1970
v Chelsea
League Cup Away
Total League
& Cup Appearances: 11 Goals: 0

Career Details:

Carnoustie Penmure		1968
Brechin City	July	1969
WEDNESDAY	2 October	1969 £5,000
St.Mirren	18 February	1971 Free
East Fife		1973
Dundee Downfield		

The rise of Willie Lawson from Scottish amateur football to England's top-flight was a real 'Roy of the Rovers' story. Early in 1969 Lawson was still enjoying his first season of senior non-league football whilst earning a living working in his father's Dundee based window cleaning business. In the summer that followed he joined Scottish Second Division side Brechin City on a part-time basis and made such an impact that scouts flocked to Glebe Park. Offers came from Aberdeen and his hometown club Dundee but when Sheffield Wednesday came calling with a huge £5,000 offer – a fortune at the time for the small club – there was only one destination for the youngster who had amazingly played only eight Scottish League games for City.

The move into the big time must have been a daunting experience for the relatively untried 21 year-old but he had little time for nerves as within seven days of signing he was given a top-flight debut when regular Tony Coleman was injured for a trip to Turf Moor. He would appear in eight league games for The Owls in that debut campaign but after relegation Willie was more of a peripheral figure, playing only twice more. With his wife unable to settle in the City, Wednesday allowed him to return to Scotland for trials in February 1971 and within a month St Mirren manager Wilson Humphries signed him. By this time Lawson had gone back to work with his father – a business he inherited and still runs today – and remained part-time at St.Mirren and East Fife before retiring from the game. After hanging up his boots Lawson did play a couple of games for Dundee junior side Downfield purely as a favour to a friend.

LAYNE, David Richard 'Bronco' 1962-64 & 72-73

Born: 29 July 1939 Sheffield
(5ft 10ins, 11st 11lbs – 1963)
Debut: 18 August 1962
v Bolton Wanderers
Division One Home
Last Appearance: 8 April 1964
v Stoke City
Division One Away
Total League
& Cup Appearances: 81 Goals: 58

Career Details:

Oaksfolds		Trial
Chesterfield		Trial
Sheffield United		Jnrs
English Steel		
Rotherham United	July	1957
Swindon Town		1959 £500
Bradford City	December	1960 £7,500
WEDNESDAY	30 May	1962 £22,500
Banned Sine Die		1964
Contract cancelled	January	1965
Thorpe Arch Open Prison	January	1965
WEDNESDAY	28 July	1972 Free
Hereford United	14 December	1972 Loan
Retired	March	1973
Matlock Town		1974-5

Regarded by many Wednesday fans as one of the greatest centre forwards in the club's long history. His top-flight goals record could only be matched by the likes of David McLean and Jack Allen but sadly the name of David Layne will always be associated with the events of April 1964 when along with Peter Swan, and ex team mate Tony Kay, he was banned sine die by the Football Association for his part in the infamous bribes scandal. Before Layne's career came to an abrupt halt he had seemed set for International honours after having made a huge impact at Wednesday after signing from Bradford City. His 52 league goals in only 74 games made him one of the most feared attackers in the British game and he was truly hero worshipped by Wednesday fans – the bustling, hard shooting Layne took fans back a decade earlier to when Derek Dooley terrorised opposition defences. Such was his popularity that when Layne was controversially sent off in the home game with Aston Villa in November 1962 the club was fined £100 – Layne being suspended for seven days - for the (minor) crowd disturbances that followed, including a barrage of blue cushions being thrown from the North Stand!

His career had started in his home City where he played alongside both John Fantham and Gordon Banks for Sheffield boys. He also appeared for Yorkshire boys but despite playing for Sheffield United's under-16 side he started work at English Steel on leaving school. He played for the works side in the Drake U-18 League but soon signed part-time forms for Rotherham United where four goals in eleven league games brought a transfer to Swindon Town. It was at Town where he first earned his nickname as after scoring with a fierce free kick he was said to have 'the hardest shot in the west' and dubbed 'Bronco' after a popular TV cowboy of the time. His tremendous scoring for Swindon – 28 goals in only 41 league games – persuaded Bradford City to break their transfer record to bring him to Valley Parade and they were not to be disappointed as in his second season Layne netted 34 league goals – a seasonal club record that has still to be beaten. It was inevitable that City would not be able to hold onto their prize asset and it was Vic Buckingham who won the chase, Wednesday paying a relatively small fee for his services – considering Albert Quixall was sold for twice the fee almost fours years earlier.

When the bribes scandal hit the news stands in April 1964 the club suspended Layne and later in the year he was jailed for four months. He played for the prison team while serving his sentence but his professional career effectively ended when being banned sine die by the F.A. on his release. His life continued to unravel when his wife was killed in a car crash in 1966 but he soon remarried and in 1967 became a publican. His attempts to have the ban lifted in 1966 failed but a change in F.A rules in 1968 gave Layne hope although it would not be until 1972 that the powers that be relented and lifted the ban. He had kept fit with Peter Swan and was soon re-signed by The Owls, given a contract to the end of the season following a successful trial period. It was hard though for the now 33 year-old player to impress back at Wednesday and after a few games for the reserves he left for a loan spell at Hereford United. Came back to Hillsborough after four league games but an ankle injury eventually led to his retirement, allowing him to concentrate on running his Bolsover public house. He made a brief comeback under the management of Peter Swan at Matlock Town in the mid-1970s and is now a publican near Meadowhall in Sheffield.

LAYTON, William "Willie" 1896-1910

Born: 1875 Gornall, Staffordshire
(5ft 7½ins, 12st 4lbs – 1907)
Died: April 1944 Australia
Debut: 8 January 1898
v Everton Division One Away
Last Appearance: 25 September 1909
v Tottenham Hotspur Division One Away
Total League
& Cup Appearances: 361 Goals: 2

Career Details:

Blackwell Colliery		
Chesterfield		
WEDNESDAY	September	1895
St.Lawrence		1910

CAPS (@SWFC)
Football League (1) v Irish League 1901

A twist of fate ensured that full back Willie Layton would spend his entire professional career as a Wednesday player. This occurred in November 1895 when Layton was working as a miner at Blackwell Colliery but was also a regular in the Owls reserve side, hoping to secure a professional contract. On the day before a game at Attercliffe, Layton should have been working his usual night shift but instead decided not to work so he would be fresh for the match. It proved a truly life saving decision as on that very same night an underground explosion on the coal seam killed seven men and from that day forward Layton vowed he would not play for any other club – he never did.

Born in the midlands, he moved to the Derbyshire village of Blackwell as a youngster and would play as a forward in the same village side as Sheffield United's legendary keeper William 'Fatty' Foulke. His form in local football – and in a solitary season for

Chesterfield - persuaded Wednesday to give the youngster a trial and after signing for the club Layton would serve a long apprenticeship in reserve team soccer, appearing in almost one hundred second team games. The Owls relegation from Division One in 1899 proved the turning point for Willie who had initially been used as a standby for Earp and Langley but had never let the team down when appearing in either of the full back positions. His rival Earp started the first game back in Division Two but Layton replaced him at right back for the next game and never looked back, being ever present as Wednesday coasted to the Championship and a quick return to the top-flight. Layton was a sturdy, dashing and plucky individual who boasted a powerful kick but was a scrupulously fair tackler and a model professional. Part of the famous three 'Ls' of Layton, Langley and Lyall he remained a rock in the club's defence for over a decade, helping Wednesday to two League Championships and an F.A.Cup win while also appearing regularly for Sheffield Association against the likes of Glasgow.

After retiring from the game in 1910 Layton – whose brother Arthur played for several league clubs and whose grandson Michael Knighton owned Carlisle United - became licensee at The Butchers Arms at Whitwell and signed as a player for the village side St.Lawrence, after rejecting an early approach from Midland League Worksop Town for his signature. His decision to stay loyal to his local team made Willie an immensely popular figure in local circles and he was appointed captain after being the first player to sign up for the season. Layton – famous for the unique scissor kicks with which he would clear his lines – then no doubt shocked the locals by leaving both his wife and children in 1912 to emigrate to Australia. He experienced another brush with death on the outward journey as his ship ran into heavy storms off South Africa and at one stage was reported lost! The vessel eventually reached its destination several weeks later and soon after docking Willie would marry the policeman's daughter, Margaret, who he fell for on the ship – perhaps forgetting that he had not divorced his first wife! He eventually settled in New South Wales – working as a miner in Sydney - but a crippling illness meant he was unable to work for the last ten years of his life.

LEACH, Thomas 'Tony' 1925-34

Born: 23 September 1903 Sheffield
(5ft 10ins, 11st 10lbs – 1929)
Died: 30 January 1968 Owston Ferry, Doncaster
Debut: 2 February 1927
v South Shields
F.A.Cup Away
Last Appearance: 3 March 1934
v Sheffield United
Division One Away
Total League
& Cup Appearances: 260 Goals: 14

Career Details:

Retford Town		
Blackburn Wesleyans		
Wath Athletic		
Rotherham County	May	1922 Trial
Liverpool	December	1923 Trial
Tankerton United		
WEDNESDAY	31 October	1925 £150
Newcastle United	16 June	1934 £1100
Stockport County	27 July	1936 £300
Carlisle United	5 February	1937 * Part exchange
Lincoln City	September	1938
Released		1939

CAPS (@SWFC)
England Full (2) v Ireland 20/10/30, v Wales 22/11/30
Football League (1) v Scottish League 1930

Member of the famous inter-war years back line of Strange-Leach-Marsden that powered Wednesday to consecutive League Championships in 1929 and 1930. At his peak Leach was arguably the finest centre back in the country, being very fast, intelligent and hard in the tackle. He was a glutton for work and as strong as a horse – a true 'old-fashioned' centre back in every sense - who guarded the middle path to goal with his iron frame and broad shoulders – not many forwards could find a way past this 'tough' stopper. He had originally arrived at Hillsborough from a Wath Athletic side that was literally swamped with talent – not only did his team mate Jack Wilkinson move to Wednesday at the same time but an amazing seven other players from the same eleven would eventually move into league football! His footballing career had started in Sheffield amateur soccer – he played in the same Wesleyans side as future Owl Len Hargreaves – and like many of his contemporaries started his working life down his local pit.

It was actually as a forward that he made his name in local football and after eighteen months in the Owls reserve side it was at inside right that he made his senior bow for the club – a shock Cup loss at Second Division South Shields. His league debut three days later also came in the same position but the real breakthrough came when being converted to centre half and replacing Arthur Lowdell at right halfback for the last few games of the 1926-7 campaign. However his true position proved to be in what was called the pivot role (the central player in a three man defensive line) and he never looked back after replacing Fred Kean in the No. 5 shirt towards the end of the following season when The Owls made one of the most dramatic escapes from relegation ever seen. His tremendous form made sure Wednesday did not regret selling Kean to Bolton in 1928 as Leach was a fixture in the side for five seasons, captaining the team on several occasions. Full caps for England soon came his way – his England debut came at Bramall Lane in a side also containing Wednesday trio Blenkinsop, Burgess & Strange – although he fell foul of the F.A. in March 1933 when he was banned for 28 days after being sent off in a home win over Wolves at Hillsborough!

He was placed on the transfer list in 1934 after a dispute over contract terms, after losing his first team place to Walt Millership part way through the 33-4 season – and eventually moved to Second Division Newcastle. He was appointed captain of a United side that also boasted an International back line consisting of Leach, Bill Imrie (Scotland) and Sam Weaver (England). However after Newcastle failed to get back into Division One he left for half a season at Stockport County – playing in enough games to win a Division Three (North) Championship medal - before a part exchange deal involving five players and £400 cash saw a move to Carlisle United. His time was relatively short at the Cumbrian club but after moving to Lincoln he was suspended for four weeks and find £20 after it was proven that while at Carlisle he had accepted money that was to be distributed between his team mates. The cash had come from a Stockport County director who wanted Carlisle to beat Lincoln in two vital matches in order to help County gain promotion. He finally retired at the end of the last pre war season and later worked as a builder in Hull before living in South Yorkshire for the rest of his life.

LEDGER H. 1880-83

Born:
Debut:
8 January 1881 v Turton F.A.Cup Away
Last Appearance:
13 January 1883 v Nottingham Forest F.A.Cup Home
Total League & Cup Appearances: 13 Goals: 0

Career Details:

WEDNESDAY	November	1880
Released		1883

Goalkeeper of the early 1880s who appeared in the club's first ever home F.A.Cup tie after having made his debut at home to Heeley in a November 1880 friendly. He initially fought with William Stacey for the No. 1 jersey and played 23 minor games for Wednesday – winning the Wharncliffe Charity Cup in 1882 –before losing his place to George Ulyett part way through the 1882-3 season. After leaving Wednesday the amateur custodian seemingly dropped out of football altogether.

LEE, George 1899-1901

Born: 3rd Quarter 1876 Northeast
Died: 28 March 1906 Rotherham
Debut:
16 September 1899 v Bolton Wanderers Division Two Home
Last Appearance:
19 February 1900 v Sheffield United F.A.Cup Home
Total League & Cup Appearances: 6 Goals: 1

Career Details:

Stockton	
Rotherham Town	
Whitworth	
WEDNESDAY	1899
Released	1901
Amberley	1904-5

Right-winger who played for the Owls around the turn of the Twentieth Century, after having arrived from Northeast non-league soccer. He provided creditable opposition, in his early weeks at the club, to Archie Brash's first team shirt but then spent several weeks out of contention until being surprisingly recalled for the F.A.Cup replay tie with Sheffield United at Owlerton. Unfortunately his return from the cold proved a false dawn as seven minutes before half time Lee fell badly on the snow covered pitch and broke his leg, just above the ankle. The fracture brought a premature end to his season and effectively ended Lee's league career, as George would be restricted solely to reserve team football in his second season – helping Wednesday to convincingly win the Sheffield Association League in 1901. He later played in the Attercliffe & District Licensed Vitualars League for Amberley.

He was tried on several occasions as a centre forward during that successful season for the second team but at the end of the campaign was released, dropping out of football altogether. Sadly within five years of leaving the club, at the age of just 29, he passed away and was said to be in 'poor circumstances' at the time of his death, leaving a widow and two children. Wednesday put aside £10 to start a benefit fund and Lee's employer - a Wednesday player in the Olive Grove years – asked for donations.

LEE, Graeme Barry 2003-

Born: 31 May 1978 Middlesbrough
(6ft 2ins, 13st 7lbs - 2003)
Debut: 9 August 2003
v Swindon Town
Division Two Away
Total League
& Cup Appearances: 57+3 Goals: 6

Career Details:

Marton Juniors		
Hartlepool United	2 July	1996
WEDNESDAY	1 July	2003 Free

It was almost inevitable that when Chris Turner moved into the Hillsborough hot seat in November 2002 players from his successful Hartlepool United side would follow. Two players duly signed, Paul Smith being the other, but it was Lee who made the greater impact, as he was almost ever present until suffering stress fractures of both legs in January 2004. Before the injury Lee had proved a rock at the heart of The Owls defence with his superb heading ability and strong defensive play - he was also forging a reputation for scoring from thunderous free kicks.

Lee had previously amassed a total of 252 games at his only other club Hartlepool United. After captaining United to promotion from Division Three in 2003 he was named in the PFA Divisional side but under freedom of contract moved south to join Wednesday. Went straight into the Owls side for the opening day win at Swindon Town and scored his first goal for the club on his home debut - ironically against his old side in a League Cup tie. He was later made captain and was an automatic choice as Wednesday struggled to climb up the league. Injury also played a large part in his second season at Hillsborough as after recovering from an early season problem he became a regular under Paul Sturrock before Lee's season came to a premature end.

LEMAN, Denis 1976-82

Born: 1 December 1954 Newcastle
(5ft 5ins, 10st 2lbs – 1977)
Debut: 4 December 1977
v Tranmere Rovers
Division Three Home
Last Appearance: 5 December 1981
v Chelsea Division Two Away
Total League
& Cup Appearances: 102+14 Goals:10

Career Details:

Manchester City	1 December	1971
WEDNESDAY	30 November	1976 £8,500
Wrexham	18 February	1982 2-month loan
Scunthorpe United	August	1982 Free
Burton Albion	January	1984
Cardiff City	March	1984 N/C

Denis Leman was a schoolboy star for both Newcastle and England boys before signing apprentice forms for Manchester City in July 1970. After being elevated to professional status the midfielder struggled to gain a regular first team place and after just seventeen league games moved to Wednesday on loan. After scoring on his debut, in a 3-1 win, he impressed sufficiently for his move to be made permanent on 4 January 1977 and Leman would be an automatic choice for eighteen months. However stiff competition from the likes of Jeff Johnson and Brian Hornsby then saw Leman slowly slip from the first team picture – starting only six league games during the 1980 promotion season – and it was no surprise when he asked for a transfer in January 1980.

He eventually moved on a month's loan to Wrexham, which was extended to the end of the season, but the Welsh side were relegated at the end of the season and he returned to Hillsborough. After rejecting a move to Swedish football Leman elected instead to join Scunthorpe on a free transfer but after helping them to promotion a serious knee injury meant he hardly played during the 1983-4 campaign. He failed to play a game for his next club, Burton Albion, before winding up his league career with ten games at Cardiff City, under old team mate Jimmy Mullen. Incidentally his playing career finally came to an end when after several games for the Manchester City Veterans team he was forced to retire due to an arthritic knee. On leaving City he spend a year selling double glazing before studying Recreation and Leisure for a further twelve months. On leaving college in 1986 Leman gained employment at the P.F.A. in the football in the community office while gaining a full F.A. coaching badge in 1991. He added a Bsc Honours degree in physiotherapist in 1995 and currently works as Deputy Chief Administrator for the P.F.A.

LESCOTT, Aaron Anthony 2000-01

Born: 2 December 1978 Birmingham
(5ft 8 ins, 10st 9lbs - 2002)
Debut: 8 October 2000
v West Bromwich Albion
Division One Home
Last Appearance: 3 November 2001
v Portsmouth
Division One Home
Total League
& Cup Appearances: 24+19 Goals: 0

Career Details:

Aston Villa	5 July	1996
Lincoln City	14 March	2000 Loan
WEDNESDAY	3 October	2000 £100,000
Stockport County	13 November	2001 £75,000
Bristol Rovers	25 March	2004 Loan
Bristol Rovers	26 August	2004 Free

Midfielder Aaron Lescott was a virtual unknown when Wednesday manager Paul Jewell brought him to Hillsborough, as in over four years as a professional at Villa Park Lescott had made just a solitary first team appearance – as a substitute in an F.A.Cup tie. His first taste of league football came during a five game loan spell at Lincoln City but after he was seemingly stranded in Villa's reserve team he jumped at the chance to move to First Division Wednesday. Overall he experienced a promising debut campaign with his versatility – appearing at fullback and in midfield - and energy a key factor. Played in 35 games in that first season but following Paul Jewell's departure he struggled to remain a regular and eventually became Carlton Palmer's first signing after taking over as manager at Stockport County.

Lescott – whose brother Joleon plays for Wolves – again made a big impact in his first season at the Edgeley Park club and was so influential that when long-term skipper Mike Flynn went out on loan to Stoke City Aaron was handed the captain's armband. He missed the last few weeks of the season due to a knee injury but bounced back to became a fans favourite in 2002-3 before joining ex-Owl Junior Agogo at Bristol Rovers after 72 league games for County.

LESTER, Frederick Charles 'Fred' 1937-44

Born: 20 February 1911 Chatham
(5ft 9½ins, 10st 11lbs – 1938)
Died: 28 June 1974 Chatham
Debut: 23 October 1937
v Manchester United
Division Two Away
Last Appearance: 28 January 1939
v Swansea Town
Division Two Away
Total League
& Cup Appearances: 21* Goals: 0
***Also appeared in 6 wartime games**

Career Details:

Chatham Town		
Gillingham	June	1932
WEDNESDAY	16 October	1937 £1150*
Shorts Sports	January	1940 Guest
Contract Cancelled	September	1944
Gravesend		1944

*Joint fee with Walker

Arrived at the club as understudy to England left back Ted Catlin, after playing 201 times for Southern League Gillingham. The former postman was a reserve regular for two seasons and enjoyed a run of fifteen consecutive first team games mid-way through the 1938-9 season when Catlin was absent. Remained on the Owls books during the majority of the Second World War although he quickly returned home to Kent and was working at a munitions factory near Rochester for the duration of the War. The Owls eventually agreed to cancel his contract in 1944 so Lester could assist non-league Gravesend. He was co-opted onto the Northfleet committee in July 1946 and was later manager until leaving in 1961.

LEVICK, Oliver 1919-26

Born: 3rd Quarter 1899 Rotherham
(6ft 0½ ins, 11st 7lbs - 1922)
Died: 1st Quarter 1965 Sheffield
Debut: 22 January 1921
v Port Vale
Division Two Home
Last Appearance: 3 May 1924
v Manchester United
Division Two Home
Total League
& Cup Appearances: 21 Goals: 0

Career Details:

Woodhouse FC		
WEDNESDAY		1919 £10/10s
Stockport County	17 May	1926 £500
York City		
Boston Town		1930

Left half back Oliver Levick first came to prominence in local football and was in fact courted by a prominent Southern League club before his father told him that he should sign for Wednesday. The Owls duly donated the princely sum of ten pounds, ten shillings to his club Woodhouse and Levick quickly became established in the Owls Midland League side. The ex-Sheffield boys player was a regular as the reserve team won the Midland League Championship in 1923 but was used sparingly in league soccer, competing with the likes of Tom Brelsford for the first team shirt.

His best season at Wednesday came during the 1923-4 campaign when Levick appeared in thirteen league games but the arrival of the future England International Billy Marsden in 1924 pushed him further down the pecking order and he eventually left for Division Three (North) side Stockport County. The native of Swallownest appeared in six games for the Lancashire side before ending his career in non-league football at York and Boston.

LEWIS, Idris 'Dai' 1938-46

Born: 26 August 1915 Trealaw
(5ft 8ins, 10st 12lbs – 1938)
Died: March 1996 Swansea
Debut: 27 August 1938
v Bury
Division Two Home
Last Appearance: 11 March 1939
v Newcastle United
Division Two Away
Total League
& Cup Appearances: 23* Goals: 8
***Also appeared in 2 wartime games**

Career Details:

Ton Boys Club		
Gelli Colliery		
Swansea Town	May	1935
WEDNESDAY	20 June	1938 £50 + R.Rhodes
Swansea Town	March	1939
Coventry City		WW2 Guest
Cardiff City		WW2 Guest
Bristol Rovers	31 July	1946
Newport County	12 November	1947
Haverfordwest County		1948
Pembroke Borough		

Since outstanding right-winger Mark Hooper had faded from the first team scene the Owls had unsuccessfully tried to find a replacement, Charlie Luke and Len Massarella both being tried on the right side before Wednesday boss Jimmy McMullan raided Swansea Town for the signature of Dai Lewis. The attacker had made 57 appearances for The Swans after joining from non-league football and went straight into the Wednesday side for the opening day win over Bury at Hillsborough. He started the first seven games of the season but then lost out to Masserella before switching briefly to the left wing. However Bill Fallon was an automatic choice on the left side and when he returned Lewis was left to fight for a place with his rival. The arrival of Ernie Toseland in March 1939 ensured Dai would spend the rest of his season in the reserves and although he started the opening two games of the following season that campaign was soon abandoned as War in Europe erupted. He subsequently returned to Wales to serve in the home forces for the duration of the war and finished his playing career back in amateur soccer.

LINDSAY, John McArthur 'Jack' 1945-46

Born: 11 December 1921
Flemington Cambuslang
(5ft 9½ins – 11st 2lbs – 1946)
Only Appearance: 2 September 1946
v Barnsley
Division Two Home
Total League
& Cup Appearances: 1* Goals: 1
***Also appeared in**
46 wartime games, scoring 25 goals

Career Details:

Redpath Brown		
Lanark United		1940
Kerrydale Celtic		1942
Greenock Morton		1944
WEDNESDAY	March	1945
Bury	31 October	1946 £875
Carlisle United	19 August	1947 £400
Southport	17 March	1951
Wigan Athletic	August	1952
Carlisle United	11 January	1955

Unfortunately for centre forward Jack Lindsay his best days at Wednesday came during the Second World War when he was a prolific scorer. He had initially arrived on trial, after scoring a hat trick the previous week, but two goals on his debut in a wartime game at Leeds United quickly persuaded Wednesday officials of his talents and he duly became only one of a handful of players to transfer to Hillsborough during the hostilities. His career had started in Scottish junior soccer – previously winning two caps for Scotland schoolboys – and it was not until his early twenties that Lindsay turned professional with Morton.

After his terrific start at Wednesday he remained a regular in wartime soccer, as well as netting twelve times during 1945-6 as the reserves won the Central League Championship for only the second time. However when national football returned he disappeared almost completely from the first team scene and even a goal on his only 'official' game for the club could not improve his fortunes. He soon asked for a transfer and in the autumn of 1946 left for Bury where he remained just a solitary season, despite netting a creditable seven goals in only eleven league games – three of those goals coming on Boxing Day 1946 against Wednesday at Hillsborough! A move to Carlisle finally ignited his English League career as in four successful seasons Lindsay scored almost a goal every two games – 46 in 103 – before dropping out of league soccer after a brief spell at then league side Southport – when scoring four goals for The Sandgrounders against Scunthorpe in February 1952 he scored a hat trick in only three minutes. After ending his league career back at Brunton Park he settled in the town and worked until his retirement for a security firm – at places like Courtaulds and Pirelli – while also scouting for Liverpool and Blackburn.

LINIGHAN, Brian 1992-97

Born: 2 November 1973 Hartlepool
(6ft 3ins, 12st 10lbs - 1996)
Debut: 11 January 1994
v Wimbledon
League Cup Away
Last Appearance: 19 January 1994
v Nottingham Forest
F.A.Cup Away
Total League
& Cup Appearances: 3 Goals: 0

Career Details:

WEDNESDAY	1 July	1992
Bury	20 June	1997 Free
Cambridge City	December	1998 Loan
Hallam	August	2000 Free
Gainsborough Trinity	December	2000 Free
Worksop Town	December	2001 £5,000
Released	May	2003
Whitby Town	8 August	2003 Free

Centre half Brian Linighan perhaps holds a unique record in professional football as his only three senior appearances for the Owls came in three different competitions, inside a nine-day period. The tall rangy defender had come through the club's youth system, along with twin brother John, after originally arriving as an apprentice in 1990. While in The Owls junior side Linighan reached the Final of the F.A.Youth Cup in 1991 and won the NIL Cup a year later before progressing into the reserve side. Unfortunately for Linighan it was in reserve team football that he would spend almost his entire Wednesday career, amassing 143 appearances over a five-year period – in a reserve game at York in September 1993 he managed to break both his fibula and nose! Although commanding in the air a lack of pace and poor distribution ensured he could not add to his flurry of first team starts – the closest being a handful of unused sub appearances – and was eventually released by David Pleat at the end of the 1996-7 season.

Incredibly it would be over three years before Linighan made his debut for The Shakers as he appeared exclusively in reserve team football until finally getting a first team chance in April 2000. He started the next two games but his subsequent release in May 2000 spelt the end of an eight-year professional career that brought the ex-Hartlepool boys player just half a dozen senior appearances. A drop into non-league soccer was next for Linighan although in October 2000 he returned to his hometown, gaining employment down the road at Sunderland with Nissan Motors. His brothers Andy and David both enjoyed long careers in league soccer – the former breaking Wednesday hearts with his last minute winner for Arsenal in the 1993 F.A.Cup Final replay – while his father also played football professionally. Since moving back to the Northeast, Brian has solely played non-league football while working, alongside his brother John, as a maintaince technician.

LLOYD, William 'Billy' 1906-13

Born: 1884/5 South Hylton
(5ft 8ins, 10st, 10 lbs – 1906)
Debut: 29 December 1906
v Bury Division One Home
Last Appearance: 5 October 1912
v Aston Villa Division One Away
Total League
& Cup Appearances: 84 Goals: 7

Career Details:

Hylton Star		
Jarrow		
WEDNESDAY	August	1906
Rotherham County	May	1913 Free

Pre First World War player Billy Lloyd would in modern parlance probably be called a utility player as in seven seasons at Wednesday he appeared in a variety of roles, including half back, winger and inside forward. A life as a professional footballer had looked unlikely from the day his father died when he was just five years old, meaning his mother and several siblings had to move out of the public house they ran and set up a shop in her front room to make ends meet. On leaving school he secured a job at the local foundry with his football activities restricted to his spare time – his first club Hylton Star produced four professional footballers from within its ranks. A move to crack local non-league side Jarrow came at the age of 20 and it was his form for this side that alerted The Owls Northeast scout Bob Brown to his promise. He got the shock of his life in 1906 when his brother came to the foundry to tell him Wednesday wanted to sign him and soon after at Brown's Hebben home the future Owls manager secured his signature.

After serving his apprenticeship in the reserves his big chance came on Boxing Day 1906 at Derby but snow meant the game was called off. However he remained in the side and played at inside right in the home defeat to Bury. He subsequently made six appearances in that debut season and was named as travelling reserve for the 1907 FA Cup Final. He spent the following season back in the reserves, except for playing the final five games of the Division One campaign at right halfback, but it was on the right wing that the slightly built winger would make a big impact in 1908 09. The remainder of his time at Hillsborough was spent in his favourite spot on the right side although when Sam Kirkman replaced him Lloyd could usually be found in the defensive line at halfback. Incidentally it was reported in November 1911 that he showed an abnormal liking for tobacco but the habit wasn't calculated to harm him! While still on the Owls books he also opened a tobacconist shops at Hillsborough tram terminus and then started to distribute Wednesday fixture cards to customers. His final appearance in a Wednesday shirt came in the club's record defeat, 10-0 at Villa Park, and in the following summer he signed for neighbours Rotherham County.

During the Great War, Lloyd served for three years in the 1st Battalion of the York and Lancs regiment, seeing active duty in Turkey and Greece, but the conflict effectively ended his career and after being demobbed in December 1920 he returned to Hillsborough when Wednesday offered him the role of assistant trainer. However the position was more labourer than coach – he had to arrive at the ground at 7am to light the fires and then had to clean the players' boots! He remained in that role until the mid-1920s although he would play once more on the Hillsborough turf when he attended a reserve match and turned out for Bradford City when they were a man short! After leaving the club he remained in the City and still said to be attending matches at the Hillsborough at the ripe old age of 84.

LOCHERTY, Joseph 'Joe' 1947-50

Born: 5 September 1925 Dundee
(5ft 10½ins, 10st 12lbs – 1948)
Died: 20 June 2000 Dundee
Debut: 11 December 1948
v Bradford Park Avenue
Division Two Home
Last Appearance: 8 October 1949
v Grimsby Town
Division Two Away
Total League
& Cup Appearances: 12 Goals: 0

Career Details:

Lochee Harp		
WEDNESDAY	15 September	1947 £200
Colchester United	August	1950 £1,000
Scarborough	July	1951
Dundee United	22 January	1954

Wednesday signed Joe Locherty from Dundee junior football and he made an immediate impact by scoring twice on his Central League debut, playing at inside right. A move to half back preceded his first team debut and a flurry of appearances in that new position followed until he dropped back into reserve team soccer. He was one of several players signed by Colchester United for their first season of league football and after a season at Layer Road dropped into non-league football at Scarborough. He returned to his roots when signing for Dundee United but his only senior game for The Tangerines was one to forget – a 12-1 loss at Motherwell, which is United's record defeat. After leaving football Joe worked for an insurance company and then a loan company before running a service station until his retirement.

LODGE, Robert William 'Bobby' 1959-61

Born: 1 July 1941 Retford
(5ft 6ins, 9st 9lbs – 1960)
Debut: 10 December 1960
v Blackburn Rovers
Division One Home
Last Appearance: 23 December 1960
v Arsenal
Division One Home
Total League
& Cup Appearances: 3 Goals: 2

Career Details:

WEDNESDAY	13 March	1959
Doncaster Rovers	8 May	1961
Buxton		1962
Sheffield F.C.		1964
Hampton Sports		

Although born in Retford, Bobby Lodge has spent all his life in Sheffield. This was because during the war pregnant women in Sheffield were sent away from the bombing until the child was born so within weeks of his birth, mother and baby son returned to the City. On leaving Firth Park Grammar School in 1956, aged fifteen, he started working as an apprentice engineer at a Sheffield company but also signed amateur forms for Wednesday in November 1958 after catching the eye of manager Harry Catterick during a trial match. He was elevated to professional status six months later and at the age of just nineteen was given a first team bow on the right wing in the home game with Blackburn Rovers. What followed was nothing more than sensational as the youngster scored twice as Wednesday won by the odd goal in nine. Unfortunately he found it impossible to follow up his debut display and after playing in the next two games gave way to regular Derek Wilkinson. This brief taste of top-flight soccer proved the highlight of Lodge's career as he dropped back into reserve team soccer before signing for Norman Curtis' Doncaster Rovers.

A further four goals in 23 games followed at Belle Vue before he moved with Curtis to non-league Buxton after the ex-Wednesday full back had resigned as manager – both Curtis and Lodge appeared against The Owls in a May 1964 friendly. At the same time Lodge joined Sheffield based company International Drill Twist and would work for them for thirteen years, ending his playing days appearing for the works team. After being promoted to export manager at Drill Twist he left in 1976 and after briefly working for Bone Cravens was employed by Presto Tools whose chairman was also the Owls chairman Bert McGee. After 23 years he was made redundant in December 1999 and later worked for the Post Office before gaining employment at Ventura Limited in June 2003.

LOFTHOUSE, James "Jimmy" 1920-23

Born: 24 March 1894 St.Helens
(5ft 4ins, 11st 4lbs – 1921)
Died: August 1954 Windsor
Debut: 28 August 1920
v Barnsley
Division Two Away
Last Appearance: 2 December 1922
v Leicester City
Division Two Away
Total League
& Cup Appearances: 98 Goals: 13

Career Details:

Cabbage Hall FC		
St.Helens Recreation		
Stalybridge Celtic		
Manchester United		WW1 Guest
Reading	May	1913
WEDNESDAY	August	1920 £650
Rotherham County	8 March	1923 £900
Bristol Rovers	1 December	1923 £350
Queens Park Rangers	May	1926 Free
Aldershot	August	1928 Free
GPO (Reading)	1 September	1934

New manager Bob Brown brought diminutive left-winger Jimmy Lofthouse to the club as he tried to rebuild after the disastrous 1919-20 campaign. He had previously combined his trade, as a glass blower, with appearing for Southern League Reading but after moving into the professional ranks was a mainstay in the Owls Second Division side for almost three seasons, appearing in 79 consecutive league games. This run ended when he lost his place to newcomer Horace Henshall in December 1922 and before the season had run its course Jimmy was sold to neighbours Rotherham County. The steady, if unspectacular, wing man made only 26 appearances for County before taking the long journey south to sign for Bristol Rovers.

Played 105 times for The Pirates before enjoying a superb two seasons at Division Three (South) side QPR where he finished top scorer and netted 27 goals in 81 games – excellent figures for an out-and-out winger. After dropping back into non-league soccer at Southern League Aldershot, Lofthouse obtained employment as the steward of the Tilehurst Constitutional Club in Reading. He later worked for the GPO (Post Office) in Reading until his retirement, ending his playing days with the works side.

LOGAN, John William 'John/Johnny' 1946-51

Born: 16 August 1912 Horden
(5ft 6½ins, 11st 5lbs – 1946)
Died: 4th Quarter 1980 Barnsley
Debut: 28 December 1946
v Luton Town Division Two Home
Last Appearance: 20 February 1947
v Preston North End F.A.Cup Home
Total League
& Cup Appearances: 6 Goals: 0

Career Details:

Horden Colliery Welfare		
Charlton Athletic	July	1934
Darlington	May	1935
Barnsley	4 March	1937 £750
Hartlepool United		1939 Guest
Huddersfield Town	April	1942 Guest
Bradford City		1942-44 Guest
Bradford Park Avenue		1943-44 Guest
Everton		1944-45 Guest
Darlington		1944-45 Guest
WEDNESDAY	28 December	1946 £2,000
Retired		1951

Despite spending over twenty years on the Owls staff, John Logan played first team football for only one season. He was already in the twilight of his career when joining from Barnsley and after just a handful of first team games took a more backseat role, signing a player-coach contract in June 1947. While coaching the 'A' team he would continue to play reserve team football until finally hanging up his boots in 1951, being appointed reserve team trainer and then assistant first team trainer in September 1952. He was on the bench when Wednesday lost the 1966 Cup Final to Everton but in February 1967 was a victim of the mass clear out by manager Alan Brown. After leaving football he gained employment at the Wilson and Longbottom foundry in Barnsley and helped coach the Athersley Social WMC and The Athersley Arms Hotel teams.

His playing career had started back in his native Northeast with his Colliery side but aged 21 he moved to London, signing for Charlton Athletic. However he grew increasingly homesick and after returning home, after two years, was out of work until being offered a contract by Darlington. He subsequently became the first signing of Barnsley manager Angus Seed (brother of Jimmy) who had previously failed to sign Logan when he was manager at Aldershot and John was at Charlton. The centre half was an almost ever present in his first season at Oakwell and although The Tykes suffered relegation they bounced back to win the Division Three (North) title in 1939 with Logan again a key player. At the outbreak of war Logan returned to Horden to work at his old colliery and started to appear as a guest for Hartlepool United. However after only two games for United, Seed persuaded him to return and work instead at Wharncliffe Woodmoor Colliery in Barnsley. During the hostilities he amassed 234 appearances for Barnsley but when peacetime football returned he lost his place following a six-nil defeat at Leicester City in November 1946 and was soon on his way to Hillsborough.

LOWDELL, Arthur Edward 'Darkie' 1922-27

Born: 7 November 1897 Edmonton
(5ft 7ins, 11st 4lbs – 1922)
Died: 29 July 1979 Canvey Island
Debut: 28 January 1922
v Wolverhampton Wanderers
Division Two Away
Last Appearance: 2 April 1927
v Bolton Wanderers
Division One Away
Total League
& Cup Appearances: 116 Goals: 6

Career Details:

Ton Pentre		1918
WEDNESDAY	19 January	1922 £1150
Tottenham Hotspur	2 August	1927*
Retired	March	1932

*Exchange for Jimmy Seed

Arthur Lowdell left school at the age of 14 but after eighteen months searching for employment joined the Hampshire Regiment and later fought in WW1 on the Somme and at Ypres, Arras, Paschendaele, Cambri & Monty le Prux, being wounded three times. Thankfully he came through the conflict relatively unscathed and after being discharged in 1915 he returned to his roots where in pre war years he had won schoolboys caps for both London and England boys. His footballing talents had flourished while in the forces and after kick starting his career with an unknown club in the London based Sunday Morning League 'Darkie' secured his first professional contract at prominent Welsh side Ton Pentre. It was here that he became inexorably linked with the name of Jimmy Seed as Lowdell's prolific scoring from the right wing alerted Spurs to his promise. They duly sent a scout to watch Ton Pentre play Mid Rhondda but it was Seed in the opposition ranks that caught their eye and for the second time in his career Lowdell missed out a move to White Hart Lane – he had initially been rejected as a schoolboy for being too small.

However he would not remain in non-league football for much longer as Wednesday manager Bob Brown clinched his transfer to Hillsborough with a cash bid and promise of a friendly at Ton Pentre. Described as "one of hardest workers and most conscientious players Wednesday have ever had" Lowdell started his Owls career at inside right and throughout his career would show his versatility by playing in several positions including centre forward and halfback – the majority of his 28 league appearances in the Owls 1926 Division Two Championship win came at right halfback. 'Darkie' was a big-hearted player who possessed great stamina and tremendous powers of recovery but when Spurs indicated they were willing to release Jimmy Seed, Wednesday quickly completed what would be one of the most inspirational signings in their history with Lowdell finally getting his transfer to White Hart Lane at the third attempt! He was a pillar of consistency and almost ever present for over two years in a Spurs shirt – appearing in 99 league and cup games - but sadly the November 1929 home game with Cardiff City would bring his career to a premature end. The leg injuries he received in that game put him on the sidelines and in March 1932 he received £600 compensation, marking the end of his professional career.

LOWE, H. G. 1893-96

Born:
Debut:
8 December 1894 v Stoke FC Division One Away
Last Appearance:
15 December 1894 v Nottingham Forest Division One Home
Total League & Cup Appearances: 2 Goals: 0

Career Details:

WEDNESDAY	1893
Released	1896

Little known left-sided player who spent three years as a professional at Wednesday in the mid 1890s. Was a regular scorer in reserve team football over the period – netting four goals in a win at Rotherham Town in September 1894 and three in the 18-0 rout of Eckington Works at Olive Grove in January 1896. Enjoyed a memorable 1894-5 campaign, making two senior appearances for Wednesday as a replacement for inside-left Alec Brady, as well as helping The Owls second team to the Championship of the Sheffield & Hallamshire Cup League.

LOWES, Arnold Richardson 1937-48

Born: 27 February 1919 Sunderland
(5ft $8^{1}/_{2}$ins, 11st, $8^{1}/_{2}$lbs – 1948)
Died: 2 July 1994 Sheffield
Debut: 10 September 1938
v Tranmere Rovers
Division Two Home
Last Appearance: 31 January 1948
v Cardiff City
Division Two Away
Total League
& Cup Appearances: 44* Goals: 10
***Also appeared in**
22 wartime games, scoring 4 times

Career Details:

Washington Chemicals		
WEDNESDAY	October	1937 £80
Doncaster Rovers	February	1948 *

*Lowes + £3000 for Clarrie Jordan

**Wartime guest for Crystal Palace, Chelsea, Clapton Orient, Millwall, Watford, West Ham United, Queens Park Rangers & Fulham

Like so many of his peers Arnold Lowes lost the best years of his career to war. He had joined the Owls from Northeast amateur football – the club fighting off interest from Charlton manager Jimmy Seed to secure his signature - and after a season of reserve team football Lowes made a goal scoring debut, at centre forward, in a win over Tranmere Rovers. He scored fourteen times in reserve team soccer during the two years immediately preceding the hostilities and secured further first team appearances at inside right before national football was suspended.

While serving during the war years in the Royal Artillery, Lowes guested for a wide variety of Southern based sides while when peace was declared Arnold played in just over half of the Owls Division Two games in the 1946-7 season, as unthinkable relegation was just averted. The ex-Sunderland boys attacker – he won the English Schools Trophy in 1934 – had actually reverted to part-time status in August 1946 in order to take employment as a salesman with a Sheffield bottling company. He remained a regular at inside right during the second season of post war soccer but was sacrificed as the Owls search for a regular goal scorer resulted in Lowes moving to Belle Vue and Clarrie Jordan transferring to Hillsborough. A Division Three (North) Championship medal followed in 1950 before Lowes played in the first thirteen games of the following season as Rovers finished eleventh in the old Second Division - the highest ever finish in their history. Sadly a serious injury received in that thirteenth game – at home to Cardiff City in October 1950 – ended his playing career prematurely after 66 games for Rovers.

LOWEY, John Anthony 1978-80

Born: 7 March 1958 Manchester
(5ft 11ins, 12st 7lbs – 1979)
Debut: 17 October 1978
v Oxford United
Division Three Home
Last Appearance: 26 August 1980
v Wimbledon
League Cup Away
Total League
& Cup Appearances: 43+7 Goals: 6

Career Details:

Manchester United	March	1975
Chicago Sting		1976 Loan
Chicago Sting	April	1977 Free
Port Vale	July	1977 3-month loan
Blackburn Rovers	September	1977 N/C
Port Vale	October	1977 N/C
California Sunshine	March	1978
WEDNESDAY	2 November	1978 Free
Blackburn Rovers	20 November	1980 £27,000
Wigan Athletic	22 July	1986 £25,000
Chesterfield	20 November	1986 Loan
York City	26 March	1987 Loan
Preston North End	13 August	1987 Free
Chester	23 March	1988 3-month loan
Brisbane Lions	June	1988 Free
Mount Gravatt		1995 Loan

Forward who experienced a nomadic career after being spotted playing for Manchester boys and signing apprentice forms for Manchester United in July 1974. When he arrived at Hillsborough Lowey had yet to make his league debut in English football, despite having been on the books of three different sides, but this was soon rectified as he impressed in Division Three football as Jack Charlton's side started to turn the corner. He had initially moved to Wednesday on trial from US club California Sunshine – they held his registration with F.I.F.A. – and would play a big part in the famous five game F.A.Cup marathon with Arsenal in 1979 after Wednesday secured a permanent transfer. However after Big Jack strengthened his side in the summer of 1979 Lowey found his opportunities limited and started only eleven games as Wednesday won promotion from Division Three in 1980.

After asking for a move in September 1980 he was duly sold to Blackburn Rovers where after dropping back into a midfield role he enjoyed a successful six-year stay that brought 156 league and cup games. Relatively unsuccessful spells at five different clubs followed before Lowey tried his luck in Australia with National League club Brisbane Lions. He later spent a loan spell at Queensland State League side Mount Gravatt and has remained 'down under' ever since, ending his playing career in September 1996.

He is still a member of the Brisbane Lions soccer club and has done some coaching in the Aussie Premier League while away from football Lowey runs two businesses in partnership with his wife – one a Beauty Therapy training school and the other a licensed securities (Investment) company.

LUCAS, David Anthony 2003-04 & 2004 -

Born: 23 November 1977 Preston
(6ft 2ins, 13st 10lbs - 2003)
Debut: 1 October 2003
v Notts County
Division Two Home
Total League
& Cup Appearances: 59 Goals: 0

Career Details:

Preston North End	12 December	1994
Darlington	14 December	1995 Loan
Darlington	3 October	1996 Loan
Scunthorpe United	23 December	1996 Loan
WEDNESDAY	1 October	2003 Loan
Loan return	1 November	2003
WEDNESDAY	12 December	2003 2-month loan
Loan return	11 February	2004
WEDNESDAY	25 May	2004 £100,000

Tall and agile goalkeeper who impressed greatly in two loan spells during the 2003-4 campaign before a medial knee ligament injury not only ended his season but also negotiations for a full transfer. However he returned to Hillsborough on a full transfer in the following summer and was ever present until a knee injury kept him out of the final stages of the league campaign. Thankfully he recovered to return to the side for the play off semi-finals against Brentford and was then between the sticks in Cardiff as Wednesday climbed back into England's second tier. The stopper had come through his hometown club's youth policy to sign professional forms in 1994 and would win representative honours for England at all age levels from U-18 to U-20 while also being named in the U-21 squad. His league debut would come during a six game loan spell at Darlington before Lucas returned to make his first senior start for Preston in the final day of the season game at Hartlepool that clinched the Third Division Championship for The Lilywhites. Still only a teenager, Lucas would gain more experience during further loan spells in the lower divisions and after representing England in the U-20 World Championships, in the summer of 1997, he seemed to have gained a foothold in the North End first team before injury curtailed his breakthrough.

However his claims for a first team jersey could not be ignored and after injury sidelined regular custodian Tepi Moilanen Lucas became first choice during the 1998-9 season, appearing in 38 league and cup games. Unfortunately a controversial sending off early in the following season saw his rival for the jersey gain his place back and over the next few seasons the pair would alternate between the sticks. Lucas - who can boast superb reflexes and terrific command of his area - recorded his 100th senior game for Preston in October 2002 but the arrival of Jonathan Gould during the January 2003 transfer window saw him relegated back to the bench, eventually prompting a move to Hillsborough when the Owls found themselves with all three of their senior goalkeepers unavailable through injury.

LUKE, Charles E. 'Charlie' 1936-38

Born: 16 March 1909 Esh Winning
(5ft 7½ ins, 10st 6lbs – 1936)
Died: 16 October 1983 Whitstable
Debut: 19 February 1936
v Derby County
Division One Away
Last Appearance: 4 December 1937
v Newcastle United
Division Two Away
Total League
& Cup Appearances: 43 Goals: 8

Career Details:

Ushaw Moor		
Portsmouth		1927 Trial
Tow Law Town		
Darlington		1928

Esh Winning		1929
Bishop Auckland		1930
Crook Town	October	1930
Huddersfield Town	31 January	1931 Amateur
Huddersfield Town	15 May	1931 Professional
WEDNESDAY	18 February	1936 £4000
Blackburn Rovers	4 February	1938 £1208
Chesterfield	December	1938
Whitstable		

After winning the F.A.Cup in 1935 The Owls experienced a poor 1935-6 campaign and found themselves at the wrong end of the table as spring approached. Manager Billy Walker's remedy was to raid the transfer market and Charlie Luke was one of his captures. On his debut, in the one-nil loss at Derby County, Luke made a new right wing partnership with fellow newcomer Thomas Grosvenor and the pair would remain in the first team until the season's end as Wednesday just avoided the dreaded drop into Division Two. Like the majority of his peers Luke had started his working life down the pit in the Durham coalfield and was one of several brothers who played for local Northeast teams on their Saturday off. This clash of families often led to problems, no better example coming when Charlie was playing for Tow Law and saw his penalty kick saved by brother George in the opposition net – Charlie did not speak to his brother for several weeks!

In those Northern League days Charlie was known as 'Chukey' Luke and he signed off his non-league days in fine style in the 1930-1 season as his 61 league and cup goals for Bishop Auckland helped his side win the Northern League Championship and reach the last four of the F.A.Amateur Cup. Mid way through that season Luke had signed amateur forms for league side Huddersfield Town but spent most of the season back in the Northeast before becoming a fully fledged pro in the following summer. He made the transition to league football with ease and made a huge impact during the 1933-4 campaign when he was ever present and his seventeen league goals helped Town to runners-up spot in the top-flight. After 47 goals in 143 games for The Terriers he moved to Hillsborough and immediately impressed fans with his pace and two-footed ball control which enabled Luke to operate on either flank. Sadly Luke – who in other sources was said to be just 5ft 3ins tall – could not prevent Wednesday from relegation in 1937 and in almost two seasons at Hillsborough he could never really claim a regular first team spot, after his initial impact. After finishing his professional playing career Luke and his whole family – parents, brothers, wives and children, all moved to Kent in search of employment. Work was secured in the mines and Charlie would end his football days at local side Whitstable.

LUNN, Frederick Levi 'Fred' 1921-22

Born: 8 November 1895 Marsden
Died: February 1972 Huddersfield
Debut: 7 January 1922
v Bradford Park Avenue
F.A.Cup Away
Last Appearance: 6 May 1922
v Leicester City
Division Two Home
Total League
& Cup Appearances: 12 Goals: 4

Career Details:

Marsden		
Huddersfield Town	September	1920
WEDNESDAY	August	1921
Bristol Rovers	19 May	1922
Southend United	June	1923
Nuneaton Town	August	1924

Centre forward who arrived on trial in August 1921, signing professional forms soon after. His form for the club's reserve side in the Midland League - he top scored for the reserve team with 24 goals - and over the 1921 Christmas period netted two hat-tricks in three games- quickly elevated Lunn to first team football and he impressed by scoring regularly. However at the end of the season Wednesday dispensed with his services and Lunn was quickly signed by Andrew Wilson's Bristol Rovers. He would top score for Rovers during 1922-3 although his tally was only ten goals as The Pirates netted only 35 league goals – a tight defence ensuring a mid table finish! After ending his league career Lunn dropped into Midlands non-league soccer.

LYALL. John 'Jack' 1901-09

Born: 16 April 1881 Dundee
(6ft 1½ins, 12st 7lbs – 1908)
Died: 17 February 1944 Detroit, USA
Debut: 21 September 1901
v Bolton Wanderers
Division One Home
Last Appearance: 29 March 1909
v Sunderland
Division One Home
Total League
& Cup Appearances: 295* Goals: 0
***Also played in 19 wartime games**

Career Details:

Jarrow		
WEDNESDAY	27 February	1901 £100*
Manchester City	15 September	1909 £650
Dundee	May	1911
Ayr United		1914
Jarrow		WW1 Guest
Palmer's (Jarrow)	March	1920

*Joint fee with Gosling

CAPS (@SWFC):
Scotland Full (1) v England 01/04/05

Jack Lyall was without doubt the finest goalkeeper to play for the Owls in their early history. After joining from Northeast junior football – previously winning both the Tyneside Alliance League and Durham Cup in the colours of Jarrow - he soon replaced Frank Stubbs in the first team after his rival famously gifted Notts County several goals in a September 1901 game, after receiving a blow on the head! After getting his chance Lyall did not look back, helping Wednesday to back-to-back Championships and F.A.Cup success in 1907. He became a hugely popular player with Owlerton regulars and such was his form that early in his Wednesday career he received an England call only for the offer to be withdrawn when the F.A. realised he was in fact Scottish! The reason for the confusion was probably that the tall custodian was brought to England when only a few months old and had played all his football outside of his birth nation – he did receive a call up for Scotland soon after. Unlike most goalkeepers Lyall could kick from his hands after only one step and was a big presence between the posts for Wednesday as they became established as a major force in the first decade of the Twentieth Century.

The arrival of Teddy Davison would effectively signal the end of Jack's Wednesday career as after losing his place to yet another outstanding Owls keeper he left for Manchester City early in the 1909-10 season. Played only a handful of games at City – winning a Division Two Championship medal in his first season - while in the summer of 1910, after being asked by the F.A to tour South Africa with their representative side, he famously said that he would rather go fishing! Spells in Scottish football at Dundee and Ayr United followed, Lyall saving a penalty on his debut for the latter, before in 1916 he joined the Army (Royal Engineers). Whilst billeted in the UK Lyall regularly played as a guest for The Owls before being posted to the Far East in 1917 – he continued to play football while serving his country and wrote to his old boss Arthur Dickinson describing how his team travelled over 2,000 miles to play a regimental cup tie!

After two and a half years in the Army, Lyall was demobbed in September 1919 and after several months without a club signed for North Eastern League club Palmer's. Sadly his health then began to suffer and in 1927 he emigrated to Canada with his wife, son and daughter, subsequently moving to the US a year later. He worked as a plasterer for the remainder of his life before passing away, aged sixty-two.

LYONS, Michael Joseph "Mick" 1982-85

Born: 8 December 1951 Liverpool
(6ft, 12st 2lbs – 1982)
Debut: 28 August 1982
v Middlesbrough
Division Two Home
Last Appearance: 19 October 1985
v Leicester City
Division One Away
Total League
& Cup Appearances: 164 Goals: 16

Career Details:

Everton	July	1969
WEDNESDAY	24 June	1982 £80,000
Grimsby Town	11 November	1985 £25,000

Mick Lyons was in the twilight of his career when he joined Wednesday in the summer of 1982. The inspirational centre half had enjoyed a tremendous career at his only other club Everton where in almost thirteen years as a professional he played 460 times for the Toffeemen, captaining the side for an amazing eight years. He was a highly competitive and combative individual and these qualities soon endeared him to Wednesday fans as Lyons captained The Owls to the 1983 F.A.Cup semi-final and promotion from Division Two a year later. He was seen by many as a short term buy by Jack Charlton but Lyons continued to belie his years as Wednesday not only consolidated in the top-flight but started to challenge in the higher reaches of the division. He was handed a new two-year contract by Howard Wilkinson in June 1984, giving him a secondary role as youth coach, but seemed to possess all the qualities to succeed in management and Lyons eventually moved to Grimsby Town – leaving Wednesday with the club sat in third position in the top division.

However great players do not automatically make outstanding managers and after The Mariners suffered relegation he was dismissed in June 1987. He then spent four years as reserve team manager back at Goodison Park before coaching briefly at both Wigan Athletic and Huddersfield Town. Then out of the blue the Sultan of Brunei, the world's richest man, offered Lyons the opportunity to manage the small country's national team in the Malaysian League. He remained for three years in the Far East before travelling further towards the Antarctic when being appointed boss at Australian League club Canberra Cosmos. In an area dominated by Rugby League he helped lift the soccer club's profile during two years in charge before a move to Singapore broke down following off the field problems. Another spell as Brunei boss followed while after a short time back home in Liverpool the globetrotting Lyons was appointed Director of Football at Southampton's Perth academy in 2000, remaining in charge until the Saints closed the facility in June 2002. In July 2002 he returned to Brunei for a third spell in charge of the National side.

MacKENZIE, Matthew Lawrence 'Laurie' 1946-49

Born: 7 July 1924
Old Kilpatrick, Glasgow
(5ft 9ins, 10st 12lbs – 1948)
Debut: 31 August 1946
v Luton Town
Division Two Away
Last Appearance: 27 August 1947
v Southampton
Division Two Away
Total League
& Cup Appearances: 6* Goals: 0
***Also appeared in 2 wartime games**

Career Details:

Clydebank Athletic		1945
WEDNESDAY	March	1946 £25
Grimsby Town	June	1949 £1,500
Gainsborough Trinity	July	1951 Free
Scarborough	July	1952

Before joining the Owls, Matt Mackenzie had started his working life at John Brown in the Glasgow shipyards as an apprentice fitter. During the war years he served in the R.A.F. - as a Flight Engineer on Lancaster bombers – and played regularly in forces football, appearing on one occasion for a full representative team in a match staged at Reading. When war in Europe came to an end he was allowed home until his discharge papers came through and during this period he played a few games for Scottish side Clydebank. Primarily a wing half Mackenzie could also perform at inside forward but it was in the former position that he made his Owls debut – in the Football League North game at home to Bolton Wanderers in March 1946.

He started the first competitive game in post war soccer but would spend almost all of his time at Wednesday playing in reserve team football – he appeared in 41 Central League games during the 1947-8 season and only failed to gain an ever-present record through having to make a first team appearance! It was the arrival of Doug Witcomb in March 1947 that effectively ended his Owls career as the Welshman became an automatic choice at right halfback and MacKenzie had to be content with an understudy role until moving to Grimsby Town. He enjoyed three seasons of first team soccer at Blundell Park – scoring 11 goals in 58 league games – before dropping into non-league football at Gainsborough Trinity. A cartilage operation disrupted his only season at the Lincolnshire club although he did start to forge a career outside of the game when going into business with his cake decorating mother-in-law, opening a bakers shop on Middlewood Road. While this business flourished Mackenzie ended his playing career with six seasons at Scarborough where he took part in the club's first ever floodlit match in 1953 and enjoyed a benefit game against a Football League Eleven in May 1957 before hanging up his boots. He then concentrated on his Sheffield bakery and worked in the shop – known as 'Dora Websters' on Middlewood Road - until handing over the reins to his son on his retirement. Since his retirement Matt has worked on lowering his golf handicap, no doubt helped by his son Malcolm who is a well-known and respected professional golfer.

MACKENZIE, Stephen "Steve" 1991

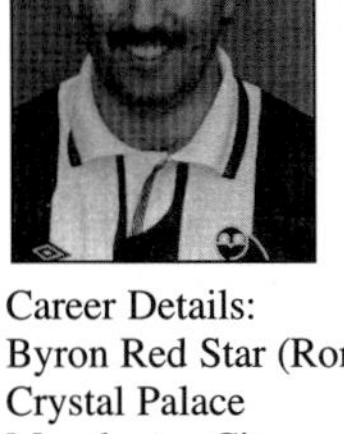

Born: 23 November 1961 Romford
(5ft 11ins, 12st 5lbs – 1991)
Debut: 2 March 1991
v Notts County
Division Two Away
Last Appearance: 3 September 1991
v Notts County
Division One Away
Total League
& Cup Appearances: 5+10 Goals: 2

Career Details:

Byron Red Star (Romford)		
Crystal Palace	29 July	1978
Manchester City	30 July	1979 £250,000
West Bromwich Albion	17 August	1981 £650,000
Charlton Athletic	30 June	1987 £300,000
WEDNESDAY	8 February	1991 £100,000

Shrewsbury Town	12 December	1991 Free to May 1994
Willenhall Town		
Stafford Rangers		
Atherstone United	June	2000 Free to April 2002
Pelsall Villa	March	2003
Gresley Rovers	24 December	2003

When seventeen year old Steve Mackenzie moved from Crystal Palace to Manchester City the transfer stunned the football world as the youngster had yet to start a first team game for Palace but the fee was an astonishing £250,000 – extravagant even by 21st Century standards. He had already won fifteen England Youth caps and helped The Eagles to F.A.Youth Cup success in 1978, before the sensational move to Maine Road. Thankfully the teenager managed to overcome the burden caused by the huge fee to settle and impress at Manchester City – repeating his Youth Cup success in 1980 – and later scoring in the 1981 F.A.Cup Final against Spurs. He appeared in a total of 75 games for City before Ron Atkinson took him to The Hawthorns for another large fee. The talented central midfielder enjoyed his best spell in league football under 'Big Ron', winning 3 England U-21 caps and appearing in over 180 games for Albion before returning to his roots when signing for London club Charlton.

It was from the East London club that Atkinson signed MacKenzie for a second time – initially on loan – to add much needed experience to The Owls promotion push from the old Second Division. At Hillsborough MacKenzie was very much a squad player – John Sheridan and Carlton Palmer being automatic choices in the Owls engine room – and even after signing on a permanent basis in March 1991 he remained a fringe player. Amazingly almost six months to the day his final appearance came on the ground of his Wednesday debut and soon after he left for a three-month loan spell at Shrewsbury Town. On deadline day 1992 – after having just returned from his Gay Meadow loan spell – he re-joined Town on a permanent basis, remaining until the end of the 1993-4 season when he was advised to quit the pro game.

While playing non-league soccer he became a lecturer in computer studies at a Stafford college before being appointed rookie manager of Dr Martens League side Atherstone United in June 2000. He continued to play while at United – he still turns out for Albion Old Stars in the summer months - and remained in charge until being dismissed from the role in April 2002. He actually announced his retirement as a player in October 2001 but in March 2003 helped an old friend by turning out for Midland Alliance club Pelsall Villa. His playing career did however experience one last hurrah when aged 42 he helped Dr Martens League Western Division side Gresley Rovers out of a striker crisis – scoring with his first touch after entering the fray as a substitute! He is now coach in the week at West Brom's school of excellence and usually works for the Press Association at the weekend covering games.

MACKEY, Thomas Scott 1929-32

Born: 22 October 1908 Cassop, County Durham
(5ft 10ins, 12st – 1929)
Died: 27 July 1969 Silsoe, Beds.
Debut: 28 April 1930 v Birmingham Division One Home
Last Appearance: 5 December 1931 v Arsenal Division One Home
Total League & Cup Appearances: 4 Goals: 0

Career Details:

Cassop Celtic		
Cassop Colliery		
Ferryhill Athletic		
Hartlepools United	April	1928
WEDNESDAY	21 December	1929 £3000*
Luton Town	June	1932 £700

* Joint fee with E.Bell

Although Thomas Mackey played only four first team games for the Owls this was negated by the fact that during his time in Sheffield, Wednesday could boast arguably the greatest side in their long history. He was brought to Hillsborough by Bob Brown as competition for the outstanding centre halfback Tony Leach and with Marsden and Strange occupying the other half back roles Mackey had to be content with being a reserve regular whilst making the occasional first team start, when his rival Leach was unavailable. After arriving from Division Three (North) side Hartlepools United in 1929 Mackey was ever present in the second team until the end of the season and for the remainder of his time in Sheffield competed with Thomas Davison for the Central League No. 5 shirt.

After almost three years of being understudy to Leach the clever defender was allowed to leave for Luton Town where he was immediately switched to left back. The change of position proved crucial for the former Durham boys player, as he was then virtually an ever present for five years, appearing in 208 league and cup games for The Hatters. However he almost failed to stay at Town for longer than a season as in August 1933 he returned home to join the Durham County Police force before an apparent change of mind saw him back at Luton and playing in the opening game of the 1933-4 season! While at the Kenilworth Road club he played in Luton's 12-2 win over Bristol Rovers in April 1936, when Joe Payne famously scored a record ten goals, and won a Division Three (South) Championship medal in 1937 before hanging up his boots to join the coaching staff as assistant trainer in August 1938.

Mackey – who started his working life as a miner while playing in amateur football – remained on the Luton coaching staff until 1959 when following relegation and defeat in the F.A.Cup Final to Nottingham Forest he was one of several staff members, including manager Syd Owen, who were released from their duties. While still employed by Town he had taken over as 'Mein Host' of the 'Battle of Arms' public house in the Bedfordshire village of Silsoe, which was in fact a general store that also contained a bar, being known locally as the 'Mouse Hole'. In 1956 he moved to another public house called 'The Star and Garter' where he remained as landlord for the remainder of his life.

MacLEAN, Steven 'Steve' 2004-

Born: 23 August 1982 Edinburgh
(5ft 10ins, 11st 1lb - 2004)
Debut: 7 August 2003
v Colchester United
League One Home
Total League
& Cup Appearances: 40+1 Goals: 20

Career Details:

Glasgow Rangers	17 September	1998
Scunthorpe United	6 August	2003 Loan
WEDNESDAY	8 July	2004 £125,000

Attacker Steve MacLean first came to the attention of Wednesday fans when he enjoyed a remarkable season on loan at Division Three Scunthorpe United in 2003-04. He was part of the United side that knocked the Owls out of the F.A.Cup at Hillsborough in December 2003 and finished the season as divisional top scorer with 25 goals - netting 28 goals in all competitions. His clinical finishing saw MacLean net hat-tricks on three separate occasions for Scunthorpe and it was obvious a move to a more senior club was next in line for the Scot. Before his fate was decided MacLean returned to his parent club Rangers where in the previous four seasons he had struggled to hold down a regular first team place. He did however win Scottish League and Cup winners medals in 2003, mainly being used as a sub, but competition from several foreign imports saw MacLean farmed out into the lower reaches of the English League.

Success at Scunthorpe alerted many clubs to his attributes and Wednesday joined Hull City and Bristol City in the race for his signature in the summer of 2004. Thankfully is was Chris Turner who persuaded MacLean a move to Sheffield would be most beneficial and he quickly showed his worth by finding the net on a regular basis in the early part of the season. His unerring accuracy from the penalty spot also proved a bonus - MacLean scoring all seven he was given - while as the season progressed he became an increasingly invaluable member of the team's vital backbone.

Although not blessed with searing pace the Scot showed a real strikers instinct in the front of goal and his hold up play was badly missed when he suffered a broken foot in the home game with Doncaster Rovers in March 2005. Four months earlier the same opposition had provided MacLean with the greatest moment of his short Owls career when at Belle Vue he became the first Wednesday player since John Sissons in 1972 to score a hat trick away from home in a league game. His nineteen goals propelled Paul Sturrock's side into the play offs but he looked set to miss the end of season competition until making a dramatic appearance on the subs bench for the Millennium Stadium final against Hartlepool United. Despite having only trained for a matter of days he entered the fray with fifteen minutes remaining and was then on hand to score the dramatic equaliser that took the Final into extra time. He therefore became the first Owls player since Mark Bright in 1993-94 to hit twenty goals and had more reason to celebrate as MacLean held the line during extra time to help Wednesday into the Championship.

* Did not play for Partick Thistle on loan in July 2002

MADDEN, Lawrence David 'Lawrie' 1983-91

Born: 28 September 1955 Hackney, London
(5ft 11ins, 13st11lbs – 1984)
Debut: 27 August 1983
v Swansea City
Division Two Away
Last Appearance: 8 May 1991
v Bristol City
Division Two Home
Total League
& Cup Appearances: 251+15 Goals: 5

Career Details:

Arsenal		1970 Amat.
Manchester University		
Mansfield Town	1 March	1975 N/C
Boston United		1977 Free
Tottenham Hotspur		1977 Trial
Charlton Athletic	January	1978 Free
Millwall	25 March	1982 £10,000
WEDNESDAY	24 August	1983 Free
Leicester City	17 January	1991 Loan
Derby County	July	1991 Trial
Wolverhampton Wanderers	15 August	1991 Free
Darlington	3 September	1993 N/C
Chesterfield	4 October	1993 Free
Emley	March	1996 Free

The signing of Lawrie Madden in the summer of 1983 was certainly a low-key event but he proved to arguably be Howard Wilkinson's best ever purchase while in charge at Hillsborough. The Londoner gave The Owls sterling service over the next eight years and although perhaps not blessed with terrific pace or outstanding passing ability his sheer consistency and non-nonsense defensive play meant that when he was absent he was invariably missed – a point perhaps no better typified when Wednesday collapsed five-nil at home to Everton in a January 1988 F.A.Cup tie when Madden was missing through injury. Despite starting over 250 games for the club Wednesday fans fondest memory of Madden probably came from a rare sub appearance when the veteran defender came off the bench in the 1991 League Cup Final to play out the final few minutes as a right-winger!

Formative years were spent playing football on Hackney Marshes while he represented North Hertfordshire district schools at U-15 and U-19 level. After touring Malta with the Roman Catholic U-15 side in 1970 he signed amateur forms for Arsenal, playing in a Gunners junior team which at the time was described as their best ever youth side. However football was not the prime driving force in the young Madden's life and he took the brave step of refusing a professional contract at Arsenal in order to attend Manchester University to gain a degree in Economics and Social Studies. It was while playing in University football that he broke into league football – signing non-contract terms for Mansfield Town – and appeared in the final seven games of the 1974-5 season as the Stags won the old Fourth Division Championship. He appeared in a handful of games in the following season but after leaving University with his B.A degree Madden then encountered Howard Wilkinson for the first time when signing for his Northern Premier League Boston United side.

His time in non-league football was brief however as after playing six reserve games for Spurs he spent three months on trial at Charlton Athletic before signing his first professional contract, aged 22. During 127 games for Charlton he helped The Addicks to promotion from the old Third Division in 1981 but was sold to rivals Millwall when his side hit serious financial problems. Fifty games and an Associate Members Cup winners medal followed before he was approached by Wilkinson to come to Hillsborough on trial. He duly impressed and was signed two weeks later, going straight into the side for the opening game of the season at Swansea – Madden was almost ever present as Wednesday won promotion back to the top-flight. In 1988 he returned to University to study part-time for an MA in Leisure Management and after being named 'player of the season' in 1988-9 he was given a deserved benefit game against neighbours United in August 1990. During the Owls glorious season of 1990-1 he played three games on loan at Leicester City but returned to Wednesday where his final appearance proved a momentous occasion as The Owls beat Bristol City at Hillsborough to secure promotion.

After finally leaving Hillsborough the no-frills defender was named 'player of the year' in his first season at Wolves. While playing at his final league club, Chesterfield, Madden appeared in his 500th league game while also starting to work on a part-time basis for local newspapers and radio stations. After leaving the Derbyshire side he registered to pay for non-league side Emley although he did not play a game for them and retired soon after to concentrate on his media career. He still appears occasionally for The Johnny Quinn Over 35 charity side while working full time for Sky T.V.

MADDIX, Daniel Shawn 'Danny' 2001-03

Born: 11 October 1967 Ashford
(5ft 10ins, 11st 7lbs – 2002)
Debut: 12 August 2001
v Burnley
Division One Home
Last Appearance: 21 April 2003
v Brighton & Hove Albion
Division One Away
Total League
& Cup Appearances: 62+4 Goals: 3

Career Details:

Tottenham Hotspur	25 July	1985
Southend United	1 November	1986 Loan
Queens Park Rangers	23 July	1987 Loan
Queens Park Rangers	August	1987 Free
WEDNESDAY	18 June	2001 Trial
WEDNESDAY	9 August	2001 Free
Released	30 June	2003
Barnet	11 July	2003 Free

Veteran defender who joined the Owls following a successful trial period, after having spent the majority of his career at Queens Park Rangers. After signing Maddix for Wednesday, Owls boss Peter Shreeves remarked that "I knew Danny from my time at Spurs – he went on loan for QPR for a month and ended up staying 14 years!" During those years at Loftus Road, Maddix became a huge crowd favourite and club captain, appearing in exactly 350 competitive games for the West London club. His debut for Rangers actually came at Hillsborough – in a 3-1 defeat – and Maddix was capped twice by Jamaica in his latter years at Loftus Road.

His final eighteen months at QPR proved a disappointment as he made only two appearances due to a foot injury and then a back problem. This poor fitness effectively ended his Rangers career and meant Wednesday only offered the experienced player a one-year deal after he had stayed injury free in the 2001 pre season. In simple terms he replaced Des Walker at the heart of the Owls defence and proceeded to give a series of commendable performances as Wednesday struggled to avoid relegation from

Division One. After being rewarded with a new one-year deal he subsequently found himself in and out of the side under new manager Chris Turner and after The Owls relegation in 2003 – Maddix's final game came at Brighton when their fate was sealed – was not offered a new deal. Later in the summer he linked up with ex-team mate Ian Hendon at Conference side Barnet and in March 2004 the duo were appointed joint-caretaker manager when Martin Allen left for Brentford.

MAGILTON, James "Jim" 1997-99

Born: 6 May 1969 Belfast
(6ft, 14st 2lbs – 1997)
Debut: 13 September 1997
v Liverpool
Premier League Away
Last Appearance: 28 November 1998
v Chelsea
Premier League Away
Total League
& Cup Appearances: 17+13 Goals: 1

Career Details:

Liverpool	14 May	1986
Oxford United	3 October	1990 £100,000
Southampton	11 February	1994 £600,000
WEDNESDAY	10 September	1997 £1.6m (T)
Ipswich Town	15 January	1999 £682,500

CAPS (@SWFC)
Northern Ireland Full (2) v Portugal 11/10/97, v Spain 03/06/98

Midfield playmaker Jim Magilton was on week-to-week terms at Southampton when Wednesday boss David Pleat fought off interest from Glasgow Celtic to secure his signature early in the 1997-8 season. Magilton had rejected a contract offer from The Saints in the previous summer and it needed a transfer tribunal to decide the fee for the 37-cap Northern Ireland International. When the formalities were complete he went straight into a struggling Wednesday side and was immediately given the captain's armband. However the arrival of Ron Atkinson a few weeks later saw Magilton fade from the first team scene – briefly returning to the fray around Easter 1998 when he netted his only goal for the club.

Under the rein of Danny Wilson he was primarily used as a substitute and after failing to shine in reserve team soccer was allowed to join Ipswich Town on loan. Magilton – brother-in-law of Steve Staunton – had started his professional career at Anfield where he was a regular in the Liverpool reserve side that swept all before them in the late 1980s. Frustratingly he failed to make a senior appearance for The Reds and it needed a move to Oxford United to truly launch his league career where after 34 goals in 150 league games he was elevated into the Premier League when signing for Southampton. His short spell at Wednesday came to an end when the transfer to Ipswich was made permanent in March 1999 and the skilful Magilton helped Town into the Premier League and then into European football before the Suffolk club fell back into the Football League in 2002. He continued to be a Northern Ireland regular as well, until retiring from International football in June 2002 due to the ill health of his son, and has now appeared in over two hundred games for the Portman Road club.

MALLINSON, W.H. 1897-1900

Born:
Debut: 5 February 1898 v Everton Division One Home
Last Appearance:
3 March 1900 v New Brighton Tower Division Two Home
Total League & Cup Appearances: 6 Goals: 0

Career Details:

Mexborough	1895
WEDNESDAY	1897
Royston	1900

Goalkeeper who spent three years at Wednesday around the turn of the Twentieth Century, mainly as back up to first choice custodian Jim Massey. He first came to prominence during two years at Mexborough where his form against Wednesday's second team no doubt persuaded Owls officials to take the keeper to Olive Grove. His first appearance in a Wednesday shirt came in a United Counties League win at Sheepbridge Works in September 1897 and he missed only a handful of games as the reserves won the League Championship. His senior debut came during that debut season and Mallinson stood in for Massey on several occasions while also helping the second team win both the Wharncliffe Charity and Sheffield Association Leagues in 1900. Dropped back into non-league soccer after The Owls first season at Hillsborough and was reportedly sent a donation of two guineas in February 1903 because he was too ill to play for his club Royston.

MALLOCH, Gavin Cooper 1931-36

Born: 18 July 1905 Glasgow
(5ft 9½ins, 11st 7lbs – 1931)
Died: 10 December 1974 Glasgow
Debut: 25 December 1931
v Liverpool
Division One Away
Last Appearance: 24 March 1936
v Grimsby Town
Division One Away
Total League
& Cup Appearances: 89 Goals: 0

Career Details:

Glasgow Benburb		
Derby County	January	1927 £140
WEDNESDAY	23 December	1931 £1400
Millwall	August	1936 Free
Barrow	August	1937 Free
Morton	August	1938

Left half back who followed in the footsteps of his father 'Jock' Malloch when playing first team football for The Owls. Malloch junior had started his career in Glasgow amateur football before being snapped up by Derby County, where after serving an apprenticeship in the reserves he broke into the first eleven when Harry Storer left – the Scot appearing in 33 games as County finished Division One runners-up to Wednesday in 1930. However he quickly found himself out of favour at the start of the following season and just before Christmas 1931 Bob Brown swooped to take him to Hillsborough. He immediately replaced Bill Smith in Wednesday's top-flight side and was an automatic choice until injury in the April 1933 home game with Birmingham ended his run in the team. It would be almost a year until Malloch returned to the side but lady luck again deserted him as an injury in December 1934 saw Horace Burrows switched to Malloch's position with Wilf Sharp taking over from Burrows – the duo staying in the side for the remainder of the season, therefore denying Malloch the chance of appearing in the F.A.Cup Final.

Malloch – who regularly played cricket in the summer months and appeared for Sheffield & Hallamshire – was not retained by Wednesday in April 1936 and duly moved south to sign for Millwall – a £1,000 March 1936 move to Bradford Park Avenue had previously broken down. He spent just a year in East London before making the long trip North to sign for League side Barrow. Within another twelve months he was back in Scotland where after ending his playing career Malloch owned his own light engineering company. He still occasionally pulled on his boots to play in charity matches – appearing in the same 'Old Crocks' veteran side as Ex-Owl Neil Dewar – while after selling his business he worked for another engineering company until retiring.

MALLOCH, John Napier 'Jock' 1900-09

Born: 3 November 1879 East Craigie, Dundee
(5ft 9ins, 10st 12lbs - 1901)
Died: December 1935 Moorthorpe
Debut: 1 September 1900
v Manchester City
Division One Away
Last Appearance: 10 April 1907
v Manchester United
Division One Away
Total League
& Cup Appearances: 154 Goals: 11

Career Details:

East Craigie		
Dundee	21 August	1896
Brighton United		1899
WEDNESDAY	30 April	1900 £50*
Barnsley	December	1908 Loan
Barnsley	May	1909 £20
South Kirkby Colliery		1909

*Fee paid to Dundee

Left sided attacker who was a Wednesday regular during the first five years of the Twentieth Century, partnering the legendary Fred Spiksley during the 1902-3 Championship win and George Simpson as the title was retained. Described as an 'extremely clever player with superb ball control' he had started his playing career in Scottish junior soccer where following a Forfarshire Cup win with East Craigie he signed for his local Scottish League side. However a dispute with Dundee then saw Malloch join long since defunct club Brighton United for the 1899-00 season although the Scottish club still held his registration. He did return briefly to his hometown to help The Dark Blues win the Dundee Charity Shield in 1900 but within weeks was again journeying south to sign for Wednesday.

He joined an Owls side that had just secured a quick return to the top-flight by winning the Division Two Championship and went straight into the side, initially replacing Spiksley on the left wing, and remained an ever present until February 1901 when Spiksley and 'Jock' Wright renewed their left wing partnership that had help lift the aforementioned Second Division title. However injury disrupted both of his rivals for a left sided berth and 'Jock' remained a first team regular until the departure of Wright in March 1902 effectively secured Malloch the No.10 shirt. The form of the outstanding Jimmy Stewart eventually saw Malloch switched back to the left wing and he challenged with George Simpson for the position for the remainder of his Owls career – his rival playing in the 1907 F.A.Cup Final success while Malloch had to be content with helping the second team to two Midland League Championships in 1906 and 1908. Over the latter part of his Wednesday career Malloch proved himself a loyal and dependable clubman who was always fit and ready to step into the breach, being rewarded with a joint benefit game with fellow Dundee native Jack Lyall in March 1908.

He was somewhat uniquely loaned to neighbours Barnsley during the 1908-9 campaign but failed to make a senior appearance for The Tykes despite the move being made permanent at the end of the season. Within a few months he dropped into local football, signing for Doncaster side South Kirkby, and would captain his new side to Sheffield Association League and Wharncliffe Charity Cup success. He retired in 1914 after spending five years in South Kirkby colours.

MALPAS, Arthur 1879-85

Born:
Debut: 18 December 1880
v Blackburn Rovers
F.A.Cup Away
Last Appearance: 8 November 1884
v Long Eaton Rangers
F.A.Cup Away
Total League
& Cup Appearances: 15 Goals: 0

Career Details:

Attercliffe	1877-78
Attercliffe/Exchange	1878-79
WEDNESDAY	1879

Defender Arthur Malpas was a key player during the Owls formative years in the F.A.Cup, appearing for Wednesday in their first ever Cup-tie at Blackburn Rovers in 1880. He would go onto play in thirteen consecutive games in the tournament for Wednesday – including the 12-2 win over Spilsby in 1881 - and was a fixture in the Wednesday team for almost six seasons as the club became the dominant force in Sheffield soccer. Malpas had first come to the fore at Attercliffe Club and after playing in the famous floodlit 'Zulus' match in 1878 he decided to throw his lot in with Wednesday in the summer of 1879.

His first appearance for Wednesday actually came in an October 1879 friendly at old club Attercliffe and he was close to winning silverware in his debut season when being on the losing side in the final of prestigious Wharncliffe Charity Cup. However success would soon follow with Malpas helping Wednesday to Sheffield Challenge Cup success in 1881, the Wharncliffe Cup a year later and then a Sheffield Cup double in 1883, as the club started to outgrow local football. He missed a large chunk of the 1884-5 campaign through injury – sadly he did play in the humiliating 12-0 friendly loss at Blackburn Olympic in November 1884 – but did comeback to enjoy a benefit game against Lockwood Brothers in April 1885. That season proved his last as a Wednesday player and he was left to concentrate on his blossoming cricket career – Malpas had played for Mexborough CC for several years, scoring fifty in an innings on one occasion. His career duly turned full circle when in 1886 he was engaged to play for the Carlton Cricket Club in Edinburgh!

He was involved in a curious incident back in January 1883 when just prior to kick off against Nottingham Forest the Owls opponents lodged a protest against Arthur's appearance on the grounds that he had been paid thirty shillings to play in an earlier fixture for Sheffield Wanderers. The protest was upheld and Willis Bentley took his place at the last minute.

MARRIOTT, John Leonard "Jackie" 1947-55

Born: 1 April 1928 Scunthorpe
(5ft 6½ins, 9st 11lbs – 1948)
Debut: 22 February 1947
v Burnley
Division Two Away
Last Appearance: 30 April 1955
v West Bromwich Albion
Division One Home
Total League
& Cup Appearances: 159 Goals: 19

Career Details:

Scunthorpe United		1944
WEDNESDAY	20 February	1947 £2500
Huddersfield Town	18 July	1955 Player exchange*
Scunthorpe United	June	1957

*Marriott and Conwell exchanged for Shiner and Staniforth

When Wednesday signed Jackie Marriott from Midland League Scunthorpe United the fee, which eventually totalled £2,500 after twenty league games, was a record for the Lincolnshire club and bought The Owls a highly promising right winger who was thrust straight into the first team. Wednesday almost missed out on his signature though as in February 1947 the big freeze meant Wednesday manager Eric Taylor and director Cyril Hemmingfield were an hour late for their appointment after a taxi ride on treacherous roads. The Scunthorpe board had promised to let Taylor know if they were ever willing to part with the Midland league club's crowd idol and this had led to the dash from Sheffield. However when arriving at the ground they found a Manchester City representative already there but thankfully Taylor spoke in such persuasive terms that before the night was out Marriott was an Owls player!

At the time the teenager was working at steel company Firth Browns as an apprentice estimator draughtsman and on moving to Sheffield he decided to remain a part-time professional, gaining employment at Firth Vickers Stainless Steel in the City. His decision to remain part-time was something he regretted in later life as Marriott could never really establish himself at Hillsborough in over seven years in Sheffield, working full time and training two evenings a week always putting him at a disadvantage. He also had to cope with a rocky start to his Wednesday career as only two months after joining, in May 1947, he broke his wrist and ankle in a motorcycle accident back in his native Scunthorpe, missing the rest of a season that did not end until mid-June. Throughout his time in Sheffield the stockily built wide man faced fierce competition from the likes of Rickett, Kilshaw and the rapidly emerging Alan Finney but was a regular in both the 1950 Division Two promotion season and the 1954-55 campaign when The Owls suffered relegation from the top-flight.

Despite being a regular, that season proved to be Marriott's last at Wednesday as in the summer he moved to neighbours Huddersfield Town in a four-player swap deal. He finally became a full time professional at the Leeds Road club and stayed for two seasons before returning to Scunthorpe who of course were now a league side – the cheque from Wednesday for his original transfer fee was framed in the Scunthorpe boardroom for many years. Remained at United until retiring in December 1963, totalling 212 league appearances and 26 goals, and then became an Oil Industry rep for the remainder of his working life.

MARRISON, Thomas 'Tom' 1902-05

Born: 1 January 1885 Rotherham
(5ft 7ins, 11st 7lbs – 1902)
Died: 21 August 1926 Sheffield
Debut: 28 March 1903
v Stoke FC
Division One Home
Last Appearance: 7 January 1905
v Wolverhampton Wanderers
Division One Away
Total League
& Cup Appearances: 5 Goals: 1

Career Details:

WEDNESDAY	10 February	1902
Rotherham Town	September	1906
Nottingham Forest	22 November	1906 £40*
Oldham Athletic	29 June	1911 £200
Bristol City	10 May	1912

*Joint fee with Levick – paid to Wednesday

Inside forward Tom Marrison was an England schoolboy International during his days at Walkley school in Sheffield and soon signed professional forms for the Owls. He made an immediate impact in reserve team football - his 21 goals during the 1902-3 season helped Wednesday to the Championship of the Midland League while they also captured the Sheffield Challenge Cup in a glorious season when the first team lifted the Football League title. He effectively formed a reserve right wing partnership with Ryalls but the duo could make little impression at first team level due to the truly outstanding form of Harry Davis and Harry Chapman – he scored on his first team debut during that aforementioned title success but was straight back into the reserves when Chapman was available.

The goals continued to flow for Marrison in second team football – he netted 26 times during the 1903-4 season – but he was never anything other than a consistent understudy to his rival Chapman and he surprisingly left for non-league Rotherham Town early in the 1906-7 season. A moulder by trade, he was out of league soccer only a matter of weeks as Nottingham Forest secured his services, the transfer fee going to The Owls who held his registration. He enjoyed a great debut season at Forest, scoring on his debut and then appearing in 25 games as his new side won the old Division Two Championship. Regularly played against Wednesday in top-flight football although in six games against his old side Marrison could only boast a single point and posted several heavy defeats! However although never a prolific scorer in league soccer – he was the only forward not to score during Forest's record league win against Leicester Fosse in April 1909 – he was a regular at Forest for five seasons and when leaving for Oldham in 1911 he had totalled 39 goals in 171 competitive games. Joined Oldham for their second season of Division One football but was only a peripheral player and netted only four times in seventeen games before ending his career at Bristol City.

MARSDEN, Christopher 'Chris/Mazza' 2004-05

Born: 3 January 1969 Sheffield
(5ft 11ins, 12st 10lbs – 2004)
Debut: 7 August 2004
v Colchester United
League One Home
Last Appearance: 30 October 2004
v Chesterfield
League One Home
Total League
& Cup Appearances: 18 Goals: 0

Career Details:

Intake Juniors		
Sheffield Rangers		
Sheffield United	6 January	1987
Huddersfield Town	15 July	1988 £10,000
Coventry City	2 November	1993 Loan
Wolverhampton Wanderers	11 January	1994 £250,000
Notts County	15 November	1994 £250,000
Stockport County	1 January	1996 £70,000
Birmingham City	9 October	1997 £500,000
Southampton	2 February	1999 £800,000
Pusan I.cons	20 January	2004 Free
WEDNESDAY	4 June	2004 £125,000
Retired injured	7 March	2005

Vastly experienced midfielder who finally joined his boyhood club when Chris Turner brought him back from a brief spell in South Korea. The former Sheffield boys player was immediately made captain by Turner and was seen as a vital player as the Owls looked to launch a promotion push from League One. However despite finally being granted his wish to end his days at Hillsborough the move would prove somewhat bittersweet for Marsden as after being a regular for the first three months of the season he was then sidelined with a serious hamstring injury that required an operation in December 2004. Sadly the surgery did not cure the problem and in March 2005 he honourably announced he would not take any more of the club's wages and instead decided to hang up his boots after scoring 29 times in 519 league games for nine different English clubs.

His retirement brought an end to a career that had began for the Gleadless youngster across the city at Bramall Lane. He signed his first professional contract for United – scoring on debut in August 1987 - before enjoying a great spell at Huddersfield Town where he overcome a cruciate knee ligament injury. A broken leg and ruptured knee ligaments ruined his short spell at Wolves but Marsden's career was on the rise and after impressing at Birmingham City he moved into the Premier League at Southampton. His calm, assured and tigerish displays at the heart of the Saints midfield soon saw Marsden appointed captain and he enjoyed an Indian summer to his career when leading the South Coast club in the 2003 F.A.Cup Final. After falling out of favour at St Mary's he moved to the Far East but Wednesday started to negotiate for his transfer with Pusan when Marsden quit South Korean soccer in May 2005, citing personal reasons for his return after his family failed to settle. The Owls eventually agreed a fee for the 35 year-old Sheffielder and he would spend the final months of his career in the blue and white shirt, much to the joy of his Wednesday mad family.

MARSDEN, William "Billy" 1924-31

Born:10 November 1901 Silksworth,
Co. Durham
(5ft 9ins, 11st 3lbs – 1924)
Died: 20 September 1983 Sheffield
Debut: 30 August 1924
v Crystal Palace Division Two Away
Last Appearance: 3 May 1930
v Manchester City
Division One Home
Total League
& Cup Appearances: 221 Goals: 9

Career Details:

Ryhope F.C.		
Silksworth Colliery		
Sunderland	1 October	1920
WEDNESDAY	17 May	1924 £450
Retired		1931

CAPS (@SWFC)
England Full (3) v Wales 20/11/29, v Scotland 05/04/30, v Germany 10/05/30

Football League (1) v Scottish League 1929

Billy Marsden was a brilliant left halfback whose career was cruelly ended after he was seriously injured while playing for England against Germany in May 1930. The match was his third consecutive appearance for his country and at the time Marsden was widely regarded as the finest halfback in the game. However during the game Billy collided with teammate Roy Goodall as he challenged for a high ball and sustained truly horrific injuries – suffering a broken neck and a spinal injury that left his life in danger. It was only the skill of a German surgeon that saved his life and Billy remained in a Berlin hospital for six weeks before returning home to salvage his career. His much-awaited comeback finally came for the reserve side in late November 1930 and Marsden would play five times in Central League football. Unfortunately he was eventually forced to retire because of the injury and received a total of £750 in compensation from the Football Association with Wednesday receiving £2000 for the loss

It signalled the end of a career that had blossomed after moving to Hillsborough from Sunderland in 1924. He had started his playing career in northeast amateur soccer – while working at his local pit – before serving as understudy for four years at Sunderland to the great Charles Buchan. Wednesday boss Bob Brown however recognised his little used talents and fought off interest from Leeds United to secure Marsden's signature. He was described as "tall, speedy and strong" when moving to Wednesday but this did little to describe a wholehearted and inspirational player who not only showed tremendous enthusiasm but proved a real example to his colleagues. He was actually signed as an inside forward but within a year had been converted to left half back and proved an outstanding success even though he was right footed – Marsden diligently practised with his left foot to adapt to his new role. He started the 1925-6 season in the No. 6 shirt and was ever present as Wednesday won the Division Two Championship and consolidated back in the top-flight. Within three years the Strange-Leach-Marsden back line had powered Wednesday to consecutive league Championships with Billy peerless on the left side of the trio.

Sadly the tragic injury occurred when Marsden was at the peak of his career and he was never replaced as The Owls tried unsuccessfully to maintain their position at the summit of the English game. After being forced onto the sidelines Marsden was awarded a benefit game at Hillsborough in September 1931 – a Sheffield XI against an F.A.team – and three months later left for a one-year contract coaching Dutch side HBS Hague. His new charges were beaten 8-1 by a touring Wednesday side in May 1932 but he remained the club's coach for three years before returning home after being appointed Gateshead trainer in July 1934. However he resigned in December 1934 to return to Holland where he coached Be Quick FC and DWS Amsterdam before the outbreak of War. Incidentally while in Holland he would play in the occasional friendly but due to his injury would never head the ball – once during a training session a ball hit him on the head and he collapsed, taking 24 hours to recover.

He was actually assistant coach to the Dutch national side when War was declared and in May 1940, with the Germans invading Holland and snipers all around, he was forced to take refuge in a barber's shop – later commenting that "nobody wanted a shave though". He dashed to the British Consul and fortunately was repatriated to England along with his wife although they were forced to leave all their possessions behind. Once back home The Owls set up a trust fund to help him and in August 1942 Billy was appointed part-time coach at Hillsborough. Between April 1944 and January 1946 he was part-time manager of Doncaster Rovers and later coached at Worksop Town while running the Crosspool Tavern public house in Sheffield. He was the last surviving member of the Wednesday team that won back-to-back League Championships when he passed away, aged 81, in The Hallamshire Hospital.

MARSON, Fred 1925-28

Born: 8 January 1900 Darlaston
(5ft 6ins, 10st 11lbs – 1925)
Died: Q/E December 1976 Lichfield
Debut: 23 October 1926 v Arsenal Division One Away
Last Appearance:
8 October 1927 v Birmingham Division One Home
Total League & Cup Appearances: 10 Goals: 0

Career Details:

Darlaston		
Wolverhampton Wanderers	May	1923
WEDNESDAY	13 June	1925
Swansea Town	7 May	1928 £350
Darlaston		1929
Wellington Town	July	1931
Shrewsbury Town	May	1932

Fast and clever attacker who spent three seasons at Hillsborough after signing from his first league club, Wolves. It was actually his outstanding performance for the Black Country's reserve side, against Wednesday's second team, during the previous season that had alerted Owls officials to his qualities and he was duly signed in the summer that followed. Four goals in eight appearances was his record at Wolves and he fared little better at Hillsborough as he was competing with Harold Hill and Arthur Prince in his debut season and then newcomer Jack Wilkinson after Wednesday had earned promotion in 1926. Primarily an inside left he could also perform admirably on the left wing – it was in the out-and-out winger role that Marson made the majority of his first team appearances for the club. Ended his league career in Wales and later played non-league soccer back in his native West-midlands until retiring.

MARTIN, John Grieve "Jack" 1954-62

Born: 20 August 1935 Dundee
(5ft 10ins, 10st 7lbs – 1954)
Debut: 19 February 1955
v Blackpool
Division One Away
Last Appearance: 31 August 1960
v Cardiff City
Division One Home
Total League
& Cup Appearances: 66 Goals: 0

Career Details:

Butterburn Boys Club		1951
Dundee North End	9 June	1953
WEDNESDAY	8 February	1954 £490
Rochdale	June	1962
Alfreton Town		1963

Right back who followed in the footsteps of his grandfather Bob Petrie when joining Wednesday from Dundee football. However unlike his more famous relation, Martin could never really earn a regular place in the first team despite spending over eight years at Hillsborough after having arrived from the same junior side that had provided Wednesday with Tom McAnearney. The full back was quick in the tackle and slowly progressed through the youth and reserves sides at Wednesday to break into the first team near the end of the 1954-55 season – one of his first senior appearances came in Derek Dooley's benefit game which was the first floodlit game played at Hillsborough.

Over the remainder of the 1950s he proved a loyal clubman who served initially as understudy to Ron Staniforth and then as reserve full back to Peter Johnson, having to be content with occasional first team appearances and reserve team football. His career was halted during the Owls Second Division Championship season of 1958-9 when damaged ankle tendons left Martin on the sidelines but he bounced back to help the second team win the Central League Championship in 1961 before dropping down the divisions to sign for Rochdale. He netted his only goal in senior football while at Spotland but spent only a season with the Lancashire club and after moving to Derbyshire club Alfreton Town played only a handful of times before retiring from the game. Moved back to Sheffield, gaining employment at British Steel at Stocksbridge and later worked in the same industry at Tinsley Park before taking early retirement.

MARWOOD, Brian 1984-88

Born: 5 February 1960 Seaham Harbour, Sunderland
(5ft 7ins, 11st – 1984)
Debut: 25 August 1984
v Nottingham Forest
Division One Home
Last Appearance: 19 March 1988
v Portsmouth
Division One Home
Total League
& Cup Appearances: 157+4 Goals: 35

Career Details:

Hull City	9 February	1978
WEDNESDAY	9 August	1984 £115,000 (T)
Arsenal	23 March	1988 £600,000
Sheffield United	21 September	1990 £350,000
Middlesbrough	18 October	1991 Loan
Swindon Town	9 March	1993 N/C
Barnet	9 August	1993 Free

Goalscoring right winger who joined the Owls from his first club for a tribunal set fee and immediately made his mark on the top-flight of English football by netting twelve times in his debut campaign. He had spent over six years at City, having signed as an apprentice in June 1976, and helped The Tigers to promotion from Division Four in 1983 – top scoring with 19 goals – and the Final of the Associate Members Cup a year later while agonisingly missing out on promotion by a single goal. Incidentally Marwood could have become a professional cricketer as he turned down a chance to play for Northamptonshire Seconds to sign apprentice forms with The Tigers. He again finished top scorer for Hull during the 1983-4 season with sixteen goals and in the summer that followed Luton Town, Sheffield United and Wednesday all vied for his services with of course Howard Wilkinson winning the race on The Owls behalf.

Although not known for beating defenders during his time at Wednesday, Marwood still supplied a constant stream of high quality crosses for the likes of Lee Chapman and Garry Thompson as well as proving a consistent scorer in his own right. He was a vital member of Wilkinson's successful side of the mid-1980s and his absence from the 1986 F.A.Cup semi-final meeting with Everton was believed by many to have denied Wednesday an appearance in the Final. When he was injured half way through the following season The Owls form slumped alarmingly and he eventually left in a club record sale to Arsenal. His consistency at Hillsborough had taken Marwood to the fringes of the England squad but it was not until he moved to North London that he gained what proved to be his one and only full cap – playing alongside Mel Sterland against Saudi Arabia in 1988. Won a Division One Championship medal in 1989 but after injuries curtailed his appearances he left for Sheffield United.

Played only 22 games for The Blades and after brief spells at three other sides he retired injured in 1994 to take up a full-time role as Chairman of the PFA, as well as working as a match summariser for Radio Five Live. He is now based in Sunderland working as a marketing executive for Sportswear company Nike while also being employed by SKY T.V. as a football analyst and co-commentator.

MASSARELLA, Leonard "Len" 1937-45

Born: 14 February 1917 Doncaster
(5ft 6ins, 10st 9lbs – 1937)
Died: 16 January 1999 Doncaster
Debut: 15 January 1938
v Swansea Town
Division Two Away
Last Appearance: 21 January 1939
v Chester FA Cup Home
Total League
& Cup Appearances: 33 Goals: 10
***Also appeared in**
51 wartime games, scoring 16 goals

Career Details:

Firbeck Main Colliery		
Bentley Colliery		
Doncaster Rovers		Amat.
Denaby United	January	1937 Amat.
WEDNESDAY	17 December	1937
Doncaster Rovers	October	1944 Guest
Bentley Thursday Amateurs		1946

Forward who came from a large family of Italian decent who were well known for breeding both horses and ponies in addition to selling ice cream. His mother and grandfather were both born in Italy and Len boasted six brothers and three sisters – his first experience of organised football came in the family football team that played in the Doncaster Thursday Amateur League and was unbeaten for two seasons!

He was spotted by Doncaster non-league outfit Denaby United and in November 1937 joined Wednesday on a month's trial. It was during a trial game for the Owls 'A' team that a watching Owls director discovered that other league sides were showing an interest in him so immediately after the game he signed the twenty year-old on professional forms. He would make a dream start to his first team career at Wednesday, scoring after just three minutes of his debut in a 1-1 draw at Swansea, and played in all but the final game of the season as Wednesday avoided the unthinkable drop into regional soccer.

New signing Idris Lewis took Massarella's place at the start of the following season but off the field events dominated the campaign for Len as in November 1938 he knocked down and killed a cyclist in Doncaster. He was subsequently cleared of any blame at the inquest a week later when it was revealed the cyclist had swerved into his path but the incident no doubt affected his form although he did net five times in only thirteen league games as Wednesday fractionally missed out on promotion. Incidentally during his time in a Wednesday shirt Len's brothers travelled to watch him in their ice cream van and on numerous occasions they collected him from training, selling ice cream to his team mates! Like many of his contemporaries the Second World War then took the best years of his playing career – at the outbreak of war Len began working as a farmer back in Doncaster and would play as a guest for his hometown club on several occasions. Despite only being in his twenties Massarella did not return to professional soccer after the war, instead playing for Bentley Thursday Amateurs where he won four trophies in 1946-7 and netted 42 times in the following season as the league title was retained. After retiring from full time football he was a farmer until his retirement at the age of 65 while he also bred horses and once won first prize at The Olympia Horse Show.

MASSEY, James 'Jimmy' 1893-1901

Born: 1869 Wolverhampton
(5ft, 10ins, 10st 9lbs – 1896) Died: December 1960 Mexborough
Debut: 3 November 1894 v Aston Villa Division One Home
Last Appearance: 9 February 1901 v Bury F.A.Cup Home
Total League & Cup Appearances: 173 Goals: 0

Career Details:

Denaby United	
Doncaster Rovers	1890
WEDNESDAY	1893
Denaby United	1901
South Kirkby Colliery	

After starting his playing career with non-league Denaby United goalkeeper Jimmy Massey moved to Wednesday after being spotted by a club official who just happened to be refereeing a cup-tie at Loughborough. He persuaded Wednesday to sign Massey and the newcomer became a reserve team regular at Olive Grove before getting his big break in January 1896 when regular keeper Bill Allan reported for a game hardly able to walk – Massey taking his place despite having a broken finger himself! Massey would remain first choice for the next four and a half seasons; despite being frequently hurt such was his sheer bravery in the area. He often rose to brilliant heights and was a major factor in The Owls first F.A.Cup win in 1896 – it was reported at the time that in the last few minutes of the win over Wolves Massey was plied with innumerable shots, all of which he repelled.

He would play in the final game at Olive Grove and then the first 29 games at Wednesday's new Owlerton Ground, helping the club to the Second Division Championship in 1900. However he suffered one too many knocks and eventually lost his place, initially to Frank Stubbs, and then to the outstanding Jack Lyall. Injury saw Massey miss the whole of the 1901-2 season before his career was re-launched back at his old club Denaby United, whilst also working at the local pit. His playing career continued at Doncaster side South Kirkby – he was still a regular as his fortieth birthday approached – while later in his life he lost an eye in a pit accident while working at Barnburgh Colliery. He was the last surviving member of the 1896 Cup Final side when he passed away at the grand old age of 91.

MATTHEWS, Ernest 1937-38

Born: 8 November 1912
Chester-le-Street
(5ft 9½ins, 11st 6lbs – 1937)
Debut: 16 September 1937
v Tottenham Hotspur
Division Two Home
Last Appearance: 5 March 1938
v Manchester United
Division Two Home
Total League
& Cup Appearances: 16 Goals: 7

Career Details:

Knibblesworth Welfare		
Bury	2 April	1934 £10
WEDNESDAY	14 September	1937 £3750
Colchester United	August	1938 £2500
Released		1939
Ashington	August	1939
Mansfield Town		1939-40 Guest

There is no doubt that centre forward Ernie Matthews was one of the quickest players to appear in a blue and white shirt, as he was both a professional sprinter and footballer. In fact when joining Colchester United from Wednesday in 1938 a United official travelled to an athletics meeting in York where he duly signed Matthews late in the evening and travelled overnight back to Colchester with his new capture! The move to Southern League United had occurred after Matthews had enjoyed a highly creditable debut season at Wednesday, netting almost a goal every two games as The Owls struggled at the foot of the old Second Division. He replaced Harry Ware in the side but after impressing the centre forward saw his career come to an abrupt end when Wednesday signed Doug Hunt in the spring of 1938.

His career had started at Durham non-league side Knibblesworth Welfare and he quickly rose to fame when netting 28 league goals in only 37 games during his debut season at Bury. He possessed tremendous pace, great ball control and a good shot in both feet – these attributes helping him net another seventeen goals in the season that followed. However a slump in attendances at the Gigg Lane club meant Bury had to sell their prize asset and he duly moved to Hillsborough with The Shakers receiving, what at the time, was the second largest fee in their history. After less than a year at Wednesday he would play only seven times for Colchester – netting four goals – before war ended his professional football career. One of his final appearances came as a guest for Mansfield Town in March 1940 when he scored a hat trick to perhaps emphasis those qualities that were not properly utilised at Hillsborough.

MATTHEWSON, Thomas James 1921-23

Born: 9 May 1903 Gateshead
(5ft 11½ins, 12st 3lbs - 1924)
Died: 19 May 1966 Sheffield
Only Appearance: 24 December 1921
v Coventry City
Division Two Away
Total League
& Cup Appearances: 1 Goals: 0

Career Details:

Gateshead Town		
Close Works		
WEDNESDAY	September	1921
South Shields	August	1923
North Shields		1931
Pelaw Athletic		
Dunston Co Op Wholesale Society FC		

It was previously thought that the Wednesday career of Tommy Matthewson – grandfather of 1980s Owls player Trevor – was confined to two seasons of reserve team football. However recent research revealed that the right-winger actually made a solitary league appearance for Wednesday on Christmas Eve 1921 when Emil Thompson dropped out of the side for the visit to Coventry City. He helped The Owls to a 2-2 draw but it would be at his next club, South Shields, that Matthewson would make a significant impact on league football. In fact during seven years at the Horsley Hill based side – who were a league club in the 1920s – he played in 219 games, netting 44 times and was captain of the club for many years. In a windswept October 1926 game against Chelsea he scored two goals direct from corners and came back to haunt Wednesday when netting the opening goal in an F.A.Cup tie at Hillsborough – the game finished 1-1 with the minnows winning the replay.

He stayed loyal when relegation from Division Two and financial problems hit South Shields but eventually left for local rivals North Shields, scoring 14 times in 48 games before hanging up his proverbial boots in 1931, after just a solitary season. Tommy, whose son Reg played for Sheffield United, Fulham and Chester, returned to Sheffield in 1938 to work for a company called Daniel Doncasters – playing in and later managing the works side until March 1951. He retired due to ill health in 1960, in the same year that his wife, Agnes, retired after having laundered The Owls kit for 25 years! Incredibly their daughter Betty then took up kit washing duties at Hillsborough, remaining in charge for an amazing 43 years before she herself retired in 2003.

MATTHEWSON, Trevor 1981-83

Born: 12 February 1963 Sheffield
(6ft 1ins, 12st – 1981)
Debut: 2 May 1981
v Watford
Division Two Away
Last Appearance: 11 January 1983
v Southend United
Division F.A.Cup Home
Total League
& Cup Appearances: 5 Goals: 0

Career Details:

WEDNESDAY	12 February	1981
Newport County	15 October	1983 Free
Stockport County	27 September	1985 Free
Lincoln City	1 August	1987 £13,000
Birmingham City	3 August	1989 £45,000
Preston North End	20 August	1993 £25,000
Bury	2 September	1994 £10,000
Witton Albion		1996
Hereford United	11 October	1996 Free
Ilkeston Town		1998
Matlock Town	December	1998 Loan
Gresley Rovers	January	1999 Loan

When Trevor Matthewson made his senior debut for Wednesday he completed an unprecedented treble which had seen three generations of the same family appear for the one of the city's professional clubs – following in the footsteps of grandad Tommy at Wednesday and uncle Reg at United. He had joined the Owls as an apprentice in June 1979 and after graduating to the Central League side was signed on professional forms, making his first team debut just three months later. He spent two full seasons at Hillsborough but the likeable centre half could not become established, facing stiff competition from the likes of Mark Smith, Peter Shirtliff and Mick Lyons. He was therefore only an occasional contributor and it was no surprise that he left on a free transfer soon after the arrival of Howard Wilkinson as manager.

He appeared in over 175 games for his next two sides before helping Lincoln City win the Conference at the first attempt. His greatest success came at Birmingham City where one of his two hundred plus games came as a winning substitute in the 1991 Leyland Daf Cup Final. After two spells in Lancashire football he dropped into non-league soccer, combining part-time football with a job in the wholesale trade. However after only three months at the Cheshire side he made a surprise return to the Football League with Hereford United but despite being ever present found himself back in non-league soccer after United were relegated on the final day of the season. Later signed for Ilkeston Town but struggled with his fitness and after a solitary game on loan at Gresley Rovers decided to retire due to a persistent knee problem. In November 1999 he opened his own retail shop about a mile from Hillsborough, which he still runs today.

MAXWELL, James Morton 1907-08

Born: New Cunnock (5ft 7ins, 11st – 1907)
Died: Killed in action - WWI
Debut:
29 March 1907 v Woolwich Arsenal Division One Away
Last Appearance:
20 April 1908 v Woolwich Arsenal Division One Away
Total League & Cup Appearances: 27 Goals: 6

Career Details:

Kilmarnock Shawbank		
Petershill Juniors		1904
Kilmarnock	December	1904
WEDNESDAY	18 March	1907 £500
Woolwich Arsenal	13 May	1908 £350
Hulford and Galstone	September	1909
Carlisle United		1910
Lanemark	August	1911
Kilmarnock	December	1912
Nithsdale Wanderers	August	1913

Right-winger James Maxwell was only nineteen years old when Wednesday brought him to Sheffield from his native Scotland. He went straight into the first team in the problematic outside right position, netting his first goal in the 2-1 derby defeat at Bramall Lane in April 1907. He also netted on his home debut against Sunderland and the pacy attacker, who also possessed great ball control, started the following season as first choice as Wednesday stormed to the summit of Division One.

However after losing his place six games into the campaign Maxwell was in and out of the side throughout the remainder of the season – sharing right-sided duties with Harry Chapman – before surprisingly moving to Woolwich Arsenal. His son Bud played for several senior clubs in Scotland and England but after just over a year in London Maxwell Snr. would play the remainder of his career in Scottish junior soccer before joining the forces during the Great War. Sadly he was subsequently killed on active service during the conflict.

MAY, Lawrence Charles 'Larry' 1987-88

Born: 26 December 1958
Sutton Coalfield
(6ft 1ins, 12st – 1988)
Debut: 28 February 1987
v Watford
Division One Home
Last Appearance: 7 May 1988
v Liverpool
Division One Home
Total League
& Cup Appearances: 37+1 Goals: 1

Career Details:

Leicester City	September	1976
New England Teamen	Jul-Aug	1978 Loan
Barnsley	August	1983 £110,000
WEDNESDAY	17 February	1987 £200,000
Brighton & Hove Albion	30 September	1988 £175,000

Started his professional career at Filbert Street where after breaking into the first team the imposing centre half became a fixture for several seasons, being named Leicester City player of the year in 1980 and 1981, while also helping City to promotion to the top-flight in 1983. However after 207 appearances he was surprisingly sold to Barnsley in the summer of 1983 where he earned the reputation as the best defender outside the top-flight. His subsequent transfer from Oakwell to Hillsborough had initially collapsed after the Barnsley board vetoed the move but 48 hours later May was an Owls player. Unfortunately for the central defender he joined an Owls side on the slide and would experience a disappointing eighteen months at the club – in February 1988 he asked for and was granted a move, duly signing for Blackpool for £125,000 on deadline day. However four days after the transfer was completed it was annulled on medical grounds, leaving May back in the reserves at Hillsborough. He did eventually move early in the following season, to Brighton, and remained on the South Coast until a serious knee injury, sustained in April 1989, eventually led to his early retirement in September of the same year. By this time he had already been appointed reserve team coach at Albion and remained on the coaching staff until November 1993 when he was a victim of stringent cost cutting as Brighton struggled to stay in business.

While still at Brighton he spent the 1993 pre season period helping out with coaching at Sussex non-league side Ringmer – May had earned his F.A. coaching badge in 1986 – before finding himself out of football for the first time. A brief career change saw May appointed Physical Education teacher at a special needs school in Sussex before returning to club football as youth team coach under Terry Fenwick at Portsmouth in February 1995. After two years at Pompey he became restless and after seeing an ad in a local paper applied and was duly appointed Football Development Officer for Crawley Boro Council. Remained in the position until April 2001 when he was appointed to his current role – coaching development manager with the Surrey Football Association.

MAYRLEB, Christian 1998

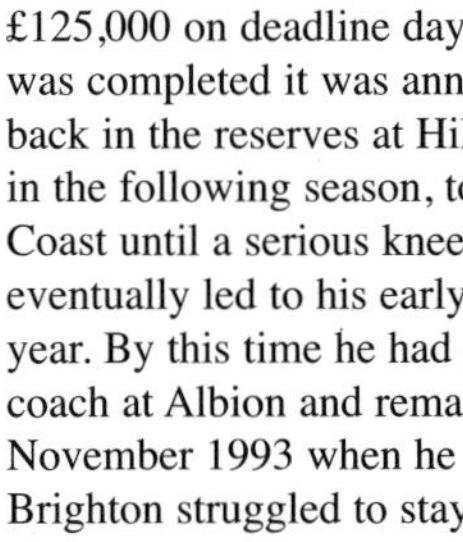

Born: 8 June 1972 Wels, Austria
(5ft 10ins, 11st 7lbs - 1998)
Debut: 31 January 1998
v Wimbledon
Premier League Home
Last Appearance: 28 February 1998
v Derby County
Premier League Away
Total League
& Cup Appearances: 0+3 Goals: 0

Career Details:

S.A.Reid		
Admira Wacker	1 August	1995
FC Tirol	1 August	1996
WEDNESDAY	26 January	1998 Loan
Austria Vienna	1 August	2000 Free
Contract cancelled	September	2002 Free
FC Superfund*	23 October	2002 Free

*Formely SV Pashing

The Wednesday career of Austrian forward Christian Mayrleb was certainly one of the strangest in the club's history as after The Owls had paid a reputed £200,000 for his loan services he duly made only three brief substitute appearances and looked totally out of sorts in both first team and reserve soccer. He was one of several foreign trialists whom Ron Atkinson brought over to Hillsborough during his second spell as manager and Mayrleb arrived as not only top scorer for his club side but with the reputation as one of the fastest forwards in Austrian football. He had impressed greatly when scoring twice for Tirol in a UEFA Cup tie against Glasgow Celtic but just could not make any impact in his short time at Hillsborough, amassing only 48 minutes of Premier League soccer in a Wednesday shirt.

However his time in Sheffield proved the only real blip on a goal-laden career that started back in his homeland at Sports Association Reid where he netted 34 times in just 63 games. Fifteen goals in 66 games followed at Admira before Mayrleb scored 17 in 53 at Tirol. After returning to Austria he instantly hit the best form of his career, scoring an outstanding 50 goals in only 91 games for Austria Vienna while also earning several full caps for the national side. After just over two years in the capital, Mayrleb transferred to top-fight new boys Pasching who had stunned the country by sitting second in the league in their first season with the 'big boys'. After gaining his mid season release from Vienna he signed a three-year deal with his new side but was unable to make his debut until the International transfer window opened in January 2003.

McANEARNEY, James 'Jim' 1952-60

Born: 20 March 1935 Lochee, Dundee
(5ft 7ins, 10st 4lbs – 1954)
Debut: 24 February 1954
v Liverpool
Division One Home
Last Appearance: 30 April 1959
v Bristol Rovers
Division Two Away
Total League
& Cup Appearances: 40 Goals: 10

Career Details:

Dundee St.Stephens		
WEDNESDAY	20 March	1952 £300
Plymouth Argyle	8 January	1960 £6,750
Watford	November	1963 £10,000
Bradford City	September	1966 Nominal

Jim McAnearney arrived at Hillsborough with his brother Tom in October 1951, after being spotted playing in Dundee junior football. He was immediately signed to amateur forms but instead of turning fully professional on his seventeenth birthday McAnearney instead signed part-time forms – on joining Wednesday the inside forward had started to work as an apprentice bricklayer, at a company owned by an Owls director, and at his father's insistence combined work with football until finally turning full time in March 1958, after serving two years of National Service. The ex-Scottish boys International played for the senior R.A.F representative side while serving in the forces while his Wednesday career had slowly progressed from youth team football – he played in the club's first ever F.A.Youth Cup game in September 1952 – to become a reserve team regular during the 1953-4 season.

He would go on to play in well over 165 second team games for Wednesday, scoring almost 80 goals (a tremendous tally in reserve soccer) and was top scorer for the reserves four times in the 1950s. However the slightly built but clever inside forward, who possessed the ability to make space in midfield and bring colleagues into the game, never really became established in the first team, due in part to the glut of outstanding midfielders at Hillsborough in the 1950s. In 1958 he became one of the youngest players to ever gain a full F.A. coaching badge but his playing career lay away from Hillsborough – Jim had rejected a £4,500 move to York City in July 1958 - and early in 1960 moved to Plymouth Argyle in a £10,000 deal that also saw George Kirby transfer to Home Park.

He enjoyed great popularity at Argyle and was considered by most fans to be the brains of the club's attack with the team said to simply not function when Jim was absent. In total he netted 37 times in 147 games for Plymouth before ending his league career with a total of 130 league games at his final two clubs – Watford and Bradford City. At City he was officially player-coach and was appointed acting manager in March 1968 when George Heir tragically died during a training session. In May of the same year he was offered the manager's job but rejected the chance, instead moving to Rotherham United as coach under Tommy Docherty. When 'The Doc' left in December 1968 Jim was elevated to manager and remained for five eventful years until resigning in May 1973. Returned to Hillsborough as second team manager in May 1974 and followed in his brother's footsteps by serving as acting manager for the club in September 1975 following Steve Burtenshaw's departure. As financial problems engulfed the club he was sacked in January 1976 as part of stringent cost-cutting measures but was immediately appointed as youth coach by Leeds United. Was later chief coach but left professional soccer in June 1978 to concentrate on his Sheffield based machine tools business that he started while on the staff at Rotherham.

He returned to the game as part-time boss of non-league Frickley Colliery in November 1980 and later spent just over a year as Scarborough manager before pressure of work forced his resignation in April 1982. Over the next seven years he scouted for a variety of managers in the professional game – as well as serving on the committee of Hallam FC – before ending his links with soccer with a season (1989-90) in charge of the first team at Hallam. In 1999 he retired from his business, handing over to his son, and now undertakes the odd after dinner speaking engagement while spending time on the golf course

McANEARNEY, Thomas 'Tom' 1951-65

Born: 6 January 1933 Lochee, Dundee
(5ft 9½ins, 10st 2lbs – 1955)
Debut: 3 September 1952
v Liverpool
Division One Home
Last Appearance: 20 February 1965
v Everton
Division One Home
Total League
& Cup Appearances: 382 Goals: 22

Career Details:

Dunkeld Amateurs U16s		1947
St.Stevens Amateurs		1949
Dundee North End		1950
WEDNESDAY	20 October	1951 £490
Peterborough United	1 November	1965 £5,000
Aldershot	11 March	1966 £5,000

Of the two McAnearney brothers who arrived at Hillsborough in October 1951 it was older sibling Tom who enjoyed the greater success. The former Scottish boys international reserve – he was named as standby on three occasions but was never capped - progressed through the Owls ranks to became an invaluable and vital performer at first team level, while also completing a bricklaying apprenticeship and spending two years in the RAF between 1956 and 1958. In total the outstanding wing back played in thirteen consecutive seasons of league football for Wednesday with his pace, superb tackling ability and thoughtful play marking Tom out as a defender of rare quality. He formed part of Harry Catterick's famous back line of Swan-Kay-McAnearney and was also captain for a spell in the early 1960s when The Owls enjoyed some of their most productive years in post war soccer. He had previously helped Wednesday to Division Two Championships honours in 1956 and 1959 and after finishing runners-up to Spurs in 1961 led the club into European football for the first time.

Eventually lost his first team place to the emerging Peter Eustace and after a brief spell at Peterborough United ended his playing career at Aldershot, who paid what was then a club record fee for the Hampshire club to secure his services. In April 1967 he was appointed player-manager at Aldershot and after taking his appearances to 106 retired from playing in the summer of 1968, returning to Hillsborough in October as assistant manager to Jack Marshall. He mirrored the career of his brother Jim when being appointed caretaker manager, in March 1969, and remained at Hillsborough under new boss Danny Williams until leaving to become manager at Bury in November 1970. A bold bid to avoid relegation by investing in players failed to save The Shakers from the drop in 1971 and a year later he returned to Aldershot for a second spell as boss. Success included promotion from Division Four in 1973 and a run to the last sixteen of the F.A.Cup in 1979 before he left in January 1981, ending his direct involvement with football after a years coaching at Chelsea. He then became a postman back in Aldershot and after retiring moved back to Sheffield where he spends many happy hours on the golf course.

McCAFFERTY, Michael 1898-99

Born:
Only Appearance: 1 April 1899 v Burnley Division One Home
Total League & Cup Appearances: 1 Goals: 0

Career Details:

Glasgow Celtic		
WEDNESDAY	20 October	1898
Released		1899

Half back who arrived during the Owls final season of football at Olive Grove. After making his debut for the reserves on Christmas Eve 1898 he was a regular for the remainder of the season while making a solitary first team start when Wednesday were hit by injuries. He helped Wednesday to a one-nil Olive Grove win – in the penultimate game at the old ground – before dropping back into second team football and being released at the end of the season.

McCALL, Stephen Harold 'Steve' 1987-92

Born: 15 October 1960 Carlisle
(5ft 11ins, 11st 3lbs – 1988)
Debut: 15 August 1987
v Chelsea
Division One Away
Last Appearance: 6 April 1991
v Portsmouth
Division Two Away
Total League
& Cup Appearances: 24+12 Goals: 2

Career Details:

Ipswich Town	5 October	1978
WEDNESDAY	3 June	1987 £250,000
Carlisle United	9 February	1990 Loan
Plymouth Argyle	26 March	1992 £25,000
Torquay United	12 July	1996 Free

When Howard Wilkinson signed Steve McCall he brought to Hillsborough an experienced top-flight player who had won England honours at Youth, U-21 and 'B' level plus won a UEFA Cup medal with Ipswich in 1981. From making his Town debut in the 1979-80 season left back McCall was almost ever present in totalling 329 games – before it was surpassed by Matt Holland he did hold the club record of 175 consecutive appearances - but sadly his move to Wednesday coincided with a terrible run of injury which totally ruined his Owls career. His problems started in only his fifth game for the club, at home to Coventry City in August 1987, when a badly broken leg kept him out of the first team picture for eighteen months. In fact he would start only eight games for Wednesday in his first three seasons at Hillsborough and it was not until the 1990-91 promotion season that the stylish player made any real impact, in a new midfield role.

The majority of his 26 appearances during that season came from the subs bench but after helping Wednesday to promotion – he just failed to make the squad for the League Cup Final – McCall fell totally out of favour under the managership of Trevor Francis and failed to make an appearance before moving to Plymouth on deadline day 1992. He became one of the first signings of new boss Peter Shilton and was named player of the year two seasons running whilst making over one hundred appearances for The Pilgrims. After Shilton was suspended in January 1996 McCall was appointed caretaker manager for two weeks and remained in charge when his boss was sacked soon after. However he resigned in late March in order to concentrate solely on playing although his injury jinx had re occurred and a move to neighbours Torquay followed. Helped United to the 1998 Division Three play off Final – playing in the Wembley Final loss to Colchester United – before moving back to Plymouth Argyle as assistant manager in July 1998. Remained at Home Park before being sacked, along with manager Kevin Hodges, in October 2000 and after working as a scout back at old club Ipswich he is now the 'Tractor Boys' reserve team manager.

McCALLIOG, James 'Jim' 1965-69

Born: 23 September 1946 Glasgow
(5ft 9ins, 10st 5lbs – 1966)
Debut: 30 October 1965
v Aston Villa
Division One Away
Last Appearance: 12 May 1969
v Tottenham Hotspur
Division One Home
Total League
& Cup Appearances: 174 Goals: 27

Career Details:

Leeds United	May	1963 Amat.
Chelsea	23 September	1963
WEDNESDAY	29 October	1965 £35,000
Wolverhampton Wanderers	21 July	1969 £70,000
Manchester United	14 March	1974 £60,000
Southampton	13 February	1975 £40,000
Chicago Sting	Apr-August	1977 Free
Lynn Oslo		1977-78
Lincoln City	September	1978
Runcorn	July	1979

CAPS (@SWFC)
Scotland Full (4) v England 15/04/67, v N.Ireland 21/10/67, v Russia 10/05/67, v Denmark 16/10/68

Scotland U-23 (2) v Wales 30/11/67, v England 01/03/67

Pencil thin inside forward who first came to prominence with Glasgow boys before attracting the attention of English scouts during two appearances for Scotland boys. He was eventually signed as an amateur by Leeds United manager Don Revie – a player could not sign pro under the age of seventeen – but it was Chelsea and not Leeds that he joined as a professional on his 17th birthday. At Stamford Bridge competition was fierce and he was unable to establish himself and only had a dozen appearances to his name before Wednesday stunned the football World when paying what was a record fee for a teenager to take McCalliog to Hillsborough. His mother, father, sister and three brothers (one brother, Freddie, also signed pro at Wednesday but was released in May 1967 after failing to make a first team start) all moved North with him to a house near Hillsborough to help the somewhat overawed youngster settle into his new surroundings.

Within a few months the fee looked money well spent as his goal against old club Chelsea helped Wednesday to the Cup Final where he netted again in the dramatic loss to Everton at Wembley. A tremendous start to his Wednesday career continued when McCalliog became the first Owls player since Jimmy Blair in 1920 to be capped at full level by Scotland – playing and scoring in the side that became the first team to beat new World Champions England when winning 3-2 at Wembley. The attacker possessed enormous energy and a tremendous capacity for running while his fitness record at Wednesday was exemplary – he missed only five of the 179 games The Owls played during his time at the club! However after the Cup Final Wednesday started to struggle and the youngster became unsettled, submitting a transfer request in May 1967, which was accepted by the club. The Owls did eventually more than double their money when selling McCalliog to Wolves and it proved a good move for the Scotsman as he netted 48 times in 210 games, captaining the side in the 1972 UEFA Cup Final defeat to Spurs.

He helped Manchester United to the Division Two Championship in 1975 and a year later was in the Southampton side that stunned United to win the F.A.Cup. A spell in US football and as player-coach at Norwegian side Oslo came next for McCalliog although a reported coaching role in Nigeria proved incorrect. On returning to these shores he appeared nine times as player-coach for Lincoln City and was caretaker manager for a short time before Colin Murphy was appointed. After being released in March 1979 he dropped into non-league football as player-manager with Runcorn, combining the role with his job as Football in the Community officer at Blackburn Rovers – he later fulfilled the same role at Halifax Town. Left the Merseyside semi-pro outfit in 1980 and began working as a publican although he did return to the game in 1990 as manager at Halifax Town. Like many men before him he was unable to turn around the Shaymen's fortunes and after being dismissed in October 1991 was left to concentrate on his George and Dragon public house at Wetherby, before moving to York in the same capacity.

McCAMBRIDGE, James 'Joseph' 1936-37

Born: 24 September 1905
Larne, Ireland
(5ft 10½ins, 11st 8lbs – 1936)
Died: 15 May 1990 Larne, Ireland
Debut: 10 October 1936
v Arsenal
Division One Away
Last Appearance: 31 October 1936
v Charlton Athletic
Division One Away
Total League
& Cup Appearances: 2 Goals: 0

Career Details:

Larne Apprenticeships		
Larne Olympic		
Ballymena United	August	1928
Everton	March	1930
Cardiff City	January	1931
Ballymena United	May	1933
Bristol Rovers	22 May	1933
Exeter City	24 September	1935 £150
WEDNESDAY	23 June	1936 £250
Hartlepools United	6 January	1937
Cheltenham Town	September	1937

Well built, strong and dashing Irish International who spent only a brief time at Hillsborough during the Owls relegation season of 1936-7. He was one of nine players who were tried in the No. 9 shirt during that season as Wednesday tried in desperation to find a winning combination. The four times capped attacker had the misfortune to break his nose during his league debut for Wednesday at Highbury and played only once more in league soccer for Wednesday before dropping back into the lower leagues when signing for Hartlepools United. During his few months at Wednesday McCambridge also netted eight goals in reserve team football – four of those coming in the 8-2 Central League win over Manchester United in September 1936. A joiner by trade and pigeon racer in his spare time, he ended his career in non-league football at Southern League club Cheltenham Town.

McCARTER, James Joseph 'Jimmy' 1946-48

Born: 19 March 1923 Glasgow
(5ft 8ins, 10st 7lbs – 1946)
Died: 22 August 2002 Weymouth
Debut: 28 September 1946
v Millwall
Division Two Away
Last Appearance: 2 November 1946
v Swansea Town
Division Two Home
Total League
& Cup Appearances: 6* Goals: 0
***Also appeared in 4 wartime games**

Career Details:

Vale of Clyde		
WEDNESDAY	24 January	1946 £75
Mansfield Town	29 July	1948 Free
Weymouth	9 August	1950 Free
Dorchester Town	28 June	1956 Free
Portland United		1957

Left-winger Jimmy McCarter started his working life as a messenger boy for a greengrocer after having left school in 1937. When war was declared two years later he had just began a five-year apprenticeship as a shoe repairer and continued his training during the war years, while also playing football for Vale of Clyde as a part time professional. In 1944 he was called up to work in the mines as part of the war effort, becoming a 'Bevin Boy'- the name being taken from a member of the government at that time. On signing amateur forms for Wednesday in 1944 he moved to work at a local pit and first appeared for the club in April of the same year, at home to York City. He was strictly classed as a guest player during his first two years at Wednesday – and therefore ineligible to play in the F.A.Cup – but eventually signed professional forms early in 1946.

After helping Wednesday's second team win the Central League Championship in 1946, McCarter made six senior appearances during the first season of peacetime football but competition from Frank Slynn and then Dennis Woodhead ensured he would remain out of the first team picture for his final two years at Hillsborough. In fact during his final season at Wednesday, McCarter struggled to even secure a run out in the reserves and it was no surprise when he moved to Mansfield Town. Enjoyed a successful two seasons at Field Mill, appearing in 67 league games, before ending his days as a professional at powerful Southern League side Weymouth. After a year at Dorchester Jimmy began working as a shoe repairer while he also spent a season as player-coach at Dorset non-league side Portland United. Later in life he worked as a postman in Weymouth – until his retirement in June 1985 – and kept involved with football by coaching the local boys club two nights a week.

McCARTHY, Jonathan David 'Jon' 2002

Born: 18 August 1970 Middlesborough
(5ft 9ins, 11st 5lbs – 2002)
Debut: 29 March 2002 v Coventry City Division One Home
Last Appearance:
13 April 2002 v Stockport County Division One Away
Total League & Cup Appearances: 4 Goals: 0

Career Details:

Hartlepool United	7 October	1987 N/C
Shepshed Charterhouse	March	1989
York City	22 March	1990 Free
Port Vale	1 August	1995 £450,000
Birmingham City	11 September	1997 £1.5m
WEDNESDAY	28 March	2002 Loan
Released	30 June	2002 Free
Port Vale	2 August	2002 Free
Doncaster Rovers	8 October	2002 Free
York City	28 October	2002 Trial
York City	7 November	2002 Free
Carlisle United	28 November	2002 Free
Released	30 June	2003
Hucknall Town	15 August	2003 Free
Northwich Victoria	12 August	2004 Free

Winger Jon McCarthy was a rare example of a player who abandoned a professional career to forward his education only to return to full time football after gaining his qualifications. He had initially broken through at Hartlepool United, signing non-contract forms in 1987, but instead of concentrating on his football career McCarthy attended Nottingham University to gain a Batchelor of Sports Science and administration degree. Whilst studying he played Northern Premier League football with Shepshed and was still in full time education when York City manager John Bird – his old boss at Hartlepool – persuaded the pacy and tricky winger to join on a part-time basis. He eventually turned professional in March 1991 – after winning a bronze medal in Sheffield at the World Student Games – and in five seasons appeared in 233 games for 'The Minstermen'. Helped City to Wembley play off success in 1995 but several big clubs were now tracking his progress and he did eventually move – only one week before the start of the 1995-6 campaign.

His star continued to rise at Port Vale- winning the first of 18 full caps for Northern Ireland - and after two outstanding seasons Birmingham City broke their transfer record to take him to St.

Andrews. However despite appearing in 142 games for City, injury – he suffered a broken leg on three occasions - and loss of form saw his career stagnate during the early part of the New Century. Terry Yorath signed him on loan until the end of the season but despite impressing on his debut in a thrilling Good Friday win over Coventry City the winger quickly dropped out of contention and was released at the end of the season. After experiencing a disappointing campaign in 2002-3 – he failed to agree terms at Carlisle United after helping the Cumbrian club escape relegation from the Football league - his league career came to end when McCarthy signed for Northern Premier League high-flyers Hucknall Town. He is now a science teacher in Cheshire.

McCONACHIE, Robert 1891-93

Born: Scotland
Only Appearance: 1 April 1893 v Stoke Division One Home
Total League & Cup Appearances: 1* Goals: 0
***Also appeared in 17 Football Alliance League games**

Career Details:

Scottish Juniors		
WEDNESDAY	March	1891
Released	April	1893

Half back who joined The Owls from Scottish junior football in the early 1890s. Made his debut for the club in the March 1891 Alliance League home win over Birmingham St. George and played in over half of the 1891-92 Alliance League fixtures in what proved to be Wednesday's final season of non-league soccer. He did actually appear in a January 1892 F.A.Cup tie against Bolton at Olive Grove but the tie was re-classified by the referee on the day of the game as bad weather and an ice bound pitch made the game somewhat of a lottery. Played only once in senior football for Wednesday – in an unaccustomed left wing role as a replacement for Fred Spiksley – and dropped out of senior football soon after.

McCONNELL, James English 'English/Irish' 1908-10

Born: 1885 Larne, Co.Antrim
(5ft 8ins, 11st 8lbs – 1909)
Died: 21 June 1928 Belfast
Debut: 1 September 1908
v Leicester Fosse
Division One Away
Last Appearance: 9 April 1910
v Chelsea
Division One Away
Total League
& Cup Appearances: 50 Goals: 0

Career Details:

Cliftonville		1903
Glentoran		1904
Sunderland	August	1905
WEDNESDAY	May	1908 £285
Chelsea	15 April	1910 £1000
South Shields	August	1912

CAPS (@SWFC)
Ireland (5) v Scotland 15/03/09, v 20/03/09, v England 12/02/10, v Scotland 19/03/10, v Wales 11/04/10

When Wednesday legend Tommy Crawshaw retired the Owls were left without a recognised pivot in the centre of their defence but this problem was quickly remedied when the stylish and polished English McConnell arrived in a big money move from First Division rivals Sunderland. He came to Hillsborough with seven Irish caps to his name and was a regular for two seasons although his time in Sheffield was not without controversy, mainly surrounding the bizarre events of a game at Villa Park in March 1910. During the game, which Wednesday lost 5-0, McConnell was said to have simply stopped playing, folded his arms and let Villa run through to score! The accusation was played down but within a few weeks he was on his way to Chelsea for a huge fee – Wednesday receiving £500 immediately and the remainder being paid by an IOU repayable six months after the transfer!

It could also be said that the Irishman was partly responsible for introducing the dreaded mascots into the game of football as in 1910 English was gifted a live monkey by a friend who had just arrived back from a trip to India. The animal was christened 'Jacko' and he led the team out – wearing a Wednesday jacket and carrying a flag – before the F.A.Cup tie with minnows Glossop North End! His hairy friend quickly earned the Wednesday defender the nickname of 'Monkey' McConnell but unfortunately 'Jacko' proved an unlucky mascot as The Owls slumped 1-0 against their Second Division visitors.

His move to Chelsea came just six days after Wednesday had lost 4-1 at Stamford Bridge and he was one of several players the Londoners signed in what proved a bold but ultimately unsuccessful attempt to stave off relegation from Division One. Incidentally The Londoners spent £3,000 in a vain attempt to escape the drop and this extravagant spending directly brought about a change in F.A. rules which saw Rule 59 introduced to set a transfer deadline day on the last Tuesday in March – a deadline that still stands today. McConnell – whose brother Victor played for Cliftonville and Belfast Celtic - appeared in 22 consecutive games for The Pensioners but a cartilage operation twelve months after his arrival brought a premature end to his Chelsea career. After a season at North-Eastern League side South Shields he retired, returning to Belfast to start his own business

McCULLOCH, Andrew "Andy" 1979-83

Born: 3 January 1950 Northampton
(6ft 2ins, 13st 6lbs – 1979)
Debut: 11 August 1979
v Hull City
League Cup Home
Last Appearance: 14 May 1983
v Crystal Palace
Division Two Home
Total League
& Cup Appearances: 146+3 Goals: 49

Career Details:

Fleet Town		
Tottenham Hotspur		Trial
Walton & Hersham		
Queens Park Rangers	October	1970
Cardiff City	27 October	1972 £45,000
Oxford United	5 July	1974 £70,000
Brentford	March	1976 £25,000
Oakland Stompers		1978 Loan
WEDNESDAY	22 June	1979 £60,000
Crystal Palace	1 August	1983 £20,000
Aldershot	December	1984 Free

Big Andy McCulloch proved to be one of Jack Charlton's most effective signings during his six years in charge at Hillsborough. The brave, bustling centre forward led the Owls attack for four seasons and his never say die attitude saw him become a crowd favourite as he netted an average of a goal every three games while also setting up countless other goals for team mates. McCulloch – whose father Adam played league soccer for several clubs including Northampton Town – was first spotted whilst playing Hampshire League soccer for non-league Fleet Town and after breaking into the Rangers first team McCulloch netted ten times in thirty appearances. However after failing to become established he moved to Ninian Park where 24 goals in 58 league games (plus his sole Scotland U-23 cap) prompted a further transfer to Oxford.

It was his consistent goal scoring at Brentford however that caught Wednesday's attention and after scoring almost fifty goals for the London club in three seasons he moved to Sheffield. Despite being usually referred to as Ian by Jack Charlton (who famously forget his players names and often confused Andy with Notts County forward Iain McCulloch!) he made sure the Wednesday fans remembered his name by spearheading the club's promotion push out of the old Third Division in 1980, scoring eighteen times. He remained a regular at Wednesday throughout the early 1980s although he was lucky to escape with his life in September 1982 when he turned over his car on the way home from a round of golf at Worksop -thankfully escaping with just minor injuries and missing only one game. A parting of the ways came soon after as after refusing a new contract in May 1983 he returned to the Capital when his Owls deal expired, joining Crystal Palace. Spent only a year at Selhurst Park and in 1985 a serious knee injury meant his playing career came to a premature end. Although possessing a civil engineering degree it was a London based soft furniture cleaning business that McCulloch then started, with his partner, which still flourishes today. He is still involved in football, managing non-league side Esher United.

McEVOY, Donald William 'Don' 1954-59

Born: 3 December 1928 Golcar, Nr Huddersfield
(5ft 10½ins, 12st 7lbs – 1954)
Died: 9 October 2004 Halifax
Debut: 18 December 1954
v Wolverhampton Wanderers
Division One Home
Last Appearance: 15 February 1958
v Chelsea
Division One Home
Total League
& Cup Appearances: 112 Goals: 1

Career Details:

Kirkheaton Rovers		
Bradley United		
Huddersfield Town	29 September	1954
WEDNESDAY	17 December	1954 £20,000
Lincoln City	28 January	1959 £1,500
Barrow	June	1960

Started his playing career in Huddersfield amateur soccer as a centre forward and remained in that role during his early years as a professional at Leeds Road. However a move to centre half during the 1950-1 season totally transformed his career and he was ever present at the back as The Terriers earned promotion to the top-flight in 1953. He was also captain during that season and was a major factor in Town's surprise third placed finish back in Division One – his robust tackling and intelligent play making Don a crowd favourite. However early in the following season, ironically against Wednesday at Hillsborough, McEvoy would play his 155th and final game for Town as he suffered an injury that the Terriers' club doctor decided would ensure that his best playing days were behind him!

However other clubs differed to that opinion and several sides, including Sheffield United and Blackpool, all tried to secure his signature before he agreed to sign for Eric Taylor at Wednesday. His leadership qualities again came to the fore at Hillsborough as after suffering relegation in 1955 he captained the club to the Second Division title a year later. The arrival of Harry Catterick as Owls boss in 1958 effectively ended McEvoy's Wednesday career as neither had seen eye to eye when they had met on the playing field and Don duly moved to Lincoln as player-coach. Stayed less than six months at Sincil Bank however before his ex-Owls team mate Ron Staniforth – then Barrow manager - signed the Yorkshireman for what proved his last hurrah in league soccer.

After hanging up his boots McEvoy spent two years as Halifax Town boss before being appointed Barrow manager in August 1964. He led the Cumbrian club to the only promotion in their entire Football League history in 1967 but a few weeks later accepted a lucrative offer to take over at Grimsby Town. Unfortunately he was not backed financially by the Town board and after just six months resigned as his position became untenable. Further short spells in charge at Southport and Barrow (again) followed before he retired from football in 1971 to take over The Crown Hotel public house in Brighouse, West Yorkshire. While working as a publican he coached in amateur football and worked occasionally for a local radio station, until retiring in 1994.

McGOVERN, Jon-Paul 2004 -

Born: 3 October 1980 Glasgow
(5ft 10ins, 12st - 2004)
Debut: 7 August 2004
v Colchester United
League One Home
Total League
& Cup Appearances: 53 Goals: 8

Career Details:

Hillwood Boys Club		
Glasgow Celtic	8 June	2000
Sheffield United	13 August	2002 Five-month loan
Livingston	28 July	2003
WEDNESDAY	25 May	2004 Free

When right-winger Jon-Paul McGovern arrived at Hillsborough in May 2004 he was hoping to finally secure a regular first team place after a somewhat stop-start beginning to his career. After progressing through boys football in his native city of Glasgow, the lively and pacy attacker signed professional forms with Celtic but in three years at Celtic Park he failed to secure the breakthrough into first team football and actually played his first senior games in Sheffield - during an impressive 18-game loan spell at neighbours Sheffield United. His appearance in the shop window at Bramall Lane did however trigger a move away from Celtic as Scottish Premier League Livingston took McGovern to West Lothian. During his only season at the club JP - as he is affectionately known by fans - began in the first team but would only start eleven league games (appearing in another 16 as sub) and despite earning a Scottish League Cup winners medal he was restless to secure first team football.

These is when Chris Turner made his move and despite still having two years to run on his contract McGovern was allowed to leave Livingston on a free transfer. After impressing in pre season football he started the new season in the starting eleven and incredibly he remained there for the whole of the campaign, playing in 53 consecutive league and cup matches to become the first player since Peter Atherton, Emerson Thome and Vim Jonk were all ever present back in the 1998-99 season. Over the season his consistent wing play and infectious personality endeared him to the Owls fans and it was perhaps fitting that it was the popular Scot that netted the first goal on that incredible day in Cardiff. He is now an invaluable member of Paul Sturrock's side and after the departure of Matt Hamshaw looks set to remain an automatic choice for the foreseeable future.

McGREGOR, James 1913-14

Born:
(5ft 10ins - 1913)
Debut: 20 December 1913
v Tottenham Hotspur
Division One Away
Last Appearance: 3 January 1914
v Burnley
Division One Home
Total League
& Cup Appearances: 6 Goals: 2

Career Details:

Coatbridge		
Albion Rovers		Trial
WEDNESDAY	September	1913
Portsmouth	August	1914 £35

Forward James McGregor spent a solitary season at Hillsborough just prior to the Great War. He had originated from Scottish junior football and was actually spotted by Wednesday player Bob McSkimming in a trial game. Enjoyed a run of six consecutive games in the Owls first team when Teddy Glennon was absent and was a regular for the club's reserve side in the Midland League – finishing the season as top scorer with eleven goals. The Owls received a small fee for his services from Southern League Portsmouth in 1914 and he later joined the Army after being released by Pompey.

McILVENNY, Patrick 'Paddy' 1925-27

Born: 18 November 1900 Belfast
(5ft 7ins, 10st 6lbs – 1925)
Died: 25 February 1955 Hinckley
Only Appearance: 19 December 1925
v Blackpool Division One Away
Total League & Cup Appearances: 1 Goals: 0

Career Details:

Highfield FC		
Belfast Distillery		
Cardiff City	May	1924
WEDNESDAY	20 November	1925 £1150*
Shelbourne		
Northampton Town	November	1927 £100
Boston Town	September	1930
Hinckley United	April	1931
Linfield		1932 Guest

* Joint fee with G.Beadles

Bustling centre forward who arrived with Cardiff teammate George Beadles for a sizable fee during The Owls 1925-26 Second Division Championship season. He had originally signed for the Welsh club after impressing for Ireland against Wales in his only full International appearance but in over two years at Hillsborough was no more than a bit player, making a solitary league start in a one-nil defeat at Blackpool and making only an occasional reserve team appearance. Believed to have played for Dublin side Shelbourne while still registered with Wednesday and later joined Northampton on trial in October 1927, signing on a permanent basis a month later. Made his debut for Midland League Boston Town in September 1930 but only stayed a few weeks while he later appeared for Leicestershire side Hinckley.

McINTOSH, David "Dave" 1947-58

Born: 4 May 1925 Girvan, Ayrshire
(5ft 10½ins, 11st 2lbs – 1947)
Died: July 1995
Debut: 3 April 1948
v Fulham
Division Two Away
Last Appearance: 7 December 1957
v Aston Villa
Division One Home
Total League
& Cup Appearances: 308 Goals: 0

Career Details:

Girvan Ayrshire		
WEDNESDAY	2 October	1947 Free
Doncaster Rovers	16 January	1958

Fearless goalkeeper who spent almost ten years as undisputed No. 1 at Hillsborough, after arriving from Scottish Junior football. He had just left the Navy when the Owls heard about him by chance – on the recommendation of a Rotherham United director - and he impressed so much during a trial period that he was quickly committed to professional forms. It was the start of a meteoric rise for the goalie who was affectionately known as 'Mac' as after starting in Yorkshire League football he was quickly promoted to reserve team duty and then to the first team – all this occurring in his debut season at Wednesday! After replacing Roy Smith in the Owls net McIntosh never looked back, missing only three games over the next two seasons that culminated in promotion from Division Two in 1950. Only injuries would deny 'Mac' an ever-present record as twice inside a year he suffered a broken arm – September 1952 at home to Liverpool and August in the following year at Preston.

However he always bounced back to regain his first team place and won Second Division Championship medals in 1952 and 1956 before falling out of favour during the infamous 1957-8 campaign when Wednesday used four different goalkeepers until Ron Springett became the next truly outstanding goalkeeper to represent the club. A move to Walsall subsequently collapsed at the last minute but Doncaster manager Peter Docherty duly signed him, as replacement for Old Trafford bound Harry Gregg, His new boss actually resigned before he saw McIntosh make his Rovers debut while 'Mac' would stay for two seasons at Belle Vue, appearing in 15 games before retiring in 1959 – his final appearance in English football rather fittingly was back at Hillsborough when he was in goal for Doncaster in an April 1959 County Cup tie. Moved back to Scotland after finishing with football and worked as a delivery driver for a Fife distillery company until his retirement.

McINTOSH, Thomas 1892-94

Born: Scotland
Debut: 7 January 1893 v Aston Villa Division One Away
Last Appearance:
9 September 1893 v Blackburn Rovers Division One Away
Total League & Cup Appearances: 9 Goals: 1

Career Details:

WEDNESDAY	1892
Released	1894

Little known forward who played a cameo role in The Owls first season of league football. Appeared in eight games during that season and appeared just once more before playing out the rest of his Wednesday career in the reserve team.

McINTYRE, John McGregor 'Johnny' 1920-22

Born: 4 January 1895 Partick
(5ft 8ins, 11st – 1920)
Died: February 1974 Blackpool
Debut: 20 March 1920
v Chelsea
Division One Away
Last Appearance: 10 December 1921
v Clapton Orient Division Two Away
Total League
& Cup Appearances: 70 Goals: 36

Career Details:

Denny Athletic Juniors			
Partick Thistle	June	1912	
Fulham	February	1917	
WEDNESDAY	16 March	1920	£1750
Blackburn Rovers	6 January	1922	£3500
Blackpool	19 January	1928	
Chorley	October	1928	
Derby Co Op Welfare	January	1935	

The arrival of Johnny McIntyre was a last desperate throw of the dice by Wednesday as they tried to stave off relegation from Division One in 1920. He was one of two big money signings in the same week – the other being George Wilson – but the newcomers failed to create the desired impact and a goal shy Wednesday scored only four goals in their final ten games to condemn themselves to the drop. Goal scoring had proved a chronic problem in a season when Wednesday had the misfortune to lose not one but two of the greatest attackers in their history – Andrew Wilson retiring and David McLean moving to Bradford Park Avenue. It was in Wilson's No. 10 shirt that McIntyre made his Wednesday debut but during that debut campaign the Scot made the majority of his appearances at left halfback.

He proved a more than capable performer in the half back line – he was truly a latter day utility player – but it would be in the forward line that McIntyre made a huge impression in his first full season at Hillsborough. The Owls again failed to score freely but incredibly of the 48 league goals they did register McIntyre netted over half, scoring 27 times in 41 games. He moved to centre forward early in the campaign – after Wednesday failed to score in their first three matches and Fletcher Welsh was sent packing back to Scotland – and grabbed ten goals during a run where he scored in six consecutive games. However his scoring alerted opposition defenders and after receiving some particularly rough treatment during a game against Birmingham at Hillsborough he was sent off after retaliating. A few weeks later he moved to inside left and enjoyed another tremendous burst of scoring, netting thirteen goals in the final thirteen games of the season as The Owls finished in mid table.

However just when manager Bob Brown started to think he could build a side around his prolific forward the two parties experienced

a dramatic parting of the ways after falling out on an undisclosed issue in December 1921. He was immediately placed on the transfer list and a few days later signed for Blackburn Rovers, supposedly in a Sheffield cinema house! Wednesday fans were stunned and disappointed by his sudden departure but perhaps it was no real surprise as McIntyre had arrived at Hillsborough after falling out with the management at Fulham – after breaking a club imposed curfew. He had originally joined the London side in 1917 as a guest player after being posted to Brooklands Air Base in Surrey soon after joining the Royal Flying Corps. The former Surgical instrument maker netted nine times in 26 games for The Cottagers before moving North to Sheffield and after eighteen months at Hillsborough he made headlines in September 1922 when scoring four goals in just five minutes during Blackburn's 5-1 home win over Everton. Whilst at Ewood Park he became publican of the 'Life Boat Inn' in Blackpool and would spend his final days in league soccer at the town's football club.

McIVER, Frederick "Fred" 1974-76

Born: 14 February 1952 Birtley
(5ft 7ins, 10st 12lbs – 1975)
Debut: 17 August 1974
v Oldham Athletic Division Two Away
Last Appearance: 19 April 1976
v Mansfield Town Division Three Away
Total League
& Cup Appearances: 39+3 Goals: 0

Career Details:

Sunderland	April	1969
Racing Jet Brussels	May	1972 Free
WEDNESDAY	28 July	1974 £11,680
Gateshead	May	1976 Free

Fred McIver started his career at Birtley Youth Club from where he signed apprentice forms for Sunderland in 1966. In three years as a professional at Roker Park the versatile and composed midfielder started just one solitary league game before securing a transfer to Belgium side Racing Jet – a previously recorded move to South African football never occurred. The ex-Chester-le-Street boys player duly arrived back in England in the summer of 1974, joining Wednesday on an initial one-month trial. This was later extended by a further month and he impressed Owls boss Steve Burtenshaw sufficiently to be awarded a contract in October 1974. He actually had to sit on the sidelines for a game while the two clubs haggled over a fee – Racing demanding an exorbitant £30,000 fee – but when a deal was agreed McIver showed 100% commitment to the cause although he could not stop Wednesday tumbling out of Division Two.

He featured less in the lower grade and it was no surprise when he was one of several players to be released during the mass clear out at the end of the worst season in the club's long history. He subsequently reverted to part-time status, playing semi-professional football for Northern Premier League Gateshead and arising at 4 a.m. every morning to complete his Durham milk round. He retired from football in April 1979 while after nine years as a milkman started to run a newsagents, a role he still fulfils today whilst also owning his own post office.

McJARROW, Hugh 1950-52

Born: 29 January 1928
New Harthill, Motherwell
(5ft 9ins, 11st 4lbs – 1950)
Died: 25 July 1987 Brigstock, Northants.
Debut: 4 March 1950
v Queens Park Rangers
Division Two Away
Last Appearance: 22 September 1951
v Rotherham United Division 2 Home
Total League
& Cup Appearances: 47 Goals: 21

Career Details:

Mary Hill Juniors		
Chesterfield	March	1946
WEDNESDAY	2 March	1950 £4,500
Luton Town	12 February	1952 £5,300
Plymouth Argyle	December	1953
Peterborough United		1956
Matlock Town		1957
Clay Cross & Danesmoor MW		1959
Chesterfield Tube Works		

During the Second World War Hugh McJarrow worked down the mines as a 'Bevin Boy' before moving into professional soccer when signing for Chesterfield in the 1946 close season. He started his Saltergate career at inside forward – scoring on his debut against Spurs in September 1946 – but it was a move to centre forward at the start of the 1949-50 campaign that transformed his career. Five goals in the opening three matches of the season alerted bigger clubs to his attributes and when Eric Taylor swooped to secure his signature for Wednesday McJarrow was top soccer for the Derbyshire side. Incidentally he was signed after The Owls had failed in an audacious bid to buy Newcastle United's Chilean forward George Roblebo while the deal for McJarrow was actually struck at St.James Park during an England versus Holland match.

The Owls new forward possessed an eye for an opening and terrific heading ability with these qualities helping Wednesday to promotion from Division Two within three months of his arrival at Hillsborough. Relegation followed a year later although McJarrow did finish joint top scorer with 14 goals and was an automatic choice until early in the 1951-2 season when a youngster by the name of Derek Dooley burst onto the scene, ensuring McJarrow would spent the rest of his Owls career in the second team. Ten goals in only fifteen league games for his next club Luton Town could not stop a subsequent transfer to Plymouth where his goals dried up with McJarrow playing his best football for the club at wing half. A move to ambitious Midland League club Peterborough United was next for the Scotsman before his playing career ended in Derbyshire amateur soccer.

McKAY, Colin Campbell 1919-20

Born: 24 August 1895 Portobello
(5ft 9ins, 11st – 1919)
Debut: 20 December 1919
v Arsenal
Division One Away
Last Appearance: 26 April 1920
v Oldham Athletic
Division One Away
Total League
& Cup Appearances: 14
Goals 3

Career Details:

Thornton Hibernians		
Raith Rovers		
Cowdenbeath		1915
Heart of Midlothian	August	1918
WEDNESDAY	13 December	1919
Huddersfield Town	June	1920
Bradford City	June	1922
Aberavon	August	1924

One of many forwards Wednesday tried during the disastrous 1919-20 season in an attempt to stave off relegation from Division One. The inside forward had started his playing career in Scottish Junior soccer – winning five Cups in one season while at Thornton Hibernians – and made a great impact at Hillsborough where he scored the only goal of the game on his home debut. He scored twice more for the club but Wednesday were in desperate straits and following the inevitable relegation he was released during a mass clear out by new manager Bob Brown. Two seasons at Huddersfield Town brought forth eighteen appearances, mainly at wing half, while his playing career ended in Welsh non-league soccer.

McKEEVER, Mark Anthony 1997-2001

Born: 16 November 1978 Derry
(5ft 9ins, 11st 8lbs – 1999)
Debut: 25 April 1999
v Chelsea
Premier League Home
Last Appearance: 3 January 2000
v Arsenal
Premier League Home
Total League
& Cup Appearances 2+5 Goals: 0

Career Details:

Moorfield Youth		
Norwich City		1989 Schoolboy
Peterborough United		1994 Trainee
WEDNESDAY	2 April	1997 £375,000
Bristol Rovers	11 December	1998 Loan
Reading	9 March	1999 Loan
Bristol Rovers	7 February	2001 £50,000
Released	30 June	2003
Weston Super-Mare	21 July	2003 Free

CAPS (@ SWFC)
Eire U-21 (4) v Czech Republic 24/03/98, v Sweden 27/04/99, v Scotland 31/05/99, v N.Ireland 02/06/99

Tricky and pacy left winger who looked set for a glittering career when moving to Premier League Wednesday for a hefty fee in the spring of 1997. He was still a YTS trainee at Peterborough United when David Pleat signed McKeever and his team mate David Billington in a deal that could have risen to £1m. It was on the recommendation of Owls back room man Lil Fuccilo that Wednesday gambled on the pair as he had witnessed the teenagers talents at first hand when assistant manager at London Road. Several clubs were courting the pair but it was Wednesday who won the race, tying the highly rated duo to five-year contracts and hoping their investment would eventually bear fruit.

Started his playing career as an associate schoolboy at Norwich City, travelling over from Ireland every second weekend, but when The Canaries youth development officer moved to Peterborough, McKeever followed in his wake. After two years on schoolboys forms at United he signed YTS forms in 1994 and would make his senior bow whilst still a trainee, aged seventeen. By this time McKeever had played one game for the Northern Ireland U-17 side before deciding to pledge his future to The Republic, subsequently being capped at U-18 and U-21 levels. He was actually on Eire U-18 duty in Portugal when on phoning his mother in Ireland – from the airport – he was shocked to learn that a move to Hillsborough was on the cards!

During his early years in Sheffield he was slowly coaxed into The Owls first team squad with two highly successful loan spells at Reading contributing greatly to that aim – during his time in Berkshire McKeever was actually called into the full Eire squad although a cap did not follow. His first team bow for Wednesday finally came as a sub in a home match with high-flying Chelsea but sadly just when he seemed on the verge of a major breakthrough, at the start of the 1999-00 season, the Irishman was hit by injury problems which would dog the remainder of his time at Hillsborough. His promising career slowly started to unravel when a move to Bristol Rovers ended with The Pirates suffering relegation to the basement division for the first time in their history. He was released in the summer of 2003 and soon after joined ambitious Dr Martens League side Weston Super-Mare.

McKEOWN, Isaac Lindsay 1976-79

Born: 11 July 1957 Belfast
(5ft 9ins, 11st – 1978)
Debut: 15 December 1976
v Darlington
F.A.Cup Away
Last Appearance: 29 April 1978
v Colchester United
Division Three Away
Total League
& Cup Appearances: 7+5 Goals: 0

Career Details:

Linfield Rangers		1973
Manchester United	11 July	1974
WEDNESDAY	November	1976 Free
Linfield	31 May	1979 Free

Despite spending almost three years at Hillsborough, Lindsay McKeown struggled to make a significant impact during a period when Wednesday struggled at the wrong end of the old Third Division. He had previously played for Northern Ireland schoolboys and spent two years as a professional at Old Trafford without making a first team appearance. The striker failed to score in a dozen senior appearances for Wednesday and it was no surprise when he was allowed to return home to Ireland, joining Linfield on a free transfer.

He certainly found Irish League soccer more to his liking, as over the next ten years Lindsay was a mainstay in the Linfield side that totally dominated domestic football in the 1980s. Honours included eight league titles (including seven in a row) and two Irish Cups as well as a multitude of other trophies. He also toured Canada in 1982 as captain of the Irish League representative side while a year earlier had been called into the full Northern Ireland squad for a game in Sweden, failing to make the final sixteen that travelled. In 1989 he became one of only two footballers to have won the Ulster player of the year twice while his playing career finally came to a close in 1991 when McKeown was appointed first team coach at Linfield. He was named assistant manager a year later and remained in the role until April 1996 when he left to join BBC Radio Ulster, reporting and acting as summariser on Irish League games. Away from football McKeown became an Electrical sales rep in 1985, a job he still holds today.

McLAREN, John James Roy 'Roy' 1958-65

Born: 12 February 1930
Auchterarder, Scotland
(6ft, 11st 13lbs – 1959)
Debut: 30 March 1959
v Fulham
Division Two Home
Last Appearance: 13 January 1965
v Everton
F.A.Cup Home
Total League
& Cup Appearances: 34 Goals: 0

Career Details:

St.Johnstone Juveniles		
St. Johnstone		1948
Bury	21 December	1955 £1,300
WEDNESDAY	22 October	1958 £4,200

Despite spending seventeen years as a professional goalie Roy McLaren's greatest achievements came during ten years as coach and then assistant manager at Aston Villa. After joining the Midlands club in 1974 as first team coach he oversaw a golden period in Villa's history which not only saw the league title come to Villa Park in 1981and the European Cup a year later but also two League Cup wins, one Super Cup and one Charity Shield success. His coaching career had started back in 1967 as second team boss at Grimsby Town – under manager and ex-Owls player Don McEvoy – although in the same year he moved to Huddersfield Town in an identical role. He was on the coaching staff at the West Yorkshire club when Town won promotion to the top-flight in 1970 and was first team coach for two years before departing for Aston Villa in 1974. Following his successful decade at Villa Park he then spent two years scouting for a variety of managers, including Bobby Robson at Ipswich and Lawrie McMenemy at Southampton, before moving to Melbourne in Australia for an intended two-year stay.

He emigrated to the Southern Hemisphere with his brother David – who was also a goalkeeper for several English and Scottish league sides including Leicester City and Wolves – and along with four other partners the siblings set up a Superannuation Consultancy business that subsequently flourished. He has remained in Australia ever since and while down under coached Northcote City, Heidelberg United, Altona Gate and lastly Moorabbin City. In 1999 he went into semi-retirement and now spends his time with his grandchildren (two of his children followed their father to Australia) and on the golf course.

His playing career had started in his native Scotland, first coming to prominence with St Johnstone boys. Between 1946 and 1951 he was a part-time player while completing an electrical engineering apprenticeship but was then called up for National Service, subsequently playing for the full Army football team whilst being stationed for a time at the Suez Canal. After returning to St.Johnstone in February 1953 Roy retained his semi-professional status but did finally turn pro in 1955 when moving south to sign for Bury. Played in 88 league games for The Shakers before the steady and reliable keeper became the first ever signing of new Wednesday manager Harry Catterick. The newcomer played in the final eight games of the season as The Owls won the Second Division Championship but during almost seven years at Hillsborough McLaren had to play the role of understudy to England International Ron Springett. In that time he never let the club down when standing in for his rival and his excellent fitness record saw Roy play in over 160 reserve team games. It was therefore ironic that a serious back injury would then force his early retirement from the game in May 1965. During his afternoons off at Wednesday, McLaren had been training as a sales rep for Sheffield based Hallamshire Electric Co. and when his career came to premature end he gained a full time position with the company, prior to starting his Australian adventure.

McLAREN, Paul Andrew 2001-04

Born: 17 November 1976 High Wycombe
(6ft, 13st, 4lbs – 2000)
Debut: 12 August 2001 v Burnley Division One Home
Last Appearance:
8 May 2004 v Queens Park Rangers Division Two Home
Total League & Cup Appearances: 92+14 Goals: 9

Career Details:

Bourne End		1988 (sun.)
Missenden		1990 (sun.)
Luton Town	5 January	1994
WEDNESDAY	7 June	2001 Free
Released	30 June	2004
Rotherham United	28 July	2004 Free

Creative midfield player who arrived on a surprise ‘Bosman’ free transfer in the summer of 2001 after Wednesday fought off competition from Cardiff City for his services. Before moving to Hillsborough McLaren had experienced a mixed time at Luton where after joining as a trainee he had progressed to become a first team regular by the mid-1990s. Injury then blighted his progress for two seasons before he bounced back to be almost ever present during the 2000-1 season - his form alerting several clubs to his qualities. After 201 games for the Kenilworth Road club the former High Wycombe and Bucks County boys player became an automatic choice as The Owls struggled to adapt to life in Division One.

His debut season at Hillsborough was solid if unspectacular while a combination of injury and inconsistent form then saw his Wednesday career disrupted over the final two years of his contract. On his day McLaren was an incisive passer of the ball who possessed a thunderous shot but despite appearing in over one hundred games for the club he failed to really stamp his authority on the midfield and could do little as The Owls slipped down the divisions and into financial crisis.

McLEAN, David Prophet ‘Davie’ 1911-19

Born: 13 December 1887 Forfar
(5ft 7½ins, 11st 10lbs – 1911)
Died: 21 December 1967 Forfar
Debut: 18 February 1911
v Bury
Division One Home
Last Appearance: 6 September 1919
v Middlesbrough
Division One Away
Total League
& Cup Appearances: 147 Goals: 100

Career Details:

Forfar Half-Holiday		1903
Forfar West End		1905
Glasgow Celtic	March	1905 Trial
Forfar Celtic		1906
Forfar Athletic	9 March	1907
Glasgow Celtic	16 April	1907 £50
Forfar Athletic	18 April	1907 Loan
Ayr F.C.	17 April	1909 Loan
Preston North End	5 November	1909 £400
WEDNESDAY	16 February	1911 £1000
Forfar Athletic	19 May	1913 Loan*
WEDNESDAY	28 December	1914 £250
Dykehead	4 September	1915 Guest
Third Lanark	18 December	1915 Guest
Glasgow Rangers	2 July	1918 Guest
Bradford Park Avenue	23 October	1919 £2,000
Dundee	October	1921
Forfar Athletic	May	1922
Dundee	4 August	1922
Forfar Athletic	20 August	1926
Dykehead		1932

*Wednesday held his registration

CAPS (@SWFC) Scotland Full (1) v England 13/03/12

Without doubt the greatest Owls centre forward of the pre Great War era and certainly rival to the likes of Allen, Dooley, Layne and Hirst for the title of Wednesday’s most outstanding No. 9 of all time. McLean was a real penalty box predator who after arriving for a club record fee would be a key figure as Wednesday competed for Championship honours in the years immediately before the First World War. The Owls agonisingly missed out on the title in 1913, finishing third, with the Scotsman’s smashing the club’s scoring records by becoming the first player to net thirty league goals in a single season. He had grabbed twenty-five goals in the previous campaign but Wednesday fans were stunned in May 1913 when their prolific scorer sensationally returned home to Forfar after The Owls declined to grant his request for a three-year contract and guaranteed benefit of £450 – in those days the power was certainly with the clubs and Wednesday had stubbornly only offered the basic one-year deal!

Incredibly he would remain in Scotland until the end of the year when Wednesday did persuade him to return to Sheffield – the club had been unsurprisingly unable to replace him and were under pressure from the Hillsborough crowd who wanted their goalscorer back. To re-sign McLean on professional forms Wednesday actually had to pay Forfar a transfer fee but it was money well spent as on his return he was straight back into the scoring groove, Davie netting his third seasonal haul in excess of twenty league goals before the War brought an end to National soccer in 1915. At the outbreak of war McLean – who was noted for the power and accuracy of his shooting – was employed in Glasgow on work of ‘national importance’ and signed professional forms for Clydebank in September 1915. However at the time Anglo-Scots were not allowed to appear for Scottish professional sides and he failed to play a game for his new team after being reported to the authorities. Instead he started to play for a Miners team called Dykehead who were based in the village of Shotts and competed in the Scottish Western League. Within a few weeks however the ban on Anglo-Scots was lifted and Davie signed for Third Lanark before making a huge impact as a guest at Rangers in the final season of wartime soccer, finishing top scorer with 29 goals as the Glasgow giants finished runners-up to Celtic but lifted the Glasgow Charity Cup.

When the hostilities came to end McLean returned to Sheffield but only appeared in the opening three games of the 1919-20 season before being sold for a club record fee – the transfer being clinched in a Sheffield Cinema house. He scored the only goal of the game on his debut for Avenue and later played alongside his brother George before returning to Scotland in 1922 after netting an outstanding 55 times in just 92 games. Back in his hometown Davie became landlord of the Strathmore Bar and spent four years playing for Dundee – earning a Scottish Cup runners-up medal in 1925 - before finally retiring from the game in his mid forties after several seasons back at Forfar Athletic and then Dykehead. He remained licensee of his public house until retiring and was also Partick Thistle assistant trainer and Scottish scout for Huddersfield Town in the 1940s and 1950s. He remained a huge celebrity in his hometown all of his life and attended Forfar matches until his death in 1967.

It was obvious from an early age that McLean would make headlines on the football field as his playing career had started at the age of just thirteen when he appeared for a team which mostly contained 18 year-olds. After playing for several local sides he moved to Celtic – being loaned back to Forfar within 48 hours - but would score eleven times in just ten games during the 1907-8 season before winning the League title with The Parkhead club a year later. He also appeared for Celtic in the infamous 'Old Firm' 1909 Scottish Cup Final replay that was abandoned after a riot with the Cup being withheld by the F.A. He eventually left Celtic on a matter of principle and started a career at Preston which eventually led to his arrival at Hillsborough.

Incidentally previously published works have stated that Davie McLean also played for Dundee and managed Bristol Rovers, East Fife and Hearts. However this was actually a totally different individual of the same name who has caused confusion amongst historians and actually passed away in February 1951.

McMAHON, Lewis 2004-05

Born: 2 May 1985 Doncaster
(5ft 10ins, 10st 1lbs - 2004)
Debut: 20 January 2004
v Scunthorpe United
A.M.S.Cup Home
Last Appearance:
12 May 2005
v Brentford
League One Play Off S/F Home
Total League
& Cup Appearances: 25+6 Goals: 2

Career Details:

Nottingham Forest		1997 Schoolboy
Edenthorpe Cougars		2001
WEDNESDAY		2001 Scholar
WEDNESDAY	1 July	2004
Notts County	5 July	2005

Attacking midfielder whose first team chance came early when The Owls were hit by horrendous injury problems part way through the 2003-4 season. His first taste of senior action came in the LDV Vans Northern Semi-Final win over Scunthorpe United at Hillsborough and the 18 year-old was subsequently named as sub, along with several fellow teenagers, for a number of league games before making a surprise and outstanding full league debut in the Hillsborough win over Barnsley in March 2004. He had initially joined the club at the age of 14 after two years at the Nottingham Forest academy where he played at right back or as a defensive midfielder. After severing his ties with Forest, McMahon scored six times in his only game for a Doncaster based Sunday League side and within a week had joined Wednesday.

He signed three-year scholarship forms in 2001 and during his first year persuaded his coach to try him in a more advanced role. His new midfield/striker role gave McMahon a new lease of life and he made his reserve team debut in November 2001 at Manchester United. A technically proficient player who is dangerous both in and out of the penalty area, McMahon progressed in every season at the club and succeeded in securing a one year professional deal when his trainee contract expired in the summer of 2004. During the early stages of the following season McMahon was a regular, netting his first senior goal during a win at Blackpool in August 2004, but after succumbing to injury he was left frustrated on the sidelines as the Owls secured a play off place. The teenager regained his squad place in April 2005 and made a sub appearance in the semi-final win over Brentford but was given a free by the Owls in the aftermath of the Cardiff celebrations.

McMORDIE, Alexander 'Eric' 1974

Born: 12 August 1946 Belfast
(5ft 7ins, 10st 4lbs – 1974)
Debut: 19 October 1974
v Hull City
Division Two Home
Last Appearance: 13 December 1974
v Oldham Athletic
Division Two Home
Total League
& Cup Appearances: 9 Goals: 6

Career Details:

Manchester United	August	1961 Trial
Glentoran		
Dundela Club		1961
Middlesbrough	7 September	1964
WEDNESDAY	16 October	1974 Two month loan
York City	May	1975
Hartlepool United	December	1976

The youngest of thirteen children, from a depressed area of East Belfast, Eric McMordie was an experienced 21-cap Northern Ireland International when he joined The Owls on a month's loan. The attacker made an immediate impact in a struggling Wednesday side, netting on his debut, and such was the club's impotence in front of goal in that nightmare 1974-5 season that McMordie's final haul of six goals made him the club's top scorer even though he only appeared in roughly twenty percent of the games! He had first crossed the Irish Sea, along with a fellow hopeful called George Best, for trials at Manchester United in the early 1960s but the pair soon returned home due to homesickness with McMordie instead signing for Belfast club Glentoran. Luckily the youngster was given a second chance by Middlesbrough three years later and after a successful trial was duly offered professional terms by the Teeside club.

McMordie – who was known by his nickname of Eric although his name was Alexander – would spend over ten years at Boro where he usually occupied an inside forward berth. In total he netted 25 times in 273 games for Middlesbrough but the arrival of Jack Charlton in 1973 saw Eric out in the cold and subsequently loaned to Wednesday. Throughout his time at Hillsborough the Irishman made it clear that he intended to return to Boro to fight for his place and despite The Owls attempts to persuade him to move permanently he did return North at the end of a highly successful loan spell. Frustratingly for Wednesday he did move to Yorkshire at the end of the season but York City was his destination and not an Owls side that without McMordie had scored a pitiful two goals in their final seventeen games of the season to slump into Division Three.

Forty-two league games followed at City before his contract was cancelled in December 1976 and McMordie wrapped up his league career with just four matches at Hartlepool United. Since the late 1960s McMordie had combined a playing career with a sales and later management position with a Northeast Builders Merchants but on retiring from football he changed careers, moving into the retail business where he now runs a food and alcoholic store in Middlesbrough.

McSKIMMING, Robert Scott 'Bob' 1910-20

Born: 1888 Hamilton
(5ft 10ins, 12st 8lbs – 1913)
Died: December 1952 Dunedin, New Zealand
Debut: 14 March 1910
v Tottenham Hotspur
Division One Home
Last Appearance: 14 February 1920
v Preston North End
Division One Away
Total League
& Cup Appearances: 194* Goals: 0
*** Also appeared in 2 wartime games**

Career Details:

Douglas Park FC		
Albion Rovers	20 September	1907
WEDNESDAY	10 February	1910 £165*
Wilshaw Thistle		1915
Motherwell	22 January	1916 Guest
Albion Rovers	23 June	1920 £35
Ayr United	January	1923
Hilenburg	29 September	1923
Auchin Sharry Juveniles	July	1928
Denny Hibs		

* Also 'donated' £35 to Albion in January 1913

Utility defensive player Bob McSkimming was a vital cog in the outstanding Wednesday side of the years immediately preceding The Great War. Equally adept at left back or half back 'Big Bob'- as he was affectionately known at Hillsborough – possessed great speed and tackling ability and was said not to "run around needlessly". Throughout his stay in Sheffield, McSkimming was an automatic choice and it was only the advent of War that brought his spell of first team football to an end – when the hostilities began Bob initially stayed in Sheffield and returned to his original trade of a moulder. As the conflict worsened he returned to Scotland to continue with his war work whilst also playing for Western League Wilshaw Thistle in Regional soccer. He later guested for Motherwell before returning to Wednesday for the first season of post war soccer.

Sadly Wednesday were ill equipped for league soccer and an over reliance on many of their 'old guard' led to relegation and the end of McSkimming's time in English soccer. His career then duly turned full circle when he rejoined Albion Rovers – his original move to Wednesday had caused such outrage amongst Rovers members that a demonstration was held at the first game following his departure, which Albion managed to lose 4-0! He later emigrated to New Zealand where he passed away in the early 1950s

McWHINNIE, William G. 1900-01

Born: (5ft 8ins)
Debut: 1 September 1900
v Manchester City
Division One Away
Last Appearance: 16 February 1901
v Blackburn Rovers
Division One Home
Total League
& Cup Appearances: 9 Goals: 0

Career Details:

Reading		
Ayr	8 June	1896
Third Lanark	4 May	1898
WEDNESDAY	1 May	1900 £75
Released		1901
Hibernian		1905
Staten Island F.C (US)		

Right-winger who arrived from Scottish side Third Lanark as a direct replacement for Archie Brash. He started the first game of the new season – a 2-2 draw at Manchester City – but could not nail down a regular first team spot and after mostly playing reserve team football was released at the end of the season. He later returned to Scottish football and after ending his professional career in the UK emigrated to New York City in the US. Over the pond he entered the silk business and in 1915 was still playing football for a local New York side.

MEGSON, Donald Harry 'Don' 1953-70

Born: 12 June 1936 Sale, Cheshire
(5ft 10ins, 11st 4lbs – 1956)
Debut: 14 November 1959
v Burnley
Division One Home
Last Appearance: 24 January 1970
v Scunthorpe United
F.A.Cup Home
Total League
& Cup Appearances: 442 Goals: 7

Career Details:

Mossley		
WEDNESDAY	21 October	1952 Amat.
WEDNESDAY	19 June	1953 £50
Bristol Rovers	14 March	1970 Free

CAPS (@SWFC)
Football League (1) v Italian League 01/11/60

When Don Megson signed as an amateur outside left from Cheshire League side Mossley in 1952 few would have guessed that 'Meg' would serve the club for eighteen years and become second only to the legendary Ernie Blenkinsop as the greatest left back to ever represent the club. The ex-Lancashire boys player served a long apprenticeship in Wednesday's youth and reserve sides, playing in several different positions before finally settling into a half back role. However after Megson completed his two-year National Service in 1959 it was the intervention of Wednesday boss Harry Catterick that would totally transform his career. The Owls manager decided to give Megson a run out at left back and after a further fifteen Central League games in his new role Megson was given his first team chance in the 1-1 draw with Burnley at Hillsborough.

After making the vital breakthrough 'Meg' was almost unchallenged for ten seasons, helping Wednesday to runners-up spot behind Spurs in 1961 and the last eight of the Fairs Cup a year later before captaining the club in the 1966 F.A.Cup Final – leading the club on an unprecedented lap of honour despite suffering a heartbreaking defeat. His passion and simple enjoyment of playing the game quickly made Megson a big favourite with Wednesday fans but it was his strong physique, robust tackling and terrific distribution that ensured the flame haired full back would remain a first choice in Division One football for Wednesday throughout the 1960s. He was perhaps unfortunate to only earn one minor representative honour – appearing for a Football League eleven in Milan – and that what proved to be his final game in a Wednesday shirt came in a shock Hillsborough Cup loss to basement club Scunthorpe United. At the start of his final season at Wednesday 'Meg' had been awarded a deserved benefit game – an International XI drawing 7-7 with Wednesday in front of 11,000 – and in March 1970 was granted a free transfer in recognition of his service to the club.

Half a dozen clubs chased his signature but the chance of becoming player-coach at Bristol Rovers secured a move to the West Country. After adding 31 appearances to his career tally Megson retired from playing and was appointed boss at Rovers in July 1972, leading The Pirates to promotion and Watney Cup success before resigning in November 1977 to take over at NASL club Portland Timbers. He returned home in 1980 and after a spell out of the game took over as Bournemouth manager in March 1983. However his new side were in trouble behind the scenes and Don stayed only six months before tendering his resignation. Financially secure after his various coaching roles, Don later scouted part-time for his son Gary for Norwich, Stockport County, Blackpool and West Brom.

MEGSON, Gary John 1981-84 & 1985-89

Born: 2 May 1959 Manchester
(5ft 10ins, 11st 6lbs – 1983)
Debut: 29 August 1981
v Blackburn Rovers
Division Two Away
Last Appearance: 2 January 1989
v Coventry City
Division One Away
Total League
& Cup Appearances: 283+3 Goals: 33

Career Details:

Frampton Rangers		
Parkway Juniors		
Mangotsfield		
Plymouth Argyle	9 May	1977
Everton	13 February	1980 £250,000
WEDNESDAY	7 August	1981 £108,500
Nottingham Forest	2 August	1984 £170,000
Newcastle United	23 November	1984 £110,000
WEDNESDAY	20 December	1985 £60,000
Manchester City	5 January	1989 £250,000
Norwich City	12 July	1992 Free
Lincoln City	26 July	1995 N/C
Shrewsbury Town	8 September	1995 N/C

Stylish midfielder who was the son of former Owls captain Don Megson. The younger Megson spent his teenage years in the South West, where his father was boss at Bristol Rovers, and first started playing organised football at his Ridings High School before being attached to several youth sides and also representing Gloucestershire boys. Although he was on schoolboy forms at Bristol Rovers it would be West Country rivals Plymouth Argyle who signed Wednesdayite Megson as a trainee in August 1975. He quickly broke into the first team after turning professional two years later and his energetic and eye-catching displays soon saw a move into the big-time at Everton after 92 games for The Pilgrims.

However, in just under two years at Goodison Park Megson was in and out of the first team and after failing to become established jumped at the chance to join his boyhood heroes Wednesday. It was this first spell at Wednesday that is most fondly remembered by Owls fans as the carrot topped Megson missed only three games in his first three seasons at Hillsborough with his tremendously consistent form helping Wednesday to the semi-final of the F.A.Cup in 1983 and a long-awaited return to the top-flight a year later. Surprisingly he then decided to join Brian Clough's Nottingham Forest but it was a move that he was soon to regret as during a nightmare four months at The City Ground Gary failed to play a league game and was even publicly criticised by his unpredictable manager. His old boss at Wednesday, Jack Charlton, then effectively saved Megson's career by taking him to Newcastle United but when 'Big Jack' left Megson was soon 'out in the cold' again and soon after was back at Hillsborough, initially on a month's loan. He was soon back in his old groove at the heart of The Owls midfield – appearing in the 1986 F.A.Cup semi-final loss to his old club Everton - but he returned to an Owls side in decline and the resignation of Howard Wilkinson and appointment of Peter Eustace effectively brought a premature end to his Wednesday career. The new manager and Megson subsequently had a very public fall out and days later the latter was transferred across The Pennines.

Played in just under one hundred games for City before a three-year spell at Norwich gave Megson his first coaching experience – he was appointed assistant manager in July 1994 and was caretaker boss from April 1995 until the end of the season. A change at boardroom level resulted in his release soon after and he played briefly as a non-contract player at both Lincoln City and Hartlepool United before being appointed First Team coach at Bradford City in November 1995. Within a month he completed a somewhat meteoric rise to management when being appointed Norwich manager but sadly at the time the club was in turmoil behind the scenes and he was handed a thankless task, eventually resigning his position in June 1996. He was not out of work long though and would polish his managerial skills at Blackpool (July 1996- July 1997), Stockport County (July 1997 – June 1999) and Stoke City (July 1999 – November 1999). He was dismissed from his role at Stoke when an Icelandic consortium took over the club but City's loss proved to be West Brom's gain as the Midlands side appointed Megson in March 2000 following the departure of Alan Little. During his time at The Hawthorns he earned a reputation as one of the brightest young managers in the English game as he led Albion to the play offs in his first season before clinching promotion to the Premier League in 2002. Despite being relegated straight back to The Football League the Baggies board persevered with Megson and he rewarded their faith by steering Albion back into the top-flight at the first attempt. However his somewhat troublesome relationship with the Albion board eventually resulted in Megson being relieved of his duties in October 2004. Three months later he was back in employment after being appointed boss as Championship strugglers Nottingham Forest

MELIA, James 'Jimmy' 1895-98

Born: Darlington
Died: February 1905 Darlington
Debut: 5 September 1896 v Everton Division One Away
Last Appearance:
1 January 1898 v Nottingham Forest Division One Home
Total League & Cup Appearances: 7 Goals: 0

Career Details:

WEDNESDAY		1895
Tottenham Hotspur	May	1898
Preston North End	July	1901 £25*

*Fee paid to Wednesday

Full back who acted as understudy to Jack Earp for two seasons, occasionally replacing his rival but mainly spending his Owls career in reserve team soccer – helping Wednesday to the United Counties League title in 1898. After joining Southern League Spurs he played 14 games during his new club's Championship success in 1900 and came back into the Football League at Preston – the Lancashire club paying Wednesday a small transfer fee as they held his registration. However he appeared in only two league games for Preston and his story has a sad ending as he passed away at the tender age of only 30 after suddenly falling ill.

MELLOR, Ian 1979-82

Born: 19 February 1950 Sale,
Manchester
(6ft 2ins, 11st 12lbs – 1981)
Debut: 11 August 1979
v Hull City
League Cup Home
Last Appearance: 8 May 1982
v Bolton Wanderers
Division Two Away
Total League
& Cup Appearances: 61+18 Goals:11

Career Details:

Blackpool		1966 Trial
Bury		1966 Amat.
Manchester City	18 December	1969
Norwich City	8 March	1973 £70,000
Brighton & Hove Albion	6 May	1974 £40,000
Chester	24 February	1978 £24,000
WEDNESDAY	11 June	1979 £50,000
Contract cancelled	31 May	1982
Bradford City	23 June	1982 Free
Tung Sing	February	1984 Free
Worksop Town	September	1984
Parramore Sports	September	1985
Matlock Town		1987
Gainsborough Trinity		1987
Burton Albion		1987
Kiverton Park		1987

Ian 'Spider' Mellor could in reality be called a one-season wonder for The Owls as the majority of his appearances, and all of his goals, came in his debut campaign as Wednesday climbed out of the old Third Division. The agile striker cum winger – who was given his nickname due to his long legs – played an integral part in that promotion campaign and will forever be remembered with affection by Wednesday fans for his spectacular long-range effort in the 'Boxing Day massacre' game against United. However his opportunities in the higher grade of football were limited and after his contract was cancelled by mutual consent he moved to West Yorkshire.

At the age of 15 Mellor had started his working life as a warehouse man and was also employed as a store man and postman before signing professional forms with hometown club Manchester City. After breaking into the first team at City, Mellor won a Charity Shield medal in 1972 but after forty senior games was signed by Brighton manager Brian Clough – at the time he was Albion's record signing. His best spell in league soccer game on the South Coast where Mellor totalled 122 games before returning north to sign for Chester. After leaving Hillsborough his spell at Bradford City was a brief and unhappy one before Mellor spent six months in Hong Kong. He was out of work for four months after returning home but then spent a year as a salesman for a Leeds Company and a year in the same role for a safety & hygiene equipment business based in Chesterfield.

While forging a career outside of the game he continued to play football on a part-time basis, appearing firstly for Northern Premier League Worksop Town before dropping way down the non-league pyramid to play for Sheffield County Senior League minnows Parramore Sports. He later played a solitary game for Gainsborough and also just one match for Burton when Neil Warnock was in charge. After finally ending his playing days Mellor – whose son Neil made his Premier League debut for Liverpool in January 2003 - became a sales rep for two sportswear manufacturers before in 1993 being appointed to his current position, working as a commercial executive at the P.F.A. in Manchester.

MELLOR, William "Billy" 1893-95

Born:
Only Appearance: 23 March 1894 v Burnley Division One Away
Total League & Cup Appearances: 1 Goals: 0

Career Details:

Heywood Central		
Sheffield United	June	1892
WEDNESDAY	June	1893
Loughborough Town	May	1895

When defender Billy Mellor made his sole appearance for The Owls during the 1893-4 season he entered the Sheffield records books as the first player to represent both of the City's professional clubs in league soccer. In 1892-3 Mellor – whose name has also been spelt as Mellars – appeared in sixteen competitive games for United and he would spend two seasons at Olive Grove, helping the Wednesday reserve side to win the Sheffield & Hallamshire Cup League in 1895. Later played for league side Loughborough before dropping out of senior football in 1896.

MELLORS, Richard Dugdale 'Dick' 1925-31

Born: Mansfield, (5ft 11ins, 12st 7lbs - 1925)
Died: October 1960 Sydney, Australia
Debut:
12 February 1927 v Huddersfield Town Division One Away
Last Appearance:
8 September 1930 v Chelsea Division One Home
Total League & Cup Appearances: 14 Goals: 0

Career Details:

Mansfield Woolhouse Exchange		1918
Welbeck Athletic		
Chesterfield		1920 Amat.
Mansfield Town	summer	1921 Amat.
WEDNESDAY	22 December	1925 £10*
Reading	21 May	1931 £150
Bournemouth & Boscombe	June	1934 Free
Queen of the South	December	1937
Lincoln City	October	1939 Guest

*Donation to Welbeck

Solid and consistent goalkeeper who spent his early playing days in Derbyshire non-league soccer, appearing for Mansfield Town in 1921-22 during their inaugural season in the Midland Counties League. He was strictly amateur at Town and initially signed for Wednesday on the same basis in May 1925, following several trial games with the Owls reserve side in the spring of 1924. When signing for the club the legendary Teddy Davison was the man in possession of the first team shirt with newcomer Jack Brown acting as understudy. However soon after Mellors signed as a professional at Hillsborough one of his rivals, Davison, was appointed player-manager at Mansfield Town and it was now a two-horse race for the first team jersey. Unfortunately for Mellors his rival Brown had been ever present during the club's 1926 Second Division title success and of course would remain an automatic choice for almost fifteen years, leaving Mellors to act as a patient understudy.

He would spend almost six years in that role, making the occasional first team start as well as helping the reserves to the 1929 Central League Championship. A move to Division Three (South) side Reading came next for Mellors where despite appearing in 92 games he is probably best remembered for a remarkable incident in January 1933 when a match versus Millwall was abandoned due to thick fog but when the Reading players returned to the dressing room they found Dick was nowhere to be seen – he was still stood between the sticks blissfully unaware that the referee had called off the game! The outbreak of the Second World War effectively ended his football career while in 1950 Mellors was appointed as Bournemouth trainer. However in 1954 he emigrated to Australia to be with his daughter – she had married old Bournemouth secretary Tommy Locks – but sadly died of lung cancer six years later.

MEREDITH, John Frederick 1961-62

Born: 23 September 1940 Dunsville, Doncaster
(5ft 8ins, 10st 10lbs – 1961)
Only Appearance: 11 March 1961 v Wolverhampton Wanderers Division One Home
Total League & Cup Appearances: 1 Goals: 0

Career Details:

Doncaster Rovers	January	1958
WEDNESDAY	6 February	1961 £7,000 + J.Ballagher
Chesterfield	1 July	1962 £1,000
Gillingham	March	1964 £4,500
Bournemouth & Boscombe	August	1969 £10,000
Hastings United	August	1972

Former Doncaster and Yorkshire boys left-winger who joined local side Doncaster Rovers as a trainee in 1955. After turning pro he broke into the first team at Belle Vue and his form persuaded The Owls to bid £5,000 for his services in January 1961. This was rejected but three weeks later Rovers accepted a player + cash bid that finally saw Meredith move to Hillsborough after eight goals in fifty-eight games for Donny. Harry Catterick signed him for Wednesday but after giving Meredith his first senior start in an Owls shirt – a nil-nil draw at Hillsborough – he resigned in April 1961 to leave the newcomer somewhat out in the cold under the new regime. In fact it marked the end of his senior career at Hillsborough and he soon transferred to Chesterfield in an attempt to kick-start his career. Incidentally while at both Wednesday and Chesterfield Meredith sold ice cream during the summer months – working for the family of ex-Owl player Len Masserella.

His career got firmly back on track at Saltergate where in a two-season stay he was almost ever present before enjoying the best years of his career at Gillingham. Developed into a superb crosser of the ball at the Kent club and from joining in March 1964 appeared in 192 consecutive league and cup games – a club record that still stands today. After 228 games for Gillingham he then spent three years at Bournemouth & Boscombe – playing in the side that knocked top-flight Wednesday out of the League Cup in

1969 – where his playing career came to abrupt halt in September 1970 when suffering a badly broken leg in a match against Workington. He never fully recovered from the injury and failed to make another senior appearance, playing only second team football at Boscombe and in non-league football during a brief four-month tenure as player-manager at Hastings United. Later he received a pay out from an insurance company with regard to his injury and when the rep called he joked that he could do his job. The rep took the comment seriously and got Meredith an interview - he was subsequently hired which enabled him to return to his Yorkshire roots. Meredith – who had not seen his father for 46 years until being reunited with him in 2000 - later worked as a Division Administrator for the Combined Insurance Company of America and now lives in York.

MILLAR, Harry 1899-1901

Born: 1874 Paisley, Scotland
(5ft 9ins. 12st)
Debut: 2 September 1899
v Chesterfield
Division Two Home
Last Appearance: 23 March 1901
v Liverpool Division Two Away
Total League
& Cup Appearances: 34 Goals: 16

Career Details:

Paisley Abercon		
Glasgow Celtic		
Preston North End		1893
Bury		1894
Reading	14 May	1898
WEDNESDAY	29 June	1899 £100
Queens Park Rangers	August	1901

Centre forward who signed from non-league Reading after having initially made his name back in his native Scotland – Wednesday paying the transfer fee to his previous club, Bury, who held his Football League registration. His debut for Wednesday came in the club's first ever game at Hillsborough and Millar made a perfect start – netting twice in a resounding 5-1 win over Chesterfield. It was the start of a tremendous debut campaign for the Scotsman as his fourteen league goals in just twenty-eight games helped his new club to run away with the Second Division Championship, twelve months after suffering relegation from the top-flight. Sadly his second season at Hillsborough could not have been of a greater contrast as not only did new signing, and fellow Scot, Andrew Wilson take his first team place but he also hit off the field problems that hastened his departure from Wednesday in the following summer – he was suspended without pay in October 1900 after failing to attend training.

MILLER, James 'Jimmy' 1909-14

Born: Glasgow
(5ft 8$^3/_4$ins, 11st 6lbs – 1913)
Debut: 4 January 1913
v Middlesbrough
Division One Away
Last Appearance: 14 February 1914
v Aston Villa
Division One Home
Total League
& Cup Appearances: 31 Goals: 0

Career Details:

Maryhill		
WEDNESDAY	May	1909
Airdrie	June	1914 £300

Former Scottish Junior International who arrived with Finlay Weir from amateur club Maryhill. He played three full seasons of reserve team football at Wednesday before finally getting a first team opportunity part way through the 1912-13 season when right halfback Tom Brittleton was absent. Helped Wednesday to a 2-0 away win on his debut and appeared in seven further league games until the end of the season as The Owls just missed out on the First Division title. Was picked ahead of stalwart Brittleton four games into the next campaign and retained his place for a run of 22 consecutive games, initially in a defensive role but later at both centre-forward and inside-left. Surprisingly after finally showing his worth in senior football for Wednesday the club's hierarchy decided his services were no longer needed and he returned to Scotland.

MILLER, John 1893-94

Born: Dumbarton
Debut: 2 September 1893 v Sunderland Division One Home
Last Appearance: 15 January 1894 v Darwen Division One Home
Total League & Cup Appearances: 13 Goals: 8

Career Details:

Dumbarton		
Liverpool		1892
WEDNESDAY	Summer	1893
Airdrie		1894 £25

Centre-forward who played a big role in the early days of Scottish League football. His club Dumbarton shared the inaugural Championship title in 1891 with Glasgow Rangers – Miller scoring twice in two appearances, including a goal in the play-off match with Rangers which ended two apiece after The Gers had been leading two-nil. The season after Miller was a regular-appearing in 24 of 26 games – and his haul of 17 goals helped Dumbarton to win the league outright. This form of course alerted clubs South of the border to his qualities but his destination was a surprise – ambitious Lancashire League side Liverpool. He found non-league soccer to his liking and netted a tremendous 27 times in only 28 league and cup games in what proved to be The Reds final season as a non-league outfit.

However he was not on Merseyside when Liverpool were elected into the Football League as The Owls had captured his signature in order to increase their firepower in advance of their second season of league soccer. He made a great start at Wednesday, netting a brace on debut, and although The Owls struggled Miller continued to net on average a goal every two games. Lost his place as the New Year dawned and appeared in only two senior games and one reserve fixture before returning home to Scotland in the summer.

The John Miller who appeared for Wednesday is now believed not to be the player of the same name who later played for Derby County and Bolton Wanderers.

MILLER, Walter 1907-08

Born: 1882 Newcastle
(5ft 10$^1/_2$ins, 11st 10lbs – 1907)
Debut: 28 March 1908
v Manchester United
Division One Away
Last Appearance: 8 April 1908
v Middlesbrough
Division One Away
Total League
& Cup Appearances: 3 Goals: 0

Career Details:

Wallsend Park Villa		
WEDNESDAY		1907
West Ham United		1908
Blackpool		1909
Lincoln City	May	1911
Merthyr Town	January	1914
Dundee	August	1914

The inflexibility of the old 3-2-5 formation was no more typified than in the experience of prolific scorer Walter Miller. The Owls had signed Miller – who played at inside or centre forward - after he had scored 40 goals for non-league club Wallsend and he became an instant success in the club's Midland League side, netting four goals on his home debut. The reserves would walk away with the Championship and Miller finished second top scorer with 25 goals but his experience of first team soccer must have left the Geordie somewhat confused. He was drafted into the side for the visit to Manchester United but with 'Andra' Wilson in possession of the No.9 jersey Miller was inexplicably given a place in the middle of Wednesday's defensive line! The Owls lost 4-1 and Miller was then given the centre forward role in the home win over Blackburn Rovers seven days later. Unbelievably though for the next game at Middlesbrough he was again picked back in defence as Wednesday crashed 6-1! This of course proved to be his final first team game and it was back to reserve team football with Walter not really being given a fair crack of the whip in League soccer.

Left Wednesday in the following summer and after a relatively unsuccessful spell at Southern League West Ham United he spent two seasons at Blackpool, playing only six league games and failing to score. Later helped Lincoln City win the Central League Championship in 1912 – scoring twenty times – and netted his first goals in league soccer during the 1913-14 season after The Imps were voted back into the Football League. However he also hit disciplinary problems at the Lincolnshire club, twice being fined for missing training and general misconduct.

MILLERSHIP, Walter 'Harry/Walt' 1930-46

Born: 8 June 1910 Warsop Vale, Notts
(5ft 10ins, 11st 9lbs – 1930)
Died: 1978 Brimington, nr Chesterfield
Debut: 5 April 1930
v Liverpool
Division One Away
Last Appearance: 15 April 1939
v Nottingham Forest
Division Two Home
Total League
& Cup Appearances: 236* Goals: 34
***Also appeared in**
155 wartime games, scoring 12 goals

Career Details:

Warsop Main		
Welbeck Athletic		1926
Shirebrook F.C.	December	1927
Bradford Park Avenue	January	1928 £10 (donation)
WEDNESDAY	10 March	1930 £2600
Doncaster Rovers		1939-40 Guest
Sheffield United		1941-42 Guest
Denaby United	24 May	1946

Started his working life as a miner – at Warsop colliery – but after being spotted by a Bradford scout he attended trials and within a month was playing centre forward in their first team. He arrived at Avenue from the relative obscurity of Midland League Shirebrook Town and made an immediate impact on league soccer – this meteoric rise occurring after Millership had previously turned down an offer from Nottinghamshire Cricket Club to join their ground staff, deciding instead to concentrate on his football in the Bassetlaw League. It was his goal against Wednesday at Hillsborough in a February 1930 F.A.Cup tie that persuaded Owls boss Bob Brown to capture his signature and he made six appearances, at inside right – as his new club clinched their second consecutive League Championship.

With the likes of Jimmy Seed and Harry Burgess blocking his path to first team football Millership was only a bit player during his first three full seasons at Wednesday, mainly playing reserve team football where he netted 48 times for the free-scoring Central League side. However it would not be as a forward that Millership would make his name as near the end of the 1932-33 campaign it was decided to try the robust and tough tackling player at half back, as a temporary replacement for Tony Leach. Played three consecutive games in his new role before returning to second team football but before 1933 was out Harry had taken over from the outstanding Leach and remained the Owls centre half pivot for the remainder of the inter-war years.

He proved truly outstanding in his new position and was soon nicknamed 'Battleship' by Wednesday fans who delighted in his no-nonsense defending – Millership was asked at times by his team mates to 'sort out' a particular player but despite this he was only booked once in his career. The old-fashioned rough and tough defender took part in a March 1935 International trial match and was tagged "the best centre half never to have played for England" after failing to win a full cap for his Country. Appeared for Wednesday in the 1935 F.A.Cup Final win over West Brom and captained the club throughout the war years whilst also working as a Forgeman in a munitions factory. Played in the 1943 War Cup Final loss to Blackpool and in April 1944 took over as licensee of a Sheffield public house after believing a foot injury would end his career.

However, he played on and when the hostilities ended signed for non-league side Denaby United. It was while playing for the Doncaster side that Wednesday would be eternally grateful to their old player as during a game against Lincoln City reserves a red haired centre-forward scored a hat-trick against him – Millership was quickly on the phone to Hillsborough to tell them about the raw boned youngster whose name was Derek Dooley! After ending his playing career he became landlord of the Bricklayer's Arms at Brimington, nr Chesterfield but in 1948 returned to his original job as a miner - at Arkwright Colliery – and remained there until his retirement in 1969.

MILLS, David John 1983

Born: 6 December 1951
Robin Hood Bay, nr.Whitby
(5ft 8ins, 11st – 1983)
Debut: 15 February 1983
v Blackburn Rovers
Division Two Home
Last Appearance: 14 May 1983
v Crystal Palace
Division Two Home
Total League
& Cup Appearances: 19 Goals: 3

Career Details:

Middlesbrough	December	1968
West Bromwich Albion	5 January	1979 £500,000
Newcastle United	January	1982 Loan
WEDNESDAY	25 January	1983 £34,327
Newcastle United	25 August	1983*
Middlesbrough	June	1984
Darlington	August	1986 N/C
Whitby Town	May	1987
Dormans Athletic Over-35s	April	1994

* Imre Varadi + £20,000

Attacking midfielder David Mills joined the Owls at a time when his career was at a crossroads after a disappointing spell at The Hawthorns. Albion boss Ron Atkinson had splashed out a then British transfer record for his services but after 97 goals in 362 games for Boro the weight of expectation at The Hawthorns weighed heavy on Mills' shoulders and he failed to live up to his price tag, netting only six times during his spell at Albion. This contrasted greatly with his time at Middlesbrough where after overcoming a career threatening back injury he had signed apprentice forms in June 1968 and became the star man of Jack Charlton's Boro side that romped to the Second Division title in 1974, playing mainly as a centre forward. The ex-Stockton and Durham boys player added six England U-23 caps to his name while at Boro and his form in the top-flight attracted the attention of many clubs, including Liverpool. He became restless and after his transfer request was accepted Boro slapped a £200,000 price tag on his head. However he remained in the Northeast and was top scorer for two consecutive seasons before the record breaking move to West Brom.

In his brief time at Hillsborough, Mills missed only two games – playing in the F.A.Cup semi-final loss to Brighton – and showed some of the qualities that had justified such a large fee just four years earlier. However two days before the start of the following season he returned to his native Northeast as part of the deal that brought Imre Varadi to Hillsborough. During Mills' only season at St.James' Park, United were promoted from the old Second

Division, although he was on the subs bench for most of the campaign, before leaving for a second spell at Middlesbrough. His fourteen goals were crucial as Boro escaped the drop but an Achilles injury and then a broken arm ensured he failed to make an appearance during the 1985-6 season as Boro slipped towards eventual bankruptcy. Instead of playing he helped manager Willie Maddren with coaching and general duties and such was the desperate state of the club that Mills was even called upon to drive the team coach on a pre season trip to Scotland! A parting of the way came soon after and Mills would play another season as a professional before retiring in 1987 to forge a career outside of the game. He did continue to play at semi-professional level after leaving Darlington – spending a time as player-coach at Whitby Town - but was stricken by tragedy in 1988 when he was seriously injured in a road traffic accident that killed his father. Despite horrendous injuries he recovered and briefly returned to action in Over-35 football at Northeast side Dormans in the mid-1990s. Off the field he started working as a sales rep for a printing firm in 1987 – a position he still holds today – while he wrote for regional newspaper The People before graduating to radio and T.V work. Later spent two years coaching at Middlesbrough's centre of excellence and since 1995 has represented Newcastle United – providing match reports and player assessments.

MILLS, Simon Ashley 1982-85

Born: 16 August 1964 Sheffield
(5ft 8ins, 11st 4lbs – 1983)
Debut: 3 January 1983
v Charlton Athletic
Division Two Home
Last Appearance: 13 April 1985
v Ipswich Town
Division One Away
Total League
& Cup Appearances: 2+4 Goals: 0

Career Details:

WEDNESDAY	16 August	1982
York City	7 June	1984 £21,000
Port Vale	24 December	1987 £35,000
Released	May	1987
Boston United	October	1994
Matlock Town		1996

CAPS (@SWFC)
England Youth (3) v Israel U-21 21/02/83,
v Israel Olympic XI 23/02/83 v Belgium 13/04/83

Simon Mills was a highly promising England Youth International who signed apprentice forms in July 1980, graduating to the professional ranks two years later. Such was Mills' early promise that he appeared as a sub on several occasions for the club's reserve side at the age of just 15. However he never really made the transformation from Youth starlet to first team material and the hard-working midfielder totalled only a handful of appearances before moving to York City. He found the lower divisions much more to his liking and appeared in 126 games for The Citizens, scoring seven times, before moving up a division to sign for Port Vale.

At Vale Park he reverted to his schoolboy position of right back and was a regular in the side that won promotion from the old Third Division in 1989. Remained a key member of the Vale side for two further campaigns before encountering serious knee problems, which required several operations, and seriously curtailed his first team appearances. During his spell in the Potteries a loan move to Walsall was aborted and at the end of the 1993-4 season he was given a free transfer – Mills deciding at this point to retire entirely from professional football. He then started working as a market trader – selling boots and shoes – and also played non-league football before hanging up his boots to concentrate on his retail business.

MIROCEVIC, Anton "Ante" 1980-83

Born: 6 August 1952 Titograd, Yugoslavia
(5ft 8ins, 12st 6lbs – 1982)
Debut: 25 October 1980
v Orient
Division Two Home
Last Appearance: 16 April 1983
v Brighton & Hove Albion
F.A.Cup semi-final
Total League
& Cup Appearances: 65+5 Goals: 7

Career Details:

Mladost*		
FC Buducnost (Titograd)	December	1971
WEDNESDAY	24 October	1980 £250,000
Released	May	1983 Free
FC Buducnost		1983

* Formerly OFK Titograd

When the Owls signed experienced midfielder Ante Mirocevic he was not only the club's first truly foreign player but his move also broke The Owls transfer record – when signing the fee was quoted as £200,000 but at an AGM in October 1983 it was confirmed that the actual amount was £50,000 higher. Despite arriving in Sheffield in August 1980 it would be almost two months before he was officially a Wednesday player as a series of delays almost saw the transfer collapse. Firstly Wednesday had to wait a month for his work permit to be granted and then the Yugoslavian FA – who effectively decided which players could leave for foreign clubs – decided they would not allow Ante to move to Sheffield. It later transpired that in May 1980 Mirocevic had actually signed a three-year pre-contract agreement with French club Metz but had done so without the sanction of the Yugoslavian FA. National coach Miljan Miljanic vetoed this and he was effectively the man behind the F.A's decision to halt Ante's move to Hillsborough. Thankfully after weeks of discussions and confusion his National federation did finally allow him to leave and 24 hours after finally becoming a Wednesday player Ante scored on his first team debut for The Owls.

His career had started as a junior at Titograd club OFK before a free transfer took him to the City's senior club – it was expected of him to move and he had no real say in the matter! Enjoyed almost nine years of first team football at Buducnost and won various representative honours including appearances for his Country at the 1980 Olympic games in Moscow. Unfortunately for Jack Charlton his big signing proved an inconsistent performer and although occasionally showing flashes of brilliance he was never a regular in the side – he will probably be best remembered for his last game in a Wednesday shirt when netting the equalising goal in the F.A.Cup semi-final at Highbury. During his time in Sheffield Ante developed a liking for the pie and peas served up after pre season training and also the Lager and Black at the Wadsley Jack at Wisewood – then ran by ex-Owls Jack Whitham. However after three years in the City the fiercely patriotic Mirocevic became worried that his small children were not talking in his native tongue – his son Mathew was born in Sheffield and still supports Wednesday from afar! He therefore decided to ask for a move and Paris St Germain were the first side to show an interest but this was dismissed by Ante as he stated he wanted to return home for family reasons. The two parties eventually agreed that if moved back to FC Buducnost then Wednesday would grant a free transfer – he left on a plane home in May 1983 clutching a bottle of champagne given to him by 'Big Jack'

He spent a year back at his old club before deciding to retire in 1984 while still at the top and then spent two years out of the game while studying for his coaching certificate. He was then manager at Buducnost for a short time before moving onto the backroom staff as coach and scout. He was still scouting in 2002 and is now president of the Juvenile Football Committee of Montenegro, sharing his time between his home in Podgorica and summerhouse on the Fijords of Montenegro.

MOBLEY, Victor John 'Vic' 1961-69

Born: 11 October 1943 Oxford
(6ft 0½ins, 13st 12lbs – 1964)
Debut: 4 April 1964
v Wolverhampton Wanderers
Division One Away
Last Appearance: 16 August 1969
v Wolverhampton Wanderers
Division One Home
Total League
& Cup Appearances: 210 Goals: 8

Career Details:

Oxford City		
WEDNESDAY	1 September	1961 £50*
Queens Park Rangers	30 September	1969 £55,000

* Donation paid in Jan 1965

CAPS (@SWFC)
England U-23 (13) v Wales 04/11/64, v Romania 25/11/64, v Scotland 24/02/65 v Czechoslovakia 07/04/65, v West Germany 25/05/65, v Czechoslovakia 29/05/65, v Austria 02/06/65, v France 03/11/65, v Yugoslavia 24/11/65, v Austria 10/05/67, v Greece 31/05/67, v Bulgaria 03/06/67, v Turkey 07/06/67

Football League (1) v League of Ireland 08/11/67

Former Oxford boys player who started his career in amateur football before joining Wednesday as a professional at the tender age of seventeen. While a schoolboy Mobley had also represented both Berkshire and Buckinghamshire boys and his move to Hillsborough certainly proved a real coup as his combination of brawn and brains made Mobley one of the finest central defenders of the 1960s. He was a commanding figure in the air and possessed excellent distribution skills but despite these qualities he played the role of understudy to Peter Swan during his early years at Hillsborough. However when his rival's career came to a sensational end in 1964 he was thrust into the team, remaining first choice for five seasons.

After breaking into the side he quickly won representative honours but lady luck then deserted Mobley as in 1964 he was denied a full England cap against Holland because of injury and was then deprived of an appearance in the 1966 F.A.Cup Final after damaging ankle ligaments on an atrocious Villa Park pitch in the semi-final. The 'gentle giant' shook off these disappointments however to remain a vital pivot at the heart of Wednesday's back line and it was only his dramatic transfer to QPR that ended a run of 111 consecutive league games. His move to West London was an almost fait accompli for the Owls as without their knowledge Mobley had travelled down to London and returned to Sheffield for the transfer forms to be counter-signed by Wednesday!

Unfortunately while at Loftus Road the onset of arthritis caused serious knee problems and after just 25 league games for Rangers he was advised to retire from the game in April 1971. He then spent two years on the QPR coaching staff before an identical tenure as manager back at his old club Oxford City- the latter role while returning to his old profession as a carpenter. In 1975 he decided to move with his family to New Zealand, gaining employment for a Brewery Company where he remained until 1982. During that time he also coached New Zealand side Eden (1975-77) and whilst coaching at Mount Wellington in the late 1970s won the National Cup and led his charges to runners-up spot in the league. After moving into the insurance business in the early 1980s he also coached Landbase Paptoetoe for two years and is now a semi-retired consultant living in Auckland, spending part of his time at his beach house on the coast.

MONAGHAN, James 1913-14

Born: Newburn (5ft 6½ins, 10st 8lbs – 1913)
Died: 15 September 1916 France
Debut:
13 December 1913 v West Bromwich Albion Division One Home
Last Appearance:
20 December 1913 v Tottenham Hotspur Division One Away
Total League & Cup Appearances: 2 Goals: 0

Career Details:

Newburn FC		
WEDNESDAY	April	1913 £25
Scunthorpe United		

Northeast born right-winger who spent a season at Hillsborough just before the Great War. Acted as understudy to the redoubtable Sam Kirkman, twice getting a taste of league action in the absence of his rival. Dropped into non-league football at Scunthorpe after leaving The Owls and after joining the Army he rose to the rank of Lance Corporal. It is believed he lost his sight in July 1916 - at the horrific battle of the Somme - only for his vision to be restored during an operation in Sunderland. Sadly on returning to active duty he was killed in action in France, Wednesday taking a collection for his dependents in April 1918.

MONK, Garry Alan 2002-03

Born: 6 March 1979 Bedford, (6ft, 13st – 2003)
Debut:
14 December 2002 v Gillingham Division One Home
Last Appearance:
15 March 2003 v Ipswich Town Division One Home
Total League & Cup Appearances: 15 Goals: 0

Career Details:

Aston Villa		Trial
Torquay United	1 August	1995 Trainee
Southampton	23 May	1997 Free
Torquay United	25 September	1998 Loan
Stockport County	9 September	1999 Loan
Oxford United	12 January	2001 Loan
WEDNESDAY	13 December	2002 3-month loan
Barnsley	20 November	2003 Free
Swansea City	1 July	2004 Free

Skilful and competent central defender who arrived on loan from Premier League Southampton during the early weeks of Chris Turner's reign as manager. Impressed immediately, forming a solid partnership at the back with Tony Crane, as Wednesday moved off the foot of the table and proved a consistent performer during a stay that was eventually extended to three months. Monk – who was on Watford's books as a schoolboy – had started less then ten league games during his time at Southampton but arrived at Hillsborough fresh from having signed a new one-year deal in the previous summer.

However his future still looked set to lie away from the South Coast and he seemed set to sign for Wednesday when his loan spell expired. Instead he decided to wait until the summer months to see if The Owls could avoid the drop from Division One. Of course they did not but it was somewhat ironic that after an initial loan spell he did move to a South Yorkshire Division Two side on a permanent basis in February 2004, signing for neighbours Barnsley. Lady luck then deserted Monk as almost immediately after signing he was injured, being ruled out for the rest of the season. After being released by Paul Hart he dropped down a division to pen a three-year deal at Swansea City.

MORALEE, Matthew Whitfield 'Matt' 1900-04

Born: 4 March 1878 Newcastle
(5ft 7ins, 11st 10lbs)
Died: 1962 Don Valley
Debut: 11 January 1902
v Notts County
Division One Home
Last Appearance: 10 October 1903
v Wolverhampton Wanderers
Division One Away
Total League
& Cup Appearances: 4 Goals: 1

Career Details:

Blyth Spartans		
Hebburn Argyle		
WEDNESDAY	12 May	1900 £35
Doncaster Rovers		1904
Mexborough Town	May	1906
Kilnhurst Town		

Half back who started his working life as a miner in his native Northeast. Arrived at Hillsborough from non-league soccer and was restricted solely to reserve team football in his first season at the club, playing regularly as the second team raced away with the Sheffield Association League Championship. Stepped into Tommy Crawshaw's shoes to make his league debut mid way through the following season – scoring in a 4-0 home win – but he would only ever be understudy to the legendary Crawshaw and had to be content with reserve team soccer. He also helped the second team to win the Midland League title in 1903 before signing for a Doncaster Rovers side that he just been elected back into the Football League after a season of Midland League soccer.

He was appointed captain but Rovers experienced a disastrous campaign, gaining a record low points total of only eight and failing to gain re-election at the season's end. After ending his professional playing career Moralee – whose son Matt played for several league clubs including Leicester City and Aston Villa – returned to non-league football, ending his career at Sheffield Association League minnows Kilnhurst Town just before the Great War. After the hostilities Matt worked as a miner and was also trainer at Mexborough Town.

MORLEY, Haydn Arthur 1889-91

Born: Q/E March 1861 Derby
(5ft 5½ins, 9st – 1890)
Died: May 1953 Hathersage
Debut: 20 January 1890
v London Swifts
F.A.Cup Home
Last Appearance: 29 March 1890
v Blackburn Rovers
F.A.Cup Final
Total League
& Cup Appearances: 7* Goals: 0
***Also appeared in**
14 Football Alliance League games

Career Details:

Derby County	1884
Notts County	1888
Derby County	1889
WEDNESDAY	1889

Right back who holds a unique place in the history of Sheffield Wednesday as the captain of the first Owls side to reach the F.A.Cup Final. He achieved the feat in 1890 during his first season at Wednesday and was carried shoulder high from the field despite Wednesday having lost 6-1! He remained strictly amateur throughout a playing career that had started at hometown club Derby County – he was the first player ever to be signed by The Rams, played in their first ever fixture while his father William and uncle William T Morley actually founded the club!

Although short in stature he proved a vital cog in the Wednesday side that reached the Kennington Oval final and also played a handful of games as the club won the inaugural Football Alliance League Championship. As well as spending his spare time on the football pitch Morley also played cricket for Derbyshire in the summer months although he did not make the first eleven. After retiring from football the 'gentleman player' entered the legal profession in Sheffield, becoming a solicitor- he was still working in that role in November 1947. When he passed away at the age of 92 Morley was the last surviving member of that historic first Cup Final side.

MORLEY, Lance A. 1883

Born:
Died: October 1935 Hornsea
Only Appearance: 1 December 1883 v Staveley F.A.Cup Away
Total League & Cup Appearances: 1 Goals: 0

Career Details:

WEDNESDAY	1883

Goalkeeper Lance Morley was a rare example of a player who appeared for both sections of The Wednesday club - football and cricket . His appearances for the former were restricted solely to a 3-1 F.A.Cup loss at neighbours Staveley in 1883 – he did not appear in any other senior football game for Wednesday.

MORRIS, Christopher Barry 'Chris' 1982-87

Born: 24 December 1963 Newquay
(5ft 8ins, 11st 6lbs – 1984)
Debut: 27 August 1983
v Swansea City
Division Two Away
Last Appearance: 9 May 1987
v Wimbledon
Division One Home
Total League
& Cup Appearances: 73+23 Goals: 2

Career Details:

Newquay AFC		
WEDNESDAY	28 September	1982
Glasgow Celtic	3 July	1987 £125,000
Middlesbrough	12 August	1992 £600,000
Bishop Auckland		1999
Billingham Synthonia		1999
St. Blazey		2002-3
Newquay		2004

Chris Morris was a real rarity – a Cornish born professional footballer. He played his early football with Newquay boys and made such an impact that he was called into the England Youth squad, appearing alongside Wednesday trainee David Mossman. It was the Owls youngster who told Wednesday chief scout John Harris about Morris' potential and he was subsequently invited to Hillsborough for a month's trial in August 1982. Incidentally Morris – who had previously been rejected by both Exeter City and Plymouth Argyle after playing in trial games – was a real all-round sportsman and also represented England Youth at Rugby Union as well as Cornwall schools at cricket. He impressed sufficiently enough during his Hillsborough trial period to be offered his first professional deal and after a season of reserve team soccer burst onto the league scene at the start of the 1983-4 season, as a right-winger.

After making thirteen appearances in the first half of the campaign Morris then dropped out of contention and it would be a year before he returned, in a new left back role. He subsequently helped Wednesday to the semi-final of the F.A.Cup in 1986 although losing his place to Peter Shirtliff for the Villa Park clash with Everton. In his later years at Wednesday Morris became a victim of the Hillsborough boo-boys and was defended on several occasions by Howard Wilkinson against what he believed to be unfair criticism. His uneasy relationship with the Wednesday fans certainly affected Morris' confidence and it was no surprise when he left in the summer of 1987 after asking for a move. However his destination was a surprise to many as he signed for Scottish giants Celtic and then saw his career take a dramatic upturn- proving his Hillsborough critics wrong. Over the next five seasons Morris made 210 appearances for Celtic, winning the Scottish League and cup double in 1988 and the Cup again a year later. Also because his mother was born in County Mayo he won 34 full caps for his adopted country of Eire – playing in the 1988

European Championship Finals in Germany and all five games during Italia '90.

On his return to England he became a crowd favourite at Middlesbrough in a new attacking wingback role and added another Eire cap to his total during 104 games in a Boro shirt. He recovered from a cruciate knee injury to help Middlesbrough to the 1995 First Division Championship but problems with his knee eventually led to his retirement from the game in May 1997. He later played a solitary game at Bishop Auckland and was still playing regularly for his home town team, Newquay, at the age of 41 in 2005. After retiring from Middlesbrough he became a successful property developer in the Northeast before returning home to help his father run the family business – consisting of two butchers shops in St.Columb, Cornwall. He is now Managing Director of the family firm and is currently setting up a franchise operation in the UK to sell his father's Cornish pasties.

MORRISON, John Owen 1998-2003

Born: 8 December 1981
Londonderry, N.Ireland
(5ft 8ins, 11st 2lbs – 2000)
Debut: 26 December 1998
v Leicester City
Premier League Home
Last Appearance: 7 January 2003
v Gillingham
F.A.Cup Away
Total League
& Cup Appearances: 40+29 Goals: 11

Career Details:

Brandywell Harps		
Trojans		
WEDNESDAY	5 January	1999
Hull City	23 August	2002 Loan
Sheffield United	21 February	2003 Free
Stockport County	21 July	2003 Free
Bradford City	October	2004 Trial
Bradford City	10 December	2004 Loan

CAPS (@SWFC)
N.Ireland U-21 (4) v Bulgaria 27/03/01, v Malta 05/10/01, v Scotland 06/09/02, v Finland 11/02/03

The career of Owen Morrison was the classic story of an outstanding talent that was effectively wasted due to his lack of self-discipline off the field of play. The pacy, exciting left winger had initially come to fore in Irish junior soccer, first playing organised football at the tender age of seven at boys club Brandywell Harps before progressing to Derry based Trojans F.C. It was here that Owls scouts spotted Morrison and became one of the first batch of players to sign the newly introduced three-year scholarship contracts attached to the Academy system. He was such a prolific scorer in Academy football during his first few months at Wednesday that his first team debut actually came before he had made a reserve team appearance – he appeared for the last few minutes of the Boxing Day game with Leicester City which should have seen Paolo Di Canio make his comeback after suspension.

A week after getting his first taste of senior football Morrison signed a professional contract but his sudden elevation from youth team player seemed to affect his form and it would be over two years before the teenager came back into first team contention. Even his return was somewhat forced upon new manager Paul Jewell who with a crippling injury list had no choice but to turn to youth. However Morrison grabbed his second chance with both hands and a series of dazzling displays and spectacular goals marked him out as one of the players of the 2000-1 campaign – finishing third top scorer with eight goals. In October 2001 he was an unused sub during Northern Ireland's full International with Malta but sadly his career then started to dramatically go off the rails, beginning in January 2002 when Morrison was fined two weeks wages after breaking the club's drinking rules the day after a reserve game at Middlesbrough. The ex-Northern Ireland schoolboy International was still a first team squad member at this point but he dropped totally out of contention in August 2002 when being sent back just eleven days into a loan spell at Hull City for disciplinary reasons. Appeared only twice under Chris Turner and in February 2003 was arrested and bailed after further investigations into incidents at the Owls Xmas Party in Leeds during December 2002

It was now obvious his career at Hillsborough was at an end and after his contract was cancelled by mutual consent he immediately became the first player to move across the City since Wilf Rostron in 1989. Made a bright start to his Sheffield United career but after a handful of league games was released in the summer, signing for ex-Owls team mate Carlton Palmer at Stockport County. Struggled to becoming established in the first team at County and after falling totally out of favour joined Bradford City on trial in October 2004, securing a loan deal until the end of the season when City finally exited administration two months later.

MORTON, Albert 1938-53

Born: 27 July 1919 Newcastle
(5ft $11^{1}/_{2}$ins, 11st $4^{1}/_{2}$lbs – 1948)
Died: July 1991 Sheffield
Debut: 23 August 1947
v Millwall
Division Two Home
Last Appearance: 17 March 1951
v Liverpool
Division One Away
Total League
& Cup Appearances: 42* Goals: 0
***Also appeared in 118 wartime games**

Career Details:

St.Peter's Albion		
WEDNESDAY	26 March	1938 £10
Rochdale	6 July	1953 Free

Goalie who arrived at Hillsborough just before the Second World War to become third choice behind Roy Smith and Derek Goodfellow. Started his career at Northern Alliance League minnows St. Peter's and signed for Wednesday after a successful trial period. Although he stayed on The Owls books for over fifteen years the records show that only 42 of his 160 games came in league football – the overwhelming majority occurring in Wartime soccer where he was between the sticks in both legs of the 1943 War Cup Final against Blackpool. In April 1943 he joined the Army and after a spell in Germany he later served at the Suez Canal whilst also continuing to play services football. After being demobbed in February 1947 he returned to Wednesday and finally made his first 'proper' appearance for the club almost ten years after having signed!

He had actually started the 1947-8 campaign as first choice and appeared in the first 23 games before a broken arm suffered in the Boxing Day home game with West Ham brought his season to a premature end. The consistency of McIntosh then kept Morton on the sidelines and ill luck again hit when during an August 1949 reserve game Albert broke his fibula. For his final two seasons at Wednesday Morton had to be content with reserve team football and eventually moved to Rochdale, playing 94 times before retiring in 1957.

MOSFORTH, William H. 'Billy' 1875-88

Born: 2 January 1858 Sheffield
(5ft 3ins, 11st – 1888)
Died: 11 July 1929 Sheffield
Debut: 18 December 1880
v Blackburn Rovers
F.A.Cup Away
Last Appearance: 30 January 1888
v Preston North End
F.A.Cup Home
Total League
& Cup Appearances: 25 Goals: 6

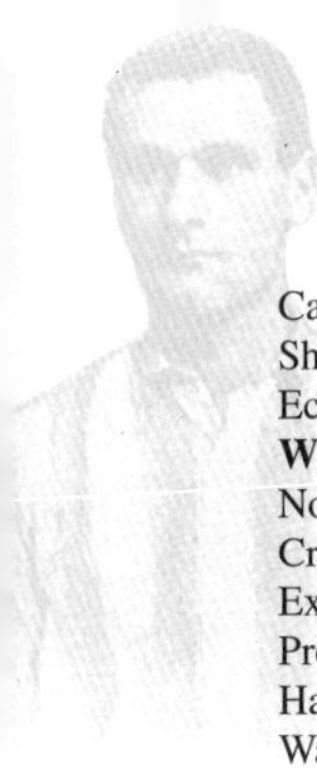

Career Details:

Sheffield Albion		1872-79
Ecclesfield		
WEDNESDAY		1875-88
Norfolk Park		1876
Crookes		1876
Exchange		1879
Providence		1879
Hallam	November	1879
Walkley		1884
Heeley		1884
Lockwood Brothers		1886
Sheffield United		1889
Owlerton		1889

CAPS - England Full (9)*
v Scotland 03/03/77, v Scotland 02/03/78, v Wales 18/01/79,
v Scotland 05/04/79, v Scotland 13/03/80, v Wales 15/03/80,
v Wales 26/02/81, v Scotland 11/03/82, v Wales 13/03/82
*Records differ as to which club Mosforth was attached to when capped for England – the above list shows all caps won in his career.

In the days of Association football when individualism was king diminutive left-winger Billy Mosforth was a pretender to the throne of England. He was a superb all round athlete, gaining prominence as a bowler for Hallam Cricket Club and as a hurdle racer who had few equals at the 150 yard dash. He also won over 200 prizes in flat racing but it was on the football field that he excelled to become without doubt the greatest Wednesday player of the pre-league era and one of the best of the Victorian age. Mosforth - nicknamed 'Little Wonder' by his adoring public – possessed marvellous speed, remarkable dribbling ability and became famous for his screw shots from the corner flag which were unerringly accurate. He first appeared in Wednesday line-ups in January 1875, aged seventeen, for a second team game but such was his impact that within a year he was representing Sheffield against London at The Oval and just over twelve months later was winning a debut cap for England.

An engraver by trade he formed a superb left wing partnership with Herbert Newbould at Wednesday and remained an integral part of the Owls side for thirteen years although being strictly amateur he did occasionally appear for other teams in the City – he had started his career as a youngster at the Albion club alongside the Clegg brothers. Although strictly amateur it did not stop Billy once changing shirts to play for Wednesday instead of against them when a supporter offered him ten shillings! During the 1880s Mosforth helped Wednesday become top dogs in the City thanks to four Sheffield Challenge Cup wins and three Wharncliffe Charity Cup triumphs while he also appeared in the club's first ever F.A.Cup tie and the opening game at Olive Grove. His England career started at the age of just 19 and he was carried shoulder high from the field after starring in England's amazing 5-4 win over Scotland in April 1879. Mosforth is generally regarded as the smallest player to play for the club but his lack of stature was Mosforth's major weapon and his dashing runs down the wing made him a real crowd entertainer for fans to whom organised football was still a novelty. His services were certainly in demand and incredibly in a ten-day period in March 1882 he not only appeared in two England Internationals and an F.A.Cup semi-final with Wednesday but also the subsequent replay!

After Wednesday failed to submit their entry for the FA.Cup in 1886-7 Mosforth helped Lockwood Brothers to the last eight of the F.A.Cup but near the end of his career at Wednesday Billy was instrumental in Wednesday turning professional as he was one of the players behind the formation of Sheffield Rovers – the new club eventually disbanding after Mosforth and Tom Cawley had persuaded Wednesday president John Holmes that professionalism was the only way forward. Billy was given a benefit game in 1888 and played his last game for Wednesday in October of the same year before moving to newly formed club Sheffield United. He appeared in United's first ever game – against Nottingham Rangers in September 1889 – and during his first season actually played in two games on the same day for two clubs! He was later a licensee in Sheffield.

MOSS, Frank 1936-38

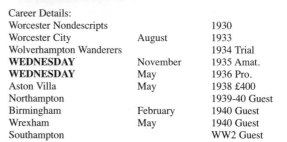

Born: 16 September 1917
Birmingham
(5ft 11ins, 11st 6lbs – 1936)
Died: May 1997 Looe, Cornwall
Debut: 14 November 1936
v Liverpool
Division One Away
Last Appearance: 18 September 1937
v Aston Villa
Division Two Home
Total League
& Cup Appearances: 23
Goals: 0

Career Details:

Worcester Nondescripts		1930
Worcester City	August	1933
Wolverhampton Wanderers		1934 Trial
WEDNESDAY	November	1935 Amat.
WEDNESDAY	May	1936 Pro.
Aston Villa	May	1938 £400
Northampton		1939-40 Guest
Birmingham	February	1940 Guest
Wrexham	May	1940 Guest
Southampton		WW2 Guest

Right wing-half who signed in 1935 after trials at both Wolves and Wednesday. The Owls were fresh from their F.A.Cup success and Moss had to play second fiddle to Wilf Sharp during his debut season, having to be content with reserve team soccer. However his rival then fell out of favour and Moss then constantly traded first team places with fellow newcomer Richard Rhodes during a campaign that sadly finished in relegation from the top-flight. He figured little in the lower grade, appearing only three times, and eventually moved to Villa Park where his father, also called Frank, had starred for Villa and England.

However he made only two appearances for Villa before war interrupted his career – Moss serving in the Royal Navy during the hostilities on gunboats and destroyers in the Middle East. Unlike many of his contemporaries the conflict did not have an adverse effect on his career and Moss would enjoy great success at Villa Park and earned a reputation as one of the toughest central defenders in the English game. In total he made 313 appearances for his hometown club before injury accelerated his retirement in June 1955. After hanging up his boots he coached the youngsters at Villa Park for a year before concentrating on his newsagents business in Kingstanding, Birmingham that he had run since 1940. Moss – whose brother Amos also played league soccer for Villa – moved to Cornwall in 1969 to run a newsagents shop in Looe and lived the remainder of his life in the County where he passed away in a nursing home.

MOSS, William 1884-85

Born: 1860/61 Heeley, Sheffield
Only Appearance:
31 October 1885 v Long Eaton Rangers F.A.Cup Away
Total League & Cup Appearances: 1 Goals: 0

Career Details:

Heeley Exchange	1878-79
Heeley	1879-87
WEDNESDAY	1884-85

Full back who made a solitary competitive appearance for Wednesday during one of the club's early forays into the F.A.Cup – a surprise 2-0 loss at Derbyshire club Long Eaton. Both William and his brother Thomas were common sights on the football field in the 1880s, playing for a variety of local sides while working as Hand File cutters. William came to prominence with local club Heeley and he was on the winning side in the 1884 Wharncliffe Charity Cup Final, beating Wednesday in the Bramall Lane final! A year later he had played several games for Wednesday and the roles were reversed when he was on the Owls side that defeated Heeley in the 1886 Final. However he soon returned to Heeley and played alongside his brother.

MULLEN, James 'Jimmy' 1970-80

Born: 8 November 1952
Hedworth, Jarrow
(5ft 10ins, 10st 6lbs – 1973)
Debut: 26 December 1970
v Hull City
Division Two Away
Last Appearance: 12 April 1980
v Bury
Division Three Away
Total League
& Cup Appearances: 254+9 Goals: 10

Career Details:

Hedworth Celtic		
WEDNESDAY	28 October	1970
Rotherham United	30 July	1980 £25,000
Preston North End	November	1981 Loan
Cardiff City	March	1982 £10,000
Newport County	June	1986 £1,500

Central defender Jimmy Mullen had trials at South Shields boys as a youngster and was told he was too small to ever make the grade. Thankfully he ignored the advice and in 1969 came to Hillsborough on trial, signing apprentice forms soon afterwards after making a big impression with the Wednesday management. The former apprentice draughtsman went on to become a firm favourite with Wednesdayites over the next decade due to his whole-hearted attitude and consistent performances. He became established despite a crazy start to his Owls career at both reserve and first team level. In his first two games for the second team Mullen experienced a 5-2 win and then a 7-1 loss but this paled against his first taste of league soccer, at Boothferry Park on Boxing Day 1970. With only seven minutes left he looked set for a winning start as Wednesday led 4-1 but those final few minutes must have left the youngster somewhat shell-shocked as Hull stormed back to grab a point in one of the greatest comebacks of all-time!

Sadly for Mullen his time at Wednesday coincided with the worst decade in the club's long history and he spent half of his time playing Third Division football – he was club captain during The Owls promotion success in 1980. A benefit game against Manchester City followed but he would not play in the higher grade for Wednesday as ex team mate Ian Porterfield took his services to Millmoor. Incidentally during his last two seasons at Hillsborough, Mullen experienced his first taste of management, being in charge of Yorkshire League club Stocksbridge Works in 1978-9 and Huddersfield Sunday League side Denby F.C. in 1979-80. He was captain as The Millers won the Third Division Championship in 1981 but after 49 games, and a solitary match on loan at Preston, he moved to Cardiff City, initially on loan. A permanent move saw Mullen appointed player-coach and was again captain as the Welsh side won promotion from the old Division Three in 1983. Stepped up to assistant manager in 1984 and was caretaker manager for the final game of the 1985-6 season after Alan Durban was sacked.

However he failed to secure the manager's post on a full-time basis and left for a four-month spell as player-manager at Newport County before in February 1987 teaming up again with Porterfield, who was then manager at Aberdeen – his playing career had ended in October 1986. While in Scotland The Dons lost the 1987 League Cup Final to Rangers and in April 1989 he was on the move again, being appointed caretaker manager at Blackpool. He was awarded the role on a permanent basis in May but after a traumatic season the Tangerines were relegated and Mullen was relieved of his duties in April 1990. He was soon back in employment as assistant manager at Burnley and after being given the manager's job in October 1991 led the Lancashire club to the old Fourth Division Championship. This was followed by promotion to the new First Division in 1994 but unfortunately relegation soon followed and after results failed to improve he left by mutual consent in February 1996 – a disgraceful incident where his wife's skirt was set on fire by a so-called fan forcing a decision.

A week after leaving Turf Moor he joined Bolton as a scout before in November became manager of Eire club Sligo Rovers. In December 1997 Mullen returned to English football as boss at Conference side Telford United but a string of poor results ended in dismissal in January 1999. He was later boss at Merthyr Tydfil (Oct 1999-Mar 2000), Little Drayton Rangers (2000) and Bridgnorth Town (2002) before being appointed in 2003 – alongside Neville Southall – as coach of the Welsh U-19 side. Mullen – who holds the highest professional qualification in professional football (the UEFA Pro licence) was appointed boss at Unibond League side Colwyn Bay in May 2003. He resigned as Colwyn boss in April 2004, citing 'personal reasons' but was soon back in the manager's chair at Bromsgrove Rovers.

MULLER, Adam 2000-02

Born: 17 April 1982 Leeds
(5ft 11ins, 12st 2lbs – 2001)
Debut: 26 August 2000
v Grimsby Town
Division One Away
Last Appearance: 17 October 2000
v Burnley
Division One Away
Total League
& Cup Appearances: 1+5 Goals: 0

Career Details:

Leeds United		
Ossett Town		
Thackley		
WEDNESDAY	18 May	2000
Worksop Town	2 March	2001 3-month loan
Released	30 June	2002 Free
Gresley Rovers	July	2002 Trial
Worksop Town		2002
Wakefield & Emley	September	2003 Loan
Wakefield & Emley	3 July	2004 Free

Pacy forward who started his playing career in Northern Counties East League football after having represented Leeds, Yorkshire and West Riding boys. Spent a spell as an associated schoolboy at Leeds United but when spotted by Wednesday was playing for Bradford club Thackley whilst attending sixth form at school. The Owls encouraged Muller to finish his studies – he gained two 'A' levels - and during that period he trained twice a week at Wednesday. After impressing in reserve team football – he scored four times in just six games during the latter part of the 1999-00 season - Muller was praised by caretaker boss Peter Shreeves and duly awarded a two-year contract in the summer of 2000.

His rapid progress continued at the start of the following campaign and Muller appeared in six first team games before dropping back into Premier Reserve League football. He ended the season on loan in Northern Premier League football, gaining valuable experience in the physical world of non-league soccer, but still finished top scorer for the reserves, albeit with only five goals. Unfortunately Adam failed to break back into the first team squad under Terry Yorath and signed for ambitious Worksop Town in 2002.

MUMFORD, Albert Corbett 'Clinks' 1886-96

Born: 1865 Wrekin, Shropshire
(5ft, 9ins, 11st, 1lbs – 1890)
Died: 30 June 1926 Loughborough
Debut: 2 February 1889
v Notts Rangers
F.A.Cup Away
Last Appearance: 9 September 1893
v Blackburn Rovers
Division One Away
Total League
& Cup Appearances: 42* Goals: 7
***Also appeared in**
58 Football Alliance League games

Career Details:

Wrackward-in-the-Wood		
Berkley Star		1881
Bethel United		1882
Bethel Reds		

WEDNESDAY/Lockwood Brothers	1886-87
WEDNESDAY	1887-96
Clinton/Park Grange	1887-88
Loughborough Town	1896

The career of 19th Century Wednesday hero 'Clinks' Mumford started at little-known Shropshire side Wrackward before he moved to Sheffield in 1881. His first club in the City was Berkley Star but after a year he joined Bethel United. The following season the younger members of the club- Mumford amongst them- broke away to form Bethel Reds and this fledgling club went the whole season losing only once – only because they had to play two matches on the same day and did not have enough players for both games! During that remarkable season Mumford netted double figures in a 27-0 win over Mexborough – as did future Owls team mate Billy Ingram – and this prolific scoring earned his side the tag of 'best minor team the City had ever seen'.

Over the next few years Mumford assisted both Wednesday and Lockwood Brothers before in 1887 he signed professional forms for the former. This was the start of a long association with the club during which time Wednesday entered their first League, reached their first F.A.Cup Final and were then elected into the Football League. Over that time 'Clinks' remained loyal to Wednesday and showed his versatility by playing in every position including goalkeeper – against Sunderland Albion in September 1891. However it was as an outstanding inside or centre-forward that Mumford is best known and in this position he scored twice in the 1890 F.A.Cup semi-final win over Bolton before appearing in the Final against Blackburn Rovers. He had previously played in The Owls first ever Football Alliance League game in September 1889 and when the club was elevated to the Football League he was one of the famous eleven that appeared in the opening fixture at Notts County.

He was a real mainspring of the side and during his time in Wednesday colours 'Clinks' played in thirteen inter-association matches although International honours proved elusive. In the latter part of his Wednesday career Mumford dropped into a more defensive role – all but one of his Football League appearances came at full back or halfback – and the arrival of Jack Earp in 1893 meant the popular Mumford spent his final three years at Olive Grove in the reserve side. He still gave his all for the club in second team football and helped the reserves to two league titles before his loyalty was rewarded in 1896 with a benefit game against Sheffield United. Soon after he moved to then Football League side Loughborough and was captain of the Leicestershire side until they disbanded at the turn of the Century. After ending his playing days he worked as a gas stoker before losing a long fight against cancer in 1926.

MURRAY, James M. 1910-11

Born: Ireland
Debut: 25 March 1910
v Bradford City
Division One Away
Last Appearance: 26 November 1911
v Blackburn Rovers
Division One Away
Total League
& Cup Appearances: 13 Goals: 4

Career Details:

Motherwell		
WEDNESDAY	March	1910 £1250*
Derry City	August	1911

*Joint fee with Robertson

CAPS (@SWFC)
Northern Ireland Full (1) v Wales 11/04/10

Centre forward James Murray arrived from Scottish football with two caps for Ireland under his belt and went straight into the Wednesday side, as replacement for the absent Andrew Wilson. The Irishman netted on his home debut – along with former Motherwell team mate George Robertson - and was then on the score sheet in a remarkable 6-0 win at Nottingham Forest in the final away game of the season. Murray – an uncertified schoolteacher – started the first four games of the following season but then dropped into reserve team soccer before the arrival of outstanding forward David McLean effectively ended his Hillsborough career. He returned to Irish football in 1911 although Wednesday retained his English league forms.

MUSTOE, Robin 'Robbie' 2003-04

Born: 28 August 1973 Witney, Oxfordshire
(5ft 11ins, 11st 12lbs – 2003)
Debut: 1 September 2003
v Wycombe Wanderers
Division Two Away
Last Appearance: 24 April 2004
v Colchester United
Division Two Home
Total League
& Cup Appearances: 26+3 Goals: 1

Career Details:

Oxford United	2 July	1986
Middlesbrough	5 July	1990 £375,000
Charlton Athletic	30 August	2002 Free
Released	30 June	2003
WEDNESDAY	30 July	2003 Free
Released	30 June	2004

Midfielder who is best known for a twelve-year stay at Middlesbrough, which accrued a mammoth 465 appearances and 35 goals. He joined Boro from his first club Oxford United where Mustoe had been an unused sub for the England U-21 team as well as playing in 98 senior games. When he arrived at Boro the club was struggling both on and off the field but over the years that followed Mustoe remained a constant in midfield as the club underwent a Steve Gibson led revolution that brought a new stadium and three Wembley Cup Finals. Sadly for Mustoe he was a loser twice in the League Cup Final (including a Hillsborough replay against Leicester in 1997) and once in the F.A.Cup although he did help Boro to promotion from Division One in 1998 and won the player of the year trophy in 1999. A series of high profile signings streamed into the Riverside but the highly consistent Mustoe saw off all his challengers and was a rock at the heart of the Teeside club's midfield, enjoying a testimonial season in 1999-2000.

After finally leaving in 2002 he moved to Premier League Charlton Athletic on an initial three-month contract. This was later extended to a year but after just seven games for The Addicks a thigh injury suffered in November 2002 put Mustoe on the sidelines and he failed to recover sufficiently to play another first team game for the London club. He subsequently left in the summer and arrived on trial at Hillsborough during the 2003 pre season as Chris Turner seeked to add experience to his midfield. He impressed sufficiently but soon after signing a one-year deal Mustoe was injured, missing the opening games of the new season, and he would experience an injury ruined season as Wednesday struggled in Division Two. When fit he showed flashes of his Premier League quality but struggled to adapt to life in the lower divisions and decided to retire from the game after his contract expired in the summer of 2004.

NAPIER, Charles Edward 'Charlie' 1938-45

Born: 8 October 1910
Bainsford, Falkirk
(5ft 9ins, 11st 9lbs – 1938)
Died: 5 September 1973 Falkirk
Debut: 19 March 1938
v Barnsley
Division Two Home
Last Appearance: 29 April 1939
v Tottenham Hotspur
Division Two Home
Total League
& Cup Appearances: 56* Goals: 10
***Also appeared in**
6 wartime games, scoring 5 times

Career Details:

Cowie Juveniles		
Grangemouth Sacred Heart Celtic		
Maryhill Hibernian		
Alva Albion Rangers		1928
Glasgow Celtic	August	1928
Maryhill Hibs		1928 Loan
Derby County	12 June	1935 £3,500
WEDNESDAY	12 March	1938 £3,000
Falkirk	September	1939 Guest
Falkirk	29 September	1945 £1100
Stenhousemuir	September	1946

Scottish inside forward who perhaps holds the unique record of twice being banned sine die by the F.A. only to have his ban lifted on both occasions. Both incidents occurred during the war years with Napier first falling foul of the authorities in February 1941 whilst playing as a guest for hometown club Falkirk. He was duly re-instated by the International Board in August 1943 but in January 1944 was again handed a life ban following the referee's report on a Wednesday versus Grimsby game played in the previous October. Incredibly the five-times capped Scottish International fell lucky again in August 1945 when as part of the celebrations surrounding VE day his ban was lifted, leaving Charlie free to pull on his boots again. Ironically he was working as an electrical engineer in Falkirk and the Labour ministry decided he could not return to Sheffield!

During the early years of his career Napier combined his job as an electrician – he qualified after a six-year apprenticeship – with playing in Scottish amateur football before signing for Glasgow giants Celtic. At Celtic Park he won the Scottish Cup in 1931 and 1933 and also became the first player from the club to play at Wembley, when representing Scotland against England in April 1932. While in Glasgow Charlie was known as 'Happy Feet' due to his tendency to score many goals from long distance but after two cartilage operations his long-range shooting days came to an end. He was also an accomplished dancer and during a Celtic tour of Canada and the US won a dancing competition although he nearly did not make the journey home after Napier – who could not swim – was thrown into a swimming pool and almost drowned!

However Charlie - whose father was a referee and also the first ever secretary-manager of Falkirk when appointed in 1922 – was soon in dispute with Celtic and refused to re-sign unless he was guaranteed a benefit in May 1935. This was rejected and after 83 goals in only 177 games he left for English football, helping Derby County to Division One runners-up spot in 1936. His next port of call was Hillsborough where Napier made a huge impression, missing only one game during the 1938-9 season when Wednesday agonisingly missed out on promotion back to the top-flight. He had been brought to Sheffield in the wake of George Drury's controversial sale to Arsenal and proved a clever player who possessed exceptional ball control. However like so many players the war then effectively ended his top-class football career with Napier returning home to work in a Glasgow munitions factory. His playing days came to an end in April 1948, after two seasons at Stenhousemuir, while four months later was appointed Scottish scout for Luton Town. He lived in Falkirk for the rest of his days and in the mid-1950s coached non-league side Bonnybridge Juniors.

NAPIER, Daniel 'Dan' 1906-10

Born: (5ft 9ins, 12st – 1906)
Debut:
26 December 1907 v Sunderland Division One Home
Last Appearance:
27 February 1909 v Preston North End Division One Away
Total League & Cup Appearances: 11 Goals: 2

Career Details:

Wallsend Park Villa		
WEDNESDAY		1906
Northampton	June	1910 £50

Little-known defensive player who spent four seasons at Hillsborough, after joining from Northeast non-league football. Although usually used in a halfback role he played several times as a forward for the reserve team during his first season at Wednesday and in fact finished top scorer with 18 goals as the Midland League side finished in third place. However it was at centre halfback that Napier made his senior bow for the club and with stalwart Tommy Crawhaw in his twilight years he appeared in eight consecutive first team games, netting in back-to-back home games over the 1907 Christmas period. It was soon back to reserve soccer though for Napier and after newcomer English McConnell became first choice at the heart of the Wednesday defence Dan asked for a transfer in February 1910. He eventually moved to Southern League Northampton Town but played only five games before being released in the summer of 1911.

NDUMBU-NSUNGU, Guylain 2003-05

Born: 26 December 1982 Kinshasa, DR Congo
(6ft 1ins, 12st 2lbs – 2003)
Debut: 13 September 2003
v Stockport County
Division Two Home
Last Appearance: 19 December 2004
v Doncaster Rovers
League One Away
Total League
& Cup Appearances: 30+14 Goals: 11

Career Details:

Amiens	1 August	2002
Bolton Wanderers	August	2003 Trial
WEDNESDAY	5 September	2003 £100,000
Preston North End	28 September	2004 Loan
Contract cancelled	18 January	2005
Colchester United	20 January	2005
Contract cancelled	31 March	2005
Darlington	5 August	2005

CAPS (@SWFC)
DR Congo U-20 (1) v Cameroon 26/10/03

Highly talented attacker who joined the Owls on a season long loan from French side Amiens early in the 2003-4 campaign. Ndumbu-Nsungu, nicknamed 'Sungu' by Owls players, was born in the Central African country of Zaire - now known as The Democratic Republic of Congo – but at the age of six moved to France with his family. He had first played football in the streets of Zaire with a homemade ball before continuing his passion for the game in the Francourville district of Paris. His first taste of organised football came with a local Paris side before earning a trial at French lower league side Amiens that led to 'Sungu' signing as a trainee in 1997. He turned professional in the summer of 2002 and after breaking into the Amiens first eleven scored once in five games, earning a June 2003 call up to the DR Congo U-20 side for their Olympic qualifying double-header against fierce rival Rwanda. It meant 'Sungu' returned to his homeland for the first time since 1989 and he made an immediate impact, scoring on his International debut.

A virtual unknown outside of France, his arrival at Hillsborough was a relatively low-key event but he quickly made headlines when scoring twice and creating one in a dazzling debut for the reserve side. He was a peripheral figure during his early weeks at Hillsborough and struggled to settle, not helped by a long absence when being called up for a DR Congo Olympic qualifying game. However he slowly started to make an impact, netting his first goal for the club in a derby draw at Barnsley in December 2003, and over the weeks that followed truly blossomed, scoring regularly whilst showing terrific ball control and exciting footwork. Although inconsistent it quickly became obvious that the Owls had signed a player of immense potential and he was quickly tied to a 2 year contract in February 2004, after Wednesday agreed a complicated compensation package with Amiens. Incidentally he was called into the full DR Congo side in January 2004 for the African Cup of Nations Finals in Tunisia but decided to stay in Sheffield to secure his future. After finishing top scorer in 2003-04 and being voted 'player of the Year' by Owls fans Sungu experienced a poor pre season and soon fell out of favour under new manager Paul Sturrock – the Scot sending Ndumbu on loan to Preston within 24 hours of taking over at Hillsborough. After regaining fitness at Deepdale he returned to Hillsborough but was just a peripheral figure although it was still a surprise to many when his contract was cancelled by mutual consent.

NEEDHAM, Liam 2002-05

Born: 19 October 1985 Sheffield
(6ft 1ins,12st 2lbs - 2005)
Only Appearance:
29 September 2004
v Chester City
LDV Trophy Home
Total League
& Cup Appearances: 0+1 Goals: 0

Career Details:

WEDNESDAY	1 July	2002 Academy
Released	30 June	2005
Notts County	28 July	2005 Trial
Gainsborough Trinity	July	2005 Trial

Born and bred Wednesdayite Liam Needham joined the Owls on a three-year scholarship in 2002 and slowly progressed through the ranks to be named as a substitute for the Division Two game at Rushden & Diamonds in February 2004. As injury disrupted Chris Turner's side Needham was one of many youngsters who were given a first team shirt, rather through necessity than choice. He failed to make a first team appearance and had to wait until Paul Sturrock's first home game in charge when the skilful forward entered the fray in the dying embers of the LDV Cup defeat at home to Chester City.

His first team appearance marked the pinnacle so far of a career that had started in the Owls junior sides and saw the highly rated Needham given an Academy debut at the tender age of 14 - he was picked for the U-17s fixture at Southampton in September 2000. His appearance was not an isolated one either as the youngster played fifteen times during the season, scoring once, and was virtually ever present in the following campaign. Just days after celebrating his sixteenth birthday he also made a bow for the U-19 side and it was no surprise when he was handed a scholarship in the summer of 2002. Unfortunately a broken leg disrupted his first season as a trainee but he returned to fitness and over the last two seasons has been a regular member of both the Academy and reserve teams, captaining the former on several occasions. Incidentally Needham is a relation of a famous Blade, Ernest Needham, and Wednesday's Mark Smith

NEVIN, George William 1930-33 & 1934-35

Born: 16 December 1907 Lintz, Co.Durham
(5ft 10½ins, 12st 7lbs – 1930)
Died: 1st Quarter 1973 Sheffield
Debut: 21 January 1933
v Blackburn Rovers
Division One Away
Last Appearance: 22 April 1933
v Middlesbrough
Division One Away
Total League
& Cup Appearances: 2 Goals: 0

Career Details:

Leazes Council School		
Lintz Institute		
Lintz Colliery		
Dipton United		
Whitehead-Le-Rangers		
Newcastle United	August	1925 Amat.
Sunderland	March	1926 Amat.
Whitehead-Le-Rangers		
Newcastle United	December	1928 £100
WEDNESDAY	5 June	1930 Free
Manchester United	29 December	1933 £1,000
WEDNESDAY	16 March	1934 £500
Burnley	May	1935
Lincoln City	May	1937
Rochdale	June	1939

Despite spending over ten years as a professional George Nevin failed to become established at any of his six league sides, amassing only 46 appearances in total. The pattern was set at his first club Newcastle United where the strong tackling left-back made only six appearances after being plucked from Northeast amateur soccer – prior to turning professional he had combined football with his job as a miner in the Durham coalfields. Bob Brown brought him to Hillsborough in 1930 although the transfer was only completed when the Football League removed the exorbitant £1,000 fee put on his head by Newcastle. He actually had two spells at Wednesday – bizarrely separated by less than four months – but stiff competition from Ernie Blenkinsop and then Ted Catlin ensured that Nevin had to be content with the role of understudy, appearing only twice in senior football for The Owls.

His initial spell at Wednesday came to an end when he moved to Old Trafford with Jack Ball as part of a deal that brought Neil Dewar to Hillsborough. However the transfer included the proviso that he would return to Wednesday if United decided not to retain his services and this duly occurred. For Nevin – whose father Ralph played for Gateshead and Exeter City– it was straight back into Central League football at Wednesday before continuing his career in Lancashire football. Later in life his son, David, was also on the Owls books but despite playing in a County Cup tie he failed to make a league appearance.

NEWBOULD, Herbert 1880-84

Born: Sheffield
Debut: 18 December 1880
v Blackburn Rovers
F.A.Cup Away
Last Appearance: 1 December 1883
v Staveley
F.A.Cup Away
Total League
& Cup Appearances: 8 Goals: 4

Career Details:

Albion Club	
WEDNESDAY	1880-84

Herbert Newbould was a real sports enthusiast, as in addition to playing football in his spare time he was also a keen and highly rated runner. He spent four years at Wednesday in the early part of the 1880s, making his debut in an October 1880 Sheffield Challenge Cup tie before becoming one of the famous eleven players to appear in the club's first ever F.A.Cup tie in December of the same year. He followed this appearance with a hat-trick in the 12-2 romp over hapless Spilsby Town in the same competition and also helped Wednesday win the Sheffield Challenge Cup in both 1881 and 1883 plus the Wharncliffe Charity Cup in 1883. As well as being a playing member of The Wednesday club he was also part of the club's committee and eventually became a director. Later in life he became President of Sheffield based athletics club Hallamshire Harriers.

NEWSOME, Jonathan 'Jon' 1989-91 & 1996-2000

Born: 6 September 1970 Sheffield
(6ft 2ins, 13st 11lbs – 1996)
Debut: 9 September 1989
v Arsenal
Division One Away
Last Appearance: 19 September 1999
v Newcastle United
Premier League Away
Total League
& Cup Appearances: 68+6 Goals: 4

Career Details:

WEDNESDAY	1 July	1989
Leeds United	28 May	1991 £300,000*
Norwich City	30 June	1994 £1,000,000
WEDNESDAY	15 March	1996 £1,600,000
Bolton Wanderers	17 November	1998 Loan
Retired	18 May	2000
Gresley Rovers	April	2002

*Joint fee with David Wetherall

Local lad Jon Newsome came through the Owls youth ranks to forge an outstanding defensive partnership with David Wetherall that was a major factor in Wednesday's Central League Championship winning campaign of 1990-91. Much was expected of both youngsters – Newsome had been with the club since signing associated schoolboy forms in June 1985 - so it was both a surprise and disappointment to Owls fans when the duo were sold, at a knock-down price, to fierce Yorkshire rivals Leeds United. The transfer was Ron Atkinson's final act during his first spell as manager at Hillsborough and was perhaps even more of a shock in Newsome's case as he had only signed a new contract at Wednesday six days earlier. Their promise would be fulfilled at Elland Road where Newsome won a League Championship medal in his debut season and appeared in 88 games before becoming Norwich City's first £1m player.

The tall and classy centre half enjoyed more success in Norfolk and took over the captaincy after becoming an integral part of The Canaries defence. However Newsome – who as a youngster played for Sheffield, South Yorkshire and Yorkshire boys – spent less than two seasons at City as David Pleat brought Jon's career full circle by bringing him back to Hillsborough. He rewarded his new manager by grabbing a crucial goal on the final day of the season to secure Wednesday's top-flight status but sadly the 1996-7 season was ruined by a combination of various ankle problems. The following campaign saw an influx of several foreign defenders increase competition and although Newsome was a regular his form was patchy with his ariel strength somewhat masking mobility problems caused by consistent ankle injuries. Unfortunately he failed to recover from a series of injuries and was forced to announce his retirement from the game in May 2000, aged 29.

After retiring he briefly worked under Clive Baker at The Owls academy before becoming a player's insurance agent. He later worked as a centre of excellence coach at Grimsby Town – as well as first team scout – before securing employment as a financial consultant. He came back into the game in April 2002 when being appointed Gresley Rovers manager for the final two games of the season, replacing ex-Bolton Wanderers attacker John McGinlay. Although he could not train Jon did make a handful of appearances for Rovers during the 2002-3 season while in February 2003 he also began working as a sales representative for a sportswear company. He combined both roles until July 2003 when after completing his UEFA coaching badge Jon resigned as Gresley boss and now owns a 'Starbucks' coffee house in Barnsley.

NIBLOE, Joseph 'Joe' 1934-39

Born: 23 November 1903
Cockerhill, Renfrewshire
(5ft 10½ins, 13st – 1934)
Died: 25 October 1976 Doncaster
Debut: 25 August 1934
v Stoke City
Division One Home
Last Appearance: 7 May 1938
v Tottenham Hotspur
Division Two Away
Total League
& Cup Appearances: 128 Goals: 0

Career Details:

Shawfield Juniors		
Rutherglen Glencairn		
Glencairn Green		
Kilmarnock	June	1924
Aston Villa	September	1932 £1,875
WEDNESDAY	10 August	1934 £2500 + George Beeson

A career as a professional footballer looked to have past Joe Nibloe by when at the age of 22 he was still employed as an apprentice moulder in the brass industry - he had worked for seven years at famous Clyde shipyard Harland and Wolfe while playing in local junior soccer. During the early part of his career Nibloe played at centre forward and even attended trials at a Scottish league side in 1923 in that position. However a move to left back then transformed his career and within a year Joe was offered professional terms by Kilmarnock. The no-nonsense, tough tackling Scot became an automatic choice at Rugby Park and helped 'Killie' to the Scottish Cup in 1929 as well as being losing finalists to Glasgow Rangers three years later. He remained at Kilmarnock for eight seasons but after 279 appearances – plus eleven full caps for Scotland - a dispute over his benefit directly led to a move to England.

After struggling to become established during his first season at Villa Park, Nibloe then became an automatic choice and his move to Hillsborough was a sensation at the time and shocked the football world. It was Billy Walker who secured his signature with the transfer no doubt helped by the fact that a few months earlier Walker and Nibloe had been teammates in the Villa side. Initially he proved a worthy successor to Ernie Blenkinsop but was soon converted to right back by Billy Walker and replaced stalwart Tommy Walker during the 1935 F.A.Cup run to Wembley - becoming one of a handful of players to win Cup winners medal in Scotland and England after helping Wednesday beat West Bromwich Albion. He would stay at Hillsborough until retiring in 1939 and during the war years worked in a munitions factory at Stocksbridge. After the hostilities Joe – whose son, John, played for several clubs including Sheffield United but was tragically killed on the Woodhead Pass on his way home after playing for Stockport County against Newport in November 1964 - remained in the Sheffield village to work at the steelworks and also coached for a few years back at Hillsborough.

NICHOLLS, Harold 'Harry' 1934-35

Born: Q/E December 1913 Hednesford
(5ft 8½ins, 11st 4lbs – 1934)
Debut: 22 September 1934
v Arsenal
Division One Home
Last Appearance: 10 November 1934
v Aston Villa
Division One Away
Total League
& Cup Appearances: 3 Goals: 0

Career Details:

Hednesford Town		
WEDNESDAY	5 May	1934 £125
Wellington Town	June	1935
Shrewsbury Town	July	1937

Halfback who spent just a solitary season at Wednesday after signing from hometown club Hednesford Town. At the time he was coveted by several league sides but it was ex-Hednesford

Town player Billy Walker who won the race for his signature. He made just three league appearances during The Owls F.A.Cup winning season and after just a handful of reserve team games transferred to non-league Wellington Town, now better known as Telford United. A move to Shrewsbury Town came two years later and he enjoyed a tremendous debut season, winning the Midland League and Welsh Cup double. Remained on 'The Shrews' books throughout the war years and played in the opening 26 games of the 1945-6 season that ended with the Midland League title returning to Gay Meadow.

NICHOLSON, George Henry 1885-86

Born: Q/E June 1863 Sheffield
Only Appearance:
31 October 1885 v Long Eaton Rangers F.A.Cup Away
Total League & Cup Appearances: 1 Goals: 0

Career Details:

Local	
WEDNESDAY	1885
Local	1886

Played only one senior game for Wednesday, a disastrous F.A.Cup defeat at Long Eaton in 1885.

NICHOLSON, Horace 1912-14

Born: 19 July 1895 Mexborough
(5ft 10ins., 12st – 1913)
Debut: 3 January 1914
v Burnley
Division One Home
Last Appearance: 14 April 1914
v Oldham Athletic
Division One Away
Total League
& Cup Appearances: 3* Goals: 0
***Also appeared in 1 wartime game**

Career Details:

Mexborough Highthorn Mission		
WEDNESDAY	May	1912 £20/10s
Mexborough Town		1914
Bradford Park Avenue	November	1920
Wath Athletic		1923
Wombwell		
Denaby United		1925

Spent two seasons at Hillsborough after joining from minor soccer. Defensive player who appeared in the half back line, signing for Wednesday at the age of 21. Stepped in for both James Campbell and Tom Brittleton during the 1913-14 campaign but returned to Mexborough football in the summer that followed. Served in the Army during the Great War and later appeared in 25 Football League games for Bradford Park Avenue.

NICHOLSON, Kevin John 1997-2001

Born: 2 October 1980 Derby
(5ft 8ins, 11st 5lbs – 2000)
Only Appearance: 28 August 2000
v Blackburn Rovers
Division One Home
Total League
& Cup Appearances: 0+1 Goals: 0

Career Details:

WEDNESDAY	22 October	1997
Northampton Town	12 November	2000 Loan
Northampton Town	24 January	2001 N/C
Forest Green Rovers	25 January	2001 Loan
Notts County	9 March	2001 Free
Scarborough	12 March	2004 Loan
Released	30 June	2004
Scarborough	9 August	2004

Kevin Nicholson was a highly promising left back who attended the old F.A.School at Lilleshall and was courted by several Premier League sides, including Arsenal. However it was Wednesday who won the race for his signature and the ex-captain of the England Youth team gave a series of assured and mature displays in the Owls reserve and junior sides. His chance of first team football came as an early sub for the stricken Andy Hinchcliffe in the 2-1 win over Blackburn Rovers in August 2000 but it proved to be his only experience of senior football at Hillsborough and within five months had signed for Northampton Town on a non-contract basis.

Within 24 hours of joining The Cobblers he was sent out to Conference side Forest Green to gain valuable experience but soon after Notts County gave Town seven days notice of approach and even though Northampton had offered Nicholson a contract he instead signed a three-year contract with the Nottingham club. Quickly became established as first choice left back at Meadow Lane and remained so until signing for Conference League side Scarborough.

NICOL, Stephen 'Steve' 1995-98

Born: 16 December 1961 Irvine
(5ft 10ins, 12st 8lbs – 1997)
Debut: 25 November 1995
v Everton
Premier League Away
Last Appearance: 1 November 1997
v Manchester United
Premier League Home
Total League
& Cup Appearances: 43+11 Goals: 0

Career Details:

Ayr Boys Club		
Ayr United		1979
Liverpool	26 October	1981 £300,000
Notts County	20 January	1995 Free
WEDNESDAY	23 November	1995 Free
West Bromwich Albion	11 March	1998 Loan
Released	30 June	1998
Hull City	August	1998 Trial
Doncaster Rovers	12 September	1998 Free
Boston Bulldogs	April	1999 Free

The name of Steve Nicol will always be inexorably linked with Liverpool where after being plucked from the relative obscurity of the Scottish lower leagues he spent a medal laden 14 years at Anfield, winning four League titles, three F.A.Cups, a European Cup and 27 caps for Scotland – appearing in the 1986 World Cup Finals in Mexico. The Scot was primarily an all-action midfielder during his time at Anfield but after his surprise capture by Owls boss David Pleat proved a more than capable performer at both full back and centre half. His vast experience often made up for a lack of pace and he played in the majority of the 1996-7 season at full back as partner to Ian Nolan. However after playing in David Pleat's final game in charge – a heavy defeat at Old Trafford – Nicol failed to figure under new boss Ron Atkinson and was eventually loaned to West Brom. He again showed his quality during two months at The Hawthorns but Albion decided against offering him a deal so Nicol returned to Wednesday to see out the remaining months of his contract.

While looking for a coaching position he trained with Wednesday during the summer of 1998 and in fact played for The Owls in August against Shrewsbury Town in the Final of the Shropshire Senior Cup. He later joined ex-Owl John Sheridan at Conference side Doncaster Rovers before flying out to North America on April Fool's Day 1999 to take up an assistant coaching role at US 'A' League club Boston Bulldogs. Also played in 19 games during his first season in The States before being appointed head coach in July 1999. Following the sacking of ex-Italian International Walter Zenga as New England Revolution manager in September 1999 Nicol was placed in temporary charge for two games – Boston were affiliated to the MLS club. After winning both games he returned to Boston and led the Bulldogs to the Division Three title in 2001 before being appointed assistant coach at New England in January 2002.

He was appointed as interim coach of Revolution in May 2002, from Fernando Clavijo, with the side having lost more games than they had won. However Nicol then performed a minor miracle as they scrapped into the play-offs and went all the way to the final staged in their own Gillette Stadium, losing 1-0 to Los Angeles Galaxy deep into overtime in front of 61,000 fans. Perhaps not surprisingly he was named 2002 MLS coach of the year and in 2003 – after being appointed head coach in November 2002 - was within a solitary goal of leading The Revs to a second consecutive MLS Cup Final. Nicol now resides in the Massachusetts town of Hopkinton with his wife and two children and is arguably the most successful British coach in US soccer since they dominated the NASL scene in the 1970s.

NILSSON, Roland Nils Lennart 1989-94

Born: 27 November 1963 Helsingborg, Sweden
(5ft 11ins, 11st 10lbs – 1989)
Debut: 9 December 1989
v Luton Town
Division One Home
Last Appearance: 7 May 1994
v Manchester City
Premier League Home
Total League
& Cup Appearances: 185+1 Goals: 3

Career Details:

Helsingborg IF		1981
IFK Gothenburg		1983
WEDNESDAY	5 December	1989 £375,000
Helsingborg IF	9 May	1994 Free
Coventry City	29 July	1997 £200,000
Helsingborg IF	1 July	1999

CAPS (@SWFC)
Sweden Full (31) v Belgium 21/02/90, v Algeria 11/04/90, v Wales 25/04/90, v Finland 27/05/90, v Brazil 10/06/90, v Scotland 16/06/90, v Costa Rica 20/06/90, v Denmark 05/09/90, v W.Germany 10/10/90, v Colombia 06/06/91, v Denmark 15/06/91, v Norway 08/08/91, v Yugoslavia 04/09/91, v Poland 07/05/92, v Hungary 27/05/92, v France 10/06/92, v Denmark 14/06/92, v England 17/06/92, v Germany 21/06/92, v Norway 26/08/92, v Israel 11/11/92, v France 28/04/93, v Austria 19/05/93, v Israel 02/06/93, v Switzerland 11/08/93, v France 22/08/93, v Bulgaria 08/09/93, v Finland 13/10/93, Austria 10/11/93, v Wales 20/04/94, v Nigeria 05/05/94

Classy and unflappable Swede Roland Nilsson is still regarded as one of the finest full backs to ever play for Wednesday and without doubt the club's best ever foreign import. Nilsson arrived in Sheffield, initially on trial, in November 1989 and was a virtual unknown to Owls fans although at the time he was a full International for Sweden. However his faultless displays soon endeared him to the Wednesday fans and he became one of the most popular players of the 1990s as The Owls challenged for honours. The right back was a defender in the true sense of the word and not many opposition players could get the better of 'Rolo' who had impeccable timing, an incredible level of fitness and was also a tremendous reader of the game. He was also remarkably consistent and in his second season at Hillsborough helped Wednesday to promotion from Division Two and played a pivotal role in the League Cup Final victory over Manchester United – with help from John Harkes he marked danger man Lee Sharpe out of the game.

Once described by his manager Ron Atkinson as the "best professional I've ever worked with" Nilsson's commitment to the cause was never in question and was no more typified than in May 1993 when 'Rolo' played for Sweden 24 hours before flying to London to appear for Wednesday in their F.A.Cup Final replay against Arsenal! It was therefore a sad day for Wednesday fans when in November 1993 Nilsson asked to be released from his contract to return home to Sweden. The Owls initially refused his request but eventually a compromise was reached where Nilsson would play out the season before leaving for his hometown club – technically on loan until his Owls contract expired in 1995. He was given a rapturous send off at his final game and Owls fans could only watch misty eyed as 'Rolo' helped Sweden to third place in the 1994 World Cup Finals.

Before signing his first professional contract with hometown club Helsingborg, Nilsson had won six caps at Swedish U-16 level and later added appearances at U-19 and U-21 level. He also appeared in Olympic qualifying games for his country before earning the first of a record breaking 116 full caps in May 1986, against Greece in Malmo. After having moved to IFK, Nilsson won the domestic league and cup double in 1983 and in 1987 added both the UEFA Cup and league title to his list of honours. After his highly successful five-year stay in English soccer Nilsson returned home and Owls fans were reminded of his qualities when he was named Swedish player of the year in 1996 and also helped Helsingborg complete a shock UEFA Cup win over Aston Villa. However in the summer of 1997 he made a surprise move back into the Premier League when old boss 'Big Ron' persuaded the Swede to sign for a cut-price fee. He was given standing ovations by Wednesday fans when appearing against The Owls over the next two seasons and would play in 69 games for the Sky Blues before suffering a punctured lung and fractured ribs at Highbury in March 1999 which effectively ended his career in England. Typically for Nilsson he recovered to make an emotional farewell appearance on the final day of the season before returning to Scandinavia to take up his appointment as player-coach of Helsingborg. A year later he led his side to the Swedish Championship and then returned to Highfield Road as coach in March 2001, playing a few games for the reserves at the end of the season due to an injury crisis. He was subsequently appointed caretaker manager in September of the same year and after a successful spell was handed the reins on a permanent basis in October 2001. After just failing to reach the Division One play offs he was surprisingly sacked in April 2002 so it was back home to Sweden where he gained employment with the Swedish F.A. as a coach. He is now in charge at Second Division club GAIS, being appointed at the Gothenburg club in November 2003.

NIMMO, Ian Wallace 1976-79

Born: 23 January 1958 Boston
(5ft 11ins, 11st 8lbs – 1977)
Debut: 13 December 1975
v Wigan Athletic
F.A.Cup Home
Last Appearance: 19 May 1979
v Hull City
Division Three Home
Total League
& Cup Appearances: 30+21 Goals: 13

Career Details:

WEDNESDAY	23 January	1976
Peterborough United	19 February	1977 Loan
Doncaster Rovers	6 June	1979 £15,000
Wyberton		

Striker Ian Nimmo signed for Wednesday on his eighteenth birthday after having initially joined straight from school in May 1974. He made a dramatic start to his first team career, netting on his debut after entering the fray as a substitute, and would make twenty appearances in his debut campaign, scoring six times as Wednesday just avoided the unthinkable drop into Division Four. Sadly this proved his best season at Hillsborough in four years as a professional as he had to be content with a handful of first and second team games until moving to Doncaster Rovers.

At Belle Vue he was a first team regular and helped Rovers to promotion from the basement division in 1981, finishing top scorer with 18 league goals. However, after 99 league and cup games injury caused his early retirement in July 1982 and Nimmo started to work as a driving instructor back in his native Lincolnshire. He also played for his local non-league side Wyberton for several years and now helps out with coaching duties as well as being Chairman of Wyberton Colts.

NIXON, Eric Walter 2003

Born: 4 October 1962 Manchester (6ft 4ins, 14st 6lbs – 2003)
Only Appearance: 27 September 2003
v Grimsby Town Division Two Home
Total League & Cup Appearances: 0+1 Goals: 0

Career Details:

Curzon Ashton		
Manchester City	12 December	1983 £1,000
Wolverhampton Wanderers	29 August	1986 Loan
Bradford City	28 November	1986 Loan
Southampton	23 December	1986 Loan
Carlisle United	23 January	1987 Loan
Tranmere Rovers	24 March	1988 £60,000
Reading	9 January	1996 Loan
Blackpool	5 February	1996 Loan
Bradford City	13 September	1996 Loan
Stockport County	28 August	1997 £100,000
Wigan Athletic	28 August	1998 Loan
Wigan Athletic	24 March	1999 Free
Tranmere Rovers	20 July	1999 Free
Kidderminster Harriers	12 October	2001 N/C
WEDNESDAY	September	2003 N/C

Veteran goalkeeper who made a surprise appearance as a substitute, when Wednesday were hit by a goalkeeping crisis in September 2003. The Owls had both Ola Tidman and Chris Stringer on the sidelines and with the senior youth goalkeeper also on the treatment table they had no choice but to register part-time goalie coach Eric Nixon as a player. He warmed the bench for two games before an injury to Kevin Pressman saw Nixon enter the record books as The Owls oldest post war player – aged 40 years, 358 days. The Mancunian had been on the Owls staff since January 2003 when he took over from Pressman as goalkeeping coach after the latter decided to concentrate on playing as Wednesday struggled to avoid the drop.

Although starting his career at Manchester City – while on City's books he became the first player to play in all four divisions in the same season, achieving the feat in 1986-87 - he is best known for a nine-year spell at Tranmere Rovers which brought forth a mammoth 440 league and cup appearances. During his time on Birkenhead he enjoyed many highs as Tranmere regularly qualified for the play-offs and also enjoyed several trips to Wembley – inside a twelve-month period he made four trips to the famous old stadium, winning the Associated Members Cup (then sponsored by Leyland Daf) in 1990, losing in the Play off Final in 1990, beating Bolton in the Second Division Play Off Final in 1991 and then losing to Birmingham City in the AMS Cup Final! The Prenton Park club also suffered play off semi-final heartbreak for three years running from 1993 to 1995. The second leg of the 1995 play off Final against Reading saw Nixon lose his place to rival Danny Coyne and it effectively signalled the end of Nixon's Tranmere career as the newcomer was ever present in the following season.

After almost eighteen years as a professional Nixon officially retired in 2001 but subsequently came out of retirement to help out Kidderminster Harriers and then made a sub appearance for Tranmere where he was now goalkeeping coach. Made more emergency appearances for Rovers during 2002-3 before spending eighteen months as part time coach at Wednesday before quitting in July 2004 after undergoing an operation to have his knee replaced. He decided to stay at his Birkenhead home and accept Tranmere's offer of extra hours coaching, enabling Nixon to also pursue his business interests in the area outside of football

NOBLE, Frank 1963-67

Born: 26 October 1945 Sheffield
(5ft 8ins, 10st 11½lbs – 1965)
Debut: 31 August 1963
v Burnley
Division One Away
Last Appearance: 30 October 1965
v Aston Villa
Division One Away
Total League
& Cup Appearances: 2 Goals: 0

Career Details:

WEDNESDAY	21 May	1963
Peterborough United	July	1967

Cool, thoughtful and two-footed full back who failed to make a lasting impression on Wednesday's first team. Sheffield born Noble, who attended Hurfield School, represented the City boys side as a youngster and initially joined Wednesday as an amateur in 1962. After helping the junior side to the last four of the F.A.Youth Cup in 1963 he signed professional forms and his reserve team debut came on the opening day of the 1963-4 campaign, at Old Trafford. Within a week he made his senior debut, as replacement for Peter Johnson, but with the likes of Brian Hill and Don Megson providing stiff competition the youngster had to knuckle down in reserve team soccer and hope for another chance. He would miss only a handful of Central League games over the next four seasons and although one more chance did come his way at Football League level a move to Peterborough proved the boost his career required. Appeared in 207 league games for United – scoring his solitary league goal – before a serious knee injury ended his playing career in 1973. Although other sources have Noble then playing for Eckington Miners Welfare this is in fact untrue as after retiring he moved into his father's building firm, which he now runs.

NOLAN, Ian Robert 1994-2000

Born: 9 July 1970 Liverpool
(6ft, 12st 11lbs – 1997)
Debut: 20 August 1994
v Tottenham Hotspur
Premier League Home
Last Appearance: 14 May 2000
v Leicester City
Premier League Home
Total League
& Cup Appearances: 197+2 Goals: 4

Career Details:

Preston North End	August	1988
Northwich Victoria		
Marine		
Tranmere Rovers	2 August	1991 £10,000
WEDNESDAY	18 August	1994 £1,700,000*
Released	30 June	2000
Bradford City	6 July	2000 Free
Wigan Athletic	9 August	2001
Released	30 June	2002
Southport	23 October	2002 N/C
Halifax Town	July	2003 Trial

*Including £200k for International cap

CAPS (@ SWFC)
N.Ireland FULL (11) v Armenia 05/10/96, v Germany 09/11/96, v Albania 14/12/96, v Portugal 29/03/97, v Ukraine 02/04/97, v Germany 20/08/97, v Portugal 11/10/97, v Germany 08/09/99, v Finland 09/10/99, v Malta 29/03/00, v Hungary 26/04/00

Ian Nolan was a rare example of a player who broke into league soccer at the second attempt. After initially failing to make a league appearance during his first taste of professional football, at Deepdale, a twist of fate earned him a second chance at Tranmere Rovers. After leaving Preston he had began working as an auto-electrician, whilst playing semi-pro for Marine, and one day Tranmere boss John King brought his car into Nolan's garage to be repaired. The duo started chatting and the outcome was that King invited Nolan for a trial and soon after he was back in the professional game. At Birkenhead he gained a reputation as a solid right-footed player who earned his crust as a left back and when in the summer of 1994 Wednesday were searching for a replacement for Nigel Worthington they fixed their eyes on Nolan.

Unfortunately with Trevor Francis determined to get his man The Owls were somewhat held to ransom by Tranmere and despite having only initially bid £750,000 for his services the fee then rose to £1m and then all the way to £1.5m! He was thrown straight into the side for the opening game of the season and would appear in 86 consecutive games, his great pace covering up any defensive frailties. However he did struggle to win over the club's fans and it was only when he gained more experience of Premier League football that his form improved. Also, due to his Irish roots, Nolan won the first of eighteen caps for Northern Ireland before he suffered a double fracture of his leg after colliding with Spurs' Justin Edinburgh in January 1998. He spent almost a year on the sidelines but on his return looked to have lost much of his speed and struggled as Wednesday were relegated in 2000. When his contract expired he left for Premier League Bradford City on a 'Bosman' free transfer

He spent only a season at the West Yorkshire club and after suffering relegation at two different sides in consecutive seasons Nolan moved to ambitious side Wigan Athletic. Unfortunately a stress fracture of his leg meant Nolan appeared in only eight first team games for The Latics and was released when his one-year deal expired. After brief spells at Conference sides Southport and Halifax Town he is now unattached.

O'BRIEN, Joseph 'Joey' 2004-05

Born: 17 February 1986 Dublin
(5ft, 11ins)
Debut: 8 December 2004
v Hull City
League One Home
Last Appearance: 26 February 2005
v Brentford
League One Away
Total League
& Cup Appearances: 14+1 Goals: 2

Career Details:

Stella Maris		
Bolton Wanderers	1 July	2004
WEDNESDAY	3 December	2004 3-month loan

CAPS (@SWFC)
Eire U-21 (1) v Portugal 08/02/05

Manager Paul Sturrock showed his sharp eye for a player when he brought inexperienced teenager Joey O'Brien to Hillsborough in December 2004. The Irishman had only appeared in one senior game for Bolton – a League Cup tie at Yeovil Town – but was captain of the club's reserve side and a Republic of Ireland Youth International. The competitive midfielder had previously represented Eire at every level from U15s to U19s and made a dream start to his league career when scoring after just nine minutes of his Owls debut. A crowd of almost 29,000 watched that game against Hull City – an attendance well in excess of the capacity at the Reebok – and it must have been an unnerving experience for the strong running player who was used to playing in front of only a handful of fans in the Premier Reserve League.

Over the weeks that followed O'Brien became more accustomed to the rough and tumble of League One and his initial loan spell was eventually extended to the maximum three months as Wednesday struggled with injuries to the heart of their midfield. Despite his tender years O'Brien became a consistent performer as the Owls embarked on a ten game unbeaten run to move into the play offs and his fine displays were rewarded when he won his first U-21 cap for Eire – playing alongside his Owls team mate Glenn Whelan. He grabbed his second goal for the club in the 2-0 win over Swindon Town in January 2005 and was handed the captain's armband for his final appearance in a Wednesday shirt. Like fellow loanee Kenwyne Jones he then returned to his mother club after having received a huge boost to his long-term aim of playing Premier League soccer for Bolton Wanderers.

O'CONNELL, Patrick 'Paddy' 1909-12

Born: 8 March 1887 Dublin
(5ft 8½ins, 11st 10lbs – 1911)
Died: 27 February 1959 London
Debut: 24 April 1909
v Bury
Division One Away
Last Appearance: 25 January 1912
v Middlesbrough
F.A.Cup Home
Total League
& Cup Appearances: 21 Goals: 0

Career Details:

Frankfort FC (Dublin)		
Belfast Celtic		
Stanville Rovers		
WEDNESDAY	March	1909 £50*
Hull City	May	1912 £250
Manchester United	May	1914 £1,000
Clapton Orient		WW1 Guest
Rochdale		WW1 Guest
Chesterfield		WW1 Guest
Dumbarton	August	1919
Ashington		1920

*Joint fee with Warren

CAPS (@SWFC)
Ireland Full (2) v England 10/02/12, v Scotland 16/03/12

Although he played league football at several English clubs and also won five caps for Ireland it was the incredible coaching career of Patrick O'Connell that made him almost unique in pre war football. It was at his final club, Ashington, that O'Connell first gained experience of coaching when being appointed player-manager in 1921 for the Northeast club's first season of League soccer. However it was his next move that was quite unexpected as in an era when coaches and players rarely ventured overseas the Dubliner was subsequently appointed manager coach at Spanish side Racing Santander in 1922 – starting an association with the country that would last the remainder of his working life. He spent seven years at Santander before going on to manage several of the greatest sides in Spanish soccer, starting with a five-year tenure at Athletico Madrid. During his only season at Betis Balompie – later renamed Real Betis – O'Connell won the Championship in 1935 which prompted an eventful three years at Catalan giants Barcelona.

He was in charge at Barca in July 1936 when a Military coup signalled the start of the Spanish civil war and is widely regarded as being a key figure in helping the Catalan giants survive the conflict. In fact the extreme mixture of sport and nationalism was nothing new for O'Connell as one of his previous clubs, Belfast Celtic, were eventually disbanded due to 'the troubles' so he was perhaps not totally unprepared for the turbulent times he experienced in Catalonia. He won the Catalonian League in 1936 and the Mediterranean League a year later and was also in charge when Barcelona embarked on a foreign tour to Mexico and the US in 1937 that would throw the cash-strapped club a financial lifeline. A party of 16 players and officials sailed for America but only four would return to war torn Barcelona with O'Connell one of the brave quartet. He remained in charge until 1938 and then spent a season back at Real Betis and the war years as manager at FC Sevilla. After the hostilities ended O'Connell remained in Spain and enjoyed a third spell at Betis and then two years back at Racing Santander before scouting for Huelva for nine years until his retirement in 1958.

His playing career had started in Irish minor soccer before his form for Belfast Celtic led to a transfer to Hillsborough. He actually joined under the strange condition that if his move proved successful Wednesday would pay a transfer fee! The Owls eventually offered £40 – for O'Connell and Peter Warren – but this was refused and in May 1911 Celtic asked the Irish F.A. to look into the matter – Wednesday finally paying £50 in April 1912. He was described as a great positional player while at Hillsborough although it was also said he would occasionally overdo his penchant for dribbling and was a somewhat rash tackler! However with McSkimming keeping him out of the side he was still considered too good a player to be stuck in the reserves so was allowed to leave for Hull City in May 1912. After leaving Wednesday he captained Ireland to the 1913-14 British Championships, playing in the first Ireland side to beat England in England, and while guesting for Rochdale in wartime soccer appeared for Ireland against Scotland in a Victory International at Ibrox in March 1919. When the hostilities ended he spent a season in Scottish soccer before starting his managerial odyssey.

O'DONNELL, Neil 1975-77

Born: 21 December 1949 Glasgow
(5ft 11ins, 11st – 1976)
Debut: 5 November 1975
v Gillingham
Division Three Home
Last Appearance: 27 October 1976
v Millwall
League Cup Away
Total League
& Cup Appearances: 47 Goals: 2

Career Details:

St. Augustine's		
Drumchapel Amateurs		
Possel Park		
Arsenal		Trial
Norwich City	30 December	1966
Gillingham	8 July	1974
WEDNESDAY	29 October	1975 Free

Ex-Scottish Youth International midfielder who started his professional career at Carrow Road, after initially joining Norwich as a trainee. At the Norfolk club O'Donnell proved a versatile and loyal player who in six years at City appeared in 64 games in addition to over 175 reserve team outings. After just over fifteen months at his next club, Gillingham, he followed his old 'Gills' boss Len Ashurst to Hillsborough although his debut proved eventful as the match at Walsall was abandoned due to a torrential downpour of rain! His 'official' debut came a few days later – ironically against the club he had just left – and he immediately became a fixture in the Wednesday side as they just avoided relegation from the Third Division.

Sadly within a few months a serious back injury had ended his playing career – he announced his intention to retire in January 1977 – and he was granted a testimonial match by The Owls with his old side Norwich City providing the Hillsborough opposition. The following season O'Donnell could still be found in football, managing Sheffield & District Sunday League side Signpost FC and later coaching Sheffield club for a short period, before opening his own betting shops. He still lives in Sheffield where he now works for a finance company.

O'DONNELL, Philip 'Phil' 1999-2003

Born: 25 March 1972 Bellshill, Scotland
(5ft 10ins, 10st 10lbs – 2000)
Debut: 11 September 1999
v Everton
Premier League Home
Last Appearance: 29 December 2001
v Norwich City
Division One Home
Total League
& Cup Appearances: 15+10 Goals: 1

Career Details:

Hamilton Colts		
Motherwell Boys Club		1985
Motherwell	30 June	1990
Glasgow Celtic	9 September	1994 £1.75m
WEDNESDAY	1 July	1999 Free
Released	30 June	2003 Free
Coventry City	1 July	2003 Trial
Motherwell	6 November	2003 Trial
Motherwell	2 January	2004 Free

Unfortunately the capture of Scottish midfielder Phil O'Donnell, on a highly lucrative 'Bosman' inspired 4-year contract in the summer of 1999, was in hindsight one of the worst signings ever made in The Owls history. His arrival, along with teammate Simon Donnelly, was much heralded by Wednesday boss at the time, Danny Wilson, but sadly for Wilson his new signing was already injured when he moved to Hillsborough and incredibly would make just a solitary sub appearance in his debut season at Wednesday. As he sat on the treatment table The Owls crashed out of the Premier League and when financial problems started to mount the salaries paid to several under-achieving players – O'Donnell amongst them - became a millstone around the club's neck. Unfortunately a catalogue of injuries over the remaining three years of his contract meant O'Donnell was a rare sight on the field of play for Wednesday fans and he astonishingly failed to make a first team appearance during the final eighteen months of his Wednesday career.

His injury record at Wednesday would have been no surprise to Celtic fans as following his big money move to Celtic Park in 1994 O'Donnell suffered his fair share of injuries although he did earn a Scottish Cup winners medal in 1995 plus a League Championship medal in 1998. He had previously enjoyed a successful spell at his first professional club Motherwell, scoring in the 4-2 Scottish Cup Final win over Dundee United in 1991 and earning his sole full cap for Scotland, against Switzerland in September 1993.

It would also be at Motherwell that O'Donnell would pick up the threads of his career after the disastrous spell in Sheffield, signing an 18-month contract in January 2004 after proving his fitness while on trial.

O'DONNELL, Ralph 'Rod' 1949-64

Born: 17 October 1931 Cudworth
(6ft 0½ins, 11st 7½lbs – 1954)
Debut: 17 November 1951
v Bury
Division Two Home
Last Appearance: 21 April 1962
v Nottingham Forest
Division One Away
Total League
& Cup Appearances: 183 Goals: 3

Career Details:

Upton Colliery		
WEDNESDAY	9 May	1949 Part-time
WEDNESDAY	12 February	1952 £30
Buxton	May	1964

Utility half back Ralph O'Donnell was spotted playing for Yorkshire League side Upton Colliery and signed amateur forms for Wednesday in February 1949, aged seventeen. Three months later he signed as a part-time professional and gained experience in The Owls youth and reserve sides before being called up for National Service in February 1950. It was while still serving in the R.A.F. that O'Donnell made his league debut although he had the misfortune to suffer a broken cheekbone in only his third senior game for Wednesday. He possessed many attributes – he was decisive in the tackle and boasted excellent distribution skills plus great positional sense - and became a mainstay of the Owls defence throughout the mid-1950s. He had the misfortune to break his leg late in 1953, after a collision with famous Manchester City keeper Bert Trautmann, but soon won his place back after returning to fitness and it was not until the emergence of Peter Swan and arrival of Don McEvoy that his first team place really came under threat. However after asking for a transfer in 1955 the resilient Yorkshireman was switched from centre halfback to left halfback and remained a regular for two more seasons, helping Wednesday to the Second Division Championship in 1956.

Unfortunately he broke his leg again and this was followed soon after by a cartilage operation that made O'Donnell reassess his career - the outcome was that in September 1957 it was announced that he had decided to turn part-time in order to attend teacher training college. He trained as a History and Physical Education teacher and remained a part-time player for the remainder of his career at Hillsborough although his commitment to Wednesday actually cost 'Rod' his job in 1961 when he took leave of absence to fly to Nigeria for the club's end of season tour. Two days before he was due to depart O'Donnell was told he could not leave as he failed to gain proper authorisation to take the requisite leave. As he had already committed himself to Wednesday O'Donnell did not let the club down but in his absence the Sheffield Education Authority dismissed him!

On his return to England he was unemployed, while still playing for Wednesday, but later found a P.E. job in West Riding. During the final years of his Owls career O'Donnell was a fixture in the club's reserve side, providing excellent cover at first team level whenever injuries struck, but a third broken leg sustained in 1963 finally brought the curtain down on his senior career. Soon after he was granted a place on the transfer list and six months later Buxton manager, and ex-Owl, Norman Curtis took Ralph to non-league Buxton. He continued to play for the Derbyshire club until May 1968 by which time 'Rod' had started a successful secondary career as a schoolboy coach – he moved to a Stoke school in 1966 and coached both Stoke and Staffordshire boys for many years. He also spent five years as England boys manager – plus three as assistant – before resigning in 1987 after a disagreement over selection policy. He retired from teaching in 1994 and still lives in Staffordshire.

O'NEILL, Harold 'Harry' 1919-22

Born: November 1894 Castle Ward, Newcastle (6ft, 11st 3lbs – 1920)
Debut: 25 October 1919
v Manchester City
Division One Away
Last Appearance: 26 November 1921
v Blackpool
Division Two Home
Total League
& Cup Appearances: 51 Goals: 0

Career Details:

Wallsend		1919
WEDNESDAY	14 October	1919 £100
Bristol Rovers	June	1922 £200
Swindon Town	16 August	1923 £100

The senior career of full back Harry O'Neill only started after he was de-mobbed from the Navy in 1919, spending two months at Northeast non-league outfit Wallsend. A move to Hillsborough quickly followed and during the Owls disastrous 1919-20 campaign he made seven appearances in a variety of defensive roles. However it was the departure of regular left back Jimmy Blair in November 1920 that opened the door for O'Neill and he remained first choice for a year until Bob Brown accepted a bid for his services from Bristol Rovers. He added 22 league appearances to his career tally while in the West Country and later netted his only goal in league soccer during a spell at Swindon Town. In the late 1920s O'Neill was in business in the Swindon area with his playing career having ended in 1928.

OAKES, Scott John 1996-2000

Born: 5 August 1972 Leicester
(5ft 10ins, 11st 13lbs – 1997)
Debut: 17 August 1996
v Aston Villa
Premier League Home
Last Appearance: 3 October 1998
v Middlesbrough
Premier League Away
Total League
& Cup Appearances: 7+20 Goals:1

Career Details:

Birstall		Sun.
Leicester City	9 May	1990
Luton Town	22 October	1991 Player-exchange
WEDNESDAY	31 July	1996 £450,000
Released	30 June	2000
Burnley	11 July	2000 Trial
Crystal Palace	August	2000 Trial
Cambridge United	29 August	2000 Trial
Cambridge United	30 October	2000 Free
Released	30 June	2001
Leyton Orient	3 July	2001 Free
St.Albans City	1 August	2002 Free
Shelbourne	April	2003 Free
St Albans City	1 July	2003 Free

When Leicester City manager David Pleat handed YTS trainee Scott Oakes his first professional contract it was the start of an association between the pair that would also see the latter signed by the former at both Luton Town and Wednesday. He had originally joined The Foxes as a trainee in August 1988 - playing his early football for a Leicestershire Sunday league team - but appeared in only four senior games for his hometown side before moving to Luton Town in an exchange deal that saw Oakes and Des Linton swapped for Steve Thompson. His brother Stefan later made the grade with both Leicester and Crewe while Scott shot to national prominence in 1994 when netting a spectacular hat-trick against top-flight West Ham United during The Hatters run to an F.A.Cup semi-final defeat against Chelsea at Wembley.

However after 27 goals in 173 league games Oakes became a free agent, arriving at Hillsborough on trial in July 1996 and within a week Pleat had secured his signature for the third time. Unfortunately it proved a wrong move for both Wednesday and Oakes as despite appearing in twenty first team games in his debut season the versatile midfielder became a peripheral figure and incredibly failed to start another game for Wednesday during the remaining three years of his contract! He was restricted almost exclusively to reserve team football in his second campaign at Wednesday and although a regular on the subs bench under Danny Wilson he became somewhat of a forgotten man – more famous for his father Trevor, who was a member of 1970s beat combo Showaddwaddy, than his own footballing skills. In simple terms the step up from a struggling First Division side to the Premier League proved too much for Oakes and on leaving Hillsborough he struggled to re-ignite a career that had stagnated at Wednesday.

He suffered a cruciate knee ligament injury in his final season at Wednesday and was still regaining full fitness when he signed non-contract terms for Cambridge United. Played alongside ex-Owls team mate Ritchie Humphreys at Cambridge before a season at Leyton Orient brought the curtain down on his Football League career. He then dropped into the Ryman League Premier Division to sign for his current club St Albans City while he later fulfilled a short term contract in Irish football.

OLIVER, Gavin Ronald 1980-85

Born: 6 September 1962 Felling, nr Gateshead (6ft 1ins, 12st 11lbs – 1981)
Debut: 6 September 1980
v Oldham Athletic
Division Two Away
Last Appearance: 2 February 1985
v Liverpool
Division One Home
Total League
& Cup Appearances: 18+11 Goals: 0

Career Details:

Redheugh Boys Club		
WEDNESDAY	6 August	1980
Tranmere Rovers	17 January	1983 Three-mnth loan
Brighton & Hove Albion	12 August	1985 Three-mnth loan
Bradford City	22 November	1985 £25,000
Matlock Town	March	1996
Sheffield Club		1997

As a youngster Gavin Oliver had a choice of signing for Wednesday or local side Middlesbrough but even though he had played for the Teeside club's nursery side it was Hillsborough that proved his destination. He signed apprentice forms in July 1979 and after breaking into the first team made a handful of appearances, primarily at right back or centre half. However despite not becoming a regular at Wednesday he would enjoy great success at Bradford City where in ten seasons he appeared in a mammoth 382 games, in a variety of defensive and midfield roles. After being granted a testimonial game against West Yorkshire rivals Leeds United he was forced to retire after three operations on his Achilles tendon and moved into non-league soccer.

After playing a few games for Sheffield FC – managed by his old friend and former Owls team mate John Pearson - he finally retired late in 1997. After ending his professional playing days Oliver spent eighteen months in the wholesale wine trade before an identical period working with the Football in the Community scheme at Bradford City. He then moved back to Sheffield to help his wife run a guest house in Hillsborough as well as working as a part-time Academy coach back at Wednesday. In July 2000 he started working for Leeds United in the same capacity and is now employed full time as Academy and Football in the Community Officer.

OLSEN, Kim 2004

Born: 11 February 1979 Herning, Denmark
(6ft 4ins, 13st 7lbs – 2004)
Debut: 7 February 2004
v Port Vale
Division Two Away
Last Appearance: 1 May 2004
v Luton Town
Division Two Away
Total League
& Cup Appearances: 7+5 Goals: 0

Career Details:

Ikast KFUM		
Ikast FS		
Holstebro		
FC Midtjylland	July	2002
Fortuna Dusseldorf	January	2004 Trial
WEDNESDAY	2 February	2004 £15,000
Contract cancelled	18 October	2004
Silkborg IF	7 December	2004

Towering, traditional style 'target man' who struggled to adapt to English football in his debut season, after arriving from Danish Superligen side FC Midtjylland on an 18-month contract. He was initially invited to Hillsborough on trial in January 2004, after being recommended by ex Wednesday player and manager Peter Eustace, and The Owls management took a gamble on the Dane who had only turned professional eighteen months earlier. He had previously played semi-professional in the Danish Second Division while working as a salesman for a clothing company that sold sportswear and workplace uniforms. However after becoming a full-time professional he failed to become established in the FC Midtjylland side and was mainly used as a substitute, scoring just five times in 24 games, before an unsuccessful trial at Fortuna from the fourth tier of German soccer – The Oberliga.

He was a regular scorer in Danish reserve team football but the form of his side's two forwards kept Olsen out of the first team starting eleven, prompting a fresh start at Hillsborough. Impressed the travelling Owls fans on his full debut at Rushden & Diamonds but overall he failed to show any real quality as Wednesday's season finished in disappointing fashion. One bright spot for the imposing attacker – who does possess a powerful shot - came in an April reserve cup-tie at Wrexham where his hat trick in a 6-0 win at least gave sceptical Owls fans a remainder why Chris Turner made him the first Dane to play for the club. However injury then saw Olsen miss the start of the next season and within a month of new manager Paul Sturrock taking the reins the two parties agreed to cancel his contract by mutual consent, after Olsen had failed to make a first team appearance under the Scot.

OWEN, Gary Alfred 1987-88

Born: 7 July 1958 St Helens
(5ft 9ins, 11st 5lbs – 1988)
Debut: 18 August 1987
v Oxford United
Division One Home
Last Appearance: 30 April 1988
v Arsenal
Division One Home
Total League
& Cup Appearances: 15+4 Goals: 0

Career Details:

Clockface Juniors		
Glazeborough		
Manchester City	May	1975
West Bromwich Albion	4 June	1979 £465,000
Panionios	July	1986 £5,000
WEDNESDAY	4 August	1987 £35,000
Released	17 May	1988
Hannerdi		
Apoel Nicosia		

Gary Owen was one of the most creative midfielders of his generation and cost West Brom a huge fee when they took him to The Hawthorns in 1979. He appeared in 124 games for City – after signing as an apprentice in August 1974 - and a further 229 for

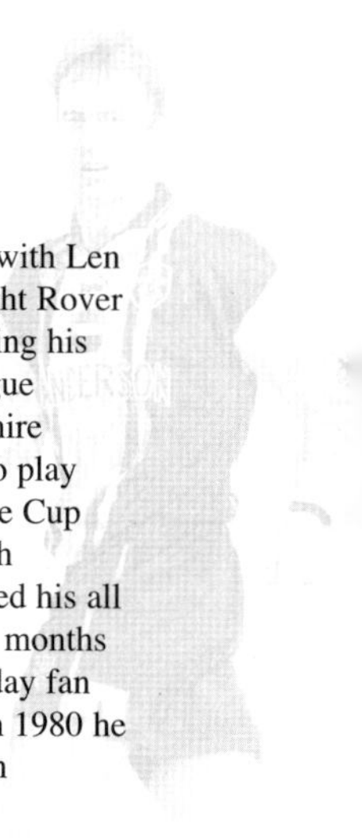

Albion but sadly a catalogue of injuries effectively ruined a blossoming career that had seen Owen appear in a record 22 games for the England U-21 side.

With his career on the ropes Owen was allowed to leave for Greek football in a cut-price move and was then surprisingly offered a trial at Wednesday by Howard Wilkinson in July 1987. He impressed sufficiently to be offered a one-year contract but his injuries had taken their toll and Owen struggled to impress in an Owls side which was short on quality due to the club's reluctance to increase their playing budget.

After a handful of appearances in Wilkinson's top-flight side he was subsequently released at the end of the season and after spells in Swedish and Cypriot football quit football in May 1990, aged only 31. After finishing with soccer he started a business buying and selling paintings – travelling thousands of miles to scour art galleries – and also ran a utilities company before starting to work as a commentator on local radio in 1997. He now works for Manchester Radio station Century FM, commentating on the big four at the weekends (the two Manchester and two Liverpool sides) and talking football alongside Graeme Sharp and Mickey Thomas during weekdays.

*As stated in other publications Owen did not play his youth football at Eccleston Youth club

OWEN, Gordon 1976-83

Born: 14 June 1959 Barnsley
(5ft 8ins, 10st 1lbs – 1978)
Debut: 27 December 1977 v Rotherham United Division Three Home
Last Appearance: 22 January 1983 v Carlisle United Division Two Home
Total League & Cup Appearances: 40+20 Goals: 7

Career Details:

West Green U-18		Sun.
West Green FC		Sat.
The Londoners		Sun.
Wolverhampton Wanderers		Trial
WEDNESDAY	19 November	1976 £50
Rotherham United	12 March	1980 3-month loan
Doncaster Rovers	6 November	1982 Loan
Chesterfield	25 March	1983 Loan
Cardiff City	4 August	1983 Free
Barnsley	24 August	1984 £27,000
Bristol City	21 August	1986 £30,000
Hull City	18 December	1987 Loan
Mansfield Town	13 January	1988 £35,000
Blackpool	2 August	1989 £15,000
Carlisle United	8 October	1990 Loan
Exeter City	13 December	1990 Free
Frickley Athletic		1991
Farsley Celtic		1992
Grimethorpe MW		1995*
Butchers Arms		1997*
Tom Treddlehoyle		Over 35s

*Only appeared in Carlsberg Pub Cup

At St.Helens school in Barnsley, Gordon Owen was the smallest player on the pitch but still played at centre half! Before joining Wednesday, aged 17, he could certainly be described as being football mad as he played for Ward Green Mens team on a Saturday afternoon, for The Londoners on a Sunday morning and then for Ward Green under 18s side on a Sunday evening! The ex-Barnsley boys player eventually metamorphosed into a winger and after scoring seven times in one game several Football League sides, including Sheffield United, Leeds and Newcastle, were after his services. However he eventually signed for Len Ashurst at Wednesday with his Saturday side Ward Green receiving a donation for his signature.

Over the next fifteen years Gordon - whose father 'Tuppeny Owen' was one of the quickest amateur wingers in South Yorkshire but sadly died before his son made the grade – appeared in 331 league games for a variety of sides although during his seven years at Hillsborough he was very much a fringe player, never able to really secure a permanent place in the starting eleven. After three loans spells – returning early from Chesterfield after they could not afford to pay his wages any more – he was re-united with Len Ashurst at Cardiff City and later played in the 1987 Freight Rover Trophy Final at Wembley when at Bristol City. After ending his league career at Exeter City, Owen dropped into non-league football and gained employment as a contractor to Yorkshire Water, a job he still holds today. However he continued to play football at minor level and won a Wragg Over-35s League Cup winners medal in 2000. He also played golf to such a high standard that at one point he played off scratch and showed his all round sporting prowess by playing cricket in the summer months for Norman Inn. Incidentally his mother is a big Wednesday fan and when Gordon moved to Rotherham United on loan in 1980 he assured her he would be fine on his own so she carried on watching The Owls!

OWEN, Niel 1976-77

Born: 14 October 1959 Bury
(5ft 5ins, 10st – 1976)
Only Appearance: 14 May 1977
v Oxford United Division Three Home
Total League
& Cup Appearances: 1 Goals: 0

Career Details:

WEDNESDAY	August	1976 App.
Rochdale	October	1977 N/C
Stalybridge Celtic		1978
Hanson Villa		Sun
Dial House		Sun.
Admiral Rodney		Sun.

Niel Owen was still a 17 year-old apprentice when he was thrust into the first team spotlight alongside fellow 'one game wonder' John Davis for the final home game of the season. The former Bury boys player helped Wednesday to a 2-0 win but this proved the highlight of the youngster's career as he failed to gain professional status at Wednesday, signing non-contract terms for Rochdale later in that year. He had originally been signed to schoolboy forms at Burnley and came to Hillsborough when The Clarets Chief Scout Dave Blakey moved to the same position at Wednesday. After playing half a season of reserve team soccer at Spotland – he failed to make a senior start for Rochdale – Owen dropped into non-league football while gaining employment in the printing industry. He later moved back to Sheffield to work in the same trade and played in local football before hanging up his boots.

*The spelling of Owen's Christian name has been confirmed with the player.

OWUSU, Lloyd 2002-03

Born: 12 December 1976 Slough
(6ft 1ins, 14st – 2002)
Debut: 1 September 2002
v Sheffield United
Division One Home
Last Appearance: 20 December 2003
v Chesterfield
Division Two Home
Total League
& Cup Appearances: 30+30 Goals: 9

Career Details:

Slough Town		
Brentford	29 July	1998 £25,000
WEDNESDAY	3 July	2002 Free
Reading	23 December	2003 Loan
Reading	25 March	2004 undisc.
Brentford	1 July	2005

When forward Lloyd Owusu became a free agent in the summer of 2002 he was courted by a multitude of Football League clubs, after netting 20 goals for Brentford as they reached the Second Division play off Final. In four years at Griffin Park the pacy attacker had become a big favourite with the Bees fans and netted 73 times in

192 league and cup games after having signed from non-league football. He gained a reputation as one of the most lethal forwards in the bottom two divisions and it was seen as a coup when Wednesday boss Terry Yorath secured his signature on a 3 year 'Bosman' inspired contract.

His debut for The Owls was delayed – he was recovering from an operation when he moved to Sheffield – but it was certainly worth waiting for as Owusu came off the subs bench against fierce rivals Sheffield United to amazingly score with his first touch, in front of an ecstatic Kop. It made Owusu an instant hit with Wednesday fans and arguably deflected any criticism when the newcomer failed to make the expected impact during the remainder of his debut campaign – he netted only four times in 34 games. His first season at Hillsborough was also badly affected by persistent bouts of sickness while on the field of play – in his next appearance after the derby game he entered the fray as a sub but after just seven minutes was himself substituted after being physically sick on the pitch. He proved only a fringe player throughout the season but in July 2003 was called into the Ghana squad for the African Nations Cup qualifying game against Rwanda – he failed to make the match day squad.

Thankfully his health problems were cured for his second season at Wednesday and early in the campaign Owusu showed signs of re-capturing his Brentford form – his best display in an Owls shirt coming in a 3-0 win at his old club in October 2003. However he could not bring consistency to his game and was in and out of the side before joining Reading on loan just before Christmas. Back in more homely surroundings his form impressed the Royals management and despite being sent off during his loan spell he moved to Berkshire on a permanent basis at the conclusion of his three-month stay.

OXLEY, Bernard 1934-35

Born: 16 June 1907 Whitwell
(5ft 9½ins, 10st 13lbs – 1934)
Died: 7 January 1975 Worksop
Debut: 5 May 1934
v Stoke City
Division One Home
Last Appearance: 4 March 1935
v Wolverhampton Wanderers
Division One Away
Total League
& Cup Appearances: 14 Goals: 4

Career Details:

Whitwell Colliery		
Whitwell Church Old Boys		
Chesterfield	December	1925
Sheffield United	May	1928 £1,350
WEDNESDAY	3 May	1934 £1,000
Plymouth Argyle	10 September	1935 £600
Stockport County	June	1936
Worksop Town	July	1938
Scunthorpe & Lindsay United	November	1938

Right-winger who is part of the select band of players to transfer directly between Sheffield's two professionals clubs. He arrived from Bramall Lane after eleven goals in 116 league games for The Blades but enjoyed only one full season at Wednesday, effectively acting as understudy to the great Mark Hooper. After failing to dislodge his rival, Oxley left for Plymouth Argyle and later played 68 league games for Stockport County before dropping into non-league soccer with Worksop Town. A move to Midland League Scunthorpe United came next before the war ended his playing career. In 1939 Bernard – whose brother Cyril played for Chesterfield, Southend United & Liverpool – moved to Holland to coach both Football and Cricket at Den Haag but in May 1940, along with his wife, had to flee the country through the port of Rotterdam as Germans parachuted in and bombs rained down. After returning home he started to work for the Worksop Fire Service and after being refused permission to join the R.A.F. he stayed in the service for the rest of his life. Away from work he was appointed Worksop Town manager in 1947, later scouted for Leyton Orient and also played cricket for Langworth.

PACKARD, Edgar 1936-52

Born: 7 March 1919 Mansfield
(5ft 10ins, 11st 6lbs – 1948)
Died: 14 January 1996 Mansfield
Debut:
2 September 1946 v Barnsley Division Two Home
Last Appearance:
10 November 1951 v Luton Town Division Two Away
Total League
& Cup Appearances: 126* Goals: 1
***Also appeared in 25 wartime games**

Career Details:

Clipstone Colliery		
WEDNESDAY	1 December	1936
Halifax Town	September	1952 £500

As a youngster Edgar Packard represented both Mansfield and Nottingham boys and arrived at Hillsborough via a playing spell at his local Colliery side. He initially joined on amateur forms in 1935 and after turning professional a year later became a regular at Central League level for The Owls. Unfortunately like many of his peers his promising career was then seriously affected by the onset of World War Two, Packard joining the Territorials just two days into the conflict - he was soon drafted and then went into the 1st Army as an artillery man. He remained on active duty for the full duration of the War and after escaping back to England from the Dunkirk beaches he returned overseas with the 46th Division, seeing active duty from Algiers to Tunis in North Africa, then in Cyprus and finally in Italy. He later served as an M.P in Rome and played for an Army side in the Olympic Stadium but his primary role as a gun layer meant that Packard hardly played any football throughout the war years, only occasionally turning out for Wednesday in the early war years.

Unfortunately when soccer returned it looked like Packard's early promise had been lost as he struggled to adapt to league soccer, despite appearing in 29 games in the first post war season. A cartilage operation during the 1948-9 season looked like it would spell the end for Packard but he bounced back and when Cyril Turton was injured at the back end of the 1948-9 season he stepped in and missed only five games until August 1951, being ever present as The Owls won promotion from the old Second Division in 1950. It had taken the fiercely loyal and determined halfback almost thirteen years to become established in the Owls first team and a broken jaw, suffered in November 1950, proved only a temporary set back. However competition from the likes of Ralph O'Donnell and Cyril Turton eventually pushed Edgar out of the limelight and despite forcing his way back into contention he left for Halifax Town.

Packard, who in his younger days was a useful amateur boxer and runner, appeared in 85 league games for Town before retiring from the game to work as a contractor to the Coal industry for the remainder of his working life. He also coached Mansfield Town colts for several years as well as coaching a variety of sides attached to the coal board.

PALETHORPE, John Thomas 'Jack' 1934-35

Born: 23 July 1909 Leicester
(5ft 11ins, 11st 2lbs – 1935)
Died: 6 June 1984 Slough
Debut: 15 December 1934
v Everton
Division One Home
Last Appearance: 28 September 1935
v Preston North End
Division One Home
Total League
& Cup Appearances: 34 Goals: 17

Career Details:

Maidenhead United		1927
Crystal Palace		Amateur
Reading	12 May	1930 Part-time
Reading	February	1931 Full-time
Stoke FC	15 March	1933 £2,500

Preston North End	16 January	1934 £1,000
WEDNESDAY	13 December	1934 £3,100
Aston Villa	14 November	1935 £2847*
Crystal Palace	16 October	1936
Chelmsford City	2 June	1938
Short Sports		1939
Colchester United		WW2 Guest

* including £97 of accrued benefit!

Although centre forward Jack Palethorpe spent only a short time at Wednesday he still made a big impression, averaging a goal every two games and scoring the opener, after just two minutes, in the 1935 F.A.Cup Final win over West Brom. After being signed by Billy Walker he took the place of crowd favourite Neil Dewar at the apex of The Owls' forward line and in only his fourth game grabbed a hat trick in a 4-0 win at Birmingham. He continued to scorer regularly but early in the following season fell out of favour, with Dewar re-claiming the No. 9 shirt. Soon after dressing room comedian Palethorpe was on his way out of Hillsborough, signing for relegation haunted Aston Villa.

He had actually started his playing career in amateur football, while working as a shoemaker, and first came to prominence at Maidenhead United where he set a club record in 1929-30 when scoring an astonishing 65 times in only 39 Spartan League games! This goal-scoring prowess eventually led to a move into League soccer where he repaid the initial faith shown by Reading with 54 goals in only 57 games and then helped Stoke to the Second Division Championship in 1933 and Preston to promotion from the same division a year later. After leaving Hillsborough he again spent only a short time at his next club – appearing in just six games for Aston Villa – before a stay of almost two years at Crystal Palace brought forth 11 goals in 39 games. In the summer of 1938 his old boss at Wednesday, Billy Walker, captured his signature for ambitious non-league side Chelmsford City while after the war he was manager and coach of North Town, a small village team just south of Maidenhead. After ending his playing days Jack – nicknamed S.O.S. – worked for Fairley Aviation Company before becoming a cabinet inspector in the Maidenhead area.

PALMER, Carlton Lloyd 1989-94, 2001

Born: 5 December 1965
Rowley Regis, Nr Oldbury
(6ft 2ins, 12st 4lbs – 1989)
Debut: 25 February 1989
v Wimbledon
Division One Away
Last Appearance: 20 October 2001
v Walsall
Division One Home
Total League
& Cup Appearances: 283+3 Goals:18

Career Details:

Whiteheath		
St. Michael's		
Oldbury		
Newton Albion		
Netherton		
Dudley Town		
West Bromwich Albion	21 December	1984
WEDNESDAY	22 February	1989 £750,000
Leeds United	1 July	1994 £2,750,000*
Southampton	26 September	1997 £1,000,000
Nottingham Forest	19 January	1999 £1,100,000
Coventry City	17 September	1999 Free
Watford	15 December	2000 Loan
WEDNESDAY	13 February	2001 Loan
Loan return	May	2001
WEDNESDAY	3 September	2001 3-month loan
Released	24 October	2001
Stockport County	6 November	2001 Free
Darlington	November	2003 Trial
Dublin City	26 August	2004

*Including £150k when Leeds qualified for Europe in first year of 4 year contract

CAPS (@SWFC)
England Full (18) v CIS 29/04/92, v Hungary 12/05/92, v Brazil 17/05/92, v Finland 03/06/92, v Denmark 11/06/92, v France 14/06/92, v Sweden 17/06/92, v Spain 09/09/92, v Norway 14/10/92, v Turkey 18/11/92, v San Marino 17/02/93, v Turkey 31/03/93, v Holland 28/04/93, v Poland 29/05/93, v Norway 02/06/93, v USA 09/06/93, v Brazil 13/06/93, v Holland 13/10/93
England 'B' (5) v Eire 27/03/90, Switzerland 20/05/91, v Spain 18/12891, v France 18/02/92, v Czechoslovakia 24/03/92
England U-21 (4) v Bulgaria 05/06/89, v Senegal 07/06/89, v Eire 09/06/89, v USA 11/06/89

The box to box running and never say die attitude of Carlton Palmer was a vital part of the successful Owls side of the early 1990s, his tigerish midfield play complimenting the silky skills of John Sheridan to create an outstanding partnership at the heart of the Wednesday side. He was Ron Atkinson's first signing as Owls boss, costing Wednesday a club record fee, and repaid the faith shown by his former manager at West Brom by being an almost ever present throughout his first spell at Hillsborough. He quickly endeared himself to the Wednesday faithful and his industrious displays also brought a multitude of representative honours, including eighteen full caps for England under the somewhat controversial reign of Graham Taylor. His only real disappointment, apart from the double Cup Final defeat in 1993, came in 1991 when a foolish red card at Portsmouth two weeks before the League Cup Final meant Carlton was suspended for the Wembley clash with Manchester United. He did however help Wednesday to promotion in 1991 and then into Europe a year later – after just missing out on a unlikely Championship medal - before a fall out with boss Trevor Francis led to his transfer up to M1 to Leeds United. Incidentally although not a renowned finisher Palmer once famously scored a first half hat trick – versus QPR in September 1991 – which left the watching Hillsborough crowd open mouthed with astonishment!

Under the stewardship of Howard Wilkinson he was a regular as Leeds qualified for Europe in his first season and appeared in 129 games, scoring 7 times, before joining old Owls team mate David Hirst on the South Coast at Southampton after falling out of favour with new Leeds boss George Graham. Although often maligned by the National media he always proved an invaluable player at club level and remained a consistent performer in top-flight football well into his 30s. He was surprisingly brought back to Wednesday by Peter Shreeves in February 2001 and his effect on the dressing room and inspirational displays on the pitch – alongside fellow veteran Trond Soltvedt - was a major factor in The Owls escape from relegation. He quickly returned for a third spell but this time there was no happy ending as an apparent fall out with caretaker manager Terry Yorath saw the remaining six weeks of his contract paid up and Palmer appointed player-manager at First Division strugglers Stockport County in early November 2001. Palmer – who started his career as a YTS player at West Brom in July 1983 and won four England U-21 caps while at The Hawthorns – failed to save County from relegation but remained in charge, dropping the player prefix of his job title in March 2003. In September 2003 his Stockport side fought back from two goals down to draw against Wednesday at Hillsborough but six days later he was sacked after winning only 25 and losing 50 of the 92 matches played under his reign. He later re-launched his playing career in Irish football and in November 2004 was placed in temporary charge at Mansfield Town after Keith Curle was suspended. He remained as temporary boss until being give the reins on a permanent basis in March 2005.

PARKER, Raymond Dennis 'Ray' 1948-49

Born: 27 January 1925 Thurcroft
(5ft 11ins, 11st 5lbs – 1948)
Only Appearance: 30 October 1948
v Fulham
Division Two Home
Total League
& Cup Appearances: 1 Goals: 0

Career Details:

Thurcroft		
Chesterfield	February	1945
WEDNESDAY	24 April	1948 £3250
Frickley Colliery		1949
Buxton		1950
Bradford City	June	1951
Wisbech Town	July	1953
Frickley Colliery		1955
Spalding United		1956
Retford Town		1957
Thurcroft		1959

Ray Parker's first experience of organised football came as a member of the Rother Valley U-9 side and after leaving school began his working life down the local pit. While working as a miner he also played amateur football for his village side and it was from here that he signed as a semi professional for Chesterfield during the latter months of the Second World War. He went on to appear in 14 league games for the Derbyshire club before Eric Taylor secured his signature for The Owls. The centre half played in half of Wednesday's reserve fixtures during the 1948-9 season but was only called upon once for first team duty, a disappointing 2-1 home defeat against Fulham at Hillsborough. He failed to impress during his sole appearance and at the end of the campaign dropped completely out of league football to sign for Frickley Colliery.

Two years later Parker was brought back into league soccer by Bradford City and would enjoy the best years of his senior career, appearing in 43 league and cup games for City and also netting his only goal – ironically the sole strike of a Valley Parade game against his old side Chesterfield. However forty of those appearances had come in his first season – playing as a left back – and after losing his place early in the next campaign Parker was stuck back in reserve team soccer until again dropping down into non-league football. He ended his playing career back in the colours of his village side and in later life spent nine years scouting for West Brom as well as several other sides including Hull City, Norwich City, Doncaster Rovers and Bolton Wanderers.

PARKES, David 1914-20

Born: 18 June 1892 Lye, Worcestershire
(5ft 11ins, 12st 4lbs – 1914)
Died: 14 June 1975 Lye, Worcestershire
Debut: 11 March 1914
v Derby County
Division One Away
Last Appearance: 7 February 1920
v Preston North End
Division One Home
Total League
& Cup Appearances: 50* Goals: 1
***Also appeared in 7 wartime games**

Career Details:

Newcastle Town (Staffs.)		
Brighton & Hove Albion	July	1912
WEDNESDAY	March	1914 £1500 + G.Beech
St.Luke's (Cradley Heath)		WW1
Stourbridge		WW1
WEDNESDAY	16 December	1919 £75
Stoke FC	May	1920 £150
Llanelly		1921
Rochdale	May	1922
Macclesfield Town	May	1928

It was his display for Brighton against Wednesday, in a February 1914 F.A.Cup tie, which led directly to the transfer of David Parkes to Hillsborough. The Owls hierarchy were so impressed by the halfback – despite Wednesday beating the South coast club 3-0 - that they paid a substantial fee for his services, which at the time was a record for Brighton. After 47 Southern League appearances for The Seagulls he was put straight into the Wednesday side, replacing Bob McSkimming in the No.5 shirt, and was a regular for two seasons as his new club just avoided relegation and then revived to finish seventh in the final season before the Great War. During the war years Parkes played non-league football but hit disciplinary problems in October 1915 when he was sent off playing for Cradley against Halesowen in the Birmingham League but refused to accept the decision, leaving the referee no option but to abandon the game. Parkes was later banned for five games, two for kicking an opponent and three for refusing to leave the pitch.

He had previously broken his leg whilst playing for Cradley during the 1914-15 season and suffered the same fate after returning from the aforementioned suspension. It was feared at that point that Parkes may not play again and he was even given a benefit, raising £79 and 10 shillings. However he recovered to play a handful of games for Wednesday in wartime football and when he re-signed in December 1919 Parkes quickly recaptured his pre-war form that had seen him established as one of the best backs in the country. Unfortunately Wednesday were experiencing one of the most dismal seasons in their long history and at the end of the season Parkes was one of many to be released as the decks were cleared for new manager Bob Brown. A short six-game spell followed at Stoke before it was back to non-league soccer with Welsh club Llanelly. He was quickly back into senior football however at Rochdale – immediately being appointed captain on signing – and played in 209 games for the Lancashire club before being given a benefit prior to joining non-league Macclesfield Town. Incidentally while at Spotland he was well known for having a few pints in 'The Church Inn' before the game!

PATERSON, Marr 1911-12

Born: 1888 Alloa, Scotland (5ft 7ins, 11st 2lbs – 1911)
Debut: 11 February 1911 v Liverpool Division One Away
Last Appearance:
23 March 1912 v Bolton Wanderers Division One Home
Total League & Cup Appearances: 21 Goals: 2

Career Details:

Leith Athletic		
WEDNESDAY	February	1911 £450*
Released		1912
Lochgelly United		

*Joint fee with Campbell

Scottish inside forward, who spent just over a year at Wednesday after signing from amateur football. He started the opening four games of the 1911-12 campaign but after Wednesday failed to gain a victory he was displaced by Teddy Glennon at inside-right and would appear only occasionally until returning home to Scotland in 1912. In November 1914 it was reported he was playing for Lochgelly United.

PEACOCK, Lee Anthony 2004 -

Born: 9 October 1976 Paisley
(6ft, 12st 8lbs - 2004)
Debut: 7 August 2004
v Colchester United
League One Home
Total League
& Cup Appearances: 22+11 Goals: 6

Career Details:

Carlisle United	19 March	1995
Mansfield Town	17 October	1997 £90,000
Manchester City	5 November	1999 £500,000
Bristol City	10 August	2000 £600,000
WEDNESDAY	1 July	2004 Free

Despite only missing seventeen league games, the 2004-05 campaign was a season of frustration for Lee Peacock as a series of major and minor injuries totally disrupted his debut season. He arrived at Wednesday with a big reputation after 63 goals in 175 games at Bristol City, following a big money move from Manchester City. Unfortunately for City he was absent through injury from their 2004 Play Off final defeat to Brighton and a few weeks later he completed a Bosman free transfer to Hillsborough. The former Scottish youth international had started his professional career at Carlisle United and enjoyed early success when winning the Associate Members Cup in 1997. While at Brunton Park he also won his solitary U-21 cap for Scotland while after a successful spell at Mansfield Town was sold to Manchester City. Just ten appearances accrued while at City and another move soon followed; Peacock signing for Danny Wilson's Bristol City in the summer of 2000. The hard running, physical target man became a big hit with Robins fans during his four years in Bristol - scoring in the 2003 Associate Members Cup Final win over Carlisle United - and it looked a coup by Chris Turner when he persuaded Peacock to make Hillsborough his next port of call.

Unfortunately for Peacock his hopes of making an early impression were rocked when he was sidelined with an ankle problem that left him on the sidelines for over three months. He was obviously not fit when he returned to action but he soldiered on to remain in the first team squad for the rest of the season, regaining some semblance of fitness to score a crucial goal in the play off semi-final at Brentford. That goal effectively meant Peacock would finally get to appear in a League One play off final - a year after he was forced to miss out - and would experience one of the highlights of his playing career as Hartlepool were beaten 4-2 to turn Peacock into a Championship forward overnight.

PEACOCK, John 1930-31

Born: 15 March 1897 Wigan
(5ft 9ins, 11st 3lbs – 1930)
Died: 4 March 1979 Ince, Lancashire
Only Appearance: 8 September 1930
v Chelsea
Division One Home
Total League
& Cup Appearances: 1 Goals: 0

Career Details:

Wigan Recreation		
Atherton FC		
Everton	June	1919
Middlesbrough	May	1927
WEDNESDAY	16 May	1930 £500
Chelsea	September	1930
Clapton Orient	May	1931

Experienced halfback John Peacock had won three England caps while at previous club Middlesbrough but was brought to Hillsborough by Bob Brown to aid the development of Wednesday's young players. He stayed in Sheffield for just one season – being a regular in the Owls Central league side – and was called upon just once at first team level for a home draw with Chelsea. The Stamford Bridge club would be Peacock's next destination but he failed to make a senior appearance for The Blues and ended his league career at fellow London club Clapton Orient. In March 1933 he left these shores to become coach of Swedish side Sleipnir, returning to the UK in July 1939 when he was appointed trainer at Wrexham.

PEARCE, Andrew John 'Andy' 1993-95

Born: 20 April 1966 Bradford on Avon
(6ft 4ins, 14st 6lbs – 1995)
Debut: 14 August 1993
v Liverpool
Premier League Away
Last Appearance: 18 November 1995
v Manchester City
Premier League Home
Total League
& Cup Appearances: 84+5 Goals: 4

Career Details:

Wednesbury Town		
Stourbridge		
Halesowen Town		
Coventry City	15 May	1990 £15,000
WEDNESDAY	14 June	1993 £500,000
Wimbledon	22November	1995 £600,000
Aldershot	12 October	1999
Released	30 June	2000

Giant defender who became the most unlikely of cult heroes in his first season at Wednesday after netting in three consecutive games, the last of the trio coming against The Blades in a 3-0 derby win at Hillsborough. He was never the most composed or refined player – he tended to clear the ball into row Z rather than play out of defence – but remained a regular for two seasons under Trevor Francis. When David Pleat was appointed manager Pearce fell out of favour and stiff competition from the likes of Des Walker, Julian Watts and Peter Atherton ensured he played only five senior games in what proved his final season at Wednesday. Incidentally his move to Hillsborough provided a £48,000 windfall for his old club Halesowen who had sensibly inserted a sell-on clause when he moved to Highfield Road.

The old-fashioned style centre half was a rare example of a player who did not turn professional until aged 24 as he worked in two factories and for a scaffolding firm before becoming a hod carrier. It was while employed on a building site that he was invited to Coventry City for trials, signing his first full-time contract after impressing the Sky Blues hierarchy. He would appear in 81 games for City before moving to Hillsborough in a deal that was overshadowed by the club record signing of Des Walker soon after. Wednesday fans were divided in their opinion of Pearce so reaction was unsurprisingly mixed when he joined Wimbledon to help ease their injury crisis. Unfortunately he experienced a nightmare spell with the Londoners and after making only eight appearances in his first season failed to play another senior game until dropping into non-league football when his contract expired in 1999 – at one point Pearce was being paid his salary but not even training with Wimbledon! After 14 games for the reformed Aldershot Town he was released in June 2000 and subsequently retired from football – he now works as a construction manager for a roofing company back in his native West Midlands.

* Never played for Tipton Town or Ludlow Town

PEARSON, John Stewart 1981-85 & 1995

Born: 1 September 1963 Sheffield
(6ft 2ins, 11st $9^1/_2$lbs – 1981)
Debut: 13 September 1980
v Bristol City
Division Two Home
Last Appearance: 24 June 1995
v FC Basel
Intertoto Cup Away
Total League
& Cup Appearances: 80+49 Goals: 27

Career Details:

Sheffield Rangers		
WEDNESDAY	12 May	1981
Charlton Athletic	20 May	1985 £100,000
Leeds United	15 January	1987 £70,000
Rotherham United	28 March	1991 Loan

Barnsley	8 July	1991 £135,000
Hull City	9 January	1992 Loan
Carlisle United	9 August	1993 Free
Mansfield Town	18 November	1994 N/C
Cardiff City	27 January	1995 Free
Released	May	1995
WEDNESDAY	June	1995 N/C
Merthyr Tydfil	August	1995
Stalybridge Celtic	August	1995
Ashfield United	August	1995
Chorley	September	1995
Hallam	December	1996
Sheffield Club	January	1997
Sheffield All Stars		

CAPS (@SWFC)
England Youth (3) v Spain 25/05/81, v Scotland 27/05/81, v Scotland 23/03/82

Sheffield born forward John Pearson perhaps holds the most unique record amongst Wednesday players as his penultimate appearance in an Owls shirt occurred an incredible ten years, one month and eighteen days before his final game! This amazing fact of course was caused by The Owls late decision to enter the UEFA Intertoto Cup in the summer 1995 which meant they had almost no senior players available for the first group game against Swiss club Basel. As well as several youngsters being drafted into the line-up The Owls also signed some veterans, for a one off match fee, with John Pearson being one of those individuals. His appearance would have brought back memories for the handful of Owls fans that travelled across Europe of a teenage Pearson who burst onto the Hillsborough scene in the early 1980s. He had started his career in Sheffield youth football as a midfielder but at the age of 14 was moved into the attack which transformed his fortunes, signing apprentice forms for Wednesday in June 1979

After representing Sheffield and South Yorkshire boys Wednesday fan Pearson – he lived just minutes from the ground - was a prominent member of the Owls successful Youth Cup side that reached the last eight in 1980. It was while still a trainee that he made a dream start, scoring on his home debut in a 1-0 win over Bristol City and in fact the lanky, tall forward scored in his first four games before returning to Central League football. However he was soon back in the first eleven and under Jack Charlton was a regular – being used in a target man role, which suited the manager's style of play. Representative honours followed for the forward nicknamed 'Bambi' by Wednesday fans – he was an unused sub for the England U-21 game against Italy in 1984 – while in September 1982 he had entered the club record books when netting the quickest ever goal at Hillsborough – 13 seconds against Bolton Wanderers. The arrival of Howard Wilkinson did not greatly affect his first team opportunities but after helping Wednesday to promotion in 1984 he figured rarely in the top-flight and eventually moved to Charlton Athletic.

An eighteen-month spell in London brought forth ten goals in 72 games before Pearson returned to Yorkshire to sign for Leeds United. While at Elland Road he was a losing F.A.Cup semi-finalist back at Hillsborough in 1987 but after leaving United led a somewhat nomadic existence, plying his trade at six other league clubs before joining Conference side Merthyr. While at Stalybridge Celtic he also played a solitary game for Ashfield United, as a favour to a friend, which was possible as both clubs were in different leagues. In March 1996 he began working as an Insurance salesman but in January 1997 made history when being appointed the first ever full time employee of Sheffield Club - his brief was team and commercial manager. He still turned out for Sheffield when injuries bit into the squad and in May 2000 also became landlord of the Coach & Horses public house that backs onto the football ground. In March of the same year he also started to work for a Sheffield based company – coaching children aged from 6 to 14 years old – but in January 2001 he resigned as Sheffield boss, severing all ties with the club to became a full time soccer agent – alongside Imre Varadi - with a Leeds based company. In addition on most Saturdays Pearson can be heard giving his totally unbiased (ahem!) opinion as co-commentator for Radio Sheffield at Wednesday games.

PEARSON, Mark 'Pancho' 1963-65

Born: 28 October 1939
Ridgeway, Derbyshire
(5ft 7ins, 11st 8lbs – 1963)
Debut: 5 October 1963
v West Bromwich Albion
Division One Away
Last Appearance: 16 January 1965
v Liverpool
Division One Away
Total League
& Cup Appearances: 42 Goals: 11

Career Details:

Manchester United	May	1957
WEDNESDAY	4 October	1963£17,000
Fulham	May	1965
Halifax Town	March	1968

After captaining North-East Derbyshire boys and playing four times for England schoolboys Mark Pearson joined Manchester United straight from school in 1955. After two years as an amateur he progressed to the professional ranks – after winning an England Youth cap - but his debut came in sad circumstances, against Wednesday in the first game after the Munich Air Disaster. Although not tall he was well built and was considered a clever and constructive inside forward who always played with enthusiasm for 90 minutes. Unfortunately he was perhaps over enthusiastic on occasion, as he was red carded twice in his Old Trafford career while his 'Teddy Boy' image constantly landed him in hot water. Rather unfairly he gained a bad reputation at United and after 14 goals in 80 games started afresh at Hillsborough after failing to become a regular at Old Trafford, despite showing immense early promise.

He went straight into the side at Wednesday, enjoying a good first season, but lady luck deserted him in the following campaign as he suffered a broken leg in the September 1964 home game with Burnley. After recovering to play four reserve games he made his comeback at Liverpool in January 1965 but incredibly fractured his leg again, which finished his Wednesday career on a sad note. Pearson – who was first nicknamed 'Pancho' while at Manchester United due to his rather unfashionable sideburns – was known as a player who could score spectacular goals and he was signed for a second time by Vic Buckingham when moving on a free transfer to Fulham in 1965 – Buckingham was previously in charge at Hillsborough. He nearly suffered relegation in his debut season at Craven Cottage but in April 1966 netted the crucial goal that saved the Londoners from relegation after they had incredibly won 9 of their final 13 games. After totalling 60 games his final league side was Halifax Town where after just five games he retired – he did not play non-league football at Bacup Boro as stated in other publications. He then worked for a Bradford engineering company for twenty years, as a driller, and from 1994 has been self-employed in the same role.

PEARSON, Nigel Graham 1987-94

Born: 21 August 1963 Nottingham
(6ft 1ins, 13st 3lbs – 1988)
Debut: 17 October 1987
v Nottingham Forest
Division One Away
Last Appearance: 18 September 1993
v Southampton
Premier League Home
Total League
& Cup Appearances: 218+6 Goals: 20

Career Details:

Heanor Town		
Shrewsbury Town	12 November	1981 £5,000
WEDNESDAY	16 October	1987 £250,000
Middlesbrough	19 July	1994 £500,000

The name of Nigel Pearson will always be linked with The Owls glory season of 1990-91 when his inspirational leadership and dozen goals from centre half powered the club to promotion and League Cup success. He won the 'Alan Hardaker' Man of the match award at Wembley and was an automatic choice at the heart of Wednesday's defence for five seasons after joining from Shrewsbury Town. He had started his career in Nottinghamshire non-league football and came to The Owls attention when giving two commanding displays for The Shrews against Wednesday in League Cup meetings between the sides early in the 1987-88 season. When at the peak of his game Pearson was the heart and soul of the Wednesday side and was badly missed during the two 1993 Wembley Cup Finals. He was absent after breaking his leg in the League Cup semi-final at Blackburn Rovers and a second shin fracture inside six months – at home to Southampton in September 1993 – effectively ended his Wednesday career as Pearson failed to play another senior game for the club.

Despite his injury problems it was still a surprise to many when he was sold to Middlesbrough and the doubters were probably proved right as Pearson immediately captained Boro to the 1995 Division One Championship. He then suffered triple heartbreak during the Teeside club's extraordinary 1996-7 campaign when losing in both domestic Cup Finals in addition to suffering relegation from the top division. He again led Boro in their 1998 League Cup Final loss and was tipped to return to Hillsborough as boss when he finally hung up his boots. However Pearson was then appointed director of coaching at Third Division strugglers Carlisle United in December 1998 but lasted only until May 1999 – ironically being sacked just ten days after he had helped the Cumbrians stay in the Football League. Pearson – whose grandad Percy Mills played for Notts County – then spent two years as assistant manager at Stoke City and after coaching the England U-16 and U-20 side he returned to club football in November 2004 when being appointed assistant manager to Bryan Robson at West Bromwich Albion.

PEARSON, Stanley 'Stan' 1917-20

Born: 1st Quarter 1896 Sheffield
Debut: 1 September 1919
v Manchester United
Division One Away
Last Appearance: 6 September 1919
v Middlesbrough
Division One Away
Total League
& Cup Appearances: 2* Goals: 0
***Also appeared in**
36 wartime games, scoring 3 goals

Career Details:

Wycliffe		
WEDNESDAY	May	1917
Released	May	1920
Malin Bridge Old Boys		1921
Huddersfield Town	18 November	1921 £175
Released	July	1922
Denaby United	August	1922

Fast and tricky right winger who joined The Owls during the Great War, impressing greatly during the 1918-19 campaign. Sadly in only the second post war game he was badly injured and his senior career looked finished before it had really begun. The fair-haired attacker did not play at all during the following season but eventually recovered sufficiently to sign for Sheffield amateur side Malin Bridge. Pearson – who possessed a great shot and loved to cut in from the wing – made a surprise return to league soccer when joining Huddersfield Town but appeared in only one league and one F.A.Cup tie for The Terriers before being released in the summer of 1922.

PEARSON, Trevor 1969-76

Born: 4 April 1952 Sheffield
(5ft 11ins, 11st 7lbs – 1972)
Debut: 28 March 1972
v Fulham
Division Two Away
Last Appearance: 8 April 1972
v Norwich City
Division Two Away
Total League
& Cup Appearances: 4 Goals: 0

Career Details:

Granville College		
WEDNESDAY		1969-76 Amat.
Heanor Town		Loan
Woodseats WMC		Sun.
Kiveton Park		1973
Stocksbridge Works		1974
Matlock Town	19 September	1974
Norton Woodseats		1976
Frecheville CA/Black Bull (Sun.)		1978
Ecclesfield Red Rose		1980
Windsor BL		1981-91
Matlock Town		1984-85

The amazing story of Trevor Pearson certainly brings hope to all those footballers who drag themselves out of bed on a Sunday morning to run around the various park pitches of Sheffield. Back in March 1972 goalkeeper Trevor Pearson was an apprentice engineer who was playing in the Sheffield Sunday League for Woodseats WMC. He had signed amateur forms for Wednesday back in 1969 but had only played in two reserve games; mainly acting as cover when the senior goalies were absent. However the 19-year old Pearson was just about to star in his own fairytale as Wednesday hit a goalkeeping crisis that put both Peter Grummitt and Peter Springett out of action for three weeks. To make matters worse the transfer deadline had passed and when the Football League stubbornly refused Wednesday permission to sign a loan keeper, Owls boss Derek Dooley had no choice but to send for Pearson.

On receiving the shock call up Pearson commented, "I was stunned. First he (Dooley) asked me if I was fit to play. I thought there must be a reserve match or something. I nearly fell over when he said he wanted me at Fulham. Good job I was in the ambulance room". The Owls England amateur International Youth player Steve Barrett was ineligible because he had not signed league forms so it was a straight choice between 16 year-old apprentice Kevin Wilson and Pearson. It was of course the older keeper who got the nod and Pearson – who trained twice at week at Hillsborough while on The Owls books – was thrown in at the deep end, conceding four goals as Wednesday were well beaten. However the youngster was not blamed for any of the goals and had the great satisfaction of conceding only one goal in the next three games before dropping out of the limelight and back into amateur football.

Almost fours years later – in January 1976 – Pearson was recalled for a reserve team game and would play in local soccer until retiring at the age of 39, after having keyhole surgery on his knee. Throughout his playing career Pearson had worked as an engineer in Sheffield but now lives in Mansfield, working as a Quality manager at British Aerospace in Nottinghamshire.

PEMBRIDGE, Mark Anthony 1995-98

Born: 29 November 1970
Merthyr Tydfil
(5ft 8ins, 11st 12lbs – 1997)
Debut: 22 July 1995
v AGF Aarhus
Intertoto Cup Home
Last Appearance: 2 May 1998
v Aston Villa
Premier League Home
Total League
& Cup Appearances: 102+5 Goals: 14

Career Details:

George Town		
Pen Y Darren Boys Club		
Hoover		
Luton Town	1 July	1989
Derby County	2 June	1992 £1.25m
WEDNESDAY	19 July	1995 £900,000
Benfica	1 July	1998 Free
Everton	6 August	1999 Free
Fulham	1 September	2003 £500,000

CAPS (@SWFC)
Wales Full (17) v Moldova 06/09/95, v Germany 11/10/95, v Albania 15/11/95, v Switzerland 24/04/96, v San Marino 02/06/96, v Faroe Islands 31/08/96, v Holland 05/10/96, v Holland 09/11/96, v Turkey 14/12/96, v Eire 11/02/97, v Belgium 29/03/97, v Scotland 27/05/97, v Belgium 11/10/97, v Brazil 11/11/97, v Jamaica 25/03/98, v Malta 03/06/98, v Tunisia 06/06/98

Welsh midfielder Mark Pembridge was one of David Pleat's first signing as boss at Hillsborough. He had managed the flame-haired player at Luton Town where Pembridge had started seventy games before a big money move to The Baseball Ground. However he experienced a decidedly mixed time at County and despite scoring 37 times in 140 games became unpopular with supporters who made his position untenable. A move to Wednesday was seen as a fresh start but his early form was poor and he again received criticism from dissatisfied fans – he was roundly condemned after a vital relegation match at Manchester City when he shot for goal instead of passing to David Hirst who was unmarked in front of goal.

Thankfully for the left-sided midfielder his fortunes then improved to such an extent that he was named 'Player of the Year' in 1997, scoring several spectacular goals with his powerful left foot. What proved to be his final season at Wednesday was a mixed campaign for the ex-Welsh schoolboy International and soon after the departure of Pleat he was involved in an aborted swap deal for Coventry City's David Burrows, which collapsed when Pembridge failed to agree personal terms. The writing was obviously on the wall but ironically he would appear in 39 games during the 1997-98 season – his highest seasonal tally while in Sheffield – and even appeared in a wing back role before rejecting The Owls offer of a new contract. He therefore became the first Wednesday player to leave under the 'Bosman' ruling when signing for Portuguese giants Benfica – at the time managed by Graeme Souness. He stayed only a year abroad before signing for Everton but injuries restricted his appearances for the Toffeemen to just short of one hundred games before moving to fellow Premier League side Fulham.

PETRESCU, Daniel Vasile 'Dan' 1994-95

Born: 22 December 1967
Bucharest, Romania
(5ft 9ins, 11st 9lbs – 1995)
Debut: 20 August 1994
v Tottenham Hotspur
Premier League Home
Last Appearance: 30 September 1995
v Leeds United
Premier League Away
Total League
& Cup Appearances: 31+11 Goals: 4

Career Details:

Steaua Bucharest	August	1985
FC Olt	August	1986 Season loan
Foggia	August	1991
Genoa	August	1993
WEDNESDAY	6 August	1994 £1.3m
Chelsea	13 October	1995 £2.6m
Bradford City	2 August	2000 £1m
Southampton	2 January	2001 £100,000
National Bucharest	23 July	2002 Free

CAPS (@SWFC)
Romania Full (9) v Azerbaijan 07/09/94, v France 08/10/94, v England 12/10/94, v Slovakia 12/11/94, v Israel 14/12/94, v Poland 29/03/95, v Azerbaijan 26/04/95, v Poland 06/09/95, v France 11/10/95

There in no doubt that Romanian Dan Petrescu was one of the most talented players to pull on a Wednesday shirt in recent years but sadly his performances on the field were overshadowed by his controversial departure to Chelsea after only fifteen months at Hillsborough. He had started his career back home with Romanian giants Steaua Bucharest and after breaking into the first eleven at right back won four consecutive league Championship medals between 1986 and 1990 as well as appearing in Steau's 4-0 European Cup Final defeat to the outstanding 1989 AC Milan side. In total he appeared in 95 League games for Steaua, scoring 27 times, before joining the outflow to Serie A when signing for Italian club Foggia. Seven goals in 55 games prompted a move to Genoa while his tremendous displays in helping Romania to the last eight in the 1994 World Cup Finals prompted interest from several clubs. However it was Wednesday boss Trevor Francis who beat off competition from Torino to capture his signature – returning to the Italian City a year after he had signed Des Walker from rivals Sampdoria.

He already had 41 caps to his name when joining The Owls but immediately flew back to Romania to train with Steaua while Wednesday awaited his work permit. It would be another two weeks before the transfer was completed and Petrescu then netted on his debut in a thrilling 4-3 home defeat to Spurs on the opening day of the season. However it soon became apparent that the skilful Petrescu was more at home in a five man defence and as the Owls stuck to a rigid 4-4-2 formation his attacking qualities were never really maximised. He made a great start to the 1995-6 campaign – netting an outstanding goal in an Intertoto Cup tie - but quickly became unsettled with Owls boss David Pleat blaming his agent for the problems. He duly asked for a move to a bigger club so he could win honours and when Chelsea came calling The Owls decided to give up the fight and doubled their money – his departure leaving a sour taste in the mouth of Wednesday fans. His actual move to Stamford Bridge was also a protracted one as two weeks after signing, the deal looked on the brink of collapse after Chelsea received conflicting medical reports. The Owls resisted attempts by the Londoners to have the fee reduced and the transfer was finally completed over three weeks after his initial move.

His wish to win honours was certainly fulfilled at Chelsea where in almost five years he earned F.A.Cup, League Cup and European Cup Winners Cup winners medals, appearing in 208 games at right wing back and then on the right side of midfield. Petrescu – who famously netted a last minute winner for Romania in France '98 against England – then spent a brief spell at Premier League Bradford City before being one of several players cleared out in a cost cutting measure when new manager Jim Jefferies took charge in January 2001. He duly rejoined his old Chelsea boss Glen Hoddle at Southampton but after Hoddle left for Spurs he was only a fringe player prior to returning home in the summer of 2002. With 95 Romania caps to his name Petrescu then played one final season for National Bucharest – playing his final game against Dinamo Bucharest on 31st May 2003 - while also fulfilling the assistant manager role to Italian Walter Zenga. After being appointed manager at Division Two side Sportul Studentesc in July 2003 he led his club to the top of the league at the winter break but in December was handed the reins at Romanian Champions Rapid Bucharest. However after just five months in charge he dramatically quit the post in April 2004, later rejoining Sportul Studentesc as head coach. He lasted until early in 2005 at Sportul, leaving after not having received any pay for five months!

PETRIE, Charles 'Charlie' 1922-25

Born: 3rd Quarter 1895 Chorlton,
Lancashire
(5ft 7½ins, 11st – 1922)
Debut: 11 February 1922
v Nottingham Forest
Division Two Away
Last Appearance: 2 October 1924
v Clapton Orient
Division Two Away
Total League
& Cup Appearances: 60 Goals: 23

Career Details:		
Openshaw		
Manchester City	September	1918 Amat.
Stalybridge Celtic	cs	1919
WEDNESDAY	10 February	1922 £1,300
Swindon Town	15 June	1925 £250
Southampton	June	1927 £150
York City	July	1929 Free

The Wednesday career of inside left Charlie Petrie was fraught with injury problems which meant he was only a regular in one season – 1923-24 – as manager Bob Brown tried to find the winning combination to lift The Owls out of Division Two. During his spell at Hillsborough the somewhat injury prone Lancastrian suffered various head injuries, underwent a cartilage operation and even contracted appendicitis! These problems meant Petrie was only a fringe player in his first full season in Sheffield – he appeared in only five reserve games as the second team lifted the Midland League title in 1923 – and it was perhaps no real surprise when he was allowed to join Swindon Town – only after the Owls asking price was reduced by the Football League!

The attacker who was said to use his head in "more ways than one" had started his playing days in the Manchester Amateur League with Openshaw before scoring 17 goals in only 22 games for Stalybridge Celtic, in their debut season of league football, prompted a move to Hillsborough. His record at the Wiltshire club was again respectable – 11 goals in 32 league games – while after hanging up his boots he moved back to Manchester to coach Gorton Celtic.

PETRIE, Robert "Bob" 1894-97

Born: December 1870 Dundee
(5ft 7½ins, 11st 3lbs – 1896)
Died: 15 March 1947 Arbroath
Debut:
1 September 1894 v Everton Division One Away
Last Appearance:
2 March 1897 v Sheffield United Division One Home
Total League & Cup Appearances: 62
Goals: 3

Career Details:		
Arbroath		
Dundee East End		
Dundee	July	1893
WEDNESDAY	April	1894
Southampton	June	1897
Dundee Wanderers	August	1900
New Brighton Tower	October	1900
Dundee Wanderers	May	1902
Arbroath	May	1903
Dundee Wanderers	October	1908
Brechin City	May	1909
Dundee Wanderers	August	1910
Arbroath	August	1911 Amat.

Versatile halfback who was a member of the famous 1896 F.A.Cup Final side that brought the old trophy back to Sheffield for the first ever time. There is no doubt that in those early league years Petrie was one of the club's outstanding halfbacks, perhaps only bettered by the likes of James Jamieson and the legendary Tommy Crawshaw, as contemporary reports likened the Scot to a rock of granite such was his dominance in defence. He was a superb athlete, possessing a splendid physique, and it was said that Bob was so proficient in the air that he could direct the ball with his head almost as skilfully as most players could with their feet. He was also pacy and tenacious but despite all these superlatives Petrie was actually never really an automatic choice at Olive Grove, usually competing with the likes of Harry Brandon for the third halfback slot behind ever presents Jamieson and Crawshaw. He also ran into trouble with club officials in October 1895 and was suspended after returning to Scotland on private business without the Owls permission. Despite those problems he regained his first team place for the Cup run and helped Wednesday beat Wolves 2-1 in the Crystal Palace final to gain a unique place in The Owls history.

He was originally a member of The East End football club – who amalgamated with Old Boys FC to form Dundee FC – and played in the first game for the newly formed team before treading the well-worn path down to English football. After leaving Wednesday he signed for Southern League Southampton where his final appearance actually came in the 1900 F.A.Cup Final when The Saints were beaten 4-0 by Bury. After 6 goals in 68 games he joined Football League club New Brighton Tower and remained a fixture in the side until they resigned from the league in September 1901, just before the season was due to commence. Petrie – whose grandson Jack Martin signed for Wednesday in 1954 – then returned home to Scotland where he played for a variety of sides and was reported to have retired in 1908 after helping Arbroath win the Scottish qualifying Cup. However he continued to play and after being reinstated as an amateur finished his career back at his first club, Arbroath, while working as a moulder at Dundee Saw Mill. A few years later he had to give up work after an accident at the sawmill but during the Second World War – with labour scare – he started to work again. After his playing career came to a close Bob was often seen at junior matches in Scotland where he gave helpful advice to young players.

*Newspaper reports (Nov 1940) & census records contradict his previously published date of birth of 25/10/74.

PICKERING, John William 1912-14

Born: 1891/92 Clowne
(5ft 7 ins, 11st – 1913)
Debut: 1 November 1913
v Derby County
Division One Home
Last Appearance: 22 November 1913
v Blackburn Rovers
Division One Away
Total League
& Cup Appearances: 4 Goals: 0

Career Details:		
Frickley Colliery		
WEDNESDAY	February	1912 £50
Rotherham County		1914

Spent two seasons at Wednesday, primarily as understudy to left-winger George Robertson. Arrived from local football and after a season of Midland League football with the club's reserve side he was given a four game run at league level when his rival Robertson was absent. However Wednesday suffered three defeats in that period and it was no surprise when Pickering returned to the reserves and then moved onto neighbours Rotherham County.

PICKERING, Michael John 'Mike' 1978-84

Born: 29 September 1956 Huddersfield
(5ft 11ins, 12st 6lbs – 1979)
Debut: 7 October 1978
v Rotherham United
Division Three Away
Last Appearance: 9 November 1982
v Crystal Palace
League Cup Away
Total League
& Cup Appearances: 123+6 Goals: 1

Career Details:		
Barnsley	18 October	1974
Southampton	11 June	1977 £35,000
WEDNESDAY	5 October	1978 £50,000
San Diego Sockers	May-July	1981 Loan
Norwich City	29 September	1983 Loan
Bradford City	3 November	1983 Loan
Barnsley	30 December	1983 Loan
Rotherham United	17 January	1984 £6,000
York City	25 July	1986 Free
Stockport County	3 August	1987 Free
Hallam		1989
Goole Town		1989
Frickley Athletic	August	1991

Mike Pickering first came to prominence with Spen Valley boys and was courted by Barnsley who wanted to sign the teenager as a trainee. However at the time Pickering wanted to become a P.E. teacher and was set to stay on at school to take 'A' levels before a change of heart meant he signed professional forms for The Tykes – he was too old to sign as an apprentice so became a professional although he played solely in the Northern Intermediate League and shared the same duties as his trainee peers. At the time Pickering was tall for his age and on several occasions played in goal – including both legs of a NIL League Cup Final against Middlesbrough – but it would be at centre half that he quickly became established in the Barnsley first team after breaking into the side. His consistency and obvious skill and strength meant that it soon proved impossible for The Tykes to hold onto him and he duly moved to Lawrie McMenemy's Southampton after over 100 league games.

At Southampton he would form an outstanding partnership with Chris Nichol and helped The Saints to promotion from the old Second Division in his debut campaign. However he was then thought not good enough for the top-flight and was allowed to join Wednesday, meaning he had the unique distinction of having played in all four divisions by the age of 22! He proved one of Jack Charlton's best signings and captained Wednesday out of the Third Division in 1980 although he then almost departed, signing a new two-year deal in June 1980 after a wages dispute. In the higher grade Pickering found his opportunities limited, through a combination of injury and competition from the emerging Peter Shirtliff, and after refusing another contract he went on week-to-week terms – in August 1982 he offered his services to any interested club after being told he was likely to start the new season in the reserves. It would be another eighteen months though before he moved to Millmoor on a permanent basis, during which time he was sent out on loan to a variety of clubs and in fact started only one senior game for Wednesday.

After over 100 games for The Millers he moved to York City while after two injury-ruined years at Stockport County he retired from professional football in 1989. He then started work as a kitchen designer before moving into the brewery trade as a salesman. While helping ex-Owl hero John Fantham with coaching duties at non-league Hallam he played a few games and later played a handful of matches for Northern Premier League Goole Town – again after being asked by an ex-Owl, this time Terry Curran. Various injuries finally brought the curtain down on his playing days in 1993, after two years at Frickley Athletic, and he now works as an Accounts Development manager for a large brewery company

PICKERING, William Henry 'Bill' 1937-48

Born: 10 December 1919 Sheffield (5ft 9½ins, 11st 5lbs – 1946)
Died: 16 November 1983 Selby
Debut: 29 October 1938 v Sheffield United Division Two Away
Last Appearance: 11 February 1946 v Stoke City F.A.Cup Home
Total League & Cup Appearances: 9* Goals: 0
***Also appeared in 129 wartime games**

Career Details:

WEDNESDAY	9 October	1937
Oldham Athletic	26 July	1948 £1000
Released	31 July	1951
Gainsborough Trinity	September	1951

Former Sheffield Boys player Bill Pickering joined The Owls as an amateur in May 1937 after having impressed greatly while representing his country at amateur level. In the summer of 1937, aged just 18, he had toured New Zealand and Australia with England and looked an excellent capture by Wednesday. The left back would act as understudy to Ted Catlin during the two years before the Second World War, making his League debut in a scoreless draw at Bramall Lane, and was a regular for the club throughout the war years while he worked in a munitions factory. Unfortunately when the hostilities ended Pickering could not break out of The Owls Central League side and failed to make a Football League appearance until being sold to Oldham Athletic. Started as a right back at Boundary Park but soon settled back into the full back role on the opposite flank and the tough tackling Pickering was a regular for three seasons, starting 87 games for Athletic. Ended his playing career in non-league football at Gainsborough Trinity and was appointed coach at Worksop Town for the 1962-3 season. He was later elevated to manager in September 1964 and was also Goole Town boss, resigning in April 1971.

PINNER, Michael John 'Mike' 1957-59

Born: 16 February 1934 Boston (6ft, 12st)
Debut: 14 December 1957 v Wolverhampton Wanderers Division One Away
Last Appearance: 28 March 1959 v Brighton Division Two Home
Total League & Cup Appearances: 7 Goals: 0

Career Details:

Boston Grammer School		
Wyberton Rangers		
Boston United		
Notts County	October	1948
Chelsea Casuals		1950-68 Sun.
Cambridge University		1952-54
Pegasus		1952-53
Aston Villa	May	1954
Arsenal		
WEDNESDAY	13 December	1957
Queens Park Rangers	July	1959
Manchester United	February	1961
Hendon		
Chelsea	October	1961
Arsenal		
Swansea Town	May	1962
Leyton Orient	October	1962
Leyton Orient	October	1963 Pro
Distillery Belfast		1965

CAPS (@SWFC)
England Amateur (9) v Scotland 29/03/58, v France 28/04/58, v Ireland 27/09/58, v Finland 11/10/58, v South Africa 25/10/58, v Wales 08/11/58, v Scotland 14/03/59, v Holland 20/05/59, v Germany 27/05/59

Mike Pinner was a rare example – particularly in post war football – of a top class player who remained amateur for almost his entire career. In a time when amateurism was on the wane and the maximum wage was abolished he remained a shining example of a player who played simply for the love of the game and not for financial reward. He combined playing with his full time job as a solicitor and enjoyed a fascinating career that spanned over twenty years and included a total of 113 league appearances for seven different Football League teams. He also played for several crack non-league sides, represented the famous Amateur touring side Middlesex Wanderers while his 52 England Amateur International caps between 1955 and 1963 set a post war record. If that was not enough to pack into a career the goalkeeper won a University 'Blue' as football captain of Cambridge and also represented Great Britain at the Melbourne Olympics in 1956 and in Rome four years later

His career had started as a 15 year-old at Boston side Wybourton and he arrived at Wednesday when The Owls ran into serious goalkeeping problems during the 1957-58 season – he was one of five different goalies used as Wednesday were relegated. Pinner was on Arsenal's books at the time and after the North London side had kindly agreed to cancel his amateur registration he was allowed to sign, with the understanding he would be able to fulfil his commitments to Pegasus in F.A. Amateur Cup games. On his Wednesday debut his brilliant interceptions and general competent display instilled confidence in the rest of the side but the 27 goals he conceded in just seven appearances suggest that perhaps he played behind a somewhat 'amateurish ' defence! Throughout his career Pinner played regularly on a Sunday for a team called Chelsea Casuals – a side run by famous sports writer Brian Granville for Fleet Street journalists – while his senior playing career finally ended in 1967 after two years in Irish Soccer. At the time of joining Wednesday he was training to be a solicitor in Spalding – taking his articles in 1959 – and in 1960 moved to a London firm where he still works today, despite now being in his early seventies.

PLATTS, Mark Anthony 1996-99

Born: 23 May 1979 Sheffield
(5ft 8ins, 11st 13lbs – 1998)
Debut: 10 February 1996
v Wimbledon
Premier League Home
Last Appearance: 24 February 1996
v Tottenham Hotspur
Premier League Away
Total League
& Cup Appearances: 0+2 Goals: 0

Career Details:

WEDNESDAY	7 October	1996
Sheffield United	5 January	1999 Trial
Torquay United	11 March	1999 Free
Worksop Town	October	2000

CAPS (@SWFC) – England U-18 (2) v Finland 11/10/96, v N.Ireland 13/10/96

The history of football is littered with examples of players who burst onto the first team scene as teenagers only for their early promise to disappear before their career had really started. Left-winger Mark Platts certainly fell into this category as after becoming the club's youngest ever outfield player – aged 16 years and 263 days – his career fell way to such an extent that within six years he had finished playing football altogether. The lightening quick youngster had started with the Young Owls side at the age of 8 and after signing associated schoolboy forms on his 14th Birthday enjoyed a meteoric rise through the ranks, which included several eye-catching displays for England, Sheffield and South Yorkshire boys during the 1994-5 season. He was highly thought of by the Hillsborough hierarchy and this was proven in 1995 pre season when Platts, having only just signed YTS forms, played in two first team friendlies before he had even played a Northern Intermediate League game!

His outstanding displays for the club's junior side soon had fans talking about the youngster and it was David Pleat who handed the youngster a place on the subs bench for the home game with Spurs in February 1996. The primarily left-footed Platts subsequently entered the record books when replacing Chris Waddle with five minutes remaining but sadly failed to build on that early promise and even dropped back into NIL football after signing professional forms in October 1996. The fall from grace was completed when he joined Sheffield United on trial and after a two-week loan at Third Division Torquay United he left Hillsborough on a permanent transfer on 25 March 1999. Despite suffering injury problems at Torquay he appeared in 41 league and cup games for the Devon club until his contract was cancelled by mutual consent in October 2000. Platts then returned north to play alongside Chris Waddle at Northern Premier League Worksop Town but appeared in only a few games and after hurting his knee in training decided to retire totally from football. He was then unemployed for a while but now works as a steel erector, working around various parts of the country.

PLLU, Charles Lamont 'Charlie' 1956-58

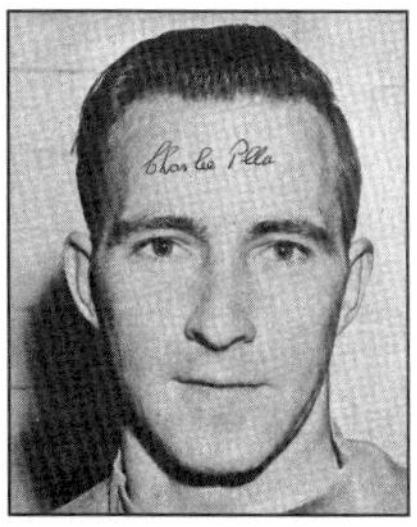

Born: 28 February 1934
Saltcoats, Ayrshire
(5ft 7½ins, 10st 2lbs – 1957)
Debut: 6 April 1957
v Everton
Division One Home
Last Appearance: 29 January 1958
v Hull City
F.A.Cup Home
Total League
& Cup Appearances: 20 Goals: 0

Career Details:

Saltcoats FC		1955
Scarborough		1956 Free
WEDNESDAY	November	1956 £1050*
Dundee	7 August	1958 Free
Portadown		

*Including £50 to Saltcoats

Goalkeeper Charlie Pllu (pronounced Ploo) was a Scot undertaking his National Service in the Tank Regiment at Catterick when the Owls invited him for a trial in December 1956. At the time he was playing Midland League football for Scarborough – he was recommended by Scarborough and ex-Owl player Laurie MacKenzie - and subsequently signed on a part-time basis before turning fully professional in January 1957, on being demobbed from the army. His first senior game for Wednesday came in a friendly at Norwich City but soon after he was given a league debut after first choice Dave McIntosh injured his knee at Spurs. After a nervous start to his senior career Charlie started to show promise and in fact retained the No. 1 shirt until November 1957, except for a five game absence due to a broken finger suffered at White Hart Lane in September 1957.

However in a crazy season the Owls used five different custodians and with competition fierce Pllu had to be content with Central League soccer. When future England International Ron Springett arrived in March 1958 Charlie must have known his time was short – he had already asked for a transfer in February – and he became so disillusioned that he decided to quit soccer at the end of the season. However after experiencing a change of heart he moved to Dundee after Owls boss Eric Taylor agreed to waive any transfer fee. He later moved into Northern Irish football but stayed only a brief time and was denied a move back into English football after Portadown refused permission when both Oldham Athletic and then Norwich City both tried to sign him as goalkeeping cover. After his playing days ended Pllu entered the building trade, becoming a contracts manager until his retirement.

PORIC, Adem 1993-98

Born: 22 April 1973 London
(5ft 9ins, 11st 13lbs – 1997)
Debut: 16 October 1993
v Wimbledon
Premier League Home
Last Appearance: 1 November 1997
v Manchester United
Premier League Away
Total League
& Cup Appearances: 4+13 Goals: 0

Career Details:

St.George Budapest		
WEDNESDAY	24 September	1993 £60,000
Southend United	5 February	1997 Loan
Contract cancelled	22 January	1998
Rotherham United	10 February	1998 Free
Notts County	26 March	1998 Free
Sydney Olympic		1998
Northern Spirit	12 December	1998 Free
Gold Coast City		2001
Gold Coast Carara		2003

Although born in London – to a Polish mother and Yugoslavian father – Adem Poric was brought up in Australia after his family emigrated when he was just two years old. Despite making the grade in soccer 'down under' the midfielder was a virtual unknown in the UK when Trevor Francis brought him to Hillsborough from Sydney club St.George Budapest. Within a week of joining The Owls he was given a first team debut from the subs bench but in his time at Wednesday the multi-lingual and tough tackling Poric was never a regular, despite showing some good form at reserve team level. His commitment could never be called into question but the Aussie did suffer from a lack of consistency and probably had the bad luck to join a Wednesday side who were established in the Premier League and had the likes of Carlton Palmer established as the 'ball winner' in midfield. In almost five years at Wednesday, Poric played just short of one hundred reserve team games, scoring on a regular basis, while his best run of league football came during a successful loan spell at then First Division club Southend United.

His final appearance came in what proved to be David Pleat's final game in charge – a 6-1 thrashing at Old Trafford – and after failing to figure under new boss Ron Atkinson his contract was cancelled by mutual consent, leaving Poric free to sign an initial one-month contract at neighbours Rotherham United. However after just a handful of appearances for The Millers he left somewhat abruptly, after being arrested for an alleged attack on a bus driver, and later signed for eventual Division Three Champions Notts County. After just four games for County he then packed his bags for home and in the summer appeared for Australia in the 1998 Olympics games in Sydney. In domestic football he appeared briefly for National League clubs Sydney Olympic (one goal in six games) and Northern Spirit (two games) before dropping into Queensland State League football with Gold Coast City. When Gold Coast finished runners-up in 2002 Poric finished second top league scorer with 16 goals while he now plies his trade with Carara while it is believed he works as a nightclub bouncer in the Queensland area.

PORTERFIELD, Ian John 1977-79

Born: 11 February 1946 Dunfermline
(5ft 11ins, 12st 8lbs – 1978)
Debut: 13 August 1977
v Doncaster Rovers
League Cup Home
Last Appearance: 8 December 1979
v Exeter City
Division Three Home
Total League
& Cup Appearances: 126+4 Goals: 6

Career Details:

Lochgelly Albert		
Lochore Welfare		
Leeds United		Apprentice
Heart of Midlothian		Trial
Glasgow Rangers		Trial
Raith Rovers		1964
Sunderland	December	1967 £43,000
Reading	1 November	1976 Loan
WEDNESDAY	26 July	1977 £15,000
Rotherham United	December	1979 Free

Ian Porterfield will forever be remembered as the man who scored the winning goal for underdogs Sunderland in their 1973 F.A.Cup Final win over hot favourites Leeds United. His career had started at Raith Rovers where after helping the Kirkcaldy club to promotion in 1967 he left for a record fee to sign for Sunderland. He would spend the majority of his career at Roker Park and totalled 266 appearances, scoring 19 goals, although his playing days almost came to a dramatic end in December 1974 when a serious car accident left him with a broken skull and jaw. However he returned to action within two months and wore a protective rugby skullcap until his injury was completely healed. He later helped Sunderland earn promotion back to Division One in 1976 but after losing his place eventually arrived at Wednesday in the summer of 1977.

In his time at Hillsborough the vastly experienced Porterfield missed only a handful of games and was a great influence on the Owls consolidation and eventual revival in the Third Division. His man management skills led to him being appointed player-coach by Jack Charlton – after much deliberation by Porterfield - in May 1979 but it was obvious a career in management beckoned and half way through the Owls 1980 promotion season Ian left to become player-boss at Rotherham United. He never actually fulfilled the player prefix of his job title at Millmoor but did achieve immediate success, leading United to the 1981 Third Division Championship in his first full season at the helm. However he then resigned for the security of a five-year contract with Sheffield United, who had just fallen into the basement division for the first time in their history. He immediately led The Blades to the Fourth Division title but experienced a mixed time at Bramall Lane – despite also getting United out of Division Three in 1984 – and it was no surprise when he was dismissed in March 1986.

He then moved back to Scotland and after a short time out of the game was appointed manager at Aberdeen in November 1986, as replacement for Alex Ferguson. He took The Dons to the 1988 League Cup Final, losing on penalties to Rangers, but was sacked in May 1988. After another sabbatical he was appointed assistant manager at Chelsea in November 1989 but bizarrely within days left for an ultimately unsuccessful 17-month spell as Reading boss. Despite his poor record at Reading Porterfield returned to Stamford Bridge as manager in June 1991 and stayed until February 1993, bringing the curtain down on his managerial career in English league football. However this was only the start of a globe trotting managerial career that would see Porterfield work in Africa, Asia and the Middle East. This all started when he was appointed coach of Zambia in April 1993 while he then spent two years as manager of Saudi Arabian club Ittihead before being appointed assistant boss back in England at Bolton Wanderers. After a brief spell as boss at non-league Worthing he was appointed Zimbabwe coach in October 1996 and was then in charge of Oman (Nov 1997 –Mar 2000) and Trindad & Tobago – being sacked by the latter in June 2001 after a poor qualifying tournament for Japan/Korea 2002. A move to Ghanaian club side Asante Kotoko came next in May 2002 but after being controversially sacked in September he sued for breach of contract and wrongful dismissal. As usual Porterfield bounced straight back and within three months signed a two-year contract at South Korean K-League club Busan Icons

POTTS, Eric Thomas 1969-77

Born: 16 March 1950 Liverpool
(5ft 6ins, 10st 2lbs – 1973)
Debut: 17 October 1970
v Charlton Athletic
Division Two Away
Last Appearance: 6 May 1977
v Tranmere Rovers
Division Three Away
Total League
& Cup Appearances: 162+20 Goals: 25

Career Details:

Old Holts		1966
Blackpool		1967 Am.
New Brighton		1968
Oswestry Town		
WEDNESDAY	17 December	1969 £4,000
Brighton & Hove Albion	9 June	1977 £12,000
Preston North End	24 August	1978 £37,000
Burnley	September	1980 £20,000
Bury	October	1982 Free
Witton Albion		

Pacy and intelligent winger Eric Potts started his career in Liverpool amateur football, being taken along by his schoolteacher to sign for Old Holts. His letter to Blackpool asking for trials eventually led to him signing as an amateur for them and Stan Mortensen said he would be the "Next Alan Ball". However he failed to make the grade at Bloomfield Road and started working as a painter and decorator before moving into non-league football at Cheshire League Oswestry Town. On hearing of The Owls interest the Oswestry boss, Fred Morris, got Potts to sign a professional contract which meant when Wednesday came calling they had to pay a fee for his services! The cash helped pay for Town's new floodlights while a friendly game – arranged as part of the deal – was postponed at the last minute due to a downpour and never rearranged.

His first senior start for Wednesday came as a one-minute substitute in a 3-2 win at The Valley but due to stiff competition from the likes of Jackie Sinclair and John Sissons it was not until the 1973-4 season that Eric secured a regular first team spot. Once he became established Potts became a crowd favourite but as with many Owls players of his era Potts was playing in a side on the slide and this tended to effect his form. During a two-year spell in the mid-1970s Potts played in close to one hundred consecutive games – he was voted player of the season in 1976 - but the arrival of new manager Len Ashurst and left-winger Paul Bradshaw combined to push Potts into the shadows during the 1976-7 season, causing his departure to Brighton.

After leaving Hillsborough Eric would total almost 200 league appearances at four league sides, helping Burnley win the Third Division Championship in 1982, before retiring from the game

after playing a few games for Witton as a favour to a friend. After a period of unemployment Potts worked for seven years for an insurance company while in 1985 he gained his full FA coaching badge. He then started to work in his current occupation, as a taxi driver, and now also helps teach youngsters for the Professional Footballers Association.
* Did not play for Clitheroe

POTTS, Harry A 1897-99

Born:
Debut:
20 November 1897 v Bury Division One Home
Last Appearance:
18 February 1899 v Sunderland Division One Home
Total League & Cup Appearances: 2 Goals: 1

Career Details:

Sheffield FC	
WEDNESDAY	1897
Sheffield FC	1899

Harry Potts was one of several amateur Sheffield Club players – the most famous being Vivian Simpson – who helped Wednesday out on occasion during their early league years. The inside left actually scored on his debut for Wednesday in a 3-0 home win over Bury but it was quickly back to local league football with Sheffield as Alec Brady regained his first team spot. Potts would make one more senior appearance for Wednesday before spending the rest of his career at the world's oldest football club – he achieved glory in 1904 when playing in Club's F. A. Amateur Cup Final win by three goals to one over Ealing at Bradford – appearing alongside fellow one-time Wednesday men Henry Bolsover and George Hoyland.

POULTER, Robert 2004-5

Born: 2 February 1986 Sheffield
(6ft 1ins, 11st 13lbs – 2004)
Only Appeance: 25 February 2004
v Blackpool
LDV Vans Trophy Home
Total League
& Cup Appearances: 0+1 Goals: 0

Career Details:

WEDNESDAY	1 July	2002 Academy
Stocksbridge Park Steels		2005 Work Ex.
Released	30 June	2005
Gretna	July	2005

Academy goalkeeper who was given a place on the subs bench on fifteen occasions during the 2003-04 season, as Wednesday suffered an injury crisis that saw all three first choice keepers sidelined at one time. The ex-Dronfield school pupil showed terrific early promise and was actually aged only 14 when he made his first Academy appearance for Wednesday - as a sub in a 3-0 defeat at Liverpool U17s in October 2000. He later represented England at U-16 level and broke into the reserve side to act as first team understudy, getting his big chance when Ola Tidman was carried off injured in the LDV Vans Northern Final tie against Blackpool at Hillsborough. The 18 year-old, who has been on The Owls books since aged 11, had a quiet evening but looked confident as he kept a clean sheet. He started the 2004-5 season as No. 3 to Lucas and Tidman but warmed the first team bench on several occasions after the latter was released just before Christmas. In March 2005 he uniquely played in two games on the same day, helping the Owls beat the Blades in a Pontins League Cup tie before playing for Stocksbridge in their Unibond League game at Ossett Albion in the evening - a feat made possible as Poulter had signed for Steels on a work experience basis.

POWELL, Darryl Anthony 2003

Born: 15 November 1971
Lambeth, London
(6ft, 12st 10lbs – 2003)
Debut: 17 January 2003
v Sheffield United
Division One Away
Last Appearance: 15 March 2003
v Ipswich Town
Division One Home
Total League
& Cup Appearances: 8 Goals: 0

Career Details:

Portsmouth	22 December	1988
Derby County	27 July	1995 £750,000
Birmingham City	13 September	2002 Free
WEDNESDAY	15 January	2003 Free
Colorado Rapids	29 May	2003 Free
Released	December	2004
Nottingham Forest	11 February	2005 Free
Released	May	2005

Combative and energetic central midfielder Darryl Powell spent only a short time at Hillsborough after being brought to the club on an 18-month contract, as new Wednesday boss Chris Turner tried to keep The Owls in Division One. The hugely experienced top-flight player was immediately handed the captain's armband and given a baptism of fire in the hostile atmosphere of a Sheffield Derby game. Sadly Owls fans saw little of his leadership qualities as after only a handful of games in a Wednesday shirt he suffered a knee injury that put him on the sidelines for the remainder of the season. It later transpired that Powell had signed his contract at Hillsborough with the proviso that he could leave on a free transfer if the Owls were relegated and it was an option he later exercised, moving to US Major Soccer League club Colorado Rapids. Unfortunately for Powell he was plagued by injuries in his first season at Rapids, missing the first four months of the season with a hamstring problem and not making his debut until October 2003. Just over a year later he left US football and after training with Championship club Forest for several weeks he was eventually handed a contract until the end of the season.

He had began his career as a trainee at Portsmouth and would make 170 appearances for the South Coast side, scoring 23 times, including a heartbreaking loss on penalties to Liverpool in the 1992 F.A.Cup semi-final. His former manager Jim Smith then took Powell to top-flight Derby County where he quickly became a fans favourite, playing in 227 games for The Rams, and captaining the side from 1997 onwards. The 1990s also saw Powell's International career begin as after becoming a Jamaican citizen he made his debut for the National team against Wales in 1998, clinching a place in The Reggae Boys squad for the 1998 World Cup Finals in France. He duly appeared as a sub in Jamaica's opening game with Croatia but was then sent off against Argentina, after two bookable offences, and in total won 17 caps for his adopted country, netting once. Back in domestic football Powell left Derby under freedom of contract and joined Premier League new boys Birmingham City, appearing in 11 games before moving to Hillsborough.

POWELL, Samuel "Sam" 1925-30

Born: 25 May 1899 Holmes, Rotherham
(5ft 9ins, 11st – 1925)
Died: 21 June 1961 Sheffield
Debut: 21 March 1925
v Middlesbrough
Division Two Away
Last Appearance: 7 March 1928
v Birmingham
Division One Away
Total League
& Cup Appearances: 26 Goals: 8

Career Details:

Thornhill United		
Leeds United	January	1921
WEDNESDAY	16 March	1925 £1400

Free scoring centre forward whose career had started in Rotherham amateur football before breaking into League soccer at Leeds United. After four years at Elland Road he was sold to raise money to buy another player and Wednesday boss Bob Brown secured his signature. Powell made an immediate impact, scoring six times in the final eight games of the 1924-5 campaign, but after starting the first six matches of the following season – in an unaccustomed inside left role – he lost his place to Harold Hill and would spend the remainder of his Owls career as understudy to the likes of Hill, Jimmy Trotter and Jimmy Seed. He pushed hard for a first team recall by finishing top scorer for the Owls reserve side for three consecutive seasons - scoring 75 times, including 33 in 1926-7 – but was used sparingly by Brown at first team level. However his career would come to abrupt halt in March 1928 when during a Central League game with Derby County at Hillsborough the attacker suffered a badly broken leg which meant twelve months in and out of hospital.

Sadly he would never play again and after finally being discharged was appointed to The Owls training staff. In September 1930 Sam became assistant trainer at Wednesday but he still struggled with his leg and in September 1932 went back into hospital for a further operation – relinquishing his role on a temporary basis to ex-team mate Sid Binks. However after four months out of action he did not return to his old job – George Irwin being appointed assistant trainer in January 1933 – but remained on the coaching staff until replacing Irwin as first team trainer in July 1937. He remained the Owls senior trainer throughout the war years and it was not until the arrival of Alan Brown in 1950 that Sam reverted back to an assistant role, remaining at Hillsborough until September 1958. He then became a part-time employee, coaching the club's Yorkshire League side until his death in Sheffield Royal Hospital.

POWELL, William Methven 'Billy' 1924-27

Born: 21 July 1901 Sutton-in-Ashfield (5ft 8ins, 11st – 1925)
Died: 2nd Quarter 1981 Sutton-in-Ashfield
Debut: 25 October 1924 v South Shields Division Two Away
Last Appearance: 11 April 1925 v Fulham Division Two Home
Total League & Cup Appearances: 22 Goals: 0

Career Details:

Retford Town		
Sutton Town	August	1923
WEDNESDAY	October	1924£10
Grimsby Town	12 May	1927
Southend United	May	1930
Sutton Town	August	1932

Although a free scoring inside forward in Hucknall Junior football and with Sutton Town it was as a forceful half back that Billy Powell appeared in league soccer for Wednesday. He was drafted straight into The Owls league side after his arrival from Midland League strugglers Sutton and was a regular in his debut campaign after replacing Bill Collier at left halfback. However like his namesake, Sam, his career at Wednesday would then be ruined by illness and after dropping out of the side Billy failed to regain his first team spot and spent two seasons in the reserves before moving to Grimsby Town.

PRENDERGAST, Michael John 'Mick/Prendo' 1967-78

Born: 24 November 1950 Denaby Main
(5ft 8ins, 12st – 1973)
Debut: 9 April 1969
v Newcastle United
Division One Away
Last Appearance: 7 March 1978
v Chester
Division Three Home
Total League
& Cup Appearances: 192+15 Goals: 59

Career Details:

WEDNESDAY	24 November	1967
Barnsley	9 March	1978 £14,000
Halifax Town	27 October	1978 Loan
Mexborough Town		
Denaby United		
The Gate		1980 Sun.

Hillsborough youth product Mick Prendergast spent over ten years at Wednesday but due to a catalogue of injuries started less than two hundred games. He was a tireless front runner but those aforementioned fitness problems – he missed almost the whole of the 1974-5 season due to a broken leg – meant the former Don and Dearne Boys player never seemed to enjoy a decent run in the side. He had originally joined Wednesday as an apprentice in October 1966 and after making his reserve team bow in September of the following year Prendergast signed professional forms on his seventeenth birthday. He finished top scorer for the Central League side in 1968-9 and duly made his league debut, scoring in a 3-2 defeat at Newcastle United. Immediately following the Owls relegation in 1970 he would enjoy his most prolific season at Wednesday, scoring sixteen times, and the player affectionately known as 'Prendo' would remain a first team regular for three seasons – he was supporters 'player of the year' in 1973 - until becoming yet another Wednesday player to suffer a broken bone at Preston.

He was probably lucky to be absent for the majority of the disastrous Division Two relegation campaign and entered the records books in August 1975 when scoring the club's first ever goal in Division Three. After turning down a transfer to Oxford United he was eventually placed on the transfer list in January 1978 and two months later severed his Wednesday ties by moving to Oakwell on transfer deadline day. The former Yorkshire boys forward scored only twice for Barnsley, in 18 games, and netted his final goal in league football whilst on loan at Halifax Town before dropping into non-league soccer. While at Denaby United he was given a second testimonial with Wednesday providing the opposition – his first had seen Leicester City visit Hillsborough – while after hanging up his boots 'Prendo' coached briefly at schoolboy level in Scunthorpe and Conisbrough before he was told to stop on medical grounds. Sadly his story has an unhappy ending as after having a hip replacement at the age of 36 he is now registered disabled and is unable to work.

PRESSMAN, Kevin Paul 1985-2004

Born: 6 November 1967 Fareham
(6ft 1in, 14st 2lbs – 1988)
Debut: 5 September 1987
v Southampton
Division One Away
Last Appearance: 8 May 2004
v Queens Park Rangers
Division Two Home
Total League
& Cup Appearances: 474+4 Goals: 0

Career Details:

Brunsmeer		Sun.
Middlewood Rovers		
WEDNESDAY	6 November	1985
Stoke City	10 March	1992 Loan
West Bromwich Albion	13 February	2004 Loan
Released	30 June	2004
Leicester City	15 July	2004 Free
Contract cancelled	26 January	2005
Leeds United	25 February	2005 N/C
Coventry City	24 March	2005 N/C
Mansfield Town	July	2005

CAPS (@SWFC)
England 'B' (3)
v N.Ireland 10/05/94, v Eire 13/12/94, v Chile 10/02/98

England U-21 (1)
v Denmark 13/09/88

England Youth (8)
v Algeria 22/04/84, v USSR 08/08/84, v Sweden 10/09/84
v Yugoslavia 12/09/84, v Brazil 29/03/86, v Hungary 30/03/86
v France 31/03/86, v China Army 09/05/86

When Kevin Pressman was released in the summer of 2004 it brought the curtain down on almost nineteen years as a professional at Hillsborough, a record of service bettered only by a handful of players in The Owls entire history. His sheer consistency and durability ensured Pressman overcame challenges to his first team shirt from the likes of Chris Turner, Chris Woods and Pavel Srnicek to remain the club's first choice goalkeeper for the majority of his time on The Owls books. A brilliant shot stopper – as any Sheffield United fan would testify – Pressman was actually born in Hampshire but after moving to Formby in Lancashire his family eventually settled in Dronfield after Kevin's father gained employment at Turner Airstreet, a company owned by Wednesday vice-president Cecil Turner. The young Pressman was eight years old when he moved into the Derbyshire village and it was his father's new employer who first took Kevin and his family to watch Wednesday, quickly making the youngster an Owls fan.

He first started to play organised football for his school team and later appeared on a Sunday for Brunsmeer before being spotted by Wednesday Scout Charlie Wain who invited Kevin for a trial at Hillsborough. After becoming attached to Wednesday, Pressman started to play for The Owls nursery side Middlewood Rovers and despite attracting interest from the likes of Manchester United, Sheffield United and Nottingham Forest signed schoolboy forms for Wednesday in November 1981. Caps for England schoolboys followed although it proved somewhat problematic when his O levels were due to be sat – his father had to drive to Switzerland on one occasion to take equipment to Kevin so he could take his Technical drawing exam!! The promising youngster also appeared for both Chesterfield and Derbyshire boys while after signing apprentice forms in June 1984 he was elevated to the professional ranks in the following year.

He made a winning debut in The Owls first team – ironically back in the County of his birth – but competition from Martin Hodge and then Chris Turner ensured the youngster remained understudy until becoming first choice under Ron Atkinson during the 1989-90 campaign. Unfortunately a cruciate Knee ligament injury, suffered on New Year's Day 1990 against Manchester City, then halted his progress and although he was back as first choice at the start of the following season Kevin missed out on Wembley glory after losing his place to Turner part way through the season. The following two seasons were without doubt the lowest point of Pressman's Hillsborough career as the purchase of England goalkeeper Chris Woods ensured Kevin appeared in only seven first team games and again missed out on several more trips to Wembley – he also played in six games on loan at Stoke City during those barren years. However the resilient keeper kept plugging away and was eventually rewarded, displacing Woods as undisputed No. 1 and showing such fine form that he received a deserved call up for the full England squad in March 1998. In July 1997 he had signed a lucrative 'double your money' four-year contract but found himself displaced by Pavel Srnicek when his old team mate Danny Wilson took over at Hillsborough. However Kevin was soon back and other than a brief challenge from Ola Tidman he remained first choice until the end of his Wednesday career. A new three-year deal in June 2001 also gave Pressman a role as goalkeeping coach – replacing Martin Hodge – but this position was relinquished in January 2003 as Pressman wanted to concentrate on The Owls battle to avoid the drop.

The arrival of loan keeper David Lucas saw Pressman granted his transfer request in January 2004 and he spent a brief spell on loan at West Brom – failing to make a senior appearance - before an injury crisis prompted his recall back into Wednesday's first team. Sadly for Pressman his final season at Wednesday proved to one of the worst in the history of the club but his service was fittingly acknowledged when he was awarded a deserved testimonial game. After leaving Hillsborough, Pressman signed a one-year deal with Championship club Leicester City and made 15 appearances for the injured Ian Walker before his contract was cancelled by mutual consent in January 2005.

PRICE, Arthur 1919-22

Born: 3rd Quarter 1892 Sheffield
(5ft 9ins, 12st – 1920)
Died: May 1954 Scarborough
Debut: 25 October 1919
v Manchester City
Division One Away
Last Appearance: 17 April 1922
v Hull City
Division Two Home
Total League
& Cup Appearances: 82 Goals: 3

Career Details:

Sheffield Boys Brigade		
Sharrow Old Boys		
Sheffield United		1912 Trial
Worksop Town	September	1912
Leeds City	December	1912 £125
WEDNESDAY	17 October	1919 £750
Southend United	November	1922 £100
Scunthorpe United	26 July	1924 – 13 Dec 1924
Bakewell		1925

Versatile player Arthur Price was a boyhood Wednesday fan who attended games with his father during his schoolboy days. His career had started as an inside forward in local football before his big break came at League side Leeds City where in 78 appearances he netted a praiseworthy 25 goals. However in October 1919 the Football League sensationally expelled City from the Football League after allegations of illegal payments in wartime football and the club immediately disbanded, giving rise to an infamous sale of City's assets, which of course included the players. It was here that Wednesday secured Price's services, along with teammate Joe Edmondson, and he was thrown straight into a struggling Owls side. Unfortunately he could not stop Wednesday from dropping out of the top-flight but was perhaps unique as he was retained at the end of the season as Wednesday had a mass clear out of players.

During the 1920-21 season Price – who was a good golfer and played cricket for Sheffield Bankers – was converted from inside-left to left halfback and appeared in 37 games as the club disappointingly failed to make a challenge to regain their First Division place. A leg injury, suffered over the 1921 Christmas period, eventually saw Price lose his first team place to Tom Brelsford and despite making a comeback in his old inside forward position Arthur eventually left for Southend United. A later spell at Scunthorpe ended when Price left to take over a Bakewell public house, also signing for the local football team, while he was appointed trainer at Scarborough in November 1927. He also became Steward of the Scarborough Conservative Club and was still trainer to the towns' football team in the mid-1930s.

PRIESTLEY, R. 1893-97

Born:
Debut: 30 March 1895 v Liverpool Division One Away
Last Appearance: 1 April 1895 v West Bromwich Albion
Division One Home
Total League & Cup Appearances: 2 Goals: 1

Career Details:

Local	
WEDNESDAY	1893
Local	1897

Little known Nineteenth Century inside forward who spent four seasons with Wednesday. The majority of that time was spent in the Owls reserve side – his second team debut coming in November 1893 – but he was given a brief taste of League soccer late in the 1894-95 campaign, scoring on his debut in a 4-2 defeat on Merseyside. Despite the defeat his services were retained for the home win over West Brom twenty-four hours later but it was then back into second team football for the remainder of his Wednesday career, helping the reserves win the Sheffield & Hallamshire Challenge Cup League in 1895.

PRINCE, Arthur 1924-28

Born: 8 December 1902 Bucknall
(5ft 9½ins, 10st 7lbs – 1924)
Died: 3rd Quarter 1980 Nuneaton
Debut: 1 September 1924
v Derby County
Division Two Home
Last Appearance: 31 March 1928
v Leicester City
Division One Away
Total League
& Cup Appearances: 54 Goals: 7

Career Details:

Bucknall		
Port Vale	January	1923
WEDNESDAY	12 May	1924
Hull City	22 June	1928 £500
Chester	September	1929
Walsall	October	1929
Bristol Rovers	August	1930
Dorden Institute	August	1932

It took Wednesday manager Bob Brown five years to build a team to take Wednesday out of the Second Division in 1926 and outstanding winger Arthur Prince was one of the final pieces of his jigsaw, signing from Port Vale after the Potteries side hit financial problems and were forced to sell their prize asset. On his day Prince was a speedy and clever forward, possessing a deceptive swerve, great crossing ability and fine stamina. He quickly displaced Joe Harron on the left wing in The Owls Division Two side and really hit top form during the promotion season, helped greatly by the tremendous form of Harold Hill – his partner in crime on the left wing.

However near the end of that promotion campaign diminutive winger Jack Wilkinson took his place and Prince quickly fell from grace, failing to play a single first team game in Wednesday's first season back in the top-flight. Being replaced by the teenage winger obviously affected his form and confidence and incredibly – especially compared to modern times where players hold most of the power – in October 1926 his wages were reduced to £6 a week after he showed "indifferent form"! His pay packet was reduced down to just £4 in September 1927 for the same reasons – this time seemingly with his consent – and it was obvious he needed a change of scenery to boost his flagging career. Prince did make one last appearance in an Owls shirt – scoring from centre forward in a 2-2 draw at Leicester in his only top-flight game – before slipping back into Central League football and then transferring to Hull City.

PRIOR, George 'Geordie' 1920-24

Born: 2 March 1898 Ashington
(5ft 9½ins, 11st 7lbs – 1920)
Died: 1 April 1977 Ashington
Debut: 30 October 1920
v Birmingham
Division Two Away
Last Appearance: 15 March 1924
v Oldham Athletic
Division Two Away
Total League
& Cup Appearances: 37 Goals: 0

Career Details:

Blyth Spartans		
WEDNESDAY	19 October	1920 £350
Watford	August	1924*
Ashington	August	1930 Free

* Part exchange for George Toone

Like so many of his Northeast contemporaries George Prior's first experience of organised football came on his Saturday afternoon off from his job at the local pit. He was employed at Ashington Colliery while playing for crack amateur side Blyth Spartans until being spotted by The Owls scouts who brought him to Hillsborough as Wednesday started to rebuild after the disastrous 1920 relegation season. He arrived as a centre forward and was quickly given a first team debut although he failed to make the initial impression he would have liked, being nothing more than a spectator in a 4-0 defeat. He was tried on the right wing for the next game and appeared in one more league match in that first season while gaining experience in the rough and tumble world of Midland League soccer.

However it was positional change that ensured Prior would enjoy two relatively successful seasons in the Wednesday first team. The first game of the new season saw George in his new position of right back and although he quickly lost his place he would return to play the final nine games of the season at left back. The tough tackling Prior was perhaps better suited to defensive duties and remained a regular at first team level for the next six months before the arrival of Ernie Blenkinsop put paid to his progress and George was back in the reserves – appearing in the Owls first ever Central League game in August 1923. He would play only one more game at league level for Wednesday before moving south to sign for Watford.

He was affectionately known as 'Geordie' Prior at Vicarage Road and proved a reliable and popular defender, scoring three times in 189 appearances, before returning home to sign as player-coach for Ashington. He added groundsman to his duties in June 1931 and later became the club masseur and physiotherapist – although self taught he reached such a high standard that the local hospital regularly sent down patients for George to help out! He continued to play for Ashington until the age of 40 and when war was declared it was decreed he could not join the services due to a childhood accident involving a cherry tree stone – one became lodged in his ear at school and attempts to remove the stone only pushed it further in. When it was finally extricated George was totally deaf in one ear – perhaps more aptly described as being stone deaf!

After leaving Ashington in 1938 he returned to the local Colliery where he gained employment as a steel sawer while he would later see his son, Ken, follow a family tradition – his brother Jack played for several league sides including Sunderland – by playing league football for Newcastle United and Millwall.

PROCTER, Mark Gerard 1987-89

Born: 30 January 1961 Middlesbrough
(5ft 10ins, 11st 13lbs – 1988)
Debut: 5 September 1987
v Southampton
Division One Away
Last Appearance: 18 March 1989
v Luton Town
Division One Away
Total League
& Cup Appearances: 69 Goals: 5

Career Details:

Nunthorpe Athletic		
Leeds United		Trial
Middlesbrough	14 September	1978
Nottingham Forest	4 August	1981 £440,000
Sunderland	March	1983 Loan
Sunderland	July	1983 £115,000
WEDNESDAY	3 September	1987 £275,000
Middlesbrough	21 March	1989 £300,000
Tranmere Rovers	15 March	1993 Loan
Tranmere Rovers	23 July	1993 Free
South Shields	May	1994 Free
St.Johnstone	22 August	1995 Free
Whitley Bay	November	1995
Blyth Spartans		1996
Hartlepool United	21 March	1997 N/C

Experienced midfielder Mark Procter was brought to Hillsborough by Howard Wilkinson and became a permanent fixture in the side under his stewardship and that of his successor Peter Eustace. However the stylish midfielder immediately fell out of favour after the arrival of Ron Atkinson and within a month made a surprise move back to the Northeast for a second spell at Middlesbrough. Procter had originally started his professional career at Ayresome Park, after impressing at schoolboy level for both Middlesbrough and Cleveland boys. An early trial spell at Leeds United was ended due to his homesickness while after signing schoolboy forms for Boro, Procter went on to captain England Youth prior to signing professional forms for Middlesbrough.

He was given a league debut by Boro aged just seventeen and quickly became a fixture in the side, earning two England U-21 caps and showing his precocious talent by appearing in over 100 competitive games whilst still a teenager. However Boro showed little ambition at the time and the youngster was cherry-picked by Brian Clough at Nottingham Forest although the move never really worked out for either party and he was soon back in the Northeast. A serious injury meant Procter missed out on Sunderland's 1985 League Cup Final against Norwich City and within two years The Black Cats had slumped into Division Three – Mark missing a crucial penalty that condemned Sunderland to the relegation play off and then to rub salt into his wounds missed from the penalty spot in the play off versus Gillingham.

It was obvious Procter was too good to play in England's third tier and a move to Hillsborough soon followed. After Atkinson sold Procter back to Middlesbrough he would return in May 1989 for a crucial relegation match but would go home disappointed as Wednesday won to send Boro tumbling out of the top-flight. However he bounced back, captaining his hometown club in the 1990 ZDS Cup Final loss to Chelsea, and then helped Boro to promotion to the newly formed Premier League in 1992. After just eleven appearances in England's new top-flight his relationship with boss Lennie Lawrence reached breaking point and Procter joined Tranmere Rovers on loan, leading to a permanent transfer. A short spell in Scottish football followed before Mark dropped into non-league soccer, back in his native Northeast, and was appointed Youth Coach at Middlesbrough. An emergency call from an ex-team mate saw Procter join Hartlepool United on non-contract terms in 1997, bringing his total league appearances to exactly 500, before he settled back into his coaching role at Boro – he led Middlesborough to the 2003 F.A.Youth Cup Final where they lost to Manchester United.

PROPHETT, Colin George 1968-73

Born: 8 March 1947 Crewe
(5ft 11ins, 11st 8lbs – 1973)
Debut: 30 August 1969
v Liverpool
Division One Home
Last Appearance: 24 April 1973
v Aston Villa
Division Two Away
Total League
& Cup Appearances: 120+9 Goals: 7

Career Details:

Crewe Junior football		
Rolls Royce		
Crewe Alexandra		1964 Amat.
WEDNESDAY	12 September	1967 Amat.
WEDNESDAY	6 June	1968
Norwich City	23 May	1973 £42,500
Swindon Town	2 October	1974 £25,000
Chesterfield	15 September	1978 £15,000
Crewe Alexandra	18 October	1979 £12,000
Matlock Town	August	1982
Heanor Town		1983
Alfreton Town	June	1983

As far as Crewe Alexandra are concerned Centre Half Colin Prophett was 'the one that got away' as he was an amateur at Gresty Road for three years, eventually leaving after Crewe decided not to offer him a professional contract. These circumstances brought him to Wednesday – ex-Crewe winger Tony Coleman recommending him to Owls boss Jack Marshall - where it was perhaps ironic that he initially signed as amateur! However this was at Prophett's insistence so he could complete his apprenticeship as a fitter and turner at Rolls Royce. His Central League debut actually came three days before he signed amateur forms and he would hardly miss a game for the following two seasons at reserve team level to earn a deserved call up to the first team bench, from where he made his senior debut.

The tall, determined central defender remained in the first team for the rest of the season and was a central figure in the final game against Manchester City, which Wednesday had to win to avoid relegation. The Owls defender and City's Mike Summerbee clashed in midfield with the latter being stretchered off, much to the anger of City boss Joe Mercer who misinterpreted the challenge – it was actually Summerbee who had committed the foul. The irate boss rushed to the touchline to urge on his previously lethargic side and sent on substitute Bowyer who netted twice to send Wednesday into Division Two. Apart from that unfortunate incident his time at Hillsborough was a success for Prophett as he was considered the 'find' of the season in 1970-1 and missed only one game in the following campaign. He was perhaps unlucky to lose his place at the start of the 1972-3 season – to the returning Peter Swan – but although he regained it a transfer to Norwich City followed in the summer.

He stayed only briefly in Norfolk, appearing 35 times, before enjoying what was arguably his best spell in league football under ex-Owls boss Danny Williams at Swindon Town. He totalled 160 games for Town – twice going in goal when goalkeepers were injured – and then played for a variety of league sides before being appointed reserve team manager at Cardiff City for the 1981-2 season. After resigning for personal reasons in April 1982 he returned to the Sheffield area to work for an insurance company and ended his playing days in non-league football. He was player-manager at Alfreton Town and later general manager while also scouting for ex-Wednesday teammate Ian Branfoot, Swansea City and then briefly for The Owls when Danny Wilson was manager. He now works as an area sales manager for a woodworking firm and although Osteoarthritis in his knee has ended his football days Prophett is a keen golfer and local league cricketer.

PROUD, Pattison 1906-07

Born: 3rd Quarter 1883 Auckland
Died: 31 March 1937 Newcastle
Only Appearance:
19 January 1907 v Middlesbrough Division One Home
Total League & Cup Appearances: 1 Goals: 0

Career Details:

Bishop Auckland		
WEDNESDAY	January	1906
Released	April	1907

Left halfback who played only a handful of games for crack northeast amateur side Bishop Auckland before being snapped up by Wednesday. He spent fifteen months at Wednesday but apart from playing reserve team football was given only one first team game, when The Owls hit injury problems part way through the 1906-07 season. Wednesday slumped to a two-nil home loss on his only appearance and Proud dropped out of the professional ranks. At the time of his death he was living back in his native northeast at Willington and working at Brancepeth Colliery.

PROUDLOCK, Adam David 2002-03 & 2003-

Born: 9 May 1981 Telford
(6ft, 13st 2lbs – 2003)
Debut: 14 December 2002
v Gillingham
Division One Home
Total League & Cup
Appearances: 49+11 Goals: 17

Career Details:

Nova United		
Wolverhampton Wanderers	15 July	1999
Clyde	1 August	2000 Loan

Nottingham Forest	3 March	2002 Loan
Tranmere Rovers	25 October	2002 Loan
WEDNESDAY	13 December	2002 Loan
Loan return	6 January	2003
WEDNESDAY	5 September	2003 £150,000

One of several loan players brought to the club by Chris Turner during the 2002-3 season as he tried to stave off relegation from Division One. The striker slowly improved with every game he played in his initial short loan spell at Wednesday, scoring in his final two games, and fans were disappointed when an injury crisis at Wolves led to his recall before the loan spell was due to expire. The ex-England and Shropshire boys player quickly came back to haunt Wednesday when netting twice in Wolves' 4-0 win at Hillsborough in February 2003 and looked set to push for a first team place after the Black Country club clinched promotion to the Premier League. However it quickly became clear he was not in Dave Jones plans for the higher grade and when a Dave Allen funded transfer fee was paid he returned to Hillsborough on a permanent basis.

Unfortunately his first season back at Hillsborough proved a big disappointment for both fans and player as Proudlock struggled to make an impact in the rough and tumble world of Division Two, scoring only three league goals in 30 appearances, as Wednesday slumped to the second worst league position in their entire history. A foolish sending off for violent conduct at Port Vale in February 2004 certainly did not help his cause and with confidence at a low ebb he was dropped for the final two games of the season. A bright pre season brought Proudlock back into contention at the start of the following campaign but it needed the arrival of new manager Paul Sturrock to bring the best out of the attacker – Proudlock enjoying his best display in an Owls shirt when netting twice in a 4-1 win at Bristol City in November 2004. Sadly though, for both club and player, a few days later he suffered a broken leg in training and then in February 2005 his comeback came to an abrupt end when it was discovered his fracture had not healed properly – ruling the striker out for the remainder of the season.

PROUDLOVE, Andrew George 'Andy' 1975-76

Born: 15 January 1955 Buxton
(5ft 10ins, 11st 9lbs – 1976)
Debut: 20 September 1975
v Grimsby Town
Division Three Home
Last Appearance: 27 December 1975
v Mansfield Town
Division Three Home
Total League
& Cup Appearances: 12+5 Goals: 1

Career Details:

Chinley		Sun.
Reading	30 September	1970 App.
Peak Dale		1971
Buxton	July	1972 Amat.
West Ham United	August	1974 3-month trial
WEDNESDAY	September	1975 Free
Norwich City	5 February	1976
Hereford United	13 May	1977
Buxton	October	1977
Port Vale	2 November	1978 £1,000
Buxton	May	1979 Free
Stafford Rangers		
Macclesfield Town		
Matlock Town		
Nykopping	June	1980
Bulova	December	1980
Atvidabergs F.F.	October	1981
Turku		1983
Rio Ave		1983

Winger Andy Proudlove experienced a varied and somewhat nomadic career, which included spells in five different countries. The former Derbyshire boys player started in local Sunday football – winning three consecutive league championships – before signing apprentice forms at Reading where whilst still a trainee he became one of The Royals youngest ever players, appearing in an F.A.Cup tie at non-league Bridgewater aged just 16 years, 309 days. After five games for the Berkshire side he was not offered a professional contract and returned home to play for Peak Dale in the dizzy heights of the Hope Valley League! He would regularly net five times on a Saturday while spending his working week as a trainee rep and it was not long before he signed amateur forms for Northern Premier League Buxton. After impressing for Buxton he was subsequently invited for a trial at West Ham by ex-Owls coach Jack Mansell, who was scouting for The Hammers.

However he could not settle in London and returned to play for Buxton where he was spotted by Wednesday during the 1975 pre season. The Owls decided to gamble on the youngster and offered him his first professional contract, which he duly signed. Despite his stay at Wednesday being brief he appeared on a regular basis and this earned a move to Second Division Norwich City where after just two substitute appearances he left for Hereford United. After failing to become established at United he rejoined Buxton before making a surprise move back into the Football League at Port Vale in 1978. His league career ended with five games for the Staffordshire side and Proudlove then moved back into non-league football before packing his case for several playing spells on foreign shores. This began with six months in Swedish football before a similar period in Hong Kong where he won a runners-up medal. It was then back to Sweden at Atvidabergs before his globetrotting came to an end after playing in Finland and then for a club near Porto, in Portugal. He then returned home to start his own business in the building trade and is now managing director of two Buxton property development companies.

PRUDHAM, Charles Edward 'Eddie' 1969-74

Born: 12 April 1952 Pelaw, nr Gateshead
(5ft 7ins, 9st 12lbs – 1973)
Debut: 9 January 1971
v Cardiff City
Division Two Away
Last Appearance: 12 October 1974
v Oxford United
Division Two Away
Total League
& Cup Appearances: 15+6 Goals: 3

Career Details:

WEDNESDAY	7 July	1969
Partick Thistle	17 October	1974 Loan
Carlisle United	18 November	1974 £35,000
Hartlepool United	9 September	1976 Loan
Workington	25 February	1977 Loan
Stockport County	July	1977 Free
Bournemouth	May	1980

Although initially attached to Wednesday from the age of 14 – he trained at Hillsborough during the school holidays – it was not until Eddie Prudham completed his education three years later that he signed professional forms for the club. During that period Eddie stayed on at school to gain six 'O' levels and therefore did not serve the usual apprenticeship undertaken by his peers. Eighteen months after joining The Owls on a full time basis the 18 year-old Prudham was given his league bow, after an injury to regular right-winger Jackie Sinclair, but it proved an inauspicious debut for Eddie as Wednesday crashed 4-0 at Ninian Park. The former Jarrow boys player had to wait until the following season to make his second appearance – this time at centre forward – and generally Prudham struggled to make a lasting impression. He finally grabbed his first goal in the 1972-3 season but could only double his seasonal appearances to a miserly two and although he played a dozen times in the following campaign it was obvious he would never be a regular and his subsequent transfer – after scoring 3 times in 4 games while on loan in Scottish football - seemed the best solution for all parties.

His eventual move, to top-flight new boys Carlisle United, was somewhat of a surprise and when making his debut at home to reigning Champions Leeds United Eddie must have thought he had fallen on his feet.

Unfortunately for Prudham he was never anything more than a fringe player at the Cumbrian club – appearing in only seventeen games - and when he left United were a Third Division club after two relegations in three seasons. He enjoyed his best spell, appearance wise, at Stockport County where in three seasons the diminutive attacker scored a commendable 22 times in 87 appearances. A short spell at Bournemouth yielded four more appearances before Eddie retired from football in April 1981 to work as Probation Hostel Warden Officer back in Sheffield. In August 1982 he joined the prison service, initially working at Her Majesty's Prison Wakefield, before being transferred at his own request in 1987 to H.M.P. Albany on the Isle of Wight. He was promoted to Senior Prison Officer in 1992 and now serves at neighbouring H.M.P. Camphill.

PRYCE, John 'Jack' 1899-1901

Born: 25 January 1874 Renton, Scotland
Died: December 1905
Debut: 4 March 1899
v Everton
Division One Home
Last Appearance: 16 February 1901
v Blackburn Rovers
Division One Home
Total League
& Cup Appearances: 59 Goals: 6

Career Details:

Renton		1893
Hibernian	May	1896
Glossop North End	September	1898
WEDNESDAY	24 February	1899
Queens Park Rangers	May	1901
Brighton & Hove Albion	October	1903

Scottish inside forward who joined The Owls at one of lowest points in their history with relegation from the top-flight imminent and the loss of their beloved Olive Grove ground just weeks away. The Owls had struggled all season and the experienced Pryce could do little to stem the tide although Wednesday did score in six consecutive games with him in their side - a feat totally unheard of before in a depressing season. The newcomer – who replaced stalwart Harry Davis at inside right - would play in the club's last ever fixture at their old ground but fortunes quickly turned around as a year later Pryce was almost ever-present as the club bounced back to win the Second Division Championship in their first season at their new Owlerton home.

Before moving south in 1898 Pryce had enjoyed a successful career in his homeland where he was a Scottish Cup Finalist with Renton in 1895 and helped Hibs to the Division One runners-up spot two years later – he was picked for Scotland against Wales in 1897 but injury denied him a full cap. He was a key player in the aforementioned 1900 promotion campaign – teaming up with Archie Brash on the right wing - but did run into trouble during the stormy F.A.Cup ties with Sheffield United when he was one of two Wednesday players sent off in the third game of the trilogy. With Wednesday back in Division One, Pryce started the first eight games of the new season but then had to compete with newcomer Harry Davis before the arrival of Harry Chapman effectively spelt the end of his Owls career. He later played in the then professional Southern League for QPR and Brighton before returning to Scotland in 1905.

PUGH, John Graham 1965-72

Born: 12 February 1948 Hoole, Chester
(5ft 7ins, 11st 7lbs – 1972)
Debut: 9 April 1966
v Tottenham Hotspur
Division One Home
Last Appearance: 29 April 1972
v Birmingham City
Division Two Home
Total League
& Cup Appearances: 149+6 Goals: 9

Career Details:

WEDNESDAY	12 February	1965
Huddersfield Town	12 May	1972 £60,000
Chester City	February	1975 £15,000
Barnsley	October	1976
Scunthorpe United	January	1980
Matlock Town	July	1981
Burton Albion		

CAPS (@SWFC)
England U-23 (1) v Wales 01/10/69

Graham Pugh burst onto the Hillsborough scene in April 1966 as a tenacious eighteen year-old winger who possessed pace and talent. His fairytale rise continued as he scored a last minute goal in the F.A.Cup semi-final win over Chelsea and then played in the young side that came so close to lifting the old trophy in that classic Final against Everton. He was a player of great promise and while still a teenager had become established in The Owls first team before a serious injury sustained in April 1967 checked his progress and kept Pugh out of the game for over a year – his injury was eventually diagnosed as cartilage damage and Pugh struggled for fitness for fully two years before regaining form and fitness during the 1969-70 campaign. He had originally arrived at Wednesday under the reign of Vic Buckingham – signing apprentice forms in August 1963 – and after making such a tremendous early impact it was always asking a lot for Pugh to fulfil all of that early promise. However he did mature into somewhat of a midfield tiger who became a big favourite at Hillsborough although his volatile persona on the field of play saw him pick up his share of bookings and in one season he was even suspended twice – almost unheard of in those days.

After relegation in 1970 Pugh was a regular for two seasons but handed in a transfer request in March 1972, which he withdrew at the end of the season. However in a shock move he was then sold to neighbours Huddersfield Town where he suffered relegation from Division Two before moving to his hometown club. After winning promotion from Division Three with Chester in 1975 he also helped Barnsley to promotion from the same division in 1979 before ending his league career with 55 games for Scunthorpe United. He later left Matlock Town after just four games when he was not paid and Pugh ended his career under Neil Warnock at Burton Albion, appearing in 25 games during the 1981-2 season prior to entering the licensing trade with his wife. He was manager of the Rising Sun at Fulwood first and then owned The Freemason Arms, in Hillsborough, for fourteen years until moving to his current position in 2001 as steward of a working mens club in Lincolnshire.

QUIGLEY, Edward 'Eddie' 1947-49

Born: 13 July 1921 Bury
(5ft 9ins, 11st 4lbs – 1947)
Died: 16 April 1997 Blackpool
Debut: 11 October 1947
v Plymouth Argyle
Division Two Away
Last Appearance: 26 November 1949
v Luton Town
Division Two Home
Total League
& Cup Appearances: 78 Goals: 52

Career Details:

Bury	September	1941
WEDNESDAY	9 October	1947 £12,000
Preston North End	December	1949 £26,000
Blackburn Rovers	17 November	1951 £20,000
Bury	29 August	1956 £1,000
Mossley	5 July	1957

During his teenage years Eddie Quigley worked for an engineering company and held high hopes of becoming a professional cricketer – he played for Radcliffe as a 16 year-old. However it would be as a professional footballer that the Lancastrian would make his name, signing for hometown club Bury during the Second World War. However he spent the majority of the war years on active service with the Royal Navy, serving on destroyers and corvettes, and was part of the first convoy to sail through the Mediterranean route after it was reopened. He joined Bury as a full back but after netting five times in a trial game as an attacker he remained in a forward role position for the rest of his career. Quigley's languid movements and big build were highly deceptive as his speed of thought and superb passing skills made him a constant threat to opposition defences. He preferred to play in a deeper lying role than most of contemporaries and specialised in long crossfield passes and accurate long range shooting. It was all these qualities that persuaded Eric Taylor to smash the club's transfer record to bring Quigley to Hillsborough – the fee was also a record sum for Bury at that time – as Wednesday tried to climb their way out of Division Two by spending heavily in the transfer market.

The Owls secretary-manager always had a good eye for a player and he was not proved wrong with Quigley as the new boy proved one of his best signings – he netted four times on two separate occasions in a Wednesday shirt and his goals per game ratio was excellent. Despite his success at Wednesday his time in Sheffield was not without problems as in March 1949 he was stripped of the captaincy, following misconduct, and told that if his future behaviour did not improve he would be put on the list! This incident may have partly explained why Wednesday were willing to sell their star inside-forward in December 1949 when big spending Preston came calling. The move stunned Wednesday fans although the British record fee paid by North End at least gave the Owls a financial war chest to finally scramble out of the second tier of the English game.

Unfortunately his move to Deepdale was not a success – although he did win two England 'B' caps and earn a Division Two Championship medal - as he failed to click with Tom Finney and left for Blackburn after 17 goals in 52 league games. He quickly found Rovers boss Johnny Carey's attacking philosophy more to his liking and was back on the goal trail – netting 95 goals in 166 league and cup games for the Ewood Park club- prior to ending his league career back at Bury. Five years as player-manager at Manchester club Mossley followed before Quigley was appointed youth team boss at Bury. He moved to Stockport County in October 1964 as Adminstration Manager and was later General manager and then team manager before moving to another of his old clubs, Blackburn Rovers, as assistant manager in November 1966. When Jack Mansell resigned in February 1967 Quigley was made caretaker boss and was appointed on a permanent basis two months later. A lack of finances meant he was hampered as Rovers failed to gained promotion and he later dropped back into a Youth Coach/Chief Scout role in October 1970 before being sacked in April 1971. He then scouted for Sheffield United and Blackpool prior to his final spell as a manager – eleven months back at Stockport County between May 1976 and April 1977. He was back at Blackburn Rovers as Chief Coach in 1979 but ended an on-off association spanning thirty years in May 1981 when he left along with Howard Kendall. Quigley – uncle of Johnny Morris who played for Manchester United, Derby County and Leicester City – finally retired after a spell as Chief Coach at Blackpool.

QUINN, Alan 1997-2004

Born: 13 July 1979 Dublin, Eire
(5ft 9ins, 10st 6lbs – 2001)
Debut: 25 April 1998
v Everton
Premier League Away
Last Appearance: 24 April 2004
v Colchester United
Division Two Home
Total League
& Cup Appearances: 169+11 Goals: 17

Career Details:

Lourdes Celtic		
Cherry Orchard		
WEDNESDAY	27 November	1997 Nominal
Sunderland	3 October	2003 3-month loan
Sheffield United	1 July	2004 Free

CAPS (@ SWFC)
EIRE Full (4) v Norway 30/04/03, v Australia 19/08/03, v Jamaica 02/06/04, v Holland 05/06/04

Eire U-21 (7) v Czech Republic 22/02/00, v Columbia 25/05/00, Ghana 27/05/00, v Portugal 29/05/00, v Holland 02/09/00, v Portugal 06/10/00, v Cyprus 23/03/01

Midfielder Alan Quinn was once described on the F.A. of Ireland website as a player who "single-handedly raises the tempo every time he plays" and this was an almost perfect description of the perpetual motion Dubliner who had originally arrived at Hillsborough on trial in October 1997, along with future first team player Derek Geary. The hard running, tough tackling Quinn was always guaranteed to give 100% commitment and it was these qualities that endeared the teenager to Owls fans during the early part of his Wednesday career. His arrival at Hillsborough came after he had impressed against an Owls youth side in a friendly, whilst playing for a Dublin Youth select team, and within weeks he was signed as a professional, immediately becoming a mainstay of the club's F.A.Premier Youth League side. A reserve team debut came in March 1998 and after starting just two second team games he was handed a shock place on the subs bench for the Premier League game at Everton, duly coming off the bench in injury time to taste top-flight football. To complete an incredible year for the youngster the summer that followed saw Quinn become a pivotal member of the Eire U-18 side that won the European Championships in Cyprus – Quinn scoring in the 1-1 draw against Germany in the Final, which the Irish won eventually 4-3 on penalties.

The following season saw Quinn become a reserve team regular and despite being played out of position on his full first team debut he bounced back to break back into the side on a more permanent basis in December 1999. He proved the only real bright spot during that relegation season – winning two player of the month awards – and cemented his popularity with fans in Division One with a series of enthusiastic displays which featured his penchant for running at panic stricken defences. Sadly his season was cut short after breaking his leg against Sheffield United in April 2001 but he was back in the side at the start of the next campaign, remaining a first choice for two seasons as The Owls slipped out of Division One. A dip in form had seen Quinn dropped by new manager Chris Turner but he came back refreshed to not only win the 2003 'player of the year' trophy but also earn his first senior cap for Eire. However 2003-4 was a decidedly mixed campaign for Quinn as a combination of poor form and a relatively unsuccessful loan spell at Sunderland saw him start only half of the Division Two fixtures. After returning from Sunderland Quinn netted the winner at Wrexham and expressed the desire that he never wanted to leave Hillsborough but the primarily left sided midfielder became a free agent in the summer of 2004 and a poor disciplinary record – he was sent off twice in 2003-4 and was suspended for five games near the end of the season – probably did not help his cause when Chris Turner decided who should be offered new deals. Sadly for Quinn, and for many Wednesday fans, the popular midfielder was surprisingly not offered a new contract and left after almost seven years at Hillsborough. He was then signed by neighbours Sheffield United and a few weeks later was joined at Bramall Lane by his teenage brothers Stephen & Keith – the Blades signing his siblings on Academy forms.

QUINN, Stephen James 'James' 2005

Born: 15 December 1974 Coventry
(6ft 1ins, 12st 10lbs - 2002)
Debut: 15 January 2005
v Bournemouth League One Away
Last Appearcnce: 29 May 2005
v Hartlepool United
League One Playoff Final
Total League
& Cup Appearances: 13+5 Goals: 2

Career Details:

Birmingham City	July	1991 YTS
Blackpool	5 July	1993 £25,000
Stockport County	4 March	1994 Loan
West Bromwich Albion	20 February	1998 £500,000
Notts County	30 November	2001 Loan
Bristol Rovers	22 March	2002 Loan
Contract cancelled	24 April	2002
Willem II	26 April	2002 Free
MK Dons	10 January	2005 Trial
WEDNESDAY	14 January	2005 Free
Released	30 June	2005
Peterborough United	5 August	2005

CAPS (@SWFC)
Northern Ireland Full (1) v Poland 30/03/05

Although capped 34 times by Northern Ireland, James Quinn was a relative unknown to Owls fans after an almost three-year spell in Dutch football. After netting 12 times in 52 games for Willem II he returned to England early in 2005 to look for a club and it was Paul Sturrock who handed Quinn a contract until the end of the season. It was acknowledged that Quinn would take time to adapt to the 'hurly burly' of life in League One - especially after playing in the slower, more technical Dutch game - and this was proved right as despite netting in his second game he struggled to impress Wednesday fans. Although there was no doubt about Quinn's commitment it looked unlikely he would be offered another deal at the end of the season but this opinion changed dramatically during the final weeks of the season - the tall forward leading the line superbly in all three play off games as Wednesday made the glorious leap into the Championship. However, after being offered a new contract the forward declined the opportunity and later signed for basement club Peterborough United.

The victory in Cardiff proved the definite highlight of a career that had started as a trainee at Birmingham City in the early 1990s. Despite four appearances for City while still on YTS forms he refused the Blues offer of a professional contract and subsequently moved to Blackpool where he became established as one of the best forwards in the lower divisions - netting 48 times in 182 games for the Seaside club. This form prompted a move to West Bromwich Albion where Quinn was a regular during his early days before falling out of favour during the reign of former Owl, Gary Megson. In total he amassed 10 goals in 123 competitive games for the Hawthorns club, prior to a move into Dutch soccer after the Baggies cancelled his contract.

QUINN, James 'Jim' 1975-76

Born: 23 November 1947
Kilsyth, North Lanarkshire
(5ft 9ins, 11st – 1975)
Died: 24 April 2002 Croy, North Lanarkshire
Debut: 31 January 1975
v York City Division Two Away
Last Appearance: 19 April 1976
v Mansfield Town Division Three Away
Total League & Cup App: 52 Goals: 1

Career Details:

St Ninian's Kirkintilloch		
Croy Amateurs		1963
Holy Cross Croy Boys Guard		
Glasgow Celtic	24 November	1963
Maryhill Harps	August	1964 Season-loan
Clyde	9 January	1969
Released	18 December	1974
WEDNESDAY	8 January	1975 Free
Melbourne	July	1975 Free
Hamilton Academicals	November	1976

Started his professional career at Celtic as a centre forward but after being farmed out to junior side Maryhill to 'toughen him up' he was then converted to full back by Jock Stein. The pacy Quinn – whose grandfather was Celtic legend Jimmy Quinn - was never anything more than a fringe player in over ten years at Celtic Park where he appeared in only 27 league games, scoring once. After being released he arrived at Hillsborough on trial in January 1975 and after signing a contract was ever present for eighteen months, showing tremendous acceleration and a willingness to go forward and support the attackers. However his consistency at left back was not matched by his team mates as The Owls slumped to their worst ever league finish in their history and he did not survive the cull that came at the end of the horrendous 1975-6 season.

After leaving Wednesday he moved to Australia to play two summer seasons for Brisbane before returning home to end his playing days at Hamilton, failing to make a senior appearance for the 'Accies'. After leaving football Quinn worked for a haulage firm as a driver but sadly aged just 54 he was taken ill in his local public house and died on the way to hospital.

QUINN, John David 1959-67

Born: 30 May 1938 St Helens
(5ft 6$^{1}/_{2}$ins, 10st 7$^{1}/_{2}$lbs – 1966)
Debut: 26 September 1959
v Luton Town
Division One Home
Last Appearance: 11 November 1967
v Chelsea
Division One Away
Total League
& Cup Appearances: 184+10 Goals: 24

Career Details:

St Helens Town		
Prescot Cables		
Burnley		3-month trial
Everton		Trial
WEDNESDAY	29 April	1959 £1250
Rotherham United	24 November	1967 £25,000
Worksop Town	summer	1976
Goole Town	June	1978

Utility forward John Quinn played only a few games for Lancashire Combination club Prescot Cables before scouts started to show serious interest in the teenager. At the time he was working as a welder but after Wednesday offered Quinn a professional contract he quit his job and moved to Hillsborough, quickly being given his first team debut by Owls boss Harry Catterick. However in his first three seasons Quinn's chances of first team football were restricted, mainly due to the terrific form of the club's more senior players and Quinn having to serve his two years National Service. However the loyal and dependable Quinn saw his patience rewarded when Alan Brown was appointed manager as the new man in charge ensured John would become an automatic choice. His sheer versatility – he played in every position at Wednesday except for centre half and goalkeeper – perhaps often worked against Quinn on occasion but he always took setbacks and disappointments in his stride and remained cheerful, earning the respect of his fellow players.

The highlight of his career was without doubt an appearance in the 1966 Wembley F.A.Cup Final against Everton but eighteen months later he became one of Tommy Docherty's first signings as Rotherham United boss, The Millers spending a club record fee to take John to Millmoor. He was immediately dubbed 'The Mighty Quinn' after the pop song of the day by Manfred Mann but could not help United avoid relegation from Division Two. He then spent almost two years on the sidelines with an Achilles tendon injury but after returning to the team as captain United only just missed out on promotion, although before the season had ended Quinn was handed a free transfer move to become player-coach at Halifax Town. He totalled 114 (7 goals) for Rotherham and played a further 92 games for Halifax Town before retiring from league football in 1975 – from September 1974 until February 1976 he was player-manager at The Shay and there was an outcry amongst Town supporters when the hard working and admired Quinn was harshly sacked.

He then returned to Sheffield but immediately signed as a player for Peter Swan's Worksop Town, later spending a year as manager before resigning in January 1978. He worked in a butchers two days a week to make ends meet while at Worksop but after a spell as player-coach at Northern Premier League Goole Town he announced his retirement in October 1978, aged 38. After hanging up his boots John opened a sports shop in Stocksbridge with Peter Eustace and later started a similar venture with Gerry Young on Middlewood Road, near Hillsborough. He eventually sold both shops and now runs a small business from home whilst playing golf on local courses and in Spain. He also continues to run his charity football team 'Johnny Quinn All Stars' which has raised thousands of pounds for worthy causes over the last thirty years.

QUIXALL, Albert 1948-58

Born: 9 August 1933 Sheffield
(5ft 7¾ins, 11st – 1954)
Debut: 24 February 1951
v Chelsea
Division One Home
Last Appearance:
17 September 1958
v Sunderland
Division Two Home
Total League
& Cup Appearances: 260
Goals: 65

Career Details:
Meynell Youth Club

WEDNESDAY	24 August	1950
Manchester United	18 September	1958 £45,000
Oldham Athletic	8 September	1964 £8,500
Stockport County	2 July	1966
Altrincham	November	1967

CAPS (@SWFC)
England Full (5) v Wales 10/10/53, v N.Ireland 11/11/53, v Rest of Europe 21/10/53, v Spain 18/05/55, v Portugal 22/05/55

England 'B' (3) v Scotland 11/03/53, v Yugoslavia 16/05/54, v Switzerland 22/05/54

England U-23 (1)v Scotland 08/02/56

Football League (3) v Irish League 23/09/53, 25/04/56, v League of Ireland 19/09/56

Former Sheffield boys player Albert Quixall first joined the Owls ground staff straight from school in May 1948, aged 14, and soon won two schoolboy caps for England to indicate his immense early promise. While playing as an amateur for Wednesday he started his working life as an apprentice joiner and later worked for Owls director George Longden's construction firm before signing part-time professional forms at Hillsborough. His first team debut came alongside fellow 'starlet' Alan Finney and his progress in the club's 'A' and reserve teams was such that Quixall quickly became a first team regular, becoming the 'golden boy' of Hillsborough thanks to his blond hair and boyish looks. Quixall possessed a superb football brain and perfect ball control and it was these attributes that brought the youngster a flood of representative honours in the early years of his fledgling career, including a full cap for England at the tender age of 20. At club level Albert helped Wednesday to two promotions in 1952 and 1956 plus an appearance in the 1954 F.A.Cup semi-finals, forming a deadly left wing partnership with Finney.

However Owls fans were desperately disappointed when their golden boy handed in a transfer request in September 1958, which Wednesday reluctantly accepted. This immediately caused a scramble for his signature between seven major clubs and within 24 hours it was Matt Busby at Manchester United who made his first post-Munich signing, paying Wednesday a British record fee to take Quixall to Old Trafford. Quixall – whose practised poise and balance with his ballet teacher wife – netted 51 times in 165 games at Manchester United and earned an F.A.Cup winners medal in 1963 before moving to Oldham Athletic. Injuries restricted his appearances for Athletic during a near two-year stay netting eleven goals in 36 league and cup games – and his league career came to close after thirteen games for Stockport County. After retiring, following a brief spell at Altrincham, he settled in the Greater Manchester area and started his own scrap metal business just a stones throw from Old Trafford, which he ran until retirement

RAMSBOTTOM, Neil 1975-76

Born: 25 February 1946 Blackburn
(6ft 1ins, 12st 4lbs – 1975)
Debut: 19 August 1975
v Darlington
League Cup Away
Last Appearance: 6 December 1975
v Colchester United
Division Three Away
Total League
& Cup Appearances: 22 Goals: 0

Career Details:

Bury	July	1964
Blackpool	4 February	1971 £13,000
Crewe Alexandra	January	1972 Loan
Fulham	31 January	1972 Trial
Coventry City	9 March	1972 £10,000
WEDNESDAY	15 August	1975 £12,750
Plymouth Argyle	6 July	1976 Free
Blackburn Rovers	16 December	1977
New Jersey Americans		1979
Chorley		1979
Sheffield United	October	1979
Miami Americans		1980
Bradford City	August	1980
Bournemouth	August	1983 N/C

When Peter Springett left Wednesday the club was left without a senior goalkeeper and turned to experienced ex-plumber Neil Ramsbottom who had already appeared in 241 league games for four different clubs. The majority of those games had come at his first club Bury who he initially joined as an amateur, making his first team debut aged just seventeen. After seven years he moved into the top-flight with Blackpool but a broken arm restricted his appearances, prompting an unsuccessful 'training' spell at Fulham were Ramsbottom decided the club was too far from his Blackburn roots to entertain a transfer. He instead moved to Coventry City and then Wednesday where he played in 22 consecutive games before being struck down with an illness that left him in hospital for a while and kept him on the sidelines for the remainder of the season.

Unfortunately when he recovered he was handed a free transfer with still a year left on his contract and so moved to Plymouth, suffering relegation in his first season but being named 'player of the year'. After a spell with his hometown club, Ramsbottom then led a somewhat nomadic career with appearances for four different English clubs plus two summers in America with the same franchise team who had moved from New Jersey to Miami in between his two playing spells! He appeared in only two games for non-league Chorley – as an emergency stand in when their regular goalkeeper was injured – and ended his league career as a non-contract player at Bournemouth. After retiring from the game Ramsbottom qualified as a Financial Consultant, working for Barclays Bank and then Allied Dunbar, and is now employed as a quality controller for an Insurance Consultant business.

RAMSBOTTOM, Thomas 1921-23

Born: 13 January 1901 Idle
(5ft 8ins, 11st 7lbs – 1921)
Died: Q/E December 1972 Idle
Debut: 10 December 1921
v Clapton Orient
Division Two Away
Last Appearance: 4 March 1922
v South Shields
Division Two Home
Total League
& Cup Appearances: 12 Goals: 0

Career Details:

Idle FC		
Bradford City	June	1920
Pontypridd FC	July	1921
WEDNESDAY	1 December	1921 £400

Thomas Ramsbottom was one of six players who occupied the left back spot during the 1921-22 season as Bob Brown tried in vain to find a winning formula. He had arrived from Welsh non-league soccer part way through the season and was handed a debut within days of joining, taking over from Harry O'Neill in the problem position. Ramsbottom, aged 24 when he signed for the club, retained his place throughout the winter months but the likes of George Prior and eventually Ernie Blenkinsop ensured he would have to settle for Midland League football for the remainder of his stay in Sheffield.

RATCLIFFE, Milton Archie 'Archie' 1921-22

Born: 30 January 1898 Blackburn
(5ft 9½ins, 12st 7lbs – 1921)
Died: 25 January 1981 Ruislip
Debut:
27 August 1921 v Barnsley Division Two Home
Last Appearance:
31 December 1921 v Stoke FC Division Two Away
Total League & Cup Appearances: 12 Goals: 4

Career Details:

Nelson		
Blackpool	August	1920
WEDNESDAY	27 May	1921
Tranmere Rovers	June	1922

One of a catalogue of forwards tried in the early 1920s, as Wednesday tried to replace the likes of pre-war stars Andrew Wilson and David McLean. Described as a "rare bustler" who possessed a tremendously powerful shot, Ratcliffe scored on his debut – in a 3-2 loss against Barnsley – and averaged a praiseworthy goal every three games during his only season at Hillsborough. He later made two league appearances during a season at Tranmere Rovers before dropping out of senior football in 1923.

REDDY, Michael 2003-04

Born: 24 March 1980 Kilkenny, Eire
(6ft 1ins, 11st 7lbs – 2003)
Debut: 1 February 2003
v Wolverhampton Wanderers Division One Home
Last Appearance:
26 December 2003 v Port Vale Division Two Home
Total League & Cup Appearances: 27+5 Goals: 5

Career Details:

Kilkenny City		
Sunderland	30 August	1999 £50,000
Swindon Town	1 January	2001 Loan
Hull City	21 September	2001 Loan
Barnsley	28 March	2002 Loan
York City	1 October	2002 Loan
WEDNESDAY	30 January	2003 3-month loan
Loan Return	April	2003
WEDNESDAY	3 October	2003 3-month loan
Loan return	January	2004
Released	30 June	2004
Grimsby Town	20 July	2004 Free

Eight times capped Republic of Ireland U-21 International who spent two spells at Wednesday over a period of eleven months. The skilful, pacy winger made a big impact during his first spell, scoring a memorable winner at promotion chasing Portsmouth as Wednesday fought gallantly to avoid the drop from Division One. After The Owls failed to secure his transfer in the summer that followed, Reddy remained a fringe player at The Stadium of Light but within a few months he was back at Wednesday on loan with Alan Quinn travelling in the opposite direction. He again made an immediate impact but generally struggled to find his best form – not withstanding a fabulous goal of the season winner against Barnsley in an LDV Cup tie – and it was no surprise when he was allowed to return to Sunderland and Wednesday dropped thoughts of securing a permanent move.

The Irishman had originally joined 'The Black Cats' from non-league soccer in his native country – a hefty fee showing his early promise – and quickly become a crowd favourite after several early first team appearances from the subs bench. However the direct forward then spent several loan periods in the lower divisions to gain valuable experience although his time at Barnsley could perhaps have been longer – he signed on deadline day 2002, pulled a hamstring in his first training session and went straight back to the northeast! Unfortunately despite impressing whilst a loanee Reddy never started a league game for Sunderland and was not offered a new contract when his deal expired in the summer of 2004.

REED, Percy 1919-21

Born: 5 December 1890 Stokesley, Northeast (5ft 6ins, 7lbs – 1919)
Died: Q/E September 1970
Debut:
13 September 1919 v Notts County Division One Home
Last Appearance: 3 February 1921 v Everton F.A.Cup Home
Total League & Cup Appearances: 18* Goals: 0
*** Also appeared in 3 wartime games**

Career Details:

Royal Navy		
WEDNESDAY	May	1919
Chesterfield	29 June	1921
Doncaster Rovers	29 October	1921
Denaby United	May	1922
York City	June	1923
Heanor Town	8 November	1927
City Surveyors	August	1928
Staveley Town	September	1929

Although short in stature Percy Reed was a real bundle of energy and was said to "run himself blind" for the team's cause. A versatile player – he appeared as a winger and half back in The Owls first team – Reed joined Wednesday direct from the Navy at the end of The Great War and was one of an amazing 42 players used during the disastrous 1919-20 season as Wednesday slid out of the top-flight. He was one of a handful of players retained at the end of that season but was only a fringe player in the lower grade and after just five appearances left for Chesterfield. After appearing in a handful of league games for the Derbyshire club Percy – who boxed in his spare time while at Hillsborough - dropped into non-league, later playing 35 games for Midland League side York City. His daughter later ran a newsagents on Leppings Lane while Wednesday donated monies to Reed in November 1953 when he fell on hard times.

REEVES, David Edward 1986-89

Born: 19 November 1967 Birkenhead (6ft, 11st 7lbs – 1989)
Debut: 24 September 1988 v Arsenal Division One Home
Last Appearance: 17 May 1989 v Norwich City Division One Home
Total League & Cup Appearances: 10+12 Goals: 3

Career Details:

Heswall		
WEDNESDAY	6 August	1986 Free
Scunthorpe United	17 December	1986 Loan
Scunthorpe United	1 October	1987 Loan
Burnley	20 November	1987 Loan
Bolton Wanderers	21 July	1989 £112,000*
Notts County	25 March	1993 £80,000
Carlisle United	1 October	1993 £121,000
Preston North End	10 October	1996 Player-exchange (Smart)
Chesterfield	6 November	1997 £100,000+(Lormor)
Oldham Athletic	21 December	2001 Loan
Oldham Athletic	8 January	2002 Free
Chesterfield	14 August	2002 Loan
Loan return	22 November	2002
Chesterfield	18 December	2002 Free
Released	30 June	2004
Ards	July	2004 Free
Released	18 September	2004
Mansfield Town	September	2004 Trial
Swindon Town	October	2004 Trial
Scarborough	28 January	2005

*£80,000 + 40% sell on clause

David Reeves had to thank an irate cat owner for his long career in league soccer! Whilst still a teenager he was working as a YTS painter and decorator in his native Birkenhead and was given the task of painting a lady's banister rail white. However the pet moggy had other ideas and kept rubbing up against the rail, prompting David to throw his brush at the offending pet. However the old lady who owned the cat, and the banister rail, complained bitterly and Reeves was sacked from his post – to rub salt into his wounds he was also made to pay for the cat to be cleaned! It left the youngster on the dole but hope was around the corner just a week later as Howard Wilkinson surprisingly invited him for a Hillsborough trial despite the fact that the ex-Wirral and Cheshire boys player was only performing in the obscurity of the West-Cheshire League. However he impressed sufficiently on trial and was considered by Wilkinson as 'one for the future' after signing a one-year professional contract.

As part of the deal Wednesday sent a side to play a pre season game against Heswall in 1987 while Reeves' league debut actually came while on loan at Scunthorpe United, one of several loan spells intended to acclimatise the inexperienced teenager to the rigours of league soccer. However his record as a loanee – 15 goals in 28 games for three sides – soon forced Reeves into Wilkinson's plans and persuaded the Owls boss to blood him in top-flight football. The tall, whole-hearted forward scored twice in first team football and acquitted himself well but decided a move to Second Division Bolton Wanderers would perhaps secure a regular first team place. He was certainly proved correct as in 174 games he grabbed 42 goals, helping the Lancashire club to promotion and becoming established as one of the most consistent scorers in the lower divisions. Over the next ten years Reeves – whose twin brother Alan played for several league clubs – proved an asset at every club who employed his services and had the pleasure of playing at Wembley with Carlisle when 78,000 saw his old side Bolton win the Associate Members Cup.

He also won a Division Three Championship medal while in Cumbria and netted 64 times before the first of three spells at Chesterfield. His second had been cut short when a three-month loan spell expired but Reeves was one of four players who accepted redundancy from cash strapped Oldham and re-joined Spireites on a permanent basis in Dec 2002, signing an 18-month contract. He had recorded his 500th League appearance – in February 2002 -while at the Boundary Park club and reached the 600 milestone in January 2004 during a season when The Spireites avoided relegation from Division Two thanks to a dramatic 88th minute goal on the final day of the season. Netted his final hat-trick in league football during the 2003-4 season but was released in the summer of 2004, later joining Northern Irish club Ards whilst also coaching on a part-time basis at youth level back at Hillsborough. However he played only four times, scoring twice, for the Newtownards club before a financial crisis meant his contract was cancelled.

REEVES, Frederick 'Fred' 1921

Born: Mexborough (5ft 8ins, 10st 10lbs – 1921)
Only Appearance: 30 April 1921 v Bury Division Two Away
Total League & Cup Appearances: 1 Goals: 0

Career Details:

Bentley Colliery		
Mexborough Town		
WEDNESDAY	11 April	1921 £100
Mexborough Town	June	1921

The first team career of right wingman Fred Reeves amounted to only thirty minutes as after twisting his knee on debut he took no further part in the game and would soon drop back into local amateur soccer. He had joined from Mexborough, just a month after he had signed from Bentley Colliery. The Owls paid a sizable fee – by 1920s standards – to obtain his services but sadly the injury meant his Owls career reached only two appearances, including a solitary Midland league fixture, before his early promise was cut short.

REGAN, William 'Bill' 1894-5 & 1896-98

Born:
Debut: 1 September 1896 v Liverpool Division One Home
Last Appearance: 11 September 1897 v Bury Division One Away
Total League & Cup Appearances: 9 Goals: 0

Career Details:

WEDNESDAY		1894
Fairfield Club		1895
WEDNESDAY	August	1896
Released	April	1898
Millwall Athletic		1900
Brentford		1901
Released	April	1902
Brentford	October	1902

The Wednesday career of Bill Regan was unique as despite failing to make a senior appearance in his first spell he was subsequently re-signed after a season in non-league football at Manchester club Fairfield. He had originally spent a season in the Owls reserve side during the 1894-95 season – playing primarily at half back – before returning to make seven Division One appearances as stand in for the likes of James Jamieson and Tommy Crawshaw. He then helped the second team to win the United Counties League Championship in 1898, adding two more senior games to his career tally, before being released. He later signed for Southern League Millwall Athletic, appearing in 22 games for the Londoners, before ending his playing career at fellow non-league side Brentford.

REILLY, John 'Paddy' 1920-21

Born:
(5ft 8½ins, 11st 4lbs – 1920)
Debut:
28 August 1920 v Barnsley Division Two Away
Last Appearance:
6 November 1920 v West Ham United Division Two Home
Total League & Cup Appearances: 2 Goals: 0

Career Details:

Ryhope Colliery		
Sheffield Tramways F.C.		
WEDNESDAY	August	1920
Castleford	Summer	1921
Sheffield Tramways F.C.	August	1924

Right-winger Paddy Reilly was a fast and plucky player who joined the professional ranks at the age of 23 from local amateur football. He was immediately given a League debut in the opening game of the 1920-1 season but despite appearing in a second senior game he was only a fringe player in reserve team football and was released after one season. He had served in the Navy during the Great War and was called up for another three months in April 1921 before signing professional forms for Midland League club Castleford. He spent three years as a professional at the West Yorkshire club before being given permission by the Football Association in August 1924 to revert back to amateur status.

REYNOLDS, John Barnard 'Jack' 1905-07

Born: 23 September 1881 Manchester
(5ft 9ins, 11st 3lbs – 1906)
Died: 8 November 1962 Amsterdam, Holland
Debut: 7 April 1906
v Sunderland
Division One Home
Last Appearance: 30 March 1907
v Stoke FC Division One Home
Total League
& Cup Appearances: 2 Goals: 0

Career Details:

Manchester City	May	1902
Burton United	May	1903
Grimsby Town	April	1904
WEDNESDAY	June	1905 £275
Watford	May	1907
New Brompton	May	1908
Rochdale		1911

The Owls had to break their transfer record to obtain the services of highly rated right-winger Jack Reynolds, signing the Lancastrian to provide competition for Harry Davis. However the move proved disappointing for both club and player as Reynolds was almost solely confined to reserve team football in two seasons at Hillsborough – joining a small band of Wednesday men to net a hat-trick of penalties in a game when achieving the feat in a Midland League game against Mexborough Town in December 1905. He netted 15 times for the second team in that season, helping the reserves to a goal tally of 111 that brought them the League title, and added another seven goals in 1906-7 before moving South to sign for non-league Watford.

After ending his playing career back in his home County, Reynolds started a highly successful coaching career when leaving these shores in 1912 to take up a position in Switzerland. Reynolds – whose brother Bill played league football for five different clubs – remained in the land of cuckoo clocks for six years before starting an association with Dutch giants Ajax Amsterdam that would see Jack remain on the coaching staff for an incredible thirty years. During that time Ajax won five Dutch league titles although Jack did spent 4 years of the Second World War imprisoned in an internment camp ran by the occupying German forces. However he returned to his role when the Allies eventually liberated Holland and when retiring in 1948 was granted a pension by Ajax as recognition of his role in making the club a major force in Dutch soccer. He lived the remainder of his life in Holland.

RHODES, E. 1880-82

Born:
Debut: 8 January 1881 v Turton F.A.Cup Away
Last Appearance: 7 February 1882 v Upton Park F.A.Cup Home
Total League & Cup Appearances: 6 Goals: 8

Career Details:

WEDNESDAY	1880

Nineteenth Century player who was mainly used by Wednesday in major Cup-ties – apart from his six F.A.Cup appearances he was conspicuous by his absence from The Owls first eleven. Back in the 1880s Wednesday were more of an all round sports club and Rhodes excelled in sprinting, finishing second and third in two 1881 races. However he was best known for his exploits on the football field and made a major impact during the 1881-2 season when Wednesday reached their first ever F.A.Cup semi-final, in only their second season in the competition. In January 1882 he became the first Wednesday player to score four goals in a competitive game, against Cup opponents Staveley, and also netted in the Quarter-Final win over Heeley which set up a semi-final clash with old foes Blackburn Rovers. However he was not selected for the last four clash and never appeared for the club again.

RHODES, Richard Alma 'Dick' 1935-38

Born: 18 February 1908 Wolverhampton
(5ft 9½ins, 12st 4lbs – 1935)
Died: 21 January 1993 Wolverhampton
Debut: 19 October 1935
v Birmingham
Division One Home
Last Appearance: 19 March 1938
v Barnsley
Division Two Home
Total League
& Cup Appearances: 59 Goals: 0

Career Details:

Redditch United		
Wolverhampton Wanderers	July	1926
WEDNESDAY	12 October	1935 £3200
Swansea Town	21 June	1938 *
Rochdale	July	1939

*Exchanged Rhodes + £50 for I.Lewis

Both England and Wolverhampton Boys capped Dick Rhodes at schoolboy level although it was as a centre forward that the Black Country youngster first came to prominence. However he was soon converted to right half-back by legendary Wolves manager Major Frank Buckley and emerged as one of the best half-backs of the early 1930s, helping Wolves to the Second Division Championship in 1932 and appearing in a total of 159 league and cup games. The Owls had to beat off competition from both Manchester City and Liverpool to secure his transfer in 1935 but Rhodes was initially no more than an understudy to regular No. 4 Wilf Sharp, starting only ten games in his debut campaign.

However he started the new season as first choice and remained a regular for two campaigns, spending his spare time breeding pigeons! Unfortunately his time at Wednesday coincided with the club's slump from F.A.Cup winners into the lower reaches of the Second Division and after being replaced by newcomer Fred Walker he left for Swansea Town in an exchange deal that brought Idris Lewis to Hillsborough. The outbreak of War effectively ended his playing days and Dick then moved back to Wolverhampton to become landlord of the 'Old Still Public House'. He was later 'Mein Host' of the 'Posada' and in his spare time became a champion canary breeder – he won the National title in 1973 – as well as a keen pigeon racer.

RICHARDS, Anthony D. 1895-99

Born:
(5ft 6½ins,)
Debut: 11 December 1895 v Stoke FC Division One Away
Last Appearance: 22 February 1896 v Bury Division One Home
Total League & Cup Appearances: 8 Goals: 1

Career Details:

Stourbridge		
WEDNESDAY	Summer	1895
Released	April	1899

After joining from Staffordshire non-league football right-winger Anthony Richards spent four years at Olive Grove, the final three being spent solely in reserve team soccer. His experience of first team football all occurred during his debut season at Wednesday - a reserve team hat trick in November 1895 against Wombwell Town no doubt helping his subsequent elevation into top-flight football. His rival for a first team jersey was Archie Brash and Richards managed to displace his rival for a run of seven consecutive games early in 1896, netting his only goal in senior football during a 3-0 home win over Blackburn Rovers. However it was then back into second team football where Richards scored regularly – winning a United Counties League Championship medal in 1898 - before departing Wednesday just prior to The Owls move to their new Owlerton ground.

RICHARDS, Frederick 'Fred' 1899

Born:
Debut:
4 March 1899 v Everton Division One Home
Last Appearance:
25 March 1899 v Aston Villa Division One Away
Total League & Cup Appearances: 3 Goals: 1

Career Details:

Burton Wanderers		
Derby County	December	1898
WEDNESDAY	1 March	1899
Burton Wanderers	August	1899
Woodville Excelsior		
Trent Rovers	January	1903

Question: Which Sheffield Wednesday player scored three goals on the same day against the same opponents but did not score a hat trick? Answer : Fred Richards

This anomaly occurred back in March 1899 when Wednesday played the second part of their infamous match with Aston Villa, which had been abandoned after 79½ minutes in the previous November. The League had, bizarrely, ordered the final 10½ minutes to be played at a later date so Villa travelled north to complete the fixture. Richards had not played in the original fixture but netted in part two to make the final score 4-1 to Wednesday before the teams played an agreed 35 minute each way benefit match for Harry Davis. The Owls inside forward then completed a unique hat trick by scoring both goals in the two-nil win over Villa. The aforementioned goal against Villa proved his only strike for the club in a league career that encompassed just two games at Derby County and a handful of appearances, in two spells, at then Football League side Burton Wanderers.

RICHARDSON, Edward 'Eddie' 1924-25

Born: 4 July 1901 Easington, Co. Durham
(5ft 8½ 11st 6lbs – 1925)
Debut: 29 November 1924 v Wolverhampton Wanderers
Division Two Home
Last Appearance: 14 February 1925 v Stoke FC
Division Two Home
Total League
& Cup Appearances: 11 Goals: 0

Career Details:

Easington Colliery		
South Shields	June	1919
Newcastle United	August	1922
Easington Colliery		
Huddersfield Town	December	1923
WEDNESDAY	28 November	1924*
South Shields		1925
York City		1925
Bradford City	September	1926
Easington Colliery	October	1928
Ashington	October	1928
Whitburn		1932

* In part-exchange for Sid Binks

Eddie Richardson played for several different league sides but it was only at Bradford City that he totalled more than fifty appearances. The fast and 'thrustful' right-winger often found himself cast in the role of understudy, a pattern that began at Newcastle United where he played second fiddle to Stan Seymour. After being kept out of the team by William Smith while at Huddersfield Town, Richardson arrived at Hillsborough as direct competition for Arthur Prince and made his senior debut within 24 hours of signing. Unfortunately despite retaining his place for the next five games a catalogue of niggling injuries then disrupted his fortunes and allowed Prince to reassert his status as first choice. This effectively marked the end of his Wednesday career as he moved onto South Shields soon afterwards before re-entering league soccer at Bradford City. His time at Ashington coincided with their short spell in the Football League before his playing career ended back in his native northeast.

RICHARDSON, R. 1891-92

Born: Ayrshire
Debut: 23 January 1892 v Bolton Wanderers F.A.Cup Home
Last Appearance: 13 February 1892
v West Bromwich Albion F.A.Cup Home
Total League & Cup Appearances: 3* Goals: 3
***Also appeared in 21 Football Alliance League games**

Career Details:

Hurlford		
WEDNESDAY	March	1891
Released	April	1892

Attacking player who was a regular during the club's final season as a non-league side in 1891-2. However despite netting seventeen times in that season, including a goal in all of his three F.A.Cup appearances, Richardson was surprisingly not retained for the club's new adventure in the Football League. He had originally arrived with a good reputation from Scottish junior football, making his debut for Wednesday in a 0-0 Alliance League game at Nottingham Forest in March 1891.

RICKETT, Walter 'Wally' 1949-52

Born: 20 March 1917 Sheffield
(5ft 4ins, 10st – 1950)
Died: 25 July 1991 Kettering
Debut: 22 October 1949
v Preston North End
Division Two Away
Last Appearance: 6 September 1952
v Charlton Athletic
Division One Home
Total League
& Cup Appearances: 97 Goals: 11

Career Details:

Manor Sports		
Kiveton Park Wire Works		
Aqueduct		
Sheffield United	May	1939
Blackpool		1948*
		Exchange for Farrow
WEDNESDAY	21 October	1949 £7,000
Rotherham United	October	1952 £2,450
Halifax Town	August	1953 Nominal
Ballymena United		1954

CAPS (@SWFC)
England 'B' (1) v Switzerland 18/01/50

Winger Wally Rickett was known as the 'Tom Thumb' of Sheffield football and at just five feet four inches was one of the smallest players to ever pull on the famous blue and white shirt. Considering his height it was perhaps no surprise that as a youngster Rickett wanted to be a jockey but after leaving school he started to work as a window cleaner before holding a variety of jobs including chimney sweep, car mechanic, steel worker and even working on a jet plane assembly line! While earning a living Rickett played for a variety of local Sheffield teams on a purely amateur basis – he had previously won a cap at Schoolboy level for England - but got his big chance when Sheffield United invited him for trial in a charity game against Rotherham. At the time Rickett was working in the steel industry and training with United after work but playing in the trial game at United meant he had to turn down the chance of a medal as his team, Aquaduct, were playing a local Cup Final on the same night. Fortunately his trial was successful and he was duly signed by United boss Teddy Davison on a £1 weekly wage.

He would enjoy eight happy years at Bramall Lane that started with a sensational debut when Wally scored with his first touch, in the first minute of a March 1940 encounter with Wednesday! He was a real bundle of energy on the right wing for The Blades and his sheer enthusiasm made him a crowd favourite and a regular for United in post war soccer. However after 16 goals in 57 games for United he moved to Blackpool in a straight swap for George Farrow and in his first season at Bloomfield Road not only won an England 'B' cap but also played alongside Stanley Matthews and Stan Mortensen in the 1948 F.A.Cup Final loss to Manchester United. Despite impressing at Blackpool he never really settled and it was no surprise when he returned to Sheffield football a year later, signing for Wednesday as Eric Taylor seeked to finally get The Owls out of the old Second Division. The newcomer became an instant hit and helped Wednesday to promotion in 1950 before winning a Division Two Championship medal two years later as The Owls bounced back after relegation. He was obviously a real character off the pitch as well as during his time at Wednesday Wally owned a green sports car which he always drove with the top down, whatever the weather!

After leaving Hillsborough he spent just one season at Millmoor – scoring in one of The Millers greatest ever games when F.A.Cup holders Newcastle United were sensationally beaten 3-1 on their own ground – before ending his league career with Halifax Town. A spell as player-manager then followed at Irish club Ballymena United before he was briefly manager at fellow Emerald Isle club Dundalk. He then returned to England where in a two-year stint as Sittingbourne boss won both the Kent League and Kent Senior Cup before winning two more trophies as Ramsgate manager between March 1959 and April 1963. He left to manage his third Kent club, Gravesend, where he even made an appearance on the wing when his side were struggling near the foot of the table. A move into the Football League finally occurred in 1966, as assistant manager to Dick Graham at Leyton Orient, but he resigned after just six weeks to bring his career in football to an abrupt end. He then returned to Kent, working for a cable manufacturing firm, before later moving to Corby where he lived as a bachelor until his death in Kettering hospital in 1991.

RIMMER, Ellis James 1928-38

Born: 2 January 1907 Birkenhead
(5ft 10ins, 11st 7lbs – 1928)
Died: 16 March 1965 Formby
Debut: 25 February 1928
v Newcastle United
Division One Home
Last Appearance: 12 March 1938
v Stockport County
Division Two Away
Total League
& Cup Appearances: 417 Goals: 140

Career Details:

Parkside F.C.		
Northern Nomads		
Everton		Amat.
Whitchurch	September	1923
Tranmere Rovers		1924
WEDNESDAY	16 February	1928 £1850
Ipswich Town	16 August	1938 £450

CAPS (@SWFC)
England Full (4) v Scotland 05/04/30, v Germany 10/05/30, v Austria 14/05/30, v Spain 09/12/31

The Owls can boast some tremendous wing players in their history but Ellis Rimmer could lay claim to being the best purely based on his phenomenal goal scoring record. In just over a decade in the club's first team the highly talented left winger not only created countless chances for his team mates but also scored a remarkable 140 goals, placing Rimmer fifth in the all time Wednesday list of scorers. Along with team mate Mark Hooper he was part of the most devastating wing duo in the Owls history, which powered the club to consecutive league championships, plus the F.A.Cup in 1935 – Rimmer joining the select band of players to have scored in every round when netting a brace in the final win over West Brom.

His successes with Wednesday were a far cry from his early days when as a boy Rimmer played in the same Birkenhead school team as legendary centre-forward Dixie Dean before signing amateur forms for Everton. He never progressed further than the third team at Goodison Park and it was not until he started to shine for Whitchurch in the Cheshire League that his local club Tranmere Rovers decided to take a risk on the seventeen year old. They were quickly rewarded as Ellis became a fixture in the Rovers first team and scored 21 goals in only 61 games before Bob Brown captured his signature for Wednesday. He joined a side that looked doomed to relegation from the top-flight but he was instrumental in the subsequent 'Great Escape' that completely changed the club's fortunes. Back to back titles followed and as Wednesday consistently finished in the higher echelons of the English League Ellis was rewarded with caps for his country, netting twice on his debut in a 5-2 win against Scotland. His 22 league goals in 1930-1, from outside left, is a club record for a winger that will never be broken although he went close when scoring one less in the following campaign!

The free scoring attacker was also a very superstitious individual who always carried his lucky mascot, a horseshoe decorated with a black cat, with him on match days. However just before the 1935 F.A.Cup Final he realised he had left his mascot back at Hillsborough and doubts entered his mind that he would be able to maintain his record of having scored in every round. Thankfully

Owls trainer Sam Powell found the horseshoe back in the Hillsborough dressing rooms and the mascot arrived at Wembley just after half time - although Rimmer did not know of its arrival he promptly netted twice in the last four minutes to bring the cup back to Sheffield! Rimmer was also an accomplished pianist in his spare time and during the summer following the Cup win he successfully toured the country's music halls.

After being a fixture for Wednesday throughout their 'golden years' he was placed on the transfer list in April 1938 and a few weeks later signed for Football League new boys Ipswich Town, appearing in four games for the Suffolk club before hanging up his boots at the onset of the Second World War. In 1943 he became a publican on Sheffield's Arbourthorne Estate and later moved back to Merseyside, running a public house in Formby.

RIPLEY, Stuart Edward — 2001

Born: 20 November 1967 Middlesbrough
(5ft 11ins, 13st – 2001)
Debut: 1 April 2001 v Sheffield United Division One Home
Last Appearance:
6 May 2001 v Crewe Alexandra Division One Home
Total League & Cup Appearances: 5+1 Goals: 1

Career Details:

Middlesbrough	23 December	1985
Bolton Wanderers	18 February	1986 Loan
Blackburn Rovers	20 July	1992 £1.3m
Southampton	10 July	1998 £1.5m
Barnsley	7 November	2000 Loan
WEDNESDAY	22 March	2001 Loan
Sheffield United	February	2002 Trial
Released	30 June	2002

Highly experienced former England winger who joined the Owls on loan near the end of the 2000-1 season. The blonde haired attacker had originally made his name at Middlesbrough where he totalled 311 appearances, winning England Youth and U-21 caps as well as helping the Teeside club into the top-flight in 1992. Ripley was an old fashioned style winger who was capable of beating his man and getting telling crosses in and it was these qualities that eventually led to a move to Blackburn Rovers; excelling as the Jack Walker funded club won the 1995 Premier League Championship. While at Ewood Park he won two full caps for England and played Champions League football before joining Southampton after 228 games for Rovers.

Unfortunately the move to the South Coast was not the success Ripley would have hoped for as a combination of injury and poor form meant he only started 36 league games – his bad luck no more typified than in October 2001 when he was recalled to the side for Gordon Strachan's first game in charge as manager but received an injury that kept him on the sideline for three months. His absence effectively brought the curtain down on his professional career as in June 2002 he announced his retirement from the game.

RITCHIE, John Henry — 1966-69

Born: 12 July 1941 Kettering
(6ft 1½ins, 13st 7lbs – 1966)
Debut: 12 November 1966
v Manchester United
Division One Away
Last Appearance: 12 May 1969
v Tottenham Hotspur
Division One Home
Total League
& Cup Appearances: 105+1 Goals: 45

Career Details:

Monn and Felton Boot & Shoe Works		
Ennannett United		
Kettering Town		
Stoke City	June	1962
WEDNESDAY	11 November	1966 £80,000
Stoke City	7 July	1969 £27,500
Stafford Rangers	January	1976

CAPS (@SWFC)
Football League (1) v League of Ireland 08/11/67

When Wednesday paid a club record fee for the tall, stylish and prolific scorer John Ritchie it must have come as a relief to Owls fans as at least it would stop him scoring against their club! He had previously netted an incredible ten times in only seven games against Wednesday while in Stoke colours, including a three and four goal haul! The centre forward had started his football career in non-league soccer while working in a Kettering shoe factory but 40 goals in a season for Southern League Kettering Town alerted Stoke to his talents and his services were quickly tied to a professional contract. After gaining experience in reserve team football he was given a first team bow in October 1963 and from that point onwards he never looked back, setting a club record in the same season when scoring in nine consecutive games as well as helping City to the Football League Cup Final.

His move to Hillsborough in 1966 was a real shock to Stoke supporters but for Wednesday fans it was a real coup as they finally had an orthodox striker to compliment their subtle but somewhat shot shy attackers. As part of the move The Owls allowed Ritchie to remain in his Ashton-under-Lyne home but the travelling did not affect his form as although the new man arrived in late November he still finished his first season as joint top scorer with fifteen goals. He was top scorer in his own right in 1967-8 but when Owls boss Alan Brown left he became unsettled and the goals dried up, eventually leading to his sale back to Stoke at a greatly reduced fee.

After returning to the Potteries he quickly got back into the goalscoring groove and took his overall City tally to a club record 176 goals in 343 first team games. He helped the club to their only major honour – the 1972 League Cup – and two F.A.Cup semi-finals although his taste of Europe will bring back memories for Owls fans as he was sent off for violent conduct after just nine seconds of a UEFA Cup game against Kaiserslautern! A double fracture of his leg, suffered against Ipswich Town in September 1974, eventually forced his retirement from the professional game although he did play a handful of games in non-league soccer before finally retiring to concentrate on his pottery business. His relationship with Stoke was sadly soured for several years when they transferred his son, David, to Stockport County while Ritchie was forced to retire from his business in 2003 due to ill health.

ROBERTS, Sean — 2001-02

Born: 2 January 1983 Durban, South Africa
(6ft 2ins, 12st, 8lbs – 2002)
Only Appearance: 19 January 2002 v Burnley Division One Away
Total League & Cup Appearances: 0+1 Goals: 0

Career Details:

Manchester City		1997 Trial
Tottenham Hotspur		Trial
Crystal Palace		2001 Trial
WEDNESDAY	15 October	2001 Free
Released	30 June	2002
St Albans City		
Harrow Borough	6 September	2002 Free
Vietnam team		
Home United	December	2003

Teenage goalkeeper Sean Roberts underwent trials at several English clubs before securing a professional contract at Wednesday in 2001. He had originally travelled from his South African homeland for trials with Manchester City when aged just 14 but returned home to finish his schooling, subsequently winning caps at U-20 and U-23 level for South Africa – he also appeared in the Olympic Games for the Springboks. He joined Wednesday as third keeper behind Kevin Pressman and Chris Stringer and mainly played Academy football and the occasional reserve team game before an injury to the latter saw Roberts elevated to the subs bench for a game at Burnley early in 2002. With just four minutes left to play Pressman was stretchered off and the raw teenager was thrust into the action – he was so nervous that Danny Maddix had to help remove his tracksuit top – to play out the final moments as Wednesday secured a 2-1 win.

However those few minutes proved to be the sum of his senior career at Wednesday as Paul Heald was immediately secured on loan and Roberts warmed the subs bench for the next six games before dropping out of the first team picture when Pressman regained his fitness. He was released at the end of the season and due to a serious spinal injury returned to South Africa to attend University but he later re-launched his career in the unlikely surroundings of Vietnam and now plies his trade with Singapore side Home United.

ROBINSON, John 'Jackie' 1934-46

Born: 10 August 1917 Shiremoor, Northumberland
(5ft 8ins, 10st 1lbs – 1935)
Died: 31 July 1972 Shiremoor
Debut: 22 April 1935
v West Bromwich Albion
Division One Away
Last Appearance: 21 September 1946
v Chesterfield Division Two Home
Total League
& Cup Appearances: 119* Goals: 39
***Also appeared in**
110 wartime games, scoring 90 goals

Career Details:
New Biggin Juniors
West Wylam Colliery
Shiremoor

WEDNESDAY	October	1934 £20,10s
Newcastle United	January	1940 Guest
Darlington	April	1940 Guest
Hartlepool United		1939-40 Guest
Middlesbrough	August	1941 Guest
Sunderland	11 October	1946 £6,800*
Lincoln City	14 October	1949 £3,000

*Original fee £7,500

CAPS (@SWFC) England Full (4)
v Finland 20/05/37, v Germany 15/05/38, v Switzerland 21/05/38, v Wales 22/10/38
Football League (1) v Irish League 1939

If the best years of Jackie Robinson's career had not been lost to war he probably would have been classed as Wednesday's greatest ever player. Unfortunately for the outstanding inside forward he was at his devastating best during the 1939-46 conflict when his astonishing scoring – he netted 35 goals in only 32 games during the 1942-3 season – marked him down as arguably the best player to appear regularly in wartime soccer. His career had started in his native northeast and was spotted almost by accident by Owls boss Billy Walker after he attended a game to watch another player but was mesmerised by the skills of Robinson. He soon moved to Hillsborough with Wednesday twice donating nominal amounts – in September 1935 and March 1937 - to West Wylam Colliery. He possessed all the skills of a truly great player – superb ball control, pace, a deceptive body swerve and a remarkable ability for goal scoring – and for Owls fans who were lucky enough to witness him at his peak he is still regarded as the best Owls player of the last sixty years. He made his first team debut for Wednesday during the 1935 F.A.Cup Final week when the two Wembley finalists had to fulfil a league fixture just five days before the showpiece occasion. The youngster borrowed Ron Starling's boots and scored the only goal of the game to immediately stake a claim for a first team place.

After gaining more experience in Central League football he became a first team regular during the 1936-7 season, being a shining light as The Owls suffered relegation from the top-flight. His form was such that Jackie was handed his first full cap for England in the close season – scoring on debut in an 8-0 win in Helsinki - and in January 1937 The Owls had turned down a huge bid for his services from Arsenal. He was also in the England team that were controversially forced to give the Nazi salute in Berlin in 1938 although Robinson netted twice in a 6-3 triumph for democracy. When war was declared in September 1939 Jackie returned to his native northeast, joining the home guard, and played as a guest for several local sides – he scored 9 goals in just 8 games during the opening weeks of the 1941-2 season for Middlesbrough. However it was for Wednesday that Robinson made his greatest impact in wartime soccer, grabbing an amazing six hat tricks in the 1942-3 season including three in an 8-2 romp over Sheffield United in February 1943. The Owls reached the Final of the Football League North War Cup in that season, losing narrowly to Blackpool over two legs, and when National football returned it was hoped Robinson could maintain his wartime form.

However after just seven post war games he was surprisingly sold to First Division Sunderland although the fee was later reduced when is was discovered he was two years older that had originally been thought – it transpired that Robinson had knocked two years off his age when joining Wednesday to enable his career to last longer! During three years at Sunderland he showed he had lost none of his talents and scored a praiseworthy 34 goals in 85 appearances before being allowed to leave for Division Three (North) club Lincoln City when age finally started to catch up with him. Five goals in eight games followed for The Imps but scoring the last of those goals effectively ended his playing career as on Christmas Eve 1949 he fell awkwardly after jumping over the Wrexham keeper, breaking his leg as a consequence. Sadly he never recovered full fitness after the fracture and at the end of the season retired from football, moving back to the northeast to work in the building trade. He later became a publican but was forced to retire due to ill health and after a two-year battle against illness passed way at the relatively young age of 55.

ROBERTSON, George 1910-19

Born: Stonefield, Lanarkshire
(5ft 9$^{3}/_{4}$ins, 12st – 1913)
Debut: 25 March 1910
v Bradford City
Division One Away
Last Appearance: 13 December 1919
v Sunderland
Division One Home
Total League
& Cup Appearances: 173* Goals: 31
***Also appeared in 4 wartime games**

Career Details:
Yoker Athletic
Motherwell

WEDNESDAY	March	1910 £1250*
Released	December	1919
East Fife	30 October	1920

*Joint fee with Murray

CAPS (@SWFC)
Scotland Full (3) v Wales 02/03/12, v Ireland 15/03/13, v England 05/04/13

Lightening quick outside left who was a mainstay of the Owls side in the years immediately preceding the Great War, forming a superb partnership with all-time record scorer Andrew Wilson. After starting his career in Scottish Junior soccer he won four full caps for Scotland during a spell at Motherwell and arrived in Sheffield with Wednesday hoping to plug the gap at No. 11 that had not been filled since the departure of George Simpson two years earlier. The newcomer was thrust immediately into the first team, scoring on his home debut, and his strength in the tackle and ability to run 'like a deer' meant he remained first choice for the remainder of the pre war years. Incidentally he was actually a schoolteacher back home in Scotland and it was said he did not transfer to Wednesday because the club impressed him but because Sheffield could boast a University!

The Scot was also effectively responsible for Wednesday obtaining their nickname of 'The Owls' as in the summer of 1912 he presented the club with an Owl mascot. Wednesday stated at the time that they hoped this would not lead to their nickname of 'The Blades' being dropped but after the Owl was placed under the North Stand in October and Wednesday won four games in a row without conceding a goal the new 'nom de plume' was born! After helping Wednesday to three top six finishes his career was then interrupted by the war with Robertson working in a munitions factory until the hostilities ended. A long- standing knee injury meant he played only a handful of games in wartime soccer and The Owls paid for an operation on the offending joint in 1919 in the hope of final curing the problem. However it seemingly was not a success as amazingly in November 1919 he was given 14 days notice to terminate his engagement due to his "palpable inefficiency"! He then returned North of the Border and after signing for Junior side East Fife he played in their first ever Scottish League game, against Bathgate Thistle in August 1921. After ending his playing career George emigrated to Canada where he returned to his original capacity as teacher.

ROBINS, Mark Gordon 2003-04

Born: 22 December 1969 Ashton-under-Lyme
(5ft 8ins, 11st 11lbs – 2003)
Debut:
9 December 2003 v Carlisle United LDV Vans Trophy Away
Last Appearance:
8 May 2004 v Queens Park Rangers Division Two Home
Total League & Cup Appearances: 17+1 Goals: 7

Career Details:

Manchester United	23 December	1986
Norwich City	14 August	1992 £800,000
Leicester City	16 January	1995 £1m
Copenhagen	18 October	1996 Loan
Reading	29 August	1997 Loan
Deportivo Orense	15 January	1998 Free
Panionios	August	1998
Manchester City	25 March	1999 Free
Walsall	5 August	1999 Free
Rotherham United	25 June	2000 Free
WEDNESDAY	8 December	2003 Free
Released	30 June	2004
Burton Albion	5 July	2004

During a career of almost twenty years attacker Mark Robins earned a reputation as the archetypical 'goal poacher'. He had started with Boundary Park Juniors and after representing Oldham boys was part of the first ever intake to the Football Association's National School at Lilleshall. England Youth caps followed for the promising youngster and after signing trainee forms for Manchester United he was elevated to professional status just a few months later. He would remain at Old Trafford for almost six years and earned an F.A.Cup winners medal in 1990, scoring in the semi-final against Oldham Athletic, as well as winning six England U-21 caps – netting five times for his country against France. However he was primarily used as a substitute by United and although he appeared in 70 first team games for the Old Trafford club 43 came from the subs bench as he was kept out of the side by the likes of Mark Hughes and Brian McClair.

A move to Norwich City saw Robins become an automatic first choice and he top scored in his first season as The Canaries confounded the critics by finishing in third place in the inaugural season of the Premier League. Injury then restricted his appearances although he was in the City line that stunned Europe by winning at Bayern Munich in an October 1993 UEFA Cup tie. Incidentally he netted on his debut for Norwich City, a feat he repeated at Leicester, Rotherham and Wednesday! A big money move to Filbert Street did not quite work out for Robins and after 17 goals in 73 games he spent time in both Spanish and Greek football before trying to resurrect a flagging career back in England at Manchester City. He could only manage two sub appearances at City but he was back in the shop window and after a season at Walsall he found his niche at Rotherham United where he helped the Millers to promotion from Division Two in 2001, finishing top scorer with 24 league goals, and then aided their consolidation in the higher grade.

During the 2003-4 season Robins became a peripheral figure at Millmoor and when Wednesday were looking to boost their firepower Chris Turner turned to the vastly experienced forward. He rewarded The Owls faith by netting twice on his debut and showed all of his goal poaching instincts to average almost a goal every two games before being sidelined for several weeks in February 2004 after suffering a serious knee injury. He returned to the side for the run in but was struggling for fitness and after being released at the end of the season took the decision to retire from the full-time game, later signing a one-year deal at Nigel Clough's ambitious Conference side Burton Albion. Further injuries gave Robins no option but to retire from playing while in January 2005 he was surprisingly appointed as assistant manager at Rotherham United – until the end of the season – following the shock departure of Millmoor legend Ronnie Moore.

ROBINSON, Carl Philips 2003

Born: 13 October 1976 Llandrudod Wells
(5ft 10ins, 12st 10lbs – 2003)
Debut:
17 January 2003 v Sheffield United Division One Away
Last Appearance:
15 February 2003 v Derby County Division One Away
Total League & Cup Appearances: 4 Goals: 1

Career Details:

Shrewsbury Town		1992 Trial
Wolverhampton Wanderers	3 July	1995
Shrewsbury Town	28 March	1996 Loan
Portsmouth	24 July	2002 Free
WEDNESDAY	16 January	2003 Loan
Walsall	18 February	2003 3-month loan
Rotherham United	18 September	2003 3-month loan
Sheffield United	30 January	2004 Loan
Sunderland	25 March	2004 Free

Welsh International midfielder who spent a month on loan at Wednesday during their relegation season of 2002-3. He made his debut in the hostile atmosphere of a Sheffield derby game but despite failing to impress Owls fans he looked set to have his loan spell extended before surprisingly moving instead to join Division One rivals Walsall. Robinson had started his professional career at Wolves and whilst on loan at Shrewsbury Town tasted Wembley when playing in the Shropshire club's Auto Windscreen Shield Final defeat to Rotherham United. During over six years as a professional at Wolves he failed to really become an established first team player, despite winning several full caps for Wales, and the workmanlike, right sided midfielder eventually left for fellow Division One side Portsmouth. Unfortunately he also struggled to win a regular place at the South Coast club, appearing in 17 games, and spent several spells on loan before his move to Sunderland was made permanent in June 2004.

ROBSON, Thomas 1930-33

Born: 1909 Morpeth (5ft 8ins, 11st – 1930)
Debut:
28 March 1931 v Leicester City Division One Home
Last Appearance:
19 December 1931 v Manchester City Division One Home
Total League & Cup Appearances: 3 Goals: 0

Career Details:

Morpeth		
Blyth Spartans	January	1926
Everton	April	1929
WEDNESDAY	29 October	1930 £3,000
Yeovil & Petters United	July	1933
Northampton Town	August	1934
Kettering Town		1937

Half Back Thomas Robson was described as a stylish player with a high skill level and spent four years in league football after being signed from non-league football by Everton. He went on to appear in 29 top-flight games for the Merseyside club and arrived at Wednesday under the reign of Bob Brown to provide competition for Alf Strange as the club attempted to complete a hat trick of League Championships. However his rival was imperious in the Owls back line and Robson had to be content as understudy until leaving for powerful Southern League side Yeovil & Petters United in 1933. He appeared in 56 games in what proved to be his only season with the Somerset club as Robson was soon back into league football, moving to Division Three (South) club Northampton Town. After 46 games for The Cobblers he ended his playing days back in Southern League football at Kettering Town. Incidentally he was once described as having two hobbies – 'good behaviour' and playing the ukelele!!

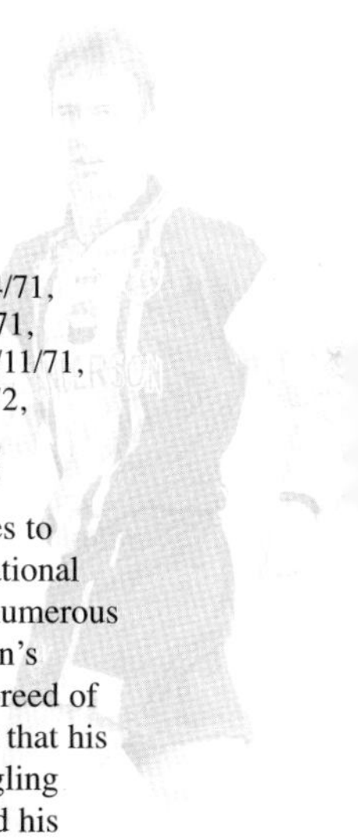

ROCASTLE, Craig 2005-

Born: 17 August 1981 Lewisham
(6ft 1in, 12st 13lbs - 2004)
Debut: 12 February 2005
v Bradford City
League One Home
Total League
& Cup Appearances: 12+2 Goals: 1

Career Details:

Gravesend & Northfleet		
Ashford Town	November	2001 Loan
Kingstonian	December	2001
Ford United	October	2002 Loan
Slough Town	February	2003
Chelsea	1 September	2003 Free
Barnsley	13 February	2004 Loan
Lincoln City	25 March	2004 Loan
Hibernian	31 August	2004 4-month loan
WEDNESDAY	3 February	2005 Free

There is no doubt that initially Craig Rocastle struggled to impress the Owls fans after completing a free transfer move from Premiership giants Chelsea. Reports of a somewhat disastrous loan spell at neighbours Barnsley had no doubt trickled through to the Wednesday supporters and his sluggish start to life in League One did little to dispel those fears. However he did slowly start to show why Paul Sturrock brought him into Hillsborough on a contract until 2007 and really came into his own during the Owls play off campaign. A combative display in the win at Brentford secured the central midfielder a place in the Cardiff starting eleven and an all action display against Hartlepool United saw the cousin of former Arsenal and England star David Rocastle show the fans why he had been plucked by Chelsea from non-league football back in September 2003.

His initial move to the London club was a dream transfer for the 22 year-old as until then he had plied his trade in local non-league football, reaching Conference football standard. The former Blackheath District boys player obviously faced huge competition for places at Stamford Bridge but just before joining Barnsley on loan he was an unused sub for the Blues home game with Charlton in February 2004. His league debut came for the Tykes but sadly he failed to sparkle at Oakwell and was probably happy to return to his parent club after fans started to barrack him before he entered the field of play! He would later play twice for Lincoln City but again he struggled to adapt to life in the lower reaches of the Football League. However a loan move to Scottish football then revitalised his career as a series of impressive performances in a 14-game spell for Edinburgh club Hibs alerted many English sides to his probable availability. The Owls were one of many teams linked to the Londoner and two weeks after that initial link was identified he duly moved to Sheffield 6. Despite playing with an injury he managed 14 games for Wednesday and after saving his best display of the season for the final game there is hope he will be able to make the step up to Championship football.

RODRIGUES, Peter Joseph 1970-75

Born: 21 January 1944 Cardiff
(5ft 9ins, 11st 6lbs – 1973)
Debut: 17 October 1970
v Charlton Athletic
Division Two Away
Last Appearance: 1 April 1975
v Nottingham Forest
Division Two Away
Total League
& Cup Appearances: 174 Goals: 2

Career Details:

Cardiff City	May	1960
Leicester City	24 December	1965 £42,000
WEDNESDAY	14 October	1970 £45,000
Southampton	July	1975 Free
Romsey Town		1977

CAPS (@SWFC)
Wales Full (17) v Romania 11/11/70, v Czechoslovakia 21/04/71, v Scotland 15/05/71, v England 18/05/71, v N.Ireland 22/05/71, v Finland 13/10/71, Czechoslovakia 27/10/71, v Romania 24/11/71, v England 20/05/72, v N.Ireland 28/05/72, v England 15/11/72, v England 24/01/73, v Poland 28/03/73, v Scotland 12/05/73, v England 15/05/73, v N.Ireland 19/05/73, v Poland 26/09/73

When Owls boss Danny Williams brought Peter Rodrigues to Hillsborough he was already an established Welsh International who at his first two clubs had amassed 23 full caps plus numerous other International honours. He was rated as one of Britain's fastest full backs at the time – he was also one of a new breed of overlapping full backs - and Williams understandably felt that his top-flight experience would prove invaluable to his struggling Second Division side. The attacking right back had started his career at hometown club Cardiff City where he had initially looked set to be released before an injury crisis thrust him into the first team picture. However this lucky break truly launched his career and City collected a hefty fee when Leicester broke their club transfer record to take Rodrigues to Filbert Street. He had totalled 85 league games for Cardiff and added a further 139 games to his tally while in Leicester colours, being described as "the master of the sliding tackle". He appeared in their 1969 F.A.Cup Final defeat to Manchester City but after helping City to the Second Division Championship in 1971 he was surprisingly allowed to leave for Wednesday – ironically playing his final game against old side Cardiff City.

Unfortunately for Rodrigues his spell at Hillsborough coincided with a slump in the club's fortunes but to his credit his own form remained consistent and he was a regular at Wednesday for five seasons until being one of several players given free transfers at the end of the disastrous 1974-5 season. Being released by a club who has just experienced the worst season in their history would not usually attract many suitors but Division Two Southampton moved quickly to sign up the experienced defender and astonishingly within two years Rodrigues was lifting the F.A.Cup as captain of the Saints side that sensationally beat Manchester United in the 1976 Cup Final.

Within a year he had retired from the professional game due to a bad knee injury and ran a public house near Southampton called the 'King Rufus' while also being player-coach at Hampshire League club Romsey Town. He remained behind the bar until 1985 when he left to spend a year in the US, coaching at San Diego University. On moving back to these shores he returned to Wales to become a licensee again – coaching a minor side Telephone Sports for a while - although in December 1990 he again packed his bags, opening a restaurant back in Hampshire. He later coached both Braishfield and Blackfield & Langley before being appointed Club Steward at a Hampshire based Conservative Club. He remained in this role until retiring to Spain in 2002.

ROGERS, Alfred 'Alf' 1942-51

Born: 10 April 1921 Sheffield
(5ft 8ins, 11st 7lbs – 1946)
Died: 28 October 1992 Sheffield
Debut: 31 August 1946
v Luton Town
Division Two Away
Last Appearance: 11 February 1950
v Coventry City
Division Two Away
Total League
& Cup Appearances: 30* Goals: 8
***Also appeared in**
98 wartime games, scoring 31 goals

Career Details:

Birley Carr		
Arsenal		1939 Trial
WEDNESDAY	May	1942 £10

Outside right Alf Rogers signed amateur forms for Wednesday just three months before the start of the Second World War, after being spotted playing against The Owls reserve team in a benefit game. As a youngster Alf was a staunch Owls fans, seeing his first game at the age of five, and was no doubt encouraged to play football by his father who ran a junior team in the Sheffield district of Walkley. After his displays for junior side Birley Carr he was invited for a trial at Arsenal in 1939 and was asked to return the next year but the war put paid to any ambitions he may have held with the London giants. Instead Rogers began playing wartime soccer for Wednesday whilst working in the dusty and dirty surroundings of Samuel Osborn's munitions factory as a fettler – the conditions caused serious breathing problems for Alf and eventually saw him hospitalised with serious illness. Thankfully he recovered to become a regular in the Wednesday side throughout the conflict, hitting the heights in August 1945 when he was one of two men – the other being Jackie Robinson - to hit hat tricks in the 6-3 Football League North win against Sunderland.

When regional football ended in 1946 Rogers struggled to become established at first team level and had to be content playing Central League football where in August 1947 he grabbed six goals in a 12-1 rout of Chesterfield. After representing the Sheffield F.A. against Eindhoven in 1949 Alf finally broke into the Wednesday first eleven and appeared in 18 games as The Owls earned promotion by finishing Division Two runners up. Sadly just when Rogers looked to have made the breakthrough he started to experience hip problems – relating to an injury suffered during the aforementioned representative game – and this was eventually diagnosed as arthritis in September 1950. Unfortunately this diagnosis brought his career to a premature end and Alf subsequently gained employment at Sheffield engineering firm Hamptons. He later worked for Arthur Lees before being appointed Sport Assistant at Sheffield University's Goodwin Centre, a job he held until retiring at the age of sixty-two.

ROLLINSON, Frank — 1905-11

Born: Q/E June 1884 Ecclesall
(5ft 7ins, 11st – 1905)
Died: 15 September 1927 Sheffield
Debut: 25 December 1906
v Derby County Division One Home
Last Appearance: 27 December 1910
v Newcastle United Division One Home
Total League & Cup Appearances: 44 Goals: 16

Career Details:

Heeley Friends		
WEDNESDAY	June	1905 £10
Leicester Fosse	June	1911 £100
Portsmouth	February	1912
Luton Town	8 October	1913

In modern parlance Frank Rollinson would be described as a squad player as in only one season as a Wednesday player did his first team appearance tally exceed ten league games. That came during the 1909-10 campaign when Rollinson kept his rival for the No.10 ten shirt, Frank Bradshaw, on the sidelines thanks to ten goals in only twenty league matches. He had started his playing career in minor Sheffield football but quickly made a big impression in Wednesday's Midland League side, scoring a dozen goals in his first season as the second team lifted the League Championship. Throughout his time at Wednesday Rollinson impressed greatly in reserve team soccer – he gained the reputation as the best ever player to have played in the Midland League – but found his first team opportunities limited due to the form of Jimmy Stewart and then Bradshaw.

After failing to become a first team regular he eventually moved to Leicester City where he was involved in an infamous game against Grimsby Town in January 1912 when despite horrendous weather conditions of rain, gale force wind and sleet the referee refused to abandon the game and six City players left the pitch, leaving the official with no alternative but to bring proceedings to a premature end. The ex-Owl was one of the six who walked off and all were later found guilty by the F.A. and fined £5 each. After leaving the Filbert Street club Rollinson played under Bob Brown at Portsmouth where he was outstanding at inside-left as Pompey won promotion to the Southern League top-flight. His career ended with Southern League Luton Town but sadly he died, aged 43, of Pneumonia after only a week's illness.

ROSTRON, John Wilfred 'Wilf' — 1989

Born: 29 September 1956 Sunderland
(5ft 6ins, 11st 1lb – 1989)
Debut: 14 January 1989
v Liverpool
Division One Home
Last Appearance: 8 April 1989
v Liverpool
Division One Away
Total League & Cup Appearances: 9 Goals: 0

Career Details:

Arsenal	October	1973
Sunderland	12 July	1977 £40,000
Watford	19 October	1979 £150,000
WEDNESDAY	12 January	1989 Free
Sheffield United	19 September	1989 Loan
Loan return	20 November	1989
Sheffield United	28 November	1989 Free
Brentford	January	1991 Free
Gateshead	September	1993
Ryhope Colliery Welfare		1994

When Peter Eustace signed veteran defender Wilf Rostron it caused puzzlement amongst Wednesday fans who questioned the long-term benefit of a 32 year-old defender who was in the twilight of his career. Unfortunately those fears proved correct as in his brief time at Wednesday Rostron played the role of understudy to undisputed left back Nigel Worthington, filling in for 'Barney' only when the Irish International was injured. Once new manager Ron Atkinson assessed his squad Rostron played only twice more and eventually moved to neighbours United on an initial two-month loan.

He returned to Hillsborough after contract talks with The Blades broke down but within eight days was back at Bramall Lane, joining a small band of players to transfer direct between the city's two professional clubs. After an initial spell as just a player he was later assistant manager at Brentford before returning to his native northeast to play for Conference side Gateshead. He was appointed player-coach at Gateshead in October 1993 and was caretaker manager for a while before playing a handful of games for Sunderland based club Ryhope Colliery, as a favour to a friend who was manager at the time. After retiring from the game he started to work in retail and is now a company buyer.

However it was his career before joining Wednesday for which Rostron is best remembered. As a teenage winger he was capped by Sunderland and Durham boys and also won eight England boys caps before signing apprentice forms for Arsenal in July 1973. After failing to win a regular first team place at Highbury he moved to Sunderland where 76 league games followed prior to his switch to Hertfordshire. He arrived at Vicarage Road as Watford were moving quickly through the divisions and after being converted into a full back he appeared in a mammoth 404 games as they became a force in the top-flight and made their one and only venture into European competition. Incidentally in the 1980s Rostron missed only one of forty consecutive F.A.Cup ties for Watford but unfortunately that game happened to be the 1984 Final! He was only suspended once in his whole professional career and sadly did not even get a medal as The Hornets lost to Everton at Wembley.

*Rostron was never assistant manager at Gateshead

ROWAN, Alexander 'Sandy' — 1892-93

Born: 1869 Scotland
(5ft $8^{1}/_{2}$ins, 11st, 7lbs – 1893)
Debut: 10 September 1892 v Accrington Stanley
Division One Home
Last Appearance: 4 September 1893 v Wolverhampton Wanderers
Division One Away
Total League & Cup Appearances: 34 Goals: 14

Career Details:

Albion Rovers	
Nottingham Forest	1890

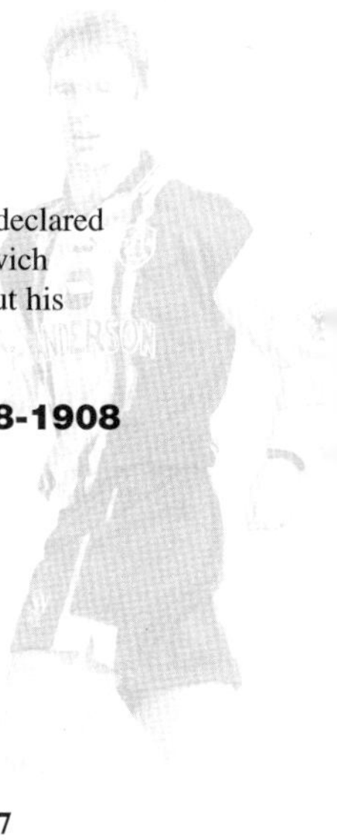

Albion Rovers		1891
WEDNESDAY	August	1892
Burton Swifts	November	1893
Ardwick	8 August	1894
Released		1896

Scottish centre forward Sandy Rowan led the Owls attack during their first ever season of league football in 1892-3. He was one of several players signed by the club after gaining election into the league and joined after winning two Charity Cup medals with Albion Rovers where he had played the majority of his football, except for a brief spell in England with Nottingham Forest. Although not selected for the club's first ever league fixture, at Notts County in September 1892, he was in the side for the first home game and scored in a 5-2 romp over Accrington Stanley. He was then ever present for the remainder of the campaign, scoring regularly, although he was absent for the final game of the season, therefore missing only two games all season – the first and last!

He had previously set a scoring record at Albion when netting six against Clydebank in October 1891 and with 14 goals for Wednesday he looked set to be a regular after The Owls consolidated in the top-flight. However he would play only one more game for the club and after being dropped to the reserves eventually signed for then league club Burton Swifts. He later spent time at Ardwick (later re-named Manchester City) and after retiring from the game stayed in the Manchester area to become a publican.

ROY, John Robin 'Jack' 1937-38

Born: 22 March 1914 Woolston, Southampton
(5ft 10ins, 11st – 1937)
Died: 24 November 1980 Bournemouth
Debut: 6 February 1937
v Preston North End
Division One Away
Last Appearance: 15 January 1938
v Swansea Town
Division Two Away
Total League
& Cup Appearances: 16 Goals: 1

Career Details:

Sholing		
Norwich City	25 August	1933
Mansfield Town	16 April	1936 Free
WEDNESDAY	5 February	1937 £1,750
Notts County	16 March	1938* exchange for Fallon
Tranmere Rovers	16 December	1938
Yeovil & Petters United	May	1939
Aberman Athletic		WW2 Guest
Southampton	24 December	1939 Guest
Ipswich Town	7 February	1946
Gravesend & Northfleet	June	1947
Yeovil Town		1948

When the careers of Wednesday wing legends Mark Hooper and Ellis Rimmer were simultaneously coming to an end the Owls started to search for players to compete with and eventually replace the almost irreplaceable duo. One such player bought for that task was Jack Roy for who Wednesday had to break Mansfield Town's transfer record to secure his services. The Hampshire born player was equally adept on either wing and initially it was Rimmer who he replaced for a six-game run during the 1936-7 relegation season. However the old maestro was not ready to give up his first team place yet and Roy was pushed back into reserve team soccer until getting another chance in the following season, this time in Hooper's favourite position on the right wing. Unfortunately for Roy he could not secure a regular place and it was not Hooper but Charlie Luke and then Len Massarella who kept him on the sidelines.

He eventually moved to Notts County on deadline day 1938 and appeared in sixteen games for the league's oldest club before transferring to Tranmere Rovers. He spent only a brief spell at the Birkenhead club and was then only a professional at powerful Southern League club Yeovil for a matter of weeks as the outbreak of war caused their ground to be closed and all contracts declared null and void! After ending his professional career at Ipswich Town he worked as an Engineering Inspector and lived out his retirement in Poole, Dorset.

RUDDLESDIN, Herrod 'Harry/Ruddy' 1898-1908

Born: 1875/6 Birdwell, Barnsley
(5ft 7ins, 11st 2lbs – 1901)
Died: 26 March 1910 Birdwell
Debut: 10 September 1898
v Nottingham Forest
Division One Home
Last Appearance: 19 October 1907
v Aston Villa
Division One Home
Total League
& Cup Appearances: 285 Goals: 7

Career Details:

Birdwell		
WEDNESDAY	April	1898
Northampton	May	1908

CAPS (@SWFC)
England Full (3) v Wales 29/02/04, v Ireland 14/03/04, v Scotland 01/04/05

When Herrod Ruddlesdin arrived at Olive Grove from village side Birdwell he was considered a promising left-winger but it was quickly discovered that his best position was in fact left halfback. He quickly jumped, with consummate ease, from minor football to playing top-flight soccer and over the next eight seasons combined with Bob Ferrier and Tommy Crawshaw to create the club's best defensive trio of the years prior to The Great War. Ruddlesdin was a very intelligent, steady and dependable player and it was these qualities that endeared him to Wednesday followers - "good old Ruddy" was a familiar cry during those early years at Hillsborough. Incidentally when he signed for Wednesday he said he would only have left Birdwell for a First Division team!

His first full season at Wednesday was hard for Ruddlesdin as not only did The Owls suffer relegation from Division One but were forced to leave their beloved Olive Grove. Thankfully he came through the disappointment and missed only a handful of games as Wednesday won the Second Division Championship in 1900 and then secured back-to-back League Championships in 1903 and 1904. His imperious form also won 'Ruddy' three full caps for England and its almost certain more honours would have come his way if not for the terrible illness of consumption which started to affect his career during the 1906-7 campaign. The ex-miner bravely fought the disease, playing a solitary game in the next season, but his top-flight career was over and he moved to non-league Northampton Town after their manager Herbert Chapman offered him the opportunity to re launch his career. Sadly when the new season started he was not well enough to take his place in The Cobblers first team and would fail to make an appearance before announcing his retirement in February 1909. His long battle against illness finally ended in 1910 when he passed away, aged only 34.

RUDI, Petter Norman 1997-2000

Born: 17 September 1973 Kristiansund, Norway
(6ft 3ins, 12st 10lbs – 1998)
Debut: 19 October 1997
v Tottenham Hotspur
Premier League Away
Last Appearance: 19 August 2000
v Huddersfield Town
Division One Home
Total League
& Cup Appearances: 81+8 Goals: 9

Career Details:

Traeff		
Molde FK		
Piacenza		1996 Loan
WEDNESDAY	1 October	1997 £800,000
Molde FK	28 August	2000 Season loan
Molde FK	1 July	2001 Free

Sporting Lokeren	September	2001 Free
Germinal Beerschot Antwerpen	18 November	2002 Free
FK Austria	1 July	2003 Free
Molde FK	1 January	2004 Free

CAPS (@SWFC)
Norway Full (10) v France 25/02/98, v Mexico 20/05/98, v Romania 19/08/98, v Latvia 06/09/98, v Egypt 18/11/98, v Italy 10/02/99, v Greece 27/03/99, v Georgia 28/04/99, v Albania 05/06/99, v Greece 04/09/99

Tall, rangy midfielder Petter Rudi was David Pleat's final signing as Owls boss and quickly endeared himself to the Hillsborough faithful with a series of dynamic displays on the left side of the Wednesday midfield. He had initially come to the fore in Norwegian football and had already spent a loan spell in Italian football before The Owls paid a relatively low fee for a player who had already won fifteen full caps for Norway. A spate of niggling injuries and tiredness – he had played a complete summer season in Norway before signing for Wednesday – meant he faded near the end of that debut season at Wednesday which also cost him a place in the Norway squad for the 1998 World Cup Finals in France. He struggled to recapture his early form under both Ron Atkinson and then Danny Wilson although on his day Rudi could dominate a game – an outstanding display and two goals in a 4-1 win at Blackburn Rovers in February 1999 perhaps being the highlight of his time in Sheffield.

During The Owls final season in the Premier League Rudi was in and out of the side, mainly due to injury, and it was no real surprise when he was allowed to return to Molde on a season long loan in August 2000. When his Owls contact expired he signed for the Norwegian club on a free but within two months was on the move again, signing for Belgium club Lokeren. He netted twice during the 2001-2 season but despite suffering injury problems he was still offered a new contract, which Rudi promptly turned down! He therefore returned to his old club Molde where he trained throughout the autumn months of 2002 after they failed to agree a contract before the transfer deadline closed. In November 2002 he did sign a new deal, with Belgian club GBA, although he could not join until the transfer window opened in January 2003. However he again failed to settle and after six months in Austrian soccer he returned home to start a third spell with Molde.

RUSHBURY, David Garreth 'Dave' 1976-79

Born: 20 February 1956 Wolverhampton
(5ft 10ins, 11st 4lbs – 1977)
Debut: 6 November 1976
v Bury
Division Three Away
Last Appearance: 11 May 1979
v Swindon Town
Division Three Home
Total League & Cup Appearances: 132+1 Goals: 9

Career Details:

St Chad's College		
West Bromwich Albion	July	1974
WEDNESDAY	4 November	1976 £22,500
Swansea Town	24 May	1979 £60,000 (T)
Carlisle United	8 August	1981 £40,000
Gillingham	21 March	1985 £15,000
Doncaster Rovers	8 July	1985 £10,000
Cambridge United	21 February	1987 Loan
Bristol Rovers	25 February	1987 Free
Goole Town	June	1987

After joining West Bromwich Albion as a trainee in December 1972 Dave Rushbury broke into the first team aged just 18, appearing in 26 consecutive league games during the 1974-5 season, after replacing Ally Robertson at halfback. However during West Bromwich Albion's promotion season of 1975-6 he was used only twice and moved to Hillsborough on loan to gain valuable league experience, plugging the gap in the Owls side at left back. He quickly became an integral part of the Owls first team and missed only a handful of games after Wednesday secured his permanent transfer in early January 1977. He was absent for only two matches during his first full season at the club and later switched to central defence when Dave Grant was introduced at full back – he was ever present during the epic F.A.Cup battles with Arsenal and scored in the thrilling 3-3 draw in game four.

Under both Len Ashurst and then Jack Charlton he was one of the first names on the team sheet and it was therefore a big disappointment to the latter when Rushbury elected to join Swansea City when his contract expired in the summer of 1979 – Charlton's mood was not helped when two months later at the newly introduced transfer tribunal (then called the Appeals Commission) set the fee at £30,000 less than Wednesday expected, causing 'Big Jack' to slam the new scheme. He joined a Swansea side on an upward curve under John Toshack and played 52 times for the Welsh club, helping them clinch promotion to the top-flight in 1981. However his chance of playing in Division One football ended when he was sold to Carlisle United although he immediately won promotion to Division Two and was named in the PFA Third Division team. He totalled 129 league games for the Cumbrians before returning to South Yorkshire after a brief spell at Gillingham. A somewhat bizarre five day loan spell at Cambridge – he played one game – was ended by a full transfer to Bristol Rovers where he wound up his league career.

He then spent a season at Northern Premier League Goole Town where he was captain and coach, helping Town to win their first trophy for thirty years when winning the League Cup. After hanging up his boots Rushbury was appointed physiotherapist /coach at Chesterfield in January 1989 although he soon concentrated solely on the physio side of his role. During the early 1990s he also worked as a co-commentator for Radio Sheffield – being behind the microphone during all of Wednesday's trips to Wembley – while on New Year's Day 2002 he was surprisingly appointed caretaker manager at Saltergate following Nicky Law's sacking 24 hours earlier. He was installed on a permanent basis in February and remained in the role until a series of poor results led to his resignation in April 2003. His son, Andy, played first team football for Chesterfield while Rushbury senior is now Director of Football at ambitious Conference North club Alfreton Town, being appointed in May 2003.

RUSSELL, David Wallace 1938-46

Born: 7 April 1914 Methil, Fife
(5ft 8ins, 11st 7lbs – 1938)
Died: 12 June 2000 Birkenhead
Debut: 27 August 1938
v Bury
Division Two Home
Last Appearance: 29 April 1939
v Tottenham Hotspur
Division Two Home
Total League & Cup Appearances: 50* Goals: 0
***Also appeared in 62 wartime games, scoring 1 goal**

Career Details:

Dundee Violet		
Dundee		1932
East Fife		1934 Free
WEDNESDAY	26 May	1938 £2000
Blackpool	September	1941 Guest
Bolton Wanderers		1941-43 Guest
Burnley		1943-44 Guest
Aberdeen	October	1944 Guest
Walsall		1944-45 Guest
Released		1946

Former Dundee boys captain who came to prominence when helping East Fife win the Scottish Cup in 1938 – their only success in Scotland's premier Cup competition. He had previously played at hometown team Dundee but after being released became an integral part of the Fifers defence before Wednesday boss Jimmy McMullen went on a scouting mission north of the border which resulted in Russell leaving Scotland for the first time in his life! The sturdy built right halfback possessed fine positional sense and was an automatic choice during the 1938-9 season, playing in every game as the club agonisingly missed out on promotion to the top-flight. He appeared in the opening game of the next season but days later war was declared and all football temporarily ceased, those early league games being expunged from the records.

The Scotsman initially joined the Home Guard and played on a regular basis for Wednesday in the first season of wartime football before joining the forces – playing for a British XI against a Football League XI at Hillsborough in 1941 and also representing the British Army Rhine team against Denmark. He later played for a British XI against Holland and in Poland while also appearing on a regular basis for Wednesday, playing in both legs of the 1943 Football League North Cup Final defeat against Blackpool. If not for the intervention of the war its almost certain Russell would have achieved International honours but like many of his contemporaries his career had to take a back seat for the greater good of his nation. When the hostilities finally ceased Russell informed Wednesday, in February 1946, that after being de-mobbed from the RAF he would become trainer to Danish club Odense, a position he held for only a few months before being appointed coach of the Danish National side. He remained in charge for three years and in 1948 led his charges to a bronze medal in the 1948 Olympic games held in London.

He returned to the UK in 1950 and after just over three years as coach at Bury he was elevated to manager in December 1953, staying at the helm until surprisingly moving to become Tranmere Rovers boss in December 1961- the Birkenhead club were two divisions below Bury at the time. He had twice won promotion while in charge at Bury and repeated the feat in 1967 when leading Rovers out of Division Three. The move to Prenton Park started an association with Tranmere what would last until the day he died as after moving to become general manager in December 1969 Russell remained on the staff until retiring in 1979 – in his final capacity he developed the club's sports centre, improved the Prenton Park facilities and was the man behind Rovers move to an all white kit from all blue after stating that if Liverpool play in all red and Everton in all blue then Rovers should be all white. He was awarded a testimonial game in 1978 - a Tranmere/Everton XI playing a Manchester City/United side – and was a regular at Rovers games for the remainder of his life.

RYALLS, Brian 1952-58

Born: 7 July 1932
Grimethorpe, Barnsley
(6ft, 10st 11lbs– 1953)
Debut: 12 September 1953
v Sheffield United
Division One Away
Last Appearance: 12 March 1958
v Birmingham City
Division One Away
Total League
& Cup Appearances: 47 Goals: 0

Career Details:

Brierley Juniors U-18s		1948-9
Wath Wanderers		1950-1
Wolverhampton Wanderers		1950-1 Amat.
Grimethorpe Athletic		1952
WEDNESDAY	8 November	1952 P-Time
WEDNESDAY	27 January	1953 £150
Frickley Colliery	July	1958 Free
Retford Town	7 August	1962
Scarborough	18 August	1963
Grimethorpe Ex Servicemen		1965-66

Despite playing his early years as a full back it was as a goalkeeper that Brian Ryalls was considered the find of the season in 1953-4 after replacing broken arm victim Dave McIntosh. He possessed exceptional anticipation and made the goalkeeping art look easy even though he had only played between the sticks for a year – he switched to the position after joining his Colliery team. He had previously failed to make the grade at Wolves – after a spell with their nursery side Wath Wanderers – and was released after an illness to seemingly end his hopes of a professional career in the game. However he was soon invited for extended trials at Hillsborough and eventually signed part-time forms in November 1952, making his Central League bow in April 1953 after leaving his Colliery post.

His performances after taking over from McIntosh were such that Wednesday discontinued negotiations with Glasgow Rangers for Scottish International Bobby Brown but injury then put Ryalls on the sidelines after 28 consecutive games. His career at Wednesday then stagnated somewhat and after just three games in 1954-55 he failed to make a senior appearance for two full seasons – during this period he served his National Service in the Army at Ripon where he played more basketball than football! The form of McIntosh and arrival of Les Williams also kept Ryalls in the shadows although he was given another run in the side during the relegation season of 1957-8, playing in the emotional F.A.Cup tie at Manchester United that immediately followed the Munich Air Disaster. However at the end of that season he was one of eight players released by Wednesday and immediately secured work at the Frickley Colliery Pit Head as well as signing for the Colliery side. He later worked at Upton Colliery and spent a short time working for an Insurance company before returning to the National Coal Board. He held several jobs for the remainder of his working life, including meter reader, and was Office Manager at South Elmsall before retiring. He is now enjoying his retirement and has been a season ticket holder at Barnsley for several seasons.

RYALLS, Joseph 'Joe' 1901-05

Born: Q/E March 1881 Sheffield
Debut: 14 March 1903
v Blackburn Rovers
Division One Home
Last Appearance: 9 April 1904
v Sheffield United
Division One Home
Total League
& Cup Appearances: 2 Goals: 0

Career Details:

Montrose Works			
WEDNESDAY		1901	
Barnsley		1905	£30
Fulham		1906	
Rotherham Town	June	1906	
Brentford	August	1908	
Nottingham Forest	June	1909	
Brentford		1910	
Chesterfield Town	September	1911	

Although winger Joe Ryalls played in both of Wednesday's League Championship winning campaigns in the early Twentieth Century he failed to win a medal as he only appeared in a solitary game in both seasons. It was in the club's reserve team that Ryalls spent the majority of his Wednesday career after having joined from Sheffield based Montrose Works where he was employed as an Electrical Engineer. Although he missed out on the major honours Ryalls had the consolation of winning back-to-back Sheffield Challenge Cups in 1902 & 1903 with the reserves while also gaining a Midland League winners medal in the glorious 1902-03 season when the club lifted four trophies.

His final game in the first team was a resounding 3-0 win over City rivals United but he could not displace Harry Davis from the right wing and eventually moved to neighbours Barnsley. He was a regular for The Tykes during the first half of the 1905-6 season, playing seventeen times, but after losing his place to Birtles he moved to Yorkshire neighbours Rotherham Town. A somewhat nomadic career then saw Joe appear for several different sides – including 74 games during two spells at Brentford - before ending his playing days at Chesterfield.

RYAN, John Bernard 1984-85

Born: 18 February 1962 Failsworth
(5ft 10ins, 11st 7lbs – 1984)
Debut: 29 September 1984
v Liverpool Division One Away
Last Appearance: 6 May 1985
v Chelsea Division One Away
Total League
& Cup Appearances: 6+3 Goals: 1

Career Details:

Mancunian Boys		Sun.
Seattle		1979-80 Loan
Oldham Athletic	February	1980
Newcastle United	5 August	1983 £225,000
WEDNESDAY	27 September	1984 £40,000 + Pat Heard
Oldham Athletic	24 August	1985 £25,000
Mansfield Town	28 October	1987 £25,000
Chesterfield	June	1989 £125,000 + Steve Prindiville
Rochdale	July	1991
Bury	December	1993
Stalybridge Celtic	July	1994
Radcliffe Boro	August	1996

When left back John Ryan joined Wednesday his career already seemed to be on the slide after dramatically falling out of favour at Newcastle United. Arguably the best form of his career – which had started in Manchester Sunday football – had come at his first club Oldham where his outstanding displays took him into the England U-21 set up. One such U-21 cap came at St.James Park and four months later he was moving to the northeast to join the Geordies after Arthur Cox paid a substantial fee for his services. He appeared in 31 games for Newcastle but after losing his place to Kenny Wharton arrived at Hillsborough hoping that Howard Wilkinson could resurrect his career like he did for so many players during his tenure as Wednesday boss.

However his time at Hillsborough perhaps reflected his overall career as he hit the heights on his debut as The Owls won at European Champions Liverpool and then scored on his home debut in a 5-0 rout of Leicester City. Then he slowly faded from the first team scene and appeared in only seven more games before returning to his first club Oldham Athletic. His career had started at Boundary Park as an apprentice – playing on loan in the NASL while still a trainee – but he could not regain his former glories and missed almost the whole of the 1986-7 season after breaking a leg in two places during an August 1986 pre season friendly. The remainder of his career was spent in the lower leagues – reaching the 1990 play off final with Chesterfield – before dropping into non-league football with Conference side Stalybridge in 1994. A cruciate ligament injury ended his playing days after six months at Manchester club Radcliffe Boro while he then worked as a labourer in the building trade before becoming a partner in a Manchester based building renovation company. He was later a director at Radcliffe (1998-2000) and after selling his share in the business in 2003 the former Manchester boys player travelled the world for a year. He is now back in the UK, awaiting an operation on his troublesome cruciate ligament.

SANETTI, Francesco 1998-99

Born: 11 January 1979 Rome
(6ft 1ins, 12st 6lbs – 1998)
Debut: 2 May 1998
v Aston Villa
Premier League Home
Last Appearance: 31 October 1998
v Leeds United
Premier League Home
Total League
& Cup Appearances: 1+6 Goals: 1

Career Details:

Genoa		Amat.
WEDNESDAY	26 March	1998 Free
Released	30 June	1999
R.S.Livorno		1999
Giorgione		1999
Lodigiani		2000
Teramo		2003
Acireale		2004

Teenage forward Francesco Sanetti won Italian U-21 caps whilst an amateur at Serie B club Genoa but after deciding not to sign professional forms it was actually the Genoa chairman who recommended the youngster to Wednesday. He had just won the player of the tournament accolade in a Youth competition in Viareggio and he was considered a loss to Italian football when Ron Atkinson swooped to capture his signature for The Owls. Although Sanetti was signed on transfer deadline day Wednesday had to wait several weeks for his International clearance as his old side dragged their heels and it was not until the intervention of UEFA that the matter was finally resolved. Virtually 24 hours after he was cleared to play the youngster was given a place on the subs bench for the final home game of the season and duly made a dream start to his professional career, netting a spectacular late goal. Incidentally his first appearance in an Owls shirt actually came in a mid-week testimonial at Glasgow Rangers where Sanetti played under the name of Wednesday youth team player Krystof Kotylo!!

It is arguable whether his outstanding goal on debut proved an advantage or hindrance to Sanetti as he struggled to make an impression on his full debut a few days later and proved a peripheral figure during the 1998-9 season, making only a handful of substitute appearances. He also looked somewhat out of his depth in reserve team football and it was no surprise when he was allowed to return home in the summer of 1999. He started his two-year military service when returning to Italy and later played on a part-time basis for Serie C1 club Livorno, making just a solitary appearance. He made eight appearances for his next club, Giorgione, before joining Rome's third club Lodigiani where he netted 20 times in 81 games in what is effectively the fourth tier of Italian soccer. After 2 goals in twelve games for Teramo he then plied his trade in the same league as ex-Owl Michele Di Piedi.

SAYER, James 'Jim' 1884-85

Born: Q/E September 1862 Mexborough
Died: 1 February 1922 Stoke
Debut:
8 November 1884 v Long Eaton Rangers F.A.Cup Away
Last Appearance:
3 January 1885 v Nottingham Forest F.A.Cup Home
Total League & Cup Appearances: 2 Goals: 1

Career Details:

Mexborough		1882
Heeley		1884
WEDNESDAY		1884
Stoke FC		1885
Mexborough	May	1890

It was with Stoke that flying winger Jim Sayer made his biggest impact during the fledgling days of competitive football. After joining the Staffordshire club in 1885 his pace quickly earned him the nickname of 'greyhound' and in February 1887 he won his solitary cap for England, setting up three goals as Ireland were beaten 7-0 at Bramall Lane. He also earned a multitude of other representative honours while on Stoke's books, including caps for the Staffordshire FA and Birmingham FA, and was one of the eleven players who represented the club in their first ever Football League game – against West Brom in September 1888. After surviving a train crash at Stafford Station in October 1889 – the train carrying the Stoke side crashed into the back of a stationery train – his career turned full circle when Sayer re-signed for his old side Mexborough.

His career had originally started at his hometown side where Sayer impressed greatly and was twice capped by the Sheffield Association. He captained the side, playing alongside his brother, and also played a handful of games for Heeley before helping Wednesday during their F.A.Cup campaign of 1884-5. The amateur status of all those pre league players meant they could play for whomever they wanted on a Saturday afternoon and this explains how 48 hours before playing for Wednesday against Nottingham Forest in the English Cup he actually faced The Owls for Mexborough in a Wharncliffe Charity Cup game! After ending his playing days at Mexborough he returned to Staffordshire to become secretary of a pottery firm in Stoke where he later became a company director.

SCOTHORN, Gary 1967-69

Born: 6 June 1950 Hoyland, Nr Barnsley
(5ft 11ins, 11st 6lbs – 1974)
Debut: 18 February 1967
v Mansfield Town
F.A.Cup Home
Last Appearance: 2 March 1968
v Newcastle United
Division One Home
Total League
& Cup Appearances: 2 Goals: 0

Career Details:

WEDNESDAY	6 June	1967
Barnsley	26 February	1969 Loan
Johannesburg Rangers	July	1969 Free
Drumcondra		1972
Sligo Rovers	June	1973 Free
Mansfield Town	August	1974 Free

Goalkeeper Gary Scothorn enjoyed a meteoric rise to senior football from the moment, just a few days after the 1966 F.A.Cup Final, that as a 15-year old rookie he appeared for Wednesday against Doncaster Rovers in Alan Finney's benefit game. Injury to senior keepers Ron Springett and Peter Wicks gave the former Yorkshire and Barnsley boys player his big chance and for the same reason he experienced the thrill of being the club's goalie when Wednesday played six games on their Far East tour – appearing in such exotic destinations as Hong Kong and Singapore. Considering he had only just turned sixteen it was a truly wonderful time for Scothorn and this was capped early in the following year when another injury crisis meant a first team debut was thrust upon him in front of a mammoth 49,049 crowd - his appearance aged 16 years and 257 days made him the youngest player at that point to play first team football for The Owls.

He kept a clean sheet as Mansfield Town were beaten and made a big impression by staying cool under pressure, showing safe handling and intelligently using his penalty area. Later in the year he toured France with the England Youth side as reserve to Peter Shilton but did not get a game – his only appearance coming for an England select side for which he did not receive a cap. Despite making his league bow in 1968 Gary found himself third choice behind Peter Springett and Peter Grummitt and simply could break into the senior squad, eventually leaving for South African football after just two years as a professional at Hillsborough. After three years in the Southern Hemisphere he signed for Southern Irish club Drumcondra but moved on when the club was sold to amateur side Home Farm.

While on the books of Sligo Rovers he appeared for the League of Ireland select side in a friendly against Pele's touring Santos side before spending a season back in the UK as understudy to Ron Arnold at Mansfield Town. He failed to make a senior appearance for The Stags and at the end of the season retired from football, buying an off licence in Sheffield. After three years he moved to London where he primarily worked as a croupier – the pull of home was still strong though as in April 1979 he travelled from his Wembley home to play in goal for crack Sunday side Hoyland Town Jags! After thirteen years in the Capital he moved back home and now runs his own Barnsley based property development business.

SCOTT, Philip Campbell 1999-2002

Born: 14 November 1974 Perth, Scotland
(5ft 9ins, 11st 2lbs – 1999)
Debut: 3 April 1999
v Coventry City
Premier League Home
Last Appearance: 5 February 2000
v Derby County
Premier League Away
Total League
& Cup Appearances: 3+8 Goals: 1

Career Details:

Scone Thistle		
St.Johnstone	30 July	1991 Free
WEDNESDAY	25 March	1999 £75,000
Released	30 June	2002

The Wednesday career of attacking midfielder Phil Scott was totally ruined by injury which incredibly saw the former Scotland U-21 International fail to make a senior appearance in the final 29 months of his lucrative Bosman inspired contract. Before joining Wednesday, Scott had spent almost no time on the treatment table and was being tracked by several clubs – both Dundee United and Glasgow Celtic had tried to sign him while Sheffield United's bid of £750,000 had been turned down by St.Johnstone a year before he joined Wednesday. It was Danny Wilson who tied Scott to a pre-contract agreement in March 1999 but the transfer was then brought forward with Wednesday paying his club a small fee to release Scott early so he could join on deadline day. He had scored 35 times in 155 games for The Saints – winning a Division One Championship medal in 1997 - and made a good early impression at Hillsborough before a niggling injury brought his season to a premature end.

Unfortunately he was absent for the majority of the 1999-00 relegation season and what proved to be his final appearance came in the disastrous game at Pride Park when Wednesday lost a two-goal lead in injury time. Sadly he failed to play any competitive football for the club in the following campaign and this was repeated in 2001-2 before his inevitable release in the summer of 2002 when his expensive contract finally expired. Despite leaving the club's payroll Scott was allowed to train with Wednesday – in an attempt to regain his fitness – but was subsequently banned from the training ground in December 2002 after being arrested and bailed following the club's Christmas party in Leeds. He was later released without charge and returned home where, somewhat ironically considering his injury nightmare at Wednesday, he now works as a fitness trainer!

SEDLOSKI, Goce 1998-99

Born: 10 April 1974 Golemo Konjari, Macedonia
(6ft 1ins, 13st 3lbs – 1998)
Debut: 14 March 1998
v Bolton Wanderers
Premier League Away
Last Appearance: 11 April 1998
v Barnsley
Premier League Away
Total League
& Cup Appearances: 3+1 Goals: 0

Career Details:

Pobeda Prilip		
Hadjuk Split		
WEDNESDAY	13 March	1998 £750,000
NK Dinamo Zagreb	22 February	1999 Free

CAPS (@ SWFC)
Macedonia Full (5) v Bulgaria 25/03/98, v Malta 06/09/98, v Croatia 14/10/98, v Malta 18/11/98, v Albania 10/02/99

The Wednesday career of Macedonian International Goce Sedloski was a brief and expensive one for the club as this three starting appearance cost The Owls a staggering £250,000 each! The burly two-footed centre half had been tracked for several months by Wednesday boss Ron Atkinson and his transfer from Croatian club Hadjuk Split was initially agreed in December 1997, for a £1.75m fee, before Sedloski failed his medical to scupper the deal. However the Owls boss returned two months later and a deal was agreed which would eventually match the original price if Sedloski appeared in one hundred games for Wednesday. His career had started back home in the ex-Yugoslavian republic of Macedonia where after breaking into the National side he earned a move to crack Croatian side Hadjuk Split. He helped his side to runners-up spot in 1997, appeared in 43 games and took his cap tally to 14 before trying his luck in the Premier League with Wednesday – he turned down offers from several clubs, including Newcastle, Napoli and Valencia, to sign for The Owls.

He was nicknamed 'The Bear' by Atkinson but experienced a highly frustrating time at Hillsborough as a serious cartilage injury curtailed his debut season before a broken nose suffered in the 1998 pre season meant he missed the start of the league campaign. With Danny Wilson now in charge the dominant defender could not force his way into the side and with the possibility of obtaining a new work permit becoming increasingly unlikely Wednesday decided to cut their losses and let Sedloski leave on a free transfer. He therefore became the first player in Owls history to record more International appearances while at Wednesday than first team games!

Since moving back to Croatian football he has become a huge favourite at Dinamo where he has now appeared in 186 games, scoring 21 times. He won the League Championship with Dinamo in 2000 and 2003 plus runners-up spot in 2004 whilst earning Cup winners medal in 2001, 2002 and 2004 – in the latter final it was his goal against Varteks in the two-legged final that won the trophy for the Croatian giants on away goals after a 1-1 scoreline.

SEED, James Marshall 'Jimmy' 1927-31

Born: 25 March 1895 Blackhill
(5ft 10ins, 11st 9lbs – 1930)
Died: 16 July 1966 Farnborough
Debut: 27 August 1927
v Everton
Division One Home
Last Appearance: 4 April 1931
v Blackpool
Division One Away
Total League
& Cup Appearances: 146 Goals: 38

Career Details:

Whitburn		
Sunderland	April	1914
Mid Rhondda	July	1919 Free
Tottenham Hotspur	January	1920 £250
WEDNESDAY	2 August	1927*

*Part-exchange for Arthur Lowdell

Every successful team needs a player who inspires and Jimmy Seed no doubt fulfilled that role during the greatest era in the club's history. His signing proved yet another master stroke from Wednesday manager Bob Brown as after taking over the club captaincy in Easter 1928 he led Wednesday to the incredible 'great escape' which proved the platform for the back-to-back League Championships that followed in the next two years. The experienced inside-forward was already in his early 30s when he joined Wednesday but such was his terrific form that he captained a touring F.A. side to South Africa in the summer of 1929 and was picked to represent Sheffield against Glasgow in September 1930. Incidentally that inter-city match went down in football folklore as during the game Seed kept accidentally passing to the referee who after taking his jacket off at half time was wearing a white shirt – the same colours as the Sheffield team. Therefore Jimmy asked the referee to leave the field and put his jacket back on with the contemporary press reporting that Seed had sent the official off!

His tremendous success at Hillsborough proved a fitting end to a playing career that had started in his native northeast at non-league side Whitburn where he played on an amateur basis while working down his local pit. Over 80 goals for Whitburn led to a successful trial at Sunderland but he was only a professional for a few months before being whisked away to the Western Front on the onset of the Great War. He joined the Army and spent four years in mainland Europe but looked to have survived the conflict relatively unscathed until he was unfortunately gassed in France during the final month of the War. Jimmy was sent home to hospital to recover and while still on the mend played for Sunderland, performing so poorly that the Wearsiders decided he was not fit enough and promptly released him. While at Sunderland he was classed as Charles Buchan's understudy – a mantle that was taken up by future Owls and England player Billy Marsden on Seed's departure. However it would not be the first time Seed was effectively placed on the soccer scrap heap and he soon re-launched his fledgling career in Welsh non-league football, quickly coming to the attention of Tottenham who captured his signature part way through the 1919-20 campaign. He would play five times near the end of the season, scoring twice, as Spurs won the Second Division Championship and a year later was in the side that beat Wolves to win the F.A.Cup. His superb passing skills and accurate shooting marked him as one of Spurs most influential players of the early 1920s and after quickly establishing a fine reputation he was capped five times by England – he was also a reserve for his country on numerous occasions.

In the summer of 1927 he was offered the player-coach job at Guilford United and after Spurs cut his weekly wage from £8 to £7 Seed looked set to quit football altogether to join Aldershot as manager. It was only Tottenham's stubborn refusal to release him that prolonged Seed's career and after several attempts by Wednesday to sign him he eventually came north as a 'lightweight' in the transfer of Lowdell to White Hart Lane. In hindsight the sale of Seed was perhaps the London club's worst ever transfer decision as when he inspired Wednesday to surge from the foot of the table it was Spurs who dropped through the relegation trap door on the final day of the season! His talent and experience was seen as vital to steady Wednesday's young forward line and when he struggled with fitness in the latter months of his Owls career it was said he still played as Seed's mere presence on the field would lift the side – his old boss Bob Brown once said "if you're not fit, Jimmy, just throw your shirt on the pitch"- as if to symbolise his value. His playing days ended at Wednesday as he retired in April 1931 after accepting an offer to manage Clapton Orient when legendary Arsenal boss Herbert Chapman's idea was to take over the London side and make it the Gunners nursery club. However when the FA vetoed the idea Seed was left with a club that had no money or players! After spending two months coaching in Sweden during the summer of 1931 he returned to manfully manage the cash starved London side for two seasons before being appointed Charlton Athletic boss in May 1933, starting a 23-year association with the Valiants.

When Bob Brown left Wednesday in September 1933 the club's number one target to replace him was Seed but he resisted the Owls overtures and showed his qualities by leading Charlton to the greatest era in their history. Within two years of winning the Third Division title in 1935 his charges were runners-up in the top-flight and secured top four finishes in the two seasons immediately preceding the War. During wartime soccer Athletic twice visited Wembley in the Final of the Southern Cup – winning in 1944 – and were then F.A.Cup finalists in 1946 and 1947, winning the trophy for the only time in their history in the latter final. Seed – who was a keen and very highly regarded cartoonist – kept Charlton in the top-flight but after losing the first five games of the 1956-7 season was somewhat harshly sacked, later moving to Bristol City in an advisory role in January 1957. He was briefly caretaker manager at City in January of the following year and spent his final years at Millwall where he served in various roles including advisor, manager and club director

SEEMLEY, Ivor John 1946-55

Born: 30 June 1929 Sheffield
(5ft 11½ins, 13st 2lbs – 1951)
Debut: 26 December 1953
v Manchester United
Division One Home
Last Appearance: 12 March 1955
v Burnley
Division One Away
Total League
& Cup Appearances: 23 Goals: 0

Career Details:

Ellsmere Park		
WEDNESDAY	1 July	1946 £10
Stockport County	June	1955 £300
Chesterfield	June	1957* Exchange for Bill Sowden
Sutton Town		1959

Ivor Seemley first played organised football at Firth Park Grammar School in Sheffield and started to train with Wednesday on two nights a week when only fourteen year old. As a teenager he occupied the halfback position and represented Sheffield boys before signing professional forms for the Owls at the end of the Second World War. However he immediately began his two-year National Service and spent time in Egypt with the R.A.F. where he played for both the services and combined services football sides.

After being de-mobbed Ivor became a regular in the club's Central League side where he eventually switched to the position – left back -where he would play the majority of his first team games for Wednesday. His league baptism actually came at halfback and after breaking into the side he enjoyed a memorable run, deputising for regular full back Norman Curtis, which included all eight games in Wednesday's run to the F.A.Cup semi-finals in 1954.

After Curtis became re-established at left back during the following campaign Seemley played only five times and at the season's end opted for a move to Stockport County where in two seasons he was almost ever present. He later moved back nearer his birthplace to sign for Chesterfield and after 78 league games for the Spireites he spent a season as a part-time professional at Sutton Town before hanging up his boots in 1960. He then worked in a sales office for a Steel Company but has not worked since being made redundant 1975, filling his time by playing badminton and until recently attending games at Hillsborough as a season ticket holder.

* Did not play for Oak Folds FC

SEWELL, John 'Jackie' 1951-55

Born: 24 January 1927 Kell, nr Whitehaven
(5ft 9ins, 10st 11lbs – 1951)
Debut: 17 March 1951
v Liverpool
Division One Away
Last Appearance: 26 November 1955
v West Ham United
Division Two Home
Total League
& Cup Appearances: 175 Goals: 92

Career Details:

Kells Centre		
Workington		WW2 Guest
Notts County	October	1944
WEDNESDAY	15 March	1951 £35,000
Aston Villa	2 December	1955 £23,000
Hull City	October	1959
City of Lusaka	September	1961
Zambia		1964

CAPS (@SWFC)
England Full (6) v N.Ireland 14/11/51, v Austria 25/05/52, v Switzerland 28/05/52, v N.Ireland 04/10/52, v Hungary 25/11/53, v Hungary 23/05/54

Football League (4) v Scottish League 31/10/51, v Irish League 24/09/52, v League of Ireland 10/02/54, v Scottish League 28/04/54

It probably seems almost unbelievable to today's younger generation but throughout the late 1940s and early 1950s Wednesday regularly broke the British transfer record to bring star players to Hillsborough. The last time this occurred came in March 1951 when Jackie Sewell arrived from Aston Villa in a move that was hoped would help Wednesday to climb out of the relegation places in Division One. Sadly despite the new boy grabbing six goals in ten games the Owls still went down but his purchase proved money well spent as over the next five years the skilful direct forward - who possessed a powerful shot, great ball control and a willingness to work for the side – scored on a regular basis and earned a multitude of representative honours. After suffering relegation with Wednesday within a few weeks of joining Sewell showed his eye for goal by netting an amazing 36 goals while on tour with an F.A. side in Australia and within a year was a key player as the club bounced back by winning the Division Two title.

The inside forward had made a relatively late start to his playing career as after leaving school in the war years he worked most Saturdays on a farm, allowing no time to play football. After his hopes of joining the Merchant Navy were vetoed by his father Sewell instead started work at the local mine, shovelling coal onto a lift to take it to the pithead. It was this employment that effectively launched his football career as it was while playing for his colliery side, Kells Centre, against Workington in the Cumberland League that he was spotted by a scout and invited for trials at Notts County. His father had never left his home area and did want to travel with the youngster to Nottingham so it was his uncle who took Sewell to County where he eventually signed as a part-time professional in 1944. Throughout the remainder of the war years he would travel down from the North West by rail, changing at several stations, after his Friday shift at the pit and would usually arrive at his lodgings in the early hours of Saturday morning. If County were at home the club's officials would allow him a lie in but if they were away he was woken up to travel with the rest of the team! After the game he would not arrive home sometimes until 8am on a Sunday morning but thankfully his regime eased when he was allowed Fridays off by his pit manager and eventually eased completely when he transferred to Bestwood Colliery in Nottinghamshire.

When the war ended he was allowed to leave the pit and quickly became a regular in post war soccer at the Meadow Lane club, forming a lethal partnership with football legend Tommy Lawton which brought Sewell a Division Three (South) Championship medal in 1950 and a total of 104 goals in just 193 league and cup games prior to his record breaking move to Hillsborough. After helping Wednesday back into the top-flight Sewell won the first of his six full caps for England although his final two appearances were memorable for all the wrong reasons as the magic Hungarian side beat England 6-3 at Wembley and 7-1 in Budapest. At Villa Park he became more of a goal maker than goal taker but was in the Villa side that beat Manchester United to win the F.A.Cup in 1957, prior to joining Hull City. He took his career figures in league soccer to a highly impressive 227 goals in 510 games before an ex Workington team mate asked him to go to Northern Rhodesia to form a new team in Lusaka. Within three months his fledgling side were in the local Cup Final but Sewell then returned to Hull where after securing a free transfer he returned to Africa on a permanent basis. Soon after Northern Rhodesia was renamed Zambia, Sewell was handed an additional role of player-coach to the National side which he continued with until returning to the UK in 1973 – in Lusaka he also managed the labour force that tended the City's flower beds before becoming a car salesman after being told his fame would make it easy to sell the vehicles! After returning to Nottingham he continued to work as a car salesman before retiring in 1987.

*Never played for Whitehaven Town or in wartime football for Carlisle United

SHADBOLT, William Henry 'Bill' 1952-53

Born: 4 August 1932 Shrewsbury
(5ft 9½ins, 11st 7lbs – 1953)
Debut: 14 February 1953 v Preston North End Division One Away
Last Appearance: 4 April 1953 v Portsmouth Division One Away
Total League & Cup Appearances: 7 Goals: 0

Career Details:

Oswestry Town		
WEDNESDAY	February	1953 £5,000
Halifax Town	16 March	1954
Contract cancelled		1954

Strong, forceful winger Bill Shadbolt made a quick first team debut after arriving from Birmingham League side Oswestry Town but unfortunately events totally overshadowed his first appearance as it came in the fateful match at Deepdale where Derek Dooley's career came to a tragic end. The newcomer would play a further half a dozen games in that debut campaign but totally dropped out of the first team picture in 1953-4, only making a handful of reserve team appearances. He eventually moved on transfer deadline day to basement club Halifax Town but after scoring once in just three league games his contract was cancelled by mutual consent in the summer of 1954.

SHAKESPEARE, Craig Robert 1989-90

Born: 26 October 1963
Great Barr, Birmingham
(5ft 10ins, 9st 5lbs – 1989)
Debut: 19 August 1989
v Norwich City
Division One Home
Last Appearance: 20 January 1990
v Everton
Division One Away
Total League
& Cup Appearances: 18+3 Goals: 1

Career Details:

Walsall	5 October	1981
WEDNESDAY	19 June	1989 £300,000
West Bromwich Albion	2 February	1990 £275,000
Grimsby Town	14 July	1993 £115,000
Scunthorpe United	7 July	1997 Free
Telford United	March	1998 Loan
Telford United	July	1998
Blakenall	September	1999
Aberystwyth Town	February	2000

Prior to his move to Hillsborough in the summer of 1989 midfielder Craig Shakespeare had enjoyed almost eight years as a professional at Walsall where he had amassed a mammoth 355 games, scoring 59 times. During those years on the Saddlers books he helped them to the semi-final of the League Cup in 1984 – losing narrowly to Liverpool – and won promotion via the play offs from the old Third Division in 1988. His consistent form soon alerted many top-flight clubs to his qualities and it was Owls boss Ron Atkinson who eventually secured his signature - Shakespeare moving along with Walsall teammate Mark Taylor. The hefty fee almost guaranteed he would start the new season in the first team but Wednesday struggled from the start and he was dropped from his left sided midfield role in late October 1989 when major team surgery saw the likes of John Sheridan, Roland Nilsson & Phil King brought to the club. The latter immediately started to forge a left-wing partnership with Nigel Worthington and condemned Shakespeare to the subs bench for the remainder of his brief and disappointing career at Wednesday. The player with the famous surname eventually joined West Brom on loan and Wednesday recouped the majority of their initial outlay when he joined the Baggies on a permanent basis in March 1990.

He quickly proved his time at Hillsborough was just a blip as Shakespeare would appear in over 100 games for West Brom over the next three years and was even appointed team captain. He later experienced relegation with Grimsby Town before ending his Football League career with just six games for Scunthorpe United. A loan spell at Conference side Telford United was then made permanent with Shakespeare also being handed the role of assistant manager. After a season at Buck's Head he returned to the Hawthorns in 1999 after being appointed to West Brom's coaching staff while his playing career ended after brief spells in Dr Martens League football at Blakehall and in Welsh non-league football. He now scouts for the Baggies while also coaching their youth side.

SHARP, Wilfred 'Wilf' 1934-36

Born: 8 April 1907 Bathgate, Scotland
(5ft 10½ins, 11st 7lbs – 1934)
Died: Q/E June 1981 Sefton South
Debut: 8 December 1934
v Leicester City
Division One Away
Last Appearance: 13 April 1936
v Middlesbrough
Division One Away
Total League
& Cup Appearances: 58 Goals: 2

Career Details:

Pumpherston Rangers		
Bathgate		
Clydebank		1925
Airdrieonians		1929
Tunbridge Wells Rangers	June	1932
Airdrieonians		
WEDNESDAY	11 August	1934 £750
Bradford Park Avenue	13 May	1936
Burton Town	August	1937

Strong and aggressive halfback Wilf Sharp was initially brought to the club by Billy Walker as a direct replacement for Alf Strange, who had departed for Bradford Park Avenue. However when the new season started the newcomer found himself in the reserves as Horace Burrows kept the No. 4 shirt and it was not until just before Christmas that the Scotsman made his senior debut. However he would then miss only one game until the end of the season and appeared in every F.A.Cup tie as Wednesday went all the way to Wembley where he of course gained a winners medal - it proved a fairytale story for Sharp as his only previous experience of English football had come during a stint as a professional at Kent non-league side Tunbridge Wells.

Unfortunately his wife never settled in Sheffield and after losing his place to Walter Millership mid-way through the 1935-6 season he asked to go on the transfer list, hoping to secure a move back to Scottish football. Before the end of the season his spouse moved back home but Wilf was not to follow her immediately as he only moved a few miles north, signing for Bradford Park Avenue. He would appear in only 17 games for the Yorkshire side and after a short spell at non-league Burton Town he did eventually return home with a Cup winners medal more than ample reward for a career in English football where he was certainly in the right place at the right time.

SHAW, Bernard L. F. 1885-86

Born:
Only Appearance:
31 October 1885 v Long Eaton Rangers F.A.Cup Away
Total League & Cup Appearances: 1 Goals: 0

Career Details:

Hallam		
WEDNESDAY		1885

Attacker who spent one season with Wednesday during the mid-1880s. His only senior appearance came in a disastrous F.A.Cup loss at minnows Long Eaton, which proved to be the Owls' last match in the old competition as an amateur club. In April 1886 he was in the side that beat Heeley 2-0 to win the Wharncliffe Charity Cup although he never achieved the fame of his father, John, who not only was one of the founder members of Hallam Football Club but was also a senior Tory politician, pioneering footballer and President of the fledgling Sheffield F.A. who at the time rivalled the London F.A in importance.

SHAW, Bernard 1973-76

Born: 14 March 1945 Sheffield
(5ft 8ins, 11st 2lbs – 1974)
Debut: 25 August 1973
v Swindon Town
Division Two Away
Last Appearance: 29 April 1976
v Southend United
Division Three Home
Total League
& Cup Appearances: 109+4 Goals: 4

Career Details:

Sheffield United	October	1962
Wolverhampton Wanderers	17 July	1969 £15,000
WEDNESDAY	21 May	1973 £34,200
Worksop Town	July	1976
Baslow		1977

After being discarded by Sheffield boys for being too small, Parson Cross born defender Bernard Shaw joined Sheffield United as an apprentice and was soon capped at Youth level by his country. He would spend seven seasons at Bramall Lane, regularly playing alongside his older brother Graham, and appeared in 136 games for the Blades whilst also earning two England U-23 caps. After United were relegated to Division Two in 1968 Shaw stayed only one season in the lower grade before transferring to Wolves where he was a regular in top-flight soccer and helped Wolves to the 1972 UEFA Cup Final. He also won the Texaco Cup while at the Black Country club but the consistent full back then moved back to Sheffield, joining the small band of players to have played for the two senior sides in the city.

In a struggling Wednesday side Shaw was a defensive rock and in three seasons at Hillsborough missed only a handful of games as the Owls experienced one of the worst periods in their history. After helping Wednesday to beat Southend United in April 1976, avoiding the unthinkable drop into Division Four, he was one of nine players handed free transfers as Len Ashurst cleared the decks after a traumatic season. By this time Shaw had bought the 'Prince of Wales' public house in the Derbyshire Peak District and also a fish and chip shop at Lodge Moor in Sheffield. After leaving Hillsborough he played a season as a semi-professional with Northern Premier League Worksop Town – he received a call up for the England non-league side in November 1976 – and then spent three seasons playing in the local Eyam League with Baslow before finally retiring from the game in 1980. He continues to run his public house today and is kept busy by various other business interests.

SHAW, John Stephen 'Jack' 1953-59

Born: 10 April 1924 Doncaster
(5ft 9¼ins, 10st 9¾lbs – 1953)
Debut: 29 August 1953
v Burnley
Division One Away
Last Appearance: 12 October 1957
v Blackpool
Division One Home
Total League
& Cup Appearances: 65 Goals: 27

Career Details:

Edlington WMC		
Yorkshire Main Colliery		
Rotherham United	March	1945
WEDNESDAY	19 June	1953 £7,800
Denaby United	June	1959
British Ropes (Balby)		1960

Despite being tracked by Wolves as a teenager it was with local club Rotherham United that Jack Shaw started his senior career. At the time he was working as a haulage hand at Yorkshire Main Colliery and agreed to join the Millers only if his pit side won their local league championship. They duly lifted the title and Shaw was drafted almost immediately into the Millmoor first team, playing alongside Wally Ardron in the five-man forward line, scoring the winning goal in the 1946 Third Division (North) Cup Final. However it was not until Ardron left for Nottingham Forest in 1949 that Shaw was switched to his natural position of centre forward and the move brought spectacular success as Shaw grabbed a club record 46 league and cup goals in 1950-1 as United walked away with the Division Three (North) Championship.

The Donny lad combined flair and abundant skill with brilliant heading ability and this brought him another 25 goals in the higher grade, eventually leading to a somewhat reluctant transfer to Hillsborough as Wednesday tried in vain to replace the phenomenon that was Derek Dooley. Before the start of the 1953-4 season Shaw was called to Millmoor and told he was being sold to Wednesday where his pay would be unchanged. He told the Millers he was happy to stay and did not want to go but was told in no uncertain terms that if he did not move he would never play for Rotherham again! After 139 goals in 365 games for United he duly moved to Hillsborough and enjoyed a good first season, netting 17 times and appearing in an F.A.Cup semi-final. He proved he was a naturally gifted forward by scoring ten more times for top-flight Wednesday in the following campaign but after being replaced by Roy Shiner in 1955 he dropped into reserve team soccer – at the suggestion of Eric Taylor he joined Clarrie Jordan in coaching the Owls youngsters. He was actually due to be released at the end of the 1955-6 campaign but was re-employed purely in a coaching capacity and was later drafted into the Owls side as a emergency attacker, over two years after his previous appearance.

The arrival of new manager Harry Catterick at Wednesday in 1958 ended his coaching days at Hillsborough and he looked set to join his old Rotherham United boss Andy Smailes at Scarborough after being offered a first team place, a house and a job. However his departure from Millmoor still rankled with Shaw and after rebuffing the offer he instead spent a season at Conisborough based side Denaby United. He then took employment as a fitters mate at a Doncaster company and played at centre half until the age of 45 in the works side, which he coached. After taking early retirement in 1980 he watched and scouted for Doncaster Rovers but will always be remembered as one of Rotherham United's all-time greats

SHAW, Jonathan 'Jon' 2003-04

Born: 10 November 1983 Sheffield
(6ft 1ins, 12st 9lbs – 2003)
Debut: 7 January 2003
v Gillingham
F.A.Cup Away
Last Appearance: 25 September 2004
v Wrexham
League One Away
Total League
& Cup Appearances: 9+15 Goals: 2

Career Details:

WEDNESDAY	3 July	2000 Academy
WEDNESDAY	1 July	2003
York City	14 November	2003 Loan
Loan return	7 January	2004
Released	5 November	2004
Oldham Athletic	November	2004 Trial
Burton Albion	19 November	2004 Free
Cheltenham Town	23 November	2004 Trial

Industrious and bustling attacker who first came to the fore when being included in a depleted squad for an F.A.Cup tie at Gillingham in January 2003. The teenager came off the bench for the final fifteen minutes for his senior debut and after continuing his progress in reserve and youth soccer was rewarded with a one-year professional contract in the following summer. The born and bred Wednesdayite had previously maintained an impressive scoring record in Academy football – he was top scorer in 2002-3 with 14 goals – and his power in the air, sharp finishing ability and terrific technique marked him as one for the future.

After missing just three reserve games in 2002-3 he continued his steady progress by netting eleven times for the second team in the following season, in addition to impressing during a loan spell at Division Three side York City. The experience gained at Bootham Crescent no doubt helped his cause at Hillsborough as on returning he was drafted into Chris Turner's senior squad, impressing greatly on his full debut at Rushden & Diamonds in February 2004. His first goals for the club in the final two league games of the season secured a second 12-month deal for Shaw but the youngster dropped out of first team contention following the arrival of Paul Sturrock and left by mutual consent. Incidentally Shaw manages his father's Sheffield based Sunday League side! After joining Conference club Burton Albion he netted on his debut and was immediately invited for a week's trial at League Two club Cheltenham Town.

SHELLEY, Albert — 1937

Born: Birmingham
(5ft 10ins, 11st 8lbs – 1935)
Debut: 2 January 1937
v Wolverhampton Wanderers
Division One Home
Last Appearance: 21 April 1937
v West Bromwich Albion
Division One Away
Total League
& Cup Appearances: 3 Goals: 2

Career Details:

Birmingham	February	1933	
Oakengates Town	August	1933	
Gloucester City	August	1935	
WEDNESDAY	January	1937	£300
Torquay United	May	1937	
Gloucester City	August	1939	
Torquay United	September	1939	

Centre forward Albert Shelley was the sixth player to be tried in the problematic No. 9 shirt during the 1936-7 season, as Wednesday struggled at the wrong end of the First Division table. He had initially arrived on trial from Birmingham League club Gloucester City in December 1936 and such was his form in Central League football for Wednesday that Billy Walker secured his services on a permanent basis – Shelley actually finished the season as top scorer for the second team with 12 goals despite playing only half of the campaign. He netted on his first team debut and also on what proved to be his final appearance – a 3-2 success at The Hawthorns – but moved to Devon in the summer that followed, scoring 15 times in 41 league and cup games for Torquay before ending his senior career.

SHELTON, Gary — 1982-87

Born: 21 March 1958 Nottingham
(5ft 7ins, 10st - 1982)
Debut: 27 March 1982
v Orient
Division Two Home
Last Appearance: 9 May 1987
v Wimbledon
Division One Home
Total League
& Cup Appearances: 237+4 Goals: 24

Career Details:

Parkhead United		
Walsall	1 March	1975
Aston Villa	18 January	1978 £80,000
Notts County	13 March	1980 Loan
WEDNESDAY	25 March	1982 £50,000
Oxford United	23 July	1987 £135,000
Bristol City	24 August	1989 Exchange for McClaren
Rochdale	11 February	1994 Loan
Chester City	22 July	1994 Free

CAPS (@SWFC)
England U-21 (1)* v Finland 16/10/84 * Over age player

Wholehearted midfielder Gary Shelton came to Hillsborough for a bargain fee and went on to become an influential, popular and vital cog in the Owls engine room during the 1980s. The skilful and creative Shelton endeared himself to Wednesday fans with a series of fiery and committed displays, which allied with his eye for an opening and proven goal touch, helped the Owls to promotion from Division Two – he was player of the year in 1983-4 - and subsequent consolidation in the top-flight. He initially joined Wednesday on loan but once in the first team became ever present with only an occasional loss of form, due to injury, restricting his appearances. Shelton's attitude to the game was no more typified than by his club nickname of 'Stretch' which referred to the excessive number of times he was stretchered off the pitch with a suspected injury only to return to the fray soon after!

As a schoolboy Shelton tended to play in a defensive or sweeper role but it was as a forward that he attended trials for Nottingham boys, netting four goals on his debut for the 'B' side. After being promoted to the 'A' side he again netted four times but it was his performances as a midfielder for his junior side Parkhead that led to Shelton signing schoolboy forms for Walsall in 1972. However, on leaving school he was not offered trainee terms and it needed a star display against a team of trialists at Walsall that finally launched his professional career. His senior career at Walsall was relatively brief as after starting just 14 league games he was snapped up by Aston Villa boss Ron Saunders for a sizeable fee. During over four years at Villa Park he was in and out of the side and after two dozen appearances was allowed to join Notts County on loan before being signed by Jack Charlton at Wednesday.

After his successful spell at Hillsborough, Gary suffered relegation during two years at Oxford United but bounced back to enjoy a terrific spell at Bristol City, being an inspirational figure in their promotion from Division Three in 1990. He added much needed steel to the Robins defence and appeared in 180 games for the West Country club before bringing the curtain down on his playing career at Chester City – he became the oldest player to appear for City when making his final league appearance in February 1998 at the age of 39 years, 10 months and 21 days. By this time Shelton had become assistant manager and remained at Chester until their relegation from the Football League in 2000. He then joined ex-Owls teammate Gary Megson at West Brom where as assistant manager/reserve team boss he helped Albion gain promotion to the Premier League in 2002 and 2004.

SHELTON, George — 1920-22

Born: Q/E September 1899 Sheffield
(5ft 9 1/2ins, 11st – 1920)
Died: 24 February 1934 Exeter
Debut: 14 February 1920
v Preston North End
Division One Away
Last Appearance: 26 December 1921
v Leeds United
Division Two Away
Total League
& Cup Appearances: 18 Goals: 0

Career Details:

Attercliffe F.C.		
Star Inn Club		
WEDNESDAY	23 January	1920 Free
Exeter City	13 May	1922
New Brighton	27 July	1926
Oakhampton	December	1927

Outside left who played in local Sheffield football before serving his country in the Great War, fighting in France and Italy for the 8th Battalion York and Lancaster Regiment. Whilst in Italy George received a large amount of Austrian money which was declared useless and the regiment used the bank notes to light their cigarettes – unfortunately after the armistice was called he discovered the notes were in fact legal! After being de-mobbed he returned to Attercliffe Alliance League football from where he was offered professional terms by Wednesday. The Owls were experiencing one of the worst seasons in their history at the time and although Shelton appeared in nine league games he could not stop Wednesday tumbling out of the top-flight.

Under new manager Bob Brown the winger competed with Smelt and Capper for the left-sided role and slowly dropped out of the first team picture as Brown completely over hauled the club's playing staff. Playing spells in Southern England followed before George retired from football to take the Bull Hotel in Exeter. Sadly he died at the tender age of 34 after a short illness.

SHEPHERD, James 1892-94

Born: 1867 Scotland
Died: December 1925 Sheffield
Debut: 23 September 1893 v Sunderland Division One Away
Last Appearance:
25 September 1893 v West Bromwich Albion Division One Home
Total League & Cup Appearances: 2 Goals: 0

Career Details:

Dundee football	
WEDNESDAY	1892
Chesterfield	1894

Halfback who was one of several signings to join Wednesday after they were elected into the Football League in 1892. He arrived from Dundee football but had to be content with reserve team football in his first season, playing regularly as the second team won the Sheffield & District League Championship. His chance at first team level came early in the following season but sadly he suffered a knee injury in only his second game and after regaining fitness he played out the final months of his Wednesday career back in the reserves before spending a brief time at Chesterfield. He passed away aged 58.

SHERIDAN, John Joseph 1989-96

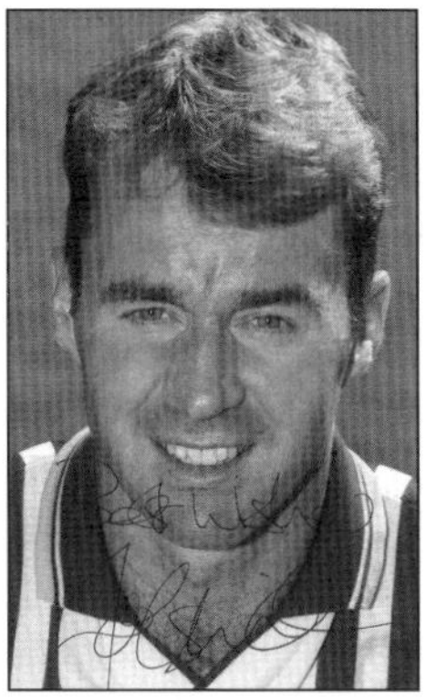

Born: 1 October 1964 Stetford, Manchester
(5ft 10ins, 10st 8lbs – 1993)
Debut: 4 November 1989
v Nottingham Forest
Division One Away
Last Appearance: 7 September 1996
v Chelsea
Premier League Home
Total League
& Cup Appearances: 233+11 Goals: 33

Career Details:

Manchester City		Trainee
Leeds United	2 March	1982
Nottingham Forest	3 August	1989 £650,000
WEDNESDAY	2 November	1989 £500,000
Birmingham City	9 February	1996 Loan
Bolton Wanderers	12 November	1996 £225,000
Huddersfield Town	August	1998 Trial
Doncaster Rovers	August	1998 Free
Oldham Athletic	20 October	1998 Free

CAPS (@SWFC)
Eire (29) v Wales 28/03/90, v Turkey 27/05/90, v Malta 02/06/90, v Italy 30/06/90 v Morocco 12/09/90, v Turkey 17/10/90, v Chile 22/05/91, v USA 01/06/91, v Hungary 11/09/91, v Latvia 09/06/93, v Spain 13/10/93, v Holland 20/04/94, v Bolivia 24/05/94, v Germany 29/05/94, v Czech Republic 05/06/94, v Italy 18/06/94, v Mexico 24/06/94, v Norway 28/06/94, v Holland 04/07/94, v Latvia 07/09/94, v Liechtenstein 12/10/94, v N.Ireland 16/11/94, v England 15/02/95, v N.Ireland 29/03/95, v Portugal 26/04/95, v Liechtenstein 03/06/95, v Austria 11/06/95, v Austria 06/09/95, v Holland 13/12/95

Eire U-23 (1) v N.Ireland 15/05/90

Creative midfielder John Sheridan is widely regarded as one of the greatest players to ever appear in a Wednesday shirt. At his peak Sheridan's superb passing skills and vision made him one of the best midfield players of his generation and he was a major influence on the Owls successful side of the early 1990s. Alongside Carlton Palmer he created one of the best midfield pairings in the club's history and Sheridan pulled all the strings as Wednesday won promotion and the League Cup in 1991, finished third in the top flight a year later, played European football in 1992 and then made four trips to Wembley.

He arrived at Wednesday after falling foul of the eccentric Brian Clough at Nottingham Forest who after paying a hefty fee for his services duly played Sheridan in just one game before Ron Atkinson ended his brief and unhappy time at the City Ground. Ironically just two days after signing for The Owls he was back at Forest and could not hide his delight after helping Wednesday to a shock one-nil win! He instantly became a Hillsborough hero after netting a spectacular winning goal in a ZDS Cup tie at home to Sheffield United and of course will always be remembered as the man whose goal won the League Cup at Wembley. Although born in Manchester he qualified for the Republic of Ireland due to his Dublin born parents and while at Wednesday 'Shezza' appeared in both the 1990 and 1994 World Cup Finals, the highlights being a quarter final appearance against hosts Italy in the former tournament and a stunning win over the Italians in New York during the latter competition. Throughout his time in the blue and white shirt Sheridan had a penchant for outstanding goals - a stunning free kick at Luton Town standing out as his best – and he remained a Wednesday regular until the arrival of David Pleat in the summer of 1995.

After losing his place in the side Sheridan spent a loan spell at Birmingham City, appearing in a League Cup semi-final against his old club Leeds, but after a permanent deal did not materialise he returned to Hillsborough where almost criminally he was back in the reserve team – gladdening the hearts of the die-hard reserve watchers! A second loan spell, at Bolton Wanderers, did eventually secure a permanent deal with the Lancashire club paying Wednesday an additional £20,000 for the loan spell on top of the £180,000 transfer fee. It marked the end of a career at Hillsborough that left such an indelible mark on the minds of Owls fans that for many years after he was given a rousing standing ovation whenever he appeared against Wednesday in opposition colours.

The playmaker had originally started his career at hometown side Manchester City but was snapped up by Leeds United before he had signed a professional contract. It proved a wise move for United as Sheridan would enjoy several successful seasons at Elland Road, scoring 52 goals in 267 games, and carved out a reputation as one of the best players outside of the top-flight. After finally playing with Wednesday in the higher grade he dropped out of the Premiership to sign for Bolton and it was a struggle initially to nail down a regular place as Bolton won promotion to the Premier League for the first time in their history in 1997 – the elevation earning Wednesday another £25,000 on Sheridan's transfer fee! However he was a mainstay in Wanderers' brave but ultimately unsuccessful attempt to stave off relegation a year later before being released, later signing for Conference new boys Doncaster Rovers. After turning down a contract offer from Rovers he was back in the Football League with Oldham Athletic and in October 2001 was appointed player-coach before registering his 500th league appearance. After supposedly retiring at the end of the 2002-3 season he was forced to re-register as a player during the summer and in December 2003 was appointed joint caretaker manager following the sudden departure of Iain Dowie to Crystal Palace. Sheridan – whose brother Darren played for several clubs including Oldham and Barnsley – did finally retire for good in March 2004, mainly due to a long standing knee injury, when he was appointed No.2 to new manager Brian Talbot. He was then appointed youth coach following a re-organisation in November 2004.

SHINER, Roy Albert James 1955-59

Born: 15 November 1924
Seaview, Isle of Wight
(5ft $8^1/_2$ins, 12st 3lbs – 1955)
Died: 28 October 1988 Isle of Wight
Debut: 20 August 1955
v Plymouth Argyle
Division Two Home
Last Appearance: 26 September 1959
v Luton Town
Division One Home
Total League
& Cup Appearances: 160 Goals: 96

SIBON, Gerald 1999-2003

Born: 19 April 1974 Dalen, Holland
(6ft 3ins, 13st 4lbs – 1999)
Debut: 7 August 1999
v Liverpool
Premier League Home
Last Appearance: 11 January 2003
v Reading
Division One Home
Total League
& Cup Appearances: 116+34 Goals: 43

Career Details:

VV Dalen		1980
FC Groningen		1989
VV Dalen		1990
FC Twente		1992
VVV Venlo		1994
JC Roda		1996 Free
Ajax Amsterdam		1997
WEDNESDAY	9 July	1999 £1,500,000
Heerenveen	15 January	2003
PSV Eindhoven	17 June	2004 € 750,000 (£493,000)

Tall forward Gerald Sibon will probably go down in Wednesday's history as the most frustrating, inconsistent, enigmatic and downright infuriating players to ever pull on the blue and white shirt. On his day Sibon would not have been out of place in one of Europe's top teams, sometimes single handily winning games for Wednesday, but unfortunately these did not come around too often and all fans were usually left with were flashes of brilliance mixed in with a tendency to over elaborate and gift the opposition possession. However in his time Gerald was top scorer on three consecutive occasions and finished with a reasonable goals to games ratio when you consider he never played in a side that wasn't struggling at the wrong end of a division.

He was one of two high profile signings made by Danny Wilson in the summer of 1999 – the other being Gilles De Bilde - but both struggled to adapt to life in the Premier League and Gerald was in and out of the side, scoring only six times as the Owls tumbled out of the top-flight. The club's fans soon started to realise that although the Dutchman possessed a considerable height advantage it was actually with the ball at his feet that he was most dangerous – he possessed one of the hardest shots seen for many years at Hillsborough – and his much improved form and 15 goals helped Wednesday avoid the unthinkable drop out of Division One in 2001. He was also named player of the year by the Owls fans and scored a spectacular hat trick at home to QPR in December 2000 to cement his growing popularity – he was also linked with a £3m move to Sunderland in the close season that followed. He was top scorer again a year later and repeated the feat in 2002-3 with 9 goals although he was actually allowed to return to Holland part way through the campaign. Unfortunately Sibon had become a luxury that Wednesday could no longer afford – he had signed a highly lucrative 4-year deal when arriving from Ajax – and it was financial rather than footballing reasons that led to his departure just six months before his contract expired.

He started playing football at the age of six and appeared - alongside his twin brother Andre - for his village side that won several Championships and reached a national cup final. At the age of 15 Sibon joined top-flight club Groningen, playing for the U-18 side, but a serious ankle injury saw him return home to re-join his village club. However after regaining fitness he signed a professional contract at FC Twente and would play alongside the likes of Michael Mols and Ronald de Boer after making his senior debut against his old side Groningen. During two years at Twente he was mainly restricted to reserve team football, making only four senior starts, but another two years at Venlo brought 34 goals and a move back into the Dutch top-flight at JC Roda. In his only season at Roda Gerald scored as they beat Heerenveen 4-2 to win the Dutch Cup and a year later he was signed by giants Ajax on a five-year contract. He would spend two years in Amsterdam but was never a regular in a star-studded Ajax side that boasted the de Boer twins, Jari Litmanan & Michael Laudrup. However he did complete a hat trick of Dutch Cup medals by winning in 1998 and 1999 as well as earning a League Championship medal in the former year when Ajax recorded a 'double dutch'. After his spell in Sheffield, Sibon found the Dutch league to his liking after returning home and in 2003-4 finished third top scorer in the First Division, with 16 goals, as Heerenveen finished 4th.

SIMMONITE, Gordon 1976-78

Born: 25 April 1957 Sheffield
(5ft 9ins, 10st 9lbs – 1977)
Only Appearance: 26 February 1977
v Chesterfield
Division Three Away
Total League
& Cup Appearances: 1 Goals: 0

Career Details:

Rotherham United	May	1974 App.
WEDNESDAY	2 April	1976
Boston United	August	1978 Free
Blackpool	September	1980 £20,000
Lincoln City	November	1982 £6,000
Gainsborough Trinity	November	1987
Lincoln City	December	1987
Gainsborough Trinity	July	1988
Matlock Town	July	1990
Buxton	October	1992

Although born in Sheffield and representing the city boys team at every level from U-11 to U-15 it was with Rotherham United that Gordon Simmonite signed apprentice forms. However after a disagreement with Millers boss Jim McGuigan he was released and arrived at Hillsborough when Owls manager Len Ashurst agreed the youngster could train with Wednesday and play for the youth team in the Northern Intermediate League. Soon after he was handed a short-term contract – running only until 30 June 1976 – but Simmonite would stay another two years to become the mainstay of the club's reserve team. In fact he was almost ever present for the Central League side and one of the few games he missed came when he made his one and only senior appearance for Wednesday, replacing the injured Dave Cusack in the 2-0 loss at Saltergate.

He eventually left for Howard Wilkinson's Boston United in 1978 where in his debut season the tough defender was named player of the year and went onto represent his county at non-league level, winning a four-team tournament against Scotland, Holland and Italy. His form soon won Simmonite a way back into league soccer at Blackpool where he totalled 63 games before moving to Sincil Bank. An ankle injury sustained in March 1985 caused his retirement from the professional game five months later and Simmonite was then appointed youth team coach at Grimsby Town in July 1986.

He stayed only four months before becoming assistant manager at Stockport County but was back at Lincoln in July 1987 when he was appointed No. 2 to Colin Murphy. Again his stay was brief as a change of career – he joined the South Yorkshire Police – meant Simmonite resigned in October 1987 before re-launching his playing career at Northern Premier League Gainsborough. However within a few weeks he had made a surprise return to Lincoln City and was part of the side that won the Conference title to ensure the Imps bounced back into the Football League at the first attempt. He later played non-league soccer at a variety of senior clubs before finally retiring in May 1993 although he still occasionally appears for the Yorkshire Police and Great Britain Police team. He has now risen through the ranks to become a Detective sergeant in the C.I.D. department.

SIMMONS, Antony John 'Tony' 1983

Born: 9 February 1965 Sheffield
(5ft 11ins, 10st 7lbs – 1983)
Debut: 15 May 1982
v Norwich City
Division Two Home
Last Appearance: 5 March 1983
v Grimsby Town
Division Two Away
Total League
& Cup Appearances: 2+3 Goals: 0

Career Details:

Middlewood Rovers		
WEDNESDAY	7 February	1983
Queens Park Rangers	15 November	1983 £50,000
Rotherham United	March	1984 Loan
Rotherham United	2 August	1984 £50,000
Lincoln City	5 September	1986*
Cardiff City	12 February	1987 Loan
Gainsborough Trinity	October	1988 Free
Spalding United	March	1990 Free
Holbeach United		1990
Lincoln United	September	1991
Grantham Town	January	2000

*Exchange for John McGinlay

CAPS (@SWFC)
England Youth (9) v Norway 13/07/82, v Denmark 15/07/82, v Poland 17/07/82, v USSR 04/09/82, v Switzerland 06/09/82, v Yugoslavia 09/09/82, v Israel U-21 21/02/83, v Israel Olympic XI 23/02/83, v Belgium 13/04/83

After joining as an apprentice in June 1981, from the club's nursery club Middlewood Rovers, forward Tony Simmons became a prolific scorer at youth and reserve team level in the early 1980s. The Owls hierarchy had high hopes that the teenager would be able to replicate his deadly finishing at senior level and while still a trainee he was given a league debut by Jack Charlton. However despite scoring an incredible 47 goals in the 1981-2 season – including 24 for the reserve side – the Owls boss only used the exciting teenager occasionally at first team level as he pondered whether the youngster deserved a prolonged run in the side. Despite being a proven finisher 'Big Jack' was not convinced and when top-flight QPR offered a substantial sum for his services he let Simmons go, to a mixed reaction from supporters.

Sadly the former Sheffield boys player experienced a disappointing and all too brief time at Rangers as injury meant he failed to make a first team appearance for the London club. Within a year he was back in South Yorkshire at Rotherham United where his eight goals helped the Millers avoid relegation. After three seasons at Millmoor he registered just five goals in nineteen games at Lincoln City before being handed a free transfer in 1988. This marked the end of Simmons' professional career as he then began working for Lincolnshire based European Gas Turbines while also playing semi-pro football. A move to Central Midlands League side Lincoln United as player/assistant manager then saw Simmons rediscover his goal touch and he was a major factor in Lincoln's rapid rise through the pyramid to the top division of the Northern Premier League. In nine years at the club he won a multitude of honours and when he finally left for neighbours Grantham Town he had become the club's all-time record scorer, with over 200 goals to his name. He moved to Grantham along with the United manager and several players and helped his new side to the top division of the Dr Martens League in 2002. He remains on the Grantham's coaching staff and now works for Parcelforce.

SIMMONS, William 1899-1902

Born: 1879 Sheffield
Only Appearance:
20 January 1900 v Loughborough Division Two Home
Total League & Cup Appearances: 1 Goals: 0

Career Details:

Parkgate United		
WEDNESDAY	July	1899
Barnsley	20 January	1900 Loan
Doncaster Rovers	11 July	1902 £10

Right-winger who signed from local football to initially provide competition for Archie Brash. However after failing to dislodge his rival Simmons was transferred to Barnsley in January 1900 as part of a unique arrangement that saw Harry Davis sign for Wednesday and Simmons move to the Tykes until the end of the 1899-00 season. He transferred to Barnsley within hours of making his senior debut for Wednesday – in a 5-0 Owlerton romp over whipping boys Loughborough – and appeared in 15 games during his spell at Barnsley, scoring six times. He returned to Wednesday in the summer of 1900 but had to be content with reserve team football for the remainder of his Owls career as Davis became established as one of the finest wingers in the country, leaving Simmons in the shadows. He later moved to Doncaster Rovers but failed to register a first team appearance for Rovers.

SIMPSON, George 'Georgie' 1902-09

Born: 1883 Jarrow
(5ft 6ins, 10st 5lbs – 1907)
Debut: 14 March 1903
v Blackburn Rovers
Division One Home
Last Appearance: 29 March 1909
v Sunderland
Division One Home
Total League
& Cup Appearances: 163 Goals: 39

Career Details:

Jarrow FC		
WEDNESDAY	2 May	1902 £10 donation
West Bromwich Albion	29 March	1909 £850*
North Shields		1910

*Joint fee with Harry Burton

It would always be a thankless task for the left winger who had to follow in the footsteps of the legendary Fred Spiksley but George Simpson proved a more than capable successor, helping Wednesday to retain their League title in 1904 and then heading the winning goal in the 1907 F.A.Cup Final against Everton. He had originally arrived from crack non-league side Jarrow, aged 20, and after playing just a solitary game in his first full season at Owlerton he became an established top-flight player and firm crowd favourite with the Wednesday faithful. He was a fast and fearless attacker and fans often wondered why he did not collide with the goal posts such was his speed when dashing for goal!

After the Cup triumph the Owls went through a period of transition but Simpson remained a constant on the wing until losing his place to Frank Foxall during the 1908-9 campaign. However despite George not being a first team regular his move to Division Two promotion chasers West Brom, along with teammate Harry Burton, caused a sensation in Sheffield football, mainly due to the large fee paid for the duo. On the day his transfer was agreed Simpson was awarded a somewhat hastily arranged benefit game against that days opponents, Sunderland, and was probably quite pleased that Wednesday happened to be at home on the day his hasty move was pushed through! In hindsight his transfer to the Hawthorns proved a wise move from the Owls point of view as Simpson struggled to find his form and appeared in only 24 games for the Baggies before dropping out of league soccer and returning to his native northeast to sign for non-league North Shields.

SIMPSON, Vivian Sumner 1900-07

Born: 1883 Sheffield
Died: 13 April 1918 Outtersteene, France
Debut: 28 March 1902 v Manchester C
Division One Away
Last Appearance: 9 March 1907
v Liverpool F.A.Cup Home
Total League
& Cup Appearances: 38 Goals: 11

Career Details:

Wadsley College		
WEDNESDAY	7 December	1900
Norwich City	November	1907
Sheffield Club		1907
Northern Nomads		1908

In the club's early days every player was strictly amateur but by the beginning of the 20th Century the Owls playing staff was totally professional, as was required to deal with the rigours of league football. However one player, Vivian Simpson, stood out as a shining example of the old guard of 'gentleman players' who played purely for pleasure while working outside of the game. The versatile attacker was employed as a Sheffield based solicitor during the week but after signing amateur forms for Wednesday he was used on a regular basis in top-flight football, showing his ability in February 1904 when grabbing a hat-trick in a 6-0 romp against Manchester United.

Despite being on the Owls books for seven years he played the majority of his football during that period for amateur club Sheffield and played in every round of their run to the F.A.Amatuer Cup Final in 1904. Unfortunately he missed out on the final due to an injury received in a Wednesday game but was still awarded a medal by the club although this differed to the ones presented to the other players. Whenever called upon by Wednesday he always gave 100% commitment and such was his displays that in January 1907 he appeared for the North against the South in an England International trial match.

He later signed amateur forms for Southern League Norwich City and played a solitary game for the Canaries before switching to famous amateur side Northern Nomads. Incidentally a week after his one game for Norwich he scored a hat-trick for Sheffield Club and in January 1908 he could have played for either City or Wednesday when the two clashed in the F.A.Cup – he instead decided to play for his first love Sheffield Club in the Amateur Cup! The demands of his legal practice and a serious injury curtailed his career at a relatively early age but sadly while fighting for his country in World War One he was killed in action in France.

SINCLAIR, John Evens Wright 'Jackie' 1969-73

Born: 21 July 1943 Dunfermline
(5ft 6ins, 10st 8lbs – 1973)
Debut: 20 December 1969
v Arsenal
Division One Home
Last Appearance: 25 November 1972
v Orient
Division Two Away
Total League
& Cup Appearances: 105+4 Goals: 16

Career Details:

Blairhall Colliery		
Dunfermline Athletic		1960 £100
Leicester City	May	1965 £25,000
Newcastle United	December	1967 £67,500
WEDNESDAY	16 December	1969 £30,000*
Chesterfield	8 March	1973 Loan
Durban City	May	1973 Loan
Dunfermline Athletic	August	1973
Stenhousemuir		1975

*Deemed value in exchange

Diminutive and direct Scottish winger Jackie Sinclair came from real football stock as his father, Chris, played for several league sides in Scotland while his brother Willie played for the likes of Huddersfield Town and Tranmere Rovers. In addition his uncle, Tommy Wright, was capped for Scotland while his cousin, also called Tommy Wright, enjoyed a long career in English soccer that included spells at Leicester City, Leeds United and Bradford City. However for young Jackie it looked like a career as a professional footballer had passed him by as after leaving school he began working at Blairhall Colliery. While working at the pit he also played for the colliery side and it was here that he was spotted by Dunfermline scouts and subsequently signed by legendary Scottish manager Jock Stein for the Fife club. After breaking into the Pars first team he quickly earned a reputation as a goal scoring winger and boasted a tremendous record of 32 goals in only 61 games prior to moving south to sign for Leicester City – he transferred a few weeks after playing in Dunfermline's Scottish Cup Final loss to Celtic.

His star continued to rise at Filbert Street where he maintained his goals record – 50 in 103 league games – and was rewarded with his only full cap for Scotland, against Portugal in June 1966. After moving to Newcastle United he helped the northeast club to their last major honour – the old Fairs Cup in 1969 – before he arrived at Hillsborough in a swap deal that saw David Ford travel in the opposite direction. The Owls were struggling at the wrong end of the First Division table when Sinclair arrived and he would play the majority of his games for Wednesday in the Second Division after relegation was suffered in April 1970. He was a fixture on the right wing for over two seasons, under both Danny Williams and then Derek Dooley, but the arrival of the incomparable Willie Henderson in the summer of 1972 effectively ended his Hillsborough career and he was allowed to join neighbours Chesterfield on loan and then try his luck in South African football. After a brief spell in Durban he returned to these shores to end his playing career back in Scottish football before reverting to his original employment for the National Coal Board. His son, Chris, later played for Dunfermline in the 1991 Scottish League Cup Final while Jackie is now assistant steward at the Dunfermline Golf Club.

SINTON, Andrew 'Andy' 1993-96

Born: 19 March 1966 Cramlington, Newcastle
(5ft 8ins, 11st 5lbs – 1996)
Debut: 21 August 1993
v Arsenal
Premier League Home
Last Appearance: 6 January 1996
v Charlton Athletic
F.A.Cup Away
Total League
& Cup Appearances: 74+7 Goals: 3

Career Details:

Cambridge United	13 April	1983
Brentford	13 December	1985 £25,000
Queens Park Rangers	23 March	1989 £350,000
WEDNESDAY	19 August	1993 £2.75m
Tottenham Hotspur	23 January	1996 £1.5m
Wolverhampton Wanderers	6 July	1999 Free
Walsall		2002 Trial
Burton Albion	16 August	2002 Free
Bromsgrove Rovers	20 March	2004 Free
Fleet Town	8 July	2004

CAPS (@SWFC)
England Full (2) v Holland 13/10/93, v San Marino 17/11/93

The arrival of England International Andy Sinton, just weeks after Des Walker had signed, looked to be the final piece in the jigsaw as Wednesday looked to mount a challenge for major honours on the back of their four Wembley appearances. Unfortunately for the Owls and the likeable Geordie his time at Hillsborough was a big disappointment as he failed to show the consistent form that had led Wednesday and Arsenal into a tug of war for his signature, eventually costing Wednesday a joint club record fee. At his peak Sinton's enthusiasm and superb close dribbling skills were a joy to watch but this sight was a rare one for Wednesday fans as a combination of injury and loss of form denied him a full season in an Owls shirt. In addition Sinton's goal scoring record at QPR – 25 goals in 190 games – was not brought north as after netting in the home game against Norwich City in September 1993 he failed to score again in the remainder of his Wednesday career!

The former England schoolboy had been courted by a multitude of clubs when he was a teenager in the Northeast, ironically including Arsenal, but decided the quickest route to first team football would come at Cambridge United. He duly moved up the league ladder and reached the top division when Trevor Francis signed him for the first time, when he was player-manager at Queens Park Rangers, and subsequently won the first of his twelve full caps for England while at Loftus Road. The left-sided attacker had looked a fine purchase when Wednesday secured his services – the deal made sweeter by the fact that he chose the Owls over Cup nemeses Arsenal – and he could never be accused of not giving one hundred percent.

He actually ended his Owls career at left wing back before a move to Spurs revived his career somewhat as after an injury lay off he became a crowd favourite at White Hart Lane – winning the 1999 League Cup against Leicester City. After the Cup success he joined Wolves on a Bosman free transfer but injuries meant he was never a regular and Sinton eventually dropped out of league soccer to sign for Nigel Clough's Burton Albion. After a spell as player and then caretaker manager at Bromsgrove Rovers he helped out with the youth and reserve sides at Bromsgrove while working as player-coach/full-time development manager at Fleet Town. Appointed Fleet Town manager in June 2005.

SISSONS, John Leslie 1970-73

Born: 13 September 1945 Hayes, Middlesex
(5ft 7ins, 11st – 1971)
Debut: 29 August 1970
v Blackburn Rovers
Division Two Home
Last Appearance: 26 December 1973
v Norwich City
Division Two Home
Total League
& Cup Appearances: 125+1 Goals: 15

Career Details:

West Ham United	2 October	1962
WEDNESDAY	1 August	1970 £65,000
Norwich City	28 December	1973 £33,333
Chelsea	15 August	1974 £50,000
Tampa Bay Rowdies	April-Aug	1975 Loan
Cape Town City	May	1976

Winger John Sissons was a teenage star at West Ham for whom he made a first team bow at the tender age of seventeen. The classy Sissons combined a brilliant left foot with a great turn of pace and the former England schools and Youth International – he netted four goals on his debut for the former – became the youngest scorer in an F.A.Cup Final when he netted, aged just 18, in the Hammers win over Preston in 1964. A year later he earned a European Cup Winners Cup medal and looked set for a glittering career in the top-flight after adding ten England U-23 caps to his roll of honours. However despite this trophy laden start to his senior career Sissons never really maintained his outstanding early standards and after 265 appearances for West Ham he was allowed to leave for Wednesday, following protracted negotiations.

He missed only a handful of games in his first three years at Wednesday and held the distinction as the last Owls player before Steve Maclean to score an away league hat trick when he grabbed a treble in the 5-3 February 1972 defeat at Burnley. In his final season at Hillsborough the left-sided attacker suffered, like so many of his team mates, with illness and injury and four days after Derek Dooley was sensationally sacked Sissons was also packing his bags, moving back to the top-flight with Norwich City. However his stay in Norfolk was brief and after just three goals in 21 games he returned to London after City were relegated from Division One. He would make only eleven appearances for his next club, Chelsea, and later swapped reserve team football for the sunnier climes of Tampa Bay where in 1975 he helped the U.S club to win both the Eastern Division Championship and the Soccer Bowl.

On his return to Chelsea his contract was cancelled and the player who ex-Hammers boss Ron Greenwood described in his autobiography as "having rare gifts, including a left foot that was a miracle" was without a club. He then accepted an offer to play in South Africa and has resided in the Southern Hemisphere ever since, playing for Cape Town until 1983 when he retired at the age of 38. He is now a partner in a motor products and warranty company and keeps fit by biking to work every day while also regularly entering cycle races, one being the Argus 65 mile race. Sadly his medals from both the F.A.Cup and Cup Winners Cup successes were stolen from his South African home to leave Sissons with just memories from a glorious spell in his playing career.

SLATER, John Brian 1951-54

Born: 20 October 1932 Sheffield
(5ft 9ins, 10st 12lbs – 1953)
Died: 13 September 1999 Sheffield
Debut: 27 December 1952
v West Bromwich Albion
Division One Away
Last Appearance: 18 April 1953
v Aston Villa
Division One Away
Total League
& Cup Appearances: 3 Goals: 0

Career Details:

Lower Handsworth Community Assoc.		1948
WEDNESDAY	16 June	1951
Grimsby Town	July	1954 £500
Rotherham United	September	1955 Free
Chesterfield	June	1957 £1,000
Burton Albion		1958
Denaby United		1959
Thorne Colliery		1962
Heeley Amateurs		1966

Pacy inside forward who first joined Wednesday in 1948 when he signed amateur forms following a successful trial. At the time he was a raw sixteen year-old kid who in the 1948-9 season would score an amazing 104 goals in just 34 games for his local side, including a ten-goal haul, eight, two sevens, six, five, six fours and five hat tricks!! While still on the Owls books he started work as an apprentice Patternmaker and continued his remarkable scoring when netting twelve times in one game for his works side in the local Drake League, receiving a Cup for his feat. His reserve team debut for Wednesday came in April 1951 and soon after Slater signed as a part-time professional at Hillsborough although it was not until the 1952-3 campaign that he became a regular at second team level. His first team debut came alongside fellow new boy David Storrar in a 1-0 win at the Hawthorns but with competition from Red Froggatt and Jackie Sewell it proved impossible for Slater to retain his first team place.

After completing his apprenticeship in 1954 Slater moved to Grimsby Town for a small fee but he then had to serve his two years National Service, restricting his appearances for the Mariners to just four games. He was eventually released on a free transfer while still serving in the forces and went on to score five times in 17 games for Rotherham United before ending his league playing days at Chesterfield. A solitary season followed at non-league Burton Albion where despite Brian scoring nine times in 31 games his new club finished bottom of the North-West Division of the Southern League. He left after financial problems caused by Burton's move to their new Eton Park home ground resulted in the club asking for the players to take substantial pay cuts. He remained a professional player at both Denaby United and Thorne Colliery before in 1966 he was granted permission by the Football Association to play as an amateur for Heeley Friends – in those days ex-professionals were required to obtain an amateur permit if they wished to play without remuneration. He was actually player-manager with Heeley and continued to turn out until a serious leg injury ended his football career in 1972.

After finishing as a professional he had gained employment as an engineering patternmaker while after his football days came to a close he turned to his other sporting love – cricket. After playing to a high standard with Hallam Cricket Club he started an association with Whiston Parish Church Cricket Club that would last for the remainder of his life, Brian being the team's star player in the South Riding Division of the Yorkshire Council competition. He also worked tirelessly behind the scenes with his wife Sheila and helped the club build their new pavilion - his spouse still helps with the teas on matchdays. He would continue to play cricket well into his fifties – representing Yorkshire in the over-50s County Championship and touring Spain on several occasions – while away from the game he worked for British Steel at Renishaw before ending his working life as a self-employed carpenter who fitted household kitchens. Sadly he lost a three-month battle against cancer just before the dawn of the new millennium.

SLAVIN, Hugh 1904-10

Born: 1883/84 Kirkdale, Liverpool
(5ft 10ins, 12st 6lbs – 1904)
Debut: 26 November 1904
v Manchester City
Division One Home
Last Appearance: 25 September 1909
v Tottenham Hotspur
Division One Away
Total League
& Cup Appearances: 55 Goals: 0

Career Details:

Birkenhead FC		
WEDNESDAY	May	1904 £120*

*Joint fee with Chris Dodds

Unlike the majority of his contemporaries Hugh Slavin began his working life in the classroom, being employed in Liverpool as a teacher at the tender age of eighteen. It was his form for his local amateur side that attracted the Owls attention and at the age of 21 he moved across the Pennines to join a Wednesday team that were celebrating their second successive league championship. However the move to Sheffield did not mean his teaching days came to an end as Slavin continued in the profession, working during his Wednesday playing career at Sheffield school St Wilfred's. During his time on the Owls books he mainly played the role of understudy to legendary right back Willie Layton – but also showed his versatility by regularly being called upon to play at left back, usually when Harry Burton was absent.

His best run in the side came during his first full season, playing thirteen games as Layton's replacement, while even though he was never a first choice Slavin gave the club loyal service before retiring from the game to concentrate on his career outside of the game. After ending his playing days Slavin became a popular teacher and sportsman in the Sheffield area – he had joined the Sheffield Schools Athletics Association in 1904 – and was trainer of the Sheffield boys side during the mid-1920s, leading the youngsters to the prestigious English Schools Trophy in 1925. His standing in the City was further enhanced when he became Chairman of the Yorkshire County Schools Association and in March 1927 he was elected to the English Schools Football Association.

SLYNN, Frank 1946-50

Born: 10 February 1924 Birmingham
(5ft 9ins, 11st 6lbs – 1948)
Debut: 23 November 1946
v Birmingham City
Division Two Away
Last Appearance: 9 September 1950
v Charlton Athletic
Division One Home
Total League
& Cup Appearances: 46 Goals: 5

Career Details:

Birmingham City		Amat.
Batchelor Sports		
WEDNESDAY	September	1946 Free
Bury	30 November	1950 £5,000
Walsall	18 September	1953 Free
Stocksbridge Works		1954

After spending fours years in the Navy during the Second World War Frank Slynn returned to his Birmingham home and was subsequently spotted by Wednesday playing in his works side. The halfback was invited to Hillsborough for a trial but in a practice game the regular outside left, Charlie Tomlinson, was injured and Frank was asked to fill the role. He revelled in the new position and after signing a professional contract he quickly made his senior debut, against his hometown club, and was an automatic choice on the left for the remainder of the 1946-7 season. He started the following season as first choice but unfortunately his Wednesday career ran aground on Boxing 1947 when he suffered a double fracture of his right leg in the home game with West Ham United.

It was not until November 1948 that Slynn returned to action, for the reserves, and fierce competition from the likes of Jackie Marriott, Dennis Woodhead and Walter Rickett meant he simply could not regain his first team place – he appeared in only two more first team games after the leg break, both at wing half. After moving to Bury he appeared in a further 41 league games, showing his versatility by playing at halfback, full back and on the left wing. After ten games at Walsall he returned to Sheffield to gain employment at Samuel Fox's Steelworks, continuing to play football for the highly successful Works side that swept all before them in the mid-1950s. He later coached Stocksbridge Works – recommending Peter Eustace to Wednesday – and worked in the Melting Shop at the Steelworks until his retirement in 1989.

SMAILES, Andrew 1922-23

Born: 21 May 1895 Radcliffe, Northumberland
(5ft 9ins, 11st 4lbs – 1922)
Died: Q/E December 1978 Shepton Mallet, Somerset
Debut: 14 October 1922
v Fulham
Division Two Away
Last Appearance: 29 September 1923
v Fulham
Division Two Away
Total League
& Cup Appearances: 40 Goals: 15

Career Details:

Blyth Spartans		
Newcastle United	October	1919 £300
WEDNESDAY	13 October	1922 £1,500
Bristol City	18 October	1923*
Rotherham United	August	1929

*Exchange for William Walker

When Wednesday manager Bob Brown signed inside forward Andy Smailes from Newcastle United it seemed his search for a long-term replacement for the sorely missed Andrew Wilson was finally at an end. However despite the newcomer netting fifteen times in his debut season he dramatically fell out of favour at the beginning of the 1923-34 campaign, losing his place to Charlie Petrie, and prior to his transfer was actually utilised at left halfback!

His career had started as an amateur at Northeast non-league giants Blyth Spartans and after serving in the Army, mainly in Egypt, during the Great War he was signed by Newcastle United. The sturdy and pacy attacker was an immediate hit at St.James' Park and netted 30 times in 77 games, including a memorable hat trick against fierce rivals Sunderland, before losing his first team place at the start of the 1922-23 season. After his brief spell at Hillsborough Smailes suffered relegation in his first season with Bristol City, despite netting seven goals, but was ever present in the next season, appearing at halfback as City finished third in the Third Division (South). In 1927 he helped City back into Division Two before returning to Yorkshire, signing for Rotherham United.

This would start a long association with the Millmoor club, which saw Andy play for a further three years before being appointed trainer in August 1932. He remained in the role for exactly twenty years, working alongside former team mate and Army colleague Reg Freeman, and helped the Millers to the Division Three (North) title in 1951. After Freeman moved to Sheffield United in 1952, Smailes was appointed manager and in 1955 led Rotherham to the highest ever league position in their entire history – they finished third in the old Second Division with only goal average stopping the Millers from joining the big boys in the top-flight. His charges struggled to emulate that high finish over the seasons that followed and eventually after a string of poor results Smailes resigned his position in October 1958, becoming the Yorkshire scout for Middlesbrough. Four months later Smailes – who was related to the famous Charlton football family through marriage – was appointed boss at non-league Scarborough where he stayed until retiring in February 1961, after almost 45 years in professional football.

SMELT, John William — 1921

Born: Q/E December 1895 Rotherham
(5ft 8ins, 11st 7lbs – 1921)
Died: Q/E September 1968
Debut:
5 February 1921 v Blackpool Division Two Away
Last Appearance:
29 August 1921 v Derby County Division Two Away
Total League & Cup Appearances: 16 Goals: 2

Career Details:

Mansfield Mechanics		
Chesterfield Municipal		1914
Rotherham County	September	1919
Portsmouth	September	1920
WEDNESDAY	January	1921 Free
Bangor City	December	1921
Barrow		1922
Thatched House FC		
Bradgate W.M.C.	November	1927

The Owls search for a quality right-winger in the early 1920s led to the arrival on trial of John Smelt in January 1921. He came to Hillsborough after spells at a variety of senior non-league sides and at his previous club, Portsmouth, had actually appeared in three games in goal as well as in his usual forward role. He impressed immediately at Wednesday and went straight into the club's Division Two side, solving the problem position that had existed since pre war days. However by the end of the year Smelt was relegated to Midland League football and eventually travelled to Bangor City with a transfer looking likely – he actually signed as player-coach for the Welsh club without the Owls permission. The move went through though and he ended his playing career at Barrow, playing alongside his brother, Len, who played league football for several clubs including Burnley and Chesterfield.

SMITH, Dean — 2003-04

Born: 19 March 1971 West Bromwich
(6ft 1ins, 12st 10lbs – 2003)
Debut: 22 February 2003
v Crystal Palace
Division One Away
Last Appearance: 8 May 2004
v Queens Park Rangers
Division Two Home
Total League
& Cup Appearances: 61+1 Goals: 1

Career Details:

Bayliss Colts		
Admiral Colts		
Vine Athletic		
Walsall	1 July	1989
Hereford United	17 June	1994 £75,000
Leyton Orient	2 June	1997 £42,500 (T)
WEDNESDAY	21 February	2003 Free
Released	30 June	2004
Port Vale	5 July	2004 Free

Old fashioned stopper who had spent his entire career in the lower divisions before he was surprisingly signed by Chris Turner to aid the Owls battle against relegation in 2003. Just six days before he signed for the Owls, Smith had appeared in his 600th senior game and was a veritable rock at the heart of Leyton Orient's defence for almost seven years, captaining them in two Division Three play off finals, losing to Scunthorpe in 1999 and Blackpool two years later. He was considered by O's boss Paul Brush as the best defender in the Third Division and in September 2001 a large fee-plus-player deal was rebuffed from ambitious league new boys Rushden & Diamonds.

His career had started as a trainee at Walsall in July 1989 and after breaking into the first team he appeared in 166 games for the Saddlers before becoming Hereford United's record signing. He spent three years at Edgar Street but following the club's last day relegation from the Football League in 1997 he was quickly snapped up by Leyton Orient although the move left Hereford boss Graham Turner furious after a transfer tribunal ordered the Londoners to pay less than a quarter of the £200,000 fee, after they took the new Bosman ruling into consideration. His no-nonsense play, allied with quick anticipation and good reading of the game, meant Smith was an almost ever present at Brisbane Road and fans were disappointed when he turned down a new one-year deal to move into the second tier of the English game for the first time in the twilight of his career – he departed after 288 appearances for Orient.

After signing an eighteen-month deal at Hillsborough he impressed Owls fans with his displays but could not help stave off relegation in that debut season and although he was a regular in the terrible 2003-4 season his form was inconsistent and it was no surprise that he was one of the thirteen players released by the club at the end of their contracts. He eventually joined Port Vale on a trial basis, later signing a one-year deal with the League One club. However he stayed only six months and in early January 2005 decided to retire from playing to take up a role as Youth Coach back at Leyton Orient – his final league game coming against the Owls at Vale Park on 28 December 2004.

SMITH, James 'Jim' — 1883-93

Born: 11 April 1863 Sheffield
(5ft 9½ins, 12st – 1890)
Died: Q/E December 1937 Sheffield
Debut: 8 November 1884
v Long Eaton Rangers F.A.Cup Away
Last Appearance: 13 February 1892
v West Bromwich Albion F.A.Cup Home
Total League
& Cup Appearances: 22* Goals: 0
***Also appeared in**
57 Football Alliance League games

Career Details:

All Saints Wanderers		
Nether Club		
WEDNESDAY	December	1883
Rotherham County		1893

Without doubt Jim Smith was the greatest Wednesday keeper of their pre league years, being an almost ever present as Wednesday became established as a major force in the North of England. His playing career had started in local Sheffield football before being drafted into the Wednesday side for a Bramall Lane friendly against Darwen in December 1883. By the end of 1880s the brave goalie – who played under the name of Smith although his surname was actually Clarke – had helped Wednesday to two Sheffield Challenge Cups and two Wharncliffe Charity Cups while also appearing in 22 consecutive F.A.Cup ties.

One of those English Cup ties was the Owls first ever appearance in the final in 1890 while he had already recorded another first when lining up for the opening game at Olive Grove three years earlier. When the Owls were founder members of Football Alliance League in 1889 Jim was ever present as the club won the inaugural Championship and he remained first choice until Wednesday were voted into the Football League in 1892. He was also a real character, as during games he would smoke a clay pipe with a broken stem and when his goal came under pressure would throw it into the back of the goal! Away from football he was also a fine cinder track runner, winning many races from 100 to 300 yards, while his popularity at Wednesday was shown when his benefit game (English v Scotch in April 1893) raised the not inconsiderable sum of almost £120. After losing his first team place Jim made the occasional reserve team appearance during the 1892-3 campaign before leaving for neighbours Rotherham County.

Throughout his football career he worked in Sheffield's East End as a steel melter at the Atlas Works of John Brown & Company. He eventually became melting shop manager and was a founder member of the Atlas & Norfolk Works sports club.

SMITH, John 'Jock' — 1893-94

Born: Ayrshire, Scotland
Died: 3 February 1911 Newcastle
Debut: 2 September 1893 v Sunderland Division One Home
Last Appearance: 26 December 1893 v Burnley Division One Home
Total League & Cup Appearances: 18 Goals: 1

Career Details:

Kilmarnock		1885
Newcastle East End		1887
Kilmarnock		1887
Sunderland	August	1889
Liverpool	May	1893
WEDNESDAY		1893
Newcastle United		1894

Inside forward who played both league and pre-league football for Sunderland after arriving from Scottish football. While in Sunderland colours he won a League Championship medal in 1892 but after failing to make a senior appearance for Liverpool he struggled to regain his form after moving to Olive Grove in 1893, scoring only one goal as Wednesday slumped to the lower reaches of the First Division. His final games were played at centre forward and his Owls career was effectively over when Harry Davis was switched to the No.9 shirt. After leaving Wednesday he played a solitary game for old side Kilmarnock, ironically against Sunderland, and in 1898 he became a licensee before his untimely death through illness.

SMITH, John Thomas 'Tom' 1935

Born: 8 April 1915 Chester Moor
(5ft 7½ins, 12st 12lbs – 1935)
Only Appearance: 28 January 1935
v Blackburn Rovers
Division One Home
Total League
& Cup Appearances: 1 Goals: 0

Career Details:

Lochside United		
Annfield Plain		
West Stanley		1931
Blyth Spartans		1931
Blackpool	February	1933
Blyth Spartans	June	1934
West Stanley	October	1934
WEDNESDAY	15 January	1935 £10
Gateshead	July	1937

Pacy attacker Tom Smith possessed a great shot and made an immediate impact after signing from non-league football, netting a hat trick in a reserve game against Newcastle at Hillsborough. He had played in the same South Northumberland schools side as Jackie Thompson and at the age of just sixteen was appearing for West Stanley in the highly competitive North-Eastern League. He was eventually snapped up by a league side in 1933 but for family reasons he returned home after just a few weeks at Blackpool, scoring 34 times for West Stanley during the remainder of the season. He netted another 21 times in the following season, which prompted Billy Walker to bring Smith to Hillsborough.

However despite making the aforementioned impact in Central League football he was given only one senior game in an Owls shirt – a 2-2 home draw with Blackburn – and over the next two seasons he became almost a forgotten man at Hillsborough, appearing only occasionally in reserve team football. A move to league club Gateshead certainly revived his career as Tom scored an impressive 33 goals in only 49 games for the northeast club, finishing top scorer in his debut season with 24 and netting two hat tricks in the following campaign despite playing only thirteen games. His career came to a close when war was declared in 1939 and Tom – who due to his bulky frame was nicknamed 'Gunboat' at Hillsborough – served in the Army for the duration. Sadly while in Italy he was run over by a tank but thankfully he recovered to take over a hotel in the Northeast and whenever Wednesday were playing in the area he would always go and support his old side.

SMITH, Mark Craig 1978-87

Born: 21 March 1960 Sheffield
(6ft, 12st 6lbs – 1978)
Debut: 29 April 1978
v Colchester United
Division Three Away
Last Appearance: 9 May 1987
v Wimbledon
Division One Home
Total League
& Cup Appearances: 349+1 Goals: 20

Career Details:

Middlewood Rovers		
WEDNESDAY	21 March	1978
Plymouth Argyle	22 July	1987 £170,000
Barnsley	16 November	1989 £145,000
Notts County	2 October	1992 £70,000
Port Vale	25 January	1993 Loan
Huddersfield Town	25 February	1993 Loan
Chesterfield	25 March	1993 Loan
Lincoln City	1 August	1993 Loan

CAPS (@SWFC)
England U-21 (5) v Eire 25/02/81, Romania 28/04/81, v Switzerland 30/05/81, v Hungary 05/06/81, v Poland 07/04/82

Stylish centre half Mark Smith started training with Wednesday at the tender age of eleven and after several seasons with the club's nursery side, Middlewood Rovers, he was elevated to apprentice status with his boyhood favourites in July 1976. The former Sheffield boys player had also trained occasionally with neighbours Sheffield United – he was a ball boy at Bramall Lane on several occasions – but after leaving school he soon became a regular at youth level for Wednesday, especially after Owls youth coach Ken Knighton switched the young Smith from midfield to defence. The positional change proved the making of Smith and after breaking into the first team under Jack Charlton he would remain a fixture in the side until the mid-1980s, helping Wednesday climb back into the top-flight of the English game.

He is perhaps best remembered for only his second season as a regular at Wednesday when a remarkable sequence saw the classy and reliable Smith score eleven times from the penalty spot, as well as missing a further two – he was also named in the Third Division PFA team. During that promotion season he netted over half of his career goals for the club and broke the seasonal club record held by pre-war star Jack Ball. His form in the higher grade then saw Mark rewarded with U-21 caps for his country and by the time Wednesday earned promotion from Division Two in 1984 Smith was a firm favourite with Owls fans and recognised as one of the best defenders outside of the top-flight. Incidentally he had almost left a year earlier after rejecting a new contract but decided to stay, signing a new three-year deal.

Competition from the likes of Mick Lyons and Lawrie Madden meant Smith was in and out of the side during the latter years of his Wednesday career but he seemed set to remain at Hillsborough after winning his team first place back at the end of the 1986-7 season. However despite having enjoying a successful testimonial season he twice asked for a transfer and after rejecting terms in June 1987 left soon after for Plymouth Argyle – the Pilgrims paying a club record fee for his services. Smith – whose grandfather Ted Green was a top amateur footballer – was a regular at the Southwest club for over two seasons, appearing in 97 games, before moving back to South Yorkshire to sign for Barnsley. He added a further 120 games to his career tally while at Oakwell and scored a goal in front of the Kop end on a rare visit back to Wednesday in April 1991. After ending his playing days at Notts County he moved into coaching at Lincoln City, being appointed youth team boss in 1994, before returning to Meadow Lane to take over as reserve team manager. He was caretaker manager for a few weeks before being appointed assistant manager to new boss Sam Allardyce in January 1997 and continued his tour of his old clubs when returning to Barnsley in August 1998 as reserve team manager. He later enjoyed great success with the Tykes Academy side –finishing league runners-up and reaching the F.A.Youth Cup semi-finals in 2003 - before coming home to

Wednesday on 1st July 2003 as Academy coach. Following Chris Turner's departure in September 2004 he was appointed caretaker manager for the second time in his career. Made a huge impression at Wednesday, leading the youth side to second place in 2005.

SMITH, Norman 1927-30

Born: 12 December 1897 Newburn
(5ft 8ins, 11st 3lbs – 1927)
Died: 18 May 1978 Newcastle
Debut: 17 December 1927
v Sunderland
Division One Home
Last Appearance: 21 April 1928
v Portsmouth
Division One Home
Total League
& Cup Appearances: 23 Goals: 0

Career Details:

Ryton United		
Mickley Athletic		
Bolton Wanderers	February	1921
Newburn	September	1921
Huddersfield Town	April	1923
WEDNESDAY	16 December	1927 £1,600
Queens Park Rangers	15 August	1930 £300
Kseuzlingen	August	1932

Despite spending almost ten years as a professional footballer it was as a trainer and coach that Norman Smith made his name, spending 23 years at Newcastle United during which time the Geordies won the F.A.Cup three times while also training both the England and Football League representative side. He was appointed trainer at St.James Park in July 1938 after returning home from a spell in Swiss football where initially he was player-coach at Kseuzlingen before training St Gallen – his time abroad meaning Smith was fluent in the German language. To reward his loyal service Smith was awarded a testimonial by Newcastle in 1959 while in October 1961, at the age of 63, he was surprisingly appointed manager after Charlie Mitten was dismissed. Despite helping United avoid relegation his tenure lasted only 25 games and after being released in June 1962 he retired from the game. After leaving St James' Park he continued to watch the team purely as a fan and in fact was walking home from a game in 1978 when he tragically collapsed and later died.

He had previously experienced a somewhat chequered playing career, which began in schools football and led to Smith representing Northumberland boys and appearing in a Schoolboy International at Leeds at the age of 12. However he then inexplicably gave up football completely until joining Durham based amateur club Ryton at the age of eighteen! A brief spell at Bolton Wanderers ended when he returned to his amateur side but Norman did eventually break into league football in the guise of a hard working halfback/utility player. He was generally a reserve team player at Huddersfield – appearing in 24 games in the three seasons when the terriers completed a hat-trick of First Division Championships – and after briefly enjoying a run of first team football at Hillsborough, Smith again had to be content with reserve team soccer, helping the Owls to the Central League title in 1928-9. After leaving Wednesday he was captain at Queens Park Rangers before launching his coaching career on mainland Europe.

SMITH, Ian Paul 2003-05

Born: 22 January 1976 Easington
(6ft, 13st 3lbs – 2003)
Debut: 25 August 2003
v Wrexham
Division Two Home
Last Appearance: 17 October 2004
v Barnsley
League One Home
Total League
& Cup Appearances: 23+8 Goals: 2

Career Details:

Burnley	10 July	1994
Oldham Athletic	22 September	2000 Loan
Torquay United		2001 Trial
Hartlepool United	1 November	2001 Free
WEDNESDAY	1 July	2003 Free
Released	30 June	2005

Left winger who was on the Owls books as a schoolboy until the club decided to sign Lee Briscoe as a trainee. In 1992 he signed apprentice forms for Burnley and after breaking into the senior ranks he appeared in 125 games for the Turf Moor club although a succession of injuries limited his opportunities. The former Peterlee boys player would be dogged by injuries throughout his career and this poor luck was apparent whilst on trial at Oldham as Smith fell down a manhole and suffered such a badly cut leg that he was forced to return to Turf Moor!

His luck finally improved after Chris Turner signed him for Hartlepool United and he was actually ever present in his debut season as United lost on penalties in the Division Three play off semi finals. His undoubted quality on the ball shone through in the lower division but the injury jinx struck again during Hartlepool's promotion season of 2002-03 – Smith starting only fifteen games plus a further nine as substitute. Considering his fitness record it was perhaps surprising when Chris Turner captured his signature for a second time and the doubts of Owls fans were proven as the totally left footed attacker spent three spells on the sidelines in an injury plagued first season at Hillsborough – a stress fracture of the foot eventually ending his season in February 2004. At Hartlepool he created 45 goals in 64 games and at times did impress in an Owls shirt, mainly with some quality centres from the left wing. However he suffered from a lack of pace and tackling ability which meant he struggled to convince a sceptical Wednesday crowd of his qualities. His injury problems continued in 2004-5 when after impressing fans with his displays from left back he suffered a knee ligament injury that eventually saw Smith miss the rest of the season.

SMITH, Royston Leonard 'Roy' 1936-48

Born: 22 September 1916 Shirebrook
(5ft 11ins, 11st 6lbs – 1936)
Debut: 26 March 1937
v Bolton Wanderers
Division One Away
Last Appearance: 29 March 1948
v Chesterfield
Division Two Home
Total League
& Cup Appearances: 97* Goals: 0
***Also appeared in 24 wartime games**

Career Details:

Selby Town		
WEDNESDAY	8 May	1936 £10
Notts County	16 December	1948 £2,500

Goalkeeper who was one of only a handful of players to appear for the Owls either side of the Second World War. He originally joined from Yorkshire League champions Selby Town, as a possible successor to the great Jack Brown, and it was Brown who he replaced for the final games of the 1936-7 campaign as Wednesday slipped out of the old First Division. However due to the excellent form of fellow new boy Derwick Goodfellow the Derbyshire born stopper then spent eighteen months in the shadows, appearing only occasionally until getting his first team chance when his rival was struck down with illness.

Unfortunately just when he seemed to have cemented his first team place the war in Europe put an end to national football and saw Roy serve abroad with the R.A.M.C. Before being posted overseas he made a handful of appearances for the club in wartime soccer and when the Football League restarted in 1946 he began as the Owls No.1, appearing in 35 games during the traumatic 1946-7 season. This remained the case until Albert Morton nudged him temporarily out of the side but then a youngster by the name of Dave McIntosh forced him into the shadows permanently and he later moved to Division Three (South) club Notts County. He would enjoy five successful years at the Meadow Lane club – apart from a return to Hillsborough in November 1951 when Derek Dooley crashed five goals past him – and won a Championship medal in 1950. After 110 league games for the league's oldest club he retired in 1952.

SMITH, Wilfred Samuel 'Wilf' 1963-70

Born: 3 September 1946 Neumünster, Germany
(5ft 10ins, 11st 3lbs – 1966)
Debut: 19 December 1964
v Blackpool
Division One Home
Last Appearance: 15 August 1970
v Charlton Athletic
Division Two Home
Total League
& Cup Appearances: 234 Goals: 5

Career Details:

WEDNESDAY	4 September	1963
Coventry City	31 August	1970 £100,000
Brighton & Hove Albion	14 October	1974 Loan
Millwall	16 January	1975 Loan
Bristol Rovers	4 March	1975 £25,000
Chesterfield	November	1976
Atherstone United	July	1977

CAPS (@SWFC)
England U-23 (6) v Portugal 16/04/69, v Holland 22/05/69, v Portugal 28/05/69, v Wales 01/10/69, v Scotland 04/03/70, v Bulgaria 08/04/70

Football League (3) v League of Ireland 08/11/67, v Scottish League 26/03/69, v Scottish League 18/03/70
Youth (6) v Scotland, Belgium, Spain, Hungary, Italy, E.Germany (64/5)

Although Wilf Smith spent the majority of his early years in Sheffield, attending Pipworth Road School, he was actually born in Germany and was originally christened Wolfgang! His father was in the Army in Germany and after marrying a native girl he returned to England where it was decided to change the infant's forename by deed poll to Wilfred, to help him settle more easily. The family duly made Sheffield their home and Wilf excelled in swimming, cricket and football – he captained Sheffield, Yorkshire and England boys in the latter discipline. His superb displays for city, county and country alerted several clubs to his talents but after turning down an approach from Sheffield United he instead decided to start his working life as an apprentice electrician for the English Steel corporation.

However soon after leaving school, aged 14, he signed amateur forms for Wednesday and on his fifteenth birthday was elevated to apprentice status. Smith was quick, strong in the tackle and loved to get forward and it was these qualities that earned him a first team call up aged just eighteen, replacing the injured Gerry Young at left halfback. However it was at right back that Smith would excel, playing in the epic 1966 F.A.Cup Final loss to Everton and appearing in over two hundred top-flight games for the Owls. A multitude of representative honours also came his way but relegation in 1970 proved a bitter blow to the Owls chances of keeping their prize asset and 24 hours after a big money move to Chelsea fell through he became Britain's costliest full back when a six-figure fee took him back into the First Division with Coventry City.

He maintained his fine form at Highfield Road, playing 151 times for the Sky Blues, before being signed by former teammate Don Megson at Bristol Rovers. His final league side proved to be Chesterfield where an ankle injury and disagreements over its treatment led to his retirement from the full time game at the relatively young age of 31, following a major operation on his ankle. He was later persuaded to return to the game at non-league Atherstone United but after six months retired completely to pursue his business interests. After severing his links with football Wilf has forged a successful career in retail and now owns two stores in the Leicestershire area, selling household and garden goods.

SMITH, William Sheil 1927-33

Born: 22 October 1903 South Shields
(5ft 8½ins, 11st 7lbs – 1927)
Debut: 1 February 1930
v Sheffield United
Division One Home
Last Appearance: 1 April 1933
v Chelsea
Division One Home
Total League
& Cup Appearances: 29 Goals: 1

Career Details:

Tyneside Juniors		
Jarrow		
WEDNESDAY	25 June	1927 £50
Brentford	May	1933 £250
Crystal Palace	27 October	1933
Burnley	May	1936
Accrington Stanley	June	1939

Halfback William Smith was yet another player to arrive from regular pre war source Jarrow FC. He was signed primarily as understudy to the great Billy Marsden and appeared on three occasions as a replacement for the England international. When Marsden was sadly forced to retire Smith was given a first team chance but he was soon disposed by Charles Wilson and then kept out of the side by newcomer Gavin Malloch, his best run in the team occurring in 1931-2 when he started seventeen games.

After failing to become a first team regular at Hillsborough he subsequently moved to Brentford but made only one appearance before transferring across London to sign for Crystal Palace. Forty-one games followed for Palace and he was also a regular at his next club, Burnley, where he was in the Clarets side that dumped Wednesday out of the F.A.Cup in January 1938. Joined Accrington Stanley in the summer of 1939 but after starting the first game of the new Football League season his career in senior football came to an end as the outbreak of war saw National soccer mothballed.

SNODIN, Glynn 1985-87

Born: 14 February 1960 Thrybergh, Rotherham
(5ft 6ins, 9st 5lbs – 1985)
Debut: 21 September 1985
v Tottenham Hotspur
Division One Away
Last Appearance: 25 April 1987
v Luton Town
Division One Away
Total League
& Cup Appearances: 65+9 Goals: 1

Career Details:

Doncaster Rovers	1 October	1977
WEDNESDAY	11 June	1985 £135,000
Leeds United	31 July	1987 £150,000
Oldham Athletic	15 August	1991 Loan
Rotherham United	28 February	1992 Loan
Heart of Midlothian	31 March	1992 Free
Barnsley	23 July	1993 Free
Carlisle United	July	1995
Gainsborough Trinity		1995

Diminutive Glynn Snodin and his brother Ian will always be inexorably associated with their first club Doncaster Rovers, the siblings playing a combined total of over 500 games for Rovers. Although later in his career Glynn was considered somewhat of a utility player he appeared as a left sided midfielder for Donny, appearing in 343 games, after having signed as an apprentice back in 1976. The former Rotherham boys player also boasted a tremendous scoring record at Belle Vue, netting 59 times, and was in fact top scorer for two seasons in the early 1980s before Howard Wilkinson took him to Hillsborough.

He had actually supported Wednesday as a youngster and his debut for the club came at left back, as replacement for the injured Nigel Worthington. He remained in the position for several games before being pushed into his usual midfield role when the Irishman returned to the side. He took the step from the lower divisions into top-flight football in his stride and enjoyed a tremendous first season as Wednesday finished fifth and reached the semi-finals of the F.A.Cup – his form was such that he was named in the provisional 40-man squad for the 1986 World Cup Finals in Mexico although he failed to make the final squad of 22. He remained an automatic choice at Hillsborough in his second season but the lure of re-joining old Rovers boss Billy Bremner at Second Division Leeds United proved too strong and Owls fans were disappointed and surprised when he left for Elland Road.

He remained for five years at United but appeared in only four games as Howard Wilkinson led the 'Whites' to the Second Division title in 1990 and failed to make an appearance two seasons later when the First Division Championship came to West Yorkshire. He eventually moved to Scottish football and proved a big hit with Hearts fans before he returned to South Yorkshire after Joe Jordan was sacked as Tyncastle manager. After starting his career at Oakwell as first choice left back a series of injuries ruined his season and after being released in the following summer he took his first step on the coaching ladder when joining Carlisle United in a player-coach role. He appeared in only a handful of reserve team games for United – also appearing for Northern Premier League Gainsborough when time allowed – whilst achieving his main aim of qualifying as an F.A.coach. In July 1996 he was appointed Youth coach at Scarborough before making an emotional return to Belle Vue, as assistant manager to his brother Ian, in September 1998. Whilst at Rovers he helped them to consecutive Conference League Cups in 1999 and 2000 but poor league form saw the 'dream' duo sacked in April 2000. Two months later he was appointed coach/reserve team manager at Premier League Charlton Athletic, a position he holds today.

SOLTVEDT, Trond Egil 2001-03

Born: 15 February 1967 Voss, Norway
(6ft 2ins, 12st 6lbs – 2000)
Debut: 13 February 2001
v Tranmere Rovers
Division One Home
Last Appearance: 11 January 2003
v Reading
Division One Home
Total League
& Cup Appearances: 81 Goals: 4

Career Details:

Dale		
NY-Krohnborg		
Viking Stavanger		
Brann Bergen		1992
Stoke City		1992 Trial
Rosenborg		1995
Coventry City	24 July	1997 £500,000
Southampton	17 August	1999 £300,000
WEDNESDAY	12 February	2001 Loan
WEDNESDAY	22 March	2001 £200,000*
Brann Bergen	June	2003
Hovding		2004

* £100k after 30 appearances & £100k after 60 games

Tall, hard-working ex-Norwegian International Trond Soltvedt must have wondered what he had walked into when joining the Owls on loan as on the day he signed both manager and chairman left the club! Although signed by Paul Jewell it was caretaker manager Peter Shreeves who gave Soltvedt his Owls debut and along with fellow new boy Carlton Palmer his influence was crucial as the Owls climbed out of relegation trouble to finish the season away from danger. He was appointed captain for the following season and although primarily a midfielder he did drop back, with great success, into central defence as Wednesday avoided the dreaded drop and also reached the semi-finals of the League Cup. Unfortunately injury meant he missed the second half of the following season and after Wednesday were relegated he left to re-join his old club Brann Bergen. He later took over as player-manager at Third Division club Hovding before retiring from playing in November 2004, at the end of the 2004 Norwegian season.

His playing career had started in his native Norway where he initially worked as bricklayer in the summer months while playing for Viking Stavanger. He later trained for two years to be an electrician but eventually signed for Brann Bergen where Trond won a league and cup double before a successful trial at the English club he supported as a boy, Stoke City. He was offered a contract by then City boss Lou Macari but decided he did not want to stay and returned home. After joining Rosenborg he became the first player to win the domestic double with two different sides – at the time he was still semi-professional, working for a computer firm. The inevitable move to English football finally occurred when he joined top-flight Coventry City and he was an almost ever present for two seasons before moving to the Dell after 69 games for the Sky Blues. He struggled with injuries at Southampton and after failing to become established moved to Hillsborough on loan after Glenn Hoddle replaced Dave Jones as Saints manager.

SONNER, Daniel James 'Danny' 1998-2000

Born: 9 January 1972 Wigan
(5ft 11ins, 12st 8lbs – 1998)
Debut: 18 October 1998
v Coventry City
Premier League Away
Last Appearance: 14 May 2000
v Leicester City
Premier League Home
Total League
& Cup Appearances: 49+14 Goals: 4

Career Details:

Wigan St Jude's		
Wigan Athletic		Trainee
Burnley	6 August	1990
Bury	21 November	1992 Loan
Preussen Köln	July	1993 Free
FC Erzgebirge	August	1995 Free
Ipswich Town	12 June	1996 Free
WEDNESDAY	14 October	1998 £75,000
Birmingham City	4 August	2000 Free
Wolverhampton Wanderers	July	2002 Trial
Walsall	5 August	2002 Free
Contract cancelled	10 April	2003
Nottingham Forest	4 August	2003 Free
Released	30 June	2004
Kidderminster Harriers	July	2004 Trial
Peterborough United	13 August	2004 Free
Port Vale	21 February	2005

CAPS (@ SWFC)
N.Ireland Full (5) v Germany 27/03/99, v Canada 27/04/99, v Luxembourg 23/02/00, v Malta 29/03/00, v Hungary 25/04/00

N.Ireland 'B' (1) v Wales 09/02/99

When Danny Sonner arrived at Wednesday he was a virtual unknown to the Hillsborough faithful and the move was questioned as the adopted Irishman arrived from the reserve team of a club in a division lower than Premier League Wednesday! At the time he was out of favour at Ipswich Town where, perhaps unsurprisingly in hindsight, he was unable to displace either Matt Holland or youngster Keiron Dyer from the 'Tractor Boys' Division One line up. His move to Hillsborough ended a frustrating time at Portman Road for Sonner who made almost half of his 69 appearances from the subs bench although he did help Town reach the play off semi-finals in consecutive seasons.

Before joining the East Anglian club Sonner had spent three seasons in mainland Europe, beginning with German club Preussen. The move was instigated by his agent at the time, ex-Forest and Cologne forward Tony Woodcock, and the combative midfielder later spent a year in neighbouring Austria before moving back to the UK. He had tried his luck abroad after failing to make an impression at three Lancashire based league clubs, the first of which he left whilst still a trainee. His league debut came at Burnley but he started only one game for the 'Clarets' before nine games on loan at Bury brought a temporary end to his English League career.

Whilst at Ipswich he won his first senior cap for Northern Ireland and looked set to stay after signing a new contract in the summer of 1998, after previously having been in dispute with the club over an alleged off the field incident. However Danny Wilson took advantage of a clause in Sonner's new deal to sign him for a cut-price fee and he initially performed well in an Owls shirt, missing only a handful of games as the Owls finished just below mid table in the top-flight. However like many of his teammates his form suffered during the relegation season a year later and after Wednesday withdrew their initial offer of a contract he was allowed to leave on a 'Bosman' transfer, later signing for Trevor Francis' Birmingham City. Reached the Division One play off semi-finals with the Blues and found himself without a club after his contract at Walsall was cancelled as part of a cost cutting measure. However he earned a new deal at Nottingham Forest and was even recalled to the Northern Ireland side by new manager Lawrie Sanchez in April 2004. Later joined Port Vale, signing permanently in June 2005.

SPIKSLEY, Frederick 'Fred' 1891-1904

Born: 25 January 1870 Gainsborough
(5ft, 6ins, 10st, 4lbs – 1896)
Died: 28 July 1948 Goodwood, Sussex
Debut: 23 January 1892
v Bolton Wanderers
F.A.Cup Home
Last Appearance: 18 April 1903
v West Bromwich Albion
Division One Home
Total League
& Cup Appearances: 321* Goals: 115
***Also appeared in**
16 Football Alliance League games

Career Details:

Gainsborough Jubilee Swifts		
Gainsborough Trinity	September	1887
WEDNESDAY	February	1891
Glossop	October	1904 Free
Leeds City	February	1905
Watford	February	1906

CAPS (@SWFC)
England Full (7) v Wales 13/03/93, v Scotland 01/04/93, v Ireland 01/03/94, v Scotland 07/04/94, v Ireland 07/03/96, v Wales 28/03/98, v Scotland 02/04/98

Football League (2) v Scottish League 21/04/94, v Scottish League 14/03/03

Of all the players to have represented Sheffield Wednesday in their 138-year history there is no doubt that Fred Spiksley was the most remarkable individual of them all. During his incredible life Spiksley reached the pinnacle of the English game as a footballer, became one of the first ever men to coach on two different continents, escaped from a German prisoner of war camp, was arrested for illegal betting and once declared bankrupt but was also multi lingual, a musician, and a writer! His life story began in Willoughby Street, Gainsborough at the Crown and Anchor Inn where a son was born to publican Edward Spiksley, a former farm worker from the Lincolnshire Fens. Over the years that followed a story emerged that Fred's two brothers were given differently spelt surnames at their baptisms, due to a combination of alcohol and their father's thick accent, but it has transpired that it was Fred's grandfather or great grandfather who was the guilty party - naming his sons Spiksley, Spicksley and Picksley!

After leaving school Fred gained employment as an apprentice printer but showed his early love for horse racing when after his boss barred him from attending Lincoln races he went anyway and was sacked for his impudence – his father having to pay another £50 bond to secure an apprenticeship at Gainsborough News! He managed to hold down his second job and gained his first experience of organised football when appearing for newly formed Gainsborough club Jubilee Swifts – named so as Queen Victoria was celebrating her Golden Jubilee. He took part in an U-18 competition promoted and sponsored by Mr Cook from Boston and helped Swifts reached the last four (out of 82 entries) with Fred getting eleven in a 13-0 win over Lincoln Avenue, he also won the prize for tournament top scorer with 31 goals. His tremendous form in youth football did not go unnoticed by the town's powerful senior team and soon after Spiksley – weighing just seven stones – joined Gainsborough Trinity. During the 1887-88 season Fred set the remarkable record of scoring in every home game played by Trinity – he was also capped by Lincolnshire and won the Gainsborough News Charity Cup - while his phenomenal speed and amazing footwork meant League clubs were soon alerted to his promise. However he received a set back on his nineteenth birthday when, ironically playing against Wednesday, in a minor cup tie he suffered a broken leg after just two minutes play, forcing Fred to miss the rest of the season.

Thankfully he recovered to win the Lincolnshire Senior Cup (1890) and Midland League Championship (1891) with Trinity before a tug of war for his signature ended when Fred signed for non-league Wednesday. His move to Wednesday was a story in itself as he had virtually arranged to sign for Accrington but on his way back to Gainsborough missed the last train home and was stranded in Sheffield late one night. While there he met Wednesday player Fred Thompson in a Sheffield hotel and promised him he would not sign for Accrington until he had spoken to Wednesday. He returned home the following day and was sent a telegram by the Owls asking him to return to Sheffield - he duly signed in the Bull and Mouth Hotel on Waingate at £3 per week and was handed a compositors job at the Sheffield Telegraph. Although now registered a Wednesday player Fred remained with Trinity for the remainder of the season, finally making his debut for 'The Blades' in a friendly at Sunderland Albion in September 1891.

He quickly became a big favourite with the Olive Grove crowd and in an age when individualism was king Spiksley was simply a genius on the left wing – it was said he was so lightening quick that many legitimate goals were chalked off for offside because no one could believe Spiksley could have got to the ball so quickly! He delighted Wednesday fans in those early years of league soccer with his nimble footwork, superb movement and tremendous shooting ability while he was a truly two-footed footballer who was quickly nicknamed 'The Olive Grove Flyer' by his adoring fans. There is no doubt he was the greatest Owls player of the Victorian age although in the summer of 1892 he was diagnosed with 'galloping consumption' and not expected to live out the year! Thankfully the doctor was proven wrong and after signing an almost unheard of three-year contract with Wednesday he appeared in the club's first ever league game – in September 1892 - before scoring both goals as Wednesday beat Wolves 2-1 in the 1896 F.A.Cup Final. He later helped Wednesday to the Second Division title in 1900 and also added a League Championship medal to his collection in 1903 while he bore comparison with a certain Wednesday right winger of 1990s as it was said Spiksley would often set off from the half way line and stop dead twice before crossing into the area! His form for Wednesday – where he combined brilliantly with Alec Brady - was also replicated with England as he netted twice on his debut – contemporary reports suggest he netted a hat trick – in a 5-2 win over Scotland and was never on the losing side when netting seven times in as many games. He was also a consummate professional who approached the game in a 'scientific' manner and never allowed his shirt to be washed with the rest of the team – he always wore two shirts during games, changing at half time, and took them home for his wife to wash. A leg injury finally ended his senior career at Wednesday in 1904 and Fred later played for a further two years before being appointed secretary at London based non-league club Southern United. He later played twelve games for Southern League Watford but missed out the manager's job when the interview coincided with a race meeting, Fred refusing to miss the racing! He left Vicarage Road in May 1906 and later, in February 1907, he showed his musical talents by playing the piano in Fred Karno's famous touring sketch show. Then after missing out on the manager's job at QPR and Spurs he was found guilty in August 1908 of 'Loitering for the purposes of betting' and fined £2. Later in the year he was appointed a referee by the Midland Counties League but times were hard for Fred and in March 1909 he was declared bankrupt with debts of £84 – he admitted to living off the charity of family and friends. At the time he was a freelance writer for various newspapers and scouted for clubs on a commission basis – neither generating much income.

Thankfully his fortunes then improved and in May 1911 he moved to Sweden where he coached teams in the Stockholm area – including AIK - and also coached the national side for one game, a 4-2 loss to Germany. He was in the running for the job to coach the Olympic side for the 1912 games but eventually left to take over at German club Munich 1860 in June 1913. A year later he was in charge of FC Nuremburg but when the Great War started Fred and his son were arrested as 'aliens' and imprisoned. However they somehow managed to escape back to England and in 1915 Fred could be found in America working as a munitions inspector! He returned to Europe in 1918 to become coach at Spanish giants Barcelona while in 1920 he was back in Sheffield when an attempt was made to revive the Sheffield handicap races – Fred entering under his pseudonym of Fred Haywood. A few months later he was back in court when being charged with deserting his wife – Fred being order to pay Ellen £2 per week – while his remarkable life story next took Fred to Mexico where his fluency with languages saw him land the job of head of the despatch department (in charge of 140 employees) at the Mexico City branch of the Canadian bank of Montreal. He combined this position initially with a player-coach role with Mexican side Real Club Espana O.D. before in 1923 he was appointed coach of The Reforma Club – a side run by the white section of the local community.

He returned to England in 1924 when being appointed to Fulham's coaching staff and stayed for two years before making a triumphant return to Nuremburg where his side won the German Cup in 1927 – Fred though was not allowed to travel with the team or see them in the final because of the war! Just before returning from Germany in September 1927 Fred was divorced from his wife after alleged misconduct with a Twickenham woman (!) while his final coaching appointment saw him spend a year at Swiss club Lausanne Sports before finally retiring in 1929. However Fred was not the sort of man to let the grass grow under his feet as at the age of 59 he married for the second time and competed in skating, rowing and swimming competitions. However he spent most of his time competing in professional handicap sprint races – competing until the age of 75 – and was regularly seen training at Bramall Lane. One such occasion was in the summer of 1939 when Fred was training for a sprint handicap to be held in Morpeth, complete with an AAA coach and stopwatch!! He was as quick as some sprinters in their 20s and confided that if he could get 20 yards handicap he would win the race and make a killing with the bookies (he was not bothered about the prize money!). Unfortunately the handicapper was far too cute and 69 year-old Fred was allowed too little a handicap to persuade him to travel north. A major internal operation meant Fred lived the final years of his life in London but he still retained his passion for Horse Racing and it was perhaps fitting that on Ladies day at Goodwood Races he should collapse and pass away whilst watching the action - the story goes that Fred backed the winner of the 3.10 Goodwood Stakes, at 100-8, but did not survive to collect his winnings.

SPOORS, James 'Jimmy' 1908-20

Born: 1887/88 Jarrow
(5ft 9½ins, 11st 4lbs – 1913)
Died: February 1960 Aston, Sheffield
Debut: 7 November 1908
v Middlesbrough
Division One Home
Last Appearance: 5 April 1920
v Bolton Wanderers
Division One Home
Total League
& Cup Appearances: 272* Goals: 5
***Also appeared in**
15 wartime games, scoring 1 goal

Career Details:

Jarrow		
WEDNESDAY	April	1908 £10
Barnsley	11 June	1920 £350

Strong and fierce tackler Jimmy Spoors was yet another player spotted by legendary Owls boss Bob Brown when he was employed purely as the club's scout in the Northeast. He arrived from regular source Jarrow and a few weeks into his Wednesday career – September 1908 - was at the centre of a bizarre incident in a reserve game against Leicester Fosse when his last minute penalty looked to have given Wednesday a 3-2 win. However it transpired that the referee had actually blown for full-time as the ball was crossing the line and insisted the game had ended in a draw! The game was ordered to be replayed with the rematch ironically ending in a draw!

His first game for Wednesday came at the pivotal centre halfback role but when long-time right back Willie Layton decided to retire in 1909 it was Spoors who took his place, his polished style and great pace meaning the stalwart was not missed. He remained an automatic choice until the beginning of the First World War when Spoors joined the Army and served in Italy where he continued to play football. On returning to Sheffield after the hostilities ended he went straight back into the first team but Wednesday experienced a dreadful season and Spoors played only eighteen times before joining neighbours Barnsley. While being employed as an emergency centre forward Jimmy became the first Tykes player to score a league hat trick away from home – at Birmingham in March 1921 – and he netted nine goals in the final 11 games of the 1920-1 season in his new role. However he never played another league game in his career – his final match being an F.A.Cup tie for Barnsley – and spent a season fulfilling his role of player-manager for the Tykes Midland League side before being released in the summer of 1922. Spoors – who married the daughter of 1880s Wednesday player Jack Hudson – later became a publican in Sheffield.

SPRINGETT, Peter John 1967-75

Born: 8 May 1946 Fulham
(5ft 10ins, 12st – 1967)
Died: 28 September 1997 Sheffield
Debut: 19 August 1967
v West Ham United
Division One Away
Last Appearance:
14 December 1974
v Oldham Athletic
Division Two Home
Total League
& Cup Appearances: 207 Goals: 0

Career Details:

Queens Park Rangers	May	1963
WEDNESDAY	22 May	1967 £40,000*
Barnsley	21 May	1975 Free
Scarborough	July	1980

*Swap deal with R.Springett

CAPS (@SWFC)
England U-23 (6) v Italy 20/12/67, v Scotland 07/02/68,
v Hungary 01/05/65, v Italy 25/05/68, v W.Germany 09/06/68,
v Belgium 'B' 25/05/69

Peter Springett will always be compared with his England International brother Ron but the younger sibling was a fine keeper in own right, winning several England U-23 caps during his early years at Hillsborough. He had started his career playing as a forward for West London schools but after converting to goalkeeper he signed apprentice forms for QPR in 1961 and later won several England Youth caps. The definite highlight of his time at Loftus Road came in the 1966-7 season when Springett was not only ever present as Rangers won the Third Division Championship but also appeared at Wembley in the League Cup Final as top-flight West Brom were stunned as the minnows came from two goals down to register a 3-2 win.

He was then involved in a unique transfer deal that saw the Springett brothers swap clubs with Wednesday paying QPR a notional fee of £40,000 – Rangers actually received a net sum of

£24,000 after the Owls deducted their fee for Springett Senior. After 160 games for Rangers his first appearance for Wednesday came in the exotic surroundings of the Aztec Stadium in Mexico City – the Owls were playing in a post-season friendly tournament – and he remained an almost ever present for three seasons until losing his place to Peter Grummitt part way through the 1970 relegation season. Springett then spent a similar amount of time in the shadows, starting only fifteen games in the lower tier, until reclaiming a first team spot early in Derek Dooley's final season as manager. However after losing his place to teenager Peter Fox half way through the nightmare 1974-5 campaign it signalled the end of his Wednesday career and a free transfer took him to neighbours Barnsley. In five years at Oakwell he was an automatic choice and helped the Tykes earn promotion from Division Three in 1979 while recording his 500th league appearance.

In December 1981 - after a season with Scarborough in the Alliance Premier League - Springett retired from the game to join the South Yorkshire Police force although he still made appearances for Johnny Quinn's Charity side as well as playing seven-a-side football every week – he also kept fit in the summer months by keeping wicket for his local cricket side. He was later Community Constable in the Highfield area of Sheffield and frequently served at both Bramall Lane and Hillsborough on match days. Sadly a serious illness later left him paralysed from the waist down and after a four-year battle against the disease he passed away at a relatively young age.

SPRINGETT, Ronald Derrick 'Ron' 1958-67

Born: 22 July 1937 Fulham
(5ft 10ins, 12st 11lbs – 1961)
Debut: 15 March 1958
v Bolton Wanderers
Division One Home
Last Appearance: 15 May 1967
v Leeds United
Division One Away
Total League
& Cup Appearances: 384 Goals: 0

Career Details:

Victoria United		
Queens Park Rangers	February	1953
WEDNESDAY	13 March	1958 £10,000
Queens Park Rangers	22 May	1967 £16,000*
Valley United		1970 (Sun.)

* Swap deal with P.Springett

CAPS (@SWFC)
England Full (33) v N.Ireland 18/11/59, v Scotland 19/04/60, v Yugoslavia 11/05/60, v Spain 15/05/60, v Hungary 22/05/60, v N.Ireland 08/10/60, v Luxembourg 19/10/60, v Spain 26/10/60, v Scotland 15/04/61, v Mexico 10/05/61, v Portugal 21/05/61, v Italy 24/05/61, v Austria 27/05/61, v Luxembourg 28/09/61, v Wales 14/10/61, v Portugal 25/10/61, v N.Ireland 22/11/61, v Austria 04/04/62, v Scotland 14/04/62, v Switzerland 09/05/62, v Peru 20/05/62, v Hungary 31/05/62, v Argentina 02/06/62, v Bulgaria 07/06/62, v Brazil 10/06/62, v France 03/10/62, v N.Ireland 20/10/62, v Wales 21/11/62, v France 27/02/63, v Switzerland 05/06/63, v Wales 02/10/65, v Austria 20/10/65, v Norway 29/06/66

Football League (9) v Irish League 23/09/59, v League of Ireland 04/11/59, v Italian League 01/11/60, v Scottish League 22/03/61, v League of Ireland 11/10/61, v Italian League 08/11/61, v Italian League 29/11/62, v Scottish League 21/03/62, v Scottish League 16/03/66

It required all Eric Taylor's powers of persuasion to convince promising goalkeeper Ron Springett to uproot from his London home and move North in March 1958. A week before his eventual move the keeper had declined the transfer, although the two clubs had agreed a fee, and only relented when Taylor made the remarkable concession of allowing Springett to live and train in London and just commute to Sheffield for games. This unusual arrangement perhaps showed how highly Wednesday rated the 20-year old stopper and that faith was rewarded as over the next nine years Springett emerged as one the greatest goalies in the Owls long history and became the club's highest capped England International – taking the record from pre war hero Ernie Blenkinsop.

His arrival at Hillsborough – after 89 league games for Rangers - ended the Owls desperate search for a quality goalkeeper as Springett was the fifth custodian to appear for Wednesday during the traumatic 1957-8 campaign, which ended with relegation to Division Two. The brilliant agile keeper, who made up for his lack of inches with tremendous bravery, lightening reflexes and almost faultless judgement, was an automatic choice from day one at Hillsborough and after helping Wednesday back to the top-flight in 1959 he was between the sticks as his new club finished in their highest post war league position and enjoyed a first taste of competitive European football. His tremendous form soon won Springett representative honours and he was almost unchallenged for four years as England No. 1, playing in his country's famous 9-3 rout of the Scots at Wembley in April 1961 and appearing in the 1962 World Cup Finals in Chile. It was not until the emergence of Gordon Banks that Ron lost his England shirt and sadly, although he was back up to Banks during the 1966 World Cup win, he did not earn a winners medal as only the eleven players on the Wembley pitch against the Germans were such honoured. The year of 1966 proved somewhat bittersweet for Ron as he was in the Owls side that famously lost the F.A.Cup Final to Everton after having led by two goals early in the second half!

The fact that Springett trained during the week alongside his brother, Peter, at Loftus Road was probably the main reason behind his transfer request for 'personal reasons' in April 1964. However he remained at Wednesday for another three years before being involved in the unique swap deal that saw the siblings swap clubs - the younger Springett being valued higher than his big brother. On leaving Hillsborough Ron presented Wednesday with his first England cap as a mark of his appreciation and happy association with the club – his popularity with Owls fans was shown later in the year when a bumper 23,070 crowd attended his Hillsborough testimonial game to contribute the not inconsiderable sum of over £5,000 to his fund. Incidentally in that game he spent the second half as a centre forward while a year earlier, in Derek Wilkinson's testimonial game, he had managed to score four times as a second half sub!

After rejoining Rangers, Ron amassed a further 45 league games before retiring from the professional game in 1969. He later played a handful of matches for Sunday club Valley United – as a centre forward – while developing his sports goods business in the shadow of Loftus Road. In 1984 he also started his own decorating and gardening business in East Sheen while his daughter, Terry, continued the family tradition by appearing for the England woman's team.

*Did not play for Ashford Town or have a middle initial of 'G'

SRNICEK, Pavel 'Pav' 1998-2000

Born: 10 March 1968 Bohumin, nr Ostrava, Czechoslovakia
(6ft 2ins, 14st 9lbs – 1999)
Debut: 14 November 1998
v Newcastle United
Premier League Away
Last Appearance: 18 March 2000
v Watford
Premier League Away
Total League
& Cup Appearances: 52 Goals: 0

Career Details:

Victoria Bohumin Juniors	
ZD Bohumin	
Dulka Tabor	1986
Dulka Prague	1987
Banik Ostrava	

Leicester City	October	1990 Trial
Newcastle United	January	1991 £350,000
Marseille	June	1992 Trial
Banik Ostrava		1998 Free
WEDNESDAY	11 November	1998 Free
Brescia	6 July	2000 Free
Cosenza		2003
Released	30 June	2003
Wolverhampton Wanderers	25 August	2003 Trial
Portsmouth	1 September	2003 Free
West Ham United	19 February	2004 Free

CAPS (@SWFC) Full (Czech Republic 15)
v Belgium 09/02/99, v Lithuania 27/03/99, v Scotland 31/03/99, v Poland 28/04/99, v Estonia 05/06/99, v Scotland 09/06/99, v Lithuania 04/09/99, v Bosnia 08/09/99, v Faroe Islands 09/10/99, v Holland 13/11/99, v Israel 26/04/00, v Germany 03/06/00, v Holland 11/06/00, v France 16/06/00, v Denmark 21/06/00

Former Eastern Block soldier who first arrived in England during October 1990 to attend a trial at Leicester City. He eventually signed, after a further trial, for Newcastle United and after acclimatising to life in the Northeast eventually took over the number one spot following the arrival of Kevin Keegan as manager. In June 1992 he was involved in a payments dispute with United and had trials with Marseille but he returned to Newcastle to become somewhat of a cult hero with the Geordie faithful, playing 32 games as United won the Second Division Championship in 1993. In total he appeared in 188 games for Newcastle before leaving on a 'Bosman' free transfer in the summer of 1998, signing a week-to-week deal at former club Banik Ostrava. However within a few weeks he was back in the English Premier League after Wednesday fought off competition from Glasgow Celtic to capture his signature on a two and a half year contract.

Ironically his debut came back at St James' Park in a 1-1 draw to complete a bizarre circle that had seen Srnicek make his debut for Newcastle against Wednesday back in April 1991! After arriving at Hillsborough the Czech Republic International, who did not need a work permit due to him holding a French passport, took over from long serving Kevin Pressman and proved a somewhat inconsistent performer for Wednesday, showing himself to be a superb shot stopper but somewhat weak in the air. He will be best remembered for saving two penalties at Aston Villa in 1999 but after Pressman reclaimed his first team spot near the end of the 1999-00 season Srnicek exercised a clause in his contract that allowed him to leave on a free transfer if he did not play a certain number of games. He duly signed a three year deal with Italian Serie A club Brescia and remained in Southern Europe – also playing at Italian side Cosenza – until returning to these shores for trials at newly promoted clubs Wolves and Portsmouth. He signed for the latter but struggled to displace Shaka Hislop from the first team, appearing in only 4 games, before joining Division One side West Ham United in March 2004 after a month's loan.

STACEY, William Heaton 1876- 83

Born: Q/E March 1848 Sheffield
Died: 5 November 1903 Sheffield
Debut: 18 December 1880
v Blackburn Rovers F.A.Cup Away
Last Appearance: 2 December 1882
v Lockwood Brothers
F.A.Cup Away
Total League
& Cup Appearances: 5 Goals: 0

Career Details:

Hallam		
WEDNESDAY		1876

Versatile player from the early years of the Owls history who has the distinction of appearing in the club's first ever F.A.Cup tie, a 4-0 win at Blackburn Rovers in 1880. He was the Owls goalkeeper on that historic occasion but usually appeared in either of the full back positions where he proved himself a quick, powerful player who was strong in the tackle. Two years earlier he recorded another first when captaining the club to their first senior trophy – the inaugural Sheffield Challenge Cup – and in total won three Sheffield Cups while with Wednesday plus a prestigious Wharncliffe Charity Cup medal in 1879.

Before joining Wednesday, Stacey – whose brother Fred regularly played for the club in goal during the 1870s – had represented Sheffield against London in one of the first ever inter-city games played between the two football powers. He had actually travelled to the capital – in January 1873 - just to watch the game but when a player called T.C.Willey failed to show he was drafted in to make up the numbers. In addition to playing football for Wednesday he was also a keen cricketer while away from sport he worked as an elementary school teacher in the city, later becoming one of Sheffield's youngest headmasters. Later in life he was made a vice-president at Wednesday and also became a senior referee.

STAINROD, Simon Allan 'Stan' 1985

Born: 1 February 1959 Sheffield
(5ft 10ins, 12st 9lbs – 1985)
Debut: 3 April 1985 v Norwich City
Division One Away
Last Appearance: 7 September 1985
v West Ham United
Division One Home
Total League
& Cup Appearances: 8+7 Goals: 2

Career Details:

Hillsborough Celtic		
Sheffield United	10 July	1976
Oldham Athletic	13 March	1979 £60,000
Queens Park Rangers	21 November	1980 £275,000
WEDNESDAY	19 February	1985 £250,000
Aston Villa	24 September	1985 £250,000
Stoke City	31 December	1987 £90,000
Racing Club Strasbourg		1989 Loan
Rouen	July	1989 £100,000
Falkirk	2 August	1990 Free
Dundee	6 February	1992 £30,000
Ayr United	26 December	1993

Although Simon Stainrod supported Wednesday as a youngster and was brought up in Grenoside - a stones throw from Hillsborough – it was with cross City neighbours United that the pacy forward would sign apprentice forms in July 1975. Soon after signing professional forms Stainrod won England Youth caps and netted fifteen times for the Blades before moving across the Pennines to Boundary Park. While in Oldham colours he incurred the wrath of Owls fans when, in September 1980, an unruly section of supporters rioted at Oldham after Terry Curran had been controversially sent off following a tussle with Stainrod. His first taste of success came at QPR where he played in the 1982 F.A.Cup Final defeat to Spurs before helping Rangers to promotion from Division Two a year later – he also toured South America with the England squad in the summer of 1984.

He eventually arrived at Hillsborough to boost Howard Wilkinson's push for a European place but unfortunately his stay at his boyhood club was extremely brief, Stainrod starting only a handful of games before seemingly being set to join Terry Venables at Spanish giants Barcelona. However the move broke down when Wednesday rejected the Catalan club's request to take him on a season long loan and the forward had to settle for the slightly less glamorous setting of Birmingham! Wednesday must have had cause to regret the move as Stainrod duly netted 21 times for Aston Villa in that debut season, helping the Villa Park club to the semi-finals of the League Cup. After a spell in French football Stainrod began a six-year stay in Scotland, beginning with a starring role in Falkirk's Division One Championship success in 1991 – he was voted by his peers as Divisional player of the season. He later joined Dundee in a player/assistant manager role and after taking over as caretaker boss in February 1992 won a second consecutive Division One title.

After being appointed Director of Football in August 1992 he stayed at Dens Park until leaving in November of the following year – Stainrod eventually being handed the player-manager role at

Ayr United on Boxing Day 1993. Stainrod – whose father Allan was a centre forward on the books of both Wednesday and Sheffield United as an amateur – was eventually given his cards at Ayr in September 1995 and briefly coached in Scotland while also working for Satellite television. He now works as a football agent and was the man behind Michele Di Piedi's move to Hillsborough.

STANIFORTH, Ronald 'Ron' 1955-59

Born: 13 April 1924 Manchester
(5ft 11ins, 11st – 1957)
Died: 5 October 1988 Barrow
Debut: 20 August 1955
v Plymouth Argyle
Division Two Home
Last Appearance: 11 April 1959
v Cardiff City
Division Two Home
Total League
& Cup Appearances: 107 Goals: 2

Career Details:

Newton Albion		
Stockport County	5 October	1946
Huddersfield Town	20 May	1952 £8,000
WEDNESDAY	18 July	1955*
Barrow	13 October	1959 £1,500

* Staniforth and Shiner swapped for Marriott and Conwell

When Ron Staniforth joined the Owls, aged 31, in an exchange deal involving four players he was already an established International with eight full and three 'B' caps to his name. The former Hague Street school and Manchester boys player was a tall, stylish and cultured full back who had looked set to join Manchester United as a teenager before the outbreak of war meant he signed up with the Royal Navy Air Service instead. After being de-mobbed in 1946 Staniforth actually started to work as a milkman in his native Manchester but after writing to Stockport County for a trial he eventually signed amateur forms for the Hatters, turning professional two months later. He would make 223 league appearances for County over the following six years and such was his outstanding form that when Stockport boss Andy Beattie moved to Huddersfield Town his first signing was Ron Staniforth.

Within two years the right back was making his debut for the full England side and was ever present during the 1954 World Cup Finals in Switzerland. He had helped Town to promotion from Division Two in his first season and looked set to remain in the top-flight before he was somewhat surprisingly allowed to join Wednesday in the summer of 1955. His many qualities, including shrewd positioning, intelligent distribution and expert tackling, meant he proved invaluable as Wednesday bounced back into Division One at the first attempt and he remained a regular until losing his first team spot to Peter Johnson.

Whilst player-manager at league club Barrow he made a further 38 appearances (the player prefix being dropped in 1961) but after having to seek re-election with the Cumbrians in 1961 and 1964 he resigned in July 1964, complaining of interference from boardroom level. He then spent six years out of the professional game during which time he gained his full coaching qualifications and coached the England schoolboys team as well as at Hull University. He eventually returned to Hillsborough in July 1970 as coach and was employed as senior coach from March 1971 until being appointed Youth team boss in May 1974. Unfortunately he was one of many staff members to suffer from stringent cost cutting measures in January 1976 and after leaving Hillsborough he returned to Barrow where he worked in a local shipyard, coaching the works football team to many local honours.

STAPLETON, William 1919-20

Born: Sheffield
(5ft 9½ins, 12st 6lbs – 1919)
Died: 15 June 1929 Sheffield
Debut: 30 August 1919
v Middlesbrough
Division One Home
Last Appearance: 1 May 1920
v Oldham Athletic
Division One Home
Total League
& Cup Appearances: 20* Goals: 0
***Also appeared in**
73 wartime games, scoring 1 goal

Career Details:

Silverwood Colliery		
Mexborough Town	Summer	1914
WEDNESDAY		
Swansea Town	22 June	1920

One of a club record 43 players who appeared for Wednesday in the disastrous 1919-20 campaign. The attacking right back had started his playing career with his Colliery side before appearing on a regular basis for Wednesday during wartime soccer. Although he always looked pale and somewhat frail he proved a more than capable defender and was often found in the opposition half of the field – he scored just once for Wednesday, in a December 1918 match at Grimsby Town. He started the first season of post war football as the club's first choice right back and competed with veteran Tom Brittleton for the role later in the season before being part of the close season cull as new manager Bob Brown cleared the decks. He subsequently joined Swansea Town but before moving to Wales was involved in a freak mishap on his way to work, when walking along Penistone Road. He somehow managed to trip over a piece of wood and crash into a plate glass window, resulting in a cut forearm and severed artery but he thankfully recovered to start the new season with the Swans!

STARLING, Ronald William 'Ronnie' 1932-37

Born: 11 October 1909 Pelaw-on-Tyne
(5ft 9½ins, 11st 5lbs – 1935)
Died: 17 December 1991 Sheffield
Debut: 27 August 1932 v Blackpool
Division One Home
Last Appearance: 2 January 1937
v Wolverhampton Wanderers
Division One Home
Total League
& Cup Appearances: 193* Goals: 30
***Also appeared in**
2 wartime games, scoring 2 goals

Career Details:

Usworth Colliery		
Washington Colliery		
Hull City		1927
Newcastle United	May	1930 £3,750
WEDNESDAY	25 June	1932 £3250
Aston Villa	6 January	1937 £6900
Northampton Town		1939-40 Guest
Walsall		1939-40 Guest
WEDNESDAY		1940-41 Guest
Nottingham Forest		1941-42 Guest
Beighton Miners Welfare		1951

CAPS (@SWFC)
England Full (1) v Scotland 01/04/33

Although commonly remembered as the last Sheffield Wednesday captain to lift the F.A.Cup this somewhat masks the fact that Ronnie Starling was an inside forward of outstanding talent. He was known as the 'man with fluttering feet' but when he initially arrived at Wednesday his unorthadox methods at inside right did not suit everyone's tastes and it was not long before his critics argued that he should be dropped. Thankfully Owls boss Billy Walker recognised his genius and took the bold step of making 24 year-old Ronnie captain and switching him to inside left, forming a partnership with Ellis Rimmer. He quickly became the most talked about inside forward in the country and fans were surprised when he failed to add to his solitary cap for England.

After representing Durham schools as a teenager Starling's senior career started at Hull City where he worked in the club's offices while playing for the Tigers as an amateur. A move into the big time at Newcastle United was not really a success for Starling as despite being recognised as a superb ball player he was only a regular for one season before being allowed to move south to sign for Wednesday. Within a year of joining the Owls, Ronnie won his solitary England cap while at Hillsborough before the definite highlight of his career came at Wembley in April 1935 when he received the Cup from the Prince of Wales following the 4-2 win over West Bromwich Albion. He added the Charity Shield to his medal haul later in the year and was twice in a Wednesday side that finished third in the top-flight but as the club struggled near the foot of the table during the 1936-7 season he was seemingly sacrificed a day after Wednesday rejected a huge Arsenal bid for their rising star Jackie Robinson.

His sale was still a then transfer record for Wednesday and he enjoyed further success at Villa Park, helping the Birmingham club to the Second Division championship in 1938 as well as the semi-final of the F.A.Cup – it was his fourth semi-final appearance after playing with Hull City in 1930, Newcastle in 1932 and of course Wednesday three years later. He continued to play throughout the war years – winning the League North with Villa in 1944 – and after almost two years as trainer at Nottingham Forest he made a playing comeback in February 1951, aged 41, for Beighton Miners Welfare in the old Yorkshire League! After his playing days ended Ronnie settled back in Sheffield and ran a newsagents shop near the Hillsborough ground- he also played in charity football matches until the age of sixty. After finally retiring he spent the majority of his final years on the golf course before passing away – aged 82 – in a Sheffield nursing home.

STEFANOVIC, Dejan 1995-99

Born: 20 October 1974 Vranje, Yugoslavia
(6ft 2ins, 12st 2lbs – 1995)
Debut: 26 December 1995
v Nottingham Forest
Premier League Away
Last Appearance: 16 May 1999
v Charlton Athletic
Premier League Away
Total League
& Cup Appearances: 65+7 Goals: 5

Career Details:

Yumco Vranje		
Red Star Belgrade		
Vradnicki Belgrade		1991 Loan
WEDNESDAY	11 December	1995 £2m
Perugia	1 July	1999 Free
OFK Belgrade		1999
Vitesse Arnhem	2 February	2000
Portsmouth	30 July	2003 £1.85m

FULL CAPS (@ SWFC)
Yugoslavia Full (4) v Romania 27/03/96, v Japan 26/05/96, v Russia 07/02/97, v Argentina 24/02/98

The early career of Dejan Stefanovic was like a dream come true as he was plucked from Third Division club Yumco by Red Star Belgrade, who at the time were one of the strongest teams in Europe. Within a year he had secured a first team place and when still only 20 the talented left-footed defender made his International debut. His superb form for Red Star meant it was inevitable that he would follow the well worn path to Western football and after 46 games this duly happened in late October 1995 when David Pleat agreed a £4.5m double deal that would bring Dejan and his team mate Darko Kovacevic to Premier League Wednesday. However red tape then seriously delayed the transfer and the Owls looked set to abandon the move as the department of Employment took seven weeks to issue a work permit – it would not be the first time Stefanovic would fall foul of the Government department. Wednesday did not give up the chase though and Dejan's star looked set to soar further after he finally secured the lucrative move.

However – like his compatriot Kovacevic – he initially struggled to settle in Sheffield and a subsequent loss of form saw him omitted from the Yugoslavian national side and fail to nail down a first team place at Hillsborough. This immediately created a big problem for the likeable Serb as in June 1996 he was refused a work permit for the 1996-7 season after failing to play in the required 75% of games at Wednesday. An Owls appeal was successful a month later and Stefanovic took full advantage to become a regular in the David Pleat side that started the season like a train and eventually finished just outside the European places. Injury problems with Jon Newsome opened the door at central defence for Dejan and he gave a series of commanding displays at the heart of the Owls defence, earning a reputation as an excellent man-marker, strong in air and adept at launching attacks. Unfortunately in the following season he was then in and out of the side under Pleat and later Ron Atkinson which meant he was again refused a work permit in summer of 1998. This time the Owls appeal, in August 1998, fell on deaf ears and the frustrated Stefanovic was left kicking his heels until the Government surprisingly relented and awarded the Wednesday defender a one-year permit in October 1998.

Unfortunately due to the lateness of his work permit award it meant Stefanovic had little chance of playing 75% of the Owls games and despite enjoying a late season spell in central midfield it was inevitable he would fail to earn another work permit. After leaving Wednesday he had difficulties finding a new club as after signing a pre-contract agreement with Italian club Perugia the deal fell through when they failed to sell the surplus of foreign players in their squad. While waiting for the right offer he joined OFK back home in Yugoslavia but stayed only a month before securing a move to Vitesse in Holland. He settled well at Arnham – playing along side ex-Owl Orlando Trustfull - where his form won a recall to the National side, now renamed Serbia & Montenegro, after a break of more than three years. He returned to the Premier League in the summer of 2003 when newly promoted Portsmouth broke their transfer record to bring Dejan to Fratton Park and he missed only a handful of games, playing at left back, as Pompey survived in the top-flight.

STEPHENSON, George Ternent 1931-33

Born: 3 September 1900 Seaton Delaval, Northumberland
(5ft 9$^1/_2$, 11st – 1935)
Died: 18 August 1971 Derby
Debut: 7 February 1931
v Bolton Wanderers
Division One Away
Last Appearance: 11 February 1933
v West Bromwich Albion
Division One Away
Total League
Cup Appearances: 45 Goals: 20

Career Details:

New Delaval Villa		
Leeds City	August	1919
Aston Villa	October	1919 £250
Stourbridge	August	1920 Season-loan
Derby County	November	1927
WEDNESDAY	7 February	1931 £4850*
Preston North End	19 July	1933 £850
Charlton Athletic	19 May	1934 £660

*Joint fee with T.Davison

CAPS (@SWFC)
England Full (1) v France 14/05/31

Whilst at Derby County George Stephenson was considered "the brains of their forward line" and there was uproar amongst Rams fans when he moved to a Wednesday side who were chasing a third consecutive League Championship. He was seen as a replacement for outstanding inside-forward Jimmy Seed, who would retire three months after Stephenson's arrival, and over the next eighteen months George was a first team regular at Wednesday, alternating between inside right and inside left. However despite earning the last of his three caps for England – playing in Paris alongside team mates Burgess, Blenkinsop & Strange – and boasting an excellent scoring record Stephenson was replaced by newcomer Ronnie Starling at the start of the 1932-33 season and was only a bit player until moving to Deepdale in July 1933.

After a short spell at Preston he ended his league career at Charlton Athletic – winning a Division Three (South) Championship medal in 1935 - where due to a succession of injuries he was forced to retire in May 1937, moving onto the Valiants coaching staff. A year later he was appointed assistant manager to Jimmy Seed at The Valley and remained in the role until being appointed Huddersfield Town manager in August 1947. He spent five years in the Leeds Road hot seat but throughout his tenure Town struggled at the wrong end of the First Division table and with relegation looking unavoidable he resigned in March 1952, later taking over the running of the Sportsman Club public house in the town. After his spell as licensee he moved back to Derby, gaining employment at Rolls Royce, and in the early 1960s was 'A' team coach back at County.

His coaching role at Derby ended a career in football that had started back in his native Northeast where the teenage Stephenson had worked in a grocer's shop, his father's blacksmith's shop and down the pit before signing for his local amateur side. A move into league football came next when Leeds City captured his signature but his stay was extremely brief as following the Yorkshire club's expulsion from the league, due an illegal payments scandal, he was sold at auction to Aston Villa. He joined his England International brother Clem at Villa Park – another brother, Jimmy, also played league soccer for several clubs including Villa and Sunderland while his son, Bob, would not only play for Derby County but also captured 661 dismissals as a wicket keeper in County cricket for Derbyshire and Hampshire! He served a real apprenticeship at Villa as after being loaned out for a season to non-league Stourbridge he was a reserve team regular for several seasons before finally breaking into the league side in the mid-1920s, going on to make 95 appearances before being sold to Derby County. His star continued to rise at the Baseball Ground where he averaged a goal every second game and matured into one of the finest attacking players of the early 1930s.

STERLAND, Melvyn 'Mel' 1979-89

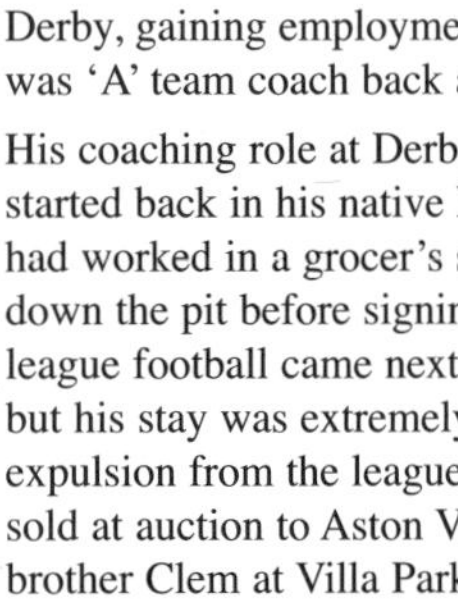

Born: 1 October 1961 Sheffield
(5ft 11ins, 12st 7lbs – 1981)
Debut: 17 May 1979
v Blackpool
Division Three Home
Last Appearance: 25 February 1989
v Wimbledon
Division One Away
Total League
& Cup Appearances: 338+9 Goals: 49

Career Details:

Three Feathers		Sun.
Lincoln City Juniors		
Middlewood Rovers		
WEDNESDAY	5 October	1979
Glasgow Rangers	3 March	1989 £800,000
Leeds United	1 July	1989 £600,000
Boston United	8 June	1994 Free
Denaby United	July	1996-Dec1997
Denaby United	August	1998
Universal Drilling		1998 Sun.
Hollinsend Amateurs	November	1998
Hallam	August	1999

CAPS (@SWFC)
England FULL (1) v Saudia Arabia 16/11/88

England 'B' (1) v Malta 14/10/87

England U-21 (7) v Denmark 20/09/83, v Hungary 11/10/83, v France 28/02/84, v France 28/03/84, v Italy 18/04/84, v Spain 17/05/84, v Spain 24/05/84

Football League (1) v Irish League 08/09/87

There is no doubt Mel Sterland is regarded as one of the most popular players to have ever worn the blue and white shirt. His rise to England honours was a classic tale of 'local boy made good' as Sterland was brought up on the Manor and started his playing career in Sheffield Sunday League football. His potential was first spotted by Lincoln City, who took Sterland to Sincil Bank as a centre forward, but it was Wednesday scout Charlie Wain who would have the most influence on the youngster's career after he invited him for a Hillsborough trial. Soon after Mel signed for the club's nursery side, Middlewood Rovers, and was a regular for Sheffield boys before signing apprentice forms for Wednesday in June 1978.

He duly became a vital member of the Owls successful youth team of the late 1970s and his first team debut came whilst still a trainee, in a 2-0 Hillsborough win over Blackpool. He soon signed professional forms for the Owls but had to wait until the 1980-1 campaign to make a real breakthrough at first team level. However when in 1981 Owls coach John Harris converted Sterland to right back it proved the catalyst to his entire career as his rampaging runs from defence and flowing locks quickly endeared him to supporters who dubbed the whole-hearted player 'Zico' after the star Brazilian forward - incidentally he also earned the nickname of 'The Flying Pig' from the Owls management which was probably a reference to his ample frame! His terrific displays during the Owls 1983-84 promotion season earned Sterland a sackful of England U-21 caps which peaked in May 1984 when he earned a European U-21 Championships winners medal as Spain were beaten over two legs. He netted many a vital goal in that season although none was more important than the penalty kick at home to Crystal Palace in April 1984 that clinched the Owls promotion back to the top-flight after an absence of fourteen years. He was by now an automatic choice and proved his versatility by starting the 1988-9 season at centre forward where his six goals must have brought back memories of his younger days when he once netted 144 goals in a single season for his two teams.

He finally won a deserved cap for England in an ill-fated friendly in Saudi Arabia – becoming the first Wednesday player since Ron Springett to achieve the honour – but this came in what proved to be his final season at Hillsborough as he was placed on the transfer list after falling out with new manager Peter Eustace over the team captaincy. He remained available for transfer after Eustace's departure and it was new manager Ron Atkinson who actually allowed Sterland to leave – for a club record fee - as he looked to raise finances to re-build a neglected Owls side. His destination was Graeme Souness' Glasgow Rangers were in a very brief spell Mel played in enough games to earn a Championship medal and also finished on the losing side in the 1989 Scottish Cup Final. On a trip home to Sheffield in the close season he discovered his services were no longer needed, after Rangers signed Trevor Steven, and he jumped at the chance to link up again with his old Wednesday boss Howard Wilkinson at Second Division Leeds United. His new side immediately won the title and he added a League Championship medal to his collection in 1992 before persistent injury problems eventually forced his early retirement from the professional game in 1994 – his testimonial game took place at Elland Road with Wednesday providing the opposition. In June 1994 he was appointed player-manager at Northern Premier League Boston United but left after two successful years after an administrative error cost the Lincolnshire club a place in the Conference League. He then helped Northern Counties East League club Denaby United to the Championship – playing at centre half – before being appointed 'football in the community officer' at Rotherham United in May 1997. He remained on Denaby's books until being appointed manager at Conference club Stalybridge Celtic in December 1997 but was sacked five months later after Celtic were relegated. It was then back to Denaby - he also played on a Sunday for Universal Drilling - while away from the game Mel starting working as a salesman, selling telephone systems and faxes. He also worked occasionally as a commentator for Radio Sheffield on Wednesday games while he secured a part in the football film 'When Saturday Comes', which was filmed mainly in Sheffield. After briefly playing alongside Chris Waddle for Hollinsend Amateurs he finally wound up his playing career at Hallam before becoming a football agent. In 2003 he underwent life saving surgery when a blood clot travelled from his leg to his lung but thankfully the died in the wool Wednesdayite survived and recently sold his medal collection to embark on a new business venture with his brother.

STEVENS, J. 1881-82

Born:
Debut: 9 January 1882
v Staveley
F.A.Cup Away
Last Appearance: 15 March 1882
v Blackburn Rovers
F.A.Cup S/F @ Manchester
Total League
& Cup Appearances: 5 Goals: 0

Career Details:

WEDNESDAY	1881

Mystery player who made only six appearances for Wednesday during the 1881-82 season, five in F.A.Cup ties. This included the club's first ever semi-final in the competition which saw Wednesday draw 0-0 with Blackburn Rovers at Huddersfield Rugby Ground before losing heavily in the replay.

STEVENSON, Thomas 1897-98

Born:
Debut: 4 September 1897 v Sunderland Division One Home
Last Appearance:
22 January 1898 v Nottingham Forest Division One Away
Total League & Cup Appearances: 2 Goals: 0

Career Details:

Clyde		
WEDNESDAY	August	1897
Released		1898

Attacker who arrived from Scottish football but failed to become established at Wednesday, appearing in only two senior fixtures whilst struggling to even become a reserve regular.

STEWART, James 'Jimmy' 1902-08

Born: 1883 Gateshead
(5ft 8ins, 10st 10lbs – 1902)
Died: 23 May 1957 Durham
Debut: 14 February 1903
v Grimsby Town
Division One Home
Last Appearance: 25 April 1908
v Everton
Division One Away
Total League
& Cup Appearances: 141 Goals: 60

Career Details:

Todds Nook (Newcastle)		
Gateshead NER		
WEDNESDAY	29 April	1902 £32
Newcastle United	1 August	1908 £1,000
Glasgow Rangers	September	1913 £600
North Shields	May	1914

CAPS (@SWFC)
England Full (2) v Wales 18/03/07, v Scotland 06/04/07

The football hotbed of the northeast provided Wednesday with a succession of high quality players in the early part of the Twentieth Century and Jimmy Stewart was no exception. His playing career had started at the nursery side of the Gateshead Railway works team and after being spotted by Wednesday he was invited down to Sheffield, along with his team mate George Simpson, for trials. It did not take Wednesday long to realise Stewart's potential and after just a solitary reserve team outing he was signed as a professional, serving an apprenticeship in reserve team football until breaking into the Owls first team during the Championship winning season of 1903-4.

Over the next four seasons 'Tadger' – a nickname given to him as a youngster – became established as one of the best inside forwards in the English game and helped Wednesday to the semi-final of the F.A.Cup in 1905 before scoring at both the semi and final stage as the Owls lifted the Cup in 1907. He also scored on his international debut, against Wales at Fulham, but stunned Wednesday fans at the end of the 1907-8 season when he refused to sign a new contract despite being offered the maximum wage allowed by FA rules.

This impasse only ended when he moved back to his native northeast where the delicate skills of Stewart helped the Geordies to the League Championship in 1909, as well as the last four of the Cup. A year later he missed out on an appearance in the F.A.Cup Final but did play in the glamour final in 1911 although his side lost in a replay to Bradford City. He later moved to Glasgow giants Rangers, along with team mate Scott Duncan, but stayed for only a season and after 10 goals in 19 league games he returned home to take over as player-manager at North Shields.The outbreak of war ended Jimmy's playing days and after the hostilities ended he worked for a time as a commercial traveller before becoming a licensee in Northallerton. In the early 1930s he was living back on Tyneside, working as an accountant while also scouting for Derby County.

STEWART, Reginald 'Reg' 1944-49

Born: 15 October 1925 Sheffield
(6ft 2 1/2ins, 12st 10lbs – 1953)
Debut: 5 January 1946
v Mansfield Town
F.A.Cup Away
Last Appearance: 16 November 1946
v West Bromwich Albion
Division Two Home
Total League
& Cup Appearances: 8* Goals: 0
***Also appeared in 1 wartime game**

Career Details:

Sheffield Y.M.C.A		
WEDNESDAY		1944
Colchester United	June	1949 £1,000
Hastings United	May	1957
Clacton Town	May	1958

It was at Colchester United that gangling centre half Reg Stewart came to the fore, appearing in almost 400 games for the Essex club after joining from Wednesday in 1949. When he moved to Layer Road his new club were actually still a non-league side and in his debut season Reg won a Southern League Cup medal, beating Bath City over two legs, while only goal average denied him a league and cup double. A few months later United were duly elected into the league, triggering a payment to Wednesday for his signature, and over the next eight seasons he was a rock at the heart of the Colchester defence, being ever present in the club's first season in Division Three (South) while in December 1951 setting an unwanted first when becoming the first ever U's player to be sent off in a league game.

He had previously spent five years at Hillsborough but failed to make a lasting impression on the first team scene, mainly due to the form of Cyril Turton – he therefore failed to follow in the footsteps of his famous relation, Ernie Blenkinsop, whose old shoes he wore in his schoolboy days. After making the grade at Colchester, Stewart dropped back into Southern League soccer at Hastings United but played only half a season before joining Clacton Town for their first ever campaign in the same competition. He was made captain at Clacton at the start of the 1959-60 season but sadly illness effectively ended his playing days and Reg was forced to retire two years later. On leaving football he started to coach local schoolboys and then ran a company's sports and leisure club for 32 years until retiring in 1991. Stewart – whose father, Frank, was a professional at Derby County until a cartilage operation finished his career – also became an accomplished after dinner speaker and now lives out his retirement in Colchester.

STEWART, Simon Andrew 1992-96

Born: 1 November 1973 Leeds
(6ft 1ins, 12st – 1993)
Debut: 10 March 1993
v Ipswich Town
Premier League Away
Last Appearance: 11 May 1993
v Queens Park Rangers
Premier League Away
Total League
& Cup Appearances: 7+1 Goals: 0

Career Details:

WEDNESDAY	16 July	1992
Shrewsbury Town	11 August	1995 Loan
Fulham	17 June	1996 Free
Woking	August	1997 Loan
Kingstonian	August	1998

Commanding central defender who performed outstandingly at youth level for Wednesday and looked set for a long career in the professional game. The inevitable pro contract soon came to the former Lincolnshire boys player- his family moved to Skegness when he was two years old – and was thrust into the first team at the latter end of the 1992-93 season when a fixture pile up forced Wednesday manager Trevor Francis to blood several youngsters. He enjoyed a superb debut at Portman Road, showing a terrific attitude and impressive defensive qualities, but lady luck then deserted the youngster as he was forced to undergo a major back operation, which left him on the sidelines for several months.

When he returned to competitive action Simon struggled to recapture his form and although appearing in four games while on loan at Shrewsbury his chances of breaking back into the Owls' Premier League squad grew increasingly unlikely and in the summer of 1996 he left for Second Division Fulham. Unfortunately his fortunes fared little better at Craven Cottage and he eventually dropped into Conference football in 1998, winning the F.A.Trophy in 1999 and 2000 under the management of Geoff Chapple at Kingstonian. After ending his professional career Stewart used his sports science degree to establish and monitor more than ten non-league football academies while he retired totally from football in 2001. Although still aged only 29 he was later appointed manager at struggling Dr Martens League side Spalding United but lasted only a few months before leaving by mutual consent in the summer of 2003 after the Tulips relegation. He now teaches in a Bedford college.

STOCKDALE, Robert Keith 'Robbie' 2000

Born: 30 November 1979 Redcar (5ft 11ins, 11st 3lbs – 2000)
Debut: 13 September 2000
v Nottingham Forest Division One Home
Last Appearance: 14 October 2000
v Portsmouth Division One Away
Total League & Cup Appearances: 6 Goals: 0

Career Details:

Middlesbrough	2 July	1998
WEDNESDAY	13 September	2000 Loan
West Ham United	23 October	2003 3-month loan
Rotherham United	18 February	2004 Loan
Rotherham United	June	2004 Free
Hull City	31 January	2005 Free

Of all the players Wednesday have signed on loan since the system was introduced Robbie Stockdale had the misfortune to experience the worst ever spell as a temporary Owls player. When the former Cleveland boys full back was brought to Hillsborough by Paul Jewell he was fresh from earning his first England U-21 cap but could not force his way into Boro's expensively assembled first eleven in what was Stockdale's third year as a professional. As a youngster Stockdale had actually attended trials at Wednesday, prior to signing trainee forms for Middlesbrough, and probably wished he had not returned to Sheffield as he joined a struggling Wednesday side who promptly lost all six games that Stockdale started – in a club record run of eight consecutive defeats. It was perhaps not surprising that Stockdale failed to make an impression with the long suffering Hillsborough faithful during his loan spell and he returned to Middlesbrough's reserves for the rest of the season.

However his fortunes at Middlesborough changed in dramatic style following the arrival of Steve McClaren as manager in the summer of 2001. He not only won a regular place in the side, initially in midfield, playing 36 league and cup games in 2001-2 but also won his first full cap for Scotland in April 2002 – his Scottish grandparents prompting Scotland boss Berti Vogts to award him senior honours. Unfortunately a series of injuries and the form of England U-21 right back Stuart Parnaby then saw the cultured right back relegated back to the club's shadow squad before eventually joining Division One side West Ham on a three-month loan. By the time Stockdale joined Rotherham United on loan, for the remainder of the 2003-4 season, he had taken his haul of Scotland caps to five and in the following summer signed on a permanent basis for the Millers.

STORRAR, David McKinnion 1952-54

Born: 16 October 1933 Lochgelly, Scotland
(5ft 9½ins, 11st 2lbs – 1953)
Debut: 27 December 1952
v West Bromwich Albion
Division One Away
Last Appearance: 17 January 1953
v Charlton Athletic
Division One Away
Total League
& Cup Appearances: 4 Goals: 0

Career Details:

Wath Wanderers		1948
Darfield Road FC		1951
WEDNESDAY	2 February	1952
Released	April	1954
Grimsby Town		1954
Hickleton Main		1956
Scunthorpe United		Trial
Frickley Colliery		
Grimethorpe Miners Welfare		

Scottish born winger David Storrar came down to England when his father moved south to work in the Yorkshire mines and his playing career started with Wolverhampton Wanderers nursery side, Wath Wanderers, who played their home games at Brampton. After three years at Wath he joined Barnsley Association League club Darfield Road and around the same time seemingly signed amateur forms for Wednesday, appearing on several occasions in the club's junior sides during the 1950-1 campaign. The following season he was a regular in the Owls Yorkshire League side and a steady progression meant he became a reserve team regular after signing professional forms for the Owls. He had played most of his football at wing half but a switch to outside left came in December 1952 and amazingly a week later he was making his First Division debut – along with fellow newcomer John Slater - in a 1-0 win at the Hawthorns. He retained the No. 11 shirt for the next three games but just when he started to acclimatise to top-flight football Storrar was promptly relegated back to Yorkshire League soccer for the remainder of the season!

He reverted back to his original wing half position for the 1953-4 season and played thirty times in reserve and 'A' team soccer before being released by the Owls at the end of season. Storrar – a cousin of Scotland international George Aitken – then joined the Army to serve his two-year National Service and although he signed professional forms for Grimsby Town he was never allowed leave to play for the Mariners. By the time he was de-mobbed Grimsby had appointed a new manager and Storrar was released, dropping into non-league soccer. He later refused the chance of signing a contract at Scunthorpe United when he considered the terms offered not sufficient and would spend the reminder of his playing days in Yorkshire non-league football, finally hanging up his boots in 1972 at the age of thirty-nine. Away from football Storrar worked for 31 years as a plate-layer on the Railways while he now plays golf to a high standard – having won the Yorkshire Senior Championship twice and the Yorkshire Veterans title.

STRANGE, Alfred Henry 'Alf' 1927-35

Born: 2 April 1900 Marehay, nr Ripley
(5ft 8ins, 11st 6lbs – 1927)
Died: October 1978 Ripley
Debut: 19 February 1927
v Sunderland
Division One Home
Last Appearance: 22 April 1935
v West Bromwich Albion
Division One Away
Total League
& Cup Appearances: 273 Goals: 22

Career Details:

Marehay Colliery		
Ripley Town		
WEDNESDAY		1918 Trial
Portsmouth	December	1922
Port Vale	26 November	1925 £500
WEDNESDAY	17 February	1927 £1230 + Harry Anstiss
Bradford Park Avenue	10 May	1935 £200
Ripley Town		1936
Raleigh	November	1936
Corsham United	cs	1945

CAPS (@SWFC)
England Full (20) v Scotland 05/04/30, v Germany 10/05/30, v Austria 14/05/30, v Ireland 20/10/30, v Wales 22/11/30, v Scotland 28/03/31, v France 14/05/31, v Belgium 16/05/31, v Ireland 17/10/31, v Wales 18/11/31, v Spain 09/12/31, v Scotland 09/04/32, v Ireland 17/10/32, v Austria 07/12/32, v Scotland 01/04/33, v Italy 13/05/33, v Switzerland 20/05/33, v Ireland 14/10/33, v Wales 15/11/33, v France 06/12/33

Football League (2) v Irish League 1930, v Scottish League 1932

Alf Strange was another truly outstanding player from the club's golden period between 1928 and 1935. Although he initially joined as a highly rated inside forward a change to right halfback, at the latter end of the 1927-8 season, altered his fortunes in dramatic style as over the next five seasons he was imperious in the position, missing only six games as Wednesday won back-to-back Championships and became established as England's top side. In that position he also won multiple England caps – only Ernie Blenkinsop and Ron Springett have won more caps while at Wednesday - and was an integral part of the famous Leach-Marsden-Strange middle line. He possessed many qualities - including superb passing skills, a tremendous long range shot and sharpness in the tackle – and while at Wednesday showed his all round sporting prowess by playing cricket for Derbyshire's second team and being a regular for his local side Ripley Wednesday.

As a youngster Strange had worked at the Butterley Company pits, near Ripley, but his chances of league football looked unlikely as most clubs thought he was too small. However in 1918 he was rushed in a taxi to Hillsborough to turn out for Wednesday's reserve side when they were short of a player but the expected invitation for a proper trial never materialised and it would be several years before Wednesday were made to pay a transfer fee to bring a player to Hillsborough who they could have signed for nothing! A successful two-week trial period at Portsmouth ended with a contract after he netted twice in a reserve game against Southampton and Alf's career began in earnest in a centre forward role for the South coast club. He would net 16 times in only 24 league games for Pompey, including a five-goal haul at home to Gillingham in January 1923, and was soon moving up a division to sign for second tier club Port Vale. He continued to impress at Vale Park and Bob Brown completed his rise through the divisions when taking Strange to Hillsborough - Harry Anstiss moving to the Potteries as part of deal. The new boy went straight into the Owls side but failed to nail down a regular place during the following season until being converted to his new defensive role and helping Wednesday pull off the 'great escape'.

He remained an automatic choice at Wednesday until suffering an injury ravaged 1933-4 season, which saw Alf first break a bone in his foot before suffering a leg fracture at Liverpool in December 1933 – incidentally Lord Derby was in the crowd on that day and was so concerned that he presented Alf with a Gold banded walking stick which he kept and treasured!. He was on the sidelines for twelve weeks but then had the misfortune to break his other leg, effectively bringing the curtain down on a frustrating campaign. The form of Horace Burrows and Wilf Sharp then kept Strange in the reserve team during the Owls F.A.Cup winning season – he made only one appearance – and was then part of Billy Walker's mass clear out at the end of the season. Unfortunately Strange was not really fit enough to sign for Park Avenue and he played only a handful of games before quitting professional football in the summer of 1936. He then played briefly for his local side Ripley Town before gaining employment at Nottingham Company Raleigh Cycle where he became player-coach of the works football team whilst also appearing for the cricket team in the close season. After the war Strange was still playing at the age of 46 for Wiltshire side Corsham United – were he was captain and 'adviser-in-chief' – and later returned to the mines before retiring in 1964. In his retirement he tended a plot of land in Ripley where he kept chickens – he did the same whilst a player at Wednesday and was popular amongst his team mates when he kept them supplied with eggs and fresh chickens at Christmas time!

STRATFORD, Charlie L 'Chas' 1877-85

Born: 1858 Sheffield
Debut: 5 February 1881
v Darwen
F.A.Cup Away
Last Appearance: 3 January 1885
v Nottingham Forest
F.A.Cup Home
Total League
& Cup Appearances: 11 Goals: 0

Career Details:

WEDNESDAY	1877

Chas Stratford was a prominent player from the club's amateur days whose family were associated with Wednesday for many years. His father, Henry, was a silver plate manufacturing by trade and officiated on several occasions at the club's athletic sports days while his brother, William, also played for Wednesday in the 1880s. Chas followed the family tradition by becoming an electro plate manager and played football for a fledgling Wednesday side for over eight years, winning both the Sheffield Challenge Cup and Wharncliffe Charity Cup on three occasions – he was in the Owls side that won the former competition for the first time in their history in March 1878.

STREETS, George Henry 1913-15

Born: 5 April 1893 Nottingham
(5ft 9ins, 11st – 1913)
Died: 25 July 1958 Nottingham
Debut: 1 September 1913
v Bolton Wanderers
Division One Away
Last Appearance: 3 January 1914
v Burnley
Division One Home
Total League
& Cup Appearances: 2* Goals: 0
***Also appeared in 26 wartime games**

Career Details:

Raleigh Athletic		
Mansfield Mechanics	March	1913
WEDNESDAY	May	1913 £50
Grantham Town		
Notts County	July	1919
Boston Town	July	1928
Newark Town	July	1931

Goalie George Streets started his career in Nottinghamshire non-league football and was snapped up by Wednesday after he had spent just eight weeks at Mansfield Mechanics. He was brought to Hillsborough to act as back up to the outstanding Teddy Davison and was given an early chance in the first team on the opening day of the 1913-14 season, when Davison was not risked after having picked up an injury in the pre season public trial game a few days earlier. He helped Wednesday to record a single goal victory but Davison was back in the side for the next game and Streets would play only one more senior game for the club – a shock 6-2 home defeat against Burnley.

He remained on the Owls books during the Great War – appearing on a regular basis in the first wartime season – but later joined hometown club Notts County where in eight years he made 140 first team appearances. He mainly acted as understudy to Albert Iremonger while at Meadow Lane but did enjoy one season as first choice before ending his playing days in non-league football.

STRINGER, Christopher 'Chris' 2000-04

Born: 16 June 1983 Grimsby
(6ft 2ins, 12st 9lbs – 2002)
Debut: 13 August 2000
v Wolverhampton Wanderers
Division One Away
Last Appearance: 26 April 2003
v Burnley
Division One Away
Total League
& Cup Appearances: 8+4 Goals: 0

Career Details:

WEDNESDAY	20 June	2000
Released	30 June	2004

Young goalkeeper whose promising career at Wednesday was totally ruined by quite horrendous injury problems which eventually forced his retirement from football in 2004, at the tender age of 21 years old. Brought up in Rotherham, after his family moved there when he was a toddler, Stringer joined the Young Owls at the U-11 stage and remained with them until in 1998 he became one of the first players to sign the newly introduced Scholarship forms. After becoming an Academy regular Stringer joined the small band of goalies to score during open play when his long punt up field, against Leeds United academy in January 2000, bounced over the startled visiting keeper.

However this goal paled into insignificance with the events of six months later when he made one of the most dramatic debuts of all time. The inexperienced youngster had played only two reserve games, conceding eight goals at Leeds, but found himself on the bench for the opening game of the season at Wolves as Wednesday had failed to replace the recently departed Pavel Srnicek. It was hoped the archetypical rookie would not be needed but after just thirteen seconds Kevin Pressman was sensationally sent off and the nervous 17-year old youngster was thrown into the fray. He duly performed heroics to help Wednesday to a draw and played seven times during the 2000-1 season to become established as back up to Pressman. Unfortunately his injury problems then began and over the next three seasons he battled against a variety of ailments, restricting his senior games to just a handful. After missing the whole of the 2003-4 season – suffering two blood clots on his thigh – he gave in to medical advice and announced his retirement in May 2004. In October 2004 he started a coaching course at Dearne Valley College but due to deep vein thrombosis he now cannot play football at all. He returned to Hillsborough early in 2005 when helping coach kids as part of the Owls' 'Football in the Community' intiative.

STRINGFELLOW, John Francis 'Frank' 1908-11

Born: Q/E March 1888
Sutton-in-Ashfield
(5ft 7ins, 10st 5lbs – 1908)
Debut: 27 February 1909
v Preston North End
Division One Away
Last Appearance: 17 April 1911
v Manchester United
Division One Home
Total League
& Cup Appearances: 21 Goals: 5

Career Details:

Ilkeston United		
WEDNESDAY	10 December	1908 £85
Mansfield Town	April	1911
Portsmouth	July	1911 £125*
Broyburn United	January	1918
Heart of Midlothian	8 February	1922
Poole Town	July	1923
Bournemouth & Boscombe United	July	1925
Scunthorpe & Lindsey Utd	September	1929

*Joint fee with Dowling

Inside forward Frank Stringfellow possessed the reputation of having the hardest shot in the Notts & Derbyshire League when Wednesday signed the 19 year-old in 1908. During three years in Wednesday colours Stringfellow fulfilled the role of understudy to the great Harry Chapman and when called upon he proved an enthusiastic if relatively inexperienced replacement.

He was later signed by future Wednesday boss Bob Brown, for ambitious Southern League Portsmouth, and spent almost a decade on the South Coast during which time Pompey won the Championship in 1920 and were elected into the Football League – Frank was captain and scored in Portsmouth's first ever league fixture. In total he appeared in 213 competitive games for Pompey, netting 91 times, before making the long trip North to sign for Edinburgh club Hearts. His stay in Scotland was brief and following a spell in Dorset with Weymouth he was signed by ex-Wednesday player and Bournemouth boss Leslie Knighton. He subsequently faced the Owls in an F.A.Cup tie at Hillsborough in 1928 and played in 117 league games for the Cherries, scoring 19 times.

STRUTT, Brian John 1977-81

Born: 21 September 1959 Malta
(5ft 9 1/2ins, 10st 7lbs – 1980)
Debut: 10 November 1979
v Blackpool
Division Three Away
Last Appearance: 23 February 1980
v Rotherham United
Division Three Away
Total League
& Cup Appearances: 2 Goals: 0

Career Details:

WEDNESDAY	19 September	1977
Matlock Town	May	1981 Free
Worksop Town		1984
Gisborne City		1986
Mount Manganui		

Former Sheffield boys player who signed apprentice forms for the club in July 1976 prior to turning professional. He progressed through the Owls youth system, making his reserve team debut in February 1976 at the age of just sixteen, but the right back appeared only twice in first team football for Wednesday before dropping into non-league football. After leaving Hillsborough Strutt's football career almost came to a complete stop as after only a few games for Matlock Town he effectively quit football to concentrate on his job working for a Rotherham clothing company. He did however later re-launch his playing career at Worksop Town and Strutt – who was born on the Mediterranean island of Malta where his father was serving in the Royal Navy – then changed his life totally when moving to New Zealand to play as a professional for Gisborne City.

He spent three years at Gisborne, who were managed by former Rotherham United player Kevin Fallon, and then another three seasons at fellow National League side Mount Manganui before deciding it was a good time to retire in 1992 when the league was re-classified as a regional competition. He then started to work for an Auckland based company called Farmers, who sell electrical and household goods, and is now settled on the North Island where he is married to a local girl and has a son and daughter.

STUBBS, Francis Lloyd 'Frank' 1900-03

Born: 13 April 1878 Woodhouse Eaves, Leicestershire
Died: 11 May1944 Loughborough
Debut: 13 October 1900
v Blackburn Rovers
Division One Away
Last Appearance: 20 December 1902
v West Bromwich Albion
Division One Away
Total League
& Cup Appearances: 18 Goals: 0

Career Details:

Woodhouse		
Coalville		
Loughborough Town		
WEDNESDAY	1 May	1900 £50
Loughborough Wednesday		1903

Goalkeeper Frank Stubbs started his playing career at minnows Loughborough Town, who were actually a Football League side in the late 1890s. However they struggled constantly during their short spell in league football and their lack of quality was no more shown that in March 1900 when, with Stubbs between the sticks, they were on the wrong end of a 12-0 score line against Arsenal – which at the time equalled the record score in a league fixture. It is thought that his appearance against Arsenal was his only senior game for Town – he mainly played for the club's reserve side called Loughborough Athletic. At the end of the 1899-00 season Loughborough folded and Stubbs moved to Hillsborough to provide competition for established first choice James Massey. The newcomer acted as understudy to Massey for the first few months of his Owls career but after breaking into the first team in January 1901 he would appear in fifteen consecutive league games until a fateful afternoon at Notts County, in September 1901, effectively ended his Wednesday career.

Various stories emerged of his performance at Meadow Lane but one fact that seems to be certain was that during the first half Stubbs received a heavy crack on the head which caused the confused goalie to ask his team mates at half time what the score was! Early in second half it was said that Frank – who was clearly concussed - proceeded to catch the ball, turn around and place it over his own goal line to gift the home side a goal! Contemporary match reports suggest these stories have been somewhat embellished although a football scribe at the time said Stubbs seemed to be "suffering from an attack of nervous excitement"! The game was lost six-nil and Stubbs played only one more first team game for the Owls before dropping out of senior football – he did leave with a Midland Counties Championship medal in his possession after Wednesday's reserve team won the title in 1903.

He duly moved back to Woodhouse Eves – where his father was the town blacksmith - and uniquely became the only Owls player to later play for another 'Wednesday' in his career! In 1904 he moved to Loughborough where he bought a butchers shop and four years later moved to new premises in the cattle market. In later years his son ran the family business while Frank was appointed Mayor of Loughborough in 1942, after being on the town council for five years.

SUNLEY, David 'Dave' 1970-76

Born: 6 February 1952 Skelton, Yorkshire
(5ft 9ins, 11st 3lbs – 1973)
Debut: 12 December 1970
v Birmingham City
Division Two Away
Last Appearance: 24 January 1976
v Swindon Town
Division Three Home
Total League
& Cup Appearances: 135+13 Goals: 26

Career Details:

WEDNESDAY	28 January	1970
Nottingham Forest	9 October	1975 Loan
Hull City	30 January	1976 £7,500
Lincoln City	1 July	1978 Free
Stockport County	13 March	1980 Free
Stafford Rangers		1982
Burton Albion	August	1982
Tsuen Wan		1982
Burton Albion		1983
Matlock Town	August	1984
Stocksbridge Works		1984
Sheffield Club		1985

The professional football career of Dave Sunley almost failed to materialise as after unsuccessful trials at Preston North End and Middlesbrough he made a final attempt to kick-start his career by dispatching a letter to Owls boss Alan Brown asking for a trial. The Wednesday supremo invited the teenager down for a trial in May 1968 and was sufficiently impressed to sign Sunley as an apprentice later in the month, promoting the youngster into reserve team football as early as October of the same year.

He finished top scorer for the second string in 1970-71 but after breaking into the first team he was unlucky when an injury sustained in a pre season friendly at Bramall Lane saw him miss the first half of the following campaign. However he regained fitness to become a fixture in the Owls Second Division side for almost three years and won representative honours in March 1973 when he played in an F.A.XI that won 8-0 in Gibralter, Sunley netting twice for a side managed by Alf Ramsey and including Gordon Banks in goal. The brave striker was in and out of the side during the disastrous 1974-5 season and was on borrowed time when he refused to sign a contract in the summer of 1975. A loan spell at Nottingham Forest followed before Sunley started a somewhat nomadic part of his career that saw the forward play for a wide variety of clubs – including a stint in Hong Kong – without really making the desired impact. His playing career finally ended in non-league soccer while he was unemployed for a period before working as a building site labourer and then in a chilled warehouse.

SURTEES, John 'Jack' 1934-36

Born: 1 July 1911 Willington-on-Tyne
(5ft 11ins, 12st – 1934)
Died: 16 July 1992 Percy Main
Debut: 25 December 1934
v Birmingham
Division One Home
Last Appearance: 12 February 1936
v Portsmouth
Division One Home
Total League
& Cup Appearances: 50 Goals: 8

Career Details:

Percy Main Amateurs		
Middlesbrough	15 March	1930
Portsmouth	27 June	1932
Bournemouth & Boscombe	June	1933*
Northampton Town	May	1934
WEDNESDAY	27 December	1934 Free
Nottingham Forest	22 October	1936 £2500
York City		WW2 Guest

*Surtees & Friar in exchange for L.Williams

If it was not for the dogged persistency of his brother, Albert, then it is highly likely that Jack Surtees would never have joined the Owls and completed a fairytale story by earning an F.A.Cup winners medal within six months of signing. His brother had played alongside Owls manager Billy Walker at Aston Villa and wrote to his former teammate at the start of the 1934-5 season stating "You used to say I was a good player. Well, he is a better player than I was". The Wednesday boss expressed a willingness to give the young Surtees a trial but in the meantime he had signed for Northampton Town.

However his spell at the Cobblers was a short and unhappy one and after the club agreed to his release he was so despondent that he obtained a passport and booked a passage to America. At that point his brother again intervened and convinced Jack to do nothing until he had spoken to Billy Walker again on his behalf. Finally in late November 1934 the brothers arrived at Hillsborough and the Wednesday boss gave Jack a month's trial. He impressed to such an extent that on Christmas Day Starling was rested and Surtees made his league debut for Wednesday. Such was his performance that he was retained for the return game 24 hours later and soon after was signed until the end of the season, missing only one game and playing in the inside-right position as Wednesday won the F.A.Cup by beating West Brom at Wembley.

He had started as an amateur with Percy Main but after turning professional with Middlesbrough started only one senior game before making a solitary appearance for Portsmouth. A drop into the lower leagues with Bournemouth saw Surtees net four goals in 21 games but he never really showed his true form until coming to Hillsborough where he was a revelation after arriving as a virtual unknown. His right wing partnership with Mark Hooper at Wednesday continued until early in 1936 when newcomer Thomas Grosvenor took his place and Surtees left for Nottingham Forest later in the year. Despite playing 93 times for Forest his relationship with the City Ground faithful deteriorated to such an extent that in December 1938 he asked to be only picked for away games! During the Second World War he played occasionally for Forest but in 1943 was appointed manager at Darlington who after closing down at the start of the conflict had re-entered competitive football. He was later, in November 1948, appointed as a scout by Wednesday at the princely sum of £4 per week and in 1966 travelled down to Wembley as a guest of the club.

SUTHERLAND, George 1894-97

Born: 1876 New Scone, Perth
(5ft 10ins, 11st 9lbs – 1894)
Debut: 17 November 1894
v Wolverhampton Wanderers Division One Home
Last Appearance: 22 April 1895
v West Bromwich Albion Division One Away
Total League & Cup Appearances: 3 Goals: 0

Career Details:

Perthshire		
WEDNESDAY	5 November	1894
Released		1897

Scottish Junior international right back who made three top-flight appearances for Wednesday, as a stand in for regular full back Jack Earp. In total he spent three years at Wednesday and was a reserve team regular before hanging up his boots and becoming a baker in the Attercliffe district of Sheffield

SWAN, Peter 1953-65 & 1972-73

Born: 8 October 1936 South Elmsall
(6ft, 11st 2lbs – 1954)
Debut: 5 November 1955
v Barnsley Division Two Away
Last Appearance:
11 November 1972
v Oxford United
Division Two Home
Total League &
Cup Appearances: 299+2 Goals: 0

Career Details:

WEDNESDAY	19 November	1953
Contract cancelled	April	1965
WEDNESDAY	28 July	1972
Bury	26 July	1973 Free
Matlock Town	11 June	1974
Worksop Town	May	1977

CAPS (@ SWFC):
England Full (19) v Yugoslavia 11/05/60, v Spain 15/05/60, v Hungary 22/05/60, v N.Ireland 08/10/60, v Luxembourg 19/10/60, v Spain 26/10/60, v Wales 23/11/60, v Scotland 15/04/61, v Mexico 10/05/61, v Portugal 21/05/61, v Italy 24/05/61, v Austria 27/05/61, v Luxembourg 28/09/61, v Wales 14/10/61, v Portugal 25/10/61, v N.Ireland 22/11/61, v Austria 04/04/62, v Scotland 14/04/62, v Switzerland 09/05/62

England U-23 (3)
v France 11/11/59, v Scotland 02/03/60, v Holland 16/03/60

England Youth (1)
v Holland 1955

Football League (6)
v League of Ireland 04/11/59, v Italian League 01/11/60, v Scottish League 22/03/61, v League of Ireland 11/10/61, v Italian League 08/11/61, v Scottish League 21/03/62

Sadly for outstanding wing half Peter Swan his name will always be associated with the infamous betting scandal that rocked the football world in April 1964. Along with several other individuals he was implicated in the case, which revolved around an Owls game at Ipswich Town in 1962, and was immediately suspended by Wednesday when the story broke before in January 1965 he was jailed for four months for his part in the scandal. He was also ordered to pay £100 costs and his career was effectively ended soon after when the Football Association banned the England International sine die.

After serving his sentence Swan tried to pick up the pieces of his life by gaining employment at Fletchers Bakeries and later entered the licensing trade before his ban was surprisingly lifted in 1972. He immediately began training back at Hillsborough and impressed Derek Dooley sufficiently to be awarded a 12-month contract in August 1972 to complete a remarkable comeback. However Swan was now in his 36th year and after taking his Wednesday tally to over three hundred games he dropped into reserve team football before moving to Bury where his Football League career finally came to a close after 35 games – ironically after failing to score for Wednesday he netted on his debut for the Shakers!

His career had started in schoolboy football and it was his outstanding form for Doncaster boys that led to Swan signing amateur forms for Wednesday in May 1952. He was quickly tied to a professional contract and the long-legged defender soon displaced Don McEvoy in the Wednesday first team, remaining an automatic choice for six seasons until his career came to a dramatic halt – his longest spell out of the first team came during the 1960-1 season when he suffered a double fracture of his left shoulder in the coach crash in which Doug McMillan lost his leg. He proved a vital member of the Owls best side since pre war years – the McAnearney-Swan-Kay back line being almost unrivalled in English soccer – and appeared in 19 consecutive games for England, including the 1962 World Cup Finals in Chile, before a bout of tonsillitis ended the run. It was therefore a huge blow to Wednesday, purely in footballing terms, when Swan and centre forward Bronco Layne were banned as they instantly lost two players who were impossible to replace.

After leaving Bury he joined non-league side Matlock Town as player-manager and enjoyed an Indian summer, appearing at Wembley in 1975 as his new side won the F.A.Trophy. He resigned from the role in the summer of 1976 and in May 1977 was appointed player-manager at Worksop Town although he failed to play a senior game for the Tigers. A year later he was boss at Buxton and his managerial career ended in December 1981 when he was sacked as Matlock Town manager. He continued to play in charity games until the age of 60 and worked as a publican until his retirement.

SWIFT, Humphrey Mills 'Hugh' 1944-51

Born: 22 January 1921 Sheffield
(5ft 11ins, 11st 8lbs – 1948)
Died: 24 January 1970 Sheffield
Debut: 5 January 1946
v Mansfield Town F.A.Cup Away
Last Appearance: 26 February 1951
v Manchester United
Division One Home
Total League
& Cup Appearances: 195* Goals: 0
***Also appeared**
in 136 wartime games, scoring 6 goals

Career Details:

Burngreave Old Boys		1937
Lopham Street W.M.C.		1939
WEDNESDAY		1944
Sheffield United	March	1945 Guest
Retired	11 August	1951

CAPS (@SWFC)
England 'B' (1) v Switzerland 18/01/50

When Hugh Swift left school, at the age of sixteen, he gained employment as an office boy at Wednesday President William Turner's Silversmith's company. A few weeks earlier he had received the prestigious Sheffield Clegg Shield – the City's top schoolboy trophy - from Mr Turner and was soon training with Wednesday while playing in local football with Burngreave Old Boys. The Wednesday mad youngster regularly trained in the evenings at Hillsborough under a scheme ran by then manager Jimmy McMullen but was never noticed and eventually stopped attending the sessions after being told he was too frail to make the grade. The former Sheffield and Yorkshire boys left winger then joined Sheffield Association League side Lopham Street but was given a second chance at Wednesday in February 1942 when he played as a guest for the club in a wartime game at Burnley.

After becoming established in the club's reserve side Hugh started the next season in the first team and after signing amateur forms in September 1942 he was almost ever present, scoring five times in the club's most successful wartime season. Near the end of the season – prior to the first leg of the War North Cup Final – Swift's career would take a completely new path as he stood in for injured left back Ted Catlin and after marking the great Stanley Matthews out of the game would remain in the position for the remainder of his career! In his new role Swift proved a quite outstanding back, proving two-footed, pacy and a great exponent of the sliding tackle, and in the immediate post war years formed an unbroken full back partnership with Frank Westlake that lasted 106 games between December 1946 and April 1949. He later captained Wednesday to promotion from Division Two in 1950 and looked set for full England honours after impressing for England 'B' but sadly a double fracture of his jaw, suffered at Coventry in 1951, proved an initial setback before knee problems forced his premature retirement in August 1951. Swift had suffered Rheumatic fever at the age of 19 and had been left with a heart murmur, which was thought to be the reason why his knees started to swell and meant his playing days came to an end.

Thankfully for Swift he was never a full time professional at Hillsborough – he continued to work at Turners Limited on Eyre Street in Sheffield where by 1946 he had risen to department manager while also owning his own general dealer's shop. After his playing career ended he was also retained by Wednesday on full wages as a scout and scouted and coached on a part-time basis for the club until February 1967 when manager Alan Brown sacked him. However he was appointed juniors coach a year later when Jack Marshall became manager and remained on the staff until passing away at the age of 59, just two days after celebrating his birthday.

SYKES, Joseph 'Joe' 1920-24

Born: 8 January 1898 Sheffield
(5ft 7ins, 10st 10lbs – 1921)
Died: 4 September 1974 Swansea
Debut: 6 March 1920
v Liverpool
Division One Away
Last Appearance: 8 March 1924
v Stockport County
Division Two Away
Total League
& Cup Appearances: 31 Goals: 1

Career Details:

Hallam		
WEDNESDAY	January	1920
Swansea Town	3 July	1924 £300

Every football club's history is littered with players who only enjoyed great success after joining another side and centre half back Joe Sykes certainly falls into that category for Wednesday. He had started his career with Sheffield based non-league side Hallam, in the period prior to the Great War, and after serving for the Army in India during the conflict he returned to Sheffield where the Owls secured his signature. Within a few weeks Sykes was making his top-flight debut and after surviving the end of season cull following relegation he stayed a further four years at Wednesday although he was never more than understudy to England International George Wilson.

He eventually departed for Swansea Town where he would become one of the Welsh club's greatest players, appearing in 314 league games over the next ten years and captained them to the Division Three (South) title in 1925 and to the semi-finals of the F.A.Cup a year later. He was known as the 'diminutive giant' by Swans fans and after his playing days ended he returned to Sheffield to start his own business only to return to Swansea to join the club's coaching staff within a few months. In the summer of 1947 he was elevated to assistant trainer and was behind the scenes when Town won the Division Three (South) title again in 1949 – during his period as trainer he was credited with bringing the likes of John Charles and Ivor Allchurch into the game after spotting them playing in local park football! In July 1960 he was appointed assistant manager and was later caretaker boss between October 1966 and February 1967 before returning to his former role until leaving the Vetch Field in June 1968.

SYMM, Colin 1965-69

Born: 26 November 1946
Dunston-on-Tyne
(5ft 9ins, 10st 7lbs – 1966)
Debut: 15 October 1966
v Everton
Division One Away
Last Appearance: 10 August 1968
v West Bromwich Albion
Division One Away
Total League
& Cup Appearances: 19+4 Goals: 1

Career Details:

Redheugh Boys Club		
Gateshead		
WEDNESDAY	14 May	1965
Sunderland	14 June	1969 Free
Lincoln City	June	1972 Free
Boston United	July	1975
Consett F.C.		1979

Colin Symm arrived at Wednesday, along with teammate Ian Branfoot, from non-league Gateshead but like Branfoot he failed to make a lasting impression on the Owls first team. The former County Durham boys and Association of boys clubs international was signed by Alan Brown and proved a neat and classy player at either inside or outside right but fierce competition meant he started fewer than twenty league games before looking set to sign for Peterborough United in 1968. However after travelling down the A1 with his wife he decided to turn down the transfer and instead remained a further year at Wednesday before returning to his roots when signing for Sunderland. His fortunes fared little better at Roker Park, starting only nine league games in three years, but he did enjoy a sustained run of games at his final Football League club, Lincoln City, where he appeared in 69 league games, scoring nine times.

While at Lincoln he attended Trent Polytechnic on a two-year part-time Leisure management course, funded by the P.F.A., and when playing at Northern Premier League Boston United he was appointed assistant manager at Bircotes Sports Centre near Worksop. He later moved back to the Northeast, initially working as assistant manager at Consett Sports Centre, and also played a handful of games for the local non-league side. His links with football continued when he scouted for a variety of clubs managed by his old team mate Branfoot while he has now worked for over twenty years for the Derwentshire District Council – he is now employed as General Manager of the Limited Company that manages the authority's two leisure centres and swimming Centre.

TALBOT, Andrew 'Drew' 2003-

Born: 19 July 1986 Barnsley
(5ft 10ins, 11st - 2004)
Debut: 20 October 2004
v Peterborough United League One Away
Total League
& Cup Appearances: 4+21 Goals: 5

Career Details:

Barnsley		Academy
Dodworth Miners Welfare		
WEDNESDAY	1 July	2003

Pacy and livewire striker who burst onto the Hillsborough scene during the early days of Paul Sturrock's reign. Over the months that followed the Owls boss had no qualms about handing Talbot a place on the subs bench and his star rose further after the teenager netted his first goal in senior football, against Doncaster Rovers in March 2005. A week later he netted a brace from the bench and the diminutive striker was quickly transformed into the darling of the Hillsborough faithful. His searing pace and running of the channels caused countless problems for opposition defenders and his ability to be in the right place at the right time ensured he netted in the crucial game at Hull City that secured a play off place for Wednesday. The campaign was proving a dream debut season for the 18 year-old and it was real fairytale stuff in Cardiff as in the last minute of extra time Talbot raced away from the Hartlepool defence to coolly slot home the Owls fourth goal and confirm a glorious promotion to the Championship in front of 40,000 plus delirious Wednesday fans.

That unforgettable day in Cardiff must have seemed an impossible dream for Talbot when as an Academy player with Barnsley he had the misfortune to suffer a broken leg on two separate occasions, at U-15 and then U-16 level. Those devastating injuries looked to have ruined his chances of a professional career and despite returning to action for the Tykes U-17 team he eventually drifted out of the senior game and unbelievably stopped playing football for several months! Thankfully he made a comeback in local non-league football and soon moved to Hillsborough after his former boss at Oakwell, Mark Smith, moved to the same role at Hillsborough. It proved a truly inspirational signing by Smith as Talbot quickly showed his qualities by netting four times in only seven games for the Owls Academy side during the second half of the 2003-04 campaign. His first goal for the reserve team came in the final match of the season and his goal for the Academy side against Sheffield United was enough to impress Paul Sturrock who duly handed the youngster a place on the subs bench for the home game against Barnsley in October 2004. His first team debut came three days later and despite being involved in a minor car accident he played on with a light plaster cast over a broken wrist. In hindsight the success of Kenwyne Jones probably helped keep the spotlight off Talbot and he was rewarded in March 2005 when Wednesday handed him a new contract, taking the teenager through to the end of June 2007.

TAYLOR, Charles Stanley 'Stan 1920-21

Born: Q/E September 1897 Sheffield
(5ft 8ins, 11st 7lbs – 1924)
Died: Q/E December 1963 Sheffield
Debut: 7 February 1920 v Preston North End Division One Home
Last Appearance:
1 May 1920 v Oldham Athletic Division One Home
Total League & Cup Appearances: 7 Goals: 0

Career Details:

Norfolk Amateurs	October	1919
WEDNESDAY	February	1920
Norton Woodseats		1921
Sheffield United	27 February	1924
Denaby United		1925
Mexborough Athletic	March	1926
Worksop Town		1926
Mexborough Athletic		1927

Forward who spent the majority of his career in local non-league football while being employed at a Sheffield based lawyer's office. However he also spent two separate spells as a professional at Wednesday and neighbours United, appearing for the Owls first during the disastrous 1919-20 relegation season. Prior to joining Wednesday he had served in the marines and then the Army during the Great War and regularly played in representative services football before being de-mobbed. He signed for Wednesday after impressing in a trial game and was one of several forwards used as the Owls desperately tried to avoid the drop from the top division.

However after failing to find the net he dropped back into reserve team football and after applying for an amateur permit from the F.A. he signed for Amateur League Norton Woodseats. After finishing league top scorer in 1923-4 he was given a second chance at the pro game by the Blades but appeared in only one game before reverting back to non-league soccer.

TAYLOR, Ian Kenneth 1994

Born: 4 June 1968 Birmingham
(6ft 1ins, 12st 4lbs – 1994)
Debut: 20 August 1994
v Tottenham Hotspur
Premier League Home
Last Appearance: 3 December 1994
v Crystal Palace
Premier League Home
Total League
& Cup Appearances: 11+7 Goals: 2

Career Details:

Shirley Crusaders		
Moor Green		
Port Vale	1 July	1992 £40,000
WEDNESDAY	12 July	1994 £1m (T)
Aston Villa	21 December	1994 £1m
Derby County	1 July	2003 Free
Northampton Town	1 July	2005 Free

When Carlton Palmer departed Hillsborough in the summer of 1994 the Owls seemed to have signed a perfect replacement when they fought off several clubs to secure the signature of Ian Taylor. The hard working box-to-box midfielder had risen to prominence at Port Vale where he netted 35 times in 106 games and won the 1993 Associate Members Cup, beating Stockport County in the Wembley final. Before joining the Staffordshire club it seemed Taylor's chances of a career as a professional had receded as after qualifying as an electrician he worked as a fork lift truck driver while playing for his works side on a Saturday and then for Shirley Crusaders on a Sunday.

However he proved a late developer and after helping Port Vale to promotion from Division Two in 1994 it was Wednesday boss Trevor Francis who won the race for his signature. Unfortunately he would experience a frustrating time at Hillsborough as the form of John Sheridan, Chris Bart-Williams and Graham Hyde meant he struggled to nail down a regular place and was often played out of position on the right side of midfield. In hindsight his subsequent move to boyhood heroes Aston Villa, after less than six months at Wednesday, proved an error of judgement by Francis as over the next eight seasons Taylor became a vital cog in the Villa midfield, appearing in almost three hundred games for the Birmingham club and winning the League Cup in 1996 – the tall, somewhat underrated midfielder netting in the 3-0 win over Leeds United. He developed into one of the most consistent performers in the top division and it was only two seasons of niggling injuries that eventually led to his move to Division One side Derby County on a 'Bosman' free transfer. He regained his fitness and form at Pride Park, finishing top scorer in 2003-4, and remained a regular for County until signing for League Two side Northampton Town.

TAYLOR, James 'Jock' 1907-10

Born:
Debut: 31 December 1907
v Woolwich Arsenal
Division One Home
Last Appearance: 9 April 1910
v Chelsea
Division One Away
Total League
& Cup Appearances: 20 Goals: 0

Career Details:

Wallsend Park Villa		
WEDNESDAY	December	1907
Leicester Fosse		1910 Trial
Doncaster Rovers	October	1911

Acted as understudy to William Bartlett for four seasons after joining from non-league soccer. Made his senior debut for Wednesday in a 6-0 home win over Arsenal on New Year's Eve 1907 and enjoyed his best run in the side during what proved to be his final campaign at Hillsborough, appearing in thirteen games as cover for his rival Bartlett. He eventually moved to neighbours Doncaster Rovers, winning the Sheffield Challenge Cup in 1912, but was released at the end of the 1913-14 season when Rovers were officially wound up after being engulfed by financial problems.

TAYLOR, Kevin 'Ticker' 1978-84

Born: 22 January 1961 Wakefield
(5ft 8ins, 11st 11lbs – 1982)
Debut: 27 January 1979
v Plymouth Argyle
Division Three Away
Last Appearance: 31 March 1984
v Leeds United
Division Two Away
Total League
& Cup Appearances: 136+9 Goals: 28

Career Details:

Ryhill Colts		
Monckton AFC		
WEDNESDAY	30 October	1978 £30 donation
Derby County	18 July	1984 £10,000
Crystal Palace	5 March	1985 £20,000
Scunthorpe United	9 October	1987 Free
Fryston Colliery Welfare		1991
Farsley Celtic	July	1993
Bradford Park Avenue		1993
Pontefract Colleries		1995
Worsbrough Bridge MW		1997
Tom Treddlehoyle		1999
Royston WMC		

Midfielder Kevin 'Ticker' Taylor was another product of the club's highly successful youth policy of the late 1970s and like many of his contemporaries went on to became a first team regular as Wednesday climbed out of the Third Division and consolidated in the higher grade. The former Royston comprehensive and Barnsley boys player had started at Wednesday as an apprentice in May 1977 and within three months of turning professional made his league bow, quickly going on to earn a niche in the side under Jack Charlton's management. He contributed vital goals during the 1980 promotion campaign, including one in the crunch win at Blackburn that practically sealed Division Two football, and was virtually an automatic choice in the Owls midfield for the first three years of the 1980s. However during that period, in January 1982, he submitted a shock transfer request and also turned down a new deal in May 1983, before having a change of heart.

He became more unsettled when Howard Wilkinson took over in the summer of 1983 and Taylor found he had only a bit part in the new manager's all running outfit, starting only two games as Wilkinson's direct football took the Owls back into the top-flight. His final appearance in a Wednesday shirt came in an unaccustomed left back role and it was no surprise when Taylor was placed on the transfer list in May 1984 and subsequently signed for Arthur Cox at Derby County. Unfortunately his move to the Baseball Ground proved a disappointment for Taylor and after just 22 games he transferred to Crystal Palace where during his 87 appearances his new side twice just missed out on promotion to Division One.

His final club in league football proved to be Scunthorpe United where he lost consecutive play off semi-finals – under the management of future Owls Chief Scout and caretaker manager Bill Green. After amassing 192 competitive games for The Iron, netting 29 goals, Taylor gained employment outside of the game and began playing non-league soccer with West Yorkshire side Fryston Colliery. After playing for a variety of Yorkshire non-league sides throughout the 1990s he appeared in the Wragg Over-35s league for Barnsley based Tom Treddlehoyle while working as a warehouse operative. After a spell at Royston WMC, Taylor retired and now scouts for Leeds United.

TAYLOR, Robert Mark 1989-91

Born: 22 February 1966 Birmingham
(5ft 8ins, 11st 8lbs – 1989)
Debut: 22 August 1989
v Luton Town
Division One Away
Last Appearance: 28 October 1989
v Wimbledon
Division One Home
Total League
& Cup Appearances: 10+1 Goals: 0

Career Details:

Newton Albion		
Walsall	24 July	1984
WEDNESDAY	16 June	1989 £50,000
Shrewsbury Town	7 February	1991 3-month loan
Shrewsbury Town	12 September	1991£50,000
Hereford United	August	1998 Free
Nuneaton Borough		2000
Halesowen Town	July	2001
Redditch United	24 October	2002 Free

The signing of Walsall duo Mark Taylor and Craig Shakespeare represented a gamble by Owls boss Ron Atkinson, as he searched the lower divisions for players capable of performing in top-flight soccer. Unfortunately neither player managed to adapt to life in the higher grade and for midfielder Taylor he spent the majority of his Owls career in reserve team football after having started the opening seven league games of the 1989-90 season. A depressing home defeat to Wimbledon proved to be his final appearance in a Wednesday shirt and after almost two years in the shadows he eventually moved to Shrewsbury Town, following a successful loan period.

During his time at Hillsborough he was utilised as either a right-sided midfielder or wing back but at Shrewsbury he became a mainstay in the former position, helping the Shropshire club to the Third Division Championship in 1994 and the final of the Associate Members Cup in 1996 – Taylor netting in the Wembley final defeat against Rotherham United. He totalled over 300 games for the Shrews before dropping into Conference football at Hereford United prior to becoming player-coach at Nuneaton Borough. He later moved to Southern League (Western Division) club Halesowen Town and after helping them to the Divisional title in 2002 he was appointed player-coach and captain of Southern League Redditch United.

TAYLOR, Paul Anthony 1971-73

Born: 3 December 1949 Sheffield
(5ft 11ins, 11st 10lbs – 1973)
Debut: 14 August 1971
v Queens Park Rangers
Division One Away
Last Appearance: 30 September 1972
v Carlisle United
Division Two Away
Total League
& Cup Appearances: 5+1 Goals: 0

Career Details:

Loughborough College		
Doncaster Rovers		Trial
WEDNESDAY	1 July	1971
York City	6 July	1973
Hereford United	January	1974 Loan
Colchester United	March	1974 2-month loan
Southport	19 July	1974
Released	30 June	1975
San José		1975
Southport	September	1975
Los Angeles Skyhawks	April	1977
Team Hawaii		

As a teenager Paul Taylor decided to put his education first and after leaving Abbeydale school in Sheffield he attended Loughborough College to gain a PE teaching certificate. While furthering his education the former Sheffield boys player signed part-time forms at Wednesday – in 1969 – and eventually turned professional after completing his teacher-training course. The powerfully built midfielder received an early boost to his fulltime career when he was handed a place in the first eleven on the opening day of the 1971-2 season. However he would only be used sparingly over the next two seasons and after failing to become established under Derek Dooley he moved to York City, initially on a month-to-month contract.

Over the next few seasons Taylor played for a variety of lower league clubs with his most productive period coming during two spells at Southport where he netted 16 times in 102 league and cup games. After his contract at Haig Avenue was cancelled late in the 1976-77 season he returned to US football and remained across the pond for several years, playing for three different sides before being appointed manager at Columbus Magic in the late 1970s. While in the States he ran soccer schools with former Owl Jim Hinch but returned home in June 1981 to take over as assistant manager at Gillingham. He later spent eleven months as manager before being dismissed in October 1988 and in 1989 started a long association with Walsall when joining the coaching staff. He was caretaker boss at Walsall in early 1990 and after being appointed General Manager in August 1990 he remained until leaving to start his own soccer consultant business in January 2002.

TAYLOR, Samuel James 'Sam' 1921-25

Born: 17 September 1893 Sheffield
(5ft 7ins, 11st – 1921)
Died: March 1973 Sheffield
Debut: 15 January 1921
v Port Vale
Division Two Away
Last Appearance: 7 February 1925
v Leicester City
Division Two Away
Total League
& Cup Appearances: 128 Goals: 39

Career Details:

Atlas & Norfolk Works		
Silverwood Colliery		
Huddersfield Town	March	1913
Rotherham County		WW1 Guest
Bradford Park Avenue		WW1 Guest
WEDNESDAY	6 January	1921 £3,500
Mansfield Town	May	1925 £1,000*
Southampton	21 May	1926 £950**
Halifax Town	June	1928
Grantham	January	1929
Chesterfield	May	1929
Llanelly	August	1930
Loughborough Corinthians	November	1932
Grantham Town		1933

*Fee set but not paid as Mansfield were non league
** £300 paid to Wednesday who held his league registration

Diminutive centre forward Sam Taylor first came to prominence in the years immediately preceding the Great War when he scored freely for Atlas & Norfolk in local Sheffield football, winning the prestigious Amateur League in 1912 when aged just eighteen. However he was not spotted by either of the city's two professional clubs and Wednesday especially would have cause for regret as Sam started his professional career with a bang at Huddersfield Town. His incredible goal haul of 35 in the 1919-20 season is still the joint record for the Terriers and it not only helped Town surge out of the Second Division but also to an F.A.Cup Final appearance against Aston Villa. In the same season a shot-shy Owls slid out of the top-flight and six months later Bob Brown made his first major signing as Owls boss – paying a club record fee to bring Taylor back to Sheffield.

He immediately formed a deadly attacking duo with Johnny McIntyre, netting almost a goal every other game as Wednesday finished the 1920-1 season in tremendous style by losing only one of their final sixteen games. Unfortunately McIntyre's surprise departure mid way through the following season ended that affiliation and Taylor dropped into an inside-right role as Sid Binks was handed the No. 9 shirt. However the change of position did not affect Taylor's proficiency in front of goal, finishing joint top scorer in 1923-24 with 13 goals, and he was later described as "the brains of the Hillsborough attack". In the summer of 1924 Sam reached the final of the Sheffield Amateur Billiards Championship but his first team place at Wednesday was now in the hands of Harold Hill and after being put on the transfer list at his own request in October 1924 he then turned down an offer to play football in the United States. In the summer that followed he refused the Owls offer of a new contract and caused a mini sensation when he dropped out of league football altogether to sign for Midland League Mansfield Town – incredibly the non-league outfit were able to offer Taylor a better financial package! To make matters worse for Wednesday his new club did not have to pay a fee because of their status although the Owls kept his registration documents in case he returned to league football. Unsurprisingly he finished the 1925-6 season as Midland League top scorer with 28 goals and helped Town to runners-up spot plus success in the Final of the Notts Senior Cup, Sam scoring a treble in the 6-0 rout of Players Athletic.

He was quickly back in league football at Southampton – part of the Saints record transfer fee making its way back to Hillsborough – and in his debut season he played in the club's F.A.Cup semi-final defeat to Arsenal. Later in his Southampton career the thoughtful and intelligent attacker moved to inside left and after 17 goals in 69 games returned to Yorkshire, signing for Halifax Town. After a handful of games in Division Three (North) for Town he dropped back into non-league soccer with Grantham but was quickly back in league soccer, being appointed player-coach at Chesterfield. An injury suffered part way through the 1930-1 season eventually ended his league career although Sam continued to play until the mid-1930s, following a second spell at Grantham. After hanging up his boots Sam returned to Sheffield – marrying at Attercliffe on Christmas Day 1938 – and along with his spouse became well known as entertainers on the local club circuit, the former Owls forward accompanying Mrs Taylor on the piano.

TAYLOR, William 'Billy' 1919-22

Born: Q/E June 1896 Crook, County Durham
(5ft $9^1/2$ins, 11st 7lbs – 1920)
Debut:
29 April 1920 v Aston Villa Division One Away
Last Appearance:
14 January 1922 v Stoke FC Division One Home
Total League & Cup Appearances: 17 Goals: 4

Career Details:

Crook Town		1918
Norfolk Amateurs	October	1919
WEDNESDAY	February	1920
Doncaster Rovers	August	1922
Mansfield Town	June	1923
Mexborough Town	July	1924
Mansfield Town	February	1926
Doncaster Rovers	June	1925
Denaby United	October	1926
Mexborough Town		1927
Worksop Town	January	1928

After serving during the First World War as an officer in the Army, forward Billy Taylor returned home to launch a football career with local side Crook Town. While in Crook colours Taylor reached the Final of the Durham Challenge Cup in 1919 but lost 8-0 to Sunderland after they decided to play their first team against the amateurs! Soon after he moved to Sheffield based side Norfolk Amateurs and then spent almost eighteen months as a professional at Wednesday, appearing occasionally as new manager Bob Brown strived to find a winning formula.

His first spell at Belle Vue lasted only a year but ended with a Wharncliffe Charity Cup winners medal and runners up spot, behind the Owls' reserves, in the Midland League. However despite Rovers subsequently being voted into the Football League in the summer of 1923 Taylor surprisingly left, dropping back into the Midland League with Mansfield Town. Again he spent only a season with the Stags – helping Town to the Championship – but was soon back to help Town retain the title in 1925. He came back into league soccer during a second spell at Doncaster Rovers, appearing in 19 games and netting 5 goals, and ended his playing days at Worksop Town.

THACKERAY, Fred 1898-1904

Born: 1878 Sheffield
Debut: 9 March 1901
v Aston Villa
Division One Away
Last Appearance: 4 April 1903
v Everton
Division One Away
Total League
& Cup Appearances: 10 Goals: 0

Career Details:

Montrose Works		
WEDNESDAY	August	1898
Gainsborough Trinity	15 June	1904 £20
Rotherham Town		

Despite spending six seasons at Hillsborough, Fred Thackeray was used sparingly at first team level, his best run in the side occurring in the 1902-03 season when he made six appearances at right-back. He had previously played all his first team football in the centre halfback position and started in this role in reserve team football for Wednesday after joining from local works team Montrose just before the dawn of the 20th Century. He experienced a highly successful debut season, winning both the Sheffield Association and Wharncliffe Charity Cup leagues with the reserves, and was then a mainstay of the second team that not only retained the Association League but also completed the season with a remarkable 100% home record as well as netting 110 goals!

A year later he helped the reserves win the inaugural season of the Midland League and overall proved a loyal and dependable club man who provided credible back up for the likes of Tommy Crawshaw and Willie Layton. Incidentally there is some doubt over Thackeray's actual christian name as no Fred appears in the 1901 census records that could possibly have played football for Sheffield Wednesday. Therefore it is more likely – considering he worked in the Sheffield steel industry - he was a called Charlie, John, William, Harry or Arthur!

THOMAS, Walter Keith 1950-52

Born: 28 July 1929 Oswestry
(5ft 9ins, 11st – 1950)
Debut: 3 March 1951
v Wolverhampton Wanderers
Division One Away
Last Appearance: 29 September 1951
v Cardiff City
Division Two Away
Total League
& Cup Appearances: 10 Goals: 1

Career Details:

Oswestry Town		
WEDNESDAY	7 September	1950 £3,000
Cardiff City	July	1952 £1,000

Plymouth Argyle	November	1953
Exeter City	March	1956
Oswestry Town		1959

Inside left Keith Thomas spent only two seasons at Wednesday, after being signed from non-league soccer, and fierce competition from the likes of Red Froggatt and Albert Quixall ensured he appeared in only a handful of first team games. His nine appearances during the 1951-2 season were unfortunately insufficient for him to gain a Division Two Championship medal and at the end of the season he moved to Cardiff City, after impressing in a public trial match for the Welsh club. While at Cardiff he made just nine league appearances but had become a part-time player whilst training to be a teacher.

He finally made a mark in league soccer while at Plymouth and then Exeter City – taking his career tally of league games to exactly 100 – before returning to his roots when being appointed player-manager back at Oswestry Town. His playing career had started with just a handful of games at the Shropshire club after initially working in a bank before serving his two years National Service in Singapore with the R.A.F. His second spell at Oswestry lasted three seasons at which point Keith left to attend Loughborough College for a year, gaining P.E. teaching qualifications and his F.A. coaching badge. He then re-joined the R.A.F. and as Flying Officer Thomas continued to captain and play for his unit football side until moving into the Army in 1966. At the age of fifty he left the services and moved to the Shrewsbury area, becoming a teacher of blind children until retiring in 1991, aged 62.

*Did not play for Hereford United

THOME, Emerson Augusto 1998-99

Born: 30 March 1972 Porto Alegre, Brazil
(6ft 1ins, 13st 4lbs – 1999)
Debut: 11 April 1998
v Barnsley
Premier League Away
Last Appearance: 18 December 1999
v Aston Villa
Premier League Away
Total League
& Cup Appearances: 69+2 Goals: 2

Career Details:

SC Internacional		
Coimbra		1993
Ferense		1994
Benfica		1995
WEDNESDAY	20 March	1998 Free
Chelsea	22 December	1999 £2.5m
Sunderland	31 August	2000 £4.5m
Glasgow Rangers	July	2003 Trial
Bolton Wanderers	29 August	2003 Free
Wigan Athletic	4 August	2004 Free

Emerson Thome was born into a poor family in Brazil's fourth largest city of Porto Alegre and played his early football in the streets before attending mammoth trials at his local club Internacional. His birthplace in Southern Brazil boasts a population bigger than London and a career as a professional footballer was certainly seen as a way out of poverty for the highly determined youngster as at the age of 12 he attended trials along with 999 other wide-eyed children, which lasted fully three days. At the conclusion Emerson signed for the highly rated Internacional Academy but despite gaining a foothold on the professional ladder those early days were still tough for the youngster as he could not afford the bus fare to the training sessions and had to fare dodge to keep his dream alive! His coach quickly nicknamed Thome 'pared'o' – Portuguese for 'The Wall' – when another boy ran into him during a training session and promptly bounced off and fell over!

After progressing into the senior side the superbly fit, tall and strong defender was a first team regular for two seasons but at the age of 21 moved to Portugal after being spotted by scouts back home in Brazil. Emerson – named after Brazilian Formula 1 racing driver Emerson Fittipaldi who won the drivers championship in his year of birth – eventually progressed to Portuguese giants Benfica where he also met his future wife. He would experience a mixed time at Benfica and after falling into dispute with the club attended a variety of trials in England but Stoke City, Huddersfield Town and Bristol Rovers all considered he was talented but simply not physically fit enough to take a risk paying a transfer fee for – he had not played competitive football for six months whilst in dispute. To stop the impasse Thome eventually paid Benfica himself to be released from his contract and in March 1998 he was yet another foreign trialist to arrive at Hillsborough during Ron Atkinson's brief second spell as manager.

After impressing for the reserves the stylish centre half was handed a contract until the end of the season – he held dual nationality so there was no work permit problems - and despite making his debut in midfield he was named man of the match. However it was at the heart of the Owls defence that Thome impressed – Atkinson later said he was a gem found by the roadside – and Wednesday had no hesitation in tying the imposing Brazilian to a three-year contract in July 1998. Over the next eighteen months he became somewhat of a cult hero amongst Owls fans while his performances alongside Des Walker ensured Wednesday retained their Premier League status in Danny Wilson's first season as manager – Thome was ever present during that 1998-99 campaign. Unfortunately he then became unsettled by talk of a possible transfer from Hillsborough and his form suffered before Wednesday and Chelsea agreed to his transfer to Stamford Bridge. The fee seemed a bargain one for the Londoners and Thome would play Champions League football in his first season although he missed out on an appearance in the 2000 F.A.Cup Final after being cup-tied whilst playing for the Owls in the Third Round.

After just 22 games for Chelsea he was then sold, for a massive profit, to Premier League Sunderland who broke their club record transfer fee to take the Brazilian to the Northeast. He enjoyed a tremendous debut season with the Black Cats but then experienced horrendous injury problems, mainly caused by a persistent medial knee ligament injury, and appeared in only a handful of games during the final two years of his three-year contract. After being released he successfully relaunched his career with Premier League Bolton Wanderers and was a regular at the Lancashire club who enjoyed one of the best seasons in their history – Thome appearing in the 2004 League Cup Final defeat to Middlesbrough.

THOMPSON, Ernest Guy 'Ernie' 1921-22

Born: Q/E December 1890 Rotherham
(5ft 8ins, 11st 4lbs – 1921)
Debut: 10 September 1921 v Notts County Division Two Away
Last Appearance: 15 April 1922 v Bury Division Two Away
Total League & Cup Appearances: 24 Goals: 0

Career Details:

South Shields		
Rotherham Town		
Portsmouth	May	1913
WEDNESDAY	20 May	1921
Bradford Park Avenue	26 August	1922 £100
Grimsby Town	May	1924
Castleford Town	August	1925
Denaby United	May	1926
Scunthorpe & Lindsey United		1926

Right winger Ernie Thompson first came to prominence when winning the prestigious Midland League with Rotherham Town in 1913 and was soon signed by future Owls boss Bob Brown for Southern League Portsmouth. He went on to appear in Pompey's first ever league game in 1920, after winning the Southern League title, and was once sent off playing against Southend United only for the referee to change his mind when both sets of players appealed against the decision! Following Portsmouth's first season of league soccer he was signed for a second time by Bob Brown – now manager at Hillsborough – and was a regular on the right wing as Wednesday finished in a mid table slot in the Second Division. Incidentally the £100 transfer fee was paid direct to Thompson as he was owed a benefit by the Fratton Park club.

The arrival of Rees Williams effectively ended his career at

Wednesday and he soon moved to Bradford Park Avenue where his new side finished runners-up in Division Three (North) to Nelson – only the champions were promoted in those days. He later appeared in eight games for Grimsby Town before dropping out of senior football altogether.

THOMPSON, Frederick 'Fred' 1887-91

Born: 1870 Sheffield
Died: May 1898 Sheffield
Debut:
15 October 1887 v Belper Town F.A.Cup Away
Last Appearance:
14 February 1891 v West Bromwich Albion F.A.Cup Home
Total League & Cup Appearances: 12* Goals: 1
***Also appeared in 30 Football Alliance League games**

Career Details:

Hastings (Sheffield)		
WEDNESDAY	February	1887
Nottingham Forest	August	1891

Although full back Fred Thompson was a regular for Wednesday for four seasons his whole career was cursed by poor health which not only denied him an appearance in the 1890 F.A.Cup Final but sadly led to his premature death at the age of only 28. He was somewhat of a teenage prodigy when he made his debut for Wednesday, in a friendly at Mexborough in February 1887, and quickly became established at right back as the club moved into the professional era, although Fred initially remained amateur. He would play in the first ever game at Olive Grove – against Blackburn Rovers in September 1887 – and over the next two seasons won the Sheffield Challenge Cup, Wharncliffe Charity Cup and Gainsborough News Charity Cup as Wednesday dominated the Sheffield football scene.

He remained a mainstay, and captain, of the Wednesday side as the club were founder members (and first winners) of the Football Alliance League – appearing in the first game in the competition – but his health then started to fail, as he was absent from Boxing Day 1889 until April of the following year. His time on the sidelines coincided with the club's run to their first ever F.A.Cup Final and his comeback game was actually a week after the club had lost heavily to Blackburn Rovers in the showpiece final. Sadly in September 1890 Fred was found in a state of 'insensibility' on his bedroom floor and despite receiving medical treatment he suffered another attack a few hours later. He recovered sufficiently to reclaim a first team place at Wednesday and after moving to Nottingham Forest won a second Football Alliance League Championship medal prior to Forest being voted into the expanded Football League. The elevation meant Fred made his first league appearance – as a halfback in Forest's first ever league home match against Stoke City in September 1892 – but unfortunately this proved to be his only senior game for the Reds and he was released in the summer of 1893.

THOMPSON, Garry Linsey 1985-86

Born: 7 October 1959 Birmingham
(6ft 2ins, 12st 11lbs – 1985)
Debut: 17 August 1985
v Chelsea
Division One Home
Last Appearance: 3 May 1986
v Ipswich Town
Division One Home
Total League
& Cup Appearances: 42+2 Goals: 8

Career Details:

Coventry City	29 June	1977
West Bromwich Albion	17 February	1983 £225,000
WEDNESDAY	12 August	1985 £450,000
Aston Villa	5 June	1986 £450,000
Watford	12 December	1988 £325,000
Crystal Palace	24 March	1990 £200,000
Queens Park Rangers	19 August	1991 £125,000
Cardiff City	15 August	1993 Free
Northampton Town	10 February	1995 Free

Aggressive and no nonsense centre forward Garry Thompson seemed the perfect target man for the Owls direct style of play in the mid-1980s and Owls boss Howard Wilkinson obviously agreed as he smashed the club's transfer record to bring 'Tommo' to Hillsborough. However despite helping Wednesday to fifth place in the top-flight and the semi-finals of the F.A.Cup his goal record was poor and this was probably the major factor in his subsequent surprise move back to Birmingham, signing for Aston Villa in a 'get your money back' deal. Prior to joining Wednesday he had finished top scorer for West Brom for two seasons running and despite his lack of goals at Wednesday he became a big favourite with Owls supporters.

As a teenager Thompson was a natural athlete and competed in the high jump as well as playing football. However a torn knee cartilage saw the young Thompson briefly lose interest in football before he eventually signed schoolboy forms for Coventry City in February 1975. He was eventually elevated to professional status but then spent a long spell on the sidelines after breaking his leg in three places during a practice game. After regaining fitness he broke back into the Sky Blues side, helping them to the semi-finals of the League Cup, and was rewarded with six England U-21 caps before Chairman Jimmy Hill controversially sold him, over the head of then manager Dave Sexton. The former South Birmingham boys player then achieved success at the Hawthorns and following his Hillsborough spell he won promotion to Division One with Villa in 1988 and then lifted the Full Members Cup in 1991 whilst at Crystal Palace. At his nine league sides Thompson netted a total of 154 times in competitive football and his first taste of coaching came at his final club, Northampton Town, where 'Tommo' was employed as player-coach.

His playing days ended when Thompson was appointed coach at Bristol Rovers in January 1999 and he later spent five months as caretaker boss before reverting back to his coaching duties in June 2001. However following the departure of Gerry Francis in December 2001 he was then appointed full-time boss on a generous five-year contract. Incredibly after just over three months in charge Thompson was then sacked and remained out of the game until being appointed assistant manager at Brentford in October 2002. He was again given the reins on a caretaker basis following Wally Downes' departure in March 2004 but 24 hours after new man Martin Allen was appointed Thompson was shown the exit door.

THOMPSON, Gavin 1891-92

Born: Scotland
Debut: 23 January 1892 v Bolton Wanderers F.A.Cup Home
Last Appearance: 13 Februry 1892 West Brom F.A. Cup Home
Total League & Cup Appearances: 3* Goals: 1
***Also appeared in 20 Football Alliance League games**

Career Details:

Third Lanark	
WEDNESDAY	1891
Stockton	

Scottish forward who spent just one season at Wednesday after arriving from Third Lanark. The campaign proved to be the Owls final season as a non-league side and Thompson was a regular in Alliance League football, scoring seven times, as Wednesday finished in fourth place. His only 'senior' football came in three F.A.Cup ties played during the season but his Wednesday career came to an abrupt halt in April 1892 when an ankle injury suffered in a friendly against St.Mirren meant he did not play for the Owls first team again and was subsequently released in 1892, prior to Wednesday being voted into the Football League.

THOMPSON, John 'Jack' 1933-46

Born: 21 March 1915 Cramlington, Northumberland
(5ft $6^1/_2$ins, 10st 1lb – 1936)
Died: November 1996 Sheffield
Debut: 25 November 1933
v Sunderland Division One Away
Last Appearance: 9 February 1946
v Stoke City F.A.Cup Away
Total League
& Cup Appearances: 40* Goals: 12
***Also appeared in**
112 wartime games. Scoring 52 goals

Career Details:

Cramlington Juniors		
Hartford Celtic		
Blyth Spartans	August	1932
WEDNESDAY	19 June	1933 Free
Doncaster Rovers	May	1946
Chesterfield		1939-40 Guest
Southport		1940-41 Guest
Halifax Town		1944-45 Guest
Doncaster Rovers	May	1946
Chesterfield	July	1948

Despite being born in the Northeast, Jack Thompson supported Wednesday as a schoolboy and after scoring over 400 goals in amateur football he eventually moved to his boyhood favourites in 1933. His playing career had started at Cramlington school where an 11-year old Jack attended a trial for the school team and promptly scored all seven goals as his side were thrashed 25-7! After leaving school he starting working with pit ponies at his local colliery but it was his tremendous goal scoring in non-league soccer that suggested an alternative career would be on the horizon. He was subsequently looked at by Sunderland but they dithered and allowed Bob Brown to capture Thompson's signature, leaving Jackie thrilled to sign for his club.

Within five months of signing for Wednesday the inside left was making a Division One debut as replacement for Harry Burgess and he would retain his place for the next game before dropping back into reserve team football to complete his 'apprenticeship'. It would be almost three years – October 1936 – before Thompson made another first team appearance for the Owls but just when he began to make an impression on the senior side he was hit with a succession of injuries including a broken nose, fractured collarbone, cartilage trouble and a rash of pulled muscles. However his natural talent meant he was always a contender for a first team jersey but like many of his contemporaries he would lose the peak years of his career to war.

When the hostilities began Jack started making crankshafts at a Sheffield based steel works and later joined the Navy for a while before a soccer related knee injury led to his release from the services. He was then employed in the munitions industry for the remainder of the war years while also being a regular for Wednesday in wartime soccer, scoring a multitude of goals and appearing for the Owls in the War North Cup Final loss to Blackpool in 1943. When peacetime soccer returned he reluctantly signed for Doncaster Rovers but was then involved in a remarkable campaign in which Rovers were virtually unbeatable, setting a new points record with future Owl Clarrie Jordan scoring 46 goals! His playing career came to a close at Chesterfield where he was pressed into first team action although he had joined with the idea of helping the club's young players. After hanging up his boots Jack worked on a building site before gaining employment at Sheffield Steel Company Samuel Fox's Stocksbridge Plant. He worked for Fox's – and British Steel when the industry was nationalised - until his retirement while also running a local amateur football club.

THOMPSON, Ronald 'Ron' 1945-47

Born: 24 December 1921 Sheffield
(5ft $10^1/_2$ins, 11st – 1946)
Died: 10 February 1988 Sheffield
Only Appearance: 25 January 1947
v Everton
F.A.Cup Home
Total League
& Cup Appearances: 1* Goals: 0
***Also appeared in**
28 wartime games, scoring 6 goals

Career Details:

Wadsley Church		
WEDNESDAY	19 April	1945 £10
Leicester City		1944-45 Guest
Rotherham United	May	1947 Free
York City	June	1949
Gainsborough Trinity	June	1950

Inside forward Ron Thompson first signed amateur forms for Wednesday in April 1940, making his first team debut at Huddersfield Town in September 1940. He played on ten occasions for the Owls during that 1940-41 season but then received his call up papers to the forces, eventually becoming a corporal in the Royal Air Force. Throughout the remainder of the war he made the occasional appearance for Wednesday while home on leave but then signed professional forms as the victory in Europe came within touching distance. However when national football returned in 1946 he found his first team opportunities were distinctly limited and made just one senior appearance - in a 2-1 F.A.Cup home win over Everton at Hillsborough – before moving to Millmoor. He spent two seasons at Rotherham, appearing in 30 league games, before ending his league career at York City prior to dropping into non-league football.

THOMPSON, William Allan 1969-76

Born: 20 January 1952 Liverpool
(5ft 11ins, 11st 10lbs –1974)
Debut:
9 September 1970 v Chelsea League Cup Home
Last Appearance:
19 April 1976 v Mansfield Town Division Three Away
Total League & Cup Appearances: 167+6 Goals: 4

Career Details:

WEDNESDAY	23 January	1969
Stockport County	21 July	1976 Free
Portland	April	1979 £25,000
Bradford City	January	1980 £15,000
Scunthorpe United	March	1982 Free – N/C
Redfern National Glass		1983

Allan Thompson was much in demand as a teenager after captaining the Liverpool boys team to the 1967 English Schools trophy. It was Wednesday who won the race to sign him as an apprentice in July 1967 and he repaid their faith in his qualities by making a first team bow at the tender age of eighteen and remaining in the first team for the remainder of the 1970-1 season. Over the next five seasons Thompson remained a regular as Wednesday slipped down the divisions and it was no surprise when the defender was part of the mass clear out at the end of the disastrous 1975-6 campaign.

Ex Owl Eddie Quigley then signed Thompson for Stockport County and in April 1977 Allan was appointed player-manager in Quigley's place. Somewhat ironically he was himself replaced as player-manager in March 1978 by one of his own signings, although Thompson remained at Edgeley Park as a player. A short playing spell in the NASL with Portland followed before Thompson ended his Football League career with 31 games for Bradford City and eleven while a non-contract player at Scunthorpe United. In 1982 he started working as a financial consultant, based in Yorkshire, while his playing days ended with Doncaster based non-league side Redfern.

*Did not play for Frickley Athletic

TIDMAN, Ola 2003-04

Born: 11 May 1979 Malmo, Sweden
(6ft 2ins, 11st 13lbs – 2003)
Debut: 9 August 2003
v Swindon Town
Division Two Away
Last Appearance: 30 October 2004
v Chesterfield
League One Home
Total League
& Cup Appearances: 15+1 Goals: 0

Career Details:

UC Kick		
Malmo FF		
AA Gent		
La Louviere		2001
Bolton Wanderers	19 November	2001 Trial
Wolverhampton Wanderers	22 November	2001 Trial
Tranmere Rovers		2002 Trial
Bradford City	12 January	2003 Trial
Stockport County	24 January	2003 Free
WEDNESDAY	1 July	2003 Free
Contract cancelled	8 December	2004
FC Midtjylland	1 February	2005 Free

Swedish goalkeeper Ola (pronounced Oola) Tidman arrived in the summer of 2003 to provide competition for first choice Kevin Pressman. After starting the season as No. 1 he lost his place when a knee injury meant surgery and when he did regain fitness he almost immediately broke his hand in training, meaning a second spell on the sidelines. His decidedly mixed debut campaign at Wednesday then saw Tidman concussed during only his second comeback game and a series of errors and subsequent loss of confidence resulted in Pressman reclaiming his first team jersey. The departure of Pressman during the following summer left Tidman as the club's only senior goalkeeper but the return of former loan player David Lucas meant the former Swedish U-21 International reverted back to an understudy role to his highly rated rival before leaving by mutual consent in December 2004. He later arrived on trial at Kim Olsen's former club in Denmark, signing a two-year contract with the top-flight club.

His career had started back home in Sweden where although Tidman wanted to be a striker as a youngster it was as a keeper that he would represent his country at every level up to U-21s. After signing professional terms at Malmo he eventually moved to Belgium club Gent and then after several trials with a variety of English clubs he eventually procured a short-term contract at Stockport County. After appearing in eighteen games for the Hatters he became a free agent and left his manager, former Owl Carlton Palmer, fuming when moving on a free transfer to Hillsborough.

TODD, Samuel John 'Sammy' 1970-74

Born: 22 September 1945 Belfast
(6ft, 11st 6lbs – 1972)
Debut: 15 August 1970
v Charlton Athletic
Division Two Home
Last Appearance: 24 April 1973
v Aston Villa
Division Two Away
Total League
& Cup Appearances: 24+2 Goals: 1

Career Details:

Glentoran		Amat.
Burnley	22 September	1962 Nominal
WEDNESDAY	12 May	1970 £44,444
Mansfield Town	22 February	1974 Loan
Released	30 June	1974
Great Harwood Town	November	1974
Padiham		1976

CAPS (@SWFC)
N.Ireland Full (3) v Spain 11/11/70, v Cyprus 03/02/71, v Cyprus 21/04/71

Tall, blonde haired Irishman Sammy Todd started his career as an amateur at hometown club Glentoran before joining Burnley on trial in October 1961. He was duly signed on his seventeenth birthday, making a first team debut at right back at the end of the 1963-64 season, but throughout his career at Turf Moor he faced fierce competition for a first team spot. In total he appeared in 108 games for the Clarets and was capped at Northern Ireland U-23 level before earning the first of eleven full caps for his country. In the summer of 1970 he agreed to drop out of the top division to sign for Danny Williams' Sheffield Wednesday but after being a regular for the first half of his debut campaign he then dropped out of first team contention and virtually spent the remainder of his four years at Wednesday in the shadows. The arrival of Derek Dooley as manager in March 1971 effectively spelt the end of his Owls career and during what should have been his best years Todd was consigned to Central League football, making just four appearances in his final three seasons at Hillsborough.

The versatile midfielder became disillusioned and after six games on loan at Mansfield Town he left Wednesday, moving back to Burnley in October 1974 where he gained employment with a local company that manufactured television parts. He then spent two seasons as a part-time player with Great Harwood Town before playing a handful of games with Padiham - as a favour to the club's manager who Todd worked alongside. While at Wednesday his knee was operated upon twice and it was this injury that eventually led to his retirement from the game in 1978. In December 1982 he moved back to Northern Ireland and gained employment at a West Belfast power station, where he is still employed today.

TOMLINSON, Charles Conway 'Charlie' 1935-39 & 44-51

Born: 2 December 1919 Sheffield
(5ft 10ins, 10st 11lbs – 1944)
Died: February 1971
Debut: 5 January 1946
v Mansfield Town
F.A.Cup Away
Last Appearance: 20 January 1951
v Middlesbrough
Division One Away
Total League
& Cup Appearances: 77* Goals: 12
***Also appeared in**
85 wartime games, scoring 21 goals

Career Details:

Tinsley Park Colliery		
Woodburn Alliance		
WEDNESDAY		1935 Amat.
Bradford Park Avenue	April	1939
Rotherham United		1940 Guest
Chesterfield		WW2 Guest
WEDNESDAY	24 August	1944 £1,500
Rotherham United	March	1951 £2,750
Worksop Town		
Langwith Colliery		
Beighton		

Diminutive winger Charlie Tomlinson will always hold a unique place in the Owls history books as the player who scored the quickest recorded goal for the club. This occurred in October 1949 when he netted after just twelve seconds of the 1-0 win at Preston North End. In his youth Charlie had looked set for a career as a goalkeeper as his only appearance for his school team came between the sticks while he later spent a complete season as goalkeeper for Tinsley Park. However he did play a solitary game on the left wing and his four goals in a 5-4 defeat changed the course of his career, Charlie switching to the wing position at his next club Woodburn Alliance. His form in the Intermediate League for Woodburn soon had scouts taking notice and just after Wednesday won the cup in 1935 he was invited for a trial at Wednesday, duly signing amateur forms. He was immediately given the nickname 'Shadows' by manager Billy Walker - due to his slight frame – but played only a few 'A' team games for the club before new manager Jimmy McMullen decided he was not good enough to make the grade.

He was quickly signed as a professional by Bradford Park Avenue but his career was then put into hibernation as war intervened. During the hostilities he divided his time between the rolling Mills in Sheffield and football – his performances while playing as a guest player for Rotherham United in 1943-44 persuading Eric Taylor to bring Charlie back to Hillsborough in August 1944. His first team debut came 48 hours later in a derby game against United and the clever winger with a powerful shot went on to enjoy a great season in the transitional campaign of 1945-6, scoring a hat trick at York City in the F.A.Cup and netting a goal of a lifetime when crashing home a spectacular volley in a League North game at Bramall Lane. He appeared in 98 consecutive games for Wednesday until injury ended the sequence in September 1946 and in post war soccer Charlie was a consistent performer when he was handed a first team place ahead of the rapidly emerging Dennis Woodhead. His best spell in peacetime soccer saw Tomlinson appear in 22 games as the Owls won promotion from Division Two in 1950 but he was never the same player after suffering a knee ligament problem at his peak. He eventually moved to neighbours Rotherham United – scoring on his debut – and appeared in the final three games of the season as the Millers lifted the Division Three (North) Championship. After only a year at Millmoor he dropped into non-league soccer and sadly, at the relatively young age of 51, passed away.

TOMLINSON, David Ian 1985-87

Born: 13 December 1968 Rotherham
(10st 7lbs – 1985)
Only Appearance: 3 January 1987
v Leicester City
Division One Away
Total League
& Cup Appearances: 0+1 Goals: 0

Career Details:

WEDNESDAY	December	1985
Rotherham United	August	1987
Gainsborough Trinity		1988
Boston United		1989
Barnet	December	1989 £25,000
Peterborough United	September	1992 Loan
Kettering Town		1992
Matlock Town		1992
Dagenham & Redbridge		1993
Witton Albion		1993
Stalybridge Celtic		1993-94
Parkgate		1998
Wickersley		
Wickersley Old Boys		
Wickersley Over 35s		2003

Winger David Tomlinson signed schoolboy forms at Hillsborough in January 1983 and the Owls looked to have an outstanding prospect on their books when he starred for England boys on nine occasions. He was subsequently elevated to apprentice status and while still at school made his reserve team debut, in April 1985. He was only an occasional member of the club's reserve side so it was therefore a major surprise when the teenager was handed a subs shirt at Filbert Street after Wednesday were hit by an injury crisis. He spent 23 minutes on the field of play – along side fellow one game wonder Kenny Brannigan - but could not stop the Owls slipping to a 6-1 defeat and subsequently failed to secure a new contract at the end of the season. After joining neighbours Rotherham United he added nine league appearances to his career tally before dropping into non-league football.

However his form in the Northern Premier League for Gainsborough prompted a move into the Conference under Barry Fry at Barnet and Tomlinson then won a Championship medal with the London club in 1991 to re-enter League soccer. He would make three sub appearances in the old Fourth Division for Barnet and played a solitary Anglo Italian game on loan at Peterborough United before Tomlinson brought the curtain down on his league career, signing for ex-Owl Dave Cusack at Kettering Town. The former Rotherham, South Yorkshire and Yorkshire boys player gained employment as a galvaniser after ending his professional playing career and later worked as a fabricator for a double glazing firm before becoming a fire-fighter for South Yorkshire Fire and Rescue, based in Rotherham. Although Tomlinson actually stopped playing in 1994 he was persuaded to return to the game by his wife – joining Parkgate – and still plays today for the Fire Service and in Over 35s soccer.

TOONE, George 1924-25

Born: 6 September 1893 Nottingham
(5ft 8$^{1}/_{2}$ins, 11st 8lbs – 1925)
Died: 21 July 1950 Nottingham
Debut: 4 October 1924
v Leicester City
Division Two Home
Last Appearance: 10 April 1925
v Oldham Athletic
Division Two Away
Total League
& Cup Appearances: 21 Goals: 0

Career Details:

Mansfield Mechanics		
Notts County	August	1913
Watford	July	1919
WEDNESDAY	9 August	1924 £240 + George Prior
Ilkeston Town	11 September	1925
Scarborough Penguins		

Halfback who arrived in the summer of 1924 to provide competition for Fred Kean. He had previously been ever present at Watford for three seasons and was described as a steady and clever player who could boast experience and no little ability – although it was said he trained on beer! His career had started at hometown club Notts County before he joined Watford in what proved their final season as a non-league side, prior to the whole Southern League top division being voted en-bloc into the League to form the new Division Three (South).

He would go on to appear in Watford's first 159 games as a Football League club before his defensive qualities led Bob Brown to secure his signature for the Owls. However despite replacing Kean for the latter end of the 1924-5 season Toone was always the future England International's understudy although it was a surprise when he was allowed to leave for non-league soccer just over twelve months after signing for Wednesday. Incidentally his father, George, won two caps for England in the 1880s and actually played against Wednesday in 1889 when playing for Notts Rangers!

TOPHAM, John H. 'Jack' 1896-1902

Born:
Debut:
22 October 1898 v Sunderland Division One Away
Last Appearance:
31 March 1900 v Leicester Fosse Division Two Home
Total League & Cup Appearances: 16 Goals: 2

Career Details:

Staveley	
WEDNESDAY	1896
Released	1902

During six seasons at Wednesday outside left Jack Topham was a prolific scorer in reserve team football, helping the second team to a variety of honours around the turn of the Century. He grabbed three hat tricks whilst appearing in reserve team soccer and was given a first team bow during the Owls final season at Olive Grove. Unfortunately his rival for the No. 11 shirt was the incomparable Fred Spiksley and Jack was restricted to only a handful of senior games although he did appear in eight games as Wednesday won the Division Two championship in 1900.

TOSELAND, Ernest 'Ernie' 1939

Born: 17 March 1905 Northampton
(5ft 6$^{1}/_{2}$ins, 10st 3lbs –1935)
Died: 19 October 1987 Northampton
Debut: 18 March 1939
v West Bromwich Albion
Division Two Home
Last Appearance: 29 April 1939
v Tottenham Hotspur
Division Two Home
Total League
& Cup Appearances: 12* Goals: 2
***Also appeared in 9 wartime games**

Career Details:

Higham Ferrers Town		
Northampton Town		Amat.
Queens Park Rangers		Amat.
Coventry City		1925
Manchester City	11 March	1929 £3,000
WEDNESDAY	14 March	1939 £1,575
Manchester City		1939-40 Guest
Manchester United		1939-40 Guest
Stockport County		1939-40 Guest
Stockport County		1940-41 Guest
Rochdale		WW2 Guest
Manchester City		1945-46 Guest

Prior to signing for Wednesday in 1939 flying winger Ernie Toseland had enjoyed a tremendous ten years at Maine Road where he amassed a mammoth 409 appearances, scoring 75 goals. At his peak he was considered one of the best uncapped wingmen in the game and he earned both League Championship and F.A.Cup winners medal while at the Moss Side club. He was noted for his speed and methodical play; he had played three-quarters for his school at rugby before concentrating on soccer, and also boasted a tremendous fitness record, which saw Toseland ever present for City in three complete seasons. His eleven goals in only 22 games for his first professional club Coventry City had originally persuaded City to sign the diminutive right-winger but the sizeable fee proved money well spent.

Unfortunately for Toseland, and Owls fans, his talents had little opportunity to shine following his move to Wednesday as after appearing in the final twelve games of the 1938-9 season and the first three of the following season his career came to an abrupt halt as football was suspended when war was declared. After a handful of games in wartime football Toseland's contract was cancelled and he returned to Manchester to work in munitions for the remainder of the conflict, appearing as a guest for a variety of northwest clubs. His fitness record continued to be exemplary and he was still playing Cheshire league football well past his fortieth birthday.

TROTTER, James William 'Jimmy' 1922-30

Born: 25 November 1899 Easington
(5ft 8ins, 11st 6lbs – 1922)
Died: 17 April 1984 St Albans
Debut: 13 February 1922
v Wolverhampton Wanderers
Division Two Home
Last Appearance: 2 February 1929
v Sheffield United
Division One Away
Total League
& Cup Appearances: 159 Goals: 114

Career Details:

Parsons Turbine Works		
Bury	November	1919
WEDNESDAY	17 February	1922 £1,907
Torquay United	5 June	1930 £500
Watford	November	1931 £375

Jimmy Trotter was the first in a line of inter war year centre forwards who propelled Wednesday to one of the greatest periods in their history. He had originally been spotted by Bury, who signed him from amateur soccer, but initially struggled to become established at Wednesday after financial problems forced the Lancashire club to let their prize asset leave for Hillsborough. He had to be play second fiddle to first team centre forward Sid Binks for over two seasons - finishing his first full season as 20-goal top scorer as the reserves won the Midland League championship - but when Binks departed for Huddersfield in September 1924 Trotter was finally given a fair crack of the whip at senior level and rewarded Bob Brown's faith with 17 goals in only 24 league games – he became the first Wednesday player to score five times in one match when achieving the feat at home to Portsmouth in December 1924.

After becoming the Owls first choice, Trotter was virtually unstoppable as Wednesday won the Second Division title in 1926 – his club record haul of 37 league goals including a five-goal feat for the second time in his Owls career – while Wednesday fans took him to their hearts with the song "Trot, Trot, Trotter, score a little goal for me" often heard ringing around Hillsborough. Incredibly in his first season of top-flight football he netted exactly the same number of league goals as in the previous season and superbly led the line as Bob Brown's charges consolidated in the higher grade. However as the decade wore on Trotter started to feature less and less at first team level, giving way to the prolific Jack Allen a few games into the 1928-9 championship season. His 21 goals duly helped the reserves to win the Central League title and he spent another season in second team football before leaving for the English Riveria. He blasted seven goals for Torquay United in an August 1930 public trial match but remained only a season in Devon before ending his playing days at Watford prior to retiring from the game in the summer of 1933.

During the 1933-4 campaign he worked as a masseur and in March 1934 was actually recommended by the Owls board for the position of trainer at Italian club Roma! However it was his old Wednesday team mate Jimmy Seed who brought Trotter back into football, appointing him trainer to Charlton's 'A' team after Seed was himself appointed manager at The Valley. Within a year Trotter was promoted to senior trainer and he remained in the role for over twenty years until taking over as manager from Seed in September 1956 – Trotter also served as England trainer under the reign of Walter Winterbottom. He was at the helm when Charlton lost their Division One status in 1958 and after failing to get them back into the top-flight he was eventually sacked in October 1961, retiring from football at the same time.

TRUSTFULL, Orlando 'Ollie' 1996-97

Born: 4 August 1970 Amsterdam, Holland
(6ft, 13st – 1997)
Debut: 24 August 1996
v Newcastle United
Premier League Away
Last Appearance: 22 April 1997
v Blackburn Rovers
Premier League Away
Total League
& Cup Appearances: 11+11 Goals: 3

Career Details:

Rivalen		
Blauw Wit		
Haarlem		
SVV		
SVV Dordrecht '90		
FC Twente		
Feyenoord		
WEDNESDAY	19 August	1996 £750,000
Vitesse Arnhem	5 August	1997 £800,000

Dutch midfielder who was actually first spotted by Owls boss David Pleat on a video of an Ajax v Feyenoord game and when Wednesday toured Holland in the 1996 pre season Pleat invited Trustfull to train with the side. A few weeks later he arrived in Sheffield on trial – famously playing in a pre season friendly at Stocksbridge under the pseudonym of Ryan Twerton – and impressed sufficiently for Wednesday to pay his club a sizeable fee to bring the tall central midfielder to Hillsborough on a permanent

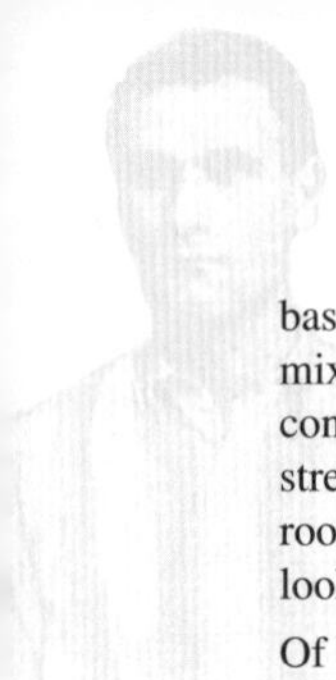

basis. However the talented player would experience a decidedly mixed time in what proved his only season at Wednesday, a lack of consistency seeming to be his major problem. His height and strength made Trustfull stand out in the middle of the Owls' engine room and a brace in the April 1997 home game with Wimbledon looked to be a catalyst to his Wednesday career.

Of course this proved incorrect and it was a surprise to most fans when he returned home after less than a year in Sheffield – on the same day his compatriot Regi Blinker left for Celtic. Trustfull – whose wife Quinty is a TV celebrity in Holland – subsequently signed for ambitious Vitesse Arnhem where he would remain a regular until joining the club's coaching staff in July 2002.

TUMMON, Oliver 'Ollie' 1903-10

Born: 3 March 1884 Sheffield
(5ft 7ins, 12st 2lbs – 1909)
Died: October 1955 Sheffield
Debut: 23 April 1906 v Everton Division One Home
Last Appearance: 5 March 1910 v Liverpool Division One Home
Total League & Cup Appearances: 46 Goals: 12

Career Details:

Sharrow Lane		
South Street New Connexion		
Gainsborough Trinity		1901
WEDNESDAY	19 March	1902 Amat.
WEDNESDAY	February	1903
Gainsborough Trinity	28 June	1910 £40
Oldham Athletic	16 July	1912 £300
Sheffield United		WW1 Guest
Sheffield United	August	1919
Barnsley	30 June	1920
Sir Albert Hawkes F.C.	May	1924 Amat.
Nether Edge	Aug	1924 Amat.

Sturdy built left-winger who was said to make up for his lack of pace with "experience, smart play and a thunderous shot". He came through Sheffield schoolboy football to join Wednesday as an amateur and became a reserve team regular at Hillsborough, netting 27 goals in his first three seasons of second team football. The form of George Simpson meant Ollie would spend the majority of his Owls career as his rival's understudy and in fact his best run in the side actually came on the right wing during the F.A.Cup winning season of 1906-07– Tummon appearing in twenty games, primarily as a replacement for the absent Harry Davis. In addition to almost fifty senior appearances Ollie was also instrumental in helping the reserves to two Midland League Championships – in 1906 & 1908 – before he signed for Football League side Gainsborough Trinity.

He was ever present for two seasons at the Lincolnshire club and then achieved great heights at Oldham where he appeared in the 1912 F.A.Cup semi-final before helping the Latics to the highest league finish in their entire history – runners up spot behind League Champions Everton in 1915. He missed only a handful of games in three seasons at Boundary Park, netting 19 goals in 108 games, and his form must have left Wednesday fans wondering if their club had been hasty in letting the local lad leave. When the Great War saw all national football grind to a halt Tummon returned to Sheffield to work in a munitions factory and guested on several occasions for Sheffield United - scoring a bizarre goal against Wednesday in May 1916 when a back pass to the goalie went astray, allowing Tummon to score into an empty net, as the keeper was tying his boot laces at the time! When wartime soccer ended he signed for the Blades and later played a solitary league game for Barnsley – ironically against Wednesday – before ending his professional career. However he retained a passion for the game and after gaining permission from the Football Association he returned to amateur football, playing until his early forties in local Sheffield soccer. Later in life he became a leading bowls player with Brincliffe Oaks.

TURLEY, Michael Douglas 'Mike' 1953-56

Born: 14 February 1936 Rotherham
(5ft 8ins, 10st 9lbs – 1955)
Debut: 1 January 1955
v Aston Villa
Division One Away
Last Appearance: 22 January 1955
v Tottenham Hotspur
Division One Away
Total League
& Cup Appearances: 4 Goals: 0

Career Details:

WEDNESDAY	March	1953
Burnley	October	1956

Halfback Mike Turley came through the Owls youth ranks to make four senior appearances for the club during the 1954-55 relegation season. He had originally joined the Owls ground staff in 1951, appearing in 19 games during the 1951-2 season in junior and 'A'team soccer – and after progressing to Central League football was given a first team bow at Villa Park on New Year's Day 1955, as injury problems bit hard. He would play in three consecutive league games for the club but then disappeared from the first team almost as quickly as he had arrived and even struggled to make the reserve side before moving across the Pennines. Unfortunately he failed to start a senior game for Burnley and soon dropped out of league football.

TURNER, Christopher Robert 'Chris' 1976-79 & 1988-91

Born: 15 September 1958 Sheffield
(5ft 10ins, 11st – 1978)
Debut: 14 August 1976
v Grimsby Town
League Cup Away
Last Appearance: 8 May 1991
v Bristol City
Division Two Home
Total League
& Cup Appearances: 205 Goals: 0

Career Details:

WEDNESDAY	1 August	1976
Lincoln City	6 October	1978 Loan
Sunderland	4 July	1979 £75,000
Manchester United	15 August	1985 £275,000
WEDNESDAY	12 September	1988 £175,000
Leeds United	15 November	1989 Loan
Leyton Orient	25 October	1991 £75,000
Leicester City		1995 Free

CAPS (@SWFC)
England Youth (5),v Wales 09/03/77, v Wales 23/03/77, v Belgium 19/05/77, v Iceland 21/05/77, v Greece 23/05/77

When Chris Turner was appointed manager at Hillsborough on 7 November 2002 he joined Peter Eustace in the select group of individuals to have not only experienced two separate playing spells at Wednesday but also return later in their career to take over the managerial reins. His first taste of coaching had come at Leyton Orient where he was assistant manager and later joint manager before being dismissed in May 1995. He then moved to Leicester City, initially as a non-contract player, where he became youth coach before being appointed joint-caretaker manager in December 1995, following Mark McGhee's resignation. After leaving the Foxes in the summer of 1996 he re-joined McGhee as youth coach at Wolves and stayed for almost three seasons before being appointed manager at struggling basement club Hartlepool United in February 1999. With fellow ex-Owl Colin West at his side Turner achieved great success at Hartlepool, on a tight budget, where he transformed the perennial strugglers into play off contenders and when he departed for Hillsborough his charges led Division Three and would go on to secure the Championship six months later.

Unfortunately for Turner he joined a Wednesday side who were already staring relegation from Division One in the face and despite steadying the ship – his side boasted a mid-table record for the remainder of his first season – the damage was already done and the Owls slipped into the third tier of English football for only the second time in their long history. Despite relegation hopes were high of an immediate promotion back into the First Division but after a good start Wednesday experienced a torrid season which eventually led to a final league position of seventeenth – the club's second lowest finish of all time. The poor results were generally blamed upon the 'old guard' of players who had got into a losing mentality and in the summer of 2004 Turner took draconian steps to correct the situation by releasing a total of thirteen players and effectively signing virtually a new first team. The new boys looked far more impressive than their predecessors and despite failing to totally gell in the first few weeks of the season it was expected Turner would remain at the helm for several more months, mainly due to his strong bond with Chairman Dave Allen. However following a poor display at home to Bournemouth – Turner perhaps showing his tactical naivety by failing to change his formation – he was dramatically fired almost on the full-time whistle as Allen's patience finally run out with the Owls sat in mid-table. After a short spell out of the game Turner was appointed boss at League One bottom club Stockport County in December 2004.

His departure marked the end of a near thirty-year on-off association with Wednesday that had started back in March 1975 when Turner signed apprentice forms at Hillsborough. He broke into the Third Division side at the tender age of seventeen and missed only one game in his debut season – appearing in 52 league and cup games - while also winning England Youth caps.

The arrival of Bob Bolder saw the new boy seemingly favoured by Jack Charlton and fierce competition ensued between the pair with Wednesday fan Turner certainly having the backing of a vocal Hillsborough crowd. However it was the bulkier and taller Bolder who effectively won the contest as Turner moved to Sunderland where he was undisputed number 1 for several seasons, appearing in 223 games for the Wearside club and appearing at Wembley in the 1985 League Cup Final loss to Norwich City. A move to Manchester United came next for Turner where competition from Gary Bailey and Jim Leighton restricted his appearances to 79 games prior to moving back across the Pennines for a second spell at Wednesday.

The former Sheffield boys player was brought to provide competition for Kevin Pressman and the pair virtually shared goalkeeping duties over the next two seasons with injury and then loss of form allowing Turner to take over from Pressman. His razor sharp reactions and brilliant shot stopping would then help Wednesday to lift their first major trophy for 56 years – his old club Manchester United being vanquished in the 1991 League Cup Final – but the surprise arrival of £1m England goalkeeper Chris Woods then saw Turner displaced from the senior side. Within a few months he asked for a transfer and after joining Leyton Orient on loan the move was made permanent in November 1991 in a deal that saw starlet Chris Bart-Williams sign for Wednesday.

TURTON, Cyril 1944-54

Born: 20 September 1921 South Kirkby
(5ft $11^{3}/_{4}$ins, 12st $11^{1}/_{2}$lbs – 1946)
Died: 31 December 1999 South Kirkby
Debut: 31 August 1946
v Luton Town
Division Two Away
Last Appearance: 26 December 1953
v Manchester United
Division One Home
Total League
& Cup Appearances: 151* Goals: 0
***Also appeared in**
52 wartime games, scoring 1 goal

Career Details:

South Kirkby Juniors		
South Kirkby Colliery		1938
Frickley Colliery		1940
Rotherham United		1942-3 Amateur
WEDNESDAY	12 October	1944 £200
Goole Town		1954

Although in his school days Cyril Turton solely played rugby at Hemsworth Grammar school it was as a footballer that he would make his name, initially coming to the fore with his village side South Kirkby alongside fellow future Owls player Clarrie Jordan. After his all conquering local side were disbanded in 1940 (the club secretary being called up into the forces) the big, strong and tenacious halfback joined Frickley Colliery and would play four games for Rotherham United during the 1942-3 season after signing amateur forms. However following his appearance for Frickley at the Owls nursery club of Norton Woodseats, Turton become one of only a few players to be transferred for money in wartime football – Wednesday paying Frickley a small fee for his signature.

After signing for Wednesday he continued to work at Frickley Colliery – he remained a part-time professional until 1948 – while after making his debut against Mansfield Town in October 1944 he remained a regular for the final two seasons of wartime soccer. During the first season of post war football he was kept in the shadows by the form of Edgar Packard but he then missed only a handful of games over the next two seasons – earning the affectionate nickname of 'Mother Turton' from Wednesday fans who reckoned Cyril was able to run quicker backwards than forwards! However for some reason he was never a big favourite with the Hillsborough crowd and often preferred to play away from critical home supporters. After almost two seasons away from the first team scene Turton regained a first team spot in the Second Division Championship winning season of 1951-2 and then missed only a handful of top-flight games in 1952-3 before eventually ending his loyal service in 1954 when moving to Goole Town.

His playing days ended after two years with Goole at which point Turton returned to his mining job at Frickley Colliery while also being appointed trainer at the pit side. After six years as trainer at the South Elmsall club he then spent two years as manager before resigning in February 1963, severing all links with the football section of the Colliery. He remained on the coalface for the rest of his working life and became secretary of the South Kirkby Coronation Working Men's Club, remaining in the South Kirkby village where he lived all his life until passing away on Millennium night.

TYNAN, Thomas Edward 'Tommy' 1976-78

Born: 17 November 1955 Liverpool
(5ft 10ins, 12st 8lbs – 1978)
Debut: 11 September 1976
v Swindon Town
Division Three Away
Last Appearance: 26 September 1978
v Bury
Division Three Home
Total League
& Cup Appearances: 105+2 Goals: 37

Career Details:

Liverpool	17 November	1972
Swansea City	17 October	1975 Loan
Dallas Tornadoes	Apr-August	1976 Loan
WEDNESDAY	9 September	1976 £8,000
Lincoln City	29 September	1978 £33,000
Newport County	23 February	1979 £25,000
Plymouth Argyle	August	1983 £55,000
Rotherham United	31 July	1985 £25,000
Plymouth Argyle	1 April	1986 Loan
Plymouth Argyle	5 September	1986 £25,000
Torquay United	May	1990
Doncaster Rovers	July	1991
Goole Town	October	1992

Tommy Tynan was one of the most prolific strikers of the lower divisions in the mid-1970s to mid-1980s, netting a mammoth total of 314 goals for a variety of clubs. During his two-year stay at Hillsborough he maintained a respectable goal record as Wednesday put the brakes on their 1970s slump down the divisions and was top scorer and 'player of the year' in 1977-78 with 21 league and cup goals. During that season, in March 1978, he was actually transfer listed after breaching club discipline and six months later became a record buy for Lincoln City.

His career had began in earnest when a competition ran by the Liverpool Echo selected Tommy in the final 20 players out of 1,000 hopefuls. In November 1971 he signed apprentice forms for Liverpool and over the next five years Tynan was a regular scorer in youth and reserve team football – he was Central League top scorer for four consecutive seasons - although he failed to make a senior appearance for the Merseyside giants. His league debut actually came whilst on loan at Swansea City and prior to moving to Sheffield he spent five months in the NASL at Dallas Tornadoes. After being sold by Jack Charlton he experienced a brief and unhappy stay at Sincil Bank and was soon transferred back into Welsh football, signing for Newport County. The fiery and talented attacker enjoyed much happier times with County where he was part of the club's best ever side, winning the Welsh Cup in 1980, scoring the promotion winning goal from the old Third Division in 1983 and also setting a post-war scoring record when finishing joint Football League top scorer.

It was only financial problems that forced County to part with their prize asset and Plymouth were the beneficiaries as in two separate spells Tynan finished top scorer at Home Park on an amazing seven occasions! He was also 'player of the year' for four seasons and his goals helped the Pilgrims to the 1984 F.A.Cup semi-final where the Third Division side narrowly lost to top-flight Watford. He netted over a century of goals for Argyle before joining neighbours Torquay United in a player-coach capacity. However after helping United to promotion from Division Four in 1991 his contract was cancelled after disciplinary problems – mainly because he made an obscene sign towards the director's box! After returning north he became landlord of the Horse and Jockey pub near Hillsborough while his playing career ended in February 1993 when he left his player-manager role at Northern Premier Leaguer Goole Town. In November 1996 he took over the tenancy of the Golden Hind public house near Home Park, Plymouth and later owned and ran the Stoke Social Club in a district of the town. Since 2001 he has worked as a cabbie in Plymouth.

ULYETT, George 1882-83

Born: 21 October 1851 Sheffield
Died: 18 June 1898 Sheffield
Only Appearance:
12 February 1883 v Notts County F.A.Cup Home
Total League & Cup Appearances: 1 Goals: 0

Career Details:

Ecclesfield	
WEDNESDAY	1882

All round sportsman George Ulyett was regarded as the greatest Yorkshire cricketer of the Nineteenth Century, scoring over 1000 runs in a season for the Tykes on 10 occasions. The ace batsman was also capped 25 times by England and his brief career with Wednesday certainly paled into significance when set against the National fame he achieved through the willow. He remained an amateur player throughout his career – working in the Sheffield steel industry as a sheet roller - and spent the 1882-3 season on the Owls books, appearing between the posts in the 4-1 home loss in the F.A.Cup to Notts County but also helping Wednesday to success in the Wharncliffe Charity Cup Final. Due to injury he retired from football around 1883 and sadly passed away at an early age after catching pneumonia when watching Yorkshire play Kent at Bramall Lane.

USHER, Brian 1965-68

Born: 11 March 1944 Belmont, Co. Durham
(5ft 11ins, 11st 5lbs – 1965)
Debut: 21 August 1965
v Manchester United
Division One Away
Last Appearance: 25 April 1968
v Manchester City
Division One Away
Total League
& Cup Appearances: 66+2 Goals: 3

Career Details:

Sunderland	11 March	1961
WEDNESDAY	2 June	1965 £20,000
Doncaster Rovers	29 May	1968 £3,500
Yeovil Town	9 July	1973
Bentley Victoria		1974

Winger Brian Usher first came to national prominence as a teenager in Alan Brown's Sunderland side that won promotion from the Second Division in 1964. He was subsequently capped at U-23 level by England and when Brown moved to take over at Hillsborough he was soon returning to Wearside to bring Usher south. At the time his signing seemed good business by Wednesday but unfortunately his three-year stay at Hillsborough was blighted by injury and loss of form and it was no surprise when he left for Doncaster Rovers in the deal that brought Alan Warboys to Wednesday. During his first season at Belle Vue he would appear in 27 games as Rovers won the Fourth Division Championship and proved a good servant, playing in 170 league games, before being released in the summer of 1973. Incidentally during his time at Rovers Usher coached a Sheffield Junior Sunday league side for several seasons.

After leaving Doncaster Rovers he moved to Southern League Yeovil Town but after playing in only two friendlies a pelvic injury he sustained at Donny flared up and he was advised by a specialist at Yeovil Hospital to take a years rest from the game. He duly moved back to Yorkshire and later spent five years as player –manager of Yorkshire club Bentley Colliery while since 1973 he has worked in insurance.

*Never played for Durham boys

VARADI, Imre 'Ray' 1983-85 & 1988-90

Born: 8 July 1959
Paddington, London
(5ft 8½ins, 11st 11lbs – 1983)
Debut:
27 August 1983
v Swansea City
Division Two Away
Last Appearance:
21 October 1989
v Tottenham Hotspur
Division One Away
Total League & Cup
Appearances: 108+13 Goals: 46

Career Details:

Letchworth Garden City		1974
Tottenham Hotspur		Trial
Cambridge United		Trial
Sheffield United	1 April	1978 Free
Everton	1 March	1979 £80,000
Benfica	July	1981 Trial
Newcastle United	27 August	1981 £100,000
WEDNESDAY	26 August	1983 £170,000*
West Bromwich Albion	19 July	1985 £285,000(T)**
Manchester City	17 October	1986 £100,000
WEDNESDAY	30 September	1988 £100,000***
Leeds United	2 February	1990 £45,000
Luton Town	26 March	1992 Loan
Oxford United	21 January	1993 Loan
Rotherham United	5 March	1993 Free
Mansfield Town	11 August	1995 N/C
Boston United	August	1995 Free
Scunthorpe United	29 September	1995 N/C
Boston United		1995
Matlock Town	November	1995
Guiseley	December	1996
Denaby United	January	1997
Stalybridge Celtic	December	1997
Universal Drilling	August	1998 Sun.
Sheffield FC	February	1999

*Including £20,000 rated David Mills
** Plus one third of any future sale
*** Exchange for C.Bradshaw

Pacy, deadly striker Ray Varadi was a crowd favourite at his many clubs, netting a total of 151 league goals in a much-travelled career. He had started in non-league football whilst working as an asphalter and trained two nights a week at Luton Town before joining Spurs for a three-month trial. After being released he played a trial game under Ron Atkinson at Cambridge United but his chances of breaking into the professional game seemed to have receded when he returned to Letchworth Garden City. However when former Luton manager Harry Haslam moved to Bramall Lane he got in touch with Varadi and the teenager jumped at the chance of moving into League football.

He made an immediate impact at United and after four goals in only ten games he moved into the top-flight, being signed by Gordon Lee at Everton. He failed to become established at Goodison Park and after a trial game for Portuguese giants Benfica he moved to Newcastle United where he became a huge favourite with the Geordie fans by scoring 42 times in only 90 games. However both player and fans were then shocked when in the 1983 close season he was sold to Wednesday – his feelings about the transfer were obvious when Varadi netted twice in the 4-2 November 1983 Hillsborough win over Newcastle United but failed to celebrate. The Geordies loss was certainly the Owls gain as Varadi – born of a Hungarian father and Italian mother – was top scorer as Wednesday gained promotion in 1984 and then netted 21 league and cup goals during the 1984-5 season. The quicksilver striker was certainly at the height of his powers but it would be the turn of Wednesday fans to be disappointed when he rejected the club's offer of a new contract and moved to the Hawthorns – a transfer tribunal setting a middle ground figure after the Owls wanted £400,000 but Albion offered only £175,000.

During the next two seasons he top scored for both Albion and then Manchester City but suffered relegation on both occasions. Howard Wilkinson then signed him for a second time for Wednesday but his return to Hillsborough proved an unhappy experience for Varadi as he quickly fell out of favour with new manager Peter Eustace – at one point Varadi was suspended by Eustace after demanding a transfer! Despite Ron Atkinson arriving Varadi's fortunes did not improve and after failing to start a first team game for ten months he was again signed by Wilkinson – now in charge at Elland Road. After helping United to the Second Division title in 1990 Varadi would then spend the remainder of his career at a multitude of different clubs, with varying degrees of success, which included finishing top scorer for Rotherham United in 1993-4 and playing just a single game for Mansfield Town and two matches for Scunthorpe United. After ending his league career at the Lincolnshire club Varadi was briefly assistant manager to Mel Sterland at Boston United before taking over as player-manager at Matlock Town. After a three-month coaching stint in the US he again joined Sterland as assistant – this time at Conference club Stalybridge Celtic –and continued to play Sunday football alongside 'Zico' in Sheffield parks football. He later signed for another ex-team mate, John Pearson, for Sheffield Club but played only one game before finally ending his competitive playing career just a few weeks short of his fortieth birthday. After ending his professional career Varadi was co-founder of a Sheffield company that coached 6 to 14 year-old children while he also worked for a boot company. However he left both jobs and now works as a football agent.

WADDLE, Christopher Roland 'Chris' 1992-96

Born: 14 December 1960
Felling
(6ft, 11st 5lbs – 1995)
Debut:
15 August 1992
v Everton
Premier League Away
Last Appearance:
5 May 1996
v West Ham United
Premier League Away
Total League
& Cup Appearances:
130+17 Goals: 15

Career Details:

Sheffield United		1974 Trial
Coventry City		1974 Schoolboy
Pelaw Juniors		1975
Whitehouse Social Club		1975 Sun.
Sunderland		1976 Trial
Pelaw Social Club		1976
Clarke Chapman		1977
Leam Lane Social Club		1977 Sun.
Tow Law Town		1978
Sunderland	January	1979 Trial
Newcastle United	28 July	1980 £500
Tottenham Hotspur	1 July	1985 £650,000
Olympic Marseille	1 July	1989 £4.25m
WEDNESDAY	17 July	1992 £1m
Falkirk	13 September	1996 Free
Bradford City	12 October	1996 Free
Sunderland	20 March	1997 £75,000
Burnley	8 July	1997
Hollinsend	August	1998
Brunsmeer		1998
Torquay United	24 September	1998 Free
Hilltop	November	1998
Davy Sports	November	1998
Brumsmeer	December	1998
Worksop Town	26 July	2000
Parkgate	November	2001 Loan
Staveley	April	2002
Glapwell	3 August	2002
South Normanton Ath.	March	2003
Stocksbridge Park Steels	April	2003
Staveley		2003
South Normanton Ath.	November	2003
Staveley	July	2004

The mercurial Chris Waddle was without doubt one of the finest players of his generation and in just over four years at Hillsborough became a huge crowd favourite amongst Owls fans. At his peak he was almost unplayable and despite joining Wednesday at the age of 31 he produced some of the best form of his illustrious career, leaving supporters calling for his recall to the England side. His time at Hillsborough left Wednesday fans with many fond memories with his astonishing goal against Sheffield United in the 1993 F.A.Cup Semi-final perhaps the highlight. He also netted in the Cup Final replay against Arsenal but it was a performance against West Ham in December 1993 that has entered into Hillsborough folklore as 'Waddle's game' as he tied full back David Burrows in knots during one of the most outstanding individual performances ever seen at Sheffield Six.

His debut campaign at Wednesday saw Waddle lauded throughout the country and he duly became the one and only Owls player to be voted the 'Football Writers Player of the Year'. The season proved somewhat bittersweet for Waddle as he suffered the heartbreak of defeats in both domestic Cup Finals but overcame the disappointment to delight Wednesday fans over the next three seasons with displays of vision, outstanding passing and superb dribbling skills not seen at Hillsborough since the days of Albert Quixall and Jackie Robinson. Soon after the arrival of David Pleat as manager in the summer of 1995 Waddle turned down the Owls offer of a player-coach role and he was left disappointed when Wednesday offered the former England International just a one-year playing deal instead of the two-year contract he had hoped for. Throughout the 1995-96 season Waddle was in and out of the side and the almost inevitable parting of the ways came early in the following season.

However his destination was a surprise to all as Waddle signed a one-month deal at Scottish Division One side Falkirk. After one goal in five games he returned to England to join Bradford City where he was top scorer before signing for boyhood heroes Sunderland. Sadly for Waddle he was unable to help the 'Black Cats' stave off relegation from the Premier League and left for an unsuccessful one-year player-manager role at Burnley. Although a win on the final day of the season saw the Clarets avoid relegation Waddle left by 'mutual consent' in May 1998 and ended his league career at Torquay United before being appointed to the Owls coaching staff in December 1998. His brief at Wednesday was to coach the club's youngsters but he was promoted to reserve team boss in July 1999 but remained only a season, resigning in June 2000 after failing to win the race for the manager's job ahead of Paul Jewell. Since leaving the professional game in 2000 Waddle has continued to play in non-league football while regularly appearing on local and national radio as a match summariser

His departure from Torquay marked the end of a career in professional football that had started as a thirteen year-old schoolboy when he attended trials at Bramall Lane. His playing days had started at Bill Quay Junior School and he represented several district sides before signing schoolboy forms at Coventry City. He travelled to the East Midlands during school holidays to train and play but City decided against offering Waddle an apprenticeship and he returned home to appear for a variety of local sides until leaving school in 1977 to sign on the dole. However he soon gained employment with Chevivot Seasoning – a company who made spices for seasoning pies and sausages – and continued to play football on Saturdays and Sundays until finally getting his first break when joining long established Northern League side Tow Law Town. With Waddle in their side Tow Law became one of the top sides in the Northeast but his hopes of a career as a professional looked doomed when he was invited to sign for Newcastle United but failed to do so when the United manager was too busy to meet the youngster after a local derby against Sunderland! Thankfully Chris put the disappointment behind him and was finally rewarded in 1980 when Newcastle returned to his door and finally secured the mazy winger to a full time playing contract.

His talent took time to refine by the United coaching staff but along with Terry McDermott and Kevin Keegan he subsequently helped Newcastle regain their top-flight place in 1984. In total he would appear in 192 games for the Geordie club, scoring 52 goals, and while at St.James Park he won the first of his 52 full caps for England. Such was his form that a big money move to Spurs followed and it was at White Hart Lane that he became an established England International although honours eluded him, losing in the 1987 F.A.Cup Final to underdogs Coventry City and suffering the heartbreak of missing the decisive penalty in the 1990 World Cup semi-final against West Germany in Rome - while at Spurs he also collaborated with team mate Glenn Hoddle to record a top ten hit with 'Diamond Lights'. He then became the most expensive British footballer when joining French club Marseille where his career seemed to reach even greater heights as his talent on the ball made him into a superstar and brought Waddle three League Championships and an appearance in the 1991 European Cup Final. While in Southern France he was nicknamed "Le Dribbleur Fou" and there was heartbreak amongst Marseille fans when their hero left for Hillsborough in the summer of 1992.

WALDEN, Richard Francis 1976-78

Born: 4 May 1948 Hereford
(6ft, 12st 12lbs – 1977)
Debut: 10 January 1976
v Hereford United
Division Three Home
Last Appearance: 3 May 1978
v Wrexham Division Three Home
Total League
& Cup Appearances: 115 Goals: 1

Career Details:

Aldershot	May	1965
WEDNESDAY	7 January	1976 Free
Newport County	26 July	1978 £3,500 (T.)
Farnborough Town		1982
Basingstoke Town		1988

Right back Richard Walden was signed by Aldershot straight from school and seemed set to play all of his career at the Hampshire club as by 1976 he had amassed a mammoth 448 appearances and was on the verge of setting a new appearance record for the club. However in January 1976 Walden made the surprise move to Hillsborough with Wednesday gaining his vastly experienced services for nothing, after Walden had attended tribunal meetings in London and Manchester to force Aldershot to grant his release. He would then be ever present at Wednesday for two whole seasons - helping the club just avoid relegation to the old Fourth Division in April 1976 - but it was then the Owls turn to be surprised when he duly walked out just before his contract expired to move to his newly purchased southern based house!

Two months later a league transfer tribunal set his fee at a giveaway price – much to Jack Charlton's anger – and ex-Owls manager Len Ashurst secured his services for Newport County. At County he played alongside John Aldridge and former Owl Tommy Tynan, winning the Welsh Cup in 1980, and appearing in County's progress to the third round of the European Cup Winners Cup in 1981. He totalled 193 competitive games for the Welsh club but became a part-time player with Farnborough Town after the new incoming manager at County expressed his disapproval of Walden training at his home close to London. After dropping into non-league soccer he gained employment as a sales representative with a sports firm, later becoming manager, while he captained Farnborough to two Hampshire Senior Cup wins. His playing days ended after two seasons at Basingstoke Town and he now combines his full-time job with working as an assessor at the weekends for the F.A Academy set up, checking that grounds and facilities are up to the required standard.

WALKER, Colin 1986-87

Born: 1 May 1958 Rotherham
(5ft 8ins, 11st 8lbs – 1987)
Debut: 6 October 1986
v Stockport County
League Cup Away
Last Appearance: 25 October 1986
v Coventry City Division One Home
Total League
& Cup Appearances: 2+1 Goals: 3

Career Details:

York City		1975 N/C
Barnsley	October	1975 Trial
Matlock Town		1979
Gisborne City	January	1980
Sutton Town	October	1980
Barnsley	November	1980
Doncaster Rovers	February	1983 Loan
Gisborne City	April	1983
Doncaster Rovers	November	1985 N/C
Cambridge United		1985 N/C
Matlock Town	January	1986
Harworth Colliery Institute	March	1986
Joker F.C.		1986 Sun.
WEDNESDAY	7 August	1986 Free
Darlington	24 December	1986 Loan
Torquay United	9 October	1987 Loan
Gisboune City	3 December	1987 Free
Doncaster Rovers		1989 Trial

Despite appearing in only three senior games for Sheffield Wednesday, Colin Walker holds a unique place in club history as the only man to score a hat-trick after entering the fray as a substitute. He recorded this feat against Stockport County – on his debut – when a League Cup tie was switched to Maine Road and he came on at half time for Carl Bradshaw with Wednesday already a goal ahead on the night and four on aggregate. His journey to the Owls first team had been somewhat meteoric as Walker, who famously named dustman as one of his former jobs, had only joined the club on trial during the pre season tour of Finland but impressed Howard Wilkinson enough for the Owls boss to award him a two-year professional contract. After his remarkable debut the diminutive attacker started two top-flight games with his final appearance coming in the home game with Coventry City when visiting keeper Steve Ozgrizovic scored past a stunned Martin Hodge. Walker then dropped into reserve team football and after two loan spells in the lower divisions he announced he was returning to New Zealand to re-join his old club Gisborne City. Incidentally back in 1970 his sister lived in the same village as Wednesday boss Danny Williams and this led to the eleven year-old Walker being the mascot for the fateful game against Manchester City in April 1970 when Wednesday were relegated from the top division!

Before joining Wednesday the former Rother Valley Boys forward had experienced mixed fortunes, initially joining York City at the age of seventeen but being too old to sign as an apprentice but unable to secure a professional contract. He subsequently had spells in both non-league and in Kiwi football before a successful trial at Oakwell resulted in Colin signing his first professional contract in English soccer. His debut came in a Cup tie at Liverpool and he would score 13 times in only 18 games for the Tykes before falling out of favour and returning to New Zealand. He signed a three-year contract with Gisborne City – working part-time in a sports shop to supplement his income – and became a National hero when scoring 18 goals in 34 games for the New Zealand National side, appearing in six World Cup qualifying games.

He returned to the UK when his family became homesick and gained employment as a gym instructor while playing on a non-contract basis with Doncaster Rovers and then Cambridge United. He eventually dropped into local non-league football – playing for Harworth on a Saturday and Joker on a Sunday – but a slice of luck then brought him to Hillsborough as a damaged knee ligament meant he visited Owls physio Alan Smith for treatment, appearing in four reserve games for Wednesday at the end of the 1985-6 season. A spell as player-manager back at Gisborne City – he scored 60 goals in 97 games for the Kiwi club - saw Walker win the last of his caps for New Zealand and he returned to England for good in 1989, joining Doncaster Rovers on trial. Unfortunately a knee ligament injury suffered whilst on trial ended his playing career soon after and Walker then spent three successful years as manager of Northern Counties East League side Maltby Miners Welfare, prior to being appointed youth team coach at Barnsley in 1993. He later became assistant manager to Glyn Hodges but when the club changed ownership in July 2003 he was one of five major figures sensationally sacked on the same day, including manager and general manager. He was appointed assistant manager at York City in May 2005

WALKER, Cyril John 1937-38

Born: 24 February 1914 Pirton, Herts.
(5ft 10ins, 11st 7lbs – 1937)
Died: 7 July 2002 Chatham, Kent
Debut: 23 October 1937 v Manchester United Division Two Away
Last Appearance: 27 December 1937
v Plymouth Argyle Division Two Home
Total League & Cup Appearances: 4* Goals: 0
***Also appeared in 2 wartime games**

Career Details:

Hitchin Town		
Watford	September	1935 Amat.
Leavesden Mental Hospital	October	1935
Watford	November	1935

Gillingham	June	1937
WEDNESDAY	9 October	1937 £1150*
Chelmsford City	May	1938
Short Sports	August	1939
Raith Rovers		Guest
WEDNESDAY		1941 Guest
Crystal Palace		1942-43 Guest
Brighton & Hove Albion		1942 Guest
Watford		1943 Guest
Norwich City	December	1942 Guest
Norwich City	23 August	1946 Free
Dartford	August	1947
Chatham	August	1949
Snowden Colliery Welfare		
Dartford	November	1952

*Joint fee with Lester

Inside forward who spent just a single season at Wednesday after being signed by his namesake Billy Walker from non-league Gillingham. The pacy inside right effectively acted as understudy to the outstanding talents of Jackie Robinson and within a year of joining Billy Walker, who had now taken over at ambitious Southern League club Chelmsford City, signed him for a second time. During the Second World War, Cyril served in the R.A.F. for five years, guesting for a variety of clubs, and was then player-manager at four Kent based non-league clubs before retiring from football in 1954. He then worked as a caretaker for a local school, until his retirement in 1979, and was married to his wife Greta for 66 years until his death in 2002.

WALKER, Desmond Sinclair 'Des' 1993-2001

Born: 26 November 1965 Hackney
(5ft 11ins, 11st 13lbs – 1997)
Debut: 14 August 1993
v Liverpool
Premier League Away
Last Appearance: 21 April 2001
v Barnsley
Division One Home
Total League
& Cup Appearances: 362
Goals: 0

Career Details:

Nottingham Forest	2 December	1983
Sampdoria	1 August	1992 £1.5m
WEDNESDAY	14 July	1993 £2.75m
Released	30 June	2001
Burton Albion	October	2001
Nottingham Forest	9 July	2002
Mansfield Town	July	2005 Trial

CAPS (@SWFC)
England Full (1) v San Marino 17/11/93

The early 1990s saw Wednesday capture the signatures of several England Internationals and outstanding central defender Des Walker was one of those big money buys in the summer of 1993, the Owls smashing their club transfer record to bring Des back from a difficult spell in Italian football. Previous to moving abroad Walker had been hailed as the best defender in English football and under the wing of Brian Clough at Nottingham Forest was an automatic choice for club and country, winning 58 caps for England and a variety of club honours. Tottenham Hotspur had initially rejected him as a youngster but his talents soon came to the fore at the City Ground and after only a handful of senior games for Forest he won the first of his seven England U-21 caps. He simply became a modern day legend amongst Forest fans and in his first spell amassed 346 games for the Nottingham club, scoring his solitary goal in senior football against Luton Town on New Year's Day 1992. Two League Cup and two Full Members Cup winners medals came his way although Walker had the misfortune to put though his own goal as Forest lost 3-1 to Spurs in the 1991 F.A.Cup Final.

Following his superb displays in the 1990 World Cup Finals in Italy a host of Italian and Spanish clubs were said to be lining up a swoop for his signature but it would be another two years before Walker did move abroad, Genoa club Sampdoria paying a hefty fee for his services. However he failed to settle in Italy – not helped by the fact that England's best centre half was often forced to play at full back – and it was Owls boss Trevor Francis who used his connections in the Italian City to secure a move back to England with Wednesday. The capture of Walker was yet another feather in the Owls cap and over the next eight years he was a veritable rock at the heart of the Owls defence, his coolness under pressure, tremendous pace, superb tackling skills and sheer consistency meaning that he seemed at times to keep the opposition at bay on his own. Unfortunately the hoped for success on the field of play did not materialise and under a succession of managers the Owls eventually slipped from Championship challengers to relegation. However Walker's form remained constant and he was a firm favourite at Hillsborough with his poor distribution just a minor quibble when compared to his other qualities – Wednesday fans were constantly amazed that Walker won only one cap while at Hillsborough. His final season proved to be the Owls first in Division One and after being named 'player of the year' he was released at the end of his contract – the club's financial problems meaning they could not afford to offer Walker a new deal.

After leaving Wednesday, Des explored his options in US football but eventually returned home and started training with ex-Forest team mate Nigel Clough at Northern Premier League club Burton Albion. He subsequently signed for Albion but played only one game – a Cup tie at Matlock Town in October 2001 – before re-joining his old club, Forest, on trial in March 2002. After Forest boss Paul Hart awarded Walker a contract he then enjoyed an Indian summer at the City Ground, captaining Forest to the Division One play-offs in 2003 where they lost to Sheffield United. His influence on the young Forest side won Walker another one-year deal in the following summer and he added 33 appearances to his Forest appearance tally before hanging up his boots in May 2004 to join the club's coaching staff. He remained on the Forest coaching staff until January 2005 when he departed after former Owl Gary Megson was appointed manager.

WALKER, Frederick 'Fred' 1937-38

Born: 3 July 1913 Wednesbury
(5ft 7ins, 10st 6lbs – 1938)
Died: Q/E March 1978 Walsall
Debut: 16 September 1937
v Tottenham Hotspur
Division Two Home
Last Appearance: 7 May 1938
v Tottenham Hotspur
Division Two Away
Total League
& Cup Appearances: 10 Goals: 1

Career Details:

Metro Shaft FC		
Wednesbury		1936
Walsall		1936
WEDNESDAY	15 September	1937
Chelmsford City	13 May	1938 Free

Versatile half back who spent a solitary season at Hillsborough after being signed following a successful trial period. He spent the majority of his sole season at Wednesday in the reserve team – he underwent a throat operation soon after signing - but did appear in the final nine senior games of the season, replacing regular right halfback Richard Rhodes. However it did not lead to a regular place in the 1938-9 season as Walker spent the campaign at non-league club Chelmsford City, under the wing of ex-Owls boss Billy Walker. The Owls actually retained Fred's registration until May 1939, when his playing career effectively ended when war intervened. In the war years he joined the Army, being injured in Ceylon, and did not play senior football after the hostilities ended.

WALKER, Thomas 'Tommy' 1926-37

Born: 4 March 1902 Cross Crols, Stirlingshire
(5ft 9½ins, 11st 8lbs – 1926)
Died: 7 March 1973 Sheffield
Debut: 3 April 1926
v Hull City Division Two Home
Last Appearance: 22 April 1935
v West Bromwich Albion
Division One Away
Total League
& Cup Appearances: 287 Goals: 3

Career Details:

Cross Crols		
Haverbridge Rechabities		
Sternburn Thistle Juveniles		
California Celtic Juniors		
Bowness		
Vale of Grange		
Bradford City	June	1924
WEDNESDAY	24 February	1926 £1900

As a player and then coach Tommy Walker spent an amazing 41 years on the Owls staff, initially being signed by Bob Brown to bolster the club's promotion challenge from the old Second Division. He duly appeared in the last seven games of the season, replacing Billy Felton, as the title was secured and over the seasons that followed formed a formidable partnership with left back Ernie Blenkinsop as Wednesday enjoyed a real 'golden age' of their long history. Walker would win back to back League Championship while at Wednesday and became known during his playing days for his 'Scotch kick' which was a type of scissors kick that he used to clear the ball from defence. The stylish and athletic Walker boasted many fine qualities – he could read the game well and was brilliant at intercepting the ball – and not only linked superbly down the right side with star winger Mark Hooper but also provided a multitude of crosses for the likes of Jack Allen and Jack Ball to feast upon. In September 1929 he became the first ever Scottish player to be picked to appear for the Sheffield FA in their annual challenge match against Glasgow and the pacy and tough tackling full back was consistency itself during a decade in the Owls first team – it was a surprise to all that he did not win some form of International recognition.

There is no doubt Walker would also have been in the 1935 Cup Final side if he had not experienced a major fall out with manager Billy Walker, just five minutes before the Third Round tie at Wolves. Incredibly the pair fell out in the dressing room after all the players had gone onto the pitch and the disagreement was such that Walker incredibly dropped Tommy on the spot and drafted Joe Nibloe into the side at the last minute. He retained his place all the way to Wembley and Tommy appeared only twice more for the club before being handed the role of 'A' team trainer in April 1936. Just over a year later – in July 1937 - he was appointed reserve team trainer when Sam Powell was promoted to senior trainer and remained on the coaching staff until March 1967 when manager Alan Brown re-organised his backroom personnel. During the war Tommy worked twelve hours shifts in a Sheffield steelworks – he remained part-time trainer at Wednesday – while in 1952 the club's doctor reported to the board that he thought Walker not fit enough to be a full-time trainer but it was not until July 1958 that Tommy was demoted from trainer to lighter duties! After retiring from the training staff the club allowed him to live in a club owned house on Carlton Road for the remaining six years of his life.

Tommy had started his life in the Scottish mining village of Cros Cols and was one of twelve children sired by his father, Bobby, who had played professional football for Hearts. At the age of thirteen Tommy started working at the pit top as a fireman boiler but before long was sent underground where he miraculously escaped a roof cave-in, crawling on his stomach for an hour to escape to safety. However he would break away from the hard life of a miner when being spotted by Bradford City although his destination could have been Highbury as he actually went to the station to catch a train for a month's trial at Arsenal before getting cold feet and returning home. On his debut for City he was actually sent off due to mistaken identity when a Fulham winger accidentally collided with the Bradford keeper but the referee thought it was Tommy's fist and ordered him off the field – the winger even said it was the goalie but the official was not ready to change his mind! He would spend two seasons at Bradford – twice going close to winning full caps for Scotland – and only left for Hillsborough when City needed to sell to raise money to meet their summer wage bill.

WALKER, William Baird 'Billy' 1923-24

Born: 5 May 1893 New Cumnock, Ayrshire
(5ft 7½ins, 11st 9lbs – 1923)
Debut:
20 October 1923 v Nelson Division Two Away
Last Appearance:
3 May 1924 v Manchester United Division Two Home
Total League & Cup Appearances: 19 Goals: 5

Career Details:

New Cumnock		
Lugar Boswell		
Lanemark		
Bradford City	August	1911
Lanemark	March	1913
Birmingham City	November	1913
Leicester Fosse		WW1 Guest
Coventry City	November	1919
Merthyr	May	1920
Bristol City	October	1922 £1,000
WEDNESDAY	18 October	1923*
Weymouth	19 July	1924 Free
Leamington Town	October	1925
Redditch Town		1927
Leamington Town		1928

*exchange for Andrew Smailes

Forward Billy Walker started his career in Scottish Junior football before moving south to join Bradford City. He scored freely in reserve team football for City but after just five senior appearances was allowed to return to his Scottish non-league side after less than two years in Yorkshire. However, soon after, Birmingham City brought him back into English football and he fared much better at St Andrews, scoring 8 times in only 12 games in his first season. He did find goals harder to come by in the season immediately preceding the Great War but did hit six hat tricks in reserve team football.

When the war started Walker joined the Army and served in the Royal Engineers, The Infantry and the Royal Field Artillery before being discharged on medical grounds. During the conflict Billy appeared in only two wartime games for City and it was not until the 1919-20 season that he returned to competitive football, starting the first eleven games of the season before a loss of form and barracking from the crowd led him to ask for a transfer - Walker moving to Coventry City soon after. He netted 7 times in 20 games for City but was soon on his travels again, appearing for League club Merthyr and then winning the Division Three (South) Championship with Bristol City before Bob Brown brought Walker to Hillsborough.

The somewhat nomadic nature of his career continued at Wednesday as although Walker appeared in eighteen league games in his debut campaign, playing at inside forward and centre forward, he was allowed to move to Weymouth when offered the player-manager role. He later joined Leamington Town in the same capacity before retiring from the game.

WALL, Andrew Arthur 1967-69

Born: 25 November 1949 Creswell, Derbyshire
(5ft 11ins, 10st 7lbs – 1968)
Debut: 6 April 1968
v Chelsea
Division One Home
Last Appearance: 15 April 1968
v Everton Division One Away
Total League
& Cup Appearances: 3 Goals: 0

Career Details:

WEDNESDAY	25 November	1966
Workington	August	1969
Boston United		1970
Goole Town		1970
Worksop Town	January	1971
Creswell Colliery		1980

Adrian Wall first came to prominence in schoolboy football with his performances for Derbyshire boys and signed apprentice forms for Wednesday in July 1965. The pacy winger signed professional forms in the following year and subsequently made three senior appearances at the age of eighteen. Unfortunately the Owls failed to register a win in those three games and Wall dropped back into reserve team football from where he never returned, joining League side Workington after a season of Central League soccer.

His league career came to a close after 24 appearances for the Northwest club and Wall then played for several non-league sides whilst working at Creswell and then Thorsby collieries. He won the Midland League title with Worksop Town in 1973 and ended his playing days with four seasons at hometown club Creswell – winning seven trophies - prior to retiring from the game in 1984. Away from the game he has also worked as a chauffer and is now a hotel night manager.

* He was not born in Clowne as other records state

WALLER, George 1887-90

Born: 3 December 1864
(5ft 10ins, 11st 2lbs – 1890)
Died: 11 December 1937 Sheffield
Debut: 15 October 1887
v Belper
F.A.Cup Away
Last Appearance: 29 March 1890
v Blackburn Rovers
F.A.Cup Final
Total League
& Cup Appearances: 16* Goals: 2
***Also appeared in**
16 Football Alliance League games

Career Details:

Pyebank		1883
Park Grange		1885
WEDNESDAY		1887
Middlesbrough Ironopolis		1890
Sheffield United	May	1892

Born in the Sheffield suburb of Pitsmoor, George Waller was an all round sportsman who played both football and cricket professionally. The unassuming utility player started his football career in Sheffield junior soccer and joined the Owls in the year they adopted professionalism, appearing in the club's opening game at their new Olive Grove ground – against Blackburn Rovers in September 1887. It was as a forward that Waller initially came to Wednesday and in his first two seasons he scored several hat tricks as the club started to outgrow local football and make an impact on the National stage. He later helped Wednesday to the inaugural Football Alliance League title in 1890 and completed a memorable season by appearing at halfback in the F.A.Cup Final loss to Blackburn Rovers.

His appearance in the Kennington Oval Cup Final proved his last for Wednesday as Waller then moved to Middlesbrough Ironopolis, signing a contract to play both football and cricket for the Teeside club. After two seasons he returned to Sheffield to take over as reserve team coach at Bramall Lane, making the occasional appearance when United found themselves short of players. It was while at United that Waller played County Cricket for Yorkshire (1893-96), taking a wicket with his first ball in first class cricket. He was a medium pace bowler in the summer game and appeared in three senior games for the White Rose County before concentrating on his coaching role at Sheffield United, working as trainer and physio until retiring in 1931 – he also ran a sports shop near Bramall Lane.

WANDS, Alexander Mitchell Doig 'Alex' 1945-47

Born: 5 December 1922 Cowdenbeath
(6ft $^{1}/_{2}$ins, 12st 1lb – 1945)
Debut: 5 January 1946
v Mansfield Town
F.A.Cup Away
Last Appearance: 22 February 1947
v Burnley
Division Two Away
Total League
& Cup Appearances: 18* Goals: 2
***Also appeared in**
17 wartime games, scoring 1 goal

Career Details:

Wallsend St Luke		
Gateshead		1939 Amat.
WEDNESDAY	12 May	1945
Doncaster Rovers	20 May	1947 £500
Boston United		1948
Peterborough United	July	1949
Corby Town		1950
Kettering Town	4 July	1952
Loughborough United		1954

Scottish halfback Alex Wands started his career as an amateur with Northeast side Gateshead before signing professional forms for Wednesday, just four days after the VE day celebrations. Wands, who moved with his parents to Gateshead when aged 12, had previously been captain of Wallsend boys and quickly broke into the Owls senior side during the transitional season of 1945-6. He also helped the reserves win the Central League Championship but was used sparingly when National football returned and after eleven league starts moved to neighbours Doncaster Rovers. He joined a Rovers side who had just ran away with the Division Three (North) title but his new side struggled in the higher grade, eventually being relegated, and Wands played in 22 games before being released in the summer.

After leaving Belle Vue he would spend the remainder of his playing career in semi-professional football, starting with Boston United and then Midland League Peterborough United. He would then enjoy great success at Corby Town – winning several trophies including back-to-back United Counties League titles in 1951 & 1952 - before refusing new terms offered to sign for Kettering Town in 1952. After hanging up his boots Wands later managed Rothwell Town while he worked at Corby Steelworks, also coaching the works football team, until his retirement in the 1980s.

WARBOYS, Alan 1968-70

Born: 18 April 1949 Goldthorpe
(6ft, 14st 5lbs – 1970)
Debut: 24 August 1968
v Tottenham Hotspur
Division One Away
Last Appearance: 19 December 1970
v Oxford United
Division Two Home
Total League
& Cup Appearances: 70+6 Goals: 13

Career Details:

Doncaster Rovers	April	1967
WEDNESDAY	29 May	1968 £20,000
Cardiff City	24 December	1970 £45,000
Sheffield United	22 September	1972 £20,000*
Bristol Rovers	6 March	1973 £35,000
Fulham	17 February	1977 £30,000
Hull City	7 September	1977 £25,000
Doncaster Rovers	12 July	1979 £12,500

*Plus Reece & Powell

Forward Alan Warboys was regarded as a player with a great future ahead of him when the Owls brought the 19 year-old to Hillsborough. His career had started as a centre half in schools football but after scoring six times on his debut at centre forward for the Don & Dearne district side he quickly carved out a reputation as a prolific scorer in junior soccer. After leaving school he worked for just three weeks at Goldthorpe Colliery before signing apprentice forms for Doncaster Rovers and would go on to make his senior debut for Rovers whilst still a trainee. After eleven goals in 39 games the big, strong and fearless "old fashioned style" attacker made the move to Wednesday, Brian Usher going in the opposite direction as part of the deal. Unsurprisingly the youngster found top-flight football a tough proposition and in his first season at Wednesday was in and out of the side, scoring just a solitary goal. He did earn a regular place in the Owls relegation season of 1969-70 but his goal ratio was poor and six months after dropping into the Second Division he was sold to divisional rivals Cardiff City – the Welsh club breaking their transfer record to sign Warboys.

Within a fortnight he came back to haunt Wednesday - netting a brace in a game at Ninian Park - and amazingly repeated the feat in the following season in a Cardiff career which saw Warboys net 27 times in 60 games, including a four goal haul against Carlisle United. While at Cardiff he helped them to Welsh Cup success in 1971 and 1972 and appeared in the European Cup Winners Cup before returning to Sheffield to sign for top-flight neighbours United. However he failed to settle at Bramall Lane and appeared in only seven games prior to a successful spell at Bristol Rovers where he formed a "smash and grab" partnership with Bruce Bannister that brought Warboys an impressive 53 goals in 144 league games. Short spells at Fulham & Hull City followed before Warboys returned to where his career had started over twelve years earlier, signing for Doncaster Rovers. He was named 'player of the season' in his debut campaign and twelve months later helped Rovers to promotion from the Fourth Division. Unfortunately a back injury – suffered in a January 1982 F.A.Cup tie against Cambridge United –then ended his playing career and in October 1982 he retired from professional football, later spending eight years as a pub landlord before becoming an HGV driver in 2002.

WARD, Thomas Alfred 'Tommy' 1937-48

Born: 6 August 1917 Tow Law
(5ft 8ins, 10st $10^1/_2$lbs – 1937)
Died: November 1992 Scunthorpe
Debut: 5 January 1946
v Mansfield Town
F.A.Cup Away
Last Appearance: 14 February 1948
v Nottingham Forest
Division Two Away
Total League
& Cup Appearances: 39* Goals: 20
***Also appeared in**
78 wartime games, scoring 25 goals

Career Details:

Tow Law Town Juniors		
Crook Town		
WEDNESDAY	1 March	1937 £50
Portsmouth		1942-3 Guest
Darlington	October	1944 Guest
Mansfield Town		1945-6 Guest
Darlington	September	1948 £1,500

Joined the Owls from Northeast amateur club Crook Town and played regularly in the first two seasons of wartime football, making his debut at Doncaster Rovers in October 1939. He subsequently joined the Navy in January 1941 and for the remainder of the war played only the occasional game for Wednesday whilst also appearing as a guest player for three other clubs. He returned to the Owls side on a permanent basis on Boxing Day 1945 and over the next eighteen months the versatile Ward – he appeared on both wings and at centre forward – was a fixture in the team, finishing top scorer in the first post war season with 18 goals from only 28 appearances. However he faced stiff competition from the likes of Red Froggatt and Jimmy Dailey and after being placed on the transfer list at his own request was eventually sold to Darlington where in six successful seasons he scored 32 times in 119 league appearances before retiring in 1954.

WARE, Harry 1937

Born: 22 October 1911 Birmingham
(6ft, 12st 4lbs – 1937)
Died: 28 October 1970 Stoke-on-Trent
Debut: 28 August 1937
v Chesterfield
Division Two Away
Last Appearance: 6 November 1937
v Barnsley
Division Two Away
Total League
& Cup Appearances: 12 Goals: 1

Career Details:

Hanley St Luke		
Cobridge Celtic		
Stoke St. Peters		
Stoke City	December	1929 Signed amateur 19/12/27
Newcastle United	September	1935 £2,400
WEDNESDAY	5 May	1937 £1,700
Norwich City	9 November	1937 £2,000
Port Vale		1940-44 Guest
Northampton Town		1940-41 Guest
Stoke City		1940-41 Guest
Nottingham Forest		1940-41 Guest
Crystal Palace		1942-43 Guest
Watford		1943-44 Guest

Just four days after Wednesday suffered relegation from the top-flight in 1937, manager Billy Walker bolstered his forward line by bringing Harry Ware to Hillsborough. Unfortunately for Walker and Ware the move proved unsuccessful for both as the Owls slumped to the lower reaches of the Second Division and 24 hours after the latter moved to Norwich City the former resigned his position as Wednesday boss. Perhaps the most surprising fact about his move to Carrow Road was that just days earlier Norwich City player Burke had been found guilty by the F.A. of breaking Ware's jaw in a league meeting between the sides earlier in the season!

Prior to joining the Owls the centre forward had forged a career in professional football after having started in local Stoke junior soccer, signing for the local Football League side after some brilliant displays. Ware was an all round sportsman – he was a fine swimmer and table tennis player – and before joining Stoke City looked set to follow in the footsteps of his outstanding Boxing father who was British and European bantamweight champion. Unsurprisingly, considering where he spent his childhood, Ware trained as a potter while a teenager but after becoming a professional footballer he spent six years at Stoke City, counting Stanley Matthews as one of his team mates. However competition was fierce and after 15 goals in 57 games for the Potters he moved to the Northeast, spending two seasons there before his brief spell at Hillsborough.

When the Second World War started Harry was on the books of Norwich City and played for a variety of clubs during wartime soccer, whilst serving as a Sergeant in the Anti-Tank platoon. During the Overlord campaign in Normandy Ware was wounded in the chest and after returning to the Norwich side in the transitional season of 1945-46 he was eventually forced to retire when the injury proved too troublesome. In September 1946 he was appointed manager at non-league Northwich Victoria and moved to Holland in August 1948 to become trainer at EDO Haarlem. After six years back at Northwich as manager Ware then returned to his roots in November 1956 when being appointed trainer at Port Vale. He was then manager at Crewe Alexandra (June 1958 – May 1960) and for the final ten years of his life was assistant trainer and then scout for Stoke City.

WARHURST, Paul 1991-93

Born: 26 September 1969 Stockport
(6ft 1ins, 12st 8lbs – 1992)
Debut: 17 August 1991
v Aston Villa
Division One Home
Last Appearance: 25 August 1993
v West Ham United
Premier League Away
Total League
& Cup Appearances 81+7 Goals: 18

Career Details:

Manchester City	1 July	1988
Oldham Athletic	27 October	1988 £10,000
WEDNESDAY	10 July	1991 £750,000
Blackburn Rovers	3 September	1993 £2.75m
Crystal Palace	31 July	1997 £1.25m
Bolton Wanderers	25 November	1998 Loan
Bolton Wanderers	7 January	1999 £800,000
Stoke City	27 March	2003 Loan
Released	30 June	2003
Bolton Wanderers	10 September	2003 Free
Released	26 September	2003
Chesterfield	16 October	2003
Released	18 November	2003
Barnsley	12 December	2003
Released	17 January	2004
Queens Park Rangers	10 February	2004
Carlisle United	20 February	2004 N/C
Released	23 February	2004
Notts County	8 March	2004 Trial
Grimsby Town	12 March	2004 N/C
Chester City	July	2004 Trial
Blackpool	2 November	2004
Released	1 March	2005
Forest Green Rovers	31 March	2005

CAPS (@SWFC)
England U-21 (1) v Germany 10/09/91

To say Paul Warhurst experienced an eventful time in his two years in a Wednesday shirt would be an understatement of colossal proportions as he progressed from an England U-21 central defender to a member of the full national squad – as a striker! The athletic and pacy Warhust had started his professional career at Manchester City, after impressing for both Stockport and Manchester boys, but was snapped up by neighbours Oldham Athletic for a nominal fee and appeared in 91 games for the Latics, mainly in an attacking right back role as Oldham won the Division Two title in 1991 and reached the League Cup Final in the previous year . After impressing against Wednesday it was Trevor Francis who equalled the Owls transfer record to bring the 21 year-old Warhurst to Hillsborough on a 4-year contract and he quickly became an automatic choice at the heart of the club's defence. At the time he could run 100m in under 11 seconds and this electric pace meant he could surge from defence and cause countless problems for opposition defences.

However it was in September 1992 that Warhurst's roller coaster journey really began when Francis experimented with a forward role for the Mancunian. The change of position paid immediate dividends as he netted at Nottingham Forest and four days later scored a brace as Luxembourg minnows Spora were put to the sword in the UEFA Cup – Warhurst having to thank Owls physio Alan Smith for saving his life during the game after he swallowed his tongue following an ariel collision. He was unconscious for twenty minutes and had a fit on the pitch but after several days in hospital made a miraculous recovery to return to the side, scoring in the return leg in Luxembourg. He soon after reverted back to a defensive position but early in the New Year reprised the striker role and over the next few months made a quite sensational impact on English football – taking his goals tally to eighteen for the season and receiving a shock call up to the full England squad in March 1993 – a groin injury forcing his withdrawal from the squad for a World Cup qualifying game against Turkey. In February 1993 he became the first Owls player since Redfern Froggatt to score in seven consecutive league games and Warhurst now considered himself to be an out and out forward. However problems then arose at the F.A.Cup Final when he initially refused to play if forced to revert to his original central defensive position and although he did pull on an Owls shirt for the showpiece occasion – complete with plaster cast over a broken wrist – it was clear his days were numbered at Wednesday and he looked set to join Blackburn Rovers in July 1993 for a £3m fee. That deal depended though on Wednesday securing Brian Deane from neighbours United as his replacement and when this move collapsed so did the Warhurst deal.

The following month he signed a new lucrative four-year contract but within a few weeks the Owls had received a club record fee as he finally moved to Ewood Park. Soon after moving to Rovers he suffered a broken leg and over the ensuing years experienced a succession of persistent injuries which restricted his appearances to just 74 games, netting only four times. He did appear in the requisite number of games to win a Premier League Championship medal in 1995 but after settling into a midfield role at Crystal Palace he suffered relegation in 1998. Financial problems at Selhurst Park led to a loan move to Bolton Wanderers – teaming up with Jon Newsome who was on loan from Wednesday – and after the move was made permanent Warhurst was a regular for the Lancashire club, helping them to two Division One play off Finals although he was not picked for either.

After leaving Bolton in the summer of 2003 Warhurst played for a wide variety of clubs over the next two years, including a second brief spell back at Bolton Wanderers. He incredibly spent just 72 hours at Carlisle United – playing only 23 minutes of first team football – and during the 2003-4 season was sent off, against Wednesday, on his Barnsley debut and netted an own goal in his first game for Grimsby Town! Incidentally Paul's father, Roy, was born in Sheffield and played league soccer for several clubs including Manchester City & Oldham Athletic while he was the grandson of Harry Stock who was the third member of the family to play for Oldham.

WARREN, Peter 1909-12

Born: Dublin
(5ft $7^1/_2$ins, 11st 7lbs – 1910)
Debut: 13 November 1909
v Woolwich Arsenal
Division One Home
Last Appearance: 16 September 1911
v Middlesbrough
Division One Home
Total League
& Cup Appearances: 7 Goals: 0

Career Details:

Belfast Celtic		
WEDNESDAY	March	1909 £50*
Shelbourne		1912
Millwall	May	1913 £75

*Joint fee with O'Connell

Left back Peter Warren spent three full seasons at Wednesday where he acted mainly as understudy to the likes of Rob McSkimming and Walter Holbem. Although born in Southern Ireland it was with Belfast Celtic that his senior career had began and he joined Wednesday on the understanding that if the move proved successful then the Owls would pay a transfer fee. Wednesday eventually offered £40 for Warren and Patrick O'Connell – after Belfast Celtic had asked the Irish F.A. to investigate their claim for a fee – and eventually agreed on a £50 payment. After leaving Hillsborough he returned to his roots to sign for Shelbourne and was capped twice by Ireland in 1912 before returning to England a year later – Millwall paying Wednesday the transfer fee for his Football League registration. He failed to make a senior appearance for the Lions before dropping out of senior football.

WATLING, Barry John 1976

Born: 16 July 1946 Walthamstow
(5ft 9ins, 11st 12lbs – 1976)
Only Appearance: 24 January 1976
v Swindon Town
Division Three Home
Total League
& Cup Appearances: 1 Goals: 0

Career Details:

Leyton Orient	July	1964
Bristol City	July	1965
Notts County	6 August	1969
Hartlepool United	July	1972
Seattle Sounder		1973-75
Chester	19 September	1975 Loan
Crewe Alexandra	18 November	1975 Loan
Rotherham United	19 December	1975 Loan
WEDNESDAY	22 January	1976 Free
Barea Park	March	1976
Charlton Athletic	September	1976
Maidstone United	October	1976
Chatham Town		1981
Bromley		1982
Sittingbourne		1983

The Owls were Barry Watling's eighth club when the goalkeeper signed a short-term deal after his contract had been cancelled at Hartlepool by mutual consent. He quickly made his debut for Wednesday but was almost immediately displaced by Peter Fox and after just two months at Hillsborough departed for a player-coach role in South African football. He later returned to the UK, signing for Charlton, but after failing to make a senior appearance he dropped into non-league football, being appointed player-coach at Maidstone United. Three months later he was elevated to the manager's chair and was also player-manager at his next three clubs before retiring in the mid-1980s. He then became a financial services consultant, a role he still occupies today.

His career had started back in 1962 when he signed apprentice forms at Leyton Orient but after being elevated to the professional ranks he failed to make a senior appearance for the Brisbane Road club. His fortunes did not improve greatly during four years at Bristol City as with Mike Gibson an almost ever-present Watling appeared in only two competitive games prior to moving North to sign for Notts County in 1969. He did eventually break into the County side early in 1970 and was an almost ever present until the end of the season – incidentally he was named as substitute for a February 1970 home game with Newport County and entered the fray as an outfield player! The following season Watling missed only three games as the Magpies won the Fourth Division Championship but after losing his place he left for a successful spell at Hartlepool United, not missing a game from joining until the final match of the 1974-5 season. He totalled 139 league games for United but after falling out of favour spent several loan spells at a variety of clubs – including two stints in US football – prior to arriving at Hillsborough.

WATSON, Donald 1954-56

Born: 27 August 1932 Barnsley
(5ft 8ins, 11st 1lb – 1955)
Debut: 22 January 1955
v Tottenham Hotspur
Division One Away
Last Appearance: 3 November 1956
v Bolton Wanderers
Division One Home
Total League
& Cup Appearances: 10 Goals: 4

Career Details:

Worsbrough Bridge MW		
WEDNESDAY	25 September	1954 £25
Lincoln City	29 November	1956 £4,250
Bury	16 November	1957 £2,250
Barnsley	January	1962 £2,850
Rochdale	July	1962
Barrow	July	1964
Buxton	October	1966

Joined the Owls from Barnsley junior football and within four months was making a goal scoring first team debut in a heavy defeat at White Hart Lane. Although inexperienced Watson was a keen, lively and all running attacker and it was these attributes that persuaded Eric Taylor to retain his services for six consecutive games as Wednesday tried desperately to find a winning formula that would alleviate their position at the wrong end of the First Division table. However when Roy Shiner and Albert Broadbent arrived on the scene in the summer of 1955 the youngster was pushed back into reserve team soccer, netting seven times in Central League football but failing to make a senior appearance in the 1955-56 Division Two Championship campaign. The former apprentice Engineer did return to the first team briefly when the Owls were back in the top-flight but just a few days after his final senior game for the club he was sold to Lincoln City.

It was at his next club, Bury, that Watson would experience his best spell in league soccer as with ex-Owl David Russell in charge he scored 69 times in 180 league and cup games, winning a Division Three Championship medal in 1961. Various playing stints in the lower leagues followed with Barrow proving his final league side prior to being released in the summer of 1966. After leaving Holker Street he played a solitary game for Buxton but decided it was time to retire and so returned to his original profession as an engineering turner. He was later made redundant and worked as a double glazing delivery driver until his retirement.

WATSON, Gordon William George 'Flash' 1991-95

Born: 20 March 1971 Sidcup
(5ft 11ins, 12st 9lbs – 1991)
Debut: 2 March 1991
v Notts County
Division Two Away
Last Appearance: 14 March 1995
v Crystal Palace
Premier League Away
Total League
& Cup Appearances: 42+46 Goals: 21

Career Details:

Kingfisher F.C.		
Charlton Athletic	1 March	1989
WEDNESDAY	14 February	1991 £250,000*
Southampton	17 March	1995 £1.2m
Bradford City	17 January	1997 £550,000
Bournemouth	20 August	1999 Free
Portsmouth		2001 N/C
Hartlepool United	21 September	2001 Free
Released	30 June	2003
WEDNESDAY	July	2003 Trial

*plus further £250,000 dependant upon appearances

CAPS (@SWFC)
England U-21 (2) v Senegal 27/05/91, v USSR 01/06/91

Popular, hard working forward Gordon Watson was brought to Hillsborough by Ron Atkinson who saw the teenager as a real prospect for the future. The Owls paid his club an initial fee, which was due to rise to £500,000 after 50 league games and if he was capped for England, and the youngster made a sensational impact by netting a sparkling hat trick for the reserve team in only his second game - he ended the season with thirteen goals from as many games as the second team won the Central League Championship and in his time at Wednesday boasted a tremendous record in reserve team football of 58 goals in only 89 games. Over the next three seasons the livewire striker made fleeting first team appearances – he was competing against the likes of David Hirst, Mark Bright & Paul Warhurst – but he moved up the pecking order in the 1993-4 season, netting 14 times to finish the campaign as second top scorer behind Bright. However after seemingly becoming established he was back on the subs bench following the return from injury of David Hirst and arrival of Guy Whittingham, prompting his sale to Premier League Southampton just ninety seconds from the end of trading on the 1995 transfer deadline day.

The sale seemed good business for Wednesday but the move proved disappointing for Watson as he encountered further frustration on the South coast, drifting in and out of the side and scoring just 14 goals in 67 competitive games for the Saints. He was allowed to leave Southampton to become Bradford City's record buy but sadly in only his third game for City he was the victim of a terrible tackle that left 'Flash' with a double fracture of his right leg, a 7" metal plate inserted in his leg and 18 months on the sidelines. In a later court case – where witness Jimmy Hill said the tackle was " the worst he had seen in 50 years of football" - Watson won over £1m in damages from Huddersfield Town player Kevin Gray. After struggling to regain fitness he left Bradford under freedom of contract in 1999 and spent a season at Bournemouth, making only a handful of appearances before being released in 2000. He then spent a year out of the game as he tried to regain full fitness and after scoring six times in eight reserve games at Portsmouth he won a contract at Hartlepool United. His 18 goals duly helped Chris Turner's side into the Division Three play-offs but bad luck struck again when he suffered another broken leg in September 2002. After being released Watson returned to Wednesday on trial in the 2003 pre season and made a big impact, scoring regularly in warm up games but just when a contract seemed on the table he suffered an injury setback that would eventually lead to his retirement in 2004. He is now a Director of Kickers Indoor Sports Limited.

WATSON, J. 1885-86

Born: Sheffield
Only Appearance: 31 October 1885 v Long Eaton Rangers F.A.Cup Away
Total League & Cup Appearances: 1 Goals: 0

Career Details:

Hallam	
WEDNESDAY	1885

Forward who played a handful of games for Wednesday during the 1885-86 season, including a shock F.A.Cup loss at Long Eaton. He scored twice in ten friendly games for the Owls before dropping back into local football.

WATTS, Julian David 1992-96

Born: 17 March 1971 Sheffield
(6ft 3ins, 13st 7lbs – 1995)
Debut: 1 October 1992
v Spora Luxembourg
UEFA Cup Away
Last Appearance: 2 March 1996
v Nottingham Forest
Premier League Home
Total League
& Cup Appearances: 16+4 Goals: 1

Career Details:

Frecheville CA		
WEDNESDAY		1986 Trial
Rotherham United	19 July	1990
Sheffield United	November	1991 Trial
WEDNESDAY	10 March	1992 £130,000*
Shrewsbury Town	18 December	1992 Loan
Leicester City	28 March	1996 £210,000 (T)
Crewe Alexandra	29 August	1997 Loan
Huddersfield Town	5 February	1998 Loan
Bristol City	6 July	1998
Lincoln City	18 December	1998
Blackpool	23 March	1999 Loan
Luton Town	6 August	1999
Northern Spirit	13 June	2001

*Initial £80k + 2 x £25k payments linked to appearances

Tall, commanding centre half Julian Watts actually started his playing career as a midfielder but was switched to his natural position whilst playing for Rotherham's Northern Intermediate League side. He helped the Millers win the NIL Cup in 1988 and after finishing his studies at Loxley College Watts signed professional forms for the Millmoor club. However after just twenty senior games for United he moved to Premier League Wednesday, being appointed captain of the reserve side, and effectively became a squad player at Hillsborough. With the likes of Des Walker and Peter Atherton automatic choices he found his first team opportunities limited but proved a solid performer when called upon. A loan spell at Shrewsbury Town added to his league experience and it was a surprise to many Wednesday fans when Watts moved to Leicester City on transfer deadline day 1996, earning promotion to the Premier League just two months later - Watts setting up Steve Claridge to net the last minute winner in the Wembley play off final.

He then enjoyed an extended run in Leicester's first season back in the top-flight but was unlucky to miss out on the League Cup Final when manager Martin O'Neil decided to change formation to man mark Middlesbrough danger man Juninho. The Foxes, in a Hillsborough replay, claimed the trophy but although Julian did not play in either game he was still awarded a winners medal. He subsequently lost his place to newcomer Matt Elliott and then appeared for a variety of clubs over the next five years before moving to Sydney in Australia to sign for Northern Spirit. His father, Graham, played for the Owls 'A' team in the 1950s and Julian was back at Wednesday in the summer of 2003 to train with the club before returning down under to complete his three-year contract at Spirit. After returning home for good in May 2004 Julian set up his own business in Worksop and retired from senior football.

WEAVER, Alexander Edward 'Alex' 1924-26

Born: 22 June 1902 Weymouth
(5ft 10ins, 11st 3lbs – 1924)
Died: 18 April 1976 Weymouth
Debut:
1 January 1925 v Oldham Athletic Division Two Home
Last Appearance:
7 March 1925 v Bradford City Division Two Away
Total League & Cup Appearances: 6 Goals: 1

Career Details:

Royal Air Force		
Wycombe Wanderers		1923
WEDNESDAY	June	1924
Released		1926
Worcester City		

Forward Alex Weaver played most of his early football in the forces, serving in the R.A.F. throughout the First World War and then in peacetime until joining non-league Wycombe Wanderers in 1923. He netted 21 times in his only season with Wanderers and this prompted a move into professional football under Bob Brown at Hillsborough. He briefly enjoyed a spell in the Wednesday first team part way through the 1924-25 season but had to be content with Midland League football for the majority of his two year stay in Sheffield. He had the misfortune to break his leg playing for the reserves in February 1926 and this effectively ended his senior career as Weaver failed to play another game for Wednesday after the injury. He later played in non-league soccer and in October 1947 was a member of the Whitehead Sports Committee.

WEBSTER, Arnold 'Arnie' 1936-37

Born: 3 March 1913 Birchover
(5ft 11ins, 12st – 1937)
Died: 26 February 1982 Matlock
Only Appearance: 5 April 1937
v Stoke City
Division One Away
Total League
& Cup Appearances: 1 Goals: 0

Career Details:

Birchover		
WEDNESDAY	December	1936 Pro.
Released		1937
Frickley Colliery		
Mill Close Mine		1946-50
Darley Dale United		1950-53

Centre Forward who signed amateur forms for Wednesday in February 1936, prior to turning professional ten months later. After gaining experience in the club's Central League side he was given a first team bow in a 1-0 loss at Stoke City in April 1937 but this proved his only senior game for Wednesday as Arnie became homesick and returned to his Derbyshire village. Southend United manager David Jack wanted to secure his services but Webster rejected his overtures and instead worked locally whilst playing for Frickley Colliery. He served in the Army during the War and after the hostilities ceased he worked in a Lead Mine and then at a flourmill until his retirement. He continued to play football until 1953, appearing for his works side and then in local amateur soccer.

WEBSTER, Frederick Joseph 1887-88

Born:
Only Appearance: 15 October 1887 v Belper Town F.A.Cup Away
Total League & Cup Appearances: 1 Goals: 0

Career Details:

WEDNESDAY	1887

Unknown centre forward who appeared in only one senior game for Wednesday, a 3-2 Cup win at minnows Belper Town in the club's first season after turning professional.

WEBSTER, John 'Johnny' 1890-95

Born:
(5ft 7 1/2ins, 10st 10lbs – 1894)
Debut:
16 September 1893 v Newton Heath Division One Home
Last Appearance:
22 April 1895 v West Bromwich Albion Division One Away
Total League & Cup Appearances: 27* Goals: 5
***Also appeared in 2 Football Alliance League games**

Career Details:

Attercliffe	
WEDNESDAY	1890

Although winger Johnny Webster spent five years at Wednesday he was only a first team regular for a solitary campaign, netting five times in 25 games during the 1893-94 season. He had previously appeared only briefly at first team level in pre-league football and failed to make a senior appearance in the club's debut season in league competition. However he made such a big impression after replacing Harry Davis on the right wing that he retained his place for almost the whole of the season before the arrival of Archie Brash pushed him back into the shadows. At his peak Webster was a superb crosser of the ball but after losing his first team place his form tailed away and he left Olive Grove in 1895, later becoming licensee of the Old Gate Inn at Attercliffe after his playing days ended.

WEIR, William Findlay 1909-12

Born: 18 April 1889 Glasgow
(5ft 6ins, 10st 7lbs – 1910)
Died: 9 July 1918
Debut: 19 February 1910
v Notts County
Division One Home
Last Appearance: 18 March 1912
v Bury
Division One Home
Total League
& Cup Appearances: 72 Goals: 1

Career Details:

Campvale		
Maryhill		
WEDNESDAY	May	1909 £20*
Tottenham Hotspur	September	1912 Trial/£350

*Joint fee with J.Miller

Versatile halfback who arrived from Scottish non-league football to comfortably adjust to life in England's top tier. The Glaswegian had won Scottish Junior International honours while at Maryhill and he was a regular first team player at Wednesday for three seasons, only losing his place to Rob McSkimming near the end of the 1911-12 campaign. In that season Weir had become one of only a handful of Wednesday players to be sent off in pre war football – receiving his marching orders at Middlesbrough in January 1912 – while he joined Spurs initially on trial before completing a permanent move. While on the White Hart Lane club's books Weir showed his qualities by appearing in 119 games but sadly during the Great War he was killed in action whilst serving for the Tottenham Royal Engineers.

WELSH, Fletcher 1920

Born: 16 August 1893 Galashiels, Scotland
(5ft 11ins, 12st 5lbs – 1920)
Debut:
17 January 1920 v Everton Division One Home
Last Appearance:
4 September 1920 v Barnsley Division Two Home
Total League & Cup Appearances: 12 Goals: 4

Career Details:

Raith Rovers		
Heart of Midlothian		
Raith Rovers	June	1914
WEDNESDAY	12 January	1920 £1,800
Third Lanark	13 October	1920 £450

Scot who was one of an amazing 43 players used during the disastrous 1919-20 season when Wednesday fought unsuccessfully to avoid relegation from the top-flight. Welsh was in fact the seventh centre forward to be used in that campaign and made an immediate impact when netting the winning goal on his debut. He certainly arrived with a goal scoring pedigree – he left Raith Rovers having netted 23 goals in only 18 games – and looked a valuable capture when scoring a brace in his second game as the Owls won back-to-back games. Unfortunately Wednesday would not win again for the remainder of the season and Welsh would only score once more for the club before returning to Scotland. He subsequently retired from the game in 1924 and worked in the Leith shipyards.

WEST, Colin 1987-89

Born: 13 November 1962 Wallsend
(6ft, 13st 11lbs – 1987)
Debut: 12 September 1987
v Watford
Division One Home
Last Appearance: 4 February 1989
v Aston Villa
Division One Away
Total League
& Cup Appearances: 55+5 Goals: 13

Career Details:

Sunderland	9 July	1980
Watford	28 March	1985 £115,000
Glasgow Rangers	23 May	1986 £180,000
WEDNESDAY	4 September	1987 £150,000
West Bromwich Albion	22 February	1989 £200,000
Port Vale	1 November	1991 Loan
Swansea City	5 August	1992 Free
Leyton Orient	26 July	1993 Free
Northampton Town	19 September	1997 Loan
Rushden & Diamonds	November	1997 Loan
Rushden & Diamonds	4 February	1998 £20,000
Northwich Victoria	13 September	1999 Free
Hartlepool United	2 October	1999 Free

Old fashioned style centre forward who failed to win over the Wednesday faithful in his time as a player and is perhaps unfortunate to be remembered more for a terrible penalty miss at home to Luton Town in November 1987 than for any of his goals. West was a tall and stocky player who was a powerful header of a ball but was part of the poor Owls side of the late 1980s and with chances and goals at a premium he failed to make the desired impact. With West not overly proficient when the ball was at his feet it was no surprise that just a few days after taking over at Hillsborough new manager Ron Atkinson used West as a makeweight in the record transfer deal that brought Carlton Palmer from the Hawthorns.

Throughout his career West had never been a prolific scorer and in fact 42 of his 128 career league goals (in 448 games) came in the twilight of his career at basement club Leyton Orient. He had started as a professional at local club Sunderland and helped the Black Cats to the 1985 League Cup Final, scoring three times in the semi-finals, although he was left out of the Wembley loss to Norwich City. A brief spell at Watford was followed by a similarly short and unsuccessful time under Graeme Souness at Glasgow Rangers where West started only four games – Wednesday and Rangers actually agreed a £120,000 fee for his transfer in February 1987 only for the blonde target man to decide against the move back to England.

After leaving Hillsborough, West dropped down the divisions to eventually end his league days at Hartlepool United, after playing a few games for Conference club Northwich as a favour to a friend. He was appointed assistant manager to Chris Turner in October 1999 at the Northeast club and the duo then gradually turned the perennial strugglers into promotion material. A week after Turner moved to Hillsborough as Owls boss his erstwhile assistant followed in his footsteps – being appointed No. 2 on 14 November 2002 – but like many before them the duo could not manage to turn the club around and West was dismissed in September 2004 after almost two years back at Hillsborough. After a spell out of the game he was again appointed No. 2 to Turner, becoming assistant manager at League One strugglers Stockport County in February 2005.

WEST, Frederick 'Fred' 1881-82

Born: Sheffield
Debut:
28 December 1881 v Staveley F.A.Cup Home
Last Appearance:
6 March 1882 v Blackburn Rovers F.A.Cup S/F Away
Total League & Cup Appearances: 7 Goals: 0

Career Details:

Heeley	1880-81
Exchange	1881-82
WEDNESDAY	1881-82
Lockwood Brothers	1882-87

Attacker Fred West was a member of the Owls side that reached the last four of the F.A.Cup in only their second season in the competition. The locally born player came into the side for the second game in that Cup run and remained an ever present as Wednesday went all the way to a Huddersfield Cup semi clash with old foes Blackburn Rovers. That tie finished nil-nil and West appeared in the 5-1 replay loss at Manchester before joining Lockwood Brothers in the following summer.

WESTLAKE, Francis Arthur 'Frank' 1938-50

Born: 11 August 1915 Bolton-on-Dearne
(5ft 10ins, 11st 9lbs – 1948)
Died: 13 February 1999 Doncaster
Debut: 26 March 1938
v Luton Town
Division Two Away
Last Appearance: 14 January 1950
v Plymouth Argyle
Division Two Home
Total League
& Cup Appearances: 117* Goals: 0
***Also appeared in 35 wartime games**

Career Details:

Thurnscoe Victoria		
WEDNESDAY	3 May	1937 £100*
Bournemouth	September	1941 Guest
Bradford City		1943-46 Guest
Leeds United	November	1945 Guest
Halifax Town	July	1950 £1,000
Denaby United		

*Joint fee with G.S.Tepper & A.Bloomfield

The Owls career of Frank Westlake had the strangest of beginnings as after making his first team debut he was subsequently banned for six months after Wednesday forget to submit his Football League registration! The League also fined the club five pounds and five shillings and the whole episode certainly did not help the 20 year-old full back as he failed to make another senior appearance before the onset of war in 1939. During the war years Westlake - who initially came to the fore with local club Thurnscoe where he won the Sheffield Association Cup in 1937 – became a PE Instructor and Drill sergeant in the Royal Air Force, appearing in several representative games for the forces and winning several honours. During the conflict he also guested occasionally for a handful of clubs before re-launching his senior career at Hillsborough during the transitional season of 1945-46.

Although he could play in both full back positions it was at right back that Westlake would make his name as a long-term partner to Hugh Swift in the mid to late 1940s. The duo appeared in 106 consecutive games together between December 1946 and April 1949 (Westlake's personal run stretching to 114 games in a row) before Vin Kenny replaced Westlake at right back. His advancing years were probably the main reason for losing his first team spot and it was no surprise when he left for Halifax Town in the summer of 1950 – after refusing an offer from Boston United to take over as player-manager. His stay at The Shay was brief, playing only two league games, and after a short spell at Denaby United he retired from the game in 1951 to become a grocer in the Denaby area. He was married to Vera for sixty years – the pair were local ballroom dancing champions – before passing away in a Doncaster nursing home at the age of eighty-three.

WESTWOOD, Ashley Michael 2000-03

Born: 31 August 1976 Bridgnorth
(6ft, 12st 9lbs – 2000)
Debut: 10 August 2000
v Wolverhampton Wanderers
Division One Away
Last Appearance: 4 May 2003
v Walsall
Division One Home
Total League
& Cup Appearances: 91+5 Goals: 9

Career Details:

Manchester United	1 July	1994
Crewe Alexandra	26 July	1995 £40,000
Bradford City	20 July	1998 £150,000
WEDNESDAY	10 August	2000 £150,000
Northampton Town	14 July	2003 Free

Centre half who started his career as a trainee at Old Trafford, playing in the same side as Terry Cooke as United won the F.A.Youth Cup in 1995. He also won two Youth caps for England but failed to play a senior game for the Manchester club prior to signing for Crewe Alexandra. After 126 games under Dario Gradi, including a play off success from Division Two in 1997, he was signed by Paul Jewell for Bradford City where he was part of the Bantams side that took City to the Premier League for the first time in their history in 1999. However a combination of injury and suspension then meant he struggled to make an impression in the top-flight and when fit could not displace the centre-half pairing of David Wetherall and Andy O'Brien.

However when Jewell left for Hillsborough Westwood was soon to follow, initially signing on loan prior to a full transfer in September 2000. Although prone to the occasional error he proved a competent defender during a difficult spell at Wednesday as the club lurched from crisis to crisis after suffering relegation from the Premier League. He proved to have a useful knack of finding the goal in that debut season – scoring after just two minutes on his home debut for the club – but an ankle injury disrupted his second season and he subsequently missed only one game during the second half of the 2002-3 relegation season. His contract was not renewed in the summer of 2003 and he duly moved to Northampton Town, being appointed captain. He helped the Cobblers to the semi-final of the 2003 Division Two play-offs but was sent off in the first leg as Town lost on aggregate to Mansfield Town.

WHALLEY, John William 'Johnny' 1920-21

Born: 17 February 1897 Bradford
(5ft 8½ins, 10st)
Died: 3 August 1972 Morecombe
Debut: 3 April 1920
v Bolton Wanderers
Division One Home
Last Appearance: 19 April 1920
v Bradford Park Avenue
Division One Home
Total League
& Cup Appearances: 5 Goals: 0

Career Details:

Crystal Palace		
Portsmouth	April	1917
Bradford		WW1 Guest
WEDNESDAY	March	1920 £100
Released		1920
Halifax Town	April	1921

Centre forward Johnny Whalley was yet another player who was tried briefly during the disastrous 1919-20 campaign. He had previously appeared in Southern League football for Portsmouth and played five league games for Wednesday, failing to find the net before being released during the mass clear out at the end of the season. He subsequently joined Halifax Town and went on to become a major player during the West Yorkshire club's early years in the Football League – appearing in their first ever home league game. He also entered the record books as the first man to appear in one hundred games for Town and was the first to hit a hat-trick in league football – in a sensational 5-5 draw at home to Crewe on the final day of the 1921-22 season. After appearing in 141 league games for the 'Shaymen' his registration was cancelled in May 1925.

WHELAN, Glenn David 2004-

Born: 13 January 1984 Dublin
(6ft, 12st 5lbs - 2004)
Debut: 21 August 2004
v Huddersfield Town
League One Home
Total League
& Cup Appearances: 42 Goals: 4

Career Details:

Manchester City	25 January	2001
Bury	29 September	2003 Loan
Bury	23 December	2003 Loan
Wycombe Wanderers		2004 Trial
WEDNESDAY	1 July	2004 Free

CAPS (@SWFC)
Eire U-21 (7) v Bulgaria 17/08/04, v Cyprus 03/09/04, v Switzerland 07/09/04,v France 08/10/04, v Portugal 08/02/05, v Israel 25/03/05, v Israel 03/06/05

Talented midfielder who came through the youth ranks at Manchester City. However after failing to break into Kevin Keegan's first team - his sole first team appearance being seventeen minutes as a substitute in an August 2003 UEFA Cup tie at Welsh club TNS - he signed a pre contract agreement to join Chris Turner's Wednesday in the summer of 2004. Unfortunately a sending off in a reserve game for Manchester City meant the Irish youngster was suspended for the opening three games of the new season and his early months at Hillsborough were further hampered when he was shown a red card in only his seventh competitive game for the club.

Despite his only league games coming while on loan at basement club Bury he was somewhat unfairly burdened with the tag of the 'next John Sheridan' by Chris Turner but since becoming a regular in the side showed a wide range of passing skills and eye for goal. While at Manchester City he won both Eire Youth and U-21 honours and after joining Wednesday was subsequently made captain of the latter side - scoring his first goal for his country against Cyprus in September 2004. He ended a terrific year at International level by being named 2004 Eire U-21 'player of the year' but it would be at club level that Whelan would enjoy the finest moment of his career as his increasingly impressive displays at the heart of the Owls midfield propelled the club into the play offs. For the youngster it meant a return to the Millennium Stadium - the scene of his only game for Manchester City - where his stunning goal in extra time against Hartlepool United capped a man of the match display that secured Championship football at Hillsborough in 2005-06.

WHITAKER, Colin 1951-53

Born: 14 June 1932 Leeds
(5ft 10ins, 11st 4lbs – 1951)
Only Appearance:
15 March 1952 v Queens Park Rangers Division Two Home
Total League & Cup Appearances: 1 Goals: 0

Career Details:

Farsley Celtic		1949
WEDNESDAY	24 November	1951
Bradford Park Avenue	19 June	1953
Shrewsbury Town	11 July	1956
Queens Park Rangers	15 February	1961
Rochdale	19 May	1961
Oldham Athletic	6 October	1962 Player-exchange
Barrow	7 August	1964
Ashton United	6 November	1964
Stalybridge Celtic		1967

In the Owls history books Colin Whitaker was just a one game wonder but this disguises the fact that he enjoyed a lengthy Football League career, which spanned seven clubs, almost 250 games and over 100 goals. Although born in Leeds, Whitaker spent much of his childhood in the Southampton area– after his Prison Officer father was transferred to Winchester – but after attending Southampton College he moved back to Yorkshire when his father was transferred back to Leeds. He subsequently started to play for local club Farsley Celtic and after impressing in Yorkshire League soccer he was snapped up by Wednesday and groomed for senior football in the club's 'A' and reserve sides. He did not have to wait long for his league debut at Hillsborough – a 2-1 home win over QPR – but his career received a major setback when in the opening reserve game of the 1952-3 season he suffered a broken leg. The injury put Colin out of the game for a year but he did recover sufficiently to effectively re-launch his career at Bradford Park Avenue. Incidentally while Colin served his National Service in the early 1950s he was posted to Germany and Wednesday used to pay for the tricky winger to be flown home on a Friday night to play in the Central League team the day after!

In three seasons at Park Avenue he appeared in 49 league games and it was only his National Service that denied Whitaker an England U-23 cap. His best spell in league soccer certainly came at his next club, Shrewsbury, where the pacy skilful winger netted 60 times in only 162 competitive games. During a short spell at Rochdale Whitaker attended an F.A.Coaching course run by England boss Walter Winterbottom – later working as a schools coach for a time - and after buying a small farm from an impoverished farmer he showed his entrepreneurial side by turning the land into a nine hole golf course! On the field of play he appeared for Rochdale in the 1962 League Cup Final defeat to Norwich City and after ending his league career at Barrow he returned to Lancashire to join Manchester non-league outfit Ashton. While based in the Red Rose County Whitaker played cricket for Castleton Moor – he had previously appeared in Minor Counties cricket for Shropshire while on Shrewsbury's books – and the all round sportsman also boasted a single figure golf handicap!

He was appointed player-manager at Stalybridge Celtic in the summer of 1967 and led them to Manchester Intermediate Cup success in 1969. The untimely death of his first wife in the same year saw Colin relinquish control of his golf course while a year later he became manager at Buxton, taking the Derbyshire club into the Northern Premier League in 1973 after lifting the Cheshire League Championship. He then left for a four-year stay at Droylsden where in 1976 he led the 'Bloods' to the First Round of the F.A.Cup for the first time in their history – the Manchester club losing 5-3 to Grimsby Town after a 0-0 draw. He returned to Buxton in 1977 before severing all ties with football in 1980 to work in the telecommunication industry. In 1982 he started his own business – computerising telephone exchanges – and employed a dozen staff before taking retirement at the age of sixty in 1992. He is still a single handicap golfer and now spends part of the year at his Spanish Villa, playing on the local courses.

* Did not play for Leeds United juniors or Heanor Town

WHITEHOUSE, John Charles 'Jack' 1929-30

Born: 4 March 1897 Smethwick
(5ft 8ins, 11st 10lbs – 1929)
Died: 3 January 1948 Halesowen
Debut: 2 March 1929
v Bury
Division One Home
Last Appearance: 7 December 1929
v Middlesbrough
Division One Away
Total League
& Cup Appearances: 10 Goals: 1

Career Details:

Grange Athletic		
Waterloo Road Wesleyans		
Smethwick		
Royal Engineers		
Blackheath Town		
Belling & Morcon		
Redditch Town		
Derby County		WW1 Guest
Chelsea		WW1 Guest
Birmingham City	August	1916
Derby County	May	1923 £500
WEDNESDAY	28 February	1929 £2,000
Bournemouth & Boscombe United	August	1930 £500
Folkestone Town	May	1933
Worcester City	June	1934

Inside forward who arrived at Wednesday with a fine reputation, after tremendous success at both Birmingham City and Derby County. He had initially joined the former during the war years, after impressing in local football, and netted 48 goals in only 87 games for the St Andrews club prior to joining Derby County. He had won a Division Two Championship medal with Birmingham in 1921 and after helping Derby to promotion in 1926 continued to score freely in the higher grade – netting four against Wednesday in an 8-0 romp for the Rams in March 1927 and totalling 86 goals in 200 games. The no-nonsense and sturdy attacker – who was difficult to knock off the ball – possessed a great shot and looked a terrific signing when Wednesday completed the deal to aid their challenge for the Championship. The transfer was actually completed at Bob Brown's house where the Wednesday manager was confined with flu and the newcomer went straight into the Owls side, replacing Harry Gregg at inside-left.

He remained in the side for five consecutive games but after contributing to the eventual title success he found competition from the likes of Gregg and Jimmy Seed – he was effectively understudy to the inspirational Seed - meant the majority of the 1929-30 season was spent in the club's reserve side where he netted twelve times for the free scoring second team. After failing to break back into the first team Whitehouse moved to the South Coast where he played many of his one hundred plus league games for Bournemouth at halfback. While at Folkstone he won both the Kent Senior and Kent Shield in 1934 before spending a season as player-manager at Worcester City, appearing in 39 games as his charges finished sixth and were unbeaten at home. However at the end of the season he left by 'mutual consent' and later in life scouted for old club Derby County.

WHITHAM, Jack 1964-70

Born: 8 December 1946 Burnley
(6ft, 12st – 1968)
Debut: 6 May 1967
v Burnley
Division One Home
Last Appearance: 22 April 1970
v Manchester City
Division One Home
Total League
& Cup Appearances: 62+9 Goals: 31

Career Details:

Holy Trinity F.C.		
Burnley		Amat.
WEDNESDAY	December	1964
Liverpool	12 May	1970 £55,000
Cardiff City	1 January	1974 Free
Reading	1 July	1975
Worksop Town	August	1977
Hallam	August	1979
Oughtibridge WMSC		1982
Hallam	December	1983

CAPS (@SWFC)
England U-23 (1) v Wales 02/10/68

As a teenager Jack Whitham was an amateur on the books of hometown club Burnley, in addition to working for a firm of accountants. He also formed and played in his own side, Holy Trinity, but after impressing in a trial period at Wednesday was snapped up by Alan Brown. After a spell in the youth team he broke into the Central League side and finished top scorer for two consecutive seasons prior to earning a place on the subs bench for the penultimate home game of the 1966-67 season. He duly entered the fray at half time and made an instant name for himself by sensationally scoring twice inside a twenty-minute period as Wednesday romped to a 7-0 win – Jack being the first Owls player to net twice as a substitute. This proved to be a taste of things to come for the tall blond striker as his natural goal scoring instincts meant he would regularly grab the headlines over the next three years. This included another two-goal substitute appearance at Old Trafford plus a treble against the same opposition on that unforgettable afternoon in August 1968 when Wednesday came from behind to beat the European Champions 5-4 at Hillsborough. Unfortunately, although he averaged roughly a goal every other game, injuries blighted his career at Wednesday and he was in and out of side until transferring back into the top-flight after Wednesday were relegated in 1970.

The former Burnley and Lancashire Boys player was used sparingly in his first season at Liverpool, two of his five appearances being as an emergency left back, but he enjoyed a ten game run in the first team in the following campaign – scoring a hat-trick at home to Derby County in January 1972. However injuries again hampered his progress and he played eighteen months of reserve team football before his contract was cancelled by mutual consent in January 1974, after 7 goals in 16 competitive games for the Merseyside giants. He duly joined Cardiff City on a month's trial but signed a contract before the end of the month and spent eighteen months in South Wales prior to ending his league career at Reading. While in Berkshire he passed his full F.A. coaching badge but returned to Sheffield in 1976 to take over as landlord of the 'Wadsley Jack'.

After spending a season out of the game Jack returned to the football scene as a part-time player with Worksop Town, managed by ex-Owl Peter Swan. He then joined Sheffield based non-league side Hallam, scoring on his debut, and found the net on a regular basis in Yorkshire league football before dropping into the Sheffield County Senior League with Oughtibridge. He top scored in 1982-3 with fifteen goals and was leading the scoring charts in the following season when he returned to Hallam to take over as player-manager. He enjoyed a successful two and half years as manager at Sandygate until work commitments forced him to relinquish the position at the end of the 1985-86 season. In 1988 he became manager of South Yorkshire Police's sports and social club at the Niagara Ground, near Hillsborough, while for twenty years played for Johnny Quinn's All Star Charity team. He appeared in over 400 games for the All Stars and also served as secretary and treasurer for the side that reached the milestone in 1999 of having raised £1m towards charitable causes. Whilst playing with the All Stars, Whitham won the National Over 35s trophy in 1990, 1991 & 1998 – the finals taking place at Wembley - while his final appearance came in April 2000, at the age of fifty-three. Incidentally, Jack's grandfather, Private Thomas Whitham of the Coldstream Guards, was awarded the Victoria Cross in July 1917 for his bravery in the Belgium trenches.

WHITHAM, Terance 'Terry' 1952-61

Born: 14 August 1935 Sheffield
(5ft 9ins, 11st 10lbs – 1953)
Debut: 13 October 1956
v Luton Town
Division One Away
Last Appearance: 20 December 1958
v Swansea Town
Division Two Away
Total League
& Cup Appearances: 4 Goals: 0

Career Details:

Stocksbridge Works		1950
WEDNESDAY	September	1952
Chesterfield	16 June	1961£750
Worksop Town		1963
Matlock Town		1966
Bridlington		
Middlewood		
Oughtibridge WMSC		

Versatile defender Terry Whitham arrived at Hillsborough as a teenager from local football and served a lengthy apprenticeship in the club's Junior and 'A' teams before breaking into the Central league side in January 1956. Whitham was almost ever present in reserve team football during the following season and was rewarded with a couple of first team games at halfback before dropping back into second team football. He appeared at right back in two further games during the Owls Second Division Championship winning season of 1958-9 before transferring to neighbours Chesterfield for a small fee after eight and a half years at Wednesday.

He spent three years at Saltergate where Whitham showed his versatility by playing in five different positions, including centre forward on one occasion, and totalled 71 games prior to dropping into non-league soccer. He remained a professional until joining Bridlington in 1969 and after becoming a part-time player held a wide variety of jobs which included working in the steel, insurance, motor and telecommunications industry before opening a car repair garage. He worked alongside the father of future Newcastle defender John Beresford at the garage while after hanging his boots up after a stint as player/trainer at Oughtibridge he served as trainer to Sheffield based non-league side Charlton.

WHITTINGHAM, Guy 1994-1999

Born: 10 November 1964 Evesham
(5ft 10ins, 12st 2lbs – 1997)
Debut: 26 December 1994
v Everton
Premier League Away
Last Appearance: 18 October 1998
v Coventry City
Premier League Away
Total League
& Cup Appearances: 105+28 Goals: 25

Career Details:

Combined Services		
Oxford City		
Waterlooville	July	1988
Yeovil Town	November	1988
Portsmouth	9 June	1989 Free
Aston Villa	1 August	1993 £1.2m
Wolverhampton Wanderers	28 February	1994 Loan
WEDNESDAY	22 December	1994 £700,000
Wolverhampton Wanderers	2 November	1998 Loan
Portsmouth	27 January	1999 Loan
Watford	17 March	1999 Loan
Released	30 June	1999
Portsmouth	13 July	1999 Free
Peterborough United	25 August	2000 Loan
Oxford United	10 October	2000 Loan
Wycombe Wanderers	22 March	2001 Free
Newport Isle of Wight	July	2001 Free
Newbury Town	May	2003 Free

Forward who famously paid £450 to buy himself out of the Army in 1989 to sign a professional contract with Portsmouth. He had joined the services at the age of seventeen and played for several non-league sides on a part-time basis whilst still in the forces. All round sportsman Whittingham, who captained his school at soccer and rugby and also excelled at cricket, basketball and skiing, maintained a high level of fitness whilst in the Army and this gave him a fighting chance when he decided to try his luck as a professional footballer at the relatively late age of 24. However he did not have cause to regret his decision as Whittingham made a huge impact at Fratton Park and in four seasons netted an astonishing 104 goals in 188 league and cup games for Pompey, including a record breaking 47-goal haul in the 1992-93 campaign. Unsurprisingly this form earned him a crack at the Premier League with Aston Villa – he had written to every top-flight club offering his services - but he struggled to become established in Birmingham and netted just six times in sixteen months prior to a successful eight goal loan spell at Midlands rivals Wolves.

Thankfully he brought that Molineux form to Wednesday when Trevor Francis secured his signature in a deal that saw Ian Taylor move in the opposite direction – the Owls receiving £300,000 from Villa after agreeing a £1m fee for Taylor. He made a dramatic start to his Wednesday career – netting a brace in a 4-1 Boxing Day win at Everton and repeating the feat on his home debut – and ended his first season with a creditable nine goals to his name as Wednesday staved off relegation. However when new manger David Pleat took over he decided to play Whittingham as an attacking midfielder and it was perhaps no surprise when his goal output started to decline. Although he could always be relied upon to give 100% wherever he was asked to play Whittingham became solely a squad player in his final months at Wednesday and after several loan spells was released, returning to Portsmouth. He later spent a short time as assistant to player-manager Steve Claridge at Pompey and then during a six-week contract at Wycombe appeared as a substitute in their F.A.Cup semi-final loss to Liverpool in April 2001.

In the latter years of his league career Whittingham collected an impressive array of coaching badges – including a UEFA 'A' licence and Coach's education certificate – and after leaving Wycombe was appointed player-manager/community officer at Dr Martens club Newport Isle of Wight, making his debut in a friendly against Portsmouth! He was relieved of the managerial duties in May 2002 but remained on the playing staff until taking over as player-manager at Wessex League side AFC Newbury. He combines his role at Newbury with his other position as S-West Regional Coach for the PFA.

WHITTON, Stephen Paul 'Steve' 1989-91

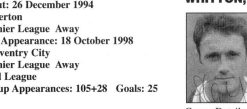

Born: 4 December 1960 East Ham
(6ft 1ins, 12st 7lbs – 1989)
Debut: 4 March 1989
v Charlton Athletic Division One Home
Last Appearance: 13 October 1990
v Plymouth Argyle Division Two Home
Total League
& Cup Appearances: 25+12 Goals: 8

Career Details:

Coventry City	9 September	1978
Seiko		1980 Loan
West Ham United	11 July	1983 £175,000
Birmingham City	1 January	1986 Loan
Birmingham City	28 August	1986 £60,000
WEDNESDAY	2 March	1989 £275,000
Halmstad	14 June	1990 Loan
Loan return	9 October	1990
Ipswich Town	4 January	1991 £150,000
Colchester United	24 March	1994 £10,000

Tall, skilful attacker Steve Whitton spent almost two years at Wednesday and in that time earned a place in the hearts of Wednesdayites by scoring the vital goal against Middlesbrough, in May 1989, that saved the Owls from relegation. He also entered the record books when netting four times in the club's biggest ever away victory – 8-0 in a League Cup tie at Aldershot in 1989 – and generally added some much needed experience to the Wednesday ranks. He was always committed to the cause and when out of the side was a consistent scorer for the reserve team, eventually prompting a summer loan move to Swedish football. On his return to the UK several clubs tracked him and 24 hours after a move to Rotherham United fell through he was snapped up by fellow Second Division side Ipswich Town.

The former Newham Boys player had originally signed apprentice forms at Coventry City in April 1977 and after finishing top scorer for the Sky Blues in 1982-83 he returned home to sign for his boyhood heroes West Ham United. After 39 games for the Hammers he arrived at Hillsborough via two spells at Birmingham City and his West Ham connection came to the fore again when it was former Hammers boss John Lyall who captured his signature for Ipswich. He duly helped the 'Tractor Boys' to the Second Division title in 1992 before moving to Colchester United in a player-coach role, being appointed caretaker manager in December 1994. He was appointed assistant-manager in June 1995 and continued to play until a back injury forced his retirement in May 1998 – playing his final game in February against Peterborough United. In August 1999 he was promoted to the manager's chair following Mick Wadsworth's resignation and remained in charge until leaving by 'mutual consent' in January 2003. After leaving Layer Road he severed all football ties and is now a partner in an Ink Cartridges business based in the Colchester area.

WICKS, Peter 1965-70

Born: 14 May 1948 Hemsworth
(6ft, 12st 8lbs -)
Debut: 16 January 1965
v Liverpool
Division One Away
Last Appearance: 20 September 1969
v West Ham United
Division One Away
Total League
& Cup Appearances: 14 Goals: 0

Career Details:

South Elmsall		
WEDNESDAY	14 May	1965
Barnsley	February	1970 Trial/Loan
Cape Town FC	1 April	1970 Free

CAPS (@SWFC)
England Youth (1) v Italy May 1966

When Peter Wicks made his debut for Wednesday in 1965 – at the tender age of 16 years, 8 months and two days - he became the club's youngest ever player (a record only beaten subsequently by Peter Fox and Mark Platts). The inexperienced goalkeeper was still only an apprentice when given his first team bow at Anfield but despite having made only six appearances for the reserve team he performed well despite conceding four goals to Liverpool. At the end of the following season he travelled with the England youth side for the European Championship in Yugoslavia and throughout the 1960s acted as reserve to both Springett brothers without managing to shake off the understudy tag. He later played a solitary game on trial at Barnsley before former Chesterfield forward Frank Lord secured his signature for South African club Cape Town. He remained in the Southern Hemisphere for just a season and when returning to England worked as a building site labourer until taking a job in the mining industry in 1981. He was eventually forced into early retirement after suffering a work related injury.

WILCOCKSON, Harold 1969-71

Born: 23 July 1943 Sheffield
(5ft 11ins, 12st 6lbs – 1970)
Debut: 20 December 1969
v Arsenal
Division One Home
Last Appearance: 2 January 1971
v Tottenham Hotspur
F.A.Cup Away
Total League
& Cup Appearances: 43 Goals: 1

Career Details:

Hillsborough Boys Club		
Rotherham United	July	1963
Doncaster Rovers	February	1968 Part-exchange
WEDNESDAY	17 December	1969*
Doncaster Rovers	20 May	1971
Goole Town		1973

* Exchange for Branfoot & Irvine

Harold Wilcockson was yet another player off the Hillsborough Boys Club production line, beginning his professional playing career at Millmoor. It was in fact Danny Williams – who was later manager at Hillsborough – who persuaded the young Wilcockson to give up his job as a tool setter to sign professional forms for the Millers and the full back later won a Fourth Division Championship medal at Doncaster Rovers before Williams signed him for a second time, this time for the Owls. Prior to moving to Wednesday he had totalled 183 league games for his first two clubs but after being an automatic choice at Hillsborough for twelve months he lost his place to Peter Rodrigues and was surprisingly given a free transfer at the end of the 1970-1 season. The all round sportsman – he also excelled at cricket, tennis and golf – ended his playing days at Goole Town and after retiring in 1976 he became a HGV driver.

WILKINSON, Derek 1953-65

Born: 4 June 1935 Stalybridge
(5ft 9ins, 10st 7lbs – 1953)
Debut: 13 November 1954
v Cardiff City
Division One Away
Last Appearance: 7 November 1964
v Manchester United
Division One Away
Total League
& Cup Appearances: 231 Goals: 57

Career Details:

Stalybridge Celtic		1951
Dukinfield Town		1952
WEDNESDAY	14 November	1953 £100

CAPS (@SWFC)
Football League (2) v Scottish League 08/10/58, v League of Ireland 17/03/59

As a teenager Derek Wilkinson was wanted by Manchester United, Huddersfield Town, Stockport County and Wednesday but it was the latter who secured his signature after a successful month's trial. At the time Wilkinson was working as a French Polisher while playing in local football and initially continued to pursue his trade outside of the game after signing as a part-time pro for Wednesday – he trained two nights a week with Stalybridge and played on a Saturday for the Owls. After becoming a full-time player at Hillsborough the fast, direct and tenacious winger was almost ever present in the Owls reserve team between January 1954 and September 1957, only absent when called up for first team duty.

As the 1950s came to a close Wilkinson became truly established on the right wing and was a vital member of the side that clinched the 1959 Division Two title, scoring eleven times in 39 league games. His boundless enthusiasm for the game and 100% attitude made him a much loved figure amongst both players and supporters and during his time at Wednesday showed his versatility by appearing all along the forward line, including centre forward. In the early 1960s he helped Wednesday to the F.A.Cup semi-finals, runners up spot in Division One and the last eight of the Fairs Cup but his career then became dogged by a succession of injuries. Sadly in May 1965, at the relatively tender age of 29, he was forced to retire on medical advice after failing to overcome a persistent groin injury and duly returned to Manchester where he restarted his career as a French Polisher. Just over a year later a 10,096 crowd attended his Hillsborough Testimonial match when a Wednesday side beat an All Star XI. He worked as a French Polisher until 1978 while until his retirement in 2000 he was employed as a fork lift truck driver at Romley Board Mill in Stockport. He now lives out his retirement in the area although a back condition meant he had to give up both golf and snooker, both sports at which he excelled.

WILKINSON, Eric 1958-59

Born: 4 June 1935 Stalybridge
(5ft 5ins, 10st 6lbs – 1958)
Only Appearance:
10 September 1958
v Sunderland
Division Two Away
Total League
& Cup Appearances: 1 Goals: 0

Career Details:

Duckinfield Town		
WEDNESDAY	25 March	1958

When left winger Eric Wilkinson was called into the first team for a game at Roker Park in 1958 he created club history as his twin brother, Derek, was also in the Wednesday side on that evening – the first and only occasion when twin siblings have played first team football together. He had initially joined Wednesday on trial in February 1958, signing professional forms after sufficiently impressing the Hillsborough coaching staff, and the diminutive Eric was a fixture in the second team for the remainder of the season.

After his moment in the spotlight Eric struggled to even regain his Central League spot and it was no real surprise when he was subsequently omitted from the traditional retained list at the end of the season. Perhaps uniquely when he left Wednesday Wilkinson totally gave up football and started to work as an engineer, a profession he did until his retirement.

WILKINSON, Harry 1881-83

Born: Sheffield
Debut: 28 December 1881
v Staveley
F.A.Cup Home
Last Appearance: 12 February 1883
v Notts County
F.A.Cup Home
Total League
& Cup Appearances: 12 Goals: 0

Career Details:

Spital Chesterfield		
WEDNESDAY		1881

Defensive player who spent two seasons with Wednesday during their early F.A.Cup adventures. It is believed he was one of three brothers who played for Derbyshire club Spital and while in Wednesday colours he appeared in the 1882 F.A.Cup semi-final and won two Wharncliffe Charity Cup medals (1882 & 1883) and one Sheffield Senior Cup (1883). In addition he won representative honours in 1883 when playing for the North against the South in an International trial match.

WILKINSON, Howard 1962-66

Born: 13 November 1943 Sheffield
(5ft 9ins, 12st 2lbs – 1964)
Debut: 9 September 1964
v Chelsea
Division One Away
Last Appearance: 19 March 1966
v Northampton Town
Division One Away
Total League
& Cup Appearances: 22 Goals: 2

Career Details:

Sheffield United		Amat.
Hallam		1962
WEDNESDAY	25 June	1962
Brighton & Hove Albion	9 July	1966 £6,000
Boston United		1970

CAPS (@SWFC)
England Youth (5) v Ireland, Scotland, Yugoslavia, Holland, Bulgaria 1961-62

Although not unique in having played and then managed Sheffield Wednesday, Howard Wilkinson is without doubt the only former player to bring tangible success to the club during his days in the manager's chair. The success he achieved at managerial level certainly eclipsed his modest playing career, which had started promisingly for the Abbeydale School educated Wilkinson when he won England Youth and Grammar School International honours. The outside right's first experience of competitive football came at Sheffield non-league club Hallam and he was later on Sheffield United's books as an amateur before signing professional forms for the Owls. After becoming established in the club's reserve side the 20-year old winger broke into the first team and enjoyed an excellent debut season, playing in exactly a third of the Owls league fixtures. However he struggled to maintain that form and after only a handful of games during the 1965-66 campaign he moved to Brighton where 19 goals in 129 league games brought the curtain down on his senior playing career.

His climb up the managerial ladder then started at Northern Premier League Boston United where Wilkinson was initially signed as a player before being appointed player-manager in 1970. While at York Street he won a variety of honours, including three League Championships, and later enjoyed a successful spell as Mossley manager (1977-79) while also managing the England semi-professional side – winning the Four Nations title in 1979. While at Boston he had competed a four-year P.E. course at Sheffield University and later become F.A.Regional coach for the Northeast before being appointed to the Notts County coaching staff in December 1979. After stepping up to the assistant manager role at Meadow Lane – almost simultaneously being given the same role with the England U-21 side – he was given the manager's seat in July 1982 but stayed in the role for less than a year, being appointed Owls boss on 24 June 1983.

His direct playing style quickly earned Wednesday promotion back to the top-flight, after a fourteen-year absence, and two years later led the Owls to the semi-final of the F.A.Cup and fifth place in Division One – only the Heysel ban denying the club European qualification. His success with Wednesday saw many clubs covet his talents and in April 1985 he turned down a reputed offer from Saudi Arabian club Aittihad Club of a £500,000 signing on fee and astonishing £1m salary over three years. Speculation in the press finally subsided when Wilkinson signed a new five-year contract in December 1985 but unfortunately his final two years at Wednesday would sour somewhat as disenchantment grew with the Owls perceived long-ball game and Wilkinson felt he was not receiving the financial backing required to import quality players to change the system. His frustration finally came to a head on 10th October 1988 – three months after rejecting a job offer from Greek club PAOK Salonika – when the born and bred

Wednesdayite resigned to take over at Yorkshire rivals Leeds United. The club's agreed a £75,000 compensation package for his services and within fours years Wilkinson not only led United to the Division Two Championship but also secured the last Football League title before the onset of the newly founded F.A.Premier League. He remained in charge at Elland Road until being sacked in September 1996 and in January 1997 made history by being appointed the Football Association's first ever Technical Director. During his tenure as F.A.supremo Wilkinson was also twice handed the reins of the full International side after the departures of Glenn Hoddle and then Kevin Keegan – his side lost 2-0 at home to France in 1999 after the former resigned and drew 0-0 in Finland after Keegan left his post in 2000.

While Technical Director he was also handed the England U-21 job after Peter Taylor was relieved of his duties but failed to continue his predecessors success and eventually came back into club management at Sunderland in October 2002. Unfortunately his fortunes went from bad to worse at the Stadium of Light as after winning only two of twenty league games he was sacked in March 2003 with Sunderland rooted to the foot of the Premier League and relegation a virtual certainty. He re-appeared as head coach at Chinese champions Shanghai Shenshua in March 2004 but left in May citing 'personal reasons' for his departure. His most recent appointment saw Wilkinson appointed temporary assistant first team coach at Leicester City, in October 2004 following the resignation of Micky Adams, although he stayed on briefly before new manager Craig Levein was handed the managerial reins. In late December 2004 he returned to Notts County in an unpaid non-executive role.

WILKINSON, Jack — 1925-30

Born: 13 June 1908 Wath-upon-Dearne
(5ft 6ins, 10st 7lbs – 1926)
Died: April 1979 Mexborough
Debut: 3 April 1926
v Hull City
Division Two Home
Last Appearance: 8 March 1930
v Leicester City
Division One Away
Total League
& Cup Appearances: 79 Goals: 17

Career Details:

Dearne Valley Old Boys		1920
Wath Athletic	February	1925
WEDNESDAY	31 October	1925 £450
Newcastle United	8 May	1930 £3,000
Lincoln City	September	1932
Sunderland	22 January	1935
Hull City	October	1936
Scunthorpe and Linsey United		1937-8
Burton Town	August	1939

In the early 1920s a team from the little mining village of Wath grabbed national headlines as their giant killing run in the F.A.Cup took them to a game against Chesterfield at Saltergate. However to the dismay of their supporters Owls manager Bob Brown had been paying particular attention to their exploits and just before the big Cup-tie he swooped to sign their two star performers – Jack Wilkinson and Tony Leach. Incredibly nine of that Wath team left within a few months to sign for league clubs but arguably Wednesday captured the best two as Leach won caps for England and diminutive winger Wilkinson was a top-flight regular for the Owls after helping them to the Second Division title in his debut season – scoring three times in the final seven games of the season after breaking into the side.

Wilkinson had started his playing career at Wath National School and was a star performer as Dearne Valley Schoolboys surprisingly reached the last four of the English Schools Trophy in 1922. The fearless and tricky left winger – he also possessed a powerful accurate shot and tremendous ball control – started work in the underground office at Manvers Main Colliery after leaving school but when his old school team was reformed as a senior side he took up his former position on the wing. He would spend five seasons with Dearne Valley Old Boys – netting over one hundred times – and this form persuaded his local Midland league club Wath to give the youngster a trial in February 1925. He signed a contract with Wath soon after and this effectively started a race for his signature amongst several league clubs as his tremendous form in the higher grade indicated he could easily hold his own in professional soccer. This particular race was of course won by Wednesday and the level headed and unassuming seventeen year-old became a tremendous favourite with Owls fans until a greater hero, Ellis Rimmer, replaced him during the season of the 'Great Escape'.

For the final two seasons of Wilkinson's Wednesday career he was effectively understudy to Rimmer and played only seven times during the back-to-back Championship wins in the late 1920s/early 1930s. After failing to dislodge his rival, Jack was transferred to Newcastle where unfortunately in his early days he received a cartilage injury that would dog the remainder of his career. He scored the only senior hat trick of his career while with United – at Derby in February 1931 – and after 7 goals in 32 games dropped out of top-flight soccer. His league career ended at Sunderland and he later won the Midland League Championship with Scunthorpe United before gaining employment at Ransome and Marles in Newark. He was honorary manager of the works team during his ten years of employment and after retiring from football he ran his own business in Halifax and then Thurnscoe. Prior to retiring he ran his own grocers shop in the Doncaster village of Staniforth.

WILLIAMS, Andrew 'Andy' — 1995

Born: 29 July 1962 Dudley
(6ft 2ins, 12st – 1997)
Only Appearance: 24 June 1995
v FC Basel
UEFA Intertoto Cup Away
Total League
& Cup Appearances: 1 Goals: 0

Career Details:

Dudley Town	July	1979
Solihull Borough	December	1983
Coventry City	24 July	1985 £20,000
Rotherham United	16 October	1986 Exchange for D.Emerson
Leeds United	11 November	1988 £175,000
Port Vale	11 December	1991 Loan
Notts County	4 February	1992 £115,000
Huddersfield Town	13 September	1993 Loan
Rotherham United	21 October	1993 Free
WEDNESDAY	June	1995 N/C
Hull City	19 July	1995 Free
Scarborough	16 August	1996 N/C
Gainsborough Trinity	August	1996
Matlock Town	February	1997
Guiseley	February	1998
Retired	May	2001
Sheffield Veterans		2004

Midfielder who was one of the five non-contract players recruited by Wednesday in June 1995 to enable them to fulfil a hastily arranged Intertoto Cup game in Switzerland. The tall and rangy Williams did not actually come into league football until the age of 23, giving up his accountancy studies to sign for Don MacKay's Coventry City, and after nine senior games for the Sky Blues moved to Millmoor. His form at Rotherham (15 goals in 106 games) persuaded Howard Wilkinson to make Andy one of his first signings for Leeds United and he would win a Second Division Championship in 1990 prior to joining Notts County, following an initial loan period. He subsequently re-joined the Millers after 43 games for County and after being released in the summer of 1995 played his solitary game for Wednesday.

After his European adventure with the Owls he returned home to sign for Hull City where to great acclaim was converted into a sweeper role. However he was surprisingly released by the Tigers after just a season and played in the opening two games of the following campaign for Scarborough before rejecting an offer of a monthly contract. His appearances for Boro proved to be his final in league soccer as Williams then combined his role as a Customer Finance Officer for Rotherham Borough Council with non-league football. He retired from semi-professional football in 2001 but still pulls on his boots to compete in over 40s football.

WILLIAMS, David Rees 'Rees' 1922-27

Born: Q/E March 1900 Abercanaid, Glamorgan
(5ft 7ins, 10st 6lbs – 1922)
Died: 30 December 1963 Abercanaid
Debut: 26 August 1922 v Rotherham United Division Two Away
Last Appearance: 29 August 1927 v Manchester United Division One Home
Total League & Cup Appearances: 173 Goals: 7

Career Details:

Abercanaid		
Pentrebach		
Merthyr Town	April	1919
WEDNESDAY	29 June	1922 £1,500
Manchester United	6 October	1927 £2,000
Thames Association	August	1929
Aldershot	July	1930
Merthyr Town	August	1931
Glenavon	August	1933

CAPS (@ SWFC)
Wales Full (4) v Scotland 17/03/23, Scotland 31/10/25, v England 14/02/27, v Ireland 09/04/27

The Owls have been blessed with many fine wingers in their history and Rees Williams was yet another example. He was brought up in his parents' public house in the Welsh village of Merthyr and first started playing organised football with local village side Abercanaid, whilst working at the local pit. He won caps at Welsh schoolboy level and was soon playing league soccer after signing for Merthyr. Such was his speed off the mark that Rees won several handicap sprints in his native Wales and was said to run the 100 yards in 10.2 seconds. He could also run fast with the ball at his feet and it was these attributes that saw Williams capped twice at full level for Wales while on Merthyr's books – succeeding the legendary Billy Meredith in the Welsh side. His form alerted many clubs to his talents and both Aston Villa and Sunderland had been rebuffed in their attempts to sign him before Owls assistant secretary S.P.Stephen recommended the winger to Wednesday manager Bob Brown. The Owls official had actually been scouting another player at the time but like the clubs before them Wednesday's offer was turned down with Merthyr under no pressure to cash in on their prize asset. However when a financial crisis hit in 1922 the two-footed attacker was on his way to Hillsborough.

He quickly made the left wing spot his own with his tremendous close control and dribbling skills confounding countless defenders and allowed him to feed the prolific Jimmy Trotter with numerous scoring chances. He won the Second Division Championship with Wednesday in 1926 and was capped four more times for Wales before losing his place to legendary winger Mark Hooper at the start of the 1927-28 season. Within a few weeks he was on his way across the Pennines to sign for Manchester United where although he was capped twice more for his country Rees was never at his best, scoring twice in 31 games prior to joining Thames Association. He helped the London club gain election into the Football League in 1930 but departed before a ball was kicked and later returned to Merthyr before ending his playing days in Irish soccer. After retiring from the game he moved back home to work for the local Hoover company, coaching the works team, but sadly his story has a tragic end as in December 1963, whilst worrying about his failing health, he took his own life.

WILLIAMS, Leonard Horace 'Len' 1923-26

Born: 17 May 1898 Dalton Brook, Rotherham
(5ft 8ins, 11st - 1923)
Died:
Debut:
26 January 1924 v Leeds United Division Two Away
Last Appearance:
24 October 1925 v Nottingham Forest Division Two Away
Total League & Cup Appearances: 9 Goals: 0

Career Details:

Silverwood Colliery		
Parkgate Christchurch		
Wath Athletic		1921
WEDNESDAY	8 May	1923
Stockport County	17 May	1926 £350
Wolverhampton Wanderers	June	1927
Swansea Town	February	1930
Oswestry Town		1931
Wellington Town	September	1931

Right back Len Williams was another product of the highly successful Wath side of the early 1920s that produced so many Football League players. He was ever present for the non-league side for two seasons prior to joining Wednesday and arrived to fill the role of understudy to first choice Billy Felton. His first game in an Owls shirt was the club's inaugural match in the Central League – away at Aston Villa in August 1923 – and he was a reserve team regular throughout his debut season while also stepping into Felton's shoes on seven occasions. However his rival's form and fitness ensured Williams would only make a solitary appearance in both of the seasons that followed and he eventually moved to Stockport County in search of first team football. After dropping out of league soccer in 1931 he eventually retired from the game in 1934.

WILLIAMS, Leslie 'Les' 1953-57

Born: 27 March 1935 Thurcroft
(6ft 1in, 10st 7½ins – 1956)
Debut: 31 August 1955 v Liverpool Division Two Home
Last Appearance: 27 October 1956 v Manchester City Division One Away
Total League & Cup Appearances: 11 Goals: 0

Career Details:

Rotherham United		Juniors
WEDNESDAY	July	1953
Swindon Town	23 January	1957 Free
Rotherham United	January	1958 Free
Boston United		1959
Corby Town		1961
Boston United		1963

Former Rother Valley Boys goalkeeper who joined Wednesday after his first club, Rotherham United, decided against offering the teenager a professional contract. He was quickly snapped up by Owls boss Eric Taylor and spent his first season at Wednesday appearing for the club's 'A' and junior sides prior to being called up to serve his two years of National Service. He was demobbed just three weeks before the start of the 1955-56 season and duly made his reserve team bow in the opening match of the campaign. He then enjoyed a somewhat meteoric rise to first team football as inside a fortnight was called up to the senior side after regular No. 1 Dave McIntosh fractured his cheekbone. He enjoyed two short spells in the league side during the season – saving a penalty against Barnsley in November 1955 – but was never considered as anything other than third choice at Wednesday and it was no surprise when he was allowed to join Division Three (South) club Swindon Town.

He spent a year in Wiltshire without making a first team appearance before returning to South Yorkshire to re-join Rotherham United. He was again unable to break into the senior side at Millmoor and dropped into non-league soccer, initially at Boston United and then Corby Town. A broken finger forced his retirement in 1968 at which point he took over as licensee of a

Sheffield public house, also managing the pub's football side. Williams – whose brother Ted played for Nottingham Forest & Northampton Town – then ran and owned his own off licence until poor health forced his early retirement. Sadly he has suffered from increasingly poor eyesight since retiring and although he thankfully has some vision is in fact registered blind.

WILLIAMS, Michael Anthony 'Mike' 1991-97

Born: 21 November 1969 Bradford
(5ft 10ins, 11st 6lbs - 1996)
Debut: 1 October 1992 v Spora Luxembourg
UEFA Cup Away
Last Appearance:
28 September 1996
v Everton Premier League Away
Total League
& Cup Appearances: 21+10 Goals: 1

Career Details:

Bradford More		
Ossett Town		
Maltby Miners Welfare		
Leeds United		Trial
WEDNESDAY	13 February	1991
Halifax Town	18 December	1992 Loan
Huddersfield Town	18 October	1996 Loan
Peterborough United	27 March	1997 Loan
Burnley	14 July	1997 Free
Oxford United	25 March	1999 Free
Halifax Town	21 November	1999
Worksop Town	July	2001
Ossett Town	January	2002
Dinnington Town		2004

In pre war soccer it was commonplace for players to jump from non-league football into the higher echelons of the Football League but in recent decades this has become a rare occurrence. However one player who bucked the trend was utility man Mike Williams who rose from the relative obscurity of Northern Counties East League side Maltby to play Premier League football with Wednesday. He was initially invited for trials at Hillsborough early in 1991 and impressed the training staff sufficiently to be offered a professional contract until the end of the season. He signed a longer deal in May 1991 and duly made his senior debut for the club in a European tie in Luxembourg. During his time at Wednesday he proved himself to be a capable deputy at first team level, appearing at right back and in midfield, but spent most of his time playing reserve team football - making a total of 139 appearances while on the Owls books. A terrible run of back luck with injury probably did not help his cause either as on returning from a loan spell at Halifax he suffered a serious knee ligament injury in a reserve game that put him out of action for several months. He subsequently broke his leg in November 1993, ruptured his anterior cruciate ligament in December 1995 (meaning six months on the sidelines) and even saw a loan spell at Huddersfield cut short due to injury!

All these injury problems, in addition to fierce competition for a first team spot, meant that Williams was never able to sustain a place in the senior squad for any length of time and it was perhaps a surprise he stayed for over six years before being signed by former team mate Chris Waddle for Burnley. In almost two years at Turf Moor he started only 15 league games and fortunes did not improve greatly when he signed for Oxford United on deadline day 1999 - his poor fitness meaning he was released after only two substitute appearances. After a period of unemployment he signed a one-month contract with Third Division Halifax Town - conceding two penalties on debut - but made only four appearances before again being released. After eighteen months on the sidelines with a serious knee injury he relaunched his career with Worksop Town in the 2001 pre season but appeared in only a handful of games before switching to Ossett Town. In May 2002 he moved to the US to fulfil a coaching appointment and after a spell back home over the Christmas period he spent almost all of 2003 across the pond. He returned to England in November 2003 and started coaching his old Sunday League side, Bradford More, where his playing career had started as a fifteen year-old. He later returned to Sheffield to work with children with behavioural disorders and re-launched his playing career with Central Midlands League Dinnington Town.

WILLIAMS, Paul Anthony 1990-92

Born: 16 August 1965 Stratford
(5ft 7ins, 10st 3lbs – 1991)
Debut: 25 August 1990
v Charlton Athletic
Division Two Away
Last Appearance: 5 September 1992
v Manchester City
Premier League Home
Total League
& Cup Appearances: 94+20 Goals: 28

Career Details:

Aveley		
Clapton		
Woodford Town		
Charlton Athletic	23 February	1987 £12,000
Brentford	20 October	1987 Loan
WEDNESDAY	2 August	1990 £600,000
Crystal Palace	11 September	1992 £500,000
Sunderland	19 January	1995 Loan
Birmingham City	13 March	1995 Loan
Charlton Athletic	29 September	1995 Free
Torquay United	28 March	1996 Loan
Southend United	30 August	1996 Free
Canvey Island	March	1997 Loan
Canvey Island	March	1998 Free
Bowers United		2002
Concord United		2003

Nippy and diminutive forward Paul Williams was never a prolific scorer but will always be remembered fondly by Wednesday fans for the superb partnership he formed with David Hirst, which produced eighty goals in two seasons as the Owls moved from the Second Division to the brink of the league Championship. The unselfish attacker – affectionately nicknamed "Willo" by Wednesday fans – was a mainstay of the Owls side during his time in Sheffield and missed only four of the 118 games played by the club, proving a more than capable replacement for the more flamboyant Dalian Atkinson. Although his time at Wednesday was relatively short the period was without doubt the most successful of his playing career as Williams won the League Cup against Manchester United in 1991, netted 17 times as the Owls were promoted from the Second Division and then scored the goal – at Crystal Palace in April 1992 – that secured European football for the club for the first time since the early 1960s. Competition from newcomer Nigel Jemson briefly saw Williams demoted to the subs bench during the 1991-2 season - causing him to ask for a move in February 1992 – but he was quickly back as an automatic choice, remaining so until his surprise transfer to Crystal Palace as part of the deal that brought Mark Bright to Hillsborough.

A West Ham fan as a youngster, Williams started his career in non-league football and gave up his accountancy studies to turn professional with Charlton Athletic in 1987. He quickly blossomed at The Valley, winning England 'B' and U-21 caps, and netted 29 times prior to moving North to Wednesday. After leaving the Owls it would be fair to say he never came close to achieving the success he enjoyed at Wednesday and although he won a Division One Championship medal in 1994 his time at Palace was a generally unhappy one. Following a brief spell back at Charlton his career was somewhat resurrected at Southend United where he was a regular during the 1996-97 season but after drifting out of the first team he returned to his non-league roots, signing for Ryman League club Canvey Island. After dropping into semi-professional football he began running his own furniture store in London while on the football field won back-to-back titles with

Canvey before dropping into the minor Essex Senior League. His playing career finally ended during the 2003-4 season due to a persistent knee injury.

* Did not play for Braintree Town as stated in other records

WILLIAMSON, Charles Harold 'Charlie' 1980-85

Born: 16 March 1962 Sheffield
(5ft 10ins, 11st 3lbs – 1981)
Debut: 21 December 1979
v Reading
Division Three Away
Last Appearance: 7 May 1984
v Manchester City
Division Two Home
Total League
& Cup Appearances: 66+1 Goals: 1

Career Details:

WEDNESDAY	15 February	1980
Lincoln City	10 February	1984 Loan
Southend United	1 March	1985 Loan
Chesterfield	27 June	1985 Free
Stafford Rangers	July	1987
Goole Town	October	1988
Gainsborough Trinity	January	1990
Matlock Town	December	1990
Eastwood Town		1992 Loan
Maltby Miners Welfare		1993
Matlock Town	November	1995

One of the highpoints of every player's career is his debut on his club's home ground. For seventeen year-old Charlie Williamson he experienced a truly astonishing first game as that debut came at home to United in the famous 'Boxing Day massacre' game of 1979. The young full back had made his senior debut just five days earlier, as replacement for regular left back Dave Grant, in a 2-0 win at Reading and coped with the pressure of the big derby atmosphere to go down in history as one of the eleven men who were involved on that pivotal days in the Owls recent history. The derby game was one of only three games Charlie would play during that promotion season and in fact he was only a regular in the side for one season (1981-82) as competition from the likes of Ian Bailey and then Nigel Worthington meant he played most of his football for Wednesday in the reserve team.

He eventually departed for neighbours Chesterfield and in the early 1990s was appointed 'Football in the Community' Officer back at Wednesday. He also continued to play in local non-league soccer until joining Imre Varadi as assistant manager at Matlock Town in November 1995. He was elevated to youth coach at Wednesday in the summer of 1997 and was placed in charge of the new U-17 side when the Academy structure was launched a year later. He saw several of his young players progress to the first team during the traumatic 2000-01 season but following the arrival of new Academy Director Jimmy Shoulder his position was put in doubt and along with fellow Academy coach Albert Phelan his contract was not renewed in the summer of 2001. In July 2002 he joined ambitious Northern Premier League club Alfreton Town as assistant manager and presided over back-to-back promotions that took the Derbyshire club to the brink of the Conference league before leaving by mutual consent in May 2005.

WILSON, Andrew 'Andra' 1900-20

Born: 10 December 1880 Lendalfoot, Ayrshire
(5ft 10ins, 13st 6lbs – 1913)
Died: 13 March 1945 Patterton Farm, nr Irvine
Debut: 1 September 1900
v Manchester City
Division One Away
Last Appearance: 10 March 1920
v Liverpool
Division One Away
Total League
& Cup Appearances: 546* Goals: 216
***Also appeared in**
75 wartime games, scoring 25 goals

Career Details:

Irvine Meadow		1897
Clyde		1899
WEDNESDAY	1 May	1900 £200

CAPS (@SWFC)
Scotland Full (6) v England 06/04/07, v England 04/04/08, v England 23/03/12v England 05/04/13, v Wales 03/03/13, v Ireland 14/03/14

Forward Andrew Wilson is unchallenged as the greatest goal scorer in the history of Sheffield Wednesday, netting 199 league goals and 17 F.A.Cup goals in his twenty-year stay at Hillsborough. In addition he is not only the club's top marksman but also holds the club record for appearances, a mark that will surely now never be beaten. He possessed many outstanding qualities, which included a thunderous shot, and his total professionalism made him probably the best value for money signing in the history of the club. There were certainly eyebrows raised when Wednesday broke their transfer record to bring the Scot to Hillsborough – paying a "stiff price" for his services – but although he was not particularly impressive on his arrival he soon blossomed into one of the greatest British players in the years preceding the Great War.

He was born in the small Scottish village of Lendalfoot but at the age of two his family moved to Colmonell before finally settling on a farm near Irvine. In his early school days 'Andra' (his nickname at Wednesday) did not play any football at all but after moving to the Irvine Royal Academy he made occasional appearances for the school team. However when he left school a football career seemed highly unlikely for Wilson as he worked as a butcher for a year before returning home to help on the family farm after his father fell ill. In total he spent three years away from the game but after scoring on his debut for Junior side Irvine Meadow his career quickly advanced although his early days were spent on the right wing and then at left back – Wilson actually considered full back his best position and thought he would have been a far better performer than at inside forward! In his second season with Irvine he lifted three locals Cups and this prompted a move into the Scottish League, joining Glasgow club Clyde on a salary of £2 per week. However he stayed just a solitary season and a few days after Clyde were relegated from the top-flight he walked the well-worn path to English football.

He arrived at Wednesday with the club newly crowned as Second Division Champions and went straight into the side at centre forward, replacing Harry Millar in the No. 9 shirt. He finished his debut season as top scorer, with 13 goals, and incredibly would net double figures in every season until the Great War brought a halt to league football in 1915! He remained at centre forward for the remainder of the decade and was an automatic choice as the Owls won back-to-back league titles (1903 & 1904) and the 1907 F.A.Cup. He was switched to inside left following the arrival of James Murray in March 1910 and revelled in his new role, forming a great partnership with lethal centre forward David McLean that took Wednesday within touching distance of another league title in 1913. Wilson – whose sheer strength and burly frame made him difficult to knock off the ball –remained at inside forward for the remainder of his career and was always relied upon to give 100%

commitment whenever he pulled on the famous blue and white shirt. Incidentally for some time after joining the Owls the Scot continued to work but was eventually persuaded to give up his job, as it was not benefiting his football - he later spent most of 1909 working as a fruit merchant!

During his twenty years at Wednesday, Wilson was awarded three benefit games (the player taking the majority of the net match receipts) but lady luck deserted him on all three occasions, an example being his third game in November 1913 when Wilson bought cigars and 'bubbly water' but found there was far too much 'ordinary water' splashing around to ensure a good gate! He remained on the Owls books during the Great War, scoring regularly in the early years of the conflict, and in July 1919 signed a new £5 per week contract which gave 'Andra' a coaching role with the reserves and a scouting position. He would make one more appearance for the Owls first team, as an emergency forward in a 1-0 defeat at Liverpool, before hanging up his boots and eventually leaving Hillsborough to become Bristol Rovers manager in June 1921. Before leaving Sheffield he was a founder member of the Hillsborough Golf Club, helping to design the course just after the war.

While in charge at Rovers he earned the reputation as a quiet, deep thinking boss but after five years he resigned after his charges only just avoided having to apply for re-election from Division Three (South). He was then appointed Oldham Athletic boss in July 1927 and agonisingly missed out on promotion to the top-flight in 1930 when his side lost their final game. He left in July 1932 to take over at neighbours Stockport County but stayed only a season despite leading County to third place in Division Three (North) - he also won his final game 8-5! Wilson – who once played with his brother David for Scotland – then returned home to Scotland and after two years of illness he passed away in 1945.

WILSON, Charles 'Tug' 1928-32

Born: 20 July 1905 Heeley, Sheffield
(5ft 9ins, 11st 8lbs – 1928)
Died: April 1985 Kidderminster
Debut: 25 February 1928
v Newcastle United
Division One Home
Last Appearance: 21 November 1931
v Sheffield United
Division One Home
Total League
& Cup Appearances: 60 Goals: 5

Career Details:

Stonehouse		
Hallam		
Sheffield United		Trial
Chesterfield	November	1920 Trial
West Bromwich Albion	December	1920 Amat.
West Bromwich Albion	November	1922 Pro.
WEDNESDAY	February	1928 £3000
Grimsby Town	9 March	1932 £2,250
Aston Villa	August	1933
Coventry City	June	1934
Kidderminster Harriers	August	1935
Peterborough & Fletton United		
Worcester City	June	1937
Kidderminster Harriers	June	1938
Brierley Hill Alliance		
Charlton Athletic		WW2 Guest
Aldershot		WW2 Guest
Kidderminster Police		1946

Although Charles Wilson was born and brought up in Sheffield it was with West Brom that the former Sheffield, Yorkshire and England Boys player started his professional career. He had initially starred for both the City boys and his school at centre halfback but proved to be a versatile player who was comfortable in several positions, including centre forward. After attending trials at Bramall Lane when aged 15 he signed amateur forms for Albion, netting five times on his debut for the Baggies in the Smethwick League, and made his First Division bow as a centre forward at the tender age of sixteen in October 1921 – he still holds the Albion record as the club's youngest ever player at 16 years and 73 days. While at the Hawthorns he carved out a reputation as an opportunist forward who could shoot with unerring accuracy from any angle, with either foot, and in total netted 45 goals in 133 games. His film star looks also earned him a reputation as somewhat of a playboy and this got him in hot water on more than one occasion during his career!

He returned to his native City to provide competition for the likes of Jimmy Seed and Jimmy Trotter but was used sparingly in his first three seasons – his only success coming in 1929 when he was a regular in the reserve side that won the Central League title. However one man's misfortune is often another man's gain and this proved the case when as injury to star halfback Billy Marsden – which would force his early retirement – saw Wilson slip into his shoes for the 1930-31 campaign and appear in 37 games as Wednesday just missed out on completing a hat-trick of League Championships. Unfortunately he was back in the reserves for the season after as Smith and then Malloch were handed the No. 6 shirt. This eventually led to his move to First Division bottom club Grimsby Town in 1932 and he later returned to the Midlands, playing for Aston Villa before ending his league career at Coventry.

He then dropped into non-league football where he appeared for a variety of clubs including a season at Worcester City where he netted 21 league and cup goals but returned to Kidderminster after just a season to avoid the extra travelling after City were elected into the Southern League. He continued to play during the war years and for a time was landlord of the Raven public house in Kidderminster but finally hung up his boots in 1947 after a few games for Kidderminster Police. He was later appointed trainer/coach at the Harriers – he was also elected onto the Board as one of two Supporters Club committee representatives – but resigned in 1948 and severed all ties with the Worcestershire club. For the reminder of his working life he worked as a wholesale tobacconists rep in the Kidderminster area.

WILSON, Daniel Joseph 'Danny/Didwell' 1990-94

Born: 1 January 1960 Wigan
(5ft 7ins, 10st 3lbs – 1990)
Debut: 25 August 1990
v Ipswich Town
Division Two Away
Last Appearance: 20 May 1993
v Arsenal
F.A.Cup Final Replay @ Wembley
Total League
& Cup Appearances: 127+10 Goals: 14

Career Details:

Wigan Athletic		
Bury	21 September	1977 Free
Chesterfield	22 July	1980 £100,000
Nottingham Forest	1 January	1983 *
Scunthorpe United	7 October	1983 Loan
Brighton & Hove Albion	30 November	1983 £100,000
Luton Town	16 July	1987 £150,000
WEDNESDAY	3 August	1990 £200,000
Barnsley	3 June	1994 £200,000

* Exchange for C. Plummer & S. Kendal

CAPS (@SWFC)
N.Ireland Full (6) v Yugoslavia 12/09/90, v Denmark 17/10/90, v Austria 14/11/90, Faroe Islands 01/05/91, v Austria 16/10/91, v Scotland 19/02/92

Tigerish midfielder who holds a unique place in the Owls history as he is one of only six former players to have managed the club but is also one of only five players whose son has also played for Wednesday. He enjoyed a tremendous three year playing career at Wednesday which saw Danny become a huge favourite amongst the Hillsborough faithful – his inspirational and never-say-die qualities endearing him to fans and players alike. He was a superb passer of the ball and his general enthusiasm lifted the side and helped Wednesday to League Cup success, promotion and four Wembley appearances in 1993. Nicknamed 'Didwell' – after Alan Parry's commentary in the 1991 League Cup semi-final win over Chelsea – he always showed great courage which was typified in

February 1993 when he insisted on playing at Manchester City despite having two broken ribs.

His career had started at Northern Premier League Wigan Athletic – Wilson leaving in their last season as a non-league club – and his league debut came at Bury where he appeared in 105 games prior to signing for Chesterfield. After a century of league games for the Spireites he moved into the top-flight at Nottingham Forest but after failing to settle he left for Brighton within a year – netting twice on his debut. At the Goldstone Ground, and his next club Luton Town, he was a vital member of the side and scored in the 1988 League Cup Final as the Hatters stunned Arsenal to win the trophy. Incidentally in July 1984 Howard Wilkinson tried to sign the Northern Ireland International (he qualified due to an Irish mother) from Brighton but the South Coast club rebuffed the Owls approach.

He left Wednesday just after the 1993 F.A.Cup Final and went with the good wishes of Owls fans after being appointed player-coach at neighbours Barnsley. Within a year he was elevated to manager - following the departure of Viv Anderson – and over the next three years carved out a reputation as one of the best young managers in the game as with limited resources he took Barnsley into the Premier League for the first time in their history. A controversial move to Wednesday followed, in July 1998, and Wilson steered the Owls to mid table security in his first season at the helm. However his signings in the summer of 1999 (the likes of De Bilde, O'Donnell & Donnelly) proved disastrous and by the following spring, with the Owls facing relegation from the top-flight, his tenure as Owls boss came to an abrupt end in March 2000 following a disastrous defeat at bottom club Watford. Wilson – whose father played for Derry City during the Second World War when stationed there with the Navy – was quickly back in work when appointed Bristol City boss in June 2000. Over the next four seasons his City side were regular play off contenders but after losing in the 2004 Final to Brighton he was controversially fired by the City board who had demanded nothing more than promotion after several near misses. After a few months scouting for various clubs and working for National Radio station 'Five Live' he was appointed manager at League One strugglers MK Dons in December 2004.

WILSON, George 1920-25

Born: 14 January 1892 Kirkham, Preston
(5ft 8½ins, 11st 7lbs – 1920)
Died: 25 November 1961 Blackpool
Debut: 13 March 1920 v Liverpool Division One Home
Last Appearance: 21 March 1925 v Middlesbrough Division Two Away
Total League & Cup Appearances: 196 Goals: 4

Career Details:

Sacred Heart School		
Catholic College		
Kirkham Sunday School League		
Willow's Rovers		
Fleetwood		
Morecambe		
Blackpool	January	1912
WEDNESDAY	11 March	1920 £2,500
Nelson	13 July	1925 £2,350

CAPS (@SWFC)

England Full (12) v Wales 14/03/21, v Scotland 09/04/21, v Belgium 21/05/21, v Ireland 22/10/21, v Scotland 08/04/22, v Ireland 21/10/22, v Wales 05/03/23, v Belgium 19/03/23, v Scotland 14/03/23 v Ireland 20/10/23, v Wales 03/03/24, v France 17/05/24

Football League (4) v Scottish League 1921, 1922 & 1923 v Irish League 1924

From a modern perspective it would seem almost unbelievable that a player from Division Two could be capped on a regular basis for England but also captain his country. However this occurred in the early 1920s when Owls centre halfback George Wilson represented the National side despite playing in a Wednesday team that was struggling to make an impression in Division Two after being relegated from the top-flight in 1920. Wilson was the son of a former detective-sergeant of the Blackpool Police and started his playing career at the age of 11 for a Kirkham Sunday School League club prior to signing for non-league Morecambe. He actually joined Blackpool as a centre forward but after being converted to halfback during the 1914-15 season he became an automatic choice. In 1917 he joined the Army and fought in France and Belgium, winning the Belgian Medal of Honour for his bravery, and after being de-mobbed in 1919 went straight back into the first team at Bloomfield Road, being handed the captaincy.

He was surprisingly placed on the Blackpool transfer list in March 1920 and this caused a chase for the signature of a highly intelligent and energetic player who was emerging as the finest pivot in the game – he was also a prodigious worker, showed remarkable energy and command of the ball in addition to being adept at spreading play out to his wingers. It was Wednesday who broke their transfer record to sign Wilson but hopes that his arrival would help stave off relegation were dashed as the Owls tumbled out of the top-flight. New manager Bob Brown quickly recognised his leadership qualities and Wilson was given the Wednesday captaincy in the following season before he impressed sufficiently in a trial match at Burnley to be awarded the first of his 12 full caps for England. He quickly emerged as the greatest centre-back at Hillsborough since the days of Tommy Crawshaw and was a rock at the heart of the Owls defence for five seasons, receiving a club record benefit of £650 at the end of the 1924-25 season. However, Wilson and Wednesday then fell into dispute over terms for the new season - the Owls offering £8 a week for his services.

It looked likely he would be on his way out of Hillsborough but his destination was a real shock as he moved to Division Three (North) minnows Nelson with his new club splashing out a huge fee which at the time was not only a record sale for Wednesday but a record fee paid by a Third Division club. Probably a major factor in the move was Nelson's offer of the licensee of the Prince of Wales public house and Wilson stayed in the Northwest for two seasons before retiring from the game and moving back to Blackpool. He took over the running of the Mere Park Hotel in his hometown and retired in 1961, sadly passing away a few months later.

WILSON, Joseph 'Joe' 1922-24

Born: Q/E June 1901 Southwick
(5ft 8½ins, 11st 4lbs – 1923)
Debut:
25 August 1923 v Bradford City Division Two Home
Last Appearance:
11 February 1924 v Leicester City Division Two Home
Total League & Cup Appearances: 3 Goals: 0

Career Details:

Southwick		
Leadgate Park		
Manchester United	15 September	1920 Amat.
Durham City	March	1921
WEDNESDAY	18 June	1923 £110
Norwich City	18 June	1924

When Joe Wilson arrived at Hillsborough in 1923 he was described as "the best winger in the Northern League" with pace and the ability to cross the ball accurately. He was bought to provide direct competition for left-sided attacker Joe Harron and started the first two games of the season in the first team. However the former Manchester United amateur was dropped into the reserves after Wednesday failed to win, or score, in those first two games of the 1923-24 season and appeared only once more before moving to Football League (South) club Norwich City. He appeared in 41 games for the Canaries, scoring four times, before dropping out of senior football.

WILSON, Laurie — 2003-04

Born: 5 December 1984 Brighton
(5ft 10ins, 10st 10lbs – 2003)
Debut:
6 December 2003 v Scunthorpe United F.A.Cup Away
Last Appearance:
17 December 2003 v Scunthorpe United F.A.Cup Home
Total League & Cup Appearances: 1+2 Goals: 0

Career Details:

WEDNESDAY	1 August	2003
Luton Town	April	2004 Trial
Burton Albion	1 July	2004 Free
Gresley Rovers	20 December	2004 Trial
Grantham Town	January	2005 Loan
Belper Town	February	2005 Loan
Kidderminster Harriers	July	2005 Free

Right-sided midfielder who showed the same grit and tenacious qualities of his father, Danny, when appearing briefly in the first team during the traumatic 2003-04 campaign. Horrendous injury problems saw the teenager given a first team bow, helping the Owls to overcome Carlisle United in the LDV Vans Trophy but appearing as a sub twice as Wednesday crashed out of the F.A.Cup to Scunthorpe United. He originally joined the club as a Scholar in the summer of 2000 and over the next three years was a regular at Academy and reserve team level – making his debut for the second team in October 2001 and netting 4 times in 37 games for the reserves. However at the end of the season he was one of 13 players released by Chris Turner and after a trial at his father's old club, Luton Town, he turned down offers from League clubs to sign for Nigel Clough's Conference side Burton Albion.

WILSON, Mark — 2004

Born: 9 February 1979 Scunthorpe (5ft 11ins, 12st 2lbs – 2003)
Debut: 24 January 2004
v Peterborough United Division Two Home
Last Appearance: 7 February 2004
v Port Vale Division Two Away
Total League & Cup Appearances: 3 Goals: 0

Career Details:

Bottesford Town		
Manchester United	9 February	1996
Wrexham	23 February	1998 Loan
Middlesbrough	9 August	2001 £1.5m
Stoke City	14 March	2003 Loan
Swansea City	12 September	2003 Loan
WEDNESDAY	22 January	2004 Loan
Loan return	9 February	2004
Doncaster Rovers	3 September	2004 Loan
Livingston	24 January	2005 Loan
Dallas Burn	July	2005

Started his career at the Grimsby Town School of Excellence where he was recommended to attend the National school of excellence at Lilleshall. The former England schoolboys International subsequently had trials with several Premier League sides, and some in the Football League, before being signed on YTS forms by Manchester United in 1995. His league debut came during a loan spell at Wrexham, scoring the winning goal, and the attacking midfielder duly returned to Old Trafford in an attempt to dislodge the several Internationals who were automatic choices in the Red Devils midfield. He did manage to appear in 11 first team games for United – in addition to earning six England U-21 caps – but with competition fierce he eventually moved with good friend Jonathan Greening to Middlesbrough when his former coach at United, Steve McClaren, moved to take over as manager.

After joining Boro he evolved into a more defensive midfielder but his first season was badly disrupted by injury and he failed to earn a niche in the Teeside club's side after regaining fitness. He joined the Owls on loan after similar spells at Stoke City and Swansea City but after struggling to make an impact he had the further misfortunes to suffer medial knee ligament damage in only his third game for Wednesday – the injury curtailing his season in early February. He returned to Boro to recuperate and hoped for better fortune with Wilson having started less then ten Premier League games for Middlesbrough during his four-year contract.

WILSON, S. — 1884-85

Born:
Debut:
8 November 1884 v Long Eaton Rangers F.A.Cup Away
Last Appearance:
3 January 1885 v Nottingham Forest F.A.Cup Home
Total League & Cup Appearances: 2 Goals: 0

Career Details:

WEDNESDAY		1884

Mystery player who played twice during the Owls early forays into the F.A.Cup. Contemporary match reports suggest his Christian name began with the letter S or G but it has been impossible to confirm either.

WINDASS, Dean — 2001

Born: 1 April 1969 Hull
(5ft 10ins, 12st 6lbs – 2002)
Debut: 8 December 2001 v Millwall Division One Home
Last Appearance:
15 December 2001 v Gillingham Division One Away
Total League & Cup Appearances: 2 Goals: 0

Career Details:

North Ferriby United	August	1990
Hull City	24 October	1991
Aberdeen	1 December	1995 £700,000
Oxford United	6 August	1998 £475,000
Bradford City	5 March	1999 £950,000
Middlesbrough	15 March	2001 £600,000
WEDNESDAY	6 December	2001 Loan
Loan return	22 December	2001
Sheffield United	13 November	2002 Loan
Loan return	16 December	2002
Sheffield United	16 January	2003 Free
Contract cancelled	20 June	2003
Bradford City	14 July	2003 Free

Hard running, physical forward Dean Windass started his career as a trainee at Hull City but after being released he dropped into local football in the Humberside region prior to being spotted and signed by Hull non-league side North Ferriby. After two seasons with the Church Street side he was back at Hull City and over the next few seasons became somewhat of a cult hero, netting 64 goals in 205 competitive games, prior to a big money move to Aberdeen. He netted 25 times in his debut season in Scotland but soon wanted to return home and eventually moved for another sizeable fee to Oxford United. Incidentally while playing for Aberdeen he was famously sent off three times in one game after initially refusing to accept his dismissal!

His stay at the University town was brief however and he soon signed for Bradford City, helping his new club into the Premier League for the first time in their history in 1999 and then finishing top scorer with ten goals as the Bantams defied the critics to retain their top-flight status a year later. He was always guaranteed to give 100% commitment wherever he was asked to play and was known as a totally fearless player who would run through a brick wall for his team. These qualities obviously made him a favourite with supporters and City fans were shocked when Windass was sold to relegation rivals Middlesbrough in March 2001. Two months later Windass had helped the Teeside club to avoid the drop – Bradford suffering the fate instead – but he was only a squad player at the Riverside and joined the Owls on loan for a chance of first team football. Unfortunately he lasted only two games and Owls fans had little chance to judge as he soon returned to the Northeast after injury cut short his stay.

Almost a year later he returned to Sheffield to sign on loan for neighbours United, subsequently signing permanently in January 2003 and playing in both legs of the Division One play-off victory over Nottingham Forest that took the Blades to Cardiff. However he was then controversially dropped by Neil Warnock for the Final and within a matter of weeks his contract was cancelled by mutual consent. He later re-joined Bradford City and after a spell playing in midfield he was switched back to the forward line although his late run of goals was not enough to stop City from tumbling out of Division One. He continued to score regularly and City turned down a large bid from Premier League Wigan Athletic in August 2005.

WINTERBOTTOM, Harry 1879-92

Born: 19 December 1861 Sheffield
(5ft 7½ins, 10st 12lbs – 1890)
Debut: 18 December 1880
v Blackburn Rovers
F.A.Cup Away
Last Appearance: 14 February 1891
v West Bromwich Albion
F.A.Cup Home
Total League
& Cup Appearances: 22* Goals: 10
***Also appeared in**
28 Football Alliance League games

Career Details:

Suffolk	1873
Parish Church/Alexander Club	1876
Heeley	1878
WEDNESDAY	1879-1892
Exchange/Providence	1879-80
Exchange/Attercliffe	1880-81
Heeley	1881-86
Lockwood Brothers	1882-87
West Bromwich Albion	1888

Flying winger Harry Winterbottom was a stalwart of the Owls pre-league days and at his peak one of the finest and quickest wingman in the English game. He remained a regular with Wednesday for thirteen years and in that time saw the Owls develop from just one of many fledgling teams in Sheffield to the dominant club in the City and a force Nationwide. His love of the game was obvious at an early age as while still at school Harry was captain, treasurer and secretary of his first club, Suffolk FC. He kept this club alive until 1876 when he moved to play for two different sides, eventually joining top ranking Sheffield side Heeley who used the Alexander Club as their nursery team. Soon after joining the Talbot Street club (Heeley) he also started to become associated with The Wednesday – first appearing for the Blue and Whites on 1st March 1879 in a fixture at Spital Chesterfield.

He made infrequent appearances for Wednesday in the early 1880s – appearing for a variety of other teams and winning the 1882 Sheffield Challenge Cup with Heeley - but was part of history when he played in the club's first ever F.A.Cup game, scoring in a 4-0 win. As the decade progressed he become more and more important to the Wednesday cause, developing into a right-winger of undoubted class who possessed pace and a fine shot. When the Owls turned professional in 1887 Harry decided to remain amateur as he was in business as a bone haft and scale cutter – a very skilled occupation of the 1880s. He did play a solitary game for professional club West Bromwich Albion but was quickly back at Wednesday, appearing in the Owls first ever Football Alliance League game in 1889 (he also played in the club's first game at Olive Grove two years earlier). He was capped thirty times by the Sheffield FA and his absence from the 1890 F.A.Cup Final, due to an ankle injury, was seen by many as a major factor in the embarrassing 6-1 loss to Blackburn Rovers. He had previously helped Wednesday lift the Sheffield Challenge and Wharncliffe Charity Cups in 1888 and his loyal service was rewarded in September 1891 when he was awarded a benefit game against Stoke FC.

WISE, F. 1887

Born:
Only Appearance: 15 October 1887 v Belper Town F.A.Cup Away
Total League & Cup Appearances: 1 Goals: 0

Career Details:

WEDNESDAY	1887

Mystery back who seemingly played only a solitary game for Wednesday – a 3-2 Cup win at minnows Belper in 1887. He failed to appear for Wednesday either before or after the Cup game.

WITCOMB, Douglas Frederick 'Doug' 1947-53

Born: 18 April 1918 Cwn, nr Ebbw Vale, Gwent
(5ft 8ins, 10st 10lbs – 1947)
Died: cs. June 1997
Debut: 1 March 1947
v Tottenham Hotspur Division Two Home
Last Appearance: 25 April 1953
v Sunderland Division One Home
Total League
& Cup Appearances: 230 Goals: 12

Career Details:

Cwm Villa (Monmouthshire)		
Tottenham Hotspur		Amateur
Northfleet FC		
Enfield		
West Bromwich Albion	October	1937
Leicester City	May	1941 Guest
Grimsby Town		1940-41 Guest
Swansea Town		1941-42 Guest
Newport County		1945-46 Guest
Lovells Athletic		WW2 Guest
WEDNESDAY	28 February	1947 £6,500
Newport County	27 November	1953 Free
Llandudno Town	August	1954
Redditch United	October	1955
IHB Alloys & Alkamatic Works		1955

CAPS (@ SWFC)
Wales Full (1) v N.Ireland 16/04/47

As with the majority of his contemporaries Doug Witcomb left school at the age of 14 to start work at his local coalmine. While at school he had played in the same team as future Welsh International captain Ronnie Burgess and the pair actually signed amateur forms with North London giants Spurs after leaving Ebbw Vale County School. However after several games with their nursery side, Northfleet, Witcomb fell ill and after being examined by the Spurs doctor he was sent home and told he would never be fit enough to play league soccer. Thankfully this diagnosis proved incorrect as Doug soon signed professional forms with West Brom, remaining at the Hawthorns for a decade. The Second World War limited his appearances with Albion to just 56 games – plus 64 in wartime soccer - while during the conflict Doug served with the RAF and also played seven times for Wales in 'unofficial' wartime internationals. When peacetime football returned Witcomb won two full caps for Wales and it was a surprise when the talented right halfback was sold to struggling Division Two side Wednesday in February 1947.

Witcomb, who was equally good in attack as in defence, made an immediate impact as Wednesday beat Spurs 5-1 at Hillsborough and six weeks later he won his third and final cap for his country. Thankfully the Owls avoided the drop and over the next fours seasons Doug hardly missed a game, helping Wednesday to promotion in 1950 and then playing in 21 games as the Second Division title was secured in 1952. The hard working halfback could pass coolly under pressure and possessed a great right-footed shot but he had lost his place part way through that Championship season – going on the transfer list at his own request in October 1951 – and after being displaced by newcomer George Davies returned to Welsh football.

After 25 league games for Newport County he retired from senior football, later spending a season as player-coach to Llandudno Town before playing just a single game for Redditch. He later became a lathe operator for an engineering firm and Doug played for the Works side until 1962 when he finally retired at the age of 44 – he won a multitude of trophies with the works team and in fact played alongside his son in a local Cup Final. After retiring from work he eventually moved back to Redditch in the West Midlands where sadly his life came to a tragic end. He disappeared from his home on 18th June 1997 and later a decomposing body was fished from the River Usk, near Newport. The body was not identified for several months – he was buried in a pauper's grave in the town – but in January 1998 DNA tests confirmed it was Witcomb; a truly sad end to the life of the former Welsh International.

WOOD, Darren Terence 1989-92

Born: 9 June 1964 Scarborough
(5ft 10ins, 11st – 1989)
Debut: 21 January 1989
v Arsenal
Division One Away
Last Appearance: 23 October 1991
v Manchester City
Full Members Cup Home
Total League
& Cup Appearances: 12+2 Goals: 0

Career Details:

Middlesbrough	July	1981
Chelsea	September	1984 £50,000 + McAndrew
WEDNESDAY	12 January	1989 £400,000
Released	30 June	1992

Experienced utility defender Darren Wood was Peter Eustace's second signing and easily the most expensive of his short tenure in the Hillsborough hot seat. Wood came with a good pedigree, which included over 200 games for Middlesbrough before the age of 21 and over 150 starts at Chelsea, but unfortunately his time at Wednesday was totally ruined by a serious of major and minor injuries that severely restricted his first team opportunities. The former England schoolboys player – his father Terry also played for and captained his country at boys level - had been tracked by Wednesday back in 1982 but both the Owls and Liverpool were rebuffed and two years later he signed for Chelsea.

After appearing in eight games for the Owls in his first season Wood then totally disappeared from the first team scene and only appeared intermittently for the reserves, playing a small part in their Central League Championship success in 1991. He had briefly returned to first team action during the 1989-90 season but simply could not reclaim any semblance of full fitness and it was no surprise when he was released when his contract expired. After leaving Wednesday he underwent several unsuccessful back operations and was eventually forced to retire from football altogether. He later returned to his home town and started a delicatessen cooked meats business which is now thriving and boasts six outlets in the Yorkshire area.

WOOD, Richard 2003-

Born: 5 July 1985 Ossett
(6ft 3ins, 11st 11lbs - 2003)
Debut: 21 April 2003
v Brighton & Hove Albion Division One Away
Total League
& Cup Appearances: 52+6 Goals: 3

Career Details:

Ossett Trinitarians		
WEDNESDAY	21 March	2003

Central defender Richard Wood was spotted playing in the Wakefield and District League at the tender age of ten and soon joined the Owls youth structure. He progressed through the club's ranks to sign three-year scholarship forms in July 2001 but within two years the Owls had secured his signature on a professional contract. The left footed and composed defender, was by now a regular in the reserve side and first came to the attention of new manager Chris Turner when Wood captained the Academy team to an F.A.Youth Cup win at Reading in December 2002. A few months later Turner blooded the 17 year old in senior football although his debut was somewhat bittersweet as it came on the day Wednesday suffered relegation from Division One. His full debut came a week later at Burnley and proved an infinitely more memorable afternoon as not only did the Owls record an astonishing 7-2 win but the teenage centre half also netted - a mis-kicked effort dribbling into the net, much to his sheer delight!

He retained his place in the first team squad during the next season, appearing in 18 league and cup games, although he missed a large chunk of the campaign after suffering a stress fracture of his foot. Although not blessed with pace, Wood possesses strength in the air and good ball distribution and these qualities endeared him to new manager Paul Sturrock who paired the youngster with Graeme Lee at the heart of the Owls defence as the club strived to fight their way out of League One. Injury meant Wood was paired with Lee Bullen as the season reached its conclusion and the teenager was outstanding on that unforgettable Cardiff day as Wednesday beat Hartlepool United to soar into the Championship.

WOODALL, Brian Harold 1965-70

Born: 6 June 1948 Chester
(5ft 6ins, 9st 9lbs – 1966)
Debut: 24 February 1968
v Coventry City
Division One Away
Last Appearance: 27 September 1969
v Derby County
Division One Home
Total League
& Cup Appearances: 22+3 Goals: 6

Career Details:

WEDNESDAY	7 June	1965
Oldham Athletic	12 February	1970 Loan
Chester City	13 June	1970
Crewe Alexandra	11 March	1971 Loan
Oswestry Town		1971
Rhyl		1975
Colwyn Bay		1977
Browns of Chester		1979 (Sun.)

Although winger Brian Woodall once scored 100 goals in a single season in schoolboy football it was just two goals that put him firmly into Hillsborough folklore. The wholehearted attacker had initially joined the Owls as an apprentice in August 1963 and for three seasons after turning professional was almost ever present in Central League football, earning a call up to the first team bench and subsequent debut at Highfield Road in February 1968. He was in and out of the side prior to a January 1969 visit to Elland Road, for an F.A.Cup replay against red-hot cup favourites Leeds United, but he firmly wrote himself into Owls history thanks to his brace that helped Wednesday to a famous 3-1 win that shocked the football world.

His double secured Woodall a mini-run in the senior side but he struggled to live up to his Cup exploits and in February 1970 joined Oldham on loan, scoring on an impressive debut. Unfortunately financial problems meant the Latics were unable to finance a permanent signing and he was given a free transfer in May 1970, moving back home to sign for Chester City. He appeared in 16 games for Chester before spending the remainder of the 1970-71 season on loan at Crewe, netting a hat trick at home to Exeter City. Despite his treble he was without a club in the summer of 1971 and duly turned his part-time employment with Ellesmere Port Borough Council into a full-time position while dropping into semi-professional football. His playing career ended when he broke his leg in three places while playing Sunday League football while he was forced to take early retirement from his job in 1996 after the onset of arthritis in both knees.

WOODHEAD, Dennis 1945-55

Born: 12 June 1925 Sheffield
(5ft 9ins, 12st 9½lbs – 1946)
Died: 26 July 1995 Sheffield
Debut: 24 May 1947
v Newcastle United
Division Two Home
Last Appearance: 5 March 1955
v Everton
Division One Home
Total League
& Cup Appearances: 226* Goals: 75
***Also appeared in 1 wartime game**

Career Details:
Edgar Allen's
Hillsborough Boys Club

WEDNESDAY	June	1942 Amateur
WEDNESDAY	19 April	1945 Free
Chesterfield	9 September	1955 £2,000
Derby County	January	1956 £1,500
Southport	February	1959 £750
Derby County	March	1959 £750
Frickley Colliery	July	1959
Worksop Town	July	1960
Retford Town	April	1964

Winger Dennis Woodhead started his playing career with the works side of Sheffield based engineering company Edgar Allen's – gaining employment as a fitter and turner after leaving school in 1939 – and signed amateur forms with Wednesday during the war years after being invited to train at Hillsborough by manager Jimmy McMullen in 1941. He actually played only one game for the Owls in wartime soccer because he volunteered for the R.A.F. at the age of 18 and served with distinction throughout the conflict, flying 31 operational bombing flights over Germany in his role as a flight engineer. The Owls were so keen to secure Woodhead on a professional contract that they sent the forms out to India – where he was serving with the R.A.F. – and he finally made his league debut after being de-mobbed from the forces in April 1947.

The pacy left-winger with a powerful shot quickly became established in the first team and netted 14 times from the left wing during the 1948-9 season, missing only two games. However his career was then interrupted when he suffered a broken leg against Leicester City in August 1949 but he returned to fitness late in the season to help Wednesday to promotion from Division Two. A grandson of Wednesday 19th Century hero Billy Betts, Woodhead formed an exciting wing partnership with Red Froggatt and won a Second Division Championship medal with Wednesday in 1952, also appearing in the 1954 F.A.Cup semi-final loss to Preston. He also experienced double relegation with the Owls in the 1950s before the former footballer and cricketer with Sheffield boys was allowed to sign for Teddy Davison's Chesterfield, making a huge impact on debut when scoring a hat trick in the Spireites 7-2 home win over Rochdale.

Within six months Dennis joined Division Three (North) side Derby County and helped the Rams to runners-up spot and then promotion a year later. He totalled 24 goals in 94 league games for the Rams and at one point was sold to Southport but on league orders was transferred back after less than a month due a knee injury! After leaving County he owned a sweet shop and then sold insurance whilst also playing for a variety of local non-league clubs – he was player-manager at both Frickley and Retford prior to hanging up his boots. He was appointed lottery manager at Chesterfield in 1967 and then commercial manager back at Hillsborough four years later, replacing his old fishing pal Derek Dooley who had been given the manager's job. He remained in the position until taking early retirement in June 1987 while the family connection remains with his son. Steve, the Owls Football in the Community Officer.

WOODS, Christopher Charles Eric 'Chris' 1991-96

Born: 14 November 1959 Swineshead, Lincs.
(6ft 1ins, 14st lbs – 1993)
Debut: 17 August 1991
v Aston Villa Division One Home
Last Appearance: 23 March 1996
v Bolton Wanderers Premier League Away
Total League
& Cup Appearances: 137+1 Goals: 0

Career Details:
Swineshead Sunday League
Priory Celtic

Nottingham Forest	1 December	1976
Queens Park Rangers	4 July	1979 £225,000
Norwich City	12 March	1981 Loan
Norwich City	June	1981 £250,000
Glasgow Rangers	1 July	1986 £600,000
WEDNESDAY	14 August	1991 £1.2m
Reading	27 October	1995 Loan
Colorado Rapids	10 May	1996 £150,000
Southampton	31 October	1996
Sunderland	26 March	1997 Free
Kansas City Wizards		1997
Burnley	17 July	1997

CAPS (@SWFC) – England Full (19)
v Turkey 16/10/91, v Poland 13/11/91, v Germany 11/09/91, v France 19/02/92, v CIS 29/04/92, v Brazil 17/05/92, v Finland 03/06/92, v Denmark 11/06/92, v France 14/06/92 v Sweden 17/06/92, v Norway 14/10/92, v Turkey 18/11/92, v San Marino 17/02/93, v Turkey 31/03/93, v Holland 28/04/93, v Poland 29/05/93, v Norway 02/06/93, v Spain 09/09/92, v USA 09/06/93

When Chris Woods became the club's first £1m player he was the current England International goalkeeper, having replaced Peter Shilton after the 1990 World Cup Finals. However to many fans his purchase from Scottish Champions Rangers seemed illogical as Wednesday already had Kevin Pressman, Chris Turner and Marlon Beresford on their books while the newcomer did not endear himself to Owls fans in his first season by conceding sloppy goals in both derby meetings with the Blades. His form did improve in his second season with his superb reflexes saving many a situation but the campaign ended badly for Woods when he conceded a poor last minute goal as Wednesday lost the F.A.Cup Final replay against Arsenal. The summer of 1993 saw Woods win the last of his 43 caps for England and although he started the new season as No. 1 at Wednesday he was soon displaced by Pressman and failed to play first team football for the Owls for almost eighteen months.

He eventually departed for US football in 1996 but soon returned to British shores when joining Premier League Southampton on a four-month loan, starring for the Saints in a draw at Hillsborough. He made six appearances for Southampton before unfortunately breaking his leg in a game at Blackburn and later signed a short-term contract at Sunderland, failing to make a senior appearance for the Wearside club. His final league game came under ex-team mate Chris Waddle at Burnley where he combined his role as goalkeeping coach with playing duties. He retired from the game in 1998 and subsequently joined Birmingham City as goalkeeping coach in July 1998 prior to joining Everton in the same capacity, where he is still employed today.

It would be fair to say that Woods' best years came prior to joining Wednesday as he had won four titles in Glasgow as well as setting a British record of 1,196 minutes without conceding a goal. His career had started back in June 1976 when he joined Nottingham Forest as an apprentice – he had worked on his father's farm while on schoolboy forms – and shot to National prominence in 1978 when he made his senior debut for Forest in the League Cup Final, winning the trophy in a replay. However he could not displace Peter Shilton from the first team and eventually left for QPR and then Norwich City, helping the Canaries to two promotions from Division Two (1982 & 1986), the League Cup in 1985 and appearing in 171 consecutive games. A big money move to Glasgow giants Rangers followed – where an ear infection affected his balance and at one point threatened his career - and after 230 games he returned South after Trevor Francis splashed out a club record fee for his services. Incidentally Woods appeared in exactly 739 league and cup games on both sides of the border.
His Great Uncle, Eric Houghton, played for Aston Villa, Notts County and England.

WOOLHOUSE, Henry 'Toddles' 1888-95

Born: 1868 Ecclesfield, Sheffield
(5ft, 6ins, 10st 8lbs - 1890)
Died: Q/E December 1911 Sheffield
Debut: 2 February 1888
v Notts Rangers F.A.Cup Away
Last Appearance: 16 March 1895
v West Bromwich Albion F.A.Cup Away
Total League
& Cup Appearances: 35* Goals: 21
***Also appeared in 45 Football Alliance League games**

Career Details:

Sheffield FC		
WEDNESDAY		1888

Versatile forward who was a stalwart of the Owls pre league days, not only appearing in the club's first ever F.A.Cup Final but also playing in the opening match in the Football Alliance League. He was a regular for two seasons in the latter - which was effectively the Football League's second tier - and netted seven times as Wednesday won the inaugural title in 1890. In January 1891 he netted five times in the club's record win - 12-0 against minnows Halliwell - but after Wednesday were elected into the Football League in 1892 'Toddles' was used infrequently although his record of 10 goals in just 16 league games perhaps suggests that his talents should have been utilised more. Competition from the likes of Harry Millar, Harry Davis and the incomparable Fred Spiksley meant 'Toddles' struggled to secure a permanent place in the League side but he did however remain somewhat of a cup specialist and played in losing F.A.Cup semi-finals in 1894 and 1895 before ending his playing days. He sadly died at the tender age of 43 in 1911.

WORRALL, John Edwin 'Teddy' 1909-19

Born: 2 October 1891 Buxton, Derbyshire
(5ft 10ins, 11st 4lbs – 1913)
Died: 24 July 1980 Chesterfield
Debut: 21 January 1911
v Preston N. E. Division One Home
Last Appearance: 20 March 1915
v Manchester City Division One Away
Total League
& Cup Appearances: 114* Goals: 0
***Also appeared in 2 wartime games**

Career Details:

Buxton College		
The Comrades		
Buxton		1908
WEDNESDAY	7 July	1909£35
Chelsea		WW1 Guest
Tottenham Hotspur		WW1 Guest
Buxton		1918-19 Guest
Fulham	June	1919
Aberdare Athletic	14 May	1923
Watford	31 January	1925
New Brighton Tower	9 June	1925
Southport	27 May	1927
Shirebrook	July	1929
Gresley Rovers	August	1930
Ripley Town		1930-31

Teddy Worrall started his working life in a Buxton bank after joining straight from Buxton College. He also played football for a local amateur side before he was given a trial by Wednesday and subsequently signed professional forms, aged just seventeen. The youngster then spent two seasons gaining experience in the Owls' Midland League side before making two appearances at right back for the absent Jimmy Spoors. When Spoors was switched to left back in November 1911 it was Teddy who took his place and would remain an automatic choice until the Great War brought an end to competitive football in 1915. Worrall- who was the nephew of legendary goalkeeper Sam Hardy – missed only two games as Wednesday came agonisingly close to the League Championship in 1913 and continued to play occasionally during the hostilities, whilst serving with the Pay Corps in Mesopotamia (part of modern day Iraq).

The war effectively signalled the end of Teddy's Wednesday career as he moved to Fulham soon after, gaining employment as a clerk in the Borough of Wandsworth council offices. He was later signed by former Owls teammate Frank Bradshaw for Welsh Division Three (South) club Aberdare and in his career played on every ground in all four sections of the Football League. His playing days ended in Derbyshire non-league football and he later worked as a schools coach for the Derbyshire FA and as a scout for Tottenham before working in the Social Security offices in Chesterfield before retiring at the age of 71.

WORTHINGTON, Nigel 1984-94

Born: 4 November 1961
Ballymena, N.Ireland
(5ft 11ins, 12st 6lbs – 1985)
Debut: 25 February 1984
v Brighton & Hove Albion
Division Two Home
Last Appearance: 7 May 1994
v Manchester City
Premier League Home
Total League
& Cup Appearances: 413+4 Goals: 15

Career Details:

Ballymena United		1976
Linfield		1981 Guest
Notts County	1 July	1981 £100,000
WEDNESDAY	7 February	1984 £100,000
Leeds United	4 July	1994 £325,000 (T)
Stoke City	18 July	1996 Free
Blackpool	14 July	1997 Free

CAPS (@SWFC)

Northern Ireland FULL (50) v Wales 22/05/84, v Finland 27/05/84, v Israel 16/10/84, v Spain 27/03/85, v Turkey 11/09/85, v Romania 16/10/85, v England 13/11/85, v Denmark 26/03/86, v Algeria 03/06/86, v Spain 07/06/86, v England 15/10/86, v Turkey 12/11/86, v Israel 18/02/87, v England 01/04/87, v Yugoslavia 29/04/87, v Yugoslavia 14/10/87, v Turkey 11/11/87, v Greece 17/02/88, v Poland 23/03/88, v France 27/04/88, v Malta 21/05/88, v Eire 14/09/88, v Hungary 19/10/88, v Spain 21/12/88, v Malta 26/04/89, v Hungary 06/09/89, v Eire 11/10/89, v Uruguay 18/05/90, v Yugoslavia 12/09/90, v Denmark 17/10/90, Austria 14/11/90, v Faroe Islands 01/05/91, v Austria 16/10/91, v Denmark 13/11/91, v Scotland 19/02/92, v Lithuania 28/04/92, v Germany 02/06/92, v Albania 09/09/92, v Spain 14/10/92, v Denmark 18/11/92, v Eire 31/03/93, v Spain 28/04/93, v Lithuania 25/05/93, v Latvia 02/06/93, v Latvia 08/09/93, v Denmark 13/10/93, v Eire 17/11/93, v Liechtenstein 20/04/94, v Colombia 04/06/94, v Mexico 11/06/94

For over a decade Nigel Worthington was a fixture in the Owls side and holds the club record as the most capped player to ever appear for Wednesday. The highly consistent and unflappable Worthington – affectionately nicknamed 'Irish' by Owls fans – originally arrived as a left back but would play the latter years of his Wednesday career on the left side of midfield, forming an outstanding partnership with Phil King which propelled the club to success in the early 1990s. Worthington had started his playing career as a part-timer with Irish club Ballymena – also working at the Michelin tyre factory – with whom he lifted the Irish Cup in 1981. Although he was tracked by several Football League clubs whilst on Ballymena's books he was not allowed to leave by his manager until a firm bid was received – his boss was quoted as saying "if he was good enough he would not need to go for trials". In fact it was while touring Holland as a guest player with Belfast club Linfield that he was spotted by Notts County manager Jimmy Sirrel who subsequently brought him to English football, in the same year Nigel was voted Northern Ireland Young Footballer of the Year.

Of course Howard Wilkinson later took over at Meadow Lane and Worthington would follow in his footsteps to Hillsborough a few months after Wilkinson departed for Sheffield 6, playing the last 14 games of the season as Wednesday won promotion to the top-flight. After the Owls consolidated in the higher grade 'Irish' represented Ireland in the 1986 World Cup Finals but he looked set to leave in May 1989 after being courted by newly crowned champions Arsenal. However he decided to stay, signing a one-year contract, although in September 1989 he asked for a transfer! However he remained an Owls player and would produce the best form his career in his new midfield role as Wednesday won a promotion and League Cup double in 1991 then reached Europe and two Cup Finals in the same season – he was also named the inaugural Northern Ireland player of the year in 1992. Although he was now playing in midfield for his club 'Irish' continued to play at left back for his country and reached the 50 cap mark in the summer of 1994 – a year earlier he had been awarded a testimonial with Derby County providing the opposition.

However in June 1994 he rejected a new contract offer and a few weeks later had joined up with former boss Wilkinson up the MI at Elland Road. Worthington was very much a squad player at Leeds – slotting into the side when required – and after two seasons (which included an appearance in the 1995 League Cup Final) moved to Stoke City where he won the final two of his 66 caps for Northern Ireland. After being released from Stoke he was handed his first managerial appointment when taking over as player-manager at Blackpool, remaining in charge until resigning two days before Christmas in 1999. He then assisted the England U-21 side before joining Norwich City as assistant manager in June 2000, becoming caretaker boss six months later, and after a successful spell in temporary charge he was handed the reins on a permanent basis on 2nd January 2001, ironically facing Wednesday four days later at Hillsborough in his first game as manager. Since taking charge Worthington has created a reputation as one of the brightest young managers in the game and led Norwich City back to the Premier League as Division One champions in 2004.

WORTLEY, George 1884-85

Born:
Only Appearance:
3 January 1885 v Nottingham Forest F.A.Cup Home
Total League & Cup Appearances: 1 Goals: 0

Career Details:

WEDNESDAY	1884

Player who appeared occasionally for Wednesday during the 1984-85 season before disappearing from the local football scene. In addition to playing in the F.A.Cup defeat to Nottingham Forest he also played in four friendly fixtures for Wednesday.

WRIGHT, Ernest Victor 'Vic' 1930-33

Born: 24 January 1909 Bloxwich nr.Walsall
(5ft 11ins, 11st 12lbs – 1930)
Died: Q/E March 1964 Wednesbury
Debut: 3 October 1931 v Aston Villa Division One Home
Last Appearance: 10 October 1931
v Leicester City Division One Away
Total League & Cup Appearances: 2 Goals: 0

Career Details:

Bloxwich Strollers		
Bristol City	February	1929 £240
Rotherham United	June	1929
WEDNESDAY	16 October	1930 £1,900
Rotherham United	9 February	1933 Exchange for G.Bratley
Liverpool	14 March	1934
Plymouth Argyle	June	1937
Chelmsford City	June	1938
Millwall		WW2 Guest
Crystal Palace		WW2 Guest
Walsall		WW2 Guest

Vic Wright was the nephew of former England International Billy Athersmith but he failed to reach the heights of his relation after starting his professional career at Bristol City. An astonishing 40 goals in just four months whilst playing for Bloxwich in Birmingham & District League had persuaded the West Country club to take a risk on the youngster but he failed to make a senior appearance prior to signing for Rotherham United. He made a far greater impact at Millmoor where playing at inside-right netted a dozen goals in his debut season and had scored eight times in only seven matches prior to the Millers receiving a record fee from Wednesday for his services – just days before moving to Hillsborough he had netted four goals in a 8-1 win over Accrington Stanley.

He possessed a powerful shot and quick reactions but he was in direct competition to Ron Starling for a place in the Owls top-flight side and would play only twice before moving back to Millmoor in a deal that brought George Bratley to Hillsborough. In the lower tier he was quickly back into the scoring groove and netted 19 times in 53 more games for United before another transfer took Wright to Anfield. He finished second top scorer for the Reds in his debut campaign and ended his playing career with ambitious Southern league club Chelmsford City.

WRIGHT, James 'Jimmy' 1935-36

Born: 11 September 1910 Okehampton
(5ft $9^{1}/_{2}$ins, 12st – 1935)
Died: Q/E December 1978 Grimsby
Debut: 20 March 1935
v Derby County
Division One Away
Last Appearance: 12 February 1936
v Portsmouth
Division One Home
Total League
& Cup Appearances: 4 Goals: 0

Career Details:

Okehampton		
Exeter City		Amat.
Torquay United	April	1930
Grimsby Town	June	1932
WEDNESDAY	2 March	1935 £600
Guildford City	May	1936
Swansea Town	June	1937
Hartlepool United	August	1938

Left back Jimmy Wright was one of only a handful of Devon born players to appear for Wednesday, perhaps the most famous being Trevor Francis. His career started with his village side and after turning professional with Torquay United he netted his only goal in league soccer prior to moving North to sign for Grimsby Town. He made 22 appearances for the Mariners in his first season on the East coast but then dropped totally out of first team contention as Town won the Second Division title in the following season. He was back on the fringes of the side during Town's First Division campaign and one of his five top-flight appearances actually came against Wednesday in December 1934 when his side won 3-1 at Blundell Park.

After moving to Hillsborough he was effectively understudy to Ted Catlin and made only the occasional senior start before dropping out of the Football League to sign for Guildford City. After a year in non-league soccer the stocky defender was back in the Football League with Swansea Town but played only four games prior to a final move to Hartlepool United where he was a regular, playing the first three games of the 1939-40 season before England declared war on Germany.

WRIGHT, John 'Jocky' 1898-1902

Born: 4 February 1873 Hamilton, Scotland
Died: 1946 Southend
Debut: 26 November 1898
v Aston Villa Division One Home
Last Appearance: 17 March 1902
v Derby County Division One Home
Total League
& Cup Appearances: 110 Goals: 42

Career Details:

Hamilton Academical		
Cylde		
Bolton Wanderers	June	1895
WEDNESDAY	October	1898 £200
Hamilton Academical	September	1902
Bolton Wanderers	October	1902 £100
Plymouth Argyle		1904
Watford	May	1907
Southend United	May	1908

There is no doubt inside-left Jocky Wright experienced one of the longest debut of all time as his first game in Wednesday colours was abandoned after $79^{1}/_{2}$ minutes with the remaining time played out fifteen weeks later! This was a bizarre introduction for the Scotsman who had risen to prominence with Bolton Wanderers where he appeared in the first ever game to be played at their former ground of Burnden Park, in addition to netting 17 times in 94 games for the Lancashire club. He suffered relegation in his first season at Wednesday but was a revelation as the club romped away with the Second Division title just twelve months later, finishing top scorer with 26 league and cup goals – he also repeated his Bolton feat of appearing in the first ever match played at Owlerton.

Known as a superb dribbler and skilful player, he added ten goals to his Wednesday tally as the Owls consolidated back in the top-flight but eventually dropped out of first team contention, losing the No. 10 shirt to Jack Malloch. After a short spell back in Scotland he returned to Bolton Wanderers for a second spell where despite appearing in 19 games in his first season back at Burnden Park he failed to find the net. He did grab five goals in the next season but his days in top-flight soccer were over and he played out his career in the lower leagues before being appointed reserve team trainer at Southend United in 1913. He was later coach of Southend Transport while his two sons, Billy and Doug, both enjoyed careers in league football with the latter being capped for England just before the Second World War.

WRIGHT, Percy Lionel — 1910-14

Born: 1890 Darley Dale
(5ft 7³/4ins, 10st 12lbs – 1913)
Died: 10 July 1971 Matlock
Debut: 22 April 1911
v Everton Division One Away
Last Appearance: 31 January 1914
v Wolverhampton Wanderers
F.A.Cup Away
Total League
& Cup Appearances: 22 Goals: 6

Career Details:

Heanor Town		
WEDNESDAY		1910 £55
West Ham United		1914 £250
Chesterfield	September	1919 Trial

Utility attacker who arrived at Wednesday for a small fee from Nottinghamshire non-league side Heanor Town. He made a scoring debut at outside left in a 1-1 draw at Everton and acted as understudy to the likes of George Robertson over the next four seasons. His best run in the side actually came in what proved to be his final season in a Wednesday shirt, scoring twice in eleven games, prior to moving to West Ham United. During the Great War he was captured and held as a prisoner of war and on his return failed to secure a league club after a trial at Chesterfield. He passed away, aged 81, in the early 1970s.

WYLDE, Rodger James — 1971-80

Born: 8 March 1954 Sheffield
(6ft 1ins, 12st – 1978)
Debut: 18 November 1972
v Middlesbrough
Division Two Home
Last Appearance: 16 February 1980
v Chesterfield
Division Three Home
Total League
& Cup Appearances: 182+12 Goals: 66

Career Details:

WEDNESDAY	1 July	1971
Burnley	13 November	1975 Loan
Oldham Athletic	29 February	1980 £75,000
Sporting Lisbon	July	1983
Sunderland	26 July	1984
Barnsley	5 December	1984 £15,000
Rotherham United	10 March	1988 Loan
Stockport County	25 July	1988

Popular striker Rodger Wylde was a Sheffield United supporter as a boy but he was signed by Wednesday on schoolboy forms in 1968 after his Owls fans teacher, Mr Frost, sent him to Hillsborough for a trial. He signed apprentice forms in July 1970 and the non-nonsense, polished forward with deft feet broke into the Wednesday first team as a teenager although it was not until the arrival of Len Ashurst in the mid-1970s that Wylde became established. He duly built up a great rapport with the Wednesday fans and rewarded them with 56 goals in a three-season spell as the Owls unsuccessfully tried to fight their way out of the Third Division. The former Sheffield Boys player eventually fell out of favour under Jack Charlton and after being transfer listed in February 1980 he soon moved, somewhat reluctantly, to Second Division Oldham Athletic.

He continued to find the net with regularity at the Boundary Park club – netting 51 times in 113 games – before a surprise move saw Wylde sign for Portuguese giants Sporting Lisbon. He spent a year in sunnier climes before returning home to South Yorkshire to play for both Barnsley and Rotherham prior to making his final transfer to Stockport County. While on the Hatters books he studied physiotherapy at Salford University and after gaining a BSc (Hons) Degree he retired from playing and was appointed at County in June 1989, a position he still holds today.

YOUNG, Gerry Morton 'Gerry' **1955-71**

Born: 1 October 1936
Harton, South Shields
(5ft $10^{1}/_{2}$ins, 11st 9lbs – 1964)
Debut: 2 March 1957
v Blackpool Division One Away
Last Appearance:
2 January 1971
v Tottenham Hotspur
F.A.Cup Away
Total League
& Cup Appearances: 342+2
Goals: 20

Career Details:

Newcastle United		Amat.
Hawthorn Leslie		
WEDNESDAY	14 May	1955

CAPS (@SWFC)
England Full (1) v Wales 18/11/64

Gerry Young represented Jarrow boys as a youngster and was on Newcastle's books as an amateur before gaining employment as an apprentice electrician with local firm Hawthorn Leslie. It was while playing for his works side in a local Cup Final that Wolves scout Bill Rochford spotted his potential – Young netted a hat trick – but after he failed to persuade the youngster to attend trials at Wolves he instead phoned Wednesday to recommend his talents to Eric Taylor. He soon joined the Owls as a part-time professional – turning full-time when he finished his apprenticeship – but it would be almost two years before Young made his first team debut, at inside forward in a 3-1 defeat at Bloomfield Road. However despite grabbing trebles against both Manchester United and A.S.Roma in 1961 he could not nail down a regular place and it was not until star wing half Tony Kay was sold to Everton that Young became an integral part of the team. In a mirror image of Paul Warhurst's exploits of 30 years later Young was then moved from the forward line into defence and took to his new position with such style that within 18 months he was capped for England – only missing a second cap against Holland when he was forced to withdraw from the squad due to a ruptured thigh, allowing a certain Bobby Moore to take his place.

A run of 80 consecutive games in the No. 6 shirt started at Blackpool in March 1963 with Young's sheer professionalism endearing him to his fellow players (he was married on a Saturday morning and then caught the train to Birmingham to play for Wednesday at St.Andrews in the afternoon!). In addition his 100% commitment, thoughtful play and good positional sense made Gerry a firm favourite with fans. He was a rock at the heart of the Owls defence throughout the mid to late 1960s but unfortunately will probably be best remembered as the player who failed to cut out a long clearance which led to Everton's winning goal in the 1966 F.A.Cup Final. Luck also deserted him when the time came for a deserved testimonial game as Wednesday had been relegated from the top-flight just three days earlier but a good crowd still attended a 3-3 draw with local rivals United.

He was appointed reserve team coach in April 1971 and three months later decided to retire from playing when he was given the role of First team coach at Hillsborough. After Derek Dooley's dismissal in December 1973 Young was caretaker manager for a time before reverting back to a coaching role when Steve Burtenshaw was appointed manager in January 1974. He remained on the Owls staff until October 1975 when he was sacked, along with Burtenshaw, to bring the curtain down on twenty years service with the Owls. He then worked for a short time on the backroom staff at Barnsley before starting to help out John Quinn at his Middlewood Road sports shop, just a stone's throw from Hillsborough. He eventually started his own business selling sporting trophies from the shop and when Quinn sold the premises in April 2001 Gerry continued his business from home.

MEN AT THE HELM

Managers 1867-2005

DICKINSON, Arthur Joshua 1876- 1920

Although strictly not classed as a manager it would be highly remiss not to include Arthur Dickinson at any point in a book dedicated to the men who made Sheffield Wednesday. In short he was a man who was totally dedicated to the club and it was often said that without his organisation skills and tireless work the Owls would not have even survived into the Twentieth Century.

He joined the Owls committee back in 1876 and was an influential member, as the club became a force in the City and become known on the national stage. When Wednesday turned professional in 1887 Dickinson was handed the role of honorary financial secretary and became full honorary secretary in 1891 - a role he combined with his job as a salesman for a Sheffield cutlery firm which saw Arthur travel to the US on over seventy occasions, in order to develop and extend sales markets. Considering his role at Wednesday was not only unpaid but also on a purely part-time basis it's quite remarkable that Dickinson became known as one of the greatest administrators in the English game - he was the only honorary secretary in the Football League.

Although he never played football as a youngster - he was a fine road cyclist - Dickinson showed undoubted enthusiasm for his role at Wednesday and in 1899 was instrumental in the club becoming a limited company, as well as moving to a new plush home at Owlerton. He was the first man to pay £5 for a share in Sheffield Wednesday Limited - receiving ticket No. 1 - and then used his talents to ensure the Owls moved across the City and effectively built a new ground before the start of the new season. Incidentally in his early days as secretary he used to take home the gate receipts and leave them under his sofa until the bank opened on the following Monday! Later he reached an agreement with the bank so they would stay open after every home game to receive the gate receipts.

After the move to Owlerton he effectively ran the club as Wednesday won back-to-back league championships and added an F.A.Cup win to their role of honour in 1907. Incredibly in addition to holding a full-time job and running the Owls the remarkable Dickinson also served as a member of the highly influential F. A. Council, the International selection committee, the Football League management committee and held a variety of roles over a 40 year period for the Sheffield & Hallamshire League! If that was not enough he was also vice-president of the powerful Midland League, served with the Sheffield & Hallamshire F.A. and boasted an almost encyclopaedic knowledge of the rules and regulations of football. After keeping the Owls open during the Great War, Dickinson would see Wednesday suffer relegation in the first season after the hostilities and it proved his final campaign at the helm, resigning from his role on 18th May 1920, after 44 years service. Just before his departure he showed he had lost none of his flair for organisation by ensuring the staging of the April 1920 England v Scotland game at Hillsborough ran smoothly.

Although Dickinson handed over the reins to Bob Brown he remained a regular sight at Hillsborough during the 1920s and was often known to still take the match receipts to the bank after games. He acted as bank courier after the November 1930 County Cup semi-final between Wednesday and United, travelling to London on the following day to attend a meeting of the Football League management committee. However after signing in at the Eastern Hotel he was walking with an Everton official when he collapsed and died instantly, without saying a word. Many officials thought he had simply fainted but sadly this was not the case and Dickinson died at the age of 79. The following day the players in the England v Scotland Inter-League match wore black arm-bands as a show of respect and Wednesday mourned the loss of one of the greatest figures in their long history.

BROWN, Robert (Bob) 1920-1933

There is no doubt that Bob Brown was the most successful of the twenty-four men to have managed Sheffield Wednesday since the club's first managerial appointment back in 1920. Before Brown arrived from Southern League Gillingham the Owls – like the majority of their contemporaries – were run on a committee basis with the club secretary and board of directors usually picking the eleven on the day before a game. However following a painful relegation from the top-flight in 1920 the Owls decided it was time for change and the resignation of secretary Arthur Dickinson provided the ideal opportunity to appoint one of the new breed of professional secretary-managers who had sole responsibility for picking the team.

The Northeast born Brown was no stranger to the Hillsborough hierarchy as back in August 1905 he had been appointed to the position of scout on wages of £10 per week (plus expenses) – duly recommending a plethora of players from the Northeast who would give the Owls sterling service. Three years later, in August 1908, he moved to Sheffield when being appointed general assistant to Arthur Dickinson and he remained in the £3 per week position until being head hunted by ambitious Southern League club Portsmouth, joining on 1 July 1911 when his Wednesday contract expired. Within a year he had taken Pompey back into Division One of the Southern League – they had been relegated in 1911 – and over the years that followed he carved out a reputation as the brightest manager outside of the Football League; an opinion strengthened further when Brown led Portsmouth to the Championship in 1920 and subsequent entry into the newly formed Division Three.

However Brown did not lead Pompey into the Football League as in May 1920, after a disagreement with the Portsmouth Chairman, he surprisingly accepted the post as Gillingham manager – the Kent club having also been elected into the League after the whole top division of the Southern League was voted in en-masse. Within a month though, Brown found the lure of Hillsborough too hard to resist and in June 1920 became boss at Wednesday. The quiet and unassuming man had spent his early working life in the Tyne Shipyards – whilst playing non-league football for the likes of Hebburn Argyle – but would spend the majority of his adult life as a football manager.

When Brown took over at Wednesday he was faced with a virtual rebuilding job as a few weeks earlier an ageing Owls side had won only four games in being relegated from Division One – the club releasing or transferring an amazing 21 players at the end of the club's worst ever season! It was a task that Brown relished and the Owls board stayed patient as Wednesday spent five seasons in Division Two without really threatening to climb back into the top-flight. However Brown had an incredible talent to spot potential and it was definitely 'his side' which eventually surged to the Second Division Championship in 1926, the likes of Ernie Blenkinsop, Jimmy Trotter, Jack Brown & Billy Marsden playing crucial roles. With centre forward Trotter finishing Division One top scorer in 1926-27 (with 39 league and cup goals) the Owls finished just below mid table in their first season back but it seemed Brown was facing relegation almost twelve months later with the club marooned at the foot of the table in a seemingly hopeless position.

The inspirational signing of Jimmy Seed proved the catalyst for Wednesday and after a truly remarkable escape from the drop the club enjoyed arguably the greatest period in their long history. With Brown at the helm and trainer Chris Craig at his side the Owls would win consecutive titles in 1929 & 1930; Owls legends Ellis Rimmer, Mark Hooper, Harry Burgess & Jack Allen all captured from lower league soccer by Brown. The club remained at the forefront of the English game in the early 1930s but it was an off the field event that would ultimately bring an end to the Brown years. In the summer of 1933 his wife tragically died while the couple were holidaying in Blackpool and from that point onwards Brown was not the same man - his own health soon beginning to deteriorate. He would eventually tender his resignation, due to ill health, on 21 September 1933 and so ended the reign of a manager whose Wednesday side had not finished out of the top three in the First Division for the previous five seasons - they had come so close to completing the elusive 'double' in 1930 when his charges were controversially beaten by Huddersfield Town in the F.A.Cup semi-final. The Owls had made a poor start to the new season – sitting down in a relatively lowly tenth place – but there was still widespread surprise when the club accepted Brown's resignation and many wondered if the board were somewhat harsh in their decision.

However the die was cast and after a spell out of the game Brown returned to football as a scout for Chelsea. Sadly on 7 March 1935, while on a scouting mission for the Pensioners, Brown collapsed on a Leeds railway station platform and was taken to the Royal Infirmary suffering from a cerebral haemorrhage, passing away on the following day. It was perhaps fitting that a few weeks later an Owls side full of players that Brown had signed won the F.A.Cup.

MCCLELLAND, J. B. 1933-34

J.B.McClelland was appointed assistant to Bob Brown on 31st July 1931 and was handed the reins on a temporary basis when Brown resigned in September 1933. He was in charge for a total of eleven games, tasting victory only twice, and reverted back to his former role when Billy Walker arrived from Villa. Previous to joining Wednesday he had helped form Halifax Town in 1911 and spent ten years as honorary secretary-manager before the Shaymen were voted into the Football League in 1921 - his role became full time following Town's election in the league. He remained at Wednesday until resigning on 30 October 1934 and then spent ten years as secretary-manager at Lincoln City (1936-46). Before joining Town he was largely responsible for the formation of the Halifax & District Football Association and was awarded a long service medal by the West Riding F.A. He was also honorary secretary of the Midland Combination

WALKER, William Henry 'BILLY' December 1933- November 1937

The man eventually chosen to following in the footsteps of Bob Brown was perhaps a surprise appointment as 35 year-old former England International Billy Walker had no previous managerial experience and was only handed the role when St Johnstone boss Tom Muirhead and then old skipper Jimmy Seed turned down the opportunity. It actually took the Owls over ten weeks to fill the post – he was appointed on 8 December 1933 - but there was no doubt that Walker was a highly respected figure in the game; having earned 18 caps for England and scored 244 times in 531 games for his only club, Aston Villa. In his playing days Walker was an outstanding inside forward who had initially developed at Kings Hill school prior to playing in amateur football for Hednesford and Darlaston – in the 1910-11 season he netted 80 goals in the Walsall boys league. He nearly died from consumption while still a teenager but he recovered to play for Wednesbury Old Park during the Great War after winning a solitary cap for England Schoolboys. Despite Birmingham wanting his signature – guesting in wartime football for the Blues - he had his heart set on joining his Villa, duly signing amateur forms at the age of just sixteen years and three months. In his first season as a professional at Villa Park, Walker scored twice on his debut and played in the 1920 F.A.Cup Final against Huddersfield Town which Villa won 1-0. In August 1920 he netted four times against Arsenal and in November 1921 scored a hat trick of penalties against Bradford City. He quickly developed into one of the star players of the 1920s, captaining England on several occasions and was idolised by Villa supporters as he set a new aggregate goals record that still stands today.

He was therefore a name that was not unknown to Owls fans when it was revealed the Staffordshire born Walker (29.10.1898) would be the club's second secretary-manager. In the weeks immediately after Brown's departure the team had been somewhat of a rudderless ship, drifting down into nineteenth position, but the new man made an immediate impact and Walker took Wednesday on an unbeaten run of twelve games, which began with four consecutive wins. The return to form secured a position of safety by the season's end while in the months that followed he showed he was not a man to curry popularity as crowd favourites Jack Ball, Harry Burgess, Ernie Blenkinsop & Tony Leach were all shown the door. Their replacements were good, solid players but in hindsight it would be Walker's record in the transfer market that would eventually lead to his downfall,

However his first full season at the helm brought glory for Walker as the Owls went all the way to Wembley, where West Brom were beaten to win the F.A.Cup for the third and last time in the club's history. The Owls also finished third in the top-flight but the honeymoon was quickly over as Wednesday escaped relegation by only three points in 1936 before finishing rock bottom twelve months later. His inability to replace the Wednesday stars of the later 1920s/early 1930s had cost Walker dear and an Owls side bereft of quality had alarmingly slumped to 21st place in the Second Division by early November 1937. At that point the Owls had just eight points to their name and after a shocking 4-1 defeat at Barnsley Walker faced an angry group of shareholders. What was said between the two parties was never published but the next day Walker met the Owls board and duly tendered his resignation on 8th November 1937.

Wednesday paid Walker £800 for the remaining eighteen months of his contract and the now ex-Owls manager would spend a few months out of the game before being appointed manager of ambitious non-league Chelmsford City in January 1938. The Essex side were in the process of moving to semi-professional status and Walker remained for ten months, signing several ex-League players including '35 Cup Final scorer Jack Palethorpe. He would lead City all the way to the Fourth Round of the F.A.Cup in 1939 – beating Darlington and Southampton on route – but eventually resigned in February 1939. After a month of inactivity he was appointed Nottingham Forest manager in March 1939 but the onset of the Second World War ruined Walker's plans to re-build the Forest side. When peacetime soccer returned his charges struggled and suffered relegation to Division Three (South) in 1949. However Walker then made several crucial signings and by 1957 Forest had climbed back into the top-flight and two years later he led them to F.A.Cup glory. After over 21 years in charge he resigned his position in June 1960 but remained at the City Ground as a member of the Forest committee. Sadly in October 1963 he suffered a stroke and he never really recovered his health, passing away in Nottingham on 28 November 1964 at the age of sixty-six.

McMULLAN, James 'JIMMY' January 1938 - April 1942

Whilst Billy Walker was an England star of the 1920s; his successor Jimmy McMullan was an International of some repute for Scotland. The Scot was born in the Stirlingshire village of Denny on 26 March 1895 and started his working life as a miner before moving into the Football League with Third Lanark. A move to Partick Thistle followed in November 1913 and the wing half remained at the Glasgow club until a dispute saw him leave to take over at Kent League club Maidstone United as player manager in 1921. After two seasons he returned to Partick but was soon back in English football when Manchester City paid a reputed £4,700 fee in February 1926. Whilst with the Maine Road club McMullan blossomed into a brilliant inside left and was part of the Scotland team that was dubbed 'Wembley Wizards' after beating England 5-1 at the national stadium in 1928. In total he won 16 full caps for his country while in club football he was twice on the losing side in an

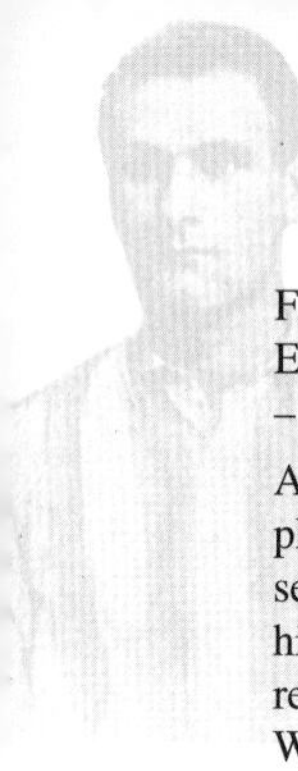

F.A.Cup Final with Manchester City (1926 v Bolton & 1933 v Everton) but did win a Second Division Championship medal 1926 – he appeared in a total of 224 games for City.

A man of considerable charm and modesty, McMullan retired from playing in May 1933 and was immediately handed his first secretary-manager job by Oldham Athletic. In what proved to be his only season with the Latics they finished in mid-table and reached the Lancashire Senior Cup Final, losing to Bolton Wanderers. In May 1934 he was handed the reins at Aston Villa but despite spending £35,000 – a considerable sum in the 1930s - on new players the Birmingham club were relegated and McMullan left in October 1936. The diminutive McMullan – he stood only 5ft 5ins tall – took over at Notts County a month later and was still in charge when interviewed for the post of Owls boss on 23 December 1937. He accepted the position and six days later County agreed to release him; McMullan officially starting work at Hillsborough on 3 January 1938. He took over an Owls side dangerously close to the Second Division relegation zone but fortunes improved greatly under the Scot and he averaged a point a game to steer the club clear of trouble. The signings of Doug Hunt and Charlie Napier then contributed towards a total transformation during the 1938-39 season as Wednesday made a determined effort to gain promotion. In fact after completing their fixtures the Owls were actually in the second promotion spot but when neighbours Sheffield United won their outstanding fixture it was the Blades who pipped their great rivals to promotion by just a single point. Unfortunately for McMullan his encouraging start to life in the Hillsborough hot seat came to an abrupt end early in the 1939-40 season as Europe was plunged into war. All contracts were declared null and void and McMullan began work in a Sheffield factory while fulfilling his duties at Hillsborough on a strictly part-time basis. However it was a difficult task for McMullan as many of his better players were called into the Armed Forces and the public appetite for football in the early war years was nothing better than luck warm. It was therefore no surprise when in April 1942 the Owls announced that his contract would not be renewed; effectively ending McMullan's managerial career as he remained in industry for the remainder of his life. He died in Sheffield on 28 November 1964 – the exact same day as Billy Walker.

TAYLOR, ERIC
April 1942 - August 1958

The fact that Eric Taylor was called "Mister Sheffield Wednesday" shows the incredible influence the master administrator bestowed on the club during his 45 years on the Owls staff. Born on a Wednesday in the Sheffield district of Birley Carr in May 1912, Taylor quickly gained a life long passion for the club by slipping into the ground to see the final few minutes after the gates were opened. His working life started in a law office but he successfully applied for the job as office boy at Hillsborough in 1929 on wages of seven shillings and sixpence (37.5p in new money!) – his appointment was said to be a reward for Bob Brown after leading Wednesday to the League Championship.

When Joe McClelland departed the youngster was elevated to assistant secretary, in November 1934, and remained in that role until being appointed temporary part-time manager in April 1942. He showed his managerial qualities by leading Wednesday to the War Cup Final in 1943 and his growing stature was rewarded when Wednesday officially handed him the position of secretary-manager on 14 June 1945. In his first full season as Owls boss he took Wednesday to sixth place in the final wartime season and when peacetime football returned he slowly built a side that would eventually earn promotion from Division Two in 1950. He certainly had a keen eye for a player and was not afraid to ask his board of directors to break the British transfer record on several occasions in the late 1940s/early 1950s – Jackie Sewell proving good value after the Owls paid £35,000 for his services. He also signed the likes of Derek Dooley, Alan Finney, Don Megson, Ron Springett, Redfern Froggatt & Gerry Young while selling Eddie Quigley for a British transfer record in 1949. Taylor was very much an office based manager during his sixteen years at the helm – leaving the training and tactical matters to his coaches such as Bill Knox, Alan Brown and Jack Marshall – but his influence on the field of player was always evident.

The Owls boss dubbed the 1950s the 'yo-yo years' as Wednesday were either relegated or promoted on six separate occasions and it was after the last of those relegations in 1958 that the Owls hierarchy decided it was time to take the pressure off Taylor and advertise for a team manager. Therefore in August 1958 Harry Catterick became the first Wednesday manager with sole responsibility for team affairs while Taylor became secretary and general manager. After being relieved of his extra responsibilities Taylor showed his remarkable vision and flair for organisation; his far-sightedness and drive helping to make Hillsborough one of the best club grounds outside Wembley by the end of the 1960s. He was always proud that Hillsborough hosted countless F.A.Cup semi-finals, a full England International and four games in the 1966 World Cup tournament – the organisation for the competition being voted the best of all the provincial grounds during England's summer of glory. Taylor was such a thorough organiser that he even travelled to the 1962 World Cup in Chile to ensure Wednesday were prepared and was even head hunted in September 1966 when the North American Soccer League offered Taylor the incredible sum, by 1960s standards, of £11,000 per year to organise their new professional soccer league. After much deliberation over the post of Executive Secretary he decided to stay at Hillsborough; much to the Owls' relief as they were faced with losing one of the finest football administrators in the game. Incidentally he also had to deal with the infamous bribes scandal in 1964 and his impassioned speech before the home game with Spurs, directly after the news story broke, is still remembered by all who were in the ground that night.

In 1967 Taylor was fighting for his life in hospital after a car crash but thankfully recovered to return to his post. By this time Taylor was chairman of both the Football League Secretaries & managers association but he would experience what he called the unhappiest night of his life when Wednesday were relegated from the top-flight in 1970. Unfortunately for Taylor the team on the pitch had not kept place with the ground developments and when he announced in January 1974 that he would retire in the following summer the Owls were struggling at the wrong end of the Second Division table. One of the outstanding personalities in the history of Sheffield football duly left his post on 30 June 1974 – he was immediately appointed vice-president and agreed to act on a consultancy basis for the club. Sadly he was not able to enjoy his retirement as just twelve weeks after retiring he died on 23 September 1974, aged just 62. The Owls held a memorial match against an England XI a few weeks later and it's certain Taylor would have appreciated that Hillsborough was graced by Internationals in his memory.

CATTERICK, HARRY
August 1958 - April 1961

Born in Darlington on 26 November 1919, Harry Catterick was relatively unknown to Wednesday fans when he arrived at Hillsborough after a five-year spell as Rochdale manager. His playing career had started as an amateur with Stockport County but the bustling centre forward was best known for a 14 year spell with Everton where the likes of Jack Dodds kept him in the Goodison shadows – Catterick appeared in only 71 games, netting 24 times. He also appeared as an amateur for Cheadle Heath Nomads and as a guest for Manchester United in the Second World War but was handed his first managerial job in December 1951, being appointed player-boss at Crewe Alexandra. The Gresty Road club would prove an ideal apprenticeship for the young manager and his growing reputation was enhanced further at Rochdale before moving to newly relegated Wednesday on 14 August 1958 – he officially started on 1 September 1958 on a £1,800 per annum contract. He quickly showed he was his own man by selling 'golden boy' Albert Quixall to Manchester United for a British transfer record but his impact on the field of play was immediate as Wednesday won the Second Division Championship in his first season at the helm. Incidentally just four days after moving to Sheffield – and having yet to sign a contract – it was reputed that Leicester City offered him a huge pay rise to take over at Filbert Street but Catterick stayed true to his word and rejected the offer.

Catterick was a single-minded, tough and uncompromising manager but earned respect amongst his playing staff and Wednesday finished fifth in their first season back in the top-flight, as well as reaching the F.A.Cup semi-finals. He was also a great wheeler-dealer in the transfer market although during his time at Hillsborough Catterick was fairly quiet on the transfer front, instead bringing the likes of John Fantham, Ron Springett, Don Megson, Peter Swan & Tony Kay into the first team and moulding a side that compared with any in the country. With their inspirational manager at the helm Wednesday proved the only creditable opposition to famous Spurs 'double' side in 1961 but sadly for Owls fans their final home game of the season saw an Everton side win 2-1 at Hillsborough. However it was not particularly the result that would have upset the Hillsborough faithful but the fact that it was Harry Catterick who had led the Toffeemen to victory, in his first game in charge after resigning from Wednesday on 10th April 1961. The parting of ways was a huge disappointment to Wednesday fans and although he cited no reason at the time it was well known that he was frustrated at a lack of transfer cash and his relationship with Eric Taylor was never a particularly happy one.

Ten days after leaving Hillsborough he was appointed manager back at Everton – his head coach Tom Eggleston later resigning and joining him at Goodison Park – and Owls fans certainly had cause to regret his departure as during the 1960s he build two Championship winning sides and even led his new club to a dramatic victory over Wednesday in the 1966 F.A.Cup Final. Playing a brand of entertaining and stylish football the Blues won the title in 1963 and during his time in charge Catterick signed a plethora of future Everton legends, such as Howard Kendall, Alan Ball, Colin Harvey – his second outstanding side sweeping to the 1970 League Championship. He also led Everton to a 1968 F.A.Cup Final loss to West Bromwich Albion but his career came to a halt when he suffered a heart attack in January 1972 while he was driving back to Merseyside from Sheffield. He returned to his managerial duties but just a year later – and with Everton struggling at the wrong end of the table – he was moved to a general manager position with four years of ten-year contract still to run. In August 1975 he left to take over at Preston North End but retired from the game in May 1977 and it was perhaps fitting that on 9 March 1985 he collapsed and died while attending the F.A.Cup tie between Everton and Ipswich Town at his beloved Goodison Park.

BUCKINGHAM, Victor Frederick 'VIC'
May 1961 - April 1964

The void left by Harry Catterick was soon filled by flamboyant Londoner Vic Buckingham, who moved from Dutch club Ajax to take over at Hillsborough on 8 May 1961- officially starting on 1 June. The Greenwich born Buckingham (b. 23.10.15) had enjoyed a long and successful playing career with Tottenham where in fourteen years as a professional the elegant defender amassed 310 senior games for the North London giants. Soon after signing pro forms for Spurs he was also loaned to nursery side Northfleet while during the war years – he served in the R.A.F. during the conflict – he guested for Crewe, Fulham, Millwall and Portsmouth. The former England boys player gained his first coaching experience when he spent the summer of 1946 coaching in Norway at Moss FC and back in the UK he was coach at London club Stanmore and then Oxford University, before spending time back at White Hart lane as youth coach. He retired from playing in 1949 and a year later was appointed coach of famous amateur side Pegasus (a combined Oxford/Cambridge University team). It was a real boom period for amateur football and in April 1951 an astonishing crowd of 100,000 packed into Wembley to see Pegasus beat Bishop Auckland to lift the much loved F. A. Amateur Cup.

His success with Pegasus earned Buckingham a shot in league soccer at Bradford Park Avenue and after two years at the helm he moved to First Division West Brom in February 1953. Success was virtually instant as the articulate and debonair Buckingham took the Baggies to F.A.Cup success in 1954, as well as runners-up spot in the league. He established a style of football that delighted fans and although he could not repeat his early successes it was still a blow when he resigned in May 1959 to accept the post of manager at Amsterdam based club Ajax. During two years in Holland he won both the Championship and domestic Cup while he is widely regarded as the man who discovered and nurtured the blossoming talent of Johann Cryuff. He decided to move back to England in March 1961 – accepting the post of Plymouth manager – but contractual problems meant he was unable to take up the position immediately and by the time he was released from his Ajax contract he moved to Hillsborough instead.

He joined a Wednesday side fresh from finishing runners-up to Spurs and expectations were high that the Owls could push for the Championship. His arrival was seen as the dawn of a new era as the maximum wage had just been abolished and Wednesday were geared for success with the ground boasting the new state of art North Stand. His debut season saw Wednesday finish in sixth place, as well as reaching the last eight of the FAIRS Cup, although in March 1962 he proved his happy-go-lucky demeanour hid a steely determination when he sensationally blasted his own side in the local media. The story made the front page with Buckingham quoted as saying "It's just not good enough" and " as a team they have got no skill and in the long run hard work will never make up for that defect". The criticism showed that Buckingham was a great believer in players expressing themselves on the field and always tried to rely on his players own experience and talent to guide through ninety minutes. This philosophy led Wednesday to sixth place for the next two seasons but the Hillsborough board were impatient for success and with no silverware in the trophy cabinet they sensationally sacked Buckingham on April 9 1964. A lack of consistency in performances was cited as a major reason for his dismissal although his relationship with the Wednesday hierarchy had certainly soured and disagreements with Chief scout Jack Mansell were becoming increasingly commonplace. Perhaps more important was the fact that in the weeks leading up to his departure several players had also appeared in court on various charges – the last being Eddie Holliday who was charged with being drunk at the wheel – and this would have counted against Buckingham as Chairman Andrew Stephen and Eric Taylor hated seeing the club's good name dragged through the tabloids.

In hindsight the Buckingham period must be deemed a success as Wednesday finished sixth in the top-flight in three consecutive seasons but the Owls were desperate for success and in the end their ambitions could not be equalled on the field of play and the club's decline as a force in the English game effectively started when Buckingham walked away from Hillsborough. Although told his contract would not be renewed it was expected that Buckingham would remain at the club until his contract expired on 31st May 1964. However he left immediately and it was Eric Taylor who stepped into the breach as caretaker manager for the remainder of the season. After leaving Hillsborough Buckingham returned to Ajax - he had turned down a double your money offer in May 1963 – and later spent three years as Fulham boss (Jan 1965 – Jan 1968) before he was sacked and replaced by Bobby Robson. After leaving Craven Cottage one of the finest coaches in the English game spent the rest of his career abroad, initially at

Greek club Ethnikos before being appointed boss at Catalan giants Barcelona on 11 January 1970. He took a revived Barca side to fourth place in 1970 and a year later Barcelona were runners-up and Buckingham led them to a 4-3 Spanish Cup Final triumph over Valencia. Unfortunately soon after the Cup Final he had to quit his post due to a recurring back problem but before leaving he set in motion the wheels that would eventually bring Johann Cryuff to the Nou Camp in 1973. In March 1972 he was appointed coach at Spanish side Seville and ended his career back in Greece at Ethnikos where his generous and out going personality made him a popular figure. He returned to the UK to live out his retirement and passed away in Chichester, Sussex on 26 January 1995.

BROWN, ALAN Winstone
August 1964 – February 1968

After the departure of Buckingham the Owls reverted back to a manager in the mould of Catterick as new man Alan Brown held a reputation of being an 'iron man' who was well known for being a tough disciplinarian. However there was genuine warmth below his steely exterior and it was this that made him well-respected and admired amongst players and his fellows managers. His move to Hillsborough caused somewhat of a sensation as Northeast born Brown had led Sunderland to promotion back to Division One at the end of the 1963-64 season and was fully expected to lead his charges back in the top-flight. However the Wednesday hierarchy had other ideas and Brown stunned the football world by walking out on Sunderland in July 1964 to sign a five-year deal at Wednesday – he officially started on 1st August 1964. He led Wednesday to a creditable eighth place in his first season in charge and then helped lift some of the gloom left behind by the infamous bribes scandal by inspiring a young team to reach the 1966 F.A.Cup Final. The Owls won away from home in every round to reach Wembley and looked set for glory in the final when they led Everton 2-0. Sadly the Harry Catterick managed side stormed back to win the Cup but Wednesday fans were still hopeful it was the dawn of a new exciting era as the Owls boasted several highly rated youngsters such as Wilf Smith, David Ford, Jack Whitham & Jim McCalliog. The post World Cup boom saw crowds flock to Hillsborough in the following season but they had to settle for a mid table finish after a late flourish ensured there was no battle against the drop. Wednesday topped the table after a great start to the 1967-68 campaign but a run of only one win in twelve games saw them slump to the lower reaches of the table by February. However despite the poor run of form there was no inclination that the popular Brown was considering his options so it was therefore a shock to Owls fans when he sensationally walked out on 8 February 1968. As he departed he vehemently denied he was set for a £10,000 a year job back at Sunderland - the Wearsiders had sacked their manager Ian McColl earlier in the day – but unsurprisingly 24 hours later he was revealed as the new Roker Park boss!

Although Alan Winstone Brown was born in the small Northeast village of Consett - on 26 August 1914 - he was brought up in Corbridge where at school he played rugby on Saturday mornings and football in the afternoon. He would excel at the latter discipline and first played club football for Durham junior side Spen Black and White before signing professional forms at Huddersfield Town in March 1933. He left the Terriers in August 1936 to join the Police Force but returned a year later, appearing in 28 league games in the two seasons immediately prior to the Second World War. He served in the R.A.F. during the hostilities – playing as a guest player for Liverpool, Manchester United & Notts County – and would enjoy the best period of his playing days after moving to Burnley for a hefty £25,000 fee in February 1946. A commanding half back, Brown was part of the Clarets defence that conceded a paltry 29 goals as they won promotion to the top-flight in 1947 and he was also captain when Burnley reached the F.A.Cup Final, only losing 1-0 to First Division Charlton Athletic. However despite playing to a high standard in league football it would be as a coach that Brown would become widely known – his career behind the scenes started when he retired as a player at Notts County and divided his time between his restaurant in Burnley and an F. A. coaching course.

It would be at Hillsborough that Brown – whose cousin Austen Campbell played for England, Blackburn & Huddersfield - served his coaching apprenticeship as he stepped into the breach on 23 January 1951, replacing the late Bill Knox as trainer-coach at Wednesday. It was not the first time Brown had coached in the city as during the war he was detached from the R.A.F. to act as a PT instructor and later coached occasionally for the Sheffield & Hallamshire County F.A. After four years working under Eric Taylor at Hillsborough he was handed the managers job at his old club Burnley, taking the reins on 31 August 1954. He struggled with a small budget at Turf Moor and success eluded Brown although along with Chairman Bob Lord he is credited with developing a fine youth policy that bore fruit in later years. Brown also earned a reputation as an astute tactical manager and when Sunderland fell on hard times they turned to their local lad, appointing Brown as manager in July 1957. Ironically despite the Sunderland board investing heavily in the side they were relegated for the first time in their history in Brown's debut season and despite several near misses it would take six years for Brown to take Sunderland back into the top-flight. After re-joining Sunderland he again concentrated on developing the youth side of the club but was criticised for neglecting other areas as the Black Cats again suffered relegation in 1970. They just missed out on promotion in 1972 but a bad start to the following season saw Brown sacked in November 1972. His coaching days looked over after he took Norwegian side Ham-Kam Hamar to the league runners up spot in 1973 as he then moved to Bodmin in Cornwall to live out his retirement. However he was soon asked to take over as Chief Coach at local club Plymouth Argyle and he duly came out of retirement to coach the Pilgrims to promotion from Division Three in 1975. He retired again in 1977 and resisted calls to take over as manager at Plymouth to live the rest of his life in the Southwest. He wrote a coaching manual in 1993 – titled 'Team Coach' – and died in the Devon town of Barnstaple on 9 March 1996.

MARSHALL, John Gilmour 'JACK'
February 1968 – March 1969

Born in Bolton on 29 May 1917, Jack Marshall was a popular figure in football circles and such was his outgoing and friendly personality that he was nicknamed "Jolly Jack" by his friends. His short spell as Owls manager was in fact his third different role behind the scenes at Hillsborough as back in January 1955 he was appointed Chief Coach and physio while despite leaving to become Rochdale boss in September 1958 he would return – in March 1967 - to act as assistant manager to Alan Brown. It was a role that Marshall enjoyed and it is probable that the former Burnley professional was a somewhat reluctant manager when he was appointed to the position on 11 February 1968, after just three days as caretaker boss. His time at the helm was not helped by a spell of illness early in the 1968-69 season – he was in hospital when Wednesday beat Manchester United 5-4 in August 1968 – and despite being fully committed to the job Marshall struggled to lift the gloom of Alan Brown's final weeks in charge and after a 5-0 home loss to Arsenal in March 1969 the proverbial writing was one the wall – Jack resigning as Wednesday manager on 18 March 1969 after learning that the club had decided not to renew his contract in the following summer.

In July 1969 Marshall was appointed manager at Bury but after just seven games in charge was controversially sacked when a new board implemented several cost cutting measures, which included Marshall's somewhat generous salary! His short tenure at Gigg

Lane would prove to be his final managerial position as from July 1970 until his retirement in 1979 he was physio at Blackburn Rovers. He subsequently moved back to his Bolton roots while later in life moved to Rotherham, passing away on 6 January 1998, aged eighty.

His football life had started as a youngster with Lancashire amateur side Bacup Boro where he was spotted and invited for a trial by Burnley. After signing professional forms for the Turf Moor club in November 1936 he struggled to hold down a regular place at full back and when in 1949 he retired through injury had made only 27 senior appearances in over 12 years as a professional. When he was forced to retire he studied massage and physiotherapy, whilst working as a scout for Bolton Wanderers, and was later coach at Bury and then Stoke City prior to his first spell at Wednesday. When Harry Catterick arrived from Rochdale in 1958 it was Marshall who moved to take over his old job at Spotland but Rochdale finished bottom of Division Three in his first season of management and he moved to neighbours Blackburn Rovers in July 1960. His Blackburn side was noted for its entertaining style in the early 1960s but as the decade progressed the team slowly broke up and relegation came in 1966 after a disastrous season. A year later – in February 1967 – he left Ewood Park to return to Wednesday for a second spell.

McANEARNEY, TOM CARETAKER
March – June 1969

- See players section

WILLIAMS, Daniel Thomas 'DANNY'
July 1969 – January 1971

When Danny Williams was appointed Wednesday boss on 17 July 1969 he was seen by many as an inspired choice as the former Silverwood Colliery miner had achieved remarkable success at Third Division Swindon Town, recording an incredible double in 1969 when leading the Wiltshire side to promotion from Division Three and a stunning League Cup Final win over Arsenal. Born on 20 November 1924 in Rotherham, he first played organised football with his colliery side before spending the whole of his eighteen years as a professional with local side Rotherham United. Initially a winger he later switched to wing half and when he retired in 1960 to became a coach at Millmoor he had amassed 461 league games – a club record that still stands today. He was part of the great Rotherham side of the early 1950s that almost gained promotion to the top-flight and when he hung up his boots coached the reserves before becoming trainer and then finally, in July 1962, manager. However he resigned in February 1965 – when his young players were sold against his will – and looked set to retire totally from the game and concentrate on his sport's outfitters shop in the town. Within two months though he was persuaded to join Swindon Town and the four years he spent at the Robins proved to be the highlight of his managerial career.

Unfortunately his eighteen months at Wednesday could not have provided a greater contrast to his Swindon experiences as his lack of knowledge of top-flight football, internal strife at Hillsborough, an unhappy dressing room and a general malaise around the club all contributed to a disastrous reign. Williams was a real happy-go-lucky character but he soon looked out of his depth at Hillsborough and seemingly lacked the guile and tactical acumen to stop the rot which led to relegation from Division One in 1970 and then saw Wednesday struggle in the lower reaches of the Second Division. His record in the transfer market certainly did not help his cause – he sold individuals of the quality of David Ford & Peter Eustace but replaced them with far inferior players. The inevitable parting came on 25 January 1971 but Williams and Wednesday would then fight for over two years with regard to compensation – the protracted dispute finally being settled in July 1973 when the former boss accepted a £10,000 'golden handshake' to finally lay the matter to rest. In November 1971 he had been appointed manager at Mansfield Town but suffered relegation from Division Three in his first season and repeated the feat back at Swindon Town after returning to the County Ground in March 1974. He remained with Town for three more seasons before taking a more backseat role, finally retiring to his Bournemouth home in the mid-1980s.

DOOLEY, DEREK
January 1971 – December 1973

See players section

McANEARNEY, James 'JIM' CARETAKER
December 1973 – January 1974

See players section

BURTENSHAW, Stephen 'STEVE'
January 1974 – October 1975

After both Danny Williams and Derek Dooley failed to wake the Owls from their slumber of the early 1970s the club turned to youth, appointing 38 year old former QPR Chief Coach Steve Burtenshaw on 28 January 1974. The highly rated Burtenshaw seemed an ideal candidate for the position after having worked behind the scenes at both Arsenal and QPR since retiring as a player in 1966. Born in Portslade-by-Sea (23.11.35) he made a league bow for local club Brighton at the tender age of seventeen and over the next fourteen years would total 237 league appearances – winning the Third Division (South) title in 1958 and the Division Four Championship in 1965 - before being appointed reserve team manager at Highbury. After winning the Football Combination twice and both the Combination & London Challenge Cups he was elevated to Chief Coach at the Gunners in July 1971 when Don Howe left the club while just over two years later swapped positions with Bobby Campbell at Loftus Road. However he spent only a few months at QPR – who at the time were the top side in the Capital – as he believed he was ready for his first managerial post and when Wednesday came calling he jumped at the chance.

At the time he was the youngest manager in the Owls history – only Trevor Francis subsequently setting a new mark – and started well enough when Wednesday beat Bristol City at Hillsborough in the club's first ever league game on a Sunday. Unfortunately the win only proved a false dawn as the Owls showed no real improvement as the season progressed and it needed a famous Ken Knighton goal, in the final home game of the season, to save Wednesday from the unthinkable drop into Division Three, Sadly though fortunes soon went from bad to worse for the now somewhat shell-shocked young manager as the 1974-75 season entered club history as the worst of all time – Wednesday winning only five games all season and failing to eek out a win from December 28 1974 until the end of a desperate season. His best move in the transfer market was probably the capture of Eric McMordie on loan during that disastrous season but with finances at Hillsborough reaching crisis point and crowds dwindling he was left in an increasingly helpless situation, forced to sell crowd favourite Tommy Craig in 1974 and having no resources at his disposal to replace the playmaker. He was in charge when Wednesday played their first ever match in Division Three, at Southend United in August 1975, but the slide continued and by the time new Chairman Bert McGee wielded the axe on 1st October 1975 the club was at its lowest ebb – languishing in the lower reaches of the old Third Division.

After leaving Hillsborough he joined the Everton coaching staff – serving as caretaker manager early in 1977 – but his managerial career received another mortal blow when his sole season in charge at QPR ended in disastrous relegation from the old First Division – he was sacked just ten months into a 3-year contract. He later rejoined Arsenal as Chief Scout but his experiences at both Wednesday and QPR made sure that when he was made caretaker manager in the spring of 1986 Burtenshaw made it clear that he did not intend to go back into management!

ASHURST, Leonard 'LEN'
October 1975 - October 1977

Although when Len Ashurst left Wednesday in October 1977 the club was bottom of the Third Division there is no doubt that he was the manager who finally laid the foundations that would see the Owls climb out of the lower reaches of the Football League. When he walked out on Gillingham - the Gills issuing a writ against Wednesday in February 1976 for illegal approach and receiving £5,000 in July 1977 in an out of court settlement - to become the Owls ninth post war manager on 16 October 1975 Ashurst must have known that the club needed to take some harsh medicine and he would have to make decisions that may prove unpopular with supporters. The first of these was to make crowd favourite Eric Potts available for transfer in December 1975 but in hindsight his two years at Wednesday saw Ashurst sign many players that would be of long-term benefit to the club – the likes of Tommy Tynan, Bob Bolder, Ian Porterfield & Jeff Johnson. He also helped to develop the youth policy that would bear fruit later in the decade but experienced mixed fortunes on the field of play after joining an Owls side facing relegation to Division Four. He is quoted as saying his first six months at Wednesday were the toughest of his whole managerial career and just eight wins in his first 35 games in charge took the Owls into a crunch relegation meeting with Southend United on the final day of the 1975-76 season. Thankfully the Owls grabbed the lifeline to avoid the drop into the basement division and in the following season it looked like Ashurst's hard work behind the scenes was paying dividends as he led Wednesday to a promising eighth place in the division. However the writing was on the wall at the start of the 1977-78 campaign as Wednesday failed to win any of their opening ten league games and he was sacked on 5 October 1977 – leaving his successor to take advantage of his restructuring of the club from the bottom upwards.

Born in Liverpool on 10 March 1939, Ashurst first came to prominence with the City's boys side – winning the prestigious English Schools Trophy in 1953 – and would spent three years as an amateur at Liverpool whilst serving an apprenticeship in the printing trade. Despite also being capped at England Youth level Ashurst was not offered a full contract by the Anfield club but after a brief spell at Prescot Cables it was Sunderland coach (and England Youth coach) George Curtis who was instrumental in Len signing as a part-time professional for Sunderland in December 1957. He joined a local printer to compete his training but it would be in the football world where he would remain for the rest of his working life, initially as a player for Sunderland where he earned the reputation of a steady, reliable left back who always gave 100% commitment for the cause. In over 13 years at Sunderland he became a naturalised 'Mackem' and hardly missed a game, amassing a mammoth 458 appearances and being ever present as Sunderland won promotion from Division Two in 1964. His form was also rewarded with an England U-23 cap against West Germany in 1961 and his loyalty repaid when Ashurst was awarded a testimonial game against Newcastle United – prior to being handed a deserved free transfer and being appointed player-manager at Hartlepool United in March 1971.

It was a tough start to his managerial career at Victoria Park as a cash crisis saw Ashurst take over the role of trainer in addition to playing and picking the side! His experiences with Hartlepool no doubt proved a benefit in hindsight and a short spell as Gillingham manager (June 1974- - October 1975) preceded his biggest appointment so far – trying to revive a floundering Owls side. His best spell as a manager arguably came after his two years at Wednesday as when appointed Newport County boss in May 1978 the Welsh side were near the foot of the old Fourth Division. However he led them to a promotion and Welsh Cup double in 1980 and a year later made national headlines as County came within a whisker of the reaching the semi finals of the European Cup Winners Cup. Despite keeping County in the Third Division he was sacked in February 1982, joining rivals Cardiff City a month later and taking the Bluebirds to promotion from the Third Division in his first full season at the helm. He left in March 1984 to return 'home' to manage Sunderland but his time in charge was not a happy one as despite the Wearside club reaching the 1985 League Cup Final he was criticised for his Wembley selection, as Norwich City lifted the trophy, and was sacked at the end of the season after Sunderland were relegated from the top-flight. His next appointment took Ashurst to the sunny climes of Kuwait where he coached the National side, before being handed the same role with Middle East neighbours Qatar. He returned to the UK in the late 1980s to become assistant manager at Blackpool and then spent two years back as boss at Cardiff City – being unable to stave off relegation from Division Three in 1990 and being handed his P45 in May 1991. Two years as Weymouth manager followed before a three-year stint coaching in Malaysia came to an end in February 1996 when taking over as manager at Southern League Weston-Super-Mare. While at the Dorset club he did his old club a favour by recommending goalie Stuart Jones to the Owls while in August 1999 he resigned to take the important role of F. A. Academy Director for the whole of Southern England – seeing Ashurst involved heavily with the Premier League and the development of the Academy system throughout his region. He now works as a Premier League match assessor.

CHARLTON, JACK OBE
October 1977 - May 1983

While Len Ashurst laid the foundations it was Jack Charlton who finally dragged the Owls out of the lower leagues and took them to the brink of the top-flight. It was thought a real coup when Bert McGee persuaded Charlton to come out of virtual retirement to take over at struggling Wednesday in 1977 as 'Big Jack' was a high profile personality in the football world and did not really need the stresses of football management – since resigning after a highly successful spell as Middlesbrough manager he had combined his love of fishing and shooting with lucrative appearances as a TV pundit and an 'after dinner' speaker.

The plain speaking and articulate Charlton was born in Ashington on 8 May 1935 and along with his younger brother Bobby would go on to enjoy a tremendous record as a player which included various club honours and memorably England's World Cup win in 1966. As a player 6ft 2ins Jack was nicknamed 'giraffe' but his career almost stalled before it had begun as when 15 year-old Jack was working down his local pit he turned down a trial with Leeds United due to homesickness. Thankfully he was given a second chance and duly signed professional forms for United in May 1952, making his league debut at the age of 17 against Doncaster Rovers in April 1953. It was just the start of a tremendous career that saw Charlton develop into one of the finest central defenders of his generation, amassing a mammoth 629 appearances for his only league club and winning 35 full caps for England. Shortly after joining United he underwent National Service in Germany and it was not until John Charles departed for Juventus in 1957 that Charlton became a first team regular. His outspoken nature saw Jack become the player's union representative at Elland Road, when the PFA was formed in the early 1960s, and he quickly fell out with new manager Don Revie. However the pair sorted out their differences and while Revie was at the helm Charlton helped United to promotion from Division Two in 1964 and won his first England cap in April 1965. He and Bobby became the first brothers to play together for England in the Twentieth Century and of course enjoyed the finest moment of their career in July 1966 when both played in the 4-2 win over West Germany at Wembley that secured the World Cup for England. A year after the victory Jack was named 'Footballer of the Year' and added a First Division

Championship medal in 1969 when Leeds were crowned Champions of England for the first time in their history – he also won two F.A.Cups, one Fairs Cup and one League Cup while at Elland Road. Incidentally he was suspended for a time in the late 1960s after admitting he kept a little black book in which he entered the names of difficult opposition players who he intended to exact revenge upon in the future!!

When he was offered the manager's job at Second Division Middlesbrough in May 1973 he decided it was time to retire and he would enjoy an incredible first season in charge – running away with the Championship to such an extent that Boro were promoted with still eight games of the season remaining. One of those eight games was an 8-0 thrashing of Wednesday at Ayresome Park and during his remaining years at Boro he stabilised the club in the top-flight and reached the last eight of the F.A.Cup in 1975 and the semi finals of the League Cup a year later. His charges did win the Anglo-Scottish Cup but in April 1977 he resigned from his post, stating that he needed a rest from the game after 25 years. When, and if, Charlton returned to management it was expected he would secure a post in the higher echelons of the English game so it was a surprise when it was rumoured that Charlton was in the running for the vacant position at Hillsborough. He duly attended the home game with Chesterfield on 8 October 1977, seeing Wednesday gain their first win of the season, but it was the crowd's reaction to his appearance in the stands that persuaded Jack to accept the job after the full time whistle.

His first task was to pull the club away from the foot of the division, after appointing John Harris as his assistant, and this he duly achieved with the Owls finishing in 14th place after losing only three times in their final 22 games. Unsurprisingly, considering his playing career, Charlton built from the back and although his early months at the club did not provide much entertainment for the long suffering fans it was a medicine that needed to be administered and a dour Owls side drew 19 times in finishing just below mid-table in 1979 – the season mainly being remembered for a remarkable F.A.Cup marathon with eventual winners Arsenal that stretched to five games and perhaps showed that the side Jack was building was slowly starting to take shape. His restructuring of the side certainly bore fruit in the following season as with the likes of Terry Curran, Andy McCulloch, Jeff King & Ian Mellor in the side the Owls enjoyed a tremendous second half of the season – starting with the famous Boxing Day win over United – and eventually finished third to secure promotion back to football's second tier. The club also made a big mark in their first season back in Division Two and were in the hunt for an unlikely promotion until falling away late in the campaign. The addition of Gary Bannister, Gary Megson and Gary Shelton turned the Owls into one of the most entertaining sides in the division and Wednesday agonisingly missed out on promotion again in 1982 – if the points system had not been altered to three points for a win in the previous summer the Owls would have beaten Norwich City to the third promotion place! A year later Charlton led Wednesday to the semi-final of the F.A.Cup but he had always stated that five years at one club was long enough for any manager so it was perhaps not really a shock when after six years at the helm he resigned in May 1983, after having dragged the club from backwaters of the lower leagues.

After leaving Hillsborough Charlton decided to take a complete break from the game and returned to management in March 1984 when he was briefly caretaker boss back at his old club Middlesbrough. He then spent a relatively unsuccessful fourteen months at Newcastle United which ended in August 1985 after he was barracked by the crowd and the club directors tried to sign a player he did not want. His resignation looked like the end for Charlton's managerial career as he vowed he would never return to full-time club management. However in February 1986 he was approached by the F.A. of Ireland, in relation to the vacant position of Eire manager and the offer of a part-time position proved too good for Jack to resist. It proved a match made in heaven as Jack trawled birth records to take advantage of new FIFA eligibility rules, introducing a variety of born and bred Englishmen such as John Aldridge and Chris Houghton plus Scot Ray Houghton. When mixed with Irish born players he produced a direct side that brought unprecedented success to Irish National football and made sure Jack would never have to buy another Guinness in Ireland! He became feted in Southern Ireland after leading the side to the European Championship Finals for the first time in their history – famously beating England during the 1988 tournament in Holland – and went one better two years later as Ireland qualified for their first World Cup Finals. They went all the way to the Quarter-Finals in 1990, before bowing out by a solitary goal to hosts Italy, but gained revenge four years later when beating the Italians in US 94 prior to being knocked out in the second round. After the finals Jack was made a Freeman of Dublin – in recognition of services to Irish sport – and he resigned in 1995 to retire back to his native Northeast. He now lives out his retirement in Ponteland, near Newcastle, although he is still a regular on the after dinner circuit and is much in demand at company seminars for his powerful motivational speeches. He remains one of the best raconteurs in the sporting world and is a much-loved figure both home and abroad.

WILKINSON, HOWARD
June 1983 - October 1988

See players section

EUSTACE, PETER
October 1988 - February 1989

- See players section

ATKINSON, Ronald Frederick 'RON'
February 1989 - June 1991 & November 1997 - May 1998

When high profile manager Ron Atkinson walked into Hillsborough on 15 February 1989 he was like a breath of fresh air to Owls fans after the disastrous rein of Peter Eustace. The flamboyant Atkinson - nicknamed 'Big Ron' by fans and media alike – made an immediate impact by selling Mel Sterland and then breaking the Owls transfer record to bring Carlton Palmer to Hillsborough. He joined an Owls side in real relegation trouble but the addition of a few experienced heads ensured survival and subsequently resulted in Atkinson penning a new one-year deal before the final home match of the season. The new manager had a reputation for playing entertaining and attractive football and over the next twelve months slowly moulded a side that contained such talents as John Sheridan, Roland Nilsson & Dalian Atkinson. However despite the quality of football improving ten fold from the dark days of late 1980s the Owls were dealt a grievous blow when Atkinson's side lost five of their final six games of the 1989-90 season and were disastrously relegated on the final afternoon. At that point Atkinson's future seemed in doubt but once he vowed to take the club back into the big time at the first attempt a roller coaster journey began that would see the Owls enjoy one of the greatest seasons of their long history. The Owls started the season playing an exciting brand of attacking football and did not lose their first game until late October, becoming established in the top three where they remained for the majority of a campaign that ended in promotion. However Atkinson – who won three manager of the month accolades - not only led the club back into the big time but he also to Wembley where his underdogs gloriously beat Manchester United to win the club's only major domestic post war trophy.

There is no doubt Atkinson was at the peak of his managerial powers and was truly adored by the club's followers who could see Wednesday had appointed one of most inspirational manager's in their history. Success looked set to follow success but on the final day of May in 1991 Owls fans were hit with a bombshell when 'Big Ron' sensationally walked out after being offered the job of managing his boyhood side Aston Villa. Distraught Wednesday supporters besieged the ground and on an emotional afternoon there were celebrations all round when Chairman Dave Richards persuaded 'Big Ron' to stay. Sadly it proved only a stay of execution as six days later Atkinson left for good with anger and betrayal the only emotions felt by heartbroken fans. His return on the opening day of the following season with Villa saw Atkinson receive an understandably hostile reception and fans were left to wonder what could have been as what was effectively Atkinson's side just missed out on the 1992 League Championship. In later years Atkinson would admit he made a mistake in leaving Hillsborough as despite winning the League Cup with Villa in 1994 he could not bring sustained glory to Villa Park and eventually moved to Coventry City as manager in February 1995. Eighteen months later he was appointed 'Director of Football' at the Highfield Road club and was instrumental in persuading former Wednesday hero Roland Nilsson to make a surprise return to English football. He left City in June 1997 but his next destination was a real surprise as he returned to Hillsborough after Wednesday had dispensed with the services of David Pleat. After being appointed, on a contract until the end of the season, on 14 November 1997 he received a mixed reception from fans but quickly won over the doubters by inspiring a four game winning streak that lifted the club out of the bottom three and ultimately secured Premier League football at the end of the season. He showed he had lost none of his skill in the transfer market – buying virtual unknown Niclas Alexandersson for a bargain fee and giant Brazilian Emerson Thome on a free transfer – but there was a further twist in the tale of the Atkinson years at Wednesday as in May 1998 the Owls announced they would not be renewing his contract and his reign came to an abrupt halt. After undertaking various media work 'Big Ron' came back into the game in January 1999 when he was appointed manager at struggling Nottingham Forest but he could not work his legendary magic this time and after Forest were relegated from the Premier League he left in June 1999. His spell at the City Ground brought his managerial career to a close as Atkinson then carved out a successful career as a TV pundit and match summariser. Sadly this ended in April 2004 when he sacked from commercial TV after an off the air comment and he now lives out his retirement in his Midlands home.

Although born in Liverpool on 18 March 1939 it was in Birmingham that Atkinson spent his formative years, first playing football for his Lea Village school team. After completing his studies he gained employment in local industry and after impressing for his B.S.A. Tools works side in the Birmingham League Atkinson was signed as a part-time professional by Aston Villa. Unfortunately he failed to make the grade at Villa Park and it required a move to non-league Headington United in July 1959 to kick-start his career. He remained at the Manor Ground for twelve years – playing alongside his brother Graham - and became an automatic choice at half back, as the club changed their name to Oxford United and were elected into the Football League. During a total of 384 appearances for Oxford he also helped them to promotion from Division Three in 1965 and then the Third Division title in 1968 before a brief spell at Witney Town preceded his first taste of management – as player-boss at Kettering Town. During three years at Kettering he led the club to two League Championships and was soon elevated to League soccer when Cambridge United appointed him boss in November 1974. The Third Division title followed in 1977 but it was his spell as West Brom boss that would elevate Atkinson into the top echelon of English managers. He took over at the Hawthorns in January 1978 and produced one of most entertaining sides in the club's history with the likes of Laurie Cunningham, Cyrille Regis & Bryan Robson taking the Baggies into the last eight of the UEFA Cup in 1979 and several top six finishes in the top-flight. He earned a reputation as a bejewelled big spending manager at Old Trafford and won the F.A.Cup in 1983 and 1985. However it was League and European success that the Old Trafford fans craved for and ironically it was Wednesday who played a part in his eventual downfall when they became the first side to beat United after the Red Devils had made a flying start to the 1985-86 season - they ended the season with nothing and Atkinson was sacked for the first time in his career in November 1986. He returned for a second spell as West Brom manager in September 1987 but controversially walked only six weeks later when offered a £250,000 per annum post at Spanish club Atletico Madrid. Incredibly he lasted only 96 days in Spain and then took a break from the game before making a comeback at Wednesday.

FRANCIS, TREVOR
June 1991 – May 1995

See players section

PLEAT, David John
June 1995 – November 1997

Born in Nottingham on 15 January 1945, David Pleat began his football career as a trainee at local club Nottingham Forest and showed great promise when earning England Schoolboy and Youth caps. However he would start only six senior games for Forest before a £6,000 fee took Pleat to Fourth Division Luton Town. He had the misfortune to break his leg in his first season but recovered to play for Shrewsbury Town, Exeter City and Peterborough United before joining non-league Nuneaton Borough as player-manager in 1971. A year later he returned to Luton Town as coach, after a spell of unemployment, and over the next few years fulfilled a variety of roles at Kenilworth Road while also briefly working as a freelance journalist. He was promoted to chief coach by manager Harry Haslam and was appointed Luton manager when Haslam took over as Sheffield United boss in January 1978. It was the start of an eight-year tenure as Hatters boss, which earned Pleat the reputation as one of the brightest young managers in the English game. After taking Luton to the Second Division Championship in 1982 he then successfully fought several battles against relegation – his be-suited manic run across the Maine Road pitch to hug his players in delight (when Luton won to stay in the division) being one of the abiding memories of the decade. After taking Town to their highest ever league placing – ninth in the top-flight - he was appointed Tottenham manager in May 1986 and enjoyed a memorable first season where his attractive style won praise from fans and critics alike. A five-man midfield formation was a definite change from the norm but with attacking players in all positions Pleat took Spurs to third in the league, the 1987 F.A.Cup Final and the last four of the League Cup. However the season ended with no silverware in the White Hart Lane trophy cabinet and Pleat was unfortunately unable to continue his bright start at Spurs after newspaper revelations about his private life, in October 1987, forced him out of the club. He was quickly back in football when being handed the reins at Leicester City in December 1987 but despite spending heavily he could not find that elusive winning formula and was shown the door in January 1991, with City on the brink of a disastrous relegation into the Third Division for the first time in their history. He returned to Luton as boss in June 1991 and introduced an attacking style of play that was reminiscent of his first spell with the Bedfordshire club. However finances were tight and as his better players were sold the Hatters dropped out of the First Division and then only just avoided a second consecutive relegation.

Town finished the 1994-95 season in the lower half of the First Division so it was therefore a surprise to many when it was announced he would replace Trevor Francis as manager at Premier League Wednesday. He was officially appointed on 14 June 1995 but Luton chairman David Kohler immediately obtained a court injunction to stop Pleat working as the respective clubs haggled over a compensation fee – Wednesday offering £100,000 and Luton demanding three times that figure. The court case was eventually dropped when the Owls agreed to take the matter to an F.A. arbitration panel and Wednesday were ordered to pay £150,000 plus costs for Pleat's services. His reputation as an honest, deep thinking and media friendly manager no doubt counted in his favour and Pleat made some excellent captures in his first few months at Hillsborough – signing Marc Degryse, Dejan Stefanovic & Darko Kovacevic. However results were poor and he struggled to establish a rapport with Owls fans as the club just escaped relegation on the final day of the 1995-96 season. Fortunes turned around completely at the start of the following campaign as Wednesday won their first four games to top the Premier League for the only time and the Owls just missed out on a UEFA Cup place when finishing in seventh place. He brought more players of undoubted quality to Hillsborough – the club record purchase of Paulo Di Canio being arguably his best capture – but his side always seemed more a team of individuals than a cohesive unit and the writing was on the wall when Wednesday slumped to the foot of the table in early Autumn 1997. He was duly sacked on 2 November - after a 6-1 loss at Manchester United – but was soon back in work when being handed the role of 'Director of Football' back at Tottenham. He stayed at Spurs until being replaced in July 2004 and after a short spell out of the game was appointed advisor to new Portsmouth manager Alain Perrin in April 2005.

WILSON, Daniel 'DANNY'
July 1998 – March 2000

See players section

JEWELL, PAUL
June 2000 – February 2001

The reign of Paul Jewell as Owls manager was certainly a case of 'right man at the wrong time' as before arriving at Hillsborough he had achieved remarkable success at Bradford City and after leaving Wednesday guided unfashionable Wigan into the Premiership. As a player Jewell had started as a trainee at home town club Liverpool but after failing to make the grade his league debut came at Wigan Athletic where the striker remained for four seasons, netting 35 times in 137 league games for the Latics. An £80,000 transfer to Bradford City followed in July 1988 and Jewell became a real crowd favourite in West Yorkshire where he ended his playing career after 53 goals in 251 games. When Chris Kamara was sacked in December 1998 it was Jewell who stepped into his shoes and he achieved immediate success as six months later City gained promotion to the Premier League for the first time in their history. His charges were tipped for immediate relegation but against the odds Jewell made City competitive and a dramatic last day Valley Parade win over Liverpool secured another season of Premier League football. However Jewell would not be at the helm as a disagreement with chairman Geoffrey Richmond saw him walk out, joining the Owls three days later on 21 June 2000.

It's highly likely that Jewell was unaware of the problems he would immediately encounter at Wednesday as the Owls were newly relegated from the top-flight and were already starting to show the first signs of financial strife. It was a poor Wednesday side that had fallen from the higher grade and with little or no money for Jewell to spend he was faced with an uphill struggle before the first ball was kicked. The likeable Scouser tried to stem the tide but an injury crisis and a club record run of eight consecutive league defeats put the club firmly in the First Division relegation zone and after a 4-1 beating at Wimbledon he was sacked on 12 February 2001 with the Owls bottom of the league. Four months later he was back in a job at ambitious Wigan Athletic who backed by the millions of JJB entrepreneur Dave Whelan were aiming to move swiftly through the divisions. He achieved immediate success as Wigan walked away with the 2003 Second Division title – amassing 100 points in the process – and then only a last minute goal on the final day of the 2003-04 season denied them a place in the First Division play offs. He went one better a year later when taking Wigan into the Premier League and became firmly established as the most successful manager in the club's relatively short league history.

SHREEVES, Peter
February 2001 – October 2001

After the short tenure of Paul Jewell the Owls initially appointed the vastly experienced Peter Shreeves on a caretaker basis. It was the third time in temporary charge for the Welshman as back in November 1997 he had been at the helm for a single game – a 5-0 home win over Bolton – between the reigns of David Pleat and Ron Atkinson. He had originally been appointed as first team coach by David Pleat in June 1996 – moving from a similar role at Chelsea – but left by mutual consent in September 1998 before returning to Hillsborough in February 2000, when being appointed as temporary replacement for the dismissed Danny Wilson. When Jewell was appointed as manager Shreeves was handed the No. 2 role, albeit on a temporary three-month contract, before signing a three-year contract in August 2000. When he took over from Jewell in February 2001 the Owls were in desperate trouble at the foot of the First Division but with the help of two inspirational signings – Trond Soltvedt and Carlton Palmer – Shreeves hauled the Owls to safety, winning the March 2001 'Manager of the Month' accolade.

He was rewarded on 4 May 2001 with a two-year contract as Wednesday's permanent manager but a poor start to the new season immediately saw the Owls in trouble and with resources severely limited the likeable Shreeves found himself operating with both hands tied behind his back. A 2-1 home defeat to Preston in mid-October saw Wednesday slump to one place off the bottom of the division and Shreeves decided it was best for all parties concerned by resigning from his position on 17 October 2001. He later spent time as manager of Conference club Barnet, resigning in March 2003, and is now one of twenty men recruited to a delegate team that attends Premier League games to report on referees, the behaviour of players and coaches plus aspects of ground security.

Although born in the South Wales village of Neath on 30 November 1940, Peter Shreeves was your archetypical Londoner as his mother had been evacuated to Wales during the Blitz of World World Two and soon returned for Shreeves to spend his formative years in Islington. As a player he started his career at amateur club Finchley, before appearing in 113 league games for Reading, and then played for Southern League clubs Chelmsford City and Wimbledon. His coaching career began at Charlton Athletic in 1974 and he was later youth coach, reserve team manager and assistant manager at Tottenham before being appointed manager in June 1984, taking over from Keith Burkinshaw. His best season in charge saw Shreeves take Spurs to third place in the top-flight but he left in March 1986, joining Queens Park Rangers as coach a few months later. He was briefly manager again at Spurs in the early 1990s and when he arrived at Hillsborough in 1996 had been part-time assistant manager for the Welsh national team for several years.

YORATH, Terry
October 2001 – October 2002

Former Welsh international Terry Yorath was first appointed to the Owls coaching staff by Paul Jewell in June 2000 and was subsequently appointed assistant manager to Peter Shreeves when Jewell was dismissed in February 2001. He signed a new two-year deal when Shreeves was confirmed as Wednesday boss in the summer of 2001 and on 17 October 2001 was named caretaker manager when Shreeves became another casualty of the Owls struggles. A month later Yorath was confirmed as manager for the remainder of the season, persuading highly-rated Manchester City coach Willie Donachie to act as his assistant. Under Yorath the Owls fortunes initially improved and a point on the final day of the season secured First Division football for another year. However Wednesday started the new campaign badly and by October 2002 the club was back in the bottom three and as pressure mounted he tendered his resignation, leaving Hillsborough on 31 October 2002.

As a player Yorath was best remembered for a period at Leeds United where the flame haired and fiery midfielder appeared in 197 games and became a regular for Wales – he totalled 59 caps in his career and captained the side in the majority of those games. He moved to Coventry City in 1976 – after winning the league title with Leeds in 1974 - and later enjoyed spells at Tottenham and Canadian club Vancover Whitecaps prior to being appointed player-coach at Bradford City in 1982. During a successful spell as Swansea City manager – winning promotion in 1988 – Yorath was appointed part-time Wales manager but caused uproar when he controversially walked out on the Swans in February 1989 to take over back at Bradford City. Arguably his time as Wales boss were the best years of his managerial career as with Peter Shreeves at his side Yorath steered the principality to within a whisker of qualification for both Euro 92 and the 1994 World Cup Finals in the US. Sadly for Yorath he suffered personal tragedy in 1992 when his teenage son – a trainee at Leeds United - died of a hitherto unknown heart condition. His daughter, Gabby, is of course a familiar face as the front girl for much of ITV's soccer output.

After a second spell as manager back at Swansea City he then took over the reins of Lebanon before coaching back in the UK at Huddersfield Town and Bradford City (again). He resigned from his post at Valley Parade to join Wednesday and is now assistant manager at Huddersfield Town – being appointed to the role in June 2003.

TURNER, Christopher 'CHRIS'
November 2002 - September 2004

See players section

STURROCK, PAUL Whitehead
September 2004 - present

When Paul Sturrock was appointed successor to Chris Turner on 23 September 2004 not even the most optimistic Owls fan would have believed that just over eight months later Wednesday would be promoted to the Championship. However this was the incredible feat achieved by the likable Scot as he inspired, cajoled, motivated and totally revitalised a playing personal that had struggled to deliver in the early stages of the season, effectively costing Turner his job. With the help of assistant Kevin Summerfield and defensive coach John Blackley the straight talking Sturrock re-shaped the Owls style of play, introducing a more direct and attack minded formation, and the changes paid immediate dividends as Wednesday surged into the play off places thanks to a tremendous run of form either side of the Christmas period. The loan signings of both Kenwyne Jones and Joey O'Brien proved a masterstroke by the new manager and Wednesday briefly threatened to catch the top two before falling away over the Easter period. A late season wobble looked to have ruined the Owls chances but when Sturrock asked his players for one last courageous display they delivered – a dramatic last minute winner at Hull City in late April ensuring Sturrock had already exceeded expectations by leading the club into the play offs. However Sturrock, who was quickly becoming a huge favourite with the long suffering Owls fans, was not finished yet as two wins over Brentford secured a trip to Cardiff and the League One play off final against Hartlepool United. Most of the 40,000 strong travelling support dared not believe that promotion could be achieved but for once Wednesday delivered and on a glorious day Sturrock led his side to the Championship in a quite remarkable first season at the helm.

The almost instant success at Wednesday contrasted greatly with his previous post at Southampton where he sensationally left by mutual consent after just two games of the 2004-05 season. In total Sturrock was in charge for only thirteen games at the St Mary's Stadium and no doubt will relish a return next season as Wednesday and the Saints meet on level terms. That ill-fated spell with Southampton followed a tremendous run of success with Plymouth which had seen the Home Park club move from the bottom division to the brink of the Championship. He took the reins in October 2000 and eighteen months later Argyle had won the old Third Division with a record points haul of 102 with Sturrock named Nationwide manager of the season. After a season of consolidation Plymouth completed a double over Wednesday on the way to the Second Division title in 2004 - a scintillating display at Hillsborough leaving the Owls a well beaten side. Sturrock had actually left for Southampton before his side clinched promotion – ironically his final match in charge came against Wednesday at Home Park – but he is rightly recognised as the man who inspired the Pilgrims to two promotions inside four seasons.

Born in the small Aberdeenshire village of Ellon on 10 October 1956, Paul Sturrock started his successful playing career with junior club Bankfoot Juniors before signing apprentice forms for Dundee United in July 1973. He turned professional in the following year and would go on to achieve legendary status with the Tannadice club, appearing in a mammoth 571 league & cup games and netting 170 goals before retiring in May 1989. During that period Sturrock – affectionately nicknamed 'Luggy' – matured into one of the best strikers in the Scottish game and led United to the League title in 1983. He had already won the first of 20 full caps for Scotland and was in the outstanding United side that reached the European Cup semi-final in 1984 and the final of the UEFA Cup in 1987 – recording a sensational win in the Nou Camp against Barcelona before losing narrowly against IFK Gothenburg. He also won two League Cups while in Dundee colours before moving onto the club's coaching staff after injury forced his early retirement from the game. His first managerial appointment came with St Johnstone in August 1993, leading the Saints to the Division One title in 1987, before returning to Tannadice as boss in September 1998. Within two seasons he moved to the South West to start a career South of the Border, which five years later would see Sturrock finally wake the sleeping giant that was dozing in the backwaters of League One.

CHAIRMEN

1899-2005

Since the club became a limited company in 1899 a total of thirteen men have been elected Chairman of the Board. The following are brief biographies of the men who have led the club through good and bad times:

SENIOR, Alderman George 1899-1915

The first ever Sheffield Wednesday club Chairman, George Senior was a self made man who rose from a humble background to become Lord Mayor of Sheffield. He was described as a man of "undoubted energy, enterprise & sterling integrity" who during his tenure at Hillsborough also served as master cutler – he was prominent in the Sheffield forging history. He presided over a tremendous period of success at Wednesday as they successfully adapted to life at their new ground and then won back-to-back league titles in 1903 and 1904 prior to F.A.Cup success in 1907. The Owls were still one of the top sides in the English game when Senior passed away, aged 77, in 1915.

CLEGG, Sir John Charles 1915-1931
(b. 15.06.1850 Sheffield, d. 26.06.37 Sheffield)

WEDNESDAY 1870/ Perseverance 1871-73/ Norfolk 1872/ Sheffield Club 1871-79/ Surrey 1873/ Broomhall 1873-75/ Sheffield Albion 1875-80

Of all the great administrators to have served the Owls, Charles Clegg was not only a giant in Sheffield football but also virtually a National Institution that towered over the English game for in excess of fifty years. Along with his brother, William, he was a dominant figure in his early days as a player – appearing for England in their first ever International match (against Scotland in 1872). A year later he played in the first ever F.A.Cup tie played by a team from the city (Sheffield Club) and then took part in the first ever inter-association game – appearing for Sheffield against Glasgow in 1874. In addition to football he achieved great fame as an amateur on the running track, winning a 120-yard handicap race in 1870 when starting from scratch. On several occasions he was known to run 100 yards in under ten seconds and once on three successive afternoons won a total of 15 races, including two Championship finals! He also won tournaments with his tennis racket and was a keen rugby player. As a footballer he first appeared for Wednesday back in 1869 – often playing alongside his brother – but it was his off the field achievements that saw Clegg become one of the most eminent figures in British football.

While still only in his early thirties Charles was elected President of the Sheffield & Hallamshire Association – astonishingly serving for in excess of 50 years – while he emerged as one of the game's top referees, officiating in the 1882 and 1892 F.A.Cup Finals in addition to England v Scotland in 1886. No big local game in the latter part of the Nineteenth Century did not see either Charles or William in the middle while the former continued to rise in status off the field, being elected to the F.A. Council in 1886. Three years later he was appointed vice-Chairman and finally in 1890 he reached the pinnacle of the English game – Chairman of the Football Association. He would remain at the apex of the game for an amazing 47 years and in 1923 was also voted President while in 1927 he was knighted "for services to the Board of Trade and the Ministry of Labour" - political speak for his contribution to football in both social and economical terms.

Throughout his life Clegg was fiercely against professionalism – he played sport for the sheer enjoyment while working alongside William as a lawyer at his father's eminent Sheffield practice – but after bowing to the inevitable he presided over England's growth as the World power in the game. He counted senior politicians and even the King himself as personal acquaintances while his integrity was never in question – he was oft quoted with the saying "Nobody ever got lost on a straight road". His tenure as Owls Chairman started when he filled the void left by George Senior's death in 1915 and Clegg was at the helm when Bob Brown took the Owls to consecutive league titles in 1930. He then resigned the chair – being appointed President - but remained involved at local and national level well into his 80s. In addition to serving the Owls he was also President of the Sheffield United cricket and Football Club while he was a board member for the Blades and later Chairman. If his football activities did not take enough of his time Clegg was also a Justice of the Peace and had enjoyed a full and rewarding life when he finally passed away, aged 87, in 1937 – a memorial being erected in the Wednesday boardroom to honour his service to the English game.

TURNER, William G. O.B.E. 1931-44

When his father, counsellor William Turner, died in 1906 it was his son of the same name who took his place on the Wednesday board of directors. He served the Owls solely in that capacity for 25 years until being chosen as Chairman in 1931, when Charles Clegg became president. Before being appointed to the position he had already been awarded an O.B.E. for his work on munitions in the Great War while he was held in great esteem in the Sheffield business community as a senior partner in William Turner & Co. – a nickel and silver merchants who were founded by his father. Under his guidance the Owls won the F.A.Cup in 1935 while away from football Turner was an active freemason and member of the institute of metals. He was also president of the Sheffield branch of the British War Graves commission and led several pilgrimages to France after the First World War. He retired as Wednesday chairman in July 1944 – at the age of 75 – and was immediately elected President, remaining so until his death at the age of 77 on 18th May 1947.

FEARNEHOUGH, William 1944-53

The Fearnehough family held strong links with Wednesday for several decades as Walter Fearnehough - father of William – was a founder member of The Wednesday football section back in 1867 and not only helped saved the club from extinction in the 1880s but then made the move to Olive Grove possible. William's brother, Whiteley, was also a board member for many years so it was no surprise when William was voted onto the board in October 1910. Like the majority of his fellow board members William was a prominent businessman in the Sheffield area while also serving as a magistrate when called upon. He was elected to the chair in July 1944 and helped the club return to peacetime football, winning promotion from Division Two in 1950. Relegation and then another promotion followed before he sadly passed away on one of the most traumatic days in the history of Sheffield Wednesday, 14th February 1953. The club Chairman died at the age of 74 on the morning of a game at Preston North End, where a few hours later the career of Derek Dooley tragically ended.

LONGDEN, James 1953-54

James Longden was the owner of Longden's Builders in Sheffield and joined the Wednesday board in 1936, stepping up to vice-chairman in July 1944 when George Senior retired as chairman. He was a member of the F.A.Council and President of Sheffield amateur side Hallam FC. Unfortunately his tenure as Owls Chairman was relatively brief as after being appointed on 5th March 1953 the big-hearted sportsman died suddenly in May of the following year.

CRAIG, Colonel R.L. 1954-55

Following the sudden death of James Londgen the baton passed to Colonel Craig whose father, Donald, and brother, Dudley, had both served on the club's board of directors. He was appointed to the chair in July 1954 but after just ten months he was forced to resign, after a long illness, on May 7th 1955 – just a few days after Wednesday had suffered relegation from the top-flight.

STEPHEN Sir Andrew 1955-73

Doctor Andrew Stephen would follow in the footsteps of his predecessor Charles Clegg when rising to Chairman of the Football Association, after giving sterling service at Hillsborough. The Scot had moved to Sheffield from Aberdeenshire in the early 1930s and was subsequently appointed the Owls medical officer on New Year's Day 1937. However he was voted onto the board of directors in March 1949 following the death of A. Francis and stepped up to vice-chairman in July 1954. When Colonel Craig resigned Stephen was appointed chairman on 16th May 1955 and along side Eric Taylor the duo would develop Hillsborough into one of England's best grounds while establishing Wednesday as Championship contenders in the early 1960s. The bribes scandal that rocked the club in April 1964 was certainly a bitter blow to the honourable Dr Stephen who was famously quoted in the local press as saying "I would rather see Sheffield Wednesday relegated to Division Four than be involved in anything shady".

He was elected F.A. chairman in January 1967 and remained in the position until 1976 – being knighted for his services to the game in June 1972. The 1970s were certainly not kind to the Owls and with the club slipping deeper into financial troubles - in addition to sliding down the divisions - Stephen decided to resign as chairman in December 1973. He accepted a vice-president role in January 1974 and passed away in 1980.

SHEPPARD, Matt 1973-76

There is no doubt the rein of Matt Shepard was the most controversial of any Wednesday chairman. He was initially appointed to the board in April 1971, causing a storm of protest from the rebel shareholders association who were angry that none of their members had been considered. However he will always be associated with the events of Christmas Eve 1973 – just 18 days after he had taken over as chairman from Sir Andrew Stephen - when Owls legend Derek Dooley was sensationally sacked from his position as team manager. The timing and nature of the dismissal was roundly criticised and it would be almost twenty years before Dooley set foot in Hillsborough again, such was his bitterness to the Wednesday regime. Unfortunately Sheppard's ascent to the chair, aged 49, coincided with probably the worst three back-to-back seasons in the history of the club as the local JP and chartered accountant had to cope with a worsening financial position and quite appalling results on the pitch.

Brought up in Firth Park, Sheppard was a born and bred Wednesdayite who first came into contact with the Owls on a professional basis when working for the club's auditors as a youngster. He later became advisor and club accountant to the Owls before the self made man (he was the son of a steel works maintenance foreman) was co-opted onto the board of directors at Hillsborough. Away from football he became a financial advisor, connected with several firms in a variety of industries, as a director and in some instances chairman. His tenure as Owls supremo came to an end on 26 September 1975 when he dropped down to vice-chairman to allow Bert McGee to take the chair. Soon after Sheppard resigned from the board completely, citing "pressure of business" as the main reason for his decision.

McGEE, Herbert E. 'Bert' 1975-90

When life long Wednesday fan Bert McGee took the Hillsborough reins in 1975 he found a club almost on its knees and close to financial ruin. Thankfully for Wednesday he proved the man for a crisis and is widely credited – along with his first managerial appointment Jack Charlton – with pulling the club around both on and off the pitch during his near fifteen years in the Wednesday chair. Like so many of his predecessors McGee was a man who had risen from humble beginnings to became a major player in the Sheffield business community – he had started his working life as an apprentice engineer after leaving Sheffield based Central secondary school.

Born in Hillsborough on 11 August 1917 his earliest memory of watching Wednesday came back in 1926 when Newcastle legend Hughie Gallagher scored past Owls keeper Jack Brown at Hillsborough while Wednesday blood certainly ran through his veins as McGee's father, Bernard, suffered a heart attack while stood on the Hillsborough terraces. His dad would live for only a few months more, before dying aged 48 in 1931, which meant the young Bert had to give up his dream of being a doctor to leave school and get a job in order to support his family. However he quickly made a success of his secondary career and rose from works manager to chairman/managing director at tool cutting company Presto Tools – turning the Penistone Road firm into one of Sheffield's most successful businesses. His rise meant he followed in the footsteps of the Owls first chairman, George Senior, by being appointed master cutler in 1980. The widely travelled and shrewd businessman also held strong links with Sheffield University and the Chamber of Commerce and joined the Owls board in December 1973, just a week after Sir Andrew Stephen had resigned as chairman.

He duly stepped up to vice-chairman in March 1975 and was then at the helm as Wednesday won promotion from Division Three in 1980 and reclaimed their place in the top-flight four years later. During his time as chairman McGee made the Owls a profitable entity but in his latter years was criticised for his tight rein on the Hillsborough purse strings – many critics believing a lack of funding directly led to Howard Wilkinson's resignation in 1988. The Hillsborough disaster proved a moment of personal sadness for McGee and in March 1990 he resigned from the board, allowing more time for his other passion of golf, before passing away on 29 April 1995, aged 77.

RICHARDS, Dave 1990-2000

When Walkley steelworker's son Dave Richards was elected chairman in March 1990 at the age of 46 he was not only a surprise choice to supporters but to Richards himself, saying at the time "when my colleagues on the board invited me to succeed to Bert McGee I was absolutely flabbergasted". The managing director of Three Star Engineering – the fourth of seven children - became the youngest chairman in the Owls history after having only been on the board since the previous October. Sheffield born Richards had started his working life as an apprentice at H.Kirk & Sons, after leaving Burgoyne School in 1958, and in 1970 joined Three Star Engineering (who were then based in Chesterfield) as general manager. He then rose through the ranks and was instrumental in their relocation to purpose built premises in Attercliffe. The reign of the diminutive Richards started badly as the Owls suffered relegation from the top-flight just two months after he was handed the chair. However a glorious season followed as the Hillsborough purse strings were loosened and Ron Atkinson's side achieved league and cup glory. The manager's subsequent defection to Villa Park – after Richards had seemingly persuaded him to stay – was a grievous blow but under Trevor Francis Wednesday enjoyed their best spell since the early 1960s with the club transfer record broken on several occasions.

The South Stand development was also a major ground improvement during his time at the helm but unfortunately for Richards an ill-advised partnership with finance house Charterhouse proved a failure and then a succession of poor managers and bad buys saw Wednesday struggle to retain their Premier League place. The big spending would eventually come back to haunt Wednesday though, plunging the club into a financial crisis that shows no sign of abating over five years later. His appointment as Premier League chairman in April 1999 – he had been elected the F.A.Council in May 1994 – led to criticism from some quarters in Sheffield with regard to his commitment to the Owls and he eventually resigned as Owls chairman on 12th February 2000. He was immediately appointed full-time chairman of the F. A. Premier League, a position he still holds today..

CULLEY, Howard 2000-01

A prominent solicitor with Sheffield based firm Irwin Mitchell, Howard Culley spent just over a year as Sheffield Wednesday chairman. The life long Owls fan had originally joined the Wednesday board in July 1995, replacing Ernest Barron, and was picked as the successor to Dave Richards on 12th February 2000. When Culley was elevated to chairman the Owls were already staring relegation from the Premier League in the face and the club's fortunes continued to wane during Culley's brief time at the helm. He would eventually resign on the same day that manager Paul Jewell was sacked and subsequently resigned from the board of directors in August 2001 to concentrate on his business interests.

HULLEY, Geoff 2001-03

When Ecclesfield born businessman Geoff Hulley was appointed Chairman in February 2001 he became, at the age of 70, the oldest man to be voted into the chair in the Owls history. He had supported the Owls since the age of five and spent his working life running the family ice cream and frozen foods business, only retiring when he was handed the Hillsborough reins. Within a month of being appointed he was one of a trio of directors who purchased the shares that had previously been owned by Charterhouse, these shares being gifted to fans organisation 'The Owls Trust' soon after. He had originally joined the board on 25 September 1980, replacing Roy Whitehead who had resigned in the summer, and remains on the board despite giving way to Dave Allen in June 2003. A keen golfer, Hulley can now claim almost 25 years service to Wednesday in the boardroom.

ALLEN, Dave 2003-

Current chairman Dave Allen is certainly unique as he is the only man who did not actively support Wednesday before joining the boardroom. He was initially invited into the club by Howard Culley to offer much needed business acumen as the club's debts started to spiral out of control. The self-made multi-millionaire duly became a non-executive director of both the football and plc board on 2nd June 2000 and quickly became a dominant figure behind the scenes at Hillsborough, being instrumental in the appointment of Chris Turner as manager in November 2002. Allen – the owner of the A & S Group, which boasts Owlerton Stadium and casinos Napoleons and Bonapartes amongst its portfolio – emerged as a single minded and determined figure in the Hillsborough boardroom and the Owls became indebted to Allen as Wednesday tried in vein to avoid relegation from the First Division. His draconian style certainly attracted its fair share of critics – supporters were banned and the Owls Trust became enemy rather than foe - and 2004 was dominated off the field by his P.R. battle with stalking horse Ken Bates. The former Chelsea supremo – backed by former chairman Dave Richards and ex-board member Joe Ashton - was involved in a war of words with Allen over several months which certainly had a de-stabilising effect on the club but eventually saw Bates give up the challenge in January 2005 and move up the M1 to buy out Championship strugglers Leeds United. A few months earlier Allen – who lives in Chesterfield and races homing pigeons as a hobby - had sacked Turner as Wednesday slumped into the lower half of League One and immediately appointed Paul Sturrock, an appointment that proved a masterstroke as the Scot forced Wednesday towards a play off place and subsequent promotion. He had taken over as chairman in June 2003 and has now certainly been bitten by the football bug, seeming determined to finish the job his way and drag Wednesday back up the divisions.

SHEFFIELD WEDNESDAY PLAYERS STATS - 1880-2005

Name		Lge. App	Lge. Sub	Lge. Goals	FAC App	FAC Sub	FAC Goals	FLC App	FLC Sub	FLC Goals	Euro App	Euro Sub	Euro Goals	Other App	Other Sub	Other Goals	TOTAL App	TOTAL Sub	TOTAL Goals
A																			
ADAMS	Steve	8	1												1		8	2	0
ADAMSON	Chris	1	1														1	1	0
AGOGO	Junior		2			1											0	3	0
ALEXANDERSSON	Niclas	73	2	8	8		2	4	1	2							85	3	12
ALJOFREE	Hasney	2												1			3	0	0
ALLAN	William	102			16												118	0	0
ALLEN	Jack	104		76	10		9										114	0	85
ANDERSON	Viv	60	11	8	8	2	2	10		1	3		2	2			83	13	13
ANSTISS	Harry	12		5													12	0	5
ANTHONY	Nudger				5		3										5	0	3
ANTOINE-CURIER	Mickael		1														0	1	0
ARANALDE	Zigor	1	1														1	1	0
ARMITAGE	Harry	3															3	0	0
ARMITAGE	Len	3															3	0	0
ARMSTRONG	Craig	29	6	1				3						2			34	6	1
ARMSTRONG	Harold	6															6	0	0
ARMSTRONG	James	7															7	0	0
ASHLEY	Jack	106		3	11												117	0	3
ATHERTON	Peter	214		9	18			16			3						251	0	9
ATKINSON	Dalian	38		10	2		1	3		3				2		1	45	0	15
AVEYARD	Walter	4		3	6		2										10	0	5
AYRES	George	26		11													26	0	11
B																			
BAILEY	Gavin											1					0	1	0
BAILEY	Ian	35			5			5									45	0	0
BAIRD	Walter	1															1	0	0
BAKER	Peter	11			1												12	0	0
BALL	Jack	132		90	3		4										135	0	94
BALLAGHER	John	3															3	0	0
BANNISTER	Gary	117	1	55	12		4	13		7							142	1	66
BANNISTER	Keith	75			3												78	0	0
BARGH	George	5															5	0	0
BARKER	Richard										1	1					1	1	0
BARRASS	Matt	48		14	1												49	0	14
BARRETT	Earl	10	5						1								10	6	0
BARRETT	Graham	5	1	1													5	1	1
BARRICK	Dean	11		2													11	0	2
BARRON	George	1															1	0	0
BARRY-MURPHY	Brian	55	3		2			1						6			64	3	0
BARTLETT	William	175		2	24		1										199	0	3
BART-WILLIAMS	Chris	95	29	16	9	3	2	10	6	4	1	2	2		1		115	41	24
BECKETT	Albert				1												1	0	0
BEDFORD	Lewis	11		2													11	0	2
BEECH	Jack	20		5	2												22	0	5
BEESON	George	74			1												75	0	0
BELL	Derek	5		1													5	0	1
BELL	Lawrie	46		10	7		3										53	0	13
BELLAS	Jack	45			6												51	0	0
BENNETT	Dave	20	8					1						2		1	23	8	1
BENNETT	Mickey				5		4										5	0	4
BENTLEY	Harry	51		3	2												53	0	3
BENTLEY	Willis				5		1										5	0	1
BERESFORD	Marlon	4															4	0	0

BESWETHERICK	Jon	9	2		2	1								1	1		12	4	0
BETTS	Billy	50		3	33		1										83	0	4
BINGLEY	Jack				2												2	0	0
BINGLEY	Walter	38			1												39	0	0
BINKS	Sid	77		29	6		4										83	0	33
BINNEY	Chas	40		6	3												43	0	6
BIRCH	Arnold	27			2												29	0	0
BIRKS	Graham	4															4	0	0
BLACKHALL	Ray	115		1	12			13									140	0	1
BLAIR	Andy	58		3	7		1	10		3							75	0	7
BLAIR	Jimmy	57			4												61	0	0
BLATSIS	Con	6			2												8	0	0
BLENKINSOP	Ernie	393		5	31												424	0	5
BLINKER	Regi	24	18	3	1			2									27	18	3
BLONDEAU	Patrick	5	1														5	1	0
BOLDER	Bob	196			12			16									224	0	0
BOLLAND	Tommy	13		1													13	0	1
BOLSOVER	Henry	2															2	0	0
BONVIN	Pablo	7	16	4		1		2	4	1							9	21	5
BOOTH	Andy	124	9	28	9	1	5	10	1	1							143	11	34
BOSWORTH	Samuel	7															7	0	0
BOWLING	Ian										1						1	0	0
BOWNS	George				2												2	0	0
BRADBURY	Lee	10	1	3													10	1	3
BRADLEY	Martin	2															2	0	0
BRADSHAW	Carl	16	16	4	6	1	3	2	2					1			25	19	7
BRADSHAW	Frank	87		38	8		2										95	0	40
BRADSHAW	Paul	62	2	9	4			6		2							72	2	11
BRADY	Alec	159		34	19		5										178	0	39
BRANDON	Harry	147		15	25		1										172	0	16
BRANDON	Robert				2		1										2	0	1
BRANDON	Tom	30		2	8												38	0	2
BRANFOOT	Ian	33	3		3	1		1									37	4	0
BRANNIGAN	Kenny	1															1	0	0
BRANSTON	Guy	10	1		1			1									12	1	0
BRASH	Archie	119		17	12		6										131	0	23
BRATLEY	George	3															3	0	0
BRAYSHAW	Teddy				21												21	0	0
BREEDON	Jack	45			2												47	0	0
BRELSFORD	Chas	6			1												7	0	0
BRELSFORD	Tom	117		6	5												122	0	6
BRETNALL	Oscar				1												1	0	0
BRIEN	Tony										1						1	0	0
BRIGHT	Mark	112	21	48	13		7	20	1	11	3		4				148	22	70
BRISCOE	James	5		3													5	0	3
BRISCOE	Lee	48	30	1		2		5	2		2	1					55	35	1
BRITTLETON	Tommy	342		30	30		3										372	0	33
BROADBENT	Albert	81		17	2												83	0	17
BROLLY	Tom	2															2	0	0
BROMBY	Leigh	98	2	2	6	1		8						5			117	3	2
BROOMES	Marlon	18	1		1												19	1	0
BROWN	Bobby	17	4	3													17	4	3
BROWN	Jack	465			42												507	0	0
BROWN	James	10															10	0	0
BROWN	Sparrow	46		7	9		1										55	0	8
BRUCE	Alex	5	1											3			8	1	0
BRUCE	Robert	5															5	0	0
BRUNT	Chris	35	16	6	1			1	1					2	2	1	39	19	7
BRYANT	Steve	2	1														2	1	0
BULLEN	Lee	46		7				2						4			52	0	7

Name		Lge. App	Lge. Sub	Lge. Goals	FAC App	FAC Sub	FAC Goals	FLC App	FLC Sub	FLC Goals	Euro App	Euro Sub	Euro Goals	Other App	Other Sub	Other Goals	TOTAL App	TOTAL Sub	TOTAL Goals
BURCHILL	Mark	4	1														4	1	0
BURGESS	Harry	215		70	18		7										233	0	77
BURGIN	Andy	1			2												3	0	0
BURKINSHAW	Jack	56		8	5		2										61	0	10
BURKINSHAW	Laurie	23		6	2		1										25	0	7
BURRIDGE	Bert	26															26	0	0
BURROWS	David	21						2									23	0	0
BURROWS	Horace	233		8	27												260	0	8
BURTON	Harry	171			27												198	0	0
BURTON	Ken	55	3	2		1		3									58	4	2
BUTLER	Barry	26		1	10												36	0	1
BUTTERY	Edward				11												11	0	0
BUTTERY	Thomas				2												2	0	0
C																			
CALLAGHAN	John	4		2													4	0	2
CAMERON	Danny	31		1	2			5									38	0	1
CAMPBELL	James	143		3	13												156	0	3
CAMPBELL	Phil		1														0	1	0
CAPEWELL	Ron	29			1												30	0	0
CAPPER	Alf	59		4	3												62	0	4
CARBONE	Benito	86	10	25	7		1	3	1								96	11	26
CARGILL	David	10			3												13	0	0
CARR	Chris		2														0	2	0
CARR	Franz	9	3		2												11	3	0
CATLIN	Ted	206			21												227	0	0
CAWLEY	Tom				37		22										37	0	22
CHALMERS	Bruce	23		1	5												28	0	1
CHAMBERLAIN	Mark	32	34	8	1	11	1	5	2	1				2	1		40	48	10
CHAMBERS	Adam	8	3											1			9	3	0
CHAPMAN	Harry	270		93	29		7										299	0	100
CHAPMAN	Lee	147	2	62	17	1	10	17		6				2	1		183	4	78
CHAPMAN	William	4															4	0	0
CHEDGZOY	Syd	4															4	0	0
CLARKE	Harry	1															1	0	0
CLARKE	Matt	2	2														2	2	0
CLEMENTS	Dave	78			6			3									87	0	0
CLOUGH	Nigel	1						1									2	0	0
COBIAN	Juan	7	2					1									8	2	0
COCKROFT	Joe	87		2	10												97	0	2
CODD	Ronnie	2															2	0	0
COLE	William	8		1	2												10	0	1
COLEMAN	Simon	11	5	1	2			3									16	5	1
COLEMAN	Tony	25	1	2	2												27	1	2
COLLIER	William	14															14	0	0
COLLINS	John	7						4									11	0	0
COLLINS	Patrick	25	3	1	1			2						1	1		29	4	1
COLLINS	Wayne	16	15	6	1			2									19	15	6
CONWELL	Tony	44			3												47	0	0
COOKE	Terry	35	5	3		1			1						1		35	8	3
COOPER	Alf	3															3	0	0
COOPER	Anthony	1															1	0	0
COOPER	Joe	1															1	0	0
COOPER	Sedley	19		4													19	0	4
COOPER	William				1												1	0	0
COX	Brian	22						4									26	0	0
COYLE	Roy	38	2	2	7		1	2	1								47	3	3

CRAIG	Jim	5	1										5	1	0
CRAIG	Robert	84		25	11		3				4		99	0	28
CRAIG	Tommy	210	4	38	9	1	1	9		1			228	5	40
CRANE	Tony	24	25	4	1	3		3	5	1			28	33	5
CRANSON	Ian	29	1		2			2				1	34	1	0
CRAPPER	Chris	1											1	0	0
CRAWSHAW	Percy	9											9	0	0
CRAWSHAW	Tommy	418		24	47		2						465	0	26
CRESSWELL	Richard	7	24	2		3		1	1	1			8	28	3
CRINSON	William	4											4	0	0
CRUICKSHANK	Alex	2											2	0	0
CUNNINGHAM	Tony	26	2	5	4	1							30	3	5
CURRAN	Terry	122	3	35	3			10		4			135	3	39
CURRY	Bob	1											1	0	0
CURTIS	Norman	310		21	14								324	0	21
CUSACK	Dave	92	3	1	7			7					106	3	1
D															
DAILEY	Jimmy	37		24	4		1						41	0	25
DARLING	Malcolm	1	1					1					2	1	0
DARROCH	Jack	17			3								20	0	0
DAVIES	Brian	3		1				1					4	0	1
DAVIES	George	98		1	11		1						109	0	2
DAVIS	Harry	160		36	24		6						184	0	42
DAVIS	Harry	213		59	22		8						235	0	67
DAVIS	John	1											1	0	0
DAVISON	Teddy	397			27								424	0	0
DAVISON	Tommy	17			1								18	0	0
DE BILDE	Gilles	50	9	13	4			5		2			59	9	15
DEGRYSE	Marc	30	4	8	1			3		4			34	4	12
DENT	Fred	4		1									4	0	1
DEWAR	Neil	84		43	11		7						95	0	50
DI CANIO	Paulo	39	2	15	3			4		2			46	2	17
DI PIEDI	Michaelli	9	30	5				1	4	2			10	34	7
DICKINSON	Wally	7			1								8	0	0
DILLON	Francis	7			2								9	0	0
DJORDJIC	Bojan	4	1										4	1	0
DOBSON	Colin	177		49	11		1	7		2			195	0	52
DODDS	Chris	1											1	0	0
DONALDSON	O'Neill	4	10	3									4	10	3
DONNELLY	Simon	27	26	8		3		3	3				30	32	8
DOOLEY	Derek	61		62	2		1						63	0	63
DOWD	Hugh	110	3		5			19					134	3	0
DOWLING	Michael	7											7	0	0
DOWNES	Steve	26	5	4				3		1			29	5	5
DRISCOLL	John	5		2	1								6	0	2
DRIVER	Allenby	6		3	6		3						12	0	6
DRURY	George	44		9	3		2						47	0	11
DRYBURGH	William	47		11	3								50	0	11
DUNGWORTH	Jack				17		2						17	0	2
DUNLOP	Walter	1											1	0	0
DUNN	John	8											8	0	0
E															
EARP	Jack	155		7	19		1						174	0	8
EATON	Walter	1											1	0	0
EDMONSON	Joe	14		3									14	0	3
EDWARDS	Len	2											2	0	0
EGGO	Robert	23											23	0	0
EKOKU	Efan	52	7	14	2	1		8	1	7			62	9	21

Name		Lge. App	Lge. Sub	Lge. Goals	FAC App	FAC Sub	FAC Goals	FLC App	FLC Sub	FLC Goals	Euro App	Euro Sub	Euro Goals	Other App	Other Sub	Other Goals	TOTAL App	TOTAL Sub	TOTAL Goals
ELLIS	Keith	102		52	14		7				2		1				118	0	60
ELLIS	Sam	155	3	1	13			11									179	3	1
EUSTACE	Peter	238	11	25	20	1		11		1							269	12	26
EVANS	Paul	7															7	0	0
EVANS	Richard	8	2	1				1									9	2	1
EYRE	Ron	1															1	0	0
EYRE	Issac	1															1	0	0
F																			
FALLON	Bill	44		12	7		1										51	0	13
FANTHAM	John	381	7	146	33	1	11	6		4	6		5				426	8	166
FAULKNER	David											1					0	1	0
FEE	Greg	16	10					3	1	1				1			20	11	1
FEELY	Peter	17	2	2				4	1								21	3	2
FELTON	Billy	158			6												164	0	0
FERGUSON	Bobby	5															5	0	0
FERGUSON	Ron	10	1	1													10	1	1
FERRIER	Bob	308		18	21		2										329	0	20
FINNEY	Alan	455		81	39		6				10		1				504	0	88
FISH	Tom	7			1												8	0	0
FLEMING	Ian	13		1				4		1							17	0	2
FLETCHER	Brough	2															2	0	0
FLETCHER	Doug	4															4	0	0
FLETCHER	Henry				1												1	0	0
FORD	David	117	5	31	10		5	3		1							130	5	37
FOX	Oscar	44		3	3		1										47	0	4
FOX	Peter	49			3												52	0	0
FOX	William	4															4	0	0
FOXALL	Frank	44		9													44	0	9
FRANCIS	Trevor	29	47	5	2	2	1	5	2	3	1			1			38	51	9
FROGGATT	Frank	91		1	5												96	0	1
FROGGATT	Redfern	434		139	24		9										458	0	148
FRYE	John				1												1	0	0
G																			
GALE	Tommy	9			4												13	0	0
GALLACHER	Kevin		4														0	4	0
GALLACHER	Paul	8															8	0	0
GALVIN	Tony	21	15	1				4	2					1	1	1	26	18	2
GANNON	Eddie	204		4	15												219	0	4
GEARY	Derek	95	9		4			12	2					5			116	11	0
GEMMELL	Duncan				3												3	0	0
GERMAN	David										1						1	0	0
GIBSON	Don	80		2	4		1										84	0	3
GILL	James	38		9	5		1										43	0	10
GILLIES	Alex	2															2	0	0
GLEN	Bob	1															1	0	0
GLENNON	Teddy	121		41	12		1										133	0	42
GOODFELLOW	Derwick	69			8												77	0	0
GOOING	William	3		1													3	0	1
GOSLING	William	5															5	0	0
GOWDY	William	1			1												2	0	0
GRANT	Dave	132	1	4	4	2		11		1							147	3	5
GRAY	George	32			1												33	0	0
GRAYSON	Simon	5															5	0	0
GREEN	Adam	3															3	0	0
GREEN	Albert	6		1													6	0	1

GREEN	Ryan	4														4	0	0
GREENSMITH	Ronald	5			1		1									6	0	1
GREENWOOD	Ross		2					1						1		1	3	0
GREGG	Robert	37		7	2											39	0	7
GREGORY	Tony	14	4	1	2				1							16	5	1
GREGORY	Bob				17		14									17	0	14
GREGSON	Colin	1	1					1								2	1	0
GRIFFIN	Billy	35		20	1						1	1				37	0	21
GROSVENOR	Tommy	22		1	1											23	0	1
GRUMMITT	Peter	121			3			6								130	0	0
H																		
HALL	Sandy	17		2	3											20	0	2
HALL	Harry	31		1												31	0	1
HAMILTON	Henry	7														7	0	0
HAMSHAW	Matt	35	39	2	2	1	2	6	3	2			2			45	43	6
HANFORD	Harry	85		1	9											94	0	1
HARDY	Robin	30		1							3					33	0	1
HARGREAVES	Len	2		1												2	0	1
HARKES	John	59	22	7	12	1	1	17		3	4		3			95	23	11
HARKNESS	Steve	28	2	1	2											30	2	1
HARPER	Alan	32	3		1			1	1				1			35	4	0
HARPER	Ted	18		13	4		3									22	0	16
HARRISON	W.				2		3									2	0	3
HARRON	Joe	61		5	3		1									64	0	6
HART	Paul	52		2	3			4		1			1			60	0	3
HARVEY	Colin	45		2	1			2								48	0	2
HARVEY	Edward	12														12	0	0
HARVEY	William	19		1	1											20	0	1
HASLAM	Steve	115	29	2	9	1		10	1				5	1		139	32	2
HATFIELD	Ernie	1														1	0	0
HAZEL	Des	5	1					1						1		6	2	0
HEALD	Paul	5						1								6	0	0
HEARD	Pat	22	3	3	6			2								30	3	3
HECKINGBOTTOM	Paul	37	1	4				1					3			41	1	4
HEDLEY	Graeme	6		1												6	0	1
HEESON	J.				1											1	0	0
HEMMINGFIELD	Bill	43		12	4		1									47	0	13
HENDERSON	Willie	42	6	5	5			3								50	6	5
HENDON	Ian	49		2	2			2								53	0	2
HENRY	Gerry	40		7												40	0	7
HENSHALL	Horace	14		1	3											17	0	1
HENSON	Phil	65	8	9	2			5								72	8	9
HERBERT	David	12	5	4				1	1							13	6	4
HIBBERT	Henry	2														2	0	0
HICKTON	John	52	1	20	3											55	1	20
HILL	Brian	116	1	1	2						3					121	1	1
HILL	Harold	91		37	8		3									99	0	40
HILL	Haydn	4														4	0	0
HILLER	Carl				5		1									5	0	1
HILLER	Walpole				1											1	0	0
HINCH	Jim		1													0	1	0
HINCHCLIFFE	Alan	2														2	0	0
HINCHCLIFFE	Alfred	1														1	0	0
HINCHCLIFFE	Andy	86		7	6			4	1							96	1	7
HIRST	David	261	33	106	12	7	6	26	9	11	3	1	7		4	309	49	128
HODDER	William				2		1									2	0	1
HODGE	Martin	197			25			24					3			249	0	0
HODGKISS	Thomas	2														2	0	0
HODGSON	David	6	5	1	1		1									7	5	2

Name		Lge. App	Lge. Sub	Lge. Goals	FAC App	FAC Sub	FAC Goals	FLC App	FLC Sub	FLC Goals	Euro App	Euro Sub	Euro Goals	Other App	Other Sub	Other Goals	TOTAL App	TOTAL Sub	TOTAL Goals
HOLBEM	Walter	86			3												89	0	0
HOLLIDAY	Eddie	55		12	2		1				5		1				62	0	14
HOLMES	Darren										1						1	0	0
HOLMES	George	20			1												21	0	0
HOLSGROVE	John	103	1	5	6			5									114	1	5
HOLT	Grant	12	12	3	2		1		1					1	2		15	15	4
HOOPER	Mark	384		124	39		11										423	0	135
HOPE	Bobby	39	3	7	2		1	2		1							43	3	9
HORNE	Barry	7															7	0	0
HORNSBY	Brian	102	4	25	10		4	8		1							120	4	30
HORROBIN	Thomas	3															3	0	0
HOUNSFIELD	Reg	2															2	0	0
HOWELLS	Peter	3		1													3	0	1
HOYLAND	George	3		1													3	0	1
HUDSON	Jack				16												16	0	0
HUKIN	Arthur	6		3													6	0	3
HULL	Gary	6	2														6	2	0
HULL	Jack	1															1	0	0
HUMPHREYS	Ritchie	34	33	4	5	4	4	4	2								43	39	8
HUNT	Doug	42		30	6		1										48	0	31
HUNT	George	32		8	3												35	0	8
HUNTER	Andy	15		3													15	0	3
HUNTER	Jack				3												3	0	0
HUTTON	Robert	5		1													5	0	1
HYDE	Graham	126	46	11	13	5	2	17	3	2	7			1		1	164	54	16
I																			
IBBOTSON	Wilf	1															1	0	0
INGESSON	Klas	12	6	2	1			2									15	6	2
INGLIS	Bill	29			2												31	0	0
INGRAM	Billy				16		8										16	0	8
IRVINE	Archie	25	3	1	4			2									31	3	1
J																			
JACKSON	Jerry	1															1	0	0
JACKSON	Norman	31															31	0	0
JACOBS	Wayne	5	1					3						1			9	1	0
JAMESON	Joe	7															7	0	0
JAMIESON	James	125		3	10												135	0	3
JARVIS	Richard	6															6	0	0
JEEVES	Jack				1												1	0	0
JEFFERSON	Derek	5						1									6	0	0
JEMSON	Nigel	26	25	9	3	3		3	4	1	1	1		1	1	1	34	34	11
JOHNSON	David	5	1														5	1	0
JOHNSON	David	7		2													7	0	2
JOHNSON	George	1		1													1	0	1
JOHNSON	Jeff	175	5	6	14		1	17		2							206	5	9
JOHNSON	Kevin		1														0	1	0
JOHNSON	Peter	181		6	19			7									207	0	6
JOHNSON	Tommy	8		3				1									9	0	3
JOHNSTON	Allan	12		2													12	0	2
JOICEY	Brian	144	1	48	7	3	4	9	2	1							160	6	53
JONES	Kenwyne	7		7													7	0	7
JONES	Ryan	36	5	6	3			4	1	1							43	6	7
JONES	Tommy	29		6													29	0	6
JONK	Wim	69	1	5	7			4									80	1	5
JONSSON	Siggi	59	8	4	1	1	1	3		1				1			64	9	6

JORDAN	Clarrie	92		36	2										94	0	36
JORDAN	John	10		2	1										11	0	2
K																	
KAY	Tony	179		10	18						6				203	0	10
KAYE	Albert	41		12	3		1								44	0	13
KEAN	Fred	230		8	17										247	0	8
KELL	George	5			1										6	0	0
KENNY	Vin	144			8										152	0	0
KENT	Mick	4						1	1						5	1	0
KEY	Lance					1									0	1	0
KILSHAW	Eddie	17		1	2										19	0	1
KING	Jeff	54	3	5	2		1	9		1					65	3	7
KING	Phil	124	5	2	9			17					4		154	5	2
KINGHORN	Henry	25													25	0	0
KINMAN					1		1								1	0	1
KIPPAX	Dennis	1													1	0	0
KIRBY	Eric	1													1	0	0
KIRBY	George	3													3	0	0
KIRKMAN	Sam	187		37	14		3								201	0	40
KIKWOOD	Dan	18		1	1										19	0	1
KITE	Percy	1													1	0	0
KNIGHT	Ian	21			5			1							27	0	0
KNIGHT	Leon	14	10	3		1		2							16	11	3
KNIGHTON	Ken	71	5	2	4		1	4		1					79	5	4
KOVACEVIC	Darko	8	8	4	1										9	8	4
KUQI	Shefki	58	6	19	1			3							62	6	19
L																	
LAMB	John	5													5	0	0
LAMB	Walter	2													2	0	0
LANG	James				5										5	0	0
LANGLEY	Ambrose	295		14	23										318	0	14
LAW	Alex	9		4											9	0	4
LAWSON	Willie	9			1			1							11	0	0
LAYNE	David	74		52	4		1				3	5			81	0	58
LAYTON	Willie	331		2	30										361	0	2
LEACH	Tony	238		12	22		2								260	0	14
LEDGER					13										13	0	0
LEE	George	5		1	1										6	0	1
LEE	Graeme	49	3	4	4			1		1			3	1	57	3	6
LEMAN	Denis	89	14	9	9		1	4							102	14	10
LESCOTT	Aaron	19	18		2			3	1						24	19	0
LESTER	Fred	17			4										21	0	0
LEVICK	Oliver	21													21	0	0
LEWIS	Idris	18		7	5		1								23	0	8
LINDSAY	Jack	1		1											1	0	1
LINIGHAN	Brian	1			1			1							3	0	0
LLOYD	Billy	79		6	5		1								84	0	7
LOCHERTY	Joe	10			2										12	0	0
LODGE	Bobby	3		2											3	0	2
LOFTHOUSE	Jimmy	95		13	3										98	0	13
LOGAN	John	4			2										6	0	0
LOWDELL	Arthur	108		6	8										116	0	6
LOWE	H.	2													2	0	0
LOWES	Arnold	42		8	2		2								44	0	10
LOWEY	John	35	7	4	7		2	1							43	7	6
LUCAS	David	51			1			2					5		59	0	0
LUKE	Charlie	42		8	1										43	0	8
LUNN	Fred	11		4	1										12	0	4

Name		Lge. App	Lge. Sub	Lge. Goals	FAC App	FAC Sub	FAC Goals	FLC App	FLC Sub	FLC Goals	Euro App	Euro Sub	Euro Goals	Other App	Other Sub	Other Goals	TOTAL App	TOTAL Sub	TOTAL Goals
LYALL	Jack	263			32												295	0	0
LYONS	Mick	129		12	15		2	20		2							164	0	16
M																			
MacKENZIE	Matt	6															6	0	0
MacKENZIE	Steve	5	10	2													5	10	2
MACKEY	Thomas	4															4	0	0
MacLEAN	Steve	36		18	1			2						1	1	2	40	1	20
MADDEN	Lawrie	200	12	2	20	1		26	2	3				5			251	15	5
MADDIX	Danny	55	4	2				7		1							62	4	3
MAGILTON	Jim	14	13	1	1			2									17	13	1
MALLINSON	W.	5			1												6	0	0
MALLOCH	Gavin	84			5												89	0	0
MALLOCH	Jock	144		11	10												154	0	11
MALPASS	Arthur				15												15	0	0
MARRIOTT	Jackie	153		19	6												159	0	19
MARRISON	Thomas	5		1													5	0	1
MARSDEN	Billy	205		9	16												221	0	9
MARSDEN	Chris	15						2						1			18	0	0
MARSON	Fred	10															10	0	0
MARTIN	Jack	63			3												66	0	0
MARWOOD	Brian	125	3	27	19		3	13		5					1		157	4	35
MASSARELLA	Len	31		10	2												33	0	10
MASSEY	Jimmy	159			14												173	0	0
MATTHEWS	Ernest	16		7													16	0	7
MATTHEWSON	Thomas	1															1	0	0
MATTHEWSON	Trevor	3			2												5	0	0
MAXWELL	James	27		6													27	0	6
MAY	Larry	30	1	1	4			3									37	1	1
MAYRLEB	Chistian		3														0	3	0
McANEARNEY	Jim	38		10	2												40	0	10
McANEARNEY	Tom	352		19	23		2				7		1				382	0	22
McCAFFERTY	Michael	1															1	0	0
McCALL	Steve	21	8	2	1			2	3						1		24	12	2
McCALLIOG	Jim	150		19	18		5	6		3							174	0	27
McCAMBRIDGE	Joseph	2															2	0	0
McCARTER	Jimmy	6															6	0	0
McCARTHY	Jon	4															4	0	0
McCONACHIE	Robert	1															1	0	0
McCONNELL	English	44			6												50	0	0
McCULLOCH	Andy	122	3	44	10		4	14		1							146	3	49
McEVOY	Don	105		1	7												112	0	1
McGOVERN	Jon-Paul	46		6	1			2						4		2	53	0	8
McGREGOR	James	6		2													6	0	2
McILVENNY	Paddy	1															1	0	0
McINTOSH	Dave	293			15												308	0	0
McINTOSH	Tom	9		1													9	0	1
McINTYRE	Johnny	67		36	3												70	0	36
McIVER	Fred	34	3		1			4									39	3	0
McJARROW	Hugh	46		21	1												47	0	21
McKAY	Colin	12		3	2												14	0	3
McKEEVER	Mark	2	3			1			1								2	5	0
McKEOWN	Lindsay	6	5		1												7	5	0
McLAREN	Roy	31			3												34	0	0
McLAREN	Paul	83	13	8	2			6	1	1				1			92	14	9
McLEAN	David	135		88	12		12										147	0	100
McMAHON	Lewis	22	3	2	1			1	1					1	2		25	6	2

McMORDIE	Eric	9		6											9	0	6
McSKIMMING	Bob	181			13										194	0	0
McWHINNIE	William	9													9	0	0
MEGSON	Don	386		6	41		1	5			10				442	0	7
MEGSON	Gary	230	3	25	27		6	23		2			3		283	3	33
MELIA	James	7													7	0	0
MELLOR	Ian	54	16	11	2	1		5	1						61	18	11
MELLOR	Billy	1													1	0	0
MELLORS	Richard	14													14	0	0
MEREDITH	John	1													1	0	0
MILLAR	Harry	32		16	2										34	0	16
MILLER	James	30			1										31	0	0
MILLER	John	13		8											13	0	8
MILLER	Walter	3													3	0	0
MILLERSHIP	Harry	210		25	26		9								236	0	34
MILLS	David	15		3	4										19	0	3
MILLS	Simon	1	4		1										2	4	0
MIROCEVIC	Ante	58	3	6	3	2	1	4							65	5	7
MOBLEY	Vic	187		8	19			4							210	0	8
MONAGHAN	James	2													2	0	0
MONK	Garry	15													15	0	0
MORALEE	Matt	4		1											4	0	1
MORLEY	Hayden				7										7	0	0
MORLEY	Lance				1										1	0	0
MORRIS	Chris	61	13	1	7	5		5	5	1					73	23	2
MORRISON	Owen	31	25	8	1	2		8	2	3					40	29	11
MORTON	Albert	41			1										42	0	0
MOSFORTH	Billy				25		6								25	0	6
MOSS	Frank	22			1										23	0	0
MOSS	William				1										1	0	0
MULLEN	Jimmy	222	8	10	9	1		23							254	9	10
MULLER	Adam	1	4						1						1	5	0
MUMFORD	Albert	23		1	19		6								42	0	7
MURRAY	James	13		4											13	0	4
MUSTOE	Robbie	22	3	1	3								1		26	3	1
N																	
NAPIER	Charlie	48		9	8		1								56	0	10
NAPIER	Dan	11		2											11	0	2
NDUMBU-NSUNGU	Guylain	24	11	10	1	1	1		1				5	1	30	14	11
NEEDHAM	Liam													1	0	1	0
NEVIN	George	2													2	0	0
NEWBOULD	Herbert				8		4								8	0	4
NEWSOME	Jon	56	5	4	6	1		6							68	6	4
NIBLOE	Joe	116			12										128	0	0
NICHOLLS	Harry	3													3	0	0
NICHOLSON	George				1										1	0	0
NICHOLSON	Horace	3													3	0	0
NICHOLSON	Kevin		1												0	1	0
NICOL	Steve	41	8		2	1			2						43	11	0
NILSSON	Roland	151		2	15			16		1	1	1	2		185	1	3
NIMMO	Ian	26	19	10	2	2	3	2							30	21	13
NIXON	Eric		1												0	1	0
NOBLE	Frank	2													2	0	0
NOLAN	Ian	164	1	4	15			15	1		3				197	2	4
O																	
OAKES	Scott	7	17	1		2			1						7	20	1
O'BRIEN	Joey	14	1	2											14	1	2
O'CONNELL	Paddy	18			3										21	0	0

Name		Lge. App	Lge. Sub	Lge. Goals	FAC App	FAC Sub	FAC Goals	FLC App	FLC Sub	FLC Goals	Euro App	Euro Sub	Euro Goals	Other App	Other Sub	Other Goals	TOTAL App	TOTAL Sub	TOTAL Goals
O'DONNELL	Neil	40		1	3			4		1							47	0	2
O'DONNELL	Phil	13	7					2	3	1							15	10	1
O'DONNELL	Ralph	170		3	13												183	0	3
OLIVER	Gavin	14	6		2	1		2	4								18	11	0
OLSEN	Kim	6	4											1	1		7	5	0
O'NEILL	Harry	49			2												51	0	0
OWEN	Gary	12	2			2		2						1			15	4	0
OWEN	Gordon	32	15	5	1	1		7	4	2							40	20	7
OWEN	Neil	1															1	0	0
OWUSU	Lloyd	24	28	8	3		1	2	1					1	1		30	30	9
OXLEY	Bernard	14		4													14	0	4
P																			
PACKARD	Edgar	124		1	2												126	0	1
PALETHORPE	Jack	28		13	6		4										34	0	17
PALMER	Carlton	226	1	14	18	1		31		3	3	1		5		1	283	3	18
PARKER	Ray	1															1	0	0
PARKES	David	47		1	3												50	0	1
PATERSON	Marr	21		2													21	0	2
PEACOCK	John	1															1	0	0
PEACOCK	Lee	18	11	4				1		1				3		1	22	11	6
PEARCE	Andy	66	3	3	6	1	1	11	1		1						84	5	4
PEARSON	John	64	41	24	8	5	2	7	3	1	1						80	49	27
PEARSON	Mark	39		9	1						2		2				42	0	11
PEARSON	Nigel	176	4	14	15		1	17	2	5	3			7			218	6	20
PEARSON	Stanley	2															2	0	0
PEARSON	Trevor	4															4	0	0
PEMBRIDGE	Mark	88	5	12	7		1	6		1	1						102	5	14
PETRESCU	Dan	28	9	3		2		2			1		1				31	11	4
PETRIE	Charles	58		22	2		1										60	0	23
PETRIE	Bob	52		3	10												62	0	3
PICKERING	John	4															4	0	0
PICKERING	Mick	106	4	1	9			8	2								123	6	1
PICKERING	William	3			6												9	0	0
PINNER	Mike	7															7	0	0
PLATTS	Mark		2														0	2	0
PLLU	Charlie	19			1												20	0	0
PORIC	Adem	3	11						2		1						4	13	0
PORTERFIELD	Ian	103	3	4	11			12	1	2							126	4	6
POTTS	Eric	142	17	21	8	2		12	1	4							162	20	25
POTTS	Harry	2		1													2	0	1
POULTER	Robert														1		0	1	0
POWELL	Darryl	8															8	0	0
POWELL	Sam	25		8	1												26	0	8
POWELL	William	20			2												22	0	0
PRENDERGAST	Mick	170	14	53	7	1	2	15		4							192	15	59
PRESSMAN	Kevin	400	4		21			46			1			6			474	4	0
PRICE	Arthur	78		2	4		1										82	0	3
PRIESTLEY	R.	2		1													2	0	1
PRINCE	Arthur	53		7	1												54	0	7
PRIOR	George	37															37	0	0
PROCTER	Mark	59		4	6		1	1						3			69	0	5
PROPHETT	Colin	111	8	7	7			2	1								120	9	7
PROUD	Pattison	1															1	0	0
PROUDLOCK	Adam	40	9	11	3		3	1	1					5	1	3	49	11	17
PROUDLOVE	Andy	10	5		2		1										12	5	1
PRUDHAM	Eddie	14	5	2		1		1		1							15	6	3

PRYCE	Jack	55		6	4												59	0	6
PUGH	Graham	136	5	7	9		1	4	1	1							149	6	9
Q																			
QUIGLEY	Eddie	74		49	4		3										78	0	52
QUINN	Alan	147	10	16	6	1		14		1				2			169	11	17
QUINN	James	46		1	3			3									52	0	1
QUINN	James	10	5	2										3			13	5	2
QUINN	John	165	8	20	14	1	3	3	1		2		1				184	10	24
QUIXALL	Albert	241		63	19		2										260	0	65
R																			
RAMSBOTTOM	Neil	18			1			3									22	0	0
RAMSBOTTOM	Tom	12															12	0	0
RATCLIFFE	Archie	12		4													12	0	4
REDDY	Michael	22	5	4	2									3		1	27	5	5
REED	Percy	14			4												18	0	0
REEVES	David	8	9	2	1	1		1	1	1					1		10	12	3
REEVES	Fred	1															1	0	0
REGAN	William	9															9	0	0
REILLY	John	2															2	0	0
REYNOLDS	John	2															2	0	0
RHODES	E.				6		8										6	0	8
RHODES	Richard	57			2												59	0	0
RICHARDS	Anthony	7		1	1												8	0	1
RICHARDS	Fred	3		1													3	0	1
RICHARDSON	Edward	9			2												11	0	0
RICHARDSON	R.				3		3										3	0	3
RICKETT	Walter	95		11	2												97	0	11
RIMMER	Ellis	381		122	36		18										417	0	140
RIPLEY	Stuart	5	1	1													5	1	1
RITCHIE	John	88	1	34	12		10	5		1							105	1	45
ROBERTS	Sean		1														0	1	0
ROBERTSON	George	163		30	10		1										173	0	31
ROBINS	Mark	14	1	3										3		4	17	1	7
ROBINSON	Carl	4		1													4	0	1
ROBINSON	Jackie	108		34	11		5										119	0	39
ROBSON	Tom	3															3	0	0
ROCASTLE	Craig	9	2	1										3			12	2	1
RODGRIGUES	Peter	162		2	7			5									174	0	2
ROGERS	Alf	30		8													30	0	8
ROLLINSON	Frank	41		16	3												44	0	16
ROSTRON	Wilf	7			1									1			9	0	0
ROWAN	Alexander	29		13	5		1										34	0	14
ROY	John	15		1	1												16	0	1
RUDDLESDIN	Herrod	259		7	26												285	0	7
RUDI	Petter	70	7	7	6	1	1	5		1							81	8	9
RUSHBURY	Dave	111	1	8	13		1	8									132	1	9
RUSSELL	David	42			8												50	0	0
RYALLS	Brian	41			6												47	0	0
RYALLS	Joe	2															2	0	0
RYAN	John	5	3	1				1									6	3	1
S																			
SANETTI	Francesco	1	4	1					2								1	6	1
SAYER	Jim				2		1										2	0	1
SCOTHORN	Gary	1			1												2	0	0
SCOTT	Phil	2	7	1	1	1											3	8	1
SEDLOSKI	Goce	3	1														3	1	0
SEED	Jimmy	134		33	12		5										146	0	38

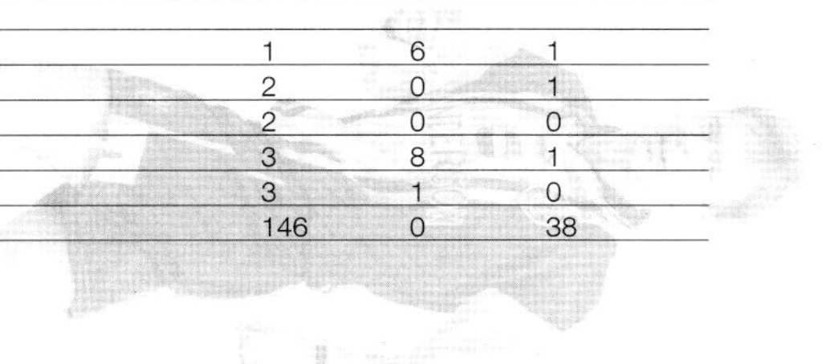

Name		Lge. App	Lge. Sub	Lge. Goals	FAC App	FAC Sub	FAC Goals	FLC App	FLC Sub	FLC Goals	Euro App	Euro Sub	Euro Goals	Other App	Other Sub	Other Goals	TOTAL App	TOTAL Sub	TOTAL Goals
SEEMLEY	Ivor	15			8												23	0	0
SEWELL	Jackie	164		87	11		5										175	0	92
SHADBOLT	Bill	7															7	0	0
SHAKESPEARE	Craig	15	2					3		1					1		18	3	1
SHARP	Wilf	48		2	10												58	0	2
SHAW	Bernard				1												1	0	0
SHAW	Bernard	100	4	3	5		1	4									109	4	4
SHAW	Jack	56		21	9		6										65	0	27
SHAW	Jon	8	10	2		2			1					1	2		9	15	2
SHELLEY	Albert	3		2													3	0	2
SHELTON	Gary	195	3	18	23	1	3	18		3				1			237	4	24
SHELTON	George	17			1												18	0	0
SHEPHERD	James	2															2	0	0
SHERIDAN	John	187	10	25	17	1	3	24		3	2		1	3		1	233	11	33
SHINER	Roy	153		93	7		3										160	0	96
SHIRTLIFF	Paul	7	2					1									8	2	0
SHIRTLIFF	Peter	292		8	25	1	4	35	2	1	1			3			356	3	13
SHORT	James	2															2	0	0
SHUTT	Carl	36	4	16	4	1	4	3		1							43	5	21
SIBON	Gerald	98	31	36	7	1	3	11	2	4							116	34	43
SIMMONITE	Gordon	1															1	0	0
SIMMONS	Tony	1	3					1									2	3	0
SIMMONS	William	1															1	0	0
SIMPSON	George	142		30	21		9										163	0	39
SIMPSON	Vivian	30		8	8		3										38	0	11
SINCLAIR	Jackie	97	4	14	3			5		2							105	4	16
SINTON	Andy	54	6	3	5			13			2	1					74	7	3
SISSONS	John	114	1	14	6			5		1							125	1	15
SLATER	Brian	3															3	0	0
SLAVIN	Hugh	48			7												55	0	0
SLYNN	Frank	44		5	2												46	0	5
SMAILES	Andy	37		13	3		2										40	0	15
SMELT	John	16		2													16	0	2
SMITH	Dean	55		1	1	1		1						4			61	1	1
SMITH	Jim				22												22	0	0
SMITH	Jock	18		1													18	0	1
SMITH	Tom	1															1	0	0
SMITH	Mark	281	1	16	39		3	29		1							349	1	20
SMITH	Norman	19			4												23	0	0
SMITH	Paul	19	8	2				1						3			23	8	2
SMITH	Roy	84			13												97	0	0
SMITH	Wilf	207		4	21		1	6									234	0	5
SMITH	William	29		1													29	0	1
SNODIN	Glynn	51	8	1	9			4	1					1			65	9	1
SOLTVEDT	Trond-Egil	74		2	1			6		2							81	0	4
SONNER	Danny	42	11	3	4	2		3	1	1							49	14	4
SPIKSLEY	Fred	292		100	29		15										321	0	115
SPOORS	Jimmy	255		5	17												272	0	5
SPRINGETT	Peter	180			16			11									207	0	0
SPRINGETT	Ron	345			28			1			10						384	0	0
SRNICEK	Pavel	44			6			2									52	0	0
STACEY	William				5												5	0	0
STAINROD	Simon	8	7	2													8	7	2
STANIFORTH	Ron	102		2	5												107	0	2
STAPLETON	William	20															20	0	0
STARLING	Ron	176		30	17												193	0	30
STEFANOVIC	Dejan	59	7	4	4		1	2									65	7	5

STEPHENSON	George	39		18	6		2								45	0	20
STERLAND	Mel	271	8	37	34	1	5	30		7		3			338	9	49
STEVENS	J.				5										5	0	0
STEVENSON	Thomas	2													2	0	0
STEWART	Jimmy	123		52	18		8								141	0	60
STEWART	Reg	6			2										8	0	0
STEWART	Simon	6							1		1				7	1	0
STOCKDALE	Robbie	6													6	0	0
STORRAR	David	4													4	0	0
STRANGE	Alf	253		22	20										273	0	22
STRATFORD	Chas				11										11	0	0
STREETS	George	2													2	0	0
STRINGER	Chris	6	3		2				1						8	4	0
STRINGFELLOW	Frank	20		5	1										21	0	5
STRUTT	Brian	2													2	0	0
STUBBS	Frank	18													18	0	0
SUNLEY	David	121	12	21	12		5	2	1						135	13	26
SURTESS	Jack	40		5	10		3								50	0	8
SUTHERLAND	George	3													3	0	0
SWAN	Peter	273	2		14			2			10				299	2	0
SWIFT	Hugh	181			14										195	0	0
SYKES	Joe	29		1	2										31	0	1
SYMM	Colin	16	3	1	2	1		1							19	4	1
T																	
TALBOT	Andrew	3	18	4	1								3	1	4	21	5
TAYLOR	Charles	7													7	0	0
TAYLOR	Ian	9	5	1				2	2	1					11	7	2
TAYLOR	Jock	20													20	0	0
TAYLOR	Kevin	118	7	21	7		2	11	2	5					136	9	28
TAYLOR	Mark	8	1					2							10	1	0
TAYLOR	Paul	5	1												5	1	0
TAYLOR	Sam	120		36	8		3								128	0	39
TAYLOR	William	16		4	1										17	0	4
THACKERAY	Fred	9			1										10	0	0
THOMAS	Walter	10		1											10	0	1
THOME	Emerson	60	1	1	4		1	5	1						69	2	2
THOMPSON	Ernie	23			1										24	0	0
THOMPSON	Fred				12		1								12	0	1
THOMPSON	Garry	35	1	7	5		1	2	1						42	2	8
THOMPSON	Gavin				3		1								3	0	1
THOMPSON	Jackie	36		9	4		3								40	0	12
THOMPSON	Ron				1										1	0	0
THOMPSON	William	150	6	3	9		1	8							167	6	4
TIDMAN	Ola	12	1		1							2			15	1	0
TODD	Sammy	22	2	1				2							24	2	1
TOMLINSON	Charlie	68		7	9		5								77	0	12
TOMLINSON	David		1												0	1	0
TOONE	George	19			2										21	0	0
TOPHAM	Jack	12		2	4										16	0	2
TOSELAND	Ernie	12		2											12	0	2
TROTTER	Jimmy	153		109	6		5								159	0	114
TRUSTFULL	Orlando	9	10	3		1		2							11	11	3
TUMMON	Oliver	40		9	6		3								46	0	12
TURLEY	Mike	3			1										4	0	0
TURNER	Chris	166			21			17				1			205	0	0
TURTON	Cyril	146			5										151	0	0
TYNAN	Tommy	89	2	31	4		1	12		5					105	2	37

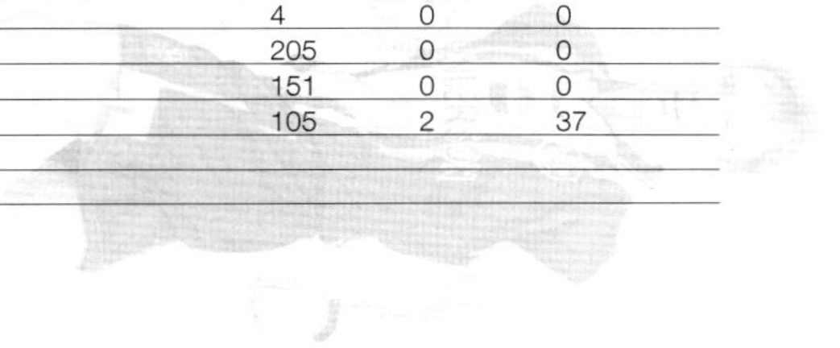

Name		Lge. App	Lge. Sub	Lge. Goals	FAC App	FAC Sub	FAC Goals	FLC App	FLC Sub	FLC Goals	Euro App	Euro Sub	Euro Goals	Other App	Other Sub	Other Goals	TOTAL App	TOTAL Sub	TOTAL Goals
U																			
ULYETT	George				1												1	0	0
USHER	Brian	55	1	2	7	1	1	4									66	2	3
V																			
VARADI	Imre	86	12	36	9		7	12	1	3				1			108	13	46
W																			
WADDLE	Chris	94	15	10	12	1	3	19			5	1	2				130	17	15
WALDEN	Richard	100			4			11		1							115	0	1
WALKER	Colin	2							1	3							2	1	3
WALKER	Cyril	4															4	0	0
WALKER	Des	307			24			28			3						362	0	0
WALKER	Fred	10		1													10	0	1
WALKER	Tommy	258		3	29												287	0	3
WALKER	William	18		5	1												19	0	5
WALL	Adrian	3															3	0	0
WALLER	George				16		2										16	0	2
WANDS	Alex	11		1	7		1										18	0	2
WARBOYS	Alan	66	5	13	2			2	1								70	6	13
WARD	Tommy	35		19	4		1										39	0	20
WARE	Harry	12		1													12	0	1
WARHURST	Paul	60	6	6	7	1	5	9		4	4		3	1			81	7	18
WARREN	Peter	7															7	0	0
WATLING	Barry	1															1	0	0
WATSON	Don	8		3	2		1										10	0	4
WATSON	Gordon	29	37	15	5	2		6	5	5	2	1	1		1		42	46	21
WATSON	J.				1												1	0	0
WATTS	Julian	12	4	1				1			3						16	4	1
WEAVER	Alex	6		1													6	0	1
WEBSTER	Arnie	1															1	0	0
WEBSTER	Fred				1												1	0	0
WEBSTER	Johnny	23		5	4												27	0	5
WEIR	Findlay	71		1	1												72	0	1
WELSH	Fletcher	12		4													12	0	4
WEST	Colin	40	5	8	6		1	6		3				3		1	55	5	13
WEST	Fred				7												7	0	0
WESTLAKE	Frank	110			7												117	0	0
WESTWOOD	Ashley	79	3	5	2			10	2	4							91	5	9
WHALLEY	Johnny	5															5	0	0
WHELAN	Glenn	36		2	1		1	2						3		1	42	0	4
WHITAKER	Colin	1															1	0	0
WHITEHOUSE	Jack	10		1													10	0	1
WHITHAM	Jack	54	9	27	6		4	2									62	9	31
WHITHAM	Terry	4															4	0	0
WHITTINGHAM	Guy	90	23	22	7	1	1	7	2	2	1	2					105	28	25
WHITTON	Steve	22	10	4		1		3		4					1		25	12	8
WICKS	Peter	13						1									14	0	0
WILCOCKSON	Harold	40		1	1			2									43	0	1
WILKINSON	Derek	212		53	15		4				4						231	0	57
WILKINSON	Eric	1															1	0	0
WILKINSON	Harry				12												12	0	0
WILKINSON	Howard	22		2													22	0	2
WILKINSON	Jack	72		16	7		1										79	0	17
WILLIAMS	Andy										1						1	0	0
WILLIAMS	David	163		7	10												173	0	7
WILLIAMS	Len	9															9	0	0
WILLIAMS	Les	11															11	0	0

WILLIAMS	Mike	16	7	1				3	2		2	1				21	10	1
WILLIAMS	Paul	78	15	25	3	2		10	3	3				3		94	20	28
WILLIAMSON	Charlie	61	1	1	1			4								66	1	1
WILSON	Andrew	502		199	44		17									546	0	216
WILSON	Charles	57		5	3											60	0	5
WILSON	Danny	91	7	11	9	1		22		2	3	1	1	2	1	127	10	14
WILSON	George	184		4	12											196	0	4
WILSON	Joe	3														3	0	0
WILSON	Laurie					2								1		1	2	0
WILSON	Mark	3														3	0	0
WILSON	S.				2											2	0	0
WINDASS	Dean	2														2	0	0
WINTERBOTTOM	Harry				22		10									22	0	10
WISE	F.				1											1	0	0
WITCOMB	Doug	224		12	6											230	0	12
WOOD	Darren	10	1					1	1					1		12	2	0
WOOD	Richard	45	4	2	1	1		1		1				5	1	52	6	3
WOODALL	Brian	19	3	4	3		2									22	3	6
WOODHEAD	Dennis	213		72	13		3									226	0	75
WOODS	Chris	106	1		10			13			6			2		137	1	0
WOOLHOUSE	Toddles	16		10	19		11									35	0	21
WORRYALL	Teddy	103			11											114	0	0
WORTHINGTON	Nigel	334	4	12	29		1	41		1	3		1	6		413	4	15
WORTLEY	George				1											1	0	0
WRIGHT	Vic	2														2	0	0
WRIGHT	Jimmy	3			1											4	0	0
WRIGHT	Jocky	103		41	7		1									110	0	42
WRIGHT	Percy	20		6	2											22	0	6
WYLDE	Rodger	157	12	54	15		4	10		8						182	12	66
Y																		
YOUNG	Gerry	307	2	13	17		2	10		1	8		4			342	2	20

Roll of Honour

Andrew Brodie
Jess Brodie
Brent Humberstone
Lee Hicklin
Andrew Bass
Richard Crooks
Matthew J.P. Elliott
Alan Fletcher
Barry Nicholson
Timothy Joseph Hartley
Philip Taylor
Mick Renshaw
George Hardy
Nigel Gunnee
David Cooper
Richard Paul Taff
Michael Liversidge
Michael H. Rudd
Michael Fellows
Jam Cooper
Daniel J. Batham
Joe Stockwell
Stephen Rogers
Ian Gregory
Keith Moulden
John M. Womersley
Nicola Jane Wroe
Tim, Ruth & Patrick McGuinness
Andrew Gray
Raymond Ward
Eddy Hogg
George Michael Clay
Roy Clifford Hurst
Peter James Ranson
Peter Law
Keith Howard
John Robinson
Doreen & Ken Dickinson
Mick Grayson
Sebastian Scothorn
Chris Edwards
Gary Spooner
Simon J. Rhodes
Mark Kappelhof
Peter Baker
Dean Calvert
John Thomas Brittleton
Jack Whitham
Trevor Robinson
Joss Wild
Colin Davies
Ian Colley
Ian Brownhill

Ralph & Clive Nicholson
Lloyd Briscoe
Robert Moody
John Grant
Robert Leek
Sean C. Mahon
Rachael Morton
Maurice H. Denton
Stephen Brunyee
Lucy Gill
Paul Massey
Scott Roberts
Stephen Needham
Andy Gouldsbrough
Roger Allan
Leon Russell
Adrian & Terry Richards
Lee White
Robert White
Alan Collins
Gary & Linda Mackender
Keith, David & Richard Mackender
Glyndon Foster
Sean Galbraith
Ashley Furo
Nick Marsden
John Simon Wrigley
Michael Howard
Chris Keeling
Russell Johnson
Simon Rodgers
Mr. Geoffrey Burgess
Peter Hurman
David (Bod) Pursehouse
Mark Bottomley
Scott Beck
Edward Gannon
Robert Callum Oldfield
Marie Askey
Ernest Swift
David Maddock
Raymond Darker
Philip J. Mead
Kieran Daniel Shaw
Lewis Wild
Timothy Matthew Fitzmaurice
Mike Andrews
Kenzie
Mick Brightmore
Brent Kyle Ford
Stephen Hill
Tony Jones
Kristian Raymond Dale

Richard Todd
Kelwin Meegan
Graham Johnson
Bob Neville
John Richard Bradley
Shaun Hunter
Andrew Millington
Dennis Millington
James D. Wragg
Norman Lewis Crooks
David Parry
John Turner
Kyle William Atkinson, 25-11-95
Pip Caselli/John Caselli
John B. Gath
Alex P. Gath
Louis Radforth
Nicholas Sanderson
Paul Kevin Ward
Michael James Ward
Stuart Hogg
Christopher Smalley
Joel Turner
Jonathan Paul Clifford Hurst
Tony Brogan
Liz, Eric & Neil Broomhead
Jarrod Baum
Alan Whitehead
Cerys Faith Jones
Keith Hall
Steve Johnson
Albert Fishwick
Matt Giles
Stephen Kieran Byrne
Alexander George Fuller
Benjamin John Taylor
Ron Tingle
Eric Brook
Joshua France
Malcolm John Anderson
Paul Greetham
Nicola Jayne Drury
Andrew Alex McCulloch
Andrew & Jack Crookes
Ernie Lockett
Rhys Luke Boughen
Colin Hunt
Steve Mitchell
Donald Randall
Steven A. Laughton
Keith King
Mick Green
Alan Howard

Roll of Honour

Chris Metcalfe
Timothy James Wild
Peter Smith
Peter Vause
Andrew P. Topham
Andrew J. Whiteley
Peter Webster
Spud Edwards
Rob Edwards
P & A Partnership
Haydn Pugh
Philip Lockwood
Andrew George
Benjamin Pashley
Ron Antcliffe
Robert Mortimer
David Mortimer
Derrick Kerrison
Mr. Edgar Loy
Steven R. Wordsworth
Mark Beresford
Geoff A. Hoyle
John Delamore
Kirk Steven Crooks
David Elliott Hoyle
Laura & Matt Herbert
George, Howard
& Christopher Mellish
Derek Booker
Mr. Philip Ortton-Smedley
Bryn Wheeldon
Kevin Wheeldon
Julian Wall & Sarah Wheeldon
Trevor Wilson
Roger Hellewell
Tony Hall
Nige Hewitt
David Barlow
Paul Ironmonger
Christopher Ironmonger
Natalia Kallai
Miklos Kallai
John Michael Lunn
Alan Ward
Keith Pearson
Philip Grant
Tony & Pat Drewett
Anthony & Julie Drewett
Karen Hulse
Malcolm Drewett
Martin & Wayne Shaw
Charles Pllu
Mark Taylor

George Dearden
Brian Turner
Steve Bower
Alan Smedley
Dennis Oldale
Jack Wells
Luke Tindall
Tim Daley
Stuart Laver
Sean P. Mahon
Peter Foster
Michael P. Axelby
Robert Metcalfe
Paul Woolfson
Matthew Hunt
Frank Roberts
Brian Tuner
John 'Eastie' Eastwood Sr.
John 'Eastie' Eastwood Jnr.
Tony Orwin
Chris Fox
Lee & Darren Ramsden
Ailsa Brookes
Bob Avery
Michael Hardy
Bob Precious
Rikki James Adshead
Gary James Adshead
John E. Jewitt
Stephen Crownshaw
Simon Crownshaw
Rodney Crownshaw
Ian Growcock
Lionel Mackender
Stephen Wade
John Tompkins
Anthony John Staniforth
Graham T. North
David North
Steve & Danny Armitage
Mick Simpson
Phil Pywell
Edward William Lee Mason
Rodney David Sharpe
Raymond J. Beckett
Ashley, Adam & Abbie Fearn
Charlie Carr
Robert Irwin Jordan
Peter William Chambers
Kelly Chambers
Wayne Roddis
Jamie M. Hall
Simon J. Hall

Paul & Lauren Thompson
Trevor Hall
Brian Moull
Neil Pieprzak
Jeremy David Swinerd
Philip Humphrey
Stephen Wainwright
Steven Peter Hurman
Peter Cyril Hurman
Daniel Plummer
Sam Walker
Richard Lightning
Andrew Yate
Malcolm Walker
Gwen Clarke
William Fieldsend
Simon Kay
Michael A. Clapham
Robert William Hanson
Christopher Dobson
Michael Stokes-Moorhouse
Norman J. Johnson
John Bellamy
Joan Jackman
Matloub Husayn-Ali-Khan
Richard Skelton
Mark Anthony Hughes
Keith Hill
Neal Wilson
Roy Hattersley
Jordan Brunyee
Tom Burton
Maurice Bulmer
Steven R. Hughes
Nicholas G. A. Wray
Matt Ruddick
Chris & Jack Ramsden
Graham Clixby
Wayne A. Brown
Stephen Ward
Rebecca Dale Garlick
Alistair Dean
Dean A. S. Headley
Tom Crowshaw
Simon Easthope
Joseph Lee Betts
Christopher Bell
Chris Dando

To:..

To:..

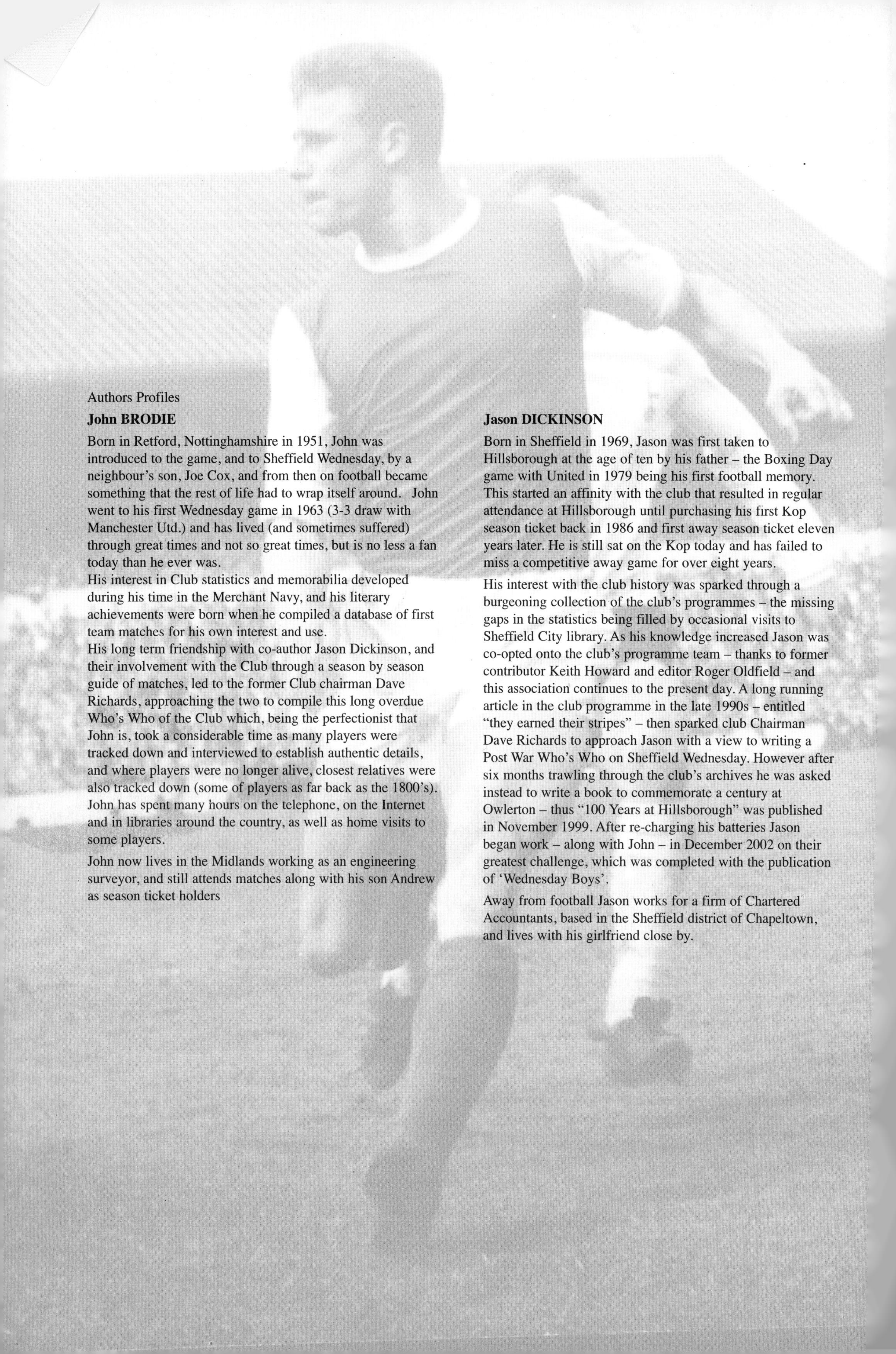

Authors Profiles

John BRODIE

Born in Retford, Nottinghamshire in 1951, John was introduced to the game, and to Sheffield Wednesday, by a neighbour's son, Joe Cox, and from then on football became something that the rest of life had to wrap itself around. John went to his first Wednesday game in 1963 (3-3 draw with Manchester Utd.) and has lived (and sometimes suffered) through great times and not so great times, but is no less a fan today than he ever was.

His interest in Club statistics and memorabilia developed during his time in the Merchant Navy, and his literary achievements were born when he compiled a database of first team matches for his own interest and use.

His long term friendship with co-author Jason Dickinson, and their involvement with the Club through a season by season guide of matches, led to the former Club chairman Dave Richards, approaching the two to compile this long overdue Who's Who of the Club which, being the perfectionist that John is, took a considerable time as many players were tracked down and interviewed to establish authentic details, and where players were no longer alive, closest relatives were also tracked down (some of players as far back as the 1800's). John has spent many hours on the telephone, on the Internet and in libraries around the country, as well as home visits to some players.

John now lives in the Midlands working as an engineering surveyor, and still attends matches along with his son Andrew as season ticket holders

Jason DICKINSON

Born in Sheffield in 1969, Jason was first taken to Hillsborough at the age of ten by his father – the Boxing Day game with United in 1979 being his first football memory. This started an affinity with the club that resulted in regular attendance at Hillsborough until purchasing his first Kop season ticket back in 1986 and first away season ticket eleven years later. He is still sat on the Kop today and has failed to miss a competitive away game for over eight years.

His interest with the club history was sparked through a burgeoning collection of the club's programmes – the missing gaps in the statistics being filled by occasional visits to Sheffield City library. As his knowledge increased Jason was co-opted onto the club's programme team – thanks to former contributor Keith Howard and editor Roger Oldfield – and this association continues to the present day. A long running article in the club programme in the late 1990s – entitled "they earned their stripes" – then sparked club Chairman Dave Richards to approach Jason with a view to writing a Post War Who's Who on Sheffield Wednesday. However after six months trawling through the club's archives he was asked instead to write a book to commemorate a century at Owlerton – thus "100 Years at Hillsborough" was published in November 1999. After re-charging his batteries Jason began work – along with John – in December 2002 on their greatest challenge, which was completed with the publication of 'Wednesday Boys'.

Away from football Jason works for a firm of Chartered Accountants, based in the Sheffield district of Chapeltown, and lives with his girlfriend close by.